The Editors

V. A. Kolve is the author of *The Play Called Corpus Christi*, a study of medieval drama, *Chaucer and the Imagery of Narrative: The First Five Canterbury Tales*, and its sequel, *Telling Images: Chaucer and the Imagery of Narrative II*. He has taught at Oxford, Stanford, the University of Virginia, and most recently at UCLA, as Foundation Professor of English (now Emeritus). He has served as president of the New Chaucer Society and of the Medieval Academy of America.

Glending Olson, Professor Emeritus of English at Cleveland State University, is the author of *Literature as Recreation in the Later Middle Ages* and of many articles on Chaucer and medieval literary theory. He has held NEH and Guggenheim fellowships.

NORTON CRITICAL EDITIONS
ANCIENT, CLASSICAL, AND MEDIEVAL ERAS

AESCHYLUS, The Oresteia
AQUINAS, St. Thomas Aquinas on Politics and Ethics
The Arabian Nights
ARISTOTLE, Poetics
Beowulf (prose)
Beowulf (verse)
The Bhagavad Gita
BOCCACCIO, The Decameron
BOETHIUS, The Consolation of Philosophy
CHAUCER, The Canterbury Tales
CHAUCER, Dream Visions and Other Poems
CHAUCER, Troilus and Criseyde
CONFUCIUS, The Analects
DANTE, Inferno
The English Bible, Vol. One: The Old Testament
The English Bible, Vol. Two: The New Testament
The Epic of Gilgamesh
EURIPIDES, Medea
HERODOTUS, The Histories
HOMER, The Odyssey
JULIAN, The Showings of Julian of Norwich
KEMPE, The Book of Margery Kempe
LANGLAND, Piers Plowman
MALORY, Le Morte Darthur
MARIE DE FRANCE, Poetry
Middle English Lyrics
Middle English Romances
OVID, Metamorphoses
ST. PAUL, The Writings of St. Paul
PIZAN, The Selected Writings of Christine de Pizan
The Qur'ān
Sir Gawain and the Green Knight
SOPHOCLES, Oedipus Tyrannus
THUCYDIDES, The Peloponnesian War

For a complete list of Norton Critical Editions, visit
wwnorton.com/nortoncriticals

A NORTON CRITICAL EDITION

Geoffrey Chaucer

THE CANTERBURY TALES

SEVENTEEN TALES AND THE GENERAL PROLOGUE

AUTHORITATIVE TEXT

SOURCES AND BACKGROUNDS

CRITICISM

THIRD EDITION

Selected and Edited by

V. A. KOLVE

THE UNIVERSITY OF CALIFORNIA AT LOS ANGELES

GLENDING OLSON

CLEVELAND STATE UNIVERSITY

W · W · NORTON & COMPANY · *New York · London*

W. W. Norton & Company has been independent since its founding in 1923, when William Warder Norton and Mary D. Herter Norton first published lectures delivered at the People's Institute, the adult education division of New York City's Cooper Union. The Nortons soon expanded their program beyond the Institute, publishing books by celebrated academics from America and abroad. By mid-century, the two major pillars of Norton's publishing program—trade books and college texts—were firmly established. In the 1950s, the Norton family transferred control of the company to its employees, and today—with a staff of four hundred and a comparable number of trade, college, and professional titles published each year—W. W. Norton & Company stands as the largest and oldest publishing house owned wholly by its employees.

Library of Congress Cataloging-in-Publication Data

Names: Chaucer, Geoffrey, -1400, author. | Kolve, V. A., editor. | Olson, Glending, editor.
Title: The Canterbury tales: seventeen tales and the general prologue: authoritative text, sources and backgrounds, criticism / Geoffrey Chaucer; selected and edited by V. A. Kolve, Glending Olson.
Description: Third edition. | New York: W. W. Norton & Company, 2018. | Series: A Norton crtical edition | Includes bibliographical references.
Identifiers: LCCN 2018006340 | **ISBN 9781324000563** (pbk.)
Subjects: LCSH: Christian pilgrims and pilgrimages—Poetry. | Storytelling—Poetry. | Tales, Medieval.
Classification: LCC PR1867 .K65 2018 | DDC 821/.1—dc23 LC record available at https://lccn.loc.gov/2018006340

W. W. Norton & Company, Inc., 500 Fifth Avenue, New York, NY 10110
wwnorton.com

W. W. Norton & Company Ltd., 15 Carlisle Street, London WID 3BS

1 2 3 4 5 6 7 8 9 0

for
Hester Lewellen
and for
Larry Luchtel

Contents

Criticism

Preface

The first part of this Norton Critical Edition of *The Canterbury Tales: Seventeen Tales and the General Prologue*—the glossed Chaucer text—is addressed specifically to students making their first acquaintance with Chaucer in his own language, and it takes nothing for granted. All difficult words and constructions are translated, in glosses at the margins of the page or in footnotes at the bottom when longer explanations are required. Because we hope the book will serve introductory courses in literature as well as more specialized courses in medieval studies, the glossing is complete for each of the tales. They may be assigned in any number and in any sequence. We have selected tales generally considered among Chaucer's finest, and whenever possible we have included from Chaucer's framing story passages that locate each tale in its immediate dramatic context.

The glossing is frankly pedagogic, intended to help the student understand Chaucer in the original language rather than to provide a steadily idiomatic modern translation. *Thou* forms of the verb, for instance, are glossed as such, though a modern translation would express them as *you*. Verbs are glossed in their exact tense, though medieval texts often shift between past and present forms in ways modern English declares ungrammatical. The glosses sometimes provide both a cognate word (which can help fix the original in mind) and a synonym that better conveys its contextual meaning. The glossing, more extensive than that in most modern editions, is intended not only to explain unfamiliar words but also to confirm students' likely guesses about more recognizable ones. Chaucer's language is not so far removed from modern English that translation need be the aim of anyone's study. The poet can be understood in his own voice from the beginning.

The text is likewise conservative and pedagogic. This has not seemed to us an appropriate occasion to attempt a radically new edition of Chaucer's text, even if there were general agreement concerning the shape such an edition should take. Although some eighty-two manuscripts of *The Canterbury Tales* survive, in full or in fragment, none is in Chaucer's own hand and none possesses his final authority. He died before the work was complete, and what has come down to us is, in even its earliest examples, scribal and implicitly editorial. Since we have neither autograph nor archetype, Chaucer's "original text" is in fact irrecoverable—and for editors attempting a definitive edition, as for critics specially concerned with Chaucerian metrics and stylistics, that is a great frustration. But the best manuscripts of *The Canterbury Tales* are, on the whole, very good, and the variations between them, word by word, reasonably few and only seldom of substantive importance. In the present case, we have used Skeat's landmark edition as our copy-text; for many specific readings we have consulted facsimile editions of the Ellesmere and Hengwrt manuscripts, the editions of Manly & Rickert, Robinson, Pratt, Fisher, Mann, Boenig & Taylor, and the *Riverside Chaucer*, 3rd ed., under the general editorship of Larry D. Benson. [See "Modern Editions and Facsimiles" in the Selective Bibliographies for full citations.] Skeat lightly normalized the spelling in the manuscripts, a feature we have retained as a convenience for beginning students, along with his use of a hyphen after the *y*-prefix in past participles. Our most systematic change has been to repunctuate the text, for the sake of clarity and in accordance with both medieval and contemporary usage. In matters of punctuation, less has seemed to us more. Finally, for ease of cross-reference, we have numbered the lines of each tale to accord with the standard numbering in virtually all modern editions and critical studies.

The second part of this book offers a collection of documents of various kinds—sources, analogues, or other medieval writings—which represent ways in which Chaucer or his first audiences might have known these stories from elsewhere or ways in which they might have thought about certain aspects of their meaning. Such documents can help students think in historically relevant ways about what Chaucer is most concerned with in these tales. In such study, they will find the differences at least as revealing as the similarities, for the differences help identify choices made, emphases added, roads taken and not taken.

To that end we have worked with a more generous definition of the relevant than do the two most important collections of sources and analogues of *The Canterbury Tales*.[1] We have brought together writings that cast an interesting and suggestive light on the tales included here and have made those writings accessible to students. Some of the translations that follow have been made specially for this volume; certain others, though previously published, have been difficult to come by and seem worth reprinting here. We have not glossed the Middle English writings in this section as extensively as we have the Chaucer texts, but even here we take for granted only a beginner's knowledge of Chaucer's language; a good deal of help is provided. Again, we have normalized certain features of these texts, substituting the appropriate modern letters for Middle English letters no longer current, regularizing *u/v* and *i/j*, eliminating certain scribal idiosyncracies, and modernizing punctuation and capitalization. We hope that both the new translations and the gathering together of what has been widely scattered or out of print will prove welcome, to teacher and student alike.

For reasons of space we have not been able to offer source and background material for every tale included in this edition. Students interested in exploring the relationship of the *Knight's Tale* to its source, Boccaccio's *Teseida*, may find a complete text with English translation in *Theseid of the Nuptials of Emilia*, trans. Vincenzo Traversa (New York: Peter Lang, 2002). There is also a full translation by Bernadette Marie McCoy, *The Book of Theseus* (Sea Cliff, NJ: Teesdale Publishing Associates, 1974), and

1. *Sources and Analogues of Chaucer's* Canterbury Tales, ed. W. F. Bryan and Germaine Dempster (1941; New York: Humanities P, 1958); *Sources and Analogues of the* Canterbury Tales, ed. Robert M. Correale and Mary Hamel, 2 vols. (Woodbridge, Suffolk, and Rochester, NY: D. S. Brewer, 2002–2005). The new *Sources and Analogues* volumes contain texts in their original languages with facing-page translations, along with extensive introductions surveying the relation of each tale to its analogues and antecedents.

extensive selections are translated in Nicholas Havely, *Chaucer's Boccaccio* (Cambridge: D. S. Brewer, 1980). A text and translation of the principal analogue to the *Summoner's Tale* appears in *The Literary Context of Chaucer's Fabliaux*, ed. and trans. Larry D. Benson and Theodore M. Andersson (Indianapolis: Bobbs-Merrill, 1971), along with multiple analogues to the Miller's and Reeve's stories. In the *Man of Law's Tale* and the *Second Nun's Tale* Chaucer translated Anglo-Norman and Latin sources, respectively; they are available, with modern English translations, in Correale and Hamel, *Sources and Analogues*, vols. 1 (for the *Second Nun's Tale*) and 2 (for the *Man of Law's Tale*). While we do not offer background texts for every tale printed here, for certain of Chaucer's richest and most widely discussed works, such as the *General Prologue*, the *Wife of Bath's Tale*, and the *Prioress's Tale*, we have tried to provide substantial contextual material.

The third part of this book brings together an updated selection of critical essays on Chaucer. Instead of trying to select a single definitive essay on each tale that we print—beyond the scope of this book, and a difficult, indeed impossible task—we have chosen influential studies that address or invite broader critical questions. Hence Donaldson on Chaucer the pilgrim, and Hoffman on the double focus, sacred and secular, of the pilgrimage. Hence the studies of Strohm and Patterson on the literary and social implications of the collection's multivocal structure and the roles of the Manciple and Parson as concluding voices. The first three essays offer an introductory framework for these literary explorations. Keen discusses the social hierarchy of late medieval England and the changes that forced adjustments to the old model of the three estates. Wetherbee provides a brief biography of Chaucer, an analysis of *The Canterbury Tales* that stresses the pilgrims' social self-awareness, and a summary of how subsequent centuries have understood the work. The addition of the Man of Law's and the Second Nun's stories to the *Canterbury Tales* selections—all four narratives in rhyme royal are now available here—has prompted us to include essays that directly address Chaucer's most serious work concerning women, religion, and Christian response to otherness: Mann on the suffering of Custance and Griselda, Schibanoff on the attitude to Islam and women in the *Man of Law's Tale*, Fradenburg on the Wife of Bath and her tale of fantasy, and Spector on the *Prioress's Tale* and Christian-Jewish relationships in the later Middle Ages. To Dinshaw's essay on the Pardoner we have added Cooper's succinct assessment of important interpretive issues concerning his *Prologue* and *Tale*.

Beyond the *Man of Law's Tale*, the *Second Nun's Tale*, and the several new critical essays, this Third Edition includes more of the *Parson's Tale* itself, a revised discussion of Chaucer's language that directs students to resources on the web for hearing and learning how to speak Middle English, a new short glossary for quick reference to some of Chaucer's most common words, and an updated and enlarged set of bibliographies both for the *Tales* as a whole and for each story we print. It will also be available in a searchable electronic edition identical in content to the printed one. Almost all of our editorial changes come in response to the seventy-seven teachers of Chaucer who took the time to provide W. W. Norton with detailed answers to survey questions on their use of the second edition. This new one will probably make few of them completely happy, partly because they teach Chaucer in varied kinds of classes, from introductory to graduate, partly because their individual preferences are widely disparate. Nevertheless, the survey made certain things quite clear, such as the importance of the *Man of Law's Tale* to current Chaucer studies, and we deeply appreciate the thoughtful attention that all the respondents gave to it.

We note as well that this edition follows not long after a totally revised second edition of the Modern Language Association's *Approaches to Teaching Chaucer's* Canterbury Tales, ed. Peter W. Travis and Frank Grady (New York, 2014), a valuable resource for students as well as teachers and testimony to the continuing appeal of *The Canterbury Tales*. In further testimony, we offer this expanded selection of seventeen tales and the *General Prologue* that introduces them as exemplifying Chaucer's remarkable achievement in the art of story. His is a Gothic art, full of variety and contradiction, tension and transcendence, an art that dared to look at life under so many guises and from so many points of view that it lays convincing claim, even in the twenty-first century, to having seen life whole.

In the making of the first edition of this book, the editors received the able assistance of Betsy Bowden, Thomas Cannon, Jr., Raymond Cormier, Rosa DelVecchio, Julie Bates Dock, Mary Dugan, Rita Hammond, Betty Hanson-Smith, and Jeanne Vanecko. Carol Bemis and Marian Johnson at W. W. Norton provided careful and cooperative editorial work. For the second edition Jane Dugan, Christina Fitzgerald, and Toni K. Thayer supplied valuable help, as did Carol Bemis, Brian Baker, and Katharine Ings at Norton. For assistance with this edition we thank Jane Dugan again for her attentive and timely work, Donna Stewart for technical assistance, and the English Department at Cleveland State University for allowing the use of some of its resources. At Norton Carol Bemis was as ever supportive and inspiring, and Rachel Goodman a prompt, lucid, and patient editor.

Chaucer's Language

There are many differences between Chaucer's Middle English and modern English, but they are minor enough that a student can learn to adjust to them in a fairly short time. We have sketched below just a few of the principal differences.

I. Pronunciation / Reading Chaucer Aloud

The chief difference between Middle English (ME) and Modern English (NE, as in "New English") is in pronunciation, and the best way to learn to pronounce Chaucer is to hear him be read—by your teacher, on a CD, or online—and then to work at getting those sounds into your own reading, whether you speak the words aloud or not. A reasonably good Chaucerian pronunciation will help you find the rhythm of his lines, as we discuss later, and also their beauty and power. Acquiring the pronunciation not only makes reading Chaucer more pleasurable but also aids in understanding him, since your ear can help you grasp words and phrases in context even when your eye becomes confused by an unusual spelling. We describe Chaucerian English below, but experiencing it is better than reading about it, so we suggest that you consult the following websites, or others like them, to begin your engagement with his work. (Our directions for access are based on site formats as of 2017.)

- Baragona, Alan. "The Criyng and the Soun: Chaucer Audio Files." alanbaragona.wordpress.com. This website offers immediate access in MP3 format to a number of short passages from *The Canterbury Tales* read in Middle English, including five different performances of the opening lines of the *General Prologue*.
- *Harvard's Geoffrey Chaucer Website*. chaucer.fas.harvard.edu. Click on "How to Read Chaucer." Then work through Lessons 1–3, which explain Middle English pronunciation, include audio examples, and allow you time to repeat what you have heard. Highly recommended.
- Jokinen, Anniina. Luminarium.org. On the homepage click first on "Medieval," then on "Geoffrey Chaucer," then on "Canterbury Tales." Scroll down to "Study Resources." This section includes Jokinen's ME readings of several passages from the *General Prologue*.
- Thomas, Paul R. *The Chaucer Studio*. chaucer.byu.edu. Readings in Middle English of every Canterbury verse tale included in this Norton Critical Edition are available through the Chaucer Studio Recordings. They are purchasable through the website at moderate prices, either as downloads or as CDs.

A. *Vowels*

Many of Chaucer's vowel sounds are quite different from their NE counterparts, not because of the oddity of ME pronunciation but because of a change that happened after Chaucer's time—one unique to English among European languages—known as the Great Vowel Shift. The result of that historical evolution, which is too complicated to describe here, is that in Chaucer the relationship between the spelling of certain vowels and their pronunciation is much more like the relationship thereof in modern Spanish or French or German than in English. What Chaucer spells "a" or "aa" represents the vowel sound in American English *pot*, Spanish *casa*, or French *bas*. It is never pronounced with the "long a" sound as when we say "a, b, c." You will not go far wrong if you just say *ah* every time you see the Middle English letter *a* in a stressed position. Similarly, what Chaucer spells "e" or "ee" represents not the vowel in NE *see* but rather the vowel sound of *bait* or *fate* (today's "long a" sound). The vowels in Chaucer's personal pronouns *he*, *she*, and *we* should be pronounced as if you were speaking the NE words *hay*, *shay*, and *way*. And what Chaucer spells "i" or "y" sounds like the *i* in Spanish *si*, not like the *i* in NE *like*. Here too pronouncing personal pronouns accurately is crucial to good spoken ME—Chaucer's first-person pronoun *I* is pronounced with the "long e" vowel sound in NE *bee*, as is his possessive pronoun *my*. And following the rule above for ME *e*, Chaucer's *me* is pronounced like NE *may*. However arbitrary these differences appear at first glance, they are part of a systematic shift that over centuries raised what are often called "long" vowel sounds higher in the mouth. But not all ME vowels shifted. The letter *i* in ME *in*, *it*, or *him* is pronounced as it is in NE; the letter *e* in ME *best* or *belt* is pronounced as it is in NE.

Beginning students can best deal with these and other differences by working backward from NE pronunciations and spellings. For example, if you see a word in Chaucer that has a "long i" sound in NE (like *I*, *wyfe*, *wyse*, *knyfe*, *whyte*), pronounce the *i* or *y* with a "long e" sound; if you see a word in Chaucer that has a "short i" sound in NE (like *sit*, *is*, *thrifty*, *simple*), pronounce it just as you normally do. The detailed table of vowel sounds that follows indicates not only Chaucer's spelling and pronunciation but also how the sounds evolved in NE, using both examples from modern American English and symbols used in the phonetic alphabet. Our table follows a traditional model; opinion on Chaucerian pronunciation is not unanimous, and without the benefit of Chaucer himself on tape we can only work toward an approximation of what he sounded like.

Two further aspects of the pronunciation of vowels may be considered in connection with Chaucer's principles of versification. Although scholars are not in complete agreement about the nature of Chaucer's metrics, most assume that his lines are basically iambic pentameter with a good deal of metrical variation. Vowels occurring in combination should all be pronounced, as the meter often makes clear:

An̆d pĺesaun̆t wás hĭs ab́sŏlúcĭoún

More complex is the question of final *e*. Originally there was no such thing as "silent e" in English: the final *e* in ME words often represents a reduction of more distinctive Old English inflections. By Chaucer's time it is likely that in normal speech the final *e* was silent, but in his poetry it is frequently pronounced, with the schwa sound [ə] that we use in unstressed syllables such as those at the end of *sofa* and the beginning of *about*. Always pronounce final *e* at the end of lines, and within lines pronounce it or not depending on the requirements of the meter. In the following example the final *e*'s that should be pronounced are italicized:

> Wĕl coúde hĕ sítte oň hórs, ănd fáir*ĕ* rýd*ĕ*,
> Hĕ cóud*ĕ* sóngeš máke ănd wél eňdyt*ĕ*

As these instances indicate, final *e* is usually not pronounced when it appears before words beginning with vowels or weakly pronounced *h*'s.

B. Consonants

ME consonants are pronounced as in NE, with some exceptions:

1. In general, pronounce all consonants in clusters: *g* and *k* before *n* (*gnawe, knife*), although *gn* in French borrowings (*digne, signe*) is [n]; *w* before *r* (*write, wroth*); *l* before *f, v, k, m* (*half* or *halve, folk, palmer*); *ng* is usually pronounced [ŋg], the consonant cluster in *finger* rather than *singer.*
2. *gh* is pronounced with the guttural sound in German *ich*. There is no comparable sound in NE, except for *loch* when pronounced with a heavy Scots accent.
3. *ch* is always pronounced [č], as in NE *church*.
4. *r* should be trilled.
5. *h* is not pronounced at the beginning of words borrowed from French (*honour, hostelrye*); it is also silent or only weakly pronounced at the beginning of short ME words like *he, his, hit, him, hem*.
6. Final *s* should not be voiced to [z] in stressed positions. At the end of lines Chaucer rhymes *was* with *glas* and *cas, is* with *this*.

II. Morphology

NOUNS: The usual ending for plural and genitive singular forms is *-es*, sometimes *-is*, generally pronounced as a separate syllable. The plural ending *-en* is more common than in NE: e.g., *eyen* instead of *eyes*.

PERSONAL PRONOUNS: Second-person pronouns have both singular forms—*thou, thy* or *thyn, the(e)*—and plural forms—*ye, youre, you* or *yow*. The latter set can be used with singular meaning in some cases.

The third-person singular neuter pronoun may be spelled *it* or *hit*; the possessive case of *it* is *his*, not *its*, which did not enter the language until the Renaissance.

CHAUCER'S SPELLING	EXAMPLES	ME PRONUNCIATION	EVOLUTION IN NE
VOWELS			
a	*after, at*	[a], as in NE *top*	usually becomes [æ], as in NE *after, at*
a, aa	*take, caas*	[a:], as in NE *father*	becomes [e], as in NE *take, case*
e	*best, hem*	[ɛ], as in NE *best*	no change
e, ee	*heeth, ese, see*	[ɛ:], as in NE *bed*	becomes [i], spelled *ea*, as in NE *heath, ease, sea*
e, ee	*swete, be, see*	[e:], as in NE *take*	becomes [i], spelled *e* or *ee*, as in NE *sweet, be, see*
i, y	*hit, in*	[ɪ], as in NE *hit, in*	no change
i, y	*I, ride*	[i:], as in NE *seed*	becomes [ai], as in NE *I, ride*
o	*of, oxe*	[ɔ], as in NE *long*	usually becomes [ə] or [a], as in NE *of, ox*
o, oo	*go, hope, so*	[ɔ:], as in NE *law*	becomes [o], as in NE *go, hope, so*
o, oo	*roote, to, good*	[o:], as in NE *note*	becomes [u] or [ʊ], as in NE *root, to, good*
u, o[1]	*up, but, come*	[ʊ], as in NE *put*	usually becomes [ʌ], as in NE *up, but, come*
ou, ow	*hous, town*	[ʉ:], as in NE *to*	becomes [au], as in NE *house, town*
u, eu, ew	*vertu, salewe*	[y], as in Fr. *tu*[2]	no NE equivalent
DIPHTHONGS			
ai, ey, ei, ey	*day, sayn, they*	[æɪ], somewhere between NE *hay* and *high*	becomes [e], as in NE *day, say, they*
au, aw	*cause, draw*	[aʊ], as in NE *out*	becomes [ɔ], as in NE *cause, draw*
eu, ew[3]	*newe, reule*	[ɪu], close to NE *few*	becomes [ɪu] or [u], as in NE *few, rule*
oi, oy	*joye, point*	[ɔɪ], as in NE *joy*	no change
ou, ow	*thought, bowe*	[ɔʊ], a glide between the vowels of NE *law* and *put*	becomes [ɔ] ir [o], as in NE *thought, bow*

1. A few words with the short [ʊ] sound in ME are spelled with *o* instead of *u*: *sone* (NE *son*), *sonne* (NE *sun*), *come*, *love*, *some*. These words were originally spelled with *u* in Old English; the *o* spelling is an orthographic change only.
2. This sound occurs only in a few words recently borrowed from French.
3. A few words—the most familiar are *fewe*, *lewed*, *shew*, *shrewe*—should be pronounced [ɛʉ] instead of [ɪʉ].

Chaucer's third-person plural forms are notably different from those in NE. *They, their,* and *them* are Scandinavian borrowings, which were assimilated into the language at different times in different ME dialects. Chaucer uses the nominative *thei* but retains the native forms for possessive and accusative case: *hir(e)* or *her(e)* instead of *their, hem* instead of *them*.

RELATIVE PRONOUNS: Chaucer uses *which, that,* or *which that* instead of *who* and *whom* when referring to human beings, as in "But I, that am exiled" and "a wyf, / Whiche that he lovede."

VERBS: The old infinitive form in *-en* appears frequently in Chaucer, but not consistently. For example, in the opening sentence of the *General Prologue* the infinitive of *seek* appears both as *to seken* and *to seke*.

The past participle is usually prefixed by *y-*, as in *hadde y-ronne*.

Verbs are inflected in the present tense as follows:

Indicative—Singular: 1. *take* 2. *takest* 3. *taketh*
Plural (all persons): *take(n)*
Subjunctive—Singular: *take*
Plural: *take(n)*

As in NE, ME verbs form past tense either by adding *-ed* or by a sound change within the word (e.g., *speke, spak*); the only difference is that some ME verbs that use a sound change have since shifted to the *-ed* form: in Chaucer the past tense of *shape*, for example, is *shop* rather than *shaped*.

ADVERBS: In addition to using *-ly* and *-liche*, Chaucer also uses the suffix *-e* to form adverbs, as in "ful loude he song."

III. Syntax

Chaucer's ME is more flexible in word order than NE, and he uses syntactic patterns no longer common today. Among the most frequent are:

object—subject—verb	But Cristes lore, and his apostles twelve, / He taughte
object—verb—subject	A Yeman hadde he
complement—subject—verb	Curteys he was
complement—verb—subject	Short was his gowne
verb—subject—object	Thus hath this pitous day a blisful ende
subject—auxiliary—object—verb	I have thy feith and thy benignitee . . . assayed

Other features of Chaucer's syntax also differ from standard NE practice. Often he shifts tense within a sentence:

And doun he *kneleth*, and with humble chere
And herte soor, he *seyde* as ye shul here . . .

The relative pronoun may be omitted:

With him ther was dwellinge a poure scoler,
Hadde lerned art . . .

As in spoken English, grammatical construction may shift in mid-sentence, or the subject may be repeated:

The reule of Seint Maure, or of Seint Beneit,
By cause that it was old and somdel streit,
This ilke monk leet olde thinges pace . . .

Upon that oother syde Palamon,
Whan that he wiste Arcite was agon,
Swich sorwe he maketh . . .

NEGATION: Chaucer has a variety of negative words, including *no* (sometimes spelled *na*), *nay*, and most prominently *ne* ("not"; pronounced *nuh*). When repeated in phrases, *ne* . . . *ne* often means "neither . . . nor." Whereas later English grammarians applied mathematical notions in their thinking about double negatives (two negatives make a positive), Chaucer's principle is that one negative element in a sentence creates denial and further negative elements reaffirm or strengthen that denial. Thus he often uses double negatives, or triple ("Ther nas no man nowher so vertuous"—literally, "There was not no man nowhere as capable"), or even quadruple negatives, as in these lines about the Knight's very careful use of language:

He *nevere* yet *no* vileinye *ne* sayde
In al his lyf, unto *no* maner wight.

Often Chaucer uses *ne* in contractions when it appears before a verb that begins with a vowel or a weakly articulated consonant, in the same way that NE uses contractions like *isn't* and *don't*. Some of these are at first not easy to recognize: *he nis* is short for *he ne is* ("he is not"); *she nas*=*she ne was* ("she was not"). *I noot* contracts *I ne woot* ("I do not know"); *she niste* contracts *she ne wiste* ("she did not know"). *I nil*=*I ne wil* ("I will not"; "I do not want to"), and similarly in the past tense, *I nolde* is a contraction of *I ne wolde*.

Finally, Chaucer uses a number of verbs in impersonal constructions that in more recent centuries have become exclusively personal. Chaucer sometimes writes *I remembre*, as in NE, but he also writes *it remembreth me* ("It comes into my memory"). *Me thinketh it* means "It seems to me." Sometimes the grammar of impersonal constructions is obscured when the subject "it" is omitted: *hire liketh* means "It pleases her"; *him oughte*="It is proper for him." Translating these impersonal phrases as "I remember," "I think," "she likes," or "he ought" conveys a roughly equivalent meaning but not the grammatical structure.

For further guidance, see the bibliography on "Chaucer's Language" at the end of this volume, p. 675.

Selections from

THE CANTERBURY TALES

The Canterbury Tales

The General Prologue

Whan that Aprill with his shoures sote° — *sweet showers*
The droghte° of Marche hath perced to the rote,° — *dryness / root*
And bathed every veyne° in swich licour,° — *vein / such moisture*
Of which vertu° engendred is the flour; — *By power of which*
Whan Zephirus° eek with his swete breeth — *the west wind*
Inspired° hath in every holt° and heeth° — *Breathed into / wood / heath*
The tendre croppes,° and the yonge sonne — *sprouts*
Hath in the Ram his halfe cours y-ronne;[1]
And smale fowles° maken melodye, — *birds*
That slepen al the night with open yë°— — *eye(s)*
So priketh hem Nature in hir corages[2]—
Than longen° folk to goon° on pilgrimages, — *Then long / go*
And palmeres for to seken straunge strondes,[3]
To ferne halwes,° couthe° in sondry londes; — *far-off shrines / known*
And specially, from every shires ende
Of Engelond to Caunterbury they wende,
The holy blisful martir[4] for to seke,° — *seek*
That hem hath holpen,° whan that they were seke.° — *helped / sick*
Bifel° that, in that seson on a day, — *It befell*
In Southwerk at the Tabard° as I lay° — *(an inn) / lodged*
Redy to wenden° on my pilgrimage — *depart*
To Caunterbury with ful devout corage,° — *heart*
At night was come into that hostelrye° — *inn*
Wel nyne and twenty in a companye
Of sondry folk, by aventure° y-falle° — *chance / fallen*
In felawshipe, and pilgrims were they alle,
That toward Caunterbury wolden° ryde. — *wished to*
The chambres° and the stables weren wyde,° — *bedrooms / spacious*
And wel we weren esed° atte beste.° — *made comfortable / in the best (ways)*
And shortly, whan the sonne was to° reste, — *at*
So hadde I spoken with hem everichon° — *every one*
That I was of hir felawshipe anon,

1. Has run his half-course in the Ram; i.e., has passed through half the zodiacal sign of Aries (the Ram), a course completed on April 11. A rhetorically decorative way of indicating the time of year.
2. Nature so spurs them in their hearts.
3. And pilgrims to seek foreign shores.
4. Thomas Becket, archbishop of Canterbury, murdered in 1170 and canonized shortly thereafter. The place of his martyrdom was the greatest shrine in England and much visited by pilgrims.

And made forward° erly for to ryse, *agreement*
To take oure wey, ther as I yow devyse.° *(will) tell*
But natheles,° whyl I have tyme and space, *nevertheless*
Er that I ferther in this tale pace,° *pass on*
Me thinketh it acordaunt to resoun[5]
To telle yow al the condicioun[6]
Of ech of hem, so as it semed me,° *seemed to me*
And whiche° they weren, and of what degree,° *what / status*
And eek in what array° that they were inne; *clothing*
And at a knight than wol° I first beginne. *will*
A KNIGHT ther was, and that a worthy man,
That fro° the tyme that he first bigan *from*
To ryden out,° he loved chivalrye, *ride (on expeditions)*
Trouthe and honour, fredom and curteisye.[7]
Ful worthy was he in his lordes werre,° *war(s)*
And therto° hadde he riden, no man ferre,° *in such / further*
As wel in Cristendom as in hethenesse,° *in pagan lands*
And evere honoured for his worthinesse.
At Alisaundre° he was whan it was wonne; *Alexandria*
Ful ofte tyme he hadde the bord bigonne° *headed the table*
Aboven alle naciouns in Pruce.° *Prussia*
In Lettow hadde he reysed and in Ruce,[8]
No Cristen man so ofte of his degree.° *rank*
In Gernade° at the sege° eek hadde he be° *Granada / siege / been*
Of Algezir,° and riden in Belmarye.° *Algeciras / Benmarin (in Morocco)*
At Lyeys° was he and at Satalye,° *Ayas / Adalia (both in Asia Minor)*
Whan they were wonne; and in the Grete See° *Mediterranean*
At many a noble armee° hadde he be. *armed expedition*
At mortal batailles[9] hadde he been fiftene,
And foughten for oure feith at Tramissene° *Tlemcen (in Algeria)*
In listes° thryes,° and ay slayn his foo.° *tournaments / thrice / foe*
This ilke° worthy knight hadde been also *same*
Somtyme with the lord of Palatye,° *Palatia*
Ageyn° another hethen in Turkye; *Against*
And everemore he hadde a sovereyn prys.° *reputation*
And though that he were worthy,° he was wys,° *i.e., valiant / prudent*
And of his port° as meke as is a mayde. *deportment*
He nevere yet no vileinye° ne sayde *rudeness*
In al his lyf, unto no maner wight.° *any sort of person*
He was a verray,° parfit,° gentil° knight. *true / perfect / noble*
But for to tellen yow of his array,
His hors° were gode, but he was nat gay.° *horses / brightly dressed*
Of fustian° he wered° a gipoun° *rough cloth / wore / tunic*
Al bismotered with° his habergeoun,° *stained by / coat of mail*
For he was late y-come° from his viage,° *recently come / expedition*
And wente for to doon° his pilgrimage. *make*

5. It seems to me reasonable (proper).
6. Character, estate, condition.
7. Fidelity, honor, generosity of spirit, and courtesy (the central chivalric virtues).
8. He had been on campaigns in Lithuania and in Russia.
9. Tournaments fought to the death.

With him ther was his sone, a young SQUYER,
A lovyere, and a lusty bacheler,[1]
With lokkes crulle, as they were leyd in presse.[2]
Of twenty yeer of age he was, I gesse.
Of° his stature he was of evene lengthe,° *In / average height*
And wonderly delivere,° and of greet strengthe. *agile*
And he hadde been somtyme in chivachye° *on expeditions*
In Flaundres,° in Artoys,° and Picardye,° *Flanders / Artois / Picardy*
And born him wel, as of so litel space,[3]
In hope to stonden° in his lady° grace. *stand / lady's*
Embrouded° was he, as it were a mede° *Embroidered / meadow*
Al ful of fresshe floures, whyte and rede.
Singinge he was, or floytinge,° al the day; *fluting (whistling?)*
He was as fresh as is the month of May.
Short was his gowne, with sleves longe and wyde.
Wel coude° he sitte on hors, and faire ryde. *knew how to*
He coude songes make and wel endyte,° *compose verse*
Juste° and eek daunce, and wel purtreye° and wryte. *Joust / draw*
So hote° he lovede that by nightertale° *hotly / at night*
He sleep° namore° than dooth a nightingale. *slept / no more*
Curteys he was, lowly, and servisable,[4]
And carf° biforn his fader at the table. *carved (meat)*
A YEMAN hadde he, and servaunts namo[5]
At that tyme, for him liste° ryde so; *it pleased him to*
And he was clad in cote and hood of grene.
A sheef of pecok arwes° brighte and kene *arrows*
Under his belt he bar° ful thriftily.° *bore / carefully*
Wel coude he dresse° his takel° yemanly: *keep in order / equipment*
His arwes drouped noght with fetheres lowe,
And in his hand he bar a mighty bowe.
A not-heed° hadde he, with a broun visage.° *closely cropped head / face*
Of wodecraft wel coude° he al the usage. *knew*
Upon his arm he bar a gay bracer,° *fine wrist guard*
And by his syde a swerd and a bokeler,° *shield*
And on that other syde a gay daggere,
Harneised° wel, and sharp as point of spere; *mounted*
A Cristofre° on his brest of silver shene.° *St. Christopher medal / bright*
An horn he bar, the bawdrik° was of grene; *shoulder strap*
A forster° was he, soothly, as I gesse. *forester*
Ther was also a Nonne, a PRIORESSE,
That of hir smyling was ful simple and coy°— *modest*
Hir gretteste ooth was but by Seynte Loy°— *Eligius (French: Eloi)*
And she was cleped° madame Eglentyne. *called*
Ful wel she song° the service divyne, *sang*
Entuned° in hir nose ful semely;° *Intoned / becomingly*

1. A lover, and a vigorous young man, one preparing to become a knight.
2. With locks as curly as if they'd been pressed (by a curling iron).
3. And conducted himself well, considering his inexperience.
4. He was courteous, humble, and willing to be of service.
5. He (the Knight) had a Yeoman (a servant one step above a groom in rank; this one seems to be a forester) with him, and no other servants.

And Frensh she spak ful faire and fetisly,° *elegantly*
After the scole of Stratford atte Bowe,[6]
For Frensh of Paris was to hire unknowe.
At mete° wel y-taught was she with alle: *i.e., At table*
She leet° no morsel from hir lippes falle, *let*
Ne wette hir fingres in hir sauce depe.° *(too) deeply*
Wel coude she carie a morsel, and wel kepe[7]
That no drope ne fille° upon hire brest. *fell*
In curteisye° was set ful muchel° hir lest.° *etiquette / much / delight*
Hir over°-lippe wyped she so clene, *upper*
That in hir coppe was no ferthing° sene° *small drop / seen*
Of grece,° whan she dronken hadde hir draughte. *grease*
Ful semely after hir mete she raughte,° *reached*
And sikerly° she was of greet disport,° *certainly / cheerfulness*
And ful plesaunt, and amiable of port,° *deportment*
And peyned hire° to countrefete chere° *took pains / imitate behavior*
Of court, and to been estatlich° of manere, *stately*
And to ben holden digne° of reverence. *considered worthy*
But, for to speken of hire conscience,° *sensibility*
She was so charitable and so pitous,° *compassionate*
She wolde wepe if that she sawe a mous° *mouse*
Caught in a trappe, if it were deed or bledde.
Of° smale houndes hadde she, that she fedde *i.e., Some*
With rosted flesh, or milk and wastel-breed.° *fine white bread*
But sore° wepte she if oon of hem were deed, *sorely*
Or if men° smoot it with a yerde° smerte;° *(some)one / stick / sharply*
And al was conscience and tendre herte.
Ful semely hir wimpel° pinched° was, *headdress / pleated*
Hir nose tretys,° hir eyen° greye as glas, *graceful / eyes*
Hir mouth ful smal, and therto softe and reed.
But sikerly° she hadde a fair forheed— *certainly*
It was almost a spanne° brood, I trowe°— *span / believe*
For hardily° she was nat undergrowe.° *certainly / undersized*
Ful fetis° was hir cloke, as I was war.° *elegant / aware*
Of smal coral° aboute hire arm she bar *i.e., small coral beads*
A peire of bedes, gauded al with grene;[8]
And theron heng a broche° of gold ful shene,° *ornament / bright*
On which ther was first write° a crowned A,[9] *written*
And after, *Amor vincit omnia*.° *Love conquers all (Latin)*
  Another NONNE with hire hadde she,
That was hir chapeleyne,° and PREESTES three. *chaplain, assistant*
  A MONK ther was, a fair for the maistrye,° *a very fine one*
An outrydere° that lovede venerye:° *estate supervisor / hunting*
A manly man, to been an abbot able.
Ful many a deyntee° hors hadde he in stable, *valuable*
And whan he rood, men mighte his brydel here° *hear*

6. I.e., in the English fashion, as it was spoken at Stratford at the Bow—a suburb some two miles east of London and home of the Benedictine nunnery of St. Leonard's.
7. She knew well how to raise a portion (to her lips) and take care.
8. A string of beads (a rosary), its groups marked off by special stones, called "gauds," of green.
9. The letter *A* with a symbolic crown fashioned above it.

Ginglen° in a whistling wind als° clere — *Jingling / as*
And eek° as loude as dooth the chapel belle, — *also*
Ther as° this lord was kepere of the celle.[1] — *Where*
The reule of Seint Maure° or of Seint Beneit,° — *Maurus / Benedict*
By cause that it was old and somdel streit,° — *somewhat strict*
This ilke° monk leet olde thinges pace,° — *same / pass away*
And held after the newe world the space.° — *course (i.e., customs)*
He yaf° nat of° that text a pulled° hen, — *gave / for / plucked*
That seith that hunters ben° nat holy men, — *are*
Ne that a monk, whan he is reccheless,° — *negligent of his vows*
Is lykned til° a fish that is waterlees° — *likened to / out of water*
(This is to seyn,° a monk out of his cloistre); — *say*
But thilke° text held he nat worth an oistre.° — *that same / oyster*
And I seyde his opinioun was good:
What° sholde he studie, and make himselven wood,° — *Why / mad*
Upon a book in cloistre alwey to poure,° — *pore over*
Or swinken° with his handes and laboure — *work*
As Austin bit?° How shal the world be served? — *Augustine bids*
Lat Austin have his swink° to him reserved! — *work*
Therfore he was a pricasour° aright:° — *hard rider / truly*
Grehoundes he hadde, as swifte as fowel° in flight; — *bird*
Of priking° and of hunting for the hare — *riding*
Was al his lust,° for no cost wolde he spare. — *pleasure*
I seigh° his sleves purfiled° at the hond — *saw / trimmed*
With grys,° and that the fyneste of a lond;° — *gray fur / land*
And, for to festne° his hood under his chin, — *fasten*
He hadde of gold y-wroght° a ful curious pin: — *made*
A love-knotte[2] in the gretter° ende ther was. — *larger*
His heed was balled,° that shoon as any glas, — *bald*
And eek his face, as° he had been anoint.° — *as if / anointed*
He was a lord ful fat and in good point,° — *condition*
His eyen° stepe° and rollinge in his heed, — *eyes / prominent*
That stemed as a forneys of a leed;[3]
His bootes souple,° his hors in greet estat°— — *supple / condition*
Now certeinly he was a fair prelat.
He was nat pale as a forpyned goost;° — *tormented spirit*
A fat swan loved he best of any roost.
His palfrey° was as broun as is a berye.° — *horse / berry*
  A Frere° ther was, a wantowne° and a merye, — *Friar / gay (one)*
A limitour,[4] a ful solempne° man. — *distinguished*
In alle the ordres foure[5] is noon that can° — *knows*
So muchel of daliaunce and fair langage.
He hadde maad° ful many a mariage — *arranged*
Of yonge wommen, at his owne cost.[6]
Unto his ordre he was a noble post.° — *pillar*

1. A priory or dependent house.
2. An elaborate knot symbolizing true love.
3. That gleamed like a furnace (a fire) under a cauldron.
4. One licensed to beg within a certain region or limit.
5. The four orders of friars (Franciscan, Dominican, Carmelite, and Augustinian).
6. I.e., he gave them dowries out of his own funds, perhaps after having first seduced them himself.

Ful wel biloved and famulier was he
With frankeleyns over al in his contree,[7]
And eek with worthy wommen of the toun;
For he hadde power of confessioun,
As seyde himself, more than a curat,° *parish priest*
For of his ordre he was licentiat.° *licensed to hear confessions*
Ful swetely herde he confessioun,
And plesaunt was his absolucioun;
He was an esy man to yeve° penaunce *give*
Ther as he wiste to have a good pitaunce.[8]
For unto a povre° ordre for to yive° *poor / give*
Is signe that a man is wel y-shrive°— *shriven*
For if he yaf,° he dorste make avaunt,° *gave / (the Friar) dared assert*
He wiste° that a man was repentaunt. *knew*
For many a man so hard is of his herte,
He may nat wepe althogh hym sore smerte:° *it sorely pain him*
Therfore, in stede of wepinge and preyeres,
Men moot° yeve silver to the povre° freres. *may / poor*
His tipet° was ay farsed° ful of knyves *scarf / always stuffed*
And pinnes, for to yeven° faire wyves. *give to*
And certeinly he hadde a murye note;° *pleasant voice*
Wel coude he singe and pleyen on a rote;° *stringed instrument*
Of yeddinges he bar outrely the prys.[9]
His nekke whyt was as the flour-de-lys;° *lily*
Therto° he strong was as a champioun. *Moreover*
He knew the tavernes wel in every toun,
And everich hostiler° and tappestere° *innkeeper / barmaid*
Bet than a lazar or a beggestere,[1]
For unto swich° a worthy man as he *such*
Acorded nat, as by his facultee,[2]
To have with seke lazars° aqueyntaunce: *sick lepers*
It is nat honest,° it may nat avaunce° *respectable / be profitable*
For to delen with no swich poraille,° *such poor people*
But al with riche and selleres of vitaille.° *victuals*
And over al,° ther as° profit sholde aryse, *everywhere / wherever*
Curteys he was, and lowely of° servyse. *humble in*
Ther nas° no man nowher so vertuous.° *was not / capable*
He was the beste beggere in his hous,
And yaf° a certeyn ferme° for the graunt: *gave / payment*
Noon of his bretheren cam ther in his haunt.° *area of begging*
For thogh a widwe° hadde noght a sho,° *widow / shoe*
So plesaunt was his *In principio*,° *In the beginning (Latin)*
Yet wolde he have a ferthing,° er he wente. *farthing*
His purchas was wel bettre than his rente.[3]

7. With rich landholders everywhere in his region.
8. Wherever he knew (that he could expect) to have a good gift in return.
9. At narrative songs, he absolutely took the prize.
1. Better than a leper or beggar woman.
2. It was not fitting, considering his position.
3. His profit from begging was much greater than "his regular income" or "the fee he paid for his exclusive begging rights." (Meaning uncertain.)

And rage he coude, as it were right a whelpe;[4]
In love-dayes° ther coude he muchel° helpe, *legal arbitrations / much*
For there he was nat lyk a cloisterer,[5]
With a thredbare cope,° as is a povre scoler. *cape*
But he was lyk a maister° or a pope: *Master of Arts*
Of double worsted was his semi-cope,° *half cape*
That rounded as a belle out of the presse.° *mold*
Somwhat he lipsed, for his wantownesse,[6]
To make his English swete upon his tonge;
And in his harping, whan that he hadde songe,
His eyen° twinkled in his heed aright *eyes*
As doon° the sterres° in the frosty night. *do / stars*
This worthy limitour was cleped° Huberd. *called*
A MARCHANT was ther with a forked berd,° *beard*
In mottelee,° and hye[7] on horse he sat; *figured cloth*
Upon his heed a Flaundrish° bever° hat, *Flemish / beaver fur*
His bootes clasped° faire and fetisly.° *tied / neatly*
His resons° he spak ful solempnely,° *opinions / impressively*
Souninge° alway th'encrees° of his winning.° *Proclaiming / increase / profit*
He wolde the see were kept for any thing[8]
Bitwixe Middleburgh° and Orewelle.° *(in Holland) / (in England)*
Wel coude he in eschaunge° sheeldes° selle. *foreign exchange / French coins*
This worthy man ful wel his wit bisette:° *used*
Ther wiste no wight° that he was in dette, *no person knew*
So estatly° was he of his governaunce,° *dignified / conduct*
With his bargaynes and with his chevisaunce.° *(possibly illegal) lending*
For sothe he was a worthy man with alle,° *indeed*
But sooth to seyn, I noot° how men him calle. *know not*
A CLERK° ther was of Oxenford° also, *student / Oxford*
That unto logik hadde longe y-go.[9]
As leene° was his hors as is a rake, *lean*
And he nas° nat right fat, I undertake,° *was not / declare*
But loked holwe° and therto° soberly. *hollow / also*
Ful thredbar was his overest courtepy,° *outer short cloak*
For he hadde geten him° yet no benefyce, *obtained for himself*
Ne was so worldly for to have offyce;° *secular employment*
For him was levere° have at his beddes heed *he would rather*
Twenty bokes, clad° in blak or reed, *bound*
Of Aristotle and his philosophye,
Than robes riche, or fithele,° or gay sautrye.° *fiddle / psaltery, harp*
But al be that° he was a philosophre,[1] *although*
Yet hadde he but litel gold in cofre;° *coffer*
But al that he mighte of his freendes hente,° *get*
On bokes and on lerninge he it spente,

4. And he knew how to play and flirt, as if he were a puppy.
5. A religious who knows only the enclosed life of the cloister.
6. He lisped a little, out of affectation.
7. On a high saddle.
8. He wanted the sea to be guarded (against pirates) at any cost. (His profits depended on it.)
9. Who had long since proceeded to (the study of) logic in the university curriculum.
1. With a pun on alchemist, another meaning of the word.

And bisily gan for the soules preye[2]
Of hem that yaf him wherwith° to scoleye.° *i.e., the means / study*
Of studie took he most cure° and most hede.° *care / heed*
Noght o° word spak he more than was nede, *Not one*
And that was seyd in forme° and reverence,° *properly / respectfully*
And short and quik, and ful of hy sentence.° *serious meaning*
Souninge° in moral vertu was his speche, *Resounding*
And gladly wolde he lerne and gladly teche.

A SERGEANT OF THE LAWE,° war° and wys, *An eminent lawyer / alert*
That often hadde been at the Parvys,[3]
Ther was also, ful riche of excellence.
Discreet he was and of greet reverence:° *worthy of great respect*
He semed swich,° his wordes weren so wyse. *such*
Justyce° he was ful often in assyse,° *Judge / local courts*
By patente° and by pleyn° commissioun; *letter of appointment / full*
For his science° and for his heigh renoun, *knowledge*
Of fees and robes hadde he many oon.° *a one*
So greet a purchasour° was nowher noon:° *speculator in land / none*
Al was fee simple to him in effect;[4]
His purchasing mighte nat been infect.° *invalidated*
Nowher so bisy a man as he ther nas;
And yet he semed bisier than he was.
In termes hadde he caas and domes alle,[5]
That from the tyme of King William[6] were falle.° *had taken place*
Therto he coude endyte,° and make a thing;° *write / draw up papers*
Ther coude no wight pinche at° his wryting, *no one find fault with*
And every statut coude° he pleyn by rote.° *knew / completely by heart*
He rood but hoomly° in a medlee° cote, *informally / figured*
Girt with a ceint° of silk, with barres° smale; *girdle / metal bars*
Of his array telle I no lenger tale.

A FRANKELEYN° was in his companye. *wealthy landowner*
Whyt was his berd as is the dayesye;° *daisy*
Of his complexioun° he was sangwyn.° *temperament / sanguine*
Wel loved he by the morwe a sop in wyn.[7]
To liven in delyt was evere his wone,° *custom*
For he was Epicurus[8] owene sone,
That heeld opinioun that pleyn° delyt *complete*
Was verray° felicitee parfyt.° *true / perfect*
An housholdere, and that a greet,° was he; *a great one*
Seint Julian[9] he was in his contree.° *region*
His breed, his ale, was alweys after oon;° *of uniform good quality*
A bettre envyned° man was nowher noon. *stocked with wine*
Withoute bake mete° was nevere his hous, *meat pies*
Of fish and flesh,° and that so plentevous° *meat / plentiful*

2. And busily did pray for the souls.
3. The porch of St. Paul's Cathedral, a favorite gathering place for lawyers.
4. I.e., he always got unrestricted possession ("fee simple") of the property.
5. He knew the exact terms (details) of all the cases and decisions.
6. I.e., since the Norman Conquest (1066).
7. In the morning he dearly loved a sop (a piece of bread or cake) in wine.
8. A Greek philosopher who held that pleasure was the highest good.
9. The patron saint of hospitality.

It snewed° in his hous of mete° and drinke. *snowed / food*
Of alle deyntees° that men coude thinke, *delicacies*
After° the sondry sesons of the yeer, *According to*
So chaunged° he his mete° and his soper. *varied / dinner*
Ful many a fat partrich° hadde he in mewe,° *partridge / coop*
And many a breem° and many a luce° in stewe.° *carp / pike / fishpond*
Wo° was his cook, but if° his sauce were *(Made) sorry / unless*
Poynaunt° and sharp, and redy al his gere.° *Pungent / utensils*
His table dormant[1] in his halle° alway *main room*
Stood redy covered° al the longe day. *set*
At sessiouns ther was he lord and sire;[2]
Ful ofte tyme he was knight of the shire.[3]
An anlas° and a gipser° al of silk *dagger / purse*
Heng° at his girdel, whyt as morne° milk. *Hung / morning*
A shirreve° hadde he been, and a countour;° *sheriff / auditor*
Was nowher such a worthy vavasour.° *landholder*
An Haberdassher and a Carpenter,
A Webbe,° a Dyere, and a Tapicer,° *weaver / tapestry maker*
Were with us eek, clothed in o liveree° *one livery (uniform)*
Of a solempne° and greet fraternitee.° *distinguished / (parish) guild*
Ful fresh and newe hir gere° apyked° was; *equipment / adorned*
Hir knyves were chaped° noght with bras, *mounted*
But al with silver; wroght ful clene and weel
Hire girdles° and hire pouches° everydeel.° *belts / purses / altogether*
Wel semed ech of hem a fair burgeys° *citizen, burgher*
To sitten in a yeldhalle° on a deys.[4] *guildhall*
Everich,° for the wisdom that he can,° *Each one / knows*
Was shaply° for to been an alderman. *fit*
For catel° hadde they ynogh and rente,° *property / income*
And eek° hir wyves wolde it wel assente;° *also / assent to*
And elles° certein were they to blame.° *otherwise / deserving of blame*
It is ful fair to been y-clept° *"Madame,"*° *called / "my lady"*
And goon to vigilyës al bifore,[5]
And have a mantel royalliche y-bore.° *royally carried*
A Cook they hadde with hem for the nones,° *occasion*
To boille the chiknes° with the mary-bones° *chickens / marrowbones*
And poudre-marchant tart and galingale.[6]
Wel coude he knowe° a draughte of London ale. *recognize*
He coude° roste, and sethe,° and broille, and frye, *knew how to / boil*
Maken mortreux,° and wel bake a pye. *stews*
But greet harm° was it, as it thoughte° me, *misfortune / seemed to*
That on his shine° a mormal° hadde he. *shin / ulcerous sore*
For blankmanger,[7] that made he with the beste.

1. Most tables were made of boards laid on trestles and were taken down after each meal; this one seems to have been permanent.
2. I.e., he presided over meetings of local justices of the peace when they gathered to hear cases.
3. Member of Parliament for his county.
4. The dais (a raised platform) on which the mayor or alderman of a city sat.
5. And go to church vigils at the head of the procession.
6. Both are spices, one tart and one sweet.
7. An elaborate dish of chicken in a sweet milk-and-rice sauce.

A SHIPMAN was ther, woninge fer by weste:[8]
For aught I woot,° he was of Dertemouthe.° *know / Dartmouth (in Devon)*
He rood upon a rouncy, as he couthe,[9]
In a gowne of falding° to the knee. *heavy wool*
A daggere hanginge on a laas° hadde he *cord*
Aboute his nekke, under his arm adoun.
The hote somer° hadde maad his hewe al broun; *summer*
And certeinly he was a good felawe.° *cheerful companion*
Ful many a draughte of wyn had he y-drawe° *drawn off*
Fro Burdeux-ward, whyl that the chapman sleep.[1]
Of nyce° conscience took he no keep:° *scrupulous / heed*
If that he faught, and hadde the hyer hond,° *upper hand*
By water he sente hem hoom° to every lond. *i.e., drowned them*
But of his craft, to rekene wel his tydes,[2]
His stremes° and his daungers him bisydes,° *currents / close to him*
His herberwe° and his mone,° his lodemenage,° *harbor / moon / pilotage*
Ther nas noon swich° from Hulle to Cartage.[3] *such*
Hardy he was, and wys to undertake;[4]
With many a tempest hadde his berd been shake.
He knew wel alle the havenes,° as they were, *harbors*
From Gootlond to the cape of Finistere,[5]
And every cryke° in Britayne° and in Spayne; *creek / Brittany*
His barge y-cleped° was the Maudelayne.° *called / Magdalen*
With us ther was a DOCTOUR OF PHISYK;° *a physician*
In al this world ne was ther noon him lyk
To speke of phisik° and of surgerye, *In regard to medicine*
For he was grounded in astronomye.° *astrology*
He kepte° his pacient a ful greet deel *watched*
In houres, by his magik naturel.[6]
Wel coude he fortunen the ascendent
Of his images for his pacient.[7]
He knew the cause of everich maladye,
Were it of hoot or cold, or moiste, or drye,[8]
And where engendred,° and of what humour; *originated*
He was a verrey° parfit practisour.° *true / practitioner*
The cause y-knowe,° and of his harm° the roote,° *known / malady / cause*
Anon° he yaf° the seke man his boote.° *Quickly / gave / remedy*
Ful redy hadde he his apothecaries[9]

8. There was a shipmaster, dwelling far off to the west.
9. He rode on a small sturdy horse, as (well as) he knew how. (A man more used to ships than horses.)
1. On the way from Bordeaux, while the (wine) merchant slept.
2. But at his craft, in calculating well the tides.
3. From Hull (in England) to Carthage (in northern Africa), or possibly Cartagena (in Spain).
4. Prudent in the risks he undertook.
5. From Gotland (an island in the Baltic Sea) to Cape Finisterre (in Spain).
6. During those hours (best for treatment), through his knowledge of natural magic (i.e., astrology).
7. He knew well how to determine the most favorable position of the stars for (making astrological) images for his patient.
8. The four fundamental qualities, which were thought to combine in pairs to form the four elements and the four humors (melancholia, cholera, phlegm, and blood); bodily health depended upon the existence of a proper equilibrium among them.
9. I.e., pharmacists.

To sende him drogges and his letuaries,° *medicinal syrups*
For ech of hem made other for to winne;° *profit*
Hir° frendschipe nas nat newe to biginne.° *Their / recently begun*
Wel knew he the olde Esculapius,
And Deiscorides, and eek Rufus,
Old Ypocras, Haly, and Galien,
Serapion, Razis, and Avicen,
Averrois, Damascien, and Constantyn,
Bernard, and Gatesden, and Gilbertyn.[1]
Of his diete mesurable° was he, *moderate*
For it was of no superfluitee
But of greet norissing° and digestible. *nourishment*
His studie was but litel on the Bible.[2]
In sangwin° and in pers° he clad was al, *bloodred / blue*
Lyned with taffata and with sendal;[3]
And yet he was but esy of dispence.° *slow to spend*
He kepte that he wan in pestilence,
For gold in phisik is a cordial;[4]
Therefore he lovede gold in special.° *particularly*
A good Wyf was ther of bisyde Bathe,° *from near Bath*
But she was somdel° deef, and that was scathe.° *somewhat / a pity*
Of clooth-making she hadde swiche an haunt,° *such practiced skill*
She passed° hem of Ypres and of Gaunt.[5] *surpassed*
In al the parisshe wyf ne was ther noon
That to the offringe° bifore hir sholde goon;° *offering in church / go*
And if ther dide, certeyn so wrooth° was she, *angry*
That she was out of alle charitee.
Hir coverchiefs° ful fyne were of ground;° *kerchiefs / texture*
I dorste° swere they weyeden° ten pound *would dare / weighed*
That on a Sonday weren upon hir heed.
Hir hosen° weren of fyn scarlet reed, *hose*
Ful streite y-teyd,° and shoos ful moiste° and newe. *tightly tied / soft*
Bold was hir face, and fair, and reed of hewe.° *hue*
She was a worthy womman al hir lyve:
Housbondes at chirche dore[6] she hadde fyve,
Withouten° other companye in youthe— *Not to mention*
But therof nedeth nat to speke as nouthe°— *at present*
And thryes° hadde she been at Jerusalem. *thrice*
She hadde passed many a straunge streem:[7]
At Rome she hadde been, and at Boloigne,° *Boulogne (France)*
In Galice at Seint Jame, and at Coloigne;[8]

1. A list of the best medical authorities, ancient and modern (e.g., John of Gaddesden, an Englishman, died ca. 1349).
2. Doctors were often held to be skeptical in religious matters.
3. With linings of taffeta and fine silk.
4. He kept what he had earned during time of plague, for gold in medicine is good for the heart. (An ironic reference to *aurum potabile*, a liquid medicine compounded of gold and held to be a sovereign remedy for disease.)
5. Cloth making in the Low Countries (here represented by Ypres and Ghent) was of high repute.
6. The medieval marriage ceremony was customarily performed by the priest on the church porch. Afterward the company entered the church to hear the nuptial mass.
7. She had crossed many a foreign river.
8. In Galicia (in Spain) at (the shrine of) St. James of Compostella, and at Cologne.

She coude° muchel of wandringe by the weye.° *knew / along the road(s)*
Gat-tothed° was she, soothly for to seye. *Gap-toothed*
Upon an amblere° esily° she sat, *saddle horse / comfortably*
Y-wimpled° wel, and on hir heed an hat *Covered with a wimple*
As brood as is a bokeler° or a targe;° *shields*
A foot-mantel° aboute hir hipes large, *outer skirt*
And on hir feet a paire of spores° sharpe. *spurs*
In felawschipe wel coude she laughe and carpe.° *talk*
Of remedyes of love she knew per chaunce,° *as it happened*
For she coude° of that art the olde daunce.° *knew / (steps of the) dance*
  A good man was ther of religioun,
And was a povre PERSOUN° of a toun, *poor parson*
But riche he was of holy thoght and werk.
He was also a lerned man, a clerk,° *scholar*
That Cristes gospel trewely wolde preche;
His parisshens° devoutly wolde he teche. *parishioners*
Benigne° he was, and wonder° diligent, *Kindly / very*
And in adversitee ful pacient,
And swich he was y-preved ofte sythes.[9]
Ful looth° were him to cursen° for his tithes, *loath / excommunicate*
But rather wolde he yeven,° out of doute,° *give / there is no doubt*
Unto his povre parisshens aboute
Of° his offring, and eek of his substaunce.° *From / income*
He coude in litel thing han suffisaunce.[1]
Wyd was his parisshe, and houses fer asonder,
But he ne lafte° nat, for reyn ne° thonder, *ceased / nor*
In siknes nor in meschief,° to visyte *misfortune*
The ferreste in his parisshe, muche and lyte,[2]
Upon his feet, and in his hand a staf.
This noble ensample° to his sheep he yaf,° *example / gave*
That first he wroghte,° and afterward he taughte. *did (what was right)*
Out of the gospel he tho° wordes caughte,° *those / took*
And this figure° he added eek therto, *metaphor, image*
That if gold ruste, what shal iren° do? *iron*
For if a preest be foul,° on whom we truste, *corrupted*
No wonder is a lewed man to ruste;[3]
And shame it is, if a preest take keep,° *heed (it)*
A shiten° shepherde and a clene sheep. *i.e., covered with excrement*
Wel oghte a preest ensample for to yive,° *give*
By his clennesse, how that his sheep sholde live.
He sette nat his benefice to hyre,[4]
And leet° his sheep encombred in the myre, *left*
And ran to London unto Seynte Poules° *St. Paul's Cathedral*
To seken him a chaunterie for soules,

9. And he was proved (to be) such many times.
1. He knew how to have enough in very little.
2. The farthest (members) of his parish, great and humble.
3. It is no wonder that an unlearned man (should go) to rust.
4. He did not hire out (i.e., engage a substitute for) his benefice (church appointment).

Or with a bretherhed to been withholde,[5]
But dwelte at hoom, and kepte° wel his folde, *took care of*
So that the wolf ne made it nat miscarie;° *come to harm*
He was a shepherde and noght a mercenarie.
And though he holy were, and vertuous,
He was to sinful men nat despitous,° *scornful*
Ne of his speche daungerous ne digne,° *haughty nor disdainful*
But in his teching discreet and benigne.
To drawen folk to heven by fairnesse,
By good ensample, this was his bisinesse;° *endeavor*
But it were° any persone obstinat, *were there*
What so° he were, of heigh or lough estat,° *Whatever / condition, class*
Him wolde he snibben° sharply for the nones.° *rebuke / on such an occasion*
A bettre preest I trowe° that nowher noon is. *believe*
He wayted after° no pompe and reverence, *looked for*
Ne maked him a spyced conscience,[6]
But Cristes lore,° and his apostles twelve, *teaching*
He taughte, and first he folwed it himselve.
  With him ther was a PLOWMAN, was his brother,
That hadde y-lad° of dong° ful many a fother.° *hauled / dung / cartload*
A trewe swinkere° and a good was he, *worker*
Livinge in pees° and parfit charitee. *peace*
God loved he best with al his hole° herte *whole*
At alle tymes, thogh him gamed or smerte,[7]
And thanne his neighebour right as himselve.
He wolde thresshe, and therto dyke° and delve,° *make ditches / dig*
For Cristes sake, for every povre wight,° *poor man*
Withouten hyre,° if it lay in his might.° *wages / power*
His tythes° payed he ful faire and wel, *tithes*
Bothe of his propre swink° and his catel.° *own work / possessions*
In a tabard° he rood upon a mere.° *smock / mare*
  Ther was also a Reve° and a Millere, *Reeve*
A Somnour° and a Pardoner also, *Summoner*
A Maunciple,° and myself—ther were namo.° *Manciple / no more*
  The MILLERE was a stout carl° for the nones;[8] *exceedingly strong man*
Ful big he was of brawn, and eek of bones—
That proved wel, for over al ther he cam,
At wrastling he wolde have alwey the ram.[9]
He was short-sholdred, brood, a thikke knarre:° *knotty fellow*
Ther nas no dore that he nolde heve of harre,[1]
Or breke it at a renning° with his heed. *(by butting it)*

5. To seek for himself an appointment as a chantry-priest singing masses for the souls of the dead or to be retained (as a chaplain) by a guild. (Both sorts of positions were relatively undemanding and paid enough for such a priest to retain a curate at home and have money to spare.)
6. Nor affected an overly scrupulous nature.
7. At all times, whether he was glad or in distress.
8. Here, a tag-ending, useful to fill out the line metrically but almost wholly devoid of meaning (cf. l. 523).
9. That (was) well proved, for everywhere he went, at wrestling contests he would always win the ram (a usual prize).
1. There was no door he wasn't willing to heave off (its) hinges.

His berd as any sowe or fox was reed,
And therto brood, as though it were a spade.
Upon the cop right° of his nose he hade — *very top*
A werte,° and theron stood a tuft of herys, — *wart*
Reed as the bristles of a sowes erys;° — *ears*
His nosethirles° blake were and wyde. — *nostrils*
A swerd and a bokeler° bar he by his syde. — *small shield*
His mouth as greet° was as a greet forneys;° — *large / furnace*
He was a janglere° and a goliardeys,° — *chatterer / teller of jests*
And that was most of sinne and harlotryes.° — *vulgarities*
Wel coude he stelen corn, and tollen thryes,[2]
And yet he hadde a thombe of gold, pardee.[3]
A whyt cote and a blew hood wered° he. — *wore*
A baggepype wel coude he blowe and sowne,° — *play*
And therwithal° he broghte us out of towne. — *with it*
  A gentil° MAUNCIPLE was ther of a temple,[4] — *worthy, proper*
Of which° achatours° mighte take exemple — *From whom / buyers*
For to be wyse in bying of vitaille,° — *provisions*
For whether that he payde, or took by taille,° — *on account*
Algate he wayted so in his achat[5]
That he was ay biforn° and in good stat. — *always ahead*
Now is nat that of God a ful fair grace,
That swich a lewed° mannes wit shal pace° — *unlearned / surpass*
The wisdom of an heep of lerned men?
Of maistres hadde he mo° than thryes ten — *more*
That weren of° lawe expert and curious,° — *in / skillful*
Of which° ther were a doseyn° in that hous — *Among whom / dozen*
Worthy to been stiwardes of rente° and lond — *income*
Of any lord that is in Engelond,
To make him live by his propre good° — *within his own income*
In honour, dettelees,° but° he were wood,° — *debtless / unless / mad*
Or live as scarsly as him list desire,[6]
And[7] able for to helpen al a shire° — *an entire county*
In any cas° that mighte falle° or happe; — *eventuality / befall*
And yit this maunciple sette hir aller cappe.° — *made fools of them all*
  The REVE was a sclendre colerik man.[8]
His berd was shave as ny° as ever he can; — *close*
His heer was by his eres° ful round y-shorn,° — *ears / cut off*
His top was dokked° lyk a preest biforn.° — *cut short / in front*
Ful longe were his legges, and ful lene,
Ylyk° a staf; ther was no calf y-sene.° — *Like / to be seen*

2. He knew well how to steal corn (grain) and take his toll (his percentage for grinding it) three times over.
3. The proverb "An honest miller hath a golden thumb" implies there are no honest millers; "pardee" is a weak form of "by God" (Fr. *par Dieu*), perhaps best translated simply as "I swear."
4. A manciple was in charge of purchasing provisions for a college or (as here) for an inn of court, where law was studied.
5. He was always so watchful in his purchasing.
6. Or live as frugally as it pleases him to wish.
7. The subject is again the "doseyn" men of l. 578 worthy to be stewards.
8. A reeve was manager and accountant of an estate or manor and was chosen from among the serfs. This one is choleric, i.e., dominated by the humor called choler (or yellow bile), and thus hot-tempered by nature.

Wel coude he kepe a gerner° and a binne— *granary*
Ther was noon auditour coude on him winne.° *catch him short*
Wel wiste° he by the droghte and by the reyn *knew*
The yeldinge of his seed and of his greyn.
His lordes sheep, his neet,° his dayerye,° *cattle / dairy cows*
His swyn, his hors, his stoor,° and his pultrye,° *livestock / poultry*
Was hoolly° in this reves governinge, *wholly*
And by his covenaunt° yaf° the rekeninge, *contract / (he) gave*
Sin that° his lord was twenty yeer of age. *Since*
Ther coude no man bringe him in arrerage.° *arrears*
Ther nas baillif, ne herde, ne other hyne,[9]
That he ne knew his sleighte° and his covyne;° *cunning / deceit*
They were adrad° of him as of the deeth.[1] *afraid*
His woning° was ful fair upon an heeth; *dwelling*
With grene trees shadwed was his place.
He coude bettre than his lord purchace.[2]
Ful riche he was astored prively;° *privately stocked*
His lord wel coude he plesen subtilly,
To yeve and lene him of his owne good,
And have a thank, and yet a cote and hood.[3]
In youthe he hadde lerned a good mister:° *trade*
He was a wel good wrighte,° a carpenter. *craftsman*
This reve sat upon a ful good stot° *farm horse*
That was al pomely° grey and highte° Scot. *dappled / named*
A long surcote° of pers° upon he hade, *outer coat / blue cloth*
And by his syde he bar° a rusty blade. *bore*
Of Northfolk° was this reve of which I tell, *Norfolk*
Bisyde° a toun men clepen° Baldeswelle. *(From) near / call*
Tukked° he was as is a frere° aboute; *Belted / friar*
And evere he rood the hindreste° of oure route.° *hindmost / company*
A SOMONOUR[4] was ther with us in that place,
That hadde a fyr-reed cherubinnes face,[5]
For sawcefleem° he was, with eyen° narwe. *pimpled / eyes*
As hoot° he was and lecherous as a sparwe,° *passionate / sparrow*
With scalled° browes blake and piled berd;° *scabby / scraggy beard*
Of his visage° children were aferd.° *face / afraid*
Ther nas quiksilver, litarge,° ne brimstoon, *lead oxide*
Boras,° ceruce,° ne oille° of tartre noon, *Borax / white lead / cream*
Ne oynement that wolde clense and byte,° *sting*
That him mighte helpen of° his whelkes° whyte, *cure / pimples*
Nor of the knobbes° sittinge on his chekes. *lumps*
Wel loved he garleek, oynons, and eek lekes,° *leeks*

9. There was no overseer, nor herdsman, nor (any) other servant.
1. Death in general, or perhaps the Black Death (plague).
2. He knew, better than his lord, how to increase one's possessions.
3. He knew well how to please his lord in sly ways, giving and lending to him from his (the lord's) own resources, and earn thanks (for it) and a coat and hood besides.
4. A summoner was an officer who cited ("summoned") malefactors to appear before an ecclesiastical court: in this case, an archdeacon's, having jurisdiction over matrimonial cases, adultery, and fornication.
5. Cherubim, the second order of angels, were sometimes painted brilliant red ("fire-red") in medieval art. The summoner resembles them, not through beatitude but through a skin disease.

And for to drinken strong wyn, reed as blood.
Thanne wolde he speke, and crye° as° he were wood;° *shout / as if / mad*
And whan that he wel dronken hadde the wyn,
Thanne wolde he speke no word but Latyn.° *(in) Latin*
A fewe termes° hadde he, two or three, *technical phrases*
That he had lerned out of som decree—
No wonder is,° he herde it al the day; *it is*
And eek ye knowen wel how that a jay° *a chattering bird*
Can clepen "Watte" as well as can the Pope.[6]
But whoso coude in other thing him grope,° *question*
Thanne hadde he spent° al his philosophye; *exhausted*
Ay *"Questio quid iuris"* wolde he crye.[7]
He was a gentil° harlot° and a kinde;° *worthy / rascal / natural one*
A bettre felawe° sholde men noght finde: *companion*
He wolde suffre,° for a quart of wyn, *allow*
A good felawe to have his concubyn
A° twelf-month, and excuse him atte fulle;° *(For) a / fully*
Ful prively a finch eek coude he pulle.[8]
And if he fond° owher° a good felawe, *found / anywhere*
He wolde techen him to have non awe° *fear*
In swich cas of the erchedeknes curs,[9]
But-if° a mannes soule were in his purs, *Unless*
For in his purs he sholde y-punisshed be.
"Purs is the erchedeknes helle," seyde he.
But wel I woot° he lyed right in dede: *know*
Of cursing oghte ech gilty man him drede—
For curs wol slee, right as assoilling saveth—
And also war him of a *significavit*.[1]
In daunger° hadde he at° his owene gyse° *his power / in / way*
The yonge girles° of the diocyse, *wenches*
And knew hir counseil,° and was al hir reed.° *their secrets / adviser to them all*
A gerland° hadde he set upon his heed, *garland*
As greet as it were for an ale-stake;° *tavern sign*
A bokeler° hadde he maad him of a cake.° *shield / round bread*
  With him ther rood a gentil PARDONER[2]
Of Rouncival,[3] his freend and his compeer,° *companion*
That streight was comen fro the court of Rome.
Ful loude he song,° "Com hider,° love, to me." *sang / hither*
This somnour bar to° him a stif burdoun,° *accompanied / sturdy bass*
Was nevere trompe° of half so greet a soun.° *trumpet / sound*
This pardoner hadde heer° as yelow as wex,° *hair / wax*

6. Knows how to say the word "Walter" as well as does the Pope.
7. He would always cry, "The question is, what point of law applies?"
8. He was skilled in secretly seducing girls. ("To pull a finch," i.e., to pluck a bird, was an obscene expression.)
9. Curse, the power of excommunication.
1. Every guilty man ought to be fearful of excommunication, for it will slay (the soul eternally), just as absolution (the forgiveness granted through the sacrament of penance) saves—and (he ought) also to beware a *significavit* (a writ of arrest).
2. A pardoner was a seller of papal indulgences (remissions of punishment for sin), whose proceeds were often intended to build or support a religious house. Many pardoners were fraudulent, and their abuses were much criticized.
3. Near Charing Cross in London.

But smothe it heng,° as dooth a strike of flex;° *hung / bunch of flax*
By ounces° henge his lokkes that he hadde, *In thin strands*
And therwith° he his shuldres overspradde;° *with it / covered*
But thinne it lay, by colpons° oon and oon; *in small bunches*
But hood, for jolitee,° wered° he noon, *sportiveness / wore*
For it was trussed° up in his walet.° *packed / pouch*
Him thoughte he rood al of the newe jet;
Dischevele, save his cappe, he rood al bare.[4]
Swiche glaringe eyen° hadde he as an hare. *staring eyes*
A vernicle[5] hadde he sowed on his cappe.
His walet lay biforn° him in his lappe, *in front of*
Bretful of pardoun comen from Rome al hoot.[6]
A voys he hadde as smal as hath a goot.° *goat*
No berd hadde he, ne nevere sholde have,
As smothe it was as it were late shave.° *recently shaved*
I trowe° he were a gelding or a mare. *believe*
But of his craft, fro Berwik into Ware,° *i.e., from north to south*
Ne was ther swich another pardoner.
For in his male° he hadde a pilwe-beer,° *bag / pillowcase*
Which that he seyde was Oure Lady veyl.° *Our Lady's veil*
He seyde he hadde a gobet° of the seyl° *piece / sail*
That seynt Peter hadde, whan that he wente° *walked*
Upon the see, til Jesu Christ him hente.° *took hold of*
He hadde a croys° of latoun,° ful of stones,° *cross / metal / gems*
And in a glas° he hadde pigges bones. *glass container*
But with thise relikes,° whan that he fond *relics*
A povre person dwellinge upon lond,[7]
Upon a° day he gat him more moneye *In one*
Than that the person gat in monthes tweye.° *two*
And thus, with feyned flaterye and japes,° *tricks*
He made the person and the peple his apes.° *fools*
But trewely to tellen, atte laste,° *after all*
He was in chirche a noble ecclesiaste.° *preacher*
Wel coude he rede a lessoun or a storie,° *religious tale*
But alderbest° he song° an offertorie; *best of all / sang*
For wel he wiste,° whan that song was songe, *knew*
He moste preche, and wel affyle° his tonge *make smooth*
To winne silver, as he ful wel coude—
Therefore he song the murierly° and loude. *more merrily*
Now have I told you soothly, in a clause,° *briefly*
Th'estaat, th'array, the nombre, and eek the cause
Why that assembled was this compaignye
In Southwerk, at this gentil° hostelrye *worthy*
That highte° the Tabard, faste° by the Belle.° *was called / close / Bell Inn*
But now is tyme to yow for to telle

4. It seemed to him he rode in the very latest fashion; (his hair) loose, he rode bareheaded except for his cap.
5. A copy of the veil St. Veronica gave to Christ when he was carrying the cross, that he might wipe his brow; it received the imprint of Christ's face.
6. Brimful of pardons, come all hot (fresh) from Rome.
7. A poor parson living in the country.

How that we baren us° that ilke° night, *conducted ourselves / same*
Whan we were in that hostelrye alight;° *alighted*
And after wol I telle of our viage,° *journey*
And al the remenaunt° of oure pilgrimage. *remainder*
But first I pray yow, of youre curteisye,
That ye n'arette it nat my vileinye,[8]
Thogh that° I pleynly speke in this matere, *Even though*
To tell yow hir° wordes and hir chere,° *their / behavior*
Ne thogh I speke hir wordes properly.° *exactly*
For this ye knowen al so wel as I:
Whoso shal telle a tale after a man,[9]
He moot reherce° as ny° as evere he can *must repeat / closely*
Everich a word, if it be in his charge,
Al speke he never so rudeliche and large;[1]
Or elles° he moot° telle his tale untrewe, *else / may*
Or feyne thing,° or finde wordes newe. *invent something*
He may nat spare,° althogh he[2] were his brother; *hold back*
He moot° as wel seye o° word as another. *must / one*
Crist spak himself ful brode° in Holy Writ, *broadly*
And wel ye woot,° no vileinye° is it. *know / churlishness*
Eek Plato seith, whoso can him rede,
The wordes mote be cosin° to the dede. *cousin*
Also I prey yow to foryeve° it me, *forgive*
Al have I nat set folk in hir degree[3]
Here in this tale, as that they sholde stonde;
My wit is short, ye may wel understonde.
  Greet chere made oure Hoste us everichon,[4]
And to the soper sette he us anon;° *immediately*
He served us with vitaille° at the beste. *victuals*
Strong was the wyn, and wel to drinke us leste.° *it pleased us*
A semely° man oure hoste was withalle *suitable*
For to been a marshal in an halle;[5]
A large man he was with eyen stepe°— *protruding eyes*
A fairer burgeys° was ther noon in Chepe.° *citizen / Cheapside (in London)*
Bold of his speche, and wys, and wel y-taught,
And of manhod him lakkede° right naught. *he lacked*
Eek therto he was right° a mery man, *truly*
And after soper pleyen° he bigan, *to jest*
And spak of mirthe amonges othere thinges—
Whan that we hadde maad oure rekeninges°— *paid our bills*
And seyde thus: "Now, lordinges, trewely,
Ye been° to me right welcome hertely.° *are / heartily*
For by my trouthe, if that I shal nat lye,
I saugh nat this yeer so mery a compaignye

8. That you do not attribute it to my churlishness.
9. I.e., repeats another man's story.
1. Every word, if that be the responsibility he's charged with, however roughly and broadly he (may) speak.
2. I.e., the original teller.
3. Although I haven't described (these) people in (the order of) their social rank.
4. Our host made great welcome to every one of us.
5. I.e., the officer in charge of the serving of meals and banquets in a great hall.

Atones° in this herberwe° as is now. — *At one time / inn*
Fayn wolde I doon yow mirthe, wiste I how,
And of a mirthe I am right now bithoght,[6]
To doon yow ese,° and it shal coste noght. — *give you pleasure*
Ye goon° to Caunterbury—God yow spede; — *are going*
The blisful martir quyte° yow your mede.° — *pay / reward*
And wel I woot, as ye goon by the weye,
Ye shapen yow to talen and to pleye;[7]
For trewely, confort° ne mirthe is noon° — *pleasure / (there) is none*
To ryde by the weye doumb as a stoon;
And therfore wol I maken yow disport,° — *amusement*
As I seyde erst,° and doon yow som confort. — *before*
And if yow lyketh° alle, by oon° assent, — *it pleases you / one*
Now for to stonden at° my jugement, — *abide by*
And for to werken° as I shal yow seye, — *do*
To-morwe, whan ye ryden by the weye—
Now by my fader° soule that is deed— — *father's*
But° ye be merye, I wol yeve° yow myn heed.° — *Unless / give / head*
Hold up youre hondes, withouten more speche."
Oure counseil° was nat longe for to seche;° — *decision / seek*
Us thoughte it was noght worth to make it wys,[8]
And graunted him withouten more avys,° — *further consideration*
And bad him seye his voirdit° as him leste.° — *verdict / it pleased him*
"Lordinges," quod° he, "now herkneth° for the beste, — *said / listen*
But tak it nought, I prey yow, in desdeyn.° — *disdain*
This is the poynt, to speken short and pleyn:
That ech of yow, to shorte with° oure weye, — *with which to shorten*
In this viage° shal telle tales tweye° — *journey / two*
To Caunterbury-ward,° I mene° it so, — *Toward Canterbury / intend*
And homward he shal tellen othere two,
Of aventures that whylom° han bifalle. — *once upon a time*
And which° of yow that bereth° him best of alle, — *whichever / conducts*
That is to seyn, that telleth in this cas° — *on this occasion*
Tales of best sentence° and most solas,° — *wisdom, instruction / delight*
Shal have a soper at oure aller cost° — *the expense of us all*
Here in this place, sittinge by this post,° — *column*
Whan that we come agayn fro Caunterbury.
And for to make yow the more mery,° — *merry*
I wol myselven goodly° with yow ryde, — *gladly*
Right at myn owne cost, and be youre gyde.
And whoso wole my jugement withseye° — *oppose*
Shal paye al that we spenden by the weye.
And if ye vouchesauf° that it be so, — *grant*
Tel me anon,° withouten wordes mo,° — *immediately / more*
And I wol erly shape me° therfore." — *prepare myself*
This thing was graunted, and oure othes° swore° — *oaths / sworn*

6. I would gladly make you (some) amusement if I knew how, and I have just now thought of some fun.
7. You plan to tell tales and to play.
8. It seemed to us (that) it was not worth pondering over.

With ful glad herte, and preyden° him also *we begged*
That he wolde vouchesauf for° to do so, *grant*
And that he wolde been oure governour
And of oure tales juge and reportour,° *referee(?)*
And sette a soper at a certeyn prys;° *price*
And we wol reuled been at his devys° *desire, will*
In heigh and lowe;° and thus, by oon assent, *In all respects*
We been acorded to his jugement.
And therupon the wyn was fet° anon;° *fetched / at once*
We dronken, and to reste wente echon,° *each one*
Withouten any lenger taryinge.
  Amorwe,° whan that day bigan to springe, *In the morning*
Up roos oure Host and was oure aller cok,[9]
And gadrede° us togidre,° alle in a flok; *gathered / together*
And forth we riden,° a° litel more than pas,° *rode / at a / walking speed*
Unto the watering of Seint Thomas,[1]
And there oure Host bigan his hors areste,° *stopped his horse*
And seyde, "Lordinges, herkneth, if yow leste.° *it may please*
Ye woot° youre forward,° and I it yow recorde.° *know / agreement / recall*
If even-song and morwe-song° acorde, *morning song*
Lat se° now who shal telle the firste tale. *Let us see*
As evere mote° I drinke wyn or ale, *may*
Whoso be rebel to my jugement
Shal paye for al that by the weye is spent.
Now draweth cut,° er that we ferrer twinne;° *lots, cut straws / go farther*
He which that hath the shortest shal biginne.
Sire Knight," quod he, "my maister and my lord,
Now draweth cut for that is myn acord.° *decision*
Cometh neer,"° quod he, "my lady Prioresse; *nearer*
And ye, sire Clerk, lat be° youre shamfastnesse,° *leave off / shyness*
Ne studieth° noght. Ley hond to, every man!" *deliberate*
Anon° to drawen every wight° bigan, *At once / person*
And shortly for to tellen as it was,
Were it by aventure,° or sort,° or cas,° *chance / fate / fortune*
The sothe° is this, the cut fil° to the Knight, *truth / fell*
Of which ful blythe and glad was every wight;
And telle he moste° his tale, as was resoun,° *must / right*
By forward° and by composicioun,° *agreement / arrangement*
As ye han herd. What nedeth wordes mo?° *more*
And whan this gode man saugh it was so,
As he that wys was and obedient
To kepe his forward by his free assent,
He seyde: "Sin° I shal biginne the game, *Since*
What,° welcome be the cut, a Goddes° name! *Why / in God's*
Now lat us ryde, and herkneth what I seye."
And with that word we riden° forth oure weye; *rode*
And he bigan with right a mery chere° *in a very merry mood*
His tale anon, and seyde as ye may heere.

9. The rooster who wakened us all.
1. St. Thomas a Watering was a brook two miles from London on the Canterbury road.

The Knight's Tale

PART ONE

Whylom,° as olde stories tellen us, *Once, formerly*
Ther was a duk that highte° Theseus; *was called*
Of Athenes he was lord and governour,
And in his tyme swich° a conquerour, *such*
That gretter was ther noon under the sonne.
Ful many a riche contree hadde he wonne;
What with his wisdom and his chivalrye,° *knightly prowess*
He conquered al the regne° of Femenye,[1] *kingdom, realm*
That whylom was y-cleped° Scithia, *called*
And weddede the quene Ipolita,° *Hippolyta*
And broghte hire hoom with him in his contree
With muchel glorie and greet solempnitee,° *pomp, ceremony*
And eek hire yonge suster Emelye.
And thus with victorie and with melodye
Lete I this noble duk to Athenes ryde,
And al his hoost, in armes, him bisyde.
And certes,° if it nere° to long to here, *certainly / were not*
I wolde have told yow fully the manere
How wonnen was the regne of Femenye
By Theseus and by his chivalrye;° *host of knights*
And of the grete bataille for the nones° *occasion, purpose*
Bitwixen Athenës and Amazones;
And how asseged° was Ipolita, *besieged*
The faire hardy quene of Scithia;
And of the feste that was at hir° weddinge, *their*
And of the tempest at hir hoomcominge;
But al that thing I moot° as now° forbere. *must / at this time*
I have, God woot,° a large feeld to ere,° *knows / harrow, plow*
And wayke° been the oxen in my plough. *weak*
The remenant of the tale is long ynough.
I wol nat letten° eek noon of this route;° *hinder / company*
Lat every felawe telle his tale aboute,° *in turn*
And lat see now who shall the soper winne;
And ther° I lefte, I wol ageyn biginne. *where*
This duk, of whom I make mencioun,
When he was come almost unto the toun,
In al his wele° and in his moste pryde, *success, happiness*
He was war,° as he caste his eye asyde, *aware*
Where that ther kneled in the hye weye
A companye of ladies, tweye and tweye,° *two by two*
Ech after other clad in clothes blake;
But swich a cry and swich a wo they make,
That in this world nis° creature livinge *(there) is not*
That herde swich another weymentinge;° *lamenting*

1. The country of the Amazons.

And of this cry they nolde° nevere stenten,° *would not / cease*
Til they the reynes of his brydel henten.° *seized*
"What folk ben ye, that at myn hoomcominge
Perturben so my feste with cryinge?"
Quod Theseus. "Have ye so greet envye
Of myn honour, that° thus compleyne and crye? *that ye*
Or who hath yow misboden° or offended? *insulted, harmed*
And telleth me if it may been amended,
And why that ye ben clothed thus in blak."
The eldeste lady of hem alle spak,
When she hadde swowned° with a deedly chere° *fainted / deathly appearance*
That it was routhe° for to seen and here. *a pity*
She seyde: "Lord, to whom Fortune hath yiven° *given*
Victorie, and as a conquerour to liven,
Noght greveth us° youre glorie and youre honour; *We do not resent*
But we biseken° mercy and socour.° *beseech / aid, comfort*
Have mercy on oure wo and oure distresse.
Som drope of pitee, thurgh thy gentillesse,
Upon us wrecched wommen lat thou falle.
For certes, lord, ther nis noon of us alle,
That she ne hath been a duchesse or a quene;
Now be we caitifs,° as it is wel sene, *wretches*
Thanked be Fortune and hire false wheel,
That noon estat assureth to be weel.[2]
And certes, lord, to abyden° your presence, *await*
Here in this temple of the goddesse Clemence° *Mercy*
We han ben waytinge al this fourtenight;° *fourteen nights*
Now help us, lord, sith° it is in thy might. *since*
I, wrecche, which that wepe and waille thus,
Was whylom° wyf to king Capaneus, *once*
That starf° at Thebes—cursed be that day! *died*
And alle we that been in this array° *condition*
And maken al this lamentacioun,
We losten alle oure housbondes at that toun,
Whyl that the sege° theraboute lay. *siege*
And yet now the olde Creon, weylaway,° *alas*
That lord is now of Thebes the citee,
Fulfild° of ire and of iniquitee, *Filled full*
He, for despyt° and for his tirannye, *malice, spite*
To do the dede bodyes vileinye,° *outrage*
Of alle oure lordes whiche that ben y-slawe,° *slain*
Hath alle the bodyes on an heep y-drawe,° *dragged*
And wol nat suffren° hem, by noon assent,° *allow / on any terms*
Neither to been y-buried nor y-brent,° *burned*
But maketh houndes ete hem in despyt."
And with that word, withouten more respyt,° *further delay*
They fillen gruf° and cryden pitously, *fell facedown*
"Have on us wrecched wommen som mercy,
And lat oure sorwe sinken in thyn herte."

2. Who ensures that no estate will be (permanently) in prosperity.

This gentil duk doun from his courser sterte° *leaped*
With herte pitous,° whan he herde hem speke. *pitying, merciful*
Him thoughte° that his herte wolde breke, *It seemed to him*
Whan he saugh hem so pitous° and so mat,° *pitiable / dejected*
That whylom° weren of so greet estat. *formerly*
And in his armes he hem alle up hente,° *took*
And hem conforteth in ful good entente;
And swoor his ooth, as he was trewe knight,
He wolde doon so ferforthly° his might *exert to such an extent*
Upon the tyraunt Creon hem to wreke,° *avenge*
That al the peple of Grece sholde speke
How Creon was of° Theseus y-served,° *by / treated*
As he that hadde his deeth ful wel deserved.
And right anoon, withouten more abood,° *delay*
His baner he desplayeth, and forth rood
To Thebes-ward,° and al his host bisyde.° *Toward Thebes / with him*
No neer° Athenës wolde he go° ne ryde, *nearer / walk*
Ne take his ese fully half a day,
But onward on his wey that night he lay,° *lodged*
And sente anoon° Ipolita the quene *at once*
And Emelye, hir yonge suster shene,° *bright, fair*
Unto the toun of Athenës to dwelle;
And forth he rit;° ther is namore to telle. *rides*
The rede statue° of Mars, with spere and targe,° *red image / shield*
So shyneth in his whyte baner large,
That alle the feeldes gliteren up and doun;
And by his baner born is his penoun° *pennant*
Of gold ful riche, in which ther was y-bete° *embroidered*
The Minotaur, which that he slough° in Crete. *slew*
Thus rit this duk, thus rit this conquerour,
And in his host of chivalrye the flour,° *the flower of knighthood*
Til that he cam to Thebes, and alighte° *alighted*
Faire in a feeld, ther as° he thoghte to fighte. *where*
But shortly for to speken of this thing,
With Creon, which that was of Thebes king,
He faught, and slough him manly° as a knight *in a manly fashion, boldly*
In pleyn° bataille, and putte the folk to flight; *open*
And by assaut° he wan° the citee after, *assault / conquered*
And rente° adoun bothe wal and sparre° and rafter; *tore / beam*
And to the ladyes he restored agayn
The bones of hir housbondes that were slayn,
To doon obsequies, as was tho° the gyse.° *then / custom*
But it were al to longe for to devyse° *tell, describe*
The grete clamour and the waymentinge° *lamentation*
That the ladyes made at the brenninge° *burning*
Of the bodyes, and the grete honour
That Theseus, the noble conquerour,
Doth to the ladyes, whan they from him wente;
But shortly for to telle is myn entente.
Whan that this worthy duk, this Theseus,
Hath Creon slayn and wonne Thebes thus,

Stille in that feeld he took al night his reste,
And dide with al the contree as him leste.° *as it pleased him*
To ransake in the tas° of bodyes dede, *pile, heap*
Hem for to strepe° of harneys° and of wede,° *strip / armor / clothing*
The pilours° diden bisinesse and cure° *pillagers / worked busily and carefully*
After the bataille and disconfiture.° *defeat*
And so bifel,° that in the tas they founde, *it happened*
Thurgh-girt° with many a grevous blody wounde, *Pierced through*
Two yonge knightes ligginge° by and by,° *lying / side by side*
Bothe in oon armes,[3] wroght° ful richely, *made*
Of whiche two, Arcita highte that oon,
And that other knight highte Palamon.
Nat fully quike° ne fully dede they were, *alive*
But by hir cote-armures[4] and by hir gere° *accoutrements*
The heraudes° knew hem best in special° *heralds / especially well*
As they that weren of the blood royal
Of Thebes, and of sustren° two y-born. *sisters*
Out of the tas the pilours han hem torn,
And han hem caried softe° unto the tente *gently*
Of Theseus, and he ful sone hem sente
To Athenës, to dwellen in prisoun
Perpetuelly: he nolde no raunsoun.° *would not (accept) ransom*
And whan this worthy duk hath thus y-don,
He took his host, and hoom he rit anon
With laurer° crowned as a conquerour; *laurel*
And there he liveth in joye and in honour
Terme° of his lyf; what nedeth wordes mo?° *The remainder / more*
And in a tour,° in angwish and in wo, *tower*
Dwellen this Palamoun and eek Arcite
For everemore; ther may no gold hem quyte.° *ransom*
This passeth yeer by yeer and day by day,
Til it fil° ones, in a morwe° of May, *befell, happened / morning*
That Emelye, that fairer was to sene° *see*
Than is the lilie upon his° stalke grene, *its*
And fressher than the May with floures newe—
For with the rose colour stroof° hire hewe,° *strove / hue, complexion*
I noot° which was the fairer of hem two— *know not*
Er° it were day, as was hir wone° to do, *Before / wont, custom*
She was arisen and al redy dight,° *promptly dressed*
For May wole have no slogardye° a-night.° *laziness / at night*
The sesoun priketh° every gentil herte, *incites, rouses*
And maketh him out of his sleep to sterte,° *start, wake up*
And seith "Arys, and do thyn observaunce."
This maked Emelye have remembraunce
To doon honour to May, and for to ryse.
Y-clothed was she fresh, for to devyse:° *as I may tell*
Hir yelow heer was broyded° in a tresse *braided*
Bihinde hir bak, a yerde long, I gesse.

3. Having the same coat of arms.
4. Coat-armor: a vest displaying a knight's heraldic emblems that is worn over armor.

And in the gardin, at the sonne upriste,° *sun's uprising*
She walketh up and doun, and as hire liste° *it pleased her*
She gadereth floures, party° whyte and rede, *particolored*
To make a sotil° gerland for hire hede, *skillfully woven*
And as an aungel hevenysshly she song.
  The grete tour, that was so thikke and strong,
Which of the castel was the chief dongeoun
(Theras the knightes weren in prisoun,
Of whiche I tolde yow and tellen shal),
Was evene joynant to° the gardin wal *directly adjoining*
Ther as this Emelye hadde hir pleyinge.° *amusement*
Bright was the sonne and cleer that morweninge,
And Palamon, this woful prisoner,
As was his wone, by leve° of his gayler,° *permission, leave / jailer*
Was risen and romed in a chambre on heigh,
In which he al the noble citee seigh,° *saw*
And eek the gardin, ful of braunches grene,
Theras this fresshe Emelye the shene° *bright, beautiful*
Was in hire walk, and romed up and doun.
This sorweful prisoner, this Palamoun,
Goth in the chambre rominge to and fro,
And to himself compleyninge of his wo.
That he was born, ful ofte he seyde, "Alas!"
And so bifel, by aventure° or cas,° *chance / accident*
That thurgh a window, thikke of° many a barre *thickset with*
Of yren greet and square° as any sparre,° *sturdy / beam*
He caste his eye upon Emelya,
And therwithal he bleynte° and cryde "A!" *flinched*
As though he stongen were unto the herte.
And with that cry Arcite anon up sterte
And seyde, "Cosin myn, what eyleth° thee, *ails*
That art so pale and deedly° on to see?° *deathly / to look at*
Why crydestow?° Who hath thee doon offence? *didst thou cry*
For Goddes love, tak al in pacience
Oure prisoun, for it may non other be;° *may not be otherwise*
Fortune hath yeven° us this adversitee. *given*
Som wikke aspect or disposicioun
Of Saturne, by sum constellacioun,
Hath yeven us this, although we hadde it sworn:[5]
So stood the hevene whan that we were born.
We moste endure it; this is the short and pleyn."
  This Palamon answerde and seyde ageyn,° *in reply*
"Cosyn, for sothe,° of this opinioun *in truth*
Thou hast a veyn imaginacioun.° *foolish, mistaken idea*
This prison caused me nat for to crye,
But I was hurt right now thurghout myn yë° *eye*
Into myn herte, that wol my bane° be. *destruction*
The fairnesse of that lady that I see

5. Some ill-omened aspect or disposition of Saturn, in relation to the other stars, has given us this (adversity), no matter what we might have done.

Yond° in the gardin romen to and fro *Yonder*
Is cause of al my crying and my wo.
I noot wher° she be womman or goddesse, *do not know whether*
But Venus is it soothly, as I gesse."
And therwithal on kneës doun he fil,° *fell*
And seyde: "Venus, if it be thy wil
Yow° in this gardin thus to transfigure *Yourself*
Bifore me, sorweful wrecched creature,
Out of this prisoun help that we may scapen.° *escape*
And if so be my destinee be shapen° *shaped, determined*
By eterne° word to dyen in prisoun, *eternal*
Of oure linage have som compassioun,
That is so lowe y-broght by tirannye."
And with that word Arcite gan° espye *did*
Wher as this lady romed to and fro;
And with that sighte hir beautee hurte him so,
That, if that Palamon was wounded sore,
Arcite is hurt as muche as he, or more.
And with a sigh he seyde pitously:
"The fresshe beautee sleeth° me sodeynly *slays*
Of hire that rometh in the yonder place;
And, but° I have hir mercy and hir grace, *unless*
That I may seen hire atte leeste weye,° *at least*
I nam but deed;° ther nis namore to seye." *I am (not) but dead*
This Palamon, whan he tho° wordes herde, *those*
Dispitously° he loked and answerde: *Angrily*
"Whether seistow° this in ernest or in pley?" *sayest thou*
"Nay," quod Arcite, "in ernest, by my fey!° *faith*
God help me so, me list ful yvele pleye."° *I have no desire to jest*
This Palamon gan knitte his browes tweye:
"It nere,"° quod he, "to thee no greet honour *were not*
For to be fals, ne for to be traytour
To me, that am thy cosin and thy brother
Y-sworn ful depe,[6] and ech of us til° other, *to the*
That nevere, for to dyen in the peyne,[7]
Til that the deeth departe° shal us tweyne,° *part / two*
Neither of us in love to hinder other,
Ne in non other cas, my leve° brother; *dear*
But that thou sholdest trewely forthren° me *assist*
In every cas, as I shal forthren thee.
This was thyn ooth, and myn also, certeyn;
I wot right wel, thou darst° it nat withseyn.° *darest / deny*
Thus artow of my counseil,° out of doute,° *in on my secrets / beyond doubt*
And now thou woldest falsly been aboute° *set about*
To love my lady, whom I love and serve,
And evere shal til that myn herte sterve.° *die*
Now certes,° false Arcite, thou shalt nat so. *surely*
I loved hire first, and tolde thee my wo

6. I.e., deeply sworn to you in blood-brotherhood.
7. Even should it mean death by torture.

As to my counseil° and my brother sworn *confidant*
To forthre me, as I have told biforn.
For which thou art y-bounden as a knight
To helpen me, if it lay in thy might,
Or elles artow fals, I dar wel seyn."
  This Arcite ful proudly spak ageyn:° *in reply*
"Thou shalt," quod he, "be rather° fals than I; *sooner*
But thou art fals, I telle thee outrely;° *plainly*
For paramour° I loved hire first er thow. *With passionate love*
What wiltow seyn? Thou woost° nat yet now *knowest*
Whether she be a womman or goddesse!
Thyn is affeccioun of° holinesse, *pertaining to*
And myn is love, as to a creature;
For which I tolde thee myn aventure
As to my cosin and my brother sworn.
I pose° that thou lovedest hire biforn:° *I put the case (hypothetically) / first*
Wostow° nat wel the olde clerkes sawe,° *Knowest thou / saying*
That 'who shal yeve° a lovere any lawe?' *give*
Love is a gretter lawe, by my pan,° *brainpan, skull*
Than may be yeve to any erthly man.
And therefore positif lawe[8] and swich decree
Is broken al day° for love in ech degree.° *every day / every social rank*
A man moot nedes love, maugree his heed.[9]
He may nat fleen° it, thogh he sholde be deed, *flee, escape*
Al be she° mayde or widwe or elles wyf. *Whether she be*
And eek it is nat lykly al° thy lyf *during*
To stonden in hir grace; namore shal I;
For wel thou woost° thyselven verraily, *knowest*
That thou and I be dampned° to prisoun *condemned*
Perpetuelly; us gayneth° no raunsoun. *we shall gain*
We stryve as dide the houndes for the boon:° *bone*
They foughte al day, and yet hir part° was noon; *their share*
Ther cam a kyte,° whyl that they were so wrothe, *kite (bird)*
And bar awey the boon bitwixe hem bothe.
And therfore, at the kinges court, my brother,
Ech man for himself: ther is non other.° *no other way*
Love if thee list;° for I love and ay° shal; *if it pleases thee / always*
And soothly, leve° brother, this is al. *dear*
Here in this prisoun mote° we endure,° *must / remain*
And everich° of us take his aventure."° *each / what befalls him*
  Greet was the stryf and long bitwixe hem tweye,
If that I hadde leyser° for to seye, *leisure, opportunity*
But to th'effect.° It happed on a day, *outcome*
To telle it yow as shortly as I may,
A worthy duk that highte Perotheus,
That felawe° was unto duk Theseus *fellow, friend*
Sin° thilke day that they were children lyte,° *Since / little*
Was come to Athenes his felawe to visyte,

8. Laws made by man rather than natural law.
9. A man must necessarily love despite his intention (not to).

And for to pleye as he was wont to do;
For in this world he loved no man so,
And he loved him as tendrely ageyn.
So wel they lovede, as olde bokes seyn,
That whan that oon was deed, sothly to telle,
His felawe wente and soghte him doun in helle;
But of that story list me nat to wryte.
Duk Perotheus loved wel Arcite,
And hadde him knowe° at Thebes yeer by° yere; *known / after*
And fynally, at requeste and preyere
Of Perotheus, withouten any raunsoun,
Duk Theseus him leet out of prisoun
Freely to goon wher that him liste over al,° *anywhere it pleased him*
In swich a gyse° as I you tellen shal. *manner*
  This was the forward,° pleynly for t'endyte,° *agreement / write*
Bitwixen Theseus and him Arcite:
That if so were, that Arcite were y-founde
Evere in his lyf, by day or night, o stounde° *one moment*
In any contree of this Theseus,
And he were caught, it was acorded° thus, *agreed*
That with a swerd he sholde lese° his heed; *lose*
Ther nas non other remedye ne reed;° *option*
But taketh his leve, and homward he him spedde;
Let him be war, his nekke lyth to wedde.° *lies as a pledge*
  How greet a sorwe suffreth now Arcite!
The deeth he feleth thurgh his herte smyte;° *smite, strike*
He wepeth, wayleth, cryeth pitously;
To sleen himself he wayteth prively.[1]
He seyde, "Allas that day that I was born!
Now is my prison worse than biforn;
Now is me shape° eternally to dwelle *it is destined for me*
Noght in purgatorie but in helle.
Allas, that evere knew I Perotheus!
For elles hadde I dwelled with Theseus
Y-fetered° in his prisoun everemo. *Fettered, confined*
Than hadde I been in blisse, and nat in wo.
Only the sighte of hire whom that I serve,
Though that I nevere hir grace may deserve,
Wolde han suffised right ynough for me.
O dere cosin Palamon," quod he,
"Thyn is the victorie of this aventure:
Ful blisfully in prison maistow dure.° *endure, remain*
In prison? certes nay, but in paradys!
Wel hath Fortune y-turned thee the dys,° *dice*
That hast the sighte of hire, and I th'absence.
For possible is, sin° thou hast hire presence, *since*
And art a knight, a worthy and an able,
That by som cas,° sin Fortune is chaungeable, *case, chance*
Thou mayst to thy desyr somtyme atteyne.° *attain*

1. He secretly looks for a chance to slay himself.

But I, that am exyled and bareyne° *barren*
Of alle grace, and in so greet despeir
That ther nis erthe, water, fyr, ne eir,° *air*
Ne creature that of hem maked is
That may me helpe or doon confort in this,
Wel oughte I sterve° in wanhope° and distresse. *die / despair*
Farwel my lyf, my lust,° and my gladnesse! *joy*
  Allas, why pleynen° folk so in commune° *complain / commonly*
On purveyaunce° of God, or of Fortune, *About the providence*
That yeveth° hem ful ofte in many a gyse *gives*
Wel bettre than they can hemself devyse?
Som man desyreth for to han° richesse, *have*
That cause is of his mordre° or greet siknesse. *murder*
And som man wolde° out of his prison fayn,° *would be / gladly*
That in his hous is of his meynee° slayn. *household, retinue*
Infinite harmes been in this matere;
We witen° nat what thing we preyen° here. *know / pray for*
We faren° as he that dronke° is as a mous: *fare, behave / drunk*
A dronke man wot° wel he hath an hous, *knows*
But he noot° which the righte wey is thider; *does not know*
And to a dronke man the wey is slider.° *slippery*
And certes, in this world so faren we;
We seken faste° after felicitee, *seek steadily*
But we goon wrong ful often, trewely.
Thus may we seyen alle, and namely° I, *especially*
That wende° and hadde a greet opinioun *thought*
That if I mighte escapen from prisoun,
Than hadde I been in joye and perfit hele,° *perfect well-being*
Ther° now I am exyled fro my wele.° *Whereas / happiness*
Sin that I may nat seen yow, Emelye,
I nam but deed; ther nis no remedye."
  Upon that other syde Palamon,
Whan that he wiste° Arcite was agon,° *knew / gone*
Swich sorwe he maketh that the grete tour
Resouneth° of his youling° and clamour. *Resounds / howling*
The pure° fettres on his shines grete° *very / swollen shins*
Weren of his bittre salte teres wete.
"Allas!" quod he, "Arcita, cosin myn,
Of al our stryf, God woot, the fruyt is thyn.
Thow walkest now in Thebes at thy large,° *freely, at large*
And of my wo thou yevest litel charge.° *care, consideration*
Thou mayst, sin thou hast wisdom and manhede,° *manliness*
Assemblen alle the folk of our kinrede,° *kindred*
And make a werre° so sharp on this citee, *war*
That by som aventure, or some tretee,° *treaty, agreement*
Thou mayst have hir to lady and to wyf,
For whom that I moste nedes lese° my lyf. *lose*
For, as by wey of possibilitee,
Sith° thou art at thy large,° of prison free, *Since / at large*
And art a lord, greet is thyn avauntage
More than is myn, that sterve° here in a cage.° *die / prison*

For I mot wepe and wayle, whyl I live,
With al the wo that prison may me yive,
And eek with peyne that love me yiveth also,
That doubleth al my torment and my wo."
Therwith the fyr of jalousye up sterte
Withinne his brest, and hente° him by the herte — *seized*
So woodly,° that he lyk was to biholde — *madly*
The boxtree or the asshen° dede and colde. — *ashes*
Thanne seyde he: "O cruel goddes, that governe
This world with binding of youre word eterne,
And wryten in the table of athamaunt° — *adamant, hardest stone*
Your parlement° and youre eterne graunt,° — *decision / grant, decree*
What is mankinde more unto yow holde
Than is the sheep that rouketh in the folde?[2]
For slayn is man right as another beste,
And dwelleth eek in prison and areste,° — *arrest, detention*
And hath siknesse and greet adversitee,
And ofte tymes giltelees, pardee!° — *certainly*
What governaunce is in this prescience[3]
That giltelees tormenteth innocence?
And yet encreseth° this al my penaunce,° — *increases / suffering*
That man is bounden to his observaunce,° — *bound to the obligation*
For Goddes sake, to letten of° his wille, — *restrain*
Ther as° a beest may al his lust° fulfille. — *Whereas / desire*
And whan a beest is deed, he hath no peyne;
But man after his deeth moot wepe and pleyne,° — *lament, complain*
Though in this world he have care and wo.
Withouten doute it may stonden so.
The answere of this I lete° to divynis,° — *leave / theologians*
But wel I woot, that in this world gret pyne° is. — *suffering*
Allas! I see a serpent or a theef,
That many a trewe man hath doon mescheef,° — *harm*
Goon at his large, and where him list may turne.
But I mot° been in prison thurgh Saturne, — *must*
And eek thurgh Juno,[4] jalous and eek wood,° — *mad, angry*
That hath destroyed wel ny° al the blood — *near*
Of Thebes, with his waste° walles wyde. — *its wasted, destroyed*
And Venus sleeth° me on that other syde — *slays*
For jalousye, and fere of him Arcite."
Now wol I stinte° of Palamon a lyte,° — *cease (to tell) / little*
And lete him to his prison stille dwelle,
And of Arcita forth I wol yow telle.
The somer passeth, and the nightes longe
Encresen double wyse° the peynes stronge — *twofold*
Bothe of the lovere and the prisoner.
I noot° which hath the wofullere mester.° — *do not know / sadder situation*

2. In what way is mankind more highly valued by you than is the sheep that cowers in the fold?
3. What sort of governing purpose is there in such foreknowledge.
4. Through the influence of the planet Saturn, whose characteristic workings are enumerated in ll. 2453–69, and through the hostility toward Thebes of the goddess Juno, occasioned by Jove's several infidelities with Theban women.

For, shortly for to seyn, this Palamoun
Perpetuelly is dampned° to prisoun, *condemned*
In cheynes and in fettres to ben deed;
And Arcite is exyled upon his heed° *on pain of losing his head*
For evermo as out of that contree,
Ne neveremo ne shal his lady see.
Yow loveres axe° I now this questioun. *ask*
Who hath the worse, Arcite or Palamoun?
That oon may seen his lady day by day,
But in prison he moot dwelle alway.
That other wher him list may ryde or go,° *walk*
But seen his lady shal he neveremo.
Now demeth° as yow liste, ye that can,° *judge, decide / know how*
For I wol telle forth as I bigan.

PART TWO

Whan that Arcite to Thebes comen was,
Ful ofte a day he swelte° and seyde "allas," *fainted*
For seen his lady shal he neveremo.
And shortly to concluden° al his wo, *briefly to sum up*
So muche sorwe hadde nevere creature
That is, or shal,° whyl that the world may dure.° *shall (be) / endure*
His sleep, his mete,° his drink is him biraft,° *(appetite for) food / bereft*
That lene he wex and drye as is a shaft.[5]
His eyen holwe,° and grisly° to biholde; *hollow / horrible*
His hewe falow° and pale as asshen colde; *faded*
And solitarie he was and evere allone,
And waillinge al the night, makinge his mone.° *moan, lament*
And if he herde song or instrument,
Thanne wolde he wepe, he mighte nat be stent.° *stopped*
So feble eek were his spirits, and so lowe,
And chaunged so, that no man coude knowe
His speche nor his vois, though men it herde.
And in his gere° for al the world he ferde° *erratic behavior / fared*
Nat oonly lyk° the loveres maladye *like (one afflicted with)*
Of Hereos,[6] but rather lyk manye° *mania*
Engendred of humour malencolyk° *Born of the melancholic humor*
Biforen,° in his celle fantastyk.[7] *In the front (of the brain)*
And shortly, turned was al up so doun° *upside down*
Bothe habit° and eek disposicioun *outward form*
Of him, this woful lovere daun° Arcite. *sir, lord*
What sholde I al day of his wo endyte?° *write*
Whan he endured hadde a yeer or two
This cruel torment and this peyne and wo,
At Thebes, in his contree, as I seyde,

5. So that he became as thin and dry as the shaft of an arrow.
6. An illness caused by passionate love. Its symptoms, according to medieval medical authorities, are those attributed to Arcite in ll. 1356–71.
7. Medieval medicine divided the brain into three cells, the front one containing the imagination (fantasy), the middle cell judgment, the back cell memory. Mania was a disease of the imagination.

Upon a night, in sleep as he him leyde,° *laid*
Him thoughte how that the winged god Mercurie
Biforn him stood and bad° him to be murye.° *bade, requested / merry*
His slepy yerde° in hond he bar uprighte; *sleep-bringing wand*
An hat he werede° upon his heres° brighte. *wore / hair*
Arrayed was this god, as he took keep,° *as (Arcite) took note*
As he was whan that Argus[8] took his sleep;
And seyde him thus: "To Athenes shaltou° wende: *shalt thou*
Ther is thee shapen° of thy wo an ende." *destined, determined*
And with that word Arcite wook° and sterte.° *woke / gave a start*
"Now trewely, how° sore that me smerte,"° *however / it may hurt me*
Quod he, "to Athenes right now wol I fare;
Ne for the drede of deeth shal I nat spare° *refrain*
To see my lady, that I love and serve.
In hire presence I recche° nat to sterve."° *care / if I die*
  And with that word he caughte° a greet mirour, *seized*
And saugh° that chaunged was al his colour, *saw*
And saugh his visage al in another kinde.° *totally altered*
And right anoon it ran him in his minde,
That, sith his face was so disfigured
Of maladye,° the which he hadde endured, *By illness*
He mighte wel, if that he bar him lowe,° *behaved humbly*
Live in Athenes everemore unknowe,° *unknown*
And seen his lady wel ny° day by day. *nearly*
And right anon he chaunged his array,
And cladde him as a povre° laborer, *poor*
And al allone, save° oonly a squyer *except for*
That knew his privetee° and al his cas,° *private affairs / condition*
Which° was disgysed povrely as he was, *Who*
To Athenes is he goon the nexte° way. *nearest*
And to the court he wente upon a day,
And at the gate he profreth his servyse
To drugge° and drawe,° what so men wol devyse.° *drudge / carry / require*
And shortly of this matere for to seyn,
He fil in office° with a chamberleyn, *got a job*
The which that dwelling was with Emelye;
For he was wys, and coude soone aspye° *discover*
Of every servaunt, which that serveth here.° *her*
Wel coude he hewen° wode and water bere, *cut*
For he was yong and mighty for the nones,° *occasion, purpose*
And therto he was strong and big of bones
To doon that° any wight can him devyse. *what*
A yeer or two he was in this servyse,
Page of the chambre of Emelye the brighte;
And Philostrate he seide that he highte.° *was named*
But half so wel biloved a man as he
Ne was ther nevere in court of his degree;° *social position*
He was so gentil of condicioun° *disposition*

8. Argus, the monster with a hundred eyes, had likewise been put to sleep by Mercury.

That thurghout al the court was his renoun.
They seyden that it were° a charitee — *would be*
That Theseus wolde enhauncen his degree° — *improve his rank*
And putten him in worshipful° servyse, — *honorable*
Ther as he mighte his vertu° excercyse. — *natural ability*
And thus withinne a whyle his name is spronge,° — *sprung up, become known*
Bothe of his dedes and his goode tonge,
That Theseus hath taken him so neer° — *so near (to himself)*
That of his chambre he made him a squyer,
And gaf him gold to mayntene his degree;
And eek men broghte him out of his contree
From yeer to yeer, ful prively, his rente;° — *income*
But honestly° and slyly° he it spente, — *fittingly / discreetly*
That no man wondred how that he it hadde.
And three yeer in this wyse° his lyf he ladde,° — *manner / led*
And bar him so in pees and eek in werre,
Ther was no man that Theseus hath derre.° — *holds more dear*
And in this blisse lete° I now Arcite, — *leave*
And speke I wol of Palamon a lyte.

In derknesse and horrible and strong prisoun
Thise seven yeer hath seten° Palamoun, — *dwelt*
Forpyned,° what for wo and for distresse; — *Wasted away*
Who feleth double soor° and hevinesse — *sorrow*
But Palamon, that love destreyneth° so — *distresses*
That wood° out of his wit he gooth for wo? — *mad*
And eek therto he is a prisoner
Perpetuelly, noght oonly for a yeer.
Who coude ryme in English proprely
His martirdom? For sothe, it am nat I;
Therefore I passe as lightly° as I may. — *quickly*

It fel° that in the seventhe yeer, of May — *befell*
The thridde night, as olde bokes seyn,
That al this storie tellen more pleyn,° — *fully*
Were it by aventure° or destinee— — *chance*
As, whan a thing is shapen,° it shal be— — *determined (in advance)*
That sone after the midnight Palamoun,
By helping of a freend, brak° his prisoun — *escaped from*
And fleeth the citee faste as he may go;
For he hadde yive his gayler° drinke so — *jailer*
Of a clarree° maad of a certeyn wyn, — *spiced wine*
With nercotikes and opie of Thebes fyn,[9]
That al that night, thogh that men° wolde him shake, — *one*
The gayler sleep,° he mighte nat awake; — *slept*
And thus he fleeth as faste as evere he may.
The night was short and faste by the day,° — *near daybreak*
That nedes cost° he moot° himselven hyde, — *of necessity / must*
And til° a grove, faste ther bisyde, — *to*

9. Fine opium from Thebes (in Egypt).

With dredful° foot thanne stalketh Palamoun. *fearful*
For, shortly, this was his opinioun:
That in that grove he wolde him hyde al day,
And in the night thanne wolde he take his way
To Thebes-ward,° his freendes for to preye *Toward Thebes*
On Theseus to helpe him to werreye;° *make war*
And shortly, outher° he wolde lese° his lyf *either / lose*
Or winnen Emelye unto his wyf.
This is th'effect° and his entente pleyn.° *substance / complete intent*
  Now wol I turne to Arcite ageyn,
That litel wiste° how ny° that was his care, *knew / near*
Til that Fortune had broght him in the snare.
  The bisy larke, messager of day,
Saluëth° in hir song the marwe° gray; *Salutes, greets / morning*
And fyry Phebus ryseth up so brighte
That al the orient° laugheth of the lighte, *eastern sky*
And with his stremes° dryeth in the greves° *beams / bushes*
The silver dropes hanginge on the leves.
And Arcite, that in the court royal
With Theseus is squyer principal,
Is risen and loketh on the myrie day.
And for to doon his observaunce to May,
Remembringe on° the poynt° of his desyr, *Holding in mind / object*
He on a courser, startlinge° as the fyr,° *leaping / fire*
Is riden into the feeldes him to pleye,
Out of the court, were it a myle or tweye;
And to the grove of which that I yow tolde,
By aventure his wey he gan to holde,
To maken him a garland of the greves,° *branches*
Were it of wodebinde or hawethorn leves,
And loude he song ageyn° the sonne shene:° *in response to / bright*
"May, with alle thy floures and thy grene,
Welcome be thou, faire fresshe May,
In hope that I som grene° gete may." *something green*
And from his courser, with a lusty herte,
Into the grove ful hastily he sterte,° *leaped*
And in a path he rometh up and doun,
Theras,° by aventure, this Palamoun *Where*
Was in a bush, that no man mighte him see,
For sore afered° of his deeth was he. *afraid*
Nothing° ne knew he that it was Arcite; *Not at all*
God wot he wolde have trowed° it ful lyte. *believed*
But sooth is seyd, go sithen many yeres,° *since many years ago*
That "feeld hath eyen° and the wode hath eres." *the field has eyes*
It is ful fair° a man to bere him evene,° *desirable (for) / with restraint*
For al day° meeteth men at unset stevene.[1] *every day*
Ful litel woot Arcite of his felawe,
That was so ny° to herknen al his sawe,° *near / speech*

1. For people are always meeting at unexpected moments.

For in the bush he sitteth now ful stille.
Whan that Arcite hadde romed al his fille,
And songen al the roundel° lustily, *song*
Into a studie° he fil sodeynly, *i.e., deep thought*
As doon thise loveres in hir queynte geres,° *strange behaviors*
Now in the croppe,° now doun in the breres,° *treetop / briars*
Now up, now doun, as boket in a welle.
Right as° the Friday, soothly for to telle, *Just as*
Now it shyneth, now it reyneth faste,
Right so can gery° Venus overcaste° *changeable / cloud over, darken*
The hertes of hir folk; right as hir day
Is gereful, right so chaungeth she array.° *the order, disposition of things*
Selde is the Friday al the wyke ylyke.[2]
Whan that Arcite had songe, he gan to syke,° *sigh*
And sette him doun withouten any more.° *without further delay*
"Alas!" quod he, "that day that I was bore!
How longe, Juno, thurgh thy crueltee,
Woltow° werreyen° Thebes the citee? *Wilt thou / make war on*
Allas! y-broght is to confusioun
The blood royal of Cadme° and Amphioun— *Cadmus*
Of Cadmus, which that was the firste man
That Thebes bulte,° or first the toun bigan, *built*
And of the citee first was crouned king.
Of his lynage° am I, and his ofspring *lineage*
By verray ligne,° as of the stok royal; *true descent*
And now I am so caitif° and so thral° *wretched / enslaved*
That he that is my mortal enemy,
I serve him as his squyer povrely.° *in a lowly manner*
And yet doth Juno me wel more shame,
For I dar noght biknowe° myn owne name; *acknowledge*
But ther as I was wont to highte° Arcite, *be called*
Now highte I Philostrate, noght worth a myte.
Allas, thou felle° Mars! allas, Juno! *cruel, deadly*
Thus hath youre ire our lynage al fordo,° *destroyed*
Save only me and wrecched Palamoun,
That Theseus martyreth in prisoun.
And over al this, to sleen me outrely,° *utterly*
Love hath his fyry dart so brenningly° *burningly*
Y-stiked° thurgh my trewe careful° herte, *stabbed / woeful*
That shapen was my deeth erst than° my sherte.° *before / shirt*
Ye sleen° me with youre eyen, Emelye! *slay*
Ye been the cause wherfore that I dye.
Of all the remenant of myn other care° *woe*
Ne sette I nat the mountaunce° of a tare,° *amount / weed*
So° that I coude don aught to your plesaunce!" *If*
And with that word he fil down in a traunce
A longe tyme; and after he up sterte.
This Palamoun, that thoughte that thurgh his herte

2. Seldom is Friday like the other days of the week.

He felte a cold swerd sodeynliche° glyde, *suddenly*
For ire he quook,° no lenger wolde he byde. *quaked*
And whan that he had herd Arcites tale,
As he were wood,° with face deed° and pale, *mad / deathly*
He sterte him up out of the buskes° thikke, *bushes*
And seyde: "Arcite, false traitour wikke,° *wicked*
Now artow hent,° that lovest my lady so, *art thou caught*
For whom that I have al this peyne and wo,
And art my blood, and to my counseil° sworn, *secret counsel*
As I ful ofte have told thee heerbiforn,
And hast byjaped° here duk Theseus, *tricked*
And falsly chaunged hast thy name thus!
I wol be deed, or elles° thou shalt dye. *else*
Thou shalt nat love my lady Emelye,
But I wol love hire only, and namo;° *no one else*
For I am Palamoun, thy mortal fo.
And though that I no wepne° have in this place, *weapon*
But out of prison am astert° by grace, *escaped*
I drede noght° that outher° thou shalt dye *doubt not / either*
Or thou ne shalt nat loven Emelye.
Chees° which thou wolt,° for thou shalt nat asterte." *Choose / wish*
  This Arcitë, with ful despitous° herte, *scornful*
Whan he him knew, and hadde his tale herd,
As fiers as leoun pulled out his swerd
And seyde thus: "By God that sit° above, *sits*
Nere it° that thou art sik and wood for love, *Were it not*
And eek that thou no wepne hast in this place,
Thou sholdest nevere out of this grove pace,° *pass, leave*
That thou ne sholdest dyen of myn hond.
For I defye° the seuretee° and the bond *scorn, disclaim / pledge*
Which that thou seyst that I have maad to thee.
What, verray° fool, I think wel that love is free, *true*
And I wol love hire maugre° al thy might! *in spite of*
But, for as muche thou art a worthy knight,
And wilnest° to darreyne hire° by batayle, *wish / decide the claim to her*
Have heer my trouthe:° tomorwe I wol nat fayle, *troth, promise*
Withoute witing° of any other wight,° *knowledge / person*
That here I wol be founden as° a knight, *(on my honor) as*
And bringen harneys° right ynough for thee; *armor*
And chees° the beste, and leve the worste for me. *(you may) choose*
And mete and drinke this night wol I bringe
Ynough for thee, and clothes for thy beddinge.
And if so be that thou my lady winne,
And slee° me in this wode ther° I am inne, *slay / where*
Thou mayst wel have thy lady, as for me."° *as far as I am concerned*
This Palamon answerde: "I graunte it thee."
And thus they been departed° til amorwe,° *parted / the next morning*
Whan ech of hem had leyd his feith to borwe.° *as a pledge*
  O Cupide, out of° alle charitee!° *devoid of / unselfish love*
O regne,° that wolt no felawe° have with thee! *sovereign rule / associate*
Ful sooth is seyd that love ne lordshipe

Wol noght, his thankes,° have no felaweshipe; *willingly*
Wel finden that Arcite and Palamoun.
Arcite is riden anon unto the toun,
And on the morwe, er it were dayes light,
Ful prively two harneys hath he dight,° *prepared*
Bothe suffisaunt° and mete° to darreyne° *sufficient / suitable / decide*
The bataille in the feeld bitwix hem tweyne.° *two*
And on his hors, allone as he was born,
He carieth al this harneys him biforn;
And in the grove, at tyme and place y-set,
This Arcite and this Palamon ben met.
  To chaungen gan the colour in hir face,
Right as the hunters° in the regne° of Trace,° *hunter's / kingdom / Thrace*
That stondeth at the gappe° with a spere, *gap (in the forest)*
Whan hunted is the leoun or the bere,° *bear*
And hereth him come russhing in the greves,° *bushes*
And breketh bothe bowes° and the leves, *boughs*
And thinketh, "Heere cometh my mortel enemy!
Withoute faile, he moot° be deed or I; *must*
For outher° I mot sleen him at the gappe, *either*
Or he mot sleen me, if that me mishappe,"°— *if it should go ill for me*
So ferden° they in chaunging of hir hewe. *acted*
  As fer as° everich° of hem other knewe, *Although / each*
Ther nas no "good day," ne no saluing;° *saluting, greeting*
But streight, withouten word or rehersing,° *restating (their pact)*
Everich of hem heelp° for to armen other *helped*
As freendly as he were his owne brother;
And after that, with sharpe speres stronge
They foynen° ech at other wonder longe. *thrust*
Thou mightest wene° that this Palamoun *suppose*
In his fighting were a wood leoun,
And as a cruel tygre was Arcite;
As wilde bores gonne they to° smyte, *they did*
That frothen whyte as foom for ire wood.° *mad anger*
Up to the ancle° foghte they in hir blood. *ankle*
And in this wyse I lete° hem fighting dwelle,° *leave / continuing to fight*
And forth I wole of Theseus yow telle.
  The destinee, ministre° general, *agent*
That executeth in the world over al° *everywhere*
The purveyaunce° that God hath seyn biforn,° *providential plan / foreseen*
So strong it is that, though the world had sworn
The contrarie of a thing by ye or nay,
Yet somtyme it shal fallen° on a day *befall, happen*
That falleth nat eft° withinne a thousand yere. *again*
For certeinly, oure appetytes° here, *desires*
Be it of werre, or pees, or hate, or love,
Al is this reuled by the sighte° above. *foresight*
This mene I now by° mighty Theseus, *in relation to*
That for to hunten is so desirous,
And namely° at the grete hert° in May, *especially / hart*
That in his bed ther daweth him° no day *dawns for him*

That he nis clad and redy for to ryde
With hunte° and horn and houndes him bisyde. — *huntsman*
For in his hunting hath he swich delyt
That it is al his joye and appetyt
To been himself the grete hertes bane;° — *slayer*
For after Mars° he serveth now Diane.° — *god of war / goddess of the hunt*
  Cleer was the day, as I have told er this,
And Theseus, with alle joye and blis,
With his Ipolita, the fayre quene,
And Emelye, clothed al in grene,
On hunting be they riden royally.
And to the grove that stood ful faste by,
In which ther was an hert, as men him tolde,
Duk Theseus the streighte wey hath holde.° — *has taken*
And to the launde he rydeth him ful right,[3]
For thider was the hert wont have his flight,
And over a brook, and so forth on his weye.
This duk wol han a cours° at him or tweye, — *chase*
With houndes swiche as that him list° comaunde. — *it pleases him*
  And whan this duk was come unto the launde,
Under the sonne he loketh, and anon
He was war of Arcite and Palamon,
That foughten breme° as it were bores two. — *furiously*
The brighte swerdes wenten to and fro
So hidously that with the leeste strook
It seemed as it wolde felle an ook;
But what° they were, no thing he ne woot. — *who*
This duk his courser with his spores° smoot,° — *spurs / struck*
And at a stert° he was bitwix hem two, — *in an instant*
And pulled out a swerd and cryed, "Ho!
Namore, up° peyne of lesinge° of youre heed! — *upon / losing*
By mighty Mars, he shal anon be deed
That smyteth° any strook that I may seen. — *strikes*
But telleth me what mister men° ye been, — *what kind of men*
That been so hardy° for to fighten here — *audacious*
Withouten juge or other officere,
As it were in a listes° royally?" — *lists (of a tournament)*
  This Palamon answerde hastily,
And seyde: "Sire, what nedeth wordes mo?
We have the deeth deserved bothe two.
Two woful wrecches been we, two caytyves,° — *captives*
That been encombred° of our owne lyves; — *weary*
And as thou art a rightful lord and juge,
Ne yeve° us neither mercy ne refuge,° — *give / protection*
But slee° me first, for seynte° charitee. — *slay / holy*
But slee my felawe eek as wel as me,
Or slee him first: for though thou knowest it lyte,° — *little*
This is thy mortal fo, this is Arcite,
That fro thy lond is banished on his heed,° — *on pain of losing his head*

3. And he rides directly to the clearing in the forest.

For which he hath deserved to be deed.
For this is he that cam unto thy gate
And seyde that he highte Philostrate.
Thus hath he japed° thee ful many a yeer, *tricked*
And thou hast maked him thy chief squyer;
And this is he that loveth Emelye.
For sith° the day is come that I shal dye, *since*
I make pleynly° my confessioun *frankly, fully*
That I am thilke° woful Palamoun *that*
That hath thy prison broken wikkedly.
I am thy mortal fo, and it am I
That loveth so hote° Emelye the brighte *fervently*
That I wol dye present° in hir sighte. *at once*
Wherfore I axe° deeth and my juwyse;° *ask (for) / just sentence*
But slee my felawe in the same wyse,° *way*
For bothe han we deserved to be slayn."
 This worthy duk answerde anon agayn,
And seyde, "This is a short conclusioun.° *quick decision*
Youre owne mouth, by your confessioun,
Hath dampned you, and I wol it recorde;° *declare it as my verdict*
It nedeth noght to pyne° yow with the corde.° *torture / rope*
Ye shul be deed, by mighty Mars the rede!"
 The quene anon, for verray° wommanhede, *true*
Gan for to wepe, and so dide Emelye,
And alle the ladies in the companye.
Gret pitee was it, as it thoughte hem° alle, *it seemed to them*
That ever swich a chaunce sholde falle;° *befall, occur*
For gentil° men they were of greet estat, *well-born, courteous*
And no thing but for love was this debat;° *conflict*
And sawe hir blody woundes wyde and sore,
And alle cryden, bothe lasse and more,° *the lesser and the greater*
"Have mercy, lord, upon us wommen alle!"
And on hir bare knees adoun they falle,
And wolde have kist his feet ther as he stood,
Til at the laste aslaked° was his mood;° *diminished / anger*
For pitee renneth° sone in gentil herte. *runs*
And though he first for ire quook° and sterte,° *quaked / started*
He hath considered shortly, in a clause,° *a brief while*
The trespas of hem bothe, and eek the cause,
And although that his ire hir gilt accused,° *blamed their offense*
Yet in his resoun he hem bothe excused,
As thus: he thoghte wel that every man
Wol helpe himself in love, if that he can,
And eek delivere himself out of prisoun.
And eek his herte had compassioun
Of wommen, for they wepen evere in oon.° *i.e., continued to weep*
And in his gentil herte he thoghte anoon,
And softe unto himself he seyde: "Fy
Upon a lord that wol have no mercy,
But been a leoun, bothe in word and dede,
To hem that been in repentaunce and drede

As well as to a proud despitous° man *scornful*
That wol maynteyne that° he first bigan! *what*
That lord hath litel of discrecioun° *discernment*
That in swich cas can° no divisioun,° *knows (how to make) / distinction*
But weyeth° pryde and humblesse after oon."° *weighs, judges / alike*
  And shortly, whan his ire is thus agoon,° *passed away*
He gan to loken up with eyen lighte,° *cheerful*
And spak thise same wordes al on highte:° *aloud*
"The god of love, a, *benedicite*,° *bless us*
How mighty and how greet a lord is he!
Ayeins° his might ther gayneth° none obstacles. *Against / prevails*
He may be cleped° a god for his miracles, *called*
For he can maken at his owne gyse° *as he chooses*
Of everich herte as that him list devyse.° *whatever it pleases him to contrive*
Lo heere, this Arcite and this Palamoun,
That quitly° weren out of my prisoun, *freely, entirely*
And mighte han lived in Thebes royally,
And witen° I am hir mortal enemy *know*
And that hir deeth lyth in my might also;
And yet hath love, maugree hir eyen two,[4]
Broght hem hider bothe for to dye!
Now loketh, is nat that an heigh° folye? *great*
Who may been a fool but if° he love? *unless*
Bihold, for Goddes sake that sit° above, *sits*
Se how they blede! be they noght wel arrayed?
Thus hath hir lord, the god of love, y-payed
Hir wages and hir fees for hir servyse!
And yet they wenen° for to been ful wyse *think (themselves)*
That serven love, for aught that may bifalle.
But this is yet the beste game° of alle: *joke*
That she, for whom they han this jolitee,° *frolic, diversion*
Can hem therfore as muche thank as me;[5]
She woot° namore of al this hote fare,° *knows / frantic business*
By God, than woot a cokkow° or an hare! *cuckoo*
But al mot been assayed,° hoot and cold; *tried, experienced*
A man mot been a fool, or yong or old;
I woot it by myself ful yore agoon,° *long ago*
For in my tyme a servant° was I oon. *i.e., of love*
And therefore, sin° I knowe of loves peyne, *since*
And woot how sore it can a man distreyne,° *distress, torment*
As he that° hath ben caught ofte in his las,° *one who / net*
I yow foryeve al hoolly° this trespas, *wholly*
At requeste of the quene that kneleth here,
And eek of Emelye, my suster dere.
And ye shul bothe anon unto me swere
That neveremo ye shul my contree dere,° *harm*
Ne make werre upon me night ne day,
But been my freendes in al that ye may.

4. Despite their two eyes (i.e., despite anything they can do).
5. I.e., has no more to thank them for than I do.

I yow foryeve this trespas every del."° *in every respect*
And they him swore his axing° fayre and wel, *request*
And him of lordshipe° and of mercy preyde, *his protection as their overlord*
And he hem graunteth grace, and thus he seyde:
"To speke of royal linage and richesse,
Though that she were a quene or a princesse,
Ech of yow bothe is worthy, doutelees,
To wedden whan tyme is, but nathelees°— *nevertheless*
I speke as for my suster Emelye,
For whom ye have this stryf and jalousye—
Ye woot yourself she may not wedden two
Atones,° though ye fighten everemo: *At one time*
That oon of yow, al be him looth or leef,° *whether he like it or not*
He moot go pypen° in an ivy leef; *go whistle*
This is to seyn, she may nat now han bothe,
Al be ye never so jalous ne so wrothe.
And forthy° I yow putte in this degree,° *therefore / condition, position*
That ech of yow shal have his destinee
As him is shape,° and herkneth in what wyse; *determined*
Lo heer your ende° of that I shal devyse. *fate*
My wil is this, for plat° conclusioun, *blunt, plain*
Withouten any replicacioun°— *reply*
If that yow lyketh, tak it for the beste:
That everich of yow shal gon wher him leste
Frely, withouten raunson° or daunger;° *ransom / control*
And this day fifty wykes, fer ne ner,° *neither later nor sooner*
Everich of yow shal bringe an hundred knightes
Armed for listes° up at alle rightes,° *tournament / points*
Al redy to darreyne hire° by bataille. *to settle claim to her*
And this bihote° I yow withouten faille, *promise*
Upon my trouthe, and as I am a knight,
That whether° of yow bothe that hath might— *whichever*
This is to seyn, that whether he or thou
May with his hundred, as I spak of now,
Sleen° his contrarie° or out of listes dryve— *Slay / opponent*
Thanne shal I yeve Emelya to wyve° *as wife*
To whom that Fortune yeveth so fair a grace.
The listes° shal I maken in this place, *tournament arena*
And God so wisly° on my soule rewe,° *surely / have pity*
As I shal even° juge been and trewe. *impartial*
Ye shul non other ende° with me maken, *agreement*
That oon of yow ne shal be deed or taken.
And if yow thinketh this is wel y-sayd,
Seyeth your avys,° and holdeth yow apayd.° *opinion / content*
This is your ende and youre conclusioun."
Who loketh lightly now but Palamoun?
Who springeth up for joye but Arcite?
Who couthe telle, or who couthe it endyte,° *write*
The joye that is maked in the place
Whan Theseus hath doon so fair a grace?
But doun on knees wente every maner wight,

And thanked him with al hir herte and might,
And namely° the Thebans often sythe.° — *especially / many times*
And thus with good hope and with herte blythe° — *glad*
They take hir leve, and homward gonne° they ryde — *did*
To Thebes, with his° olde walles wyde. — *its*

PART THREE

I trowe° men wolde deme it necligence — *believe*
If I foryete° to tellen the dispence° — *forget / spending*
Of Theseus, that goth so bisily
To maken up the listes royally,
That swich a noble theatre° as it was, — *amphitheater*
I dar wel seyn that in this world ther nas.
The circuit a myle was aboute,
Walled of stoon, and diched° al withoute. — *ditched*
Round was the shap, in manere of compas,° — *circle*
Ful of degrees,° the heighte of sixty pas,° — *steps / paces*
That whan a man was set on o° degree, — *one*
He letted° nat his felawe for to see. — *hindered*
Estward ther stood a gate of marbel whyt,
Westward right swich another in the opposit.
And shortly to concluden, swich a place
Was noon in erthe, as in so litel space;° — *(built) in such a short time*
For in the lond ther was no crafty° man — *skilled*
That geometrie or ars-metrike° can,° — *arithmetic / knows*
Ne purtreyour,° ne kervere° of images, — *painter / carver*
That Theseus ne yaf° him mete and wages — *gave*
The theatre for to maken and devyse.
And for to doon his ryte and sacrifyse,
He estward hath, upon the gate above,
In worshipe of Venus, goddesse of love,
Don make° an auter° and an oratorie; — *Had made / altar*
And on the gate westward, in memorie
Of Mars, he maked hath right swich another,
That coste largely of gold a fother.° — *load, large quantity*
And northward, in a touret° on the wal, — *turret*
Of alabastre whyt and reed° coral, — *red*
An oratorie riche for to see,
In worshipe of Dyane° of chastitee, — *Diana*
Hath Theseus don wroght° in noble wyse. — *had constructed*
But yet hadde I foryeten to devyse
The noble kerving and the portreitures,° — *representations*
The shap, the countenaunce, and the figures,
That weren in thise oratories three.
First in the temple of Venus maystow° see — *mayest thou*
Wroght on the wal, ful pitous to biholde,
The broken slepes and the sykes° colde,° — *sighs / chilling, fatal*
The sacred teres and the waymentinge,° — *lamenting*
The fyry strokes of the desiringe
That loves servaunts in this lyf enduren;

The othes that hir covenants assuren;° *bind their vows*
Plesaunce and Hope, Desyr, Foolhardinesse,
Beautee and Youthe, Bauderie,° Richesse, *Pandering*
Charmes and Force, Lesinges,° Flaterye, *Deceits*
Dispense,° Bisynesse, and Jalousye, *Expense*
That wered of yelwe goldes° a gerland, *marigolds*
And a cokkow sittinge on hir hand;
Festes,° instruments, caroles,° daunces, *Feasts / songs sung dancing*
Lust° and array, and alle the circumstaunces *Pleasure*
Of love, whiche that I rekned° and rekne shal, *reckoned, considered*
By ordre weren peynted on the wal,
And mo than I can make of mencioun.° *i.e., make mention of*
For soothly, al the mount of Citheroun,° *Cithaeron*
Ther° Venus hath hir principal dwellinge, *Where*
Was shewed on the wal in portreyinge,
With al the gardin and the lustinesse.
Nat was foryeten the porter, Ydelnesse,
Ne Narcisus the faire of yore agon,° *long ago*
Ne yet the folye of king Salamon,
Ne yet the grete strengthe of Hercules,
Th'enchauntements of Medea and Circes,
Ne of Turnus, with the hardy fiers corage,° *proud heart*
The riche Cresus, caytif in servage.° *wretched in bondage*
Thus may ye seen that wisdom ne richesse,
Beautee ne sleighte,° strengthe ne hardinesse,° *cleverness / boldness*
Ne may with Venus holde champartye,° *equal power*
For as hir list the world than may she gye.° *guide, govern*
Lo, alle thise folk so caught were in hir las,° *net*
Til they for wo ful ofte seyde "Allas!"
Suffyceth heer ensamples oon or two,
And though° I coude rekne a thousand mo. *Although*
The statue of Venus, glorious for to see,
Was naked fletinge° in the large see, *floating*
And fro the navele doun all covered was
With wawes° grene, and brighte as any glas. *waves*
A citole° in hir right hand hadde she, *cithara (a stringed instrument)*
And on hir heed, ful semely° for to see, *seemly, comely*
A rose gerland, fresh and wel smellinge;
Above hir heed hir dowves flikeringe.° *doves fluttering*
Biforn hir stood hir sone Cupido,
Upon his shuldres winges hadde he two,
And blind he was, as it is ofte sene.
A bowe he bar° and arwes brighte and kene. *carried*
Why sholde I noght as wel eek telle yow al
The portreiture that was upon the wal
Withinne the temple of mighty Mars the rede?
Al peynted was the wal, in lengthe and brede,° *breadth*
Lyk to the estres° of the grisly place *like the interior*
That highte° the grete temple of Mars in Trace,° *is called / Thrace*
In thilke° colde frosty regioun *that*
Ther as° Mars hath his sovereyn mansioun. *Where*

First on the wal was peynted a foreste,
In which ther dwelleth neither man ne beste,
With knotty knarry° bareyne° treës olde, *gnarled / barren*
Of stubbes° sharpe and hidouse to biholde, *With stublike branches*
In° which ther ran a rumbel in a swough,° *Through / sough, noise (of wind)*
As though a storm sholde bresten° every bough. *break*
And downward from an hille, under a bente,° *below a grassy slope*
Ther stood the temple of Mars armipotente,° *powerful in arms*
Wroght al of burned° steel, of which the entree° *burnished / entrance*
Was long and streit,° and gastly for to see. *narrow*
And therout cam a rage° and such a vese° *roar (of wind) / blast*
That it made al the gate for to rese.° *shake*
The northren light in at the dores shoon,° *shone*
For windowe on the wal ne was ther noon,
Thurgh which men mighten any light discerne.
The dore was al of adamant eterne,
Y-clenched° overthwart° and endelong° *Braced / crosswise / lengthwise*
With iren tough; and for to make it strong,
Every piler,° the temple to sustene, *pillar*
Was tonne-greet,° of iren bright and shene.° *big as a cask / shiny*
Ther saugh I first the derke imagining
Of Felonye,° and al the compassing;° *Crime, Treachery / plotting*
The cruel Ire, reed as any glede;° *live coal*
The pykepurs,° and eek the pale Drede; *pick-purse, pickpocket*
The smylere with the knyf under the cloke;
The shepne° brenning° with the blake smoke; *stable, shed / burning*
The treson of the mordring° in the bedde; *murdering*
The open werre, with woundes al bibledde;° *bloodstained*
Contek,° with blody knyf and sharp manace.° *Strife / menace, threat*
Al ful of chirking° was that sory place. *harsh noises*
The sleere of himself° yet saugh I ther: *i.e., the suicide (self-slayer)*
His herte-blood hath bathed al his heer;° *hair*
The nayl y-driven in the shode[6] a-night;
The colde deeth, with mouth gaping upright.
Amiddes of° the temple sat Meschaunce,° *In the middle of / Misfortune*
With disconfort° and sory contenaunce. *discouragement*
Yet saugh I Woodnesse° laughing in his rage, *Madness*
Armed Compleint, Outhees,° and fiers Outrage; *Outcry*
The careyne° in the bush, with throte y-corve;° *corpse / cut*
A thousand slayn, and nat of qualm y-storve;° *dead by plague*
The tiraunt, with the prey° by force y-raft;° *plunder / seized*
The toun destroyed, ther was nothing laft.
Yet saugh I brent the shippes hoppesteres;° *dancing, bobbing*
The hunte° strangled with° the wilde beres; *hunter / killed by*
The sowe freten° the child right in the cradel; *devour*
The cook y-scalded, for al his longe ladel—
Noght was foryeten by the infortune of Marte[7]—
The carter overriden with° his carte, *run over by*

6. The top of the head, where the hair parts.
7. Nothing was forgotten concerning the evil influence of Mars.

Under the wheel ful lowe he lay adoun.
Ther were also, of Martes divisioun,° *company, category*
The barbour and the bocher° and the smith, *butcher*
That forgeth sharpe swerdes on his stith.° *anvil*
And al above, depeynted° in a tour, *depicted*
Saw I Conquest, sitting in greet honour,
With the sharpe swerde over his heed
Hanginge by a sotil twynes threed.° *thin thread of twine*
Depeynted was the slaughtre of Julius,° *Julius Caesar*
Of grete Nero, and of Antonius;° *Mark Antony*
Al be that thilke tyme they were unborn,
Yet was hir deeth depeynted ther-biforn
By manasinge of Mars, right by figure.[8]
So was it shewed in that portreiture,
As is depeynted in the sterres° above *stars*
Who shal be slayn or elles deed for love.
Sufficeth oon ensample in° stories olde: *from*
I may not rekene hem alle, thogh I wolde.

The statue of Mars upon a carte stood
Armed, and loked grim as he were wood;
And over his heed ther shynen° two figures *shine*
Of sterres, that been cleped° in scriptures° *called / writings*
That oon Puella, that other Rubeus:[9]
This god of armes was arrayed thus.
A wolf ther stood biforn him at his feet
With eyen rede, and of a man he eet.° *ate*
With sotil° pencel was depeynted this storie *subtle*
In redoutinge° of Mars and of his glorie. *fearful reverence*

Now to the temple of Diane the chaste,
As shortly as I can, I wol me haste
To telle yow al the descripcioun.
Depeynted been the walles up and doun
Of hunting and of shamfast° chastitee. *modest*
Ther saugh° I how woful Calistopee,° *saw / Callisto*
Whan that Diane agreved° was with here,° *aggrieved, angry / her*
Was turned from a womman til° a bere,° *into / bear*
And after was she maad the lode-sterre;° *lodestar (North Star)*
Thus was it peynted, I can say yow no ferre;° *further*
Hir sone is eek a sterre, as men may see.
Ther saugh I Dane,° y-turned til a tree— *Daphne*
I mene nat the goddesse Diane,
But Penneus doughter, which that highte Dane.
Ther saugh I Attheon° an hert° y-maked, *Actaeon / hart*
For vengeaunce that he saugh Diane al naked;
I saugh how that his houndes have him caught
And freten° him, for that they knewe him naught. *devoured*
Yet° peynted was a litel forther moor,° *In addition / along*

8. Yet their death through the menacing influence of Mars was depicted beforehand, in an image.
9. Puella and Rubeus are the names of two patterns of dots (not stars) used in geomancy—a form of divination—to determine astrological influences.

How Atthalante° hunted the wilde boor, *Atalanta*
And Meleagre,° and many another mo, *Meleager*
For which Diane wroghte him care and wo.
Ther saugh I many another wonder storie,
The whiche me list nat drawen to memorie.° *remember*
This goddesse on an hert ful hye° seet,° *high / sat*
With smale houndes al aboute hir feet;
And undernethe hir feet she hadde a mone,° *moon*
Wexinge it was, and sholde wanie° sone. *wane*
In gaude° grene hir statue clothed was, *yellowish*
With bowe in honde, and arwes in a cas.° *quiver*
Hir eyen caste she ful lowe adoun,
Ther Pluto hath his derke regioun.
A womman travailinge° was hir biforn, *in labor*
But for° hir child so longe was unborn, *because*
Ful pitously Lucyna[1] gan she calle,
And seyde, "Help, for thou mayst best of alle."
Wel koude he peynten lyfly° that it wroghte; *in a lifelike way*
With many a florin he the hewes° boghte. *colors, pigments*
Now been thise listes maad, and Theseus,
That at his grete cost arrayed° thus *adorned*
The temples and the theatre every del,° *in every part*
Whan it was doon, him lyked° wonder wel. *it pleased him*
But stinte° I wole of Theseus a lyte, *stop (talking)*
And speke of Palamon and of Arcite.
The day approcheth of hir retourninge,
That everich° sholde an hundred knightes bringe *each*
The bataille to darreyne,° as I yow tolde; *decide*
And til Athenes, hir covenant for to holde,
Hath everich of hem broght an hundred knightes
Wel armed for the werre at alle rightes.° *points*
And sikerly,° ther trowed° many a man *surely / believed, thought*
That never, sithen that the world bigan,
As for to speke of knighthod of hir hond,[2]
As fer as God hath maked see or lond,
Nas of so fewe so noble a companye.
For every wight that lovede chivalrye,
And wolde, his thankes,° han a passant° name, *gladly / outstanding*
Hath preyed that he mighte ben of that game;
And wel was him that therto chosen was.
For if ther fille° tomorwe swich a cas,° *befell / case, situation*
Ye knowen wel that every lusty knight
That loveth paramours° and hath his might,° *passionately / the power*
Were it in Engelond or elleswhere
They wolde, hir thankes, wilnen° to be there. *wish*
To fighte for a lady, *benedicite!*° *bless us*
It were° a lusty° sighte for to see. *would be / joyful*
And right so ferden° they with Palamon. *fared, did*

1. Lucina, goddess of childbirth, a role attributed to Diana.
2. I.e., the deeds of knighthood.

With him ther wenten knightes many oon;° *a one*
Som° wol ben armed in an habergeoun,° *One / hauberk, coat of mail*
And in a brest plate and a light gipoun;° *tunic (worn under hauberk)*
And som wol have a peyre° plates large; *pair, suit of*
And som wol have a Pruce° sheeld or a targe;° *Prussian / light shield*
Som wol ben armed on his legges weel,° *well*
And have an ax, and som a mace of steel.
Ther nis no newe gyse that it nas old.[3]
Armed were they, as I have you told,
Everich after his opinioun.
Ther maistow° seen, coming with Palamoun, *mayest thou*
Ligurge° himself, the grete king of Trace.° *Lycurgus / Thrace*
Blak was his berd, and manly was his face.
The cercles° of his eyen in his heed, *irises*
They gloweden bitwixen yelow and reed;
And lyk a griffon loked he aboute,
With kempe° heres on his browes stoute;° *shaggy / large*
His limes° grete, his braunes° harde and stronge, *limbs / muscles*
His shuldres brode, his armes rounde and longe;
And as the gyse was in his contree,
Ful hye upon a char° of gold stood he, *chariot*
With foure whyte boles° in the trays.° *bulls / traces*
In stede of cote-armure[4] over his harnays,° *armor*
With nayles° yelewe and brighte as any gold *claws*
He hadde a beres skin, col-blak for old.° *because of age*
His longe heer was kembd° bihinde his bak— *combed*
As any ravenes fethere it shoon° for° blak; *shone / very*
A wrethe of gold arm-greet,° of huge wighte,° *thick as an arm / weight*
Upon his heed, set ful of stones brighte,
Of fyne rubies and of dyamaunts.° *diamonds*
Aboute his char ther wenten whyte alaunts,° *wolfhounds*
Twenty and mo, as grete as any steer,
To hunten at the leoun or the deer,
And folwed him with mosel° faste y-bounde, *muzzle*
Colered° of gold, and tourettes[5] fyled° rounde. *Wearing collars / filed*
An hundred lordes hadde he in his route,° *retinue*
Armed ful wel, with hertes sterne and stoute.
With Arcita, in stories as men finde,
The grete Emetreus, the king of Inde,° *India*
Upon a steede bay° trapped in steel,° *bay-colored / with steel trappings*
Covered in cloth of gold diapred weel,° *finely patterned*
Cam ryding lyk the god of armes, Mars.
His cote-armure was of cloth of Tars,° *Tarsia, in Turkestan*
Couched° with perles whyte and rounde and grete. *Set, overlaid*
His sadel was of brend° gold newe y-bete;° *burnished / hammered, crafted*
A mantelet° upon his shuldre hanginge *short cloak*
Bret-ful° of rubies rede as fyr sparklinge. *Brimful*

3. There is no new fashion (in arms) that did not exist long ago.
4. See ll. 1016–19 and n. 4.
5. Rings on the collar for attaching a leash.

His crispe° heer lyk ringes was y-ronne,° *curly / i.e., hung down*
And that was yelow, and glitered as the sonne.
His nose was heigh, his eyen bright citryn,° *lemon-colored*
His lippes rounde, his colour was sangwyn;° *blood-red*
A fewe frakenes° in his face y-spreynd,° *freckles / scattered*
Betwixen yelow and somdel blak y-meynd;° *mingled*
And as a leoun he his loking caste.
Of fyve and twenty yeer his age I caste:° *estimate*
His berd was wel bigonne for to springe.
His voys was as a trompe° thunderinge. *trumpet*
Upon his heed he wered of laurer° grene *laurel*
A gerland fresh and lusty for to sene.
Upon his hand he bar for his deduyt° *delight*
An egle tame, as any lilie whyt.
An hundred lordes hadde he with him there,
Al armed, sauf° hir heddes, in al hir gere,° *except / gear, armor*
Ful richely in alle maner thinges.
For trusteth wel that dukes, erles, kinges
Were gadered° in this noble companye *gathered*
For love and for encrees° of chivalrye. *increase*
Aboute this king ther ran on every part° *side*
Ful many a tame leoun and leopart.
And in this wyse° thise lordes, alle and some,° *way / one and all*
Ben on the Sonday to the citee come
Aboute pryme,° and in the toun alight. *between 6 and 9 A.M.*
 This Theseus, this duk, this worthy knight,
Whan he had broght hem into his citee,
And inned° hem, everich in his degree,° *housed / each according to his rank*
He festeth hem, and dooth so greet labour
To esen° hem and doon hem al honour, *set at ease*
That yet men wenen° that no mannes wit *think*
Of noon estat ne coude amenden° it. *improve on*
The minstralcye, the service at the feste,
The grete yiftes° to the moste and leste,° *gifts / highest and lowest (in rank)*
The riche array of Theseus paleys,
Ne who sat first ne last upon the deys,° *dais, platform*
What ladies fairest been or best daunsinge,
Or which of hem can dauncen best and singe,
Ne who most felingly° speketh of love; *sensitively*
What haukes sitten on the perche above,
What houndes liggen° on the floor adoun— *lie*
Of al this make I now no mencioun;
But al° th'effect, that thinketh me° the beste. *only / seems to me*
Now comth the poynt, and herkneth if yow leste.° *it please you*
 The Sonday night, er day bigan to springe,
When Palamon the larke herde singe
(Although it nere° nat day by houres two, *were*
Yet song the larke) and Palamon right tho
With holy herte and with an heigh corage,° *spirit*
He roos° to wenden on his pilgrimage *arose*
Unto the blisful Citherea benigne—

I mene Venus, honurable and digne.° *worthy*
And in hir houre[6] he walketh forth a pas° *slowly, at a footpace*
Unto the listes ther° hir temple was, *where*
And doun he kneleth, and with humble chere
And herte soor,° he seyde as ye shul here: *sore (with love)*
"Faireste of faire, O lady myn, Venus,
Doughter to Jove and spouse of Vulcanus,
Thou gladere° of the mount of Citheroun. *gladdener*
For thilke love thou haddest to Adoun,° *Adonis*
Have pitee of my bittre teres smerte,
And tak myn humble preyere at thyn herte.
Allas! I ne have no langage to telle
Th'effectes ne the torments of myn helle;
Myn herte may myne harmes nat biwreye;° *reveal*
I am so confus° that I can noght seye *bewildered*
But mercy, lady bright, that knowest weele
My thought, and seest what harmes that I feele.
Considere al this, and rewe° upon my sore,° *have pity / pain*
As wisly° as I shal for everemore, *surely*
Emforth° my might, thy trewe servant be *To the extent of*
And holden werre° alwey with chastitee. *war*
That make I myn avow,° so ye me helpe. *vow*
I kepe° noght of armes for to yelpe,° *dare / boast*
Ne I ne axe nat tomorwe to have victorie,
Ne renoun in this cas,° ne veyne glorie *event*
Of pris° of armes blowen up and doun, *reputation, praise*
But I wolde have fully possessioun
Of Emelye, and dye in thy servyse.
Find thou the manere how, and in what wyse:
I recche° nat but° it may bettre be *care / whether*
To have victorie of hem, or they of me,
So that I have my lady in myne armes.
For though so be that Mars is god of armes,
Youre vertu is so greet in hevene above,
That if yow list, I shal wel have my love.
Thy temple wol I worshipe everemo,
And on thyn auter,° where° I ryde or go,° *altar / whether / walk*
I wol don sacrifice and fyres bete.° *kindle*
And if ye wol nat so, my lady swete,
Than preye I thee, tomorwe with a spere
That Arcita me thurgh the herte bere.° *pierce*
Thanne rekke I noght, whan I have lost my lyf,
Though that Arcita winne hire to his wyf.
This is th'effect° and ende of my preyere: *essence*
Yif° me my love, thou blisful lady dere." *Give*
Whan the orison° was doon of Palamon, *prayer*

6. An hour of the day assigned astrologically to Venus. The hours were assigned to the planets in rotation, beginning at sunrise with the planet specially associated with that day. All three characters pray to their deities at the appropriate hours: Palamon to Venus two hours before Monday's sunrise; Emily to Diana during the first hour of Monday, the moon's day (ll. 2271–74); and Arcite to Mars during the fourth hour (ll. 2367–69).

His sacrifice he dide, and that anon,° *promptly*
Ful pitously, with alle circumstaunces,° *attendant details*
Al° telle I noght as now his observaunces. *Although*
But atte laste the statue of Venus shook,
And made a signe, wherby that he took
That his preyere accepted was that day.
For thogh the signe shewed a delay,
Yet wiste° he wel that graunted was his bone;° *knew / boon, request*
And with glad herte he wente him hoom ful sone.
The thridde houre inequal[7] that° Palamon *after*
Bigan to Venus temple for to goon,
Up roos the sonne, and up roos Emelye,
And to the temple of Diane gan hye.° *hastened*
Hir maydens, that she thider with hir ladde,° *led*
Ful redily with hem the fyr they hadde,
Th'encens,° the clothes,° and the remenant al *incense / cloths, hangings*
That to the sacrifyce longen shal;° *should belong*
The hornes fulle of meth,° as was the gyse,° *mead / fashion*
Ther lakked noght to doon hir sacrifyse.
Smokinge the temple, full of clothes faire,[8]
This Emelye, with herte debonaire,° *gracious, humble*
Hir body wessh° with water of a welle,° *washed / spring*
But how she dide hir ryte I dar nat telle,
But° it be any thing in general; *Unless*
And yet it were a game° to heren al; *pleasure*
To him that meneth wel it were no charge,° *it wouldn't matter*
But it is good a man ben at his large.° *at liberty (to speak or not)*
Hir brighte heer was kembd,° untressed° al; *combed / loose*
A coroune° of a grene ook cerial° *garland / a species of oak*
Upon hir heed was set ful fair and mete.° *fitting*
Two fyres on the auter gan she bete,
And dide hir thinges, as men may biholde
In Stace° of Thebes and thise bokes olde. *Statius*
Whan kindled was the fyr, with pitous chere° *countenance*
Unto Diane she spak as ye may here:
"O chaste goddesse of the wodes grene,
To whom bothe hevene and erthe and see is sene,° *visible*
Quene of the regne° of Pluto derk and lowe, *realm*
Goddesse of maydens, that myn herte hast knowe
Ful many a yeer, and woost° what I desire, *knowest*
As keepe me fro thy vengeaunce and thyn ire,
That Attheon° aboughte° cruelly. *Actaeon / suffered for*
Chaste goddesse, wel wostow° that I *knowest thou*
Desire to been a mayden al my lyf,
Ne never wol I be° no love° ne wyf. *do I wish to be / lover*
I am, thou woost, yet of thy companye,

7. The hours assigned to the planets (see n. 6 above) were based on a system that divided them into twelve each of daylight and darkness. Hence they would almost always be unequal in duration, since day and night are the same length only at the equinoxes.
8. Censing the temple, full of beautiful cloth hangings.

A mayde, and love hunting and venerye,° — *hunting, the chase*
And for to walken in the wodes wilde,
And noght to been a wyf and be with childe.
Noght wol I knowe companye of man.
Now help me, lady, sith ye may and can,
For tho° thre formes[9] that thou hast in thee. — *those*
And Palamon, that hath swich love to me,
And eek Arcite, that loveth me so sore,
This grace I preye thee withoute more:
As sende love and pees° bitwixe hem two, — *peace*
And fro me turne awey hir hertes so
That al hir hote love and hir desyr,
And al hir bisy° torment and hir fyr, — *intense*
Be queynt° or turned in another place.° — *quenched / direction*
And if so be thou wolt° not do me grace, — *will*
Or if my destinee be shapen° so, — *shaped, determined*
That I shal nedes° have oon of hem two, — *must necessarily*
As sende me him that most desireth me.
Bihold, goddesse of clene chastitee,
The bittre teres that on my chekes falle.
Sin° thou art mayde° and kepere° of us alle, — *Since / a virgin / guardian*
My maydenhede thou kepe and wel conserve,
And whyl I live a mayde, I wol thee serve."
  The fyres brenne° upon the auter° clere,° — *burn / altar / brightly*
Whyl Emelye was thus in hir preyere.
But sodeinly she saugh a sighte queynte,° — *strange*
For right anon oon of the fyres queynte,° — *died out*
And quiked° agayn, and after that anon — *became alive, flamed up*
That other fyr was queynt, and al agon;° — *gone*
And as it queynte, it made a whistelinge,
As doon thise wete brondes° in hir brenninge, — *pieces of burning wood*
And at the brondes ende out ran anoon
As it were° blody dropes many oon; — *What seemed like*
For which so sore agast was Emelye
That she was wel ny° mad, and gan to crye, — *near*
For she ne wiste what it signifyed;
But only for the fere° thus hath she cryed, — *fear*
And weep,° that it was pitee for to here. — *wept*
And therwithal Diane gan appere,
With bowe in hond, right as an hunteresse,
And seyde: "Doghter, stint° thyn hevinesse.° — *stop / sorrow*
Among the goddes hye° it is affermed, — *high*
And by eterne word writen and confermed,
Thou shalt ben wedded unto oon of tho° — *those*
That han° for thee so muchel care and wo; — *have*
But unto which of hem I may nat telle.
Farwel, for I ne may no lenger dwelle.
The fyres which that on myn auter brenne

9. The goddess appears as Diana on earth, Luna in heaven, and Proserpina in the underworld (the "regne of Pluto" referred to in l. 2299).

Shulle thee declaren, er that thou go henne,°	*hence*
Thyn aventure° of love, as in this cas."	*What will befall thee*
And with that word, the arwes in the cas°	*quiver*
Of the goddesse clateren faste and ringe,	
And forth she wente, and made a vanisshinge;	
For which this Emelye astoned° was,	*stunned, astonished*
And seyde, "What amounteth° this, allas!	*means*
I putte me in thy proteccioun,	
Diane, and in° thy disposicioun."°	*at / disposing*
And hoom she gooth anon the nexte° weye.	*nearest*
This is th'effect, ther is namore to seye.	
The nexte houre of Mars folwinge this,	
Arcite unto the temple walked is°	*has walked*
Of fierse Mars, to doon his sacrifyse,	
With alle the rytes of his payen wyse.°	*pagan customs*
With pitous herte and heigh devocioun,	
Right thus to Mars he seyde his orisoun:°	*prayer*
"O stronge god, that in the regnes° colde	*realms*
Of Trace° honoured art and lord y-holde,°	*Thrace / considered*
And hast in every regne and every lond	
Of armes al the brydel° in thyn hond,	*i.e., control*
And hem fortunest as thee list devyse,[1]	
Accepte of me my pitous sacrifyse.	
If so be that my youthe may deserve,	
And that my might be worthy for to serve	
Thy godhede, that I may be oon of thyne,	
Thanne preye I thee to rewe° upon my pyne.°	*take pity / suffering*
For thilke° peyne and thilke hote fyr	*that same*
In which thou whylom° brendest° for desyr,	*once / burned*
Whan that thou usedest° the beautee	*enjoyed*
Of fayre yonge fresshe Venus free,°	*noble, generous*
And haddest hir in armes at thy wille—	
Although thee ones° on a tyme misfille°	*once / it went wrong with*
Whan Vulcanus hadde caught thee in his las,°	*net*
And fond° thee ligginge° by his wyf, allas!—	*found / lying*
For thilke sorwe that was in thyn herte,	
Have routhe° as wel upon my peynes smerte.°	*pity / sharp*
I am yong and unkonning,° as thou wost,°	*ignorant / knowest*
And, as I trowe,° with love offended° most	*believe / assailed*
That evere was any lyves° creature;	*living*
For she that dooth° me al this wo endure,	*makes*
Ne reccheth° nevere wher° I sinke or flete.°	*cares / whether / float*
And wel I woot, er she me mercy hete,°	*promise*
I moot with strengthe winne hire in the place;°	*i.e., the tournament lists*
And wel I woot, withouten help or grace	
Of thee, ne may my strengthe noght availle.	
Than help me, lord, tomorwe in my bataille,	
For thilke fyr that whylom brente° thee,	*burned*

1. And give them (whatever) fortune it pleases you to devise.

As wel as thilke fyr now brenneth me;
And do° that I tomorwe have victorie. *bring it about*
Myn be the travaille,° and thyn be the glorie! *labor*
Thy soverein temple wol I most honouren
Of any place, and alwey most labouren
In° thy plesaunce° and in thy craftes° stronge, *For / pleasure / activities*
And in thy temple I wol my baner honge,° *hang*
And alle the armes of my companye;
And everemo, unto that day I dye,
Eterne fyr I wol biforn thee finde.° *provide*
And eek° to this avow I wol me binde: *also*
My berd, myn heer, that hongeth long adoun,
That never yet ne felte offensioun° *damage*
Of rasour nor of shere,° I wol thee yive, *shears*
And ben thy trewe servant whyl I live.
Now lord, have routhe upon my sorwes sore:
Yif° me the victorie, I aske thee namore." *Give*
The preyere stinte° of Arcita the stronge, *being ended*
The ringes on the temple dore that honge,
And eek the dores, clatereden ful faste,
Of which Arcita somwhat him agaste.° *took fright*
The fyres brenden up on the auter brighte,
That it gan al the temple for to lighte;
And swete smel the ground anon up yaf,° *gave*
And Arcita anon his hand up haf,° *lifted*
And more encens° into the fyr he caste, *incense*
With othere rytes mo; and atte laste
The statue of Mars bigan his hauberk° ringe. *coat of mail*
And with that soun he herde a murmuringe
Ful lowe and dim, that sayde thus, "Victorie,"
For which he yaf to Mars honour and glorie.
And thus with joye and hope wel to fare,
Arcite anon unto his in° is fare,° *dwelling / gone*
As fayn° as fowel° is of the brighte sonne. *glad / fowl, bird*
And right anon swich stryf ther is bigonne,
For thilke graunting, in the hevene above,
Bitwixe Venus, the goddesse of love,
And Mars, the sterne god armipotente,° *strong in arms*
That Jupiter was bisy it to stente;° *stop*
Til that the pale Saturnus the colde,[2]
That knew so manye of aventures olde,
Fond° in his olde experience an art *Found*
That he ful sone hath plesed every part.° *side*
As sooth is sayd, elde° hath greet avantage; *old age*
In elde is bothe wisdom and usage;° *experience*
Men may the olde atrenne° and noght atrede.° *outrun / outwit*
Saturne anon, to stinten stryf and drede,
Al be it that it is agayn° his kynde,° *against / nature*

2. In describing Saturn, the word not only indicates his imbalance of humors but also means ominous, baleful.

Of al this stryf he gan remedie fynde.
"My dere doghter Venus," quod Saturne,
"My cours,° that hath so wyde for to turne, *orbit*
Hath more power than wot° any man: *knows*
Myn is the drenching° in the see so wan;° *drowning / pale, colorless*
Myn is the prison° in the derke cote;° *imprisonment / hut, cell*
Myn is the strangling and hanging by the throte;
The murmure and the cherles° rebelling, *churls', peasants'*
The groyninge° and the pryvee° empoysoning. *grumbling / secret*
I do vengeance and pleyn° correccioun° *full / punishment*
Whyl I dwelle in the signe of the leoun.[3]
Myn is the ruine of the hye halles,
The falling of the toures and of the walles
Upon the mynour° or the carpenter. *miner*
I slow° Sampsoun, shakinge the piler; *slew*
And myne be the maladyes colde,
The derke tresons, and the castes° olde; *plots, deceits*
My loking° is the fader of pestilence. *aspect*
Now weep namore, I shal doon diligence
That Palamon, that is thyn owne knight,
Shal have his lady, as thou hast him hight.° *promised*
Though Mars shal helpe his knight, yet nathelees
Bitwixe yow ther moot be som tyme pees,° *peace*
Al be ye noght of o complexioun,° *the same temperament*
That causeth al day swich divisioun.
I am thin ayel,° redy at thy wille; *grandfather*
Weep now namore, I wol thy lust° fulfille." *desire*
Now wol I stinten° of the goddes above, *cease (to tell)*
Of Mars and of Venus, goddesse of love,
And telle yow as pleynly as I can
The grete effect° for which that I bigan. *outcome*

PART FOUR

Greet was the feste in Athenes that day,
And eek the lusty seson of that May
Made every wight to been in swich plesaunce,° *pleasure*
That al that Monday justen° they and daunce, *joust*
And spenden it in Venus heigh servyse.
But by the cause that° they sholde ryse *i.e., because*
Erly, for to seen the grete fight,
Unto hir reste wenten they at night.
And on the morwe, whan that day gan springe,
Of hors and harneys° noyse and clateringe *equipment*
Ther was in hostelryes al aboute;
And to the paleys rood ther many a route° *company*
Of lordes upon stedes and palfreys.
Ther maystow seen devysing° of harneys *fashioning, preparation*
So uncouth° and so riche, and wroght so weel° *curious, unusual / well*

3. Saturn is most malign while in the astrological house of Leo.

Of goldsmithrie, of browdinge,° and of steel; *embroidery*
The sheeldes brighte, testeres,° and trappures;° *headpieces / trappings*
Gold-hewen helmes, hauberkes, cote-armures;
Lordes in paraments° on hir courseres,° *decorated robes / coursers, chargers*
Knightes of retenue,° and eek squyeres *in service*
Nailinge the speres,[4] and helmes bokelinge;
Gigginge of° sheeldes with layneres° lacinge— *Putting straps on / thongs*
Ther as° need is, they weren no thing ydel; *Wherever*
The fomy steedes on the golden brydel
Gnawinge, and faste the armurers also
With fyle and hamer prikinge° to and fro; *riding*
Yemen° on foote and communes° many oon *Yeomen / common people*
With shorte staves, thikke as they may goon;
Pypes, trompes,° nakers,° clariounes *trumpets / kettledrums*
That in the bataille blowen blody sounes,° *warlike sounds*
The paleys ful of peple up and doun,
Heer three, ther ten, holding hir questioun,
Divyninge of° thise Thebane knightes two. *Speculating about*
Somme seyden thus, somme seyde it shal be so;
Somme helden with° him with the blake berd, *sided with*
Somme with the balled,° somme with the thikke herd;° *bald / haired*
Somme sayde he° loked grim, and he wolde fighte— *that one*
"He hath a sparth° of twenty pound of wighte."° *battle-ax / weight*
Thus was the halle ful of divyninge,
Longe after that the sonne gan to springe.
The grete Theseus, that of° his sleep awaked *out of*
With minstralcye and noyse that was maked,
Held yet the chambre of his paleys riche,
Til that the Thebane knightes, bothe yliche° *equally*
Honoured, were into the paleys fet.° *summoned*
Duk Theseus was at a window set,
Arrayed right as he were a god in trone.° *throne*
The peple preesseth thiderward ful sone
Him for to seen, and doon heigh reverence,
And eek to herkne° his heste° and his sentence.° *hear / command / decision*
An heraud on a scaffold made an "Oo!"
Til al the noyse of peple was ydo;° *done, finished*
And whan he saugh the peple of noyse al stille,
Thus showed he the mighty dukes wille:
"The lord hath of his heigh discrecioun° *acumen*
Considered that it were destruccioun
To gentil blood to fighten in the gyse° *manner*
Of mortal bataille now in this empryse.° *undertaking*
Wherfore, to shapen° that they shal not dye, *arrange things so*
He wol his firste purpos modifye.
No man therfore, up° peyne of los of lyf, *upon*
No maner shot,° ne polax,° ne short knyf *arrow, missile / battle-ax*
Into the listes sende,° or thider bringe; *may send*

4. I.e., nailing the head to the shaft.

Ne short swerd, for to stoke° with poynt bytinge,° *stab / piercing*
No man ne drawe ne bere it by his syde.
Ne no man shal unto his felawe° ryde *against his opponent*
But o cours° with a sharp y-grounde spere; *one charge*
Foyne,° if him list, on fote, himself to were.° *He may parry / defend*
And he that is at meschief° shal be take,° *in trouble / taken, captured*
And noght slayn, but be broght unto the stake
That shal ben ordeyned° on either syde; *set up*
But thider he shal by force, and ther abyde.[5]
And if so falle° the chieftayn be take *befall, happen*
On either syde, or elles° sleen° his make,[6] *else / slay*
No lenger shal the turneyinge laste.
God spede yow! goth forth, and ley on faste.
With long swerd and with mace fighteth youre fille.
Goth now youre wey—this is the lordes wille."
  The voys of peple touchede the hevene,
So loude cryde they with mery stevene:° *voice*
"God save swich a lord, that is so good,
He wilneth° no destruccioun of blood!" *desires*
  Up goon the trompes° and the melodye, *trumpets*
And to the listes rit° the companye, *rides*
By ordinaunce,° thurghout the citee large, *In order*
Hanged with cloth of gold and nat with sarge.° *serge*
Ful lyk a lord this noble duk gan ryde,
Thise two Thebans upon either syde;
And after rood the quene and Emelye,
And after that another companye
Of oon and other, after hir degree.° *according to their rank*
And thus they passen thurghout the citee,
And to the listes come they bytyme.° *promptly*
It nas° not of the day yet fully pryme° *was / 9 A.M.*
Whan set was Theseus ful riche and hye,
Ipolita the quene and Emelye,
And othere ladies in degrees° aboute. *tiers*
Unto the seetes preesseth al the route.° *crowd*
  And westward, thurgh the gates under Marte,° *Mars*
Arcite, and eek the hundred of his parte,° *on his side*
With baner° reed is entred right anon; *banner*
And in that selve° moment Palamon *same*
Is under Venus, estward in the place,
With baner whyt, and hardy chere° and face. *countenance*
In al the world, to seken up and doun,
So evene° withouten variacioun, *equal*
Ther nere° swiche companyes tweye. *were not*
For ther was noon so wys that coude seye
That any hadde of other avauntage
Of° worthinesse, ne of estaat ne age, *In*
So evene were they chosen, for to gesse.° *one would guess*

5. But there he must be brought by force, and there remain.
6. I.e., the opposing leader.

And in two renges° faire they hem dresse.° *rows / place themselves*
Whan that hir names rad° were everichoon,° *read / every one*
That° in hir nombre gyle° were ther noon, *So that / deception*
Tho° were the gates shet,° and cryed was loude: *Then / shut*
"Do now your devoir,° yonge knightes proude!" *duty*
  The heraudes lefte hir priking° up and doun; *their riding*
Now ringen trompes loude and clarioun.
Ther is namore to seyn, but west and est
In goon the speres ful sadly° in th'arest;° *firmly / into the spear rests*
In goth the sharpe spore° into the syde. *spur*
Ther seen men who can juste° and who can ryde; *joust*
Ther shiveren shaftes upon sheeldes thikke;
He° feleth thurgh the herte-spoon° the prikke. *One / breastbone*
Up springen speres twenty foot on highte;° *on high*
Out goon the swerdes as the silver brighte.
The helmes they tohewen and toshrede;° *hew and shred to pieces*
Out brest° the blood, with sterne° stremes rede. *bursts / powerful, violent*
With mighty maces the bones they tobreste.° *smash to bits*
He thurgh the thikkeste of the throng gan threste;° *thrust*
Ther stomblen stedes stronge, and doun goth al;
He rolleth under foot as dooth a bal.
He foyneth° on his feet with his *parries*
  tronchoun,° *truncheon, shattered spear*
And he him hurtleth° with his hors adoun. *strikes*
He thurgh the body is hurt and sithen° y-take, *then*
Maugree his heed,° and broght unto the stake. *In spite of all he could do*
As forward° was, right ther he moste abyde; *agreement*
Another lad° is on that other syde. *led, carried off*
And som tyme dooth° hem Theseus to reste, *causes*
Hem to refresshe and drinken, if hem leste.° *if it please them*
  Ful ofte a day° han thise Thebanes two *during this day*
Togidre y-met, and wroght his felawe wo;° *done harm to each other*
Unhorsed hath ech other of hem tweye.° *twice*
Ther nas no tygre° in the vale of Galgopheye,[7] *tigress*
Whan that hir whelp is stole whan it is lyte,° *little*
So cruel on the hunte° as is Arcite *toward the hunter*
For jelous herte upon° this Palamoun. *toward*
Ne in Belmarye ther nis so fel° leoun *fierce*
That hunted is, or for° his hunger wood,° *because of / enraged*
Ne of his praye desireth so the blood,
As Palamon to sleen° his foo Arcite. *slay*
The jelous strokes on hir helmes byte;
Out renneth° blood on bothe hir sydes rede. *runs*
  Som tyme an ende ther is of every dede.
For er the sonne unto the reste wente,
The stronge king Emetreus gan hente° *seize*
This Palamon, as he faught with Arcite,

7. Probably the valley of Gargaphie, where according to Ovid's *Metamorphoses* Actaeon was killed by his hounds. Chaucer describes the event in ll. 2065–68. For Belmarye (l. 2630), see *General Prologue*, l. 57.

And made his swerd depe in his flesh to byte;
And by the force of twenty is he take
Unyolden° and y-drawe° unto the stake. — *Not having yielded / drawn, dragged*
And in the rescus° of this Palamoun — *(attempted) rescue*
The stronge king Ligurge is born adoun;
And king Emetreus, for al his strengthe,
Is born° out of his sadel a swerdes lengthe, — *carried, knocked*
So hitte him Palamon er he were take.
But al for noght: he was broght to the stake.
His hardy herte mighte him helpe naught;
He moste abyde, whan that he was caught,
By force° and eek by composicioun.° — *necessity / agreement*
Who sorweth now but woful Palamoun,
That moot° namore goon agayn to fighte? — *may*
And whan that Theseus had seyn this sighte,
Unto the folk that foghten thus echoon
He cryde, "Ho! namore, for it is doon!
I wol be trewe juge, and nat partye.° — *partisan*
Arcite of Thebes shal have Emelye,
That by his fortune hath hir faire° y-wonne." — *fairly*
Anon ther is a noyse of peple bigonne
For joye of this, so loude and heighe° withalle, — *great*
It semed that the listes sholde falle.
What can now faire Venus doon above?
What seith she now? what dooth this quene of love
But wepeth so, for wanting° of hir wille, — *lacking*
Til that hir teres in the listes fille?° — *fell*
She seyde, "I am ashamed,° doutelees." — *shamed, disgraced*
Saturnus seyde, "Doghter, hold thy pees.° — *peace*
Mars hath his wille: his knight hath al his bone;° — *request*
And, by myn heed,° thou shalt ben esed° sone." — *head / eased, satisfied*
The trompours° with the loude minstralcye,° — *trumpeters / music*
The heraudes that ful loude yelle and crye,
Been in hir wele° for joye of daun° Arcite. — *happiness / sir, master*
But herkneth me, and stinteth° noyse a lyte,° — *cease / little*
Which° a miracle ther bifel anon. — *What*
This fierse° Arcite hath of° his helm y-don,° — *bold / off / taken*
And on a courser, for to shewe his face,
He priketh endelong° the large place, — *the length of*
Loking upward upon this Emelye;
And she agayn° him caste a freendlich yë — *toward*
(For wommen, as to speken in comune,° — *generally*
They folwen alle the favour of fortune)
And she was al his chere,° as in his herte. — *happiness*
Out of the ground a furie infernal sterte,° — *started, leaped*
From Pluto sent at requeste of Saturne,
For which his hors for fere° gan to turne — *fear*
And leep° asyde, and foundred° as he leep; — *leaped / foundered, stumbled*
And er that Arcite may taken keep,° — *heed*
He pighte° him on the pomel° of his heed, — *pitched / crown, top*
That in the place he lay as he were deed,

His brest tobrosten° with° his sadel-bowe.[8] *broken, shattered / by*
As blak he lay as any cole° or crowe, *coal*
So was the blood y-ronnen in° his face. *into*
Anon he was y-born out of the place,
With herte soor, to Theseus paleys.
Tho° was he corven° out of his harneys,° *Then / cut / armor*
And in a bed y-brought ful faire and blyve,° *quickly*
For he was yet in memorie° and alyve, *conscious*
And alway crying after Emelye.
Duk Theseus, with al his companye,
Is comen hoom to Athenes his citee,
With alle blisse and greet solempnitee.
Al be it that this aventure° was falle,° *accident / had occurred*
He nolde noght disconforten° hem alle. *dishearten*
Men seyde eek that Arcite shal nat dye;
He shal ben heled of his maladye.
And of another thing they were as fayn:° *glad*
That of hem alle was ther noon y-slayn,
Al° were they sore y-hurt, and namely° oon, *Although / especially*
That with a spere was thirled° his brest-boon. *pierced*
To° othere woundes and to broken armes *For*
Some hadden salves, and some hadden charmes;
Fermacies° of herbes, and eek save° *Medicines / a drink made of herbs*
They dronken, for they wolde hir limes° have.° *limbs / keep, preserve*
For which this noble duk, as he wel can,° *knows how*
Conforteth and honoureth every man,
And made revel al the longe night
Unto the straunge° lordes, as was right. *foreign*
Ne ther was holden no disconfitinge
But as a justes or a tourneyinge;
For soothly ther was no disconfiture,
For falling nis nat but an aventure.[9]
Ne to be lad° with fors unto the stake *led, carried*
Unyolden,° and with twenty knightes take, *Not having yielded*
O° persone allone, withouten mo, *One*
And haried° forth by arme, foot, and to,° *dragged / toe*
And eek his steede driven forth with staves
With° footmen, bothe yemen and eek knaves°— *By / servants*
It nas aretted° him no vileinye,° *attributed to / disgrace*
Ther may no man clepen° it cowardye.° *call / cowardice*
For which anon duk Theseus leet crye,° *caused to be proclaimed*
To stinten° alle rancour and envye,° *stop / bad will*
The gree° as wel of o syde as of other, *worthiness*
And either syde ylyk° as otheres brother; *alike*
And yaf hem yiftes after hir degree,
And fully heeld a feste dayes three;

8. The high-arched front of a saddle. Arcite's horse, after rearing and pitching him off, falls backward on top of him.
9. Nor was anything accounted a defeat except as is proper to a jousting or a tournament; for truly there was no dishonor, since falling (in a joust) is nothing but an accident.

And conveyed the kinges worthily
Out of his toun a journee° largely.° *a day's journey / fully*
And hoom wente every man the righte way.
Ther was namore but "Farewel, have good day!"
Of this bataille I wol namore endyte,° *tell, make verses*
But speke of Palamon and of Arcite.
  Swelleth the brest of Arcite, and the sore
Encreesseth at his herte more and more.
The clothered° blood, for° any lechecraft,° *clotted / despite / medical care*
Corrupteth and is in his bouk° y-laft,° *body / left*
That neither veyne-blood,° ne ventusinge,° *bloodletting / cupping*
Ne drinke of herbes may ben his helpinge.
The vertu expulsif, or animal,
Fro thilke vertu cleped natural[1]
Ne may the venim voyden° ne expelle. *void, remove*
The pypes° of his longes° gonne to swelle, *tubes / lungs*
And every lacerte° in his brest adoun *muscle*
Is shent° with venim and corrupcioun.° *damaged / decay*
Him gayneth° neither, for to gete° his lyf, *It helps him / save*
Vomyt upward ne dounward laxatif;
Al is tobrosten° thilke regioun. *shattered*
Nature hath now no dominacioun;° *dominion, power*
And certeinly, ther nature wol nat wirche,° *work*
Farewel, phisyk;° go ber the man to chirche. *medicine*
This al and som,° that Arcita mot° dye; *This is the entire matter / must*
For which he sendeth after Emelye
And Palamon, that was his cosin dere.
Than seyde he thus, as ye shul after here:
  "Naught may the woful spirit in myn herte
Declare o poynt° of alle my sorwes smerte° *one part / painful*
To yow, my lady, that I love most;
But I biquethe° the service of my gost° *bequeath / spirit, soul*
To yow aboven every creature,
Sin° that my lyf may no lenger dure.° *Since / last*
Allas, the wo! allas, the peynes stronge,
That I for yow have suffred, and so longe!
Allas, the deeth! allas, myn Emelye!
Allas, departinge° of oure companye! *separation*
Allas, myn hertes quene! allas, my wyf!
Myn hertes lady, endere of my lyf!
What is this world? what asketh men° to have? *does one ask*
Now with his love, now in his colde grave
Allone, withouten any companye.
Farewel, my swete fo, myn Emelye!
And softe tak me in your armes tweye,
For love of God, and herkneth what I seye:

1. Medieval medicine thought three powers ("virtues") controlled the functions of the body. Here the animal virtue, located in the brain, is unable to force the muscles to expel the corrupted blood from the natural virtue, located in the liver. Hence the natural virtue is powerless to perform one of its normal tasks, cleansing the lungs of corrupt substances.

I have heer with my cosin Palamon
Had stryf and rancour many a day agon,° *past*
For love of yow and for my jalousye.
And Jupiter so wis° my soule gye,° *wise / guide*
To speken of° a servant° proprely, *about / servant (of love)*
With alle circumstaunces° trewely— *necessary qualities*
That is to seyn, trouthe,° honour, knighthede, *fidelity*
Wisdom, humblesse,° estaat,° and heigh kinrede,° *humility / position* *kindred*
Fredom,° and al that longeth° to that art— *Generosity / belongs*
So Jupiter have of my soule part,° *i.e., receive after death*
As in this world right now ne knowe I non
So worthy to ben loved as Palamon,
That serveth yow and wol don al his lyf.
And if that evere ye shul been a wyf,
Foryet nat Palamon, the gentil° man." *noble, virtuous*
And with that word his speche faille gan,° *began to*
For from his feet up to his brest was come
The cold of deeth, that hadde him overcome,
And yet moreover, in his armes two
The vital strengthe is lost and al ago.
Only° the intellect, withouten more,° *Only then / without delay*
That dwelled in his herte syk and sore,
Gan faillen when the herte felte deeth.
Dusked° his eyen two, and failled breeth, *Became dim*
But on his lady yet caste he his yë;
His laste word was, "Mercy, Emelye!"
His spirit chaunged hous and wente ther
As° I cam never, I can nat tellen wher. *Where*
Therfor I stinte,° I nam no divinistre;° *stop / diviner, theologian*
Of soules finde I nat in this registre,° *register, list*
Ne me ne list° thilke° opiniouns to telle *It does not please me / those*
Of hem, though that they wryten wher they dwelle.
Arcite is cold, ther° Mars his soule gye.° *wherefore may / guide*
Now wol I speken forth of Emelye.

Shrighte° Emelye and howleth Palamon, *Shrieked*
And Theseus his suster took anon
Swowninge, and bar° hire fro the corps away. *bore, carried*
What helpeth it to tarien forth the day[2]
To tellen how she weep° bothe eve and morwe? *wept*
For in swich cas wommen have swich sorwe,
Whan that hir housbondes been from hem ago,° *gone*
That for the more part they sorwen so,° *thus, in that manner*
Or elles fallen in swich a maladye
That at the laste certeinly they dye.

Infinite been the sorwes and the teres
Of olde folk and folk of tendre yeres
In al the toun, for deeth of this Theban;

2. What does it serve to while away the day.

For him ther wepeth bothe child and man.
So greet weping was ther noon, certayn,
Whan Ector° was y-broght, al fresh y-slayn, *Hector*
To Troye. Allas, the pitee that was ther:
Cracchinge° of chekes, renting° eek of heer. *Scratching / rending, tearing*
"Why woldestow° be deed," thise wommen crye, *didst thou wish to*
"And haddest gold ynough, and Emelye?"
No man mighte gladen Theseus
Savinge° his olde fader Egeus, *Except*
That knew this worldes transmutacioun,° *mutability*
As he had seyn it chaunge bothe up and doun—
Joye after wo, and wo after gladnesse—
And shewed hem ensamples and lyknesse.° *i.e., analogies*
"Right as ther deyed° nevere man," quod he, *died*
"That he ne livede in erthe in some degree,
Right so ther livede never man," he seyde,
"In al this world, that som tyme he ne deyde.
This world nis but a thurghfare° ful of wo, *thoroughfare, roadway*
And we ben pilgrimes, passinge to and fro:
Deeth is an ende of every worldly sore."° *pain, sorrow*
And over° al this yet seyde he muchel more *beyond*
To this effect, ful wysely to enhorte° *exhort*
The peple that they sholde hem reconforte.° *be comforted*
Duk Theseus, with al his bisy cure,° *diligent concern*
Caste° now wher that the sepulture° *Considered / burial*
Of goode Arcite may best y-maked be,
And eek most honurable in° his degree.° *according to / rank*
And at the laste he took conclusioun,
That ther as° first Arcite and Palamoun *where*
Hadden for love the bataille hem bitwene,
That in that selve° grove, swote° and grene, *same / sweet*
Ther as he hadde his amorouse desires,
His compleynte,° and for love his hote fires, *lament*
He wolde make a fyr, in which the office° *duties, rites*
Funeral he mighte al accomplice;
And leet comaunde° anon to hakke and hewe *had commands given*
The okes olde, and leye hem on a rewe° *row*
In colpons° wel arrayed° for to brenne.° *pieces / arranged / burn*
His officers with swifte feet they renne° *run*
And ryde anon at his comaundement.
And after this, Theseus hath y-sent
After a bere,° and it al overspradde° *bier / covered*
With cloth of gold, the richeste that he hadde;
And of the same suyte° he cladde Arcite. *material*
Upon his hondes hadde he gloves whyte,
Eek on his heed a croune of laurer° grene, *laurel*
And in his hond a swerd ful bright and kene.
He leyde him, bare the visage,° on the bere; *with face uncovered*
Therwith he weep° that pitee was to here. *wept*
And for° the people sholde seen him alle, *so that*
Whan it was day he broghte him to the halle,

That roreth of the crying and the soun.
Tho cam this woful Theban Palamoun,
With flotery° berd and ruggy,° asshy° heres, — *fluttering / unkempt / ash-covered*
In clothes blake, y-dropped° al with teres; — *wet*
And, passinge othere of° weping, Emelye, — *surpassing others in*
The rewfulleste° of al the companye. — *most rueful, sorrowful*
In as muche as the service sholde be
The more noble and riche in° his degree, — *according to*
Duk Theseus leet° forth three stedes bringe,° — *caused / to be brought*
That trapped° were in steel al gliteringe — *outfitted*
And covered with the armes° of daun Arcite. — *coat of arms*
Upon thise stedes, that weren grete and whyte,
Ther seten° folk, of which oon bar° his sheeld, — *sat / bore*
Another his spere up in his hondes heeld,
The thridde bar with him his bowe Turkeys°— — *Turkish*
Of brend° gold was the cas° and eek the harneys;° — *refined / quiver / fittings*
And riden° forth a pas° with sorweful chere° — *(they) rode / at a walk / countenance*
Toward the grove, as ye shul after here.
The nobleste of the Grekes that ther were
Upon hir shuldres carieden the bere,
With slakke pas° and eyen rede and wete, — *slow pace*
Thurghout the citee by the maister° strete, — *principal*
That sprad° was al with blak; and wonder hye° — *spread / wondrously high*
Right of the same is the strete y-wrye.[3]
Upon the right hond wente old Egeus,
And on that other syde duk Theseus,
With vessels in hir hand of gold ful fyn,
Al ful of hony, milk, and blood, and wyn;
Eek Palamon, with ful greet companye;
And after that cam woful Emelye,
With fyr in honde, as was that tyme the gyse,° — *custom*
To do the office of funeral servyse.
Heigh° labour and ful greet apparaillinge° — *Great / preparation*
Was at the service and the fyr-makinge,
That with his° grene top the hevene raughte,° — *its / reached*
And twenty fadme of brede the armes straughte[4]—
This is to seyn, the bowes° were so brode. — *boughs*
Of stree° first ther was leyd ful many a lode; — *straw*
But how the fyr was maked upon highte,° — *in height*
Ne eek the names how the treës highte°— — *were called*
As ook, firre, birch, aspe,° alder, holm,° popler, — *aspen / holm oak (holly)*
Wilow, elm, plane, ash, box, chasteyn,° lind,° laurer, — *chestnut / linden*
Mapul, thorn, beech, hasel, ew,° whippeltree°— — *yew / dogwood*
How they weren feld shal nat be told for me;
Ne how the goddes° ronnen° up and doun, — *i.e., tree spirits / ran*
Disherited° of hire habitacioun, — *Disinherited*

3. With the same material the street fronts were draped.
4. And twenty fathoms in breadth the sides stretched.

In which they woneden° in reste and pees— *dwelled*
Nymphes, faunes, and amadrides,° *hamadryads (forest nymphs)*
Ne how the bestes and the briddes alle
Fledden for fere whan the wode was falle,° *felled*
Ne how the ground agast was of the light,
That was nat wont° to seen the sonne bright; *accustomed*
Ne how the fyr was couched° first with stree,° *laid / straw*
And thanne with drye stikkes cloven a° three, *in*
And thanne with grene wode and spycerye,° *spices*
And thanne with cloth of gold and with perrye,° *jewels*
And gerlandes hanginge with ful many a flour,
The mirre,° th'encens,° with al so greet odour; *myrrh / incense*
Ne how Arcite lay among al this,
Ne what richesse aboute his body is;
Ne how that Emelye, as was the gyse,° *custom*
Putte in° the fyr of funeral servyse; *i.e., Lit*
Ne how she swowned whan men made the fyr,
Ne what she spak, ne what was hir desyr;
Ne what jeweles men in the fyr caste,
Whan that the fyr was greet and brente° faste; *burned*
Ne how som caste hir sheeld, and som hir spere,
And of hire° vestiments whiche that they were,° *part of their / were wearing*
And cuppes ful of milk and wyn and blood,
Into the fyr that brente as it were wood;° *mad*
Ne how the Grekes with an huge route° *company*
Thryës° riden al the fyr aboute *Thrice*
Upon the left hand, with a loud shoutinge,
And thryës with hir speres clateringe;
And thryës how the ladies gonne crye;° *cried out*
Ne how that lad° was homward Emelye; *led*
Ne how Arcite is brent to asshen colde;
Ne how that liche-wake° was y-holde° *funeral wake / held*
Al thilke night; ne how the Grekes pleye
The wake-pleyes,° ne kepe° I nat to seye— *funeral games / care*
Who wrastleth best naked with oille enoynt,° *anointed*
Ne who that bar him best in no disjoynt.° *in any difficulty*
I wol nat tellen eek how that they goon
Hoom til° Athenes whan the pley is doon; *to*
But shortly to the poynt than wol I wende,° *proceed*
And maken of my longe tale an ende.

By processe° and by lengthe of certeyn° yeres *In due course / a certain number of*
Al stinted° is the moorninge and the teres *ceased*
Of Grekes, by oon general assent.
Thanne semed me ther was a parlement
At Athenes, upon certeyn poynts and cas;° *matters*
Among the whiche poynts y-spoken was
To have with certeyn contrees alliaunce,
And have fully of Thebans obeisaunce.° *submission*
For which this noble Theseus anon
Leet° senden after gentil Palamon, *Caused*

Unwist of° him what was the cause and why; *Unknown to*
But in his blake clothes sorwefully
He cam at his comaundement in hye.° *haste*
Tho sente Theseus for Emelye.
Whan they were set, and hust° was al the place, *hushed*
And Theseus abiden hadde a space° *space of time*
Er any word cam from his wyse brest,
His eyen sette he ther as was his lest,° *pleasure*
And with a sad visage he syked stille,° *sighed quietly*
And after that right thus he seyde his wille:
"The Firste Moevere of the cause above,
Whan he first made the faire cheyne of love,
Greet was th'effect, and heigh° was his entente. *noble*
Wel wiste he why, and what thereof he mente,° *intended*
For with that faire cheyne of love he bond° *bound*
The fyr, the eyr, the water, and the lond
In certeyn boundes, that they may nat flee.
That same Prince and that Moevere," quod he,
"Hath stablissed° in this wrecched world adoun° *established / below*
Certeyne[5] dayes and duracioun
To al that is engendred in this place,
Over° the whiche day they may nat pace,° *Beyond / pass*
Al mowe they° yet tho dayes wel abregge.° *Although they may / abridge, shorten*
Ther needeth non auctoritee to allegge,° *cite*
For it is preved° by experience, *proved*
But that me list° declaren my sentence.° *it pleases me / thought*
Than may men by this ordre wel discerne
That thilke Moevere stable is and eterne.° *eternal*
Wel may men knowe, but it be a fool,
That every part deryveth° from his hool.° *derives, descends / its own whole*
For nature hath nat taken his beginning
Of no partye° or cantel° of a thing, *part / portion*
But of° a thing that parfit is and stable, *from*
Descendinge so° til it be corrumpable.° *i.e., from heaven / corruptible*
And therfore, of his wyse purveyaunce,° *providence, foresight*
He hath so wel biset° his ordinaunce° *arranged / plan*
That speces° of thinges and progressiouns° *species / natural changes*
Shullen enduren by successiouns° *succession of generations*
And nat eterne,° withouten any lye. *by being eternal*
This maistow° understonde and seen at eye:° *mayest thou / by looking*
Lo, the ook that hath so long a norisshinge° *growth*
From tyme that it first biginneth springe,
And hath so long a lyf, as we may see,
Yet at the laste wasted is the tree.
Considereth eek, how that the harde stoon
Under oure feet, on which we trede and goon,
Yet wasteth it, as it lyth by the weye.

5. I.e., a certain number of.

The brode river somtyme wexeth dreye;° *becomes dry*
The grete tounes see we wane and wende.° *pass away*
Than may ye see that al this thing hath ende.
Of man and womman seen we wel also
That nedes,° in oon of thise termes° two, *by necessity / times*
This is to seyn, in youthe or elles age,
He moot be deed, the king as shal a page;
Som° in his bed, som in the depe see, *One*
Som in the large feeld, as men may see.
Ther helpeth noght: al goth that ilke° weye. *same*
Thanne may I seyn that al this thing moot deye.° *must die*
What° maketh this but Jupiter the king, *Who*
That is prince and cause of alle thing,
Convertinge al unto his° propre welle° *its / source*
From which it is deryved, sooth to telle?
And here-agayns° no creature on lyve,° *against this / alive*
Of no degree, availleth° for to stryve. *it avails*
Thanne is it wisdom, as it thinketh° me, *seems to*
To maken vertu of necessitee,
And take it wel that° we may nat eschue,° *what / eschew, avoid*
And namely° that to us alle is due. *especially*
And whoso gruccheth° ought,° he dooth folye, *grouches, complains / in any way*
And rebel is to him that al may gye.° *govern*
And certeinly a man hath most honour
To dyen in his excellence and flour,
Whan he is siker° of his gode name; *sure*
Than hath he doon his freend ne him° no shame. *himself*
And gladder oghte his freend ben of his deeth
Whan with honour up yolden° is his breeth, *yielded*
Than whan his name apalled° is for age, *faded, dimmed*
For al forgeten is his vasselage.° *prowess*
Than is it best, as for a worthy fame,
To dyen whan that he is best of name.
The contrarie of al this is wilfulnesse.
Why grucchen we, why have we hevinesse,° *sorrow*
That goode Arcite, of chivalrye flour,° *the flower*
Departed is with duetee° and honour *due respect*
Out of this foule prison of this lyf?
Why grucchen heer his cosin and his wyf
Of his welfare, that loveth hem so weel?
Can he hem thank? Nay, God wot, never a deel,° *not a bit*
That° bothe his soule and eek hemself° offende,° *Who / themselves / hurt*
And yet they mowe° hir lustes° nat amende.° *can / happiness / advance*
What may I conclude of this longe serie,° *sequence of arguments*
But after wo I rede° us to be merie, *advise*
And thanken Jupiter of al his grace;
And er that we departen from this place,
I rede° that we make of sorwes two *advise*
O° parfyt joye, lastinge everemo; *One*
And loketh now, wher most sorwe is herinne,

Ther wol we first amenden and biginne.
Suster," quod he, "this is my fulle assent,° *desire*
With al th'avys° heer of my parlement: *advice*
That gentil Palamon, your owne knight,
That serveth yow with wille, herte, and might,
And ever hath doon sin° ye first him knewe, *since*
That ye shul of your grace upon him rewe,° *take pity*
And taken him for housbonde and for lord.
Leene° me your hond, for this is our acord.° *Give / agreement*
Lat see now of youre wommanly pitee.
He is a kinges brother° sone, pardee;° *brother's / indeed (French: par Dieu)*
And though he were a povre bacheler,° *young knight*
Sin he hath served yow so many a yeer,
And had for yow so greet adversitee,
It moste been considered, leveth° me; *believe*
For gentil mercy oghte to passen° right."° *surpass, prevail over / justice*
Than seyde he thus to Palamon the knyght:
"I trowe° ther nedeth litel sermoning° *believe / preaching, persuading*
To make yow assente to this thing.
Com neer, and tak your lady by the hond."
Bitwixen hem was maad anon° the bond *at once*
That highte matrimoigne° or marriage, *matrimony*
By al the counseil° and the baronage. *council*
And thus with alle blisse and melodye
Hath Palamon y-wedded Emelye.
And God, that al this wyde world hath wroght,
Sende him his love that hath it dere aboght.° *who has paid dearly for it*
For now is Palamon in alle wele,° *happiness*
Livinge in blisse, in richesse, and in hele,° *health, well-being*
And Emelye him loveth so tendrely,
And he hir serveth so gentilly
That nevere was ther no word hem bitwene
Of jalousye or any other tene.° *trouble, vexation*
Thus endeth Palamon and Emelye;
And God save al this faire companye! Amen.

The Miller's Prologue and Tale

The Prologue

Whan that the Knight had thus his tale y-told,
In al the route° nas° ther yong ne old *company / was not*
That he ne seyde it was a noble storie,
And worthy for to drawen to° memorie, *hold in*
And namely the gentils everichoon.[1]
Oure Hoste lough° and swoor, "So moot I goon,[2] *laughed*
This gooth aright;° unbokeled° is the male.° *well / opened / bag*

1. And particularly the well-born (pilgrims), every one.
2. Roughly, "As I may hope to live."

Lat see now who shal telle another tale,
For trewely, the game is wel bigonne.
Now telleth ye, sir Monk, if that ye conne,° *know how*
Sumwhat° to quyte with° the Knightes tale." *Something / match (repay)*
The Miller, that fordronken° was al pale, *totally drunk*
So that unnethe° upon his hors he sat, *with difficulty*
He nolde avalen° neither hood ne hat, *take off*
Ne abyde° no man for his° curteisye, *wait for / out of*
But in Pilates vois he gan to crye,[3]
And swoor, "By armes° and by blood and bones, *(Christ's) arms*
I can° a noble tale for the nones,° *know / occasion*
With which I wol now quyte° the Knightes tale." *repay*
  Oure Hoste saugh that he was dronke of° ale, *drunken from*
And seyde, "Abyd,° Robin, my leve° brother, *Wait / dear*
Som bettre man shal telle us first another:
Abyd, and lat us werken thriftily."° *proceed properly*
  "By Goddes soul," quod° he, "that wol nat I; *said*
For I wol speke or elles° go my wey." *else*
Oure Hoste answerde, "Tel on, a devel wey!° *what the devil*
Thou art a fool, thy wit is overcome."
  "Now herkneth,"° quod the Miller, "alle and some!° *listen / one and all*
But first I make a protestacioun
That I am dronke, I knowe it by my soun.° *the sound of my voice*
And therfore, if that I misspeke or seye,° *speak or talk amiss*
Wyte it° the ale of Southwerk, I yow preye;° *Blame it on / beseech*
For I wol telle a legende and a lyf
Bothe of a carpenter and of his wyf,
How that a clerk hath set the wrightes cappe."[4]
  The Reve[5] answerde and seyde, "Stint thy clappe!° *Stop your chatter*
Lat be thy lewed° dronken harlotrye.° *coarse / ribaldry*
It is a sinne and eek° a greet folye° *also / folly*
To apeiren° any man, or him diffame, *injure*
And eek to bringen wyves in swich fame.° *into such (bad) repute*
Thou mayst ynogh of othere thinges seyn."° *speak*
  This dronken Miller spak ful sone ageyn,° *in response*
And seyde, "Leve brother Osewold,
Who hath no wyf, he is no cokewold.° *cuckold*
But I sey nat therfore that thou art oon;
Ther been ful gode wyves many oon,° *a one*
And ever a thousand gode ayeyns° oon badde. *(to set) against*
That knowestow wel thyself, but if thou madde.[6]
Why artow° angry with my tale now? *art thou*
I have a wyf, pardee,° as well as thou, *by God*
Yet nolde° I, for the oxen in my plogh,° *would not / plow*
Take upon me more° than ynogh,° *more (cares) / necessary*

3. He cried aloud in a voice like Pilate's (familiar from the mystery plays: a ranting voice conventionally high and hoarse).
4. How a student made a fool of the carpenter.
5. The Reeve is the general manager of an estate; see the *General Prologue*, ll. 587–622.
6. Thou knowest that well thyself, unless thou art mad.

As demen of myself that I were oon;[7]
I wol beleve wel that I am noon.
An housbond shal nat been inquisitif
Of Goddes privetee,° nor of his wyf. *secrets*
So he may finde Goddes foyson° there, *plenty*
Of the remenant nedeth nat enquere."[8]
What sholde I more seyn, but this Millere
He nolde° his wordes for no man forbere,° *would not / spare*
But tolde his cherles° tale in his manere. *churl's*
M'athynketh° that I shal° reherce it here. *I regret / must*
And therfore every gentil wight° I preye,° *person / beg*
For Goddes love, demeth° nat that I seye° *judge / speak*
Of° evel entente, but that I moot° reherce *From / must*
Hir° tales alle, be they bettre or werse, *Their*
Or elles falsen° som of my matere. *falsify*
And therfore, whoso list° it nat y-here,° *desires / to hear*
Turne over the leef,° and chese° another tale; *page / choose*
For he shal finde ynowe,° grete and smale, *enough*
Of storial° thing that toucheth° gentillesse, *historical / treats of*
And eek° moralitee and holinesse. *also*
Blameth nat me if that ye chese amis.
The Millere is a cherl,° ye knowe wel this; *churl, rude fellow*
So was the Reve eek and othere mo,° *more*
And harlotrye° they tolden bothe two. *ribaldry*
Avyseth yow° and putte me out of blame; *Think (before you choose)*
And eek men shal nat maken ernest of game.[9]

The Tale

Whylom° ther was dwellinge at Oxenford° *Once / Oxford*
A riche gnof,° that gestes heeld to bord,° *churl / took in lodgers*
And of his craft° he was a carpenter. *by trade*
With him ther was dwellinge a povre scoler,° *poor student*
Hadde lerned art, but al his fantasye[1]
Was turned for to lerne astrologye,
And coude a certeyn of conclusiouns
To demen by interrogaciouns,[2]
If that men asked him in certein houres
Whan that men sholde have droghte or elles shoures,° *else showers*
Or if men asked him what sholde bifalle
Of every thing, I may nat rekene hem° alle. *count them*
This clerk was cleped hende Nicholas.[3]
Of derne° love he coude° and of solas;° *secret / knew / pleasure*
And therto he was sleigh° and ful privee,° *sly / secretive*
And lyk a mayden meke for to see.° *meek to look at*
A chambre hadde he in that hostelrye° *lodging house*

7. As to think that I am one (i.e., a cuckold).
8. There is no need to inquire about the rest.
9. And furthermore one should not treat play as something serious.
1. Who had studied the liberal arts, but all his fancy.
2. And he knew a certain (number) of propositions by which to arrive at an opinion on questions.
3. This scholar was called gentle (pleasant) Nicholas.

Allone, withouten any companye,
Ful fetisly y-dight° with herbes swote;° *neatly arrayed / sweet*
And he himself as swete as is the rote° *root*
Of licorys, or any cetewale.[4]
His Almageste[5] and bokes grete and smale,
His astrelabie,° longinge for° his art, *astrolabe / belonging to*
His augrim-stones[6] layen faire apart
On shelves couched° at his beddes heed; *placed*
His presse y-covered with a falding reed.[7]
And al above ther lay a gay sautrye,[8]
On which he made a-nightes° melodye *by night*
So swetely, that al the chambre rong,° *rang*
And *Angelus ad virginem*° he song, *(an Annunciation hymn)*
And after that he song the kinges note;° *(an unidentified song)*
Ful often blessed was his mery throte.
And thus this swete clerk his tyme spente
After his freendes finding and his rente.[9]
This carpenter hadde wedded newe° a wyf *recently*
Which that he lovede more than his lyf;
Of eightetene yeer she was of age.
Jalous he was, and heeld hire narwe in cage,° *confined, as in a cage*
For she was wilde and yong, and he was old
And demed himself ben lyk° a cokewold.° *likely to be / cuckold*
He knew nat Catoun, for his wit was rude,[1]
That bad° man sholde wedde his similitude.° *bade / his like*
Men sholde wedden after hire estaat,° *according to their condition*
For youthe and elde° is often at debaat.° *old age / strife*
But sith that° he was fallen in the snare, *since*
He moste° endure, as other folk, his care. *must*
Fair was this yonge wyf, and therwithal
As any wesele° hir body gent° and smal. *weasel / graceful*
A ceynt° she werede° barred° al of silk; *belt / wore / striped*
A barmclooth eek as whyt as morne milk[2]
Upon hir lendes,° ful of many a gore.° *loins / very fully cut*
Whyt was hir smok,° and broyden° al bifore *dress / embroidered*
And eek bihinde, on hir coler° aboute, *collar*
Of col-blak silk, withinne and eek withoute.
The tapes° of hir whyte voluper° *strings / bonnet*
Were of the same suyte of° hir coler;° *kind as / collar*
Hir filet° brood of silk and set ful hye.° *headband / high*
And sikerly° she hadde a likerous yë.° *certainly / lecherous eye*
Ful smale y-pulled° were hire browes° two, *plucked / eyebrows*
And tho° were bent, and blake as any sloo.[3] *they*

4. A spice of the ginger family.
5. An astronomical treatise by Ptolemy.
6. Counters for doing arithmetic.
7. His clothes chest covered with red wool cloth.
8. Psaltery: a flat, stringed instrument.
9. In accordance with the money provided (for him) by his relatives, and his income.
1. He didn't know Cato (the *Distichs*, a Latin reader used in the schools), for his intelligence was untutored.
2. An apron also, as white as morning milk.
3. Sloeberry, a purple-black fruit.

She was ful more blisful on to see° *to look on*
Than is the newe pere-jonette° tree; *newly (blossomed) pear*
And softer than the wolle° is of a wether.° *wool / sheep*
And by hir girdel heeng° a purs of lether *hung*
Tasseled with silk, and perled with latoun.° *studded with metal*
In al this world, to seken up and doun,
There nis° no man so wys° that coude thenche° *is not / wise / imagine*
So gay a popelote,° or swich° a wenche. *plaything (puppet-doll) / such*
Ful brighter was the shyning of hir hewe° *complexion*
Than in the Tour° the noble° y-forged° newe. *Tower of London / gold coin / minted*
But of° hir song, it was as loude and yerne° *in regard to / lively*
As any swalwe° sittinge on a berne.° *swallow / barn*
Therto she coude skippe and make game,° *play*
As any kide or calf folwinge his dame.° *mother*
Hir mouth was swete as bragot or the meeth,[4]
Or hord of apples leyd in hey or heeth.° *heather*
Winsinge° she was, as is a joly colt, *Skittish*
Long as a mast, and upright° as a bolt.° *straight / crossbow bolt*
A brooch she baar° upon hir lowe coler,° *wore / collar*
As brood as is the bos of a bocler;[5]
Hir shoes were laced on hir legges hye.° *high*
She was a prymerole,° a piggesnye,° *primrose / cuckooflower*
For any lord to leggen° in his bedde, *lay*
Or yet for any good yeman° to wedde. *yeoman*
Now sire, and eft° sire, so bifel the cas,° *again / affair*
That on a day this hende° Nicholas *gracious, gentle, clever*
Fil with this yonge wyf to rage° and pleye, *dally*
Whyl that hir housbond was at Oseneye,° *Osney (a town near Oxford)*
As clerkes ben ful subtile and ful queynte.° *sly*
And prively he caughte hire by the queynte,[6]
And seyde, "Ywis, but if ich° have my wille, *Surely, unless I*
For derne° love of thee, lemman,° I spille,"° *hidden / sweetheart / perish*
And heeld hire harde° by the haunche-bones,° *firmly / hips*
And seyde, "Lemman, love me al atones,° *immediately*
Or I wol dyen, also° God me save!" *as*
And she sprong as a colt doth in the trave,[7]
And with hir heed she wryed° faste awey, *twisted*
And seyde, "I wol nat kisse thee, by my fey.° *faith*
Why, lat be,"° quod° she, "lat be, Nicholas, *leave off / said*
Or I wol crye 'out, harrow'° and 'allas.' *help*
Do wey your handes° for your curteisye!" *Take your hands away*
This Nicholas gan° mercy for to crye, *began*
And spak so faire, and profred him° so faste,° *offered himself / eagerly*
That she hir love him graunted atte laste,° *at (the) last*
And swoor hir ooth, by Seint Thomas of Kent,° *Thomas Becket*

4. "Bragot" and "meeth" (mead) are drinks made of ale and honey.
5. And broad as is the boss (the central fitting) of a shield.
6. And when they were alone he grabbed her between her legs. ("Queynte" puns on ME "cunte.")
7. A stall for shoeing unruly horses.

That she wol been at his comandement,
Whan that she may hir leyser° wel espye.° *chance, opportunity / perceive*
"Myn housbond is so ful of jalousye,
That but ye wayte° wel and been privee,° *watch out / secretive*
I woot° right wel I nam but° deed," quod she. *know / I'm as good as*
"Ye moste been ful derne,° as in this cas." *secret*
   "Nay, therof care thee noght," quod Nicholas.
"A clerk had litherly biset his whyle,° *poorly used his time*
But if° he coude a carpenter bigyle."° *Unless / trick*
And thus they been acorded and y-sworn
To wayte a tyme, as I have told biforn.
Whan Nicholas had doon thus everydeel,° *all this so*
And thakked° hire aboute the lendes° weel, *stroked / loins*
He kiste° hire swete, and taketh his sautrye,° *kissed / psaltery*
And pleyeth faste, and maketh melodye.
   Thanne fil° it thus, that to the parish chirche, *befell*
Cristes owene werkes for to wirche,° *perform*
This gode wyf wente on an haliday;° *holy day*
Hir forheed shoon as bright as any day,
So was it wasshen whan she leet° hir werk. *left*
   Now was ther of that chirche a parish clerk,[8]
The which that was y-cleped° Absolon. *called*
Crul° was his heer, and as the gold it shoon, *Curly*
And strouted° as a fanne large and brode; *spread out*
Ful streight and evene lay his joly shode.° *the part in his hair*
His rode° was reed, his eyen greye as goos;° *complexion / a goose*
With Powles window corven on his shoos,[9]
In hoses rede° he wente fetisly.° *red stockings / neatly*
Y-clad he was ful smal° and properly, *tightly*
Al in a kirtel° of a light waget°— *coat / blue*
Ful faire and thikke° been the poyntes° set— *close together / laces*
And therupon he hadde a gay surplys° *loose robe*
As whyt as is the blosme upon the rys.° *twig*
A mery child° he was, so God me save. *young man*
Wel coude he laten° blood and clippe° and shave, *let / cut hair*
And make a chartre° of lond or acquitaunce.° *charter / deed of release*
In twenty manere° coude he trippe and daunce *ways*
After the scole° of Oxenforde° tho,° *fashion / Oxford / then*
And with his legges casten to and fro,
And pleyen songes on a small rubible,° *fiddle*
Therto he song som tyme a loud quinible;° *high treble*
And as wel coude he pleye on a giterne.° *guitar*
In al the toun nas° brewhous ne taverne *there was no*
That he ne visited with his solas,° *entertainment*
Ther° any gaylard tappestere° was. *Where / gay barmaid*
But sooth to seyn, he was somdel squaymous° *somewhat squeamish*
Of farting, and of speche daungerous.° *fastidious*
   This Absolon, that jolif° was and gay, *jolly, amorous*

8. Assistant to the parish priest.
9. With (a design like) the window of St. Paul's (Cathedral) cut into the leather of his shoes.

Gooth with a sencer° on the haliday,° *(incense) censer / holy day*
Sensinge the wyves of the parish faste,° *diligently*
And many a lovely look on hem° he caste, *them*
And namely° on this carpenteres wyf: *especially*
To loke on hire him thoughte a mery lyf.
She was so propre° and swete and likerous,° *comely / flirtatious*
I dar wel seyn, if she had been a mous,
And he a cat, he wolde hire hente anon.° *seize immediately*
This parish clerk, this joly Absolon,
Hath in his herte swich° a love-longinge, *such*
That of° no wyf ne took he noon offringe; *from*
For curteisye, he seyde, he wolde noon.° *wanted none*
  The mone, whan it was night, ful brighte shoon,
And Absolon his giterne hath y-take;
For paramours he thoghte for to wake.[1]
And forth he gooth, jolif and amorous,
Til he cam to the carpenteres hous
A litel after cokkes° hadde y-crowe,° *cocks / crowed*
And dressed him up by a shot-windowe[2]
That was upon the carpenteres wal.° *wall*
He singeth in his vois gentil and smal,° *high, thin*
"Now, dere lady, if thy wille be,
I preye yow that ye wol rewe° on me," *have pity*
Ful wel acordaunt to his giterninge.[3]
This carpenter awook and herde him singe,
And spak unto his wyf, and seyde anon,
"What, Alison, herestow° nat Absolon *hearest thou*
That chaunteth° thus under oure boures° wal?" *sings / bedroom's*
And she answerde hir housbond therwithal,
"Yis, God wot,° John, I here it every deel."° *knows / every bit*
  This passeth forth; what wol ye bet than wel?° *what more do you want?*
Fro day to day this joly Absolon
So woweth hire, that him is wo bigon.[4]
He waketh° al the night and al the day; *remains awake*
He kembeth° hise lokkes brode, and made him gay; *combs*
He woweth hire by menes and brocage,[5]
And swoor he wolde been hir owene page;
He singeth, brokkinge° as a nightingale; *quavering*
He sente hire piment,° meeth,° and spyced ale, *spiced wine / mead*
And wafres,° pyping hote out of the glede;° *wafer cakes / embers*
And for° she was of toune, he profred mede.° *because / money, bribes*
For som folk wol ben wonnen for° richesse, *by*
And som for strokes,° and som for gentillesse. *blows*
  Somtyme, to shewe his lightness° and maistrye,° *agility / skill*
He pleyeth Herodes on a scaffold hye.[6]

1. For love's sake, he intended to stay awake.
2. And took a place up near a casement window, one that opens and closes.
3. In fine harmony with his guitar-playing.
4. Woos her so that he is utterly wretched (woebegone).
5. Through (the use of) go-betweens and agents, intermediaries.
6. He plays Herod (in a mystery play) high on a scaffold (stage).

But what availleth him as in this cas?
She loveth so this hende Nicholas,
That Absolon may blowe the bukkes horn;[7]
He ne hadde for his labour but a scorn.
And thus she maketh Absolon hire ape,° *monkey*
And al his ernest turneth til° a jape.° *into / joke*
Ful sooth is this proverbe, it is no lye,° *lie*
Men seyn right thus, "Alwey the nye slye° *nearby sly (one)*
Maketh the ferre leve to be looth."[8]
For though that Absolon be wood° or wrooth,° *mad / angry*
By cause that he fer° was from hir sighte, *far*
This nye° Nicholas stood in his lighte. *nearby*
Now bere thee wel, thou hende Nicholas!
For Absolon may waille and singe "allas."
And so bifel it on a Saterday,
This carpenter was goon til° Osenay,° *gone to / Osney*
And hende Nicholas and Alisoun
Acorded been to° this conclusioun, *Were agreed on*
That Nicholas shal shapen him a wyle° *prepare a stratagem*
This sely° jalous housbond to bigyle;° *foolish, simple / trick*
And if so be the game wente aright,
She sholde slepen in his arm al night,
For this was his desyr and hire° also. *hers*
And right anon,° withouten wordes mo,° *at once / more*
This Nicholas no lenger wolde tarie,
But doth ful softe° unto his chambre carie° *quietly / carry*
Bothe mete and drinke for a day or tweye,° *two*
And to hire housbonde bad° hire for to seye, *bade*
If that he axed after° Nicholas, *asked about*
She sholde seye she niste° where he was, *did not know*
Of° al that day she saugh him nat with yë; *During*
She trowed° that he was in maladye,° *believed / sickness*
For for no cry hir mayde coude him calle
He nolde° answere, for thing° that mighte falle.° *wouldn't / anything / befall*
This passeth forth° al thilke° Saterday, *goes on / that same*
That Nicholas stille in his chambre lay,
And eet° and sleep, or dide what him leste,° *ate / pleased*
Til Sonday, that° the sonne gooth to reste. *when*
This sely carpenter hath greet merveyle° *marveled greatly*
Of Nicholas, or what thing mighte him eyle,° *ail*
And seyde, "I am adrad,° by Seint Thomas, *afraid*
It stondeth nat aright with Nicholas.
God shilde° that he deyde° sodeynly! *forbid / should die*
This world is now ful tikel,° sikerly:° *unstable / surely*
I saugh to-day a cors° y-born° to chirche *corpse / carried*
That now, on Monday last, I saugh him wirche.° *work*
Go up," quod he unto his knave° anoon,° *servant / at once*
"Clepe° at his dore, or knokke with a stoon, *Call*

7. I.e., doesn't have a chance.
8. Makes the far-off dear (one) to be hated.

Loke how it is, and tel me boldely."° *straightway*
This knave gooth him up ful sturdily,
And at the chambre dore, whyl that he stood,
He cryde and knokked as that° he were wood:° *as if / insane*
"What! how! what do ye, maister Nicholay?
How may° ye slepen al the longe day?" *can*
But al for noght, he herde nat a word.
An hole he fond, ful lowe upon a bord,
Ther as the cat was wont in for to crepe;[9]
And at that hole he looked in ful depe,
And at the laste he hadde of him a sighte.
This Nicholas sat evere caping uprighte,° *staring upward*
As he had kyked on the newe mone.[1]
Adoun° he gooth, and tolde his maister sone° *Down / at once*
In what array° he saugh this ilke° man. *state / same*
This carpenter to blessen him° bigan, *cross himself*
And seyde, "Help us, Seinte Frideswyde!° *patron saint of Oxford*
A man woot° litel what him shal bityde.° *knows / happen to*
This man is falle, with his astromye,[2]
In som woodnesse° or in som agonye;° *madness / fit*
I thoghte ay° wel how that it sholde be!° *ever / might happen*
Men sholde nat knowe of Goddes privetee.° *secrets*
Ye, blessed be alwey a lewed° man *unlearned*
That noght but oonly his bileve° can!° *creed / knows*
So ferde° another clerk° with astromye: *fared / scholar*
He walked in the feeldes for to prye° *spy*
Upon the sterres, what ther sholde bifalle,
Til he was in a marle-pit[3] y-falle—
He saugh nat that. But yet, by Seint Thomas,
Me reweth sore of° hende Nicholas. *I pity greatly*
He shal be rated of° his studying, *berated for*
If that I may, by Jesus, hevene° king! *heaven's*
Get me a staf, that I may underspore,° *pry up*
Whyl that thou, Robin, hevest up° the dore. *push on*
He shal° out of his studying, as I gesse." *shall (come)*
And to the chambre dore he gan him dresse.° *directed his attentions*
His knave was a strong carl° for the nones,° *fellow / for this purpose*
And by the haspe he haf it up atones;° *heaved it off at once*
Into° the floor the dore fil anon.° *On to / straightway*
This Nicholas sat ay° as stille as stoon, *ever*
And ever caped° upward into the eir.° *stared / air*
This carpenter wende° he were in despeir, *thought*
And hente° him by the sholdres mightily, *seized*
And shook him harde, and cryde spitously,° *violently*
"What, Nicholay! what, how! what, loke adoun!
Awake, and thenk on Cristes passioun!

9. There where the cat was accustomed to creep in.
1. As if he were gazing (half-crazed) at the new moon.
2. This man has fallen, because of his astronomy (John mispronounces "astronomye").
3. A pit from which clay is dug.

I crouche thee from elves and fro wightes!"[4]
Therwith the night-spel[5] seyde he anon-rightes° *at once*
On foure halves° of the hous aboute, *sides*
And on the threshfold° of the dore withoute:° *threshold / outside*
"Jesu Crist, and Seynte Benedight,° *Benedict*
Blesse this hous from every wikked wight,° *creature*
For nightes verye, the white *pater-noster!*[6]
Where wentestow, seynt Petres soster?"[7]
  And atte laste° this hende Nicholas *finally*
Gan for to syke° sore,° and seyde, "Allas! *began to sigh / deeply*
Shal al the world be lost eftsones° now?" *so soon again*
  This carpenter answerde, "What seystow?° *sayest thou*
What! thenk on God, as we don, men that swinke!"° *labor*
  This Nicholas answerde, "Fecche me drinke;
And after wol I speke in privitee° *secretly*
Of certeyn thing that toucheth me and thee;
I wol telle it non other man, certeyn."
  This carpenter goth doun and comth ageyn,
And broghte of mighty ale a large quart;
And whan that ech of hem° had dronke his part, *them*
This Nicholas his dore faste shette,° *shut*
And doun the carpenter by him he sette.
  He seyde, "John, myn hoste lief° and dere, *beloved*
Thou shalt upon thy trouthe° swere me here, *honor*
That to no wight° thou shalt this conseil° wreye;° *person / secret / betray*
For it is Cristes conseil that I seye,
And if thou telle it man,° thou art forlore;° *to anyone / lost*
For this vengeaunce thou shalt han therfore,
That if thou wreye° me, thou shalt be wood!"° *betray / go mad*
"Nay, Crist forbede it, for° his holy blood!" *by*
Quod tho this sely man, "I nam no labbe,
Ne, though I seye, I nam nat lief to gabbe.[8]
Sey what thou wolt, I shal it nevere telle
To child ne wyf, by him° that harwed° helle!" *i.e., Christ / harrowed*
  "Now John," quod Nicholas, "I wol nat lye.
I have y-founde in myn astrologye,
As I have loked in the mone bright,
That now, a Monday next, at quarter night,° *about 9 P.M.*
Shal falle a reyn° and that so wilde and wood,° *rain / furious*
That half so greet was nevere Noës° flood. *Noah's*
This world," he seyde, "in lasse° than in an hour *less*
Shal al be dreynt,° so hidous is the shour;° *drowned / shower, storm*
Thus shal mankynde drenche° and lese° hir lyf." *drown / lose*
  This carpenter answerde, "Allas, my wyf!

4. I make the sign of the cross over thee (to protect thee) from elves and from (other such) creatures.
5. A charm against evil spirits, said at night.
6. A bedtime blessing, "white" because black magic plays no part in it.
7. The sense of these lines is confused and comically intended: they represent a carpenter's version of "white" magic. Line 3486 means literally "Where didst thou go, St. Peter's sister?"
8. This foolish man said then, "I am no blabbermouth, nor, though I say (it myself), am I fond of chattering."

And shal she drenche?° allas, myn Alisoun!"   *drown*
For sorwe of this he fil almost adoun,
And seyde, "Is ther no remedie in this cas?"
"Why, yis, for° Gode," quod hende Nicholas,   *before*
"If thou wolt werken after lore and reed;[9]
Thou mayst nat werken after thyn owene heed;°   *head, wits*
For thus seith Salomon, that was ful trewe,°   *trustworthy*
'Werk al by conseil,° and thou shalt nat rewe.'°   *advice / be sorry*
And if thou werken wolt by good conseil,
I undertake,° withouten mast and seyl,°   *promise / sail*
Yet shal I saven hire and thee and me.
Hastow° nat herd° how saved was Noë,°   *Hast thou / heard / Noah*
Whan that Oure Lord hadde warned him biforn
That al the world with water sholde be lorn?"°   *lost*
"Yis," quod this carpenter, "ful yore° ago."   *long*
"Hastow nat herd," quod Nicholas, "also
The sorwe of Noë with his felawshipe?[1]
Er that° he mighte gete his wyf to shipe,   *Before*
Him hadde be levere, I dar wel undertake,[2]
At thilke° tyme than alle hise wetheres° blake   *that same / sheep*
That she hadde had a ship hirself allone.
And therfore, wostou° what is best to done?°   *knowest thou / do*
This asketh° haste, and of an hastif° thing   *requires / urgent*
Men may nat preche or maken tarying.
Anon° go gete us faste into this in°   *At once / dwelling*
A kneding trogh° or elles a kymelyn°   *(dough-)kneading trough / shallow tub*
For ech of us, but loke that they be large,
In whiche we mowe swimme° as in a barge,   *may float*
And han therinne vitaille suffisant°   *provisions sufficient*
But for a day; fy on the remenant!
The water shal aslake° and goon away   *diminish*
Aboute pryme° upon the nexte day.   *near sunrise*
But Robin may nat wite° of this, thy knave,°   *know / servant*
Ne eek° thy mayde° Gille I may nat save.   *Nor / maid*
Axe° nat why, for though thou aske me,   *Ask*
I wol nat tellen Goddes privetee.°   *secret things*
Suffiseth thee, but if° thy wittes madde,°   *unless / are gone (insane)*
To han as greet a grace as Noë hadde.
Thy wyf shal I wel saven, out of° doute.   *without*
Go now thy wey, and speed thee heer-aboute.
But whan thou hast, for hire and thee and me,
Y-geten us thise kneding tubbes three,
Than shaltow° hange hem in the roof ful hye,°   *must thou / high*
That no man of oure purveyaunce° espye.°   *provision / catch sight*
And whan thou thus hast doon, as I have seyd,
And hast oure vitaille faire in hem y-leyd,°   *laid*
And eek an ax, to smyte the corde atwo°   *in two*

9. If thou wilt work according to learning and good counsel.
1. The trouble(s) of Noah and his companions (as portrayed in the mystery plays).
2. He would have rather, I dare declare.

When that the water comth, that we may go,
And breke an hole an heigh° upon the gable *on high*
Unto the gardin-ward,° over the stable, *Toward the garden*
That we may frely passen forth our way
Whan that the grete shour° is goon away— *shower, storm*
Than shaltow swimme as myrie, I undertake,[3]
As doth the whyte doke° after hire° drake. *duck / its*
Thanne wol I clepe,° 'How, Alison! how, John! *call*
Be myrie, for the flood wol passe anon!'° *at once*
And thou wolt seyn, 'Hayl, maister Nicholay!
Good morwe, I se thee wel, for it is day.'
And thanne shul we be lordes al oure lyf
Of al the world, as° Noë and his wyf. *as (were)*
  But of o thyng I warne thee ful right:
Be wel avysed° on that ilke° night *forewarned / same*
That we ben entred into shippes bord° *on board the ship*
That noon of us ne speke nat a word,
Ne clepe, ne crye, but been in his preyere;[4]
For it is Goddes owene heste° dere. *commandment*
  Thy wyf and thou mote° hange fer atwinne,° *must / far apart*
For that° bitwixe yow shal be no sinne *So that*
No more in looking than ther shal° in dede; *shall (be)*
This ordinance is seyd, go, God thee spede!° *give thee success*
Tomorwe at night, whan men ben alle aslepe,
Into oure kneding tubbes wol we crepe,
And sitten ther, abyding° Goddes grace. *awaiting*
Go now thy wey, I have no lenger space° *no more time*
To make of this no lenger sermoning.
Men seyn thus, 'Send the wyse, and sey no thing.'
Thou art so wys, it nedeth thee nat teche;[5]
Go, save oure lyf, and that I thee biseche."
  This sely carpenter goth forth his wey.
Ful ofte he seith "allas" and "weylawey,"
And to his wyf he tolde his privetee;° *secret*
And she was war,° and knew it bet° than he, *aware / better*
What al this queynte cast was for to seye.[6]
But nathelees she ferde as° she wolde deye,° *acted as if / die*
And seyde, "Allas! go forth thy wey anon,° *immediately*
Help us to scape,° or we ben dede echon.° *escape / each one*
I am thy trewe verray° wedded wyf; *real*
Go, dere spouse, and help to save oure lyf."
  Lo, which° a greet thyng is affeccioun!° *what / emotion*
Men may dyen° of imaginacioun, *die*
So depe may impressioun be take.° *taken*
This sely° carpenter biginneth quake; *foolish, simple*
Him thinketh verraily° that he may see *truly*

3. Then shalt thou swim as merrily, I declare.
4. Nor call, nor cry out, but be at his prayer(s).
5. It's not necessary to teach thee.
6. What all this elaborate stratagem meant.

Noës flood come walwing° as the see° *rolling / sea*
To drenchen° Alisoun, his hony dere. *drown*
He wepeth, weyleth, maketh sory chere,° *a long face*
He syketh° with ful many a sory swogh.° *sighs / groan*
He gooth and geteth him a kneding trogh,° *kneading trough*
And after that a tubbe and a kymelyn,° *shallow tub*
And prively° he sente hem to his in,° *secretly / house*
And heng° hem in the roof in privetee.° *hung / secret*
His owene° hand he made laddres three, *(With) his own*
To climben by the ronges° and the stalkes° *rungs / shafts*
Unto the tubbes hanginge in the balkes,° *beams*
And hem vitailled,° bothe trogh and tubbe, *provisioned*
With breed and chese, and good ale in a jubbe,° *jug*
Suffysinge right ynogh as for a day.
But er that° he had maad al this array,° *before / preparation*
He sente his knave° and eek his wench° also *servant / maid*
Upon his nede° to London for to go. *business*
And on the Monday, whan it drow° to night, *drew near*
He shette° his dore withoute candel-light, *shut*
And dressed° al thing as it sholde be. *arranged*
And shortly, up they clomben° alle three; *climbed*
They sitten stille wel a furlong-way.° *short time*
"Now, *Pater-noster*, clom!" seyde Nicholay,[7]
And "clom," quod John, and "clom," seyde Alisoun.
This carpenter seyde his devocioun,
And stille he sit,° and biddeth° his preyere, *sits / offers*
Awaytinge on° the reyn,° if he it here. *Waiting for / rain*
The dede sleep, for wery bisinesse,[8]
Fil° on this carpenter right as I gesse *Fell*
Aboute corfew°-tyme, or litel more; *curfew (8 P.M.)*
For travail of his goost° he groneth sore, *spirit*
And eft he routeth, for his heed mislay.[9]
Doun of° the laddre stalketh° Nicholay, *from / creeps*
And Alisoun, ful softe adoun she spedde;° *hastened*
Withouten wordes mo,° they goon to bedde *more*
Theras° the carpenter is wont to lye. *Where*
Ther was the revel and the melodye;
And thus lyth° Alison and Nicholas *lie*
In bisinesse of mirthe and of solas,° *pleasure*
Til that the belle of Laudes gan to ringe,[1]
And freres° in the chauncel° gonne° singe. *friars / chancel / began to*
This parish clerk, this amorous Absolon,
That is for love alwey so wo bigon,
Upon the Monday was at Oseneye
With compaignye him to disporte° and pleye, *to amuse himself*
And axed upon cas a cloisterer[2]

7. "Now, (an) 'Our Father' (and then) 'mum!'" said Nicholas.
8. A dead sleep, because of (his) tiring labor.
9. And also he snores, for his head lay uncomfortably.
1. Till the chapel bell began to ring Lauds (a canonical hour, about 4 A.M.).
2. And asked by chance a resident of the cloister.

Ful prively after John the carpenter;
And he drough° him apart° out of the chirche, *drew / aside*
And seyde, "I noot,° I saugh him here nat wirche° *don't know / work*
Sin° Saterday. I trow° that he be went *Since / believe*
For timber, ther° oure abbot hath him sent, *where*
For he is wont for timber for to go,
And dwellen at the grange° a day or two; *monastery's farmhouse*
Or elles° he is at his hous, certeyn.° *else / for sure*
Wher that he be, I can nat sothly° seyn." *truly*
  This Absolon ful joly was and light,° *joyous*
And thoghte, "Now is tyme to wake° al night; *to stay awake*
For sikirly° I saugh him nat stiringe *surely*
Aboute his dore sin° day bigan to springe. *since*
So moot I thryve,° I shal, at cokkes° crowe, *So may I thrive / cock's*
Ful prively° knokken at his windowe *secretly*
That stant° ful lowe upon his boures° wal. *stands / bedroom's*
To Alison now wol I tellen al
My love-longing, for yet I shal nat misse
That at the leste wey° I shal hire kisse. *at least*
Som maner° confort shal I have, parfay.° *kind of / by my faith*
My mouth hath icched al this longe day;
That is a signe of kissing atte leste.° *at the least*
Al night me mette eek, I was at a feste.[3]
Therfore I wol gon slepe an houre or tweye,° *two*
And al the night than wol I wake and pleye."
  Whan that the firste cok hath crowe, anon° *immediately*
Up rist° this joly lovere Absolon, *rises*
And him arrayeth gay, at point-devys.° *to perfection*
But first he cheweth greyn° and lycorys *an aromatic spice*
To smellen swete, er° he had kembd° his heer. *before / combed*
Under his tonge a trewe-love he beer,[4]
For therby wende° he to ben gracious. *thought*
He rometh to the carpenteres hous,
And stille he stant° under the shot-windowe— *stood*
Unto his brest it raughte,° it was so lowe— *reached*
And softe he cougheth with a semi-soun:° *small sound*
"What do ye, hony-comb, swete Alisoun,
My faire brid,° my swete cinamome?° *bird / cinnamon*
Awaketh, lemman° myn, and speketh to me! *sweetheart*
Wel litel thenken ye upon my wo,
That for youre love I swete° ther° I go. *sweat / wherever*
No wonder is thogh that I swelte° and swete; *swelter*
I moorne° as doth a lamb after the tete.° *yearn / teat*
Ywis,° lemman, I have swich° love-longinge, *Truly / such*
That lyk a turtel° trewe is my moorninge;° *turtledove / mourning*
I may nat ete na more than a mayde."
  "Go fro the window, Jakke fool,"° she sayde, *you Jack-fool*

3. Also I dreamed all night (that) I was at a feast.
4. He bore a true-love (the leaf of a plant evidently thought to bring good fortune in love) under his tongue.

"As help me God, it wol nat be 'com pa me.'° *come kiss me*
I love another, and elles° I were to blame, *otherwise*
Wel bet° than thee, by Jesu, Absolon! *Much better*
Go forth thy wey or I wol caste a ston,
And lat me slepe, a twenty devel wey!"° *in the devil's name*
"Allas," quod Absolon, "and weylawey,
That trewe love was evere so yvel biset!° *ill bestowed*
Thanne kisse me, sin° it may be no bet,° *since / better*
For Jesus love and for the love of me."
"Wiltow thanne go thy wey therwith?" quod she.
"Ye, certes,° lemman,"° quod this Absolon. *truly / lover*
"Thanne make thee redy," quod she, "I come anon;"° *at once*
And unto Nicholas she seyde stille,° *quietly*
"Now hust,° and thou shalt laughen al thy fille." *hush*
This Absolon doun sette him on his knees,
And seyde, "I am a lord at alle degrees;[5]
For after this I hope ther cometh more.
Lemman, thy grace, and swete brid, thyn ore!"° *mercy*
The window she undoth,° and that in haste, *opens*
"Have do,"° quod she, "com of,° and speed thee faste, *done / on*
Lest that oure neighebores thee espye."
This Absolon gan° wype his mouth ful drye: *did*
Derk was the night as pich,° or as the cole,° *pitch / coal*
And at the window out she putte hir hole,
And Absolon, him fil no bet ne wers,[6]
But with his mouth he kiste hir naked ers° *arse*
Ful savourly, er° he was war° of this. *before / aware*
Abak he stirte,° and thoghte it was amis, *leaped*
For wel he wiste a womman hath no berd;° *beard*
He felte a thing al rough and long y-herd,° *haired*
And seyde, "Fy! allas, what have I do?"° *done*
"Tehee!" quod she, and clapte the window to;° *shut*
And Absolon goth forth a sory pas.° *with a sad step*
"A berd,° a berd!" quod hende Nicholas, *trick, joke*
"By Goddes *corpus*,° this goth faire and weel!" *body*
This sely° Absolon herde every deel,° *poor / bit*
And on his lippe he gan° for anger byte; *began*
And to himself he seyde, "I shal thee quyte."° *repay*
Who rubbeth now, who froteth° now his lippes *chafes*
With dust,° with sond,° with straw, with clooth, with chippes,° *dirt / sand* *bark*
But Absolon, that seith ful ofte, "Allas!
My soule bitake° I unto Sathanas,° *commit / Satan*
But me wer levere° than al this toun," quod he, *If I would not rather*
"Of this despyt° awroken° for to be. *insult / avenged*
Allas!" quod he, "allas, I ne hadde y-bleynt!"° *that I did not abstain*
His hote love was cold and al y-queynt;° *quenched*
For fro that tyme that he had kiste hir ers,

5. I am (equal to) a lord, in every way.
6. And Absolom, it befell him neither better nor worse.

Of paramours he sette nat a kers,[7]
For he was heeled° of his maladye. *cured*
Ful ofte paramours he gan deffye,° *denounce*
And weep° as dooth a child that is y-bete.° *wept / beaten*
A softe paas° he wente over the strete *(With) a soft step*
Until° a smith men cleped daun° Gerveys, *To / sir, mister*
That in his forge smithed plough harneys:° *parts*
He sharpeth shaar and culter[8] bisily.
This Absolon knokketh al esily,° *quietly*
And seyde, "Undo,° Gerveys, and that anon." *Open up*
  "What, who artow?"° "It am I, Absolon." *art thou*
"What, Absolon! for Cristes swete tree,° *cross*
Why ryse ye so rathe,° ey, *benedicite!*° *early / bless us all*
What eyleth° yow? som gay gerl, God it woot,° *ails / knows*
Hath broght yow thus upon the viritoot;° *astir(?)*
By Seynt Note,° ye woot wel what I mene." *St. Neot*
  This Absolon ne roghte° nat a bene° *cared / bean*
Of° al his pley. No word agayn° he yaf;° *For / in response / gave*
He hadde more tow on his distaf[9]
Than Gerveys knew, and seyde, "Freend so dere,
That hote culter in the chimenee° here, *forge*
As lene° it me: I have therwith to done, *Do lend*
And I wol bringe it thee agayn ful sone."
  Gerveys answerde, "Certes,° were it gold, *Truly*
Or in a poke° nobles alle untold,° *sack / coins uncounted*
Thou sholdest have,° as I am trewe smith. *have (it)*
Ey, Cristes foo!° what wol ye do therwith?" *i.e., the devil*
  "Therof," quod Absolon, "be as be may:
I shal wel telle it thee tomorwe day,"
And caughte the culter by the colde stele.° *handle*
Ful softe out at the dore he gan to stele,° *stole away*
And wente unto the carpenteres wal.
He cogheth first, and knokketh therwithal
Upon the windowe, right as° he dide er.° *just as / before*
  This Alison answerde, "Who is ther
That knokketh so? I warante it° a theef." *believe it (is)*
  "Why, nay," quod he, "God woot, my swete leef,° *dear one*
I am thyn Absolon, my dereling.° *darling*
Of gold," quod he, "I have thee brought a ring—
My moder yaf° it me, so God me save— *gave*
Ful fyn it is, and therto wel y-grave.° *engraved*
This wol I yeve° thee, if thou me kisse!" *give*
  This Nicholas was risen for to pisse,
And thoghte he wolde amenden° al the jape;° *improve / joke*
He sholde kisse his ers° er that° he scape.° *arse / before / escape*
And up the windowe dide° he hastily, *put*
And out his ers he putteth prively

7. For stylish love affairs he didn't care a cress (a common waterweed).
8. A plowshare and colter (the front part of a plow).
9. I.e., more business in hand.

Over the buttok, to the haunche-bon;
And therwith spak this clerk, this Absolon,
"Spek, swete brid,° I noot° nat wher thou art." *bird / know not*
  This Nicholas anon° leet fle° a fart, *at once / fly*
As greet as it had been a thonder-dent,° *thunderclap*
That with the strook he was almost y-blent;° *blinded*
And he was redy with his iren hoot,
And Nicholas amidde the ers he smoot.° *struck*
  Of gooth the skin an hande-brede aboute,[1]
The hote culter brende° so his toute,° *burned / rump*
And for the smert he wende° for to dye. *expected*
As° he were wood,° for wo he gan to crye°— *As if / mad / cried out*
"Help! water! water! help, for Goddes herte!"
  This carpenter out of his slomber sterte,
And herde oon° cryen "water" as he were wood, *someone*
And thoghte, "Allas! now comth Nowelis flood!"[2]
He sit° him up withouten wordes mo,° *sits / more*
And with his ax he smoot the corde atwo,° *in two*
And doun goth al; he fond° neither to selle *found time*
Ne breed ne ale, til he cam to the celle° *floorboards*
Upon the floor; and ther aswowne° he lay. *in a faint*
  Up sterte hire° Alison and Nicholay, *leaped*
And cryden "out" and "harrow"° in the strete. *help*
The neighebores, bothe smale and grete,
In ronnen° for to gauren° on this man, *ran / stare*
That yet° aswowne lay, bothe pale and wan; *still*
For with the fal he brosten° hadde his arm. *broken*
But stonde he moste unto his owene harm.[3]
For whan he spak, he was anon° bore doun° *at once / shouted down*
With° hende Nicholas and Alisoun. *By*
They tolden every man that he was wood,° *crazy*
He was agast so of "Nowelis flood"
Thurgh fantasye,° that of his vanitee° *delusion / foolish pride*
He hadde y-boght him kneding tubbes three,
And hadde hem hanged in the roof above;
And that he preyed hem, for Goddes love,
To sitten in the roof, *par*° *compaignye*. *for the sake of*
  The folk gan laughen° at his fantasye; *laughed heartily*
Into the roof they kyken° and they cape,° *gaze / gape*
And turned al his harm° unto a jape.° *misfortune / joke*
For what so that this carpenter answerde,
It was for noght; no man his reson° herde. *explanation*
With othes° grete he was so sworn adoun, *oaths*
That he was holden° wood° in al the toun. *considered / mad*
For every clerk° anonright° heeld° with other: *scholar / at once / agreed*
They seyde, "The man is wood, my leve° brother;" *dear*

1. Off goes the skin (from an area) a hand's-breadth around.
2. John confuses "Noah" with "Nowell" (Noel, or Christmas).
3. But he must accept responsibility for his own misfortune.

And every wight° gan laughen at this stryf. *person*
Thus swyved° was this carpenteres wyf *made love to*
For al his keping° and his jalousye; *watchfulness*
And Absolon hath kist hir nether yë;° *lower eye*
And Nicholas is scalded in the toute.° *rump*
This tale is doon, and God save al the route!° *company*

The Reeve's Prologue and Tale

The Prologue

Whan folk had laughen at this nyce cas° *foolish matter*
Of Absolon and hende° Nicholas, *courteous, gentle*
Diverse folk diversely they seyde,
But, for the more° part, they loughe° and pleyde;° *greater / laughed / jested*
Ne at this tale I saugh no man him greve,° *become vexed*
But° it were only Osewold the Reve. *Except*
By cause he was of carpenteres craft,
A litel ire° is in his herte y-laft.° *anger / left*
He gan° to grucche° and blamed it a lyte.° *began / grumble / little*
"So theek," quod he, "ful wel coude I thee quyte
With blering of a proud milleres yë,[1]
If that me liste° speke of ribaudye.° *it pleased me / ribaldry*
But ik° am old; me list not pley for° age; *I / because of*
Gras-tyme is doon, my fodder° is now forage,[2] *food*
This whyte top wryteth° myne olde yeres. *declares*
Myn herte is also mowled° as myne heres,° *as moldy / hair(s)*
But if° I fare as dooth an open-ers;[3] *Unless*
That ilke° fruit is ever lenger the wers,° *same / the older the worse*
Til it be roten in mullok° or in stree.° *muck / straw*
We olde men, I drede,° so fare we: *fear*
Til we be roten, can we nat be rype;
We hoppen alwey whyl that the world wol pype.
For in oure wil ther stiketh evere a nayl,[4]
To have an hoor° heed and a grene tayl *hoary*
As hath a leek,[5] for thogh our might° be goon,° *power, force / gone*
Oure wil desireth folie evere in oon.° *always the same*
For whan we may nat doon,° than wol we speke; *act*
Yet in oure asshen° olde is fyr y-reke.° *ashes / raked up*
Foure gledes° han we, whiche I shal devyse:° *burning coals / mention*
Avaunting,° lying, anger, coveityse.° *Boasting / avarice*
Thise foure sparkles° longen° unto elde.° *sparks / belong / old age*
Our olde lemes° mowe° wel been unwelde,° *limbs / may / weak*

1. "So may I thrive," said he, "I could very well pay you back with (a story of) the deceiving of a proud miller" (*lit.*, "the blearing of his eye").
2. Hay laid up for winter.
3. The medlar fruit, inedible until it is mushy and decayed.
4. We dance on always, as long as the world will pipe. For in our will (desire), there is always an obstruction (literally, a nail sticking up).
5. A kind of onion.

But wil ne shal nat faillen, that is sooth.
And yet ik have alwey a coltes tooth,[6]
As many a yeer as it is passed henne° *hence*
Sin that my tappe of lyf bigan to renne.[7]
For sikerly,° whan I was bore,° anon° *truly / born / at once*
Deeth drogh the tappe° of lyf and leet it gon;° *drew the tap / run*
And ever sithe° hath so the tappe y-ronne, *afterward*
Til that almost al empty is the tonne.° *tun, cask*
The streem of lyf now droppeth on the chimbe.° *rim of the cask*
The sely° tonge° may wel ringe and chimbe° *foolish / tongue / chime*
Of wrecchednesse that passed is ful yore;° *long ago*
With olde folk, save° dotage, is° namore." *except for / there is*
Whan that oure Host hadde herd this sermoning,° *preaching*
He gan to speke as lordly as a king.
He seide, "What amounteth al this wit?[8]
What shul° we speke alday of Holy Writ? *Why must*
The devel made a reve for to preche,
Or of a soutere° a shipman or a leche.° *shoemaker / doctor*
Sey forth thy tale, and tarie° nat the tyme; *delay*
Lo, Depeford, and it is half-way pryme!
Lo, Grenewich, ther many a shrewe is inne![9]
It were al tyme thy tale to biginne."
"Now, sires," quod this Osewold the Reve,
"I pray yow alle that ye nat yow greve,° *take (it) amiss*
Thogh I answere and somdel sette his howve;[1]
For leveful is with force force of-showve.[2]
This dronke millere hath y-told us heer
How that bigyled° was a carpenteer, *deceived*
Peraventure° in scorn for I am oon. *Perhaps*
And, by youre leve,° I shal him quyte° anoon; *permission / pay back*
Right in his cherles° termes wol I speke. *churl's*
I pray to God his nekke mote tobreke°— *may break*
He can wel in myn yë seen a stalke,° *straw*
But in his owne he can nat seen a balke."° *beam*

The Tale

At Trumpyngtoun,° nat fer° fro Cantebrigge,° *Trumpington / far / Cambridge*
Ther goth a brook and over that a brigge;° *bridge*
Upon the whiche brook ther stant a melle;° *mill*
And this is verray soth° that I yow telle. *the real truth*
A millere was ther dwelling many a day;
As eny pecok° he was proud and gay. *peacock*
Pypen he coude and fisshe, and nettes bete,

6. And even now I have in every way the desire of youth (literally, a colt's tooth).
7. Since my tap of life began to run. (The figure is that of a wine cask.)
8. He said, "What does all this wisdom amount to?"
9. Lo, Deptford, and it's half past seven in the morning! Lo, Greenwich, wherein there is many a rascal! (Both are suburbs of London; Chaucer lived in Greenwich for a time.)
1. Somewhat adjust his hood (i.e., make a fool of him).
2. For it is lawful to repel force with force.

And turne coppes, and wel wrastle and shete;[3]
Ay by his belt he baar a long panade,° *cutlass*
And of a swerd ful trenchant° was the blade. *sharp*
A joly popper° baar he in his pouche— *dagger*
Ther was no man for peril dorste° him touche— *dared*
A Sheffeld thwitel° baar he in his hose. *knife*
Round was his face, and camus° was his nose; *flat, pug*
As piled° as an ape was his skulle. *bald*
He was a market-betere atte fulle.[4]
Ther dorste no wight hand upon him legge,° *lay*
That he ne swoor he sholde anon abegge.° *pay for it*
A theef he was for sothe° of corn° and mele,° *truly / grain / meal*
And that a sly,° and usaunt for° to stele. *sly one / accustomed*
His name was hote° deynous° Simkin. *called / scornful, proud*
A wyf he hadde, y-comen of noble kin:
The person of the toun hir fader was.[5]
With hire he yaf° ful many a panne° of bras, *gave / pan (as dowry)*
For that Simkin sholde in his blood allye.[6]
She was y-fostred° in a nonnerye *raised*
For Simkin wolde° no wyf, as he sayde, *desired*
But° she were wel y-norissed° and a mayde,° *Unless / brought up / virgin*
To saven his estaat of yomanrye.[7]
And she was proud, and pert as is a pye.° *magpie*
A ful fair sighte was it upon hem two;[8]
On halydayes° biforn hire wolde he go *holy days*
With his tipet° wounde about his heed, *scarf*
And she cam after in a gyte of reed;° *red gown*
And Simkin hadde hosen° of the same. *stockings*
Ther dorste no wight clepen° hire but "Dame."° *call / Lady*
Was noon so hardy that wente by the weye
That with hir dorste rage° or ones° pleye, *dally / once*
But if° he wolde° be slayn of Simkin *Unless / wished (to)*
With panade,° or with knyf, or boydekin,° *cutlass / dagger*
For jalous folk ben perilous° everemo— *dangerous*
Algate they wolde hire wyves wenden so.[9]
And eek, for she was somdel smoterlich,[1]
She was as digne° as water in a dich, *dignified, worthy*
And ful of hoker° and of bisemare.° *scorn / disdain*
Hir thoughte that a lady sholde hire spare,[2]
What for hire kinrede° and hir nortelrye° *family / education*
That she had lerned in the nonnerye.

3. He knew how to play bagpipes and fish and mend (fishing) nets and turn (wooden) cups on a lathe and wrestle well and shoot.
4. He was a great swaggerer at markets.
5. The parson of the town was her father. (She was therefore born out of wedlock.)
6. I.e., marry her (with a pun on "alloy").
7. To preserve his rank as a freeman.
8. It was a handsome sight (to look) upon the two of them.
9. At any rate, they would like their wives to believe so.
1. And also, because she was somewhat besmirched (i.e., by her illegitimate birth).
2. It seemed to her that a lady ought to treat her with respect.

A doghter hadde they bitwixe hem two
Of twenty yeer, withouten any mo,° *more*
Savinge° a child that was of half-yeer age; *Except for*
In cradel it lay and was a propre page.° *fine boy*
This wenche thikke° and wel y-growen was, *stout*
With camuse° nose and eyen greye as glas, *pug*
With buttokes brode and brestes rounde and hye;
But right fair was hire heer,° I wol nat lye. *hair*
The person° of the toun, for° she was feir, *parson / because*
In purpos was to maken hire his heir
Bothe of his catel° and his messuage,° *property / house*
And straunge he made it of hir mariage.[3]
His purpos was for to bistowe hire hye° *in a high place*
Into som worthy blood of auncetrye;° *old lineage*
For holy chirches good° moot° been despended° *goods / must / spent*
On holy chirches blood, that is descended.
Therfore he wolde his holy blood honoure,
Though that he holy chirche sholde devoure.
Gret soken° hath this miller, out of doute,° *monopoly / doubtless*
With° whete and malt of al the land aboute; *On*
And nameliche ther was a greet collegge
Men clepen° the Soler Halle° at Cantebregge;° *call / Solar Hall / Cambridge*
Ther was hir whete and eek° hir malt y-grounde. *also*
And on a day it happed, in a stounde,° *at one time*
Sik lay the maunciple on a maladye:[4]
Men wenden wisly° that he sholde dye, *expected for certain*
For which this millere stal° bothe mele and corn *stole*
An hundred tyme more than biforn;
For ther-biforn he stal but curteisly,[5]
But now he was a theef outrageously.
For which the wardeyn chidde and made fare,[6]
But therof sette° the millere nat a tare;° *cared / whit*
He craketh boost,° and swoor it was nat so. *talks loudly*
Than were ther yonge povre scolers° two *poor scholars*
That dwelten in this halle of which I seye.° *speak*
Testif° they were, and lusty for to pleye, *Headstrong*
And, only for hire mirthe and revelrye,
Upon the wardeyn bisily they crye
To yeve° hem leve° but a litel stounde° *give / permission / while*
To goon to mille and seen hir corn° y-grounde; *grain*
And hardily° they dorste leye° hir nekke, *boldly / wager*
The millere shold nat stele hem° half a pekke° *from them / peck*
Of corn by sleighte, ne by force hem reve;° *rob*
And at the laste the wardeyn yaf hem leve.° *gave them permission*
John highte° that oon, and Aleyn highte that other; *was named*
Of o° toun were they born, that highte Strother, *one*

3. And he made (the question of) her marriage difficult.
4. The college steward lay sick with an illness.
5. For previously he stole only in a polite fashion.
6. On account of which the warden (the college head) chided (him) and made a fuss.

Fer in the north—I can nat telle where.[7]
  This Aleyn maketh redy al his gere,° *gear, equipment*
And on an hors the sak° he caste anon.° *sack (of grain) / at once*
Forth goth Aleyn the clerk,° and also John, *scholar*
With good swerd and with bokeler° by hir syde. *buckler, shield*
John knew the wey, hem nedede° no gyde, *they needed*
And at the mille the sak adoun he layth.
Aleyn spak first, "Al hayl, Symond, y-fayth!° *in faith*
How fares thy faire doghter and thy wyf?"
  "Aleyn, welcome," quod° Simkin, "by my lyf! *said*
And John also, how now, what do ye heer?"° *here*
  "Symond," quod John, "by God, nede has na peer.° *need has no equal*
Him boes serve himselve that has na swayn,[8]
Or elles he is a fool, as clerkes sayn.
Oure manciple, I hope° he wil be deed, *expect*
Swa werkes ay the wanges in his heed.[9]
And forthy° is I come, and eek° Alayn, *therefore / also*
To grinde our corn and carie it ham° agayn; *home*
I pray yow spede us hethen° that° ye may." *hence / as much as*
  "It shal be doon," quod Simkin, "by my fay.° *faith*
What wol ye doon whyl that it is in hande?"° *being processed*
  "By God, right by the hopur° will I stande," *hopper*
Quod John, "and se how that the corn gas° in. *goes*
Yet saugh I never, by my fader° kin, *father's*
How that the hopur° wagges til and fra."° *hopper / to and fro*
  Aleyn answerde, "John, and wiltow swa?° *wilt thou (do) so*
Than wil I be bynethe, by my croun,° *head*
And se how that the mele° falles doun *meal*
Into the trough; that sal° be my disport. *shall*
For John, in faith, I may° been of youre sort: *must*
I is as ille° a millere as are ye." *bad*
  This miller smyled of° hir nycetee,° *at / foolishness*
And thoghte, "Al this nis doon but for a wyle.° *only as a trick*
They wene° that no man may hem bigyle,° *think / beguile, trick*
But, by my thrift, yet shal I blere hire yë° *blur their eye(s)*
For al the sleighte° in hir philosophye. *craftiness*
The more queynte crekes° that they make, *sly tricks*
The more wol I stele whan I take.
In stide of flour, yet wol I yeve° hem bren.° *give / bran*
'The gretteste clerkes been noght wysest men,'
As whylom° to the wolf thus spak the mare;[1] *once*
Of al hir° art counte I noght a tare."° *their / whit*
  Out at the dore he gooth ful prively,° *secretly*

7. The town has not been identified, though there was a Strother castle in Northumberland. The speech of the students firmly characterizes them as Northerners: words such as "boes," "lathe," "fonne," "hethyng," "taa"; the substitution of long *a* for normal long *o* (as in "gas," "swa," "ham"); present indicative verbs in *-es* or *-s*, and so on, are used to create a distinct and slightly comic dialect.
8. It behooves him who has no servant to serve himself.
9. The molars in his head keep aching so.
1. Refers to a fable in which the wolf, very hungry, is kicked by a mare while trying to read on her hind foot the price of her foal.

Whan that he saugh his tyme, softely;
He loketh up and doun til he hath founde
The clerkes hors, ther as° it stood y-bounde *where*
Bihinde the mille, under a levesel.° *leafy arbor*
And to the hors he gooth him faire and wel;
He strepeth of° the brydel right anon. *strips off*
And whan the hors was laus,° he ginneth gon° *loose / dashes off*
Toward the fen,° ther° wilde mares renne,° *marsh / where / run*
Forth with "wehee,"° thurgh thikke and thurgh thenne.° *a whinny / thin*
  This miller gooth agayn, no word he seyde,
But dooth his note,° and with the clerkes pleyde,° *job / jested*
Til that hir corn° was faire and wel y-grounde. *grain*
And whan the mele° is sakked° and y-bounde,° *flour / sacked / tied*
This John goth out and fynt° his hors away, *finds*
And gan to crye "harrow" and "weylaway![2]
Oure hors is lorn!° Alayn, for goddes banes° *lost / bones*
Step on thy feet! com of, man, al atanes!° *right now*
Allas, our wardeyn has his palfrey° lorn!"° *riding horse / lost*
This Aleyn al forgat bothe mele and corn;
Al was out of his mynde his housbondrye.° *shrewd management*
"What, whilk° way is he geen?"° he gan to crye.° *which / gone / cried out*
  The wyf cam lepinge inward with a ren;° *run*
She seyde, "Allas! youre hors goth to the fen
With wilde mares, as faste as he may go.
Unthank° come on his hand that boond him so, *Bad luck*
And he that bettre sholde han knit the reyne."° *tied the reins*
  "Allas," quod John, "Aleyn, for Cristes peyne,° *pain*
Lay doun thy swerd, and I will myn alswa.° *also*
I is ful wight,° God waat,° as is a raa;° *swift / knows / roe*
By Goddes herte he sal° nat scape° us bathe!° *shall / escape / both*
Why ne had thou pit° the capul° in the lathe?° *put / horse / barn*
Il-hayl,° by God, Aleyn, thou is a fonne!"° *Bad luck / fool*
  This sely clerkes° han ful faste y-ronne *These poor scholars*
Toward the fen, bothe Aleyn and eek John.
  And whan the millere saugh° that they were gon, *saw*
He half a busshel of hir flour hath take,
And bad his wyf go knede it in a cake.[3]
He seyde, "I trowe° the clerkes were aferd,° *believe / afraid, suspicious*
Yet can a millere make a clerkes berd° *outwit a scholar*
For al his art; now lat hem goon hir weye.
Lo, wher he gooth! ye, lat the children pleye.
They gete him nat so lightly, by my croun!"[4]
  Thise sely clerkes rennen up and doun
With "Keep! keep! stand! stand! jossa! warderere![5]
Ga° whistle thou, and I shal kepe him here!" *Go*
But shortly,° til that it was verray° night, *in short / real*

2. And cried out "help" and "alas-alack."
3. And told his wife to go knead it into a loaf.
4. They won't catch him so easily, by my head!
5. Down here! look out behind!

They coude nat, though they dide al hir might,° *their best*
Hir capul cacche,° he ran alwey so faste, *Catch their horse*
Til in a dich they caughte him atte laste.
  Wery and weet,° as beest° is in the reyn,° *wet / animal / rain*
Comth sely John, and with him comth Aleyn.
"Allas," quod John, "the day that I was born!
Now are we drive til hething° and til scorn. *driven into derision*
Oure corn° is stole, men wil us foles° calle, *grain / fools*
Bathe° the wardeyn and our felawes° alle, *Both / companions*
And namely° the millere, weylaway!"° *especially / alas*
  Thus pleyneth° John as he goth by° the way *complains / on*
Toward the mille, and Bayard° in his hond. *the horse's name*
The millere sitting by the fyr he fond,
For it was night, and forther° mighte they noght. *go farther*
But for the love of God they him bisoght
Of herberwe° and of ese,° as for hir peny.° *lodging / rest / money*
  The millere seyde agayn,° "If ther be eny, *in response*
Swich° as it is, yet shal ye have youre part. *Such*
Myn hous is streit,° but ye han lerned art: *narrow, small*
Ye conne° by argumentes make a place *know how to*
A myle brood of° twenty foot of space. *out of*
Lat see now if this place may suffyse—
Or make it roum° with speche, as is youre gyse."° *roomy / way*
  "Now, Symond," seyde John, "by Seint Cutberd,° *Cuthbert*
Ay° is thou mery, and this is faire answerd. *Ever*
I have herd seyd, 'man sal taa of twa thinges:
Slyk as he fyndes, or taa slyk as he bringes.'[6]
But specially, I pray thee, hoste dere,
Get us som mete and drinke and make us chere,° *good cheer*
And we will payen trewely atte fulle;
With empty hand men may na haukes tulle.° *lure no hawks*
Lo, here oure silver, redy for to spende."
  This millere into toun his doghter sende° *sent*
For ale and breed, and rosted hem° a goos, *roasted for them*
And bond hir hors, it sholde namoore go loos;
And in his owene chambre hem made a bed
With shetes and with chalons° faire y-spred, *bedspreads*
Noght from his owene bed ten foot or twelve.
His doghter hadde a bed, al by hirselve,
Right in the same chambre, by and by.° *side by side*
It mighte be no bet, and cause why,[7]
Ther was no roumer° herberwe° in the place. *larger / lodgings*
They soupen° and they speke, hem to solace,° *sup / for amusement*
And drinken evere strong ale atte beste.° *of the best*
Aboute midnight wente they to rest.
  Wel hath this millere vernisshed his heed:[8]

6. I have heard said, "a man must take one of two things: such as he finds, or take such as he brings."
7. No better could be (arranged), and (this is the) reason why.
8. Literally, varnished his head (with ale).

Ful pale he was fordronken,° and nat reed; *very drunk*
He yexeth,° and he speketh thurgh the nose *hiccups*
As he were on the quakke,° or on the pose.° *hoarse / had a cold*
To bedde he gooth, and with him goth his wyf—
As any jay she light° was and jolyf,° *cheerful / jolly*
So was hir joly whistle wel y-wet.
The cradel at hir beddes feet is set,
To rokken° and to yeve° the child to souke.° *rock / give / suck*
And whan that dronken al was in the crouke,° *jug*
To bedde went the doghter right anon;
To bedde gooth Aleyn and also John;
Ther nas na more, hem nedede no dwale.° *sleeping potion*
This millere hath so wisly° bibbed° ale, *deeply / imbibed*
That as° an hors he fnorteth° in his sleep, *like / snorts*
Ne of his tayl bihinde he took no keep.° *heed*
His wyf bar him a burdon,° a ful strong: *bass accompaniment*
Men mighte hir routing° here two furlong; *snoring*
The wenche routeth eek *par compaignye*.° *to keep (them) company*
  Aleyn the clerk, that herd this melodye,
He poked John, and seyde, "Slepestow?° *Art thou asleep?*
Herdestow evere slyk° a sang° er° now? *such / song / before*
Lo, swilk° a compline° is y-mel° hem alle! *such / evening song / among*
A wilde fyr[9] upon thair bodyes falle!
Wha herkned° ever slyk° a ferly° thing? *Who heard / such / weird*
Ye, they sal have the flour of il ending.[1]
This lange° night ther tydes° me na° reste; *long / comes to / no*
But yet, na fors,° al sal° be for the beste. *no matter / shall*
For John," seyde he, "als evere moot I thryve,° *may I thrive*
If that I may, yon wenche wil I swyve.° *lie with*
Som esement° has lawe y-shapen° us. *redress / provided*
For John, ther is a lawe that says thus,
That gif° a man in a° point be agreved,° *if / one / aggrieved*
That in another he sal be releved.° *relieved*
Oure corn is stoln, sothly, it is na nay,° *there is no denial*
And we han had an il fit° al this day. *sorry time of it*
And sin° I sal have neen amendement° *since / no amends*
Agayn my los,° I wil have esement.° *loss / redress*
By Goddes saule, it sal neen other be!"[2]
  This John answerde, "Alayn, avyse thee,° *consider*
The miller is a perilous° man," he seyde, *dangerous*
"And gif° that he out of his sleep abreyde,° *if / awake*
He mighte doon us bathe° a vileinye."° *both / harm*
  Aleyn answerde, "I count him nat a flye."
And up he rist,° and by the wenche he crepte. *rises*
This wenche lay upright,° and faste° slepte *face up / soundly*
Til he so ny° was, er° she mighte espye,° *near / before / see (him)*

9. A painful skin disease.
1. The best of bad ending(s).
2. By God's soul, it shall not be otherwise!

That it had been to° late for to crye, *too*
And shortly for to seyn, they were aton;° *at one, united*
Now pley, Aleyn! for I wol speke of John.
This John lyth stille a furlong-wey or two,[3]
And to himself he maketh routhe° and wo: *lamentation*
"Allas!" quod he, "this is a wikked jape.° *joke*
Now may I seyn° that I is but an ape. *say*
Yet has my felawe° somwhat° for his harm: *companion / something*
He has the milleris° doghter in his arm. *miller's*
He auntred him,° and has his nedes sped,° *took a chance / satisfied*
And I lye as a draf-sak° in my bed. *bag of straw or refuse*
And when this jape is tald° another day, *told*
I sal been halde° a daf,° a cokenay!° *held / fool / milksop*
I wil aryse and auntre° it, by my fayth! *chance*
Unhardy is unsely,[4] thus men sayth."
And up he roos° and softely he wente *arose*
Unto the cradel, and in his hand it hente,° *took*
And baar° it softe unto his beddes feet. *bore*
Sone after this the wyf hir routing leet,° *ceased snoring*
And gan awake,° and wente hir out to pisse, *woke up*
And cam agayn, and gan hir cradel misse,
And groped heer and ther, but she fond noon.
"Allas!" quod she, "I hadde almost misgoon;° *gone amiss*
I hadde almost gon to the clerkes bed—
Ey, *benedicite*, thanne hadde I foule y-sped!"[5]
And forth she gooth til she the cradel fond;
She gropeth alwey° forther with hir hond, *ever*
And fond the bed, and thoghte noght but good,° *everything was well*
By cause that the cradel by it stood,
And niste° wher she was, for it was derk; *knew not*
But faire and wel she creep° in to the clerk,° *crept / scholar*
And lyth° ful stille, and wolde han caught a sleep.° *lies / fallen asleep*
Withinne a whyl this John the clerk up leep,° *leapt*
And on this gode wyf he leyth on sore.° *sets to it vigorously*
So mery a fit ne hadde she nat ful yore;[6]
He priketh harde and depe as he were mad.
This joly lyf han thise two clerkes lad° *led*
Til that the thridde cok[7] bigan to singe.
Aleyn wex° wery in the daweninge,° *grew / at dawn*
For he had swonken° al the longe night, *labored*
And seyde, "Fare weel, Malyne, swete wight!
The day is come; I may no lenger byde;° *remain*
But everemo, wher so° I go° or ryde, *wherever / walk*
I is thyn awen clerk, swa have I seel!"[8]

3. This John lies still for a moment or two (literally, the length of time it takes to walk a furlong or two. A furlong is an eighth of a mile).
4. (He who is) not bold is unlucky.
5. Aye, bless me! then I would have fared badly.
6. She hadn't had so merry a bout for a long time.
7. The third crow of the cock that heralds dawn.
8. I'm your very own scholar, as I hope to have bliss.

"Now, dere lemman,"° quod she, "go, far weel! *sweetheart*
But er° thou go, o° thing I wol thee telle: *before / one*
Whan that thou wendest homward by the melle,° *mill*
Right at the entree of the dore bihinde,
Thou shalt a cake° of half a busshel finde *loaf*
That was y-maked of thyn owene mele,° *meal*
Which that I heelp° my sire for to stele. *helped*
And, gode lemman, God thee save and kepe!"
And with that word almost she gan to wepe.° *fell to weeping*
Aleyn up rist,° and thoughte, "Er° that it dawe,° *rises / Before / dawns*
I wol go crepen in by my felawe,"
And fond the cradel with his hand anon.° *at once*
"By God," thoghte he, "al wrang° I have misgon.° *wrong / gone amiss*
Myn heed is toty° of° my swink° tonight: *dizzy / from / labor*
That maketh me that I go nat aright.
I woot° wel by the cradel I have misgo— *know*
Heere lyth the miller and his wyf also."
And forth he goth, a twenty devel way,° *straight to the devil*
Unto the bed ther as° the miller lay— *there where*
He wende have cropen by his felawe John[9]—
And by the millere in he creep° anon, *crept*
And caughte hym by the nekke, and softe he spak.
He seyde, "Thou, John, thou swynes-heed,° awak *swine's head*
For Cristes saule, and heer a noble game.° *great joke*
For by that lord that called is Seint Jame,° *James*
As° I have thryes° in this shorte night *So / thrice*
Swyved the milleres doghter bolt upright,[1]
Whyl thow hast as a coward been agast.° *afraid*
"Ye, false harlot,"° quod the millere, "hast? *rascal*
A! false traitour! false clerk!" quod he,
"Thou shalt be deed, by Goddes dignitee!
Who dorste° be so bold to disparage° *would dare / dishonor*
My doghter, that is come of swich linage?"° *such (high) birth*
And by the throte-bolle° he caughte Alayn; *Adam's apple*
And he hente hym despitously agayn,[2]
And on the nose he smoot him with his fest°— *fist*
Doun ran the blody streem upon his brest.
And in° the floor, with nose and mouth tobroke,° *on / smashed*
They walwe° as doon two pigges in a poke. *wallow*
And up they goon, and doun agayn anon,° *immediately*
Til that the miller sporned at a stoon,[3]
And doun he fil bakward upon his wyf,
That wiste° no thing of this nyce° stryf, *Who knew / foolish*
For she was falle aslepe a lyte wight° *little bit*
With John the clerk, that waked hadde al night;
And with the fal, out of hir sleep she breyde.° *started*

9. He thought to have crept in alongside his friend John.
1. Made love to the miller's daughter (as she lay) flat on her back.
2. And he (Alan) grabbed him fiercely in return.
3. Until the miller tripped on a stone.

"Help, holy croys of Bromeholm," she seyde,[4]
"*In manus tuas!*° Lord, to thee I calle! *Into thy hands*
Awak, Symond! the feend° is on me falle,° *fiend / fallen*
Myn herte is broken, help, I nam but° deed! *am just about*
There lyth oon upon my wombe° and on myn heed. *belly*
Help, Simkin, for the false clerkes fighte."
This John sterte° up as faste as ever he mighte, *leaped*
And graspeth by° the walles to and fro, *gropes along*
To finde a staf; and she sterte° up also, *leape*
And knew the estres° bet° than dide this John, *interior / better*
And by the wal a staf she fond anon,
And saugh° a litel shimering of a light— *saw*
For at an hole in shoon the mone bright—
And by that light she saugh hem bothe two,
But sikerly° she niste° who was who, *truly / knew not*
But as° she saugh a whyt° thing in hir yë. *Except that / white*
And whan she gan° this whyte thing espye, *did*
She wende the clerk hadde wered a volupeer,[5]
And with the staf she drough° ay neer° and neer, *drew / ever nearer*
And wende han hit this Aleyn at the fulle,[6]
And smoot the millere on the pyled° skulle *bald*
That° doun he gooth and cryde, "Harrow!° I dye!" *So that / Help!*
Thise clerkes bete° him weel and lete him lye, *beat*
And greythen hem,° and toke hir hors anon, *get themselves ready*
And eek hire mele,° and on hir wey they gon. *meal*
And at the mille yet they toke hir cake
Of half a busshel flour, ful wel y-bake.° *baked*
Thus is the proude millere wel y-bete,° *beaten*
And hath y-lost the grinding of the whete,
And payed for the soper everideel° *completely*
Of Aleyn and of John, that bette° him weel; *beat*
His wyf is swyved, and his doghter als.[7]
Lo, swich it is° a millere to be fals! *thus it is for*
And therefore this proverbe is seyd ful sooth,
"Him thar nat wene wel that yvel dooth;[8]
A gylour° shal himself bigyled° be." *beguiler, deceiver / deceived*
And God, that sitteth heighe in magestee,
Save al this compaignye grete and smale!
Thus have I quit° the Millere in my tale. *repaid*

4. "Help, holy cross of Bromholm," she said (a famous relic, supposed to be a piece of the true cross of Christ, brought to Bromholm in Norfolk in 1223).
5. She thought the scholar had worn a nightcap.
6. And thought to have hit this Alan square-on.
7. His wife's been made love to, and his daughter as well.
8. He need not expect good who does evil.

The Cook's Prologue and Tale

The Prologue

The Cook of London, whyl the Reve spak,
For joye him thoughte he clawed him on the bak.[1]
"Ha ha!" quod he, "for Cristes passioun,
This millere hadde a sharp conclusioun
Upon° his argument of herbergage!"° *To / discussion about lodging(s)*
Wel seyde Salomon° in his langage, *Solomon*
'Ne bringe nat every man into thyn house.'° *(cf. Ecclesiasticus 11:31)*
For herberwinge° by nighte is perilous. *lodging*
Wel oghte a man avysed° for to be *cautious*
Whom that he broughte into his privetee.° *privacy*
I pray to God, so yeve° me sorwe and care *give*
If ever, sith I highte Hogge of Ware,[2]
Herde I a millere bettre y-set a-werk.° *set to work, tricked*
He hadde a jape° of malice in the derk. *joke*
But God forbede that we stinten° here, *leave off*
And therfore, if ye vouchesauf to here° *agree to hear*
A tale of me, that am a povre man,
I wol you telle as wel as evere I can
A little jape that fil° in our citee." *befell, occurred*
Our Host answerde and seide, "I graunte it thee;° *i.e., I agree*
Now telle on, Roger, loke that° it be good; *see to it that*
For many a pastee° hastow laten blood,[3] *meat pie*
And many a Jakke of Dover[4] hastow sold
That hath been twyes° hoot and twyes cold. *twice*
Of many a pilgrim hastow Cristes curs,° *curse, i.e., been damned*
For of thy persly° yet they fare the wors,° *parsley / worse*
That they han eten° with thy stubbel-goos,[5] *have eaten*
For in thy shoppe is many a flye loos.
Now telle on, gentil° Roger, by thy name. *noble*
But yet I pray thee, be nat wrooth for game.[6]
A man may seye ful sooth° in game and pley." *say the whole truth*
"Thou seist ful sooth," quod Roger, "by my fey,° *faith*
But 'sooth pley, quaad pley,' as the Fleming seith.[7]
And therfore, Herry° Bailly, by thy feith, *i.e., Harry*
Be thou nat wrooth, er we departen° heer, *before we part company*
Though that my tale be of an hostileer.° *innkeeper*
But nathelees° I wol nat telle it yit,° *nevertheless / yet*
But er we parte, ywis,° thou shalt be quit."° *certainly / paid back*

1. For the joy (he felt), it seemed to him the Reeve was scratching him on the back.
2. If ever, since I first was called Hodge (Roger) of Ware (in Hertfordshire).
3. Thou hast let blood, i.e., drawn off the gravy from unsold pies (to keep them from getting soggy).
4. Probably a name for some kind of reheated pie.
5. Goose fed only on stubble, stalks, and stumps of harvested grain.
6. Do not be wroth, angry, (at what is said) in sport.
7. "A true jest is a bad jest," as the Flemish say.

And therwithal he lough° and made chere,° *laughed / acted cheerfully*
And seyde his tale, as ye shul after here.

The Tale

A prentis whylom° dwelled in our citee, *An apprentice once*
And of a craft of vitaillers° was he. *victualers, foodsellers*
Gaillard° he was as goldfinch in the shawe,° *Lively / wood, thicket*
Broun° as a berie, a propre° short felawe, *Dark-complexioned / handsome*
With lokkes blake, y-kempt° ful fetisly.° *combed / elegantly*
Dauncen he coude so wel and jolily
That he was cleped° Perkin Revelour.° *called / Reveler*
He was as ful of love and paramour° *sexual desire*
As is the hyve° ful of hony° swete; *beehive / honey*
Wel was the wenche with him mighte mete.° *i.e., who might encounter him*
At every brydale° wolde he singe and hoppe.° *wedding party / dance*
He loved bet° the taverne than the shoppe. *better*
For whan ther any ryding° was in Chepe,[8] *procession, parade*
Out of the shoppe thider° wolde he lepe.° *thither, to that place / leap*
Til that he hadde al the sighte y-seyn° *seen*
And daunced wel, he wolde nat come ageyn.° *i.e., come back to work*
And gadered him a meinee of his sort[9]
To hoppe and singe and maken swich disport.° *have such entertainment*
And ther they setten steven for to mete° *set a time to meet*
To pleyen at the dys° in swich a strete,° *dice / a certain street*
For in the toune nas ther no° prentys *there was no*
That fairer° coude caste a paire of dys *more skillfully*
Than Perkin coude, and therto° he was free° *in that (activity) / unrestrained*
Of his dispense,° in place of privetee.° *spending / in private place(s)*
That fond° his maister wel in his chaffare,° *i.e., discovered that fact / business*
For often tyme he fond his box° ful bare. *money box*
For sikerly° a prentis revelour *certainly*
That haunteth dys, riot, or paramour,[1]
His maister shal it in his shoppe abye,° *pay for*
Al° have he no part of the minstralcye.° *Even though / i.e., entertainment*
For thefte and riot, they ben convertible,° *interchangeable*
Al conne he pleye on giterne or ribible.[2]
Revel and trouthe, as in a low degree,
They been ful wrothe al day, as men may see.[3]
This joly prentis with his maister bood,° *stayed*
Til he were ny° out of his prentishood,° *nearly / apprenticeship*
Al were he snibbed° bothe erly and late, *Even though he was rebuked*
And somtyme lad with revel to Newgate.[4]

8. Cheapside, a busy market area of London with many shops.
9. And (he) gathered around him a group of (people of) his type.
1. Who haunts (pursues) dicing, riotous living, or womanizing.
2. However well he (the apprentice) can play a cittern (guitar) or a rebec (fiddle); i.e., whatever his charms and skills. Some critics think "he" in this line refers to the master, whose musical accomplishments contrast with the "minstrelsy" of Perkin and his friends.
3. Revelry and honesty in a person of low social standing are always at odds, as people can see.
4. And sometimes led away to Newgate Prison with revelry. (Minstrels often accompanied people led off to prison in order to shame them publicly.)

But atte laste his maister him bithoghte,° *thought to himself*
Upon a day whan he his paper soghte,[5]
Of a proverbe that seith this same word:
"Wel bet° is roten appel out of hord° *better / hoard, barrel*
Than that it rotie al the remenaunt."° *cause all the rest to rot*
So fareth it by° a riotous servaunt— *So it is in regard to*
It is ful lasse° harm to lete him pace,° *much less / go, leave*
Than he shende° alle the servants in the place. *ruin*
Therefore his maister yaf° him acquitance,° *gave / discharge*
And bad him go, with sorwe and with meschance.° *bad luck (to him)*
And thus this joly prentis hadde his leve.° *permission to go*
Now lat him riote al the night or leve.° *leave off*
And for° ther is no theef withoute a louke,° *since / accomplice*
That helpeth him to wasten° and to souke° *spend lavishly / suck, extract*
Of that° he brybe° can or borwe may, *Whatever (money) / steal*
Anon° he sente his bed and his array° *Quickly / clothing*
Unto a compeer° of his owne sort, *comrade*
That lovede dys and revel and disport,
And hadde a wyf that heeld for countenance° *for the sake of appearances*
A shoppe, and swyved° for hir sustenance.°[6] *had sex / livelihood*

The Man of Law's Introduction, Prologue, and Tale

The Introduction

Our Hoste saugh° wel that the brighte sonne *saw*
The ark° of his artificial day hath ronne° *arc / has run*
The fourthe part and half an houre and more,[1]
And though he were not depe y-stert in lore,° *deeply grounded in learning*
He wiste° it was the eightetethe° day *knew / eighteenth*
Of April, that is messager° to May; *forerunner*
And saugh wel that the shadwe° of every tree *shadow*
Was as in lengthe the same quantitee
That° was the body erect that caused it; *i.e., just as long as*
And therfore by the shadwe he took his wit° *i.e., concluded*
That Phebus,° which that shoon so clere and brighte, *Phoebus (the sun)*
Degrees was fyve and fourty clombe on highte, ° *Had climbed 45°*
And for° that day, as in that latitude, *on*
It was ten at the clokke, he gan conclude,° *concluded*
And sodeynly° he plighte his hors *suddenly*
aboute.° *pulled his horse around*

5. One day when he (Perkin) sought his certificate (that would indicate release from his contract as an apprentice).
6. Most scholars believe that for one reason or another Chaucer never finished the Cook's Tale. Scribes of *The Canterbury Tales* seem to have expected something more—one wrote in the margin of an early manuscript, "Of this Cokes tale maked Chaucer na moore." In some cases scribes added short endings to the tale or substituted the non-Chaucerian outlaw romance, the *Tale of Gamelyn*.
1. I.e., the Host saw that the sun had traversed one fourth of its arc across the sky (plus an additional thirty-some minutes) during its time above the horizon (the "artificial" day, calculated from sunrise to sunset). The elaborate time-telling in these and the following lines appears to be awkward or wrong in some respects and has prompted much scholarly debate.

"Lordinges," quod he, "I warne yow, al this route,°	*this whole company*
The fourthe party° of this day is goon.°	*part / has gone, elapsed*
Now, for the love of God and of Seint John,	
Leseth° no tyme, as ferforth° as ye may.	*Lose / far*
Lordinges, the tyme wasteth° night and day	*wastes away*
And steleth° from us—what prively slepinge°	*departs / secretly as we sleep*
And what thurgh° necligence in our wakinge—	*also through*
As dooth the streem° that turneth never agayn,°	*river / never turns back*
Descending fro the montaigne into playn.°	*the plain*
Wel can Senek° and many a philosophre	*Seneca*
Biwailen° tyme more than gold in cofre,°	*Lament (the loss of) / coffer*
For los of catel° may recovered be,	*goods (chattel)*
But los of tyme shendeth° us," quod he.	*ruins, shames*
"It wol nat come agayn, withouten drede,°	*doubt*
Na more than wol Malkins maydenhede,[2]	
Whan she hath lost it in hir wantownesse.°	*wantoness*
Lat° us nat moulen° thus in ydelnesse.	*Let / grow moldy*
Sir Man of Lawe," quod he, "so have ye blis,°	*so may you thrive*
Tel us a tale anon,° as forward° is.	*at once / our agreement*
Ye been submitted,° thurgh your free assent,	*You are under obligation*
To stonden in this cas at° my jugement.	*act in this case according to*
Acquiteth yow° now of your biheeste,°	*Make good on / promise*
Than have ye doon your devoir° atte leste."	*duty*
"Hoste," quod he, "*depardieux*,° ich assente.	*in God's name*
To breke forward° is not myn entente.	*break an agreement*
Biheste is dette,° and I wol holde fayn°	*debt, obligation / gladly keep*
Al my biheste. I can no better seyn.°	*say*
For swich° lawe as a man yeveth another wight°	*such / applies to another person*
He sholde hymselven usen it,° by right.	*apply it to himself*
Thus wol our text.° But natheles, certeyn,	*That's what our (legal) text says*
I can right now no thrifty° tale seyn	*profitable*
That Chaucer, though he can but lewedly°	*has only a limited understanding*
On metres° and on ryming craftily,°	*Of meters / skillfully*
Hath seyd hem° in swich English as he can	*Hasn't already told*
Of olde tyme,° as knoweth many a man.	*Over a long period of time*
And if he have not seyd hem, leve° brother,	*dear*
In o° book, he hath seyd hem in another;	*one*
For he hath told of loveres up and doun	
Mo than Ovyde made of mencioun°	*More than Ovid mentioned*
In his Epistelles,° that been ful olde.°	*Epistles (the* Heroides*) / ancient*
What° sholde I tellen hem, sin° they ben tolde?	*Why / since*
In youthe he made of° Ceys and Alcione,	*wrote about*
And sithen° hath he spoke of everichon,°	*since then / everybody*
Thise noble wyyes and thise loveres eek.°	*also*
Whoso that° wol his large volume seek,°	*Whoever / search through*

2. No more than Malkin's virginity will (return). Malkin was a stock name for a lower-class woman; Chaucer uses it for the miller's daughter in the *Reeve's Tale*.

Cleped° the Seintes Legende of Cupyde,[3]	*Called*
Ther may he seen the large woundes wyde	
Of Lucresse° and of Babilan Tisbee;°	*Lucretia / Thisbe of Babylon*
The swerd° of Dido for° the false Enee;°	*sword / because of / Aeneas*
The tree of Phillis for hir Demophon;	
The pleinte° of Dianire° and Hermion,°	*complaint(s) / Deianira / Hermione*
Of Adriane° and of Isiphilee°	*Ariadne / Hypsipyle*
(The bareyne yle° stonding in the see),	*barren island*
The dreynte° Leander for his Erro;°	*drowned / Hero*
The teres of Eleyne,° and eek the wo°	*tears of Helen / woe*
Of Brixseyde, and of thee, Ladomea;°	*Laodamia*
The crueltee of thee, queen Medea,	
Thy litel children hanging by the hals°	*neck*
For° thy Jason, that was of love so fals!	*Because of*
O Ypermistra,° Penelopee, Alceste°—	*Hypermnestra / Alcestis*
Your wyfhod° he comendeth with the beste!	*wifely virtue*
But certeinly no word ne wryteth he	

3. Chaucer's youthful account of Ceys and Alcione, based on a story in *Metamorphoses* XI, 410ff., opens his first major poem, *The Book of the Duchess* (ll. 45–209). The book that the Man of Law calls *Cupid's Saints' Lives*, known today as Chaucer's *Legend of Good Women*, draws chiefly on Ovid for its stories of women, the men they loved, and the misery that often followed. In the surviving manuscripts the collection is less "large" than the Man of Law's list implies.

What follows is a brief summary of the stories of the women from classical legend mentioned by the Man of Law in lines 63–76. Asterisks identify those who appear in the *Legend of Good Women*. Chaucer's versions sometimes differ from their classical sources.

(a) *Lucretia, attacked by young Tarquinius, son of the king, stabbed herself rather than have dishonor brought on her husband.
(b) *Thisbe committed suicide after discovering that her lover Pyramus had killed himself, mistakenly thinking that she had been killed by a lion.
(c) *Dido, Queen of Carthage, fell in love with Aeneas and killed herself with his sword when he stole away from her one night to continue on his destined journey to found the city of Rome.
(d) *Phyllis hanged herself on a tree when her lover Demophon, the son of Theseus (see [g] below), sailed off to his homeland but failed to return at the time he had promised.
(e) Deianira lamented the death of her husband Hercules, which she had unintentionally caused.
(f) Hermione, daughter of Helen and Menelaus (see [j] below), was in love with Orestes but was forced into marrying someone else.
(g) *Ariadne loved Theseus and helped him kill the Minotaur, but he sailed off with her sister while she was asleep on an island (see l. 68).
(h) *Hypsipyle, Queen of the island of Lemnos, remained loyal to her husband Jason (see [m] below) even after he abandoned her.
(i) Hero's lover Leander often swam across the Hellespont to be with her; one night he drowned during a storm, and in grief she threw herself into the water.
(j) Helen of Troy, wife of Menelaus, was abducted by Paris, the act that led to the Trojan War.
(k) In Homer's *Iliad*, Briseis is a young Trojan woman given to the Greek warrior Achilles; she ultimately becomes, in the course of various retellings, Criseyde in Chaucer's *Troilus and Criseyde*.
(l) Laodamia was the wife of a Greek warrior killed in the Trojan War; she stabbed herself in order to join him in the Underworld.
(m) *Medea, Jason's second wife, killed their two sons to avenge his infidelity to her.
(n) *Hypermnestra was ordered by her father, on pain of death, to cut her husband's throat. She helped him escape instead.
(o) Penelope is the loyal wife of Odysseus in Homer's *Odyssey*.
(p) *Alcestis gave up her own life in order that her husband Admetus might live. Her story is not in the *Legend of Good Women* as we have it, but she appears as the God of Love's consort in its Prologue, and orders Chaucer to write (as an act of penance) narratives about "good wymmen" who were "trew in lovyng" and the "false men" who betrayed them.

Of thilke wikke° ensample of Canacee,° *that wicked / Canace*
That° lovede hir owne brother sinfully. *Who*
Of swiche cursed stories I sey fy!° *fie*
Or elles of Tyro Apollonius:° *Apollonius of Tyre*
How that the cursed king Antiochus
Birafte° his doghter of hir maydenhede,° *Took from / virginity*
That is so horrible a tale for to rede,
Whan he hir threw upon the pavement.° *paved floor*
And therfor he, of ful avysement,° *he (Chaucer), duly deliberating*
Nolde never write in none of his sermouns° *discourses*
Of swiche unkinde° abhominaciouns, *such unnatural*
Ne I wol noon reherse,° if that I may.[4] *retell*
  But of my tale—how shal I doon this day?
Me were looth be lykned,° doutelees, *I would hate to be compared*
To Muses that men clepe° Pierides[5]— *call*
Metamorphoseos wot° what I mene— *Ovid's* Metamorphoses *knows*
But nathelees I recche noght a bene° *don't care a bean*
Though I come after him with hawebake.° *baked hawthorn berries*
I speke in prose, and lat him rymes make."
  And with that word he, with a sobre chere,° *serious expression*
Bigan his tale, as ye shal after here.

The Prologue

  O hateful harm,° condicion of poverte— *misfortune*
With thurst, with cold, with hunger so confounded!° *overcome*
To asken° help thee shameth° in thyn herte. *ask for / shames thee*
If thou noon aske,° so soore artow y-wounded *ask no one*
That verray nede° unwrappeth al thy wounde *true need*
    hid.° *hidden wounds*
Maugree thyn heed,° thou most for indigence *In spite of all thou canst do*
Or stele,° or begge or borwe thy despence.° *Either steal / what thou spendest*

Thou blamest Crist, and seyst ful bitterly
He misdeparteth richesse temporal.° *unfairly distributes worldly goods*

4. After implying that Chaucer has told practically every love story there is to tell, and focusing on those with sad or violent outcomes, the Man of Law does at least absolve him of writing about incest. He mentions two "abominable" tales of that sort; both appear in the *Confessio Amantis*, a long and heavily moralized collection of stories in English by Chaucer's friend John Gower, whom he honors at the end of *Troilus and Criseyde* as "moral Gower" (V, 1856). At the end of the *Confessio*, in some first-version manuscripts, Venus speaks of Chaucer as "mi disciple and mi poete," who in his "youthe" filled the land with love poetry but who is now "olde" and needs to compose some culminating "testament of love" (Book VIII, 2941*–2957*). This part of the *Man of Law's Introduction* suggests some playful literary sparring between Chaucer and Gower.
5. Although the Man of Law disparaged Chaucer's poetic skill in lines 46–49, as he gets ready to tell a tale himself he admits he would hate to be judged in that regard as were the nine daughters of Pierus against the Muses. (They challenged the Muses to a singing contest, lost, and were turned into magpies; see *Metamorphoses* V, 305ff.) The Man of Law then professes not to care if his tale appears to be poor rustic food relative to Chaucer's fancier literary fare. After all, Chaucer has had experience in rhyming, whereas, he says, "I speke in prose." These four words have been variously interpreted. Most critics think they refer to an earlier plan of Chaucer's to give the Man of Law a tale in prose, probably the *Tale of Melibee*, which he later assigned to himself without revising this earlier passage. Or the Man of Law could mean that prose is his normal medium of expression rather than the rhyming of a prolific versifier like Chaucer. On either reading his literary self-consciousness is clear.

Thy neighebour thou wytest° sinfully, *blamest*
And seyst thou hast to lyte° and he hath al. *too little*
"Parfay," seistow, "somtyme he rekne shal,[6]
Whan that his tayl shal brennen in the glede° *his tail is burning in the coals*
For° he noght helpeth needfulle° in hir nede." *Because / the needy*

Herkne° what is the sentence° of the wyse: *Harken, listen to / maxim*
"Bet is° to dyen than have indigence. *It is better (Ecclesiasticus 40:29)*
Thy selve° neighebour wol thee despyse." *very own (Proverbs 14:20)*
If thou be povre,° farwel thy reverence!° *poor / respect from others*
Yet° of the wyse man tak this sentence:° *Also / wise saying*
"Alle the dayes of povre men ben wikke."° *wicked, miserable (Proverbs 15:15)*
Be war,° therfore, er° thou come to that prikke.° *wary / before / point*

If thou be povre, thy brother hateth thee,
And alle thy freendes fleen° fro thee, alas! *flee (Proverbs 19:7)*
O riche marchaunts, ful of wele° ben ye, *wealth, well-being*
O noble, o prudent folk as in this cas.° *in this regard*
Your bagges been nat filled with ambes as,° *double aces*
But with sys cynk,° that renneth for your chaunce.[7] *six-five*
At Cristemasse merie° may ye daunce! *merrily*

Ye seken lond and see° for your winninges. *seek (over) land and sea*
As wyse folk ye knowen al th'estaat° *state, condition*
Of regnes.° Ye ben fadres of tydinges° *kingdoms/ the fathers of news*
And tales° bothe of pees and of debat.° *stories / dispute, war*
I were° right now of tales desolat,° *would be / destitute*
Nere° that a marchaunt, goon is many a yere,° *Were it not / many years ago*
Me taughte a tale, which that ye shal here.

The Tale

In Surrie° whylom dwelte° a companye *Syria / once lived*
Of chapmen° riche, and therto sadde° and trewe, *merchants / also steadfast*
That wyde-wher° senten her spycerye,° *far and wide / their spices*
Clothes of gold, and satins riche of hewe.° *hue, color*
Her chaffare was so thrifty° and so newe *Their merchandise was so worthy*
That every wight hath deyntee to chaffare° *everyone likes doing business*
With hem, and eek to sellen hem hir ware.° *their own wares*

Now fel it° that the maistres of that sort° *it happened / company*
Han shapen hem to Rome for to wende,° *Arranged to travel to Rome*
Were it for chapmanhode or for disport.° *Whether for business or pleasure*
Non other message° wolde they thider° sende *messenger / thither*
But comen hemself to Rome—this is the ende°— *outcome*

6. "By my faith," thou sayest, "someday he will pay for it (come to a reckoning)."
7. Your bags are not filled with double aces (a losing dice throw) but with six and five (a winning throw), which increases your good fortune.

And in swich place as thoughte hem avantage° — *as seemed to them convenient*
For her entente,° they take her herbergage.° — *For their purpose / their lodging*

Sojourned han thise marchants° in that toun — *These merchants have stayed*
A certein tyme as fel to hir plesance;° — *as it pleased them*
And so bifel that th'excellent renoun° — *renown, reputation*
Of th'Emperoures doghter, dame Custance,[8]
Reported was with every circumstance° — *in all details*
Unto thise Surrien marchants in swich wyse,° — *in such a way*
Fro day to day, as I shal yow devyse.° — *explain to you*

This was the commune vois° of every man: — *voice, judgment*
"Our Emperour of Rome—God him see°— — *may God watch over him*
A doghter hath that, sin° the world bigan, — *since*
To rekne° as wel hir goodnesse as beautee — *reckon, take account of*
Nas° never swich another as is she. — *(There) was*
I prey to God in honour hir sustene
And wolde she were of al Europe the quene.

In hir is heigh beautee withoute pryde,
Yowthe withoute grenehede° or folye. — *greenness (immaturity)*
To° alle hir werkes vertu is hir gyde.° — *In / her guide*
Humblesse° hath slayn in hir al tirannye. — *Humility*
She is mirour of alle curteisye.
Hir herte is verray chambre° of holinesse, — *a true chamber*
Hir hand ministre of fredom for almesse."[9]

And al this vois was soth,° as God is trewe. — *true*
But now to purpos° lat us turne agayn: — *to the subject (the story)*
Thise marchants han doon fraught hir
shippes newe,° — *have had their ships loaded anew*
And whan they han this blisful mayden seyn,° — *seen, observed*
Hoom to Surrye° been they went ful fayn,° — *Syria / gladly*
And doon her nedes° as they han don yore,° — *do their business / previously*
And liven in wele.° I can sey° yow no more. — *prosperity / tell*

Now fel it° that thise marchants stode in
grace° — *it happened / enjoyed the favor*
Of him that was the Sowdan° of Surrye; — *Sultan*
For whan they came from any strange° place, — *foreign*
He wolde, of° his benigne° curteisye, — *out of / benign, kind*

8. Lady Constance. The distant historical source for Chaucer's heroine is Constantia, the daughter of the Eastern Roman (Byzantine) emperor Tiberius Constantine (520–582). After Tiberius's death, his successful general, Maurice, became emperor and married Constantia. Various legends eventually developed around the empress, some influenced by stories of persecuted queens. In the 1330s the Dominican friar Nicholas Trevet wrote a universal history in Anglo-Norman that included a long narrative account of her life. Chaucer's tale is a free translation/adaptation of that part of Trevet's *Cronicles*. He follows Trevet in making Maurice the son of Constance rather than her husband.
9. Her hand an agent (an administrator) of generosity in almsgiving.

Make hem good chere° and bisily espye° — *Entertain them / eagerly ask for*
Tydings of sondry regnes,° for to lere° — *News of diverse kingdoms / learn*
The wondres that they mighte seen or here.° — *might see or hear*

Amonges othere thinges, specially,
Thise marchants han him told of dame Custance
So gret noblesse° in ernest, ceriously,° — *Such fine things / in orderly detail*
That this Sowdan hath caught so gret plesance° — *has taken such great pleasure*
To han hir figure° in his remembrance, — *have her image*
That al his lust° and al his bisy cure° — *desire / constant care*
Was for to love hir whyl° his lyf may dure.° — *as long as / last*

Paraventure° in thilke large book — *Perhaps*
Which that men clepe the heven,° y-writen was° — *call heaven* / *it was written, fated*
With sterres, whan that he his birthe took,° — *In the stars when he was born*
That he for love shulde han his deeth, allas!
For in the sterres, clerer° than is glas, — *more clearly*
Is writen, God wot,° whoso coude it rede,° — *knows / for one who can read it*
The deeth of every man, withouten drede.° — *doubt*

In sterres many a winter therbiforn° — *many years beforehand*
Was writen the deeth of Ector,° Achilles, — *Hector of Troy*
Of Pompey, Julius,° er° they were born; — *Julius Caesar / before*
The stryf° of Thebes and of Ercules,° — *strife, war / Hercules*
Of Sampson, Turnus,° and of Socrates — *enemy of Aeneas in the* Aeneid
The deeth; but mennes wittes been so dulle
That no wight can wel rede it atte fulle.° — *fully*

This Sowdan for his privee conseil° sente, — *private counselors*
And, shortly of this mater for to pace,° — *to speak briefly on this matter*
He hath to hem declared his entente,
And seyd hem, certein, but° he mighte have grace — *unless*
To han Custance withinne a litel space,° — *time*
He nas but deed,° and charged hem in hye° — *was as good as dead / in haste*
To shapen° for his lyf som remedye. — *make, find*

Diverse men diverse thinges seyden:
They argumenten, casten up and doun;° — *debated back and forth*
Many a subtil resoun forth they leyden;° — *they laid out*
They speken of magik and abusioun;° — *deception*
But finally, as in conclusioun,
They can not seen in that non avantage,
Ne in non° other wey, save mariage. — *i.e., any*

Than sawe they therin° swich difficultee — *therein (i.e., in marriage)*
By wey of resoun, for to speke al playn,
By cause that ther was swich diversitee
Bitwene hir bothe lawes,° that they sayn — *their two (religious) laws*
They trowe° that "No Cristen prince wolde fayn° — *believe / willingly*

Wedden his child° under oure lawes swete *Give his child in marriage*
That us were taught by Mahoun,° our prophete." *were taught to us by Mohammed*

And he answerde, "Rather than I lese° *lose*
Custance, I wol be cristned,° doutelees. *christened, baptized*
I mot ben hires.° I may non other chese.° *I must be hers / choose*
I prey yow, holde your arguments in pees.° *keep your opinions to yourselves*
Saveth my lyf, and beeth noght recchelees° *do not be negligent*
To geten hir° that hath my lyf in cure,° *In getting her / in her power*
For in this wo I may not longe endure."

What nedeth gretter dilatacioun?° *rhetorical dilation, further words*
I seye, by tretis and embassadrye,° *treaty and negotiation*
And by the popes mediacioun,° *mediation*
And al the chirche and al the chivalrye,° *knighthood*
That in destruccioun of maumetrye° *Mohammedan idolatry*
And in encrees° of Cristes lawe dere *to the advancement*
They ben acorded° (so as ye shal here)° *came into agreement / hear*

How that the Sowdan and his baronage° *barons, i.e., followers of high rank*
And alle his liges° shulde y-cristned be, *lieges, subjects*
And he shal han Custance in mariage,
And certein° gold (I noot° what quantitee), *a fixed amount of / do not know*
And herto founden suffisant seurtee.[1]
This same acord was sworn on eyther syde.
Now, faire Custance, almighty God thee gyde!° *guide*

Now wolde som men waiten,° as I gesse, *expect*
That I shulde tellen° al the purveyance° *describe / preparations*
That th'Emperour, of his grete noblesse,° *nobility, magnificence*
Hath shapen° for his doghter, dame Custance. *Has arranged*
Wel may men knowen that so gret ordinance° *such extensive provisions*
May no man tellen in a litel clause° *briefly*
As was arrayed° for so heigh a° cause. *arranged / such an important*

Bisshopes ben shapen° with hir for to wende, *appointed*
Lordes, ladyes, knightes of renoun,
And other folk ynowe°—this is the ende.° *enough / outcome*
And notifyed is° thurghout the toun *it is proclaimed*
That every wight with gret devocioun
Shulde preyen Crist that he this mariage
Receyve in gree° and spede this viage.° *favorably / assist this journey*

The day is comen of hir departinge,
I sey, the woful day fatal° is come, *predestined day*
That° ther may be no lenger taryinge,° *So that / tarrying, delay*
But forthward they hem dressen, alle and some.° *prepare (to go), one and all*

1. And thereto provided sufficient surety, safeguards.

Custance, that was with sorwe al overcome,
Ful pale arist° and dresseth hir° to wende, *arises / gets ready*
For wel she seeth ther is non other ende.

Allas, what wonder is it though° she wepte, *that*
That° shal be sent to strange nacioun° *She who / foreign country*
Fro° freendes that so tendrely hir kepte,° *(Away) from / took care of her*
And to be bounden under subjeccioun° *bound in subjection*
Of° oon, she knoweth not his condicioun?° *To / character, qualities*
Housbondes been alle goode, and han ben yore;° *have been so / for a long time*
That knowen wyves°—I dar say yow no more. *Wives know that*

"Fader," she sayde, "thy wrecched child Custance,
Thy yonge doghter fostred up so softe,° *fostered, brought up, so gently*
And ye, my moder, my soverayn plesance° *supreme pleasure*
Over alle thing, out-taken° Crist on lofte,° *except for / on high*
Custance, your child, hir recomandeth° ofte *commends herself*
Unto your grace, for I shal to Surrye,° *(go) to Syria*
Ne shal I never seen yow more with ye.° *with my eyes*

Allas, unto the Barbre° nacioun *Saracen, heathen*
I moste anon,° sin that it is your wille. *now (go)*
But Crist, that starf° for our redempcioun, *died*
So yeve° me grace his hestes° to fulfille. *give / commands*
I, wrecche° womman—no fors though I spille.° *wretched / no matter if I perish*
Wommen are born to thraldom° and penance,° *servitude / suffering*
And to ben under mannes governance."

I trowe° at Troye, whan Pirrus brak° the wal *believe / Pyrrhus broke through*
Or Ylion brende,° at° Thebes the citee, *Before Troy burned / (or) at*
N'at° Rome for the harm thurgh Hanibal,° *Or at / caused by Hannibal*
That° Romayns hath venquisshed° tymes thre, *Whom / vanquished*
Nas° herd swich tendre weping for pitee *There was never heard*
As in the chambre was for hir departinge;
Bot forth she moot, wher-so° she wepe or singe. *forth she must go, whether*

O firste moevyng, cruel firmament,[2]
With thy diurnal sweigh that crowdest ay° *daily motion that always drivest*
And hurlest al from Est til Occident,° *from east to west*
That naturelly wolde holde° another way, *take*
Thy crowding° set the heven in swich array° *pushing / in such a configuration*

2. O First Mover, cruel heavenly sphere. This and the following stanza are based on medieval astronomy/astrology. The Man of Law addresses the *primum mobile*, the outermost sphere of the nine concentric spheres believed to constitute the universe. Its powerful rush sets everything in motion east to west, but the eight inner spheres, the fixed stars and the planets, move west to east in varying ways, creating different trajectories across the sky. Constance departs on a day when Mars has a particularly dire influence on earthly events. In the next stanza, the first four lines exclaim about the unfortunate position of Mars in the sky, and the last three about the moon's equally disadvantageous position.

At the beginning of this fiers viage° — *fierce, dangerous journey*
That cruel Mars hath slayn this mariage.

Infortunat ascendent tortuous
Of which the lord is helples falle, allas,
Out of his angle into the derkest hous!
O Mars, O atazir as in this cas![3]
O feble mone,° unhappy been thy pas!° — *feeble moon / thy steps are unlucky*
Thou knittest thee ther thou art nat receyved.
Ther thou were weel, fro thennes artow weyved.[4]

Imprudent Emperour of Rome, allas!
Was ther no philosophre° in al thy toun? — *i.e., astrologer*
Is no tyme bet than other° in swich cas? — *Is not one time better than another*
Of viage is ther noon eleccioun,
Namely to folk of heigh condicioun,° — *high station*
Nat whan a rote is of a birthe y-knowe?[5]
Allas! we ben to lewed° or to slowe. — *too ignorant*

To shippe is brought this woful faire mayde
Solempnely,° with every circumstance.° — *Solemnly / all the formalities*
"Now Jhesu Crist be with yow alle," she sayde.
Ther nis namore but "Farewel, faire Custance!"
She peyneth hir° to make good countenance;° — *takes pains / appear composed*
And forth I lete hir sayle° in this manere, — *leave her to sail*
And turne I wol agayn to my matere.° — *subject matter, story*

The moder of the Sowdan, welle of vyces,
Espyed hath hir sones pleyn entente:° — *clear intentions*
How he wol lete° his olde sacrifyces. — *forsake, abandon*
And right anon she for hir conseil° sente, — *council*
And they ben come to knowe what she mente,° — *intended*
And when assembled was this folk in-fere,° — *together*
She sette hir doun and sayde as ye shal here.

"Lordes," quod she, "ye knowen everichon,° — *every one of you knows*
How that my sone in point is for to lete° — *is about to leave, renounce*

3. Oblique ascendent, portending misfortune, from which your lord has helplessly fallen out of his house into the least favorable house. O Mars! Alas for your influence in this position! Medieval astronomy/astrology divided the heavens into twelve parts or houses. The influence of planets on earthly affairs depended on their positions within the houses. The "ascendent" is a house rising above the horizon; the "lord" of the ascendent is the dominant planet in that house. In this case the ascendent rises at an oblique angle while its lord has fallen out of its usual "angle" (a type of house) into a house that bodes evil. The influence ("atazir," borrowed from Arabic) of Mars at this time will be particularly bad. Mars is generally a planet of evil influence, associated with many kinds of death and destruction (see *Knight's Tale*, ll. 1967–2040).

4. Thou movest into a position where thou art not accepted (i.e., not able to exercise influence). Thou art banished from where thou wouldst have been powerful. The moon was thought to be influential in regard to travel, so its weak astrological position is a second reason why Constance's date of departure is ominous.

5. Is there no (possibility of) choosing a time for travel, especially for people of high social standing, when the root of a birth is known? Knowing the "root" of a birth, i.e., its precise time and place, permits astrological calculations of the best and worst days for travel; and of course an emperor might well have had astrologers at court.

The holy lawes of our Alkaron,° *Qur'ān*
Yeven° by Goddes message Makomete.° *Given / messenger Mohammed*
But oon avow° to grete God I hete:° *one vow / promise*
The lyf shal rather° out of my body sterte° *sooner / start, go*
Than Makometes lawe out of myn herte!

What shulde us tyden° of° this newe lawe *befall us / from*
But thraldom to° our bodies and penance, *Except servitude for*
And afterward in° helle to be drawe° *into / drawn*
For we reneyed Mahoun° our creance?° *renounced in Mohammed / belief*
But, lordes, wol ye maken assurance° *pledge (to do)*
As I shal seyn, assenting to my lore,° *wisdom, advice*
And I shall make us sauf° for evermore?" *safe*

They sworen and assenten, every man,
To live with hir and dye, and by hir stonde;° *stand*
And everich,° in the beste wyse° he can, *each one / way*
To strengthen hir shal alle his freendes fonde;° *try (to engage) all his friends*
And she hath this empryse y-take on honde,° *has undertaken this enterprise*
Which° ye shal heren that° I shal devyse.° *About which / hear what / tell*
And to hem alle she spak right in this wyse:

"We shul first feyne us° Cristendom to take *feign, pretend*
(Cold water shal not greve us but a lyte°), *will grieve us only a little*
And I shal swich a feste and revel make° *create such a feast and celebration*
That, as I trowe,° I shal the Sowdan quyte.° *believe / repay*
For though his wyf be cristned never° so whyte, *i.e., ever*
She shal have nede to wasshe awey the rede,° *red*
Thogh she a font-ful water with hir lede."[6]

O Sowdanesse, rote of iniquitee!° *root of iniquity*
Virago, thou Semyram the secounde![7]
O serpent under femininitee,[8]
Lyk to the serpent° depe in helle y-bounde! *i.e., Satan*
O feyned° womman, al that may confounde *feigned, false*
Vertu and innocence, thurgh thy malyce,
Is bred in thee, as nest of every vyce!

O Sathan, envious sin thilke day° *since the very day*
That thou were chased from our heritage,° *i.e., expelled from heaven*
Wel knowestow° to wommen the olde way: *dost thou know*
Thou madest Eva° bringe us in servage.° *Eve / into servitude*
Thou wolt fordoon° this Cristen mariage. *destroy*
Thyn instrument—so weylawey° the whyle!— *alas*
Makestow of wommen, whan thou wolt bigyle.[9]

6. Even if she brings with her a (baptismal) font full of water.
7. A virago is a shrewish and masculine woman (as the Latin root *vir* implies), as was Semiramus, Queen of Assyria. Legend held that Semiramus gained royal power by pretending to be her young son and kept it by her prowess as a leader of armies.
8. In the guise of a woman. In medieval art, the serpent of the Temptation often shows itself with a woman's face so as not to frighten Eve.
9. Thou makest women thy instrument—alas the while!—when thou wishest to deceive.

This Sowdanesse, whom I thus blame and warie,° *curse*
Leet prively hir conseil goon hir way.° *Had her council depart secretly*
What° sholde I in this tale lenger tarie? *Why*
She rydeth° to the Sowdan on a day, *rides*
And seyde him that she wolde reney hir ley° *wished to renounce her law*
And Cristendom of preestes handes fonge,° *receive from the priests' hands*
Repenting hire she hethen° was so longe, *heathen*

Biseching° him to doon hir° that honour *Beseeching / grant to her*
That she moste han° the Cristen folk to feste:° *might invite / to a banquet*
"To plesen hem I wol do my labour."
The Sowdan seith, "I wol don at your heste,"° *I will do what you ask*
And kneling° thanketh hir of that requeste. *kneeling*
So glad he was, he niste° what to seye. *knew not*
She kiste hir sone, and hoom she gooth hir weye.

PART TWO

Arrived ben this Cristen folk to londe
In Surrie, with a greet solempne route,° *large, impressive company*
And hastily this Sowdan° sente his sonde,° *Sultan / messenger*
First to his moder and al the regne aboute,° *realm around*
And seyde his wyf was comen, out of doute,° *had arrived, without doubt*
And preyde hir for to ryde agayn° the quene, *asked her to ride to meet*
The honour of his regne to sustene.° *sustain, keep*

Gret was the prees,° and riche was th'array° *press, crowd / appearance*
Of Surriens° and Romayns met yfere.° *Syrians / together*
The moder of the Sowdan, riche and gay,° *finely dressed*
Receyveth° hir with also glad a chere° *Receives / as happy a face*
As any moder mighte hir doghter dere.
And to the nexte° citee ther bisyde *nearest*
A softe pas° solempnely° they ryde. *At a gentle pace / ceremoniously*

Noght trowe I the triumphe of Julius,
Of which that Lucan maketh swich a bost,[1]
Was royaller° ne more curious° *more regal / elaborate*
Than was th'assemblee of this blisful host.° *joyful group*
But this scorpioun, this wikked gost,° *spirit*
The Sowdanesse, for al hir flateringe,
Caste° under this ful mortally° to stinge. *Schemed / i.e., to death*

The Sowdan comth himself sone after this
So royally that wonder is to telle,
And welcometh hir with alle joye and blis,
And thus in merthe and joye I lete hem dwelle.

1. I do not believe that Julius Caesar's ceremonial triumph (over Pompey), about which Lucan makes such a boast. . . . In Lucan's *Pharsalia*, in fact, it is Caesar, not the Roman poet in his own voice, who makes the boast.

The fruyt° of this matere is that° I telle. — *fruit, important part / what*
Whan tyme cam, men thoughte it for the beste
That revel stinte° and men goon to hir reste. — *the revelry be ended*

The tyme cam, this olde Sowdanesse
Ordeyned hath this feste° of which I tolde, — *Has arranged the feast*
And to the feste Cristen folk hem dresse° — *direct themselves*
In general, ye,° bothe yonge and olde. — *One and all, indeed*
Here may men feste,° and royaltee biholde — *enjoy the banquet*
And deyntees mo° than I can yow devyse.° — *more good food and drink / tell*
But al to dere° they boughte° it er° they ryse. — *at too high a cost / paid for / before*

O sodeyn wo,° that ever art successour — *sudden woe*
To worldly blisse, spreynd° with bitternesse, — *sprinkled, mingled*
Th'ende of the joye of our worldly labour!
Wo occupieth the fyn° of our gladnesse. — *seizes the end (Proverbs 14:13)*
Herke° this conseil for thy sikernesse:° — *Listen to / security, safety*
Upon thy glade day have in thy minde
The unwar° wo or harm that comth bihinde.° — *unexpected / follows (you) behind*

For shortly for to tellen, at o word,° — *in one word, briefly*
The Sowdan and the Cristen everichone° — *every one of the Christians*
Ben al tohewe° and stiked° at the bord,° — *hewn to pieces / stabbed / table*
But it were° only dame Custance allone. — *Except for*
This olde Sowdanesse, cursed crone,
Hath with hir frendes doon this cursed dede,
For she hirself wolde al the contree lede.° — *lead, rule*

Ne ther was Surrien noon that was converted° — *There was no Syrian convert*
That of the conseil of the Sowdan woot,° — *Who knew of the Sultan's purpose*
That he nas al tohewe er he asterted.° — *started up, could escape*
And Custance han they take anon, foot-hoot,° — *they have taken then, hastily*
And in a shippe al sterelees,° God woot, — *rudderless*
They han hir set, and bidde hir lerne sayle° — *told her to learn to sail*
Out of Surrye agaynward to Itayle.° — *back again to Italy*

A certein tresor° that she thider ladde,° — *treasure / (had) carried there*
And, sooth to sayn, vitaille gret plentee° — *plenty of provisions (victuals)*
They han hir yeven,° and clothes eek° she hadde; — *have given to her / also*
And forth she sayleth in the salte see.
O my Custance, ful of benignitee,° — *kindness*
O Emperoures yonge doghter dere,
He that is lord of fortune be thy stere!° — *rudder (i.e., steersman, guide)*

She blesseth hir,° and with ful pitous° voys — *crosses herself / pitiable, sad*
Unto the croys° of Crist thus seyde she: — *cross*
"O clere,° o welful auter,° holy croys, — *clear, bright / blessed altar*
Reed of° the Lambes° blood full of pitee, — *Red with / i.e., Christ's*
That wesh° the world fro the olde iniquitee,° — *washed / original sin*

Me fro the feend° and fro his clawes kepe,° *fiend, devil / keep*
That day that I shal drenchen in the depe.° *drown in the deep sea*

Victorious tree, proteccioun of trewe,° *true, faithful (Christians)*
That only° worthy were for to bere° *alone / bear*
The King of Heven with his woundes newe,
The whyte Lamb that hurt was with the spere,° *spear*
Flemer° of feendes out of him and here° *Driver-out / i.e., man and woman*
On which thy limes° feithfully extenden, *Over whom thy limbs, arms*
Me keep, and yif° me might° my lyf t'amenden."° *give / strength / to amend*

Yeres° and dayes fleet° this creature *Years / floats, drifts*
Thurghout the see of Grece° unto the Strayte° *i.e., Mediterranean Sea / Strait*
Of Marrok,° as it was hir aventure.° *Morocco (Gibraltar) / fortune*
On many a sory meel° now may she bayte.° *wretched meal / feed*
After her deeth ful often may she wayte,° *expect*
Er that the wilde wawes° wole hir dryve° *waves / drive*
Unto the place ther° she shal arryve. *there where*

Men mighten asken why she was not slayn
Eek° at the feste. Who mighte hir body save? *i.e., she too*
And I answere to that demaunde agayn,° *in response to that question*
Who saved Daniel° in the horrible cave,° *(see Daniel 6:16–24) / pit*
Ther every wight save he,° maister and knave,° *except him / master and servant*
Was with° the leoun frete° er he asterte?° *by / eaten / could escape*
No wight but God, that he bar° in his herte. *whom he bore*

God liste° to shewe his wonderful miracle *It pleased God*
In hir for° we sholde seen his mighty werkes. *so that*
Crist, which that is to every harm triacle,° *balm, medicine*
By certein menes° ofte, as knowen clerkes,° *means / scholars*
Doth thing for certein ende° that ful derk° is *a certain purpose / very obscure*
To mannes wit,° that for° our ignorance *understanding / which because of*
Ne conne not knowe his prudent purveyance.° *wise providence, foresight*

Now sith° she was not at the feste y-slawe,° *since / slain*
Who kepte hir fro the drenching° in the see? *drowning*
Who kepte Jonas° in the fisshes mawe° *Jonah (see Jonah 2) / belly*
Til he was spouted up° at Ninivee?° *spewed out / Nineveh*
Wel may men knowe it was no wight but he
That kepte peple Ebraik° from hir drenchinge, *the Hebrew people*
With drye feet thurghout the see° passinge. *the Red Sea (Exodus 14:21–22)*

Who bad° the foure spirits of tempest,° *commanded / angels of the winds*
That power han t'anoyen° land and see *to trouble*
Bothe north and south and also west and est,
"Anoyeth neither see, ne land, ne tree"?° *(see Apocalypse 7:1–3)*
Sothly,° the comaundour of that was he *Truly*
That fro the tempest ay this womman kepte
As wel° whan she wook° as whan she slepte. *surely / was awake*

Wher° mighte this womman mete° and drinke have — *From what source / food*
Three yeer and more? How lasteth hir vitaille?° — *supplies*
Who fedde the Egipcien Marie in the cave
Or in desert?[2] No wight but Crist, sans faille.° — *without fail*
Fyve thousand folk it was as gret mervaille° — *as great a marvel*
With loves° fyve and fisshes two to fede. — *loaves (see, e.g., Matthew 14:14–21)*
God sente his foison° at hir grete nede. — *plenty*

She dryveth forth° into our occean° — *i.e., is driven / the Atlantic*
Thurghout° our wilde see, til° atte laste, — *Across / until*
Under an hold° that nempnen° I ne can, — *stronghold, castle / name*
Fer in Northumberlond° the wawe° hir caste, — *(county in northeast England) / wave*
And in the sond° hir ship stiked so faste° — *sand / stuck so firmly*
That thennes wolde it noght of al a tyde.[3]
The wille of Crist was that she shulde abyde.° — *abide, remain*

The constable° of the castel doun is fare° — *warden / has walked down*
To seen this wrak,° and al the ship he soghte,° — *wreck / searched through*
And fond° this wery womman ful of care. — *found*
He fond also the tresor that she broghte.
In hir langage mercy she bisoghte°— — *beseeched, begged for*
The lyf out of hir body for to twinne°— — *take*
Hir to delivere of wo° that she was inne. — *To free her from the woe*

A maner Latin corrupt° was hir speche, — *A sort of corrupted Latin (Italian?)*
But algates° therby was she understonde. — *nevertheless*
The constable, whan him list no lenger seche,° — *wishing to search no longer*
This woful womman broghte he to the londe.
She kneleth doun, and thanketh Goddes sonde.° — *gives thanks for / what God has sent*
But what° she was she wolde no man seye,° — *who / reveal to no one*
For foul ne fair,° thogh that she shulde deye. — *i.e., no matter what*

She seyde she was so mased° in the see — *dazed, confused*
That she forgat hir minde,° by hir trouthe. — *lost her memory*
The constable hath of hir so greet pitee,
And eek his wyf, that they wepen for routhe.° — *pity*
She was so diligent, withouten slouthe,° — *sloth, idleness*
To serve and plesen everich in that place,
That alle hir loven° that loken on hir face. — *everyone loves her*

This constable and dame Hermengild, his wyf,
Were payens,° and that contree° everywhere. — *pagans / people of that region*
But Hermengild lovede hir right as hir° lyf, — *as much as her own*
And Custance hath so longe sojourned° there — *dwelled, remained*
In orisons,° with many a bitter tere,° — *In prayers / painful tear*

2. According to medieval legend, St. Mary of Egypt, after repenting her evil life, took just a few loaves of bread with her into the desert but survived there for forty-seven years.
3. That from there it would not (move) whether the tide was high or low.

Til Jhesu hath converted thurgh his grace
Dame Hermengild, constablesse° of that place. *wife of the warden*

In al that lond no Cristen durste route.° *dared join in a group*
Alle Cristen folk ben fled° fro that contree *have fled*
Thurgh payens,° that conquereden al aboute° *Due to the pagans / around*
The plages° of the north, by land and see. *coastal regions*
To Walis° fled the Cristianitee° *Wales / Christian believers*
Of olde Britons° dwellinge in this yle;° *Among the ancient Britons / isle*
Ther was hir refut° for the mene whyle.° *place of refuge / the time being*

But yet nere° Cristen Britons so exyled *were not*
That ther nere somme that in hir privetee° *in secret*
Honoured Crist and hethen folk bigyled,° *deceived the heathens*
And ny° the castel swiche° ther dwelten three. *near / of this kind*
That oon° of hem was blind and mighte nat see *One*
But it were° with thilke° eyen of his minde, *Except / those*
With whiche men seen after that they ben° blinde. *once they have become*

Bright was the sonne as in that someres day,
For which the constable and his wyf also
And Custance han y-take the righte° way *direct*
Toward the see, a furlong wey° or two, *(=an eighth of a mile)*
To pleyen° and to romen° to and fro, *enjoy themselves / roam, stroll*
And in hir walk this blinde man they mette,
Croked° and old, with eyen faste y-shette.° *Crooked, bent over / shut*

"In name of Crist," cryde° this blinde Britoun, *cried out*
"Dame Hermengild, yif° me my sighte agayn." *give*
This lady wex affrayed of the soun,° *grew fearful of those words*
Lest that hir housbond (shortly for to sayn)° *to speak briefly*
Wolde hir for Jhesu Cristes love° han slayn, *for her love of Jesus Christ*
Til Custance made hir bold and bad hir werche° *told her to work*
The wil of Crist, as doghter of his chirche.

The constable wex abasshed of° that sight, *grew troubled by*
And seyde, "What amounteth al this fare?"° *What does all this mean*
Custance answerde, "Sire, it is Cristes might° *power*
That helpeth folk out of the feendes° snare." *fiend's, devil's*
And so ferforth° she gan oure lay declare° *so fully / explain our law*
That she the constable, er that it was eve,
Converteth, and on Crist made him bileve.

This constable was nothing lord° of this place *not the lord*
Of which I speke, ther° he Custance fond, *there where*
But kepte° it strongly many wintres space° *guarded / over many years' time*
Under Alla, king of al Northumberlond,[4]

4. Here Chaucer follows Trevet in giving the *Man of Law's Tale* another historical coordinate (see l. 151, n. 8). King Aella (or Aelle) ruled over Deira from 560–588, a realm that later became part of the kingdom of Northumbria.

That° was ful wys and worthy of his hond° *Who / valiant in action*
Agayn the Scottes,° as men may wel here. *Against the Scots*
But turne I wol agayn to my matere.

Sathan,° that ever us waiteth to bigyle,° *Satan / lies in wait to deceive us*
Saugh° of Custance al hir perfeccioun, *Saw*
And caste° anon how he mighte quite hir whyle,° *calculated / get back at her*
And made a yong knight that dwelte in that toun
Love hir so hote,° of foul affeccioun,° *hotly, intensely / sinful passion*
That verraily him thoughte° he shulde spille° *truly / die*
But° he of hir mighte ones have his wille.° *Unless / once satisfy his desire*

He woweth° hire, but it availleth noght:° *woos / it is useless*
She wolde do no sinne by no weye.° *in any way*
And for despyt° he compassed° in his thoght *in retaliation / plotted*
To maken hir on shamful deth to deye.° *die a shameful death*
He wayteth whan° the constable was aweye, *waits until*
And prively upon a night° he crepte *secretly one night*
In Hermengildes chambre whyl she slepte.

Wery for-waked in her orisouns[5]
Slepeth Custance and Hermengild also.
This knight, thurgh Sathanas temptaciouns,
Al softely is to the bed y-go,° *Very quietly has gone to the bed*
And kitte° the throte of Hermengild atwo,° *cut / in two*
And leyde° the blody knyf by dame Custance *laid*
And wente his wey—ther God yeve him meschance!° *may God give him misfortune*

Sone after cometh this constable hoom agayn,
And eek Alla, that king was of that lond,
And saugh his wyf despitously y-slayn,° *cruelly slain*
For which ful ofte he weep and wrong his hond;° *wept and wrung his hands*
And in the bed the blody knyf he fond
By dame Custance. Allas, what mighte she seye?
For verray wo hir wit was al aweye.° *her mind was completely gone*

To king Alla was told al this meschance,
And eek the tyme, and where, and in what wyse° *way, manner*
That in a ship was founden this Custance,
As heerbiforn that° ye han herd devyse.° *previously / heard tell*
The kinges herte of pitee gan agryse° *began to tremble in pity*
Whan he saugh so benigne° a creature *kind*
Falle in disese° and in misaventure.° *into distress / misfortune*

For as the lomb° toward his° deeth is broght, *a lamb / its*
So stant° this innocent bifore the king. *stands*

5. Exhausted from loss of sleep in saying their prayers.

This false knight that hath this tresoun wroght
Berth hir on hond° that she hath doon this thing. — *Falsely says of her*
But nathelees° ther was greet moorning° — *nevertheless / sadness*
Among the peple, and seyn° they can not gesse° — *(they) say / believe*
That she hath doon so greet a wikkednesse;

For they han seyn° hir ever so vertuous — *have seen*
And lovinge Hermengild right as her lyf.° — *as much as her own life*
Of this bar° witnesse everich° in that hous° — *bore / everyone / household*
Save° he that Hermengild slow° with his knyf. — *Except / slew, murdered*
This gentil° king hath caught a gret motyf° — *noble / sensed an important issue*
Of this witnesse,° and thoghte he wolde — *In their testimony*
enquere° — *inquire*
Depper in this,° a trouthe for to lere.° — *More deeply into it / learn*

Allas,° Custance, thou hast no championn,° — *Alas / defender*
Ne fighte canstow nought,° so weylawey!° — *Nor canst thou fight / alas*
But he that starf° for our redempcioun — *who died*
And bond Sathan (and yit lyth ther he lay)[6]
So be° thy stronge champioun this day! — *So (may he) be*
For but if° Crist open miracle kythe,° — *unless / openly shows a miracle*
Withouten gilt° thou shalt be slayn as swythe.° — *guilt / immediately be slain*

She sette her doun on knees,° and thus she sayde: — *i.e., kneeled*
"Immortal God, that savedest Susanne[7]
Fro false blame, and thou, merciful mayde,° — *maiden, virgin*
Mary I mene, doghter to° Seint Anne, — *of*
Bifore whos child aungeles° singe Osanne,° — *angels / hosanna (a cry of praise)*
If I be giltlees of this felonye,
My socour be,° for elles I shal dye." — *Be my succor, help*

Have ye nat seyn° somtyme a pale face — *seen*
Among a prees,° of him that hath be lad° — *crowd / one who has been led*
Toward his deeth, wher as him gat no grace,° — *where he received no mercy*
And swich a colour in his face hath had
Men mighte knowe his face that was bistad° — *deeply troubled*
Amonges alle the faces in that route?° — *crowd*
So stant° Custance, and loketh hir aboute. — *stands*

O quenes,° livinge in prosperitee, — *queens*
Duchesses, and ye ladies everichone,
Haveth som routhe° on hir adversitee. — *pity*
An emperoures doghter stant allone.
She hath no wight to whom to make hir mone.° — *speak her grief*
O blood royal that stondest in this drede,° — *fear*
Fer ben° thy freendes at thy grete nede! — *Far away are*

6. And bound Satan (in hell), who still lies where he first lay.
7. The story of Susannah, also falsely accused, is found in the thirteenth chapter of the book of Daniel in the Vulgate Bible.

This Alla king hath swich compassioun,
As gentil herte° is fulfild° of pitee, *Since a noble heart / filled full*
That from his eyen ran the water doun.
"Now hastily do fecche a book,"° quod he, *have a (sacred) book brought here*
"And if this knight wol sweren how that she
This womman slow,° yet wole we us avyse° *slew, killed* / *then we will consider*
Whom that we wole that shal ben our justyse."° *want to be our judge*

A Briton book writen with Evangyles° *containing the Gospels*
Was fet,° and on this book he swoor anoon° *fetched / swore at once*
She gilty was, and in the mene whyles° *meanwhile*
A hand him smoot° upon the nekke-boon° *smote / collarbone*
That doun he fil atones° as a stoon,° *fell at once / like a stone*
And bothe his eyen broste° out of his face *eyes burst*
In sight of every body in that place.

A vois was herd in general audience,° *heard by everyone assembled*
And seyde, "Thou hast desclaundred,° giltelees,° *slandered / without guilt*
The doghter of holy chirche in heigh presence.° *i.e., in God's presence*
Thus hastou doon,° and yet° holde I my pees."° *Thus hast thou done / still* / *peace*
Of this mervaille° agast° was al the prees.° *marvel / aghast / crowd*
As mazed folk° they stoden everichone *people in a daze*
For drede of wreche,° save° Custance allone. *In fear of vengeance / except*

Greet was the drede and eek the repentance
Of hem that° hadden wrong suspeccioun *those who*
Upon this sely° innocent Custance; *holy*
And for° this miracle, in conclusioun, *because of*
And by Custances mediacioun,
The king and many another in that place
Converted was, thanked be Cristes grace.

This false knight was slayn for his untrouthe° *lying, treachery*
By jugement of Alla hastifly,° *promptly*
And yet Custance hadde of his deeth gret routhe.° *pity*
And after this, Jhesus, of his mercy,
Made Alla wedden ful solempnely° *ceremoniously*
This holy mayden that is so bright and shene,° *beautiful and radiant*
And thus hath Crist y-maad° Custance a quene. *made*

But who was woful, if I shal nat lye,
Of this wedding but Donegild (and namo°), *no one else*
The kinges moder, ful of tirannye?
Hir thoughte hir cursed herte brast atwo.° *would burst in two*
She wolde noght hir sone had do° so: *done*
Hir thoughte a despit° that he sholde take *It seemed to her an insult*
So strange° a creature unto his make.° *foreign, strange / as his mate*

Me list nat of the chaf° nor of the stree° — *chaff, husks / straw*
Maken so long a tale as of the corn.[8]
What° sholde I tellen of the royaltee° — *Why / royal splendor*
At mariage, or which cours gooth biforn,° — *which course is served first*
Who bloweth in a trompe° or in an horn? — *trumpet*
The fruit of every tale is for to seye:
They ete and drinke and daunce and singe and pleye.

They goon to bedde, as it was skile° and right. — *reasonable*
For thogh that wyves been ful holy thinges,
They moste take in pacience° at night — *must patiently put up with*
Swich maner necessaries as been — *Such necessary*
plesinges° — *acts as give delight*
To folk that han° y-wedded hem with ringes, — *To those who have*
And leye a lyte hir holinesse asyde
As for the tyme—it may no bet bityde.[9]

On hir he gat° a knave° child anon, — *fathered / male*
And to a bishop and his constable eke° — *also*
He took his wyf, to kepe° whan he is goon — *to take care of (her)*
To Scotland-ward, his foomen for to seke.[1]
Now faire Custance, that is so humble and meke,
So longe is goon with childe° til that stille° — *has been pregnant / quietly*
She halt° hir chambre, abyding Cristes wille. — *keeps to*

The tyme is come a knave child she ber.° — *gave birth to*
Mauricius at the font-stoon° they him calle.° — *baptismal font / name*
This constable dooth forth come a messager,° — *has a messenger brought forth*
And wroot unto° his king, that cleped was Alle,° — *wrote to / Alla*
How that this blisful tyding is bifalle,° — *event has occurred*
And othere tydings speedful° for to seye. — *other happenings useful*
He takth° the lettre and forth he gooth his weye. — *takes (=taketh)*

This messager, to doon his avantage,° — *better his own standing*
Unto the kinges moder rydeth swythe° — *rides quickly*
And salueth hir° ful faire in his langage. — *greets her*
"Madame," quod he, "ye may be glad and blythe,
And thanketh God an hundred thousand sythe.° — *times*
My lady quene hath child, withouten doute,
To joye and blisse of al this regne aboute.° — *throughout all this realm*

Lo, heer° the lettres seled° of this thing, — *here (are) / sealed*
That I mot bere° with al the haste I may. — *must bear (to Alla)*
If ye wol aught° unto your sone the king, — *want anything (sent)*
I am your servant, bothe night and day."

8. Grain. The Man of Law uses language often applied to fables and stories in medieval poetic theory. "Chaf" (chaff, husk) and "stree" (straw) can refer both to the narrative itself and to rhetorical embellishment. Beneath these pleasurable features of fiction lies the "corn" (grain) or "fruit" (l. 706), the meaning of a story, whether literal, moral, or allegorical.
9. And set aside their holiness a little, at least for a while—nothing better is going to happen.
1. Toward Scotland, to seek out his enemies.

Donegild answerde, "As now at this tyme, nay.
But heer al night I wol thou take thy reste.
Tomorwe wol I seye thee what me leste."° *tell thee what I wish*

This messager drank sadly° ale and wyn, *deeply*
And stolen were his lettres prively° *secretly*
Out of his box, whyl he sleep as a swyn,° *slept like a pig*
And countrefeted° was ful subtilly° *forged / very skillfully*
Another lettre, wroght° ful sinfully, *contrived*
Unto the king direct° of this matere *Addressed to the king*
Fro his constable, as ye shul after here.° *hear next*

The lettre spak° the queen delivered was *said that*
Of so horrible a feendly° creature *fiend-like, devilish*
That in the castel noon so hardy was° *there was no one so brave*
That any whyle dorste ther endure.° *Who dared stay there any longer*
The moder was an elf,° by aventure° *elf, demon / i.e., perhaps*
Y-come° by charmes or by sorcerye, *Come there*
And every wight° hateth hir companye. *every person*

Wo° was this king whan he this lettre had seyn,° *Woeful / seen*
But to no wighte he tolde his sorwes sore,° *painful*
But of° his owene honde he wroot ageyn:° *with / in response*
"Welcome the sonde of Crist° for evermore *whatever Christ sends*
To me, that am now lerned in his lore.° *instructed in his wisdom*
Lord, welcome be thy lust° and thy plesaunce. *will, desires*
My lust I putte al° in thyn ordinaunce.° *entirely / command*

Kepeth° this child, al be it° foul or fair, *Protect / whether it be*
And eek my wyf, unto myn hoom-cominge.
Crist, whan him list, may sende me an heir
More agreable° than this to my lykinge."° *pleasing / desires*
This lettre he seleth,° prively° wepinge, *seals / privately, secretly*
Which to the messager was take sone,° *promptly delivered*
And forth he gooth—ther is na more to done.° *i.e., to say*

O messager, fulfild of dronkenesse,° *besotted with drink*
Strong is thy breeth,° thy limes faltren ay,° *breath / limbs shake constantly*
And thou biwreyest alle secreenesse.° *betrayest every secret*
Thy mind is lorn,° thou janglest as a jay,° *gone / chatterest like a jaybird*
Thy face is turned in a newe array.° *i.e., is changed, distorted*
Ther° dronkenesse regneth° in any route,° *Where / reigns / company*
Ther is no conseil hid,° withouten doute. *There are no secrets*

O Donegild, I ne have noon English digne° *adequate*
Unto° thy malice and thy tirannye, *To (describe)*
And therfore to the feend I thee resigne.° *consign thee to the devil*
Let him endyten of thy traitorye.° *describe thy treachery*
Fy, mannish,° fy!—O nay, by God, I lye— *unwomanly (woman)*
Fy, feendly spirit, for I dar wel telle,° *dare well say*
Though thou heer° walke, thy spirit is in helle! *i.e., here on earth*

This messager comth fro the king agayn,
And at the kinges modres court he lighte,° *dismounted*
And she was of this messager ful fayn,° *very welcoming*
And plesed him in al that ever she mighte.° *whatever way she could*
He drank and wel his girdel underpighte.° *stuffed (his belly under) his belt*
He slepeth and he fnorteth in his gyse° *snorts in his usual way*
Al night, until the sonne gan aryse.° *rose*

Eft° were his lettres stolen everichon,° *Again / every one*
And countrefeted lettres in this wyse:° *manner*
"The king comandeth his constable anon,
Up peyne of hanging and on heigh juyse,[2]
That he ne sholde suffren° in no wyse *should not allow*
Custance in-with his regne for t'abyde° *to remain within his realm*
Thre dayes and a quarter of a tyde.[3]

But in the same ship as he hir fond,
Hir and hir yonge sone and al hir gere° *belongings*
He sholde putte, and croude° hir fro the lond, *drive*
And charge° hir that she never eft come there." *command*
O my Custance, wel may thy goost have fere° *soul be fearful*
And, sleping, in thy dreem been in penance,° *be tormented in thy dreams*
When Donegild caste al this ordinance.° *contrived this whole plan*

This messager, on morwe° whan he wook, *in the morning*
Unto the castel halt the nexte wey,° *takes the most direct route*
And to the constable he the lettre took,
And whan that he this pitous lettre sey,° *saw*
Ful ofte he seyde allas and weylawey.
"Lord Crist," quod he, "how may this world endure?
So ful of sinne is many a creature!

O mighty God, if that it be thy wille,
Sith thou art rightful juge,° how may it be *a righteous judge*
That thou wolt suffren° innocents to spille° *allow / perish*
And wikked folk regne° in prosperitee? *reign*
O good Custance, allas, so wo is me
That I mot° be thy tormentour, or deye *must*
On shames deeth°—ther is noon other weye." *A shameful death*

Wepen° bothe yonge and olde in al that place *Wept*
Whan that the king this cursed lettre sente;
And Custance, with a deedly° pale face, *deathly*
The ferthe° day toward hir ship she wente. *fourth*
But natheles° she taketh in good entente° *nevertheless / with good will*
The wille of Crist, and kneling on the stronde° *kneeling on the shore*
She seyde, "Lord, ay welcom be thy sonde!° *what thou sendest*

2. On pain of hanging and of high judicial punishment. In Trevet's *Cronicles*, Chaucer's source for this tale, the forged letter's threat of judicial punishment involves the loss of inheritance rights for the constable's wife and family.
3. I.e., three days and one quarter of the time between one high or low tide and another.

He that me kepte° fro the false blame — *protected*
Whyl I was on the londe amonges yow,
He can me kepe from harme and eek fro shame
In salte see, althogh I se nat° how. — *don't see*
As strong as ever he was, he is yet° now. — *still*
In him triste° I and in his moder dere, — *trust, believe*
That is to me my seyl° and eek my stere."° — *sail / rudder*

Hir litel child lay weping in hir arm,
And kneling pitously° to him she seyde, — *kneeling with pity*
"Pees,° litel sone, I wol do thee non harm." — *Peace*
With that hir coverchief of° hir heed she breyde° — *headscarf from / snatched*
And over his litel eyen° she it leyde,° — *eyes / laid*
And in hir arm she lulleth it ful faste,° — *lulls him in her arms*
And into° heven hir eyen up she caste. — *unto*

"Moder," quod she, "and mayde bright,° Mary, — *radiant virgin*
Sooth is that thurgh wommannes eggement
Mankind was lorn and damned ay to dye,[4]
For which thy child was on a croys y-rent.° — *torn, pierced*
Thy blisful eyen sawe al his torment.
Than is ther no comparisoun bitwene
Thy wo and any wo man may sustene.° — *sustain, experience*

Thou sawe thy child y-slayn° bifor thyn eyen, — *slain*
And yet now liveth my litel child, parfay.° — *by my faith (indeed)*
Now lady bright, to whom alle woful° cryen, — *all who are woeful*
Thou glorie of wommanhede, thou faire may,° — *maiden*
Thou haven of refut,° brighte sterre° of day, — *refuge / morning star*
Rewe° on my child, that of thy gentillesse — *Take pity*
Rewest on every rewful° in distresse. — *pitiable person*

O litel child, allas! What is thy gilt,
That never wroughtest sinne as yet, pardee,
Why wil thyn harde fader° han thee spilt?° — *cruel father / killed*
O mercy, dere constable," quod she,
"As lat° my litel child dwelle heer with thee, — *Let*
And if thou darst° not saven him, for blame,° — *darest / (fear of) blame*
So kis him ones° in his fadres name." — *Kiss him one time*

Therwith° she loketh bakward to the londe — *With that*
And seyde, "Farewel, housbond routhelees!"° — *ruthless, pitiless*
And up she rist° and walketh doun the stronde — *rises*
Toward the ship—hir folweth al the prees°— — *all the throng*
And ever she preyeth° hir child to holde his pees,° — *begs / be calm*
And taketh hir leve, and with an holy entente° — *devout intent*
She blesseth hir,° and into ship she wente. — *crosses herself*

4. It is true that through woman's enticement mankind was lost and condemned forever to die. In Genesis 3, Eve eats of the apple, offers it to Adam, and after he has eaten both are expelled from Eden.

Vitailled° was the ship, it is no drede, — *Provisioned*
Habundantly° for hir ful longe space,° — *Abundantly / space of time (at sea)*
And other necessaries that sholde nede° — *would be required*
She hadde ynogh, heried° be Goddes grace. — *praised*
For wind and weder almighty God purchace° — *provide*
And bringe hir hoom—I can no bettre seye.° — *say*
But in the see she dryveth forth hir weye.° — *drifts forth on her way*

PART THREE

Alla the king comth hoom sone after this
Unto his castel, of the which I tolde,
And axeth° wher his wyf and his child is. — *asks*
The constable gan aboute his herte colde,° — *grew cold*
And pleynly al the maner° he him tolde — *the whole story*
As ye han herd—I can telle it no bettre—
And sheweth° the king his seel° and his lettre, — *shows / royal seal*

And seyde, "Lord, as ye comaunded me
Up peyne of deeth, so have I doon, certein."
This messager tormented° was til he — *tortured*
Moste biknowe° and tellen, plat° and plein, — *Had to make known / flatly*
Fro night to night in what place he had leyn.° — *lain, stayed*
And thus by wit° and subtil enqueringe° — *reasoning / careful interrogation*
Ymagined was° by whom this harm° gan springe. — *It was guessed / wrongdoing*

The hand was knowe° that the lettre wroot, — *recognized*
And al the venim° of this cursed dede,° — *venom / deed*
But in what wyse,° certeinly, I noot.° — *exactly how / do not know*
Th'effect° is this: that Alla, out of drede,° — *outcome / beyond doubt*
His moder slow° (that men may pleinly rede°) — *slew, killed / i.e., read elsewhere*
For that she traitour was to hir ligeaunce.° — *allegiance (i.e., her country)*
Thus endeth olde Donegild, with meschaunce!° — *bad luck to her*

The sorwe that this Alla night and day
Maketh for his wyf and for his child also—
Ther is no tonge that it telle may.
But now wol I unto Custance go,° — *turn*
That fleteth° in the see in peyne and wo — *Who floats, drifts*
Fyve yeer and more, as lyked Cristes sonde,° — *it suited Christ's plan*
Er that° hir ship approched unto londe. — *Before*

Under an hethen° castel atte laste, — *heathen*
Of which the name in my text noght I finde,° — *do not find*
Custance and eek hir child the see up caste.° — *the sea cast up*
Almighty God, that saveth al mankinde,
Have on Custance and on hir child som minde,° — *thought*
That fallen is in° hethen land eft-sone,° — *has come to / once again*
In point to spille,° as I shal telle yow sone.° — *On brink of death / soon*

Doun from the castel comth ther many a wight° *come many people*
To gauren on° this ship and on Custance. *gaze at*
But shortly, from the castel on a night° *one night*
The lordes styward°—God yeve° him meschaunce!°— *steward / give* *misfortune*
A theef that had reneyed our creaunce,° *renounced our religion*
Com° into ship allone, and seyde he sholde *Came*
Hir lemman° be, wher-so° she wolde or nolde.° *lover / whether* *was willing or not*

Wo° was this wrecched womman tho bigon.° *(With) woe / then beset*
Hir child cryde, and she cryde pitously.
But blisful Marie heelp° hir right anon, *blessed Mary helped*
For with hir strugling° wel and mightily, *as a result of her struggling*
The theef fil° over bord al sodeinly, *fell*
And in the see he dreynte° for vengeance.° *drowned / in retribution*
And thus hath Crist unwemmed° kept Custance. *unblemished, pure*

O foule lust of luxurie,° lo, thyn ende: *loathsome delight in lechery*
Nat only that thou feyntest° mannes minde, *weakenest*
But verraily thou wolt his body shende.° *ruin, destroy*
Th'ende of thy werk° or of thy lustes° blinde *outcome of thy acts / desires*
Is compleyning.° How many oon° may men finde *lamentation / many a one*
That noght for werk° sometyme but for th'entente° *Who not for the act* *intention*
To doon° this sinne ben outher sleyn or shente?° *commit* *are either killed or ruined*

How may this wayke° womman han this strengthe *weak*
Hir° to defende agayn° this renegat?° *Herself / against / renegade*
O Golias,° unmesurable of lengthe,° *Goliath (see 1 Samuel 17) / in height*
How mighte David make thee so mat,° *bring thee to such defeat*
So yong° and of armure so desolat?° *So young / so lacking in armor*
How dorste° he loke upon thy dredful° face? *dared / fearsome*
Wel may men seen it nas but° Goddes grace. *it was only by*

Who yaf° Judith corage° or hardinesse° *gave / courage / strength*
To sleen him Olofernus° in his tente, *Holofernes*
And to deliveren out of wrecchednesse
The peple of God?[5] I seye for this entente,° *purpose*
That right° as God spirit of vigour° sente *just / a vigorous spirit*
To hem and saved hem out of meschance,° *from misfortune*
So sente he might and vigour to Custance.

Forth goth hir ship thurghout the narwe mouth
Of Jubaltar and Septe, dryving ay[6]

5. Holofernes was leading an Assyrian siege of the Israelites when one of them, Judith, managed to gain his confidence and, when they were alone, cut off his head. This led to the defeat of the Assyrians. See Judith 8–13, in the Vulgate Bible. Protestant Bibles treat the book as apocryphal.

6. Her ship sails forth through the narrow strait of Gibraltar (in Spain) and the Seven Brothers (points on a mountain ridge in Morocco), always drifting.

Somtyme west, somtyme north and south,
And somtyme est, ful many a wery° day, *wearying*
Til Cristes moder—blessed be she ay!—
Hath shapen° thurgh hir endelees goodnesse *Has conceived a way*
To make an ende of° al hir hevinesse.° *bring an end to / sorrow*

Now lat us stinte° of Custance but a throwe,° *stop speaking / for just a while*
And speke we of the Romain Emperour,
That out of Surrie hath by lettres knowe° *learned by letters from Syria*
The slaughtre° of Cristen folk and dishonour *(Of) the slaughter*
Don° to his doghter by a fals traitour, *Done*
I mene the cursed wikked Sowdanesse,° *Sultaness*
That at the feste leet sleen both more and lesse.° *caused everyone to be slain*

For which this Emperour hath sent anoon
His senatour, with royal ordinance,° *by royal decree*
And othere lordes, God wot,° many oon, *knows*
On Surriens to taken heigh vengeance.
They brennen,° sleen,° and bringe hem to meschance° *burn / slay / bad end*
Ful many a day; but shortly this is th'ende:° *outcome*
Homward to Rome they shapen hem to wende.° *prepare to depart*

This senatour repaireth° with victorie *returns*
To Rome-ward,° sayling ful royally, *Toward Rome*
And mette the ship dryving,° as seith the storie, *drifting*
In which Custance sit° ful pitously. *sits, is placed*
Nothing ne knew he what° she was, ne° why *who / nor*
She was in swich array;° ne she nil seye° *such a state / nor would she speak*
Of hir estaat,° althogh she sholde deye. *(high) rank*

He bringeth hir to Rome, and to his wyf
He yaf° hir and hir yonge sone also, *gave*
And with the senatour she ladde° her lyf. *led*
Thus can our Lady bringen out of wo
Woful Custance and many another mo.° *more, also*
And longe tyme dwelled she in that place,
In holy werkes ever,° as was hir grace. *ever active*

The senatoures wyf hir aunte was,
But for al that she knew hir never the more.° *not at all*
I wol no lenger tarien° in this cas, *linger*
But to king Alla, which I spak of yore,° *earlier, before*
That wepeth for his wyf and syketh sore,° *sighs painfully*
I wol retourne, and lete° I wol Custance *leave*
Under the senatoures governance.

King Alla, which that hadde his moder slayn,
Upon a day fil in° swich repentance *fell into*
That—if I shortly tellen shal and plain°— *plainly*

To Rome he comth to receyven° his penance, *receive, obtain*
And putte him in the Popes ordinance° *submit to the Pope's command*
In heigh and low,° and Jhesu Crist bisoghte° *i.e., in all respects / he beseeched*
Foryeve° his wikked werkes that he wroghte. *(To) forgive*

The fame° anon thurgh Rome toun is born— *news*
How Alla king shal come in pilgrimage—
By herbergeours[7] that wenten him biforn.
For which the senatour, as was usage,° *the custom*
Rood him ageyn,° and many of his linage,° *Rode out to meet him / lineage*
As wel° to shewen his heighe magnificence *As much*
As to don any king a reverence.[8]

Greet chere° dooth this noble senatour *hospitality*
To king Alla, and he to him also.
Everich° of hem doth other greet honour. *Each*
And so bifel that in a day or two
This senatour is to king Alla go
To feste,° and shortly, if I shal nat lye, *For a feast, banquet*
Custances sone° wente in his companye. *son*

Som men wolde seyn° at requeste of Custance *Some folk would say that*
This senatour hath lad° this child to feste. *has led*
I may nat tellen every circumstance.° *every detail*
Be as be may, ther was he at the leste.° *Be as it may, he was surely there*
But soth is this: that at his modres heste,° *mother's behest*
Biforn Alla during the metes space° *while they were dining*
The child stood loking in° the kinges face. *into, directly at*

This Alla king hath of this child greet wonder,
And to the senatour he seyde anon,
"Whos° is that faire° child that stondeth yonder?" *Whose / handsome*
"I noot,"° quod he, "by God and by seint John. *do not know*
A moder he hath, but fader hath he non
That I of woot."° And shortly in a stounde° *I know of / quickly and at once*
He tolde Alla how that this child was founde.

"But God wot," quod this senatour also,
"So vertuous a livere° in my lyf *living creature*
Ne saugh I never as she, ne herde of mo
Of worldly wommen, mayde ne of wyf.[9]
I dar wel seyn hir hadde lever° a knyf *she would rather have*
Thurghout° her breste than been a womman wikke. *(Run) through*
Ther is no man coude bringe hir to that
prikke."° *bring her to that state (point)*

7. Harbingers were members of a royal entourage sent in advance to make arrangements for food and lodgings.
8. As much to demonstrate his own noble magnificence as to pay homage to any king. In Aristotle's *Nicomachean Ethics*, "magnificence" is a moral virtue involving the proper use of great wealth, notably in public displays of political or ceremonial import.
9. In my life I never saw as virtuous a person as she, nor (have I) heard of any other among secular women, whether maiden or wife.

Now was this child as lyk unto Custance	
As possible is a creature to be.	
This Alla hath the face in remembrance	
Of dame Custance, and theron mused he	
If that the childes moder were aught° she	*in any possible way*
That was his wyf, and prively he sighte°	*sighed*
And spedde him fro° the table that he	*quickly left*
mighte.°	*as soon as he could*
"Parfay,"° thoghte he, "fantome is in myn	*By my faith*
heed!°	*I'm imagining things*
I oghte deme of skilful jugement°	*ought to know by*
That in the salte see my wyf is deed."	*rational judgment*
And afterward he made his argument:°	*i.e., reasoned thus*
"What woot I if that° Crist have hider y-sent	*How do I know but that*
My wyf by see, as wel as he hir sente	
To my contree fro thennes that she wente?"[1]	
And after noon, hoom with the senatour	
Goth° Alla for to seen this wonder chaunce.°	*Goes / wondrous possibility*
This senatour dooth Alla greet honour,°	*shows Alla great respect*
And hastifly° he sente after° Custaunce.	*promptly / for*
But trusteth weel, hir liste nat to daunce°	*she had no wish to dance*
Whan that she wiste wherefor was that sonde.°	*knew why she was sent for*
Unnethe° upon hir feet she mighte stonde.°	*Barely / could she stand*
When Alla saugh his wyf, faire he hir grette°	*he greeted her courteously*
And weep° that it was routhe° for to see.	*wept / pity*
For at the firste look he on hir sette	
He knew wel verraily° that it was she.	*truly*
And she for sorwe as domb stant° as a tree,	*stands as dumb (silent)*
So was hir herte shet° in hir distresse	*shut fast*
Whan she remembred his unkindenesse.	
Twyes° she swowned° in his owne sighte.	*Twice / swooned, fainted*
He weep and him excuseth° pitously:	*wept and asks to be forgiven*
"Now God," quod he, "and his halwes° brighte	*saints*
So wisly° on my soule as have° mercy,	*As surely / as (they may) have*
That of your harm° as giltelees° am I	*suffering / guiltless*
As is Maurice my sone, so lyk your face—	
Elles° the feend me fecche° out of this place!"	*Otherwise (may) / take me*
Long was the sobbing and the bitter peyne	
Er that hir° woful hertes mighte cesse.°	*their / cease, become calm*
Greet was the pitee for to here hem pleyne,°	*hear them lament*
Thurgh whiche pleintes gan hir wo encresse.°	*their grief increased*
I prey° yow al my labour to relesse:°	*beg / to release me from my labor*

1. What if Christ has sent my wife here by sea, just as he sent her to my country from the place she left?

I may nat telle° hir wo until tomorwe,° *describe / i.e., all day long*
I am so wery° for to speke of sorwe. *weary*

But fynally, when that the sooth is wist° *truth is known*
That Alla giltelees was of hir wo,
I trowe° an hundred tymes been they kist,° *believe / they have kissed*
And swich a blisse is ther bitwix° hem two *between*
That, save° the joye that lasteth evermo, *except for*
Ther is non lyk° that any creature *nothing comparable*
Hath seyn or shal° whyl that the world may dure.° *Has seen or will see / last*

Tho preyde° she hir housbond mekely,° *Then begged / meekly*
In relief of hir longe pitous pyne,° *pitiable pain*
That he wold preye hir fader specially° *in particular*
That of his magestee° he wolde enclyne° *in his majesty / consent*
To vouche sauf° som day with him to dyne.° *grant / dine*
She preyde him eek he sholde by no weye° *in no case*
Unto hir fader no word of hir seye.° *say anything about her*

Som men wold seyn how that the child Maurice
Doth° this message unto this Emperour. *Delivers*
But as I gesse, Alla was nat so nyce° *i.e., discourteous*
To him that° was of so sovereyn° honour *Toward one who / such supreme*
(As he that is of Cristen folk the flour°) *the flower of Christendom*
Sente° any child; but it is bet to deme° *To have sent / better to suppose*
He wente himself, and so it may wel seme.° *seem, appear*

This Emperour hath graunted gentilly° *nobly agreed*
To come to diner, as he him bisoghte,° *as he (Alla) asked him to*
And wel rede I,° he loked bisily° *I have read (in a book) / intently*
Upon this child and on his doghter thoghte.
Alla goth to his in° and, as him oghte, *goes to his lodging*
Arrayed° for this feste in every wyse° *Prepared / in all respects*
As ferforth as his conning may suffyse.° *far as his knowledge would allow*

The morwe cam, and Alla gan him dresse,° *got ready*
And eek his wyf, this Emperour to mete,° *meet*
And forth they ryde in joye and in gladnesse,
And whan she saugh hir fader in the strete,° *street, road*
She lighte doun,° and falleth him to fete.° *dismounted / falls at his feet*
"Fader," quod she, "your yonge child Custance
Is now ful clene out of° your remembrance. *completely gone from*

I am your doghter Custance," quod she,
"That whylom° ye han sent unto Surrye. *Whom once*
It am I, fader, that in the salte see
Was put allone and dampned for to dye.° *condemned to die*
Now, gode fader, mercy I yow crye!
Send me namore° unto non hethenesse,° *no more / heathen lands*
But thonketh my lord heer of his kindenesse."

Who can the pitous joye tellen al
Bitwix hem three, sin° they ben thus y-mette?° *after / brought together*
But of my tale make an ende I shal.
The day goth faste—I wol no lenger lette.° *delay*
This glade folk to diner they hem sette;° *sat down*
In joye and blisse at mete I lete hem dwelle
A thousand fold wel more than° I can telle. *beyond anything*

This child Maurice was sithen° Emperour *later*
Maad° by the Pope, and lived *Made, crowned*
cristenly.° *a Christian life*
To Cristes chirche he dide greet honour,
But I lete al his storie passen by.
Of Custance is my tale specially.
In olde Romayn gestes° may men finde *histories of the Roman empire*
Maurices lyf—I bere it noght in minde.° *don't hold it in memory*

This king Alla, whan he his tyme sey,° *saw*
With his Custance, his holy wyf so swete,
To Engelond been they come the righte wey,° *by the shortest route*
Wher as° they live in joye and in quiete. *There where*
But litel whyl it lasteth,° I yow hete,° *it lasts (only) a short time / assure*
Joye of this world, for tyme wol nat abyde.° *because time will not stand still*
Fro day to night it changeth as the tyde.

Who lived ever in swich delyt o day° *such delight for a single day*
That him ne moeved outher° conscience, *That he was not moved either by*
Or ire,° or talent,° or som kin affray,° *anger / lust / some sort of trouble*
Envye, or pryde, or passion, or offence?
I ne seye but for this ende this sentence:[2]
That litel whyl in joye or in plesance
Lasteth the blisse of Alla with Custance.

For deeth, that taketh of heigh and low° his rente, *from everyone*
When passed was a yeer, even as I gesse,° *or so I guess*
Out of this world this king Alla he hente,° *took*
For whom Custance hath ful gret hevinesse.° *sadness*
Now lat us preyen God his soule blesse.
And dame Custance, fynally to seye,
Towards the toun of Rome gooth hir weye.

To Rome is come this holy creature,
And fyndeth ther hir frendes hole° and sounde.° *whole, unhurt / healthy*
Now is she scaped° al hir aventure.° *has she escaped from / misfortunes*
And whan that she hir fader hath y-founde,
Doun on hir knees falleth she to grounde.
Weping for tendrenesse in herte blythe,° *joyous*
She herieth° God an hundred thousand sythe.° *praises / times*

2. I say these wise things only for this reason.

In vertu and in holy almes-dede°   *alms deeds, charity*
They liven alle, and never asonder wende.°   *part asunder*
Til deeth departeth° hem this lyf they lede.°   *separates / lead*
And fareth now weel°—my tale is at an ende.   *now farewell*
Now Jhesu Crist, that of his might° may sende   *who through his power*
Joye after wo, governe us in his grace,
And kepe° us alle that ben in this place. Amen.   *preserve, protect*

The Wife of Bath's Prologue and Tale

The Prologue

"Experience, though noon auctoritee[1]
Were in this world, is right ynough° for me   *certainly enough*
To speke of wo that is in mariage:
For, lordinges, sith° I twelf yeer was of age,   *since*
Thonked be God that is eterne on lyve,°   *alive eternally*
Housbondes at chirche dore I have had fyve[2]
(If I so ofte myghte have y-wedded be)
And alle were worthy men in hir degree.°   *within their station*
But me was told, certeyn,° nat longe agon is,°   *truly / not long ago*
That sith that Crist ne wente nevere but onis°   *once*
To wedding in the Cane° of Galilee,   *Cana*
That by the same ensample° taughte he me   *example*
That I ne sholde wedded be but ones.°   *once*
Herkne eek, lo, which a sharp word for the nones[3]
Besyde a welle, Jesus, God and man,
Spak in repreve° of the Samaritan: *reproof*
'Thou hast y-had fyve housbondes,' quod he,
'And that ilke° man that now hath thee   *that same*
Is noght thyn housbond'—thus seyde he certeyn.
What that he mente therby, I can nat seyn,°   *say*
But that° I axe,° why that the fifthe man   *Except / ask*
Was noon housbond to the Samaritan?
How manye mighte she have in mariage?
Yet herde I nevere tellen in myn age°   *in all my days*
Upon° this nombre diffinicioun.°   *Of / definition, explanation*
Men may devyne° and glosen° up and doun,   *guess / interpret, comment upon*
But wel I woot expres,° withoute lye,°   *know particularly / lie*
God bad us for to wexe° and multiplye: *wax, increase*
That gentil° text can I wel understonde.   *noble*
Eek° wel I woot° he seyde myn housbonde   *Also / know*
Sholde lete° fader and moder and take to me;   *leave*
But of no nombre mencioun made he

1. The authoritative truths of learned tradition, preserved in writings from the past.
2. Medieval marriages were performed at the church door. Only the nuptial mass was within the church.
3. (And) lo, hear also what a sharp word on the matter ("for the nones" is a tag-ending: "for the occasion," "to the purpose," but often nearly meaningless). The incident referred to can be found in John 4:5–42, printed on pp. 415–17.

Of bigamye or of octogamye.[4]
Why sholde men thanne speke of it vileinye?° *rude things, reproach*
Lo, here the wyse king, daun Salomon;[5]
I trowe° he hadde wyves mo than oon. *believe*
As wolde° God it leveful° were unto me *Would to / lawful*
To be refresshed° half so ofte as he! *i.e., sexually*
Which yifte° of God hadde he for alle his wyvis! *What a gift*
No man hath swich° that in this world alyve is. *such*
God woot° this noble king, as to my wit,° *knows / understanding*
The firste night had many a mery fit° *bout, turn*
With ech of hem, so wel was him on lyve![6]
Blessed be God that I have wedded fyve,
44a Of whiche I have pyked out° the beste,[7] *extracted*
Bothe of here nether purs and of here cheste.[8]
Diverse scoles° maken parfyt clerkes,° *schools / perfect scholars*
And diverse practyk° in many sondry° werkes *practice / sundry, varied*
Maketh the werkman parfyt sekirly:° *assuredly*
44f Of fyve husbondes scoleiyng° am I. *schooling*
Welcome the sixte, whan that evere he shall!° *shall (come along)*
For sothe I wol nat kepe me chast in al.° *entirely chaste*
Whan myn housbond is fro the world y-gon,
Som Cristen man shal wedde me anon;° *at once*
For thanne th'Apostle° seith that I am free *St. Paul*
To wedde, a Goddes half,° where it lyketh° me. *on God's behalf / pleases*
He seith that to be wedded is no sinne:
Bet° is to be wedded than to brinne.° *Better / burn*
What rekketh me° thogh folk seye vileinye° *do I care / speak ill*
Of shrewed Lameth° and his bigamye? *accursed Lamech*
I woot° wel Abraham was an holy man, *know*
And Jacob eek, as ferforth° as I can;° *far / know*
And ech of hem° hadde wyves mo° than two, *each of them / more*
And many another holy man also.
Wher can ye seye,° in any manere age,° *say / any age whatever*
That hye° God defended° mariage *high / forbade*
By expres word? I pray you, telleth me.
Or where comanded he virginitee?
I woot as wel as ye, it is no drede,° *no doubt about it*
Th'Apostel,° whan he speketh of maydenhede, *St. Paul*
He seyde that precept° therof hadde he noon. *i.e., commandment*
Men may conseille° a womman to been oon, *advise*
But conseilling is no comandement:
He putte it in oure owene° jugement. *own*
For hadde God comanded maydenhede,
Thanne hadde he dampned° wedding with the° dede. *damned / in that*
And certes, if ther were no seed y-sowe,° *sown*

4. Here, marriages in succession.
5. Consider the wise king, lord Solomon. (According to 1 Kings 11:3, he had seven hundred wives and three hundred concubines.)
6. With each of them, so fortunate was his life.
7. Lines 44a–44f are probably a late addition; the best manuscripts exclude them.
8. Both from their lower purse (i.e., testicles) and from their (money-)chest.

Virginitee, thanne wherof sholde it growe?
Poul dorste nat comanden, atte leste,[9]
A thing of which his maister yaf noon heste.° *gave no order*
The dart° is set up for virginitee; *dart (given as prize)*
Cacche who so may: who renneth best lat see.[1]
But this word is nat take of every wight,
But ther as God list give it of his might.[2]
I woot° wel that th'Apostel was a mayde,° *know / virgin*
But natheless,° thogh that he wroot° and sayde *nevertheless / wrote*
He wolde° that every wight° were swich° as he, *wished / person / such*
Al nis° but conseil to virginitee, *All (this) is nothing*
And for to been a wyf, he yaf° me leve° *gave / leave, permission*
Of° indulgence. So nis it no repreve° *By / reproach*
To wedde me, if that my make dye,
Withoute excepcioun of bigamye,[3]
Al° were it good no womman for to touche— *Although*
He mente as in his bed or in his couche—
For peril is bothe fyr and tow t'assemble;[4]
Ye knowe what this ensample° may resemble. *example*
This al and som: he heeld virginitee
More parfit than wedding in freletee.
Freletee clepe I, but if that he and she[5]
Wolde leden° al hir lyf in chastitee. *Should wish to lead*
I graunte it wel, I have noon envye
Thogh maydenhede preferre° bigamye. *be preferred over*
Hem lyketh° to be clene, body and goost.° *They wish / soul, spirit*
Of myn estaat° I nil nat° make no boost: *condition / will not*
For wel ye knowe, a lord in his houshold
He hath nat every vessel al of gold;
Somme been of tree,° and doon hir lord servyse. *wood*
God clepeth° folk to him in sondry wyse,° *calls / various ways*
And everich hath of God a propre yifte,° *his own special gift*
Som this, som that, as Him lyketh shifte.° *it pleases Him to ordain*
Virginitee is greet perfeccioun,
And continence eek with devocioun.[6]
But Crist, that of perfeccioun is welle,° *the well, the source*
Bad° nat every wight° he sholde go selle *Commanded / person*
All that he hadde and give it to the pore,° *poor*
And in swich wyse° folwe him and his fore.° *such a way / footsteps*
He spak to hem that wolde live parfitly,
And lordinges, by youre leve,° that am nat I. *leave*
I wol bistowe the flour° of al myn age *the flower, the best part*
In the actes and in fruit of mariage.
Telle me also, to what conclusioun° *end, purpose*

9. (St.) Paul did not dare in the least command.
1. Catch (win) it whoever may: let's see who runs the best.
2. But this counsel (i.e., the preference for virginity) is not required of every person but (only) there where God is pleased to impose it by His might.
3. To wed (again) if my mate die, without being criticized for bigamy.
4. For it is perilous to bring together both fire and flax.
5. "Frailty" I call it, unless he and she.
6. And continence also (when) accompanied by devotion.

Were membres maad of generacioun
And of so parfit wys a wright y-wroght?[7]
Trusteth right wel, they were nat maad for noght.
Glose° whoso wole,° and seye bothe up and doun *Interpret / will*
That they were maked for purgacioun
Of urine, and oure bothe° thinges smale *both our*
Were eek to knowe° a femele from a male, *to distinguish*
And for noon other cause: sey ye no?
The experience° woot° wel it is noght so. *experience (in general) / knows*
So that the clerkes be nat with me wrothe,° *wroth, angry*
I sey this, that they maked been for bothe—
This is to seye, for office,° and for ese° *natural duty / pleasure*
Of engendrure,° ther° we nat God displese. *In procreation / there where*
Why sholde men elles° in hir bokes sette *otherwise*
That man shal yelde° to his wyf hire dette?° *pay / what is owing her*
Now wherwith° sholde he make his payement *by what means*
If he ne used his sely° instrument? *simple, blessed*
Thanne° were they maad upon a creature *Therefore*
To purge uryne, and eek for engendrure.
But I seye noght that every wight is holde,° *beholden, bound*
That hath swich harneys° as I to yow tolde, *such equipment*
To goon and usen hem in engendrure:
Thanne sholde men take of chastitee no cure.[8]
Crist was a mayde° and shapen as° a man, *virgin / formed like*
And many a seint, sith that° the world bigan, *since*
Yet lived they evere in parfit chastitee.
I nil° envye no virginitee: *will not*
Lat hem be breed° of pured whete-seed,° *bread / finest wheat*
And lat us wyves hoten° barly-breed.° *be called / barley bread*
And yet with barly-breed, Mark° telle can, *St. Mark*
Oure Lord Jesu refresshed° many a man. *i.e., fed*
In swich estaat° as God hath cleped° us *condition / called*
I wol persevere, I nam nat precious.[9]
In wyfhode I wol use myn instrument
As frely° as my Makere hath it sent. *generously*
If I be daungerous,° God yeve° me sorwe! *standoffish / give*
Myn housbond shal it have bothe eve and morwe,° *morning*
Whan that him list° com forth and paye his dette. *it pleases him to*
An housbonde I wol have, I wol nat lette,° *will not leave off*
Which shal be bothe my dettour and my thral,° *thrall, slave*
And have his tribulacioun withal° *besides*
Upon his flessh, whyl that I am his wyf.
I have the power duringe al my lyf
Upon° his propre° body, and noght he: *Over / own*
Right thus th' Apostel° tolde it unto me, *St. Paul*
And bad oure housbondes for to love us weel.
Al this sentence me lyketh every deel."[1]

7. And by so perfect and wise a workman (i.e., God)?
8. Then people wouldn't be concerned about chastity.
9. I will continue; I'm not overly fastidious.
1. All this lesson pleases me, every bit (of it).

Up sterte the Pardoner, and that anon.[2]
"Now dame," quod he, "by God and by Seint John,
Ye been a noble prechour° in this cas!° — *preacher / matter*
I was aboute to wedde a wyf. Allas,
What° sholde I bye° it on my flesh so dere? — *Why / pay for*
Yet hadde I levere° wedde no wyf to-yere!"° — *rather / this year*
"Abyde!"° quod° she, "my tale is nat bigonne. — *Wait / said*
Nay, thou shalt drinken of another tonne° — *tun, cask*
Er that I go, shal savoure wors than ale.[3]
And whan that I have told thee forth my tale
Of tribulacioun in mariage,
Of which I am expert in al myn age[4]—
This° to seyn, myself° have been the whippe— — *This is / (I) myself*
Than maystow chese° whether thou wolt sippe° — *mayst thou choose / sip*
Of thilke° tonne that I shal abroche.° — *that same / open*
Be war° of it, er thou to ny° approche, — *wary / too near*
For I shall telle ensamples° mo° than ten. — *examples / more*
'Whoso that nil be war° by othere men, — *Whoever will not be warned*
By him shul othere men corrected be.'
The same wordes wryteth Ptholomee:° — *Ptolemy*
Rede in his Almageste,° and take it there." — *an astronomical treatise*
"Dame, I wolde praye yow, if youre wil it were,"
Seyde this Pardoner, "as ye bigan,
Telle forth youre tale, spareth° for no man, — *hold back*
And teche us yonge men of youre praktike."° — *practice*
"Gladly," quod she, "sith it may yow lyke.° — *please*
But yet I praye to al this companye,
If that I speke after my fantasye,° — *according to my fancy*
As taketh not agrief of that I seye;[5]
For myn entente° nis° but for to pleye. — *intention / is not*
Now sires, now wol I telle forth my tale.
As evere mote° I drinken wyn or ale, — *might*
I shal seye sooth,° tho° housbondes that I hadde, — *tell the truth / (of) those*
As three of hem were gode and two were badde.
The three men were gode, and riche, and olde;
Unnethe mighte they the statut holde[6]
In° which that they were bounden unto me. — *By*
Ye woot° wel what I mene of this, pardee!° — *know / by God*
As help me God, I laughe whan I thinke
How pitously° a-night° I made hem swinke,° — *pitiably / at night / labor*
And by my fey, I tolde of it no stoor.[7]
They had me yeven° hir lond and hir tresoor;° — *given / wealth*
Me neded nat do lenger diligence[8]
To winne hir love, or doon hem reverence.° — *to honor them*
They loved me so wel, by God above,

2. The Pardoner broke in (literally, started up) at once.
3. Before I go, (which) shall taste worse than ale.
4. About which I have been expert all my life.
5. Not to take amiss that (which) I say.
6. They could scarcely observe the statute (law).
7. And by my faith, I set no store by it.
8. It wasn't necessary that I be diligent any longer.

That I ne tolde no deyntee of° hir love! — *took no pleasure in*
A wys womman wol bisye hire evere in oon[9]
To gete hire love, ye, ther as° she hath noon. — *there where*
But sith I hadde hem hoolly° in myn hond, — *wholly*
And sith they hadde me yeven° all hir lond, — *given*
What° sholde I taken keep° hem for to plese, — *Why / heed*
But° it were for my profit and myn ese?° — *Unless / comfort*
I sette hem so a-werke,° by my fey,° — *working / faith*
That many a night they songen° 'weilawey!'° — *sang / woe is me*
The bacoun was nat fet for hem, I trowe,[1]
That som men han in Essex at Dunmowe.
I governed hem so wel after° my lawe — *according to*
That ech° of hem ful blisful° was and fawe° — *each / happy / fain, eager*
To bringe me gaye thinges fro the fayre.° — *fair*
They were ful glad whan I spak to hem fayre,° — *nicely*
For God it woot, I chidde° hem spitously.° — *chided, scolded / spitefully*
  Now herkneth° how I bar me° proprely: — *listen / conducted myself*
Ye wyse° wyves, that can understonde, — *prudent*
Thus shul ye speke and bere hem wrong on honde,° — *put them in the wrong*
For half so boldely can ther no man
Swere and lyen as a womman can.
I sey nat this by° wyves that ben wyse, — *concerning*
But if° it be whan they hem misavyse.° — *Unless / act ill-advisedly*
A wys wyf, if that she can hir good,
Shal beren him on hond the cow° is wood,[2] — *chough (in the crow family)*
And take witnesse of° hir owene mayde — *take as witness*
Of° hir assent.° But herkneth° how I sayde: — *With / consent / listen*
  'Sire olde kaynard, is this thyn array?[3]
Why is my neighebores wyf so gay?° — *gaily dressed*
She is honoured over al ther° she goth:° — *everywhere / goes*
I sitte at hoom, I have no thrifty cloth.° — *suitable clothing*
What dostow° at my neighebores hous? — *dost thou*
Is she so fair?° artow° so amorous? — *beautiful / art thou*
What rowne° ye with oure mayde? *benedicite!*° — *whisper / God bless us*
Sire olde lechour, lat thy japes be!° — *leave off thy pranks*
And if I have a gossib° or a freend, — *gossip, confidante*
Withouten gilt, thou chydest as a feend,[4]
If that I walke or pleye unto his hous!
Thou comest hoom as dronken as a mous,° — *mouse*
And prechest on thy bench, with yvel preef![5]
Thou seist° to me, it is a greet meschief° — *sayst / misfortune*
To wedde a povre womman, for costage.° — *because of expense*
And if that she be riche, of heigh parage,° — *parentage, blood*

9. A prudent woman will exert herself constantly.
1. The bacon wasn't fetched for them I'm sure. (A side of bacon was awarded annually at Dunmow in Essex to couples who could claim they had not quarreled or been unhappy in their marriage that year.)
2. A prudent (skillful) wife, if she knows her (own) good, shall trick him into believing the chough is mad. (Refers to common stories—the crow in Chaucer's own *Manciple's Tale* is an example—in which a speaking bird tells tales to the husband of a wife's infidelity.)
3. Old dotard, sir, is this how you dress me?
4. Without guilt (on our part), thou scoldest like a devil.
5. And preachest (sermons, sitting) on thy bench—bad luck to you!

Thanne seistow° that it is a tormentrye° — *sayst thou / torment*
To suffre° hire pryde and hire malencolye.° — *endure / melancholy, moodiness*
And if that she be fair,° thou verray knave,° — *pretty / true rascal*
Thou seyst that every holour° wol hire have: — *lecher*
She may no whyle in chastitee abyde° — *abide, remain*
That° is assailled upon ech a syde.° — *Who / on every side*
  Thou seyst som folk desyren us for richesse,° — *(our) money*
Somme for oure shap,° and somme for oure fairnesse,° — *figure / beauty*
And som for° she can outher° singe or daunce, — *because / either*
And som for gentillesse° and daliaunce,° — *good breeding / flirtatiousness*
Som for hir handes and hir armes smale;° — *slender*
Thus goth al to the devel, by thy tale.° — *according to thy account*
Thou seyst men may nat kepe° a castel wal, — *hold*
It may so longe assailled been over al.° — *everywhere*
  And if that she be foul,° thou seist that she — *ugly*
Coveiteth° every man that she may se; — *Desires*
For as a spaynel° she wol on him lepe, — *spaniel*
Til that she finde som man hire to chepe.° — *to buy her wares*
Ne noon so grey goos goth ther in the lake[6]
As, seistow,° that wol been withoute make.° — *sayst thou / a mate*
And seyst, it is an hard thing for to welde° — *control*
A thing that no man wol, his thankes,° helde.° — *willingly / hold*
Thus seistow, lorel,° whan thow goost to bedde, — *you wretch*
And that no wys man nedeth for to wedde,
Ne no man that entendeth unto° hevene. — *aims to get to*
With wilde thonder-dint° and firy levene° — *thunderclap / fiery lightning*
Mote° thy welked° nekke be to-broke!° — *May / withered / broken*
  Thow seyst that dropping° houses and eek smoke — *leaking*
And chyding wyves maken men to flee
Out of hir owene hous; a, *benedicite!*° — *God bless us*
What eyleth° swich an old man for to chyde? — *ails*
Thow seyst we wyves wol oure vyces° hyde — *vices*
Til we be fast,° and thanne we wol hem shewe°— — *secure (married) / show*
Wel may that be a proverbe of a shrewe!° — *(fit) for a villain*
  Thou seist that oxen, asses, hors,° and houndes, — *horses*
They been assayed° at diverse stoundes;° — *tested / various times*
Bacins,° lavours,° er° that men hem bye,° — *Basins / washbowls / before / buy*
Spones° and stoles,° and al swich
    housbondrye,° — *Spoons / stools / all such housewares*
And so been pottes, clothes, and array;° — *ornament(s)*
But folk of wyves maken noon assay° — *test*
Til they be wedded. Olde dotard shrewe!° — *wretched rascal*
And thanne, seistow,° we wol oure vices shewe. — *sayst thou*
  Thou seist also that it displeseth me
But if that° thou wolt preyse° my beautee, — *Unless / praise*
And but° thou poure° alwey upon my face, — *unless / gaze intently*
And clepe° me "faire dame" in every place; — *call*
And but thou make a feste° on thilke° day — *feast / that same*
That I was born, and make me fresh and gay,

6. There swims in the lake no goose so gray.

And but thou do to my norice° honour, *nurse*
And to my chamberere° withinne my bour,° *chambermaid / bower, bedroom*
And to my fadres folk° and his allyes°— *relatives / connections*
Thus seistow, olde barel ful of lyes!° *lies (pun on lees, or dregs)*
  And yet of oure apprentice Janekyn,
For his crispe heer,° shyninge as gold so fyn, *curly hair*
And for° he squiereth° me bothe up and doun, *because / escorts*
Yet hastow caught a fals suspecioun.[7]
I wol hym noght,° thogh thou were deed tomorwe. *I don't want him*
  But tel me this, why hydestow, with sorwe,[8]
The keyes of thy cheste° awey fro me? *for storing valuables*
It is my good° as wel as thyn, pardee.° *property / by God*
What, wenestow make an idiot of oure dame?[9]
Now by that lord that called is Seint Jame,° *St. James*
Thou shalt nat bothe, thogh that thou were wood,° *mad (with rage)*
Be maister of my body and of my good;° *goods, possessions*
That oon thou shalt forgo, maugree thyne yën;[1]
What helpith thee of me to enquere° or spyën? *inquire*
I trowe,° thou woldest loke° me in thy chiste!° *believe / lock / chest*
Thou sholdest seye, "Wyf, go wher thee liste;° *it pleases thee*
Tak your disport,° I wol nat leve no talis.° *pleasure / believe any tales*
I knowe yow for a trewe wyf, dame Alis."° *Alice*
We love no man that taketh kepe or charge° *takes heed or cares*
Wher that we goon; we wol ben at oure large.° *liberty*
  Of alle men y-blessed moot° he be, *may*
The wyse astrologien° Daun Ptholome,° *astrologer / Lord Ptolemy*
That seith this proverbe in his Almageste:
"Of alle men his wisdom is the hyeste,° *greatest*
That rekketh° nevere who hath the world in honde."° *cares / in (his) control*
By this proverbe thou shalt understonde,
Have thou ynogh, what thar thee recche or care[2]
How merily that othere folkes fare?° *get along*
For certeyn, olde dotard, by youre leve,° *leave*
Ye shul have queynte° right ynough at eve. *i.e., sex (punning on ME "cunte")*
He is to° greet a nigard that wol werne° *too / refuse*
A man to lighte a candle at his lanterne;
He shal have never the lasse° light, pardee. *less*
Have thou ynough, thee thar nat pleyne thee.° *thou needst not complain*
  Thou seyst also that if we make us gay
With clothing and with precious array,° *ornaments*
That it is peril of° oure chastitee; *a danger to*
And yet, with sorwe, thou most enforce thee,[3]
And seye thise wordes in th'Apostles° name: *St. Paul's*
"In habit° maad with chastitee and shame, *garment(s)*
Ye wommen shul apparaille yow,"° quod he, *dress yourselves*

7. I.e., become wrongly suspicious.
8. But tell me this, why dost thou hide (may you have sorrow).
9. What, do you think to make an idiot of our mistress? (She here uses a kind of royal plural: she means herself.)
1. Thou shalt give up one (of them), despite thy eyes (i.e., despite anything you can do).
2. As long as thou hast enough, what need for thee to take heed or care.
3. And further—sorrow beset thee!—thou must strengthen thyself (in the argument).

"And noght in tressed heer° and gay perree,° *braided hair / precious stones*
As° perles, ne with gold, ne clothes riche." *Such as*
After thy text, ne after thy rubriche
I wol nat wirche as muchel as a gnat.[4]
  Thou seydest this, that I was lyk a cat:
For whoso wolde senge° a cattes skin,° *singe / i.e., fur*
Thanne wolde the cat wel dwellen in his in;° *lodgings*
And if the cattes skin be slyk° and gay, *sleek*
She wol nat dwelle in house half a day,
But forth she wole, er° any day be dawed,° *before / has dawned*
To shewe hir skin and goon a-caterwawed.° *caterwauling*
This is to seye, if I be gay, sire shrewe,° *wretch*
I wol renne out,° my borel° for to shewe. *run about / clothing*
  Sire olde fool, what helpeth thee to spyën?
Thogh thou preye° Argus, with his hundred yën,° *beg / eyes*
To be my warde-cors,° as he can° best, *bodyguard / knows how*
In feith, he shal nat kepe me but me lest;° *unless I wish*
Yet coude I make his berd, so moot I thee.[5]
  Thou seydest eek that ther ben thinges three,
The whiche thinges troublen al this erthe,
And that no wight ne may endure the ferthe.° *fourth*
O leve° sire shrewe, Jesu shorte° thy lyf! *dear / may Jesus shorten*
Yet prechestow° and seyst an hateful wyf *Still thou preachest*
Y-rekened° is for° oon of thise meschances.° *Counted / as / misfortunes*
Been ther none othere maner° resemblances *kind of*
That ye may lykne° youre parables to, *liken*
But if° a sely° wyf be oon of tho?° *Unless / innocent / those*
  Thou lykenest eek wommanes love to helle,
To bareyne° lond, ther° water may not dwelle; *barren / where*
Thou lyknest it also to wilde fyr.[6]
The more it brenneth,° the more it hath desyr *burns*
To consume every thing that brent wol be.° *can be burned*
Thou seyst that right° as wormes shende° a tree, *just / damage*
Right so a wyf destroyeth hire housbonde;
This knowe they that been to wyves bonde.'° *bound*
  Lordinges, right thus, as ye have understonde,
Bar I stifly myne olde housbondes on honde[7]
That thus they seyden in hir dronkenesse;
And al was fals, but that° I took witnesse *and yet*
On° Janekin and on my nece° also. *From / niece*
O Lord, the peyne I dide° hem and the wo, *suffering I caused*
Ful giltelees, by Goddes swete pyne!° *suffering*
For as° an hors I coude byte° and whyne.° *like / bite / whinny*
I coude pleyne,° thogh I were in the gilt,° *complain / wrong*
Or elles° often tyme hadde I ben spilt.° *otherwise / ruined*
Whoso that first to mille comth, first grint.° *grinds (his grain)*

4. I will not behave according to thy text or thy rubric (i.e., interpretation) as much as (would) a gnat.
5. I could still trick him, as I hope to thrive.
6. "Greek fire," a highly inflammable compound used in sea warfare.
7. I firmly deceived my old husbands into thinking.

I pleyned first: so was oure werre° y-stint.° *strife / concluded*
They were ful glad to excusen hem° ful blyve° *themselves / quickly*
Of thing of which they nevere agilte° hir lyve. *were guilty (in)*
Of wenches wolde I beren hem on honde,° *accuse them (falsely)*
Whan that for syk° unnethes° mighte they stonde. *illness / scarcely*
  Yet tikled° I his herte, for that he *tickled, pleased*
Wende° that I hadde of him so greet chiertee.° *Thought / affection*
I swoor that al my walkinge out by nighte
Was for t'espye° wenches that he dighte.° *to spy out / lay with*
Under that colour° hadde I many a mirthe,° *pretense / merry time*
For al swich wit° is yeven° us in oure birthe. *such cleverness / given*
Deceite, weping, spinning God hath yive° *given*
To wommen kindely° whyl they may live. *by nature*
And thus of o° thing I avaunte° me: *one / boast*
Atte° ende I hadde the bettre in ech degree,° *At the / in every way*
By sleighte,° or force, or by som maner° thing, *trick / kind of*
As by continuel murmur or grucching.° *grumbling*
Namely abedde° hadden they meschaunce:° *Especially in bed / misfortune*
Ther wolde I chyde° and do° hem no plesaunce;° *scold / give / pleasure*
I wolde no lenger in the bed abyde,
If that I felte his arm over my syde,
Til he had maad his raunson° unto me; *paid his ransom*
Thanne wolde I suffre° him do his nycetee.° *endure, allow / foolishness, lust*
And therfore every man this tale I telle,
Winne whoso may, for al is for to selle.[8]
With empty hand men may none haukes° lure. *hawks*
For winning° wolde I al his lust endure, *profit*
And make me a feyned° appetyt— *feigned*
And yet in bacon° hadde I nevere delyt. *old meat (aged men)*
That made me that evere I wolde hem chyde.
For thogh the Pope had seten hem biside,° *sat next to them*
I wolde nat spare hem at hir owene bord.° *table*
For by my trouthe,° I quitte° hem word for word. *troth / requited, paid back*
As° help me verray° God omnipotent, *So / true*
Thogh I right now sholde make my testament,° *will*
I ne owe hem nat a word that it nis quit.° *is not paid back*
I broghte it so aboute, by my wit,° *cleverness*
That they moste yeve it up,° as for the beste, *give up*
Or elles° hadde we nevere been in reste. *else*
For thogh he loked as a wood leoun,° *like a mad lion*
Yet sholde he faille of his conclusioun.° *fail in the end*
  Thanne wolde I seye, 'Godelief,° tak keep° *Sweetheart / heed*
How mekely loketh Wilkin oure sheep!
Com neer, my spouse, lat me ba° thy cheke! *kiss*
Ye sholde been al pacient and meke,
And han a swete spyced conscience,° *sweetly seasoned disposition*
Sith° ye so preche of Jobes° pacience. *Since / Job's*
Suffreth° alwey, sin° ye so wel can preche; *Endure / since*
And but° ye do, certein we shal yow teche *unless*

8. Profit whoever may, for all is for sale.

That it is fair° to have a wyf in pees.° *good / peace*
Oon of us two moste bowen,° doutelees, *bow (to the other's will)*
And sith° a man is more resonable *since*
Than womman is, ye moste been suffrable.° *patient*
What eyleth° yow to grucche° thus and grone?° *ails / grumble / groan*
Is it for ye wolde have my queynte° allone? *(cf. ME "cunte")*
Why taak it al! lo, have it every-deel!° *every bit of it*
Peter!° I shrewe° yow but ye love it weel! *(By St.) Peter / curse*
For if I wolde° selle my *bele chose*,° *wished to / pretty thing*
I coude walke as fresh as is a rose;
But I wol kepe it for your owene tooth.[9]
Ye be to blame. By God, I sey yow sooth.'° *tell you the truth*
Swiche manere° wordes hadde we on honde. *kind of*
Now wol I speken of my fourthe housbonde.
  My fourthe housebonde was a revelour°— *reveler, rioter*
This is to seyn, he hadde a paramour°— *mistress*
And I was yong and ful of ragerye,° *wantonness, passion*
Stiborn° and strong, and joly as a pye.° *Stubborn / magpie*
Wel coude I daunce to an harpe smale,
And singe, ywis,° as any nightingale, *truly*
Whan I had dronke a draughte of swete wyn.
Metellius, the foule cherl, the swyn,° *swine*
That with a staf birafte° his wyf hir lyf *bereft*
For she drank wyn, thogh° I hadde been his wyf, *if*
He sholde nat han daunted° me fro drinke! *frightened*
And after wyn on Venus moste° I thinke, *must*
For al so siker° as cold engendreth° hayl,° *surely / engenders / hail*
A likerous mouth moste han a likerous tayl.[1]
In wommen vinolent° is no defence°— *full of wine / resistance*
This knowen lechours by experience.
  But, Lord Crist! whan that it remembreth me° *I think*
Upon my yowthe, and on my jolitee,° *gaiety*
It tikleth° me aboute myn herte rote.° *tickles / heart's root*
Unto this day it dooth myn herte bote° *good*
That I have had my world as in my tyme.
But age, allas! that al wol envenyme,° *poison*
Hath me biraft° my beautee and my pith.° *bereft of / vigor*
Lat go,° farewel! the devel go therwith! *Let it go*
The flour is goon, ther is namore to telle:
The bren,° as I best can, now moste I selle; *bran, husks*
But yet to be right mery wol I fonde.° *try*
Now wol I tellen of my fourthe housbonde.
  I seye, I hadde in herte greet despyt° *malice*
That he of any other° had delyt. *other woman*
But he was quit,° by God and by Seint Joce!° *repaid / a Breton saint*
I made him of the same wode° a croce°— *wood / cross*
Nat of my body in no foul° manere, *unclean*
But certeinly, I made folk swich chere° *such good cheer*

9. I.e., your own sexual appetite.
1. A gluttonous mouth must have (i.e., necessarily implies) a lecherous tail.

That in his owene grece° I made him frye — *grease*
For angre and for verray° jalousye. — *pure*
By God, in erthe° I was his purgatorie, — *on earth*
For which I hope his soule be in glorie.
For God it woot,° he sat ful ofte and song° — *knows / sang*
Whan that his shoo° ful bitterly him wrong.° — *shoe / hurt*
Ther was no wight,° save° God and he, that wiste° — *person / except / knew*
In many wyse° how sore° I him twiste.° — *ways / sorely / tormented*
He deyde whan I cam fro° Jerusalem, — *from (a pilgrimage to)*
And lyth y-grave under the rode-beem,[2]
Al° is his tombe noght so curious° — *Although / elaborate*
As was the sepulcre° of him Darius, — *a very famous tomb*
Which that Appelles wroghte subtilly;° — *made skillfully*
It nis but wast to burie him preciously.[3]
Lat him° farewel, God yeve his soule reste! — *May he*
He is now in the grave and in his cheste.° — *coffin*
Now of my fifthe housbond wol I telle—
God lete his soule nevere come in helle!
And yet was he to me the moste shrewe.° — *worst rascal*
That fele° I on my ribbes al by rewe,° — *feel / in a row*
And evere shal unto myn ending day.° — *i.e., dying day*
But in oure bed he was so fresh and gay,
And therwithal so wel coude he me glose° — *cajole, flatter*
Whan that he wolde han my *bele chose*,° — *pretty thing*
That thogh he hadde me bet° on every boon,° — *beaten / bone*
He coude winne agayn my love anoon.° — *at once*
I trowe° I loved him beste for that he — *believe*
Was of his love daungerous° to me. — *standoffish, grudging*
We wommen han, if that I shal nat lye,
In this matere a queynte fantasye:° — *an odd fancy*
Wayte what° thing we may nat lightly have, — *Whatever*
Thereafter wol we crye al day and crave.
Forbede us thing,° and that desyren we; — *something*
Prees on° us faste,° and thanne wol we flee. — *Crowd, pursue / hard*
With daunger° oute° we al oure chaffare:° — *haughtiness / set out / wares*
Greet prees° at market maketh dere° ware, — *press, crowd / expensive*
And to° greet cheep° is holde at litel prys.° — *too / a bargain / worth*
This knoweth every womman that is wys.
My fifthe housbonde, God his soule blesse!
Which that I took for love and no richesse,
He som tyme° was a clerk° of Oxenford,° — *once / scholar / Oxford*
And had left scole, and wente at hoom to bord° — *to board at home*
With my gossib,° dwellinge in oure toun— — *gossip, intimate friend*
God have hir soule! hir name was Alisoun.
She knew myn herte and eek° my privetee° — *also / secrets*
Bet° than oure parisshe preest, so moot I thee!° — *Better / as I may thrive*
To hire biwreyed° I my conseil° al, — *disclosed / thoughts*

2. And lies buried under the rood-beam (a timber separating the nave from the chancel in a church).
3. It is (i.e., would have been) nothing but a waste to bury him expensively.

For had myn housebonde pissed on a wal,
Or doon a thing that sholde han cost his lyf,
To hire and to another worthy wyf,
And to my nece,° which that I loved weel, *niece*
I wolde han told his conseil° every deel.° *secrets / (in) every detail*
And so I dide ful often, God it woot,° *knows*
That made his face ful often reed and hoot
For verray° shame, and blamed himself for° he *pure / because*
Had told to me so greet a privetee.° *secret*
  And so bifel° that ones° in a Lente°— *it happened / once / at Lent*
So often tymes I to my gossib wente,
For evere yet I lovede to be gay,
And for to walke in March, Averille,° and May, *April*
Fro hous to hous, to here° sondry talis°— *hear / various tales*
That Jankin clerk° and my gossib dame Alis *Jankin (the) clerk*
And I myself into the feldes° wente. *fields*
Myn housbond was at London al that Lente:
I hadde the bettre leyser° for to pleye, *leisure, opportunity*
And for to see, and eek° for to be seye° *also / seen*
Of lusty folk. What wiste I wher my grace
Was shapen for to be, or in what place?[4]
Therefore I made my visitaciouns,° *visits*
To vigilies and to processiouns,[5]
To preching eek and to thise pilgrimages,
To pleyes° of miracles, and mariages, *(stage) plays*
And wered upon° my gaye scarlet gytes.° *wore / gowns*
Thise wormes, ne thise motthes,° ne thise mytes,° *moths / mites*
Upon my peril, frete hem never a deel;[6]
And wostow° why? for° they were used weel. *knowest thou / because*
  Now wol I tellen forth what happed° me. *befell*
I seye that in the feeldes walked we,
Til trewely we hadde swich daliance,[7]
This clerk and I, that of my purveyance° *by my foresight*
I spak to him and seyde him how that he,
If I were widwe,° sholde wedde me. *a widow*
For certeinly, I sey for no bobance,° *not as a boast*
Yet was I nevere withouten purveyance° *(future) provision*
Of° mariage, n'of° othere thinges eek. *Concerning / nor concerning*
I holde a mouses herte nat worth a leek° *leek, onion*
That hath but oon hole for to sterte° to, *run*
And if that faille,° thanne is al y-do.° *fails / done for*
  I bar him on honde° he hadde enchanted me— *made him believe*
My dame° taughte me that soutiltee°— *mother / subtlety, trick*
And eek I seyde I mette° of him al night: *dreamed*
He wolde han slayn° me as I lay upright,° *wanted to slay / face-up*

4. By pleasure-loving folk. How could I know where grace was destined to befall me, or in what place?
5. *Vigilies*: vigils (services on the eve of a feast day); *processiouns*: ceremonial processions within a church service.
6. On peril (of my soul), ate into them not at all.
7. I.e., were getting along so well.

And al my bed was ful of verray° blood; *real*
But yet I hope that he shal do me good,
For blood bitokeneth gold, as me was taught.
And al was fals—I dremed of it right naught,
But as° I folwed ay° my dames lore° *But / ever / teaching*
As wel of° this as of othere thinges more. *concerning*
But now sire, lat me see, what I shal seyn?
Aha! by God, I have my tale ageyn.
Whan that my fourthe housbond was on bere,° *(his) bier*
I weep algate, and made sory chere[8]
As wyves moten,° for it is usage,° *must / the custom*
And with my coverchief° covered my visage; *kerchief / face*
But for that° I was purveyed of° a make,° *because / provided with / mate*
I wepte but smal,° and that I undertake.° *little / declare*
To chirche was myn housbond born° a-morwe° *borne / in the morning*
With° neighebores, that for him maden sorwe; *By*
And Jankin oure clerk was oon of tho.° *them*
As° help me God! whan that I saugh° him go° *So / saw / walk*
After the bere, me thoughte he hadde a paire
Of legges and of feet so clene° and faire, *neat*
That al myn herte I yaf° unto his hold.° *gave / possession*
He was, I trowe,° twenty winter old, *believe*
And I was fourty, if I shal seye sooth;° *tell the truth*
But yet I hadde alwey a coltes tooth.° *i.e., youthful appetites*
Gat-tothed I was, and that bicam me weel;[9]
I hadde the prente of Seynte Venus seel.[1]
As help me God, I was a lusty° oon, *vigorous*
And faire, and riche, and yong, and wel bigoon;° *well-off*
And trewely, as myne housbondes tolde me,
I had the beste *quoniam*° mighte be. *i.e., pudendum*
For certes, I am al Venerien
In felinge, and myn herte is Marcien:[2]
Venus me yaf° my lust, my likerousnesse,° *gave / lecherousness*
And Mars yaf me my sturdy hardinesse;° *boldness*
Myn ascendent was Taur, and Mars therinne.[3]
Allas! allas! that evere love was sinne!
I folwed ay° myn inclinacioun *ever*
By vertu of my constellacioun;[4]
That made me I coude noght withdrawe° *withhold*
My chambre of Venus from a good felawe.° *companion*
Yet have I Martes° mark upon my face, *Mars's*
And also in another privee° place. *secret*
For, God so wis be my savacioun,° *salvation*

8. I wept, of course, and put on a sad look.
9. I was gap-toothed, and that suited me well. (In medieval handbooks of physiognomy, gap teeth are said to indicate a bold and lascivious nature.)
1. I had the print of St. Venus's seal—i.e., Venus had given me a birthmark (again indicative of amorousness).
2. *Venerien*: under the influence of the planet Venus; *Marcien*: under the influence of the planet Mars. Together they determine her appetites for love and marital strife.
3. (When I was born) the sign of Taurus was ascendant, and Mars was in it.
4. Through the influence of my horoscope (the planets reigning over my birth).

I ne loved nevere by no discrecioun,° — *with any wisdom*
But evere folwede myn appetyt:
Al° were he short or long,° or blak or whyt, — *Whether / tall*
I took no kepe, so that he lyked me,[5]
How pore he was, ne eek° of what degree.° — *nor / social rank*
   What sholde I seye but, at the monthes ende,
This joly clerk Jankin, that was so hende,° — *pleasant*
Hath wedded me with greet solempnitee,° — *ceremony*
And to him yaf° I al the lond° and fee° — *gave / land / property*
That evere was me yeven° therbifore. — *given (by earlier husbands)*
But afterward repented me° ful sore;° — *I regretted it / deeply*
He nolde suffre nothing of my list.[6]
By God, he smoot° me ones° on the list° — *hit / once / ear*
For that° I rente° out of his book a leef,° — *Because / tore / leaf, page*
That of the strook myn ere wex al deef.[7]
Stiborn° I was as is a leonesse,° — *Stubborn / lionness*
And of my tonge a verray jangleresse,° — *real ranter*
And walke I wolde, as I had doon biforn,
From hous to hous, although he had it sworn.[8]
For which he often tymes wolde preche,
And me of° olde Romayn gestes° teche, — *from / Roman stories*
How he Simplicius Gallus lefte his wyf,
And hire forsook for terme° of al his lyf, — *the duration*
Noght but for open-heveded he hir say[9]
Lokinge out at his dore upon a day.
   Another Romayn tolde he me by name,
That, for° his wyf was at a someres game° — *because / summer's revel*
Withoute his witing,° he forsook hire eke.° — *knowledge / also*
And thanne wolde he upon° his Bible seke — *in*
That ilke° proverbe of Ecclesiaste° — *same /* Ecclesiasticus
Wher he comandeth and forbedeth faste° — *firmly*
Man shal nat suffre° his wyf go roule° aboute; — *allow / to go roaming*
Thanne wolde he seye right thus, withouten doute:
   'Whoso that° buildeth his hous al of salwes,° — *Whoever / willow twigs*
And priketh° his blinde hors over the falwes,° — *spurs / fallow (plowed) land*
And suffreth° his wyf to go seken halwes,° — *allows / shrines*
Is worthy to been hanged on the galwes!'° — *gallows*
But al for noght; I sette noght an hawe° — *haw (hawthorn berry)*
Of his proverbes n'of his olde sawe,° — *saw, proverb*
Ne I wolde nat of° him corrected be. — *by*
I hate him that° my vices telleth me, — *the one who*
And so do mo,° God woot,° of us than I. — *more / knows*
This made him with me wood° al outrely:° — *mad / completely*
I nolde noght forbere him in no cas.[1]
   Now wol I seye yow sooth,° by Seint Thomas, — *tell you the truth*

5. I took no heed, as long as he was pleasing to me.
6. He wouldn't allow (me) anything I wanted.
7. So that from the blow my ear grew wholly deaf.
8. I.e., he had sworn I shouldn't.
9. Only because he saw her bareheaded.
1. I wouldn't give way to him on any occasion.

Why that I rente° out of his book a leef,° *tore / leaf*
For which he smoot° me so that I was deef. *struck*
He hadde a book that gladly, night and day,
For his desport° he wolde rede alway. *amusement*
He cleped it Valerie and Theofraste,[2]
At which book he lough° alwey ful faste.° *laughed / strongly*
And eek ther was somtyme° a clerk° at Rome, *once / scholar*
A cardinal, that highte° Seint Jerome, *was called*
That made a book agayn Jovinian;
In which book eek ther was Tertulan,
Crisippus, Trotula, and Helowys,[3]
That was abbesse nat fer fro Parys;° *Paris*
And eek the Parables° of Salomon, *Proverbs*
Ovydes Art,° and bokes many on,° *Ovid's* Art (of Love) */ a one*
And alle thise were bounden in o° volume. *one*
And every night and day was his custume,
Whan he hadde leyser° and vacacioun° *leisure / free time*
From other worldly occupacioun,
To reden on this book of wikked° wyves. *wicked*
He knew of hem mo° legendes and lyves *more*
Than been° of gode wyves in the Bible. *there are*
For trusteth wel, it is an impossible° *impossibility*
That any clerk wol speke good of wyves,
But if° it be of holy seintes lyves, *Unless*
Ne of noon other womman never the mo.° *in any way*
Who peyntede the leoun, tel me, who?[4]
By God, if wommen hadde writen stories,
As clerkes han withinne hir oratories,° *chapels, studies*
They wolde han writen of men more wikkednesse
Than all the mark° of Adam may redresse. *sex*
The children[5] of Mercurie and of Venus
Been in hir wirking° ful contrarious:° *actions / contrary*
Mercurie loveth wisdom and science,° *knowledge*
And Venus loveth ryot° and dispence;° *revelry / spending*
And, for° hire diverse disposicioun, *because of*
Ech° falleth in otheres exaltacioun,° *Each / moment of highest ascent*
And thus, God woot, Mercurie is desolat° *without influence*
In Pisces wher Venus is exaltat,° *in her greatest influence*
And Venus falleth ther° Mercurie is reysed;° *there where / has risen*
Therfore no womman of° no clerk is preysed. *by*
The clerk, whan he is old and may noght do
Of Venus werkes worth° his olde sho°— *to the value of / shoe*
Thanne sit he doun and writ in his dotage

2. Jankyn's "book of wikked wyves" includes several antifeminist works: Walter Map's *Letter of Valerius*, Theophrastus's *On Marriage*, and St. Jerome's *Against Jovinian*; they quote other authorities in turn (Tertullian, Chrysippus, et al.). For these texts, see the Sources and Backgrounds section on *The Wife of Bath's Prologue and Tale*.
3. *Trotula*: the supposed woman author of a well-known medieval treatise on the diseases of women; *Helowys*: Eloise, who loved the great scholar Abelard but argued in her letters against marrying him; she later became a nun and abbess.
4. In the *Fables* of Marie de France (#37), a peasant shows a lion a painting of a lion being killed by a peasant; the lion asks pointedly who painted that picture, a man or a lion.
5. Those born under the sign.

That wommen can nat kepe° hir mariage! *i.e., be faithful in*
But now to purpos why I tolde thee
That I was beten° for a book, pardee.° *beaten / by God*
Upon a night Jankin, that was our syre,° *lord, husband*
Redde on his book as he sat by the fyre
Of Eva° first, that for hir wikkednesse *Eve*
Was al mankinde broght to wrecchednesse,
For which that Jesu Crist himself was slayn,
That boghte us with his herteblood agayn.
Lo, here expres° of womman may ye finde *specifically*
That womman was the los° of all mankinde. *destruction*
Tho° redde he me how Sampson loste his heres:° *Then / hair(s)*
Slepinge, his lemman° kitte° hem° with hir sheres, *lover / cut / it (them)*
Thurgh whiche tresoun loste he bothe his yën.° *eyes*
Tho° redde he me, if that I shal nat lyen, *Then*
Of Hercules and of his Dianyre,° *Deianira*
That caused him to sette himself afyre.° *on fire*
Nothing forgat he the sorwe and the wo
That Socrates had with hise wyves two—
How Xantippa caste pisse upon his heed:
This sely° man sat stille, as° he were deed; *poor / as if*
He wyped his heed; namore dorste° he seyn *dared*
But 'Er° that thonder stinte,° comth a reyn.'° *Before / ceases / rain, shower*
Of Phasipha[6] that was the quene of Crete—
For shrewednesse° him thoughte the tale swete— *Out of cursedness*
Fy! spek namore, it is a grisly thing,
Of hire horrible lust and hir lyking.° *desire*
Of Clitermistra,[7] for hire lecherye,
That falsly made hire housband for to dye,
He redde it with ful good devocioun.
He tolde me eek for what occasioun
Amphiorax[8] at Thebes loste his lyf.
Myn housbond hadde a legende of his wyf,
Eriphilem, that° for an ouche° of gold *Eryphile, who / brooch*
Hath prively° unto the Grekes told *secretly*
Wher that hir housbonde hidde him in a place,
For which he hadde at Thebes sory grace.° *ill fortune*
Of Lyvia tolde he me, and of Lucye.[9]
They bothe made hir housbondes for to dye,
That oon for love, that other was for hate.
Lyvia hir housbond, on an even° late, *evening*
Empoysoned° hath, for that she was his fo.° *Poisoned / foe*
Lucya, likerous,° loved hire housbond so, *lecherous*
That, for° he sholde alwey upon hire thinke, *so that*
She yaf° him swich a manere° love-drinke, *gave / such a kind of*

6. Pasiphaë, who loved a bull and gave birth to the Minotaur.
7. Clytemnestra, who murdered her husband, Agamemnon, to keep Aegisthus, her lover.
8. Amphiaraus, a soothsayer who prophesied his own death if he fought at Thebes; he was persuaded into battle by his wife.
9. Livia poisoned her husband, Drusus, at Sejanus's instigation; Lucilia, wife of the poet Lucretius, poisoned him with a love potion meant to increase his amorousness.

That he was deed er° it were by the morwe;° *before / morning*
And thus algates° housbondes han sorwe. *in every way*
  Thanne tolde he me how oon Latumius
Compleyned unto his felawe° Arrius, *companion*
That in his gardin growed swich a° tree *a certain*
On which he seyde how that his wyves three
Hanged hemself° for herte despitous.° *themselves / spiteful*
'O leve° brother,' quod this Arrius, *dear*
'Yif° me a plante° of thilke° blissed tree, *Give / slip / that same*
And in my gardin planted shal it be!'
  Of latter date, of wyves hath he red
That somme han slayn hir housbondes in hir bed,
And lete hir lechour° dighte° hire al the night *lecher, lover / lie with*
Whyl that the corps lay in° the floor upright.° *on / faceup*
And somme han drive° nayles° in hir brayn° *driven / nails / brain*
Whyl that they slepte, and thus they han hem slayn.
Somme han hem yeve° poysoun in hire drinke. *given*
He spak more harm than herte may bithinke,° *imagine*
And therwithal° he knew of mo° proverbes *in addition / more*
Than in this world ther growen gras or herbes.° *plants*
'Bet is,'° quod he, 'thyn habitacioun *Better it is (that)*
Be with a leoun or a foul dragoun,
Than with a womman usinge for° to chyde. *accustomed*
Bet is,' quod he, 'hye in° the roof abyde° *high on / to stay*
Than with an angry wyf doun in the hous;
They been so wikked and contrarious° *contradictory*
They haten that° hir housbondes loveth ay.'° *what / ever*
He seyde, 'A womman cast° hir shame away *casts*
Whan she cast of° hir smok;° and forthermo,° *off / smock, underdress / furthermore*
'A fair° womman, but° she be chaast also, *beautiful / unless*
Is lyk a gold ring in a sowes° nose.' *sow's*
Who wolde wene,° or who wolde suppose° *think / imagine*
The wo that in myn herte was, and pyne?° *suffering*
  And whan I saugh° he wolde nevere fyne° *saw / finish*
To reden on this cursed book al night,
Al sodeynly° three leves° have I plight° *suddenly / pages / plucked*
Out of his book, right° as he radde,° and eke° *just / read / also*
I with my fist so took° him on the cheke *hit*
That in oure fyr he fil° bakward adoun. *fell*
And he upstirte° as dooth a wood leoun,° *jumped up / mad lion*
And with his fist he smoot° me on the heed *struck*
That in° the floor I lay as° I were deed. *(So) that on / as if*
And when he saugh° how stille that I lay, *saw*
He was agast,° and wolde han fled his way, *frightened*
Til atte laste out of my swogh° I breyde.° *swoon, faint / started up*
'O! hastow° slayn me, false theef?° I seyde, *hast thou / criminal*
'And for my land thus hastow mordred° me? *murdered*
Er° I be deed, yet wol I kisse thee.' *Before*
  And neer he cam, and kneled faire° adoun, *courteously*
And seyde, 'Dere suster Alisoun,

As° help me God, I shall thee nevere smyte;° *So / strike*
That I have doon, it is thyself to wyte.[1]
Foryeve° it me, and that I thee biseke'°— *Forgive / beseech*
And yet eftsones° I hitte him on the cheke *again*
And seyde, 'Theef! thus muchel° am I wreke.° *much / avenged*
Now wol I dye: I may no lenger speke.'
But atte laste, with muchel care and wo,
We fille acorded° by us selven two. *came to an agreement*
He yaf me al° the brydel° in myn hond, *completely / bridle*
To han the governance° of hous and lond, *direction*
And of his tonge and of his hond also;
And made him brenne his book anon right tho.[2]
And whan that I hadde geten unto me,° *gotten for myself*
By maistrie,° al the soveraynetee,° *mastery / supremacy, sovereignty*
And that he seyde, 'Myn owene trewe wyf,
Do as thee lust° the terme° of al thy lyf; *please / (to the) end*
Keep° thyn honour, and keep eek myn estaat'°— *Preserve / public position*
After that day we hadden never debaat.° *contention*
God help me so, I was to him as kinde
As any wyf from Denmark unto Inde,° *India*
And also° trewe, and so was he to me. *equally as*
I prey to God that sit° in magestee,° *who sits / majesty*
So blesse his soule for his° mercy dere! *by his*
Now wol I seye my tale, if ye wol here."

Biholde the wordes bitween the Somonour and the Frere.

The Frere° lough° whan he hadde herd al this. *Friar / laughed*
"Now, dame," quod° he, "so have I° joye or blis, *said / as I may have*
This is a long preamble of° a tale!" *i.e., introduction to*
And whan the Somnour herde the Frere gale,° *exclaim aloud*
"Lo,"° quod the Somnour, "Goddes armes two,° *Behold / by God's two arms*
A frere wol entremette him° everemo! *intrude himself*
Lo, gode men, a flye and eek a frere
Wol falle in every dish and eek matere.° *subject*
What spekestow° of preambulacioun?° *Why speakest thou / preambling*
What!° amble, or trotte, or [pace,]° or go sit doun! *Lo / walk*
Thou lettest° oure disport° in this manere." *hinderest / pleasure*
"Ye, woltow so,° sire Somnour?" quod the Frere; *wouldst thou (have it) so*
"Now by my feith, I shal, er that I go,
Telle of a somnour swich° a tale or two *such*
That alle the folk shal laughen in this place."
"Now elles,° Frere, I wol bishrewe° thy face," *otherwise / curse*
Quod this Somnour, "and I bishrewe me
But if° I telle tales two or thre *Unless*
Of freres, er I come to Sidingborne,[3]
That° I shal make thyn herte for to morne°— *So that / mourn*

1. For what I've done, it's thyself (who is) to blame.
2. And (I) made him burn his book then at once.
3. Sittingbourne, a town roughly two-thirds of the way to Canterbury.

For wel I woot° thy pacience is goon." *know*
Oure Hoste cryde "Pees!° and that anoon!"° *Peace / at once*
And seyde, "Lat the womman telle hire tale.
Ye fare° as folk that dronken been of ale. *act*
Do, dame, tel forth youre tale, and that is best."
"Al redy, sire," quod she, "right as yow lest,[4]
If I have licence° of this worthy Frere." *the permission*
"Yis, dame," quod he, "tel forth, and I wol here."° *listen*

The Tale

In th'olde dayes of the King Arthour,
Of which that Britons speken greet honour,
All was this land fulfild of fayerye.° *filled with fairy people*
The elf-queen with hir joly companye
Daunced ful ofte in many a grene mede.° *meadow*
This was the olde opinion, as I rede—
I speke of manye hundred yeres ago—
But now can no man see none elves mo.° *more*
For now the grete charitee and prayeres
Of limitours[5] and othere holy freres,
That serchen° every lond and every streem, *visit*
As thikke° as motes in the sonne-beem,° *thick / sunbeam*
Blessinge halles, chambres, kichenes, boures,° *bowers, sleeping rooms*
Citees, burghes,° castels, hye toures,° *towns / high towers*
Thropes, bernes, shipnes, dayeryes[6]—
This maketh° that ther been no fayeryes. *is the cause*
For ther as wont to walken was an elf,[7]
Ther walketh now the limitour himself
In undermeles° and in morweninges,° *afternoons / mornings*
And seyth his Matins° and his holy thinges *morning service*
As he goth in his limitacioun.° *licensed begging area*
Wommen may go now saufly° up and doun: *safely*
In every bush or under every tree[8]
Ther is noon other incubus[9] but he,
And he ne wol doon hem but dishonour.[1]
And so bifel° that this King Arthour *it happened*
Hadde in his hous a lusty bacheler,° *young knight*
That on a day cam rydinge fro river;[2]
And happed that, allone as he was born,
He saugh° a mayde walkinge him biforn, *saw*
Of whiche mayde anon, maugree hir heed,[3]
By verray force° he rafte° hire maydenheed. *force itself / took*

4. "(I am) all ready, sir," she said, "just as you wish."
5. Friars given exclusive rights by license to beg within a certain area, or "limits."
6. Villages, barns, sheds, dairies.
7. For there where an elf was accustomed to walk.
8. Places popularly thought to be haunted by fairies.
9. An evil spirit supposed to lie upon women in their sleep and have intercourse with them.
1. Shame, dishonor; as opposed to the begetting of devils upon them.
2. From hawking; riverbanks were favorite places for the sport.
3. (And) from this maid at once, in spite of anything she could do.

For which oppressioun° was swich° clamour *wrong / such*
And swich pursute° unto the King Arthour, *suing (for justice)*
That dampned° was this knight for to be deed *condemned*
By cours of lawe, and sholde han° lost his heed— *was to have*
Paraventure° swich was the statut° tho°— *By chance / statute, law / then*
But that° the quene and othere ladies mo° *Except / besides*
So longe preyeden° the king of° grace *begged / for*
Til he his lyf him graunted in the place,
And yaf° him to the quene al at hir wille, *gave*
To chese whether she wolde him save or spille.° *destroy*
The quene thanketh the king with al hir might,
And after this thus spak she to the knight
Whan that she saugh hir tyme, upon a day:
"Thou standest yet," quod she, "in swich array° *such a condition*
That of thy lyf yet hastow° no suretee.° *hast thou / security, guarantee*
I grante thee lyf, if thou canst tellen me
What thing is it that wommen most desyren.
Be war, and keep thy nekke-boon from yren.[4]
And if thou canst nat tellen it anon,° *right away*
Yet wol I yeve° thee leve° for to gon *give / leave*
A twelf-month and a day, to seche° and lere° *seek out / learn*
An answere suffisant° in this matere.° *sufficient / subject*
And suretee° wol I han, er that thou pace,° *a pledge, security / walk off*
Thy body for to yelden° in this place." *yield up, return*
Wo° was this knight and sorwefully he syketh.° *Woeful / sighs*
But what! he may nat do al as him lyketh,[5]
And at the laste he chees him for to wende,° *decided to go off*
And come agayn, right° at the yeres ende, *exactly*
With swich answere as God wolde him purveye;° *provide for him*
And taketh his leve and wendeth forth his weye.
He seketh every hous and every place
Wheras° he hopeth for to finde grace,° *Where / good fortune*
To lerne what thing wommen loven most;
But he ne coude arryven in no cost° *coast, country*
Wheras he mighte finde in this matere° *subject*
Two creatures accordinge in-fere.° *agreeing together*
Somme seyde wommen loven best richesse,
Somme seyde honour, somme seyde jolynesse;
Somme riche array,° somme seyden lust abedde,° *adornment / pleasure in bed*
And ofte tyme to be widwe° and wedde.° *widowed / (re)married*
Somme seyde that oure hertes been most esed
Whan that we been y-flatered and y-plesed.
He gooth ful ny the sothe,° I wol nat lye: *very near the truth*
A man shal winne us best with flaterye;
And with attendance° and with bisinesse° *attention / diligence*
Been we y-lymed, bothe more and lesse.[6]
And somme seyn how that we loven best

4. Be wary, and keep thy neck from the ax (literally, iron).
5. But lo! he cannot do everything just as he pleases.
6. We are ensnared (caught, as with birdlime), both great and small.

For to be free and do right as us lest,° *just as we please*
And that no man repreve us of° oure vyce, *reproach us for*
But seye that we be wyse, and no thing nyce.° *not at all foolish*
For trewely, ther is noon of us alle,
If any wight wol clawe° us on the galle,° *scratch / sore spot*
That we nil kike for he seith us sooth:[7]
Assay,° and he shal finde it that so dooth. *Try*
For be we never so vicious withinne,
We wol been holden° wyse, and clene of sinne. *wish to be considered*
  And somme seyn that greet delyt han we
For to ben holden stable° and eek secree,° *steadfast / discreet*
And in o° purpos stedefastly to dwelle, *one*
And nat biwreye° thing that men us telle— *reveal*
But that tale is nat worth a rake-stele.° *rake handle*
Pardee, we wommen conne nothing hele:[8]
Witnesse on Myda°—wol ye here the tale? *Midas*
  Ovyde,° amonges othere thinges smale, *Ovid*
Seyde Myda hadde under his longe heres,° *hair*
Growinge upon his heed two asses eres,° *ears*
The whiche vyce° he hidde as he best mighte° *deformity / could*
Ful subtilly° from every mannes sighte, *cleverly*
That, save his wyf, ther wiste of it namo.[9]
He loved hire most, and trusted hire also;
He preyede° hire that to no creature *begged*
She sholde tellen of his disfigure.° *disfigurement*
  She swoor him nay, for al this world to winne,
She nolde° do that vileinye° or sinne, *would not / bad deed*
To make hir housbond han so foul a name.
She nolde nat telle it for° hir owene shame. *i.e., to spare*
But nathelees, hir thoughte that she dyde[1]
That° she so longe sholde a conseil° hyde. *If / secret*
Hir thoughte it swal° so sore° aboute hir herte *swelled / painfully*
That nedely som word hire moste asterte,[2]
And sith° she dorste° telle it to no man, *since / dared*
Doun to a mareys° faste by° she ran. *marsh / close by*
Til she came there hir herte was afyre,° *on fire*
And as a bitore bombleth in the myre,[3]
She leyde° hir mouth unto the water doun: *laid*
"Biwreye° me nat, thou water, with thy soun,"° *Betray / sound*
Quod she, "to thee I telle it, and namo;° *no one else*
Myn housbond hath longe asses eres° two! *ears*
Now is myn herte all hool,° now is it oute. *whole (again)*
I mighte no lenger kepe it, out of doute."
Heer° may ye se, thogh we a tyme abyde,° *Here / wait for a time*
Yet out it moot,° we can no conseil° hyde. *must / secret*

7. Who will not kick back, because he tells us the truth. (The metaphor is of horses.)
8. By heaven, we women don't know how to conceal anything.
9. So that no one else knew about it except his wife.
1. But nonetheless, it seemed to her that she would die.
2. That of necessity some word must burst out of her.
3. And as a bittern (a marsh bird) booms in the mire.

The remenant of the tale[4] if ye wol here,
Redeth Ovyde,° and ther ye may it lere.° *Read Ovid / learn*
This knight of which my tale is specially,
Whan that he saugh he mighte nat come therby,° *i.e., learn the answer*
This is to seye, what wommen loven moost,
Withinne his brest ful sorweful was the goost,° *spirit*
But hoom he gooth, he mighte nat sojourne.° *linger*
The day was come that hoomward moste° he tourne, *must*
And in his wey it happed him to ryde
In al this care under a forest-syde,° *on the edge of a forest*
Wheras he saugh° upon a daunce go° *saw / moving in a dance*
Of ladies foure and twenty and yet mo;
Toward the whiche daunce he drow° ful yerne,° *drew / eagerly*
In hope that som wisdom sholde he lerne.
But certeinly, er° he came fully there, *before*
Vanisshed was this daunce, he niste° where. *knew not*
No creature saugh he that bar° lyf, *bore*
Save on the grene° he saugh sittinge a wyf°— *grass / woman*
A fouler wight° ther may no man devyse.° *An uglier being / imagine*
Agayn° the knight this olde wyf gan ryse,° *i.e., to meet / rose up*
And seyde, "Sire knight, heerforth° ne lyth no wey. *through here*
Tel me what that ye seken,° by youre fey!° *seek / faith*
Paraventure° it may the bettre be: *By chance*
Thise olde folk can muchel thing," quod she.[5]
"My leve° mooder," quod this knight, "certeyn° *dear / certainly*
I nam but deed, but if that I can seyn[6]
What thing it is that wommen most desyre.
Coude ye me wisse,° I wolde wel quyte your *inform*
hyre."° *repay your trouble*
"Plighte° me thy trouthe,° heer in myn hand," *Pledge / promise*
quod she,
"The nexte thing that I requere° thee, *request of*
Thou shalt it do, if it lye in thy might,° *power*
And I wol telle it yow er it be night."
"Have heer my trouthe,"° quod the knight, "I grante."° *pledge / grant (it)*
"Thanne," quod she, "I dar me wel avante° *dare well boast*
Thy lyf is sauf,° for I wol stonde therby.° *safe / i.e., I guarantee it*
Upon my lyf, the queen wol seye as I.
Lat see which is the proudeste of hem alle,
That wereth° on a coverchief° or a calle,° *wears / kerchief / hairnet*
That dar° seye nay of that° I shal thee teche. *dares to / to that which*
Lat us go forth withouten lenger speche."
Tho rouned° she a pistel° in his ere,° *Then whispered / message / ear*
And bad him to be glad and have no fere.
Whan they be comen to the court, this knight
Seyde he had holde° his day, as he hadde hight,° *kept to / promised*

4. In Ovid's conclusion—his version differs in several ways from the Wife of Bath's—the marsh reeds whisper the secret aloud whenever the wind blows.
5. "These old folk (i.e., *we* old folk) know many things," said she.
6. I'm as good as dead unless I can say.

And redy was his answere, as he sayde.
Ful many a noble wyf, and many a mayde,
And many a widwe°—for that° they ben wyse— *widow / because*
The quene hirself sittinge as a justyse,° *judge*
Assembled been, his answere for to here;
And afterward this knight was bode appere.° *bidden to appear*
  To every wight° comanded was silence, *person*
And that the knight sholde telle in audience° *in open hearing*
What thing that worldly wommen loven best.
This knight ne stood nat stille as doth a best,° *beast*
But to his questioun anon° answerde *at once*
With manly voys,° that° al the court it herde: *voice / so that*
  "My lige° lady, generally," quod he, *liege*
"Wommen desyren to have sovereyntee° *sovereignty, domination*
As wel over hir housbond as hir love,[7]
And for to been in maistrie° him above. *mastery, control*
This is youre moste° desyr, thogh ye me kille. *greatest*
Doth as yow list°—I am heer at your wille." *it please you*
In al the court ne was ther wyf, ne mayde,
Ne widwe that contraried° that° he sayde, *opposed / what*
But seyden he was worthy han° his lyf. *to have*
And with that word up stirte° the olde wyf, *started up*
Which that the knight saugh° sittinge in the grene: *saw (had seen)*
"Mercy," quod she, "my sovereyn lady quene!
Er that youre court departe, do me right.° *give me justice*
I taughte this answere unto the knight;
For which he plighte me his trouthe there:
The firste thing I wolde of him requere° *request*
He wolde it do, if it lay in his might.° *power*
Bifore the court thanne preye I thee, sir knight,"
Quod she, "that thou me take unto thy wyf,
For wel thou wost° that I have kept° thy lyf. *knowest / preserved*
If I sey fals, sey nay, upon thy fey!"° *faith*
  This knight answerde, "Allas and weylawey!° *woe is me*
I woot° right wel that swich° was my biheste.° *know / such / promise*
For Goddes love, as chees° a newe requeste: *choose*
Tak al my good,° and lat my body go." *goods, property*
  "Nay thanne," quod she, "I shrewe° us bothe two! *curse*
For thogh that I be foul° and old and pore, *ugly*
I nolde° for al the metal ne for ore *would not*
That under erthe is grave° or lyth° above *buried / lies*
But if° thy wyf I were, and eek thy love." *(Have anything) except*
  "My love?" quod he, "Nay, my dampnacioun!° *damnation*
Allas! that any of my nacioun° *birth, lineage*
Sholde evere so foule disparaged° be!" *disgracefully degraded*
But al for noght, the ende° is this, that he *outcome*
Constreyned was: he nedes moste° hire wedde, *needs must*
And taketh his olde wyf and gooth to bedde.
  Now wolden som men seye, paraventure,° *perchance*

7. Over their husband(s) as well as over their lover(s).

That for° my necligence I do no cure° *out of / omit*
To tellen yow the joye and al th'array° *the pomp*
That at the feste° was that ilke° day. *feast / same*
To whiche thing shortly° answere I shal: *in brief*
I seye ther nas° no joye ne feste at al; *was not*
Ther nas but° hevinesse and muche sorwe, *was only*
For prively° he wedded hire on morwe,° *privately / in the morning*
And al day after hidde him as an oule,° *like an owl*
So wo was him, his wyf looked so foule.[8]
   Greet was the wo the knight hadde in his thoght,
Whan he was with his wyf abedde° y-broght; *to bed*
He walweth,° and he turneth to and fro. *tosses about*
His olde wyf lay smylinge everemo,° *all the while*
And seyde, "O dere housbond, *benedicite!*° *bless us*
Fareth° every knight thus with his wyf as ye? *Acts, behaves*
Is this the lawe of King Arthures hous?
Is every knight of his so dangerous?° *haughty, reluctant*
I am youre owene love and eek youre wyf;
I am she which that saved hath youre lyf;
And certes yet dide I yow nevere unright.° *wrong*
Why fare° ye thus with me this firste night? *act*
Ye faren lyk a man had° lost his wit! *(who) had*
What is my gilt?° for Goddes love, tel me it, *error*
And it shal been amended, if I may."° *can*
   "Amended?" quod this knight, "allas! nay, nay!
It wol nat been amended nevere mo!° *more*
Thou art so loothly,° and so old also, *loathsome, ugly*
And therto comen of so lowe a kinde,° *such low birth*
That litel wonder is° thogh I walwe and winde.° *it is / toss and turn*
So wolde God myn herte wolde breste!"° *burst*
   "Is this," quod she, "the cause of youre unreste?"
   "Ye, certainly," quod he, "no wonder is."° *it is*
   "Now, sire," quod she, "I coude amende al this,
If that me liste, er it were dayes three,
So wel ye mighte bere yow unto me.[9]
   But for ye speken of swich gentillesse[1]
As is descended out of old richesse°— *wealth*
That therfore sholden ye be gentil men[2]—
Swich° arrogance is nat worth an hen. *Such*
Loke who that° is most vertuous alway, *See who*
Privee and apert, and most entendeth ay[3]
To do the gentil dedes that he can,
And tak him for the grettest gentil man.

8. So woeful was he, (because) his wife looked so ugly.
9. If it pleased me, before three days were past, if you could behave well toward me.
1. "Gentillesse" implies the kind of behavior and sensibility proper to good ("gentil") birth—openness, generosity, compassion, courtesy—but as the Wife points out (with learned authority to support her), a high ancestry is no guarantee of these things, nor does low birth necessarily preclude them.
2. That because of this, you must necessarily be "gentle"-men.
3. In private and in public, and always seeks most diligently.

Crist wol° we clayme of° him oure gentillesse, *desires (that) / from*
Nat of oure eldres° for hire old richesse. *elders, ancestors*
For thogh they yeve° us al hir heritage— *give*
For which we clayme to been of heigh parage°— *parentage, birth*
Yet may they nat biquethe,° for no thing,° *bestow / by any means*
To noon of us hir vertuous living
That made hem gentil men y-called be,
And bad us folwen hem in swich degree.° *in a similar condition*
  Wel can the wyse poete of Florence,
That highte Dant, speken in this sentence.[4]
Lo, in swich maner rym° is Dantes tale: *this sort of rhyme*
'Ful selde° up ryseth by his branches[5] smale *seldom*
Prowesse° of man, for God of° his goodnesse *The excellence / out of*
Wol° that of° him we clayme oure gentillesse.' *Desires / from*
For of oure eldres may we no thing clayme
But temporel thing, that man may hurte and mayme.[6]
  Eek° every wight° wot° this as wel as I, *Also / being / knows*
If gentillesse were planted naturelly° *by nature*
Unto a certeyn linage doun the lyne,
Privee and apert, than wolde they nevere fyne° *cease*
To doon of gentillesse the faire offyce°— *function(s)*
They mighte° do no vileinye or vyce.° *could / vicious act*
  Tak fyr, and ber it in° the derkeste hous *bear it into*
Bitwix this° and the Mount of Caucasus, *here*
And lat men shette° the dores and go thenne,° *shut / away*
Yet wol the fyr as faire lye and brenne,° *burn*
As° twenty thousand men mighte it biholde: *As when*
His office° naturel ay° wol it holde,° *Its function / ever / perform*
Up° peril of my lyf, til that it dye.° *Upon / die out*
  Heer may ye see wel how that genterye° *nobility*
Is nat annexed° to possessioun, *attached*
Sith° folk ne doon hir operacioun° *Since / perform their function*
Alwey, as dooth the fyr, lo, in his kinde.° *according to its nature*
For, God it woot, men may wel often finde
A lordes sone° do° shame and vileinye; *son / doing*
And he that wol han prys of° his gentrye *have praise (esteem) for*
For° he was boren° of a gentil hous, *Because / born*
And hadde his eldres noble and vertuous,
And nil° himselven do no gentil dedis, *will not*
Ne folwe his gentil auncestre° that deed is,° *ancestry / which is dead*
He nis nat° gentil, be he duk or erl; *is not*
For vileyns° sinful dedes make a cherl.° *villainous / churl*
For gentillesse nis° but renomee° *is nothing / the renown*
Of thyne auncestres, for hire heigh bountee,° *their great goodness*
Which is a straunge thing° to thy persone. *a thing foreign*
Thy gentillesse cometh fro God allone.
Thanne comth oure verray gentillesse of grace:

4. Who is called Dante, speak on this theme.
5. I.e., of the family tree.
6. But temporal (worldly) things, which can harm and maim man.

It was nothing biquethe us with oure place.[7]
Thenketh how noble, as seith Valerius,° *Valerius Maximus*
Was thilke Tullius Hostilius,[8]
That out of povert° roos° to heigh noblesse. *poverty / rose*
Redeth Senek,° and redeth eek° Boëce:° *Seneca / also / Boethius*
Ther shul ye seen expres° that it no drede° is *explicitly / doubt*
That he is gentil that doth gentil dedis.° *deeds*
And therfore, leve° housbond, I thus conclude: *dear*
Al were it that° myne auncestres were rude,° *Even though / humble*
Yet may the hye° God, and so hope I, *high*
Grante me grace to liven vertuously.
Thanne am I gentil, whan that I biginne
To liven vertuously and weyve° sinne. *put aside*
And ther as ye of povert° me repreve,° *poverty / reproach*
The hye God, on° whom that we bileve, *in*
In wilful° povert chees° to live his lyf. *voluntary / chose*
And certes every man, mayden, or wyf,
May understonde that Jesus, hevene king,
Ne wolde nat chese a vicious living.° *way of living*
Glad° povert is an honest thing, certeyn;° *Contented / certainly*
This wol Senek and othere clerkes seyn.
Whoso that halt him payd of his poverte,[9]
I holde him riche, al° hadde he nat a sherte.° *although / shirt*
He that coveyteth° is a povre wight,° *covets / poor creature*
For he wolde han that° is nat in his might.° *what / power*
But he that noght hath, ne coveyteth have,° *desires (to) have*
Is riche, although ye holde him but a knave.° *one of low estate*
Verray° povert, it singeth proprely.° *True / by its nature*
Juvenal seith of povert merily:
'The povre man, whan he goth by the weye,
Bifore the theves he may singe and pleye.'
Poverte is hateful good,° and as I gesse, *a hated good*
A ful greet bringere out of bisinesse;° *anxiety, care*
A greet amendere eek of sapience° *wisdom*
To him that taketh it in° pacience. *accepts it with*
Poverte is this, although it seme elenge,° *miserable*
Possessioun that no wight wol chalenge;° *claim (as his own)*
Poverte ful ofte, whan a man is lowe,
Maketh° his God and eek himself to knowe; *Makes (him)*
Poverte a spectacle° is, as thinketh me, *eyeglass*
Thurgh which he may his verray frendes see.
And therfore, sire, sin that I noght yow greve,[1]
Of° my povert namore ye me repreve.° *For / reproach*
Now, sire, of elde° ye repreve me: *old age*
And certes, sire, thogh° noon auctoritee *even if*
Were in no book, ye gentils of honour° *who are honorable*

7. Then our real *gentillesse* comes from (God's) grace; it was in no way bestowed upon us with our social position.
8. Third legendary king of Rome.
9. Whosoever considers himself satisfied with his poverty.
1. And therefore, sir, since I don't trouble you (with it).

Seyn that men sholde an old wight° doon favour *(to) an old person*
And clepe° him fader, for° youre gentillesse; *call / out of*
And auctours° shal I finden, as I gesse. *authorities (for this opinion)*
  Now ther ye seye that I am foul° and old, *ugly*
Than drede° you noght to been a cokewold,° *fear / cuckold*
For filthe and elde, also moot I thee,° *as I may prosper*
Been grete wardeyns upon° chastitee. *guardians of*
But nathelees, sin° I knowe youre delyt,° *since / pleasure, wish*
I shal fulfille youre worldly appetyt.° *appetite, lust*
  Chese° now," quod she, "oon of thise thinges tweye:° *Choose / two*
To han me foul and old til that I deye° *die*
And be to yow a trewe° humble wyf, *faithful*
And nevere yow displese in al my lyf,
Or elles° ye wol han me yong and fair, *else*
And take youre aventure of° the repair° *chance with / i.e., the crowd*
That shal be to youre hous, by cause of me,
Or in som other place, may wel be.° *(it) may well be*
Now chese yourselven whether that yow lyketh."° *whichever pleases you*
  This knight avyseth him and sore syketh,[2]
But atte laste he seyde in this manere:
"My lady and my love, and wyf so dere,
I put me in youre wyse governance:° *under your wise control*
Cheseth° youreself which may be most *Choose*
    plesance° *the greatest pleasure*
And most honour to yow and me also.
I do no fors the whether of the two,
For as yow lyketh, it suffiseth me."[3]
  "Thanne have I gete of° yow maistrye,"° quod she, *gotten from / mastery*
"Sin° I may chese and governe as me lest?"° *Since / I please*
  "Ye, certes,° wyf," quod he, "I holde° it best." *certainly / consider*
  "Kis me," quod she. "We be no lenger wrothe,° *longer wroth (angry)*
For by my trouthe,° I wol be to yow bothe, *i.e., I swear*
This is to seyn, ye,° bothe fair and good. *yes*
I prey to God that I mot sterven wood,° *may die mad*
But° I to yow be also° good and trewe *Unless / just as*
As evere was wyf, sin° that the world was newe. *since*
And but I be to-morn as fair to sene[4]
As any lady, emperyce,° or quene, *empress*
That is bitwixe the est and eke the west,
Doth with my lyf and deeth right as yow lest.° *just as you please*
Cast° up the curtin:° loke how that it is." *Lift / (bed-)curtain*
  And whan the knight saugh° verraily° al this, *saw / in truth*
That she so fair was and so yong therto,
For joye he hente° hire in his armes two; *clasped*
His herte bathed in a bath of blisse.
A thousand tyme a-rewe° he gan hire kisse,° *in a row / did kiss her*
And she obeyed him in every thing

2. This knight thinks it over and sorrowfully sighs.
3. I don't care which of the two (it be), for as it is pleasing to you, (so) it suffices me.
4. And unless I am in the morning as fair to look upon.

That mighte doon° him plesance° or lyking.° *give / pleasure / delight*
And thus they live unto hir lyves ende
In parfit° joye. And Jesu Crist us sende *perfect*
Housbondes meke,° yonge, and fresshe abedde,° *meek / in bed*
And grace t'overbyde hem that we wedde.[5]
And eek I preye Jesu shorte hir lyves° *to shorten their lives*
That° noght wol be governed by hir wyves; *Who*
And olde and angry nigardes of dispence,° *niggards with their money*
God sende hem sone° verray° pestilence! *soon / a real*

The Friar's Prologue and Tale

The Prologue

This worthy limitour,° this noble Frere, *(see General Prologue, l. 209 and note)*
He made alwey a maner louring chere° *a sort of glowering expression*
Upon° the Somnour, but for honestee° *Toward / for (the sake of) propriety*
No vileyns° word as yet to him spak he. *churlish, indecent*
But atte laste he seyde unto the Wyf,
"Dame," quod he, "God yeve° yow right good lyf! *give*
Ye han° heer touched, also moot I thee,° *have / as I may thrive*
In scole-matere greet difficultee.° *Upon scholastic questions of great difficulty*
Ye han seyd muchel thing° right wel, I seye. *many things*
But dame, here as we ryden by the weye
Us nedeth nat to speken but of game,° *entertaining subjects*
And lete auctoritees,° on° Goddes name, *leave (citing) authorities / in*
To preching and to scoles of clergye.° *to the learned schools*
But if it lyke to° this companye, *please*
I wol yow of a somnour telle a game.° *jest, funny story*
Pardee,° ye may wel knowe by the name° *By God / the term itself*
That of a somnour may no good be sayd.
I praye that noon of you be yvel apayd.° *be offended*
A somnour is a renner° up and doun *runner*
With mandements° for fornicacioun, *summonses*
And is y-bet° at every tounes ende." *beaten, assailed*
Our Host tho° spak, "A, sire, ye sholde be hende° *then / polite*
And curteys, as° a man of your estaat;° *as (befits) / position*
In companye we wol have no debaat.° *quarreling, strife*
Telleth your tale, and lat the Somnour be."
"Nay," quod° the Somnour, "lat him seye to me *said*
What so him list.° Whan it comth to my lot,° *Whatever pleases him / turn*
By God, I shal him quyten° every grot.° *repay / groat (a coin)*
I shal him tellen which° a greet honour *what*
It is to be a flateringe limitour,
And of many another manere crime
Which nedeth nat rehercen for° this tyme. *mention at*
And his offyce I shal him telle, ywis."[1]

5. And the grace to outlive them that we wed.
1. And I will reveal to him, indeed, (the true nature) of his office (his official duties).

Our Host answerde, "Pees,° namore of this." *Peace*
And after this he seyde unto the Frere,
"Tel forth your tale, leve° maister deere." *dear*

The Tale

Whilom° ther was dwellinge in my contree° *Once / district*
An erchedeken,[2] a man of heigh degree,° *rank*
That boldely dide execucioun° *carried out (church) law*
In punisshinge of fornicacioun,
Of wicchecraft and eek° of bauderye,° *also / pandering*
Of diffamacioun° and avoutrye,° *slander / adultery*
Of chirche-reves and of testaments,
Of contractes and of lakke of sacraments,[3]
Of usure° and of symonye[4] also. *usury*
But certes,° lechours° dide he grettest wo— *certainly / lechers*
They sholde singen° if that they were hent.° *sing, i.e., lament / caught*
And smale tytheres weren foule y-shent:
If any persone wolde upon hem pleyne,
Ther mighte asterte him no pecunial peyne.[5]
For smale tythes and for smal offringe,
He made the peple pitously to singe.
For er° the bisshop caughte hem with his hook,° *before / staff, crozier*
They weren in the erchedeknes book.
Thanne hadde he, thurgh his jurisdiccioun,
Power to doon on hem correccioun.° *inflict punishment on them*
He hadde a somnour redy to his hond.° *ready to do his bidding*
A slyer boy° nas noon in Engelond, *knave*
For subtilly° he hadde his espiaille° *subtly, cunningly / spies*
That taughte him wher that him mighte availle.° *he would profit*
He coude spare of lechours oon or two,
To techen° him to foure and twenty mo. *direct, lead*
For thogh this Somnour wood° were as an hare, *crazy*
To telle his harlotrye° I wol nat spare, *evildoings, immorality*
For we been out of his correccioun.[6]
They han of us no jurisdiccioun,
Ne never shullen,° terme of alle hir lyves.° *shall / for as long as they live*
"Peter!° so been the wommen of the styves,"° *By St. Peter / brothels*
Quod the Somnour, "y-put out of my cure!"° *beyond my authority*
"Pees, with mischance and with misaventure,"° *bad luck (to you)*
Thus seyde our Host, "and lat him telle his tale.

2. The archdeacon was a church official in charge of local ecclesiastical courts in a diocese. The list of offenses that follows indicates what sorts of behavior were typically tried in church courts rather than secular ones.
3. Of churchwardens' misbehavior, and of (violations in regard to) wills and marriage contracts, and of failing to perform the sacraments (most likely confession and communion).
4. Simony is the buying and selling of church offices, the corruption of spiritual benefits and responsibilities by financial motives.
5. And those who did not pay all the tithes they owed (ten percent of one's income) were dealt with severely: if any parish priest complained about them, they could not escape financial pain (punishment).
6. For we are outside of his authority. (Charges against friars were handled within their orders, not by the ecclesiastical courts.)

Now telleth forth, thogh that the Somnour gale.° *protest*
Ne spareth nat, myn owene maister dere."
  This false theef, this somnour, quod the Frere,
Hadde alwey baudes redy to his hond,° *pimps ready at hand (cf. l. 1321)*
As any hauk to lure in Engelond,[7]
That° tolde him al the secree° that they knewe, *Who / secrets*
For hir acqueyntance was nat come of newe.° *had not come about recently*
They weren hise approwours° prively.° *agents / privately, secretly*
He took himself a greet profit therby.
His maister knew nat alwey what he wan.° *won, gained*
Withouten mandement,° a lewed° man *a summons / ignorant*
He coude somne,° on peyne of Cristes curs,° *summon / excommunication*
And they were gladde for to fille his purs,
And make him grete festes atte nale.° *entertain him at the ale(house)*
And right° as Judas hadde purses smale *just*
And was a theef,[8] right swich a theef was he.
His maister hadde but half his duetee.° *amount due him*
He was, if I shal yeven him his laude,° *give him the praise (he deserves)*
A theef, and eek° a somnour, and a baude. *also*
He hadde eek wenches at his retenue,° *at his command*
That—whether that sir Robert or sir Huwe,
Or Jakke or Rauf or whoso° that it were *whoever*
That lay by hem—they tolde it in his ere.
Thus was the wenche and he of oon assent,° *in collusion*
And he wolde fecche a feyned mandement° *bring a fake summons*
And somne hem to the chapitre° bothe two, *i.e., the ecclesiastical court*
And pile° the man, and lete the wenche go. *rob, plunder*
Thanne wolde he seye, "Frend, I shal for thy sake
Do stryken hire out of° our lettres blake. *have her (name) erased from*
Thee thar° namore as in this cas travaille.° *need / labor, go to any trouble*
I am thy freend, ther° I thee may availle."° *where / help*
Certeyn° he knew of bryberyes mo° *Certainly / more ways to extort money*
Than possible is to telle in yeres two.
For in this world nis dogge for the bowe,° *hunting dog*
That can an hurt deer from an hool° knowe, *healthy (one)*
Bet° than this somnour knew a sly lechour *Better*
Or an avouter° or a paramour.° *adulterer / lover*
And, for° that was the fruit° of al his rente,° *since / major part / income*
Therfore on it he sette al his entente.° *intentions*
  And so bifel° that ones on a day° *it befell, happened / one day*
This somnour, ever waiting on° his pray,° *always on watch for / prey*
Rood for to somne an old widwe,° a ribybe,[9] *widow*
Feynynge a cause,° for he wolde brybe.° *charge / extort money*
And happed° that he saugh bifore him ryde *it happened*
A gay yeman, under a forest syde.[1]

7. Just as in England any hawk (returns) to the lure (a feathered device a falconer uses to call back a hawk).
8. Judas, as the purse keeper for the poor apostles, would have had only a small amount of money; John 12:6 says he was a thief.
9. Rebec, fiddle, a derogatory term for an old woman; see l. 1573.
1. A merry yeoman (see *General Prologue*, ll. 101–17), by the edge of a forest.

A bowe he bar,° and arwes° brighte and kene.° — *bore / arrows / keen, sharp*
He hadde upon a courtepy of grene,° — *wore a short green jacket*
An hat upon his heed with frenges° blake. — *fringes*
"Sir," quod this somnour, "hayl and wel atake!"° — *well met*
"Welcome," quod he, "and every good felawe!
Wher rydestow° under this grene-wode shawe?"° — *dost thou ride / grove*
Seyde this yeman. "Wiltow fer° to day?" — *Wilt thou (ride) far*
This somnour him answerde and seyde, "Nay.
Heer faste by,"° quod he, "is myn entente — *Close to here*
To ryden, for to reysen up a rent° — *collect some revenue*
That longeth° to my lordes duetee."° — *belongs / what is due my lord*
"Artow thanne a bailly?"[2] "Ye,"° quod he. — *Yes*
He dorste° nat, for verray° filthe and shame, — *dared / true, sheer*
Seye that he was a somnour, for the name.° — *due to the word (being hateful)*
"*Depardieux*,"° quod this yeman, "dere brother, — *By God*
Thou art a bailly and I am another.
I am unknowen as in° this contree.° — *in / region*
Of thyn aqueyntance I wolde praye thee,
And eek of brotherhede,° if that yow leste.° — *sworn brotherhood / it please you*
I have gold and silver in my cheste;
If that thee happe° to comen in our shyre,° — *happen / shire*
Al shal be thyn, right as thou wolt desyre."° — *whatever thou wilt desire*
"Grant mercy,"° quod this somnour, "by my feith." — *Thank you*
Everich in otheres hand his trouthe leith,[3]
For to be sworne bretheren til they deye.
In daliance° they ryden forth and pleye. — *friendly conversation*
This somnour, which that was as ful of jangles,° — *idle, inappropriate speech*
As ful of venim° been thise wariangles,° — *venom / shrikes, butcherbirds*
And ever enquering upon° every thing, — *always inquiring about*
"Brother," quod he, "where is now your dwelling,
Another day if that I sholde yow seche?"° — *seek*
This yeman him answerde in softe° speche, — *quiet, easygoing*
"Brother," quod he, "fer in the north contree,[4]
Wher as I hope° som tyme I shal thee see. — *Where I hope (or expect)*
Er we departe,° I shal thee so wel wisse° — *part company / inform*
That of myn hous ne shaltow never misse."° — *thou shalt not fail to find*
"Now, brother," quod this somnour, "I yow preye,
Teche me, whyl that we ryden by the weye,
Sin° that ye been a baillif as am I, — *Since*
Som subtiltee,° and tel me feithfully — *clever stratagem*
In myn offyce how I may most winne.° — *gain*
And spareth nat° for conscience ne sinne, — *do not hold back*
But as my brother tel me—how do ye?"° — *how do you (operate)?*
"Now, by my trouthe,° brother dere," seyde he, — *troth*

2. A bailiff. The term was used for local magistrates and for sheriffs' officers but here probably refers to an agent who collects rents for the lord of a manor.
3. Each lays his hand in the other's to pledge his troth.
4. Hell was often thought to be in the north. These lines, plus the earlier detail of his green coat, hint at the yeoman's soon-to-be-revealed identity.

"As I shal tellen thee a feithful tale,° *accurate account*
My wages been ful streite° and ful smale. *very limited*
My lord is hard to me and daungerous,° *haughty, ungenerous*
And myn offyce° is ful laborous,° *position / laborious*
And therfore by extorcions I live.
For sothe,° I take al that men wol me yive.° *Truly / give*
Algate,° by sleyghte° or by violence, *Always / sleight, trickery*
Fro yeer to yeer I winne° al my dispence.° *earn / living expenses*
I can no bettre telle, feithfully."
"Now, certes,"° quod this somnour, "so fare I. *certainly*
I spare nat to taken, God it woot,° *knows*
But if° it be to hevy° or to hoot.° *Unless / too heavy / too hot*
What° I may gete in conseil prively,° *Whatever / in secret*
No maner conscience of that have I.
Nere° myn extorcioun, I mighte nat liven, *If it were not for*
Ne of swiche japes wol I nat be shriven.[5]
Stomak° ne conscience ne knowe I noon. *Stomach, i.e., feeling*
I shrewe thise shrifte-fadres everichoon.[6]
Wel be we met, by God and by Seint Jame!° *St. James*
But, leve° brother, tel me than thy name," *dear*
Quod this somnour. In this mene whyle° *Meanwhile*
This yeman gan° a litel for to smyle. *began*
"Brother," quod he, "wiltow° that I thee telle? *wilt thou*
I am a feend.° My dwelling is in helle, *fiend, devil*
And here I ryde about my purchasing,° *for my acquisitions*
To wite wher° men wolde yeve me any thing. *know whether*
My purchas° is th'effect° of al my rente.° *What I take / sum / income*
Loke how thou rydest for the same entente,
To winne good,° thou rekkest° never how; *goods, profit / carest*
Right so fare I, for ryde wolde I now
Unto the worldes ende for a preye."° *prey, victim*
"A," quod this somnour, "*benedicite!*° What sey ye? *bless us*
I wende° ye were a yeman trewely. *thought*
Ye han a mannes shap° as wel as I. *shape, appearance*
Han ye a figure than determinat
In helle, ther ye been in your estat?"[7]
"Nay, certeinly," quod he, "ther have we noon;° *none*
But whan us lyketh, we can take us oon,° *assume one (shape)*
Or elles make yow seme° we ben shape *make it seem to you*
Somtyme lyk a man, or lyk an ape,
Or lyk an angel can I ryde or go.° *ride or walk, i.e., move*
It is no wonder thing thogh it be so.
A lousy jogelour° can deceyve thee, *lice-ridden conjurer*
And pardee,° yet can I more craft° than he." *by God / I know more tricks*
"Why," quod the somnour, "ryde ye thanne or goon
In sondry shap,° and nat alwey in oon?" *various shapes*

5. Nor do I want to be absolved of such tricks through confession.
6. I curse every one of these confessors. (A proper confession would include the summoner's making restitution for his extortions.)
7. Do you then have a fixed shape in hell, where you are in your normal state?

"For° we," quod he, "wol us swich formes *Because*
make° *take such shapes*
As most able° is our preyes° for to take."° *effective / victims / seize*
"What maketh° yow to han al this labour?" *causes*
"Ful many a cause, leve sir somnour,"
Seyde this feend, "but alle thing hath tyme.° *(see Ecclesiastes 3:1)*
The day is short, and it is passed pryme,° *prime, 9:00 A.M.*
And yet° ne wan° I nothing in this day. *as yet / won, gained*
I wol entende° to winnen, if I may, *concentrate, focus upon*
And nat entende our wittes to declare.° *discussing our talents*
For, brother myn, thy wit° is al to bare° *intelligence / all too bare, inadequate*
To understonde, althogh I tolde hem thee.° *them (to) thee*
But for thou axest° why labouren we: *since thou askest*
For somtyme we ben Goddes instruments
And menes to don° his comandements, *(the) means of enacting*
Whan that him list,° upon his creatures, *it pleases him*
In divers art° and in diverse figures.° *methods / shapes*
Withouten him we have no might,° certayn, *power*
If that him list to stonden ther-agayn.° *oppose (our actions)*
And somtyme, at our prayere,° han we leve° *prayer, request / leave, permission*
Only the body and nat the soule greve;° *grieve, torment*
Witnesse on° Job, whom that we diden wo. *Take as evidence*
And somtyme han we might of° bothe two, *power over*
This is to seyn, of soule and body eke.° *also*
And somtyme be we suffred° for to seke *permitted*
Upon° a man and doon his soule unreste° *i.e., harass / disturb his soul*
And nat his body, and al is for the beste.
Whan he withstandeth our temptacioun,
It is a cause of his savacioun,° *salvation*
Al be it° that it was nat our entente *Albeit, although*
He sholde be sauf° but that we wolde him hente.° *saved / seize, take*
And somtyme be we servant unto man,
As to the erchebisshop Seint Dunstan,
And to the apostles servant eek was I."[8]
"Yet tel me," quod the somnour, "feithfully,
Make ye yow° newe bodies thus alway *for yourselves*
Of elements?"° The feend answerde, *Out of the elements (earth, air, fire, water)*
"Nay.
Somtyme we feyne,° and somtyme we aryse *i.e., produce an illusion*
With° dede bodies in ful sondry wyse,° *enter into / many ways*
And speke as renably° and faire and wel *reasonably*
As to the Phitonissa dide Samuel.[9]
(And yet wol som men seye it was nat he;
I do no fors of° your divinitee.)° *do not care about / theology*
But o° thing warne I thee, I wol nat jape:° *one / jest*
Thou wolt algates° wite° how we ben shape. *in any case / know*

8. Medieval stories tell of the power over demons or devils possessed by Saint Dunstan, a tenth-century Archbishop of Canterbury, and by various apostles.
9. As Samuel did to the Witch of Endor. (See 1 Samuel 28:7–19; the Witch of Endor is referred to elsewhere in the Vulgate Bible as "pythonissam" [1 Par. 10:13].)

Thou shalt herafterward, my brother dere,
Com ther° thee nedeth nat of me to lere.° — *where / learn from me*
For thou shalt by thyn owene experience
Conne in a chayer rede of this sentence[1]
Bet° than Virgyle,° whyl he was on lyve,° — *Better / Virgil / alive*
Or Dant also.[2] Now lat us ryde blyve,° — *ride on quickly*
For I wol holde companye with thee
Til it be so that thou forsake me."
"Nay," quod this somnour, "that shal nat bityde.° — *happen*
I am a yeman, knowen is ful wyde.
My trouthe° wol I holde as in this cas. — *troth, promise (see ll. 1404–05)*
For though thou were the devel Sathanas,° — *Satan (himself)*
My trouthe wol I holde to my brother,
As I am sworn—and ech of us til other—
For to be trewe brother in this cas.
And bothe we goon abouten our purchas.° — *acquisitions*
Tak thou thy part, what that° men wol thee yive, — *whatever*
And I shal myn. Thus may we bothe live.
And if that any of us have more than other,
Lat him be trewe and parte° it with his brother." — *share*
"I graunte,"° quod the devel, "by my fey."° — *agree (to that) / faith*
And with that word they ryden forth hir wey.
And right at the entring of the tounes ende° — *town limits*
To which this somnour shoop him for to wende,° — *intended to go*
They saugh° a cart, that charged° was with hey,° — *saw / loaded / hay*
Which that a carter droof° forth in his wey. — *drove*
Deep° was the wey, for which the carte stood.° — *Deep (in mud) / stuck, stood still*
The carter smoot° and cryde as he were wood,° — *smote, struck / mad*
"Hayt, Brok! Hayt, Scot! What, spare ye° for the stones?[3] — *do you hold back*
The feend," quod he, "yow fecche,° body and bones, — *May the devil take you*
As ferforthly° as ever were ye foled,° — *surely / foaled (born)*
So muche wo as I have with yow tholed!° — *suffered*
The devel have al, bothe hors and cart and hey!"
This somnour seyde, "Heer shal we have a pley,"° — *some amusement*
And neer the feend he drough, as noght ne were,[4]
Ful prively,° and rouned° in his ere: — *privately / whispered*
"Herkne,° my brother, herkne, by thy feith. — *Harken, listen*
Herestow nat° how that the carter seith?° — *Dost thou not hear / speaks*
Hent it anon,° for he hath yeve° it thee, — *Seize it immediately / given*
Bothe hey and cart, and eek hise caples° three." — *also his horses*
"Nay," quod the devel, "God wot,° never a deel.° — *knows / not at all*
It is nat his entente,° trust me weel. — *intention*

1. Be able to lecture on this subject from a professorial chair.
2. These lines allude to the famous descriptions of the underworld in the *Aeneid* and *The Divine Comedy*.
3. "Hayt" is a word used to drive horses, like our modern "Giddyap!" "Brok" and "Scot" are the horses' names. The carter accuses them of not pulling hard enough because of the stones in the road.
4. And he drew nearer to the fiend as if it were nothing (i.e., very nonchalantly).

Axe° him thyself, if thou nat trowest° me, *Ask / dost not believe*
Or elles stint° a while and thou shalt see." *stop, hold off*
This carter thakketh° his hors upon the croupe,° *slaps / rump*
And they bigonne drawen° and to stoupe.° *to draw, pull / stoop, strain*
"Heyt, now!" quod he, "ther° Jesu Crist yow blesse, *i.e., may*
And al his handwerk,° bothe more and lesse! *handiwork, creation*
That was wel twight,° myn owene lyard° boy. *pulled / dappled gray*
I pray God save thee and Seynte Loy.[5]
Now is my cart out of the slow,° pardee."° *slough, mud / by God*
"Lo, brother," quod the feend, "what tolde I thee?
Heer may ye see, myn owene dere brother,
The carl° spak oo° thing, but he thoghte another. *churl, fellow / one*
Lat us go forth abouten our viage.° *on our journey*
Heer winne I nothing upon cariage."° *by my (feudal) rights*
Whan that they comen somwhat out of toune,
This somnour to his brother gan to roune.° *whisper*
"Brother," quod he, "heer woneth° an old rebekke° *dwells* *fiddle (i.e., woman)*
That hadde almost as lief to lese° hir nekke *would be almost as willing to lose*
As for to yeve° a peny of hir good.° *give, surrender / goods*
I wol han twelf pens, though that she be wood,° *mad*
Or I wol sompne° hir unto our offyce.° *summon / court*
And yet, God woot,° of hir knowe I no vyce.° *knows / nothing wrong*
But for° thou canst nat, as in this contree, *since*
Winne thy cost,° tak heer ensample of me." *Cover thy expenses*
This somnour clappeth° at the widwes gate. *raps*
"Com out," quod he, "thou olde viritrate!° *hag, witch*
I trowe° thou hast som frere or preest with thee." *believe*
"Who clappeth?" seyde this widwe. "*Benedicite!*° *Bless us*
God save you, sire, what is your swete wille?"
"I have," quod he, "of somonce here a bille.° *a writ of summons*
Up peyne of cursing,° loke that thou be *On pain of excommunication*
Tomorn° bifore the erchedeknes knee *In the morning*
T'answere to the court of° certeyn thinges." *in regard to*
"Now, Lord," quod she, "Crist Jesu, king of kinges,
So wisly° helpe me, as I ne may.° *Surely / I cannot (go to court)*
I have been syk, and that ful many a day.
I may nat go° so fer," quod she, "ne ryde, *walk*
But I be deed,° so priketh it° in my syde. *Without dying / it is so painful*
May I nat axe a libel,° sir somnour, *request a written copy of the charge*
And answere there by my procutour° *agent, proxy*
To swich thing as men wol opposen me?"° *charge me with*
"Yis," quod this somnour, "pay anon°—lat se°— *now / let us see*
Twelf pens to me, and I wol thee acquyte.
I shall no profit han therby but lyte;° *except a little*
My maister hath the profit and nat I.
Com of,° and lat me ryden hastily. *Come on, i.e., hurry*

5. St. Eligius, the patron saint of carters. See also *General Prologue*, l. 120.

Yif me twelf pens. I may no lenger tarie."° *tarry, delay*
"Twelf pens!" quod she, "Now lady Seinte Marie
So wisly help me out of care and sinne,
This wyde world thogh that I sholde winne,° *win, gain*
Ne have I nat twelf pens withinne myn hold.° *possession*
Ye knowen wel that I am povre° and old. *poor*
Kythe your almesse on° me, povre wrecche." *Show your charity to*
"Nay than," quod he, "the foule feend me fecche° *fetch, take*
If I th'excuse, though thou shul be spilt!"° *ruined*
"Alas," quod she, "God woot,° I have no gilt!" *knows*
"Pay me," quod he, "or by the swete Seinte Anne,° *(Mary's mother)*
As I wol° bere awey thy newe panne *i.e., I will*
For dette which that thou owest me of old.
Whan that thou madest thyn housbond cokewold,° *cuckold*
I payde at hoom for thy correccioun."° *punishment, fine*
"Thou lixt!"° quod she. "By my savacioun,° *liest / salvation*
Ne was I nevere er° now, widwe ne wyf, *before*
Somoned unto your court in al my lyf,
Ne nevere I nas° but of my body trewe. *Nor was I ever*
Unto the devel blak and rough of hewe° *in appearance*
Yeve° I thy body and my panne also!" *Give*
And whan the devel herde hir cursen so
Upon hir knees, he seyde in this manere,
"Now, Mabely, myn owene moder dere,
Is this your wil° in ernest that ye seye?" *will, wish*
"The devel," quod she, "so fecche him er he deye,[6]
And panne and al, but° he wol him repente!" *unless*
"Nay, olde stot,° that is nat myn entente," *(you) old horse*
Quod this somnour, "for to repente me
For any thing that I have had of° thee. *gotten from*
I wolde I hadde thy smok and every clooth!"[7]
"Now, brother," quod the devel, "be nat wrooth.° *wroth, angry*
Thy body and this panne ben myne by right.
Thou shalt with me to helle yet tonight,
Where thou shalt knowen of oure privetee° *secrets*
More than a maister of divinitee."° *theology*
And with that word this foule feend him hente.° *seized*
Body and soule, he with the devel wente
Wher as° that somnours han hir heritage.° *There where / inheritance*
And God, that maked after his image
Mankinde, save and gyde us, alle and some,
And leve° thise somnours good men to bicome. *let*
Lordinges, I coude han told yow, quod this Frere,
Hadde I had leyser for° this Somnour here, *Were I given (enough) time by*
After the text° of Crist, Poul,° and John, *teaching / (St.) Paul*
And of oure othere doctours° many oon, *authorities on theology*
Swiche peynes° that your hertes mighte
agryse,° *Such pains, torments / shudder*

6. She said, "May the devil carry him off before he dies."
7. I wish I had thy shift (undergarment) and every (bit of thy) clothing.

Al be it so° no tonge may devyse°— *Even though / describe*
Thogh that I mighte a thousand winter° telle— *winters, i.e., years*
The peynes of thilke cursed hous of helle.
But for to kepe us fro that cursed place,
Waketh,° and preyeth Jesu for his grace *Be awake, watchful*
So kepe us fro the temptour Sathanas.° *Satan*
Herketh this word, beth war° as in this cas: *be aware, wary*
"The leoun sit in his await° alway *lies in ambush*
To slee the innocent, if that he may."[8]
Disposeth ay° your hertes to withstonde° *always / resist*
The feend, that yow wolde make thral° and bonde.° *captive / enslaved*
He may nat tempte yow over youre might,° *beyond your power*
For Crist wol be your champion[9] and knight.
And prayeth that thise somnours hem repente° *repent (themselves)*
Of hir misdedes, er that the feend hem hente.° *before the devil seizes them*

The Summoner's Prologue and Tale

The Prologue

This Somnour in his stiropes° hye° stood. *stirrups / high up*
Upon this Frere° his herte was so wood° *Friar / angry*
That lyk an aspen leef he quook° for yre.° *trembled / ire*
"Lordinges," quod° he, "but o° thing I desyre. *said / just one*
I yow biseke° that, of your curteisye, *beseech*
Sin° ye han° herd this false Frere lye,° *Since / have / lie*
As suffereth° me I may my tale telle. *Permit*
This Frere bosteth° that he knoweth helle, *boasts*
And God it woot° that it is litel wonder: *God knows*
Freres and feendes° been but lyte asonder.° *fiends, devils / not far apart*
For, pardee,° ye han ofte tyme herd telle *by God*
How that a frere ravisshed° was to helle *carried off*
In spirit ones° by a visioun.° *once / in a dream*
And as an angel ladde° him up and doun *led*
To shewen him the peynes° that ther were, *pains*
In al the place saugh° he nat a frere. *saw*
Of other folk he saugh ynowe° in wo.° *enough / woe, torment*
Unto this angel spak the frere tho:° *then*
'Now, sire,' quod he, 'han° freres swich° a grace *have / such*
That noon° of hem° shal come to this place?' *none / them*
'Yis,'° quod this angel, 'many a millioun!' *Yes (indeed)*
And unto Sathanas° he ladde° him doun. *Satan / led*
'And now hath Sathanas,' seith he, 'a tayl
Brodder° than of a carrik° is the sayl. *Broader / large sailing ship*
Hold up thy tayl, thou Sathanas,' quod he.
'Shewe forth thyn ers,° and lat the frere see *arse*
Wher is the nest of freres in this place.'

8. See Psalm 10:8–9.
9. One who fights on behalf of someone else in a judicial duel.

And er that half a furlong wey of space,[1]
Right so as bees out swarmen from an hyve,
Out of the develes ers ther gonne dryve° *did rush*
Twenty thousand freres in a route,° *crowd*
And thurghout helle swarmeden aboute,
And comen° agayn as faste as they may gon, *came, returned*
And in° his ers they crepten everichon.° *into / every one*
He clapte° his tayl agayn, and lay ful stille. *clapped shut*
This frere, whan he loked hadde his fille
Upon the torments of this sory° place, *sorrowful*
His spirit God restored of° His grace *by*
Unto his body agayn, and he awook.° *awoke*
But natheles° for fere yet° he quook,° *nevertheless / still / trembled*
So was the develes ers ay° in his minde, *always*
That is his heritage° of verray kinde.° *inheritance / by true nature*
God save° yow alle, save° this cursed Frere! *protect / except (with pun on prior meaning)*
My prologe wol I ende in this manere."

The Tale

Lordinges, ther is in Yorkshire, as I gesse,
A mersshy contree° called Holdernesse,° *marshy region / (in southeast Yorkshire)*
In which ther wente a limitour° aboute *begging friar (see* General Prologue, *l.* 209)
To preche and eek° to begge, it is no doute. *also*
And so bifel° that on a day this frere *it happened*
Had preched at a chirche in his manere,
And specially, aboven every thing,
Excited° he the peple in his preching *Exhorted*
To trentals,[2] and to yeve,° for Goddes sake, *give (money)*
Wherwith° men mighten holy houses make° *With which / build*
Ther as° divyne service is honoured, *Where*
Nat ther as° it is wasted and devoured, *where*
Ne ther° it nedeth nat for to be yive,° *Nor where / given*
As to possessioners,[3] that mowen° live— *who are able to*
Thanked be God—in wele° and habundaunce. *prosperity*
Trentals, seyde he, deliveren fro penaunce
Hir° freendes soules, as wel olde as yonge, *Their*
Ye,° whan that they been hastily° y-songe, *Yes / without delay*
Nat for to holde° a preest joly° and gay: *keep, support / jolly, merry*
He singeth nat but o° masse in a day. *only one*
"Delivereth out,"° quod he, "anon° the soules! *Release (from Purgatory) / at once*
Ful hard it is with fleshhook° or with oules° *meathooks / awls*
To been y-clawed,° or to brenne° or bake. *torn, lacerated / burn*
Now spede yow° hastily, for Cristes sake!" *help yourselves*

1. And in a few moments (literally, the time it takes to walk half a furlong, or about 100 yards).
2. The purchase of thirty requiem masses ("trentals") sung for a soul in Purgatory.
3. Monks and clergy living on endowments and regular income, unlike the mendicant friars, who are supposed to have no property and so must beg for alms.

And whan this frere had seyd al his entente,
With *qui cum patre*[4] forth his wey he wente.
Whan folk in chirche had yeve° him what hem leste,° *given / they wished*
He wente his wey, no lenger wolde he reste.
With scrippe and tipped staf, y-tukked hye,[5]
In every hous he gan to poure° and prye, *look about*
And beggeth mele° and chese or elles corn.° *meal, flour / grain*
His felawe° hadde a staf tipped with horn, *companion friar*
A peyre of tables al of yvory,[6]
And a poyntel° polisshed fetisly,° *stylus / elegantly*
And wroot the names alwey, as he stood,
Of alle folk that yaf hem° any good,° *gave them / goods*
Ascaunces° that he wolde for hem preye. *As if*
"Yeve us a busshel whete, malt, or reye,° *rye*
A Goddes kechil° or a trip° of chese, *small alms cake / bit, morsel*
Or elles what yow list—we may nat chese°— *choose*
A Goddes halfpeny or a masse-peny,[7]
Or yeve us of your brawn,° if ye have eny, *meat*
A dagon° of your blanket,° leve dame,° *piece / woolen cloth / dear lady*
Our suster dere—lo, here I write your name—
Bacon or beef, or swich thing as ye finde."
A sturdy harlot° wente ay° hem bihinde, *fellow / always*
That was hir hostes man,[8] and bar° a sak, *bore, carried*
And what men yaf hem,° leyde it on his bak. *whatever people gave them*
And whan that he was out at dore, anon° *at once*
He planed° awey the names everichon *smoothed*
That he biforn had writen in his tables.
He served hem with nyfles° and with fables.° *trifles / lies*
"Nay, ther thou lixt,° thou Somnour!" quod the Frere. *liest*
"Pees!"° quod our Host, "for Cristes moder° dere! *Peace / mother*
Tel forth thy tale and spare it nat at al."
"So thryve I,"° quod this Somnour, "so I shal." *As I may thrive*
So longe he wente, hous by hous, til he
Cam til an hous ther° he was wont° to be *where / accustomed*
Refresshed° more than in an hundred placis. *i.e., with food and drink*
Sik lay the gode man° whos that the place is. *goodman, head of household*
Bedrede° upon a couche lowe he lay. *Bedridden*
"*Deus hic*,"° quod he, "O Thomas, freend, good day," *God be here*
Seyde this frere curteisly° and softe.° *courteously / quietly*
"Thomas," quod he, "God yelde° yow! Ful ofte *reward*
Have I upon this bench faren ful weel.° *fared very well, prospered*
Here have I eten many a mery meel."
And fro the bench he droof° awey the cat, *drove*
And leyde adoun his potente° and his hat *staff*
And eek° his scrippe,° and sette him softe adoun. *also / satchel*

4. "Who with the Father" (a liturgical formula for concluding prayers and sermons).
5. With satchel and a staff tipped with metal and with his robe tucked up high (for easier walking).
6. A folding pair of writing tablets made of ivory. The tablets were wax-coated, written on with a stylus ("poyntel"), and could be easily erased by scraping (see ll. 1757–59).
7. A half-penny as alms or a penny for saying mass.
8. Possibly the servant of the host at the inn where the two friars were staying (see ll. 1778–80).

His felawe was go walked° into toun — *had gone walking*
Forth with his knave,° into that hostelrye° — *servant / inn*
Whereas° he shoop him° thilke° night to lye. — *Where / intended / that*
"O dere maister," quod this syke° man, — *sick*
"How han ye fare sith° that March bigan? — *since*
I saugh° yow noght this fourtenight° or more." — *saw / fortnight (two weeks)*
"God woot,"° quod he, "laboured have I ful sore,° — *knows / exceedingly*
And specially for thy savacioun° — *salvation*
Have I seyd many a precious orisoun,° — *prayer*
And for our othere frendes, God hem° blesse. — *them*
I have today been at your chirche at messe° — *mass*
And seyd a sermon after my simple wit,
Nat al after° the text of holy writ, — *according to*
For it is hard to yow,° as I suppose, — *for you (to understand)*
And therfore wol I teche° yow al the glose.[9] — *teach*
Glosinge° is a glorious thing, certeyn, — *Interpretation*
For lettre sleeth,° so as we clerkes° seyn. — *slays, kills / scholars*
Ther° have I taught hem to be charitable — *I.e., in church*
And spende hir good ther° it is resonable, — *their money where*
And ther I saugh our dame°—a! wher is she?" — *i.e., your wife*
"Yond in the yerd° I trowe° that she be," — *yard, garden / believe*
Seyde this man, "and she wol come anon."° — *at once*
"Ey, maister! Welcome be ye, by Seint John,"
Seyde this wyf. "How fare ye, hertely?"° — *(I ask it) sincerely*
The frere aryseth up ful curteisly,
And hir embraceth in his armes narwe,° — *closely*
And kiste° hir swete,° and chirketh° as a sparwe° — *kissed / sweetly / chirps / sparrow*
With his lippes. "Dame," quod he, "right weel,
As he that is your servant every deel,° — *every bit, completely*
Thanked be God, that yow yaf° soule and lyf. — *gave*
Yet saugh° I nat this day so fair° a wyf — *saw / lovely*
In al the chirche, God so save me!"
"Ye, God amende defautes,° sir," quod she. — *repair (my) faults*
"Algates,° welcome be ye, by my fey."° — *In any case / faith*
"Graunt mercy,° dame, this have I founde alwey. — *Many thanks*
But of your grete goodnesse, by your leve,° — *with your permission*
I wolde prey yow that ye nat yow greve°— — *get angry*
I wol with Thomas speke a litel throwe.° — *while*
Thise curats° been ful necligent and slowe° — *parish priests / slothful*
To grope tendrely° a conscience — *search sensitively*
In shrift.° In preching is my diligence, — *confession*
And studie in Petres° wordes and in Poules.° — *St. Peter's / St. Paul's*
I walke and fisshe° Cristen° mennes soules — *fish for / Christian*
To yelden° Jesu Crist his propre rente.° — *give to / due tribute*
To sprede his word is set al myn entente."

9. The "glose" (gloss) offers a spiritual interpretation of a sacred text rather than a literal reading. "The letter killeth, but the spirit giveth life" (2 Corinthians 3:6, paraphrased below, l. 1794). But "glossing" came also to mean wilfully misinterpreting a text for ulterior purposes; see ll. 1918–28 for an example.

"Now, by your leve, o dere sir," quod she,
"Chydeth° him weel, for seinte Trinitee.° *Admonish / Holy Trinity*
He is as angry as a pissemyre,° *pismire, ant*
Though that he have al that he can desyre.
Though I him wrye° a-night and make him warm *cover*
And on hym leye my leg outher° myn arm, *or*
He groneth lyk our boor,° lyth° in our sty. *pig / that lies*
Other desport° right noon of him have I. *pleasure*
I may nat plese him in no maner cas."° *in any way*
"O Thomas! *Je vous dy*,° Thomas, Thomas, *I tell you*
This maketh the feend.° This moste ben amended. *This is the work of the devil*
Ire° is a thing that hye God defended,° *Anger (a deadly sin) / forbade*
And therof wol I speke a word or two."
"Now maister," quod the wyf, "er° that I go, *before*
What wol ye dyne?° I wol go theraboute."° *eat for dinner / see about it*
"Now dame," quod he, "*Je vous dy sanz doute*,° *I say to you indeed*
Have I° nat of a capon but the livere,° *If I were to have / just the liver*
And of your softe breed nat but° a shivere,° *nothing but / sliver*
And after that a rosted pigges heed
(But that I nolde no beest for me were deed),[1]
Thanne hadde I with yow hoomly suffisaunce.° *plain food enough*
I am a man of litel sustenaunce.° *who eats little*
My spirit hath his fostring° in the Bible. *its nourishment*
The body is ay so redy and penyble
To wake that my stomak is destroyed.[2]
I prey yow, dame, ye be nat anoyed,
Though I so freendly yow my conseil° shewe. *secrets*
By God, I wolde nat telle it° but a fewe." *tell it (to)*
"Now sir," quod she, "but o word er I go.
My child is deed° withinne thise wykes° two, *died / weeks*
Sone° after that ye wente out of this toun." *Soon*
"His deeth saugh° I by revelacioun," *saw*
Seith this frere, "at hoom in our dortour.° *dormitory (in the convent)*
I dar wel seyn that er° that half an hour *before*
After his deeth, I saugh him born to blisse° *carried to heaven*
In myn avisioun,° so God me wisse.° *vision / guide*
So dide our sexteyn° and our fermerer,° *sacristan / infirmary keeper*
That han° been trewe freres fifty yeer. *Who have*
(They may now—God be thanked of his lone—
Maken hir jubilee and walke allone.)[3]
And up I roos° and al our covent eke,° *rose / also*
With many a tere° trikling on my cheke, *tear*
Withouten noyse or clateringe of belles.
Te deum[4] was our song and nothing elles,

1. But I would not want any animal killed (just) for me.
2. [My] body is always so ready and inured to staying awake (at prayers and vigils) that my appetite has been destroyed.
3. They may now—thank God for his gift—celebrate their jubilee (fiftieth year in the convent) and go about alone (instead of in pairs).
4. A hymn of praise, usually sung at Matins.

Save° that to Crist I seyde an orisoun° *Except / prayer*
Thankinge him of his revelacioun.
For, sir and dame,° trusteth me right weel, *dear sir and madam*
Our orisons been more effectueel,° *valid, effective*
And more we seen of Cristes secree° thinges *secret, hidden*
Than burel° folk, although they weren kinges. *secular*
We live in poverte and in abstinence,
And burel folk in richesse and despence° *(wasteful) expenditure*
Of mete and drinke, and in hir foul delyt.° *their foul pleasure(s)*
We han° this worldes lust° al in despyt.° *hold / pleasure / contempt*
Lazar and Dives liveden° diversly,[5] *lived*
And diverse guerdon° hadden they therby.° *different rewards / as a result*
Whoso wol preye, he moot° faste and be clene,° *must / chaste*
And fatte° his soule and make his body lene.° *fatten / lean*
We fare as seith th'apostle:[6] cloth° and fode° *clothing / food*
Suffysen° us, though they be nat ful gode. *Suffice for*
The clennesse° and the fastinge of us freres *chaste living*
Maketh that° Crist accepteth our preyeres. *Is the reason why*
  Lo, Moyses° fourty dayes and fourty night *Moses*
Fasted, er° that the heighe God of might *before*
Spak with him in the mountain of Sinay.° *Sinai (cf. Exodus 34:28)*
With empty wombe,° fastinge many a day, *stomach*
Receyved he the lawe that was writen
With Goddes finger; and Elie,° wel ye witen,° *Elijah / know*
In mount Oreb,° er he hadde any speche *Horeb*
With hye° God, that is our lyves leche,° *high / healer, physician*
He fasted longe and was in contemplaunce.° *contemplation (cf. 1 Kings 19:8)*
  Aaron, that hadde the temple in governaunce,
And eek° the othere preestes everichon,° *also / every one*
Into the temple whan they sholde gon
To preye for the peple and do servyse,
They nolden° drinken in no maner wyse° *would not / in any way*
No drinke which that mighte hem dronke make,
But there in abstinence preye and wake,
Lest that they deyden.° Tak heed what I seye. *died (cf. Leviticus 10:8–11)*
But° they be sobre that for the peple preye, *Unless*
War° that—I seye namore, for it suffyseth. *Beware*
  Our lord Jesu, as holy writ devyseth,° *relates*
Yaf° us ensample of fastinge and preyeres. *Gave*
Therfor we mendinants,° we sely° freres, *mendicants / good, simple*
Been° wedded to poverte and continence, *Are*
To charitee, humblesse, and abstinence,
To persecucion for rightwisnesse,° *for the sake of righteousness*
To wepinge, misericorde,° and clennesse.° *mercy / chastity*
And therfor may ye see that our preyeres—
I speke of us, we mendinants, we freres—

5. In Jesus's parable (Luke 16:19–31), Lazarus, a beggar denied even the crumbs from the rich man's (Dives's) table, is carried by angels after his death to Abraham's bosom, while the rich man suffers horribly in hell.
6. St. Paul (in 1 Timothy 6:8).

Ben to the hye God more acceptable
Than youres, with your festes° at the table. *feasts*
Fro Paradys first, if I shal nat lye,
Was man out chaced° for his glotonye; *chased*
And chaast° was man in Paradys, certeyn. *chaste*
But herkne now, Thomas, what I shal seyn.° *say*
I ne have no text° of it, as I suppose, *i.e., biblical source*
But I shall finde it in a maner glose,° *a kind of gloss (see ll. 1792–94)*
That specially our swete lord Jesus
Spak this by° freres, whan he seyde thus: *concerning*
'Blessed be they that povre° in spirit been.' *poor (cf. Matthew 5:3)*
And so forth al the gospel may ye seen,
Wher it be lyker our professioun,
Or hirs that swimmen in possessioun.[7]
Fy on hir° pompe and on hir glotonye! *their*
And for hir lewednesse° I hem diffye.° *ignorance / scorn them*
Me thinketh they ben lyk Jovinian,[8]
Fat as a whale and walkinge as° a swan, *waddling like*
Al vinolent° as botel° in the spence.° *full of wine / bottle / pantry*
Hir° preyer is of ful gret reverence, *Their*
Whan they for soules seye the psalm of Davit:° *David*
Lo, 'Buf!'° they seye, '*cor meum eructavit.*'[9] *(sound of a belch)*
Who folweth Cristes gospel and his fore° *footsteps (i.e., example)*
But we that humble been and chast° and pore, *chaste*
Werkers° of Goddes word, not auditours?° *Doers / (merely) listeners*
Therfore, right° as an hauk up at a sours° *just / in rising flight*
Up springeth into th'eir,° right so prayeres *air*
Of charitable and chaste bisy freres
Maken hir sours° to Goddes eres° two. *upward flight / ears*
Thomas, Thomas, so mote° I ryde or go,° *may / walk*
And by that lord that clepid is Seint Yve,
Nere thou our brother, sholdestou nat thryve.[1]
In our chapitre° praye we day and night *In devotions at our friary*
To Crist, that he thee sende hele° and might,° *health / strength*
Thy body for to welden hastily."° *quickly (re)gain the use of*
"God woot,"° quod he, "nothing therof° fele° I. *knows / from that / feel*
As help me Crist, as° I in fewe yeres *i.e., although*
Have spended upon dyvers maner° freres *many sorts of*
Ful many a pound, yet fare I never the bet.° *better*
Certeyn, my good° have I almost biset.° *goods, wealth / used up*
Farwel my gold, for it is al ago!"
The frere answerde, "O Thomas, dostow° so? *dost thou*

7. And so you can see throughout the gospel whether it (as a statement of Christian principles) is more like our (fraternal) orders or theirs (the beneficed clergy) that swim in endowments.
8. Jovinian was a fourth-century monk whose heretical views on marriage and the good life prompted St. Jerome's *Adversus Jovinianum*, to which the Wife of Bath responds in her Prologue; see esp. ll. 673–75 and the excerpts from Jerome reprinted in the Sources and Backgrounds section of this Norton Critical Edition.
9. "My heart hath uttered [a good word]." This is the opening of Psalm 45, but *eructare* can also mean to belch.
1. And by that great man called St. Ivo, wert thou not our brother, thou shouldst not prosper. Thomas is a "brother" by having been admitted to lay-brotherhood in the friar's order. Scholars disagree about the identity of St. Ivo.

What nedeth yow diverse° freres seche?° *different / seek out*
What nedeth him that hath a parfit leche° *perfect doctor*
To sechen othere leches in the toun?
Your inconstance° is your confusioun.° *inconstancy / ruin*
Holde ye than° me or elles our covent° *Do you then consider / convent, friary*
To praye for yow ben insufficient?
Thomas, that jape° nis nat worth a myte.° *foolish notion / coin of small value*
Your maladye is for° we han to lyte.° *because / too little (from you)*
'A! yif° that covent half a quarter otes.° *give / quarter-load of oats*
A! yif that covent four and twenty grotes.° *groats (coin worth four pence)*
A! yif that frere a peny, and lat him go.'
Nay, nay, Thomas! It may no thing° be so! *not at all*
What is a ferthing° worth parted in twelve? *farthing*
Lo, ech thing that is oned° in himselve° *united / itself*
Is more strong than whan it is toscatered.° *scattered, dispersed*
Thomas, of° me thou shalt nat been y-flatered:° *by / flattered*
Thou woldest han° our labour al for noght.° *have / nothing*
The hye God, that al this world hath wroght,° *made*
Seith that the werkman worthy is his hyre.° *is worthy of his wages (Luke 10:7)*
Thomas, noght of your tresor I desyre
As for myself, but that al our covent
To preye for yow is ay° so diligent, *always*
And for to builden Cristes owene chirche.
Thomas, if ye wol lernen for to wirche,° *to do good works*
Of° buildinge up of chirches may ye finde *Concerning*
If it be good in Thomas lyf of Inde.[2]
Ye lye heer° ful of anger and of yre,° *lie here / ire, wrath*
With which the devel set° your herte afyre, *sets*
And chyden° heer this sely° innocent, *scold / poor, simple*
Your wyf, that° is so meke and pacient. *who*
And therfor, Thomas, trowe° me if thee leste,° *believe / will*
Ne stryve° nat with thy wyf, as for thy beste;° *argue, fight / for thy own good*
And ber° this word awey now, by thy feith. *bear*
Touchinge° swich thing, lo, what the wyse man seith: *Concerning*
'Within thyn hous ne be thou no leoun.° *lion (cf.* Ecclesiasticus 34:5)
To thy subgits° do noon oppressioun, *subjects*
Ne make thyne aqueyntances nat to flee.'
And Thomas, yet eftsones° I charge° thee, *again / command*
Be war from° ire that in thy bosom slepeth, *Beware of*
War fro the serpent that so slyly crepeth° *creeps*
Under the gras and stingeth subtilly.° *secretly*
Be war, my sone, and herkne° paciently *harken, hear*
That twenty thousand men han lost hir lyves
For stryving with hir lemmans° and hir wyves. *their lovers*
Now sith° ye han so holy° meke a wyf, *since / wholly, entirely*
What nedeth yow, Thomas, to maken stryf?° *create strife*
Ther nis,° ywis,° no serpent so cruel *is not / indeed*
Whan man tret° on his° tayl, ne half so fel° *treads / its / dangerous*

2. The saint's life of the apostle Thomas, some versions of which tell of his building churches in India.

As womman is whan she hath caught an ire.° *become angry*
Vengeance is thanne al that they desyre.
Ire is a sinne, oon of the grete of sevene,° *chief of the seven (deadly sins)*
Abhominable unto the God of hevene,
And to himself° it is destruccion. *a man himself*
This every lewed viker° or person° *ignorant vicar / parson*
Can seye—how Ire engendreth homicyde.
Ire is, in sooth,° executour° of pryde. *truth / i.e., agent*
I coude of ire seye so muche sorwe,
My tale sholde laste til tomorwe.
And therfor preye I God bothe day and night:
An irous° man, God sende° him litel might!° *angry / may God send / power*
It is greet harm and certes° gret pitee *certainly*
To sette an irous man in heigh degree.° *social rank*
  Whilom° ther was an irous potestat,° *Once / potentate*
As seith Senek,° that, duringe his estaat,° *Seneca / term of office*
Upon a day out riden° knightes two, *rode*
And as fortune wolde° that it were so, *willed, desired*
That oon of hem° cam hoom, that other noght.° *one of them / did not*
Anon° the knight bifore the juge° is broght, *Promptly / judge*
That seyde thus: 'Thou hast thy felawe° slayn, *fellow, companion*
For which I deme° thee to the deeth, certayn.' *condemn*
And to another knight comanded he,
'Go lede° him to the deeth, I charge thee.' *lead, bring*
And happed,° as they wente by the weye *it happened*
Toward the place ther° he sholde deye,° *where / die*
The knight cam which men wenden° had be deed. *thought*
Thanne thoughte they it was the beste reed° *plan*
To lede hem bothe to the juge agayn.
They seiden, 'Lord, the knight ne hath nat slayn
His felawe; here he standeth hool° alyve.' *whole, unharmed*
'Ye shul° be deed,' quod he, 'so moot° I thryve, *shall / may*
That is to seyn bothe oon and two and three!'
And to the firste knight right thus spak he,
'I dampned° thee. Thou most algate° be deed. *condemned / therefore*
And thou also most nedes° lese° thyn heed, *necessarily / lose*
For thou art cause why thy felawe deyth.'
And to the thridde knight right thus he seyth,
'Thou hast nat doon that° I comanded thee.' *what*
And thus he dide don sleen hem alle *caused all three of them*
    three.° *to be slain*
  Irous Cambyses was eek dronkelewe,[3]
And ay delyted him° to been a shrewe.° *always took pleasure / evil person*
And so bifel, a lord of his meynee,° *household*
That lovede vertuous moralitee,
Seyde on a day bitwix hem two° right thus: *i.e., confidentially*
'A lord is lost if he be vicious,° *given to vice*
And dronkenesse is eek a foul record° *shameful reputation*
Of° any man, and namely° in a lord. *For / especially*

3. Angry Cambises (a king of Persia) was also addicted to drink.

Ther is ful many an eye and many an ere° *ear*
Awaiting on° a lord—he noot nat° where. *Watching / does not know*
For Goddes love, drink more attemprely!° *temperately, moderately*
Wyn maketh man to lesen° wrecchedly *lose*
His minde and eek his limes° everichon.' *(control of) his limbs*
'The revers° shaltou° se,' quod he anon, *reverse / shalt thou*
'And preve° it by thyn owene experience *prove*
That wyn ne dooth to folk no swich offence.° *harm*
Ther is no wyn bireveth me my might° *(that) deprives me of my control*
Of hand ne foot ne of myn eyen sight.'
And for despyt° he drank ful muchel more— *out of spite*
An hondred part°—than he had doon bifore; *a hundred times (more)*
And right anon this irous° cursed wrecche *angry*
Leet° this knightes sone° bifore him fecche,° *Caused / son / to be brought*
Comandinge him he sholde bifore him stonde.
And sodeynly he took his bowe in honde,
And up the streng° he pulled to his ere,° *bowstring / ear*
And with an arwe he slow° the child° right there. *slew, killed / young man*
'Now whether have I a siker hand or noon?'[4]
Quod he. 'Is al my might and minde agoon?
Hath wyn bireved me myn eyen sight?'° *bereft me of my eyesight*
What sholde I telle th'answere of the knight?
His sone was slayn, ther is namore to seye.
Beth war° therfor with lordes how ye pleye. *Beware*
Singeth *Placebo*° and 'I shal if I can,' *I shall please (Psalm 114:9)*
But if° it be unto a povre° man. *Unless / poor*
To a povre man men sholde hise vyces telle,
But nat to a lord, thogh he sholde go to helle.
  Lo irous Cirus, thilke Percien,° *angry Cyrus the Great, the Persian*
How he destroyed the river of Gysen° *river Gyndes*
For that an hors of his was dreynt° therinne, *drowned*
Whan that he wente Babiloigne to winne.° *to conquer Babylon*
He made that the river was so smal[5]
That wommen mighte wade it over al.
Lo, what seyde he° that so wel teche° can? *i.e., Solomon / teach*
'Ne be no felawe to an irous man,
Ne with no wood° man walke by the weye, *mad, crazy*
Lest thee repente.'° I wol no ferther seye. *regret it (cf. Proverbs 22:24–25)*
  Now, Thomas, leve° brother, lef° thyn ire. *dear / leave*
Thou shalt me finde as just° as is a squire.° *exact, true / carpenter's square*
Hold nat the develes knyf ay° at thyn herte— *always*
Thyn angre dooth thee al to sore smerte°— *makes thee suffer all too painfully*
But shewe to me al thy confessioun."° *all you need to confess*
  "Nay," quod the syke° man, "by Seint Simoun!° *sick / Simon (the apostle)*
I have be shriven° this day at° my curat.° *confessed / by / local priest*
I have him told hoolly° al myn estat.° *wholly / spiritual condition*
Nedeth namore to speke of it, seith he,

4. Now (tell me) whether I have a steady hand or not.
5. I.e., he diverted the river into so many small channels.

But if me list° of myn humilitee." *Unless I choose*
"Yif° me thanne of thy gold to make our cloistre," *Give*
Quod he, "for many a muscle and many an oistre,[6]
Whan other men han ben ful wel at eyse,° *ease*
Hath been our fode, our cloistre for to reyse.° *build*
And yet, God woot, unnethe the fundement
Parfourned is, ne of our pavement
Nis nat a tyle yet withinne our wones.[7]
By God, we owen° fourty pound for stones. *owe*
Now help, Thomas, for Him° that harwed° helle, *i.e., Christ / harrowed*
For elles° moste° we our bokes selle. *otherwise / must*
And if ye lakke our predicacioun,° *preaching*
Than gooth the world al to destruccioun.
For whoso wolde us fro this world bireve°— *remove*
So God me save, Thomas, by your leve°— *leave*
He wolde bireve out of this world the sonne.° *sun*
For who can teche and werchen° as we conne? *work, do good deeds*
And that is nat of litel tyme,"° quod he, *i.e., not just recently*
"But sith° Elie° was, or Elisee,° *since / Elijah / Elisha*
Han freres been—that finde I of record°— *recorded, written down*
In charitee, y-thanked be our Lord.[8]
Now Thomas, help, for seinte charitee!"
And doun anon° he sette him on his knee.° *at once / i.e., he kneeled*
This syke man wex wel ny wood for ire.° *went nearly insane out of anger*
He wolde° that the frere had been on fire *wished*
With his false dissimulacioun.° *dissimulation, hypocrisy*
"Swich thing as is in my possessioun,"° *i.e., owned by me*
Quod he, "that may I yeven,° and non other.° *give / nothing else*
Ye sey me thus, how that I am your brother?"° *lay brother of your order*
"Ye, certes," quod the frere, "trusteth weel.
I took our dame our lettre with our seel."[9]
"Now wel," quod he, "and somwhat° shal I yive° *something / give*
Unto your holy covent whyl I live,
And in thyn hand thou shalt it have anoon,° *at once*
On this condicioun and other noon:° *no other*
That thou departe it so,° my dere brother, *divide it in such a way*
That every frere have as muche as other.
This shaltou° swere on thy professioun,° *shalt thou / religious vows*
Withouten fraude or cavillacioun."° *quibbling*
"I swere it," quod this frere, "upon my feith."
And therwithal his hand in his he leith.° *lays*
"Lo, heer my feith!° In me shal be no lak."° *here is my pledge / lack, fault*
"Now thanne, put thyn hand doun by my bak,"
Seyde this man, "and grope wel bihinde.

6. In the Middle Ages, mussels and oysters were held in some disdain as part of a meatless diet associated with Lenten abstinence, poverty, and penance.
7. And still, God knows, the foundation has scarcely been completed, nor has a tile yet been laid on the floor where we live.
8. The Carmelites, a thirteenth-century order of friars, claimed they were founded by the prophet Elijah and his successor, Elisha.
9. I carried a letter of confraternity (i.e., brotherhood) to our lady (your wife) with our official seal.

Bynethe my buttok° ther shaltow finde *buttocks*
A thing that I have hid in privetee."° *secrecy*
"A!" thoghte this frere, "that shal go with me!"
And doun his hand he launcheth° to the clifte° *thrusts / cleft*
In hope for to finde ther a yifte.° *gift*
And whan this syke man felte this frere
Aboute his tuwel° grope there and here, *rectum*
Amidde his hand he leet° the frere a fart. *let, released*
Ther nis no capul° drawinge in a cart, *horse*
That mighte have lete a fart of swich a soun.° *such a sound*
The frere up stirte° as doth a wood leoun.° *started, leaped / maddened lion*
"A! false cherl,"° quod he, "for Goddes bones! *churl, fellow*
This hastow for despyt doon,° for the nones.° *done for spite / on purpose*
Thou shalt abye° this fart, if that I may!" *pay for*
His meynee,° whiche that herden this affray,° *servants / disturbance*
Cam lepinge in and chaced out the frere,
And forth he gooth with a ful angry chere,° *appearance*
And fette his felawe theras lay his stoor.[1]
He looked as° he were a wilde boor; *as though*
He grinte with° his teeth, so was he wrooth. *ground, gnashed*
A sturdy pas° doun to the court° he gooth, *(At) a furious pace / manor house*
Wheras° ther woned° a man of greet honour, *Where / dwelt*
To whom that he was alwey confessour.
This worthy man was lord° of that village. *i.e., feudal lord*
This frere cam, as he were in a rage,
Wheras this lord sat eting at his bord.° *table*
Unnethes° mighte the frere speke a word, *Scarcely*
Til atte laste he seyde, "God yow see."° *May God watch over you*
This lord gan loke and seide, "*Benedicite*!° *Bless us*
What, frere John, what maner world is this?° *i.e., what's wrong*
I see wel that som thing ther is amis.° *amiss*
Ye loken as the wode° were ful of thevis.° *woods / thieves*
Sit doun anon and tel me what your greef° is, *grievance*
And it shal been amended, if I may."
"I have," quod he, "had a despyt° this day— *insult (spite)*
God yelde yow°—adoun in your village, *May God reward you*
That in this world is noon so povre a page° *so lowly a serving boy*
That he nolde° have abhominacioun° *would not / loathing, disgust*
Of that° I have receyved in your toun. *For what*
And yet ne greveth me nothing so sore° *sorely, deeply*
As that this olde cherl with lokkes hore° *white hair*
Blasphemed hath our holy covent eke."° *also*
"Now maister,"° quod this lord, "I yow biseke°—" *master / beseech*
"No maister, sire," quod he, "but servitour,° *servant*
Thogh I have had in scole that honour.° *i.e., a master of arts degree*
God lyketh nat that 'Raby'° men us calle, *rabbi (cf. Matthew 23:8)*

1. And fetched his companion friar (at the lodging) where there was all his store (what he had collected from begging).

Neither in market ne in your large halle."
"No fors,"° quod he, "but tel me al your grief."   *No matter*
"Sire," quod this frere, "an odious meschief°   *wrong*
This day bitid is° to myn ordre and me,   *has happened*
And so *per consequens*° to ech degree   *consequently*
Of holy chirche. God amende it sone!"
"Sir," quod the lord, "ye woot° what is to done.   *know*
Distempre yow noght.° Ye be my confessour;   *Do not lose your temper*
Ye been the salt of the erthe and the savour.°   *savor, taste (cf. Matthew 5:13)*
For Goddes love, your pacience ye holde.°   *i.e., calm yourself*
Tel me your grief." And he anon him tolde
As ye han herd biforn—ye woot wel what.
The lady of the hous ay° stille sat,   *all the time*
Til she had herd what the frere sayde.
"Ey, Goddes moder,"° quod she, "blisful mayde!   *mother*
Is ther oght elles?° Telle me feithfully."   *anything else*
"Madame," quod he, "how thinketh yow herby?"°   *about this*
"How that me thinketh?" quod she. "So God me speede,
I seye a cherl° hath doon a cherles dede.   *churl, common fellow*
What shold I seye? God lat him never thee!°   *thrive, prosper*
His syke heed is ful of vanitee.°   *foolishness*
I hold him° in a maner frenesye."°   *believe him (to be) / kind of madness*
"Madame," quod he, "by God, I shal nat lye,
But I on other wise° may be wreke:°   *in another way / avenged*
I shal diffame° him overal ther° I speke,   *defame / everywhere*
This false blasphemour, that charged me
To parte that° wol nat departed be   *divide that which*
To every man yliche,° with meschaunce!"°   *alike (equally) / curse him*
The lord sat stille as he were in a traunce,°   *trance*
And in his herte he rolled up and doun,°   *turned over (the question)*
"How hadde this cherl imaginacioun°   *the ingenuity*
To shewe° swich a probleme° to the frere?   *present / logical problem*
Never erst er° now herde I of swich matere.°   *before / such an affair*
I trowe° the devel putte it in his minde.   *believe*
In ars-metryke° shal ther no man finde,   *arithmetic (with pun on "arse")*
Biforn this day, of swich a questioun.°   *problem*
Who sholde make a demonstracioun°   *provide a logical proof*
That every man sholde have yliche his part
As of the soun° or savour° of a fart?   *sound / odor*
O nyce,° proude cherl, I shrewe° his face!   *foolish / curse*
Lo, sires," quod the lord, "with harde grace!°   *bad luck to him*
Who ever herde of swich a thing er° now?   *before*
To every man ylyke?° Tel me how.   *alike (equally)*
It is an inpossible°—it may nat be!   *logical impossibility*
Ey, nyce cherl, God lete him never thee!°   *thrive, prosper*
The rumblinge of a fart and every soun
Nis but of eir reverberacioun,°   *Is only reverberation of air*
And ever° it wasteth lyte and lyte° awey.   *always / diminishes little by little*
Ther is no man can demen,° by my fey,°   *judge / faith*
If that it were departed° equally.   *divided*

What, lo, my cherl, lo yet how shrewedly° *wickedly*
Unto my confessour today he spak.
I holde him certeyn a demoniak!° *madman (demon-possessed)*
Now ete your mete and lat the cherl go pleye.
Lat him go hange himself a devel weye!"° *in the devil's name*
  Now stood the lordes squyer° at the bord,° *squire / table*
That carf° his mete, and herde word by word *Who carved*
Of alle thinges of which I have yow sayd.
"My lord," quod he, "be ye nat yvel apayd,° *if you were not displeased*
I coude telle, for a goune-clooth,° *cloth for a gown*
To yow, sir frere, so ye be nat wrooth,° *wroth, angry*
How that this fart sholde even deled° be *evenly distributed*
Among your covent, if it lyked me."
  "Tel," quod the lord, "and thou shalt have anon
A goune-cloth, by God and by Seint John."
  "My lord," quod he, "whan that the weder° is fair, *weather*
Withouten wind or perturbinge° of air, *disturbance*
Lat bringe° a cartwheel here into this halle. *Let there be brought*
But loke° that it have his° spokes alle. *see to it / its*
Twelf spokes hath a cartwheel comunly.° *commonly, usually*
And bring me than twelf freres. Woot ye° why? *Do you know*
For thrittene° is a covent, as I gesse. *thirteen (twelve and a superior)*
Youre confessour heer, for his worthinesse,
Shal parfourne up° the nombre of his covent. *complete*
Than shal they knele doun, by oon assent,° *by one accord, in concord*
And to every spokes ende, in this manere,
Ful sadly° leye° his nose shal a frere. *firmly, steadily / lay, place*
Your noble confessour—ther God him save°— *may God preserve him*
Shal holde his nose upright° under the nave.° *upward / hub*
Than shal this cherl, with bely stif and toght° *taut*
As any tabour,° hider° been y-broght; *drum / hither*
And sette him on the wheel right of this cart,
Upon the nave,° and make him lete a fart. *hub*
And ye shul seen, up peril of my lyf,° *i.e., I stake my life on it*
By preve° which that is demonstratif,° *proof / demonstrable*
That equally the soun° of it wol wende,° *sound / travel*
And eek° the stink, unto the spokes ende— *also*
Save° that this worthy man, your confessour, *Except*
By cause° he is a man of greet honour, *Because*
Shal have the firste fruit, as reson is.° *as is right*
The noble usage° of freres yet° is this: *custom / still*
The worthy men of hem° shul first be served; *among them*
And certeinly he hath it weel deserved.
He hath today taught us so muchel° good *much*
With° preching in the pulpit ther° he stood, *Through / where*
That I may vouchesauf, I sey for me,° *would grant, speaking for myself*
He hadde the firste smel of fartes three.
And so wolde al his covent hardily,° *assuredly*
He bereth him° so faire and holily."° *bears himself, behaves / devoutly*
  The lord, the lady, and ech man save° the frere *except*
Seyede that Jankin spak in this matere° *on this problem*

As wel as Euclide or Ptholomee.[2]
Touchinge° this cherl, they seyde subtiltee° *As for / cleverness*
And heigh wit° made him speken as he spak; *intelligence, ingenuity*
He nis no fool ne no demoniak.° *madman (see l. 2240)*
And Jankin hath y-wonne a newe goune.
My tale is doon; we been almost at toune.

The Clerk's Prologue and Tale

The Prologue

"Sir Clerk of Oxenford,"° our Hoste sayde, *scholar from Oxford*
"Ye ryde as coy° and stille as dooth a mayde *shy*
Were newe spoused, sittinge at the bord.[1]
This day ne herde I of° your tonge a word. *from*
I trowe ye studie aboute som sophyme,[2]
But Salomon seith, 'every thing hath tyme.'
For Goddes sake, as beth° of bettre chere. *be*
It is no tyme for to studien here.
Telle us som mery tale, by youre fey!° *faith*
For what man that is entred in a pley,[3]
He nedes moot° unto the pley assente. *needs must*
But precheth nat,° as freres° doon in Lente, *don't preach / friars*
To make us for our olde sinnes wepe,
Ne that thy tale make us nat to slepe.
Telle us som mery thing of aventures.
Youre termes, youre colours, and youre figures,[4]
Kepe hem in stoor til so be ye endyte[5]
Heigh° style, as whan that men to kinges wryte. *High*
Speketh so pleyn° at this time, we yow preye,° *plain / beseech*
That we may understonde what ye seye."
This worthy Clerk benignely° answerde: *graciously*
"Hoste," quod he, "I am under your yerde;° *rod, rule*
Ye han° of us as now the governaunce,° *have / the governing*
And therfor wol I do yow obeisaunce° *obey you*
As fer° as reson axeth,° hardily.° *far / demands / certainly*
I wol yow telle a tale which that I
Lerned at Padowe° of a worthy clerk, *Padua*
As preved° by his wordes and his werk. *(was) proved*
He is now deed° and nayled° in his cheste;° *dead / nailed / coffin*
I prey to God so yeve° his soule reste! *give*
Fraunceys Petrark,° the laureat poete, *Francis Petrarch*
Highte° this clerk, whos rethoryke° sweete *Was called / rhetoric*
Enlumined° al Itaille° of° poetrye, *Illumined / Italy / with*

2. As well as Euclid (the Greek geometrician) or Ptolemy (the astronomer and mathematician).
1. (Who) is newly wed, sitting at the (wedding) table.
2. I believe you're pondering over some sophism (i.e., clever, specious argument).
3. For whoever has entered into a game.
4. Various learned devices of rhetoric.
5. Keep them in store until you (have occasion to) compose in.

As Linian° dide of philosophye   *(Giovanni da) Legnano*
Or lawe, or other art° particuler;   *field of knowledge*
But deeth, that wol nat suffre° us dwellen heer°   *allow / here*
But as it were a twinkling of an yë,°   *eye*
Hem° bothe hath slayn, and alle shul we dye.°   *Them / shall die*
But forth to tellen of this worthy man
That taughte me this tale, as I bigan,
I seye that first with heigh style he endyteth,°   *composes*
Er° he the body° of his tale wryteth,   *Before / main part*
A proheme, in the which discryveth he[6]
Pemond,° and of Saluces° the contree,   *Piedmont / Saluzzo*
And speketh of Apennyn,° the hilles hye,°   *the Apennines / high*
That been the boundes° of West Lumbardye,°   *boundaries / Lombardy*
And of Mount Vesulus° in special,   *Viso*
Where as the Poo,° out of a welle° smal,   *Po River / spring*
Taketh his firste springing and his sours,°   *source*
That estward ay encresseth in his cours
To Emelward, to Ferrare, and Venyse:[7]
The which a long thing were to devyse,°   *relate*
And trewely, as to my jugement,
Me thinketh it a thing impertinent,°   *irrelevant*
Save that he wol conveyen his matere.[8]
But this° his tale, which that ye may here."°   *this is / hear*

The Tale

PART ONE

Ther is, at the west syde of Itaille,
Doun at the rote° of Vesulus° the colde,   *base / Mount Viso*
A lusty playne, habundant of vitaille,[9]
Wher many a tour° and toun thou mayst biholde   *tower*
That founded were in tyme of fadres olde,°   *forefathers*
And many another delitable° sighte,   *delightful*
And Saluces° this noble contree highte.°   *Saluzzo / was called*

A markis° whylom° lord was of that londe,   *marquis / at one time*
As were his worthy eldres° him bifore;   *elders*
And obeisant,° ay° redy to his honde   *obedient / ever*
Were alle his liges, bothe lasse and more.[1]
Thus in delyt he liveth, and hath don yore,°   *for a long time*
Biloved and drad,° thurgh° favour of Fortune,   *feared / through*
Bothe of° his lordes and of his commune.°   *by / common people*

Therwith° he was, to speke as of linage,°   *In addition / lineage*
The gentilleste° y-born of Lumbardye,   *i.e., the highest*
A fair° persone, and strong, and yong of age,   *handsome*

6. A proem (introduction) in which he describes.
7. That eastward ever grows larger in its course, toward Emilia, Ferrara, and Venice.
8. Except that he wishes to introduce his (main) subject.
9. A pleasant plain, abounding in food.
1. Were all his vassals, both small and great.

And ful of honour and of curteisye;° *courtesy*
Discreet ynogh his contree for to gye[2]—
Save in somme thinges that° he was to blame°— *wherein / at fault*
And Walter was this yonge lordes name.

I blame him thus, that he considered noght
In tyme cominge° what mighte him bityde, *In future time*
But on his lust present° was al his thoght, *immediate pleasure*
As for to hauke° and hunte on every syde; *hawk*
Wel ny alle othere cures leet he slyde,[3]
And eek° he nolde°—and that was worst of alle— *also / would not*
Wedde no wyf, for noght° that may bifalle. *whatever*

Only that point his peple bar so sore° *took so hard*
That flokmele° on a day they to him wente, *in flocks, droves*
And oon of hem, that wysest was of lore,° *in learning*
Or elles that° the lord best wolde assente *Or because*
That he sholde telle him what his peple mente,
Or elles coude he shewe wel swich matere,[4]
He to the markis seyde as ye shul here.

"O noble markis, your humanitee
Assureth us and yeveth° us hardinesse,° *giveth / the boldness*
As ofte as tyme is of necessitee,° *it is necessary*
That we to yow mowe° telle our hevinesse. *may*
Accepteth, lord, now of youre gentillesse,
That we with pitous° herte unto yow pleyne,° *sorrowful / make complaint*
And lete youre eres nat my voys disdeyne.[5]

Al° have I noght to done in this matere *Although*
More than another man hath in this place,
Yet for as muche as ye, my lord so dere,
Han alwey shewed me favour and grace,
I dar the better aske of yow a space° *opportunity*
Of audience, to shewen° our requeste, *put forward*
And ye, my lord, to doon right as yow leste.[6]

For certes, lord, so wel us lyketh yow[7]
And al your werk, and ever han doon, that we
Ne coude nat us self° devysen° how *ourselves / imagine*
We mighte liven in more felicitee,° *happiness*
Save o° thing, lord, if it youre wille be, *one*
That for to been a wedded man yow leste:[8]
Than° were your peple in sovereyn hertes reste.° *Then / supreme happiness*

2. Wise enough to guide (govern) his country.
3. He let slide almost all other responsibilities.
4. Or else (because) he knew well how to put forward such a subject.
5. And let your ears not disdain (to hear) my voice.
6. And you, my lord, to do just as you please.
7. For truly, lord, you please us so well.
8. That it may please you to become a married man.

Boweth youre nekke under that blisful yok
Of soveraynetee, noght of servyse,
Which that men clepeth spousaille° or wedlok; *call marriage*
And thenketh, lord, among your thoghtes wyse,
How that oure dayes passe in sondry wyse;° *various ways*
For though we slepe or wake, or rome,° or ryde, *wander about*
Ay fleeth the tyme, it nil no man abyde.[9]

And though youre grene youthe floure° as yit,° *flower / yet*
In crepeth age alwey, as stille as stoon,[1]
And deeth manaceth° every age, and smit° *threatens / smites*
In each estaat,° for ther escapeth noon.° *every rank / no one*
And al so° certein as we knowe echoon° *even as / each one*
That we shul deye,° as uncerteyn we alle *die*
Been of that day whan deeth shal on us falle.

Accepteth than of us the trewe entente,° *loyal intention*
That never yet refuseden youre heste,° *command*
And we wol, lord, if that ye wol assente,
Chese yow a wyf in short tyme, atte leste,° *at (the) least*
Born of the gentilleste and of the meste° *greatest*
Of al this lond, so that it oghte seme
Honour to God and yow, as we can deme.° *judge*

Delivere us out of al this bisy drede° *anxious fear*
And tak a wyf, for hye° Goddes sake; *high*
For if it so bifelle, as God forbede,° *i.e., may God forbid*
That thurgh your deeth your lyne sholde slake,° *cease*
And that a straunge° successour sholde take *unknown*
Youre heritage, O, wo were us alyve!
Wherfor we pray you hastily to wyve."° *take a wife*

Hir° meke preyere and hir pitous chere° *Their / appearance*
Made the markis herte° han pitee. *marquis's heart*
"Ye wol,"° quod he, "myn owene peple dere, *wish*
To that° I never erst° thoghte streyne° me. *what / before / constrain*
I me rejoysed of my libertee
That selde tyme° is founde in mariage; *seldom*
Ther I was free, I moot been in servage.[2]

But nathelees° I see your trewe entente, *nevertheless*
And truste upon youre wit,° and have don ay; *judgment*
Wherfore of my free wil I wole assente
To wedde me, as sone as evere I may.
But theras° ye han profred° me today *where / offered*
To chese° me a wyf, I yow relesse° *choose / release*
That choys, and prey yow of that profre cesse.[3]

9. Time always flees, it will not wait for any man.
1. Age creeps in steadily, as quietly as (a) stone.
2. Where I (once) was free, I must be in servitude.
3. (From) that choice and ask you to withdraw that offer.

For God it woot,° that children ofte been *knows*
Unlyk hir worthy eldres° hem bifore;° *ancestors / before them*
Bountee° comth al of God, nat of the streen° *Goodness / strain, lineage*
Of which they been engendred and y-bore.° *born*
I truste in Goddes bountee and therfore
My mariage and myn estaat° and reste° *noble station / quiet peace*
I him bitake; he may don as him leste.[4]

Lat me alone in chesinge° of my wyf— *the choosing*
That charge° upon my bak I wol endure; *load*
But I yow preye, and charge upon youre lyf,
That what° wyf that I take, ye me assure *whatever*
To worshipe hire° whyl that hir lyf may dure,° *revere her / last*
In word and werk,° bothe here and everywhere, *deed*
As° she an emperoures doghter were. *As if*

And forthermore this shal ye swere,° that ye *swear*
Agayn my choys shul neither grucche° ne stryve;° *grumble / oppose*
For sith° I shal forgoon° my libertee *since / forgo*
At your requeste, as ever moot I thryve,° *I may prosper*
Ther as° myn herte is set, ther wol I wyve.° *There where / marry*
And but° ye wole assente in swich manere, *unless*
I prey yow, speketh namore of this matere."

With hertely° wil they sworen and assenten *sincere, good*
To al this thing—ther seyde no wight° nay— *person*
Bisekinge him of grace, er that they wenten,[5]
That he wolde graunten hem° a certein day *grant (to name) them*
Of° his spousaille, as sone as evere he may; *For*
For yet alwey° the peple somwhat dredde° *still / feared*
Lest that this markis no wyf wolde wedde.

He graunted hem a day, swich as him leste,[6]
On which he wolde be wedded sikerly,° *certainly*
And seyde he dide al this at hir° requeste. *their*
And they, with humble entente, buxomly,° *submissively*
Knelinge upon hir knees ful reverently,
Him thanken alle; and thus they han an ende
Of hire entente,° and hoom agayn they wende. *purpose*

And heerupon he to his officeres° *household officials*
Comaundeth for the feste° to purveye,° *feast / provide*
And to his privee° knightes and squyeres *personal*
Swich charge yaf as him liste on hem leye;[7]
And they to his comandement obeye,
And ech of them doth al his diligence
To doon unto the feste reverence.° *honor*

4. I entrust to him; he may do as it pleases him.
5. Beseeching him of (his) grace, before they departed.
6. Such as it pleased him.
7. (He) gave such responsibility as it pleased him to lay on them.

PART TWO

Noght fer fro thilke paleys honurable
Wheras this markis shoop his mariage,[8]
Ther stood a throp,° of site delitable,° *village / pleasant*
In which that povre° folk of that village *poor*
Hadden hir bestes° and hir herbergage,° *animals / lodgings*
And of° hire labour took hir sustenance *by*
After that the erthe yaf hem habundance.[9]

Amonges thise povre folk ther dwelte a man
Which that was holden° povrest of hem alle; *Who was held to be*
But hye° God somtyme senden can *high*
His grace into a litel oxes stalle.
Janicula men of that throp him calle;
A doghter hadde he, fair ynogh to sighte,° *to the eye*
And Grisildis this yonge mayden highte.° *was named*

But for to speke of vertuous beautee,
Than was she oon the faireste° under sonne; *one of the loveliest*
For povreliche y-fostred up was she,
No likerous lust was thurgh hire herte y-ronne.[1]
Wel ofter of the welle° than of the tonne° *spring / (wine) cask*
She drank; and for she wolde vertu plese,
She knew wel labour, but non ydel ese.° *no idle ease*

But thogh this mayde tendre were of age,° *i.e., young in years*
Yet in the brest of hir virginitee
Ther was enclosed rype and sad corage;° *a mature and firm heart*
And in greet reverence and charitee
Hir° olde povre fader fostred° she. *Her / cared for*
A fewe sheep, spinninge, on feeld she kepte;[2]
She wolde noght been ydel til she slepte.

And whan she hoomward cam, she wolde bringe
Wortes° or othere herbes tymes ofte, *Plants*
The whiche she shredde and seeth° for hir° livinge, *boiled / their*
And made hir° bed ful harde and nothing softe; *her*
And ay she kepte hir fadres lyf on lofte° *sustained her father's life*
With everich° obeisaunce and diligence *every*
That child may doon to fadres reverence.

Upon Grisilde, this povre creature,
Ful ofte sythe° this markis sette his yë *oftentimes*
As he on hunting rood paraventure;° *rode by chance*
And whan it fil° that he mighte hire espye,° *befell / see*

8. Not far from that same worthy palace where this marquis prepared for his marriage.
9. In whatever abundance the earth yielded them.
1. Because she was raised in poverty, no wanton desire had run through her heart.
2. (While) spinning, she watched over a few sheep in the field.

He noght with wantoun loking of folye[3]
His eyen° caste on hire, but in sad° wyse *eyes / serious*
Upon hir chere° he wolde him ofte avyse,° *countenance / often ponder*

Commendinge in his herte hir wommanhede,
And eek hir vertu, passinge° any wight° *surpassing / person*
Of so yong age, as wel in chere° as dede. *appearance*
For thogh the peple have no greet insight
In vertu, he considered ful right
Hir bountee,° and disposed° that he wolde *goodness / decided*
Wedde hire only, if ever he wedde sholde.

The day of wedding cam, but no wight° can *nobody*
Telle what womman that it sholde be;
For which merveille wondred many a man,
And seyden, whan they were in privetee,° *private*
"Wol nat our lord yet leve his vanitee?° *foolishness*
Wol he nat wedde? allas, allas the whyle!
Why wol he thus himself and us bigyle?"° *deceive*

But natheles this markis hath don make° *has had made*
Of gemmes, set in gold and in asure,° *azure, blue*
Broches and ringes, for Grisildis sake,
And of hir clothing took he the mesure
By a mayde, lyk to hire stature,
And eek of othere ornamentes° alle *adornments*
That unto switch° a wedding sholde falle. *such*

The tyme of undern° of the same day *midmorning*
Approcheth, that this wedding sholde be;
And al the paleys° put was in array,° *palace / order*
Bothe halle and chambres, ech in his° degree; *its*
Houses of office[4] stuffed with plentee
Ther maystow° seen, of deyntevous vitaille° *mayest thou / dainty foods*
That may be founde as fer as last Itaille.° *Italy extends*

This royal markis, richely arrayed,
Lordes and ladyes in his companye,
The whiche unto the feste were y-prayed,° *asked*
And of his retenue the bachelrye,° *young knights*
With many a soun° of sondry° melodye, *sound / various*
Unto the village of the which I tolde,
In this array the righte wey° han holde.° *direct way / taken*

Grisilde of this, God woot,° ful innocent° *knows / entirely unaware*
That for hire shapen° was al this array, *prepared*
To fecchen water at a welle is went,° *has gone*
And cometh hoom as sone as ever she may.

3. He did not with wanton, foolish looks.
4. Service buildings (storerooms, kitchens, etc.).

For wel she hadde herd seyd that thilke° day *that same*
The markis sholde wedde, and, if she mighte,
She wolde fayn° han seyn some of that sighte. *gladly*

She thoghte, "I wol with othere maydens stonde,
That been my felawes,° in our dore and see *companions*
The markisesse,° and therfor wol I fonde° *marchioness / try*
To doon° at hoom as sone as it may be *i.e., To finish*
The labour which that longeth° unto me; *belongs*
And than I may at leyser° hire biholde, *leisure*
If she this wey unto the castel holde."° *takes*

And as she wolde over hir threshfold° goon, *threshold*
The markis cam and gan hire for to calle,° *did call her*
And she sette doun hir water pot anoon° *at once*
Bisyde the threshfold, in an oxes stalle,
And doun upon hir knees she gan to falle,° *fell*
And with sad° contenance kneleth stille *earnest*
Til she had herd what was the lordes wille.

This thoghtful° markis spak unto this mayde *pensive*
Ful sobrely,° and seyde in this manere: *gravely*
"Wher is your fader, Grisildis?" he sayde,
And she with reverence, in humble chere,° *manner*
Answerde, "Lord, he is al redy° here." *right at hand*
And in she gooth withouten lenger lette,° *delay*
And to the markis she hir fader fette.° *fetched*

He by the hond than took this olde man,
And seyde thus whan he him hadde asyde,° *off to the side*
"Janicula, I neither may ne can
Lenger the plesance° of myn herte hyde. *pleasure, desire*
If that thou vouche sauf, what so bityde,[5]
Thy doghter wol I take er that° I wende° *before / depart*
As for my wyf, unto hir lyves ende.

Thou lovest me, I woot it wel, certeyn,
And art my feithful lige man y-bore;[6]
And al that lyketh° me, I dar wel seyn *all that which pleases*
It lyketh thee; and specially therfore
Tel me that poynt that I have seyd bifore:[7]
If that thou wolt unto that purpos drawe° *incline*
To take me as for thy sone-in-lawe."

This sodeyn cas this man astoned so
That reed he wex; abayst and al quaking

5. If thou will permit (it), whatever may happen.
6. And were born my faithful vassal.
7. Answer me in that particular that I have named before.

He stood.[8] Unnethes° seyde he wordes mo,° *Scarcely / more*
But only thus: "Lord," quod he, "my willinge
Is as ye wole, ne ayeines° your lykinge *contrary to*
I wol° no thing, ye be my lord so dere. *wish*
Right as yow lust° governeth this matere." *Just as you please*

"Yet wol I," quod this markis softely,
"That in thy chambre I and thou and she
Have a collacion,° and wostow° why? *conference / knowest thou*
For I wol axe° if it hire wille be *ask*
To be my wyf, and reule hire after me.[9]
And al this shal be doon in thy presence—
I wol noght speke out of thyn audience."° *hearing*

And in the chambre whyl they were aboute
Hir tretis,° which as ye shal after here, *Their contract*
The peple cam unto the hous withoute,° *outside*
And wondred hem in how honest manere
And tentifly she kepte hir fader dere.[1]
But outerly° Grisildis wondre mighte, *truly*
For never erst° ne saugh° she swich° a sighte. *before / saw / such*

No wonder is thogh that she were astoned° *bewildered*
To seen so greet a gest° come in that place; *guest*
She never was to swiche gestes woned,° *accustomed*
For° which she loked with ful pale face. *On account of*
But shortly forth this matere for to chace,° *pursue*
Thise arn° the wordes that the markis sayde *are*
To this benigne,° verray,° feithful mayde. *gracious / true*

"Grisilde," he seyde, "ye shul wel understonde
It lyketh to° your fader and to me *It pleases*
That I yow wedde, and eek° it may so stonde,° *also / be the case*
As I suppose, ye wol that it so be.
But thise demandes axe I first," quod he,
"That sith° it shal be doon in hastif wyse,° *since / hastily*
Wol ye assente, or elles yow avyse?° *deliberate*

I seye this, be ye redy with good herte
To al my lust,[2] and that I frely may,
As me best thinketh, do yow laughe or smerte,[3]
And never ye to grucche° it, night ne day? *grumble about*
And eek° whan I sey 'ye,'° ne sey nat 'nay,' *also / yes*
Neither by word ne frowning contenance?
Swere this, and here I swere our alliance."

8. This sudden event astonished this man so much that he grew red; he stood abashed and trembling all over.
9. To be my wife and govern herself according to my will.
1. And they marveled at how decently and attentively she cared for her dear father.
2. To (honor) my every wish.
3. As it seems best to me, make you laugh or suffer.

Wondringe upon this word,° quakinge for drede, *speech*
She seyde, "Lord, undigne° and unworthy *undeserving*
Am I to thilke° honour that ye me bede;° *that same / offer*
But as ye wol yourself, right so wol I.
And heer I swere that nevere willingly
In werk° ne thoght I nil° yow disobeye, *deed / will not*
For to be deed, though me were looth to deye."[4]

"This is ynogh, Grisilde myn!" quod he.
And forth he gooth with a ful sobre chere
Out at the dore, and after that cam she,
And to the peple he seyde in this manere:
"This is my wyf," quod he, "that standeth here.
Honoureth hire and loveth hire I preye
Whoso° me loveth; ther is namore to seye." *Whosoever*

And for that° nothing of hir olde gere° *in order that / apparel*
She sholde bringe into his hous, he bad
That wommen sholde dispoilen° hire right there; *strip*
Of which thise ladyes were nat right glad
To handle hir clothes wherinne she was clad.
But natheles,° this mayde bright of hewe° *nevertheless / hue*
Fro foot to heed they clothed han al newe.

Hir heres° han they kembd,° that lay untressed° *hair / combed / all loose*
Ful rudely,° and with hir° fingres smale *Artlessly / their*
A corone° on hire heed they han y-dressed,° *crown / set*
And sette° hire ful of nowches° grete and smale. *adorned / jewels*
Of hire array what sholde I make a tale?
Unnethe° the peple hir knew for hire fairnesse, *Scarcely*
Whan she translated° was in swich richesse. *transformed, elevated*

This markis hath hire spoused° with a ring *married*
Broght for the same cause, and thanne hire sette
Upon an hors, snow-whyt and wel ambling,° *paced*
And to his paleys,° er° he lenger lette,° *palace / before / delayed*
With joyful peple that hire ladde° and mette, *led*
Conveyed hire; and thus the day they spende
In revel, til the sonne gan descende.° *did set*

And shortly forth this tale for to chace,° *pursue*
I seye that to this newe markisesse° *marchioness*
God hath swich° favour sent hire of his grace, *such*
That it ne semed nat by lyklinesse° *likely*
That she was born and fed in rudenesse,° *lowliness*
As in a cote° or in an oxe-stalle, *cottage*
But norished in an emperoures halle.

4. Even to die, though I would be loath to die.

To every wight° she woxen is° so dere *person / has grown*
And worshipful, that folk ther she was bore[5]
And from hire birthe knewe hire yeer by yere,
Unnethe trowed they—but dorste han swore[6]—
That to Janicle, of which I spak bifore,
She doghter were, for, as by conjecture,
Hem thoughte° she was another creature. *It seemed to them*

For thogh that evere vertuous was she,
She was encressed in swich excellence
Of thewes° gode, y-set in heigh bountee,° *qualities / goodness*
And so discreet° and fair of eloquence,° *wise / speech*
So benigne° and so digne° of reverence,° *gracious / worthy / honor*
And coude so the peples herte embrace,[7]
That ech hire lovede that loked on hir face.

Noght only of Saluces° in the toun *Saluzzo*
Publiced° was the bountee° of hir name, *Made known / goodness*
But eek° bisyde in many a regioun: *also*
If oon° seyde wel, another seyde the same. *one*
So spradde° of hire heighe bountee the fame *spread*
That men and wommen, as wel yonge as olde,
Gon to Saluce upon hire to biholde.

Thus Walter lowly—nay but royally—
Wedded with fortunat honestetee,° *honor*
In Goddes pees° liveth ful esily *God's peace*
At hoom, and outward grace ynogh had he;
And for° he saugh° that under low degree *because / saw*
Was ofte vertu hid, the peple him helde
A prudent man, and that is seyn° ful selde.° *seen / seldom*

Nat only this Grisildis thurgh hir wit
Coude al the feet of wyfly hoomlinesse,[8]
But eek,° whan that the cas requyred it, *also*
The commune profit° coude she redresse.° *general welfare / amend*
Ther nas° discord, rancour, ne hevinesse° *was not / i.e., of heart*
In al that lond that she ne coude apese,° *appease*
And wysly bringe hem alle in reste and ese.

Though that hire housbonde absent were, anoon° *at once*
If gentil men or othere of hire contree
Were wrothe,° she wolde bringen hem atoon;° *angered / into accord*
So wyse and rype° wordes hadde she, *mature*
And jugements of so greet equitee,° *fairness*
That she from heven sent was, as men wende,° *they supposed*
Peple to save and every wrong t'amende.° *to amend*

5. And worthy of honor, that people where she was born.
6. They could scarcely believe—though they'd have dared to swear it.
7. And so (well) knew how to hold fast the hearts of the people.
8. Knew all the feats (skills) of a wife's household duties.

Nat longe tyme after that this Grisild
Was wedded, she a doughter hath y-bore.° *borne*
Al had hire levere have born a knave child,[9]
Glad was this markis and the folk therfore;
For though a mayde child come al bifore,
She may unto a knave child atteyne
By lyklihed, sin she nis nat bareyne.[1]

PART THREE

Ther fil, as it bifalleth tymes mo,[2]
Whan that this child had souked° but a throwe,° *nursed / short time*
This markis° in his herte longeth so *marquis*
To tempte his wyf, hir sadnesse° for to knowe, *steadfastness*
That he ne mighte out of his herte throwe
This merveillous° desyr, his wyf t'assaye;° *strange / to test*
Needless,° God woot,° he thoughte hire for t'affraye.° *Needlessly / knows* *to frighten*

He hadde assayed hire ynogh bifore
And fond hire evere good. What needed it
Hire for to tempte and alwey° more and more, *continually*
Though som men preise it for a subtil wit?
But as for me, I seye that yvel it sit[3]
T'assaye a wyf whan that it is no nede,
And putten hire in anguish and in drede.

For which this markis wroghte in this manere:
He cam alone a-night,° ther as° she lay, *by night / there where*
With sterne face and with ful trouble chere,° *troubled countenance*
And seyde thus: "Grisilde," quod he, "that day
That I yow took out of your povre array° *condition of poverty*
And putte yow in estaat of heigh noblesse,
Ye have nat that forgeten, as I gesse.

I seye, Grisild, this present dignitee,
In which that I have put yow, as I trowe,° *believe*
Maketh yow nat foryetful° for to be *forgetful*
That I yow took in povre estaat ful lowe.
For any wele° ye moot° yourselven knowe, *happiness / may*
Take hede of every word that I yow seye:
Ther is no wight° that hereth it but we tweye.° *no one / two*

Ye woot° yourself wel how that ye cam here *know*
Into this hous, it is nat longe ago,
And though to me that ye be lief° and dere, *beloved*
Unto my gentils° ye be no thing° so; *gentlefolk / not at all*

9. Although she had rather have borne a male child.
1. Quite probably, since she is not barren.
2. It happened, as it often happens.
3. It ill becomes (a man), i.e., is evil.

They seyn, to hem it is greet shame and wo
For to be subgets° and ben in servage° — *subjects / waiting, servitude*
To thee, that born art of a smal village.

And namely sith thy doghter was y-bore° — *born*
Thise wordes han they spoken, douteless;
But I desyre, as I have doon bifore,
To live my lyf with hem in reste and pees;° — *peace*
I may nat in this caas° be recchelees.° — *matter / heedless*
I moot° don with thy doghter for the beste, — *must*
Nat as I wolde, but as my peple leste.[4]

And yet, God wot,° this is ful looth° to me. — *knows / hateful*
But nathelees° withoute your witing° — *nevertheless / knowledge*
I wol nat doon;° but this wol I," quod he, — *act*
"That ye to me assente as in this thing.
Shewe now youre pacience in youre werking° — *deeds*
That ye me highte° and swore in your village — *promised*
That day that maked was oure mariage."

Whan she had herd al this, she noght ameved° — *made no motion*
Neither in word or chere° or countenaunce; — *manner*
For as it semed, she was nat agreved.
She seyde, "Lord, al lyth° in youre plesaunce; — *lies*
My child and I with hertely° obeisaunce — *sincere*
Ben youres al,° and ye mowe° save or spille° — *wholly / may / destroy*
Youre owene thing: werketh after° youre wille. — *according to*

Ther may no thing, God so my soule save,
Lyken to yow° that may displese me; — *Please you*
Ne I desyre no thing for to have,
Ne drede for to lese, save only ye;
This wil is in myn herte and ay° shal be. — *ever*
No lengthe of tyme or deeth may this deface,
Ne chaunge my corage° to another place." — *heart*

Glad was this markis of° hire answering, — *for*
But yet he feyned° as he were nat so; — *feigned*
Al drery° was his chere° and his loking — *sad / face*
Whan that he sholde out of the chambre go.
Sone after this, a furlong wey or two,[5]
He prively° hath told al his entente° — *secretly / plan, intention*
Unto a man, and to his wyf him sente.

A maner sergeant was this privee man,[6]
The which that feithful ofte he founden hadde
In thinges grete, and eek° swich° folk wel can — *also / such*

4. Not as I would wish, but as my people desire.
5. I.e., within a little while (the length of time it takes to walk a furlong—one-eighth of a mile—or two).
6. This trusted man was a kind of sergeant-at-law.

Don execucioun in° thinges badde. *Perform*
The lord knew wel that he him loved and dradde;° *feared*
And whan this sergeant wiste° his lordes wille, *knew*
Into the chambre he stalked him ful stille.° *crept very quietly*

"Madame," he seyde, "ye mote foryeve° it me, *must forgive*
Thogh I do thing to which I am constreyned.
Ye ben so wys that ful wel knowe ye
That lordes hestes° mowe° nat been y-feyned;° *commands / may / avoided*
They mowe wel been biwailled or compleyned,° *lamented*
But men mot nede° unto hire lust° obeye, *needs must / their will*
And so wol I; ther is na more to seye.

This child I am comanded for to take"—
And spak na more, but out the child he hente° *seized*
Despitously,° and gan a chere make° *Cruelly / i.e., acted*
As though he wolde han slayn it er° he wente.° *before / left*
Grisildis mot° al suffren and al consente; *must*
And as a lamb she sitteth meke and stille,
And leet this cruel sergeant doon his wille.

Suspecious was the diffame° of this man, *bad reputation*
Suspect[7] his face, suspect his word also;
Suspect the tyme in which he this bigan.
Allas! hir doghter that she lovede so,
She wende° he wolde han slawen° it right tho.° *thought / slain / then*
But natheles she neither weep ne syked,° *wept nor sighed*
Conforminge hire to that the markis lyked.[8]

But atte laste° speken she bigan, *finally*
And mekely she to the sergeant preyde,° *begged*
So as he was a worthy gentil man,
That she moste° kisse hire child er° that it deyde;° *might / before / died*
And in hir barm° this litel child she leyde° *lap / laid*
With ful sad face, and gan the child to blisse[9]
And lulled it, and after gan it kisse.

And thus she seyde in hire benigne voys,° *gracious voice*
"Far weel, my child; I shal thee nevere see.
But, sith° I thee have marked with the croys° *since / cross*
Of thilke° Fader, blessed mote he be, *that same*
That for us deyde upon a croys of tree,° *wood*
Thy soule, litel child, I him bitake,° *entrust to Him*
For this night shaltow° dyen for my sake." *shalt thou*

I trowe° that to a norice° in this cas *believe / nurse*
It had ben hard this rewthe° for to se; *pitiful sight*

7. I.e., ominous, foreboding (causing suspicion).
8. Conforming her (conduct) to what was pleasing to the marquis.
9. With a most somber face, and blessed the child.

Wel° mighte a mooder than han cryed "allas!" — *i.e., Well more*
But nathelees so sad° stedfast was she — *firmly*
That she endured all adversitee,
And to the sergeant mekely she sayde,
"Have heer agayn your litel yonge mayde.

Goth now," quod she, "and dooth my lordes heste.° — *command*
But o° thing wol I preye yow of youre grace, — *one*
That, but° my lord forbad yow, atte leste° — *unless / at (the) least*
Burieth this litel body in som place
That bestes ne no briddes it torace."[1]
But he no word wol to that purpos seye,
But took the child and wente upon his weye.

This sergeant cam unto his lord ageyn,
And of Grisildis wordes and hire chere° — *behavior*
He tolde him point for point, in short and playn,° — *briefly and clearly*
And him presenteth with his doghter dere.
Somwhat this lord hath rewthe in his manere,[2]
But nathelees his purpos heeld he stille,
As lordes doon whan they wol han hir wille.

And bad this sergeant that he prively° — *in secret*
Sholde this child softe winde and wrappe° — *i.e., cover with clothing*
With alle circumstances° tendrely, — *In every detail*
And carie it in a cofre° or in a lappe;° — *box / cloth*
But, upon peyne his heed of for to swappe,[3]
That no man sholde knowe of his entente,° — *purpose*
Ne whenne° he cam, ne whider° that he wente; — *whence / whither*

But at Boloigne° to his suster° dere, — *Bologna / sister*
That thilke° tyme of Panik[4] was countesse, — *(at) that same*
He sholde it take, and shewe hire° this matere, — *explain*
Bisekinge hire to don hire bisinesse
This child to fostre in alle gentilesse;[5]
And whos child that it was he bad hire hyde
From every wight, for oght that may bityde.[6]

The sergeant gooth, and hath fulfild this thing;
But to this markis now retourne we.
For now goth he ful faste imagining° — *intently wondering*
If by his wyves chere° he mighte see, — *countenance*
Or by hire word aperceyve,° that she — *perceive*
Were chaunged; but he never hire coude finde
But ever in oon ylyke sad° and kinde. — *consistently steadfast*

1. (So) that no beasts or birds tear it to pieces.
2. This lord showed something of pity in his behavior.
3. But on pain of having his head struck off.
4. Panico, near Bologna.
5. Beseeching her to give her careful attention to the raising of this child, in all things proper to gentle birth.
6. From every man, no matter what might happen.

As glad, as humble, as bisy in servyse,
And eek° in love as she was wont° to be, *also / accustomed*
Was she to him in every manner wyse;° *sort of way*
Ne of hir doghter noght a word spak she.
Non accident° for noon adversitee *outward sign*
Was seyn in hire, ne never hir doghter° name *daughter's*
Ne nempned° she, in ernest nor in game.° *named / play*

PART FOUR

In this estaat° ther passed been foure yeer *condition*
Er° she with childe was; but, as God wolde, *Before*
A knave° child she bar° by this Walter, *male / bore*
Ful gracious and fair° for to biholde. *handsome*
And whan that folk it to his fader tolde,
Nat only he, but al his contree, merie
Was for this child, and God they thanke and herie.° *praise*

When it was two yeer old and fro the brest
Departed of his norice,° on a day *nurse*
This markis caughte° yet another lest° *conceived / desire*
To tempte his wyf yet ofter,° if he may. *more often*
O needles was she tempted in assay!° *trial*
But wedded men ne knowe no mesure° *moderation*
Whan that they finde a pacient creature.

"Wyf," quod this markis, "ye han herd er° this, *before*
My peple sikly berth° oure mariage, *bear ill, dislike*
And namely, sith° my sone y-boren° is, *since / born*
Now is it worse than ever in al our age.° *time*
The murmur sleeth° myn herte and my corage,° *slays / spirit*
For to myne eres° comth the voys so smerte° *ears / sharply*
That it wel ny° destroyed hath myn herte. *well nigh, almost*

Now sey they thus, 'Whan Walter is agoon,° *gone, dead*
Thanne shal the blood of Janicle succede
And been our Lord, for other have we noon.'
Swiche wordes seith my peple, out of drede.° *there is no doubt*
Wel oughte I of swich° murmur taken hede, *such*
For certeinly, I drede swich sentence,° *opinion*
Though they nat pleyn° speke in myn audience.° *plainly / hearing*

I wolde live in pees° if that I mighte; *peace*
Wherfor I am disposed outerly,° *entirely*
As I his suster servede° by nighte, *dealt with*
Right so thenke I to serve him prively.° *in secret*
This warne I yow, that ye nat sodeynly
Out of youreself for no wo sholde outraye.[7]
Beth pacient, and therof I yow preye."

7. Should lose control of yourself for any sorrow.

"I have," quod she, "seyd thus, and ever shal,
I wol no thing ne nil° no thing, certayn, *desire not*
But as yow list; noght greveth me at al,[8]
Thogh that my doghter and my sone be slayn—
At your comandement, this is to sayn.
I have noght had no part of children tweyne° *the two children*
But first siknesse,° and after wo and peyne. *i.e., in childbearing*

Ye been oure lord, doth with youre owene thing
Right as yow list; axeth no reed at me.[9]
For as I lefte at hoom° al my clothing *home*
Whan I first cam to yow, right so," quod she,
"Left I my wil and al my libertee,
And took your clothing. Wherfore I yow preye,
Doth your plesaunce; I wol youre lust° obeye. *desire*

And certes,° if I hadde prescience° *certainly / foreknowledge*
Your will to knowe er° ye youre lust° me tolde, *before / pleasure, will*
I wolde it doon withouten necligence.
But now I woot° youre lust and what ye wolde, *know*
Al youre plesaunce ferme° and stable° I holde; *firmly / steadfastly*
For wiste I° that my deeth wolde do yow ese,° *if I knew / give you pleasure*
Right gladly wolde I dyen, yow to plese.

Deth may noght make no comparisoun
Unto youre love." And whan this markis sey° *saw*
The constance° of his wyf, he caste adoun *constancy*
His eyen two,° and wondreth that she may *two eyes*
In pacience suffre al this array.° *all these things*
And forth he gooth with drery° contenaunce, *doleful*
But to his herte it was ful greet plesaunce.

This ugly° sergeant, in the same wyse° *fearsome / way*
That he hire doghter caughte,° right so he— *took away*
Or worse, if men worse can devyse—
Hath hent° hire sone that ful was of beautee. *seized*
And evere in oon° so pacient was she *always*
That she no chere° made of hevinesse,[1] *appearance*
But kiste° hir sone, and after gan it blesse.° *kissed / blessed him*

Save this:° she preyede him that if he mighte *Except for this*
Hir litel sone he wolde in erthe grave,° *bury*
His tendre limes,° delicat to sighte, *limbs*
Fro foules° and fro bestes for to save. *birds*
But she non answer of him mighte have.
He wente his wey, as him nothing ne roghte,[2]
But to Boloigne he tendrely it broghte.

8. But as it pleases you; it doesn't grieve me at all.
9. Just as you please; ask no advice from me.
1. I.e., of a heavy heart.
2. He went on his way as though he didn't care at all.

This markis wondreth evere lenger the more° *i.e., increasingly*
Upon hir pacience, and if that he
Ne hadde soothly° knowen ther-bifore *truly*
That parfitly hir children loved she,
He wolde have wend° that of° som subtiltee,° *thought / out of / trick*
And of malice or for cruel corage,° *heart*
That she had suffred this with sad visage.° *unchanged countenance*

But wel he knew that next himself, certayn,° *certainly*
She loved hir children best in every wyse.
But now of wommen wolde I axen fayn,[3]
If thise assayes° mighte nat suffyse? *trials*
What coude a sturdy° housbond more devyse *cruel*
To preve° hir wyfhod and hir stedfastnesse, *prove, test*
And he continuinge evere in sturdinesse?° *cruelty*

But ther ben folk of swich condicioun° *such disposition*
That, whan they have a certein purpos take,° *decided on*
They can nat stinte° of hire entencioun;° *stop short / intention*
But right as° they were bounden to a stake, *just as if*
They wol nat of that firste purpos slake.° *leave off*
Right so this markis fulliche° hath purposed° *fully / intended*
To tempte his wyf as he was first disposed.

He waiteth° if by word or contenance *watches*
That she to him was changed of corage,° *in her heart*
But never coude he finde variance:
She was ay° oon in herte and in visage. *ever*
And ay the forther° that she was in age, *i.e., older*
The more trewe, if that it were possible,
She was to him in love, and more penible.° *painstaking*

For which it semed thus, that of hem two° *for them both*
Ther nas° but o° wil; for, as Walter leste,° *was not / one / wished*
The same lust° was hire plesance also; *desire*
And, God be thanked, al fil° for the beste. *turned out*
She shewed wel for no worldly unreste[4]
A wyf, as of hirself,° no thing ne sholde *for her own sake*
Wille in effect° but as hir housbond wolde. *Wish in fact*

The sclaundre° of Walter ofte and wyde spradde° *scandalous report / spread*
That of a cruel herte he wikkedly,
For° he a povre womman wedded hadde, *Because*
Hath mordred° bothe his children prively.° *murdered / secretly*
Swich° murmur was among hem comunly.° *Such / them generally*
No wonder is, for to the peples ere° *ear*
Ther cam no word but that they mordred were.

3. But now I would like to ask of (you) women.
4. (That) for no earthly distress.

For which, wher as his peple therbifore
Had loved him wel, the sclaundre of his diffame° — *ill repute*
Made hem that they him hatede therfore:° — *for it*
To been a mordrer is an hateful name.
But natheles, for ernest ne for game,
He of his cruel purpos nolde stente.° — *would not desist*
To tempte his wyf was set al his entente.

Whan that his doghter twelf yeer was of age,
He to the court of Rome, in subtil wyse° — *secretly*
Enformed of his wil, sente his message,° — *messenger(s)*
Comaundinge hem swiche bulles to devyse[5]
As to his cruel purpos may suffyse:
How that the Pope, as for his peples reste,
Bad° him to wedde another if him leste.° — *Bid / if he wished*

I seye, he bad they sholde countrefete° — *counterfeit*
The Popes bulles, makinge mencioun
That he hath leve° his firste wyf to lete,° — *permission / to leave*
As by the Popes dispensacioun,
To stinte° rancour and dissencioun — *stop*
Bitwixe his peple and him—thus seyde the bulle,
The which they han publiced atte fulle.° — *published widely*

The rude° peple, as it no wonder is, — *ignorant*
Wenden° ful wel that it had been right so; — *Thought*
But whan thise tydinges cam to Grisildis,
I deme° that hire herte was ful wo. — *i.e., am certain*
But she, ylyke sad° for evermo, — *uniformly steadfast*
Disposed was, this humble creature,
Th'adversitee of Fortune al t'endure,° — *wholly to endure*

Abydinge evere° his lust and his plesaunce, — *Waiting ever upon*
To whom that she was yeven° herte and al, — *given*
As to hire verray worldly suffisaunce.[6]
But shortly if this storie I tellen shal,
This markis writen hath in special
A lettre in which he sheweth° his entente, — *reveals*
And secrely he to Boloigne it sente.

To the Erl° of Panik,° which that hadde tho° — *Earl / Panico / then*
Wedded his suster, preyde° he specially — *requested*
To bringen hoom agayn his children two
In honurable estaat° al openly. — *state*
But o° thing he him preyede outerly,° — *one / above all*
That he to no wight,° though men wolde enquere,° — *nobody / inquire*
Sholde nat telle whos° children that they were, — *whose*

5. Commanding them (i.e., those at the court of Rome) to contrive such (papal) bulls.
6. As (being) her true, earthly contentment (refers back to "his lust and his plesaunce" in l. 757).

But seye the mayden sholde y-wedded be° *was to be wed*
Unto the Markis of Saluce° anon.° *Saluzzo / immediately*
And as this erl was preyed, so dide he,
For at day set° he on his wey is goon *on the day appointed*
Toward Saluce, and lordes many oon° *many a lord*
In riche array, this mayden for to gyde,° *conduct*
Hir yonge brother rydinge hire bisyde.

Arrayed was toward° hir mariage *for*
This fresshe mayde, ful of gemmes clere;° *shining jewels*
Hir brother, which that seven yeer was of age,
Arrayed eek° ful fresh in his manere. *also*
And thus in greet noblesse° and with glad chere,° *magnificence / aspect*
Toward Saluces shapinge° hir journey, *making*
Fro day to day they ryden in hir° wey. *on their*

PART FIVE

Among al this, after his wikke usage,° *wicked custom*
This markis yet his wyf to tempte more
To the uttereste preve° of hir corage,° *utmost proof / heart, spirit*
Fully to han experience and lore° *knowledge*
If that she were as stedfast as bifore,
He on a day in open audience° *assembly*
Ful boistously° hath seyd hire this sentence:° *roughly / decision*

"Certes,° Grisilde, I hadde ynough plesaunce *Truly*
To han yow to my wyf for youre goodnesse—
As for youre trouthe and for youre obeisaunce—
Nought for youre linage ne for your richesse.
But now knowe I in verray soothfastnesse° *certain truth*
That in gret lordshipe, if I wel avyse,° *discern*
Ther is gret servitute in sondry wyse.° *in sundry ways*

I may nat don as every° plowman may. *any*
My peple me constreyneth° for to take *constrain*
Another wyf, and cryen° day by day; *call (for it)*
And eek the Pope, rancour for to slake,° *appease*
Consenteth it,° that dar I undertake,° *Consents to it / declare*
And treweliche thus muche I wol yow seye,
My newe wyf is coming by° the weye. *along*

Be strong of herte, and voyde anon° hir place; *vacate at once*
And thilke° dowere that ye broghten me *that same*
Tak it agayn, I graunte it of my grace.
Retourneth to your fadres hous," quod he.
"No man may alwey han prosperitee;
With evene° herte I rede° yow t'endure *steady / advise*
The strook° of Fortune or of aventure."° *stroke / chance*

And she agayn answerde in pacience,
"My lord," quod she, "I woot,° and wiste° alway, *know / knew*
How that bitwixen° youre magnificence *between*
And my poverte no wight° can ne may *no one*
Maken comparison; it is no nay.° *it cannot be denied*
I ne heeld me nevere digne° in no manere *worthy*
To be youre wyf, no, ne youre chamberere.° *chambermaid*

And in this hous ther° ye me lady made— *where*
The heighe God take I for my witnesse,
And also wisly° he my soule glade°— *as surely / may gladden*
I nevere heeld me° lady ne maistresse, *considered myself*
But humble servant to youre worthinesse,
And ever shal, whyl that my lyf may dure,° *last*
Aboven every worldly creature.

That ye so longe of youre benignitee° *graciousness*
Han holden me in honour and nobleye,° *nobleness*
Wher as I was noght worthy for to be,
That thonke I God and yow, to whom I preye
Foryelde° it yow. There is namore to seye. *Repay*
Unto my fader gladly wol I wende,° *go*
And with him dwelle unto my lyves ende.

Ther I was fostred of° a child ful smal, *raised from*
Til I be deed, my lyf ther wol I lede:
A widwe clene,° in body, herte, and al. *widow pure*
For sith I yaf° to yow my maydenhede, *gave*
And am youre trewe wyf, it is no drede,° *without doubt*
God shilde° swich a lordes wyf to take *forbid*
Another man to housbonde or to make.° *as mate*

And of youre newe wyf, God of his grace
So graunte yow wele° and prosperitee! *happiness*
For I wol gladly yelden hire° my place, *yield to her*
In which that I was blisful wont° to be. *accustomed*
For sith it lyketh yow,° my lord," quod she, *since it pleases you*
"That° whylom° weren al myn hertes reste, *Who / formerly*
That I shal goon,° I wol gon whan yow leste. *must go*

But ther as ye me profre swich dowaire° *such a dowry*
As I first broghte, it is wel in my minde
It were my wrecched clothes, nothing° faire, *in no way*
The which to me were hard now for to finde.
O gode God! how gentil and how kynde
Ye semed by youre speche and youre visage° *face, appearance*
The day that maked was oure mariage!

But sooth is seyd—algate I finde it trewe,[7]
For in effect it preved is on° me— *is proven in*

7. But it is truly said—in any case, I find it true.

Love is noght° old as whan that it is newe. *not (the same)*
But certes, lord, for noon adversitee,
To dyen in the cas, it shal nat be[8]
That evere in word or werk° I shal repente *deed*
That I yow yaf° myn herte in hool entente.° *gave / wholeheartedly*

My lord, ye woot° that in my fadres place *know*
Ye dide me strepe out of my povre wede,[9]
And richely me cladden, of° youre grace. *by*
To yow broghte I noght elles, out of drede,° *there is no doubt*
But feyth° and nakednesse and maydenhede. *loyalty*
And here agayn your clothing I restore,
And eek° your wedding ring, for everemore. *also*

The remenant of your jewels redy be° *is prepared*
Inwith° your chambre, dar I saufly° sayn. *Within / safely*
Naked out of my fadres hous," quod she,
"I cam, and naked moot° I turne° agayn. *must / return*
Al youre plesaunce wol I folwen fayn.° *follow willingly*
But yet I hope it be nat youre entente
That I smoklees[1] out of youre paleys wente.° *should go*

Ye coude nat doon so dishoneste a thing
That thilke wombe in which youre children leye° *lay*
Sholde biforn the peple, in my walking,
Be seyn al bare;° wherfore I yow preye, *naked*
Lat me nat lyk a worm go by° the weye. *along*
Remembre yow, myn owene lord so dere,
I was youre wyf, thogh I unworthy were.

Wherfore in guerdon° of my maydenhede, *recompense*
Which that I broghte, and noght agayn I bere,° *bear*
As voucheth sauf to yeve me to my mede[2]
But swich° a smok as I was wont° to were, *Only such / used*
That I therwith may wrye° the wombe of here° *hide / her*
That was youre wyf. And heer take I my leve° *leave*
Of yow, myn owene lord, lest I yow greve."° *vex*

"The smok," quod he, "that thou hast on thy bak,
Lat it be° stille, and bere° it forth with thee." *remain / bear*
But wel unnethes° thilke° word he spak *hardly / that same*
But wente his wey for rewthe° and for pitee. *compassion*
Biforn the folk hirselven strepeth° she, *strips*
And in hir smok, with heed and foot al bare,
Toward hir fader hous forth is she fare.[3]

8. (Even) if I should die in this affair, it shall not be.
9. You had me stripped out of my poor clothing.
1. Smockless, without even an undergarment.
2. Just allow me to be given as my reward (my pay).
3. She has journeyed forth toward her father's house.

The folk hire folwe wepinge in hir weye,° *on their way*
And Fortune ay they cursen as they goon.
But she fro weping kepte hire eyen dreye,° *eyes dry*
Ne in this tyme word ne spak she noon.
Hir fader, that this tydinge° herde anoon, *news*
Curseth the day and tyme that nature
Shoop° him to been a lyves° creature. *Created / living*

For out of doute° this olde povre man *certainly*
Was evere in suspect° of hir mariage; *doubtful*
For evere he demed,° sith° that it bigan, *thought / since*
That whan the lord fulfild hadde his corage,° *desire*
Him wolde thinke it were a disparage[4]
To his estaat° so lowe for t'alighte,° *rank / to settle*
And voyden° hire as sone as ever he mighte. *(would) get rid of*

Agayns° his doghter hastilich° goth he, *Toward / hastily*
For he by noyse of folk knew hire cominge,
And with hire old cote, as it mighte be,[5]
He covered hire ful sorwefully wepinge.
But on° hire body mighte he it nat bringe, *around*
For rude was the cloth and she more of age
By dayes fele° than at hire mariage. *many*

Thus with hire fader for a certeyn space° *space of time*
Dwelleth this flour° of wyfly pacience, *flower*
That neither by hire wordes ne hire face
Biforn° the folk, ne eek in hire° absence, *In front of / their*
Ne shewed she that hire° was doon offence; *to her*
Ne of hire heighe estaat no remembraunce
Ne hadde she, as by° hire countenaunce. *to judge by*

No wonder is, for in hire grete° estaat *high*
Hire goost° was evere in pleyn° humylitee: *spirit / perfect*
No tendre mouth, noon herte delicaat,
No pompe, no semblant° of royaltee, *semblance*
But ful of pacient benignitee,° *graciousness*
Discreet and prydeles,° ay° honurable, *without pride / ever*
And to hire housbonde evere meke and stable.° *constant*

Men speke of Job and most° for his humblesse,° *above all / humbleness*
As clerkes, whan hem list, can wel endyte,° *write*
Namely of men; but as in soothfastnesse,° *with regard to truth*
Thogh clerkes preyse wommen but a lyte,° *very little*
Ther can no man in humblesse him acquyte° *acquit himself*
As womman can, ne can ben half so trewe
As wommen been, but it be falle of newe.[6]

4. It would seem to him that it was a disgrace.
5. And with her old cloak, as well as he could.
6. Unless it has happened just recently.

PART SIX

Fro Boloigne is this Erl of Panik come,
Of which the fame up sprang° to more and lesse,° *arose / great and small*
And in the peples eres° alle and some° *ears / i.e., one and all*
Was couth eek° that a newe markisesse *It was known also*
He with him broghte, in swich pompe and richesse,
That never was ther seyn with mannes yë° *eye*
So noble array in al West Lumbardye.

The markis, which that shoop° and knew al this, *planned*
Er that° this erl was° come sente his message° *Before / had / messenger*
For thilke° sely° povre Grisildis; *that same / good*
And she with humble herte and glad visage,
Nat with no swollen° thoght in hire corage,° *i.e., prideful / heart*
Cam at his heste,° and on hire knees hire sette, *command*
And reverently and wysly° she him grette.° *discreetly / greeted*

"Grisild," quod he, "my wille is outrely° *completely*
This mayden, that shal wedded been to me,
Receyved be tomorwe as royally
As it possible is in myn hous to be,
And eek that every wight° in his degree *person*
Have his estaat in sitting° and servyse *proper place at table*
And heigh plesaunce, as I can best devyse.

I have no wommen suffisaunt,° certayn, *not women enough*
The chambres for t'arraye in ordinaunce° *to put in order*
After my lust, and therfor wolde I fayn[7]
That thyn° were al swich maner governaunce; *thine*
Thou knowest eek of old al my plesaunce.
Though thyn array° be badde and yvel biseye,° *apparel / poor to see*
Do thou thy devoir° at the leeste weye."° *duty / all the same*

"Nat only, lord, that I am glad," quod she,
"To doon youre lust, but I desyre also
Yow for to serve and plese in my degree° *according to my station*
Withouten feynting,° and shal everemo. *weariness*
Ne nevere, for no wele ne no wo,
Ne shal the gost° withinne myn herte stente° *spirit / cease*
To love yow best with al my trewe entente."

And with that word she gan° the hous to dighte,° *began / to make ready*
And tables for to sette and beddes make;
And peyned hir° to doon al that she mighte, *she took pains*
Preying the chambereres,° for Goddes sake, *Urging the chambermaids*
To hasten hem,° and faste swepe and shake. *To hurry*
And she, the most servisable° of alle, *diligent*
Hath every chambre arrayed and his halle.

7. According to my desire, and therefore I would be pleased.

Abouten undern gan this erl alighte,[8]
That with him broghte thise noble children tweye,
For which the peple ran to seen the sighte
Of hire° array, so richely biseye;° *their / rich to see*
And thanne at erst amonges hem they seye[9]
That Walter was no fool thogh that him leste° *it pleased him*
To chaunge his wyf, for it was for the beste.

For she is fairer, as they demen° alle, *judge*
Than is Grisild, and more tendre° of age, *young*
And fairer fruit° bitwene hem sholde falle, *offspring*
And more plesant, for hire heigh linage;[1]
Hir brother eek so fair was of visage
That hem° to seen the peple hath caught° plesaunce, *them / taken*
Commendinge now the markis governaunce.° *conduct*

"O stormy peple! unsad and evere untrewe!
Ay undiscreet and chaunging as a vane![2]
Delytinge evere in rumbel° that is newe, *rumor*
For lyk the mone ay wexe° ye and wane! *wax, grow larger*
Ay ful of clapping, dere ynogh a jane![3]
Youre doom is fals, youre constance yvel preveth,[4]
A ful greet fool is he that on yow leveth!"° *believes in you*

Thus seyden sadde° folk in that citee, *steadfast*
Whan that the peple gazed up and doun,
For they were glad, right° for the noveltee, *just*
To han a newe lady of hir toun.
Namore of this make I now mencioun,
But to Grisilde agayn wol I me dresse,° *address myself*
And telle hir constance and hir bisinesse.

Ful bisy was Grisilde in every thing
That to the feste was apertinent;° *appertained*
Right noght was she abayst° of hire clothing, *ashamed*
Though it were rude and somdel eek torent.° *also somewhat torn*
But with glad chere to the yate° is went° *gate / has gone*
With other folk, to grete the markisesse,
And after that doth forth° hire bisinesse. *continues*

With so glad chere his gestes she receyveth,
And so conningly, everich in his degree,
That no defaute no man aperceyveth;[5]
But ay they wondren what she mighte be

8. About midmorning this earl arrived (literally, dismounted).
9. And then for the first time they say amongst themselves.
1. Because of her noble birth (lineage).
2. Ever unwise, and changeable as a weather vane.
3. Ever full of chatter, not worth a penny (a "jane").
4. Your judgment is false, your constancy proves poor.
5. She receives his guests in so happy a mood and (so) skillfully—every one according to his rank—that no one (could) discover anything lacking.

That in so povre array was for to see,
And coude° swich honour and reverence; *understood*
And worthily they preisen° hire prudence. *praise*

In al this mene whyle she ne stente° *did not cease*
This mayde and eek hir brother to commende
With al hir herte, in ful benigne entente,
So wel that no man coude hir prys° amende.° *praise / improve*
But atte laste,° whan that thise lordes wende° *at (the) last / thought*
To sitten doun to mete,° he gan to calle *to the meal*
Grisilde, as she was bisy in his halle.

"Grisilde," quod he, as° it were in his pley, *as if*
"How lyketh thee my wyf and hire beautee?"
"Right wel," quod she, "my lord, for in good fey,° *faith*
A fairer say° I nevere noon than she. *saw*
I prey to God yeve° hire prosperitee, *give*
And so hope I that he wol to yow sende
Plesance ynogh unto youre lyves ende.

O° thing biseke° I yow, and warne also, *One / beseech*
That ye ne prikke° with no tormentinge *goad*
This tendre mayden, as ye han don mo.° *others*
For she is fostred° in hire norishinge° *raised / upbringing*
More tendrely, and to my supposinge,
She coude nat adversitee endure
As coude a povre fostred° creature." *raised in poverty*

And whan this Walter saugh° hire pacience, *saw*
Hir glade chere and no malice at al—
And he so ofte had doon to hire offence,
And she ay sad° and constant as a wal, *ever firm*
Continuinge evere hire innocence overal°— *in every respect*
This sturdy markis gan his herte dresse[6]
To rewen° upon hire wyfly stedfastnesse. *take pity*

"This is ynogh,° Grisilde myn," quod he, *enough*
"Be now namore agast° ne yvel apayed;° *afraid / ill pleased*
I have thy feith° and thy benignitee, *faithfulness*
As wel as ever womman was, assayed° *tested*
In greet° estaat and povreliche° arrayed. *high / poorly*
Now knowe I, dere wyf, thy stedfastnesse,"
And hire in armes took and gan hire kesse.° *kissed her*

And she for wonder took of it no keep;° *heed*
She herde nat what thing he to hire seyde;
She ferde as° she had stert° out of a sleep, *acted as if / started*
Til she out of hir masednesse° abreyde.° *bewilderment / awoke*

6. This cruel (stern) marquis did turn his heart.

"Grisilde," quod he, "by God that for us deyde,
Thou art my wyf, ne noon other I have,
Ne never hadde, as God my soule save!

This is thy doghter which thou hast supposed
To be my wyf; that other feithfully
Shal be myn heir, as I have ay disposed;° *ever intended*
Thou bare° him in thy body trewely. *bore*
At Boloigne have I kept hem prively;° *secretly*
Tak hem agayn, for now maystow° nat seye *mayest thou*
That thou hast lorn° non of thy children tweye. *lost*

And folk that otherweyes° han seyd of me, *otherwise*
I warne hem wel that I have doon this dede
For no malice ne for no crueltee,
But for t'assaye in thee thy wommanhede,
And nat to sleen° my children, God forbede! *slay*
But for to kepe hem prively and stille,° *quietly*
Til I thy purpos knewe and al thy wille."

Whan she this herde, aswowne° doun she falleth *in a faint*
For pitous joye, and after hire swowninge
She bothe hire yonge children to hire calleth,
And in hire armes, pitously wepinge,
Embraceth hem, and tenderly kissinge,
Ful lyk a mooder, with hire salte teres
She batheth bothe hire visage° and hire heres.° *their faces / hair*

O, which a° pitous thing it was to see *what a*
Hir swowning, and hire humble voys° to here! *voice*
"Grauntmercy,° lord, God thanke° it yow," quod she, *Great thanks / reward*
"That ye han saved me my children dere!
Now rekke I never to ben deed right here;[7]
Sith° I stonde in youre love and in youre grace, *Since*
No fors of deeth, ne whan my spirit pace.[8]

O tendre, o dere, o yonge children myne,
Your woful mooder wende° stedfastly *thought*
That cruel houndes or som foul vermyne° *low animal*
Hadde eten yow; but God of his mercy,
And youre benigne° fader, tendrely *gracious*
Hath doon yow kept," and in that same stounde[9]
Al sodeynly she swapte° adoun to grounde. *fell*

And in her swough° so sadly° holdeth she *faint / firmly*
Hire children two, whan she gan hem t'embrace,° *embraced them*
That with greet sleighte° and greet difficultee *skill*

7. Now I do not care if I should die right here.
8. Death is of no consequence, nor (the time) when my spirit (shall) go hence.
9. Have had you cared for," and in that same moment.

The children from hire arm they gonne arace.° *tore away*
O many a teer on many a pitous face
Doun ran of hem that stoden hire bisyde;
Unnethe° abouten hire mighte they abyde.° *Scarcely / remain*

Walter hire gladeth° and hire sorwe slaketh;° *cheers her / eases*
She ryseth up, abaysed,° from hire traunce, *embarrassed*
And every wight hire joye and feste maketh[1]
Til she hath caught° agayn hire contenaunce.° *got / composure*
Walter hire dooth so feithfully plesaunce
That it was deyntee° for to seen the chere° *delight / happiness*
Bitwixe hem two, now they ben met yfere.° *together*

Thise ladyes, whan that they hir° tyme say,° *their / saw*
Han taken hire and into chambre goon,
And strepen° hire out of hire rude array, *undress*
And in a cloth of gold that brighte shoon,
With a coroune° of many a riche stoon° *crown / stone, jewel*
Upon hire heed, they into halle hire broghte,
And ther she was honoured as hire oghte.° *was due her*

Thus hath this pitous day a blisful ende,
For every man and womman dooth his might
This day in murthe and revel to dispende° *spend*
Til on the welkne° shoon the sterres light. *in the sky*
For more solempne° in every mannes sight *splendid*
This feste was, and gretter of costage,° *cost*
Than was the revel of hire mariage.

Ful many a yeer in heigh prosperitee
Liven thise two in concord and in reste,
And richely his doghter maried he
Unto a lord, oon of the worthieste
Of al Itaille; and than in pees° and reste *peace*
His wyves fader in his court he kepeth,
Til that the soule out of his body crepeth.

His sone succedeth in his heritage,
In reste and pees, after his fader° day, *father's*
And fortunat was eek in mariage,
Al° putte he nat his wyf in greet assay. *Although*
This world is nat so strong, it is no nay,° *it cannot be denied*
As it hath been in olde tymes yore.° *long ago*
And herkneth° what this auctour° seith therfore: *listen to / Petrarch*

This storie is seyd, nat for that wyves sholde
Folwen Grisilde as in humilitee,
For it were importable, though they wolde;[2]

1. And every person makes joy for her and good cheer.
2. For it would be intolerable (literally, unbearable), even if they should wish to.

But for that every wight° in his degree *person*
Sholde be constant in adversitee
As was Grisilde. Therfore Petrark wryteth
This storie, which with heigh style he endyteth.° *composes*

For sith° a womman was so pacient *since*
Unto a mortal man, wel more us oghte
Receyven al in gree° that God us sent. *good will*
For greet skile is he preve that he wroghte,[3]
But he ne tempteth° no man that he boghte°— *tempts / redeemed*
As seith Seint Jame,° if ye his pistel° rede. *James / epistle*
He preveth folk al day, it is no drede,° *doubtless*

And suffreth° us, as for our excercyse,° *allows / discipline*
With sharpe scourges of adversitee
Ful ofte to be bete° in sondry wyse,° *beaten / ways*
Nat for to knowe oure wil; for certes he,
Er we were born, knew al oure freletee.° *frailty*
And for our beste is al his governaunce:
Lat us than live in vertuous suffraunce.° *patience*

But o word, lordinges, herkneth° er I go: *listen*
It were ful hard to finde now-a-dayes
In al a° toun Grisildes three or two; *In an entire*
For if that they were put to swiche assayes,
The gold of hem hath now so° badde alayes° *such / alloys*
With bras, that thogh the coyne be fair at yë,° *to the eye*
It wolde rather breste a-two° than plye.° *break in two / bend*

For which heer, for the Wyves love of Bathe[4]—
Whos lyf and al hire secte° God mayntene *sect*
In heigh maistrye,° and elles were it scathe°— *mastery / a pity*
I wol with lusty° herte fresshe and grene *vigorous*
Seyn yow a song to glade° yow, I wene,° *gladden / think*
And lat us stinte of ernestful matere.[5]
Herkneth my song, that seith in this manere:

THE ENVOY

Grisilde is deed, and eek° hire pacience, *also*
And bothe atones° buried in Itaille. *together*
For which I crye in open audience:° *hearing*
No wedded man so hardy° be t'assaille *bold*
His wyves pacience, in hope to finde
Grisildes, for in certein he shall faille!

O noble wyves, ful of heigh prudence,
Lat noon humilitee your tonge naille,° *nail down*

3. For there is good reason why he (should) test what he created.
4. For which right now, for love of the Wife of Bath.
5. And let's stop (talking) of serious matters.

Ne lat no clerk have cause or diligence
To wryte of yow a storie of swich mervaille
As of Grisildis, pacient and kinde,
Lest Chichevache yow swelwe in hire entraille![6]

Folweth Ekko,° that holdeth no silence, — *Echo*
But evere answereth at the countretaille;° — *in counterreply*
Beth nat bidaffed for your innocence,[7]
But sharply tak on yow the governaille.° — *control*
Emprinteth wel this lesson in youre minde
For commune profit, sith it may availle.

Ye archewyves, stondeth at defence![8]
Sin° ye be stronge as is a greet camaille,° — *Since / camel*
Ne suffreth° nat that men yow doon offence. — *allow*
And sclendre° wyves, feble as in bataille, — *slender*
Beth egre° as is a tygre yond° in Inde;° — *fierce / yonder / India*
Ay clappeth as a mille, I yow consaille.[9]

Ne dreed° hem nat, doth hem no reverence;° — *fear / honor*
For though thyn housbonde armed be in maille,° — *mail*
The arwes° of thy crabbed eloquence — *arrows*
Shal perce his brest, and eek his aventaille.° — *helmet's faceplate*
In jalousye I rede eek° thou him binde, — *advise also*
And thou shalt make him couche° as dooth a quaille. — *cower*

If thou be fair, ther° folk ben in presence,° — *where / present*
Shew thou thy visage and thyn apparaille;° — *clothing*
If thou be foul, be free of thy dispence;° — *spending*
To gete thee freendes ay do thy travaille.° — *take thy pains*
Be ay of chere as light as leef on linde,[1]
And lat him care,° and wepe, and wringe, and waille! — *worry*

[THE WORDS OF THE HOST

This worthy Clerk, whan ended was his tale,
Our Hoste seyde and swoor, "By Goddes bones,
Me were lever than a barel ale[2]
My wyf at hoom had herd this legende ones.° — *once*
This is a gentil tale for the nones,° — *occasion*
As to my purpos, wiste ye° my wille; — *if you know*
But thing that wol nat be, lat it be stille."][3]

6. Lest Chichevache swallow you into her entrails. (Chichevache was a fabled cow who fed only on patient wives and hence was very lean.)
7. Don't be made a fool of because of (your) simplemindedness.
8. You archwives (dominating women), stand up in self-defense!
9. Always be noisy (clatter, chatter), I advise you, like a mill.
1. In behavior, always be as light as a leaf of the linden tree.
2. I'd sooner than a barrel of ale (that).
3. This stanza appears in some manuscripts and seems to have been an earlier draft canceled when Chaucer chose to have the Merchant respond directly to the Clerk's tale.

The Merchant's Prologue and Tale

The Prologue

"Weping and wayling, care and other sorwe
I know ynogh, on even and a-morwe,"° *i.e., by night and day*
Quod the Marchant, "and so doon othere mo° *many others*
That wedded been. I trowe° that it be so, *believe*
For wel I woot° it fareth so° with me. *know / that's how it goes*
I have a wyf, the worste that may be;
For thogh the feend° to hir y-coupled were, *devil*
She wolde him overmacche,° I dare wel swere. *overmatch, master*
What° sholde I yow reherce in special° *Why / rehearse in detail*
Hir hye° malice? She is a shrewe at al.° *proud / in every respect*
There is a long and large difference
Bitwix° Grisildis grete pacience *Between*
And of my wyf the passing° crueltee. *surpassing*
Were I unbounden, also moot I thee,[1]
I wolde nevere eft° comen in the snare. *again*
We wedded men live in sorwe and care.
Assaye° whoso wol, and he shal finde *Test (it)*
That I seye sooth, by Seint Thomas of Inde,[2]
As for the more part°—I sey nat alle. *i.e., the majority*
God shilde° that it sholde so bifalle! *forbid*
A! Goode sire Host, I have y-wedded be
Thise monthes two—and more nat, pardee°— *no more, by God*
And yet, I trowe, he that all his lyve
Wyflees° hath been, though that men wolde him ryve° *i.e., A bachelor / stab*
Unto the herte, ne coude in no manere
Tellen so muchel sorwe as I now heere
Coude tellen of my wyves cursednesse."° *shrewishness*
"Now," quod our Hoost, "Marchaunt, so God yow blesse,
Sin° ye so muchel knowen of that art, *Since*
Ful hertely° I pray yow telle us part." *heartily*
"Gladly," quod he, "but of myn owene sore,° *misery*
For sory° herte, I telle may namore." *(a) vexed*

The Tale

Whylom° ther was dwellinge in Lumbardye° *Once / Lombardy*
A worthy knight that born was of Pavye,° *Pavia (near Milan)*
In which he lived in greet prosperitee.
And sixty yeer a wyflees° man was he, *wifeless*
And folwed ay° his bodily delyt° *always pursued / pleasure, desire*
On° wommen, ther as° was his appetyt, *In / where*
As doon thise foles° that ben seculeer.° *As these fools do / secular, i.e., laymen*
And whan that he was passed sixty yeer—
Were it for° holinesse or for dotage° *Whether it was due to / senility*

1. Were I freed of the marriage bond, so may I thrive.
2. St. Thomas of India ("Doubting Thomas," who tested Christ's wounds).

I can nat seye—but swich a greet corage° *spirit, desire*
Hadde this knight to been a wedded man
That day and night he dooth al that he can
T'espyen° where he mighte wedded be, *To spy out, discover*
Preyinge our Lord to graunten him that he
Mighte ones knowe of thilke° blisful lyf *Might once experience that*
That is bitwixe an housbond and his wyf,
And for to live under that holy bond
With which that first° God man and womman bond.° *originally / bound*
"Non other lyf," seyde he, "is worth a bene,° *bean*
For wedlok is so esy° and so clene° *easy, comfortable / pure*
That in this world it is a paradys."
Thus seyde this olde knight, that was so wys.
  And certeinly, as sooth° as God is king, *truly*
To take a wyf it is a glorious thing,
And namely° whan a man is old and hoor;° *especially / white-haired*
Thanne is a wyf the fruit° of his tresor.° *best part / treasure, wealth*
Thanne sholde he take a yong wyf and a feir,° *fair one*
On which he mighte engendren him an heir,
And lede his lyf in joye and in solas,° *solace, pleasure*
Wheras thise bacheleres singe "Allas!"
Whan that they finden any adversitee
In love, which nis but° childish vanitee. *is only*
And trewely it sit wel° to be so, *it is fitting*
That bacheleres have often peyne and wo:
On brotel° ground they builde, and brotelnesse *brittle, fragile*
They finde whan they wene sikernesse.° *expect security*
They live but° as a brid° or as a beest,° *merely / bird / beast*
In libertee and under non arreest,° *restraint*
Ther as° a wedded man in his estaat° *Whereas / state, condition*
Liveth a lyf blisful and ordinaat,° *well-ordered*
Under the yok° of mariage y-bounde. *yoke*
Wel may his herte in joye and blisse habounde.° *abound*
For who can be so buxom° as a wyf? *obedient*
Who is so trewe and eek° so ententyf° *also / eager, attentive*
To kepe° him, syk and hool,° as is his make?° *look after / healthy / mate*
For wele or wo° she wol him nat forsake. *In joy or sorrow*
She nis nat wery° him to love and serve, *i.e., never gets tired*
Thogh that he lye bedrede° til he sterve.° *bedridden / die*
And yet somme clerkes seyn° it nis nat so, *scholars (authorities) say*
Of whiche he, Theofraste,[3] is oon of tho.° *those*
What force though° Theofraste liste° lye? *What does it matter that / liked to*
"Ne take no wyf," quod he, "for housbondrye,° *frugality, i.e., economy's sake*
As for to spare° in houshold thy dispence.° *to be sparing / expenditure*
A trewe servant dooth more diligence
Thy good° to kepe than thyn owene wyf, *goods, wealth*
For she wol clayme half part al hir lyf.

3. Theophrastus, author of *The Golden Book on Marriage*, a tract (now lost) satirically attacking marriage, excerpted by St. Jerome in his *Against Jovinian*, an important source for Chaucer's *Wife of Bath's Tale*. See A. G. Rigg's translation, pp. 395–97.

And if that thou be syk, so God me save,
Thy verray° frendes or a trewe knave° *true / male servant*
Wol kepe thee bet° than she that waiteth ay° *take better care of thee / always*
After° thy good and hath don many a day. *i.e., To inherit*
And if thou take a wyf unto thyn hold,° *into thy keeping*
Ful lightly° maystow been a cokewold."° *Very easily / cuckold*
This sentence° and an hundred thinges worse *opinion*
Wryteth this man—ther° God his bones corse!° *may / curse*
But take no kepe° of al swich vanitee.° *heed / nonsense, foolishness*
Deffye° Theofraste and herke° me. *Defy, reject / listen to*
  A wyf is Goddes yifte, verraily.° *truly*
Alle other maner yiftes, hardily,° *All other sorts of gifts, certainly*
As° londes, rentes,° pasture, or commune,[4] *Such as / income*
Or moebles,° alle ben yiftes of Fortune, *movable goods*
That passen as a shadwe° upon a wal. *shadow*
But dredelees,° if pleynly speke I shal, *doubtless*
A wyf wol laste and in thyn hous endure,
Wel lenger than thee list,° paraventure.° *it please thee / perhaps*
  Marriage is a ful gret sacrement.
He which that hath no wyf, I holde him shent:° *ruined, lost*
He liveth helplees and al desolat° *lonely*
(I speke of folk in seculer estaat).° *layfolk (as opposed to clergy)*
And herke why—I sey nat this for noght—
That womman is for mannes help y-wroght:° *made*
The hye God, whan he hadde Adam maked
And saugh° him al allone, bely-naked,° *saw / stark naked*
God of his grete goodnesse seyde than,
"Lat us now make an helpe° unto this man *helpmate*
Lyk to himself," and thanne he made him Eve.
Heer may ye se, and heerby may ye preve,° *prove*
That wyf is mannes help and his confort,
His paradys terrestre° and his disport.° *earthly paradise / delight*
So buxom° and so vertuous is she, *submissive, obedient*
They moste nedes° live in unitee. *must necessarily*
O° flesh they been, and o flesh as I gesse° *One / suppose*
Hath but on° herte, in wele° and in distresse. *one / happy times*
  A wyf—a,° Seinte Marie, *benedicite!*° *ah, oh / bless us all*
How mighte a man han° any adversitee *have*
That hath a wyf? Certes,° I can nat seye. *Certainly*
The blisse which that is bitwixe hem tweye° *the two of them*
Ther may no tonge telle or herte thinke.
If he be povre,° she helpeth him to swinke.° *poor / work*
She kepeth° his good° and wasteth never a *looks after / goods*
    deel.° *not a bit*
Al that hir housbonde lust° hir lyketh weel.° *desires / pleases her greatly*
She seith not ones° "nay" whan he seith "ye."° *once / yes*
"Do this," seith he; "Al redy, sir," seith she.
O blisful ordre of wedlok precious,
Thou art so mery and eek° so vertuous, *also*

4. Rights to use land held in common, for grazing, woodcutting, etc.

And so commended and appreved eek,
That every man that halt him° worth a leek° — *considers himself* / *i.e., anything*
Upon his bare knees oghte al his lyf
Thanken his God that him hath sent a wyf,
Or elles preye to God him for to sende
A wyf to laste unto his lyves ende,
For thanne his lyf is set in sikernesse.° — *security*
He may nat be deceyved, as I gesse,
So that° he werke after° his wyves reed.° — *Provided / act according to / advice*
Than may he boldly beren up° his heed. — *hold up*
They been so trewe and therwithal so wyse,
For which, if thou wolt werken as the wyse,° — *act as wise men (do)*
Do alwey so as° wommen wol thee rede.° — *just as / advise*
  Lo, how that Jacob, as thise clerkes rede,° — *tell, lecture on*
By good conseil° of his moder Rebekke,° — *counsel / Rebecca*
Bond° the kides° skin aboute his nekke, — *Bound, fastened / goat kid's*
Thurgh which his fadres benisoun° he wan. — *blessing*
  Lo Judith, as the storie eek° telle can, — *also*
By wys conseil she Goddes peple kepte,° — *protected*
And slow° him Olofernus° whyl he slepte. — *slew / Holofernes*
  Lo Abigayl, by good conseil how she
Saved hir housbonde Nabal whan that he
Sholde han be slayn; and loke, Ester also
By good conseil delivered out of wo
The peple of God, and made him Mardochee
Of Assuere enhaunced for to be.[5]
  Ther nis no thing in gree superlatyf,° — *superior in degree*
As seith Senek,° above an humble wyf. — *Seneca*
  Suffre° thy wyves tonge, as Caton bit;° — *Endure / Cato bids*
She shal comande and thou shalt suffren it,
And yet she wol obeye of° curteisye. — *out of*
A wyf is keper of thyn housbondrye.° — *domestic affairs*
Wel may the syke man biwaille and wepe,
Ther as° ther nis no wyf the hous to kepe. — *Wherever*
I warne thee, if wisely thou wolt wirche,° — *work, act*
Love wel thy wyf, as Crist loveth his chirche.
If thou lovest thyself, thou lovest thy wyf.
No man hateth his flesh, but in his lyf
He fostreth° it, and therfore bidde I thee — *nourishes*
Cherisse thy wyf, or thou shalt never thee.° — *prosper*
Housbond and wyf, what so° men jape° or pleye, — *however much / joke*
Of worldly° folk holden the siker° weye. — *Among secular / surer*
They been so knit° ther may noon harm bityde,° — *united / happen*
And namely° upon the wyves syde. — *especially*
For which this Januarie, of whom I tolde,

5. And look, Esther also, by good counsel, delivered from their woe the people of God and caused Mordecai (her uncle) to be advanced by Ahasuerus (her husband). For these biblical examples of feminine deception, violence, and skillful pleading, see Genesis 27:1–29 (Rebecca, Jacob, and Esau); Judith, chaps. 10–13 (Judith and Holofernes, whom she beheads); 1 Samuel 25:1–35 (Abigail, Nabal, and King David); and Esther, chaps. 7–8 (Esther and Ahasuerus).

Considered hath, inwith his dayes olde,° *in his old age*
The lusty° lyf, the vertuous quiete, *pleasurable*
That is in mariage hony-swete;
And for his freendes on a day° he sente, *one day*
To tellen hem th'effect° of his entente. *the substance*
With face sad° his tale he hath hem told. *sober, solemn*
He seyde, "Freendes, I am hoor° and old *white-haired*
And almost, God wot,° on my pittes brinke.° *knows / the edge of my grave*
Upon my soule somwhat moste I thinke.
I have my body folily despended°— *foolishly wasted*
Blessed be God that it shal been amended!
For I wol be, certeyn, a wedded man,
And that anoon° in al the haste I can, *promptly*
Unto som mayde fair and tendre of age.
I prey yow, shapeth° for my mariage *prepare*
Al sodeynly,° for I wol nat abyde,° *At once / wait*
And I wol fonde t'espyen,° on my syde,° *try to discover / for my part*
To whom I may be wedded hastily.
But forasmuche as ye ben mo° than I, *more (in number)*
Ye shullen rather° swich a thing espyen *sooner*
Than I, and wher me best were to allyen.° *ally myself, marry*
But o° thing warne I yow, my freendes dere, *one*
I wol non old wyf han in no manere.° *i.e., in any way*
She shal nat passe twenty yeer, certayn.
Old° fish and yong flesh° wolde I have fayn.° *Fully grown / meat / eagerly*
Bet is," quod he, "a pyk° than a pikerel,° *pike / young pike*
And bet than old boef° is the tendre veel.° *beef / veal*
I wol no womman thritty yeer of age;
It is but bene-straw° and greet forage.° *dry beanstalks / coarse animal food*
And eek° thise olde widwes,° God it woot,° *also / widows / knows*
They conne so muchel craft,° on Wades boot,[6] *have so much cunning*
So muchel broken harm,° whan that *petty wickedness*
hem leste,° *it pleases them*
That with hem sholde I never live in reste.
For sondry scoles maken sotil clerkis;
Womman of manye scoles half a clerk is.[7]
But certeynly, a yong thing may men gye,° *guide*
Right as men may warm wex° with handes plye.° *wax / ply, shape*
Wherfore I sey yow pleynly, in a clause,° *in a few words*
I wol non old wyf han right for this cause.
For if so were I hadde swich mischaunce° *bad luck*
That I in hir ne coude han no plesaunce,° *sexual pleasure*
Thanne sholde I lede my lyf in avoutrye° *adultery*
And go streight to the devel whan I dye,
Ne children sholde I none upon hir geten.° *beget*
Yet were me levere° houndes had me eten° *I would rather / eaten*
Than that myn heritage° sholde falle *inheritance*

6. By Wade's boat. Wade was a legendary hero, but the meaning of this oath or allusion is unclear.
7. For different schools make students (scholars) clever; a woman who's been to many schools (i.e., been married often) is half a scholar.

In straunge hand,° and this I tell yow alle. — *To anyone not my kin*
I dote nat.° I woot° the cause why — *do not dote / know*
Men sholde wedde, and forthermore woot I
Ther speketh many a man of mariage
That woot namore of it than woot my page° — *serving boy*
For whiche causes man sholde take a wyf:
If he ne may nat liven chast° his lyf, — *chastely*
Take him° a wyf with greet devocioun — *Let him take*
By cause° of leveful° procreacioun — *For the purpose / lawful*
Of children to th'onour° of God above, — *the honor*
And nat only for paramour° or love; — *amorous feeling*
And for° they sholde lecherye eschue° — *so that / eschew, avoid*
And yelde hir dettes whan that they ben due;[8]
Or for that ech of hem sholde helpen other
In meschief,° as a suster shal the brother, — *misfortune*
And live in chastitee ful holily.
But sires, by your leve,° that am nat I. — *by your leave, with your allowance*
For God be thanked, I dar make avaunt,° — *boast*
I fele my limes° stark° and suffisaunt — *limbs / strong*
To do al that a man bilongeth to.° — *is proper for a man to (do)*
I woot myselven best what I may do.
Though I be hoor,° I fare as dooth a tree — *hoar, white-haired*
That blosmeth er that fruyt y-woxen be,° — *blossoms before the fruit has grown*
And blosmy° tree nis neither drye ne deed. — *(a) blossoming*
I fele me nowher hoor but on myn heed.
Myn herte and alle my limes been as grene
As laurer° thurgh the yeer is for to sene.° — *laurel (an evergreen) / see*
And sin° that ye han herd al myn entente,° — *since / intentions, desires*
I prey yow to my wil ye wole assente."
  Diverse men diversely him tolde
Of mariage manye ensamples olde.
Somme blamed it, somme preysed it, certeyn.
But atte laste, shortly for to seyn,
As al day falleth° altercacioun — *all the time happens*
Bitwixen freendes in disputisoun,° — *debate, discussion*
Ther fil a stryf° bitwixe his bretheren two, — *An argument took place*
Of whiche that oon was cleped° Placebo; — *named*
Justinus soothly° called was that other.[9] — *truly*
  Placebo seyde, "O Januarie, brother,
Ful litel nede had ye, my lord so dere,
Conseil to axe° of any that is here, — *To ask the counsel*
But° that ye been so ful of sapience° — *Except / wisdom*
That yow ne lyketh, for your heighe prudence,
To weyven fro° the word of Salomon. — *depart from*
This word seyde he unto us everichon:° — *every one of us*
'Wirk alle thing by conseil,' thus seyde he,

8. And pay their debts when they are due. "Dettes" here echoes the biblical language for sexual intercourse as a marital obligation (1 Corinthians 7:3).
9. *Placebo*: "I shall please," "I shall be found pleasing" (Latin); *Justinus* evokes Latin *justus*: "just," "rightful," "the just one."

'And thanne shaltow° nat repente thee.' *shalt thou*
But though that Salomon spak swich a word,
Myn owene dere brother and my lord,
So wisly God° my soule bringe at reste, *As surely as God (may)*
I hold° your owene conseil is the beste. *believe, affirm*
For, brother myn, of me tak this motyf:° *idea, thought*
I have now been a court-man° al my lyf, *courtier*
And God it woot,° though I unworthy be, *knows*
I have stonden in ful greet degree° *very high rank*
Abouten lordes of ful heigh estaat,
Yet hadde I never with noon of hem° debaat.° *them / disagreement*
I never hem contraried,° trewely. *contradicted*
I woot wel that my lord can° more than I. *knows*
What that he seith, I holde it ferme° and stable. *firm, true*
I seye the same or elles thing semblable.° *something like it*
A ful gret fool is any conseillour
That serveth any lord of heigh honour
That dar presume or elles thenken it° *even imagine*
That his conseil sholde passe° his lordes wit.° *surpass / reason, intelligence*
Nay, lordes been no fooles, by my fay.° *faith*
Ye han yourselven shewed heer today
So heigh sentence,° so holily° and weel, *Such good judgment / virtuously*
That I consente and conferme everydeel° *completely*
Your wordes alle and your opinioun.
By God, ther nis no man in al this toun
Ne in Itaille that coude bet han sayd.° *could have spoken better*
Crist halt him° of this conseil wel apayd.° *considers himself (i.e., is) / pleased*
And trewely, it is an heigh corage° *a high-spirited deed*
Of any man that stapen° is in age *advanced (literally, stepped)*
To take a yong wyf. By my fader° kin, *father's*
Your herte hangeth on a joly pin!° *i.e., is jolly, lively*
Doth now in this matere right as yow leste,° *exactly as it pleases you*
For finally I holde it for the beste."
  Justinus, that ay° stille sat and herde, *all this time*
Right in this wyse° he to Placebo answerde: *manner*
"Now, brother myn, be pacient, I preye,
Sin ye han seyd,° and herkneth what I seye. *Since you have spoken*
Senek,° among his othere wordes wyse, *Seneca*
Seith that a man oghte him right wel avyse° *to consider very carefully*
To whom he yeveth° his lond or his catel.° *gives / chattels, property*
And sin I oghte avyse me right wel
To whom I yeve my good awey fro me,
Wel muchel more I oghte avysed be
To whom I yeve my body for alwey.
I warne yow wel, it is no childes pley
To take a wyf withoute avysement.° *deliberation*
Men moste enquere—this is myn assent°— *opinion*
Wher° she be wys or sobre or dronkelewe,° *Whether / given to drunkenness*
Or proud or elles otherweys a shrewe,° *wicked person*
A chydester° or wastour° of thy good, *scold / waster*
Or riche or poore, or elles mannish wood.° *man-crazy, a virago (?)*

Al be it so that° no man finden shal — *Even though*
Noon° in this world that trotteth hool — *No one*
in al°— — *trots (i.e., acts) perfectly*
Ne° man ne° beest, swich as men coude devyse°— — *Neither / nor / imagine*
But nathelees° it oghte ynough suffise — *nevertheless*
With any wyf if so were that she hadde
Mo° goode thewes° than hir vyces badde; — *More / qualities*
And al this axeth leyser for t'enquere.° — *requires leisure (time) to look into*
For God it woot,° I have wept many a tere — *knows*
Ful prively° sin° I have had a wyf. — *secretly / since*
Preyse° whoso wole a wedded mannes lyf, — *Praise*
Certein° I finde in it but cost° and care — *Certainly / only expense*
And observances° of alle blisses bare.° — *duties / i.e., joyless*
And yet, God woot,° my neighebores aboute,° — *knows / round about*
And namely of wommen many a route,° — *throng*
Seyn° that I have the moste stedefast wyf — *Say*
And eek° the mekeste° oon that bereth lyf. — *also / meekest*
But I wot best wher wringeth me my sho.° — *my shoe pinches me*
Ye mowe,° for me,° right as yow lyketh do. — *may / as far as I'm concerned*
Avyseth yow°—ye been a man of age— — *Think carefully*
How that ye entren into mariage,
And namely with a yong wyf and a fair.
By Him that made water, erthe, and air,
The yongest man that is in al this route° — *company*
Is bisy ynogh to bringen it aboute
To han his wyf allone.° Trusteth me, — *have his wife solely to himself*
Ye shul nat plese hir fully yeres three
(This is to seyn, to doon hir ful plesaunce).° — *sexual pleasure*
A wyf axeth° ful many an observaunce.° — *asks, requires / much attention*
I prey yow that ye be nat yvel apayd."° — *displeased*
"Wel," quod this Januarie, "and hastow sayd?° — *i.e., have you finished?*
Straw for thy Senek and for thy proverbes!
I counte nat a panier ful of herbes
Of scole-termes.[1] Wyser men than thow,
As thou hast herd, assenteden right now
To my purpos. Placebo, what sey ye?"
"I seye it is a cursed man," quod he,
"That letteth° matrimoine, sikerly."° — *hinders / surely*
And with that word they rysen sodeynly,
And been assented fully that he sholde
Be wedded whanne him list° and wher he wolde. — *it pleased him*
Heigh fantasye and curious bisinesse° — *obsessive preoccupation*
Fro day to day gan° in the soule impresse° — *did / make a mark*
Of Januarie aboute° his mariage. — *concerning*
Many fair shape and many a fair visage
Ther passeth thurgh his herte, night by night.
As whoso toke° a mirour polished bright — *If someone took*
And sette it in a commune market-place,
Than sholde he see many a figure pace

1. I value this scholar-talk no more than a basket full of greens.

By his mirour; and in the same wyse° *manner*
Gan Januarie inwith° his thoght devyse° *within / fantasize*
Of° maydens whiche that dwelten him bisyde.° *About / nearby*
He wiste° nat wher that he mighte abyde,° *knew / (best) settle*
For if that oon° have beaute in hir face, *if one*
Another stant° so in the peples grace *stands*
For hir sadnesse° and hir benignitee° *seriousness / graciousness*
That of the peple grettest voys° hath she. *praise*
And somme were riche and hadden badde name.° *i.e., reputation*
But nathelees, bitwixe ernest and game,° *jest*
He atte laste apoynted him° on oon, *decided*
And leet alle othere° from his herte goon, *others*
And chees° hir of° his owene auctoritee;° *chose / on / authority, judgment*
For love is blind al day° and may nat see. *always*
And whan that he was in his bed y-broght,
He purtreyed° in his herte and in his thoght *pictured*
Hir fresshe beautee and hir age tendre,
Hir myddel° smal, hir armes longe and sclendre,° *waist / slender*
Hir wyse governaunce,° hir gentillesse,° *behavior / gentility*
Hir wommanly beringe and hir sadnesse.° *seriousness*
And whan that he on hir was condescended,° *settled*
Him thoughte his chois mighte nat ben amended.° *bettered*
For whan that he himself concluded hadde,
Him thoughte ech other mannes wit so badde
That impossible it were to replye° *speak*
Agayn° his chois—this was his fantasye. *Against*
His freendes sente he to at his instaunce° *request*
And preyed hem° to doon him that plesaunce, *asked them*
That hastily they wolden to him come.
He wolde abregge° hir° labour, alle and some: *abridge, shorten / their*
Nedeth namore for him to go ne ryde;° *i.e., to search about on his behalf*
He was apoynted° ther° he wolde abyde.° *had decided / where (i.e., on whom) / settle*
Placebo cam and eek his freendes sone,° *soon*
And alderfirst° he bad hem alle a bone,° *first of all / asked them all a favor*
That noon of hem° none argumentes make *none of them*
Agayn the purpos which that he hath take,° *has decided on*
Which purpos was plesant° to God, seyde he, *pleasing*
And verray ground° of his prosperitee. *true foundation*
He seyde ther was a mayden in the toun,
Which that of beautee hadde greet renoun.
Al were it so° she were of smal degree,° *Although / low rank*
Suffyseth him hir youthe and hir beautee.
Which mayde, he seyde, he wolde han to° his wyf, *have as*
To lede in ese° and holinesse his lyf, *ease, comfort*
And thanked God that he mighte han hire al,° *entirely*
That no wight° his blisse parten° shal, *person / share*
And preyed hem to laboure in this nede° *business*
And shapen° that he faille nat to spede.° *arrange matters / succeed*
For thanne, he seyde, his spirit was at ese.
"Thanne is," quod he, "no thing may me displese,

Save o° thing priketh in my conscience, — *But one*
The which I wol reherce in your presence.
  I have," quod he, "herd seyd ful yore ago° — *a long time ago*
Ther may no man han parfite° blisses two, — *perfect*
This is to seye, in erthe and eek° in hevene. — *also*
For though he kepe him fro the sinnes sevene,° — *seven deadly sins*
And eek from every branche of thilke tree,° — *that tree (of sins)*
Yet is ther so parfit felicitee° — *such perfect happiness*
And so greet ese and lust° in mariage — *pleasure*
That ever° I am agast° now in myn age — *constantly / terrified*
That I shal lede now so mery a lyf,
So delicat,° withouten wo and stryf, — *delightful*
That I shal have myn hevene in erthe here.
For sith that° verray° hevene is boght so deere° — *since / the real* — *at such expense*
With tribulacioun and greet penaunce,
How sholde I thanne, that live in swich plesaunce
As alle wedded men don° with hir wyvis, — *do*
Come to the blisse ther° Crist eterne on lyve° is? — *where / eternally alive*
This is my drede,° and ye, my bretheren tweye, — *fear*
Assoilleth me this questioun,° I preye." — *Resolve this problem for me*
  Justinus, which that hated his folye,° — *folly*
Answerde anon,° right° in his japerye,° — *at once / directly / mockery*
And for° he wolde his longe tale° abregge,° — *because / speech / abridge*
He wolde noon auctoritee allegge° — *cite, appeal to*
But seyde, "Sire, so° ther be noon obstacle — *as long as*
Other than this, God of his hye miracle° — *miraculous power*
And of his mercy may so for yow wirche° — *work*
That, er° ye have your right° of holy chirche, — *before / last rites*
Ye may repente of wedded mannes lyf,
In which ye seyn ther is no wo ne stryf.
And elles,° God forbede but° he sente — *further / but (that)*
A wedded man him grace° to repente — *i.e., reasons*
Wel ofte rather° than a sengle man! — *more often*
And therfore, sire, the beste reed I can:° — *advice I know*
Dispeire yow noght, but have° in your memorie, — *hold*
Paraunter° she may be your purgatorie! — *By chance, perhaps*
She may be Goddes mene° and Goddes whippe. — *means, instrument*
Than shal your soule up to hevene skippe
Swifter than dooth an arwe° out of the bowe. — *arrow*
I hope to God herafter shul ye knowe
That ther nis no so greet felicitee
In mariage, ne never mo shal be,
That yow shal lette of° your savacioun, — *shall keep you from*
So that° ye use, as skile is and resoun,° — *Provided / as is proper and reasonable*
The lustes° of your wyf attemprely,° — *pleasures / moderately*
And that ye plese hir nat to° amorously, — *too*
And that ye kepe yow eek° from other sinne. — *also*
My tale is doon, for my wit is thinne.° — *weak*
Beth nat agast herof,° my brother dere. — *Do not be afraid of this*
But lat us waden° out of this matere. — *wade, go*

The Wyf of Bathe, if ye han understonde,
Of mariage, which we have on honde,° *i.e., is our present subject*
Declared hath ful wel in litel space.
Fareth now wel; God have yow in his grace."
  And with this word this Justin and his brother
Han take hir leve, and ech of hem of other.
For whan they sawe it moste nedes be,
They wroghten° so by sly° and wys tretee° *arranged it / skillful / negotiation*
That she, this mayden which that Mayus highte,° *who was called May*
As hastily as ever that she mighte
Shal wedded be unto this Januarie.
I trowe it were to° longe yow to tarie° *too / delay*
If I yow tolde of every scrit° and bond *writ, legal document*
By which that she was feffed° in his lond, *enfeoffed, put in possession of*
Or for to herknen° of hir riche array,° *hear / clothing*
But finally y-comen is the day
That to the chirche bothe be they went
For to receyve the holy sacrement.° *i.e., of marriage*
Forth comth the preest, with stole° aboute his nekke, *(a liturgical vestment)*
And bad hir be lyk Sarra and Rebekke
In wisdom and in trouthe° of mariage,[2] *troth, fidelity*
And seyde his orisons° as is usage,° *prayers / customary*
And croucheth hem,[3] and bad° God sholde hem blesse, *prayed*
And made al siker° ynogh with holinesse. *secure*
  Thus been they wedded with solempnitee,
And at the feste° sitteth he and she *feast*
With other worthy folk upon the deys.° *dais*
Al ful of joye and blisse is the paleys,
And ful of instruments and of vitaille,° *food*
The moste deyntevous° of al Itaille. *choice, delicious*
Biforn hem stoode instruments of swich soun° *of such sound*
That Orpheus ne of Thebes Amphioun
Ne maden never swich a melodye.[4]
At every cours° than cam loud minstralcye *course of the meal*
That never tromped° Joab for to here,° *trumpeted / hear*
Nor he Theodomas yet half so clere
At Thebes whan the citee was in doute.° *danger*
Bacus° the wyn hem skinketh° al aboute, *Bacchus, god of wine / pours*
And Venus° laugheth upon every wight°— *goddess of love / person*
For Januarie was bicome hir knight
And wolde bothe assayen his corage° *test his spirit (and sexual potency)*
In libertee° and eek in mariage— *i.e., bachelorhood*
And with hir fyrbrond° in hir hand aboute *her (Venus's) torch*
Daunceth biforn the bryde and al the route.° *company*

2. These lines refer to a prayer in the medieval marriage ceremony: the priest asks that the wife be as wise as Rebecca and as faithful as Sarah.

3. And makes the sign of the cross over them.

4. Orpheus won Euridyce back from the underworld (for a time) by the power of his music. Amphion raised the walls of Thebes by the same means. Joab (l. 1719) was the chief general of King David and blew the trumpet for his army. The auguries of Thiodamas (l. 1720) at the siege of Thebes were answered by the sound of trumpets.

And certeinly, I dar right wel seyn this,
Ymeneus,° that god of wedding is, *Hymen*
Saugh never his lyf° so mery a wedded man. *in his life*
Hold thou thy pees,° thou poete Marcian,[5] *Hold thy peace (keep silent)*
That wrytest us that ilke° wedding murie° *very same / merry*
Of hir, Philologye, and him, Mercurie,
And of the songes that the Muses songe.
To smal° is bothe thy penne and eek thy tonge *Too small, inadequate*
For to descryven of this mariage.
Whan tendre youthe hath wedded stouping° age, *stooping, bent*
Ther is swich mirthe that it may nat be writen.
Assayeth° it yourself; than may ye witen° *Try / know*
If that I lye or noon° in this matere. *or not*
  Mayus,[6] that sit with so benigne a chere,° *so gracious an expression*
Hir to biholde it semed fayerye.° *something enchanting, like a fairy tale*
Quene Ester° loked never with swich an yë° *Esther / eye*
On Assuer,° so meke a look hath she. *Ahasuerus (see ll. 1371–74 and note)*
I may yow nat devyse° al hir beautee, *describe*
But thus muche of hir beautee telle I may,
That she was lyk the brighte morwe° of May, *morning*
Fulfild of alle beautee and plesaunce.
  This Januarie is ravisshed in a traunce
At every time he loked on hir face;
But in his herte he gan hir to manace° *menace, threaten*
That he that night in armes wolde hir streyne° *clasp*
Harder than ever Paris dide Eleyne.[7]
But nathelees yet hadde he greet pitee
That thilke night offenden° hir moste he, *hurt physically*
And thoughte, "Allas! O tendre creature,
Now wolde God ye mighte wel endure
Al my corage,° it is so sharp and kene.° *desire / keen*
I am agast° ye shul it nat sustene.° *afraid / endure*
(But God forbede that I dide al my might!)
Now wolde God that it were woxen night° *had become night*
And that the night wolde lasten evermo.
I wolde that al this peple were ago."° *had gone, departed*
And finally he doth al his labour° *i.e., all he can*
As he best mighte, savinge his honour,° *without injuring his reputation*
To haste° hem fro the mete° in subtil wyse. *hasten / (wedding) feast*
  The tyme cam that reson was° to ryse, *it was appropriate*
And after that men° daunce and drinken
    faste, *i.e., folk (impersonal pronoun)*
And spyces al aboute the hous they caste,° *scattered*
And ful of joye and blisse is every man—
All but a squyer highte° Damian, *named*
Which carf° biforn the knight ful
  many a day. *Who carved (cf. General Prologue, l. 100)*

5. Martianus Capella, author of *The Marriage of Philology and Mercury*, an allegory of the seven liberal arts.
6. Chaucer here calls her by the Latin name for the month of May; cf. l. 2157.
7. Paris, a Trojan prince, ravished Helen of Troy, originally Greek, thus initiating the Trojan War.

He was so ravisshed on° his lady May — *by*
That for the verray peyne° he was ny wood.° — *sheer agony / almost crazy*
Almost he swelte° and swowned ther he stood, — *fainted*
So sore hath Venus hurt him with hir brond,
As that she bar it° daunsinge in hir hond; — *When she bore it*
And to his bed he wente him hastily.
Namore of him at this tyme speke I,
But ther I lete him wepe ynough and pleyne,° — *make complaints*
Til fresshe May wol rewen° on his peyne. — *have pity*
  O perilous fyr° that in the bedstraw bredeth!° — *fire / breeds, begins*
O famulier[8] foo that° his servyce bedeth!° — *foe who / offers*
O servant traitour, false hoomly hewe,° — *faithless domestic servant*
Lyk to the naddre° in bosom sly° untrewe, — *adder, serpent / deceitful*
God shilde us alle from your aqueyntaunce!
O Januarie, dronken in plesaunce° — *pleasure*
Of mariage, see how thy Damian,
Thyn owene squyer and thy borne man,° — *i.e., servant from birth*
Entendeth for to do thee vileinye.° — *wrong*
God graunte thee thyn hoomly fo t'espye,° — *to see (spy out)*
For in this world nis worse pestilence
Than hoomly foo al day in thy presence.
  Parfourned° hath the sonne° his ark diurne.° — *Completed / sun / daily arc*
No lenger may the body of him° sojurne° — *(i.e., the sun) / remain*
On th'orisonte° as in that latitude. — *the horizon*
Night with his mantel° that is derk and rude° — *mantle, cloak / rough*
Gan oversprede the hemisperie° aboute, — *hemisphere*
For which departed is this lusty route° — *joyful company*
Fro Januarie, with thank on every syde.
Hom to hir houses lustily they ryde,
Wher as they doon hir thinges as hem leste,° — *whatever pleased them*
And whan they sye hir° tyme, goon to reste. — *saw their*
Sone after that this hastif° Januarie — *eager, impatient*
Wolde go to bedde—he wolde no lenger tarie.
He drinketh ipocras, clarree, and vernage[9]
Of spyces hote, t'encresen his corage,° — *desire*
And many a letuarie° hadde he, ful fyn,° — *medicine / quite choice*
Swiche as the cursed monk dan[1] Constantyn
Hath writen in his book, *De Coitu*.
To eten hem° alle he nas no thing — *consume them*
    eschu.° — *was in no way averse*
And to his privee° freendes thus seyde he: — *closest*
"For Goddes love, as sone as it may be,
Lat voyden° al this hous in curteys° wyse." — *Clear out / courteous*
And they had doon right° as he wol devyse. — *exactly*
Men drinken, and the travers[2] drawe anon.

8. Intimate, belonging to one's household.
9. Hippocras, clary, and vernaccia are all strongly spiced sweet wines, thought to increase sexual desire.
1. *Dan* or *don*: *dominus*, a familiar title for a monk. Constantinus Africanus's treatise on sexual intercourse, *De Coitu*, written ca. 1080, contained recipes for aphrodisiacs.
2. A curtain drawn to divide the room, creating a private bedchamber.

The bryde was broght abedde as stille as stoon,
And whan the bed was with° the preest y-blessed, *by*
Out of the chambre hath every wight him dressed,° *removed himself*
And Januarie hath faste° in armes take *quickly, firmly*
His fresshe May, his paradys, his make.° *mate*
He lulleth° hir, he kisseth hir ful ofte. *soothes*
With thikke bristles of his berd unsofte—
Lyk to the skin of houndfish,° sharp as brere,° *dogfish / briar*
For he was shave al newe° in his manere— *had recently shaved*
He rubbeth hir aboute hir tendre face
And seyde thus: "Allas! I moot trespace° *commit offense*
To yow, my spouse, and yow gretly offende,° *displease, hurt*
Er tyme come that I wil doun descende.° *get down (or off)*
But nathelees, considereth this," quod he,
"Ther nis no werkman, whatsoever he be,
That may bothe werke wel and hastily.
This wol° be doon at leyser° parfitly.° *must / leisure / perfectly*
It is no fors° how longe that we pleye. *It does not matter*
In trewe wedlok coupled be we tweye,° *two*
And blessed be the yok° that we been inne, *yoke*
For in our actes we mowe° do no sinne. *may*
A man may do no sinne with his wyf,
Ne hurte himselven with his owene knyf,
For we han leve to pleye us by the lawe."[3]
Thus laboureth he til that the day gan dawe,° *began to dawn*
And than he taketh a sop in fyn clarree,° *piece of bread dipped in wine*
And upright in his bed than sitteth he,
And after that he sang ful loude and clere,
And kiste his wyf and made wantoun chere.° *behaved amorously*
He was al coltish,° ful of ragerye,° *frisky as a colt / wantonness*
And ful of jargon° as a flekked pye.° *chatter / spotted magpie*
The slakke° skin aboute his nekke shaketh *loose*
Whyl that he sang, so chaunteth° he and craketh.° *sings / croaks*
But God wot° what that May thoughte in hir herte, *knows*
Whan she him saugh up sittinge in his sherte,° *nightshirt*
In his night-cappe, and with his nekke lene.° *lean, skinny*
She preyseth° nat his pleying° worth a bene. *values / i.e., lovemaking*
Than seide he thus, "My reste wol I take.
Now day is come, I may no lenger wake."
And doun he leyde his heed and sleep° til pryme.° *slept / 9 A.M.*
And afterward, whan that he saugh his tyme,
Up ryseth Januarie; but fresshe May
Held hir chambre° unto the fourthe day, *Remained in her bedroom*
As usage° is of wyves for the beste. *the custom*
For every labour somtyme moot han° reste, *must have*
Or elles longe may he nat endure—
This is to seyn,° no lyves° creature, *say / living*
Be it of fish or brid° or beest or man. *bird*

3. For we have permission to enjoy ourselves (sexually) by law.

Now wol I speke of woful Damian,
That languissheth for love, as ye shul here.
Therfore I speke to him in this manere:
I seye, "O sely° Damian, allas! *hapless, unfortunate*
Answere to my demaunde,° as in this cas. *question*
How shaltow to thy lady, fresshe May,
Telle thy wo? She wole alwey seye 'nay.'
Eek° if thou speke, she wol thy wo biwreye.° *And / reveal, betray*
God be thyn help—I can no bettre seye."
This syke° Damian in Venus fyr *sick, sorrowful*
So brenneth° that he dyeth for desyr, *burns*
For which he putte his lyf in aventure.° *at risk*
No lenger mighte he in this wyse endure,
But prively° a penner° gan he borwe, *secretly / pen case*
And in a lettre wroot he al his sorwe,
In manere of a compleynt° or a lay,° *a poetic lament / song*
Unto his faire, fresshe lady May.
And in a purs of silk, heng° on his sherte, *which hung*
He hath it put and leyde it at his herte.
The mone that at noon was thilke day
That Januarie hath wedded fresshe May
In two of Taur, was into Cancre gliden.[4]
So longe hath Maius in hir chambre biden,° *stayed*
As custume is unto thise nobles alle.
A bryde shal nat eten° in the halle *eat, dine*
Til dayes foure, or three dayes atte leste,
Y-passed been; than lat hir go to feste.
The fourthe day compleet° fro noon to noon, *being completed*
Whan that the heighe masse° was y-doon, *High Mass*
In halle sit this Januarie and May,
As fresh as is the brighte someres day.
And so bifel how that this gode man
Remembred him upon this Damian
And seyde, "Seinte Marie! How may this be
That Damian entendeth nat° to me? *does not attend (wait on)*
Is he ay syk,° or how may this bityde?"° *Has he been sick*
His squyeres whiche that stoden ther bisyde *all this time / happen*
Excused him bycause of his siknesse,
Which letted° him to doon his bisinesse.° *prevented / duties*
Noon other cause mighte make him tarie.
"That me forthinketh,"° quod this Januarie, *worries me*
"He is a gentil° squyer, by my trouthe! *noble*
If that he deyde,° it were harm° and routhe.° *died / grief / pity*
He is as wys, discreet, and as secree° *able to keep secrets*
As any man I woot° of his degree,° *know / rank*
And therto manly and eek servisable,° *also willing to serve*
And for to been a thrifty° man right able. *successful*

4. The moon, which at noon on the day of the wedding was in the second degree of Taurus, had (four days later) slid (through Gemini) into Cancer.

But after mete,° as sone as ever I may, *dinner*
I wol myself visyte him, and eek May,
To doon him al the confort that I can."
And for that word him blessed every man,
That of° his bountee° and his gentillesse° *out of / goodness / nobility*
He wolde so conforten in siknesse
His squyer, for it was a gentil dede.
"Dame," quod this Januarie, "tak good hede,° *heed*
At after-mete° ye with your wommen alle, *After dinner*
Whan ye han been in chambre° out of this halle, *i.e., go to your chamber*
That alle ye go see this Damian.
Doth him disport°—he is a gentil man— *Provide him (some) amusement*
And telleth him that I wol him visyte,
Have I no thing but° rested me a lyte;° *When I have merely / little*
And spede yow faste,° for I wole abyde° *go quickly / wait*
Til that ye slepe faste by° my syde." *close to*
And with that word he gan to him to calle
A squyer that was marchal° of his halle, *i.e., in charge of arrangements*
And tolde him certeyn thinges what he wolde.
This fresshe May hath streight hir wey y-holde,° *taken*
With alle hir wommen, unto Damian.
Doun by his beddes syde sit° she than, *sits*
Confortinge him as goodly° as she may. *pleasantly*
This Damian, whan that his tyme he say,° *saw*
In secree wise his purs and eek his bille,° *letter*
In which that he y-writen hadde his wille,° *desire*
Hath put into hir hand, withouten more,° *without more ado*
Save° that he syketh° wonder° depe and sore, *Except / sighs / wondrously*
And softely to hir right thus seyde he:
"Mercy—and that ye nat discovere° me! *reveal*
For I am deed° if that this thing be kid."° *dead / known*
This purs hath she inwith hir bosom hid,
And wente hir wey; ye gete namore of me.
But unto Januarie y-comen is she,
That on his beddes syde sit ful softe.
He taketh hir and kisseth hir ful ofte
And leyde him doun to slepe, and that anon.° *soon*
She feyned hir° as that she moste gon° *pretended / must go*
There as ye woot that every wight mot nede.[5]
And whan she of this bille hath taken hede,° *has taken heed, attended to*
She rente° it al to cloutes° atte laste, *tore / bits*
And in the privee° softely° it caste. *privy / quietly*
Who studieth° now but faire fresshe May? *ponders*
Adoun by olde Januarie she lay,
That sleep° til that the coughe hath him awaked. *Who slept*
Anon° he preyde° hir strepen hir al naked. *At once / beseeched*
He wolde of hir, he seyde, han som plesaunce,
And seyde hir clothes dide him encombraunce,° *got in his way*

5. There where you know every person must needs go (i.e., to the privy).

And she obeyeth, be hir lief or looth.° *whether she likes it or not*
But lest that precious° folk be with me wrooth,° *fussy, prudish / angry*
How that he wroghte° I dar nat to yow telle, *How he did what he did*
Or whether hir thoughte it° paradys or helle; *it seemed to her*
But here I lete hem werken in hir wyse° *in their fashion*
Til evensong° rong and that they moste aryse. *the bell for Vespers*
  Were it by destinee or aventure,° *chance*
Were it by influence° or by nature *(of the stars)*
Or constellacion,° that in swich *astrological disposition*
    estat° *such condition*
The hevene stood that tyme fortunat
Was for to putte a bille of° Venus werkes *present a petition for*
(For alle thing hath tyme,° as seyn thise clerkes) *its time*
To any womman, for to gete hir love,
I can nat seye—but grete God above,
That knoweth that non act is causelees,
He deme° of al, for I wol holde my pees. *May he judge*
But sooth° is this: how that this fresshe May *the truth*
Hath take swich impression° that day *i.e., has been so moved*
For pitee of this syke Damian
That from hir herte she ne dryve can
The remembraunce for to doon him ese.° *make him comfortable*
"Certeyn," thoghte she, "whom that this thing displese
I rekke° noght, for here I him assure° *care / promise*
To love him best of any creature,
Though he namore hadde than his sherte."° *undershirt*
Lo, pitee renneth sone in° gentil herte. *flows quickly in*
  Heer may ye se° how excellent franchyse° *see / generosity*
In wommen is whan they hem narwe avyse.° *think things through closely*
Som tyrant is, as ther be many oon[6]
That hath an herte as hard as any stoon,° *stone*
Which wolde han lete him sterven° in the place *Who would have let him die*
Wel rather than han graunted him hir grace;
And hem reioysen° in hir cruel pryde, *And (such women) rejoice*
And rekke nat to been° an homicyde. *do not care if they are*
  This gentil May, fulfilled of pitee,
Right of hir hande a lettre made she,
In which she graunteth him hir verray grace.
Ther lakketh noght but only day and place
Wher that she mighte unto his lust suffyse,° *satisfy his desire*
For it shal be right° as he wol devyse.° *exactly / arrange*
And whan she saugh hir time upon a day,
To visite this Damian goth May,
And sotilly° this lettre doun she threste° *craftily / thrust*
Under his pilwe°—rede it if him leste.° *pillow / it pleased him*
She taketh him by the hand and harde him twiste° *squeezed*
So secrely that no wight° of it wiste,° *person / knew*
And bad° him been al hool,° and forth she wente *told / well, healthy*

6. Some (women) are tyrants; indeed, there is many a one.

To Januarie, whan that he for hir sente.
Up ryseth Damian the nexte morwe.° *morning*
Al passed was his siknesse and his sorwe.
He kembeth° him, he proyneth° him and pyketh,° *combs / preens / prinks*
He dooth al that his lady lust° and lyketh, *desires*
And eek° to Januarie he gooth as lowe° *also / humbly, obediently*
As ever dide a dogge for the bowe.[7]
He is so plesant unto every man
(For craft° is al, whoso that do it can°) *skill, trickery / knows how to use it*
That every wight is fayn° to speke him° good, *eager / of him*
And fully in his lady grace he stood.
Thus lete° I Damian aboute his nede, *let go*
And in my tale forth I wol procede.
Somme clerkes holden that felicitee° *supreme happiness*
Stant in delyt,° and therefor certeyn he, *Consists of pleasure*
This noble Januarie, with al his might,
In honest wyse,° as longeth to° a knight, *honorable manner / befits*
Shoop him° to live ful deliciously.° *Arranged / very sumptuously*
His housinge, his array,° as honestly° *clothing / worthily*
To his degree° was maked as a kinges. *For his rank*
Amonges othere of his honest° thinges *worthy, suitable*
He made a gardin, walled al with stoon.
So fair a gardin woot° I nowher noon.° *know / none*
For out of doute, I verraily° suppose *truly*
That he° that wroot the Romance of the Rose *i.e., Guillaume de Lorris*
Ne coude of it the beautee wel devyse;° *describe*
Ne Priapus[8] ne mighte nat suffyse,
Though he be god of gardins, for to telle
The beautee of the gardin and the welle° *spring*
That stood under a laurer° alwey grene. *laurel*
Ful ofte tyme he Pluto° and his quene *god of the underworld*
Proserpina and al hir fayerye° *their band of fairies*
Disporten hem and maken melodye
Aboute that welle, and daunced, as men tolde.
This noble knight, this Januarie the olde,
Swich deintee hath° in it to walke and pleye *Takes such pleasure*
That he wol no wight suffren bere° the keye *allow no person to bear, carry*
Save he himself—for of the smale wiket° *gate*
He bar alwey of silver a smal cliket,° *small latchkey*
With which, whan that him leste,° he it unshette.° *it pleased him / unlocked*
And whan he wolde paye his wyf hir dette° *marital debt (see l. 1452 and note)*
In somer seson, thider° wolde he go, *thither, to that place*
And May his wyf, and no wight but they two.
And thinges whiche that were nat doon abedde
He in the gardin parfourned° hem and spedde.° *performed / i.e., successfully so*

7. A dog trained to track game wounded by arrows from archers' bows.
8. A phallic god of gardens, fruitfulness, and fecundity.

And in this wyse° many a mery day *manner*
Lived this Januarie and fresshe May.
But worldly joye may nat alwey dure° *last*
To Januarie, ne to no creature.
O sodeyn hap!° O thou Fortune unstable, *sudden chance*
Lyk to the scorpion so deceivable,
That flaterest with thyn heed when thou wolt stinge;
Thy tayl is deeth thurgh thyn enveniminge.° *through thy poisoning*
O brotil° joye! O swete venim queynte![9] *brittle, fragile*
O monstre, that so subtilly canst peynte° *disguise*
Thy yiftes° under hewe° of stedfastnesse, *gifts / color*
That° thou deceyvest bothe more and lesse!° *So that / great and small*
Why hastow Januarie thus deceyved,
That haddest him for thy ful frend receyved?
And now thou hast biraft him° bothe hise yën,° *deprived him of / eyes*
For sorwe of which desyreth he to dyen.
Allas! this noble Januarie free,° *gracious*
Amidde his lust° and his prosperitee *pleasure*
Is woxen° blind, and that al sodeynly. *Has become*
He wepeth and he wayleth pitously,
And therwithal° the fyr of jalousye°— *following upon that / fire of jealousy*
Lest that his wyf sholde falle in som folye°— *into some folly*
So brente° his herte that he wolde fayn° *burned / very much wanted*
That som man bothe him and hir had slayn.
For neither after his deeth nor in his lyf
Ne wolde he that she were love° ne wyf, *(anyone else's) sweetheart*
But ever live as widwe° in clothes blake, *widow*
Soul° as the turtle° that lost hath hir make.° *Solitary / turtledove / mate*
But atte laste, after a monthe or tweye
His sorwe gan aswage,° sooth to seye; *began to lessen*
For whan he wiste it may noon other° be, *not otherwise*
He paciently took his adversitee,
Save,° out of doute, he may nat forgoon° *Except that / refrain*
That he nas° jalous evermore in oon.° *From being / continually*
Which jalousye it was so outrageous° *excessive*
That neither in halle n'in° noon other hous, *nor in*
Ne in noon other place, neverthemo° *no longer*
He nolde suffre° hir for to ryde or go *would not allow*
But if° that he had hand on hir alway. *Unless*
For which ful ofte wepeth fresshe May,
That loveth Damian so benignely° *graciously*
That she mot outher° dyen sodeynly *must either*
Or elles she mot han him as hir leste.° *have him as she desired*
She wayteth° whan hir herte wolde breste.° *waits for (the time) / burst*
Upon that other syde Damian
Bicomen is the sorwefulleste man
That ever was, for neither night ne day
Ne mighte he speke a word to fresshe May

9. *Queynte*: "strange," "curious"; also a slang word for female genitalia.

As to his purpos, of no swich matere,° *on no subject of that sort*
But if that Januarie moste it here,° *Without January hearing it*
That° hadde an hand upon hir evermo. *Who*
But nathelees, by wryting to and fro
And privee° signes, wiste° he what she mente, *hidden, secret / knew*
And she knew eek° the fyn° of his entente. *also / end, aim*
  O Januarie, what mighte it thee availle° *avail, benefit*
Thou mightest° see as fer as shippes saille? *(Even) if thou couldst*
For as good is blind deceyved be
As to be deceyved whan a man may se.
Lo Argus,[1] which that hadde an hondred yën,° *eyes*
For al that ever he coude poure or pryen,° *pore over or pry into (=see)*
Yet was he blent,° and God wot° so ben mo° *deceived / knows / others*
That wenen wisly° that it be nat so. *confidently believe*
Passe over° is an ese;° I sey namore. *To ignore (such deceptions) / relief*
  This fresshe May, that I spak of so yore,° *earlier*
In warme wex° hath emprented the cliket° *wax / made an imprint of the key*
That Januarie bar of the smale wiket° *gate*
By which into his gardin ofte he wente.
And Damian, that knew al hir entente,
The cliket countrefeted prively.° *copied secretly*
Ther nis namore to seye, but hastily
Som wonder by° this cliket shal bityde,° *because of / happen*
Which ye shul heren if ye wole abyde.° *wait, be patient*
  O noble Ovyde,° ful sooth seystou,° God woot! *Ovid / truly thou speakest*
What sleighte is it,° thogh it be long and hoot,° *What trick is there / difficult*
That he° nil finde it out° in som manere? *i.e., Love / will not discover it*
By Piramus and Tesbee° may men lere:° *Thisbe / people learn (this)*
Thogh they were kept ful longe streite overal,° *guarded strictly in every way*
They been accorded, rouninge thurgh a wal,[2]
Ther no wight° coude han founde out swich a sleighte. *Where no one*
  But now to purpos:° er that° dayes eighte *i.e., Back to the story / before*
Were passed er the monthe of Juil,° bifil° *July / it happened*
That Januarie hath caught so greet a wil°— *will, desire*
Thurgh egging° of his wyf—him for to pleye *incitement*
In his gardin, and no wight but they tweye,
That in a morwe° unto this May seith he: *So that one morning*
"Rys up, my wyf, my love, my lady free!° *gracious*
The turtles° vois is herd, my douve° swete. *turtledove's / dove*
The winter is goon, with alle his reynes wete.° *its wet rains*
Com forth now, with thyn eyen columbyn.° *eyes like a dove's*
How fairer been thy brestes than is wyn.° *wine*
The gardin is enclosed al aboute;
Com forth, my whyte° spouse. Out of doute *chaste; clothed in white (?)*
Thou hast me wounded in myn herte, o wyf.
No spot° of thee ne knew I al my lyf. *blemish, flaw*
Com forth, and lat us taken our disport.

1. Juno, jealous of Jupiter's love for Io, charged Argus, a monster with a hundred eyes, to keep watch over her. Argus did not succeed.
2. They communicated (reached an understanding) by whispering through (a chink in) a wall.

I chees° thee for my wyf and my confort." *choose*
  Swiche olde lewed[3] wordes used he.
On° Damian a signe made she *To*
That he sholde go biforen with his cliket.° *key*
This Damian thanne hath opened the wiket° *gate*
And in he stirte,° and that in swich manere *went quickly*
That no wight mighte it see neither y-here,° *nor hear*
And stille he sit° under a bush anoon. *sits*
  This Januarie, as blind as is a stoon,
With Maius in his hand and no wight mo,
Into his fresshe gardin is ago° *has gone*
And clapte to° the wiket sodeynly. *closed shut*
  "Now, wyf," quod he, "heer nis but thou and I,
That art the creature that I best love.
For, by that Lord that sit in heven above,
Lever ich hadde° dyen on a knyf *I would rather*
Than thee offende, trewe dere wyf!
For Goddes sake, thenk how I thee chees:° *chose*
Noght for no coveityse,° doutelees, *greed (for any dowry)*
But only for the love I had to thee.
And though that I be old and may nat see,
Beth to me trewe, and I shal telle yow why.
Three thinges, certes,° shul ye winne therby: *certainly*
First, love of Crist, and to yourself honour,
And al myn heritage,° toun and tour,° *inheritance / tower*
I yeve it yow, maketh chartres° as yow leste.° *charters, deeds / it pleases you*
This shal be doon tomorwe er sonne reste,° *before sunset*
So wisly God° my soule bringe in blisse. *As surely as God may*
I prey yow first in covenant° ye me kisse, *i.e., to seal our union*
And thogh that I be jalous, wyte° me noght. *blame*
Ye been so depe enprented° in my thoght *deeply imprinted*
That whan that I considere your beautee
And therwithal the unlykly elde° of me, *unsuitable age*
I may nat, certes, thogh I sholde dye,
Forbere to been out of your companye
For verray° love—this is withouten doute. *true*
Now kis me, wyf, and lat us rome° aboute." *roam, stroll*
  This fresshe May, whan she thise wordes herde,
Benignely° to Januarie answerde, *Graciously*
But first and forward° she bigan to wepe.° *first of all / weep*
"I have," quod she, "a soule for to kepe
As wel as ye, and also myn honour,
And of my wyfhod thilke° tendre flour° *that / flower*
Which that I have assured in° your hond *entrusted to*
Whan that the preest to yow my body bond.° *bound*
Wherfore I wole answere in this manere
By the leve of yow,° my lord so dere: *With your permission*

3. *Lewed*: "stupid," "ignorant," "unlearned," and here perhaps "lascivious" as well, meanings all ironically inappropriate to January's speech of invitation, which resounds with echoes from the biblical *Song of Songs*.

I prey to God that never dawe the day° *the day may never dawn*
That I ne sterve° as foule° as womman may, *die / shamefully*
If ever I do unto my kin that shame,
Or elles° I empeyre° so my name° *otherwise / injure / reputation*
That I be° fals. And if I do that lakke,° *i.e., by being / misdeed*
Do strepe° me and put me in a sakke *strip*
And in the nexte° river do me drenche.° *nearest / have me drowned*
I am a gentil° womman and no wenche. *well born, decent*
Why speke ye thus? But men ben ever untrewe,
And wommen have repreve of yow ay newe.° *reproof from you always*
Ye han non other contenance,° I leve,° *way of behaving / believe*
But° speke to us of untrust° and repreve."° *Except (to) / distrust / reproof*
  And with that word she saugh wher Damian
Sat in the bush, and coughen° she bigan, *to cough*
And with hir finger signes made she
That Damian sholde climbe upon a tree
That charged° was with fruit; and up he wente, *loaded*
For verraily° he knew al hir entente *truly*
And every signe that she coude mak
Wel bet° than Januarie, hir owene make. *Much better*
For in a lettre she had told him al
Of this matere, how he werchen shal.° *i.e., what he must do*
And thus I lete him sitte upon the pyrie,° *up in the pear tree*
And Januarie and May rominge myrie.° *roaming merrily*
  Bright was the day, and blew° the firmament. *blue*
Phebus° hath of gold his stremes° doun y-sent *God of the sun / beams, rays*
To gladen every flour with his warmnesse.
He was that tyme *in Geminis*, as I gesse,
But litel fro his declinacioun
Of Cancer, Jovis exaltacioun.[4]
And so bifel that brighte morwe-tyde° *morning time*
That in that gardin, in the ferther syde,
Pluto, that is the king of Fayerye,° *the fairy world (also of Hades)*
And many a lady in his companye
Folwinge his wyf, the quene Proserpyna,° *Proserpina*
Which that he ravysshed out of Ethna° *Whom he abducted from Mt. Etna*
Whil that she gadered floures in the mede.° *meadow*
(In Claudian ye may the story rede,
How in his grisly carte he hir fette.)[5]
This king of Fairye thanne adoun him sette
Upon a bench of turves° fresh and grene, *pieces of turf*
And right anon thus seyde he to his quene:
  "My wyf," quod he, "ther may no wight° sey nay. *person*
Th'experience so preveth° every day *indeed proves*
The tresons° whiche that wommen doon to man. *treasons, betrayals*
Ten hondred thousand stories telle I can

4. The sun was in the sign of Gemini (the Twins), just short of entering Cancer on June 12, the sign over which Jupiter exerted his maximum influence ("Jove's exaltacioun").
5. You may read the story in Claudian, how Pluto carried her off in his frightening chariot. Claudius Claudianus wrote an unfinished poem, *The Rape of Proserpina*, ca. 400.

Notable of your untrouthe and brotilnesse.° *frailty, fickleness*
O Salomon,° wys, richest of richesse,° *Solomon / in wealth*
Fulfild of sapience° and of worldly glorie, *Filled with wisdom*
Ful worthy been thy wordes to memorie° *to (hold in) memory*
To every wight that wit and reson can.° *has intelligence and reason*
Thus preiseth° he yet the bountee° of man: *appraises / goodness*
'Amonges a thousand men yet fond I oon,° *I found but one (good one)*
But of wommen alle fond I noon.'° *(see Ecclesiastes 7:29)*
  Thus seith the king that knoweth your wikkednesse.
And Jesus *filius Syrak*, as I gesse,
Ne speketh of yow but selde reverence.[6]
A wilde fyr° and corrupt pestilence° *burning skin disease / infectious*
So falle upon your bodies yet tonight! *plague*
Ne see ye nat this honurable knight?
Bycause, allas, that he is blind and old,
His owene man° shal make him cokewold.° *manservant / cuckold*
Lo, heer he sit,° the lechour,° in the tree. *sits / lecher (with a pun on "healer")*
Now wol I graunten, of my magestee,° *through my majesty*
Unto this olde, blinde, worthy knight
That he shal have ayeyn° his eyen sight, *again*
Whan that his wyf wold doon him vileinye.° *bring him dishonor*
Than shal he knowen al his harlotrye° *wickedness*
Both in repreve° of hir and othere mo." *reproof / other (women) more*
  "Ye shal?" quod Proserpyne. "Wol ye so?
Now, by my modres sires soule,[7] I swere
That I shal yeven° hir suffisant answere— *give*
And alle wommen after, for hir sake—
That though they be in any gilt y-take,° *caught in any offense*
With face bold° they shulle hemself° excuse, *assured, brazen / themselves*
And bere hem doun° that wolden hem accuse. *beat down those*
For lakke of answer noon of hem shal dyen.
Al hadde man seyn° a thing with bothe his yën,° *Even if one had seen / eyes*
Yit shul we wommen visage it hardily° *put a bold face on it*
And wepe and swere and chyde subtilly,° *complain cleverly*
So that ye men shul been as lewed as gees.° *ignorant as geese*
  What rekketh me of° your auctoritees? *What do I care about*
I woot° wel that this Jew, this Salomon, *know*
Fond of° us wommen foles many oon.° *Found among / many a fool*
But though that he ne fond no good womman,
Yet hath ther founde many another man
Wommen ful trewe, ful gode and vertuous.
Witnesse on hem° that dwelle in Cristes hous: *them*
With martirdom they preved hir constance.° *proved their constancy*
The Romayn gestes° eek maken *Roman histories*
    remembrance° *also remind us*
Of many a verray,° trewe wyf also. *faithful*
But sire—ne be nat wrooth°—al be it so *angry*

6. And I think Jesus the son of Sirach (the Jewish author of the book known to Christians as *Ecclesiasticus*, canonical in the Catholic but not in the Protestant Bible) spoke of you (women) only seldom with respect.
7. By the soul of my mother's father. The father of Ceres, Proserpina's mother, was Saturn.

Though that he seyde he fond no good womman,
I prey yow take the sentence° of the man. *meaning*
He mente thus: that in sovereyn bontee° *supreme goodness*
Nis noon but God, but neither he ne she.° *man nor woman*
  Ey! For verray° God that nis but oon,° *true / i.e., the one and only*
What° make ye so muche of Salomon? *Why*
What though° he made a temple, Goddes hous? *So what if*
What though he were riche and glorious?
So made he eek a temple of° false goddis. *to*
How mighte he do a thing that more forbode° is? *forbidden*
Pardee,° as faire° as ye his name emplastre,° *Certainly / favorably* *whitewash*
He was a lechour and an ydolastre,° *idolater*
And in his elde° he verray God forsook. *old age*
And if that God ne hadde, as seith the book,[8]
Y-spared him for his fadres° sake, he sholde *father's*
Have lost his regne° rather than he wolde.° *kingdom / sooner* *than he wanted*
I sette right noght, of al the vileinye
That ye of wommen wryte, a boterflye.[9]
I am a womman—nedes moot° I speke *necessarily must*
Or elles swelle til myn herte breke.
For sithen° he seyde that we ben jangleresses,° *since / chattering women*
As ever hool I mote brouke my tresses,[1]
I shal nat spare, for no curteisye,
To speke him harm° that wolde us vileinye."° *speak ill of him / do us shame*
  "Dame," quod this Pluto, "be no lenger° wrooth. *longer*
I yeve it up.° But sith° I swoor myn ooth *give up, yield / since*
That I wolde graunten him his sighte ageyn,
My word shal stonde, I warne yow, certeyn.
I am a king; it sit° me noght to lye."° *suits, befits / lie, i.e., break my word*
  "And I," quod she, "a queene of Fayerye.° *the fairy world*
Hir answere shal she have, I undertake.° *declare*
Lat us namore wordes heerof make,° *Let's have no more debate about this*
For sothe° I wol° no lenger yow contrarie."° *truly / wish, want / argue with*
  Now lat us turne agayn to Januarie,
That in the gardin with his faire May
Singeth ful merier° than the papejay,° *more merrily / parrot*
"Yow love I best, and shal, and other noon."° *no one else*
So longe aboute the aleyes° is he goon° *garden paths (alleys) / has he walked*
Til he was come agaynes thilke pyrie° *in front of that very pear tree*
Wher as° this Damian sitteth ful myrie *Where*
An heigh° among the fresshe leves grene. *On high*
  This fresshe May, that is so bright and shene,° *fair, beautiful*
Gan for to syke° and seyde, "Allas, my syde! *Began to sigh*
Now sir," quod she, "for aught that may bitydе,° *whatever may happen*
I moste han of the peres° that I see *must have (some) of the pears*

8. I.e., the Bible. See 3 Kings 11:1–13 (Vulgate) or 1 Kings 11:1–13 (Authorized Version).
9. I don't care a bit (literally, a butterfly) for all the villainous things you men write about women.
1. Literally, "as surely as I mean to keep all my hair," i.e., stay alive.

Or I mot° dye, so sore longeth me° *must / intensely I long*
To eten° of the smale peres grene. *eat*
Help, for hir love that is of hevene quene!° *i.e., the Virgin Mary*
I telle yow wel, a womman in my plyt° *condition (implying pregnancy)*
May han to fruit so greet an appetyt
That she may dyen but° she of it have." *unless*
"Allas," quod he, "that I ne had heer a knave° *servant*
That coude climbe! Allas, allas," quod he,
"That I am blind!" "Ye, sir, no fors,"° quod she, *no matter*
"But wolde ye vouchesauf,° for Goddes sake, *But if you would agree*
The pyrie inwith° your armes for to take *within*
(For wel I woot° that ye mistruste me), *know*
Thanne sholde I climbe wel ynogh," quod she,
"So° I my foot mighte sette upon your bak." *Provided that*
"Certes," quod he, "theron shal be no lak,° *i.e., I will not fail to do that*
Mighte° I yow helpen with myn herte blood." *I.e., even if it meant that*
He stoupeth doun, and on his bak she stood,
And caughte hir by a twiste,° and up she gooth— *grabbed hold of a branch*
Ladies, I prey yow that ye be nat wrooth;° *angry*
I can nat glose;° I am a rude° man— *gloss over with fine words / rough, plain*
And sodeynly anon this Damian
Gan pullen° up the smok, and in he throng.° *Began to pull / thrust*
And whan that Pluto saugh this grete wrong,
To Januarie he gaf° agayn his sighte *gave*
And made him see as wel as ever he mighte.
And whan that he hadde caught his sighte agayn,
Ne was ther never man of thing so fayn.° *happy*
But on his wyf his thoght was evermo;
Up to the tree he caste his eyen two
And saugh that Damian his wyf had dressed° *dealt with*
In swich° manere it may nat ben expressed *such*
But if° I wolde speke uncurteisly.° *Unless / crudely*
And up he yaf a roring and a cry
As doth the moder° whan the child shal dye. *mother*
"Out! Help! Allas! Harrow!"° he gan to crye. *Help*
"O stronge lady store,° what dostow?"° *bold, brazen woman / doest thou*
And she answerde, "Sir, what eyleth° yow? *ails*
Have pacience and reson in your minde.
I have yow holpe° on bothe your eyen blinde. *helped*
Up° peril of my soule I shal nat lyen: *Upon*
As me was taught, to hele° with your yën *heal*
Was nothing bet° to make yow to see *better, more effective*
Than strugle° with a man upon a tree. *wrestle*
God woot° I dide it in ful good entente." *knows*
"Strugle?" quod he. "Ye, algate° in it wente! *nevertheless*
God yeve° yow bothe on shames deeth° to dyen! *give / a shameful death*
He swyved° thee! I saugh it with myne yën,° *had sex with / eyes*
And elles° be I hanged by the hals!"° *Or else / neck*
"Thanne is," quod she, "my medicyne al fals.° *wrong, useless*
For certeinly, if that ye mighte° see, *were able to*
Ye wolde nat seyn thise wordes unto me.

Ye han° som glimsing° and no parfit° sighte." *have / glimpse, fleeting look / perfect*
"I see," quod he, "as wel as ever I mighte,
Thonked be God, with bothe myne eyen two,
And by my trouthe, me thoughte° he dide thee so." *it seemed to me*
"Ye maze,° maze, gode sire," quod she. *are confused, dazed*
"This thank have I for I have maad° yow see. *made*
Allas," quod she, "that ever I was so kinde!"° *(with pun on "natural")*
"Now, dame," quod he, "lat al passe out of minde.
Com doun, my lief,° and if I have missayd,° *love / misspoken*
God help me so, as I am yvel apayd.° *sorry*
But by my fader soule, I wende han seyn° *thought I saw*
How that this Damian had by thee leyn,° *i.e., pressed against*
And that thy smok had leyn upon his brest."
"Ye, sire," quod she, "ye may wene° as yow lest;° *believe / wish*
But, sire, a man that waketh out of his sleep,
He may nat sodeynly wel taken keep° *take good notice*
Upon a thing, ne seen it parfitly° *perfectly*
Til that he be adawed verraily.° *truly awakened*
Right so a man that longe hath blind y-be
Ne may nat sodeynly so wel y-see
First,° whan his sighte is newe come ageyn, *At first*
As he that hath a day or two y-seyn.
Til that your sighte y-satled° be a whyle, *settled*
Ther may ful many a sighte yow bigyle.° *deceive*
Beth war,° I prey yow, for by hevene° king, *Be aware / heaven's*
Ful many a man weneth to seen° a thing, *thinks to have seen*
And it is al another° than it semeth. *completely other*
He that misconceyveth,° he misdemeth."° *misapprehends / misjudges*
And with that word she leep° doun fro the tree. *leaped*
This Januarie, who is glad but he?
He kisseth hir and clippeth° hir ful ofte, *embraces*
And on hir wombe° he stroketh hir ful softe, *stomach*
And to his palays° hoom he hath hir lad.° *palace / led*
Now, gode men, I pray yow to be glad.
Thus endeth heer my tale of Januarie.
God bless us, and his moder Seinte Marie!

The Epilogue

"Ey! Goddes mercy!" seyde our Hoste tho.° *then*
"Now swich° a wyf I pray God kepe me fro! *such*
Lo, whiche sleightes° and subtilitees *what tricks*
In wommen been, for ay° as bisy as bees *always*
Ben they, us sely° men for to deceyve, *simple, innocent*
And from a sothe° ever wol they weyve.° *truth / turn away, avoid*
By this Marchauntes tale it preveth weel.° *surely proves true*
But doutelees,° as trewe as any steel *without doubt*
I have a wyf, though that she povre° be; *poor*
But of hir tonge a labbing° shrewe is she, *blabbing*
And yet° she hath an heep° of vyces mo.° *also / heap, great number / more*

Therof no fors°—lat alle swiche thinges go. *no matter*
But wite ye what?° In conseil° be it seyd, *do you know what / confidence*
Me reweth sore° I am unto hir teyd.° *It grieves me painfully / tied*
For and° I sholde rekenen° every vyce *if / reckon, count up*
Which that she hath, ywis I were to nyce.° *truly I would be too foolish*
And cause why? It sholde reported be
And told to hir of° somme of this meynee,° *by / company*
Of° whom it nedeth nat for to declare, *By*
Sin° wommen connen outen° *Since / know how to spread*
swich chaffare.° *wares, matters*
And eek° my wit suffyseth nat therto *also*
To tellen al, wherfor my tale is do."° *done*

The Franklin's Prologue and Tale

The Introduction

"In feith, Squier, thou hast thee wel y-quit° *acquitted*
And gentilly.° I preise wel thy wit," *i.e., like a gentleman*
Quod the Frankeleyn. "Consideringe thy youthe,
So feelingly thou spekest, sire, I allow the:° *commend thee*
As to my doom,° there is non that is here *judgment*
Of eloquence that shal be thy pere,° *peer, equal*
If that thou live. God yeve° thee good chaunce,° *give / fortune*
And in vertu sende thee continuaunce,
For of thy speche I have greet deyntee.° *pleasure*
I have a sone, and by the Trinitee,
I hadde levere than twenty pound worth lond[1]—
Though it right now were fallen in myn hond—
He were a man of swich discrecioun
As that ye been. Fy on possessioun,° *property, wealth*
But if° a man be vertuous withal! *Unless*
I have my sone snibbed,° and yet shal, *rebuked*
For he to vertu listeth nat entende;[2]
But for to pleye at dees,° and to despende,° *dice / spend freely*
And lese° al that he hath, is his usage.° *lose / custom*
And he hath levere° talken with a page° *rather / young servant*
Than to comune° with any gentil wight° *talk / gentlemanly person*
Where he mighte lerne gentillesse° aright." *gentility*
"Straw for your gentillesse!" quod our Host.
"What, Frankeleyn! pardee,° sire, wel thou wost° *by God / knowest*
That eche of yow mot° tellen atte leste° *must / at (the) least*
A tale or two, or breken his biheste."° *promise*
"That knowe I wel, sire," quod the Frankeleyn;
"I prey yow, haveth me nat in desdeyn° *don't disdain me*
Though to this man I speke a word or two."
"Telle on thy tale withouten wordes mo."° *more*

1. I would rather than land worth twenty pounds a year.
2. Because he does not care to concern himself with (the development of his) capacities. (*Vertu* involves notions of power, strength, and efficacy as well as moral goodness.)

"Gladly, sire Host," quod he, "I wol obeye
Unto your wil; now herkneth° what I seye. *listen to*
I wol yow nat contrarien° in no wyse *oppose*
As fer as that my wittes wol suffyse.
I prey to God that it may plesen yow:
Thanne woot I wel that it is good ynow."° *enough*

The Prologue

Thise olde gentil Britons° in hir° dayes *Bretons / their*
Of diverse aventures maden layes,° *lays, poems*
Rymeyed° in hir firste° Briton tonge; *Rhymed / original*
Which layes with hir instruments they songe,
Or elles redden hem° for hir plesaunce;° *else read them / pleasure*
And oon of hem have I in remembraunce,
Which I shal seyn with good wil as I can.
But, sires, by cause° I am a burel° man, *because / plain, untutored*
At my biginning first I yow biseche
Have me excused of my rude° speche. *crude, inartistic*
I lerned nevere rethoryk,° certeyn:° *rhetoric / in truth*
Thing that I speke, it moot° be bare and pleyn.° *must / plain*
I sleep° nevere on the Mount of Pernaso,° *slept / Parnassus*
Ne lerned Marcus Tullius Cithero.° *Cicero*
Colours ne knowe I none, withouten drede,[3]
But swiche° colours as growen in the mede,° *Only such / meadow*
Or elles swiche as men dye or peynte.° *paint*
Colours of rethoryk ben to me queynte:° *too abstruse for me*
My spirit feleth noght of° swich matere. *has no feeling for*
But if yow list,° my tale shul ye here. *it pleases you*

The Tale

In Armorik,° that called is Britayne,° *Armorica / Brittany*
Ther was a knight that loved and dide his payne° *took pains*
To serve a lady in his beste wyse;
And many a labour, many a greet empryse° *undertaking, exploit*
He for his lady wroghte,° er° she were wonne. *performed / before*
For she was oon the faireste° under sonne, *one of the loveliest*
And eek° therto come of so heigh kinrede,° *also / high lineage*
That wel unnethes dorste° this knight, for drede,° *scarcely dared / fear*
Telle hire his wo, his peyne, and his distresse.
But atte laste° she, for his worthinesse, *at (the) last*
And namely° for his meke obeysaunce,° *especially / obedience*
Hath swich° a pitee caught of° his penaunce° *such / felt for / suffering*
That prively° she fil of his accord° *secretly / i.e., consented*
To take him for hir housbonde and hir lord,
Of swich lordshipe as men han over hir wyves.
And for to lede° the more in blisse hir° lyves, *lead / their*
Of his free wil he swoor hire° as a knight *swore to her*

3. I don't know any rhetorical "colors" (ornaments)—no fear of that. (The Franklin's modest apology is of a traditional kind, recommended by the very art he claims not to know.)

That nevere in al his lyf he, day ne night,
Ne sholde upon him take no maistrye° *mastery, domination*
Agayn hir wil, ne kythe hire° jalousye, *display to her*
But hire obeye and folwe hir wil in al
As any lovere to his lady shal°— *must*
Save that the name° of soveraynetee, *title, appearance*
That wolde he have for shame of his degree.[4]
  She thanked him, and with ful greet humblesse
She seyde, "Sire, sith° of youre gentillesse *since*
Ye profre me to have so large° a reyne,° *free / rein*
Ne wolde nevere God bitwixe us tweyne,
As in my gilt, were outher werre or stryf.[5]
Sire, I wol be youre humble trewe wyf:
Have heer my trouthe,° til that myn herte breste."° *loyal pledge / burst*
Thus been they bothe in quiete and in° reste. *at*
  For o° thing, sires, saufly° dar I seye, *one / safely*
That frendes everich other° moot° obeye, *each other / must*
If they wol longe holden companye.
Love wol nat ben constreyned by maistrye.[6]
When maistrie comth, the God of Love anon° *at once*
Beteth° hise winges, and farewel, he is gon! *Beats*
Love is a thing as° any spirit free. *like*
Wommen of kinde° desiren libertee, *by nature*
And nat to ben constreyned as a thral;° *thrall, slave*
And so don men, if I soth° seyen shal. *truth*
Loke who that° is most pacient in love: *Consider the man who*
He is at his avantage al above.° *above all others*
Pacience is an heigh vertu, certeyn,
For it venquisseth,° as thise clerkes° seyn, *vanquishes / scholars*
Thinges that rigour° sholde° never atteyne. *harshness, strictness / could*
For every word men may nat chyde or pleyne.° *complain*
Lerneth to suffre, or elles, so moot I goon,° *as I may live*
Ye shul it lerne, wher so ye wole or noon.° *whether you wish to or not*
For in this world, certein, ther no wight° is *person*
That he ne dooth or seith somtyme amis.° *wrongly*
Ire,° siknesse, or constellacioun,° *Anger / fate, his stars*
Wyn, wo, or chaunginge of complexioun[7]
Causeth ful ofte to doon amis or speken.
On every wrong a man may nat be wreken:° *avenged*
After° the tyme moste be temperaunce° *According to / moderation*
To every wight that can on governaunce.° *understands self-control*
And therfore hath this wyse worthy knight,
To live in ese, suffrance hire bihight,° *promised her (his) forbearance*
And she to him ful wisly gan to swere° *truly did swear*

4. That would he retain, lest it reflect on his rank.
5. God would not wish that there should ever be either war or strife between us two for any fault (guilt) of mine.
6. Love will not be constrained by mastery (i.e., by one partner exercising absolute power over the other).
7. Wine, woe, or a change in the balance of humors ("complexioun") that determine a man's temperament.

That nevere sholdè ther be defaute in here.° *a lacking in her*
Heere may men seen an humble wys accord:
Thus hath she take hir servant and hir lord,
Servant in love, and lord in mariage;
Thanne was he bothe in lordship and servage.° *servitude*
Servage? Nay, but in lordshipe above,
Sith he hath bothe his lady and his love;
His lady, certes,° and his wyf also, *certainly*
The which that lawe of love acordeth to.
And whan he was in this prosperitee,
Hoom with his wyf he gooth to his contree,° *region*
Nat fer fro Pedmark, ther his dwelling was,[8]
Where as he liveth in blisse and in solas.° *solace, joy*
Who coude telle, but he hadde wedded be,° *unless he'd been married*
The joye, the ese, and the prosperitee
That is bitwixe an housbonde and his wyf?
A yeer and more lasted this blisful lyf,
Til that the knight of which I speke of thus,
That of Kayrrud° was cleped° Arveragus, *from Kerru / called*
Shoop him° to goon and dwelle a yeer or tweyne° *Prepared himself / two*
In Engelond, that cleped was eek° Briteyne,° *also / Britain*
To seke in armes worshipe and honour—
For al his lust° he sette° in swich° labour— *pleasure / took / such*
And dwelled ther two yeer; the book seith thus.
Now wol I stinten of° this Arveragus, *cease concerning*
And speken I wole of Dorigene his wyf,
That loveth hire housbonde as hire hertes lyf.
For his absence wepeth she and syketh,° *sighs*
As doon thise noble wyves whan hem lyketh.° *it pleases them*
She moorneth, waketh,° wayleth, fasteth, pleyneth;° *stays awake / laments*
Desyr of his presence hire so distreyneth° *afflicts*
That al this wyde world she sette at noght.° *holds to be nothing*
Hire frendes, whiche that knewe hir hevy thoght,
Conforten hire in al that ever they may:
They prechen° hire, they telle hire night and day, *preach to*
That causelees she sleeth° hirself, allas! *is killing*
And every confort possible in this cas
They doon to hire with al hire bisinesse,° *their diligence*
Al for to make hire leve hire hevinesse.
By proces,° as ye knowen everichoon,° *In the course of time / every one*
Men may so longe graven in° a stoon *engrave*
Til som figure therinne emprented be.
So longe han° they conforted hire til she *have*
Receyved hath, by hope and by resoun,
The emprenting° of hire° consolacioun, *imprint / their*
Thurgh which hir grete sorwe gan aswage:° *was assuaged*
She may nat alwey duren° in swich rage.° *continue / passion*
And eek° Arveragus, in al this care, *also*
Hath sent hire lettres hoom of his welfare,° *well-being*

8. Not far from Penmarch (on the coast of Finistère, in Brittany), where his dwelling was.

And that he wol come hastily agayn;
Or elles hadde this sorwe hir herte slayn.
Hire freendes sawe hir sorwe gan to slake,° *began to lessen*
And preyde hire on knees, for Goddes sake,
To come and romen hire° in companye, *walk about*
Awey to dryve hire derke fantasye.° *dark imagining(s)*
And finally, she graunted that requeste,
For wel she saugh° that it was for the beste. *saw*
Now stood hire castel faste° by the see, *close*
And often with hire freendes walketh she
Hire to disporte° upon the bank an heigh,° *amuse / on high*
Where as she many a ship and barge seigh° *saw*
Seilinge hir° cours, where as hem liste go. *their*
But thanne was that a parcel° of hire wo, *portion*
For to hirself ful ofte "Allas!" seith she,
"Is ther no ship, of so manye as I see,
Wol bringen hom my lord? Thanne were myn herte
Al warisshed° of his bittre peynes smerte."° *cured / smart, sharp*
Another tyme ther wolde she sitte and thinke,
And caste hir eyen dounward fro the brinke.° *edge*
But whan she saugh the grisly rokkes blake,° *black rocks*
For verray fere° so wolde hir herte quake *Out of real fear*
That on hire feet she mighte hire noght sustene.
Than wolde she sitte adoun upon the grene,° *grass*
And pitously into the see biholde,
And seyn right thus, with sorweful sykes° colde: *sighs*
"Eterne God, that thurgh thy purveyaunce° *foresight, providence*
Ledest° the world by certein governaunce,° *Guidest / rule*
In ydel,° as men seyn, ye no thing make. *vain*
But Lord, thise grisly feendly° rokkes blake, *hostile, devilish*
That semen° rather a foul confusioun *seem (to be)*
Of werk, than any fair creacioun
Of swich a parfit wys° God and a stable,° *wise / steadfast*
Why han ye wroght this werk unresonable?° *i.e., that confounds reason*
For by this werk, south, north, ne west, ne eest,
Ther nis y-fostred° man, ne brid, ne beest. *is not served, supported*
It dooth no good, to my wit,° but anoyeth.° *understanding / injures*
See ye nat, Lord, how mankinde it destroyeth?
An hundred thousand bodies of mankinde
Han rokkes slayn, al be they nat in minde:° *although they be not remembered*
Which mankinde is so fair part of thy werk
That thou it madest lyk to thyn owene merk.° *image*
Thanne semed it ye hadde a greet chiertee° *affection*
Toward mankinde; but how thanne may it be
That ye swiche meenes° make it to destroyen, *such means*
Which meenes do no good, but evere anoyen?
I woot wel clerkes° wol seyn as hem leste,° *scholars / they please*
By arguments,° that al is for the beste, *i.e., of philosophy*
Though I ne can the causes nat y-knowe.
But thilke° God that made wind to blowe, *that same*
As kepe° my lord! This° my conclusioun. *May he protect / This is*

To clerkes lete° I al disputisoun,° *leave / debate*
But wolde° God that alle thise rokkes blake *would (to)*
Were sonken° into helle for his sake! *sunken*
Thise rokkes sleen° myn herte for the fere."° *slay / fear*
Thus wolde she seyn, with many a pitous tere.
Hire freendes sawe that it was no disport° *pleasure (for her)*
To romen by the see, but disconfort,
And shopen° for to pleyen somewher elles.° *arranged / else*
They leden hire by riveres and by welles,° *springs*
And eek in othere places delitables;° *pleasant*
They dauncen, and they pleyen at ches° and tables.° *chess / backgammon*
So on a day, right in the morwe-tyde,° *morning*
Unto a gardin that was ther bisyde,
In which that they hadde maad hir ordinaunce° *their arrangements*
Of vitaille° and of other purveyaunce,° *For food / provisions*
They goon and pleye hem al the longe day.
And this was on the sixte morwe° of May, *morning*
Which May had peynted° with his softe shoures° *painted / showers*
This gardin ful of leves and of floures;
And craft of mannes hand so curiously° *skillfully*
Arrayed° hadde this gardin, trewely, *Adorned*
That nevere was ther gardin of swich prys,° *so priceless*
But if° it were the verray Paradys.° *Unless / Paradise itself*
The odour of floures and the fresshe sighte
Wolde han maked any herte lighte
That evere was born, but if to gret° siknesse *too great*
Or to gret sorwe helde it in distresse,
So ful it was of beautee with plesaunce.° *delight*
At after-diner gonne they to daunce,[9]
And singe also, save° Dorigen allone, *except*
Which made alwey hir compleint° and hir mone,° *lament / moan*
For she ne saugh° him on the daunce go, *saw*
That was hir housbonde and hir love also.
But nathelees° she moste° a tyme abyde, *nevertheless / must*
And with good hope lete hir sorwe slyde.° *pass*
Upon° this daunce, amonges othere men, *In*
Daunced a squyer biforen Dorigen,
That fressher was and jolyer of array,° *dress*
As to my doom,° than is the monthe of May. *judgment*
He singeth, daunceth, passinge° any man *surpassing*
That is, or was, sith° that the world bigan. *since*
Therwith he was, if men sholde him discryve,° *describe*
Oon of the beste faringe° man on lyve:° *handsomest / alive*
Yong, strong, right vertuous, and riche and wys,
And wel biloved, and holden in gret prys.° *held in great esteem*
And shortly, if the sothe° I tellen shal, *truth*
Unwiting of° this Dorigen at al, *Unknown to*
This lusty° squyer, servant to Venus, *vigorous, joyful*

9. After dinner (the first big meal of the day, between 9 A.M. and noon), they began to dance.

Which that y-cleped° was Aurelius, *called*
Hadde loved hire best of any creature
Two yeer and more, as was his aventure,° *lot*
But never dorste° he telle hire his grevaunce:° *dared / sorrow*
Withouten coppe he drank al his penaunce.[1]
He was despeyred;° no thing dorste° he seye, *in despair / dared*
Save in his songes somwhat wolde he wreye° *disclose*
His wo, as in a general compleyning;° *lamentation*
He seyde he lovede, and was biloved no thing.° *not at all*
Of swich matere° made he manye layes, *such substance*
Songes, compleintes, roundels, virelayes,[2]
How that he dorste nat his sorwe telle,
But languissheth as a furie dooth in helle;
And dye he moste, he seyde, as dide Ekko
For Narcisus, that dorste nat telle hir wo.[3]
In other manere than ye here me seye,
Ne dorste he nat to hire his wo biwreye,° *reveal*
Save that, paraventure,° somtyme at daunces, *by chance*
Ther° yonge folk kepen hir observaunces,° *Where / perform their devotions*
It may wel be he loked on hir face
In swich a wyse as man that asketh grace,
But nothing wiste° she of his entente.° *knew / purpose(s)*
Nathelees, it happed, er they thennes wente,° *before they departed thence*
By cause that he was hire neighebour,
And was a man of worshipe and honour,
And hadde y-knowen him of tyme yore,[4]
They fille in speche;° and forth more and more *fell into conversation*
Unto his purpos drough° Aurelius, *drew*
And when he saugh° his tyme, he seyde thus: *saw*
"Madame," quod he, "by God that this world made,
So that° I wiste° it mighte youre herte glade,° *If only / knew / gladden*
I wolde that day that youre Arveragus
Wente over the see, that I, Aurelius,
Had went ther° nevere I sholde have come agayn. *there where*
For wel I woot° my service is in vayn: *know*
My guerdon° is but bresting° of myn herte. *reward / breaking*
Madame, reweth° upon my peynes smerte,° *take pity / sharp*
For with a word ye may me sleen° or save. *slay*
Heere at your feet God wolde that I were grave!° *buried*
I ne have as now no leyser° more to seye: *leisure, opportunity*
Have mercy, swete, or ye wol do me deye!"° *make me die*
She gan to loke upon° Aurelius: *stared at*
"Is this youre wil," quod she, "and sey ye thus?
Nevere erst,"° quod she, "ne wiste° I what ye mente. *before / knew*
But now, Aurelie, I knowe youre entente,

1. Literally, "He drank all his penance without cup," but the exact meaning is unclear: perhaps "He had to swallow his pain," being unable to speak of it to her.
2. Various forms of lyric.
3. Echo, unable to speak in her own right, could not tell Narcissus of her love for him; she died in despair, ever faithful to that love.
4. The subject "she" must be supplied; *of tyme yore*: for a long time past.

By thilke° God that yaf° me soule and lyf, *that same / gave*
Ne shal I nevere been untrewe° wyf, *unfaithful*
In word ne werk,° as fer as I have wit. *deed*
I wol ben his to whom that I am knit:° *i.e., in matrimony*
Tak this for fynal answere as of me."
But after that in pley thus seyde she:
"Aurelie," quod she, "by heighe God above,
Yet wolde I graunte yow to been youre love,
Sin° I yow see so pitously complayne. *Since*
Loke what° day that, endelong° Britayne, *Whatever / along the edge of*
Ye remoeve alle the rokkes, stoon by stoon,
That they ne lette° ship ne boot to goon°— *prevent / from passing*
I seye, whan ye han maad the coost so clene
Of rokkes, that ther nis° no stoon y-sene— *is not*
Thanne wol I love yow best of any man;
Have heer my trouthe,° in al that evere I can." *pledge*
"Is ther non other grace° in yow?" quod he. *mercy*
"No, by that Lord," quod she, "that maked me!
For wel I woot° that it shal never bityde.° *know / happen*
Lat swiche° folies out of youre herte slyde.° *such / pass*
What deyntee° sholde a man han in his lyf *delight*
For to go love another mannes wyf,
That hath hir body whan so that him lyketh?"[5]
Aurelius ful ofte sore syketh;° *painfully sighs*
Wo was Aurelie, whan that he this herde,
And with a sorweful herte he thus answerde:
"Madame," quod he, "this were an inpossible!° *impossibility*
Than° moot° I dye of sodein deth horrible." *Then / must*
And with that word he turned him anoon.° *at once*
Tho° come hir othere freendes many oon, *Then*
And in the aleyes° romeden° up and doun, *garden walks / strolled*
And nothing wiste° of this conclusioun;° *knew / outcome*
But sodeinly bigonne revel newe° *began new revelry*
Til that the brighte sonne loste his hewe,° *hue*
For th'orisonte° hath reft° the sonne his light— *the horizon / taken from*
This is as muche to seye as it was night—
And hoom they goon in joye and in solas,
Save only wrecche° Aurelius, allas! *wretched*
He to his hous is goon with sorweful herte.
He seeth° he may nat fro his deeth asterte:° *sees / escape*
Him semed that he felte his herte colde.[6]
Up to the hevene° his handes he gan holde,° *heavens / did raise*
And on his knowes° bare he sette him doun, *knees*
And in his raving seyde his orisoun.° *prayer*
For verray wo out of his wit he breyde.[7]
He niste° what he spak, but thus he seyde; *knew not*
With pitous herte his pleynt° hath he bigonne *complaint*

5. Who possesses her body (in the act of love) whensoever it pleases him.
6. It seemed to him that he felt his heart grow cold.
7. For sheer grief he went out of his mind.

Unto the goddes, and first unto the sonne:° — *sun*
He seyde, "Appollo, god and governour
Of every plaunte,° herbe, tree and flour, — *plant*
That yevest, after thy declinacioun,[8]
To ech of hem° his tyme and his sesoun, — *each of them*
As thyn herberwe° chaungeth lowe or hye, — *lodging, zodiacal position*
Lord Phebus, cast thy merciable yë° — *merciful eye*
On wrecche Aurelie, which that am but lorn.° — *lost*
Lo, lord! my lady hath my deeth y-sworn
Withoute gilt, but° thy benignitee° — *unless / kindness*
Upon my dedly° herte have som pitee! — *dying*
For wel I woot,° lord Phebus, if yow lest,° — *know / if it please you*
Ye may me helpen, save° my lady, best. — *except for*
Now voucheth sauf° that I may yow devyse° — *grant / describe*
How that I may been holpe° and in what wyse.° — *helped / way*
Youre blisful suster, Lucina the shene,° — *bright*
That of the see° is chief goddesse and quene[9]— — *sea*
Though Neptunus have deitee in the see,
Yet emperesse aboven him is she—
Ye knowen wel, lord, that right as hir desyr
Is to be quiked and lighted of youre fyr,[1]
For which she folweth yow ful bisily,
Right° so the see desyreth naturelly — *Just*
To folwen hire, as she that is goddesse
Bothe in° the see and riveres more and lesse. — *i.e., goddess of*
Wherfore, lord Phebus, this is my requeste:
Do this miracle—or do° myn herte breste°— — *make / burst*
That now, next at this opposicioun,° — *opposition (of the sun and moon)*
Which in the signe° shal be of the Leoun,° — *(zodiacal) sign / Lion (Leo)*
As preyeth hire so greet a flood to bringe
That fyve fadme° at the leeste it overspringe° — *fathoms / tower over*
The hyeste rokke in Armorik Briteyne;
And lat this flood endure yeres tweyne.° — *two*
Thanne certes to my lady may I seye:
'Holdeth youre heste,° the rokkes been aweye.' — *promise*
Lord Phebus, dooth this miracle for me!
Preye hire she go no faster cours than ye;
I seye, preyeth your suster° that she go — *sister*
No faster cours than ye thise yeres two.[2]
Than shal she been evene atte fulle° alway, — *just at the full*
And spring-flood laste bothe night and day.
And but° she vouche sauf° in swiche manere° — *unless / grant / such a way*
To graunte me my sovereyn lady dere,
Prey hire to sinken every rok adoun
Into hir owene derke regioun[3]

8. That givest, according to thy distance from the equator ("declinacioun").
9. Lucina is the goddess of light, here identified with Diana, the moon.
1. *Quiked*: given life; *lighted of*: illumined by. The simple fact referred to here is that the moon depends on the sun for its light. (Cf. the explanation of tides in ll. 1052–54.)
2. The miracle requested would keep the sun and moon in perfect opposition for two years, so that the high tide covering the rocks might not wane.
3. Lucina is here also identified with Proserpina, Pluto's queen in the underworld.

Under the ground, ther° Pluto dwelleth inne, *where*
Or nevere mo shal I my lady winne.
Thy temple in Delphos wol I barefoot seke.° *seek (visit)*
Lord Phebus, see the teres on my cheke,
And of my peyne have som compassioun."
And with that word in swowne° he fil adoun, *a faint*
And longe tyme he lay forth° in a traunce. *thereafter*
His brother, which that knew of his penaunce,° *suffering*
Up caughte him and to bedde he hath him broght.
Dispeyred° in this torment and this thoght *Filled with despair*
Lete I this woful creature lye:
Chese he, for me, wher he wol live or dye.[4]
Arveragus, with hele° and greet honour, *in health*
As he that was of chivalrye the flour,
Is comen hoom, and othere worthy men.
O blisful artow° now, thou Dorigen, *art thou*
That hast thy lusty° housbonde in thyne armes, *vigorous, merry*
The fresshe° knight, the worthy man of armes, *lively*
That loveth thee as his owene hertes lyf.
No thing list him to been imaginatyf[5]
If any wight° hadde spoke, whyl he was oute,° *person / away*
To hire of love; he hadde of it no doute.° *fear*
He noght entendeth° to no swich matere, *paid no attention*
But daunceth, justeth,° maketh hire good chere; *jousts*
And thus in joye and blisse I lete hem dwelle,
And of the syke° Aurelius wol I telle. *sick*
In langour° and in torment furious *sickness*
Two yeer and more lay wrecche Aurelius,
Er° any foot he mighte on erthe goon.° *Before / walk*
Ne confort in this tyme hadde he noon,
Save of his brother, which that was a clerk:° *scholar*
He knew of al this wo and al this werk,° *affair*
For to non other creature, certeyn,° *certainly*
Of this matere he dorste° no word seyn. *dared*
Under° his brest he bar it more secree *Within*
Than evere dide Pamphilus for Galathee.[6]
His brest was hool° withoute for to sene,° *whole / seen from outside*
But in his herte ay was the arwe° kene; *arrow*
And wel ye knowe that of a sursanure[7]
In surgerye is perilous the cure,
But° men mighte touche the arwe, or come therby.° *Unless / near to it*
His brother weep° and wayled prively,° *wept / secretly*
Til atte laste him fil in remembraunce,° *it occurred to him*
That whiles he was at Orliens° in Fraunce, *Orléans (university)*
As yonge clerkes that been likerous° *desirous*
To reden artes that been curious° *recondite, subtle*

4. Let *him* choose, for my part, whether he will live or die.
5. He has no wish at all to be suspicious (full of imaginings).
6. Pamphilus and Galatea were lovers in a widely circulated twelfth-century dialogue, *Pamphilus de Amore*.
7. A wound healed only on the surface.

Seken in every halke° and every herne° *nook / corner*
Particuler° sciences for to lerne— *Little-known*
He him remembred that, upon a day,
At Orliens in studie a book he say° *saw*
Of magik naturel,[8] which his felawe,° *companion*
That was that tyme a bacheler of lawe—
Al° were he ther to lerne another craft— *Although*
Had prively° upon his desk y-laft:° *secretly / left*
Which book spak muchel of the operaciouns
Touchinge the eighte and twenty mansiouns° *positions in the heavens*
That longen° to the mone°—and swich folye *belong / moon (in a month)*
As in oure dayes is nat worth a flye;° *fly*
For holy chirches feith in our bileve
Ne suffreth noon illusion° us to greve.° *deception / vex*
And whan this book was in his remembraunce,
Anon° for joye his herte gan° to daunce, *Immediately / began*
And to himself he seyde prively:° *secretly*
"My brother shal be warisshed° hastily; *cured*
For I am siker° that ther be sciences° *certain / kinds of knowledge*
By whiche men make diverse apparences° *apparitions*
Swiche as thise subtile tregetoures° pleye.° *illusionists / perform*
For ofte at festes° have I wel herd seye *feasts*
That tregetours withinne an halle° large *(dining) hall*
Have maad come in a water° and a barge, *some water*
And in the halle rowen° up and doun; *rowed*
Somtyme hath semed come a grim leoun;° *lion*
And somtyme floures springe as in a mede;° *meadow*
Somtyme a vyne, and grapes whyte and rede;
Somtyme a castel,° al of lym° and stoon— *castle / lime*
And whan hem lyked, voyded it anoon.[9]
Thus semed it to every mannes sighte.
  Now thanne conclude I thus, that if I mighte
At Orliens som old felawe° y-find *companion*
That hadde this° mones mansions in minde, *these*
Or other magik naturel above,° *i.e., even higher*
He sholde wel make my brother han his love.
For with an apparence° a clerk° may make *illusion / scholar*
To mannes sighte, that alle the rokkes blake
Of Britaigne weren y-voyded° everichon,° *removed / every one*
And shippes by the brinke° comen and gon, *coast*
And in swich forme endure a wowke° or two. *week*
Than were my brother warisshed° of his wo; *cured*
Than moste she nedes holden hir biheste,[1]
Or elles he shal shame hire atte leste."
  What° sholde I make a lenger tale of this? *Why*
Unto his brotheres bed he comen is,

8. I.e., employing astronomy.
9. And when it pleased them, caused it at once to disappear. (The *tregetours* are as much artisans as magicians, working the kind of "magic" ordinarily associated with stage sets and properties. A feast given by Charles V in Paris in 1378 included an entertainment much like this.)
1. Then she needs must keep her promise.

And swich confort he yaf° him for to gon *gave*
To Orliens, that he up stirte anon,° *jumped up at once*
And on his wey forthward thanne is he fare,° *has he traveled*
In hope for to ben lissed° of his care. *eased*
  Whan they were come almost to that citee,
But if it were a two furlong or three,[2]
A yong clerk rominge° by himself they mette, *strolling*
Which that in Latin thriftily hem grette,° *suitably greeted them*
And after that he seyde a wonder° thing: *wondrous*
"I knowe," quod he, "the cause of youre coming."
And er° they ferther any fote° wente, *before / a foot farther*
He tolde hem al that was in hire entente.
  This Briton clerk him asked of felawes
The whiche that he had knowe in olde dawes;° *days*
And he answerde him that they dede were,
For which he weep° ful ofte many a tere. *wept*
  Doun of his hors Aurelius lighte° anon, *alighted*
And forth with this magicien is he gon
Hoom to his hous, and maden hem° wel at ese. *made themselves*
Hem lakked° no vitaille° that mighte hem plese; *They lacked / food*
So wel arrayed° hous as ther was oon *furnished (a)*
Aurelius in his lyf saugh nevere noon.
  He shewed him, er° he wente to sopeer,° *before / supper*
Forestes, parkes ful of wilde deer:
Ther saugh he hertes° with hir hornes hye,° *harts / tall antlers*
The gretteste° that evere were seyn with yë,° *largest / eye*
He saugh of hem an hondred slayn with houndes,
And somme with arwes° blede of° bittre woundes. *arrows / bled from*
He saugh, whan voided° were thise wilde deer, *departed*
Thise fauconers° upon a fair river,° *Some falconers / riverbank*
That with hir haukes han the heron slayn.
  Tho saugh° he knightes justing° in a playn; *Then saw / jousting*
And after this he dide him swich plesaunce
That he him shewed his lady on° a daunce *in*
On which himself he daunced, as him thoughte.° *so it seemed to him*
And whan this maister° that this magik wroughte *Master of Arts*
Saugh it was tyme, he clapte his handes two,
And farewel! al oure revel was ago.° *gone*
And yet remoeved° they nevere out of the hous *moved*
Whyl they saugh al this sighte merveillous,
But in his studie, ther as° his bookes be, *where*
They seten stille, and no wight but they three.
  To him this maister called his squyer,
And seyde him thus: "Is redy oure soper?
Almost an houre it is, I undertake,° *declare*
Sith° I yow bad° oure soper for to make, *Since / ordered*
Whan that thise worthy men wenten with me
Into my studie, ther as my bookes be."
  "Sire," quod this squyer, "whan it lyketh yow,° *it pleases*

2. Unless it was two or three furlongs before. (A furlong is one-eighth of a mile.)

It is al redy, though ye wol° right now." *wish (it)*
"Go we than soupe,"° quod he, "as for the beste: *to eat supper*
This° amorous folk somtyme mote° han reste." *These / must*
At after-soper fille° they in tretee° *fell / negotiations*
What somme° sholde this maistres guerdon° be, *sum / reward*
To remoeven alle the rokkes of Britayne,
And eek from Gerounde to the mouth of Sayne.[3]
He made it straunge,° and swoor,° so God him save, *difficult / swore*
Lasse° than a thousand pound he wolde nat have, *Less*
Ne gladly for that somme he wolde nat goon.[4]
Aurelius with blisful herte anoon° *at once*
Answerde thus, "Fy on a thousand pound!
This wyde world, which that men seye is round,
I wolde it yeve,° if I were lord of it. *give*
This bargayn is ful drive,° for we ben knit.° *driven, concluded / agreed*
Ye shal be payed trewely, by my trouthe!° *loyalty, fidelity*
But loketh now, for no necligence or slouthe,° *sloth*
Ye tarie us heer° no lenger than tomorwe." *delay us here*
"Nay," quod this clerk, "have heer my feith to borwe."° *i.e., as pledge*
To bedde is goon Aurelius whan him leste,° *it pleased him*
And wel ny° al that night he hadde his reste: *well nigh, almost*
What for his labour and his hope of blisse,
His woful herte of penaunce° hadde a lisse.° *suffering / relief*
Upon the morwe,° whan that it was day, *morning*
To Britaigne toke they the righte° way, *direct*
Aurelius and this magicien bisyde,° *at his side*
And been descended° ther° they wolde *have dismounted / where*
abyde;° *stay*
And this was, as thise bokes me remembre,° *remind me*
The colde frosty seson of Decembre.
Phebus wex old, and hewed lyk latoun,[5]
That in his hote declinacioun[6]
Shoon as the burned° gold with stremes° brighte; *burnished / beams*
But now in Capricorn adoun he lighte,° *alighted*
Where as he shoon ful pale, I dar wel seyn.
The bittre frostes, with the sleet and reyn,° *rain*
Destroyed hath the grene in every yerd.° *garden, yard*
Janus[7] sit by the fyr with double berd,
And drinketh of his bugle-horn° the wyn; *goblet made of ox horn*
Biforn him stant° brawen° of the tusked swyn,° *stands / brawn, meat / boar*
And "Nowel"° cryeth every lusty man. *Noel, Christmas*
Aurelius, in al that evere he can,
Doth° to this maister chere° and reverence, *Makes / good cheer*
And preyeth him to doon his diligence

3. And also from the Gironde to the mouth of the Seine.
4. I.e., the price is his absolute minimum, nothing to cause him delight.
5. Phoebus (the sun) grew old, and colored like brass.
6. I.e., in the Tropic of Cancer.
7. The two-headed Roman god (hence double-bearded), who looks both forward and backward, to the future and the past. The month of January is named for him, and medieval calendars (in the Books of Hours) often show him feasting, in the character of a medieval prince or rich landowner.

To bringen him out of his peynes smerte,
Or with a swerd that he wolde slitte his herte.
This subtil° clerk swich routhe° had of this man *skillful / compassion*
That night and day he spedde him that° he can, *hurried as much as*
To wayten a tyme of his conclusioun;[8]
This is to seye, to maken illusioun,
By swich an apparence° or jogelrye°— *apparition / magic, jugglery*
I ne can no° termes of astrologye— *I know no*
That she and every wight° sholde wene° and seye *person / suppose*
That of Britaigne the rokkes were aweye,
Or elles they were sonken under grounde.
So atte laste he hath his tyme y-founde
To maken his japes° and his wrecchednesse° *tricks / miserable actions*
Of swich° a supersticious cursednesse. *From such*
His tables Toletanes[9] forth he broght,
Ful wel corrected, ne ther lakked noght,
Neither his collect ne his expans yeres,[1]
Ne his rotes° ne his othere geres,° *statistics / gear*
As been his centres and his arguments,
And his proporcionels convenients
For his equacions in every thing.[2]
And by his eighte spere[3] in his wirking
He knew ful wel how fer Alnath° was shove° *the star / advanced*
Fro the heed° of thilke fixe° Aries above *head / that same fixed (constellation)*
That in the ninthe speere considered is:[4]
Ful subtilly he calculed at this.
Whan he had founde his firste mansioun,° *position (of the moon)*
He knew the remenant° by proporcioun, *remainder*
And knew the arysing° of his mone° weel, *rising / moon*
And in whos face, and terme,[5] and everydeel;
And knew ful weel the mones mansioun,
Acordaunt to his operacioun,
And knew also his othere observaunces° *ceremonies*
For swiche illusiouns and swiche meschaunces° *mischief*
As hethen° folk used in thilke° days. *heathen / those same*
For which no lenger maked he delayes,
But thurgh his magik, for a wyke or tweye,° *week or two*
It semed that alle the rokkes were aweye.
Aurelius, which that yet despeired° is *despairing*
Wher° he shal han his love or fare amis, *Whether*
Awaiteth night and day on this miracle;
And whan he knew that ther was noon obstacle—
That voided° were thise rokkes everichon°— *removed / every one*
Doun to his maistres feet he fil anon° *fell at once*

8. To watch for a time to conclude the matter.
9. Astronomical tables calculated for the city of Toledo, which gives them their name.
1. The "collect" recorded movements of the planets over long periods of years; the "expans yeres" for shorter periods of up to twenty years.
2. Astronomical instruments and formulae used to determine astrological positions.
3. The eighth sphere, of the fixed stars.
4. That is held to be in the ninth sphere (the Primum Mobile).
5. Divisions, even and uneven, of zodiacal signs.

And seyde, "I woful wrecche, Aurelius,
Thanke yow, lord, and lady myn Venus,
That me han holpen fro my cares colde."° — *bitter, fatal*
And to the temple his wey forth hath he holde,
Where as he knew he sholde his lady see.
And whan he saugh° his tyme, anonright° he, — *saw / right away*
With dredful° herte and with ful humble chere,° — *fearful / appearance*
Salewed° hath his sovereyn lady dere: — *Greeted*
  "My righte° lady," quod this woful man, — *own true*
"Whom I most drede° and love as I best can, — *fear*
And lothest° were of al this world displese, — *most loath*
Nere it° that I for yow have swich disese° — *Were it not / misery*
That I moste° dyen heer at youre foot anon, — *must*
Noght wolde I telle how me is wo bigon.° — *woebegone I am*
But certes outher° moste I dye or pleyne;° — *either / speak my grief*
Ye slee° me, giltelees, for verray° peyne. — *slay / real*
But of my deeth, thogh that ye have no routhe,° — *compassion*
Avyseth yow,° er° that ye breke your trouthe.° — *Take heed / before / pledge*
Repenteth yow, for thilke God above,[6]
Er ye me sleen° by cause that I yow love. — *slay*
For, madame, wel ye woot what ye han hight°— — *promised*
Nat that I chalange° any thing of right° — *claim / by rights*
Of yow, my sovereyn lady, but youre grace°— — *mercy, favor*
But in a gardin yond,° at swich a place, — *yonder*
Ye woot right wel° what ye bihighten° me; — *know full well / promised*
And in myn hand youre trouthe plighten° ye — *pledged*
To love me best. God woot, ye seyde so,
Al be° that I unworthy be therto. — *Although*
Madame, I speke it for the honour of yow
More than to save myn hertes lyf right now.
I have do° so as ye comanded me; — *done*
And if ye vouchesauf,° ye may go see. — *(will) grant (it)*
Doth as yow list, have youre biheste in minde,
For, quik° or deed, right there ye shul me finde. — *living*
In yow lyth al to do° me live or deye: — *make*
But wel I woot the rokkes been aweye!"
  He taketh his leve, and she astonied° stood; — *astonished*
In al hir face nas° a drope of blood. — *was not*
She wende° never han come in swich a trappe. — *thought*
"Allas!" quod she, "that evere this sholde happe!° — *occur*
For wende I nevere, by possibilitee,
That swich a monstre° or merveille mighte be! — *strange thing*
It is agayns the proces° of nature." — *course*
And hoom she gooth a sorweful creature.
For verray fere° unnethe° may she go.° — *deep fear / scarcely / walk*
She wepeth, wailleth, al a day° or two, — *a whole day*
And swowneth,° that it routhe° was to see; — *faints / pity*

6. Repent you, for (the sake of) that same God on high.

But why it was, to no wight° tolde she, — *person*
For out of toune was goon Arveragus.
But to hirself she spak, and seyde thus,
With face pale and with ful sorweful chere,° — *countenance*
In hire compleynt,° as ye shul after here: — *lament*
"Allas," quod she, "on thee, Fortune, I pleyne,° — *make complaint*
That unwar° wrapped has me in thy cheyne,° — *unawares / chain*
Fro which t'escape woot° I no socour° — *know / help*
Save only deeth or elles° dishonour; — *else*
Oon of thise two bihoveth me° to chese. — *it's necessary for me*
But nathelees yet have I lever to lese° — *would I rather lose*
My lyf, than of my body to have a shame,
Or knowe° myselven fals, or lese my name; — *acknowledge*
And with my deth I may be quit,° ywis. — *freed (from the debt)*
Hath ther nat many a noble wyf er this,° — *before now*
And many a mayde, y-slayn hirself, allas!
Rather than with hir body doon trepas?° — *commit a sin*
Yis, certes, lo, thise stories[7] beren witnesse;
Whan thretty° tyraunts, ful of cursednesse, — *thirty*
Hadde slayn Phidoun in Athenes atte feste,° — *at (the) feasting*
They commanded his doghtres for t'areste,° — *to be seized*
And bringen hem biforn hem in despyt° — *scorn*
Al naked, to fulfille hir foul delyt,° — *pleasure*
And in hir fadres blood they made hem daunce
Upon the pavement, God yeve hem mischaunce!° — *give them misfortune*
For which thise woful maydens, ful of drede,° — *fear*
Rather than they wolde lese hir maydenhede,
They prively° ben stirt° into a welle, — *secretly / have leaped*
And dreynte° hemselven, as the bokes telle. — *drowned*
They of Messene lete enquere and seke[8]
Of Lacedomie° fifty maydens eke,° — *From Sparta / also*
On whiche they wolden doon° hir lecherye; — *perform*
But was ther noon of al that compaignye
That she nas° slayn, and with a good entente° — *was not / will, purpose*
Chees° rather for to dye than assente — *Chose*
To been oppressed° of hir maydenhede. — *ravished*
Why sholde I thanne to dye been in drede?
Lo eek the tiraunt Aristoclides° — *a tyrant of Arcadia*
That loved a mayden, heet° Stimphalides, — *named*
Whan that hir fader slayn was on a night,
Unto Dianes temple goth she right,° — *directly*
And hente° the image° in hir handes two, — *clasped / of the goddess*
Fro which image wolde she nevere go.
No wight° ne mighte hir handes of it arace,° — *person / tear away*
Til she was slayn right in the selve place.
Now sith that° maydens hadden swich despyt° — *since / disdain, scorn*

7. The examples of virtuous women she brings to mind, from Phidon's daughters on, are all found in St. Jerome's treatise against Jovinian.
8. The men of Messene (in the Peloponnesus) had inquiries made and sought.

To been defouled with mannes foul delyt,
Wel oghte a wyf rather hirselven slee
Than be defouled,° as it thinketh me.° *defiled / it seems to me*
What shal I seyn of Hasdrubales° wyf, *Hasdrubal's*
That at Cartage° birafte° hirself hir lyf? *Carthage / took from*
For whan she saugh° that Romayns wan° the toun, *saw / won*
She took hir children alle, and skipte° adoun *jumped*
Into the fyr, and chees rather to dye
Than any Romayn dide° hire vileinye. *should do*
Hath nat Lucresse° y-slayn hirself, allas! *Lucretia*
At Rome, whanne she oppressed° was *violated*
Of° Tarquin, for hire thoughte° it was a shame *By / it seemed to her*
To liven whan she hadde lost hir name?
The sevene maydens of Milesie° also *Miletus (in Asia Minor)*
Han slayn hemself,° for verray° drede and wo, *themselves / great*
Rather than folk of Gaule° hem sholde oppresse. *the Galatians*
Mo than a thousand stories, as I gesse,
Coude I now telle as touchinge this matere.
When Habradate° was slayn, his wyf so dere *Abradates, king of the Susi*
Hirselven slow,° and leet hir blood to glyde *slew*
In Habradates woundes depe and wyde,
And seyde, 'My body, at the leeste way,° *at least*
Ther shal no wight defoulen, if I may.'° *if I can help it*
What sholde I mo ensamples heerof sayn,
Sith that so manye han hemselven slayn
Wel rather than they wolde defouled be?
I wol conclude that it is bet° for me *better*
To sleen myself than been defouled thus.
I wol be trewe unto Arveragus,
Or rather sleen myself in som manere—
As dide Demociones° doghter dere, *Demotion's*
By cause that she wolde nat defouled be.
O Cedasus!° it is ful greet pitee *Scedasus, of Boeotia*
To reden how thy doghtren° deyde, allas! *daughters*
That slowe hemself for swich manere cas.° *such a kind of occurrence*
As greet a pitee was it, or wel more,
The Theban mayden that for Nichanore° *Nichanor, an Alexandrian*
Hirselven slow° right for swich manere wo. *slew*
Another Theban mayden dide right so:
For° oon of Macedoine° hadde hire *Because / Macedonia*
oppressed,° *violated*
She with hire deeth hir maydenhede redressed.° *made amends for*
What shal I seye of Nicerates° wyf *Niceratus's, an Athenian*
That for swich cas birafte hirself hir lyf?
How trewe eek was to Alcebiades° *Alcibiades, friend of Socrates*
His love, that rather for to dyen chees° *chose*
Than for to suffre° his body unburied be! *allow*
Lo, which° a wyf was Alceste,"[9] quod she. *what*
"What seith Omer° of gode Penalopee?° *Homer / Penelope, Ulysses' wife*

9. Alcestis, wife of Admetus, out of love for him volunteered to die in his place.

Al Grece knoweth of hire chastitee.
Pardee, of Laodomya° is writen thus, *Laodamia*
That whan at Troye was slayn Protheselaus,° *Protesilaus*
No lenger wolde she live after his day.
The same of noble Porcia° telle I may: *Portia*
Withoute Brutus coude she nat live,
To whom she hadde al hool° hir herte yive.° *completely / given*
The parfit wyfhod of Arthemesye[1]
Honoured is thurgh al the Barbarye.° *heathendom*
O Teuta,° queen! thy wyfly chastitee *queen of Illirica*
To alle wyves may a mirour be.
The same thing I seye of Bilia,° *wife of Gaius Duillius*
Of Rodogone, and eek Valeria."[2]
  Thus pleyned° Dorigene a day or tweye, *lamented*
Purposinge evere that she wolde deye.° *die*
But natheless, upon the thridde night,
Hom cam Arveragus, this worthy knight,
And asked hire why that she weep° so sore;° *wept / painfully*
And she gan wepen ever lenger the more.° *ever more and more*
"Allas!" quod she, "that ever was I born!
Thus have I seyd," quod she, "thus have I sworn,"
And told him al as ye han herd bifore;
It nedeth nat reherce it yow namore.° *repeat it again to you*
This housbonde, with glade chere,° in freendly wyse, *expression, countenance*
Answerde and seyde as I shal yow devyse.° *relate*
"Is ther oght elles, Dorigen, but this?"
  "Nay, nay," quod she, "God help me so as wis;° *indeed*
This is to° muche, and° it were Goddes wille." *too / even if*
  "Ye, wyf," quod he, "lat slepen that° is stille.° *what / quiet*
It may be wel, paraventure,° yet today. *by chance*
Ye shul youre trouthe holden,° by my fay! *keep your pledge*
For God so wisly° have mercy on me, *surely*
I hadde wel levere° y-stiked° for to be, *rather / stabbed*
For verray° love which that I to yow have, *true*
But if ye sholde youre trouthe kepe and save.° *guard and preserve*
Trouthe is the hyeste thing that man may kepe."[3]
But with that word he brast anon to wepe,[4]
And seyde, "I yow forbede, up° peyne of deeth, *on*
That nevere, whyl thee lasteth lyf ne breeth,
To no wight° tel thou of this aventure— *person*
As I may best, I wol my wo endure—
Ne make no contenance of hevinesse,° *i.e., look sorrowful*

1. Artemesia, queen of Caria, built a famous tomb for her husband.
2. Rhodogune, wife of Darius; Valeria, daughter of Diocletian.
3. "Trouthe" is a central concept in this poem, for which no single modern equivalent can be found. In certain idioms, it can be defined as "pledge" or "promise"; but its larger sense (as here) is fidelity, steadfastness, integrity—the capacity to embody a single "entente" without variance, whatever the circumstances. The keeping of a promise is only symptomatic of the presence of this deeper, pervasive moral quality.
4. But with that word, he burst at once into tears.

That folk of yow may demen° harm or gesse."° *suppose / guess (at it)*
  And forth he cleped° a squyer and a mayde: *called*
"Goth forth anon° with Dorigen," he sayde, *at once*
"And bringeth hire to swich a° place anon." *a certain*
They take hir° leve, and on hir wey they gon, *their*
But they ne wiste° why she thider° wente: *knew / thither*
He nolde° no wight tellen his entente. *would not*
  Paraventure° an heep° of yow, ywis,° *Perhaps / many / certainly*
Wol holden him a lewed° man in this, *thoughtless, foolish*
That he wol putte his wyf in jupartye.° *jeopardy*
Herkneth the tale, er ye upon hire crye.[5]
She may have bettre fortune than yow semeth,° *i.e., expect*
And whan that ye han herd the tale, demeth.° *judge*
  This squyer, which that highte° Aurelius, *was called*
On Dorigen that was so amorous,
Of aventure° happed hire to mete *By chance*
Amidde the toun, right in the quikkest° strete, *busiest*
As she was boun° to goon the wey forth right° *ready / directly*
Toward the gardin ther as she had hight;° *promised*
And he was to the gardinward° also, *(going) toward the garden*
For wel he spyed° whan she wolde go *he watched closely*
Out of hir hous to any maner° place. *kind of*
But thus they mette, of aventure or grace;° *by chance or good fortune*
And he saleweth° hire with glad entente,° *greets / cheerfully*
And asked of hire whiderward she wente;
And she answerde, half as she were mad,
"Unto the gardin, as myn housbond bad,
My trouthe for to holde, allas! allas!"
  Aurelius gan wondren° on this cas,° *fell to wondering / event*
And in his herte hadde greet compassioun
Of° hire and of hire lamentacioun, *For*
And of Arveragus, the worthy knight,
That bad hire holden° al that she had hight,° *keep / promised*
So looth him was[6] his wyf sholde breke hir trouthe.
And in his herte he caughte of this greet routhe,° *took great pity on this*
Consideringe the beste on every syde,
That fro his lust yet were him levere abyde[7]
Than doon so heigh° a cherlish wrecchednesse° *great / churlish, miserable act*
Agayns franchyse° and alle gentillesse;° *Against generosity / nobleness*
For which in fewe wordes seyde he thus:
  "Madame, seyth to youre lord Arveragus,
That sith° I see his grete gentillesse *since*
To yow, and eek° I see wel youre distresse, *also*
That him were levere han shame (and that were routhe)° *would be a pity*
Than ye to me sholde breke thus youre trouthe,
I have wel levere° evere to suffre wo *would much rather*

5. Hear the (whole) tale, before you complain about her.
6. So hateful to him was (the notion that).
7. (So) that he thought it better to abstain from his desire.

Than I departe° the love bitwix yow two. — *(that) I divide*
I yow relesse,° madame, into youre hond, — *release*
Quit° every serement° and every bond — *Discharged of / oath*
That ye han maad to me as heerbiforn,
Sith thilke tyme which that ye were born.[8]
My trouthe I plighte, I shal yow never repreve° — *reproach*
Of no biheste,° and here I take my leve, — *promise*
As of the treweste and the beste wyf
That evere yet I knew in al my lyf.
But every wyf be war° of hire biheste! — *be careful*
On Dorigene remembreth atte leste.° — *at (the) least*
Thus can a squyer doon a gentil dede
As well as can a knight, withouten drede."° — *doubt*
She thonketh him upon hir knees al bare,
And hoom unto hir housbond is she fare,° — *has she gone*
And tolde him al as ye han herd me sayd;
And be ye siker,° he was so weel apayd° — *sure / pleased*
That it were inpossible me to wryte.
What° sholde I lenger of this cas endyte?° — *Why / relate*
Arveragus and Dorigene his wyf
In sovereyn° blisse leden forth° hir lyf. — *supreme / lead on*
Never eft° ne was ther angre hem bitwene: — *again*
He cherisseth hire as though she were a quene,
And she was to him trewe for everemore.
Of° thise two folk ye gete of° me namore. — *Concerning / i.e., hear from*
Aurelius, that his cost° hath al forlorn,° — *expense / lost*
Curseth the tyme that evere he was born:
"Allas," quod he, "allas! that I bihighte° — *promised*
Of pured° gold a thousand pound of wighte° — *refined / by weight*
Unto this philosophre! How shal I do?
I see namore but that I am fordo.° — *done in, ruined*
Myn heritage° moot I nedes° selle — *inheritance / I needs must*
And been a beggere; heer may I nat dwelle,
And shamen al my kinrede° in this place, — *kindred, family*
But° I of him may gete bettre grace.° — *Unless / i.e., better terms*
But natheless, I wol of him assaye° — *try (to arrange with) him*
At certeyn dayes, yeer by yeer, to paye,
And thanke him of his grete curteisye;
My trouthe wol I kepe, I wol nat lye."
With herte soor° he gooth unto his cofre,° — *painful / money chest*
And broghte gold unto this philosophre
The value of fyve hundred pound, I gesse,° — *guess*
And him bisecheth of° his gentillesse — *(out) of*
To graunte him dayes of the remenaunt,[9]
And seyde, "Maister, I dar wel make avaunt,° — *boast*
I failled nevere of my trouthe as yit;
For sikerly° my dette shal be quit° — *surely / repaid*

8. Since that same time (in) which.
9. To grant him days (i.e., some time) in which to pay the remainder.

Towardes yow, howevere that I fare° *although I may go off*
To goon a-begged° in my kirtle° bare. *begging / tunic*
But wolde ye vouche sauf,° upon seuretee,° *grant / surety, pledge*
Two yeer or three for to respyten me,° *to give me a delay*
Than were I wel; for elles° moot° I selle *otherwise / must*
Myn heritage; ther is namore to telle."
This philosophre sobrely° answerde, *gravely*
And seyde thus, whan he thise wordes herde:
"Have I nat holden° covenant unto thee?" *kept*
"Yes, certes,° wel and trewely," quod° he. *certainly / said*
"Hastow° nat had thy lady as thee lyketh?" *Hast thou*
"No, no," quod he, and sorwefully he syketh.° *sighs*
"What was the cause? tel me if thou can."
Aurelius his tale anon bigan,
And tolde him al, as ye han herd bifore:
It nedeth nat to yow reherce it more.° *recite it again*
He seide, "Arveragus, of gentillesse,
Hadde levere° dye in sorwe and in distresse *rather*
Than that his wyf were of hir trouthe fals."
The sorwe of Dorigen he tolde him als,° *also*
How looth° hire was to been a wikked wyf, *loath*
And that she levere had lost that day hir lyf,
And that hir trouthe° she swoor° thurgh innocence: *pledge / swore*
She nevere erst° herde speke of apparence.° *before / illusion, magic*
"That made me han of hire so greet pitee;
And right as frely° as he sente hire me, *generously*
As frely sente I hire to him ageyn.
This al and som,° ther is namore to seyn." *This is the whole*
This philosophre answerde, "Leve° brother, *Dear*
Everich° of yow dide gentilly til other.° *Everyone / toward the other*
Thou art a squyer, and he is a knight;
But God forbede, for his blisful might,
But if° a clerk° coude doon a gentil dede *Unless / scholar*
As wel as any of yow, it is no drede!° *doubt*
Sire, I relesse thee thy thousand pound,
As° thou right now were cropen° out of the ground, *As if / had crept*
Ne nevere er° now ne haddest knowen me. *before*
For sire, I wol nat take a peny of thee
For al my craft, ne noght for my travaille.° *labor*
Thou hast y-payed wel for my vitaille;° *food, entertainment*
It is ynogh.° And farewel, have good day." *enough*
And took his hors, and forth he gooth his way.
Lordinges, this question thanne wolde I aske now:
Which was the moste free,° as thinketh yow?[1] *generous*
Now telleth me, er that° ye ferther wende.° *before / travel*
I can namore:° my tale is at an ende. *know no more*

1. I.e., in your judgment.

The Pardoner's Prologue and Tale

The Introduction

* * *

"By corpus bones![1] but° I have triacle,° — *unless / medicine*
Or elles a draught of moyste° and corny° ale, — *fresh / malty*
Or but° I here anon° a mery tale, — *unless / at once*
Myn herte is lost for pitee of this mayde.[2]
Thou bel amy,° thou Pardoner," he seyde, — *sweet friend*
"Tel us som mirthe or japes° right anon." — *jokes*
"It shall be doon," quod° he, "by Seint Ronyon![3] — *said*
But first," quod he, "heer at this ale-stake° — *tavern sign*
I wol both drinke and eten° of a cake." — *eat*
But right anon thise gentils gonne to crye,[4]
"Nay! lat him telle us of no ribaudye;° — *ribaldry*
Tel us som moral thing, that we may lere° — *learn*
Som wit,° and thanne wol we gladly here."° — *Something instructive / listen*
"I graunte,° ywis,"° quod he, "but I mot° thinke — *agree / certainly / must*
Upon som honest° thing whyl that I drinke." — *decent, decorous*

The Prologue

"Lordinges," quod he, "in chirches whan I preche,
I peyne me° to han an hauteyn° speche, — *take pains / elevated*
And ringe it out as round as gooth° a belle, — *sounds*
For I can al by rote° that I telle. — *know all by memory*
My theme° is alwey oon,° and evere was— — *text / always the same*
Radix malorum est Cupiditas.[5]
First I pronounce° whennes° that I come, — *proclaim / whence, from where*
And thanne my bulles[6] shewe I, alle and somme.° — *one and all*
Oure lige lordes seel° on my patente,° — *i.e., bishop's seal / license*
That shewe I first, my body° to warente,° — *person / authorize*
That no man be so bold, ne preest ne clerk,° — *neither priest nor scholar*
Me to destourbe of Cristes holy werk;
And after that thanne telle I forth my tales.
Bulles of popes and of cardinales,
Of patriarkes,° and bishoppes I shewe, — *heads of churches*
And in Latyn I speke a wordes fewe,
To saffron with my predicacioun,[7]
And for to stire° hem to devocioun. — *stir*
Thanne shewe I forth my longe cristal stones,° — *glass cases*
Y-crammed ful of cloutes° and of bones— — *rags*

1. I.e., Christ's bones.
2. The Host is speaking to the Physician, who has just concluded his sad tale of a young Roman girl who allows her father to kill her rather than submit to the lust of a corrupt judge.
3. St. Ronan or St. Ninian, with a possible pun on "runnion," meaning loins (including the sexual organs).
4. But immediately these gentlefolk raised a cry.
5. Avarice (the love of money) is the root of all evil (1 Timothy 6:10).
6. Bulls—writs of indulgence for sin, purchasable in lieu of other forms of penance.
7. With which to season my preaching. (Saffron is a yellow spice.)

Reliks been they, as wenen they echoon.[8]
Thanne have I in latoun[9] a sholder-boon
Which that was of an holy Jewes shepe.
'Goode men,' seye I, 'tak of my wordes kepe:° *heed*
If that this boon be wasshe° in any welle, *washed, dunked*
If cow, or calf, or sheep, or oxe swelle,° *swell (up)*
That any worm hath ete, or worm y-stonge,[1]
Tak water of that welle, and wash his tonge,
And it is hool° anon;° and forthermore, *healed / at once*
Of pokkes° and of scabbe and every sore *pox*
Shal every sheep be hool,° that of this welle *healed*
Drinketh a draughte. Tak kepe° eek° what I telle: *heed / also*
If that the good man that the bestes° oweth° *animals / owns*
Wol every wike,° er° that the cok him croweth, *week / before*
Fastinge,° drinken of this welle a draughte— *(While) fasting*
As thilke° holy Jewe° oure eldres taughte— *that same / i.e., Jacob*
His bestes and his stoor° shal multiplye. *stock*
  And, sires, also it heleth° jalousye: *heals*
For though a man be falle in jalous rage,
Let maken with this water his potage,[2]
And nevere shal he more his wyf mistriste,° *mistrust*
Though he the sooth° of hir defaute° wiste°— *truth / erring / should know*
Al° had she taken° preestes two or three. *Even if / taken (as lovers)*
  Heer is a miteyn° eek, that ye may see: *mitten*
He that his hond wol putte in this miteyn,
He shal have multiplying of his greyn° *grain*
Whan he hath sowen, be it whete° or otes,° *wheat / oats*
So that he offre pens, or elles grotes.[3]
  Goode men and wommen, o° thing warne° I yow: *one / tell*
If any wight° be in this chirche now, *person*
That hath doon sinne horrible, that he
Dar° nat for shame of it y-shriven[4] be, *Dare*
Or any womman, be she yong or old,
That hath y-maked hir housbonde cokewold,° *a cuckold*
Swich° folk shul have no power ne no grace *Such*
To offren° to my reliks in this place. *To offer (money)*
And whoso findeth him out of swich blame,° *not deserving such blame*
He wol com up and offre a° Goddes name, *make an offering in*
And I assoille° him by the auctoritee° *(will) absolve / authority*
Which that by bulle y-graunted was to me.'
  By this gaude° have I wonne,° yeer° by yeer, *trick / earned / year*
An hundred mark sith I was pardoner.[5]
I stonde lyk a clerk° in my pulpet, *scholar*
And whan the lewed° peple is doun y-set, *ignorant, unlearned*
I preche, so as ye han herd bifore,

8. They are (saints') relics, or so they all suppose.
9. Latten, a metal like brass.
1. Who has eaten any (poisonous) worm or whom a snake has stung (bitten).
2. Have his soup made with this water.
3. Provided that he offers (to me) pennies or else groats (coins worth fourpence).
4. I.e., confessed and absolved.
5. A hundred marks (coins worth thirteen shillings fourpence) since I became a pardoner.

And telle an hundred false japes° more. *tricks, stories*
Thanne peyne I me° to strecche forth the nekke, *I take pains*
And est and west upon the peple I bekke° *nod*
As doth a dowve,° sittinge on a berne.° *dove / in a barn*
Myn hondes and my tonge goon so yerne° *rapidly*
That it is joye to see my bisinesse.
Of avaryce and of swich° cursednesse *such*
Is al my preching, for° to make hem free° *in order / generous*
To yeven hir pens, and namely unto me.[6]
For myn entente° is nat but for to winne,° *intention / profit*
And nothing° for correccioun of sinne: *not at all*
I rekke° nevere, whan that they ben beried,° *care / buried*
Though that hir soules goon a-blakeberied![7]
For certes,° many a predicacioun° *certainly / sermon*
Comth ofte tyme of yvel° entencioun: *evil*
Som for plesaunce° of folk and flaterye, *the entertainment*
To been avaunced by ypocrisye,[8]
And som for veyne glorie,° and som for hate. *vainglory*
For whan I dar non other weyes debate,[9]
Than wol I stinge him[1] with my tonge smerte° *sharp*
In preching, so that he shal nat asterte° *leap up (to protest)*
To been° defamed falsly, if that he *At being*
Hath trespased to° my brethren[2] or to me. *wronged*
For, though I telle noght his propre° name, *own*
Men shal wel knowe that it is the same
By signes and by othere circumstances.
Thus quyte° I folk that doon us displesances;° *requite / offenses*
Thus spitte I out my venim under hewe° *hue, coloring*
Of holynesse, to semen° holy and trewe. *seem*
But shortly° myn entente I wol devyse:° *briefly / describe*
I preche of no thing but for coveityse.° *out of covetousness*
Therfore my theme is yet, and evere was,
Radix malorum est cupiditas.
Thus can I preche agayn° that same vyce *against*
Which that I use,° and that is avaryce. *practice*
But though myself be gilty in that sinne,
Yet can I maken other folk to twinne° *part*
From avaryce, and sore° to repente. *ardently*
But that is nat my principal entente:
I preche nothing but for coveityse.
Of this matere° it oughte ynogh suffyse. *subject*
Than telle I hem ensamples many oon° *examples many a one*
Of olde stories longe tyme agoon,° *past*
For lewed° peple loven tales olde; *unlearned*
Swich° thinges can they wel reporte° and holde.° *Such / repeat / remember*

6. In giving their pence, and particularly to me.
7. Blackberrying, i.e., wandering.
8. (Thus) to seek advancement through hypocrisy.
9. For when I dare enter into contest (argument) no other way.
1. I.e., some enemy.
2. I.e., fellow pardoners.

What, trowe ye, the whyles I may preche[3]
And winne° gold and silver for° I teche, *obtain / because*
That I wol live in povert° wilfully?° *poverty / willingly*
Nay, nay, I thoghte° it nevere, trewely! *considered*
For I wol preche and begge in sondry° londes; *various*
I wol nat do no labour with myn hondes,
Ne make baskettes,[4] and live therby,
By cause I wol nat beggen ydelly.° *without profit*
I wol non of the Apostles counterfete:° *imitate*
I wol have money, wolle,° chese, and whete, *wool*
Al° were it yeven of° the povereste page,° *Even if / given by / servant*
Or of° the povereste widwe° in a village, *by / poorest widow*
Al sholde hir children sterve for famyne.[5]
Nay! I wol drinke licour° of the vyne, *liquor, wine*
And have a joly wenche in every toun.
But herkneth,° lordinges, in conclusioun: *listen*
Youre lyking is that I shall telle a tale.
Now have I dronke a draughte of corny° ale, *malty*
By God, I hope I shal yow telle a thing
That shal by resoun° been at° youre lyking. *with reason / to*
For though myself be a ful vicious° man, *evil, vice-ridden*
A moral tale yet I yow telle can,
Which I am wont to preche for to winne.[6]
Now holde youre pees,° my tale I wol beginne." *peace*

The Tale

In Flaundres whylom was° a compaignye *once (there) was*
Of yonge folk, that haunteden folye—
As ryot, hasard, stewes, and tavernes,[7]
Where as° with harpes, lutes, and giternes,° *There where / guitars*
They daunce and pleyen at dees° bothe day and night, *dice*
And eten also and drinken over hir might,° *beyond their capacity*
Thurgh which they doon the devel sacrifyse° *make sacrifice to the devil*
Withinne that develes temple,° in cursed wyse,° *i.e., the tavern / way*
By superfluitee° abhominable. *excess*
Hir othes° been so grete and so dampnable,° *oaths; curses / condemnable*
That it is grisly for to here hem swere.
Our blissed Lordes body they totere°— *tear apart*
Hem thoughte° Jewes rente° him noght ynough— *It seemed to them / tore*
And ech° of hem at otheres sinne lough.° *each / laughed*
And right anon thanne comen tombesteres° *female tumblers, dancers*
Fetys and smale, and yonge fruytesteres,[8]
Singeres with harpes, baudes,° wafereres,° *bawds / girls selling cakes*
Whiche been the verray° develes officeres *the very*

3. What? do you believe (that) as long as I can preach.
4. St. Paul was said to have been a basket maker.
5. Even though her children should die of hunger.
6. Which I am in the habit of preaching to make some money.
7. Of young folk who gave themselves up to folly—(such) as excessive revelry, gambling with dice, (visiting) brothels and taverns.
8. Shapely and slender, and young girls selling fruit.

To kindle and blowe the fyr of lecherye
That is annexed° unto glotonye: — *joined (as a sin)*
The Holy Writ take I to my witnesse
That luxurie° is in wyn and dronkenesse. — *lechery*
Lo, how that dronken Loth° unkindely° — *Lot / unnaturally*
Lay by his doghtres two, unwitingly;° — *unknowingly*
So dronke he was, he niste° what he wroghte.° — *knew not / did*
Herodes,° whoso wel the stories soghte,° — *Herod / should seek out*
Whan he of wyn was repleet° at his feste, — *replete, full*
Right at his owene table he yaf° his heste° — *gave / command*
To sleen the Baptist John ful giltelees.° — *guiltless (innocent)*
Senek° seith a good word doutelees: — *Seneca*
He seith, he can no difference finde
Bitwix a man that is out of his minde
And a man which that is dronkelewe,° — *drunken*
But that woodnesse, y-fallen in a shrewe,[9]
Persevereth lenger° than doth dronkenesse. — *Continues longer*
O glotonye,° ful of cursednesse! — *gluttony*
O cause first° of oure confusioun!° — *first cause / ruin*
O original° of oure dampnacioun, — *origin*
Til Crist had boght us with his blood agayn!
Lo, how dere,° shortly for to sayn,° — *costly / to speak briefly*
Aboght was thilke cursed vileinye;[1]
Corrupt° was al this world for glotonye! — *Corrupted*
Adam oure fader and his wyf also
Fro Paradys to labour and to wo
Were driven for that vyce, it is no drede.° — *doubt*
For whyl that Adam fasted, as I rede,° — *read*
He was in Paradys; and whan that he
Eet of the fruyt defended° on the tree, — *forbidden*
Anon° he was outcast to wo and peyne.° — *Immediately / pain*
O glotonye, on thee wel oghte us pleyne![2]
O, wiste a man° how manye maladyes — *(if) a man knew*
Folwen of° excesse and of glotonyes, — *Follow on*
He wolde been the more mesurable° — *measured, temperate*
Of his diete, sittinge at his table.
Allas! the shorte throte, the tendre mouth,[3]
Maketh that,° est and west, and north and south, — *Causes*
In erthe, in eir,° in water, men to swinke° — *air / labor*
To gete a glotoun deyntee° mete and drinke! — *dainty*
Of this matere,° O Paul, wel canstow trete:° — *subject / canst thou treat*
"Mete° unto wombe,° and wombe eek unto mete, — *Food / belly*
Shal God destroyen bothe," as Paulus seith.[4]
Allas! a foul thing is it, by my feith,
To seye this word, and fouler is the dede,
Whan man so drinketh of the whyte and rede° — *i.e., wines*

9. Except that madness, having afflicted a miserable man.
1. Bought was that same cursed, evil deed.
2. Oh, gluttony, we certainly ought to complain against you.
3. I.e., the brief pleasure of swallowing, the mouth accustomed to delicacies.
4. 1 Corinthians 6:13.

That of his throte he maketh his privee,° *privy (toilet)*
Thurgh thilke° cursed superfluitee.° *that same / excess*
The apostel,[5] weping, seith ful pitously,
"Ther walken manye of whiche yow told have I"—
I seye it now weping with pitous voys—
"They been enemys of Cristes croys,° *cross*
Of which the ende is deeth: wombe° is her° god!" *belly / their*
O wombe! O bely! O stinking cod,[6]
Fulfild of donge and of corrupcioun![7]
At either ende of thee foul is the soun.° *sound*
How° greet labour and cost is thee to finde!° *What / to provide for*
Thise cookes, how they stampe,° and streyne,° and grinde, *pound / strain*
And turnen substance into accident,[8]
To fulfille al thy likerous talent!° *lecherous (here, gluttonous) appetite*
Out of the harde bones knokke they
The mary,° for they caste noght° awey *marrow / nothing*
That may go thurgh the golet° softe and swote;° *gullet / sweet*
Of spicerye° of leef, and bark, and rote° *spices / root(s)*
Shal been his sauce y-maked by delyt,° *to give pleasure*
To make him yet a newer° appetyt. *renewed*
But certes, he that haunteth swich delyces[9]
Is deed, whyl that° he liveth in tho° vyces. *while / those*
A lecherous thing is wyn, and dronkenesse
Is ful of stryving° and of wrecchednesse. *quarreling*
O dronke man, disfigured is thy face,
Sour is thy breeth, foul artow° to embrace, *art thou*
And thurgh thy dronke nose semeth the soun° *sound*
As though thou seydest ay° "Sampsoun, Sampsoun";[1] *ever*
And yet, God wot,° Sampsoun drank nevere no wyn. *knows*
Thou fallest,° as it were a stiked swyn;° *i.e., down / stuck pig*
Thy tonge is lost, and al thyn honest cure,° *care for decency*
For dronkenesse is verray sepulture° *the true tomb*
Of mannes wit° and his discrecioun.° *understanding / discretion*
In whom that° drinke hath dominacioun, *In him whom*
He can no conseil° kepe, it is no drede.° *secrets / doubt*
Now kepe yow fro the whyte and fro the rede—
And namely° fro the whyte wyn of Lepe° *especially / near Cádiz*
That is to selle° in Fishstrete° or in Chepe.° *for sale / Fish Street / Cheapside*
This wyn of Spaigne crepeth subtilly
In othere wynes growinge faste by,[2]
Of° which ther ryseth swich fumositee,° *From / vapor*
That whan a man hath dronken draughtes three
And weneth° that he be at hoom in Chepe, *thinks*

5. St. Paul. See Philippians 3:18–19.
6. Bag, i.e., the stomach.
7. Filled up with dung and with decaying matter.
8. And turn substance into accident (a scholastic joke: *substance* means essence, essential qualities; *accident*, external appearances).
9. But truly, he that gives himself up to such pleasures.
1. A witty kind of onomatopoeia: the snoring sound seems to say "Samson," who was betrayed (see *Wife of Bath's Prologue*, ll. 721–23).
2. That is, the wines sold as French are often mixed with the cheaper wines of Spain.

He is in Spaigne, right at the toune of Lepe,
Nat at The Rochel,° ne at Burdeux° toun; *La Rochelle / Bordeaux*
And thanne wol he seye, "Sampsoun, Sampsoun."
  But herkneth,° lordinges, o° word I yow preye, *listen / one*
That alle the sovereyn actes,° dar I seye, *supreme deeds*
Of victories in the Olde Testament,
Thurgh verray° God, that is omnipotent, *true*
Were doon in abstinence and in preyere:
Loketh the Bible, and ther ye may it lere.° *learn*
  Loke Attila,° the grete conquerour, *the Hun*
Deyde° in his sleep, with shame and dishonour, *Died*
Bledinge ay° at his nose in dronkenesse: *continually*
A capitayn shoulde live in sobrenesse.
And over al this, avyseth yow right wel° *be well advised*
What was comaunded unto Lamuel°— *Lemuel*
Nat Samuel, but Lamuel, seye I—
Redeth the Bible, and finde it expresly
Of wyn-yeving to hem that han justyse.[3]
Namore of this, for it may wel suffyse.
  And now that I have spoke of glotonye,
Now wol I yow defenden° hasardrye.° *forbid / gambling at dice*
Hasard is verray moder° of lesinges,° *the true mother / lies*
And of deceite and cursed forsweringes,° *perjuries*
Blaspheme of Crist, manslaughtre, and wast° also *waste*
Of catel° and of tyme; and forthermo, *goods*
It is repreve° and contrarie of honour *a reproach*
For to ben holde a commune hasardour.° *gambler*
And ever the hyer° he is of estaat° *higher / in social rank*
The more is he y-holden desolaat:° *considered debased*
If that a prince useth° hasardrye, *practices*
In alle governaunce and policye
He is, as by commune opinioun,
Y-holde the lasse in reputacioun.
  Stilbon, that was a wys° embassadour, *wise*
Was sent to Corinthe in ful greet honour,
Fro Lacidomie° to make hire alliaunce.° *Lacedaemon (Sparta) / their alliance*
And whan he cam, him happede par chaunce° *it happened by chance*
That alle the grettest° that were of that lond, *greatest (men)*
Pleyinge atte° hasard he hem fond. *at (the)*
For which, as sone as it mighte be,° *could be*
He stal him° hoom agayn to his contree, *stole away*
And seyde, "Ther wol I nat lese° my name,° *lose / (good) name*
Ne I wol nat take on me so greet defame,° *dishonor*
Yow for to allye° unto none hasardours.° *to ally / gamblers*
Sendeth othere wyse embassadours—
For by my trouthe, me were levere dye° *I would rather die*
Than I yow sholde to hasardours allye.
For ye that been so glorious in honours
Shul nat allyen yow with hasardours

3. Concerning the giving of wine to those responsible for the law (see Proverbs 31:4–5).

As by my wil, ne as by my tretee."°   *negotiations*
This wyse philosophre, thus seyde he.
Loke eek° that to the king Demetrius   *also*
The king of Parthes,° as the book seith us,[4]   *Parthia*
Sente him a paire of dees° of gold in scorn,   *dice*
For he hadde used hasard ther-biforn;
For which he heeld his glorie or his renoun°   *renown*
At no value or reputacioun.
Lordes may finden other maner pley
Honeste° ynough to dryve the day awey.   *Honorable*
Now wol I speke of othes° false and grete   *oaths, curses*
A word or two, as olde bokes trete.
Gret swering° is a thing abhominable,   *cursing*
And false swering° is yet more reprevable.°   *i.e., of oaths / reproachable*
The heighe° God forbad swering at al—   *high*
Witnesse on Mathew—but in special
Of swering seith the holy Jeremye,°   *Jeremiah*
"Thou shalt swere sooth° thyn othes° and nat lye,   *truly / oaths*
And swere in dome,° and eek in rightwisnesse;"°   *(good) judgment* / *righteousness*
But ydel° swering is a cursednesse."°   *vain / wickedness*
Bihold and see, that in the first table°   *tablet (of Moses)*
Of heighe Goddes hestes° honurable,   *commandments*
How that the seconde heste of him is this:
"Tak nat my name in ydel° or amis."°   *in vain / amiss (wrongly)*
Lo, rather° he forbedeth swich° swering   *earlier (in the list) / such*
Than homicyde or many a cursed thing—
I seye that, as by ordre,° thus it stondeth—   *in terms of the order*
This knoweth, that his hestes understondeth,[5]
How that the second heste of God is that.
And forther over,° I wol thee telle al plat°   *moreover / flatly*
That vengeance shal nat parten° from his hous   *depart*
That° of his othes is to° outrageous.   *Who / too*
"By Goddes precious herte," and "By his nayles,"
And "By the blode of Crist that is in Hayles,[6]
Seven is my chaunce,[7] and thyn is cink° and treye;"°   *five / three*
"By Goddes armes, if thou falsly pleye,
This dagger shal thurghout thyn herte go!"
This fruyt cometh of the bicched bones two[8]—
Forswering,° ire,° falsnesse, homicyde.   *Perjury / anger*
Now for the love of Crist that for us dyde,
Lete° youre othes, bothe grete and smale.   *Cease*
But, sires, now wol I telle forth my tale.
Thise ryotoures° three of which I telle,   *rioters, revelers*
Longe erst er° pryme° rong of any belle,   *before / 9 A.M.*

4. The *Policraticus* of John of Salisbury, which also contains the preceding story.
5. (He) knows this, who understands his commandments.
6. An abbey in Gloucestershire supposed to possess (as a high relic) some of Christ's blood.
7. I.e., throw.
8. This fruit, i.e., result, comes from the two cursed dice. (Dice were made of bone; hence "bones" here.)

Were set hem° in a taverne for to drinke; *Had set themselves down*
And as they sat, they herde a belle clinke
Biforn a cors° was° caried to his grave. *corpse / (that) was (being)*
That oon of hem gan callen to his knave,
"Go bet," quod he, "and axe redily,[9]
What cors is this that passeth heer forby;° *by here*
And looke that thou reporte his name wel."° *i.e., correctly*
"Sire," quod this boy, "it nedeth never-a-del.° *it isn't at all necessary*
It was me told, er° ye cam heer two houres. *before*
He was, pardee,[1] an old felawe° of youres; *companion*
And sodeynly he was y-slayn tonight,
Fordronke,° as he sat on his bench upright. *Dead drunk*
Ther cam a privee° theef men clepeth° Deeth, *secret / call*
That in this contree° al the peple sleeth,° *region / kills*
And with his spere he smoot his herte atwo,[2]
And wente his wey withouten wordes mo.° *more*
He hath a thousand slayn this pestilence.° *(during) this plague*
And maister, er° ye come in his presence, *before*
Me thinketh° that it were necessarie *It seems to me*
For to be war° of swich an adversarie: *aware, careful*
Beth redy for to mete him everemore.° *always*
Thus taughte me my dame,° I sey namore." *mother*
"By Seinte Marie," seyde this taverner,° *tavernkeeper*
"The child seith sooth, for he hath slayn this yeer,
Henne° over a myle, withinne a greet village, *Hence, from here*
Bothe man and womman, child, and hyne,° and page;° *laborer / servant*
I trowe° his habitacioun be there. *believe*
To been avysed° greet wisdom it were, *forewarned*
Er that° he dide a man a dishonour." *Before*
"Ye,° Goddes armes," quod° this ryotour,° *Aye, yes / said / reveler*
"Is it swich peril with him for to mete?
I shal him seke by wey° and eek° by strete, *road / also*
I make avow to° Goddes digne° bones! *avow (it) by / worthy*
Herkneth felawes, we three been al ones:° *all of one mind*
Lat ech° of us holde up his hond til other,° *each / to the other*
And ech of us bicomen otheres° brother, *the others'*
And we wol sleen° this false traytour Deeth. *slay*
He shal be slayn, he that so manye sleeth,
By Goddes dignitee,° er it be night." *worthiness*
Togidres° han thise three hir trouthes plight° *Together / plighted their troth*
To live and dyen ech of hem for other,° *one another*
As though he were his owene y-boren° brother. *born*
And up they sterte,° al dronken in this rage,° *leaped / passion*
And forth they goon towardes that village
Of which the taverner hadde spoke biforn,

9. The one of them proceeded to call to his servant-boy, "Go quickly," he said, "and ask straightway."
1. A weak form of the oath "by God," based on the French *par Dieu*.
2. And with his spear he struck his heart in two. (Death was often shown in the visual arts as a hideous skeleton menacing men with a spear or arrow.)

And many a grisly ooth thanne han they sworn,
And Cristes blessed body they to-rente°— *tore apart*
Deeth shal be deed, if that they may him hente.° *seize*
  Whan they han goon nat fully half a myle,
Right° as they wolde han troden° over a style,° *Just / stepped / stile*
An old man and a povre° with hem mette. *poor (one)*
This olde man ful mekely° hem grette,° *meekly / greeted them*
And seyde thus, "Now, lordes, God yow see!"° *may God protect you*
  The proudest of thise ryotoures three
Answerde agayn, "What, carl,° with sory grace!° *Hey, fellow / confound you*
Why artow al forwrapped save thy face?[3]
Why livestow° so longe in so greet age?" *livest thou*
  This olde man gan loke in° his visage, *scrutinized*
And seyde thus, "For° I ne can nat finde *Because*
A man, though that I walked into Inde,° *India*
Neither in citee nor in no village,
That wolde chaunge his youthe for myn age;
And therfore moot° I han myn age stille, *must*
As longe time as it is Goddes wille.
Ne Deeth, allas! ne wol nat han my lyf.
Thus walke I, lyk° a restelees caityf,° *like / captive*
And on the ground, which is my modres° gate, *mother's*
I knokke with my staf bothe erly and late,
And seye, 'Leve° moder, leet me in! *Dear*
Lo, how I vanish,° flesh, and blood, and skin! *waste away*
Allas! whan shul my bones been at reste?
Moder, with yow wolde I chaunge° my cheste° *exchange / chest (of clothes)*
That in my chambre longe tyme hath be,° *been*
Ye, for an heyre clout° to wrappe me!' *haircloth (for burial)*
But yet to me she wol nat do that grace,
For which ful pale and welked° is my face. *withered*
  But sires, to yow it is no curteisye[4]
To speken to an old man vileinye,° *rudeness*
But° he trespasse° in worde or elles° in dede. *Unless / offend / else*
In Holy Writ ye may yourself wel rede,° *read*
'Agayns° an old man, hoor° upon his heed, *Before / hoary, white*
Ye sholde aryse.' Wherfor I yeve yow reed:[5]
Ne dooth unto an old man noon harm now,
Namore than that ye wolde men did to yow
In age, if that ye so longe abyde.° *remain (alive)*
And God be with yow, wher ye go° or ryde; *walk*
I moot° go thider as° I have to go." *must / thither where*
  "Nay, olde cherl, by God, thou shalt nat so,"
Seyde this other hasardour° anon;° *gambler / at once*
"Thou partest° nat so lightly, by Seint John! *departest*
Thou spak right now of thilke° traitour Deeth *that same*
That in this contree alle oure frendes sleeth.

3. Why art thou all wrapped up except for thy face?
4. But, sirs, it is not courteous of you.
5. "You should stand up (in respect)." Therefore I give you (this) advice.

Have heer my trouthe,° as° thou art his espye,° *pledge / since / spy*
Telle wher he is, or thou shalt it abye,° *pay for*
By God, and by the holy sacrament!
For soothly thou art oon of his assent° *in league with him*
To sleen us yonge folk, thou false theef!"
"Now, sires," quod he, "if that yow be so leef° *desirous*
To finde Deeth, turne up this croked° wey, *crooked*
For in that grove I lafte° him, by my fey,° *left / faith*
Under a tree, and there he wol abyde:° *stay*
Nat for youre boost he wole him nothing hyde.[6]
See ye that ook?° right ther ye shul him finde. *oak*
God save yow, that boghte agayn° mankinde, *redeemed*
And yow amende!"° Thus seyde this olde man. *make you better*
And everich° of thise ryotoures° ran, *each / revelers*
Til he cam to that tree, and ther they founde
Of florins° fyne of golde y-coyned° rounde *florins, coins / coined*
Wel ny an° eighte busshels, as hem thoughte.° *nearly / it seemed to them*
No lenger thanne° after Deeth they soughte, *No longer then*
But ech° of hem so glad was of that sighte— *each*
For that the florins been so faire and brighte—
That doun they sette hem by this precious hord.
The worste of hem he spake the firste word.
"Brethren," quod he, "take kepe° what that I seye: *heed*
My wit° is greet, though that I bourde° and pleye. *understanding / jest*
This tresor° hath Fortune unto us yiven° *treasure / given*
In mirthe and jolitee° our lyf to liven, *merriment*
And lightly as it comth, so wol we spende.
Ey! Goddes precious dignitee!° who *worthiness*
wende° *would have supposed*
Today that we sholde han so fair a grace?° *favor*
But° mighte this gold be caried fro this place *If only*
Hoom to myn hous—or elles unto youres—
For wel ye woot° that al this gold is oures— *know*
Thanne were we in heigh felicitee.° *supreme happiness*
But trewely, by daye it may nat be:° *be (done)*
Men wolde seyn that we were theves stronge,° *flagrant*
And for oure owene tresor doon us honge.° *have us hanged*
This tresor moste y-caried be by nighte,
As wysly° and as slyly° as it mighte.° *prudently / craftily / can (be)*
Wherfore I rede° that cut° among us alle *advise / lots, straws*
Be drawe,° and lat se wher the cut wol falle; *drawn, pulled*
And he that hath the cut with herte blythe
Shal renne° to the toune, and that ful swythe,° *run / quickly*
And bringe us breed and wyn ful prively.° *secretly*
And two of us shul kepen° subtilly° *guard / carefully*
This tresor wel; and if he wol nat tarie,° *tarry*
Whan it is night we wol this tresor carie,
By oon assent, where as us thinketh best."[7]

6. He won't conceal himself at all because of your boasting.
7. By common assent, wherever seems to us best.

That oon of hem the cut broughte in his fest,° *fist*
And bad hem drawe, and loke wher it wol falle;
And it fil on the yongeste of hem alle,
And forth toward the toun he wente anon.
And also sone as° that he was agon, *as soon as*
That oon of hem° spak thus unto that other: *The one of them*
"Thou knowest wel thou art my sworne brother;
Thy profit° wol I telle thee anon. *Something to your advantage*
Thou woost° wel that oure felawe is agon,° *knowest / gone*
And heer is gold, and that° ful greet plentee, *that (in)*
That shal departed° been among us three. *divided*
But natheles,° if I can shape° it so *nonetheless / arrange*
That it departed were among us two,
Hadde I nat doon a freendes torn° to thee?" *turn*
  That other answerde, "I noot° how that may be: *know not*
He woot how that the gold is with us tweye.
What shal we doon? what shal we to him seye?"
  "Shal it be conseil?"° seyde the firste shrewe;° *a secret / wretch*
"And I shal tellen in a wordes fewe
What we shal doon, and bringe it wel aboute."
"I graunte,"° quod that other, "out of doute,[8] *grant (it)*
That, by my trouthe, I wol thee nat biwreye."° *betray*
  "Now," quod the firste, "thou woost° wel we be tweye,° *knowest / two*
And two of us shul strenger° be than oon. *stronger*
Looke whan that he is set,° that right anoon° *has sat down / right away*
Arys° as though thou woldest with him pleye; *Arise (get up)*
And I shal ryve° him thurgh the sydes tweye° *stab / through his two sides*
Whyl that thou strogelest° with him as in game,° *strugglest / as if in play*
And with thy dagger looke° thou do the same; *take heed*
And thanne shall al this gold departed° be, *divided*
My dere freend, bitwixen me and thee.
Thanne may we bothe oure lustes° al fulfille, *desires*
And pleye at dees° right at oure owene wille." *dice*
And thus acorded° been thise shrewes° tweye *agreed / cursed fellows*
To sleen the thridde, as ye han herd me seye.
  This yongest, which that wente unto the toun,
Ful ofte in herte he rolleth up and doun° *i.e., thinks on*
The beautee of thise florins newe and brighte.
"O Lord!" quod he, "if so were that I mighte
Have al this tresor to myself allone,
Ther is no man that liveth under the trone° *throne*
Of God that sholde live so mery as I!"
And atte laste° the feend,° our enemy, *at (the) last / devil*
Putte in his thought that he shold poyson beye,° *buy poison*
With which he mighte sleen his felawes tweye°— *two companions*
For-why the feend fond him in swich lyvinge[9]
That he had leve° him to sorwe bringe: *permission (from God)*
For this was outrely° his fulle entente,° *completely / purpose*

8. I.e., you can be sure.
9. Because the fiend (the devil) found him living in such a way.

To sleen hem bothe, and nevere to repente.
And forth he gooth—no lenger wolde he tarie—
Into the toun, unto a pothecarie,° *apothecary, pharmacist*
And preyed° him that he him wolde selle *asked*
Som poyson, that° he mighte his rattes quelle,° *so that / kill his rats*
And eek° ther was a polcat° in his hawe,° *also / weasel / yard*
That, as he seyde, his capouns° hadde y-slawe,° *capons / killed*
And fayn° he wolde wreke him,° if he mighte, *gladly / avenge himself*
On vermin that destroyed° him by nighte. *were ruining*
The pothecarie answerde, "And thou shalt have
A thing that, also° God my soule save, *so (may)*
In al this world ther nis no° creature, *is not any*
That ete or dronke hath of this confiture° *mixture*
Noght but the mountance of a corn of whete,[1]
That he ne shal his lyf anon° forlete.° *at once / lose*
Ye,° sterve° he shal, and that in lasse whyle° *Yes / die / shorter time*
Than thou wolt goon a paas° nat but° a myle, *walk at normal pace / only*
This poyson is so strong and violent."
This cursed man hath in his hond y-hent° *grasped*
This poyson in a box, and sith° he ran *afterward*
Into the nexte strete unto a man
And borwed [of] him large botels° three, *bottles (probably of leather)*
And in the two his poyson poured he—
The thridde he kepte clene for his° drinke— *his (own)*
For al the night he shoop him° for to swinke° *was preparing himself / work*
In caryinge of the gold out of that place.
And whan this ryotour, with sory grace,° *i.e., blessed by evil*
Hadde filled with wyn his grete botels three,
To his felawes agayn repaireth° he. *returns*
What nedeth it to sermone° of it more? *speak*
For right as they hadde cast° his deeth bifore, *planned*
Right so they han him slayn, and that anon.° *immediately*
And whan that this was doon, thus spak that oon:
"Now lat us sitte and drinke, and make us merie,
And afterward we wol his body berie."° *bury*
And with that word it happed° him, par cas,° *befell / by chance*
To take the botel ther° the poyson was, *where*
And drank, and yaf° his felawe drink also, *gave*
For which anon they storven° bothe two. *died*
But certes, I suppose that Avicen
Wroot nevere in no canon, ne in no fen,
Mo wonder signes of empoisoning[2]
Than hadde thise wrecches two, er° hir° ending. *before / their*
Thus ended been thise homicydes two,
And eek° the false empoysoner° also.° *also / poisoner / as well*
O cursed sinne of alle cursednesse!
O traytours° homicyde, O wikkednesse! *traitorous*

1. No more than the quantity of a grain of wheat.
2. But truly, I would guess that Avicenna (an Islamic physician and author) never described, in any treatise or chapter, more terrible symptoms of poisoning.

O glotonye, luxurie,° and hasardrye! *lechery*
Thou blasphemour of Crist with vileinye° *vile speech*
And othes grete, of usage° and of pryde! *out of habit*
Allas! mankinde, how may it bityde° *happen*
That to thy Creatour which that thee wroghte,
And with his precious herte-blood thee boghte,° *redeemed*
Thou art so fals and so unkinde,° allas! *unnatural*
  Now, goode men, God forgeve° yow youre trespas, *may God forgive*
And ware yow fro° the sinne of avaryce. *make you beware of*
Myn holy pardoun may yow alle waryce°— *cure*
So that ye offre nobles or sterlinges,[3]
Or elles silver broches, spones,° ringes. *spoons*
Boweth youre heed° under this holy bulle! *head*
Cometh up, ye wyves, offreth of youre wolle!° *wool*
Youre names I entre heer in my rolle° anon:° *roll, list / at once*
Into the blisse of hevene shul ye gon.
I yow assoile,° by myn heigh power— *absolve*
Yow that wol offre°—as clene and eek as cleer° *make an offering / pure*
As ye were born.—And, lo, sires, thus I preche.
And Jesu Crist, that is our soules leche,° *healer, doctor*
So graunte° yow his pardon to receyve, *May he grant*
For that is best; I wol yow nat deceyve.
  But sires, o° word forgat I in my tale: *a, one*
I have relikes and pardon in my male° *pouch*
As faire as any man in Engelond,
Whiche were me yeven° by the Popes hond. *given*
If any of yow wol of devocioun° *out of devotion*
Offren and han myn absolucioun,
Cometh forth anon, and kneleth heer adoun,
And mekely receyveth my pardoun;
Or elles, taketh pardon as ye wende,° *travel*
Al newe and fresh, at every myles ende—
So that ye offren alwey newe and newe[4]
Nobles or pens,° which that be gode and trewe. *pence*
It is an honour to everich° that is heer *every one*
That ye mowe° have a suffisant° pardoneer *may / capable*
T'assoille° yow, in contree as ye ryde, *To absolve*
For aventures whiche that may bityde.[5]
Peraventure° ther may falle oon or two *By chance*
Doun of his hors, and breke his nekke atwo.° *in two*
Look which a seuretee° is it to you alle *what a security*
That I am in youre felaweship y-falle,
That may assoille yow, bothe more and lasse,° *great and small*
Whan that the soule shal fro the body passe.
I rede° that oure Host heer shal biginne, *advise*
For he is most envoluped° in sinne. *enveloped, wrapped up*
Com forth, sire Hoste, and offre first anon,° *first now*

3. As long as you offer nobles (gold coins) or silver pennies.
4. As long as you make offering anew each time (of).
5. In respect to things that may befall.

And thou shalt kisse the reliks everichon,° *every one*
Ye, for a grote:° unbokel° anon thy purs." *groat (four pence) / unbuckle*
"Nay, nay," quod° he, "thanne have I Cristes curs! *said*
Lat be," quod he, "it shal nat be, so theech!° *as I hope to prosper*
Thou woldest make me kisse thyn olde breech° *breeches*
And swere it were a relik of a seint,
Thogh it were with thy fundement° depeint!° *fundament (rectum) / stained*
But by the croys° which that Seint Eleyne° fond, *(true) cross / St. Helena*
I wolde I hadde thy coillons° in myn hond *testicles*
In stede of relikes or of seintuarie.° *i.e., holy things*
Lat cutte hem of! I wol thee helpe hem carie.[6]
Thay shul be shryned° in an hogges tord!"° *enshrined / turd*
This Pardoner answerde nat a word;
So wrooth° he was, no word ne wolde he seye. *wroth, angered*
"Now," quod our Host, "I wol no lenger pleye
With thee, ne with noon other angry man."
But right anon the worthy Knight bigan,
Whan that he saugh that al the peple lough,° *laughed*
"Namore of this, for it is right ynough!° *quite enough*
Sire Pardoner, be glad and mery of chere;° *mood*
And ye, sire Host, that been to me so dere,
I prey yow that ye kisse the Pardoner.
And Pardoner, I prey thee, drawe thee neer,
And, as we diden, lat us laughe and pleye."
Anon° they kiste, and riden forth hir weye.° *At once / (on) their way*

The Prioress's Prologue and Tale

The Introduction

"Well seyd, by *corpus dominus*,"° quod° oure Hoste, *the Lord's body / said*
"Now longe moot° thou sayle by the coste,° *may / sail along the coast*
Sire gentil maister, gentil marineer![1]
God yeve this monk a thousand last quad yeer![2]
A ha! felawes!° beth ware of swiche° a jape!° *companions / such / trick*
The monk putte in the mannes hood an ape,[3]
And in his wyves eek,° by Seint Austin!° *as well / Augustine*
Draweth° no monkes more unto youre in.° *Take / lodging*
But now passe over,° and lat us seke aboute, *on*
Who shal now telle first, of al this route,° *company*
Another tale;" and with that word he sayde,
As curteisly as it had been a mayde,[4]
"My lady Prioresse, by your leve,
So that I wiste° I sholde yow nat greve,° *knew / vex*

6. Have them cut off! I'll help thee carry them.
1. The Shipman has just told his tale of a merchant, his wife, and a lecherous monk.
2. God give this monk a thousand cartloads of bad years.
3. The monk put an ape in the man's hood, i.e., made a fool of him.
4. As courteously as if it had been a maiden (speaking).

I wolde demen° that ye tellen sholde *would decide*
A tale next, if so were that ye wolde.° *were willing*
Now wol ye vouche sauf,° my lady dere?" *agree*
"Gladly," quod she, and seyde as ye shal here.

The Prologue

Domine, dominus noster.° *Oh Lord, our lord*

O Lord, oure Lord, thy name how merveillous° *marvelously*
Is in this large worlde y-sprad°—quod° she— *spread / said*
For noght only thy laude° precious *praise*
Parfourned° is by men of dignitee, *Celebrated, performed*
But by the mouth of children thy bountee° *goodness*
Parfourned is, for on the brest soukinge° *sucking*
Somtyme shewen° they thyn heryinge.° *show forth / praise*

Wherfore in laude,° as I best can or may, *praise*
Of thee, and of the whyte lily flour° *i.e., the Virgin*
Which that thee bar,° and is a mayde° alway, *Who bore thee / virgin*
To telle a storie I wol do my labour;
Not that I may encresen° hir honour, *increase*
For she hirself is honour, and the rote° *root*
Of bountee, next° hir sone, and soules bote.° *next (to) / help*

O moder mayde! o mayde moder free!° *gracious, bountiful*
O bush unbrent, brenninge in Moyses sighte,[5]
That ravysedest° doun fro the deitee, *ravished*
Thurgh thyn humblesse, the goost° that in th'alighte,° *(Holy) Spirit / alighted in thee*
Of whos vertu, whan he thyn herte lighte,
Conceived was the Fadres sapience,[6]
Help me to telle it in thy reverence!

Lady, thy bountee, thy magnificence,
Thy vertu, and thy grete humilitee,
Ther may° no tonge expresse in no science;° *can / whatever its learning*
For somtyme, lady, er° men praye to thee, *before*
Thou goost biforn° of thy benignitee, *proceedest*
And getest us the light, of° thy preyere, *by means of*
To gyden° us unto thy Sone so dere. *guide*

My conning° is so wayk,° o blisful Quene, *skill / weak*
For to declare thy grete worthinesse,
That I ne may the weighte nat sustene;
But as a child of twelf monthe old, or lesse,
That can unnethes° any word expresse, *hardly*

5. Oh, bush unburned, burning in Moses's sight (a common figure for the miracle of Mary's virginity, preserved even in her motherhood of Christ; ultimately based on Exodus 3:1–5).
6. Through whose power, when he illumined thy heart, was conceived the Wisdom of the Father, i.e., Christ, the Logos.

Right so fare I, and therfor I yow preye,
Gydeth° my song that I shal of yow seye. *Guide*

The Tale

Ther was in Asie,° in a greet citee, *Asia (Minor)*
Amonges Cristen folk, a Jewerye° *Jewish quarter*
Sustened by a lord of that contree
For foule usure° and lucre of vileynye,° *usury / wicked financial gain*
Hateful to Crist and to his compaignye;° *i.e., Christians*
And thurgh° the strete men mighte ryde or wende,° *through / go*
For it was free, and open at either ende.

A litel scole° of Cristen° folk ther stood *school / Christian*
Doun at the ferther ende, in which ther were
Children an heep,° y-comen° of Cristen blood, *many, a crowd / come*
That lerned in that scole yeer by yere
Swich manere doctrine as men used there[7]—
This is to seyn,° to singen and to rede,° *say / read*
As smale children doon in hire childhede.

Among thise children was a widwes° sone, *widow's*
A litel clergeoun,° seven yeer of age, *schoolboy*
That day by day to° scole was his wone,° *i.e., to go to / custom*
And eek also, where as° he saugh° th'ymage *wherever / saw*
Of Cristes moder, hadde he in usage,° *he was accustomed*
As him was taught, to knele adoun and seye
His *Ave Marie*,° as he goth by the weye. *Hail, Mary*

Thus hath this widwe hir litel sone y-taught
Our blisful Lady, Cristes moder dere,
To worshipe ay;° and he forgat it naught, *always*
For sely child wol alday sone lere.[8]
But ay,° whan I remembre° on this matere, *ever / i.e., think, meditate*
Seint Nicholas[9] stant° evere in my presence, *stands*
For he so yong to Crist did reverence.° *honored*

This litel child, his litel book lerninge,
As he sat in the scole at his prymer,[1]
He *Alma redemptoris*[2] herde singe,
As children lerned hire antiphoner,° *their anthem book*
And, as he dorste, he drough him ner and ner,[3]
And herkned ay° the wordes and the note,° *ever / music*
Til he the firste vers coude° al by rote.° *knew / by heart*

7. Such kinds of subjects as were usual there.
8. For a good child will always learn quickly.
9. St. Nicholas is said to have fasted even as an infant; he took the breast only once on Wednesdays and Fridays. He is also the patron saint of schoolboys.
1. A prayerbook used as an elementary school text.
2. For text and translation of this anthem, see p. 484.
3. And, as (much as) he dared, he drew nearer and nearer.

Noght wiste° he what this Latin was to seye,° *knew / meant*
For he so yong and tendre was of age;
But on a day his felaw gan he preye[4]
T'expounden him this song in his langage,° *his own language*
Or telle him why this song was in usage;° *used*
This preyde he him to construe° and declare *interpret*
Ful ofte tyme upon his knowes° bare. *knees*

His felawe, which that elder was than he,
Answerde him thus: "This song, I have herd seye,
Was maked of° our blisful Lady free,° *about / generous*
Hire to salue,° and eek° hire for to preye *salute, greet / also*
To been oure help and socour° whan we dye.° *succor, aid / die*
I can no more expounde in this matere:
I lerne song, I can° but smal° grammere." *know / little*

"And is this song maked in reverence
Of Cristes moder?" seyde this innocent.
"Now certes,° I wol do my diligence *certainly*
To conne° it al, er° Cristemasse be went.° *learn / before / is passed*
Though that I for my prymer[5] shal be shent,° *scolded*
And shal be beten thryes° in an houre, *thrice*
I wol it conne, oure Lady for to honoure."

His felaw taughte him homward prively,[6]
Fro day to day, til he coude° it by rote, *knew*
And thanne he song° it wel and boldely° *sang / forcefully*
Fro word to word, acording with the note;
Twyes° a day it passed thurgh his throte, *Twice*
To scoleward° and homward whan he wente. *Toward school*
On Cristes moder set was his entente.° *(heart's) intent*

As I have seyd, thurghout the Jewerye
This litel child, as he cam to and fro,
Ful merily than wolde he singe and crye° *cry out*
O Alma redemptoris everemo.
The swetnesse his herte perced° so *pierced*
Of Cristes moder, that, to hire to preye,
He can nat stinte of° singing by° the weye. *cease from / along*

Oure firste fo,° the serpent Sathanas,° *foe / Satan*
That hath in Jewes herte his waspes nest,
Up swal° and seide, "O Hebraik peple, allas! *swelled*
Is this to yow a thing that is honest,° *honorable, seemly*
That swich° a boy shal walken as him lest° *such / it pleases him*
In youre despyt, and singe of swich sentence,[7]
Which is agayn° oure lawes reverence?"[8] *against*

4. But one day he begged his companion.
5. I.e., for failing to study my primer.
6. His companion taught him (on the way) homeward, privately.
7. In scorn of you, and sing of such a subject.
8. The best manuscripts read "oure," as here; some read "youre."

Fro thennes forth° the Jewes han° conspyred *thenceforth / have*
This innocent out of this world to chace:° *drive*
An homicyde° therto han they hyred,° *murderer / hired*
That in an aley° hadde a privee° place; *alley / secret*
And as the child gan forby for to pace,° *was walking by*
This cursed Jew him hente° and heeld him faste, *seized*
And kitte° his throte, and in a pit him caste. *cut*

I seye that in a wardrobe° they him threwe *privy*
Where as these Jewes purgen hir entraille.[9]
O cursed folk of Herodes° al newe,° *Herod / always renewed*
What may youre yvel entente° yow availle? *evil plan*
Mordre° wol out, certein, it wol nat faille, *Murder*
And namely ther° th'onour of God shal sprede, *there where*
The blood out cryeth on your cursed dede.

O martir souded to° virginitee, *made fast in*
Now maystou° singen, folwinge evere in oon° *mayest thou / forever*
The Whyte Lamb celestial—quod she—
Of which the grete evangelist Seint John
In Pathmos[1] wroot, which seith that they that goon° *walk*
Biforn° this Lamb and singe a song al newe,° *Before / wholly new*
That nevere, fleshly,° wommen they ne knewe. *carnally*

This povre widwe° awaiteth al that night *poor widow*
After hir litel child, but he cam noght;
For which, as sone as it was dayes light,
With face pale of drede° and bisy thoght,° *fear / anxiety*
She hath at scole and elleswhere him soght,
Til finally she gan so fer espye° *found out this much*
That he last seyn° was in the Jewerye. *seen*

With modres pitee in hir brest enclosed,
She gooth, as° she were half out of hir minde, *as if*
To every place wher she hath supposed
By lyklihede hir litel child to finde.
And evere on Cristes moder meke and kinde
She cryde, and atte laste thus she wroghte:[2]
Among the cursed Jewes she him soghte.

She frayneth° and she preyeth° pitously *inquires / begs*
To every Jew that dwelte in thilke° place, *that same*
To telle hire if hir child wente oght forby.° *by at all*
They seyde "Nay"; but Jesu, of° his grace, *by*
Yaf in hir thought, inwith a litel space,[3]
That° in that place after hir sone she cryde° *So that / called*
Where he was casten in a pit bisyde.° *nearby*

9. Where these Jews empty their bowels.
1. The isle of Patmos in Greece, where St. John wrote the Book of Revelation.
2. She called, and in the end she did thus.
3. Gave her an idea, within a little while.

O grete God, that parfournest thy laude[4]
By mouth of innocents, lo heer° thy might! *behold here*
This gemme of chastitee, this emeraude,° *emerald*
And eek° of martirdom the ruby bright, *also*
Ther he with throte y-corven lay upright,[5]
He *Alma redemptoris* gan° to singe *began*
So loude that al the place gan to ringe.° *resounded*

The Cristen folk, that thurgh the strete wente,
In coomen° for to wondre upon this thing, *came*
And hastily they for the provost° sente; *magistrate*
He cam anon withouten tarying,
And herieth° Crist that is of heven king, *praises*
And eek° his moder, honour of mankinde, *also*
And after that the Jewes leet he binde.° *he had bound*

This child with pitous lamentacioun
Up taken was, singing his song alway;
And with honour of greet processioun
They carien him unto the nexte abbay.° *nearest abbey*
His moder swowning° by his bere° lay. *swooning / bier*
Unnethe° might the peple that was there *Scarcely*
This newe Rachel[6] bringe fro his bere.

With torment° and with shamful deth echon° *torture / each one*
This provost dooth° thise Jewes for to sterve° *causes / die*
That of this mordre wiste,° and that anon;° *knew / immediately*
He nolde no swich cursednesse observe.[7]
"Yvel shal have that yvel wol deserve:"[8]
Therfore with wilde hors° he dide hem drawe,° *horses* / *had them drawn, dragged*
And after that he heng° hem by the lawe. *hanged (probably on pikes)*

Upon his bere al lyth° this innocent *still lies*
Biforn the chief auter,° whyl the masse° laste, *altar / the mass*
And after that, the abbot with his covent° *monks*
Han sped hem° for to burien him ful faste; *have hastened*
And whan they holy water on him caste,
Yet spak this child, whan spreynd° was holy water, *sprinkled*
And song° O *Alma redemptoris mater!* *sang*

This abbot, which that was an holy man
As monkes been°—or elles oghten° be— *are / else ought to*
This yonge child to conjure° he bigan, *entreat*
And seyde, "O dere child, I halse° thee, *beg*

4. Oh, great God, that (hast) thy praise performed.
5. There where he lay face-up, with his throat cut.
6. This second Rachel (a grieving Jewish mother, in Jeremiah 31:15, who was said to prefigure the grieving mothers of the innocents slain by command of Herod, in Matthew 2:18).
7. He would not tolerate such evil doings.
8. "He who will deserve evil shall have evil."

In vertu of the Holy Trinitee,
Tel me what is thy cause for to singe,
Sith that° thy throte is cut, to my seminge?"° *Since / it seems to me*

"My throte is cut unto my nekke-boon,"
Seyde this child, "and, as by wey of kinde,° *nature*
I sholde have deyed, ye,° longe tyme agoon,° *yea, yes / ago*
But Jesu Crist, as ye in bokes finde,
Wil° that his glorie laste and be in minde; *Wills*
And for the worship of his moder dere
Yet° may I singe O *Alma* loude and clere. *Still*

This welle° of mercy, Cristes moder swete, *spring*
I lovede alwey as after my conninge;° *as best I could*
And whan that I my lyf sholde forlete,° *was to leave*
To me she cam, and bad me for to singe
This antem° verraily° in my deyinge, *hymn / truly*
As ye han herd; and whan that I had songe,
Me thoughte she leyde a greyn° upon my tonge. *seed*

Wherfore I singe, and singe moot certeyn,° *indeed must*
In honour of that blisful mayden free,° *generous*
Til fro my tonge of° taken is the greyn; *off*
And afterward thus seyde she to me,
'My litel child, now wol I fecche° thee *fetch*
Whan that the greyn is fro thy tongue y-take;
Be nat agast,° I wol thee nat forsake.'" *afraid*

This holy monk, this abbot, him mene I,
His tongue out caughte and took awey the greyn,
And he yaf° up the goost ful softely. *gave*
And whan this abbot had this wonder seyn,° *seen*
His salte teres° trikled doun as reyn,° *tears / like rain*
And gruf° he fil al plat° upon the grounde, *face downward / flat*
And stille° he lay as° he had been y-bounde. *(as) quietly / as if*

The covent° eek° lay on the pavement, *monks / also*
Weping and herying° Cristes moder dere, *praising*
And after that they ryse, and forth ben went,° *have gone*
And toke awey this martir fro his bere,° *bier*
And in a tombe of marbulstones clere° *bright, splendid*
Enclosen they his litel body swete.
Ther° he is now, God leve° us for to mete.° *Where / grant / meet*

O yonge Hugh of Lincoln,[9] slayn also
With° cursed Jewes, as it is notable°— *By / well known*
For it nis° but a litel whyle ago— *is not*

9. In 1255, when a young boy named Hugh was found dead in the city of Lincoln, a story developed that he had been killed by Jews in a mock-crucifixion. (The first English ritual murder libel of this sort had appeared about a century earlier.) Authorities extracted a confession from one Jew and later killed him, imprisoned many other Jews in the Tower of London, and ultimately

Preye eek° for us, we sinful folk unstable,° *also / unsteadfast*
That, of his mercy, God so merciable° *merciful*
On us his grete mercy multiplye,
For reverence of his moder Marye. Amen.

The Prologue and Tale of Sir Thopas

The Prologue

Whan seyd was al this miracle,° every man *i.e., the Prioress's tale of a miracle*
As sobre was° that wonder was to se. *Was so grave, serious*
Til that our Hoste japen tho bigan,° *began then to jest, joke*
And than at erst° he loked upon me *for the first time*
And seyde thus: "What man artow?"° quod he. *art thou*
"Thou lokest as° thou woldest finde an hare, *as if*
For ever upon the ground I see thee stare.

Approche neer° and loke up merily. *nearer*
Now war yow,° sirs, and lat this man have place. *pay attention*
He in the waast° is shape as wel as I. *waist*
This were a popet° in an arm t'enbrace° *little doll / to embrace*
For any womman, smal and fair of face.
He semeth elvish by his contenaunce,[1]
For unto no wight° dooth he daliaunce.° *person / is he sociable*

Sey now somwhat, sin° other folk han sayd.° *since / have spoken*
Tel us a tale of mirthe, and that anoon."
"Hoste," quod I, "ne beth nat yvel apayd,° *do not be displeased*
For other tale certes° can° I noon, *certainly / know*
But of° a ryme I lerned longe agoon." *Except*
"Ye, that is good," quod he. "Now shul we here
Som deyntee° thing, me thinketh by his chere."° *pleasant / look, expression*

The Tale

[THE FIRST FIT][2]

Listeth,° lordes, in good entent,° *Listen / with good will*
And I wol telle verrayment° *truly*
Of mirthe and of solas:
Al of a knyght was fair and gent° *noble, elegant*
In bataille and in tourneyment;
His name was sir Thopas.° *topaz (a yellow semiprecious stone)*

---

executed eighteen under the direction of King Henry III. Chronicles and other narratives perpetuated the libel. Roger Dahood has recently argued (see the Selective Bibliography for the *Prioress's Tale*) that certain details from these accounts enter into the Prioress's miracle tale.

1. He seems elfish, from the look of him. "Elvish" is often glossed as "distracted, abstracted" but literally means someone mysterious, from another world of being; cf. the realm of "Fairye" (l. 802).
2. We follow John Burrow's argument that the *Tale of Sir Thopas* is divided into three parts or "fits" (see l. 888), the second fit roughly half as long as the first, the third roughly half as long as the second.

Y-born he was in fer° contree,	*far, distant*
In Flaundres° al biyonde the see,	*Flanders (Belgium)*
At Popering,° in the place.	*a Flemish market town*
His fader was a man ful free,°	*noble, generous*
And lord he was of that contree,	
As it was Goddes grace.	
Sir Thopas wex a doghty swayn.°	*grew into a bold young man, squire*
Whyt was his face as payndemayn,°	*fine white bread*
His lippes rede as rose.	
His rode° is lyk scarlet in grayn,°	*complexion / scarlet dye*
And I yow telle in good certayn,°	*in certainty*
He hadde a semely° nose.	*seemly, handsome*
His heer, his berd was lyk saffroun,°	*saffron (deep yellow)*
That to his girdel° raughte° adoun;	*belt / reached*
His shoon° of Cordewane.°	*shoes / cordovan (Spanish) leather*
Of Brugges° were his hosen broun,°	*Bruges (in Flanders) / brown tights*
His robe was of ciclatoun,°	*costly embroidered silk*
That coste many a jane.°	*a silver coin of Genoa*
He coude° hunte at wilde deer,°	*knew how to / animals*
And ryde an hauking for riveer°	*go hawking for waterfowl*
With grey goshauk° on honde.	*a kind of hawk*
Therto° he was a good archeer;	*In addition*
Of wrastling was ther noon his peer,°	*equal*
Ther° any ram shal stonde.°	*Where / be put up as a prize (see General Prologue, l. 548)*
Ful many a mayde, bright in bour,°	*bedchamber*
They moorne° for him paramour,°	*yearn / with love-longing*
Whan hem were bet° to slepe.	*it would be better for them*
But he was chast° and no lechour,°	*chaste / lecher*
And sweet as is the bremble-flour°	*bramble flower (dog rose)*
That bereth the rede hepe.°	*rose hip*
And so bifel° upon a day,	*it happened*
For sothe,° as I yow telle may,	*In truth*
Sir Thopas wolde out ryde.°	*decided to ride out*
He worth upon° his stede° gray,	*gets up on / steed*
And in his honde a launcegay,°	*a light lance*
A long swerd by his syde.	
He priketh° thurgh a fair forest,	*pricks, spurs his horse*
Therinne is many a wilde best,	
Ye, bothe bukke° and hare;	*buck, male deer*
And as he priketh north and est,	
I telle it yow, him° hadde almest°	*(to) him / almost*
Bitid° a sory care.°	*Happened / sad misfortune*
Ther springen herbes grete and smale,	
The lycorys° and cetewale,°	*licorice / zedoary (like ginger)*

And many a clowe-gilofre;° *clove*
And notemuge° to putte in ale, *nutmeg*
Whether it be moyste° or stale,° *fresh / stale, old*
Or for to leye in cofre.°[3] *put in a chest*

The briddes singe, it is no nay,° *it cannot be denied*
The sparhauk° and the papeiay,° *sparrow hawk / parrot*
That joye it was to here.° *hear (them)*
The thrustelcok° made eek his lay,° *male thrush / also sang (composed) his song*
The wodedowve° upon the spray° *wood pigeon / branch*
She sang ful loude and clere.

Sir Thopas fil° in love-longinge *fell*
Al whan he herde the thrustel° singe, *thrush*
And priked° as he were wood.° *rode / mad*
His faire stede° in° his prikinge *steed / because of*
So swatte° that men mighte him wringe;° *sweated / wring out*
His sydes were al blood.° *covered with blood*

Sir Thopas eek so wery was
For prikinge on the softe gras
(So fiers° was his corage°) *fierce, ferocious / heart, spirit*
That doun he leyde him in that plas° *place*
To make° his stede som solas,° *give / respite, comfort*
And yaf° him good forage.° *gave / feeding*

"O seinte Marie, *benedicite!*° *bless me*
What eyleth this love at me° *does love have against me*
To binde me so sore?
Me dremed al this night, pardee,° *by God*
An elf-queen° shal my lemman° be, *fairy queen / lover, sweetheart*
And slepe under my gore.° *robe, cloak*

An elf-queen wol I love, ywis,° *indeed*
For in this world no womman is
Worthy to be my make° *mate, match*
In toune.° *in (any) town*
Alle othere wommen I forsake,
And to an elf-queen I me take
By dale° and eek by doune."° *valley / hill*

Into his sadel he clamb anoon° *quickly climbed*
And priketh over style° and stoon *stile*
An elf-queen for t'espye,° *to discover*
Til he so longe had riden and goon
That he fond, in a privee woon,° *secret place*
The contree of Fairye
So wilde.

3. None of the spice-bearing plants named in this stanza would be found growing in Flanders. Like many other details in the story, they are part of the exotic landscape of romance that Chaucer playfully invokes throughout.

For in that contree was ther noon
That to° him dorste° ryde or goon— *against / dared*
  Neither wyf ne childe—

Til that ther cam a greet geaunt;° *giant*
His name was sir Olifaunt,° *Sir Elephant*
  A perilous man of dede.° *in (his) actions*
He seyde, "Child,° by Termagaunt,° *Noble youth / (supposedly a Saracen god)*
But if° thou prike° out of myn haunt,° *Unless / ride / territory*
  Anon I slee° thy stede *will slay*
    With mace.° *a spiked warclub*
Heer is the queen of Fayerye,° *the magical otherworld*
With harpe and pype and simphonye° *a stringed instrument*
  Dwelling in this place."

The child seyde, "Also mote I thee,° *So may I thrive (I swear)*
Tomorwe wol I mete thee
  Whan I have myn armoure;
And yet I hope, *par ma fay*,° *by my faith*
That thou shalt with this launcegay° *light lance*
  Abyen it ful soure.° *Pay for it very sourly, bitterly*
    Thy mawe° *stomach, belly*
Shal I percen,° if I may, *pierce*
Er it be fully pryme° of day, *9 A.M.*
  For heer thou shalt be slawe."° *slain*

Sir Thopas drow° abak ful faste; *drew*
This geaunt at him stones caste
  Out of a fel staf-slinge.° *terrifying slingshot*
But faire° escapeth child Thopas, *fairly, safely*
And al it was thurgh Goddes gras° *grace*
  And thurgh his fair beringe.° *behavior, conduct*

[THE SECOND FIT]

Yet listeth,° lordes, to my tale *listen*
Merier than the nightingale,
  For now I wol yow roune° *tell (whisper)*
How sir Thopas, with sydes smale,° *slender waist*
Priking over hil and dale,
  Is come agayn to toune.

His merie men° comanded he *companions in arms*
To make him bothe game and glee,° *entertainment and music*
  For nedes moste he fight
With a geaunt with hevedes° three, *heads*
For paramour° and jolitee° *love / pleasure*
  Of oon° that shoon ful brighte. *i.e., the elf queen*

"Do come,"° he seyde, "my minstrales, *Summon*
And gestours° for to tellen tales— *storytellers*

Anon in myn arminge—
Of romances that been royales,
Of popes and of cardinales,
And eek° of love-lykinge."° — *also / love delights*

They fette° him first the swete wyn, — *fetched*
And mede° eek in a maselyn,° — *mead / mazer (wooden bowl)*
And royal spicerye° — *mixtures of spices*
Of gingebreed° that was ful fyn, — *preserved ginger*
And lycorys,° and eek comyn,° — *licorice / cumin*
With sugre that is trye.° — *choice, excellent*

He dide° next° his whyte lere° — *put on / next to / flesh*
Of clooth of lake° fyn and clere° — *fine linen / bright*
A breech° and eek a sherte; — *pair of trousers*
And next his sherte an aketoun,° — *padded jacket*
And over that an habergeoun° — *coat of mail*
For° percinge of his herte; — *To prevent*

And over that a fyn hauberk° — *armor for chest and back*
Was al y-wroght of° Jewes werk, — *made, crafted by*
Ful strong it was of plate;° — *plate armor*
And over that his cote-armour° — *heraldic surcoat*
As whyt as is a lily-flour,
In which he wol debate.° — *fight*

His sheeld was al of gold so reed,° — *red*
And therin was a bores° heed, — *boar's*
A charbocle° bisyde; — *carbuncle (a red gemstone)*
And there he swoor on ale and breed
How that the geaunt shal be deed,
Bityde what bityde.° — *Come what may*

His jambeux° were of quirboilly,° — *leg armor / hardened leather*
His swerdes shethe° of yvory, — *sheath*
His helm° of laton° bright. — *helmet / latten, brass*
His sadel was of rewel-boon,° — *whalebone, ivory*
His brydel as the sonne shoon,° — *shone*
Or as the mone light.

His spere was of fyn ciprees,° — *cypress*
That bodeth werre° and nothing pees,° — *forebodes war / in no way peace*
The heed ful sharpe y-grounde.
His stede was al dappel gray,
It gooth an ambel° in the way — *goes at a slow walk*
Ful softely and rounde° — *easily*
In londe.

Lo, lordes myne, heer is a fit!° — *canto or section of a poem*
If ye wol any more of it,
To telle it wol I fonde.° — *strive, try*

[THE THIRD FIT]

Now hold your mouth, *par charitee*,° — *for charity's sake*
Bothe knight and lady free,° — *noble, generous*
  And herkneth to my spelle.° — *listen to my story*
Of bataille and of chivalry,
And of ladyes love-drury° — *love service, courtship*
  Anon I wol yow telle.

Men speken of romances of prys,° — *worthy, excellent*
Of Horn child and of Ypotys,
  Of Bevis and sir Gy,
Of sir Libeux and Pleyn-damour.
But sir Thopas—he bereth the flour° — *bears the prize*
  Of royal chivalry.[4]

His gode stede al he bistrood,° — *bestrode*
And forth upon his wey he glood° — *glided, traveled*
  As sparkle° out of the bronde.° — *sparks / burning brand, torch*
Upon his crest° he bar a tour,° — *the top of his helmet / bore a tower ornament*
And therin stiked° a lily-flour— — *stuck, was fixed*
  God shilde his cors fro shonde!° — *keep his body from harm*

And for° he was a knight auntrous,° — *because / adventurous*
He nolde° slepen in non hous, — *would not*
  But liggen° in his hode.° — *lie / hood (i.e., outdoors)*
His brighte helm° was his wonger,° — *helmet / pillow*
And by him baiteth° his dextrer° — *feeds, grazes / warhorse*
  Of herbes° fyne and gode. — *On grasses*

Himself drank water of the wel,° — *spring*
As did the knight sir Percivel,° — *Percival (a chaste romance hero)*
  So worly under wede,° — *worthy in his armor, clothing*
Til on a day—[5]

From The Prologue and Tale of Melibee

The Prologue

  "No more of this, for Goddes dignitee,"
Quod oure Hoste, "for thou makest me
So wery of thy verray lewednesse° — *sheer incompetence*
That, also wisly° God my soule blesse,° — *as surely as / may bless*

4. Chaucer claims that his hero surpasses those of the popular romances that he parodies in this tale: King Horn (also known as Child Horn), Ypotis (a pious child, Epictetus, who instructs the emperor Hadrian in the Christian faith), Bevis of Hampton and Guy of Warwick, who furnished Chaucer much to satirize here, along with Lybeaux Desconus ("sir Lybeux"), whose disguise-name means "The Fair Unknown," and the almost wholly unknown "Pleyndamour," whose name means "full of love."
5. After this line the Hengwrt MS has the following statement: "Here the hoost stynteth [stops] Chaucer of his tale of Thopas and biddeth hym telle another tale."

Myn eres° aken of° thy drasty° speche. *ears / ache from / foul, vile*
Now swiche a rym° the devel I biteche!° *rhyme, tale in verse / consign to*
This may wel be rym dogerel,"° quod he. *doggerel verse*
"Why so?" quod I. "Why wiltow lette° me *wilt thou prevent*
More of my tale than another man,
Sin° that it is the beste rym I can?"° *Since / know*
"By God," quod he, "for pleynly at a word,
Thy drasty ryming is nat worth a tord.° *turd*
Thou doost nought elles but despendest° tyme. *waste*
Sir, at o word,° thou shalt no lenger ryme. *in short*
Lat see wher thou canst tellen aught in geste[1]
Or telle in prose somwhat° at the leste, *something*
In which ther be som mirthe or som doctryne."° *useful teaching*
"Gladly," quod I, "By Goddes swete pyne,° *pain, i.e., Passion*
I wol yow telle a litel thing in prose
That oghte lyken° yow, as I suppose, *please*
Or elles, certes,° ye been to daungerous.° *surely / too disdainful, hard to please*
It is a moral tale vertuous,
Al be it° told somtyme in sondry wyse° *Although / in different ways*
Of° sondry folk, as I shal yow devyse° *By / explain to you*
As thus:° ye woot° that every evangelist° *As follows / know / Gospel writer*
That telleth us the peyne° of Jesu Crist *pain, suffering*
Ne saith nat al thing as his felaw° dooth, *fellow evangelist*
But natheles° hir sentence is al sooth, *nevertheless*
And alle acorden as in hir sentence,[2]
Al be ther° in hir telling difference; *Although there is*
For somme of hem seyn more and somme lesse
Whan they his pitous° passioun expresse *piteous, sad*
(I mene of Marke, Mathew, Luk and John),
But doutelees hir sentence is al oon.° *their meaning is the same*
Therfor, lordinges alle, I yow biseche,° *beseech, ask*
If that ye thinke I varie as in my speche,
As thus,° thogh that I telle somwhat more *In this way*
Of proverbes than ye han herd bifore
Comprehended° in this litel tretis here, *Contained*
To enforce with° the'effect of my matere,° *To strengthen / material*
And thogh I nat the same wordes seye
As ye han herd, yet to yow alle I preye,
Blameth me nat; for as in my sentence° *for in my meaning*
Shul ye nowher fynden difference
Fro the sentence of this tretis lyte° *little treatise*
After the which° this mery° tale I wryte. *Which is the source of / pleasant*
And therfor herkneth what that I shal seye,
And lat me tellen al my tale, I preye."

1. "Let (us) see whether thou canst tell something in alliterative verse."
2. But nevertheless their essential meaning is true, and they all agree on that meaning. In these and the following lines Chaucer uses the different renderings in the four gospels of a single set of events to explain how his proverb-laden tale of Melibee contains the same basic meaning as other versions of that story.

From *The Tale*

A yong man called Melibeus, mighty and riche, bigat° upon his wyf, that called was Prudence, a doghter which that called was Sophie.° /

begot / (evoking "Sophia," wisdom)

Upon a day bifel° that he for his desport° is went into the feeldes° him to pleye.° / His wyf and eek° his doghter hath he left inwith° his hous, of which the dores° weren fast y-shette.° / Thre of his olde foos° han it espyed° and setten laddres° to the walles of his hous and by the windowes been entred, / and betten° his wyf and wounded his doghter with fyve mortal woundes in fyve sondry° places / (this is to seyn, in hir feet, in hir handes, in hir eres,° in hir nose, and in hir mouth) and leften hir for deed,° and wenten awey. /

it happened / disport, pleasure; fields / to enjoy himself; also; inside / doors; firmly shut / foes; saw it / put up ladders; (they) beat, struck; different; ears; as though dead

Whan Melibeus retourned was into his hous and saugh° al this meschief,° he, lyk a mad man rendinge his clothes, gan to wepe and crye. /

saw / harm, misfortune

Prudence his wyf, as ferforth° as she dorste,° bisoghte° him of his weping for to stinte,° / but nat forthy° he gan to crye and wepen ever lenger the more.° /

far; dared / begged; stop / nevertheless; more and more intensely

This noble wyf Prudence remembered hir upon° the sentence° of Ovide, in his book that cleped is° The Remedie of Love,° wher as° he seith, / "He is a fool that destourbeth° the moder to wepen in the deeth of hir child til she have wept hir fille° as for a certein tyme, / and thanne shal man doon his diligence° with amiable wordes hir to reconforte,° and preyen° hir of hir weping for to stinte."/ For which resoun this noble wyf Prudence suffred° hir housbond for to wepe and crye as for a certein space,° / and whan she saugh° hir tyme, she seyde him° in this wyse:° "Allas, my lord," quod° she, "why make ye yourself for to be lyk a fool? / For sothe,° it aperteneth nat to° a wys man to maken swiche a sorwe. / Your doghter, with the grace of God, shal warisshe° and escape. / And al were it° so that she right now were deed, ye ne oghte nat as for hir deeth yourself to destroye. / Senek° seith, 'The wise man shal nat take to° greet disconfort for the deeth of his children, / but certes° he sholde suffren° it in pacience, as wel as

i.e., recalled / maxim; is titled / Ovid's Remedia Amoris*; in which; who prevents; as much as she desires; a person make every effort; to comfort her / beg; allowed; space of time; saw / spoke to him; way / said; truly / is not suitable for; recover; even if it were; Seneca; too; certainly; endure*

he abydeth° the deeth of his owene propre persone.' "° /

This Melibeus answerde anon° and seyde: "What man," quod he, "sholde of his weping stinte° that hath so greet a cause for to wepe? / Jesu Crist, our Lord, himself wepte for the deeth of Lazarus his freend." / Prudence answerde, "Certes, wel I woot° attempree° weping is no thing defended° to him that sorweful is amonges folk in sorwe, but it is rather graunted him to wepe. / The Apostle Paul unto the Romayns wryteth, 'Man shal rejoyse with hem that° maken joye and wepen with swich folk as wepen.' / But thogh attempree weping be y-graunted, outrageous° weping certes is defended. / Mesure of° weping sholde be considered after the lore° that techeth us Senek: / 'Whan that thy freend is deed,' quod he, 'lat nat thyne eyen° to° moyste been of teres, ne to muche drye. Althogh the teres come to thyne eyen, lat hem nat falle. / And whan thou hast forgoon° thy freend, do diligence° to gete another freend. And this is more wysdom° than for to wepe for thy freend which that thou hast lorn,° for therinne is no bote.'° / And therfore, if ye governe yow° by sapience,° put awey sorwe out of your herte. / Remembre yow that° Jesus Syrak[3] seith: 'A man that is joyous and glad in herte, it him conserveth florisshing° in his age; but soothly sorweful herte maketh his bones drye.' / He seith eek thus that sorwe in herte sleeth ful many a man. / Salomon seith that right as motthes° in the shepes flees° anoyeth° to the clothes, and the smale wormes to the tree, right so anoyeth sorwe to the herte. / Wherfore us oghte,° as wel in the deeth of our children as in the losse of our othere goodes temporels,° have pacience. / Remembre yow upon the pacient Job. Whan he hadde lost his children and his temporel substance,° and in his body endured and receyved ful many a grevous

waits for
i.e., his own death
immediately
cease
know (that)
moderate / not at all forbidden
those who
excessive
Moderation in
according to the wisdom
do not let thine eyes / too
lost / make every effort
i.e., wiser
lost
benefit, remedy / yourself
wisdom
Remember what
keeps him healthy
just as moths
fleece / do damage
we ought to
temporal, transitory
worldly wealth

3. Jesus, son of Sirach, was the Jewish author of the book known to Christians as *Ecclesiasticus* (a canonical book in the Catholic but not the Protestant Bible). The passage quoted here is actually from Proverbs 17:22. The mistake is in Chaucer's source, *Le Livre de Mellibee et Prudence*, by the fourteenth-century friar Reynaud de Louens. Chaucer's *Tale of Melibee* is a rather close translation of Reynaud's work, which itself is a translation/adaptation of a Latin work by the thirteenth-century Italian orator Albertano of Brescia.

tribulacioun, yet seyde he thus: / 'Our Lord hath yeven it me,° our Lord hath biraft it me.° Right as our Lord hath wold,° right so it is doon. Blessed be the name of our Lord.' " /

given it to me
taken it from me / willed

To thise foreseide thinges answerde Melibeus unto his wyf Prudence: "Alle thy wordes," quod he, "been sothe and therto° profitable, but trewely myn herte is troubled with this sorwe so grevously that I noot what to done."° /

on that (subject)
know not what to do

"Lat calle,"° quod Prudence, "thy trewe freendes alle and thy linage° whiche that been wyse. Telleth your cas° and herkneth° what they seye in conseiling, and yow governe° after hir sentence.° Salomon seith, 'Werk alle thy thinges by conseil,° and thou shalt never repente.' " /

i.e., Call, summon
kinfolk
case, situation / listen to
conduct yourself
according to their opinion
Do everything through counsel

Thanne° by the conseil of his wyf Prudence, this Melibeus leet callen° a greet congregacioun of folk, / as surgiens,° phisiciens, olde folk and yonge, and somme of hise olde enemys reconciled (as by hir semblaunt°) to his love and into his grace; / and therwithal ther comen somme of hise neighebores that diden him reverence° more for drede° than for love, as it happeth ofte. / Ther comen also ful many subtile flatereres and wyse advocates° lerned in the lawe. /

Then
i.e., summoned
such as surgeons
as it appeared
showed him respect
out of fear
lawyers

And whan this folk togidre° assembled weren, this Melibeus in sorweful wyse shewed hem his cas,° and by the manere of his speche it semed that in herte he bar° a cruel ire,° redy to doon° vengeaunce upon hise foos,° and sodeynly° desired that the werre° sholde biginne; / but nathelees yet axed he hir conseil° upon this matere. /

together
revealed to them what happened
carried
anger / take
foes / impetuously
war, conflict
he asked their advice

[*Summary of lines 1010–1805*: The majority of these friends and kin support Melibee's wish to take vengeance. Prudence advises him not to act hastily and to listen to her counsel. Melibee says he will not listen to her, for reasons chiefly based on her status as a woman and a wife. Prudence refutes each of these arguments, and Melibee then agrees to follow her counsel. Prudence first addresses the issue of taking counsel, discussing how counselors should be chosen and calling into question the advice he received. Melibee, seeing the direction of her argument, gives various reasons why taking vengeance is necessary and appropriate, but Prudence challenges all of them. She counsels Melibee to make peace with his enemies, and when he claims that she does not care about his "honor," she pretends to be angry with him, prompting Melibee to see that his own anger has clouded his judgment. He promises Prudence that he will follow her counsel. She tells him first to make peace between himself and God. Having secured his good will, she talks privately with his three enemies, who acknowledge they have done wrong, and persuades them to submit themselves to Melibee's judgment. Melibee agrees to pardon them if they are repentant but does not want to act without the counsel of others. This time, to Prudence's pleasure, the counselors invited to his court are "trewe and wyse" rather than self-interested friends. They advise him to pursue peace. Following his wife's counsel, Melibee asks his enemies to come to him to discuss a peaceful resolution of their conflict.]

And right anon they token hir wey° to the — *took their way*
court of Melibee / and token with hem
somme of hir trewe freendes to maken
feith° for hem and for to been hir borwes.° / — *stand surety / guarantors*
And whan they were comen to the presence
of Melibee, he seyde hem° thise wordes: / — *spoke to them*
"It standeth thus," quod Melibee, "and
sooth° it is, that ye / —causeless and with- — *true*
outen skile° and resoun / —han doon grete — *grounds*
injuries and wronges to me and to my wyf
Prudence and to my doghter also. / For ye
han entred into myn hous by violence /
and have doon swich outrage that alle
men knowen wel that ye have deserved
the deeth; / and therfore wol I knowe
and wite° of yow / whether ye wol putte the — *understand*
punissement and the chastysinge and the
vengeance of this outrage in the wil of
me° and of my wyf Prudence, or ye wol — *in my will, choice*
nat?" /

Thanne the wysest of hem thre° answerde — *the three of them*
for hem alle and seyde: / "Sire," quod he,
"we knowen wel that we been unworthy to
comen unto the court of so greet a lord and
so worthy as ye been. / For we han so greetly
mistaken us° and han offended and agilt in — *acted wrongly*
swich a wyse agayn° your heigh lordshipe / — *done such wrong against*
that trewely we han deserved the deeth.° / — *i.e., to die*
But yet, for the grete goodnesse and
debonairetee° that all the world witnesseth — *kindness*
of your persone,° / we submitten us to the — *i.e., in yourself*
excellence and benignitee° of your gracious — *goodness*
lordshipe / and been° redy to obeie to alle — *are*
your comandements, / bisekinge° yow that — *beseeching*
of° your merciable° pitee ye wol considere — *out of / merciful*
our grete repentaunce and lowe° submis- — *humble*
sioun / and graunten us foryevenesse° of — *forgiveness*
our outrageous trespas and offence. / For
wel we knowe that your liberal grace and
mercy strecchen hem ferther° into good- — *extend farther*
nesse than doon° our outrageouse giltes — *do*
and trespas into wikkednesse, / al be it that° — *even though*

cursedly and dampnably we han agilt agayn your heigh lordshipe." /

Thanne Melibee took hem up fro the ground ful benignely° / and receyved hir obligaciouns and hir bondes by hir othes upon hir plegges and borwes,[4] / and assigned hem a certeyn day to retourne unto his court / for to accepte and receyve the sentence° and jugement that Melibee wolde comande to be doon° on hem by° the causes aforeseyd. / Whiche thinges ordeyned,° every man retourned to his hous. /

very graciously; decision; imposed / for; ordained, arranged

And whan that dame Prudence saugh° hir tyme, she freyned° and axed hir lord Melibee / what vengeance he thoughte to taken of° hise adversaries. /

saw; inquired; against

To which Melibee answerde and seyde: "Certes,"° quod he, "I thinke and purpose me fully / to desherite° hem of al that ever they han and for to putte hem in exil° for ever." /

Surely; dispossess; exile

"Certes," quod dame Prudence, "this were a cruel sentence and muchel° agayn resoun. / For ye been riche ynough and han no nede of other mennes good,° / and ye mighte lightly in this wyse gete yow a coveitous name,° / which is a vicious thing and oghte been eschewed of° every good man. / For after the sawe° of the word of the apostle, 'Coveitise is rote of all harmes.'[5] / And therfore it were bettre for yow to lese° so muchel good of your owene than for to taken of hir good in this manere. / For bettre it is to lesen good with worshipe° than it is to winne good with vileinye° and shame, / and every man oghte to doon his diligence and his bisinesse to geten him° a good name. / And yet shal he nat only bisie him in kepinge of his good name, / but he shal also enforcen him° alwey to do somthing by which he may renovelle° his good name, / for it is writen that the olde good loos° or good name of a man is sone goon° and passed whan it is nat newed° ne renovelled. / And as touchinge° that ye seyn° ye wole exile your adversaries, / that thinketh me

much; goods, property; a reputation for greed; shunned by; according to the maxim; lose; honor; dishonor; himself; strive; renew; reputation; soon lost; renewed; considering / say

4. And accepted the obligations and commitments they made by oath, supported by their pledges and sureties.

5. Avarice is the root of all evil (1 Timothy 6:10). This is the text on which the Pardoner says he always preaches (see p. 259, ll. 423–26).

muchel agayn resoun and out of mesure,° / considered° the power that they han yeve° yow upon° hemself. / And it is writen that he is worthy to lesen° his privilege that misuseth the might and the power that is yeven him. / And I sette cas° ye mighte enjoyne hem that peyne° by right and by lawe / (which I trowe° ye mowe° nat do), / I seye ye mighte nat putten it to execucioun° peraventure,° / and thanne were it lykly° to retourne to the werre° as it was biforn. / And therefore if ye wole° that men do yow obeisance,° ye moste demen° more curteisly° / —this is to seyn, ye moste yeven° more esy° sentences and jugements. / For it is writen that he that most curteisly comandeth, to him men most obeyen. / And therfore I prey° yow that in this necessitee and in this nede ye caste yow° to overcome your herte.° / For Senek[6] seith that he that overcometh his herte overcometh twyes.° / And Tullius° seith ther is no thing so comendable in a greet lord / as whan he is debonaire° and meke° and appeseth him lightly.° / And I prey yow that ye wole forbere° now to do vengeance / in swich a manere that your goode name may be kept and conserved, / and that men mowe° have cause and matere° to preyse° yow of° pitee and of mercy, / and that ye have no cause to repente yow of thing that ye doon. / For Senek seith, 'He overcometh in an yvel° manere that° repenteth him of his victorie.'[7] / Wherfore I pray yow, lat mercy been in your minde and in your herte, / to th'effect and entente° that God Almighty have mercy on yow in His laste jugement. / For Seint Jame seith in his epistle, 'Jugement withouten mercy shal be doon to° him that hath no mercy of° another wight.'"° /

Whanne Melibee hadde herd the grete skiles° and resouns of dame Prudence and hir wise informaciouns° and techinges, / his herte gan enclyne° to the wil of his wyf, consideringe hir trewe entente, / and conformed him anon° and assented fully to werken after° hir conseil, / and thonked God, of° whom procedeth al vertu and alle

excessive
considering / have given
over
lose
i.e., supposing
impose that punishment on them
believe / may
carry it out / by (some) chance
the situation would be likely
conflict
will, wish
obey you / pass judgments / gently
must give / lenient
beg
make an effort / desire
twice / Cicero
kind
meek / is easily appeased
refrain
may
reason / praise / for
evil / who
for the purpose
inflicted on / on
person
arguments
instruction
incline, bend
resolved promptly
act according to
from

6. Seneca; but the author here and in line 1866 is actually Publilius Syrus.
7. He who has cause to repent his victory has won it in an evil [dishonorable] way.

goodnesse, that him sente a wyf of so greet discrecioun.° / And whan the day cam that hise adversaries sholde apperen° in his presence, / he spak unto hem ful goodly° and seyde in this wyse: / "Al be it so that° of° your pryde and presumpcioun and folie,° and of your necligence and unconninge,° / ye have misborn yow° and trespassed unto me, / yet for as much as I see and biholde your grete humilitee / and that ye been sory and repentant of your giltes,° / it constreyneth me to doon° yow grace and mercy. / Therfore I receyve yow to° my grace / and foryeve yow outrely° alle the offences, injuries, and wronges that ye have doon agayn° me and myne, / to this effect and to this ende: that God of his endelees mercy / wole at the time of our dyinge foryeven us our giltes that we han trespassed to° him in this wrecched world. / For doutelees,° if we be sory and repentant of the sinnes and giltes whiche we han trespassed in the sighte of our Lord God, / he is so free° and so merciable° that he wole foryeven us our giltes / and bringen us to his blisse that never hath ende." Amen. /

discernment, understanding
appear
kindly, sensibly
Although / out of
foolishness, sin
ignorance
misbehaved
sins
i.e., I am compelled to grant
accept you (back) into
forgive you utterly, completely
against
sinned against
without doubt
generous
merciful

The Nun's Priest's Prologue and Tale

The Prologue

"Ho!"° quod° the Knight, "good sir, namore of this; — *Stop / said*
That° ye han seyd is right ynough, ywis,[1] — *What*
And mochel more; for litel hevinesse[2]
Is right ynough to mochel° folk, I gesse. — *for many*
I seye for me it is a greet disese,° — *discomfort*
Where as° men han ben in greet welthe and ese, — *There where*
To heeren° of hire sodeyn° fal, allas! — *hear / sudden*
And the contrarie is joie° and greet solas,° — *joy / comfort*
As whan a man hath been in povre estaat,° — *a condition of poverty*
And clymbeth up, and wexeth° fortunat, — *becomes increasingly*
And ther abydeth in prosperitee—
Swich° thing is gladsome, as it thinketh me, — *Such*
And of swich thing were goodly for to telle."
"Ye," quod our Hoste, "by Seinte Poules° belle, — *St. Paul's (Cathedral)*
Ye seye right sooth:° this Monk, he clappeth loude.° — *truly / chatters loudly*

1. Indeed. The Knight here breaks off the Monk's tale, a recital of "tragedies," i.e., stories of the fall of great ones from high fortune into misery.
2. And much more (than enough); for a little seriousness.

He spak 'how Fortune covered with a cloude'—
I noot° never what. And als° of a 'tragedie' *know not / besides*
Right now ye herde, and pardee,° no remedie *by God*
It is for to biwaille° ne compleyne *bewail*
That that° is doon, and als° it is a peyne, *which / besides*
As ye han seyd, to heere° of hevinesse. *hear*
Sire Monk, namore of this, so God yow blesse!
Your tale anoyeth al this compaignye.
Swich talking is nat worth a boterflye,° *butterfly*
For therinne is ther no desport° ne game. *pleasure*
Wherfore sir Monk, or daun° Piers by youre name, *sir*
I preye yow hertely° telle us somewhat elles,° *heartily / something else*
For sikerly, nere clinking of youre belles[3]
That on your brydel hange on every side,
By hevene° king that for us alle dyde,° *heaven's / died*
I sholde er° this han fallen doun for slepe, *before*
Althogh the slough° had never been so depe. *mire*
Than had your tale al be° told in vayn; *been*
For certainly, as that° thise clerkes seyn, *just as*
'Whereas° a man may have noon audience, *There where*
Noght helpeth it to tellen his sentence.'° *meaning*
And wel I woot the substance is in me,[4]
If any thing shal wel reported be.
Sir, sey somewhat of hunting, I yow preye."
"Nay," quod this Monk, "I have no lust° to pleye; *desire*
Now let another telle, as I have told."
Than spak our Host, with rude speche and bold,
And seyde unto the Nonnes Preest° anon, *Nun's Priest*
"Com neer,° thou preest, com hider, thou sir John, *nearer*
Tel us swich thing as may oure hertes glade.° *gladden*
Be blythe,° though thou ryde upon a jade!° *cheerful / a poor horse*
What though thyn hors be bothe foule and lene?° *lean*
If he wol serve thee, rekke nat a bene.° *don't care a bean*
Look that thyn herte be mery evermo."
"Yis, sir," quod he, "yis, Host, so mote I go,° *as I may thrive*
But° I be mery, ywis,° I wol be blamed." *Unless / truly*
And right anon° his tale he hath attamed,° *right away / begun*
And thus he seyde unto us everichon,° *every one*
This sweete preest, this goodly man sir John.

The Tale

A povre widwe, somdel stape in age,[5]
Was whylom° dwelling in a narwe° cotage, *once / small*
Bisyde a grove, stondinge in a dale.° *valley*
This widwe of which I telle yow my tale,
Sin thilke° day that she was last a wyf, *Since that same*

3. For certainly, were it not for the clinking of your bells.
4. Sense uncertain: either "I know well I have the capacity to understand"; or "I know I've got the meaning (if it's been well told)."
5. A poor widow, somewhat advanced in years.

In pacience ladde° a ful simple lyf, *led*
For litel was hir catel° and hir rente.° *property / income*
By housbondrye° of such as God hire sente *careful management*
She fond° hirself and eek° hir doghtren° two. *provided for / also / daughters*
Three large sowes hadde she and namo,° *no more*
Three kyn,° and eek a sheep that highte° Malle. *cows / was called*
Ful sooty was hire bour, and eek hir halle,[6]
In which she eet ful many a sclendre° meel. *lean*
Of poynaunt° sauce hir neded never a deel:° *pungent / not a bit*
No deyntee morsel passed thurgh hir throte.
Hir diete was accordant° to hir cote°— *matched / cottage*
Repleccioun° ne made hir never syk. *Surfeit*
Attempree diete was al hir phisyk,[7]
And exercyse, and hertes suffisaunce.° *heart's contentment*
The goute lette° hire nothing for to daunce,° *hindered / from dancing*
N'apoplexye shente° nat hir heed. *Nor did apoplexy injure*
No wyn° ne drank she, neither whyt° ne reed;° *wine / white / red*
Hir bord° was served most with whyt and blak— *table*
Milk and broun breed—in which she fond no lak,° *found no fault*
Seynd° bacoun, and somtyme an ey or tweye,° *Broiled / egg or two*
For she was as it were a maner deye.° *kind of dairymaid*
  A yerd° she hadde, enclosed° al aboute *yard / fenced*
With stikkes,° and a drye dich° withoute, *palings / ditch*
In which she hadde a cok hight° Chauntecleer: *called*
In al the land of° crowing nas° his peer. *at / there was not*
His voys was merier than the mery orgon° *organ*
On messe-dayes° that in the chirche gon;° *feast days / plays*
Wel sikerer° was his crowing in his logge° *more certain / lodgings*
Than is a clokke or an abbey orlogge.° *(great) clock*
By nature knew he ech ascencioun
Of the equinoxial in thilke toun:[8]
For whan degrees fiftene were ascended,
Thanne crew he, that it mighte nat ben amended.° *improved*
His comb was redder than the fyn coral,
And batailed° as it were a castel wal. *notched (like battlements)*
His bile° was blak, and as the jeet° it shoon; *bill / jet (semiprecious stone)*
Lyk asur° were his legges and his toon;° *azure / toes*
His nayles° whytter than the lilie flour,° *claws / lily flower*
And lyk the burned° gold was his colour. *burnished*
This gentil cok hadde in his governaunce° *in his care*
Sevene hennes,° for to doon al his plesaunce, *hens*
Whiche were his sustres° and his paramours,° *sisters / lovers*
And wonder lyk to him, as of colours;
Of whiche the faireste hewed° on hir throte *hued, colored*
Was cleped° faire damoysele° Pertelote. *named / (ma)demoiselle*

6. Her "bed chamber" and her "banquet hall" were grimy with soot. (The terms are being used ironically; her humble cottage lacks such rooms and offers implicit moral criticism of such grandeur.)
7. A temperate diet was her only medicine.
8. By natural instinct he knew each revolution of the equinoctial circle—the celestial equator—in that same town (a complicated astronomical description of how the hours pass and are numbered).

Curteys° she was, discreet, and debonaire,° *Courteous / gracious*
And compaignable,° and bar hirself so faire, *sociable*
Sin thilke day that she was seven night old,
That trewely she hath the herte in hold
Of Chauntecleer, loken° in every lith;° *locked / limb*
He loved hire so, that wel was him therwith.
But such a joye was it to here hem° singe, *them*
Whan that the brighte sonne gan to springe,° *began to rise*
In swete acord, "my lief is faren in londe."[9]
For thilke tyme,° as I have understonde, *in those days*
Bestes° and briddes° coude speke and singe. *Beasts / birds*
   And so bifel that in a daweninge,[1]
As Chauntecleer among his wyves alle
Sat on his perche that was in the halle,
And next him sat this faire Pertelote,
This Chauntecleer gan gronen° in his throte *did groan*
As man that in his dreem is drecched sore.° *severely troubled*
And whan that Pertelote thus herde him rore,
She was agast,° and seyde, "Herte dere, *afraid*
What eyleth° yow to grone in this manere? *ails*
Ye been a verray sleper,° fy for shame!" *You're a fine sleeper*
   And he answerde and seyde thus, "Madame,
I pray yow, that ye take it nat agrief:° *amiss*
By God, me mette° I was in swich meschief° *I dreamed / trouble*
Right now, that yet myn herte is sore afright.
Now God," quod he, "my swevene recche aright,[2]
And keep my body out of foul prisoun!
Me mette how that I romed° up and doun *roamed*
Withinne our yerde, wher as I saugh° a beste, *saw*
Was lyk an hound and wolde han maad areste° *laid hold*
Upon my body, and wolde han had me deed.° *dead*
His colour was bitwixe yelow and reed,° *red*
And tipped was his tail and bothe his eres° *ears*
With blak, unlyk the remenant° of his heres;° *rest / hair(s)*
His snowte° smal, with glowinge eyen tweye.° *snout / two eyes*
Yet° of his look for fere° almost I deye:° *Still / fear / die*
This caused me my groning, doutelees."
   "Avoy!"° quod she, "fy on yow, hertelees!° *Go on / faint heart*
Allas!" quod she, "for, by that God above,
Now han ye lost myn herte and al my love.
I can nat love a coward, by my feith!
For certes, what so any womman seith,
We alle desiren,° if it mighte be, *desire*
To han housbondes hardy,° wyse, and free,° *bold / generous*
And secree,° and no nigard,° ne no fool, *discreet / miser*
Ne him that is agast° of every tool,° *afraid / weapon*
Ne noon avauntour.° By that God above, *boaster*

9. In sweet harmony, "my love has gone to the country" (a popular song).
1. And so it happened, one morning at dawn.
2. "Now God," he said, "(help) interpret my dream correctly."

How dorste° ye seyn for shame unto your love — *dare*
That any thing mighte make yow aferd?° — *afraid*
Have ye no mannes herte, and han a berd?° — *beard*
Allas! and conne ye been agast of swevenis?° — *dreams*
Nothing, God wot, but vanitee° in sweven is. — *foolishness, illusion*
Swevenes[3] engendren of replecciouns,° — *are born of surfeits*
And ofte of fume,° and of complecciouns, — *vapor(s)*
Whan humours been to habundant° in a wight.° — *too abundant / person*
Certes° this dreem, which ye han met tonight, — *Certainly*
Cometh of the grete superfluitee
Of youre rede *colera*,° pardee, — *choler (a humor)*
Which causeth folk to dreden° in hir° dremes — *fear / their*
Of arwes,° and of fyr with rede lemes,° — *arrows / flames*
Of rede bestes, that they wol hem byte,
Of contek,° and of whelpes° grete and lyte;° — *strife / pups, cubs / little*
Right as the humour of malencolye° — *melancholy (black bile)*
Causeth ful many a man in sleep to crye
For fere of blake beres,° or boles° blake, — *bears / bulls*
Or elles, blake develes wole hem take.
Of othere humours coude I telle also
That werken° many a man in sleep ful wo;° — *cause / great woe*
But I wol passe as lightly as I can.
  Lo Catoun,° which that was so wys a man, — *Cato*
Seyde he nat thus, 'Ne do no fors of° dremes'? — *Pay no attention to*
Now, sire," quod she, "whan we flee° fro the bemes, — *fly*
For Goddes love, as tak some laxatyf.
Up° peril of my soule and of my lyf — *On*
I counseille yow the beste, I wol nat lye,
That bothe of colere and of malencolye
Ye purge yow; and for° ye shul nat tarie,° — *so that / delay*
Though in this toun is noon apothecarie,
I shal myself to herbes techen° yow, — *direct*
That shul ben for youre hele° and for youre prow;° — *health / benefit*
And in oure yerd tho° herbes shal I finde — *those*
The whiche han of hire propretee by kinde° — *nature*
To purgen yow binethe and eek above.
Forget not this, for Goddes owene love!
Ye been ful colerik of compleccioun.° — *temperamentally dominated by choler*
Ware° the sonne in his ascencioun — *Beware*
Ne fynde yow nat repleet° of humours hote; — *Does not find you full*
And if it do, I dar wel leye° a grote,° — *bet / Dutch coin*
That ye shul have a fevere terciane,[4]
Or an agu,° that may be youre bane.° — *ague / destruction*
A day or two ye shul have digestyves
Of wormes, er° ye take your laxatyves, — *before*
Of lauriol,° centaure,° and fumetere,° — *spurge laurel / centaury / fumitory*

3. Pertelote's discussion of the causes of dreams and her insistence that Chauntecleer's dream is of physiological rather than supernatural origin (with the conclusion that it therefore need not be heeded) are informed by medieval dream theory. On the humours, see p. 12, n. 8, in the *General Prologue*: "complecccioun" refers to the existing balance between them.
4. A fever recurring every third day.

Or elles of ellebor° that groweth there, *hellebore*
Of catapuce,° or of gaytres beryis,° *caper spurge / dogwood's berries*
Of erbe yve,° growing in oure yerd, ther mery is.° *ivy / where it is pleasant*
Pekke hem° up right as they growe, and ete° hem in. *Peck them / eat*
Be mery, housbond, for youre fader kin!° *father's kin*
Dredeth no dreem: I can say yow namore."
"Madame," quod he, "*graunt mercy*° of youre lore. *many thanks*
But nathelees, as touching daun Catoun,
That hath of wisdom swich a greet renoun,° *such great fame*
Though that he bad° no dremes for to drede, *commanded*
By God, men may in olde bokes rede
Of many a man, more of auctoritee
Than ever Catoun was, so mote I thee,° *as I may thrive*
That al the revers° seyn of his sentence, *reverse, opposite*
And han wel founden° by experience, *established*
That dremes ben significaciouns° *meaningful signs*
As wel of joye° as tribulaciouns *joy*
That folk enduren in this lyf present.
Ther nedeth make of this noon argument:
The verray preve° sheweth it in dede. *true proof*
Oon of the gretteste auctours° that men rede *authorities, writers*
Seith thus, that whylom° two felawes° wente *once / companions*
On pilgrimage, in a ful good entente;
And happed so thay come into a toun,
Wher as° ther was swich congregacioun° *Where / such a gathering*
Of peple, and eek so streit of herbergage,° *such scarcity of lodgings*
That they ne founde as muche as o° cotage *one*
In which they bothe mighte y-logged° be. *lodged*
Wherfor thay mosten° of necessitee, *had to*
As for that night, departen° compaignye; *part*
And ech of hem goth° to his hostelrye,° *goes / lodging place*
And took his logging as it wolde falle.
That oon of hem° was logged in a stalle, *The one of them*
Fer° in a yerd, with oxen of the plough; *Far off*
That other man was logged wel ynough,
As was his aventure° or his fortune, *chance*
That us governeth alle as in commune.° *in general*
And so bifel that, longe er° it were day, *before*
This man mette° in his bed, ther as he lay, *dreamed*
How that his felawe gan° upon him calle, *began*
And seyde, 'Allas! for in an oxes stalle
This night I shal be mordred ther° I lye. *murdered where*
Now help me, dere brother, or I dye;
In alle haste com to me,' he sayde.
This man out of his sleep for fere abrayde,° *started up*
But whan that he was wakened of his sleep,
He turned him, and took of this no keep:° *heed*
Him thoughte his dreem nas but a vanitee.[5]
Thus twyes° in his sleping dremed he; *twice*

5. It seemed to him his dream was nothing but foolishness.

And atte thridde° tyme yet his felawe *at the third*
Cam, as him thoughte, and seide, 'I am now slawe.° *slain*
Bihold my blody woundes, depe and wyde!
Arys° up erly in the morwe tyde,° *Arise / morning*
And at the west gate of the toun,' quod he,
'A carte ful of donge° ther shaltow° see, *dung / shalt thou*
In which my body is hid ful prively:° *secretly*
Do thilke carte aresten° boldely. *Have that cart stopped*
My gold caused my mordre, sooth to sayn;'° *the truth to tell*
And tolde him every poynt how he was slayn,
With a ful pitous face, pale of hewe.
And truste wel, his dreem he fond ful trewe,
For on the morwe, as sone as it was day,
To his felawes in° he took the way; *companion's inn*
And whan that he cam to this oxes stalle,
After his felawe he bigan to calle.
The hostiler° answered him anon,° *innkeeper / immediately*
And seyde, 'Sire, your felawe is agon:° *gone*
As sone as day° he wente out of the toun.' *daybreak*
This man gan fallen in suspecioun,° *became suspicious*
Remembringe on his dremes that he mette,
And forth he goth, no lenger wolde he lette,° *delay*
Unto the west gate of the toun, and fond
A dong-carte, wente as it were to donge lond,[6]
That was arrayed in the same wyse° *way*
As ye han herd the dede man devyse.° *describe*
And with an hardy° herte he gan to crye, *bold*
'Vengeaunce and justice of this felonye!
My felawe mordred is this same night,
And in this carte he lyth° gapinge upright.° *lies / face up*
I crye out on the ministres,'° quod he, *officers*
'That sholden kepe and reulen° this citee, *care for and rule*
Harrow!° allas! heer lyth my felawe slayn!' *Help*
What sholde I more unto this tale sayn?
The peple out sterte,° and caste the cart to grounde, *came forth*
And in the middel of the dong they founde
The dede man, that mordred was al newe.° *just recently*
O blisful God, that art so just and trewe!
Lo, how that thou biwreyest° mordre alway! *revealest*
Mordre wol out, that see we day by day.
Mordre is so wlatsom° and abhominable *loathsome*
To God, that is so just and resonable,
That he ne wol nat suffre it heled be.° *to be concealed*
Though it abyde° a yeer, or two, or three, *remain (hidden)*
Mordre wol out, this my conclusioun.
And right anoon,° ministres of that toun *right away*
Han hent° the carter and so sore him pyned,° *seized / tortured*
And eek the hostiler so sore engyned,° *racked*
That thay biknewe° hir wikkednesse anoon, *acknowledged*

6. A dung-cart, going out as if to manure the land.

And were anhanged by the nekke-boon.° *neck(bone)*
Here may men seen that dremes been to drede.° *are to be feared*
And certes,° in the same book I rede, *certainly*
Right in the nexte chapitre after this—
I gabbe° nat, so have I° joye or blis— *lie / as I may have*
Two men that wolde han passed° over see, *wished to travel*
For certeyn cause, into a fer° contree, *far-off*
If that the wind ne hadde been contrarie:
That made hem in a citee for to tarie
That stood ful mery upon an haven° syde. *harbor*
But on a day, agayn the even-tyde,° *toward evening*
The wind gan chaunge, and blew right as hem leste.° *just as they wished*
Jolif° and glad they wente unto hir reste, *Jolly*
And casten hem° ful erly for to saille; *they planned*
But herkneth! To that oo° man fil° a greet mervaille. *one / befell*
That oon of hem, in sleping as he lay,
Him mette° a wonder dreem, agayn the° day: *He dreamed / toward*
Him thoughte° a man stood by his beddes syde, *It seemed to him*
And him comaunded that he sholde abyde,° *wait*
And seyde him thus, 'If thou tomorwe wende,° *travel*
Thou shalt be dreynt:° my tale is at an ende.' *drowned*
He wook,° and tolde his felawe what he mette, *awoke*
And preyde him his viage for to lette;[7]
As° for that day, he preyde him to byde. *Just*
His felawe, that lay by his beddes syde,
Gan for° to laughe, and scorned him ful faste.° *Began / very hard*
'No dreem' quod he, 'may so myn herte agaste° *frighten*
That I wol lette° for to do my thinges.° *leave off / business*
I sette not a straw by thy dreminges,
For swevenes° been but vanitees and japes.° *dreams / follies*
Men dreme alday of owles or of apes,
And eke° of many a mase° therwithal; *also / maze, bewilderment*
Men dreme of thing that nevere was ne shal.° *nor shall (be)*
But sith° I see that thou wolt heer abyde, *since*
And thus forsleuthen° wilfully thy tyde,° *slothfully waste / time*
God woot it reweth me;[8] and have good day.'
And thus he took his leve, and wente his way.
But er that° he hadde halfe his cours y-seyled,° *before / sailed*
Noot° I nat why, ne what mischaunce it eyled,° *Know not / ailed*
But casuelly° the shippes botme rente,° *by chance / tore open*
And ship and man under the water wente
In sighte of othere shippes it byside,° *alongside it*
That with hem seyled at the same tyde.
And therfore faire Pertelote so dere,
By swiche ensamples olde maistow lere[9]
That no man sholde been to recchelees° *heedless*
Of dremes, for I sey thee, doutelees,

7. And begged him to put off his voyage.
8. God knows it makes me sorry.
9. By such ancient examples thou mayest learn.

That many a dreem ful sore° is for to drede.° *greatly / to be dreaded*
  Lo, in the lyf° of Seint Kenelm I rede, *life*
That was Kenulphus sone,[1] the noble king
Of Mercenrike,° how Kenelm mette° a thing *Mercia / dreamed*
A lyte er° he was mordred on a day. *A little before*
His mordre in his avisioun° he say.° *vision / saw*
His norice° him expouned every del° *nurse / part of*
His sweven, and bad him for to kepe him wel° *guard himself carefully*
For traisoun;° but he nas but° seven yeer old, *Against treason / was only*
And therfore litel tale hath he told° *he took little note*
Of any dreem, so holy was his herte.
By God, I hadde lever° than my sherte *rather*
That ye had rad his legende as have I.[2]
  Dame Pertelote, I sey yow trewely,
Macrobeus,[3] that writ the avisioun° *vision*
In Affrike° of the worthy Cipioun,° *Africa / Scipio*
Affermeth° dremes, and seith that they been *Affirms (the validity of)*
Warninge of thinges that men after seen.° *afterward see*
And forthermore, I pray yow loketh wel
In the Olde Testament, of Daniel,
If he held dremes any vanitee.
Reed eek of Ioseph,[4] and ther shul ye see
Wher dremes ben somtyme (I sey nat alle)
Warninge of thinges that shul after falle.° *occur*
Loke of Egipte the king, daun Pharao,° *Sir Pharaoh*
His bakere and his boteler° also, *butler*
Wher° they ne felte noon effect° in dremes. *Whether / significance*
Whoso wol seken actes of sondry remes[5]
May rede of° dremes many a wonder thing. *about*
Lo Cresus,° which that was of Lyde° king, *Croesus / Lydia*
Mette he nat° that he sat upon a tree, *Did he not dream*
Which signified he sholde anhanged° be? *hanged*
Lo heer Andromacha,° Ectores° wyf, *Andromache / Hector's*
That day that Ector sholde lese° his lyf, *was to lose*
She dremed on the same night biforn,
How that the lyf of Ector sholde be lorn° *lost*
If thilke° day he wente into bataille; *that same*
She warned him, but it mighte nat availle;
He wente for to fighte natheless,° *nevertheless*
But he was slayn anoon° of Achilles. *immediately*
But thilke tale is al to long° to telle, *all too long*
And eek it is ny° day, I may nat dwelle. *near*
Shortly I seye, as for conclusioun,

1. When King Cenwulf of Mercia died in 821, his seven-year-old son Kenelm took the throne but was murdered by agents of his older sister. Shortly before death, Kenelm had a warning dream in which he climbed a tree that was then cut down, and saw himself fly to heaven in the shape of a bird.
2. By God, I'd give my shirt if you had (could have) read his story, as I have.
3. At the end of the fourth century, Macrobius wrote a commentary on Cicero's *Dream of Scipio* that became for the Middle Ages a standard authority on the nature of dreams. See pp. 496–98.
4. For the story of Joseph, see Genesis 37, 40, and 41.
5. Whosoever wishes to seek (knowledge of) the histories of various realms.

That I shal han of this avisioun° *vision*
Adversitee; and I seye forthermore,
That I ne telle of laxatyves no store,[6]
For they ben venimous,° I woot° it wel; *poisonous / know*
I hem defye,° I love hem never a del.° *defy them / not a bit*
  Now let us speke of mirthe and stinte° al this; *stop*
Madame Pertelote, so have I blis,
Of o° thing God hath sent me large° grace: *one / bounteous*
For whan I see the beautee of your face—
Ye ben so scarlet reed about your yën°— *eyes*
It maketh al my drede° for to dyen. *fear*
For, also siker° as *In principio,* *just as sure*
Mulier est hominis confusio.[7]
Madame, the sentence° of this Latin is *meaning*
'Womman is mannes joye and al his blis.'
For whan I fele° a-night° your softe syde, *feel / at night*
Al be it that I may nat on you ryde,
For that° our perche is maad° so narwe,° alas! *Because / made / narrow*
I am so ful of joye and of solas° *comfort*
That I defye bothe sweven° and dreem." *vision*
And with that word he fley° doun fro the beem, *flew*
For it was day, and eek° his hennes alle, *i.e., so did*
And with a chuk° he gan hem for to calle,° *cluck / called them*
For he had founde a corn° lay° in the yerd. *grain / (which) lay*
Real° he was, he was namore aferd;° *Regal / afraid*
He fethered° Pertelote twenty tyme, *covered with outspread wings*
And trad hir eke as ofte, er it was pryme.[8]
He loketh as it were° a grim leoun,° *as if he were / lion*
And on his toos° he rometh up and doun— *toes*
Him deyned° not to sette his foot to grounde. *deigned*
He chukketh whan he hath a corn y-founde,
And to him rennen thanne° his wyves alle. *run then*
Thus royal, as a prince is in his halle,
Leve I this Chauntecleer in his pasture;° *feeding*
And after wol I telle his aventure.
  Whan that the month in which the world bigan,
That highte° March, whan God first maked man, *is called*
Was complet, and passed were also,
Sin° March bigan, thritty dayes and two, *Since*
Bifel° that Chauntecleer, in al his pryde, *It came to pass*
His seven wyves walkinge by his syde,
Caste up his eyen to the brighte sonne,
That in the signe° of Taurus hadde y-ronne° *zodiacal sign / run*
Twenty degrees and oon, and somwhat more;
And knew by kynde,° and by noon° other lore,° *nature / no / learning*
That it was pryme, and crew with blisful stevene.° *voice*

6. That I set no store by laxatives.
7. "In the beginning" (the opening of the Gospel of St. John); "woman is man's ruin" (a much-used Latin proverb). Chauntecleer tactfully mistranslates it for Pertelote.
8. And trod (i.e., copulated with) her just as often, before it was nine o'clock (the canonical hour of prime).

"The sonne," he sayde, "is clomben° up on hevene — *has climbed*
Fourty degrees and oon, and more, ywis.
Madame Pertelote, my worldes blis,
Herkneth° thise blisful briddes° how they singe, — *Harken to / birds*
And see the fresshe floures how they springe;
Ful is myn herte of revel and solas."° — *joy*
But sodeinly him fil° a sorweful cas,° — *befell / happening*
For ever the latter ende of joye is wo.
God woot° that worldly joye is sone ago;° — *knows / soon gone*
And if a rethor° coude faire endyte,° — *rhetorician / write well*
He in a cronique° saufly° mighte it wryte — *chronicle / safely*
As for a sovereyn notabilitee.° — *supremely noteworthy fact*
Now every wys° man, lat him herkne me: — *wise*
This storie is also° trewe, I undertake,° — *just as / declare*
As is the book of Launcelot de Lake,[9]
That wommen holde in ful gret reverence.
Now wol I torne agayn° to my sentence.° — *turn again / main subject*
   A col-fox,[1] ful of sly iniquitee,
That in the grove hadde woned° yeres three, — *dwelt*
By heigh imaginacioun forncast,[2]
The same night thurghout° the hegges brast° — *through / burst*
Into the yerd, ther° Chauntecleer the faire — *where*
Was wont,° and eek his wyves, to repaire;° — *accustomed / to retire to*
And in a bed of wortes° stille he lay, — *herbs*
Til it was passed undren° of the day, — *midmorning*
Waytinge° his tyme on Chauntecleer to falle, — *Watching for*
As gladly doon° thise homicydes° alle, — *usually do / murderers*
That in awayt liggen° to mordre men. — *lie in wait*
O false mordrour, lurkinge in thy den!
O newe Scariot, newe Genilon![3]
False dissimilour,° O Greek Sinon,[4] — *dissembler*
That broghtest Troye al outrely° to sorwe! — *quite utterly*
O Chauntecleer, acursed be that morwe,° — *morning*
That thou into that yerd flough° fro the bemes! — *flew*
Thou were ful wel y-warned by thy dremes
That thilke day was perilous to thee.
But what that God forwoot mot nedes be,° — *that which God foreknows must needs be*
After the opinioun of certeyn clerkis.° — *scholars*
Witnesse on him° that any perfit clerk is — *Let him be witness*
That in scole° is gret altercacioun — *in (the) school(s)*
In this matere, and greet disputisoun,° — *disputation*
And hath ben of an hundred thousand men.
But I ne can not bulte it to the bren,[5]

9. Launcelot was the lover of Guinevere, wife of King Arthur—an entirely fictitious story.
1. A coal-fox, i.e., one with black markings (like the animal Chauntecleer saw in his dream).
2. Foreseen (preordained) by a supreme (divine) intelligence (an idea much too grand for the fate of a chicken). It leads to the problem of free will within the context of divine foreknowledge that is worried over in ll. 3234–50).
3. Oh, new (Judas) Iscariot, new Ganelon (the traitor in the *Chanson de Roland*).
4. Through Sinon's lies the wooden horse carrying Greek soldiers entered Troy.
5. But I cannot sift it down to the bran (i.e., argue the fine points).

As can the holy doctour Augustyn,° *St. Augustine*
Or Boece,° or the bishop Bradwardyn,° *Boethius / Bradwardine (of England)*
Whether that Goddes worthy forwiting° *excellent foreknowledge*
Streyneth° me nedely° for to doon a thing *Constrains / necessarily*
("Nedely" clepe° I simple necessitee); *call*
Or elles, if free choys° be graunted me *choice, will*
To do that same thing or do it noght,
Though God forwoot° it er° that I was wroght; *foreknows / before*
Or if his witing° streyneth never a del° *knowing / not at all*
But by necessitee condicionel.[6]
I wol not han to do of swich matere;
My tale is of a cok, as ye may here,
That took his counseil of° his wyf, with sorwe, *advice from*
To walken in the yerd upon that morwe° *morning*
That he had met° the dreem that I yow tolde. *dreamt*
Wommennes counseils been ful ofte colde;° *fatal*
Wommannes counseil broghte us first to wo,
And made Adam fro Paradys to go,[7]
Ther as° he was ful mery and wel at ese. *There where*
But for I noot° to whom it mighte displese, *since I know not*
If I counseil of wommen wolde blame,
Passe over, for I seyde it in my game.
Rede auctours,° wher they trete° of swich matere, *the authorities / treat*
And what thay seyn of wommen ye may here.
Thise been the cokkes wordes, and nat myne;
I can noon harm of no womman divyne.[8]
　Faire in the sond,° to bathe hire merily, *sand*
Lyth° Pertelote, and alle hire sustres° by,° *Lies / sisters / nearby*
Agayn° the sonne; and Chauntecleer so free *In*
Song° merier than the mermayde in the see— *Sang*
For Phisiologus[9] seith sikerly
How that they singen wel and merily—
And so bifel that, as he caste his yë° *eye*
Among the wortes,° on a boterflye, *herbs*
He was war° of this fox that lay ful lowe. *became aware*
Nothing ne liste him thanne for to crowe,[1]

6. Except by conditional necessity ("e.g., the sort of 'necessity' found in such a conditional sentence as 'If I see him standing, he must of necessity be standing'"—R. A. Pratt). The perplexity, at its simplest, might be put so: if God is all-knowing (that is, having a perfect knowledge of what *was, is, and will be*), He must know in advance every man's every moral choice. But if He knows how a man will choose, that man is not free to choose the alternative, for then God would be wrong (in a condition of ignorance, not omniscience). Theologians have struggled with the problem for centuries. The Middle Ages, for the most part, agreed to Boethius's resolution of it in *The Consolation of Philosophy*: to know is not necessarily to cause, particularly if you postulate a complex difference between the orders of time and eternity. After devoting considerable time to the question, the Nun's Priest announces with a certain ironic glee, "I will not have anything to do with such a subject; my story concerns a rooster" (in ll. 3251–52).
7. The fall of Adam and Eve was, naturally, the central event in discussions concerning man's free will.
8. I cannot conceive of harm in any woman (with a possible secondary meaning, "I know nothing to the discredit of any holy woman," referring to the Prioress whom he accompanies).
9. Physiologus was the supposed author of a Greek work on natural history, which was a distant source of the numerous medieval bestiaries: popular compilations of lore concerning animals and other creatures, some (as here with the mermaids) imaginary. In the medieval version, almost every description was moralized.
1. He had no wish at all to crow then.

But cryde anon, "Cok cok!" and up he sterte,° *leaped*
As man° that was affrayed° in his herte. *Like someone / frightened*
For naturelly a beest desyreth flee° *desires to flee*
Fro his contrarie,° if he may it see, *opposite*
Though he never erst° had seyn it with his yë.° *before / eye*
  This Chauntecleer, whan he gan him espye,° *caught sight of him*
He wolde han fled, but that the fox anon° *immediately*
Seyde, "Gentil sire, allas! wher wol ye gon?
Be ye affrayed of me that am your freend?
Now certes, I were worse than a feend,° *devil*
If I to yow wolde° harm or vileinye.° *wished / wrong*
I am nat come your counseil for t'espye,[2]
But trewely, the cause of my cominge
Was only for to herkne° how that ye singe. *listen to*
For trewely ye have as mery a stevene° *pleasant a voice*
As eny° aungel hath that is in hevene; *any*
Therwith ye han in musik more feelinge
Than hadde Boece,[3] or any that can singe.
My lord your fader (God his soule blesse!)
And eek your moder, of° hire gentilesse, *because of*
Han in myn hous y-been, to my gret ese;° *satisfaction*
And certes, sire, ful fayn° wolde I yow plese. *very willingly*
But for° men speke of singing, I wol saye, *since*
So mote I brouke° wel myn eyen tweye,° *profit by / two eyes*
Save° yow, I herde never man so singe *Except*
As dide your fader in the morweninge.° *morning*
Certes,° it was of herte,° al that he song. *Truly / from the heart*
And for to make his voys the more strong,
He wolde so peyne him° that with bothe his yën° *take such pains / eyes*
He moste winke,° so loude he wolde cryen, *had to shut*
And stonden on his tiptoon therwithal,[4]
And strecche forth his nekke long and smal.° *thin*
And eek he was of swich discrecioun° *wisdom*
That ther nas no man° in no regioun *was no man*
That him in song or wisdom mighte passe.
I have wel rad° in 'Daun Burnel the Asse,'[5] *read*
Among his vers,° how that ther was a cok, *its (the book's) verses*
For that° a preestes sone yaf° him a knok° *Because / gave / blow*
Upon his leg, whyl he was yong and nyce,° *foolish*
He made him for to lese° his benefyce. *lose*
But certeyn, ther nis no° comparisoun *is not any*
Bitwix the wisdom and discrecioun
Of youre fader, and of his° subtiltee. *i.e., that other rooster's*
Now singeth, sire, for seinte° charitee! *holy*

2. I've not come to spy on your private affairs.
3. Boethius, in addition to *The Consolation of Philosophy* referred to above, wrote a work on the theory of music that was used as a text in the schools.
4. And stand on (his) tiptoes at the same time.
5. *Burnellus*, or the *Speculum Stultorum*, a twelfth-century Latin satire in verse by Nigel Wireker: in one episode, a cock takes revenge on a certain Gundulfus, who injured him in his youth, by crowing so late on the morning that Gundulfus is to be ordained that he oversleeps and loses his benefice.

Let see, conne ye your fader countrefete?”° *imitate*
This Chauntecleer his winges gan to bete,° *did beat*
As man° that coude his tresoun° nat espye,° *one / betrayal / perceive*
So was he ravisshed with his flaterye.
Allas! ye lordes, many a fals flatour° *flatterer*
Is in your courtes, and many a losengeour,° *liar*
That plesen° yow wel more, by my feith, *Who please*
Than he that soothfastnesse° unto yow seith. *truthfulness*
Redeth Ecclesiaste of° flaterye; Ecclesiasticus *on*
Beth war,° ye lordes, of hir trecherye. *Beware*
This Chauntecleer stood hye° upon his toos, *high*
Strecching his nekke, and heeld his eyen cloos,° *closed*
And gan to crowe loude for the nones;° *for the occasion*
And daun Russel the fox sterte up at ones° *at once*
And by the gargat° hente° Chauntecleer, *throat / seized*
And on his bak toward the wode° him beer,° *woods / bore*
For yet ne was ther no man that him sewed.° *pursued*
O destinee, that mayst nat been eschewed!° *avoided*
Allas, that Chauntecleer fleigh° fro the bemes! *flew*
Allas, his wyf ne roghte nat° of dremes! *took no heed*
And on a Friday fil° al this meschaunce. *befell*
O Venus, that art goddesse of plesaunce,° *(amorous) pleasure*
Sin° that thy servant was this Chauntecleer, *Since*
And in thy service dide al his poweer,° *expended all his force*
More for delyt than world to multiplye,
Why woldestow° suffre him on thy day[6] to dye? *wouldst thou*
O Gaufred,[7] dere mayster soverayn,
That whan thy worthy king Richard° was slayn *Richard I*
With shot,° compleynedest his deth so sore, *an arrow*
Why ne hadde I now thy sentence° and thy lore, *wisdom*
The Friday for to chide, as diden ye?
(For on a Friday soothly° slayn was he.) *truly*
Than wolde I shewe yow how that I coude pleyne° *lament*
For Chauntecleres drede, and for his peyne.
Certes,° swich cry ne lamentacioun *Truly*
Was never of ladies maad° when Ilioun° *made by ladies / Ilium (Troy)*
Was wonne, and Pirrus° with his streite° swerd, *Pyrrhus / drawn*
Whan he hadde hent° king Priam by the berd, *seized*
And slayn him (as saith us *Eneydos*),° *the* Aeneid
As maden alle the hennes in the clos,° *enclosure, yard*
Whan they had seyn of Chauntecleer the sighte.
But sovereynly° dame Pertelote shrighte° *above all / shrieked*
Ful louder than dide Hasdrubales° wyf, *Hasdrubal's*
Whan that hir housbond hadde lost his lyf,
And that the Romayns hadde brend Cartage:° *burned Carthage*
She was so ful of torment and of rage

6. Friday is Venus's day.
7. Geoffrey of Vinsauf, author of a treatise on the writing of poetry, the *Poetria Nova* (ca. 1210). Chaucer refers to one of Geoffrey's examples of how to lament in a rhetorically elaborate style; see pp. 498–99.

That wilfully into the fyr she sterte,° *leaped*
And brende hirselven° with a stedfast herte. *i.e., to death*
O woful hennes, right so° cryden ye *in like manner*
As, whan that Nero brende the citee
Of Rome, cryden senatoures wyves,
For that hir° housbondes losten alle hir lyves; *their*
Withouten gilt this Nero hath hem° slayn. *them*
Now wol I torne to my tale agayn.
This sely° widwe and eek hir doghtres two *good, simple*
Herden thise hennes crye and maken wo,
And out at dores sterten they anoon,° *they leap at once*
And syen° the fox toward the grove goon,° *saw / go*
And bar° upon his bak the cok away; *bore, carried*
And cryden, "Out! harrow!° and weylaway!° *help / alas*
Ha, ha, the fox!" and after him they ran,
And eek with staves° many another man; *sticks*
Ran Colle our dogge, and Talbot, and Gerland,[8]
And Malkin, with a distaf° in hir hand; *for spinning*
Ran cow and calf, and eek the verray hogges,
So fered° for the berking of the dogges *frightened*
And shouting of the men and wimmen eke,
They ronne so hem thoughte hir herte breke.[9]
They yelleden as feendes° doon in helle; *fiends*
The dokes° cryden as° men wolde hem quelle;° *ducks / as though / kill*
The gees for fere° flowen° over the trees; *fear / flew*
Out of the hyve cam the swarm of bees;
So hidous was the noyse, a! *benedicite!*° *bless us*
Certes, he Jakke Straw and his meynee[1]
Ne made nevere shoutes half so shrille
Whan that they wolden any Fleming kille,
As thilke° day was maad upon the fox. *that same*
Of bras thay broghten bemes,° and of box,° *trumpets / boxwood*
Of horn, of boon,° in whiche they blewe and pouped,° *bone / puffed*
And therwithal thay shryked° and they houped:° *shrieked / whooped*
It seemed as that heven sholde falle.
Now, gode men, I pray yow herkneth° alle! *listen*
Lo, how Fortune turneth° sodeinly *overturns*
The hope and pryde eek of hir enemy!
This cok, that lay upon the foxes bak,
In al his drede unto the fox he spak,
And seyde, "Sire, if that I were as ye,
Yet sholde I seyn,° as° wis God helpe me, *say / may*
'Turneth agayn, ye proude cherles° alle! *churls*
A verray° pestilence upon yow falle! *real*
Now I am come unto this wodes syde,
Maugree your heed,° the cok shal heer abyde; *Despite your efforts*

8. All are common names for dogs.
9. They ran so (hard), it seemed to them their hearts would burst.
1. Jack Straw was a leader of the Peasants' Revolt ("his meynee," or company) in 1381; many Flemish, most of them weavers, were killed in London in that uprising (see l. 3396).

I wol him ete° in feith, and that anon.'" — *eat*
The fox answerde, "In feith, it shal be don,"
And as he spak that word, al sodeinly
This cok brak° from his mouth deliverly,° — *broke / nimbly*
And heighe upon a tree he fleigh° anon. — *flew*
And whan the fox saugh that the cok was gon,
"Allas!" quod he, "O Chauntecleer, allas!
I have to yow," quod he, "y-doon trespas,° — *wrong*
In as muche as I maked yow aferd
When I yow hente° and broghte out of the yerd. — *seized*
But, sire, I dide it in no wikke entente;° — *with no wicked intent*
Com doun, and I shal telle yow what I mente.
I shal seye sooth° to yow, God help me so." — *tell the truth*
"Nay, than," quod he, "I shrewe° us bothe two, — *curse*
And first I shrewe myself, bothe blood and bones,
If thou bigyle° me ofter° than ones.° — *deceive / more / once*
Thou shalt namore, thurgh thy flaterye,
Do° me to singe and winke with myn yë.° — *Cause / shut my eyes*
For he that winketh whan he sholde see,
Al wilfully, God lat° him never thee!"° — *let / prosper*
"Nay," quod the fox, "but God yeve° him meschaunce, — *give*
That is so undiscreet of governaunce° — *self-control*
That jangleth° whan he sholde holde his pees."° — *chatters / peace, silence*
Lo, swich it is for to be recchelees° — *reckless*
And necligent, and truste on flaterye.
But ye that holden this tale a folye,° — *silly thing*
As of a fox, or of a cok and hen,
Taketh the moralitee,° goode men. — *moral (of it)*
For Seint Paul seith that al that writen is,
To our doctryne° it is y-write, ywis.° — *instruction / indeed*
Taketh the fruyt,° and lat the chaf° be stille. — *i.e., grain / husks*
Now, gode God, if that it be thy wille,
As seith my lord,° so make us alle good men, — *my bishop*
And bringe us to his heighe° bliss. Amen. — *high*

The Epilogue

"Sir Nonnes Preest," our Hoste seyde anoon,[2]
"Y-blessed be thy breche° and every stoon!° — *buttocks / stone, testicles*
This was a mery tale of Chauntecleer.
But by my trouthe, if thou were seculer,° — *a layman*
Thou woldest been a trede-foul[3] aright.
For if thou have corage° as thou hast might,° — *spirit / strength*
Thee were nede of° hennes, as I wene,° — *You would need / suppose*
Ya, mo° than seven tymes seventene. — *more*
See, whiche braunes° hath this gentil preest, — *what brawn, muscles*

2. This epilogue occurs in nine manuscripts only: it is not in Ellesmere, for example, and may have been rejected by Chaucer at some later stage in his work on the *Tales*.
3. "Tread-fowl," a sexually potent rooster.

So greet a nekke, and swich a large breest!
He loketh as a sperhauk° with his yën;° *sparrow hawk / eyes*
Him nedeth nat his colour° for to dyen° *complexion / dye*
With brasile, ne with greyn of Portingale.[4]
Now sire, faire falle° yow for youre tale!" *may good befall*

* * *

The Second Nun's Prologue and Tale

The Prologue

The ministre and the norice unto vyces° *servant and nurse of vices*
Which that men clepe° in English ydelnesse,° *call / idleness*
That porter of the gate° is of delyces°— *gatekeeper / to carnal delights*
To eschue and by hir contrarie hir oppresse,
That is to seyn, by leveful bisinesse,
Wel oghten we to doon al our entente,[1]
Lest that the feend° thurgh ydelnesse us hente.° *fiend, devil / capture*

For he that with his thousand cordes slye° *artfully made cords*
Continuelly us waiteth to biclappe,° *waits in order to seize us*
Whan he may man in ydelnesse espye.° *espy, notice*
He can so lightly° cacche him in his trappe° *easily / trap*
Til that° a man be hent right by the lappe,° *That until / hem (of a garment)*
He nis nat war° the feend hath him in honde. *is not aware that*
Wel oughte us werche° and ydelnes withstonde.° *work, be active / oppose*

And though men dradden never for° to dye, *do not fear*
Yet seen men° wel by reson, doutelees, *people understand*
That ydelnesse is roten slogardye° *rotten sluggishness*
Of which ther never comth no° good n'encrees,° *neither / nor profit*
And seen that slouthe hir holdeth in a lees° *sloth keeps (idleness) on a leash*
Only° to slepe and for to ete and drinke *(Permitting her) only*
And to devouren al that othere swinke.° *everything that others work for*

And for to putte us fro° swich ydelnesse, *from*
That cause is of so greet confusioun,° *calamity, ruin*
I have heer doon my feithful bisinesse,
After the legende, in translacioun
Right of thy glorious lyf and passioun:[2]

4. With red powder or red dye from Portugal.
1. We certainly ought to do our utmost to avoid and suppress her (i.e., Idleness, personified) by her contrary, that is to say, by lawful good works. In medieval moral theology, Idleness is a branch of *Accidia*, Sloth, one of the seven deadly sins, each of which is to be fought against by a "contrarie" virtue. Idleness as personified here includes not only inactivity but also the pursuit of vain sensual pleasures.
2. I have here done my faith-full work by translating, in careful accord with the story, thy glorious life and passion (martyrdom). The terms *legende*, *lyf*, and *passioun* all identify the tale as belonging to a familiar medieval genre, that of a saint's life. Sherry Reames (see the Selective Bibliography) has shown that the *Second Nun's Tale* is a close translation of two Latin abridgements of a life of St. Cecilia composed in the fifth or sixth century. Cecilia lived in the third century; there is little historical evidence to verify the events recounted in her "lyf."

Thou with thy gerland wroght of° rose *garland made of*
and lilie,° *(see ll. 220ff.)*
Thee mene I,° mayde and martir, seint Cecilie! *I mean*

Invocacio ad Mariam.[3] *Invocation to Mary*

And thou that flour° of virgines art alle, *the flower, the finest*
Of whom that Bernard list so wel to wryte,[4]
To thee at my biginning first I calle:
Thou comfort of us wrecches, do me endyte° *help me narrate*
Thy maydens deeth, that wan° thurgh hir meryte *who won*
The eternal lyf, and of the feend° victorie, *over the devil*
As man° may after° reden in hir storie. *one / soon after (presently)*

Thou mayde and mooder, doghter of thy sone,
Thou welle° of mercy, sinful soules cure, *well*
In whom that God for bountee chees to wone,° *out of goodness chose to dwell*
Thou humble and heigh over° every creature, *exalted above*
Thou nobledest so ferforth° our nature *so greatly*
That no desdeyn the maker hadde of kinde° *no disdain the maker of (our) kind*
His sone in blode and flesh to clothe and winde.° *enwrap*

Withinne the cloistre° blisful of thy sydes° *cloister / sides, i.e. womb*
Took mannes shap the eternal love and pees° *peace*
That of the tryne compas lord and gyde° is, *threefold world lord and guide*
Whom erthe and see and heven out of relees° *without pause*
Ay herien.° And thou, virgin wemmelees,° *Ever praise / spotless*
Bar of° thy body (and dweltest mayden° pure) *Carried in / remained a virgin*
The creatour of every creature.

Assembled° is in thee magnificence *Brought together*
With mercy, goodnesse, and with swich pitee° *such pity, compassion*
That thou, that art the sonne° of excellence, *sun*
Nat only helpest hem that preyen thee° *those who pray to thee*
But ofte tyme of thy benignitee,° *often out of kindness*
Ful frely er that° men thyn help biseche,° *Most generously before / beseech*
Thou goost biforn° and art hir lyves leche.° *goest first / their lives' physician*

Now help, thou meke° and blisfil fayre mayde, *meek*
Me, flemed wrecche,° in this desert of galle.° *wretched exile / bitterness*
Think on the womman Cananee,° that sayde *of Canaan (Matthew 15:21–28)*
That whelpes eten° somme of the crommes° alle *dogs eat / crumbs*

3. The Latin headnotes here and before line 85 appear as glosses in the margins of the Hengwrt and Ellesmere manuscripts, the two earliest and best manuscripts of *The Canterbury Tales*.
4. About whom Bernard was so pleased to write. St. Bernard (1090–1153), who founded the Benedictine monastery of Clairvaux, was famed as a contemplative and devotee of the Virgin Mary. He was canonized in 1173. At the end of Dante's *Divine Comedy*, he replaces Beatrice as Dante's guide and says a prayer to Mary. Chaucer translates/adapts this prayer (*Paradiso* XXXIII, 1–21) in the three stanzas that follow.

That from hir lordes table been y-falle;° *have fallen from their*
And though that I, unworthy sone of Eve,[5] *masters' table*
Be sinful, yet° accepte my bileve.° *nevertheless / faith*

And for° that feith is deed° withouten werkes, *since / dead*
So for to werken yif° me wit and space,° *give / i.e., time*
That I be quit fro thennes° that most derk is. *So that I may be*
O thou that art so fayr and ful of grace, *free of the place*
Be myn advocat in that heighe place
Ther as° withouten ende is songe Osanne°— *Where / hosanna*
Thou, Cristes mooder, doghter dere of Anne! *(a cry of praise)*

And of thy light° my soule in prison *with thy (spiritual) light*
lighte,° *illumine*
That troubled is by the contagioun° *contagion (disease)*
Of my body and also by the wighte° *weight, burden*
Of erthly luste and fals affeccioun.° *desire*
O haven of refut,° o salvacioun° *refuge / salvation*
Of hem that been in sorwe and in distresse,
Now help, for to my werk I wol me dresse.° *turn*

Yet preye I yow that reden that° I wryte, *who read what*
Foryeve° me that I do no diligence° *Forgive / make no special effort*
This ilke° storie subtilly to endyte.° *same / subtly (artfully) to compose*
For both have I the wordes and sentence[6]
Of him that° at the seintes reverence *the person who*
The storie wroot,° and folwe° hir legende, *wrote / (so I) follow*
And prey yow that ye wol my werk amende.° *make better*

Interpretacio nominis Cecilie quam ponit frater Jacobus Januensis in Legenda Aurea.[7]

First wolde I yow the name of seint Cecilie
Expoune,° as men may in hir storie see. *Expound, interpret*
It is to seye° in English "hevenes lilie,"° *It means / (Latin* celi+lilia*)*
For pure chastnesse° of virginitee; *chastity*
Or, for° she whytnesse hadde of honestee,° *because / chastity*

5. Unworthy son of Eve. Various explanations have been offered for the Second Nun's reference to herself as a son. The most likely is that Chaucer translated the story before he started writing *The Canterbury Tales*, in which case the narrative voice would be his own; later he assigned it to the Nun without attending to the gender discrepancy. Another is that the Nun may be borrowing language from liturgical services that refers to all human beings as sons of Eve.
6. For I keep to both the (specific) words and the (larger) meaning.
7. Interpretation of the name "Cecilia" that brother Jacob of Genoa puts forward in the *Golden Legend*. The remainder of the prologue, offering possible etymological meanings of St. Cecilia's name, comes from the thirteenth-century *Golden Legend* of Jacobus de Voragine, the best-known collection of saints' lives in the later Middle Ages. Chaucer translated its version of Cecilia's life through line 358; for the remainder he translated an anonymous Latin version that appears in some liturgies for St. Cecilia's feast day. Etymologizing was a frequent medieval strategy, usually much less concerned with accurate linguistic history than with creating connections between words and the things they signify. In the glosses we give the Latin words that Jacobus identifies as possible sources for Cecilia's name.

And grene° of conscience, and of good fame° — *greenness / reputation*
The sote savour,° "lilie" was hir name. — *sweet fragrance*

Or Cecile is to seye "the wey to blinde,"° — *path for the blind* (cecis+via)
For she ensample was° by good techinge; — *set an example*
Or elles Cecile, as I writen finde,° — *i.e., in learned books*
Is joyned° by a maner conjoininge — *compounded*
Of "hevene" and "Lia,"° and heer in figuringe° — (celum+Lia) / *symbolically*
The "heven" is set for° thoght of holinesse — *stands for*
And "Lia" for hir lasting bisinesse.° — *continual activity*

Cecile may eek be seyd° in this manere: — *also be explained*
"Wanting of° blindnesse,"° for hir grete light — *Lacking in* / (cecitate+carens)
Of sapience° and for hir thewes° clere; — *wisdom / moral virtues*
Or elles,° lo, this maydens name bright° — *else / shining*
Of "hevene" and "leos"° comth, for which by right — (celum+leos)
Men mighte hir wel "the heven of peple" calle,
Ensample° of gode and wyse werkes alle. — *Exemplar*

For "leos" "peple" in English is to seye,
And right as men may in the hevene see
The sonne and mone and sterres every weye,° — *on every side*
Right so men gostly° in this mayden free° — *spiritually / generous*
Seyen° of feith the magnanimitee° — *See / greatness, nobility*
And eek the cleernesse hool° of sapience, — *complete clarity*
And sondry werkes brighte of excellence.

And right so° as thise philosophres wryte — *just so*
That heven is° swift and round and eek brenninge,° — *heaven's spheres are* / *burning*
Right so was fayre Cecilie the whyte
Ful swift and bisy ever in good werkinge,
And round and hool° in good perseveringe, — *whole*
And brenning ever in charitee ful brighte.
Now have I yow declared what she highte.° — *she was called (i.e., her name)*

The Tale

This mayden bright Cecilie, as hir lyf° seith, — *official life ("Legend")*
Was comen of Romayns and of noble kinde,° — *from a noble family*
And from hir cradel up fostred° in the feith — *brought up*
Of Crist, and bar° his gospel in hir minde. — *bore*
She never cessed,° as I writen finde, — *ceased*
Of hir preyere,° and God to love and drede,° — (*to say*) *her prayers / fear*
Biseking° him to kepe hir maydenhede.° — *Begging / preserve her virginity*

And when this mayden sholde unto a man
Y-wedded be, that was ful yong of age,
Which that y-cleped was° Valerian, — *Who was called*
And day was comen of hir° mariage, — *the day had arrived for their*
She, ful devout and humble in hir corage,° — *heart*

Under hir robe of gold that sat ful fayre,° *suited her so beautifully*
Had next hir flesh y-clad hir in an heyre.[8]

And whyl the organs maden melodye,
To God alone in herte thus sang she:[9]
"O lord, my soule and eek° my body gye° *also / keep*
Unwemmed,° lest that I confounded° be." *Immaculate / i.e., damned*
And for his love that deyde upon a tree,° *who died on the cross*
Every seconde and thridde day she faste,° *fasted*
Ay biddinge° in hir orisons° ful faste.° *Always begging / prayers / intently*

The night cam, and to bedde moste° she gon *must*
With hir housbonde, as ofte is the manere,° *custom*
And prively° to him she seyde anon, *privately*
"O swete and wel biloved spouse dere,° *dear*
Ther is a conseil,° and ye wolde it here,° *secret / if you wish to hear it*
Which that right fain° I wolde unto yow seye, *most willingly*
So that° ye swere ye shul me nat biwreye."° *Provided that / betray*

Valerian gan faste° unto hir swere *did earnestly*
That for no cas° ne thing that mighte be, *in no case*
He sholde never mo biwreyen here;
And thanne at erst° to him thus seyde she: *for the first time*
"I have an angel which that loveth me,
That with greet love, wherso° I wake or slepe, *whether*
Is redy ay° my body for to kepe.° *Is always ready / protect*

And if that he may felen, out of drede,° *sense, have no doubt*
That ye me touche or love in vileinye,° *sinfully, in a carnal way*
He right anon wol slee yow with the dede,° *kill you in the act*
And in your yowthe thus ye shulden dye.
And if that ye in clene love me gye,° *preserve me in chaste love*
He wol yow loven as me, for your clennesse,
And shewen yow his joye and his brightnesse."° *(heavenly) radiance*

Valerian, corrected as God wolde,° *willed*
Answerde agayn:° "If I shal trusten° thee, *in response / am to believe*
Lat me that angel se° and him biholde, *see*
And if that it a verray° angel be, *true, genuine*
Than wol I doon as thou hast preyed° me; *asked*
And if thou love another man, for sothe,° *in truth, indeed*
Right° with this swerd than wol I slee yow bothe." *Directly, right there*

Cecile answerde anon right in this wyse:
"If that yow list,° the angel shul ye see, *it please you*

8. Next to her flesh she had clothed herself in a hair shirt—an animal hide whose rough outer side scratches against the wearer's skin. A hair shirt is familiar in many saints' lives, signifying their preoccupation with the spirit and disdain for physical comfort. Biographies of St. Thomas Becket state that after he was killed in Canterbury Cathedral he was found wearing a hair shirt under his clerical garments.
9. The reference to music here is the only indication in the poem of what has since become the most celebrated aspect of Cecilia, her role as patron saint of music and musicians.

So° that ye trowe on° Crist and yow *Provided / believe in*
baptyse.° *are baptized*
Goth° forth to Via Apia,"° quod she, *Go / the Appian Way*
"That fro this toun ne stant but° myles three, *lies only*
And to the povre folkes° that ther dwelle, *poor folk*
Sey hem right thus as that° I shal yow telle. *Tell them just what*

Telle hem that I, Cecile, yow to hem sente,
To shewen yow the gode Urban the olde
For secree nedes° and for good entente.° *secret reasons / purpose*
And whan that ye seint Urban han biholde,
Telle him the wordes whiche I to yow tolde,
And whan that he hath purged yow fro sinne,
Thanne shul ye see that angel er ye twinne."° *before you leave*

Valerian is to the place y-gon,
And right as him was taught by his lerninge° *i.e., just as instructed by Cecilia*
He fond° this holy olde Urban anon *found*
Among the seintes buriels lotinge.[1]
And he anon, withouten taryinge,
Dide° his message, and whan that° he it tolde, *Delivered / when*
Urban for joye his hondes gan up holde.

The teres° from his eyen leet he falle. *tears*
"Almighty lord, O Jhesu Crist," quod he,
"Sower of chast conseil,° herde° of us alle, *chaste counsel / shepherd*
The fruit of thilke° seed of chastitee *that same*
That thou hast sowe° in Cecile, tak to thee!° *sown / take to thyself*
Lo, lyk a bisy bee withouten gyle,° *guile*
Thee serveth ay° thyn owene thral° Cecile! *always / servant*

For thilke spouse that she took but now° *just now*
Ful lyk a fiers leoun,° she sendeth here *Very like a fierce lion*
As meke° as ever was any lamb to yow." *meek*
And with that worde anon ther gan appere° *at once there did appear*
An old man, clad in whyte clothes clere,° *bright*
That hadde a book with lettre of golde° in honde *letters painted in gold*
And gan° biforn Valerian to stonde. *went*

Valerian as deed fil doun for drede° *fell down as if dead from fear*
Whan he him saugh, and he up hente *he (the angel)*
him tho,° *then raised him up*
And on his book right thus he gan to rede:° *read aloud*
"O° lord, o feith, o God withouten mo,° *One / more*
O Cristendom, and fader of alle also,

1. Hiding among saints' tombs. Old Urban, later referred to as a pope (l. 217), must refer to Urban I (Pope from 222 to 230). He and other poor Christians are hiding out because of persecution; Christianity did not become legal in the Roman empire until the fourth century. The Appian Way was (and is) a major road beginning just south of central Rome; the catacombs along it appear two or three miles out from the city.

Aboven alle and over al everywhere.”[2]
Thise wordes al with gold y-writen were.

When this was rad,° than seyde this olde man, *read*
“Levestow° this thing or no? Sey ye or nay. *Dost thou believe*
“I leve° al this thing,” quod Valerian, *believe*
“For sother° thing than this, I dar wel say, *a truer*
Under the hevene no wight thinke may.”° *no person can conceive of*
Tho° vanisshed this olde man, he niste° where, *Then / (Valerian) knew not*
And Pope Urban him cristened° right there. *baptized*

Valerian goth hoom and fint° Cecilie *finds*
Withinne his chambre with an angel stonde.° *standing*
This angel hadde of roses and of lilie° *lilies*
Corones° two, the which he bar° in honde. *Crowns, garlands / bore*
And first to Cecile, as I understonde, *which he held*
He yaf that oon,° and after gan he take *gave one*
That other to Valerian, hir make.° *her mate*

“With body clene° and with unwemmed° thoght *chaste / unblemished*
Kepeth ay wel° thise corones,” quod he. *Cherish*
“Fro Paradys to yow have I hem broght,
Ne nevermo ne shal they roten be° *wither*
Ne lese her sote savour,° trusteth me, *Nor lose their sweet fragrance*
Ne never wight shal seen hem° with his eye *Nor will any person*
ever see them
But° he be chaast° and hate vileinye.° *Unless / chaste / lechery*

And thou, Valerian, for° thou so sone° *because / quickly*
Assentedest to good conseil also,
Sey what thee list,° and thou shalt han thy *pleases / have thy*
bone.”° *boon (request)*
“I have a brother,” quod Valerian tho,
“That in this world I love no man so.° *so much*
I pray yow that my brother may han grace
To knowe the trouthe, as I do in this place.”

The angel seyde, “God lyketh thy requeste,
And bothe, with the palm of martirdom,
Ye shullen come unto his blisful feste.”[3]
And with that word Tiburce his brother com,° *came*
And whan that he the savour undernom° *perceived the fragrance*
Which that the roses and the lilies caste,
Withinne his herte he gan to wondre faste° *intently*

2. Because these lines translate St. Paul's Letter to the Ephesians 4:5–6, the mysterious old man reading these words has been thought by many critics to be St. Paul; but Reames has noted that in some liturgies for St. Cecilia's Day the old man is identified as an angelic figuration of Urban.
3. And both of you, with the palm of martyrdom, shall come to his joyous banquet. The palm leaf was a traditional symbol of victory.

And seyde, "I wondre, this tyme of the yeer,
Whennes° that sote° savour cometh so — *Whence, from where / sweet*
Of rose and lilies that I smelle heer;
For though° I hadde hem in myn hondes two, — *even if*
The savour mighte in me no depper go.° — *could not penetrate*
The sote smel that in myn herte I finde — *more deeply*
Hath chaunged me al in another kinde."° — *into another kind of person*

Valerian seyde, "Two corones han we,
Snow-whyte and rose-reed, that shynen clere,° — *shine brightly*
Whiche that thyn eyen han no might° to see; — *have no power*
And as thou smellest hem thurgh my preyere,° — *because of my prayer*
So shaltow seen hem,° leve° brother dere, — *wilt thou see them / beloved*
If it so be thou wolt° withouten slouthe° — *willest / without sloth (delay)*
Bileve aright° and knowen° verray trouthe." — *correctly / acknowledge*

Tiburce answerde, "Seistow° this to me — *Dost thou say*
In soothnesse,° or in dreem I herkne° this?" — *In reality / in a dream do I hear*
"In dremes," quod Valerian, "han we be
Unto° this tyme, brother myn, ywis.° — *Until / indeed*
But now at erst° in trouthe our dwelling is." — *for the first time*
"How woostow° this?" quod Tiburce. "In what wyse?"° — *dost thou know / way*
Quod Valerian, "That shal I thee devyse.° — *explain*

The angel of God hath me the trouthe y-taught,
Which thou shalt seen if that thou wolt reneye° — *renounce*
The ydoles° and be clene,° and elles naught."° — *idols / chaste / otherwise not*
(And of° the miracle of thise corones tweye° — *concerning / these two crowns*
Seint Ambrose in his preface list to seye.° — *is pleased to speak*
Solempnely° this noble doctour° dere — *Solemnly / Doctor (of the Church)*
Commendeth it and seith in this manere:[4]

"The palm of martirdom for° to receyve,° — *in order / receive, merit*
Seinte Cecile, fulfild of Goddes yifte,° — *filled full with God's gift*
The world and eek hir chambre gan she weyve.[5]
Witnes° Tyburces and Valerians shrifte,° — *Witness / confession(s) of faith*
To° whiche God of his bountee° wolde shifte° — *For / in his goodness / provide*
Corones two of floures wel smellinge,
And made his angel hem the corones bringe.

The mayde° hath broght thise men to blisse — *maiden, virgin*
above.° — *joy on high*
The world hath wist° what it is worth, certeyn, — *has known*
Devocioun of chastitee to love."°) — *i.e., to love chastity with devotion*
Tho shewede° him Cecile al open and pleyn — *Then showed*
That alle ydoles nis but a thing in veyn,° — *i.e., are but vain things*

4. Faithfully translating the *Golden Legend*, Chaucer cites a "preface" to a mass for St. Cecilia's Day widely attributed to Ambrose. This passage interrupts the dramatic action to remind us of what the Second Nun calls her tale's "sentence" (l. 81). The white and red flowers in the crowns symbolize, respectively, chastity and martyrdom.

5. She gave up the world and also her bedchamber (i.e., her marital duties).

For they been dombe° and therto° they been deve,°   *dumb / also / deaf*
And charged° him his ydoles for to leve.°   *ordered / abandon*

"Who so that troweth nat° this, a beste°   *Whoever does not*
he is,"   *believe / beast*
Quod tho Tiburce, "if that I shal nat lye."
And she gan kisse his brest, that herde° this,   *(she) who heard*
And was ful glad he coude trouthe espye.°   *perceive*
"This day I take thee for myn allye,"°   *ally, comrade, kinsman*
Seyde this blisful fayre mayde dere,
And after that she seyde as ye may here:

"Lo, right so as the love of Crist," quod she,
"Made me thy brotheres wyf, right in that wyse°   *manner*
Anon° for myn allye heer take I thee,   *Right now*
Sin that° thou wolt° thyn ydoles despyse.°   *Because / willest / despise*
Go with thy brother now and thee baptyse,
And make thee clene so that thou mowe biholde°   *may behold*
The angels face of which thy brother tolde."

Tiburce answerde and seyde, "Brother dere,
First tel me whider I shal° and to what man."   *where I should (go)*
"To whom?" quod he. "Com forth with right
good chere.°   *cheerfully*
I wol thee lede unto the Pope Urban."
"Til° Urban, brother myn Valerian?"   *To*
Quod tho Tiburce. "Woltow me thider lede?°   *Wilt thou lead me there*
Me thinketh that it were a wonder dede!°   *wondrous (strange) thing (to do)*

Ne menestow nat° Urban," quod he tho,   *(Surely) thou dost not mean that Urban*
"That is so ofte dampned to be deed,°   *condemned to death*
And woneth in halkes° alwey to and fro,   *dwells in hiding places*
And dar nat ones° putte forth his heed?   *dares not once to*
Men sholde him brennen° in a fyr so reed   *would burn him*
If he were founde or that men mighte him
spye°—   *or someone should spot him*
And we also to bere° him company!   *And we (burned) as well to keep*

And whyl° we seken thilke divinitee°   *while / seek out that divinity*
That is y-hid° in hevene prively,°   *hidden / secretly*
Algate y-brend° in this world shul we be!"   *All the same burned*
To whom Cecile answerde boldely:
"Men mighten dreden° wel and skilfully°   *fear / with good reason*
This lyf to lese,° myn owene dere brother,   *lose*
If this were livinge only° and non other.   *the only form of life*

But ther is better lyf in other° place   *another*
That never shal be lost, ne drede thee noght,°   *fear thee not*
Which Goddes Sone us tolde° thurgh his grace.   *revealed to us*
That Fadres Sone hath alle thinges wroght,°   *made, created*
And al that wroght is with a skilful thoght

The Goost that fro the Fader gan procede
Hath sowled hem,[6] withouten any drede.

By word and by miracle° he, Goddes Sone, *Through (his) words and miracles*
Whan he was in this world, declared here
That ther was other lyf ther° men may wone."° *another life where / dwell*
To whom answerde° Tiburce: "O suster dere, *responded*
Ne seydestow° right now in this manere *Didst thou not say*
Ther nis but o° God, lord in soothfastnesse? *is only one*
And now of three how maystow bere witnesse?"° *how canst thou speak of three*

"That shal I telle," quod she, "er I go.° *before I finish*
Right° as a man hath sapiences three°— *Just / three mental faculties*
Memorie, engyn and intellect° also— *Memory, imagination and reason*
So in o being of divinitee° *a single divine being*
Three persones° may ther right wel be." *persons (of the Trinity)*
Tho gan she him° ful bisily to preche *she began to him*
Of Cristes come° and of his peynes teche° *coming / teach about his suffering*

And many pointes of his passioun:° *particulars of his Passion*
How Goddes Sone in this world was withholde° *placed, constrained*
To doon° mankinde pleyn remissioun° *In order to give / full remission*
That° was y-bounde in sinne and cares colde. *Who*
Al this thing she unto Tiburce tolde.
And after this, Tiburce in good entente
With Valerian to Pope Urban he wente,

That° thanked God, and with glad herte and light *Who*
He cristned him, and made him in that place
Parfit° in his lerninge,° Goddes knight. *Perfect / understanding*
And after this Tiburce gat° swich grace *got, received*
That every day he saugh° in tyme and space *saw*
The angel of God, and every maner bone° *sort of boon (favor)*
That he God axed,° it was sped ful sone.° *asked of God / immediately granted*

It were ful hard by ordre for to seyn° *to describe in sequence*
How many wondres Jhesus for hem wroghte,° *accomplished for them*
But atte laste, to tellen short and pleyn,
The sergeants° of the toun of Rome hem soghte *Officials*
And hem biforn Almache, the prefect,° broghte, *Almachius, the magistrate*
Which hem apposed° and knew al hir entente, *Who interrogated them*
And to the image° of Jupiter hem sente, *statue, effigy*

And seyde, "Who so° wol nat sacrifyse,° *Whoever / make sacrifice*
Swap of his heed.° This is my sentence° here." *Cut off his head / decision*
Anon thise martirs that I yow devyse,° *whom I describe*
Oon° Maximus, that was an officere° *One, a certain / a subordinate*

6. And the Holy Spirit that proceeded from the Father has given souls to all those created with the power to reason.

Of the prefectes° and his corniculere,° *prefect's / chief assistant*
Hem hente;° and whan he forth the seintes ladde,° *Seized them / led*
Himself he weep° for pitee that he hadde. *wept*

Whan Maximus had herd° the seintes lore,° *listened to / wisdom*
He gat him of the tormentoures leve° *got the consent of the executioners*
And ladde hem° to his hous withoute more;° *took them / directly*
And with hir preching, er that it were eve,° *before evening came*
They gonnen° fro the tormentours to reve°— *did / remove, take away*
And fro Maxime and fro his folk echone°— *from all his household*
The false feith, to trowe° in God allone. *believe*

Cecilie cam whan it was woxen night,° *when night fell*
With preestes that hem cristned alle yfere;° *all together*
And afterward whan day was woxen light,
Cecile hem seyde° with a ful stedefast chere:° *spoke to them / very seriously*
"Now, Cristes owene knightes leve° and dere, *beloved*
Caste alle awey the werkes of derknesse° *(see Romans 13:12)*
And armeth yow° in armure of brightnesse.° *yourselves / armor of light*

Ye han for sothe y-doon° a greet bataille. *have truly finished*
Your cours is doon,° your feith han ye conserved.° *race is over / kept*
Goth to the corone° of lyf that may nat faille. *crown (see 2 Timothy 4:7–8)*
The rightful juge which that° ye han served *righteous judge whom*
Shall yeve it yow° as ye han it deserved." *give it to you*
And whan this thing was seyd, as I devyse,
Men ladde hem° forth to doon the sacrifyse. *led them*

But whan they weren to the place broght,
To tellen shortly the conclusioun,
They nolde encense° ne sacrifice right *would not burn incense*
noght,° *anything*
But on hir knees they setten hem adoun° *set themselves down*
With humble herte and sad° devocioun, *steadfast*
And losten bothe hir hedes° in the place. *both lost their heads*
Hir soules wenten to the king of grace.

This Maximus, that saugh this thing bityde,° *happen*
With pitous teres tolde it anon-right° *spoke out immediately*
That he hir soules saugh to heven glyde,° *glide, travel*
With angels ful of cleernesse° and of light, *brightness*
And with his word converted many a wight,° *person*
For which Almachius dide him so bete° *ordered him beaten so (harshly)*
With whippe of leed[7] til he his lyf gan lete.° *until he gave up his life*

Cecile him took and buried him anoon
By° Tiburce and Valerian softely,° *Alongside / tenderly*
Withinne hir° burying-place under the stoon.° *their / tombstone*
And after this Almachius hastily

7. A whip with lead balls attached at the end.

Bad his ministres fecchen openly[8]
Cecile, so that she mighte in his presence
Doon sacrifyce and Jupiter encense.° *burn incense for Jupiter*

But they, converted at hir wyse lore,° *by her wise teaching*
Wepten ful sore and yaven° ful credence *gave*
Unto hir word, and cryden more and more,
"Crist, Goddes sone, withouten difference[9]
Is verray° God—this is al our sentence°— *the true / our whole belief*
That° hath so good a servant him to serve. *Who*
This with o voys we trowen,° thogh we sterve."° *This we unanimously affirm / die*

Almachius, that herde of this doinge,
Bad fecchen Cecile,° that he might hir see, *Had Cecilia brought forward*
And alderfirst,° lo, this was his axinge:° *first of all / what he asked*
"What maner° womman artow?"° tho quod he. *sort of / art thou*
"I am a gentil° womman born," quod she. *noble*
"I axe° thee," quod he, "thogh it thee greve,° *ask / distress thee*
Of° thy religioun and of thy bileve."° *About / belief, faith*

"Ye han bigonne your question folily,"° *foolishly*
Quod she, "that wolden two answeres conclude° *include*
In o° demande. Ye axed lewedly."° *one single / ignorantly*
Almache answerde unto° that similitude,° *responded to / charge*
"Of whennes comth° thyn answering so rude?" *From where comes*
"Of whennes?" quod she whan that she was freyned.° *questioned*
"Of conscience and of good feith unfeyned."° *unfeigned, sincere*

Almachius seyde, "Ne takestow non hede° *takest thou no heed*
Of my power?" and she answerde him this:
"Your might," quod she, "ful litel is to drede,° *to be feared*
For every mortal mannes power nis° *i.e., is nothing more*
But° lyk a bladdre ful of wind, ywis: *Than / bladder, balloon*
For with a nedles° poynt, whan it is blowe,° *needle's / blown up, inflated*
May al the boost° of it be leyd° ful lowe." *boast, pride / laid*

"Ful wrongfully bigonne° thou," quod he, *began*
"And yet in wrong° is thy perseveraunce. *still wrongful*
Wostow nat° how our mighty princes free° *Knowest thou not / "generous"*
Han thus comanded and maad ordinaunce° *given an order, decreed*
That every Cristen wight shal han penaunce° *person shall be punished*
But if° that he his Cristendom withseye,° *Unless / renounce*
And goon al quit° if he wol it reneye?"° *(shall) go completely free / deny*

"Your princes erren, as your nobley dooth,"° *err, as do your nobles*
Quod tho Cecile, "and with a wood sentence° *crazy judgment*

8. Ordered his servants publicly to bring.
9. I.e., without any difference in substance between the Son and the Father. The difference is in the "person" only. See the earlier discussion of the Trinity in lines 323–46.

Ye make us gilty, and it is nat sooth.° *true*
For ye, that knowen wel our innocence,
For as muche as° we doon a reverence *Simply because*
To Crist and for we bere a Cristen name,
Ye putte on° us a cryme and eek a blame.° *impute to / also a fault*

But we that knowen thilke° name so° *that / so well*
For vertuous,° we may it nat withseye." *To be virtuous*
Almache answerde, "Chees oon of thise two:
Do sacrifyce or Cristendom reneye,
That° thou mowe° now escapen by that weye."° *So that / may / way, means*
At which the holy blisful fayre mayde
Gan for to laughe, and to the juge° seyde: *judge*

"O juge, confus° in thy nycetee,° *confused / folly*
Woltow° that I reneye innocence *Wilt thou*
To make me° a wikked wight?"° quod she. *of myself / person*
"Lo, he dissimuleth here in audience:
He stareth and woodeth in his advertence!"[1]
To whom Almachius: "Unsely wrecche,° *Miserable wretch*
Ne woostow nat° how far my might may strecche? *Dost thou not know*

Han noght° our mighty princes to me yeven,° *Have not / given*
Ye,° bothe power and auctoritee° *Yea / authority*
To maken folk to dyen° or to liven? *die*
Why spekestow° so proudly than° to me?" *dost thou speak / then*
"I speke noght but stedfastly,"° quod she, *only firmly, with assurance*
"Nat proudly, for I seye, as for my syde,° *part*
We haten deedly° thilke vyce of pryde. *have deadly hate for*

And if thou drede nat a sooth to here,° *to hear a truth*
Than wol I shewe al openly, by right,° *clearly, with reason*
That thou hast maad a ful gret lesing° here. *lie*
Thou seyst thy princes han thee yeven might
Bothe for to sleen° and for to quiken a wight.° *slay / give life to someone*
Thou, that ne mayst but only lyf bireve,° *who mayest only take away life*
Thou hast non other power ne no leve.° *nor permission*

But thou mayst seyn thy princes han thee maked
Ministre of deeth;° for if thou speke of mo *A minister of death*
Thou lyest, for thy power is ful naked."° *i.e., nakedly exposed*
"Do wey° thy boldnes," seyde Almachius tho, *Cease*
"And sacrifyce to our goddes er° thou go. *before*
I recche nat° what wrong° that thou me profre,° *do not care / insult / offer*
For I can suffre° it as a philosophre, *suffer, endure*

But thilke° wronges may I nat endure *those*
That thou spekest of our goddes here," quod he.
Cecile answerede, "O nyce° creature, *foolish*

1. Behold! He dissembles here in open court; he stares (wildly) and goes crazy in his mind!

Thou seydest no word sin thou spak° to me *since thou (first) spoke*
That I ne knew therwith thy nycetee
And that thou were, in every maner wyse,° *in every respect*
A lewed° officer and a veyn justyse.° *ignorant / worthless judge*

Ther lakketh nothing to thyn utter eyen° *outward eyes*
That thou nart blind,° for thing that we seen alle *Yet thou art blind*
That it is stoon°—that men may wel espyen°— *a stone / clearly observe*
That ilke stoon a god thou wolt it calle.
I rede° thee: lat° thyn hand upon it falle, *advise / let*
And taste it wel, and stoon thou shalt it finde,
Sin° that thou seest nat with thyn eyen blinde.[2] *Since*

It is a shame that the peple shal
So scorne thee and laughe at thy folye.
For comunly men woot it wel overal° *it's common knowledge everywhere*
That mighty God is in his hevenes hye,° *high*
And thise images—wel thou mayst espye—
To thee ne to hemself mowe nought profyte,° *May not help thee nor themselves*
For in effect° they been nat worth a myte."° *in efficacy* / *a mite, i.e., anything*

Thise wordes and swiche othere° seyde she, *others like them*
And he weex wroth° and bad° men sholde hir lede *grew angry / ordered*
Hom til hir hous. "And in hir hous," quod he,
"Brenne° hir right in a bath of flambes rede."° *Burn / red flames*
And as he bad, right so was doon in dede:
For in a bath they gonne hir faste shetten,° *shut her in securely*
And night and day greet fyr they under betten.[3]

The longe night and eek a day also,
For al the fyr and eek the bathes hete,
She sat al cold and felede no wo.
It made hir nat a drope for to swete.° *sweat*
But in that bath hir lyf she moste lete,° *must give up*
For he, Almachius, with ful wikke entente,° *intentions*
To sleen hir in the bath his sonde sente.° *sent his messenger*

Three strokes in the nekke he smoot hir tho,° *struck her then*
The tormentour,° but for no maner chaunce° *executioner / by no means*
He mighte noght smyte al hir nekke atwo.° *could not cut her neck in two*

2. Medieval discussions of the five senses often distinguish touch and taste, the most animalistic, from the more "spiritual" senses of smell, hearing, and especially sight, which provide knowledge without immediate contact between perceiver and object. Cecilia suggests that since Almachius's sense of sight is not serving him well, he needs to descend to his lower senses to recognize what a stone really is.
3. And night and day they stoked a great fire from below. Cecilia's bath is a separate room in her house. In ancient Rome the room would have been heated from underneath the floor. But medieval illustrations of Cecilia's martyrdom imagine her in something closer to a modern hot tub, in water heated by a fire directly below it. For illustrations and an interpretation of the change see V. A. Kolve, *Telling Images: Chaucer and the Imagery of Narrative II* (Stanford: Stanford UP, 2009), pp. 199–222.

And for° ther was that° tyme an ordinaunce° *because / at that / law*
That no man sholde doon man swich penaunce
The ferthe strook to smyten, softe or sore,[4]
This tormentour ne dorste do namore.° *did not dare to do more*

But half-deed, with hir nekke y-corven° there, *cut*
He lefte hir lye,° and on his wey he went. *left her to lie*
The Cristen folk which that aboute° hir were *around*
With shetes° han the blood ful faire y-hent.° *cloths / gathered up*
Thre dayes lived she in this torment
And never cessed° hem the feith to teche *ceased*
That she hadde fostred.° Hem° she gan to preche, *fostered, nourished / (To) them*

And hem she yaf° hir moebles° and hir thing,° *gave / goods / possessions*
And to the Pope Urban bitook hem tho,° *entrusted them then*
And seyde, "I axed° this of hevene king, *asked*
To han respyt° three dayes and namo° *respite for / no more*
To recomende° to yow, er that I go,° *In order to commend / before I die*
Thise soules, lo, and that° I mighte do werche° *so that / cause to be built*
Here of myn hous perpetuelly a cherche."

Seint Urban with his deknes° prively° *deacons / secretly*
The body fette,° and buried it by nighte *fetched, brought back*
Among his othere seintes honestly.° *honorably*
Hir hous the chirche of seint Cecilie highte.° *(is) called*
Seint Urban halwed° it, as he wel mighte, *hallowed, consecrated*
In which, into° this day, in noble wyse° *unto / in a proper manner*
Men doon° to Crist and to his seint servyse.[5] *People offer*

The Manciple's Prologue and Tale

The Prologue

Woot° ye nat wher ther stant° a litel toun *Know / stands*
Which that y-cleped is Bob-up-and-doun,
Under the Blee in Caunterbury weye?[1]
Ther gan our Hoste for to jape° and pleye, *jest, joke*
And seyde, "Sirs, what! Dun is in the myre![2]
Is ther no man for preyere° ne for hyre° *prayer / wages, money*
That wol awake our felawe° al bihinde?° *companion / (lagging) behind*
A theef mighte him ful lightly° robbe and binde. *very easily*
See how he nappeth!° See how, for cokkes bones,[3] *naps, dozes*

4. That no one should inflict on any person such punishment as a fourth stroke, whether weak or strong.
5. Services. The church of St. Cecilia in Rome functions to this day.
1. Which is called Bob-up-and-Down (probably a playful reference to Harbledown, two miles from Canterbury), by the Blean Forest on the Canterbury road.
2. Dun (name for a horse) is stuck in the mud. The Host uses this refrain from a popular game to say that things are at a standstill, it's time to get the tale-telling restarted.
3. For cock's bones, a euphemistic oath just this side of "for God's bones."

That he wol falle from his hors atones.° *at once*
Is that a cook of Londoun, with meschaunce?° *bad luck to him*
Do him° come forth. He knoweth his penaunce, *Have him*
For he shal telle a tale, by my fey,° *faith*
Although it be nat worth a botel hey.° *small clump of hay*
Awake, thou Cook," quod he, "God yeve° thee sorwe!° *give / sorrow*
What eyleth° thee to slepe by the morwe?° *ails / through the morning*
Hastow° had fleen° al night, or artow° dronke, *Hast thou / fleas / art thou*
Or hastow with som quene° al night y-swonke,° *quean, prostitute / labored*
So that thou mayst nat holden up thyn heed?"
This Cook, that was ful pale and no thing reed,° *not at all red, ruddy*
Seyde to our Host, "So God my soule blesse,
As ther is falle on me swich hevinesse,° *drowsiness*
Noot I nat° why, that me were lever° slepe *I know not / I would rather*
Than° the beste galoun wyn° in Chepe."° *Than (have) / gallon of wine / Cheapside (in London)*
"Wel," quod the Maunciple, "if it may doon ese° *bring comfort*
To thee, sir Cook, and to no wight° displese *person*
Which that heer rydeth in this companye,
And that our Host wol,° of his curteisye, *wills (it), is agreeable*
I wol as now excuse thee of thy tale.
For, in good feith, thy visage is ful pale,
Thyn eyen daswen eek,° as that me thinketh, *are dazed also*
And wel I woot° thy breeth ful soure stinketh. *know*
That sheweth wel thou art not wel disposed.° *not in good health*
Of me, certein, thou shalt nat been y-glosed.° *glossed (over), flattered*
Se how he ganeth,° lo, this dronken wight, *yawns*
As though he wolde swolwe° us anonright.° *swallow / immediately*
Hold cloos° thy mouth, man, by thy fader° kin. *Keep shut / father's*
The devel of helle sette his foot therin!
Thy cursed breeth infecte wol us alle.
Fy, stinking swyn,° fy! Foule moot thee falle!° *swine / May evil befall thee*
A! taketh heed, sirs, of this lusty man.
Now, swete sir, wol ye justen atte fan?[4]
Therto° me thinketh ye been wel y-shape°— *For that / in good shape*
I trowe° that ye dronken han wyn ape, *believe*
And that is whan men pleyen with a straw."[5]
And with this speche the Cook wex wrooth and wraw,° *angry*
And on the Maunciple he gan nodde° faste *shook his head*
For lakke of speche—and doun the hors him caste,
Wher as he lay, til that men up him took.
This was a fayr chivachee° of a cook! *feat of horsemanship*
Allas, he nadde holde him by his ladel![6]
And er° that he agayn were in his sadel, *before*
Ther was greet showving° bothe to and fro *shoving, pushing*

4. Joust at the quintain, a demanding jousting exercise far beyond the station and condition of the drunken Cook.
5. "Win ape" probably refers to a medieval classification of different types of drunkenness. The Manciple says the Cook has drunk wine that renders him apelike, capable only of silly play with straw rather than being able to joust like a knight.
6. Alas, that he hadn't stuck to his cooking ladle.

To lifte him up, and muchel care° and wo, *much trouble*
So unweldy° was this sory palled gost.° *unwieldy / pallid ghost*
And to the Maunciple thanne spak our Host.
"Bycause drink hath dominacioun
Upon this man, by my savacioun,° *salvation*
I trowe he lewedly° wolde telle his tale. *ignorantly, crudely*
For—were it° wyn or old or moysty° ale *whether it were / new*
That he hath dronke—he speketh in° his nose, *through*
And fneseth° faste, and eek he hath the pose.° *sneezes / head cold*
He hath also to do more than ynough
To kepe him and his capel° out of the slough;° *cart horse / mud*
And if he falle from his capel eftsone,° *again*
Than shul we alle have ynough to done° *do*
In lifting up his hevy dronken cors.° *body*
Telle on thy tale. Of him make I no fors.° *i.e., I've had enough of him*
But yet, Maunciple, in feith thou art to nyce° *too foolish*
Thus openly repreve him of° his vyce. *reprove, reproach him for*
Another day he wol, peraventure,° *perhaps, by chance*
Reclayme thee and bringe thee to lure.[7]
I mene, he speke wol of smale thinges,
As for to pinchen at thy rekeninges,° *find fault with thy accounts*
That were not honeste, if it cam to preef."° *to proof, to the test*
"No," quod the Maunciple, "that were a greet
mescheef!° *misfortune*
So mighte he lightly° bringe me in the snare. *easily*
Yet hadde I lever° payen for the mare *I would rather*
Which he rit° on than he sholde with me stryve.° *rides / strive, quarrel*
I wol nat wratthe° him, also mote I thryve.° *anger / so may I thrive, prosper*
That that° I spak, I seyde it in my bourde.° *That which / jesting*
And wite° ye what? I have heer in a gourde° *know / gourd-shaped flask*
A draught of wyn—ye,° of a rype grape— *yes (indeed)*
And right anon ye shul seen a good jape.° *joke*
This Cook shal drinke therof, if I may.° *if I may (offer him some)*
Up peyne° of deeth, he wol nat seye me nay." *Upon pain*
And certeinly, to tellen as it was,
Of this vessel the Cook drank faste. Allas,
What neded him? He drank ynough biforn.
And whan he hadde pouped° in this horn, *puffed, blown (i.e., taken a gulp)*
To the Maunciple he took the gourde agayn;° *gave the gourd back*
And of that drinke the Cook was wonder fayn,° *wonderfully happy*
And thanked him in swich wyse° as he coude. *in such a way*
Than gan our Host to laughen wonder loude,
And seyde, "I see wel it is necessarie,
Wher that we goon,° good drink we with us carie, *Wherever we go*
For that wol turne rancour° and disese° *rancor / dis-ease, discomfort*
T'acord° and love, and many a wrong apese.° *To accord / appease, remedy*
O Bachus,° y-blessed be thy name, *Bacchus, god of wine*
That so canst turnen ernest into game.

7. Call thee back with a lure (as one does a hawk); i.e., get back at you.

Worship and thank be to thy deitee!° *deity, godship*
Of that matere° ye gete namore of° me. *On that subject / from*
Tel on° thy tale, Maunciple, I thee preye." *forth*
"Wel, sir," quod he, "now herkneth° what I seye." *listen to*

The Tale

When Phebus° dwelled here in this erthe adoun, *Phoebus Apollo*
As olde bokes maken mencioun,
He was the moste lusty bachiler° *vigorous young knight*
In al this world and eek° the beste archer. *also*
He slow Phitoun,° the serpent, as he lay *slew the Python*
Slepinge agayn the sonne° upon a day, *in the sun*
And many another noble worthy dede
He with his bowe wroghte,° as men may rede. *worked, performed*
Pleyen he coude on every minstralcye° *musical instrument*
And singen, that it was a melodye° *sweet music*
To heren of his clere vois the soun.° *sound*
Certes° the king of Thebes, Amphioun, *Certainly*
That with his singing walled° that citee, *built the walls of*
Coude never singen half so wel as he.
Therto° he was the semelieste° man *In addition / most handsome*
That is or was, sith° that the world bigan. *since*
What nedeth it his fetures to discryve?° *describe*
For in this world was noon so fair on lyve.° *alive*
He was therwith° fulfild of gentillesse,° *also / full of nobility*
Of honour, and of parfit° worthinesse. *perfect*
This Phebus, that was flour of bachelrye° *the flower of knighthood*
As wel in fredom° as in chivalrye,° *generosity / knightly deeds*
For his desport,° in signe eek of victorie *amusement, delight*
Of Phitoun,° so as telleth us the storie, *Over Python*
Was wont to beren° in his hand a bowe. *accustomed to carrying*
Now had this Phebus in his hous a crowe,
Which in a cage he fostred° many a day, *fostered, cared for*
And taughte it speke° as men teche a jay. *to speak*
Whyt was this crowe, as is a snow-whyt swan,
And countrefete° the speche of every man *imitate (literally, counterfeit)*
He coude, whan he sholde telle a tale.
Therwith in al this world no nightingale
Ne coude, by an hondred thousand deel,° *thousandth part*
Singen so wonder merily and weel.
Now had this Phebus in his hous a wyf,
Which that he lovede more than his lyf,
And night and day dide ever his diligence
Hir for to plese and doon hir reverence,° *show her respect*
Save° only (if the sothe° that I shal sayn) *Except / truth*
Jalous° he was and wolde have kept hir fayn,° *Jealous / was eager to keep her guarded*
For him were looth° byjaped° for to be. *he did not like / deceived*
And so is every wight° in swich degree,° *person / in such a situation*
But al in ydel,° for it availleth noght.° *in vain / does not help*

A good wyf that is clene of werk° and thoght *pure in action*
Sholde nat been kept in noon await,° certayn; *under any surveillance*
And trewely the labour is in vayn
To kepe a shrewe, for it wol nat be.° *cannot be done*
This holde I for a verray nycetee:° *true folly*
To spille° labour for to kepe° wyves. *waste / trying to guard*
Thus writen olde clerkes° in hir lyves. *scholars, learned men*
 But now to purpos, as I first bigan:
This worthy Phebus dooth all that he can
To plesen hir, weninge° by swich plesaunce,° *thinking / pleasure*
And for his manhede° and his *because of manliness*
 governaunce,° *behavior*
That no man sholde han put him from hir grace.° *out of favor with her*
But God it woot,° ther may no man embrace° *knows / i.e., succeed*
As to destreyne° a thing which that nature *restrain*
Hath naturelly set in a creature.
 Tak any brid° and put it in a cage, *bird*
And do al thyn entente° and thy corage° *give all thy attention / energy*
To fostre° it tendrely with mete° and drinke *foster, raise / food*
Of alle deyntees° that thou canst bithinke,° *delicacies / imagine*
And keep it also clenly° as thou may: *as cleanly, neatly*
Although his cage of gold be never so gay,° *i.e., ever so splendid*
Yet hath° this brid, by twenty thousand fold,° *would / times*
Lever° in a forest that is rude° and cold *Rather / wild*
Gon ete° wormes and swich wrecchednesse. *Go eat*
For ever this brid wol doon his bisinesse° *busy himself*
To escape out of his cage if he may.
His libertee this brid desireth ay.° *always*
 Lat take° a cat, and fostre him wel with milk *Take (for instance)*
And tendre flesh,° and make his couche° of silk, *meat / bed*
And lat him seen a mous go by the wal:
Anon° he weyveth° milk and flesh and al, *Immediately / abandons*
And every deyntee that is in that hous,
Swich appetyt hath he to ete a mous.
Lo, here hath lust° his dominacioun, *desire*
And appetyt flemeth discrecioun.° *drives out (rational) judgment*
A she-wolf hath also a vileins kinde:° *churlish, base nature*
The lewedeste° wolf that she may finde, *lowest, most uncouth*
Or leest° of reputacion, wol she take *least*
In tyme whan hir lust to han a make.° *she desires to have a mate*
 Alle thise ensamples speke I by° thise men *concerning*
That been untrewe, and no thing° by wommen. *not at all*
For men han ever a likerous° appetyt *lecherous*
On lower thing to parfourne hir delyt° *take their pleasure*
Than on hir wyves, be they never so faire,
Ne never so trewe ne so debonaire.° *kind, gracious*
Flesh is so newefangel,° with meschaunce,° *fond of novelty / a curse upon it*
That we ne conne in no thing han plesaunce° *take pleasure*
That souneth into° vertu any whyle.° *is in accord with / to any extent*
 This Phebus, which that thoghte upon no
 gyle,° *who suspected no deceit*

Deceyved was, for al his jolitee,° *pleasing nature*
For under° him another hadde she, *in addition to*
A man of litel reputacioun,
Noght worth° to Phebus in comparisoun. *Worth nothing*
The more harm is° it happeth ofte so, *is (that)*
Of which ther cometh muchel harm and wo.
  And so bifel, whan Phebus was absent,
His wyf anon hath for hir lemman° sent. *lover*
Hir "lemman"? Certes,° this is a knavish speche!° *Certainly / vulgar language*
Foryeveth it me, and that I yow biseche.° *beseech, beg*
  The wyse Plato seith, as ye may rede,
The word mot nede° accorde with the dede. *ought to*
If men shal telle proprely a thing,
The word mot cosin° be to the werking.° *cousin / deed*
I am a boistous° man, right thus seye I: *plain, uncultivated*
Ther nis no difference, trewely,
Bitwixe a wyf that is of heigh degree,° *high social rank*
If of hir body dishonest° she be, *unchaste, immoral*
And a povre wenche,° other than this— *poor lower-class woman*
If it so be they werke bothe amis°— *they both act wrongly*
But° that the gentile,° in estaat° above, *Only / noblewoman / class, status*
She shal be cleped° his lady, as in love. *called*
And for° that other is a povre womman, *because*
She shal be cleped his wenche or his lemman.
And God it woot,° myn owene dere brother, *knows*
Men leyn° that oon as lowe as lyth° that other. *lay / lies (in intercourse)*
  Right so bitwixe a titlelees tiraunt° *i.e., a usurper tyrant*
And an outlawe or a theef erraunt,° *roving*
The same,° I seye, ther is no difference. *(They are) the same*
To Alisaundre° was told this sentence:° *Alexander the Great / observation*
That, for° the tyrant is of gretter° might *because / greater*
By force of meynee° for to sleen° dounright *power of his retinue / slay*
And brennen° hous and hoom and make al plain,° *burn / level everything to the ground*
Lo, therfor is he cleped° a capitain; *called*
And for° the outlawe hath but smal meynee *because*
And may nat doon so greet an harm as he,
Ne bringe a contree to so greet mescheef,° *misfortune, damage*
Men clepen him an outlawe or a theef.
But for I am a man noght textuel,° *book-learned*
I wol noght telle of textes° never a del.° *authorities / (not) a bit*
I wol go to my tale, as I bigan.
  Whan Phebus wyf had sent for hir lemman,
Anon they wroghten al hir lust volage.° *took all their reckless pleasure*
The whyte crowe, that heng° ay in the cage, *lived (literally, hung)*
Biheld hir werk and seyde never a word.
And whan that hoom was come Phebus, the lord,
This crowe sang "Cokkow! Cokkow! Cokkow!"[8]

8. The word "cuckold" is derived from the cry of the cuckoo, which lays its eggs in other birds' nests and thus has long symbolized sexual infidelity.

"What, brid?"° quod Phebus. "What song — *bird*
singestow?° — *dost thou sing*
Ne were thow wont° so merily to singe — *accustomed*
That to myn herte it was a rejoisinge
To here thy vois? Allas, what song is this?"
"By God," quod he, "I singe nat amis.° — *amiss, wrongly*
Phebus," quod he, "for al thy worthinesse,
For al thy beautee and thy gentilesse,
For al thy song and al thy minstralcye,° — *music making*
For al thy waiting°—blered° is thyn ye° — *watching / blurred (tricked) / eye*
With oon° of litel reputacioun, — *By one*
Noght worth to thee as in comparisoun
The mountance° of a gnat, so mote I thryve.° — *value / so may I prosper*
For on thy bed thy wyf I saugh° him swyve."° — *saw / copulate with*
What wol ye more? The crowe anon° him tolde, — *at once*
By sadde tokenes° and by wordes bolde, — *trustworthy evidence*
How that his wyf had doon hir lecherye,
Him to° gret shame and to gret vileinye,° — *To his / dishonor*
And tolde him ofte he saugh it with his yën.° — *eyes*
This Phebus gan aweyward for to wryen.° — *to turn away*
Him thoughte his sorweful herte brast a-two.° — *had burst in two*
His bowe he bente and sette therinne a flo,° — *arrow*
And in his ire° his wyf thanne hath he slayn. — *anger*
This is th'effect,° ther is namore to sayn, — *outcome*
For sorwe of which he brak° his minstralcye,° — *broke / musical instruments*
Bothe harpe and lute and giterne° and — *cittern*
sautrye;° — *psaltery (stringed instruments)*
And eek° he brak his arwes° and his bowe. — *also / arrows*
And after that thus spak he to the crowe:
"Traitour," quod he, "with tonge of scorpioun,
Thou hast me broght to my confusioun!° — *destruction*
Allas, that I was wroght!° Why nere I — *made, created*
deed?° — *Why should I not be dead*
O dere wyf, o gemme of lustiheed,° — *delight*
That were to me so sad° and eek so trewe, — *steadfast*
Now lystow deed,° with face pale of hewe, — *thou liest dead*
Ful giltelees, that dorste° I swere, ywis.° — *dare / indeed*
O rakel° hand, to doon so foule amis! — *rash, impetuous*
O trouble wit,° o ire recchelees,° — *troubled mind / reckless*
That unavysed° smytest giltelees!° — *thoughtless / kills the innocent*
O wantrust,° ful of fals suspecioun, — *distrust*
Where was thy wit and thy discrecioun?
O every man, be war° of rakelnesse.° — *beware / rash action*
Ne trowe° no thing withouten strong witnesse. — *believe*
Smyt nat to sone,° er that ye witen° — *Strike not too quickly / before you know*
why,
And beeth avysed° wel and sobrely — *take thought*
Er ye doon any execucioun° — *take any action*
Upon° your ire, for suspecioun. — *Because of*
Allas, a thousand folk hath rakel ire° — *rash anger*
Fully fordoon,° and broght hem° in the mire. — *destroyed / them*

Allas, for sorwe I wol myselven slee.”° *slay*
And to the crowe, “O false theef,” seyde he,
“I wol thee quyte anon° thy false tale! *repay at once*
Thou songe whylom° lyk a nightingale. *sang formerly*
Now shaltow,° false theef, thy song forgon° *thou shalt / lose*
And eek° thy whyte fetheres everichon,° *also / every one*
Ne never in al thy lyf ne shaltou speke.
Thus shal men on a traitour been awreke.° *avenged*
Thou and thyn ofspring ever° shul be blake,° *forever / black*
Ne never swete noise° shul ye make, *sound*
But ever crye agayn° tempest and rayn, *in anticipation of*
In tokeninge° that thurgh thee my wyf is slayn.” *As a sign*
And to the crowe he stirte,° and that anon,° *leaped / at once*
And pulled° his whyte fetheres everichon, *plucked*
And made him blak, and refte him° al his song, *deprived him of*
And eek his speche, and out at dore him slong° *slung, threw*
Unto the devel, which I him bitake.° *to whom I commend him*
And for this caas° ben alle crowes blake. *cause*
Lordings, by this ensample I yow preye,
Beth war° and taketh kepe° what I seye. *Be alert / heed*
Ne telleth never no man in your lyf
How that another man hath dight° his wyf. *had intercourse with*
He wol yow haten mortally, certeyn.
Daun° Salomon, as wyse clerkes seyn, *Master (a title of respect)*
Techeth a man to kepe his tonge° wel. *hold his tongue (cf. Proverbs 21:23)*
But as I seyde, I am noght textuel.° *learned in texts*
But nathelees, thus taughte me my dame:° *mother*
“My sone, thenk on the crowe, a° Goddes name! *in*
My sone, keep wel thy tonge and keep thy freend.
A wikked tonge is worse than a feend,° *fiend, demon*
My sone: from a feend men may hem blesse.° *cross (protect) themselves*
My sone, God of° his endelees goodnesse *out of*
Walled a tonge with teeth and lippes eke,° *also*
For° man sholde him avyse° what he speke. *So that / consider*
My sone, ful ofte for to° muche speche *too*
Hath many a man ben spilt,° as clerkes teche, *ruined*
But for a litel speche avysely° *discreetly, advisedly*
Is no man shent,° to speke generally. *hurt*
My sone, thy tonge sholdestow restreyne° *thou shouldst restrain*
At alle tyme but whan° thou doost thy peyne° *except when / devotest thyself*
To speke of God in honour and preyere.
The firste vertu,° sone, if thou wolt lere,° *First among the virtues / learn*
Is to restreyne and kepe wel thy tonge.
Thus lerne children whan that they ben yonge.
My sone, of° muchel speking yvel-avysed,° *from / ill-considered*
Ther lasse° speking hadde ynough suffysed,° *Where less / been sufficient*
Comth muchel harm; thus was me told and taught.
In muchel speche sinne wanteth naught.° *is not wanting, lacking*
Wostow° wherof° a rakel° tonge serveth? *Dost thou know / for what / rash*
Right as a swerd° forcutteth and forkerveth° *sword / cuts and hacks*
An arm a-two,° my dere sone, right so *in half*

A tonge cutteth frendship al a-two.° *in two*
A jangler° is to God abhominable. *talebearer, loose talker*
Reed° Salomon, so wys and honurable; *Read*
Reed David in his psalmes; reed Senekke.° *Seneca*
My sone, spek nat, but with thyn heed° thou bekke.° *head / nod*
Dissimule as° thou were deef,° if that thou here° *Pretend that / deaf / hear*
A jangler speke of perilous matere.
The Fleming seith°—and lerne it if thee leste— *i.e., People from Flanders say*
That litel jangling causeth muchel reste.
My sone, if thou no wikked word hast seyd,
Thee thar° nat drede for to be biwreyd;° *need / betrayed*
But he that hath misseyd,° I dar wel sayn, *spoken wrongly*
He may by no wey clepe° his word agayn.° *call / back*
Thing that is seyd is seyd, and forth it gooth,
Though him repente, or be him leef or looth.° *whether he likes it or not*
He is his thral° to whom that he hath sayd *slave*
A tale of which he is now yvel apayd.° *displeased, regretful*
My sone, be war, and be non auctour° newe *author*
Of tydinges,° whether they ben false or trewe. *tidings, news, stories*
Wherso thou come, amonges hye or lowe,° *high or low (social rank)*
Kepe wel thy tonge, and thenk upon the crowe."

From The Parson's Prologue and Tale

The Prologue

By that° the Maunciple hadde his tale al ended, *By the time that*
The sonne fro the south lyne° was descended *prime meridian*
So lowe, that he nas° nat, to my sighte, *was not*
Degrees nyne and twenty as in highte.° *height (above the horizon)*
Foure of the clokke it was tho,° as I gesse; *then*
For elevene foot, or litel more or lesse,
My shadwe° was at thilke° tyme, as there,° *shadow / that same / at that place*
Of swiche° feet as° my lengthe parted° were *such / as if / divided*
In six feet equal of proporcioun.[1]
Therwith the mones exaltacioun,° *position of greatest influence*
I mene Libra, alwey gan ascende,° *steadily kept ascending*
As we were entring° at a thropes ende;° *entering / village's edge*
For which oure Host, as he was wont° to gye,° *accustomed / guide*
As in this caas,° oure joly companye, *case*
Seyde in this wyse: "Lordings everichoon,° *every one*
Now lakketh us no tales mo than oon.° *one*
Fulfild is my sentence and my decree;
I trowe° that we han herd of ech degree.° *believe / from each (social) rank*
Almost fulfild is al myn ordinaunce.
I prey to God, so yeve him° right good chaunce,° *may he give him / fortune*
That telleth this tale to us lustily.° *pleasantly*

1. I.e., if Chaucer's height were divided into sixths, his shadow would be roughly as long as eleven of those units.

"Sire preest," quod he, "artow° a vicary?° *art thou / vicar*
Or art a person?° Sey sooth,° by thy fey!° *parson / Tell the truth / faith*
Be what thou be,° ne breke thou nat oure *Whatever thou mayest be*
pley;° *game*
For every man, save thou,° hath told his tale. *except for thee*
Unbokele,° and shewe us what is in thy male.° *Unbuckle / bag*
For trewely, me thinketh by thy chere,° *appearance*
Thou sholdest knitte up° wel a greet matere.° *bring to conclusion / subject*
Telle us a fable anon,° for cokkes bones!"° *immediately / (see p. 321, n. 3)*
This Persone him answerde, al at ones,° *at once*
"Thou getest fable noon y-told for° me; *by*
For Paul, that wryteth unto Timothee,[2]
Repreveth hem that weyven° soothfastnesse° *put aside / truthfulness*
And tellen fables and swich wrecchednesse.° *such miserable things*
Why sholde I sowen draf° out of my fest,° *chaff / fist (hand)*
Whan I may sowen whete,° if that me lest?° *wheat / it pleases me*
For which I seye, if that yow list to here° *it pleases you to listen to*
Moralitee and vertuous matere,
And thanne that ye wol yeve° me audience,° *give / hearing*
I wol ful fayn,° at Cristes reverence, *willingly*
Do yow pleasaunce leefful, as I can.[3]
But trusteth wel, I am a Southren man:
I can nat geste—rum, ram, ruf—by lettre.[4]
Ne, God wot,° rym° holde I but litel bettre. *knows / rhyme*
And therfore, if you list, I wol nat glose.° *be elaborate or subtle*
I wol yow telle a mery tale in prose
To knitte up al this feeste° and make an ende. *feast, festival*
And Jesu, for his grace, wit° me sende *wisdom, intelligence*
To shewe yow the wey, in this viage,° *journey*
Of thilke° parfit° glorious pilgrimage *that same / perfect*
That highte° Jerusalem celestial. *is called*
And, if ye vouchesauf,° anon I shal *permit*
Biginne upon my tale, for whiche I preye
Telle youre avys,° I can no bettre seye. *Make known your wish*
But nathelees, this meditacioun
I putte it ay° under correccioun *ever*
Of clerkes,° for I am nat textuel;° *scholars / textually learned*
I take but° the sentence,° trusteth wel. *only / meaning*
Therfor I make protestacioun
That I wol stonde to° correccioun." *submit to*
Upon this word we han assented sone,° *at once*
For, as us semed, it was for to-done,[5]
To enden in som vertuous sentence,
And for to yeve° him space° and audience,° *give / the time / a hearing*
And bade oure Host he sholde to him seye
That alle we to telle his tale him preye.° *ask respectfully*

2. Cf. 1 Timothy 1:4 and 4:7; 2 Timothy 4:4.
3. Give you lawful (permissible) pleasure, to the degree that I know how.
4. I do not know how to compose a romance in the alliterative style, "rum, ram, ruf" (nonsense syllables).
5. For, as it seemed to us, it was the thing to do.

Oure Host hadde the wordes° for us alle: — *was spokesman*
"Sire preest," quod he, "now fayre yow bifalle!° — *may good (chance) befall you*
Sey what yow list, and we wol gladly here."
And with that word he seyde in this manere:
"Telleth," quod he, "youre meditacioun.
But hasteth yow,° the sonne wol adoun;° — *hurry along / will set*
Beth fructuous,° and that in litel space,° — *fruitful / a short time*
And to do wel God sende yow his grace!"[6]

From *The Tale*

Jer. 6.° State super vias et videte et interrogate de viis antiquis que sit via bona, et ambulate in ea, et invenietis refrigerium animabus vestris, etc.

(*Jeremiah 6:16 (translated below, l. 77)*)

Our swete Lord God of hevene—that° no man wole perisse,° but wole that we comen alle to the knoweleche of him and to the blisful lyf that is perdurable°— / amonesteth° us by the prophete Jeremie, that seith in this wyse: / "Stondeth upon the weyes,° and seeth° and axeth° of olde pathes (that is to seyn, of olde sentences°) which is the goode wey; / and walketh in that wey, and ye shul finde refresshinge° for your soules," etc. / Manye been the weyes espirituels that leden° folk to oure Lord Jhesu Crist and to the regne° of glorie. / Of whiche weyes ther is a ful noble wey and a ful covenable,° which may nat faile to man ne to womman that thurgh sinne hath misgoon° fro the righte wey of Jerusalem celestial. / And this wey is cleped° Penitence, of° which man sholde gladly herknen° and enquere° with al his herte / to witen° what is Penitence, and whennes° it is cleped Penitence, and in how manye maneres been the accions° or werkinges of Penitence, / and how manye spyces° ther been of Penitence, and whiche thinges apertenen° and bihoven° to Penitence, and whiche thinges destourben° Penitence. /

who · *wants no man to perish* · *everlasting / admonishes* · *ways, roads* · *look / ask* · *teachings* · *refreshment, renewal* · *lead* · *realm* · *highly suitable (one)* · *gone astray* · *called / concerning* · *listen / inquire* · *know* · *why* · *actions* · *sorts (species)* · *appertain / are necessary* · *impede*

Seint Ambrose seith that Penitence is the pleyninge° of man for the gilt° that he hath doon, and namore° to do any thing for which him oghte to pleyne. / And som doctour° seith, "Penitence is the waymentinge° of man that sorweth for his sinne and pyneth°

lamenting / guilt, sins · *never again* · *doctor (of the Church)* · *lamentation* · *torments*

6. All MSS agree on this order of the final lines, although modern editors generally move lines 69–70 to the end.

85 himself for° he hath misdoon."° / Penitence, with certeyne circumstances,[7] is verray° repentance of a man that halt himself° in sorwe and other peyne° for his giltes. / And for he shal be° verray penitent, he shal first biwailen° the sinnes that he hath doon, and stidefastly purposen° in his herte to have shrift of mouthe,° and to doon satisfaccioun,[8] / and never to doon thing for which him oghte more° to biwayle or to compleyne, and to continue in goode werkes; or elles° his repentance may nat availle. / For as seith Seint Isidre:° "He is a japer° and a gabber° and no verray repentant that eftsoone° dooth thing for which him oghte repente." / Wepinge and nat for to stinte° to
90 doon sinne may nat avaylle. / But nathelees,° men shal hope that every tyme that man falleth, be it never so ofte,° that he may arise thurgh Penitence, if he have grace; but certeinly it is greet doute.° / For, as seith Seint Gregorie, "Unnethe° aryseth he out of sinne that is charged° with the charge of yvel usage."° / And therfore repentant folk, that stinte for° to sinne and forlete sinne er that° sinne forlete hem, holy chirche holdeth hem siker° of hir savacioun. / And he that sinneth and verraily repenteth him in his laste ende,° holy chirche yet hopeth° his savacioun, by the grete mercy of oure Lord Jhesu Crist, for° his repentaunce.
94 But tak the siker wey.° / . . . .

Now shaltow understande what is bihovely° and necessarie to verray parfit° Penitence. And this stant° on three thinges: / Contricioun of Herte, Confessioun of Mouth, and Satisfaccioun. / For which seith Seint John Crisostom, "Penitence destreyneth° a man to accepte benignely° every peyne that him is enjoyned° with contricion of herte, and shrift of mouth, with satisfaccion and in werkinge of alle maner° humilitee." / And this is fruitful Penitence agayn° three thinges in whiche we wratthe° oure Lord
110 Jhesu Crist: / this is to seyn, by delyt° in thinkinge, by recchelesnesse° in spekinge, and by wikked sinful werkinge.[9] /

because / done ill; sincere; i.e., lives; grief; in order to be; lament; firmly intend; make oral confession; i.e., he needs again; else; Isidore of Seville / trickster; loose talker; soon after (confession); but not ceasing; nevertheless; no matter how often; that is very doubtful; With difficulty; burdened; evil habits; who cease; forsake sin before; considers them assured; at the last moment of his life; even so expects; because of; certain (secure) way

befitting; truly perfect; depends; compels; graciously; penalty imposed on him; deeds of every kind of; against; anger; (sensual) pleasure; carelessness

7. With circumstances specifically detailed.
8. "Satisfaction" requires making reparation or compensation for the sins one has committed.
9. The traditional medieval division of evil into sins of thought, word, and deed.

[*Summary of lines 112–835*: In his Prologue the Parson calls his tale a "meditacioun" rather than a "fable" or fiction, and it is not only the longest of *The Canterbury Tales* but also the only one that is expository rather than narrative in form. Translated from Latin treatises on penitence, vices, and virtues, it is divided into three parts: contrition, oral confession, and satisfaction. Part One concentrates on six causes that lead to remorse for one's sins: remembrance of sinfulness, contempt for sin, fear of the Day of Judgment and of hell, sorrow for having neglected good works, remembrance of Christ's Passion, and hope for forgiveness, grace, and heavenly reward. Part Two treats confession. It discusses the nature of sin and the difference between mortal and venial sins, then provides detailed descriptions of the seven deadly sins, each one followed by its remedy, the virtue that counteracts or opposes it: pride by humility, envy by love, anger by meekness and patience, sloth by fortitude, avarice by mercy and pity, gluttony by abstinence, lechery by chastity and continence. We print this last section, which brings a strict doctrinal perspective to the subjects of love, sex, and marriage, subjects at the heart of many of Chaucer's tales.]

* * *

Sequitur de Luxuria°

After Glotonye° thanne comth Lecherie, for thise two sinnes been so ny cosins° that ofte tyme they wol nat departe.° / God woot,° this sinne is ful displesaunt° thing to God, for He seyd Himself, "Do no lecherie." And therfore He putte grete peynes agayns° this sinne in the olde lawe.° / If womman thral° were taken° in this sinne, she sholde be beten° with staves° to the deeth; and if she were a gentil° womman, she sholde be slayn with stones; and if she were a bisshoppes doghter, she sholde been brent,° by Goddes comandement. / Forther over,° by° the sinne of Lecherie God dreynte° al the world at the diluge,° and after that He brente fyve citees with thonder-leyt[1] and sank hem into helle. /

Concerning Lechery / Gluttony / such close cousins / part company / knows / displeasing / set great penalties for / i.e., Old Testament / a servant woman / caught / beaten / clubs / well-born / burned / Moreover / for / drowned / deluge, flood

Now lat us speke thanne of thilke° stinkinge sinne of Lecherie that men clepe avoutrie° of wedded folk, that is to seyn,° if that oon of hem° be wedded or elles bothe. / Seint John seith that avoutiers shullen° been in helle in a stank brenninge° of fyr and of brimston°—in fyr for the lecherie, in brimston for the stink of hir ordure.° / Certes° the brekinge of this sacrement is an horrible thing. It was maked of° God Himself in paradys and confermed by Jesu Crist, as witnesseth Seint Mathew in the gospel: "A man shal lete° fader and moder and

that same / call adultery / say / one of them / adulterers will / burning pool / brimstone (sulfur) / their defilement / Certainly / by / leave

1. He burned five cities with thunderbolts. The reference is to the destruction of Sodom and Gomorrah and the surrounding area in Genesis 19:24–25.

	taken him° to his wyf, and they shullen be	*betake himself*
	two in o° flesh." / This sacrement bitokneth°	*one / symbolizes*
	the knittinge togidre° of Crist and of holy	*together*
	chirche. / And nat only that God forbad°	*prohibited*
	avoutrie in dede,° but eek° He comanded	*deed / also*
	that thou sholdest nat coveite° thy neighe-	*covet*
	bores wyf. / In this heeste,° seith Seint Au-	*commandment*
	gustin, is forboden alle manere coveitise° to	*any sort of desire*
	doon° lecherie. Lo what seith Seint Mathew	*commit*
	in the gospel, that "whoso seeth° a wom-	*looks at*
	man to coveitise of his lust,° he hath doon	*with lustful desire*
845	lecherie with hir in his herte." / Here may	
	ye seen that nat only the dede° of this sinne	*commission*
	is forboden but eek the desyr to doon that	
	sinne. / This cursed sinne anoyeth° grevous-	*damages*
	liche hem that it haunten.° / And first to hir	*those who practice it*
	soule, for he° oblygeth° it to sinne and to	*i.e., Lechery / compels*
	peyne of deeth that is perdurable.° / Unto	*eternal*
	the body anoyeth it grevously also, for it	
	dreyeth him,° and wasteth° and shent° him,	*dries him up / wastes / ruins*
	and of his blood° he maketh sacrifyce to the	*(here = semen)*
	feend° of helle. It wasteth eek his catel° and	*devil / property*
	his substaunce.° And certes, if it be a foul	*wealth*
	thing a° man to waste his catel on wommen,	*(for) a*
	yet is it a fouler thing whan that, for swich	
	ordure, wommen dispenden upon° men hir	*squander on*
	catel and substaunce. / This sinne, as seith	
	the prophete, bireveth° man and womman	*steals from*
	hir gode fame° and al hir honour, and it is	*reputation*
	ful pleasaunt to the devel, for therby win-	
850	neth he the moste partie° of this world. /	*greatest part*
	And right° as a marchant delyteth him° most	*just / delights*
	in chaffare° that he hath most avantage of,°	*trade / profit from*
	right so delyteth the feend in this ordure. /	
	This is that other hand of the devel,	
	with fyve fingres to cacche° the peple to°	*catch, lure / into*
	his vileinye. / The firste finger is the fool	
	lookinge° of the fool womman and of the	*lecherous gazing*
	fool man, that sleeth° right as the basilicok°	*slays, kills / basilisk*
	sleeth folk by the venim° of his sighte; for	*i.e., deadliness*
	the coveitise of eyen° folweth the coveit-	*desire of the eyes*
	ise of the herte. / The second finger is the	
	vileyns° touchinge in wikkede manere.	*shameful, evil*
	And therfore seith Salomon that whoso°	*whosoever*
	toucheth and handleth a womman, he	
	fareth° lyk him that° handleth the scorpioun	*fares, behaves / one who*
	that stingeth and sodeynly° sleeth thurgh his	*suddenly*
	enveniminge;° as whoso toucheth warm	*poisoning*
	pich,° it shent° hise fingres. / The thridde is	*pitch, tar / defiles*
	foule° wordes, that fareth lyk fyr that right	*dirty, sinful*
855	anon brenneth° the herte. / The fourthe	*quickly burns*

finger is the kissinge; and trewely he were° a greet fool that wolde kisse the mouth of a brenninge ovene or of a fourneys.° / And more fooles been they that kissen in vileinye,° for that mouth is the mouth of helle, and namely° thise olde dotardes holours:° yet° wol they kisse (though they may nat do°) and smatre hem.° / Certes, they been lyk to houndes; for an hound, whan he comth by the roser° or by othere busshes, though he may nat pisse, yet wole he heve° up his leg and make a contenaunce° to pisse. / And for that° many man weneth° that he may nat sinne for no likerousnesse° that he doth° with his wyf—certes, that opinion is fals. God woot,° a man may sleen° himself with his owene knyf, and make himselven dronken of his owene tonne.° / Certes, be it wyf, be it child, or any worldly thing that he loveth biforn° God, it is his maumet° and he is an ydolastre.° / Man sholde loven his wyf by discrecioun,° paciently and atemprely,° and thanne is she as though it were his suster. / The fifthe finger of the develes hand is the stinkinge dede of Lecherie. / Certes, the fyve fingres of Glotonie the feend put in the wombe° of a man, and with hise fyve fyngres of Lecherie he gripeth° him by the reynes° for to throwen him into the fourneys of helle, / ther as° they shul han° the fyr and the wormes that evere shul lasten, and wepinge and wailinge, sharp hunger and thurst, and grimnesse° of develes that shullen al totrede° hem, withouten respit° and withouten ende. /

would be
furnace
sinfully
especially
senile lechers / still
perform (sexually) / defile themselves
rosebush
heave, lift
pretend
while / believes
no matter what lecherous acts
performs
knows / slay, kill
from his own wine cask
above / idol
idolater
rationally / moderately
belly
grasps
loins
there where / have, experience
savagery
trample on / relief

Of° Lecherie, as I seyde, sourden° diverse speces,° as fornicacioun that is bitwixe man and womman that been nat maried, and this is deedly sinne and agayns° nature. / Al that is enemy and destruccioun to nature is agayns nature. / Parfay,° the resoun of a man telleth eek° him wel that it is deedly sinne, for as muche as God forbad° Lecherie. And Seint Paul yeveth hem the regne that nis dewe to no wight but to hem that doon deedly sinne.[2] /

Out of / arise
kinds
against
Indeed
also
prohibited

Another sinne of Lecherie is to bireve° a mayden of hir maydenhede,° for he that so

deprive
virginity

2. I.e., St. Paul gives to them (lechers) the kingdom (of hell), which is reserved only for those who commit deadly sins. See Galatians 5:19–21.

dooth,° certes, he casteth a mayden out of the hyeste degree° that is in this present lyf / and bireveth hir° thilke precious fruit that the book clepeth° "the hundred fruit." I ne can seye it noon otherweyes° in English, but in Latin it highte° *centesimus fructus.*[3] / Certes,° he that so dooth is cause of manye damages and vileinyes,° mo° than any man can rekene,° right as he° somtyme is cause of alle damages that bestes° don in the feeld that breketh° the hegge° or the closure,° thurgh which he destroyeth that° may nat been restored. / For certes, namore° may maydenhede be restored than an arm that is smiten° fro the body may retourne agayn to wexe.° / She may have mercy (this woot° I wel) if she do penitence; but nevere shal it be that she nas corrupt.° /

And al be it so that° I have spoken somwhat of avoutrie,° it is good to shewen mo perils that longen to° avoutrie, for to eschue° that foule sinne. / Avoutrie in Latin is for to seyn° approchinge of other° mannes bed, thurgh which tho that whylom° weren o° flessh abaundone° hir bodyes to othere persones. / Of° this sinne, as seith the wyse man, folwen° manye harmes. First, brekinge of feith, and certes in feith is the keye of Cristendom. / And whan that feith is broken and lorn,° soothly° Cristendom stant veyn° and withouten fruit. / This sinne is eek a thefte, for thefte generally is for to reve a wight his thing° agayns° his wille. / Certes, this is the fouleste° thefte that may be, whan a womman steleth hir body from hir housbonde and yeveth° it to hire holour° to defoulen° hir, and steleth hir soule fro Crist and yeveth it to the devel. / This is a fouler thefte than for to breke° a chirche and stele the chalice, for thise avoutiers breken the temple of God spiritually, and stelen the vessel of grace (that is, the body and the soule), for which Crist shal destroyen hem, as seith Seint Paul. / Soothly, of this thefte douted gretly Joseph whan that his lordes wyf preyed him of vileinye,[4]

does that
highest rank, status
steals from her
the Bible calls
otherwise
is called
Certainly
evils / more
reckon / just as a man
animals
break out of / hedge / fence
that which
no more
cut off
grow / know
has not been corrupted
although
adultery
more dangers inherent in
in order to avoid
means / another
those who once
one / give
From
follow
lost / truly
stands empty
take someone's possession / against
most wicked
gives / lecher, lover
defile
break into

3. The hundredfold fruit. From Matthew 13:8 in Jesus's parable of the sower, taken in medieval exegesis of the Bible to refer to the highest state for women (virginity).
4. Truly, Joseph feared greatly (to commit) this sort of theft when his master's wife invited him to sin (with her). The Parson is referring to the story of Joseph and Potiphar's wife in Genesis 39. Potiphar had entrusted to Joseph the management of all his land and property.

whan he seyde, "Lo,° my lady, how my
lord hath take° to me under my warde° al
that he hath in this world, ne no thing of
hise thinges is out of my power but° only ye
880 that been his wyf. / And how sholde I
thanne do this wikkednesse and sinne so
horribly agayns God and agayns my lord?
God it forbede!" Allas, al to litel° is swich
trouthe° now y-founde. / The thridde harm
is the filthe thurgh which they breken the
comandement of God and defoulen the
auctour° of matrimoine, that is Crist. / For
certes, in so muche as the sacrement of
mariage is so noble and so digne,° so muche
is it gretter° sinne for to breken it, for God
made mariage in paradys in the estaat°
of innocence, to multiplye mankinde to
the service of God. / And therfore is the
brekinge therof more grevous;° of° which
brekinge comen false heires° ofte tyme that
wrongfully occupyen° folkes heritages.° And
therfore wol Crist putte hem out of the
regne° of hevene, that is heritage to gode
folk. / Of this brekinge comth eek ofte tyme
that folk unwar° wedden or sinnen with hir
owene kinrede,° and namely thilke harlottes°
that haunten bordels° of thise fool wom-
men,° that mowe be lykned° to a com-
mune gonge° where as° men purgen hir
885 ordure.° / What seye we eek of putours° that
liven by the horrible sinne of putrie° and
constreyne° wommen to yelden to hem a
certeyn rente of° hir bodily puterie—
ye,° somtyme of his owene wyf or his
child—as doon this baudes?° Certes, thise
been cursede sinnes. / Understond eek that
avoutrie is set gladly° in the ten comande-
ments bitwixe thefte and manslaughtre, for
it is the gretteste thefte that may be, for it is
thefte of body and of soule. / And it is lyk to
homicyde, for it kerveth a-two° and breketh
a-two hem that first° were maked o° flesh,
and therfore, by the olde lawe of God, they
sholde be slayn. / But nathelees, by the lawe
of Jesu Crist (that is, lawe of pitee°), whan
he seyde to the womman that was founden°
in avoutrie and sholde han been° slayn with
stones, after° the wil of the Jewes, as was
hir lawe: "Go," quod Jesu Crist, "and have
namore wil to sinne," or, "wille namore to
do sinne." / Soothly, the vengeaunce° of

Look
given / in my charge
except
all too seldom
such loyalty, integrity
creator, authorizer
honorable
a greater
state
serious / from
heirs
usurp / people's inheritances
kingdom
unknowingly
relatives / those same lechers
frequent brothels
whores / may be compared
public latrine / where
their excrement / pimps
prostitution
force
give them part of the income from
indeed
bawds, pimps
appropriately
cuts in two
previously / one
mercy
discovered
about to be
by
punishment

avoutrie is awarded° to the peynes of helle, *assigned*
but if so be that° it be destourbed° by peni- *unless / prevented*
890 tence. / Yet been ther mo speces° of this *more types*
cursed sinne, as whan that oon of hem is
religious or elles bothe; or of folk that been
entred into ordre,° as subdekne,° or dekne, *a religious order / subdeacon*
or preest, or hospitaliers.° And evere the *Knights Hospitalers*
hyer° that he is in ordre, the gretter is the *higher*
sinne. / The thinges that gretly agreggen hir
sinne° is the brekinge of hir avow of chasti- *make their sin worse*
tee whan they receyved the ordre. / And
forther over,° sooth is that holy ordre is *furthermore*
chief of al the tresorie° of God and his espe- *treasury*
cial signe and mark of chastitee to shewe
that they been joyned to chastitee, which
that is most precious lyf that is. / And thise
ordred folk° been specially tytled° to God *people in orders / dedicated*
and of the special meynee° of God, for *household*
which, whan they doon° deedly sinne, they *commit*
been the special traytours of° God and of *traitors to*
his peple; for they liven of° the peple to *get their living from*
preye for the peple, and whyle they been
suche traitours, hir preyers availen nat° to *are of no avail*
the peple. / Preestes been aungeles° as by° *angels / through*
the dignitee of hir misterye;° but for sothe° *profession / in truth*
Seint Paul seith that Sathanas transformeth
895 him° in° an aungel of light. / Soothly, the *himself / into*
preest that haunteth° deedly sinne, he may *repeatedly engages in*
be lykned to the aungel of derknesse trans-
formed in° the aungel of light: he semeth *into*
aungel of light but for sothe he is aungel of
derknesse. / Swiche° preestes been the *Such*
sones of Helie,° as sheweth in the book of *sons of Eli (1 Kings 2:12)*
Kinges that they weren the sones of Belial,
that is, the devel. / Belial is to seyn° "with- *means*
outen juge,"[5] and so faren they: hem thin-
keth° they been free and han° no juge, *it seems to them / have*
namore than hath a free bole° that taketh *bull*
which° cow that him lyketh° in the toun. / *whichever / pleases him*
So faren they by° wommen. For right as a *they act toward*
free bole is ynough for al a toun,° right so is *an entire town*
a wikked preest corrupcioun ynough for
al a parisshe or for al a contree.° / Thise *country, district*
preestes, as seith the book, ne conne nat
the misterie° of preesthode to the peple, ne *do not know the duties*
God ne knowe they nat. They ne helde hem
nat apayd,° as seith the book, of soden *They were not satisfied*
flesh° that was to hem offred, but they toke *boiled meat*

5. Without judge. The biblical source (Judges 19:22) reads in the Vulgate *absque iugo*, "without yoke." Chaucer possibly misread an intermediate French source.

900 by force the flesh that is rawe. / Certes, so
thise shrewes° ne holden hem nat apayed of
rosted flesh and sode flesh, with which the
peple fedden hem in greet reverence, but
they wole have raw flesh of folkes wyves
and hir doghtres. / And certes° thise wom-
men that consenten to hir harlotrie° doon
greet wrong to Crist, and to holy chirche,
and alle halwes,° and to alle soules; for they
bireven alle thise him° that sholde worshipe
Crist and holy chirche and preye for Chris-
tene soules. / And therfore han swiche
preestes, and hir lemmanes° eek that
consenten to hir lecherie, the malisoun°
of al the court Cristen,° till they come to
amendement.° / The thridde spece of
avoutrie° is somtyme bitwixe a man and his
wyf, and that is whan they take no reward°
in hir assemblinge° but only° to hire fleshly
delyt, as seith Seint Jerome, / and ne rekken
of nothing but° that they been assembled.
Bycause that they been maried, al is good
905 ynough, as thinketh to hem.° But in° swich
folk hath the devel power, as seyde the
aungel Raphael to Thobie;° for in hir
assemblinge they putten Jesu Crist out
of hir herte and yeven hemself° to alle
ordure.°

The fourthe spece° is the assemblee of
hem that been of hire kinrede,° or of hem
that been of oon affinitee,° or elles with
hem with whiche° hir fadres or hir kinrede
han deled° in the sinne of lecherie. This
sinne maketh hem lyk to houndes, that
taken no kepe° to kinrede. / And certes, par-
entele° is in two maneres, outher goostly°
or fleshly; goostly, as for to delen with hise
godsibbes.° / For right so as he that engen-
dreth a child is his fleshly fader, right so is
his godfader his fader espirituel. For which
a womman may in no lasse° sinne assem-
blen with hir godsib[6] than with hir owene
fleshly brother. /

The fifthe spece is thilke° abhominable
sinne of which that no man unnethe oghte°
speke ne wryte. Nathelees, it is openly re-
910 herced° in holy writ. / This cursednesse° doon
men and wommen in diverse entente° and in

scoundrels
surely
their wickedness
all the saints
deprive all these of him
lovers
curse
ecclesiastical court
correction
kind of adultery
pay no attention
coupling (sexual intercourse) / except
care about nothing except
as it seems to them / over
Tobias (Tobit 6:17)
give themselves over
filth
kind (of lechery)
their own family
related by marriage
whom
copulated
pay no attention
kinship / either spiritual
godparents or spiritual siblings
with no less
that same
scarcely any man should
mentioned / i.e., sodomy
for various reasons

6. That is, have sex with someone who is a child of her godparents or someone for whom her parents served as godparents.

diverse manere; but though that holy writ speke of horrible sinne, certes holy writ may nat been defouled,° namore than the sonne that shyneth on the mixen.° /

stained, polluted
dunghill

Another sinne aperteneth° to lecherie that comth in slepinge, and this sinne cometh ofte to hem that been maydenes° and eek to hem that been corrupt; and this sinne men clepen pollucioun,° that comth in foure maneres: / somtyme of languissinge° of body, for the humours° been to ranke° and habundaunt in the body of man; somtyme of infermetee for the feblesse of the vertu retentif,[7] as phisik° maketh mencioun; somtyme for surfeet° of mete° and drinke; and somtyme of vileyns° thoghtes that been enclosed in mannes minde whan he goth to slepe, which may nat been withoute sinne, for° which men moste kepen hem wysely° or elles may men sinnen ful grevously. /

belongs
virgins
i.e., noctural emission
through weakness / bodily fluids
too profuse
medical science
excess
food / shameful, evil
against
firmly guard themselves

Remedium contra peccatum Luxurie.°

The Remedy Against the Sin of Lechery

Now comth the remedie agayns Lecherie, and that is, generally, Chastitee and Continence, that restreyneth alle the desordeynee moevinges° that comen of fleshly talentes.° / And evere the gretter merite shal he han,° that most restreyneth the wikkede eschaufinges° of the ordure° of this sinne. And this is in two maneres,° that is to seyn, chastitee in mariage, and chastitee of widwehode.° / Now shaltow° understonde that matrimoine is leefful° assemblinge of man and of womman, that receyven by vertu of the sacrement the bond thurgh which they may nat be departed° in al hir lyf, that is to seyn, whyl that they liven bothe. / This, as seith the book, is a ful greet sacrement. God maked it, as I have seyd, in paradys, and wolde himself be born in mariage. / And for to halwen° mariage, he was at a weddinge° whereas he turned water into wyn;° which was the firste miracle that he wroghte° in erthe° biforn hise disciples. / Trewe° effect of mariage clenseth° fornicacioun and replenisseth° holy chirche of good linage; for that is the ende° of mariage;

disorderly stirrings
desires
have
burnings / filth
kinds
widowhood / shalt thou
allowable
separated
hallow, make holy
(in Cana; see John 2:1–11) / wine
performed / on earth
True / purifies
replenishes
goal

7. Sometimes through infirmity caused by weakness in the (body's) power to retain (fluids).

and it chaungeth deedly sinne into venial sinne[8] bitwixe hem that been y-wedded, and maketh the hertes° al oon° of hem that been y-wedded, as wel as the bodies. / This is verray° mariage, that was establissed by God er° that sinne bigan, whan naturel lawe was in his right point° in paradys; and it was ordeyned that o° man sholde have but o womman, and o womman but o man, as seith Seint Augustin, by manye resouns. /

First, for mariage is figured° bitwixe Crist and holy chirche. And that other is, for a man is heved° of a womman; algate,° by ordinaunce it sholde be so. / For if a womman had mo° men than oon,° thanne sholde she have mo hevedes° than oon, and that were an horrible thing biforn God; and eek° a womman ne mighte nat plese° to many folk at ones.° And also ther ne sholde nevere be pees° ne reste amonges hem; for everich° wolde axen° his owene thing. / And fortherover,° no man ne sholde knowe his owene engendrure,° ne who sholde have his heritage; and the womman sholde been the lasse° biloved, fro the time that she were conioynt° to many men. /

Now comth, how that a man sholde bere him° with his wyf; and namely in two thinges, that is to seyn in suffraunce° and reverence, as shewed Crist whan he made first womman. / For he ne made hir nat of the heved° of Adam, for° she sholde nat clayme to greet° lordshipe. / For theras the womman hath the maistrie, she maketh to muche desray;° ther neden none ensamples° of this. The experience of day by day oghte suffyse.° / Also certes, God ne made nat womman of° the foot of Adam, for she ne sholde nat been holden to° lowe; for she can nat paciently suffre:° but God made womman of the rib of Adam, for womman sholde be felawe° unto man. / Man sholde bere him to° his wyf in feith, in trouthe,° and in love, as seith seint Paul: that "a man sholde loven his wyf as Crist loved holy chirche, that loved it so wel that he deyde°

hearts / all one
true
before
its rightful position
one
symbolizes the relation
the head / in every way
more / one
more heads
also
please
once
peace / each one
ask for
moreover
offspring
less
conjoined
conduct himself
patience
head / so that
claim too much
disorder
examples
ought to suffice
from
too
endure
a companion
conduct himself toward / loyalty
died

8. Deadly or mortal sins, committed in full understanding of their seriousness, are directly contrary to charity and the love of God; venial sins, less serious or less deliberately committed, impede or weaken charity but do not alienate a person from God. The Parson uses this distinction also in lines 939–43 in his evaluation of motives for sexual intercourse within marriage.

for it." So sholde a man for his wyf, if it were nede.° /

Now how that a womman sholde be subget° to hir housbonde, that telleth seint Peter. First, in obedience. / And eek, as seith the decree,° a womman that is a wyf, as longe as she is a wyf, she hath noon auctoritee to swere° ne bere witnesse withoute leve° of hir housbonde, that is hir lord; algate,° he sholde be so by resoun. / She sholde eek serven him in alle honestee,° and been attempree° of hir array.° I wot° wel that they sholde setten hir entente° to plesen hir housbondes, but nat by hir queyntise° of array. / Seint Jerome seith that wyves that been apparailled in silk and in precious purpre° ne mowe nat clothen hem in Jesu Crist. What seith Seint John eek in this matere? / Seint Gregorie eek seith that no wight° seketh precious array but only for veyne glorie,° to been honoured the more biforn the peple. / It is a greet folye, a womman to have a fair array outward and in hir self be foul inward.° / A wyf sholde eek° be mesurable in lokinge and in beringe° and in laughinge, and discreet in alle hir wordes and hir dedes.° / And aboven alle worldly thing she sholde loven hir housbonde with al hir herte, and to him be trewe of hir body; / so sholde an housbonde eek be to his wyf. For sith° that al the body is the housbondes, so sholde hir herte been, or elles ther is bitwixe hem two, as in that,° no parfit mariage. / Thanne shal men understonde that for three thinges a man and his wyf fleshly mowen assemble.° The firste is in entente of engendrure of° children to° the service of God, for certes that is the cause fynal° of matrimoine. / Another cause is to yelden° everich of hem to other the dette of hir bodies, for neither of hem hath power over his owene body.[9] The thridde is for to eschewe lecherye and vileinye. The ferthe is, for sothe,° deedly sinne. / As to the firste, it is meritorie,° the seconde also, for, as seith the decree, that she hath merite of chastitee that yeldeth to hir housbonde

necessary
subject
ecclesiastical law
swear (legal) oaths
permission
at least
modesty, chastity
modest / clothing / know
i.e., seek, intend
refinement
purple
person
i.e., pride
within / also
bearing
deeds
since
as far as that is concerned
may have intercourse
engendering / in
ultimate purpose
pay
in truth
meritorious

9. The idea of the marital debt, the selfless giving of one's body to one's spouse, is based on St. Paul's statements in 1 Corinthians 7:3–4 (see p. 417). This text is referred to by both the Wife of Bath (*Wife of Bath Prologue*, ll. 154–62) and January (*Merchant's Tale*, l. 1452).

the dette of hir body, ye, though it be agayn hir lykinge and the lust° of hir herte. / The thridde manere is venial sinne, and, trewely, scarsly may ther any of thise be withoute venial sinne, for the corrupcion and for the delyt.° / The fourthe manere is, for to understonde, if they assemble° only for amorous love and for noon of the forseyde causes, but for to accomplice° thilke brenninge° delyt, they rekke° nevere how ofte. Sothly it is deedly sinne; and yet, with° sorwe, somme folk wol peynen hem° more to doon than to hir appetyt suffyseth.° /

The seconde manere of chastitee is for to been a clene° widewe, and eschue the embracinges of man, and desyren the embracinge of Jesu Crist. / Thise been tho that han been wyves and han forgoon° hir housbondes, and eek wommen that han doon° lecherie and been releeved° by Penitence. / And certes, if that a wyf coude kepen hir al chaast by licence° of hir housbonde, so that she yeve° nevere noon occasion that he agilte,° it were to hire a greet merite. / Thise manere wommen that observen° chastitee moste° be clene in herte as well as in body and in thoght, and mesurable° in clothinge and in contenaunce; and been abstinent in etinge and drinkinge, in spekinge, and in dede.° They been the vessel or the boyste° of the blissed Magdelene, that fulfilleth° holy chirche of° good odour. / The thridde manere of chastitee is virginitee, and it bihoveth° that she be holy in herte and clene of body. Thanne is she spouse to Jesu Crist, and she is the lyf° of angeles. / She is the preisinge of° this world, and she is as thise martirs in egalitee;° she hath in hir that° tonge may nat telle ne herte thinke. / Virginitee baar° oure lord Jesu Crist, and virgine was himselve. /

Another remedie agayns Lecherie is specially to withdrawen° swiche thinges as yeve occasion to thilke vileinye, as ese,° etinge and drinkinge; for certes, whan the pot boyleth strongly, the best remedie is to withdrawe the fyr. / Slepinge longe in greet quiete is eek a greet norice° to Lecherie. /

Another remedie agayns Lecherie is that a man or a womman eschue the companye of hem by whiche he douteth° to be tempted;

desire
pleasure (of it)
i.e., have intercourse
accomplish, satisfy
burning / care
to their
exert themselves
suffices for their sexual needs
chaste
lost
practiced
relieved (of guilt)
permission
give
sin (with her)
practice
must
moderate, modest
deed(s) / box (of ointments)
fills
with
is necessary
beloved
i.e., most praiseworthy in
equal to the martyrs / that which
gave birth to
take away, avoid
such as ease
nurse
fears

for al be it so that the dede is withstonden,° yet is ther greet temptacioun. / Soothly a whyt wal, although it ne brenne° noght fully by stikinge of° a candele, yet is the wal blak° of the leyt.° / Ful ofte tyme I rede that no man truste° in his owene perfeccioun, but° he be stronger than Sampson, and holier than Daniel, and wyser than Salomon. /

resisted / *burn* / *holding against it* / *blackened* / *by the flame* / *should trust* / *unless*

[*Summary of lines 956–1075*: Part Two then discusses the circumstances that aggravate or mitigate sins and the factors involved in making a sincere and accurate confession to a priest, the only way a Christian can attain "salvacioun" after sinning (lines 979–81). Part Three, by far the shortest, concerns "satisfaction" or restitution for sins committed and confessed. The principal forms of restitution are alms-giving, works of charity, and bodily discomforts: prayers, vigils, fasting, and more extreme kinds of "discipline" such as wearing a hair shirt or being whipped. After cautioning against both overconfidence in salvation and the danger of despair, the treatise concludes with an ecstatic vision of heaven:]

Thanne shal men understonde what is the fruit° of penaunce: and after° the word of Jhesu Crist, it is the endelees blisse of hevene, / ther° joye hath no contrarioustee° of wo ne grevaunce,° ther alle harmes been passed of this present lyf; ther as° is the sikernesse° fro the peyne of helle; ther as is the blisful companye that rejoysen hem everemo, everich° of otheres joye; / ther as the body of man, that whylom° was foul and derk, is more cleer than the sonne;° ther as the body, that whylom was syk, freele,° and feble and mortal, is inmortal, and so strong and so hool° that ther may no thing apeyren° it; / ther as ne is neither hunger, thurst, ne cold, but every soule replenissed° with the sighte of the parfit knowinge of God. / This blisful regne° may men purchace by poverte espirituel, and the glorie by lowenesse,° the plentee° of joye by hunger and thurst, and the reste° by travaille,° and the lyf by deeth and mortificacion of synne. /

fulfillment, reward / *according to* / *where* / *contrary* / *grief, sorrow* / *where* / *security* / *each one* / *formerly* / *sun* / *frail* / *healthy* / *harm* / *replenished, made full* / *realm* / *humility* / *abundance* / *peace, repose* / *labor*

Chaucer's Retraction

Here taketh the makere of this book his leve.

Now preye I to hem alle that herkne° this litel tretis or rede,° that if ther be any thing in it that lyketh hem,° that therof they thanken oure lord Jesu Crist, of° whom procedeth al wit° and al goodnesse. / And if

listen to / *read (it)* / *pleases them* / *from* / *understanding* ther be any thing that displese hem, I preye hem also that they arrette° it to the defaute° of myn unconninge° and nat to my wil, that wolde ful fayn° have seyd bettre if I hadde had conninge.° / For oure boke seith, "al that is writen is writen for oure doctrine";° and that is myn entente.° / Wherfore I biseke° yow mekely,° for the mercy of God, that ye preye for me, that Crist have mercy on me and foryeve° me my giltes;° / and namely of° my translacions and endytinges° of° worldly vanitees, the whiche I revoke in my retracciouns: / as is the book of Troilus; The book also of Fame; The book of the XXV Ladies;[1] The book of the Duchesse; The book of seint Valentynes day of the Parlement of Briddes;° The tales of Caunterbury, thilke° that sounen into° sinne; / The book of the Leoun;° and many another book, if they were in my remembrance;° and many a song and many a lecherous lay; that Crist for his grete mercy foryeve me the sinne. / But of the translacion of Boece de Consolacione,[2] and othere bokes of Legendes of seintes, and omelies,° and moralitee and devocioun, / that thanke I oure lord Jesu Crist and his blisful moder and alle the seintes of hevene; / bisekinge hem that they from hennes forth,° unto my lyves ende, sende me grace to biwayle° my giltes, and to studie to° the salvacioun of my soule; and graunte me grace of verray penitence,° confessioun and satisfaccioun to doon° in this present lyf, / thurgh° the benigne grace of him that is king of kinges and preest over alle preestes, that boghte° us with the precious blood of his herte; / so that I may been oon of hem at the day of dome° that shulle be saved. *Qui cum patre*, & c.[3]

Here is ended the book of the Tales of Caunterbury, compiled by Geffrey Chaucer, of° whos soule Jesu Crist have mercy. Amen.

attribute
fault / unskillfulness
very willingly
the skill
instruction / purpose
beseech / meekly
forgive
sins / especially for
compositions / concerning
Birds
those same / tend toward
Lion
memory
homilies
henceforth
bewail
for
true penance
perform / through
Who redeemed
Doomsday, Judgment Day
on

1. I.e., *The Legend of Good Women*.
2. Boethius's *Consolation of Philosophy*.
3. Who (lives) with the Father, etc. (the benedictional close).

SOURCES AND BACKGROUNDS

The General Prologue

The *General Prologue* is first of all a framing device for the stories that follow. Among the many story collections in the Middle Ages, the one most relevant to *The Canterbury Tales* is Giovanni Boccaccio's *Decameron*. Its long introduction describes the plague in Florence and the decision of ten young men and women to leave the city and indulge in various recreations, including storytelling. This frame narrative concludes briefly with the return of the storytellers to Florence.

Chaucer complicated Boccaccio's recreational frame by setting his storytelling game within a pilgrimage to Canterbury. The Christian idea of life as a pilgrimage to God was prominent throughout the Middle Ages, and it is expressed succinctly and eloquently in a well-known passage from St. Augustine's *On Christian Doctrine*. The spiritual implications of pilgrimage are discussed in the essay by Arthur Hoffman on pp. 533–43. But pilgrimage was also a social undertaking as well as a symbol, and by the late fourteenth century reformers argued that its spiritual purposes were being subverted by the worldliness of its participants; the selection from *The examinacion of master W. Thorpe* reveals both Lollard censure and orthodox defense of pilgrimages.

The form of the portraits in the *General Prologue* is indebted to traditional rhetorical modes of character description. For many details of the pilgrims themselves, Chaucer draws heavily on what is known as estates literature: descriptions, usually satiric, of various classes and occupations (see Maurice Keen, "Social Hierarchy and Social Change," pp. 507–12, in this volume). Thomas Wimbledon's sermon, probably delivered in London about the time Chaucer was beginning *The Canterbury Tales*, offers a religious perspective on the estates and their purposes. The passages from William Langland and John Gower suggest both what is conventional and what is original in Chaucer's portrait of the Monk. Much social criticism in Chaucer's time came from John Wyclif and his followers in the Lollard movement, some of whom Chaucer doubtless knew; two passages from Wycliffite tracts offer background to Chaucer's portraits of the Merchant, Pardoner, and Parson.

The principal critical work on the relation of the *General Prologue* to the tradition of estates literature is Jill Mann's *Chaucer and Medieval Estates Satire* (Cambridge: Cambridge UP, 1973). For analogues in the estates tradition and other relevant literary background to each pilgrim described in the *General Prologue*, see Robert R. Raymo's chapter in *Sources and Analogues of the* Canterbury Tales, Vol. 2, ed. Robert M. Correale and Mary Hamel (Woodbridge: D. S. Brewer, 2005), pp. 1–85. For material relevant to the Friar, see the passage from *The Romance of the Rose*, pp. 467–72; for the source of Chaucer's treatment of the Prioress's table manners, see the *Romance* passage on pp. 392–93.

GIOVANNI BOCCACCIO

From The Decameron, Day 1†

Introduction

HERE BEGINS THE FIRST DAY OF *THE DECAMERON*, IN WHICH THE AUTHOR EXPLAINS HOW IT CAME ABOUT THAT THE INDIVIDUALS, WHO WILL SOON MAKE THEIR APPEARANCE, WERE INDUCED TO COME TOGETHER IN ORDER TO CONVERSE WITH ONE ANOTHER, AND HOW, UNDER THE RULE OF PAMPINEA, THEY SPEAK ON WHATEVER TOPIC EACH ONE FINDS MOST AGREEABLE.

Most gracious ladies, whenever I contemplate how compassionate you all are by nature, I recognize that, in your judgment, the present work will seem both somber and painful, for its opening contains the sad record of the recent, deadly plague, which inspired so much horror and pity in all who actually saw it or otherwise came to know of it. But I do not want you to be afraid of reading beyond this introduction, as though you would always be going forward amid continual sighs and tears. You will be affected by this horrific beginning no differently than travelers are by a steep and rugged mountain,[1] for beyond it there lies a most beautiful and delightful plain, which will supply them with pleasure that matches the difficulty of both their ascent and their descent. And thus, just as happiness at its limit turns into sadness, so misery is ended by the joy that follows it.[2]

This brief pain—I call it brief because it is contained in just a few words—will be quickly followed by the sweetness and pleasure that I have just promised you and that such a beginning would not, perhaps, have led you to expect, had I not explained what is about to happen. And truly, if in all honesty I could have led you where I want to go by any route other than by such a difficult path as this one will be, I would have done so gladly. But because, without recalling these events, I could not explain the origins of the things you will read about later on, I have been forced by necessity, as it were, to write it all down.

Let me say, then, that one thousand, three hundred, and forty-eight years had passed since the fruitful Incarnation of the Son of God when the deadly plague arrived in the noble city of Florence, the most beautiful of any in Italy.[3] Whether it descended on us mortals through the influence of the heavenly bodies or was sent down by God in His righteous anger to chastise us because of our wickedness, it had begun some years before in the East, where it deprived countless beings of their lives before it headed to the West, spreading ever-greater misery as it moved relentlessly from

† From *The Decameron: A Norton Critical Edition*, trans. and ed. Wayne Rebhorn (New York: W. W. Norton, 2015), pp. 5–18. We have omitted some of Rebhorn's notes. Boccaccio probably wrote this account of the Black Death in Florence during or shortly after the event, ca. 1349–51.

1. Recalls the opening of *The Divine Comedy* in which Dante is trying without success to climb a mountain (Purgatory).
2. Cf. Proverbs 14:13. [Boccaccio rephrases Proverbs 14:13: "Laughter shall be mingled with sorrow, and mourning taketh hold of the end of joy"—*Editors.*]
3. For Florentines in this period, the year began on March 25, the date of the Incarnation or Annunciation, and in fact, the plague did appear for the first time in Florence in April 1348.

place to place.[4] Against it all human wisdom and foresight were useless. Vast quantities of refuse were removed from the city by officials charged with this function, the sick were not allowed inside the walls, and numerous instructions were disseminated for the preservation of health—but all to no avail.[5] Nor were the humble supplications made to God by the pious, not just once but many times, whether in organized processions or in other ways, any more effective. For practically from the start of spring in the year we mentioned above, the plague began producing its sad effects in a terrifying and extraordinary manner. It did not operate as it had done in the East, where if anyone bled through the nose, it was a clear sign of inevitable death. Instead, at its onset, in men and women alike, certain swellings would develop in the groin or under the armpits, some of which would grow like an ordinary apple and others like an egg, some larger and some smaller. The common people called them *gavoccioli*,[6] and within a brief space of time, these deadly, so-called *gavoccioli* would begin to spread from the two areas already mentioned and would appear at random over the rest of the body. Then, the symptoms of the disease began to change, and many people discovered black or livid blotches on their arms, thighs, and every other part of their bodies, sometimes large and widely scattered, at other times tiny and close together.[7] For whoever contracted them, these spots were a most certain sign of impending death, just as the *gavoccioli* had been earlier and still continued to be.

Against these maladies the advice of doctors and the power of medicine appeared useless and unavailing. Perhaps the nature of the disease was such that no remedy was possible, or the problem lay with those who were treating it, for their number, which had become enormous, included not just qualified doctors, but women as well as men who had never had any training in medicine, and since none of them had any idea what was causing the disease, they could hardly prescribe an appropriate remedy for it. Thus, not only were very few people cured, but in almost every case death occurred within three days after the appearance of the signs we have described, sometimes sooner and sometimes later, and usually without fever or any other complication. Moreover, what made this pestilence all the more virulent was that it was spread by the slightest contact between the sick and the healthy just as a fire will catch dry or oily materials when they are placed right beside it. In fact, this evil went even further, for not only did it infect those who merely talked or spent any time with the sick, but it also appeared to transfer the disease to anyone who merely touched the clothes or other objects that had been handled or used by those who were its victims.

What I have to tell is incredible, and if I and many others had not seen these things with our own eyes, I would scarcely dare to believe them, let

4. The plague started in Asia—to be precise, in the Crimea—from which it was brought by sea to Sicily in 1346. Boccaccio offers two conventional explanations for the disease: the influence of the stars and God's anger at the sins of humans.
5. Boccaccio's description of the plague, although pretending to be an eyewitness account, is generally based on earlier accounts such as that by Paulus Diaconus in his 8th-century *Historia Longobardorum* (*History of the Lombards*).
6. Swellings or protuberances (Tuscan). *Gavocciolo* (sing.) is a diminutive and derives from the late Latin *gaba* (Italian *gozzo*), meaning goiter, crop, throat, or even stomach. These swellings are called *bubboni* in modern Italian and buboes in English (from the Greek word for groin or gland), and it is from this term that we get the name of the sickness, the bubonic plague.
7. The black spots on the body were due to internal bleeding and led to the term the Black Death.

alone write them down, no matter how trustworthy the person was who told me about them. Let me just say that the plague I have been describing was so contagious as it spread that it did not merely pass from one man to another, but we frequently saw something much more incredible, namely that when an animal of some species other than our own touched something belonging to an individual who had been stricken by the disease or had died of it, that animal not only got infected, but was killed almost instantly. With my own eyes, as I have just said, I witnessed such a thing on many occasions. One day, for example, two pigs came upon the rags of a poor man that had been thrown into the public street after he had died of the disease, and as they usually do, the pigs first poked at them with their snouts, after which they picked them up between their teeth and shook them against their jowls. Thereupon, within a short time, after writhing about as if they had been poisoned, both of them fell down dead on the ground, splayed out upon the rags that had brought about their destruction.

These things and many others like them, or even worse, caused all sorts of fears and fantasies in those who remained alive, almost all of whom took one utterly cruel precaution, namely, to avoid the sick and their belongings, fleeing far away from them, for in doing so they all thought they could preserve their own health.

Some people were of the opinion that living moderately and being abstemious would really help them resist the disease. They, therefore, formed themselves into companies and lived in isolation from everyone else. Having come together, they shut themselves up inside houses where no one was sick and they had ample means to live well, so that, while avoiding overindulgence, they still enjoyed the most delicate foods and the best wines in moderation. They would not speak with anyone from outside, nor did they want to hear any news about the dead and the dying, and instead, they passed their time playing music and enjoying whatever other amusements they could devise.

Others, holding the contrary opinion, maintained that the surest medicine for such an evil disease was to drink heavily, enjoy life's pleasures, and go about singing and having fun, satisfying their appetites by any means available, while laughing at everything and turning whatever happened into a joke. Moreover, they practiced what they preached to the best of their ability, for they went from one tavern to another, drinking to excess both day and night. They did their drinking more freely in private homes, however, provided that they found something there to enjoy or that held out the promise of pleasure. Such places were easy to find, because people, feeling as though their days were numbered, had not just abandoned themselves, but all their possessions, too. Most houses had thus become common property, and any stranger who happened upon them could treat them as if he were their rightful owner. And yet, while these people behaved like wild animals, they always took great care to avoid any contact at all with the sick.

In the midst of so much affliction and misery in our city, the respect for the reverend authority of the laws, both divine and human, had declined just about to the vanishing point, for, like everyone else, their officers and executors, who were not dead or sick themselves, had so few personnel that they could not fulfill their duties. Thus, people felt free to behave however they liked.

There were many others who took a middle course between the two already mentioned, neither restricting their diet so much as the first, nor letting themselves go in drinking and other forms of dissipation so much as the second, but doing just enough to satisfy their appetites. Instead of shutting themselves up, they went about, some carrying flowers in their hands, others with sweet-smelling herbs, and yet others with various kinds of spices. They would repeatedly hold these things up to their noses, for they thought the best course was to fortify the brain with such odors against the stinking air that seemed to be saturated with the stench of dead bodies and disease and medicine. Others, choosing what may have been the safer alternative, cruelly maintained that no medicine was better or more effective against the plague than flight. Convinced by this argument, and caring for nothing but themselves, a large number of both men and women abandoned their own city, their own homes, their relatives, their properties and possessions, and headed for the countryside, either that lying around Florence or, better still, that which was farther away. It was as if they thought that God's wrath, once provoked, did not aim to punish men's iniquities with the plague wherever it might find them, but would strike down only those found inside the walls of their city. Or perhaps they simply concluded that no one in Florence would survive and that the city's last hour had come.

Of the people holding these varied opinions, not all of them died, but, by the same token, not all of them survived. On the contrary, many proponents of each view got sick here, there, and everywhere. Moreover, since they themselves, when they were well, had set the example for those who were not yet infected, they, too, were almost completely abandoned by everyone as they languished away. And leaving aside the fact that the citizens avoided one another, that almost no one took care of his neighbors, and that relatives visited one another infrequently, if ever, and always kept their distance, the tribulation of the plague had put such fear into the hearts of men and women that brothers abandoned their brothers, uncles their nephews, sisters their brothers, and very often wives their husbands. In fact, what is even worse, and almost unbelievable, is that fathers and mothers refused to tend to their children and take care of them, treating them as if they belonged to someone else.

Consequently, the countless numbers of people who got sick, both men and women, had to depend for help either on the charity of the few friends they had who were still around, or on the greed of their servants, who would only work for high salaries out of all proportion to the services they provided. For all that, though, there were few servants to be found, and those few tended to be men and women of limited intelligence, most of whom, not trained for such duties, did little more than hand sick people the few things they asked for or watch over them as they died. And yet, while performing these services, they themselves often lost their lives along with their wages.

As a result of the abandonment of the sick by neighbors, friends, and family, and in light of the scarcity of servants, there arose a practice hardly ever heard of before, whereby when a woman fell ill, no matter how attractive or beautiful or noble, she did not object to having a man as one of her attendants, whether he was young or not. Indeed, if her infirmity made it necessary, she experienced no more shame in showing him every part of her body than she would have felt with a woman, which was the reason why those women who were cured were perhaps less chaste in the period that followed. Moreover, a great many people chanced to die who might have survived if they had had any sort of assistance. In general, between the inadequacy of the means to care for the sick and the virulence of the plague, the number of people dying both day and night was so great that it astonished those who merely heard tell of it, let alone those who actually witnessed it.

As a result of the plague, it was almost inevitable that practices arose among the citizens who survived that went contrary to their original customs. It used to be the case, as it is again today, that the female relatives and next-door neighbors of a dead man would come to his house and mourn there with the women of the household, while his male neighbors and a fair number of other citizens would assemble in front of the house with his male relatives. After that, the clergymen would arrive, their number depending on the social rank of the deceased, who would then be carried on the shoulders of his peers, amid all the funeral pomp of candles and chants, to the church he had chosen before his death. As the ferocity of the plague began to increase, such practices all but disappeared in their entirety, while other new ones arose to take their place. For people did not just die without women around them, but many departed this life without anyone at all as a witness, and very few of them were accorded the pious lamentations and bitter tears of their families. On the contrary, in place of all the usual weeping, mostly there was laughing and joking and festive merrymaking—a practice that women, having largely suppressed their feminine piety, had mastered in the interest of preserving their health. Moreover, there were few whose bodies were accompanied to church by more than ten or twelve of their neighbors, nor were they carried on the shoulders of their honored and esteemed fellow citizens, but by a band of gravediggers, come up from the lower classes, who insisted on being called *sextons* and performed their services for a fee. They would shoulder the bier and quick-march it off, not to the church that the dead man had chosen before his demise, but in most cases, to the one closest by. They would walk behind four or six clergymen who carried just a few candles—and sometimes none at all—and who did not trouble themselves with lengthy, solemn burial services, but instead, with the aid of those *sextons*, dumped the corpse as quickly as they could into whatever empty grave they found.

The common people and most of those of the middling sort presented a much more pathetic sight, for the majority of them were constrained to stay in their houses either by their hope to survive or by their poverty. Confined thus to their own neighborhoods, they got sick every day by the thousands, and having no servants or anyone else to attend to their needs, they almost invariably perished. Many expired out in the public streets both day and night, and although a great many others died inside their houses, the stench of their decaying bodies announced their deaths to their neighbors well before anything else did. And what with these, plus the others who were dying all over the place, the city was overwhelmed with corpses.

For the most part, the neighbors of the dead always observed the same routine, prompted more by a fear of contamination from the decaying bodies than by any charity they might have felt. Either by themselves or with the aid of porters, whenever any could be found, they carried the bodies of the recently deceased out of their houses and put them down by the front doors, where anyone passing by, especially in the morning, could have seen them by the thousands. Then the bodies were taken and placed on biers that had been sent for or, for lack of biers, on wooden planks. Nor was it unusual for two or three bodies to be carried on a single bier, for on more than one occasion, they were seen holding a wife and a husband, two or three brothers, a father and a son, or other groups like that. And countless were the times when a couple of priests bearing a cross would go to fetch someone, and porters carrying three or four biers would fall in behind them, so that whereas the priests thought they had one corpse to bury, they would have six or eight, and sometimes more. Even so, however, there were no tears or candles or mourners to honor the dead; on the contrary, it had reached the point that people who died were treated the same way that goats would be treated nowadays. Thus, it is quite clear that things which the natural course of events, with its small, infrequent blows, could never teach the wise to bear with patience, the immensity of this calamity made even simple people regard with indifference.

There was not enough consecrated ground to bury the enormous number of corpses that were being brought to every church every day at almost every hour, especially if they were going to continue the ancient custom of giving each one its own plot. So, when all the graves were full, enormous trenches were dug in the cemeteries of the churches, into which the new arrivals were put by the hundreds, stowed layer upon layer like merchandise in ships, each one covered with a little earth, until the top of the trench was reached.

But rather than go on recalling in elaborate detail all the miseries we experienced in the city, let me just add that the baleful wind blowing through it in no way spared the surrounding countryside. The fortified towns there fared just like the city, though on a smaller scale, and in the scattered villages and farms the poor, wretched peasants and their families died at all hours of the day and night. Without the aid of doctors or help from servants, they would expire along the roads and in their tilled fields and in their homes, dying more like animals than human beings. They, too, became as apathetic in their ways as the city dwellers were, neglecting their property and ignoring the work they had to do. Indeed, since they thought every day was going to be their last, they consumed what they already had on hand, neglecting what they might get in the future from their animals and fields and from all their past labors. Thus it came about that oxen, asses, sheep, goats, pigs, chickens, and even dogs, who are so loyal to men, were driven from their homes and left to roam freely through fields in which the wheat had not even been reaped, let alone gathered in. Nevertheless, many of the animals, as if they were rational beings, would eat well there during the day and then return home full at night, needing no shepherd to guide them.

To leave the countryside and return to the city: what more can be said except that the cruelty of the heavens—and perhaps, in some measure, that of men, too—was so great and so malevolent that from March to the following July, between the fury of the pestilence and the fact that many of the sick were poorly cared for or abandoned in their need because of the fears of those who were healthy, it has been reliably calculated that more than one hundred thousand human beings were deprived of their lives within the walls of the city of Florence, although before the outbreak of the plague perhaps no one would have thought it contained so many.[8]

Oh, how many great palaces, beautiful houses, and noble dwellings, once filled with lords and ladies and their retainers, were emptied of all their inhabitants, down to the last little serving boy! Oh, how many famous families, how many vast estates, how many notable fortunes were left without a legitimate heir! How many valiant men, how many beautiful women, how many lovely youths, whom Galen, Hippocrates, and Aesculapius[9]—not to mention others—would have judged perfectly healthy, dined in the morning with their families, companions, and friends, only to have supper that evening with their ancestors in the next world!

Since my own grief will be increased if I continue to meditate any longer on so much misery, I want to pass over what I can suitably omit and tell what happened one Tuesday morning while our city was in these straits and had been practically deserted. As I later learned from a trustworthy person, seven young women, who had just attended divine services and who, in keeping with the requirements of the times, were dressed in mourning attire, found themselves in the venerable Church of Santa Maria Novella, which was otherwise almost empty. Each one was the friend, neighbor, or relative of one of the others, none had reached her twenty-eighth year or was under eighteen, and all were intelligent, wellborn, attractive, and graced with fine manners and marvelous honesty. I would tell you their real names, but there is a good reason that prevents me from doing so, which is that I do not want any of them to feel shame in the future because of the ensuing stories, which they either listened to or told themselves. For the rules concerning pleasure, which are rather strict today, were then, for the reasons I have already given, very lax, not just for women of their age, but even for those who were much older. Nor do I wish to supply the envious, who are ready to censure the most praiseworthy life, with material that might allow them to denigrate the honesty of these worthy ladies in any way by means of their filthy gossip. However, so that what each one said may be understood without confusion, I intend to identify them by means of names that are either wholly, or partially, adapted to their characters. We shall call the first of them, who was also the oldest, Pampinea, and the second Fiammetta; the third and fourth, Filomena and Emilia; then let us say that the fifth is Lauretta and the sixth Neifile; and to the last, not without reason, we will give the name Elissa.[1]

By chance rather than some prior agreement, they had all come together in one part of the church and were sitting down more or less in a circle. After finishing their prayers, they heaved a deep sigh and began talking among themselves about the terrible times they were going through. After a while, when all the others had fallen silent, Pampinea began to speak as follows:

8. Boccaccio's estimate of the number of deaths due to the plague is somewhat exaggerated, perhaps for the sake of rhetorical effect. Historians, relying on various 14th-century chroniclers, think that about 60 percent of the population, or anywhere from fifty to eighty thousand people, perished in Florence and the surrounding countryside. Boccaccio's interest in rhetorical effect is also evident in the heightened language of the following paragraph.

9. The Greco-Roman god of medicine (Asclepios in Greek). Galen (2nd century C.E.) and Hippocrates (5th century B.C.E.) were the two most famous doctors of the ancient Greek world.

1. [For interpretations of these names and of the names of the young men who leave Florence, see Rebhorn's introduction, pp. xliv–v—*Editors.*]

"My dear ladies, we have all heard many times that there is no harm in exercising our rights in an honest way. Now, every person on earth has a natural right to maintain, preserve, and defend his life to the best of his ability. In fact, the proof that we all take this for granted is that men are judged innocent if they sometimes kill others in self-defense. Thus, if the laws, to which the welfare of every human being has been entrusted, concede such a thing, how can it be wrong, provided no one is harmed, for us or for anyone else to use whatever remedies we can find in order to preserve our lives? When I pause to consider what we have been doing this morning as well as on previous mornings, and when I think about the subjects we have discussed and what we have had to say about them, I realize, just as you must realize, too, that each of us fears for her life. I am not surprised by this, but considering that we all have the natural feelings shared by women, what really does surprise me is why you have not taken any steps to protect yourselves from what each of you has a right to fear.

"Instead, here we sit, in my opinion, as if our sole purpose were to count the number of corpses being carried to their graves; or to hear whether the friars inside the church, whose numbers have practically dwindled away to nothing, are chanting their offices at the specified hours; or to exhibit, by means of our clothing, the quality and quantity of our miseries to anybody who might show up here. And if we go outside, either we see the dead and the sick being carried everywhere about us; or we see people, once condemned and sent into exile for their misdeeds by the authority of the civil law, mocking that law as they rampage through the city committing acts of violence, knowing that those who enforce the law are either sick or dead; or we are tormented by the dregs of our city who, thirsting for our blood, call themselves *sextons* now and go about everywhere, both on horseback and on foot, singing scurrilous songs to add insults to our injuries. And all we ever hear is 'So-and-so is dead' and 'So-and-so is about to die.' If there were anyone left to grieve, we would hear nothing but doleful laments everywhere.

"And when we return home, I do not know whether you have the same experience that I do, but since, out of a large household of servants, there is no one left except my maid, I get so frightened that I feel as if all the hairs on my head were standing on end. And what terrifies me even more is that wherever I go in the house, wherever I pause for a moment, I see the shades of those who have passed away, and their faces are not the ones I was used to, but they have strange, horrible expressions on them that come from who knows where. For these reasons, whether I am here or outside or in my house, I am always anxious, and all the more so, because it seems to me that there is no one possessing sufficient means and having some place to go to, as we do, who is left in the city except us. And as for the few people still around, they make no distinction, as I have often heard and seen for myself, between what is honest and what is not, and prompted only by their appetites, they do what promises them the most pleasure, both day and night, alone and in groups. Moreover, I am not speaking only of laymen but also of those cloistered in monasteries, who have convinced themselves that such wicked behavior is suitable for them and only improper for others. Breaking their vows of obedience, they have given themselves over to carnal pleasures, and in the belief that they will thereby escape death, they have become wanton and degenerate.

"And if this is so—and it most manifestly *is* so—then what are we doing here, what are we waiting for, what are we dreaming about? Why are we lazier and slower than all the other inhabitants of this city in providing for our safety? Do we consider ourselves less valuable than they are? Or do we believe that our lives, unlike those of others, are tied to our bodies by chains so strong that we need not worry about all these things that have the power to harm them? We are mistaken, we are deceived, what bestial stupidity for us to think this way! The clearest argument against us is the frequency with which we are forced to recall the names and conditions of the young men and women who have been struck down by this cruel pestilence.

"Although I do not know if things appear to you the way they do to me, for my part I have come to the conclusion that the best thing for us to do in our present situation would be to leave the city, just as many have done before us and many are still doing, lest we fall prey through timidity or complacency to what we might possibly avoid if we desired to do so. We should go and stay on one of our various country estates, shunning the wicked practices of others like death itself, but having as much fun as possible, feasting and making merry, without ever overstepping the bounds of reason in any way.

"There we will hear the little birds sing and see the hills and plains turning green, the fields full of wheat undulating like the sea, and thousands of kinds of trees. There we will have a clearer view of the heavens, for, even if they are sullen, they do not for all that deny us their eternal beauties, which are so much more attractive to look at than are the walls of our empty city. Moreover, the air is much fresher in the country, the necessities of life are more abundant, and the number of difficulties to contend with is smaller. Although the peasants are dying there in the same way that the city dwellers are here, our distress will be lessened if only because the houses and the people are fewer and farther between. Besides, if I am right, we will not be abandoning anyone here. Rather, we can truly say that we are the ones who have been abandoned, for our relatives, by dying or fleeing from death, have left us alone in the midst of this great affliction as if we were no kin of theirs. Nor will anyone reproach us if we adopt this plan, whereas if we do not, we will be facing sorrow and grief and possibly death itself.

"Consequently, if you please, I think it would be a good idea for us to do what I suggest, taking our maidservants with us and having everything we need sent after. We can live in one place today and another tomorrow, pursuing whatever pleasures and amusements the present times offer. And if death does not claim us before then, let us go on living this way until such time as we can perceive the end that Heaven has decreed for these events. Just remember that it is no less unseemly for us to go away and thus preserve our honor than for the great majority of the others to stay here and lose theirs."

Having listened to Pampinea, the other women not only applauded her advice, but were so eager to take it that they were already beginning to work out the details among themselves, as though they were going to get right up out of their seats and set off at once. But Filomena, who was very prudent, declared: "Ladies, although what Pampinea has argued is very well said, that is no reason for us to rush into it, as you seem to want to do. Remember, we are all women, and every one of us is sufficiently adult to recognize how women, when left to themselves in a group, can be quite irrational, and how, without a man to look after them, they can be terribly disorganized. Since we are fickle, quarrelsome, suspicious, weak, and fearful, I am really worried that if we take no guide along with us other than ourselves, this company will fall apart much more quickly, and with much less credit to ourselves, than would otherwise be the case. We would be well advised to deal with this problem before we start."

"It is certainly true," said Elissa, "that man is the head of woman,[2] and without a man to guide us, only rarely does anything we do accord us praise. But how are we to get hold of these men? As we all know, the majority of our male relatives are dead, and the others who remain alive not only have no idea where we are, but are fleeing in scattered little groups from exactly the same thing we seek to avoid ourselves. Nor would it be seemly for us to take up with those who are not our kin. Therefore, if self-preservation is the purpose of our flight, we must find a way to arrange things so that no matter where we go in quest of fun and relaxation, trouble and scandal do not follow us there."

The ladies were engaged in their discussion, when lo and behold, who should come into the church but three young men, though none so young as to be under twenty-five, in whom neither the horrors of the times, nor the loss of friends and relatives, nor fear for their own lives had been able to cool down, let alone extinguish, the love they felt. The first was named Panfilo, the second Filostrato, and the last Dioneo, all of them very pleasant and well bred. In the midst of all this turbulence, they were seeking the solace, sweet beyond measure, of catching a glimpse of the ladies they loved, all three of whom just so happened to be among the seven previously mentioned, while several of the others were close relatives of one or another of the men. No sooner did they catch sight of the ladies than the ladies caught sight of them, whereupon Pampinea smiled and began: "Look how Fortune favors us right from the start in placing before us three discreet and worthy young men who will gladly guide us and serve us if we are not too proud to ask them to do so."

Neifile's entire face had turned scarlet with embarrassment because she was the object of one of the youths' affections. "Pampinea, for the love of God," she said, "be careful about what you are saying. I know for certain that nothing but good can be said of any one of them, and I believe they are more than competent to carry out this task. I also think they would provide good, honest company not only for us but for many women more beautiful and finer than we are. But since it is perfectly obvious that they are in love with some of us here, I am afraid that if we were to take them with us, through no fault of theirs or of our own, we would be exposed to censure and disgrace."

"That really does not matter in the least," said Filomena. "If I live like an honest woman and my conscience is clear, let people say what they like to the contrary, for God and Truth will take up arms on my behalf. Now, if only they were disposed to accompany us, then we could truly claim, as Pampinea has said, that Fortune favors our plan."

Having heard what Pampinea had to say, the other ladies stopped talking and unanimously agreed that the men should be called over, told about

2. [See Ephesians 5:23: ". . . the husband is the head of the wife, as Christ is the head of the Church. . . ." This important theological statement on the marriage relationship is printed in full below, pp. 419–20—*Editors.*]

their intentions, and asked if they would like to accompany them on their expedition. And so, without another word, Pampinea, who was related by blood to one of the men, got up and went over to where they stood gazing at the women. After giving them a cheerful greeting, Pampinea explained their plan and asked them on behalf of all the women if, in a spirit of pure, brotherly affection, they might be disposed to accompany them.

At first the young men thought they were being mocked, but when they saw that Pampinea was speaking in earnest, they replied happily that they were ready to go. In order to avoid delaying their project, they all made arrangements then and there for what they had to do before their departure. The next day, which was a Wednesday, after having carefully prepared everything they needed down to the last detail and sent it all on ahead to the place where they were going, they left the city at the crack of dawn and started on their way, the ladies traveling with a few of their maids, the three youths with three of their servants. Nor did they go more than two short miles from the city before they arrived at their first destination.

The place in question was some distance from any road, situated on a little mountain that was quite a pleasant sight to see with all its shrubs and trees decked out in their green foliage. At the top there was a palace, built around a large, lovely courtyard, containing loggias, great halls, and bedchambers, all of which were beautifully proportioned and adorned with charming paintings of happy scenes. Surrounded by meadows and marvelous gardens, the palace had wells of the coolest water and vaulted cellars stocked with precious wines, wines more suitable for connoisseurs than for honest, sober ladies. When they got there, the company discovered to their great delight that the palace had been swept clean from top to bottom, the beds had been made up in their chambers, every room had been adorned with seasonal flowers, and the floors had been carpeted with rushes.

Soon after reaching the palace, they sat down, and Dioneo, who was the merriest of the young men and had the readiest wit, said: "Ladies, we have been led here more by your good sense than by our own foresight. Now, I do not know what you intend to do with all your troubles, but I left mine inside the city gates when I passed through them with you just a short while ago. Hence, you must either prepare to have fun and to laugh and sing along with me—as much as is consistent, of course, with your dignity—or you should give me leave to go back there to reclaim my troubles and stay in our afflicted city."

As though she, too, had gotten rid of such thoughts herself, Pampinea replied to him gaily: "Very well said, Dioneo. We should have fun while we are living here, for that is the very reason we fled our sorrows back there. But since things that lack order will not last long, and since I am the one who initiated the discussions that led to the formation of this fair company, I think that if we are to preserve our happiness, we have to choose a leader from among ourselves, someone whom we will honor and obey as our superior and whose every thought will be aimed at enabling us to pass our time together agreeably. Moreover, to allow us all to experience the heavy burden as well as the pleasure of being in command, and thereby to prevent those who are not in charge from envying the person who is, I think that the burden and the honor should be assigned to each of us in turn for just one day. The first ruler is someone we should all elect, but as for those who follow, the person who has been in charge on a particular day should, when the hour of vespers[3] approaches, choose his or her successor. Then this new ruler will be free to determine the place where we will go and to dictate the manner in which we are to live during the period of his or her reign."

They were all quite happy with Pampinea's proposal and unanimously elected her Queen for the first day, whereupon Filomena quickly ran over to a laurel tree, for she had often heard people say that its leaves were quite venerable and conferred great honor on those worthy individuals who were crowned with them.[4] Having gathered a few branches, she made a magnificent garland of honor, which, during the time the company remained together, was placed on each person's head as a clear sign of royal sovereignty and authority.

Once she had been crowned Queen, Pampinea summoned the servants of the three men as well as the women's maids, who were four in number. She then ordered everyone to be silent, and when they were, she said:

"So that I may begin by setting an example for you all that will allow our company to be able to live free from shame and will make our experience here an ever more orderly and pleasurable one for as long as we choose to stay together, let me first appoint Parmeno, Dioneo's servant, as my steward and entrust him with the care and management of our entire household as well as everything pertaining to the service of our dining hall. I want Sirisco, Panfilo's servant, to be our buyer and treasurer and to carry out Parmeno's orders. Tindaro, who is in Filostrato's service, shall take care of his master's bedchamber as well as those of the other two men whenever their own servants are prevented by their duties from doing so. My maid Misia will be in the kitchen full-time with Filomena's maid Licisca, where they will diligently prepare all the dishes ordered by Parmeno. We want Chimera, Lauretta's maid, and Stratilia, Fiammetta's, to act as the ladies' chambermaids and to clean all the places we frequent. Finally, if they wish to stay in our good graces, we desire and command all of the servants to take care that, no matter what they see or hear in their comings and goings, no news from the outside world should ever reach us unless that news[5] is good."

Having summarily given out her orders, which everyone commended, she rose gaily to her feet and declared: "Here there are gardens and meadows and lots of other truly delightful spots in which we are free to walk and enjoy ourselves. However, at the stroke of tierce,[6] let us all return here so that we can eat while it is still cool."

After the merry company was given leave to go by the Queen, the young men and their lovely companions set off on a leisurely walk through one of the gardens, talking of pleasant matters, making lovely garlands out of various types of foliage for one another, and singing songs of love. Then, when they had spent as much time there as the Queen had allotted them,

3. Evening, as in the canonical hours.
4. Crowning a victorious athlete or a poet with leaves from the laurel tree, which was sacred to Apollo, was an ancient Greek custom; the Romans awarded such a wreath to a victorious general. The custom of crowning writers and poets with laurel wreaths was revived in 1315 by the citizens of Padua for the humanist scholar Albertino Mussato. More famously, on April 8, 1341, Petrarch was crowned poet laureate by the Roman Senate on the Capitoline Hill.
5. Translates Boccaccio's *novelle*, which can also mean "stories."
6. Midmorning, as in the canonical hours.

they returned to their lodging where they found Parmeno had been quite diligent in carrying out his duties, for when they entered one of the great halls on the ground floor, they saw that tables had been set up, laid with the whitest tablecloths on which there were goblets gleaming like silver, and that the whole room had been adorned with broom blossoms. At the Queen's behest they rinsed their hands in water and went to sit in the places Parmeno had assigned them.

Exquisitely prepared dishes were brought in, the finest wines were at the ready, and without a sound the three servants began waiting on them. The entire company was delighted that everything was so beautiful and so well presented, and all through the meal there was a great deal of pleasant talk and much good cheer. Since everyone knew how to dance, as soon as the tables were cleared away, the Queen sent for musical instruments so that a few of their number who were well versed in music could play and sing, while all the rest, the ladies together with the young men, could dance a *carola*.[7] At her request, Dioneo took up a lute and Fiammetta a viol, and the pair began playing a melodious dance tune together, whereupon the Queen, having sent the servants away to eat, formed a circle with the other ladies and the two young men, and all began dancing at a stately pace. After that, they sang a number of pleasant, happy little songs and continued to entertain themselves in this manner until the Queen, thinking it was time for a nap, dismissed them. The three young men consequently retired to their bedchambers, which were separated from those of the ladies. There they found not merely that their beds had been neatly made, but that their rooms were as full of flowers as the hall had been, and the ladies made a similar discovery, whereupon the entire company undressed and lay down to rest.

Not long after nones[8] had struck, the Queen got up and had the young men and all the other women awakened, declaring that it was harmful to sleep too much during the day. They then went off to a little meadow where the grass, shaded everywhere from the sun, grew lush and green, and where, feeling a gentle breeze wafting over them, the Queen asked them to sit down in a circle on the green grass. She then spoke to them as follows:

"As you can see, the sun is high, the heat is intense, and nothing can be heard but the cicadas up in the olive trees. To take a walk and go somewhere else right now would be the height of folly, since it is so lovely and cool here, and besides, as you can see, there are boards set up for backgammon and chess. However, although we are free to amuse ourselves in whatever way we like, if you would take my advice in this, we should not spend the hot part of the day playing games, for they necessarily leave one of the players feeling miffed, without giving that much pleasure either to his opponent or to those who are watching. Rather, we should tell stories, for even though just one person is doing the talking, all the others will still have the pleasure of listening. And by the time each one of you will have told his or her little tale, the sun will be setting,

7. A dance in which the dancers joined hands and moved in a clockwise direction, usually accompanied by music and the singing of the dancers themselves.
8. Midafternoon, as in the canonical hours.

the heat will have abated, and we will be able to go and amuse ourselves wherever you choose. Now, if you like what I am proposing, let us put it into effect, but if you dislike it, since my only desire is to carry out your wishes, let us all go and spend our time doing whatever we please until the hour of vespers."

The entire company, the ladies and the young men alike, praised the idea of telling stories.

"Then, if that is your pleasure," said the Queen, "my wish is that, on this first day, we should all be free to speak on whatever topic each of us finds most agreeable."

Turning to Panfilo, who was seated to her right, the Queen graciously asked him to start things off with one of his stories. Upon hearing her command, Panfilo responded with alacrity, and as all the others listened, he began speaking as follows.

GIOVANNI BOCCACCIO

From The Decameron, Day 10†

Conclusion

When Dioneo's story was done, the ladies inclined to one side or the other in their responses, some criticizing one detail in it, some praising another. After they had discussed it at length, the King glanced up at the sky, and seeing that the sun was already quite low and the hour of vespers was at hand, he began, without getting up from his seat, to speak to them as follows:

"Elegant ladies, as I believe you know, the wisdom we mortals possess does not merely consist of remembering things past and apprehending the present, but on the basis of these two activities being able to predict the future, which is considered by serious men to be the highest form of human intelligence. Tomorrow, as you are aware, will be the fifteenth day since we left Florence in pursuit of recreation, seeking both to preserve our health and our lives, and to avoid the melancholy, grief, and anguish that have been inescapable in our city ever since the plague first began. In my estimation, we have managed to achieve this goal without any loss of honor, because as far as I have been able to observe, although the merry stories we have told could have been conducive to arousing carnal desire, and although we have continually enjoyed good food and drink as well as playing music and singing songs—all of which are apt to incite weak minds to less than proper behavior—I have never noted a deed or a word or anything else that is blameworthy, either on your part or on that of us men. Considering what I have seen and heard, it seems to me that our activities have been marked from start to finish by a sense of propriety, harmony, and fraternal friendship, all of which certainly gives me great pleasure and redounds to your honor and credit as well as to my own.

† From *The Decameron: A Norton Critical Edition,* trans. and ed. Wayne Rebhorn (New York: W. W. Norton, 2015), pp. 339–41. We have omitted Rebhorn's notes.

"Accordingly, to keep things from becoming tedious because of an established custom too long observed, and to prevent people from being able to raise frivolous objections to our having stayed here all this time, I think it proper, since all of us have had a day's share of the regal honor I still possess, that with your approval we should go back to the place from which we came. Furthermore, if you examine the matter carefully, there is also the fact that our company has already become known to many people around here, with the result that our numbers could increase to such an extent that it would take away all our pleasure. And so, if my advice meets with your approval, I will keep the crown that was given to me until our departure, which I propose should take place tomorrow morning. But if you should decide otherwise, I already have someone in mind to bestow it on for the next day."

The ladies and the young men debated the matter at great length, but finally, having judged the King's counsel to be both sensible and proper, they decided to do what he had recommended. He therefore summoned the steward and spoke with him about the arrangements for the following morning. Then, after dismissing the company until suppertime, he got to his feet.

The ladies and the other two men rose as well, and just as they always did, they devoted themselves to a variety of different pastimes. When the hour for supper arrived, they attended to it with the greatest pleasure, after which they started singing, playing music, and dancing *carole*,[1] and while Lauretta was leading them in a round, the King called for a song from Fiammetta, which she began singing very pleasantly. * * *

* * *

After Fiammetta's song, the company sang many another until the night was already almost half gone. Then, at the King's command, they all went off to rest.

The next day, they arose at dawn, by which time the steward had already sent all their baggage on ahead, and following the lead of their prudent King, they all walked back to Florence. There, taking their leave of the seven women in Santa Maria Novella, from which they had all set out, the three young men went off to pursue other pleasures of theirs, while the ladies in due course returned to their homes.

ST. AUGUSTINE

[Human Life as a Pilgrimage][†]

* * *

There are some things which are to be enjoyed, others which are to be used, others still which enjoy and use. Those things which are objects of enjoyment make us happy. Those things which are objects of use assist and (so to speak) support us in our efforts toward happiness, so that we can attain the things that make us happy and rest in them. We ourselves, who

1. [For a description of carol dances, see above, p. 362, n. 7—*Editors.*]

† From *On Christian Doctrine* I.3–4 (397 C.E.). Adapted from the translation of J. F. Shaw in *A Select Library of the Nicene and Post-Nicene Fathers of the Christian Church,* First Series, vol. 2 (Buffalo: Christian Literature Co., 1887), p. 523.

enjoy and use these things, being placed among both kinds of objects, if we set ourselves to enjoy those which we ought to use, are hindered in our course and sometimes even led away from it; so that, getting entangled in the love of lower gratifications, we lag behind in or even altogether turn back from the pursuit of the real and proper objects of enjoyment.

For to enjoy a thing is to rest with satisfaction in it for its own sake. To use, on the other hand, is to employ whatever means are at one's disposal to obtain what one desires, if it is a proper object of desire; for an unlawful use ought rather to be called an abuse. Suppose, then, we were wanderers in a strange country and could not live happily away from our fatherland, and that we felt wretched in our wandering and, wishing to put an end to our misery, determined to return home. We find, however, that we must make use of some mode of conveyance, either by land or water, in order to reach that fatherland where our enjoyment is to commence. But the beauty of the country through which we pass and the very pleasure of the motion charm our hearts, and turning these things which we ought to use into objects of enjoyment, we become unwilling to hasten the end of our journey; and becoming engrossed in a factitious delight, our thoughts are diverted from that home whose delights would make us truly happy. Thus in this mortal life, wandering from God [see 1 Cor. 5:6], if we wish to return to our Father's home, this world must be used, not enjoyed, so that the invisible things of God may be clearly seen, being understood by the things that are made [see Rom. 1:20]—that is, that by means of what is material and temporary we may take hold of that which is spiritual and eternal.

* * *

SIR WILLIAM THORPE

[On Pilgrimage][†]

* * *

And than he [Archbishop Arundel] said to me, "What saist thou to the thirde poynte that is certified° against the:° preching openly in Shrewisbery that pilgrimage is not lefull?° And over° this thou saidist that those men and women that go on pilgrimagis to Canturbery, to Beverley, to [Bridlington], to Walsingame° and to ony soche other placis, ar acursed and

certified: officially testified / the: thee / lefull: lawful / over: beyond / Walsingame: Walsingham

† Text based on *The examinacion of master W. Thorpe* [1530]. The work is William Thorpe's own account of the inquiry conducted against him by Thomas Arundel, archbishop of Canterbury, for preaching Lollard doctrines in a sermon in Shrewsbury in 1407. The only manuscript in English of Thorpe's account has been edited by Anne Hudson in *Two Wycliffite Texts,* Early English Text Society, original series 301 (Oxford: Oxford UP, 1993). The manuscript is closer to Thorpe's original, but the [1530] printing possesses independent authority, and its updating of spelling and vocabulary makes it more accessible for students. Where needed, we have adapted and put in brackets some readings from Hudson's edition to emend or clarify the meaning of the [1530] text. Unless otherwise indicated, all glosses in this and the following selections are by the editors of this Norton Critical Edition. For background on the Lollard movement, see Anne Hudson, *The Premature Reformation: Wycliffite Texts and Lollard History* (Oxford: Clarendon P, 1988).

made foolisch, spending their goodes in waste."

And I said, "Sir, by this certificacion° I am accused to you that I sholde teache that no pilgrimage is lefull. But I said never thus, for I knowe that ther be trew pilgrimagis and lefull and full plesaunt to God. And therfore, sir, how so ever myne enemies have certified you of me, I tolde at Shrewisbery of two maner of pilgrimagis, [saying that ther be trew pilgrimes and fals pilgrimes]."

official testimony

And the Archebisshop said to me, "Whome callest thou trewe pilgrimes?"

And I said, "Sir, with my protestacion,° I call them trew pilgremis travelyng toward the blisse of heven which—in the state, degre, or ordre that God calleth them [to]—doo besy them° feithfully for to occupie all their wittes, bodely and gostely,° to knowe trewly and to keape feithfully the biddinges of God, hatyng and fleyng all the seven dedely synnes and every braunche of them; reulyng them° verteuously, as it is said before, with all their wittes; doyng discretely, wilfully, and gladly all the werkis of mercy, bodely and gostely,[1] after° their connyng° and power; ablyng them to° the gyftes of the Holy Goste; disposing them to receyve in their soules and to holde therin the eight blessinges of Christe;° beseyng them° to knowe and to kepe the sevene principall vertues. And so than° they shall obteyne herethorow° grace for to use thankfully to God all the condicions of charite; and than they shall be moovyd with the good spirite of God for to examyne ofte and diligently their conscience that nother wilfully nor wittingly they erre° in ony article of beleve,° havyng continually, as frailte will suffer,° all their besinesse to drede and to flee the offence of God, and to loove over all thing and to seke ever to doo his plesaunt will.

solemn, public affirmation
busy themselves
spiritual
governing themselves
according to
knowledge
preparing themselves for
the beatitudes (Matthew 5:3–11)
busying themselves
then
through these (actions)
err / faith
allow

"Of these pilgremis," I said, "what so ever goode thoughte that they ony tyme thinke, what verteuous worde that they speake, and what frutefull worke that they worke: every soche thoughte, worde, and werke is a steppe

1. Thorpe is referring to the traditional categories of the seven corporal acts of mercy (feeding the hungry, giving drink to the thirsty, clothing the naked, helping the sick, visiting the prisoner, sheltering the homeless, burying the dead) and the seven spiritual acts of mercy (admonishing the sinner, instructing the ignorant, counseling the doubtful, comforting the afflicted, bearing wrongs patiently, forgiving injuries, praying for the living and the dead).

noumbered of° God toward hym into hevene. Thes forsaid pilgremis of God delyte sore° whan they heare of seyntis or of verteuous men and women: how they forsoke wilfully the prosperite of this lyfe; how they withstode the suggestion of the fende; how they restreined their fleschly lustes; how discrete they wer in their penaunce doying; how pacient they wer in all their adversites; how prudent they wer in counseling of men and women, moovyng them to hate all synnes and to flye° them, and to shame° ever greatly thereof, and to love all vertues and to drawe to them, ymaginyng how Christe and his folowers—by example of hym—suffered skornis and sclaunders; and how paciently they abode° and toke the wrongfull manasyng° of tyrauntis; how homely° they wer and servisable to poore men to relieve and comforte them, bodely and gostely,° after their power and connyng; and how devote they wer in praiers, how fervent they wer in hevenly desyres, and how they absented them fro spectacles of veyne seyngis° and hearingis; and how stable [of contenaunce they were, how heartely they wailed and sorrowed for synne, how besy] they wer to lett° and to destroye all vices, and how laborious and joifull they wer to sowe and to plante vertues. Thes hevenly condicions and soche other have the pilgremis, or endever them for to have, whose pilgrimagie God acceptith."

by
greatly
flee, avoid
be ashamed
endured
hostility / kindly, modest
spiritually
idle sights
prevent, hinder

"And ageyne[ward],"° I saide, "as their werkis shew, the moste parte of men and women that go now on pilgrimagis have not thes forsaid condicions, nor loveth to besy them feithfully for to have. For as I well know syns I have full ofte assaide:° examyne who so ever will twentie of thes pilgremis, and he shall not fynde thre men or women that knowe surely° a commaundment of God,° nor can say their Pater Noster and Ave Maria nor their Credo redely, in ony maner of langage.[2] And as I have learnid and also know somwhat by experience of thes same pilgremis tellying the cause why that many men and women go hither and thither now on pilgrimagis, it is more for the helthe of their bodies than of their soules, more for to have richesse and prosperite of

on the contrary
tested (it)
correctly
one of the Ten Commandments

2. I.e., either in Latin or in the vernacular.

thys worlde than for to be enryched with vertues in their soules, more to have here worldely and fleschely frendship than for to have frendship of God and of his seintis in heven. For what so ever thing man or woman dothe, the frendship of God nor of ony other seynt can not be hadde without keaping of Goddis commaundementis.

"Forther with my protestacion, I say now as I said in Shrewisbery: though they that have fleschely willes travell [sore]° their bodies and spende mekill° money to seake and to visite the bonys or ymagis (as they say they do) of this seynte or of that, soche pilgrimage-goyng is nother praisable nor thankefull to God nor to ony seinte of God, syns in effect all soche pelgrimes despise God and all his commaundmentis and seyntis. For the commaundmentis of God they will nother knowe nor keape, nor conforme them° to lyve verteously by example of Christe and of his seyntis. Wherfor, syr, I have prechid and taucht openly [and privately]—and so I purpose all my lyfetime to do, with Gods helpe—saing that soche fonde° people wast° blamefully Gods goods in their veyne pilgrimagis, spending their goodes upon vicious hostelars° [and upon tapsters]° which ar ofte unclene° women of their bodies, and at the leste those goodes with the which thei sholde doo werkis of mercie, after° Goddis bidding, to poore nedy men and women.

greatly exert
much
themselves
foolish
waste
innkeepers / barmaids
unchaste
according to

"Thes poore mennis goodes and their lyvelode° thes runnars about° offer to riche priestis, which have mekill more lyvelode than they neade. And thus those goodes they waste wilfully and spende them unjustely, ageinst Goddis bidding, upon straungers, with which thei sholde helpe and releve, after° Goddis will, their poore nedy neighbours at home. Ye, and over° this foly, ofte tymes diverse men and women of thes runners° thus madly hither and thither in to pilgrimage borowe hereto° other mennis goodes—ye, and some tyme they stele mennis goodes hereto—and they pay them never agein.

livelihood, sustenance
wanderers
according to
beyond
"runners about"
for this (purpose)

"Also, sir, I know well that whan diverse men and women will go thus after their own willes, and fynding out one pilgrimage, they will orden° with them before° to have with them bothe men and women that can well synge wanton songes; and some other pilgremis will have with them baggepipes, so that every

arrange / in advance

towne that they come throwe°—what with the noyse of their syngyng, and with the sounde of their piping, and with the jangelyng of their Canterbery bellis, and with the barkyng out of doggis after them—that they make more noyse than if the kyng came there awaye° with all his clarions° and many other menstrelles. And if thes men and women be a monethe° out in their pilgrimage, many of them shall be, an halfe yeare after, greate jangelers,° tale tellers, and lyers."°

through
along that route
trumpeters
month
chatterers
liars

And the Archebishop said to me, "Leude losell,° thou seest not ferre ynough in this mater, for thou considerest not the great travell° of pilgremys, therfore thou blamest that thing that is praisable. I say to the° that it is right well done that pilgremys have with them bothe syngers and also pipers, that whan one of them that goeth barfote striketh his too° upon a stone and hurteth hym sore and maketh hym to blede, it is well done that he or his felow begyn than° a songe, or els take out of his bosome a baggepype, for to dryve away with soche myrthe the hurte of his felow. For with soche salace° the travell and werinesse off pylgremes is lightely and merily broughte forthe."°

Ignorant scoundrel
travail
thee
toe
then
solace
relieved

And I said, "Sir, Seynt Paule teacheth men to wepe with them that wepe [Romans 12:15]."

And the Archebishoppe [scorned me and] saide, "What janglist thou° ageinst mennis devocion? Whatsoever thou or soch other say, I say that the pilgrimage that now is used° is to them that doo it a praysable and a good meane to come the rather° to grace. But I holde the unable to know this grace, for thou enforsest the to lett° the devocion of the people, syns by authorite of Holy Scripture men maye lefully° have and use soche solace as thou reprovest. For David in his laste psalme teacheth men to have diverse instrumentes of musike for to prayse therwith God."

Why dost thou chatter
practiced
sooner, more readily
attemptest to hinder
lawfully

And I saide, "Sir, by the sentence° of diverse doctours expounding the psalmes of David, the musike and menstrelcy that David and other seyntes of the olde lawe spake of owe° now nother to be taken nor used by the letter.° But thes instrumentes with theire musike ought to be interpreted gostely,° for all those figures are called vertues and grace, with which vertues men shold please God and prayse his

according to the understanding
ought
literally
spiritually

name. For Saynt Paule saith, 'All soche thynges befell to them in figure.'[3] Therfore, sir, I understonde that the letter of this psalme of David, and of soche other psalmes and sentences, dothe slee them that take them now letterally. This sentence I understond, sir, Christ approveth him self, putting out the menstrelles or° that he wolde quycken° the deade damsell."

before

bring to life

And the Archebishop saide to me, "Leude losell, is it not lefull to us to have organes in the chirche for to worship therwithall God?"

And I said, "Ye, syr, by mannys ordynaunce;° but by the ordinaunce of God a goode sermonne to the peoples understondying were mekill more plesaunt to God."

decree

And the Archebisshoppe sayde that organes and goode delectable songe quyckened° and sharpened more mennys wyttes than sholde ony sermonne. But I said, "Sir, lusty° men and worldly lovers delyte and covete and travell to have all theire wittes quickened and sharpened with diverse sensible° solace; but all the feithfull lovers and folowers of Christe have all their delyte to heare Goddis worde, and to understond it truely, and to worke therafter faithfully and continually. For no doute, to dreade to offende God and to love to please him in all thing quyckeneth and sharpeneth all the wittes of Christes chosen people, and ableth° them so to grace that they joye greatly to withdrawe [their eyes], their eares and all their wittes and membres frome all worldly delyte and frome all fleschly solace. For Seynt Jerome, as I thinke, saith, 'Nobody may joye with this worlde and reigne with Christe.'"[4]

(have) awakened

pleasure-loving

sensual

aids

And the Archebishop, as yf he had ben displeased with myne answere, said to his clerkes, "What gesse ye this ydiote will speke ther wher he hath none dreade, syns he speaketh thus nowe, here in my presence? Well, well, by God thou shalt be ordened for!"°

dealt with

* * *

3. By "figures" Thorpe means the details in Psalm 150 that invite an allegorical rather than a literal reading. His interpretation is consistent with those of many medieval "doctours," such as St. Augustine, who in his *Enarrationes in psalmos* explains that the instruments named in the psalm refer to various aspects of the human soul or the community of souls that worship God. They are "figures" of virtues. After citing 1 Corinthians 10:11, Thorpe alludes to Paul's famous teaching that "the letter killeth, but the spirit giveth life" (2 Corinthians 3:6). His allusion to Christ putting out the minstrels refers to Matthew 9:23–25, part of the story of Jairus's daughter, which is told more fully but without the mention of minstrels in Mark 5:22–43.
4. As Hudson's note explains, this quotation is actually from St. Gregory.

THOMAS WIMBLEDON

[On the Estates]†

My dere ferendis, ye shullen undirstonde that Crist Jesus, auctour and doccour° of trewthe, in his book of the gospel liknyng° the kyngdom of hevene to an housholdere, seith on this maneres:° "Lik is the kyngdom of hevene to an housholdynge man that wente out first on the morwe° to hire werkemen into his vine.° Also aboute the thridde,° sixte, nyenthe, and elevene houris he wente out and fond men stondynge ydel° and sey to hem: Go yee into my vyne and that right is° I wole yeve° yow. Whanne the day was ago, he clepid° his styward and heet° to yeve eche man a peny."

teacher / *comparing* / *in this way* / *morning / vineyard* / *third* / *idle* / *what is just / give* / *called* / *commanded (him)*

To spiritual undirstondyng this housholdere is oure lord Jesu Crist, that "is heed of the houshold of holi chirche."[1] And thus he clepith men in diverse houris of the day, that is in diverse ages of the world; os° in tyme of lawe of kynde° he clepide by enspirynge Abel, Ennok, Noe,° and Abraham; in tyme of the olde lawe Moyses, David, Ysaye,° and Jeremie;° and in tyme of grace apostelis, martiris, and confessoures,[2] and virgines. Also he clepeth men in diverse ages: summe in childhood, as Jon Baptist; summe on stat° of wexenge,° as Jon the Evangelist; summe in stat of manhod, as Petir and Andrew; and summe in old age, as Gamaliel and Josep of Aramathie.° And alle these he clepith to travayle on his vyne, that is the chirche, and that on diverse maneres.

as / *nature* / *Noah* / *Isaiah / Jeremiah* / *in the process / maturing* / *Joseph of Arimathea*

For right as yee seeth that in tilienge° of the material vine there beeth diverse laboreris: for summe kuttyn awey the voyde° braunchis; summe maken forkes° and rayles to beren up the veyne; and summe diggen awey the olde erthe fro the rote and leyn° there fattere.° And alle theise offices° ben so nescessarie to the veyne that yif eny of hem fayle° it schal harme gretly or distroye the vyne. For but yif° the

tilling / *unproductive* / *forked stakes* / *put / richer (soil)* / *duties* / *are lacking* / *unless*

† Text based on *Wimbledon's Sermon "Redde Rationem Villicationis Tue": A Middle-English Sermon of the Fourteenth Century*, ed. Ione Kemp Knight (Pittsburgh: Duquesne UP, 1967), pp. 61–66. Reprinted with permission of the editor. This opening passage of the sermon is based on the parable of the vineyard (Matthew 20:1–10). Notes are by the editors of this Norton Critical Edition.

1. Colossians 1:18.
2. Christians who heroically affirm their faith in the face of persecution but escape martyrdom.

vine be kut, he° schal wexe wilde; but yif she *it*
be rayled, she shal be overgoo° with netles and *overrun*
wedis; and but yif the rote be fettid° with *enriched*
donge, she for feblenesse shold wexe barayne.

Ryght so in the chirche beeth nedeful° thes *necessary*
thre offices: presthod, knyghthod, and labore-
ris. To prestis it fallith° to kutte awey the voide *it is proper*
braunchis of synnis with the swerd of here
tonge. To knyghtis it fallith to lette° wrongis *stop*
and theftis to be do,° and to mayntene Goddis *from being done*
lawe and hem that ben techeris ther-of, and
also to kepe the lond fro enemyes of other
londes. And to laboreris it falleth to travayle
bodily and with here sore swet geten out of the
erthe bodily liflode° for hem and for other par- *sustenance*
ties. And these statis° beth also° nedeful to the *estates / so*
chirche that non may wel ben withouten other.
For yif presthod lackede,° the puple for *were missing*
defaute° of knowyng of Goddis lawe shulde *lack*
wexe wilde on vices and deie gostly.° And yif *die spiritually*
the knythod lackid and men to reule the puple
by lawe and hardnesse,° theves and enemies *resoluteness*
shoden so encresse that no man sholde lyven
in pes.° And yif the laboreris weren not, bothe *peace*
prestis and knyghtis mosten bicome acremen° *plowmen*
and heerdis,° and ellis° they sholde for defaute *shepherds / or otherwise*
of bodily sustenaunce deie.

And herfore seith a gret clerk,° Avycenne,[3] *scholar*
that every unresonable beest, yif he have that
that kynde° hath ordeyned for hym as kynde *nature*
hath ordeyned it, he is sufficiaunt to lyve by
hymself withouten eny other of the same
kynde.° As yif there were but one hors other° *species / or*
oon sheep in the world, yit yif he hadde graas
and corn° as kynde hath ordeyned for suche *grain*
bestes, he shulde lyve wel inow.° But yif ther *enough*
were but oon man in the world, though he
hadde all that good that is therin, yit for
defaute he scholde die, or his life shulde be
worse than yif he were nought.° And the cause *did not exist*
is this: for thyng that kynde ordeyneth for a
mannis sustinaunce, withoutyn other araying° *preparation*
than it hath of kynde, acordith° nought to *suits*
hym. As though a man have corn as it cometh
fro the erthe, yit it is no mete acordynge to° *suitable food for*
hym into° it be by mannis craft chaungid into *until*
bred. And though he have flesche other fis-
sche, yit while it is raw, as kynde ordeyneth it,

3. This paragraph follows closely the beginning of Avicenna's *Liber de anima seu sextus de naturalibus*, part 5, chapter 1.

forto° it be by mannis travayle sothen,° rosted, other bake, it acordith not to mannis liflode. And ryght so wolle° that the sheep berith mot,° by many diverse craftis and travaylis, be chaungid er° it be able to clothe eny man. And certis° o° man bi hymsilf shulde nevere don alle thise labouris. And therfore seith this clerk, it is nede that summe beth acremen,° summe bakeris, summe makeris of cloth, and summe marchaundis to fecche that that o lond fauteth° from another ther it is plente.

until / boiled · *wool / must* · *before* · *certainly / one* · *plowmen* · *lacks*

And certis this shulde be o cause why every staat shul love other and men of o craft shulde neither hate ne despise men of another craft, sith° they beth so nedeful everych to other. And ofte thilke° craftis that semen most unhonest myghthen worst° be forbore.° And o thyng y dar wel seye: that he that is neither traveylynge in this world on prayeris and prechynge for helpe of the puple, as it fallith to prestis; neither° in fyghtinge ayenis tyrauntis and enemyes, as it fallith to knyghtis; neither travaylynge on the erthe, as it fallith to laboreris—whanne the day of his rekenyng° cometh (that is, the ende of this lif), ryght as he lyvede here withoutyn travayle, so he shal there lacke the reward of the peny (that is, the endeles joye of hevene). And as he was here lyvynge aftir noon staat° ne ordre, so he shal be put thanne "in that place that noon ordre is inne, but evere-lastynge horrour"[4] and sorwe (that is, in helle).

since · *those* · *least well / dispensed with* · *nor* · *accounting* · *according to no estate*

WILLIAM LANGLAND

[On Monks]†

"Amonges rightful religious this rule shulde be holde.[1]
Gregory, the grete clerke° and the goode Pope,
Of religiouns the rule reherseth° in his *Moralia*,[2]
And seith it in ensample° that thei shulde do°
therafter:

scholar · *rehearses, expounds* · *as an example / follow*

4. Job 10:22.

† From *Piers Plowman: A Norton Critical Edition*, trans. E. Talbot Donaldson, ed. Elizabeth Robertson and Stephen H. A. Shepherd (New York: W. W. Norton, 2006), p. 154 (B text, Passus X, lines 297–327). Copyright © 2006 by W. W. Norton & Company, Inc. Used by permission of W. W. Norton & Company, Inc. This version of the poem was probably written in the late 1370s. We have altered the text and punctuation slightly; the notes and glosses are ours.

1. Among righteous members of the religious orders (monks, friars, and nuns), this rule should be kept. The speaker is "Clergy," a personification of Learning.

2. The *Moralia*, a long commentary on the Book of Job and one of the best-known works of Pope Gregory the Great (ca. 540–604).

'Whan fisshes faillen the flode° or the fressh water, *lack the river*
Thei deye for drought whan thei drye ligge;° *lie dry*
Right so by religioun, it roileth° and sterveth° *wanders / dies*
That out of covent° and cloistre° coveiten *convent / cloister, i.e., monastery*
to libbe.'° *desires to live*
For if Hevene be on this erthe and ese° to any soule, *ease, rest*
It is in cloistre or in scole,[3] by many skiles° I fynde. *for many reasons*
For in cloistre cometh no man to carpe° ne to fighte, *talk, chatter*
But al is buxumnesse° there and bokes, to rede and to lerne. *obedience*
In scole there is scorne but if° a clerke wil lerne, *unless*
And grete love and lykynge, for eche loweth hym° to *humbles himself*
other.
Ac now is Religioun a ryder, a renner bi stretes,[4]
A leder of lovedayes[5] and a londe-bugger,° *purchaser of land*
A priker° on a palfray fro place° to maner,° *rider / house / manor*
An heep of houndes at his ers° as° he a lorde were, *arse / as if*
And but if his knave° knele that shal his cuppe bringe, *serving boy*
He loureth on° hym and lakketh° hym: 'Who *scowls at / criticizes*
lered° hym curteisye?' *taught*
Litel had lordes to donn to yyve londe fram her heires[6]
To religious that have no reuthe° though it reyne° *do not care / rain*
on here auteres.° *their altars*
In many places ther thei persones ben,° *where they are appointed parsons*
be thei purelich at ese,° *when they are wholly at their ease*
Of the pore have thei no pité, and that is her
pure charite;° *(their idea of) perfect charity*
Ac thei leten hem as lordes,° her land lith *think of themselves as lords*
so brode.° *extends so far*
Ac there shal come a kyng and confesse° yow *to hear a confession from*
religiouses,
And bete° yow as the Bible telleth, for brekynge of *beat, chastise*
yowre reule,
And amende monyales,° monkes, and chanouns,° *nuns / canons*
And putten hem to her penaunce, *Ad pristinum statum ire*;[7]
And barounes with erles° beten hem thorugh *barons together with earls*
Beatus virres techynge;[8]
Bynymen that here barnes claymen° and *Seize what their children claim*
blame yow foule."° *shamefully*

3. Monastic school, or university.
4. But now Religion (i.e., the monastic orders) is a rider of horses and a roamer in the streets.
5. An arbitrator on lovedays, days when disputes were heard out of court. See *General Prologue*, l. 258.
6. Lords had little reason to transfer property from their heirs.
7. Latin: In order to return (them) to their original state (within the rule).
8. According to the teaching "Blessed is the man." Clergy refers to the opening words of Psalm 1 in the Vulgate Bible. King David was thought to be the divinely inspired author of all (or most of) the Psalms.

JOHN GOWER

[On Monks][†]

We now consider the estate of the religious orders, and first those that hold property. They should be attentive in praying to the glorious God, within their cloisters and monasteries, for us secular people. That is the function of their order, for which they are abundantly endowed with a full measure of goods so that they do not desire to seek elsewhere for money. St. Augustine says in his teaching that just as a fish lives only in water, so Religion must lead its life according to the rule of the convent, fully obedient and cloistered. For if it lives in the world, then it alters the nature of the order that was first established, and consequently respect for the profession is lost.

In following the original order, monks took vows against the pleasures of the flesh and endured the pain of a harsh life. But now those observances have been completely abandoned. Gluttony guards all the doors so that hunger and thirst do not enter in there to make the fat paunches lean. With fur cloaks they have kept out the agonies of cold weather, for they do not wish to make its acquaintance. The old rule regularly ate fish, but this one wants to change that: when meat that has been finely chopped or well pounded in a mortar is prepared and served, the new rule maintains that such ground meat is not flesh. It hopes to deceive God but is itself deceived, for it cherishes the belly so much that rather than lose a single meal, which might make the body grow thinner, it neglects the well-being of the soul. I do not know if the monks dance or joust, but I know well that when one of them takes his large flagon filled with wine, he downs it with great boisterousness and says that is the proper rule. I do not mean St. Augustine's: it is the rule of Robin,[1] who leads the life of a raven, searching first for what he can gulp down to fill himself and giving no thought to his neighbor, just the way a mastiff devours everything down to the crumbs and crust. * * *

The monk who has been made guardian or steward of any outside property is not a good cloisterer, for then he needs a horse and saddle to get around the countryside, and he spends lavishly. He takes the best part of the grain for himself and leaves the chaff for others, such as peasants; and thus the foolish, proud monk behaves like a lord. But an empty barn and a full belly do not yield an even balance. When he is guardian of an estate,

† Translated by Glending Olson, from *Mirour de l'omme,* lines 20833–92 and 20953–1060, in *The Works of John Gower,* ed. G. C. Macaulay (Oxford: Clarendon P, 1899–1902), vol. 1, pp. 235–37. There is a complete English translation by William Burton Wilson (East Lansing: Colleagues P, 1992). These two excerpts contain the closest parallels to Chaucer's portrait of the Monk; they constitute about half of Gower's criticism of the monastic orders. The poem, whose title means *Mirror of Man,* is a didactic one in French, of which 29,444 lines survive; it was written ca. 1376–78. It begins with an allegory on the origins of sin, treats at length the seven vices and seven virtues, and then offers a critical survey of London life in the 1370s. Chaucer was a close friend of Gower, naming him as one of two persons legally authorized to act on his behalf during his second trip to Italy in 1378 and codedicating *Troilus and Criseyde* to him ("O moral Gower") and the "philosophical Strode" (Ralph Strode, a renowned Oxford logician).

1. Robin is a standard medieval name for a man of the lower classes and often carries the suggestion of low morals as well. It is the name of Chaucer's Miller and, in the *Miller's Tale,* of John's servant.

the monk says "Everything is ours" out of twisted charity; he speaks the truth in part, but only a little, for with his wicked appetite he wants for himself more than what seven others get. Surely the cloister is better for such a guardian than ownership of property, which only takes income away from others. As St. Bernard says, it is repugnant to see an overseer in a monk's habit. The monk who acts this way is half worldly, and he comes close to apostasy when he has taken possession of the world again and dispossessed himself of the cloister. I do not know how he can justify himself for this failure of rule, nor do I think that his control of land and income can be security for him before God, to whom he first pledged his faith when he became a monk.

St. Jerome tells us that the filthiness of the habit a monk wears is an outward sign that he is without pride and haughtiness, that his inner spirit is of a pure white spotlessness. But our monk of today regularly seeks fancy adornment for his body and disfigures his soul. Although he wears the habit of suffering, he also has, in his vanity, a coat adorned with fur. There is a story that a great nobleman loved by God dressed himself in wretched haircloth when King Manasses married his daughter; even on that occasion he would not sacrifice his simplicity but rather directed his actions more to pleasing God than man. Thus he set an example for others: one should not attend to the body so much that he becomes proud. I do not know how monks will react to this story, but the example should disquiet that monk who behaves luxuriously because of worldliness. He seeks not haircloth but the very best wool he can find, trimmed with gray squirrel fur, for he disdains fleece. Nor does he forget a silver pendant but gaily displays it hanging from his hood on his breast. That is the kind of simplicity we see now in monks and their dress.

A monk should nurture his religion through discretion, humility, and simplicity; but ours does not want to do that. He hates to hear the name of monk, which he vowed to take, even though his mother was a shepherdess and his father without high rank, perhaps a servant. But when those of low status rise to the heights, and poverty becomes wealthy, there is nothing in the world so villainous. The monk who seeks property sins greatly against the rule, but he has nevertheless amassed great sums for himself, wealth which he procured from the world just like a merchant. And moreover, to entertain himself, he goes along the river with game birds, falcon and molted hawk, with swift greyhounds as well, and fine high-spirited horses—all that is missing is a wife. And on the subject of wives, what can I do but wonder, for I have heard about the children that our monk accumulated while he was running around here and there, day after day. But they cannot inherit from him, so he must pass along great sums in order to enrich them. I leave it to you to decide if this is the way charity acts.

* * *

Wycliffite Estates Criticism†

[*On Merchants*]

* * *

Also marchauntis and riche men of this wikked world fallen in moche ypocrise; for thei traveilen nyght and day, bi watir and lond, in cold and in hete, bi false sotilis° and cautelis° and grete sweringes nedles° and false, for to gete muche drit° or muk of this world, to gete riche wyves, and purchase° londis and rentis,° and dewelle° in pore mennus dette after that thei han desceyved hem in byynge of here catel.° And yit ben° so bisi in thought and speche, in goyng and rydyng abouten this muk, that unnethe° may thei onys° thenke on God and han mynde of° here false robberie that thei usen° bi false wettes° and mesures to amende hem.° Yif alle here° bisinesse and love goo thus wrongly to the world and nought or to litel to hevene and hevenely thingis, thei failen foule of° holy lif; and yit holden hem self holy and coveiten to ben holden holy of° other men, and ben wode° yif men speken treuly ayenst here cursed synnes. But certes this is ypocrisie.

tricks / wiles
needless
dirt, filth
acquire / revenues / linger
goods / they are
scarcely
once / reflect on
practice
weights / prosper / their
in
by / mad, angry

[*On Pardoners and Priests*]

Thei [curates, clergymen in charge of a parish] assenten° to pardoners disceyvynge the peple in feith and charite and worldly goodis for to have part of here gederynge,° and letten° prestis to preche° the gospel for drede laste° here synne and ypocrisie be knowen and stoppid. For whanne there cometh a pardoner with stollen bullis and false relekis,° grauntynge mo yeris of pardon than comen bifore domes day for yevynge° of worldly catel° to riche placis where is no nede, he schal be sped° and resceyved of° curatis for to have part of that° he

consent
winnings / prevent
from preaching / lest
relics
giving / goods
aided
received by / what

† Text based on *The English Works of John Wyclif Hitherto Unprinted,* ed. F. D. Matthew, 2nd ed., Early English Text Society, original series 74 (London, 1902), pp. 24–25, 154. Wyclif (ca. 1329–1384) was briefly Master of Balliol College, Oxford (1361) and, as philosopher, theologian, and reformer, a most controversial figure in his time. He was first prosecuted for heresy in 1377 and again in 1382, when he was condemned for ten heresies and fourteen theological errors. But his criticism of corruption in the church and in the estates expressed attitudes shared by many of his contemporaries, including those—a majority—who did not necessarily interest themselves in, or subscribe to, his views on the powers of the Pope, "dominion by Grace," or his denial of the truth of Transubstantiation. Many of the English tracts credited to him are in fact by his followers.

getith. But a preste that wole telle the trewthe to alle men withouten glosynge° and frely withouten beggynge of° the pore peple, he schal be lettid by sotil cavyllacions° of mannus lawe, for drede last° he touche the sore of here conscience and cursed lif. And this pardoner schalle telle of more power than evere Crist grauntid to Petir or Poul or ony apostle, to drawe the almes fro pore bedrede° neigheboris that ben knowen feble and pore, and to gete it to hem self and wasten it ful synfulli in ydelnesse and glotonye and lecherie, and senden gold out of oure lond to riche lordis and housis where is no nede, and make oure lond pore by many sotile weies. And here bi° the peple is more bold to lien° stille in her synne, and weneth° not to have as myche thank and reward of Crist for to do° here almes to pore feble men—as Crist biddith in the gospel—as whanne thei don here almes to riche housis aftir graunt° of synful foolis. And this is opyn errour ayenst Cristene feith.

glossing, distorting
from
subtle cavils
lest
bedridden
hereby
remain
think
give
following the advice

The Miller's Prologue and Tale

Although there are a number of analogues to individual motifs in the *Miller's Tale*, only one story that survives from Chaucer's age contains all the major plot elements. It is a Flemish fabliau, titled *The Three Guests of Heile of Bersele* in Constance B. Hieatt's translation (New York: Odyssey Press, 1970). In *Sources and Analogues of the* Canterbury Tales, Vol. 2, ed. Robert M. Correale and Mary Hamel (Woodbridge: D. S. Brewer, 2005), pp. 249–75, Peter G. Beidler prints *Heile* and an English translation by Henk Aertsen; he argues that Chaucer probably knew enough Middle Dutch to have been able to read the story, and that even though neither tale can be dated precisely, *Heile* probably antedated the *Miller's Tale* and influenced its composition. More distant and partial analogues are available in *Sources and Analogues of Chaucer's* Canterbury Tales, ed. W. F. Bryan and Germaine Dempster (New York: Humanities Press, 1958), pp. 106–23, and in *The Literary Context of Chaucer's Fabliaux*, ed. Larry D. Benson and Theodore M. Andersson (Indianapolis: Bobbs-Merrill, 1971), pp. 3–77. Chaucer's story is rich with personal and domestic details usually lacking in the fabliau tradition, of which *Heile* is a fairly typical representative.

The Three Guests of Heile of Bersele†

You have often heard tales of all manner of things, told or sung to the tune of a fiddle or harp; but I think few will have heard of such a strange case as one which happened here in Antwerp some time ago. I will tell you about it at the request of a boon companion of mine; he wouldn't let me off.

Here in the market street in Antwerp, there lived, I recall, a fine wench, and she was called Heile of Bersele. She often made love, for a price, with good fellows to whom she displayed her arts. It fell out once, as I heard the story, that three such fellows came to her on the same day, one after the other, all three asking her that for the sake of friendship she would let them come where she lived: each wanted to speak to her alone, in secret. This was good business for Heile, who determined to satisfy all three.

The first one she made an appointment with was a miller called William Hoeft. She told him to come as soon as evening fell. The second was a priest; she told him to come when the curfew-bell rang. She told the third, a smith who was a neighbor of hers, to come when the clock struck midnight. This satisfied all three, and they all went their way happily, awaiting the proper time.

At twilight, William came promptly. Heile received him graciously and made him quite at home. They played the game of love—she knew that

† From Constance B. Hieatt, ed., *The Miller's Tale*, by Geoffrey Chaucer (New York: Odyssey Press, 1970), pp. 51–54.

business well—and thus they lay taking their pleasure until it was time for curfew.

As the bell rang out for curfew, the priest came, all eagerness, saying, "Heile, let me in! I am here: you know who."

"Good heavens, Heile," said William, "who is that there?"

"I don't know, William," she answered, "but it seems to me it's the priest. He is supposed to instruct me and mend my faults."

"Oh, dear Heile," William cried, "quick—where can I run so that the priest can't see me?"

Heile said, "Up above there is a trough which I have found useful at various times before. It is tied to the rafters with a good sound rope. You'll be better off there than anywhere else."

William hid himself in the trough and told her to let the priest in. Heile then made her second guest comfortable. After they had done the wide-awake dance three times, the priest began to discourse on the gospels. He said that the time would soon come when God would bring judgment upon the world, coming with water and fire; and that everyone—high and low, young and old—should drown.

William, sitting overhead in the trough, heard all this, and believed that it might well be true: the priests taught it, and the gospel bore witness to it.

But meanwhile Hugh, the smith, came; he thought he had waited quite long enough, and a good deal longer than he had wished. He gave a soft knock at the door. Heile said, "Who is there?"

"Why indeed, Heile, it's me," he replied.

Heile answered, "You can't come in."

"But Heile, my love, are you going to break your promise? I have to speak to you!"

"That you shall not," said Heile, "right now, for I am unwell. You cannot come in at this time."

"Ah, dear Heile, then I beg you, let me at least kiss your mouth right now."

Then Heile said to the priest, "Now, sir, let this fellow kiss your behind: he will certainly think it's me, and nobody else."

"Marvelous!" said the priest. "A splendid jest!" And he jumped right up and quickly put his tail out the window. Hugh, thinking that it was Heile, kissed the priest's arse with such ardour that his nose pushed right inside and he was caught, it seemed to him, like a mouse in a trap. He was thrown into a frenzy of rage: he was not so dull that he could not tell, from the feel and smell of the thing, that he had kissed an arse, for the mouth seemed to be set the wrong way between cheeks above and below.

"By Christ," he said to himself, "I'll come back!"

He ran as though he were mad to his house nearby and quickly picked up a huge iron. He thrust it into the fire until it was so hot that it glowed brightly, then ran with it to Heile's door, crying, "Heile, my love, let me in now, or at least let me kiss your little mouth: one or the other, or I'll stand here all night. The strength of my love for you forces me to it!"

The priest, hearing his cue, again put his hind passage out where it had been before. Without hesitating, the smith struck the glowing iron into his arse. Then the priest sang his verse loud and clear: "Water, water! Oh, I am dead," he cried at length, until the words died out in his mouth.

William, who lay hidden above, was greatly alarmed for he thought, "What the priest predicted tonight has now come true—surely the water has come and all the earth shall now be drowned! But if I can float away from here, the trough will save my life." Grasping his knife, he cut through the rope by which the trough was hanging, and said, "Now may God and good fortune aid William Hoeft in his voyage!"

Down to the ground came William, trough and all, with such a crash that he was badly hurt—both his arm and his thigh were broken. Now the priest, thinking that the devil had come, scooted off into a corner, where he fell into a privy. They say that he came home covered with filth, burned in the arse, and held up to scorn and shame. It would have been far better for him if he had stayed home and said his prayers!

That was what happened to Heile's guests. The smith had a setback, but he found good consolation for that in burning the priest's hole—he was well revenged.

Saving your dignity, let it be said that whoever keeps company with whores will surely find strife, harm, shame, and sorrow coming upon him. The guests of Heile found this out.

The Reeve's Prologue and Tale

The cradle-trick story that forms the central episode of the *Reeve's Tale* was popular throughout the later Middle Ages and Renaissance, and a number of analogues survive. *The Miller and the Two Clerics*, a thirteenth-century French fabliau, is the closest to Chaucer. For texts and translations of other medieval versions, including a story from Boccaccio's *Decameron*, see *The Literary Context of Chaucer's Fabliaux*, ed. Larry D. Benson and Theodore M. Andersson (Indianapolis: Bobbs-Merrill, 1971), pp. 79–201, and Peter G. Beidler's chapter on the *Reeve's Tale* analogues in *Sources and Analogues of the* Canterbury Tales, vol. 1, ed. Robert M. Correale and Mary Hamel (Woodbridge: D. S. Brewer, 2002), pp. 23–73.

The Miller and the Two Clerics†

There were once two poor fellows of the minor clergy who were born in the same region and in the same city. They were friends and deacons of a woodland church, where they found a living, until, as happens often and again, they fell on hard times, which is a great pity for poor people. They were heavy at heart when they considered their state of affairs, nor did they see any way out of it. For they did not know how to earn their living, either in their own country or anywhere else, and they were ashamed to beg their bread out of regard for their order, as well as for other reasons. They had no possessions by which they might keep themselves alive, and they didn't know where to turn.

One Sunday they met outside the church, and they went for a walk about the town in order to talk things over. "Listen to me," one of them said to the other, "we are helpless because we cannot earn our livings; and now hunger, which vanquishes everything, has got hold of us. Nobody can defend us against it, and we have nothing to draw upon. Have you put by anything at all by which we might keep ourselves going?" The other one answered: "By Saint Denis, I can't think of anything except that I have a friend to whom I suggest we go and ask for a bushel of wheat at the current price; he will very willingly give me credit, and at long term, until Saint John's Day, to tide us over this bad year." Then the first one said: "That's a piece of luck for us; for I have a brother who owns a fat mare. I'll go get her while you get the wheat, and we'll become bakers. There is no load too shameful to bear if it will get us through this bad year." And they did this without further delay.

† From *Fabliaux: Ribald Tales from the Old French*, trans. Robert Hellman and Richard O'Gorman, (New York: HarperCollins, 1965), pp. 51–57. Copyright © 1965 by Robert Hellman and Richard O'Gorman. Reprinted by permission of HarperCollins Publishers Inc.

Then they brought their wheat to the mill, which was at a great distance, more than two leagues away. It was a mill with a millrace near a little wood. There was no town or farm or any house nearby except the house of the miller, who knew his trade only too well. The clerics undid the gate at once and threw their sacks inside. Then they put their mare in a meadow by the millrace. One of them remained outside to keep an eye on things, and the other went in to get the miller started at their work. But the miller had gone into hiding. He had indeed seen the clerics coming, and I think he wanted a part of their wheat.

When the cleric came running into the miller's house, he found his wife at her spinning. "Lady," he said, "by Saint Martin, where is the owner of the mill? He ought to come and help us." "Sir cleric," said she, "it's no trouble at all. You will find him in that wood right near the mill, if you will be so kind as to go there." And the cleric set out quickly to find him. His friend, who was waiting for him, grew impatient that he stayed so long and came running into the house. "Lady," he said, "for the love of God, where has my companion gone?" "Sir," said she, "on my honor, he went in search of my husband who has just left the house." So she sent one cleric after the other, while the miller came around quickly to the mill. With his wife's help he took both sacks and mare and hid them in his barn. Then he returned to the mill.

The two clerics looked everywhere, and finally they also returned to the mill. "Miller," they said, "God be with you! For the love of God, help us out." "My lords," said he, "how may I do so?" "In faith, with the wheat we have here." But, when they went to get the wheat, they found neither sacks nor mare. They looked at one another. "What's this?" said one. "We are robbed!" "Yes," said the other, "so it seems to me. For our sins we are undone!" Then both cried out: "Alas! Alas! Help us, Nicholas!" "What's wrong with you?" said the miller. "Why do you cry so loud?" "Miller, we have surely lost everything. A misfortune has befallen us, for we have neither mare nor anything. And that was our whole fortune." "Lords," said the miller, "I know nothing about this." "Sir," they said, "there's nothing you can do except to tell us where we may go to look for what we have lost." "Lords," he said, "I can't help you very much, but go look in that wood there near the mill." The two clerics set out and at once went into the woods; and the miller went his way.

They looked high and low until the sun had set; and then one of the clerics said to the other: "Surely it is truly said that he's a fool who puts himself out for nothing. Wealth comes and goes like straws blown by the wind. Let's go find a lodging for the night." "And where shall we go?" "To the miller's, in whose mill we were. May God grant us lodging in Saint Martin's name!"

They went straight to the miller's house; but he was not pleased at their coming. At once he asked them: "What has Saint Nicholas done for you?" "Miller," they said, "not one thing or another." "Then," said he, "you'd better earn other goods. For what you've lost is a long way off; you won't have it for present needs." "Miller," they said, "that may well be. But put us up for Saint Sylvester's sake. We don't know where else to go at this hour." The miller took thought and decided that he would be worse than a dog if he didn't provide something for them out of their own belongings, as he was well able. "My lords," he said, "I have nothing but the floor to offer you; that you shall have and nothing more." "Miller," they said, "that is enough."

The peasant did not have many in his household. With himself there were only four: his daughter, who deserves to be mentioned first, his wife, and a little baby. The daughter was beautiful and charming, and to protect her against her own warmth, the miller put her in a cupboard every night, and there she slept. The miller would lock her in and pass her the key through an opening, and then he would go to bed.

But let us return to our clerics. In the evening at suppertime, the miller brought bread and milk and eggs and cheese, country fare, and he gave each of the clerics a good share. One of them supped with the maiden and the other with the miller and his wife. In the hearth was a little andiron with a ring on it that could be taken off and put back again. The cleric who ate with the maiden took the ring from the andiron and hid it well. That night, when they went to bed, the cleric watched the daughter carefully and saw how the miller locked her in the cupboard and threw her the key.

When they had settled down for the night, the cleric nudged his companion and said: "Friend, I want to go and speak to the miller's daughter, who is locked up in the cupboard." "Do you want to start a quarrel," said the other, "and stir up a tempest in the house? Truth is you are a rogue. Evil can soon come of this." "Even if I die," said the first, "I must go and see if I can make anything of her." He quickly jumped out of bed and went straight to the cupboard. He drew near it and scratched on it a little, and she heard him. "Who is it out there?" she said. "It is he who for your sake is so grieved and so unhappy that, unless you have pity on him, he will never feel joy again. It is he with whom you supped and who brings you a gold ring—you never had such a treasure. It is known and proved that its stone has such power that any woman, no matter how light she may be or how she may wanton about, will remain a virgin if she has it on her finger in the morning. Here, I make you a gift of it." At once she held out the key to him; and he quickly unlocked the chest. He got in and she squeezed over. And so they could take their pleasure, for there was no one to disturb them.

Before daybreak the miller's wife got up from beside her husband and all naked went into the courtyard. And she passed before the cleric where he lay abed. When he saw her go by, he thought of his friend who was taking his pleasure in the cupboard, and he had a great longing for the same kind of pleasure. He thought he would trick the wife on her way back. But then he thought he would not, for fear of what mad consequences might ensue. And then again he thought of a new stratagem. He jumped out of bed and went straight to the bed where the miller lay. He carried away the child in its cradle; and when the wife came in the door, the cleric pinched the baby's ear, whereupon it awoke and cried out. The wife, who had been going to her own bed, when she heard the cry turned about and went in that direction. When she found the cradle she was reassured, and she lifted the cover and lay down beside the cleric, who hugged her tight. He drew her to him and squeezed her so tight in his pleasure that he quite crushed her. In amazement she allowed him to do what he liked.

Meanwhile, the other cleric, when he heard the cock crow, felt he had been lingering too long. He made himself ready, took his leave of the maiden, and slipped out of the chest. He went straight to his own bed where his companion lay, but when he found the cradle he was dismayed, and no wonder. He was frightened, but nonetheless he felt a little further; and when he came on two heads he knew he must be wrong. So he went quickly to the bed where the miller was lying and lay down beside him. The miller had not yet awakened and noticed nothing. "Comrade," said the cleric, "what are you doing? He who never has anything to say is worth nothing. On my word, I've had a fine night, God save me! She's a warm little girl, the miller's daughter. That kind of pleasure is very wicked indeed, but there is great pleasure in the cupboard. Go, my friend, slip in now yourself and get your share of the bacon. There's plenty left before you get to the rind. I've bent her back seven times tonight, but she still hasn't got her fill. All she got in return was the ring from the andiron. I've done a good job."

When the miller heard this trick, he seized the cleric by the collar; and the cleric, when he saw what was up, grabbed the miller and treated him so roughly that he almost strangled him. The wife began to kick the other cleric who was lying beside her. "Husband," she said, "what's going on? Please, let's get up at once. Those clerics are strangling each other over there." "Never you mind," said the cleric, "let them be, let the fools kill each other." (He knew very well that his companion was the stronger of the two.)

When the miller managed to break loose, he ran at once to light the fire. And when he saw his wife lying with the cleric, he shouted: "Get up, you brazen whore. How did you get in there? Now it's all up with you." "Husband," she said, "it's not quite as you say. For if I am a brazen whore, I was tricked into it. But you're a bold-faced thief, for you have made away with these clerics' sacks of wheat and their mare, for which you will be hanged. It's all stuck away in your barn."

The two clerics took hold of the miller and came little short of milling him like wheat, so hard did they beat and bruise him. They kicked and cuffed him until he gave them back all their wheat. Then they went to another mill to get their wheat ground. They got Saint Martin's lodging, and they worked so well at their new trade that they got through the bad year and gave thanks up and down to God and to Saint Nicholas.

The Wife of Bath's Prologue and Tale

The Wife of Bath is inimitable but not unprecedented. She is one of a number of sexually experienced older women in classical and medieval literature. Chaucer's largest debt to this tradition may be seen in the long speech of the Old Woman in *The Romance of the Rose*, from which he derived many of the Wife's traits and even a few of her lines.

The Wife's *Prologue* is also built up from a vast medieval repertoire of antifeminist literature and debate. We include A. G. Rigg's translation of sections from the principal sources: Theophrastus, St. Jerome, and Walter Map. Various passages from the Bible, used not only by Jerome but by the Wife herself, are the central authorities for medieval ideas on marriage, remarriage, and widowhood. Further commentary may be found in Chaucer's Parson's own treatment of the sin of lechery and its remedy, which appears on pp. 333–44.

There are a number of analogues to the Wife's *Tale*, the closest being the *Tale of Florent*, one of many exempla in the *Confessio Amantis* by Chaucer's friend John Gower. It has been argued that Chaucer based his tale on Gower's treatment alone, but many scholars believe the exact relationship remains unclear.

Major and minor sources for the Wife's *Prologue* are printed in the chapter by Ralph Hanna and Traugott Lawler in *Sources and Analogues of the* Canterbury Tales, vol. 2, ed. Robert M. Correale and Mary Hamel (Woodbridge: D. S. Brewer, 2005), pp. 351–403. John Withrington and P. J. C. Field print the three closest analogues to her *Tale* in Correale and Hamel, pp. 405–48.

JEAN DE MEUN

From The Romance of the Rose†

[*The Old Woman's Speech*]

* * *

"Know then, that if only, when I was your age, I had been as wise about the games of Love as I am now! For then I was a very great beauty, but now I

† From Guillaume de Lorris and Jean de Meun, *The Romance of the Rose*, trans. Charles Dahlberg (Princeton: Princeton UP, 1971), pp. 222–33, 241–42, 247–48. The Old Woman (La Vieille) is advising a young lady on how to deal with men; the "son" she addresses is Fair Welcoming (Bel Accueil), a personification of part of the lady's psyche. This episode occurs in Jean de Meun's part of the poem, written ca. 1275. We know from the prologue to *The Legend of Good Women* that Chaucer had himself "translated the Romaunce of the Rose"; but the surviving Middle English version is in three fragments, not all of them thought to be by Chaucer, and together they amount to only about one-third of the French poem. The Old Woman's speech translated here is not represented in the extant Middle English text, though we may be certain Chaucer knew it in its original French and nearly as certain he had once translated it himself.

must complain and moan when I look at my face, which has lost its charms; and I see the inevitable wrinkles whenever I remember how my beauty made the young men skip. I made them so struggle that it was nothing if not a marvel. I was very famous then; word of my highly renowned beauty ran everywhere. At my house there was a crowd so big that no man ever saw the like. At night they knocked on my door: I was really very hard on them when I failed to keep my promises to them, and that happened very often, for I had other company. They did many a crazy thing at which I got very angry. Often my door was broken down, and many of them got into such battles as a result of their hatred and envy that before they were separated they lost their members and their lives. If master Algus, the great calculator, had wanted to take the trouble and had come with his ten figures, by which he certifies and numbers everything, he could not, however well he knew how to calculate, have ascertained the number of these great quarrels. Those were the days when my body was strong and active! As I say, if I had been as wise then as I am now, I would possess the value of a thousand pounds of sterling silver more than I do now, but I acted too foolishly.

"I was young and beautiful, foolish and wild, and had never been to a school of love where they read in the theory, but I know everything by practice. Experiments, which I have followed my whole life, have made me wise in love. Now that I know everything about love, right up to the struggle, it would not be right if I were to fail to teach you the delights that I know and have often tested. He who gives advice to a young man does well. Without fail, it is no wonder that you know nothing, for your beak is too yellow. But in the end, I have so much knowledge upon which I can lecture from a chair that I could never finish. One should not avoid or despise everything that is very old; there one finds both good sense and good custom. Men have proved many times that, however much they have acquired, there will remain to them, in the end, at least their sense and their customs. And since I had good sense and manners, not without great harm to me, I have deceived many a worthy man when he fell captive in my nets. But I was deceived by many before I noticed. Then it was too late, and I was miserably unhappy. I was already past my youth. My door, which formerly was often open, both night and day, stayed constantly near its sill.

"'No one is coming today, no one came yesterday,' I thought, 'unhappy wretch! I must live in sorrow.' My woeful heart should have left me. Then, when I saw my door, and even myself, at such repose, I wanted to leave the country, for I couldn't endure the shame. How could I stand it when those handsome young men came along, those who formerly had held me so dear that they could not tire themselves, and I saw them look at me sideways as they passed by, they who had once been my dear guests? They went by near me, bounding along without counting me worth an egg, even those who had loved me most; they called me a wrinkled old woman and worse before they had passed on by.

"Besides, my pretty child, no one, unless he were very attentive or had experienced great sorrows, would think or know what grief gripped my heart when in my thought I remembered the lovely speeches, the sweet caresses and pleasures, the kisses and the deeply delightful embraces that were so soon stolen away. Stolen? Indeed, and without return. It would have been better for me to be imprisoned forever in a tower than to have been born so soon. God! Into what torment was I put by the fair gifts which had failed me, and how wretched their remnants had made me! Alas! Why was I born so soon? To whom can I complain, to whom except you, my son, whom I hold so dear? I have no other way to avenge myself than by teaching my doctrine. Therefore, fair son, I indoctrinate you so that, when instructed, you will avenge me on those good-for-nothings; for if God pleases, he will remind you of this sermon when he comes. You know that, because of your age, you have a very great advantage in retaining the sermon so that it will remind you. Plato said: 'It is true of any knowledge that one can keep better the memory of what one learns in one's infancy.'

"Certainly, dear son, my tender young one, if my youth were present, as yours is now, the vengeance that I would take on them could not rightly be written. Everywhere I came I would work such wonders with those scoundrels, who valued me so lightly and who vilified and despised me when they so basely passed by near me, that one would never have heard the like. They and others would pay for their pride and spite; I would have no pity on them. For with the intelligence that God has given me—just as I have preached to you—do you know what condition I would put them in? I would so pluck them and seize their possessions, even wrongly and perversely, that I would make them dine on worms and lie naked on dunghills, especially and first of all those who loved me with more loyal heart and who more willingly took trouble to serve and honor me. If I could, I wouldn't leave them anything worth one bud of garlic until I had everything in my purse and had put them all into poverty; I would make them stamp their feet in living rage behind me. But to regret it is worth nothing; what has gone cannot come. I would never be able to hold any man, for my face is so wrinkled that they don't even protect themselves against my threat. A long time ago the scoundrels who despised me told me so, and from that time on I took to weeping. O God! But it still pleases me when I think back on it. I rejoice in my thought and my limbs become lively again when I remember the good times and the gay life for which my heart so strongly yearns. Just to think of it and to remember it all makes my body young again. Remembering all that happened gives me all the blessings of the world, so that however they may have deceived me, at least I have had my fun. A young lady is not idle when she leads a gay life, especially she who thinks about acquiring enough to take care of her expenses.

* * *

"O fair, most sweet son," said the Old Woman, "O beautiful tender flesh, I want to teach you of the games of Love so that when you have learned them you will not be deceived. Shape yourself according to my art, for no one who is not well informed can pass through this course of games without selling his livestock to get enough money. Now give your attention to hearing and understanding, and to remembering everything that I say, for I know the whole story.

"Fair son, whoever wants to enjoy loving and its sweet ills which are so bitter must know the commandments of Love but must beware that he does not know love itself. I would tell you all the commandments here if I did not certainly see that, by nature, you have overflowing measure of those that you should have. Well numbered, there are ten of them that you ought to know. But he who encumbers himself with the last two is a great fool; they are not worth a false penny. I allow you eight of them, but whoever follows Love in the other two wastes his study and becomes mad. One should not study them in a school. He who wants a lover to have a generous heart and to put love in only one place has given too evil a burden to lovers. It is a false text, false in the letter. In it, Love, the son of Venus, lies, and no man should believe him; whoever does will pay dearly, as you will see by the end of my sermon.

"Fair son, never be generous; and keep your heart in several places, never in one. Don't give it, and don't lend it, but sell it very dearly and always to the highest bidder. See that he who buys it can never get a bargain: no matter how much he may give, never let him have anything in return; it were better if he were to burn or hang or maim himself. In all cases keep to these points: have your hands closed to giving and open to taking. Certainly, giving is great folly, except giving a little for attracting men when one plans to make them one's prey or when one expects such a return for the gift that one could not have sold it for more. I certainly allow you such giving. The gift is good where he who gives multiplies his gift and gains; he who is certain of his profit cannot repent of his gift. I can indeed consent to such a gift. * * *

"But I can tell you this much: if you want to choose a lover, I advise you to give your love, but not too firmly, to that fair young man who so prizes you. Love others wisely, and I will seek out for you enough of them so that you can amass great wealth from them. It is good to become acquainted with rich men if their hearts are not mean and miserly and if one knows how to pluck them well. Fair Welcoming may know whomever he wishes, provided that he gives each one to understand that he would not want to take another lover for a thousand marks of fine milled gold. He should swear that if he had wanted to allow his rose, which was in great demand, to be taken by another, he would have been weighed down with gold and jewels. But, he should go on, his pure heart was so loyal that no man would ever stretch out his hand for it except that man alone who was offering his hand at that moment.

"If there are a thousand, he should say to each: 'Fair lord, you alone will have the rose; no one else will ever have a part. May God fail me if I ever divide it.' He may so swear and pledge his faith to them. If he perjures himself, it doesn't matter; God laughs at such an oath and pardons it gladly.

"Jupiter and the gods laughed when lovers perjured themselves; and many times the gods who loved *par amour* perjured themselves. When Jupiter reassured his wife Juno, he swore by the Styx to her in a loud voice and falsely perjured himself. Since the gods give them, such examples should assure pure lovers that they too may swear falsely by all the saints, convents, and temples. But he is a great fool, so help me God, who believes in the oaths of lovers, for their hearts are too fickle. Young men are in no way stable—nor, often times, are the old—and therefore they belie the oaths and faith that they have given.

"Know also another truth: he who is lord of the fair should collect his market-toll everywhere; and he who cannot at one mill—Hey! to another for his whole round! The mouse who has but one hole for retreat has a very poor refuge and makes a very dangerous provision for himself. It is just so with a woman: she is the mistress of all the markets, since everyone works to have her. She should take possessions everywhere. If, after she had reflected well, she wanted only one lover, she would have a very foolish idea. For, by Saint Lifard of Meun, whoever gives her love in a single place has a heart neither free nor unencumbered, but basely enslaved. Such a woman, who takes trouble to love one man alone, has indeed deserved to have a full measure of pain and woe. If she lacks comfort from him, she has no one to comfort her, and those who give their hearts in a single place are those who most lack comfort. In the end, when they are bored, or irritated, all these men fly from their women.

* * *

"Briefly, all men betray and deceive women; all are sensualists, taking their pleasure anywhere. Therefore we should deceive them in return, not fix our hearts on one. Any woman who does so is a fool; she should have several friends and, if possible, act so as to delight them to the point where they are driven to distraction. If she has no graces, let her learn them. Let her be haughtier toward those who, because of her hauteur, will take more trouble to serve her in order to deserve her love, but let her scheme to take from those who make light of her love. She should know games and songs and flee from quarrels and disputes. If she is not beautiful, she should pretty herself; the ugliest should wear the most coquettish adornments.

* * *

"If she has a lovely neck and white chest, she should see that her dressmaker lower her neckline, so that it reveals a half foot, in front and back, of her fine white flesh; thus she may deceive more easily. And if her shoulders are too large to be pleasing at dances and balls, she should wear a dress of fine cloth and thus appear less ungainly. And if, because of insect bites or pimples, she doesn't have beautiful, well-kept hands, she should be careful not to neglect them but should remove the spots with a needle or wear gloves so that the pimples and scabs will not show.

"If her breasts are too heavy she should take a scarf or towel to bind them against her chest and wrap it right around her ribs, securing it with needle and thread or by a knot; thus she can be active at her play.

"And like a good little girl she should keep her chamber of Venus tidy. If she is intelligent and well brought up, she will leave no cobwebs around but will burn or destroy them, tear them down and sweep them up, so that no grime can collect anywhere.

"If her feet are ugly, she should keep them covered and wear fine stockings if her legs are large. In short, unless she's very stupid she should hide any defect she knows of.

"For example, if she knows that her breath is foul she should spare no amount of trouble never to fast, never to speak to others on an empty stomach, and, if possible, to keep her mouth away from people's noses.

"When she has the impulse to laugh, she should laugh discreetly and prettily, so that she shows little dimples at the corners of her mouth. She should avoid puffing her cheeks and screwing her face up in grimaces. Her lips should be kept closed and her teeth covered; a woman should always laugh with her mouth closed, for the sight of a mouth stretched like a gash across the face is not a pretty one. If her teeth are not even, but ugly and quite crooked, she will be thought little of if she shows them when she laughs.

"There is also a proper way to cry. But every woman is adept enough to cry well on any occasion, for, even though the tears are not caused by grief or shame or hurt, they are always ready. All women cry; they are used to crying in whatever way they want. But no man should be disturbed when he sees such tears flowing as fast as rain, for these tears, these sorrows and lamentations flow only to trick him. A woman's weeping is nothing but a ruse; she will overlook no source of grief. But she must be careful not to reveal, in word or deed, what she is thinking of.

"It is also proper to behave suitably at the table. Before sitting down, she should look around the house and let everyone understand that she herself knows how to run a house. Let her come and go, in the front rooms and in back, and be the last to sit down, being sure to wait a little before she finally takes her seat. Then, when she is seated at table, she should serve everyone as well as possible. She should carve in front of the others and pass the bread to those around her. To deserve praise, she should serve food in front of the one who shares her plate. She should put a thigh or wing before him, or, in his presence, carve the beef or pork, meat or fish, depending upon what food there happens to be. She should never be niggardly in her servings as long as there is anyone unsatisfied. Let her guard against getting her fingers wet up to the joint in the sauce, against smearing her lips with soup, garlic, or fat meat, against piling up too large morsels and stuffing her mouth. When she has to moisten a piece in any sauce, either *sauce verte, cameline,* or *jauce*, she should hold the bit with her fingertips and bring it carefully up to her mouth, so that no drop of soup, sauce, or pepper falls on her breast. She must drink so neatly that she doesn't spill anything on herself, for anyone who happened to see her spill would think her either very clumsy or very greedy. Again, she must take care not to touch her drinking cup while she has food in her mouth. She should wipe her mouth so clean that grease will not stick to the cup, and should be particularly careful about her upper lip, for, when there is grease on it, untidy drops of it will show in her wine. She should drink only a little at a time, however great her appetite, and never empty a cup, large or small, in one breath, but rather drink little and often, so that she doesn't go around causing others to say that she gorges or drinks too much while her mouth is full. She should avoid swallowing the rim of her cup, as do many greedy nurses who are so foolish that they pour wine down their hollow throats as if they were casks, who pour it down in such huge gulps that they become completely fuddled and dazed. Now a lady must be careful not to get drunk, for a drunk, man or woman, cannot keep anything secret; and when a woman gets drunk, she has no defenses at all in her, but blurts out whatever she thinks and abandons herself to anyone when she gives herself over to such bad conduct.

"She must also beware of falling asleep at the table, for she would be much less pleasant; many disagreeable things can happen to those who take such naps. There is no sense in napping in places where one should remain awake, and many have been deceived in this way, have many times fallen, either forward or backward or sideways, and broken an arm or head or ribs. Let a woman beware lest such a nap overtake her; let her recall Palinurus, the helmsman of Aeneas's ship. While awake, he steered it well, but when sleep conquered him, he fell from the rudder into the sea and drowned within sight of his companions, who afterward mourned greatly for him.

"Further, a lady must be careful not to be too reluctant to play, for she might wait around so long that no one would want to offer her his hand. She should seek the diversion of love as long as youth deflects her in that direction, for, when old age assails a woman, she loses both the joy and the assault of Love. A wise woman will gather the fruit of love in the flower of her age. The unhappy woman loses her time who passes it without enjoying love. And if she disbelieves this advice of mine, which I give for the profit of all, be sure that she will be sorry when age withers her. But I know that women will believe me, particularly those who are sensible, and will stick to our rules and will say many paternosters for my soul, when I am dead who now teach and comfort them. I know that this lesson will be read in many schools.

"O fair sweet son, if you live—for I see well that you are writing down in the book of your heart the whole of my teaching, and that, when you depart from me, you will study more, if it please God, and will become a master like me—if you live I confer on you the license to teach, in spite of all chancellors, in chambers or in cellars, in meadow, garden, or thicket, under a tent or behind the tapestries, and to inform the students in wardrobes, attics, pantries, and stables, if you find no more pleasant places. And may my lesson be well taught when you have learned it well!

"A woman should be careful not to stay shut up too much, for while she remains in the house, she is less seen by everybody, her beauty is less well-known, less desired, and in demand less. She should go often to the principal church and go visiting, to weddings, on trips, at games, feasts, and round dances, for in such places the God and Goddess of Love keep their schools and sing mass to their disciples.

"But of course, if she is to be admired above others, she has to be well-dressed. When she is well turned out and goes through the streets, she should carry herself well, neither too stiffly nor too loosely, not too upright nor too bent over, but easily and graciously in any crowd. She should move her shoulders and sides so elegantly that no one might find anyone with more beautiful movements. And she should walk daintily in her pretty little shoes, so well made that they fit her feet without any wrinkles whatever.

* * *

"And what I say about the black mare, about the sorrel horse and mare and the gray and black horses, I say about the cow and bull and the ewe and ram; for we do not doubt that these males want all females as their wives. Never doubt, fair son, that in the same way all females want all males. All women willingly receive them. By my soul, fair son, it is thus with every man and every woman as far as natural appetite goes. The law restrains them little from exercising it. A little! but too much, it seems to me, for when the law has put them together, it wants either of them, the boy or the girl, to be able to have only the other, at least as long as he or she lives. But at the same time they are tempted to use their free will.

I know very well that such a thing does rise up, only some keep themselves from it because of shame, others because they fear trouble; but Nature controls them to that end just as she does the animals that we were just speaking of. I know it from my own experience, for I always took trouble to be loved by all men. And if I had not feared shame, which holds back and subdues many hearts, when I went along the streets where I always wanted to go—so dressed up in adornments that a dressed-up doll would have been nothing in comparison—I would have received all or at least many of those young boys, if I had been able and if it had pleased them, who pleased me so much when they threw me those sweet glances. (Sweet God! What pity for them seized me when those looks came toward me!) I wanted them all one after the other, if I could have satisfied them all. And it seemed to me that, if they could have, they would willingly have received me. I do not except prelates or monks, knights, burgers, or canons, clerical or lay, foolish or wise, as long as they were at the height of their powers. They would have jumped out of their orders if they had not thought that they might fail when they asked for my love; but if they had known my thought and the whole of our situations they would not have been in such doubt. And I think that several, if they had dared, would have broken their marriages. If one of them had had me in private he would not have remembered to be faithful. No man would have kept his situation, his faith, vows, or religion unless he were some demented fool who was smitten by love and loved his sweetheart loyally. Such a man, perhaps, would have called me paid and thought about his own possessions, which he would not have given up at any price. But there are very few such lovers, so help me God and Saint Amand; I certainly think so. If he spoke to me for a long time, no matter what he said, lies or truth, I could have made him move everything. Whatever he was, secular, or in an order, with a belt of red leather or of cord, no matter what headdress he wore, I think that he would have carried on with me if he thought that I wanted him or even if I had allowed him. Thus Nature regulates us by inciting our hearts to pleasure. For this reason Venus deserves less blame for loving Mars.

* * *

"By my soul, if I had been wise, I would have been a very rich lady, for I was acquainted with very great people when I was already a coy darling, and I certainly was held in considerable value by them, but when I got something of value from one of them, then, by the faith that I owe God or Saint Thibaut, I would give it all to a rascal who brought me great shame but pleased me more. I called all the others lover, but it was he alone that I loved. Understand, he didn't value me at one pea, and in fact told me so. He was bad—I never saw anyone worse—and he never ceased despising me. This scoundrel, who didn't love me at all, would call me a common whore. A woman has very poor judgment, and I was truly a woman. I never loved a man who loved me, but, do you know, if that scoundrel had laid open my shoulder or broken my head, I would have thanked him for it. He wouldn't have known how to beat me so much that I would not have had him throw himself upon me, for he knew very well how to make his peace, however much he had done against me. He would never have treated me so badly, beaten me or dragged me or wounded my face or bruised it black, that he would not have begged my favor before he moved from the place. He would never have said so many shameful things to me that he would not have counseled peace to me and then made me happy in bed, so that we had peace and concord again. Thus he had me caught in his snare, for this false, treacherous thief was a very hard rider in bed. I couldn't live without him; I wanted to follow him always. If he had fled, I would certainly have gone as far as London in England to seek him, so much did he please me and make me happy. He put me to shame and I him, for he led a life of great gaiety with the lovely gifts that he had received from me. He put none of them into saving, but played everything at dice in the taverns. He never learned any other trade, and there was no need then for him to do so, for I gave him a great deal to spend, and I certainly had it for the taking. Everybody was my source of income, while he spent it willingly and always on ribaldry; he burned everything in his lechery. He had his mouth stretched so wide that he did not want to hear anything good. Living never pleased him except when it was passed in idleness and pleasure. In the end I saw him in a bad situation as a result, when gifts were lacking for us. He became poor and begged his bread, while I had nothing worth two carding combs and had never married a lord. Then, as I have told you, I came through these woods, scratching my temples. May this situation of mine be an example to you, fair sweet son; remember it. Act so wisely that it may be better with you because of my instruction. For when your rose is withered and white hairs assail you, gifts will certainly fail."

* * *

THEOPHRASTUS

From The Golden Book on Marriage†

[Theophrastus was a Greek philosopher (371–287 B.C.E.), who succeeded Aristotle as head of the Peripatetic school. He wrote many works on philosophy but is best known for his *Characters*, brief sketches of types of men. His work *The Golden Book on Marriage* has not survived in the original but has been preserved in translation into Latin in Jerome's treatise *Against Jovinian* (see pp. 398–410). It is better to treat it as a separate work from Jerome's in that it presents a purely pagan attitude toward the subject of marriage. The introductory words are by Jerome.]

* * *

[Jerome] I feel that in my catalogue of women [see p. 407], I have exceeded the customary space given to examples, and may rightly be censured by a critical reader. But what else can I do, when women of our own time attack the authority of Paul, and, when the funeral of their first

† This excerpt and the ones from St. Jerome and Walter Map following were prepared for the first Norton Critical Edition by A. G. Rigg. Because of the length and complexity of these texts, Professor Rigg has used a combination of summary, translation, and annotation to present them to the reader. Reprinted by permission of the translator, A. G. Rigg.

husband is not yet over, start to recite arguments for a second marriage?[1] As they despise belief in Christian chastity, let them at any rate learn chastity from the pagans. There is a book by Theophrastus on the subject of marriage, called *The Golden Book*, in which he discusses whether the wise man should take a wife. After concluding that if the woman is beautiful and virtuous, her parents noble, and the husband healthy and rich, then a wise man may sometimes marry, he immediately adds:

[THEOPHRASTUS] However, it is very unusual for all these conditions to be present in a marriage, and therefore the philosopher[2] ought not to take a wife. Firstly, the pursuit of Philosophy is impeded: no one can serve both books and a wife at the same time.[3] There are many things which women require—fine clothes, gold, jewels, money, maidservants, all kinds of furniture, litters, and gilded coaches. And then there is the ceaseless chatter and grumbling all through the night—"So-and-so has smarter clothes to go out in than I do. Everyone admires *her*, but when I meet other women they all look down on me, poor thing. Why were you looking at the girl next door? What were you saying to our serving girl? What did you bring me from the market?"[4]

We are not allowed a friend or companion, for she suspects that friendship for another means hatred of her.[5] If a learned lecturer is at some nearby city, we can neither leave our wives behind nor burden ourselves with them. It is difficult to look after a poor wife, but torture to put up with a rich one.[6]

Moreover, there is no choice in the matter of a wife: one has to take whatever comes along. If she's nagging, stupid, ugly, proud, smelly—whatever fault she has, we find out *after* marriage. Now a horse, an ass, a cow, a dog, the cheapest slaves, clothes, kettles, a wooden chair, a cup, a clay pot—all these are tested first, and *then* purchased. Only a wife is not put on display—in case her faults are discovered before we take her.[7]

We always have to be noticing her appearance and praising her beauty, in case she thinks that we don't like her if we ever look at another woman. She has to be called "Madam"; we have to celebrate her birthday and make oaths by her health, saying "Long may you live!" We have to honor her nurse, her old nanny, her father's servant, her foster son, her elegant follower, her curly-haired go-between, some eunuch (cut short for the sake of a long and carefree pleasure!)—all of them are adulterers under another name. Whoever has her favors, you have to love them, like it or not.[8]

If you give the whole management of the house to her, she complains "I'm just a servant"; if you keep any part of it to yourself, "You don't trust me!"[9] She begins to hate you and quarrel with you, and if you don't watch out she'll be mixing poison. If you allow into the house old dames,

1. Cf. the *Wife of Bath's Prologue* 587ff. (hereafter cited as *WBP*) and Deschamps, *Miroir de Mariage* (cited in *Sources and Analogues of Chaucer's* Canterbury Tales, ed. W. F. Bryan and Germaine Dempster [Chicago: U of Chicago P, 1941], p. 220).
2. In all these discussions, "wise man, philosopher," etc. (Lat. *sapiens*) are equivalent to the Middle English *clerk* (i.e., Jankyn, the Wife's fifth husband).
3. The remark is echoed by Cicero, cited by both Jerome and Walter Map (below, pp. 407, 413).
4. *WBP*, 235–42.
5. Chaucer seems to have taken this as part of the woman's speech.
6. *WBP*, 248–52.
7. *WBP*, 282–92.
8. *WBP*, 293–306.
9. *WBP*, 308–10.

sooth-sayers, fortune-tellers, and gem-setters and silkworkers, she says, "You're endangering my virtue!"; but if you don't, "Why are you so suspicious?" But what good is it to keep a careful watch over her?—if a wife is unchaste, she can't be guarded, and if she isn't she doesn't need guarding. In any case, the compulsion to be chaste is an untrustworthy guard—the woman really to be called "chaste" is the one who could sin if she wanted to. Men are quick to desire a beautiful woman: an ugly one is herself lecherous. It is difficult to guard what everyone is after: it is misery to possess what no one thinks worth having. However, there's less misery in having an ugly wife than in trying to keep a beautiful one. Nothing is safe which the whole population has set its heart on—one man uses his handsome figure to court her, another his intellect, another his witticisms, another his generosity: some day, in some way, the castle besieged on all sides must surrender.[1]

Now some people marry in order to have someone to run the home, or to cheer them up, or to avoid loneliness: but (i) a faithful servant, obedient to his master's authority and conforming to his wishes, is a better majordomo than a wife, who only considers herself mistress of the house if she goes against her husband's wishes; that is, she does what she pleases, not what she's told. (ii) At the side of a sick man friends, and servants bound by ties of old benefits, do more good than a wife: she puts her tears on our charge sheet, and sells her flood of tears in the hope of the inheritance: by her show of solicitude she upsets the sick man's temper by her despair. On the other hand, if our wife herself is sick, we have to be sick in sympathy and are never allowed to leave her bedside. Or, if she is a good and gentle wife (a rare bird!), then we suffer agony with her in her birthpangs, and are in anguish when she is in danger. (iii) The philosopher can never be alone: he has with him all men who are or ever were good, and can send his free mind where he wishes. What he cannot reach in the flesh, he embraces in contemplation. And if there is a shortage of men, he speaks with God. He will never be less lonely than when he is alone.

Further, to take a wife in order to have children, either to make sure that our name survives, or to have supports in our old age and be sure of having heirs—this is the most stupid of all. For what does it matter to us as we leave this world if someone else has the same name as we did? The son does not immediately assume his father's name (?),[2] and there are countless people who are called by the same name. Why bring up at home aids for your old age, who may either die before you, or may turn out to have bad characters (or at the least, when your son reaches maturity, he will certainly think you are taking a long time to die)? Better and more certain heirs are your friends and neighbors whom you can choose judiciously, than heirs whom you have to have, whether you like it or not. Even if your heredity is sufficiently secure, it is better to use up your wealth while you still live, rather than to abandon to uncertain uses what you have collected by your own hard work.

1. *WBP*, 253–72 (with the arguments in a different order).
2. Translation doubtful.

ST. JEROME

From Against Jovinian†

[This treatise, written ca. 393 C.E., was the principal source for the medieval Church in its arguments for clerical celibacy. It is referred to by the Wife of Bath thus:

> And eek ther was somtyme a clerk at Rome,
> A cardinal, that highte Seint Jerome,
> That made a book agayn Jovinian.
> (673–75)

It is, however, primarily a refutation of heresy rather than an antifeminist tract: in two books (ed. J. P. Migne, *Patrologia Latina* 23, cols. 211–338), Jerome answers the following points made by the monk Jovinian:

> (i) that virgins, widows, and married women, once they have been baptized, are of the same merit, as long as they do not differ because of other actions; (ii) those who are purified by baptism cannot be overcome by the devil; (iii) there is no distinction between fasting and the grateful receiving of food; (iv) all who have been baptized and have kept the Faith obtain the same reward in heaven.

The first of these heresies is dealt with in the first book and is the only one that concerns us here. Quotations are selected below only insofar as they contribute to the general antifeminist debate, the arguments of the Wife of Bath, and the status of the Wife in the eyes of the Church. Omissions are indicated by * * * where the argument is irrelevant for the present purpose. Translations of biblical quotations (in Jerome's Latin) sometimes follow the wording of the King James Bible of 1611; often, however, the Latin presents a different sense from the original Hebrew on which the 1611 version was based—for instance, 1 Corinthians 7:3, the King James version has "Let the husband render unto the wife due benevolence," but the Latin here reads *Uxori vir debitum reddat*, "man shal yelde to his wyf hire dette" (*Wife of Bath's Prologue* 130). In all such cases I have translated Jerome's Latin.

After some introductory remarks, Jerome presents Jovinian's arguments:]

[i, 5: col. 215-] First he says that it is God's decree that "for this reason a man shall leave his father and his mother, and shall cleave unto his wife, and the two shall be in one flesh" (Gen. 2:24). In case we object that this is only an Old Testament saying, he adds that it was confirmed by God himself in the Gospels, "What God has joined together, let no man put asunder" (Matt. 19:5–6).[1] He then adds the quotation, "Be fruitful, and multiply, and replenish the earth" (Gen. 1:28), and lists in order Seth, Enos, Cainam, Malaleel, Jared, Enoch, Mathusalem, Lamech, and Noah, all of whom had wives and produced children according to God's decree. * * * "There was Enoch, who walked with God and was snatched up into Heaven. There was Noah, who, despite all those who must have been virgins by their age, went into the ark alone with his sons and wives, and was saved in the shipwreck of the world. Again, after the flood, pairs of men and women were joined together in, as it were, a second beginning of the human race, and

† Prepared for an earlier edition of this volume by A. G. Rigg; see note, p. 395.

1. For the whole of this section, cf. the *Wife of Bath's Prologue* (hereafter cited as *WBP*), 27–29.

the blessing 'Be fruitful, and multiply, and replenish the earth' was renewed (Gen. 8:17, etc.)." * * * He runs to Abraham, Isaac, and Jacob, of whom the first had three wives, the second one, and the third four. * * * He says that because of his faith Abraham received a blessing in the birth of a son. * * * [His examples include, among others] Rebecca, * * * Jacob, * * * Rachel, * * * Joseph (the most holy and chaste), * * * and all the patriarchs who had wives and were equally blessed by God. * * * [He continues with many more, e.g.,] Sampson, * * * he says that there was no difference between Jephta and his daughter who was sacrificed to God. * * * Samuel, he says, produced children, and his priestly honor was not diminished by his embracing a wife. * * * Need I mention Solomon[2] whom he places in his catalogue of married men, asserting that he was a figure of the Savior? * * *

Passing on to the New Testament, he gives us Zacharias, Elizabeth, Peter and his mother-in-law, and the rest of the Apostles, and then adds, "In case my opponents hope to put up a vain defense, and claim that all this was because the early world needed populating, let them hear what Paul has to say!" [From Paul, he quotes:] "Therefore my wish is that the younger widows marry and produce children" (1 Tim. 5:14), "Marriage is honorable in all, and the bed undefiled" (Heb. 13:4), "The wife is bound to her husband as long as he lives, but if he dies, let her marry whom she wishes, only in the Lord" (1 Cor. 7:39). * * *

Finally he makes an apostrophe to a virgin, and says, "I wish no harm to you, virgin: you chose chastity because of the present necessity (cf. 1 Cor. 7:26); it pleased you to be holy in body and spirit, but do not be proud—you are a member of the same Church as married women."

> [(i, 6, col. 217-): Jerome now begins his reply. His main authority is St. Paul, 1 Cor. 7, on which his argument depends. The Christians of Corinth have written to Paul asking, among other things, whether they should remain celibate after becoming Christians and, for the sake of continence, leave their wives. Jerome begins by quoting the opening of Paul's reply, 1 Cor. 7:1–9, and then continues:]

[i, 7, col. 218-] Let us go back to the beginning of the quotation: "It is better for a man not to touch a woman." Now if it is good not to touch a woman, it is bad to do so, for the only opposite to "good" is "bad." Now if it is bad and yet pardoned, it is allowed only lest anything worse than bad results. Now what kind of "good" is that which is only allowed because of the risk of something worse? Paul would never have said "let each one have his wife" (1 Cor. 7:2) if he had not first made the premise "because of (the danger of) fornication." Remove this last phrase, and he will not then say "let each one have his wife." It is as though one were to say, "It is good to be fed on the purest wheat and to eat the finest bread, but in case anyone is forced by starvation to eat cow-dung I concede the eating of barley-bread."[3] Now does wheat lose its purity if barley is preferred to cow-dung? That thing is good by nature which does not have to be compared with evil, and which is not overshadowed by merely being preferred to something else.

Note also the wisdom of the Apostle: he did not say that it is good not to have a wife, but "it is good not to touch a woman," implying that the

2. *WBP*, 35–43.
3. Cf. *WBP*, 143–46.

danger is in the act of touching: whoever touches her cannot escape, for "she snatches the precious souls of men" (cf. Prov. 6:26) and makes the hearts of young men fly. "Can a man take fire in his bosom, and not be burned? Can one go upon hot coals, and not be burned?" (Prov. 6:27–28). Just as anyone is burnt if they touch a fire, so the touch of a man and a woman senses their nature, and realizes the difference between the sexes. * * *

He did not say, "On account of fornication let each one *take* a wife"; otherwise he would by this excuse have given a free rein to lust—whenever a wife died, one would take another to avoid fornication! He said, "let each man *have* his wife." * * *[4]

[Jerome comments on the instruction that wives taken before conversion to Christianity should not be set aside and goes on to elaborate on the implications of 1 Cor. 7:5 and 1 Peter 3:7, that prayer is impeded by sexual activities.]

Do you want to know what the Apostle favors? Then take his remark, "I would that all men were even as I myself" (1 Cor. 7:7).[5] Blessed is the man who is like Paul. Fortunate is the man who listens to Paul not when he is pardoning but when he is giving instruction. "This I want," he said, "this I long for, that you should be imitators of me, just as I am an imitator of Christ." * * *

[i, 9, col. 222-] Having conceded to married people the practice of intercourse, and having shown them what he wants (or rather, what he allows), Paul passes on to the unmarried and the widows; he sets himself as an example, and says that they are blessed if they remain in their present state. * * * He gives the reason why he said "if they cannot contain themselves, let them marry"—namely "for it is better to marry than to burn." This is why is it better to marry—because burning is worse; if you remove the fervence of passion, he will not then say "it is better to marry." He considers it better only by comparison with the worse, not because it is inherently good. It is as though one were to say, "it is better to have one eye than none; it is better to go on one foot supported by a stick, than to crawl with both one's legs broken." * * *

[(i, 10–11, cols. 223–26): Jerome here expounds the doctrines in 1 Cor. 7:10–24. Most of this is not relevant to our purpose, but in cols. 223–24 he prophetically says:]

I know that many women will be furious with me, and that with the same lack of shame that they showed in their contempt for Christ they will rave against me, a miserable flea, the lowest Christian. Nevertheless, I shall say what the Apostle taught me, that they are on the side of iniquity, not of justice, of the dark rather than the light, of Belial rather than Christ; they are not temples of the living God, but idols and empty shrines of the dead! * * * [i, 12, cols. 226–29] After the discussion of the married and the continent, Paul finally comes to the subject of virgins: "On virgins, I have no order from God, but I give advice, having obtained the mercy of the Lord to be faithful. I think, therefore, that this is good,

4. Cf. *WBP*, 47–52 (ignoring Jerome's argument).
5. Cf. *WBP*, 80ff.

because of the present need, for it is good for man to be so (virgin)" (1 Cor. 7:25–26).[6] At this our adversary [Jovinian] goes wild with rejoicing, shattering open the wall of virginity with this powerful battering-ram: "You see," he says, "the Apostle says that he has no order from God about virgins; he who made orders with authority about married men and wives, dare not command what God did not order, and rightly: what is ordered, is commanded; what is commanded must be done; what must be done must carry some penalty if it is not done. For a command which is left within the authority of the person to whom it is given is a useless command."

[Jerome's answer:] If God had commanded virginity, he would have seemed to condemn marriage, and to take away the human seedbed from which virginity itself grows.[7] If he cut away the root, how would he get the fruit? If he did not first lay the foundations, how could he raise up the building and set a roof over everything? Mountains are brought down by great labor of ditch-digging: the depths of the earth are penetrated with difficulty in the search for gold. When a necklace is made from the finest pebbles, first in the blast of the furnace, and then set by the skillful hand of the craftsman, it is not the man who refined the gold from the mud who is called beautiful, but the person who uses the beauty of the gold.

Do not be surprised if, amid all the titillations of the flesh and the incentives to sin, we are not commanded to follow the life of the angels but merely recommended to do so. For when advice is given, the decision is left with the person who is freely making the offering to God [or: it is merely the authority of the suggestor],[8] but a command is an obligation imposed on a servant. Paul said, "I do not have an order from God, but I give advice, having obtained the mercy of the Lord." If you do not have a command from God, [one might ask,] why do you dare to give advice? The Apostle will answer, "Do you think I should order what God did not command, but merely suggested? He is the creator, the potter who knows how fragile is the vessel which he made; he left virginity in the power of the person who hears his words. Should I, teacher of peoples, 'made all things to all men,' (1 Cor. 9:22) attempt to win everyone, and right from the start impose a burden of perpetual chastity on the necks of weak believers? Let them enjoy for a while the holiday of marriage, and give some time to prayer; so that having had a taste of chastity they may continue to long for that which they have only delighted in for a short while."

When Christ was tempted by the Pharisees who asked if it was right according to the Law of Moses to put aside one's wife, he forbade it entirely. His disciples, considering this, said, "If this is the case of a man and his wife, it is advisable not to marry." He replied, "All men cannot receive this saying, save they to whom it is given. For there are some eunuchs which were born this way from their mothers' wombs, some who were castrated by men, and some who castrated themselves for the sake of the kingdom of heaven. He that is able to receive it, let him receive it" (Matt. 19:2–12). This is why the Apostle says he has no command, because God had said "All men cannot receive this saying, save they to whom it is given," and "He that is able to receive it, let him receive it." He

6. *WBP*, 63–70, 82–86, and frequently.
7. *WBP*, 69–72.
8. Either is possible: the Latin is *offerentis arbitrium est*.

sets out the reward for the contest, he invites to the race, he holds in his hand the prize for virginity;[9] he shows the purest fountain, and says, "If any man thirst, let him come and drink (John 7:37); He who can receive, let him receive." He does not say that you *must* drink, and run the race, whether you want to or not, but that he who wishes to, and can, run and drink, will win the race and will be sated. For this reason Christ loves virgins the more, because they pay voluntarily what they were not ordered to pay. It is of greater grace to offer what you do not owe than to hand over what you are forced to pay. The Apostles considered the burdens of a wife and said, "If this is the case of a man and his wife, it is advisable not to marry." God approved their decision, and said, "You are right: marriage is not expedient for a man reaching for heaven, but it is a difficult matter, and not all receive this word, only those to whom it is given." * * *

What is the "immediate necessity" (1 Cor. 7:26) for rejecting the ties of marriage and pursuing the freedom of virginity?—"Woe on those who are pregnant and giving suck on that day!" (Matt. 24:19). Here it is not the prostitute or whore who is condemned (their damnation is not in doubt), but those whose wombs swell, the squalling children, the fruits and works of marriage. * * *

> [Jerome argues that virgins who have consecrated themselves to God are guilty of incest if they marry. Marriage is a short-term prospect, for it ends with death. He demonstrates the spiritual distinction between a virgin who thinks only of God and a wife whose thought is on how to please her husband.]

[i, 14, col. 233-] In the same way that Paul allowed virgins to marry because of the danger of fornication, excusing that which is not sought after for its own sake, so, for the same reason (the avoidance of fornication), he allowed widows to marry again, for it is better to have knowledge of one man, even if he is the second or third, than of many: that is, it is more tolerable to be prostituted to one man than to many. The Samaritan woman in the Gospel of John said that her present husband was her sixth, but Christ told her that he was not her husband (John 4:17–18), for where there was a succession of spouses, this one ceased to be her husband, for properly speaking only one man can be the husband.[1] In the beginning one rib was turned into one wife, "and the two will be in one flesh" (Gen. 2:24)—not three, not four, for otherwise there are not two of them, if there are more.

First of all Lamech,[2] who was a man of blood and a homicide, divided one flesh into two wives; the same punishment of the flood destroyed both homicide and bigamy [Jerome means by this marrying a second time]. * * * The holiness of monogamy is illustrated by the fact that a bigamist cannot be chosen as a priest. It is for this reason that Paul writes "let a widow be chosen if she is not less than sixty years old, and has been the wife of one husband only" (1 Tim. 5:9): this instruction concerns those widows who are fed on the charity of the Church—an age limit is prescribed, so that the food of the poor can only be given to those who

9. *WBP*, 75–76.
1. *WBP*, 14–25.
2. *WBP*, 53–54.

can no longer work. At the same time, note that a woman who has had two husbands, even if she is old and decrepit and starving, does not deserve to receive the alms of the Church. Now if she is refused the bread of alms, how much more will she lack the bread which comes from heaven—anyone who eats this unworthily is guilty of violating the body and blood of Christ! * * *

[(i, 16, col. 234-) Jerome moves away from a discussion of Paul's teachings, and demonstrates that chastity has *always* been preferred to marriage; he proceeds to take each of the figures of the Old Testament cited by Jovinian, and to show how they are variously to be interpreted. He begins with Adam:]

It should be said of Adam and Eve, that in Paradise, before their offense, they were virgins; it was after their sin, and outside the garden, that marriage took place. * * *[3]

[The biblical instruction "Be fruitful, and multiply, and replenish the earth" (Gen. 1:28) is explained by Jerome thus:]

It was necessary first to plant trees and to increase, so that there would be something which could be cut away later. Also, consider the meaning of "replenish the earth"—marriage fills the earth, but paradise is filled by virginity.

[Jerome notes that the phrase "God saw that it was good" was not applied to the second day of Creation (Gen. 1:6–8), indicating a disapproval of the number 2, a symbol of marriage. The various married figures proposed by Jovinian are each dealt with in turn: some of them are interpreted typologically (Isaac, for instance, is a figure of the Church rather than a physical reward given to Sarah, Moses signifies the Law, etc.). Of Solomon (i, 24, col. 243) he notes that it was his wives and concubines that turned his heart from God—he built the Temple in his youth, at the beginning of the reign. Jerome asks the reader not to criticize those who lived under the Old Law—"they served their own times and conditions, and fulfilled the injunction of the Lord to increase and multiply and fill the earth; more than this, they gave us figures of the future. * * *" Further, he notes (i, 26, col. 245) that the married Apostles, etc., all married *before* the arrival of the New Law.

At i, 28 (col. 249) Jerome moves into the attack with quotations from the Proverbs of Solomon:]

Above, when my adversary mentioned the many-wived Solomon, the builder of the Temple, I replied specifically to his arguments, so that I could quickly go through the remaining questions. Now, in case he shouts that Solomon and the other patriarchs, prophets and holy men who lived under the Old Law have been insulted by me, I will set out Solomon's sentiments on marriage—the very man who himself had so many wives and concubines—for no one can know better what a woman or wife is really like than someone who has suffered one. In Proverbs (9:13)[4] he says, "A

3. Note that Walter Map (below, p. 412) cites Eve as an example of disobedience *within* the garden.
4. Note that the text of the *Proverbs of Solomon* used by Jerome is often very different from that used by the King James version, and sometimes even from the Vulgate (see p. 404, n. 8).

woman is foolish and bold, and is made lacking in bread." What bread is this?—The bread of heaven! He immediately adds, "The people of earth perish in her, and rush into the depths of hell." Who are these "people of earth"?—Those who follow the first Adam, who was of earth, not the second Adam, who was from heaven. Again, in another place Solomon says, "Just as a worm in wood, so does an evil woman destroy her husband" (25:20).[5] If you argue that this was said only of *evil* women, I will reply shortly, "Why should I be compelled to wonder whether my bride is going to turn out good or bad?"

"It is better," Solomon says, "to live in the desert than with a nagging and angry woman" (21:9).[6] As to how rare it is to find a wife who lacks these vices—he knows who is married. As that fine orator Varius Geminus neatly puts it, "The man who doesn't quarrel is the single man."

"It is better to live in the corner of the roof than in a house shared with an evil-tongued woman" (Prov. 25:24). If a house shared by man and wife makes the wife proud and brings shame on her husband, how much more so if the woman is the richer, and the husband lives in *her* house! For rather than behaving as a wife, she begins to have the mastery of the house—if she takes exception to her husband, *he* has to go. "On a winter day a dripping roof drives a man from his house—so does an evil-tongued woman" (27:15)[7]—she makes the house flow with her continual abuse and daily chattering, and throws him out of his own house—that is, from the Church. * * *

We must not fail to mention the riddling saying, "The blood-sucking leech had three daughters, beloved in love, and they could not be satisfied; the fourth could never say 'Enough!': Hell, the love of a woman, the earth which cannot be sated by water, fire which never says, 'Enough!'"[8] (Prov. 30:15–16). The leech is the devil; those "beloved in love" are the devil's daughters who cannot be satisfied with the blood of those they have slain—Hell, a woman's love, dry earth, and burning fire. Here he is not talking about just a whore or an adulteress—the love of woman is accused in general: it is always insatiable; when quenched it burns; after a supply it is still hungry; it enfeebles a virile spirit and does not let it think of anything but the passion which it sustains. We read of something similar in the following proverb: "By three things is the earth moved, and the fourth cannot be tolerated: if a slave rules, if a foolish man is sated with bread, if a hateful wife has a good husband, and if a serving-wench throws out her own mistress" (Prov. 30:21–23).[9] In this heap of evils is numbered a wife; if you reply that it specifies "a *hateful* wife," I will say what I said above. * * * he who takes a wife is in doubt whether he is marrying a hateful wife or a loving one. If the former, she cannot be borne; if she is loving, her love is compared to Hell, to dry earth and to fire.

5. Not in the King James (=*WBP*, 376–77).
6. Not in the King James (=*WBP*, 778–81).
7. Chaucer (*WBP*, 278–80, *Melibee*, VII, 1085ff.) used a combined version of the "three-things" proverb: see Robinson's note to *Melibee*, VII, 1086, in Chaucer, *Works* (Boston: Houghton Mifflin, 1957), p. 742. I have found this "new" proverb frequently in medieval Latin texts.
8. Jerome's Latin text of the Proverb makes little sense: it is the text neither of (his own) Vulgate Latin translation nor of the King James version. I have modified my translation according to the Vulgate version: the alteration does not affect Jerome's interpretation (=*WBP*, 371–75).
9. *WBP*, 362–67.

[Jerome continues with an argument based on Ecclesiastes 3:1 ("To everything there is a season . . .") and an interpretation of the role of sex in Paradise. In i, 30 (col. 251) he digresses in order to stress the point that the highly erotic Song of Songs is not to be interpreted literally, but is a symbol of the marriage of the Old and New Law through the visitation of Christ. He emphasizes the choice of a virgin to be mother of Christ, demonstrating the importance of virginity in the Christian religion. In i, 33 (col. 255) he reverts to the topic of widows and virgins:]

If, because baptism makes a man new, there is no difference between a virgin and a widow once they are baptized, by the same argument prostitutes and whores, once baptized, will be equated with virgins. For if past marriage does not harm a baptized widow, then the past pleasures of a prostitute, the exposure of her body to everyone's lust, will after baptism obtain the same reward as virginity! It is one thing to join to God a mind which is pure and is not polluted by any memories; it is quite another thing to remember the vile necessity of the embraces of a man, and to simulate in one's memory what one does not do physically.

[In i, 34 (col. 256-), he says that the early church was given lighter instructions by Paul because it was still weak, like a child that can drink only milk. To be perfect, however, is more difficult: he cites the story of the man who was told by Christ to give away all his goods.[1] Married men are only chosen as priests *faute de mieux*: there may be no one else available, or those who are celibate may have other faults. He then turns to a difficult problem:]

[i, 36, cols. 259–61] But you will say, "If everyone becomes a virgin, how is the human race to survive?" I will reply with an analogy: if all women were widows, or chaste in marriage, how would mortal progeny be propagated? According to this argument, it would cease to exist altogether.[2] Now, if everyone was a philosopher, there would be no farmers; and not only farmers—there would be no orators, no lawyers, no teachers of any subjects. If everyone was a king, who would be a soldier? If everyone were head, what would we say they were head of, if all the limbs were removed? Are you really afraid that if more people pursued virginity, prostitution and adultery would cease to exist, and that there would be no children squalling in the towns and villages? Every day the blood of lechers is spilled, acts of adultery are condemned, and in the very law-courts and tribunals lust dominates. There is no need to fear that all will become virgins: virginity is hard, and therefore rare—"many are called, but few are chosen" (Matt. 20:16, etc.). Many people can begin, but few persevere, and therefore those who do persevere win a great reward. If everyone could be a virgin, God would never have said, "Let him receive who can receive" (Matt. 19:12), and the Apostle Paul would not have hesitated in his advice when he said, "But on virgins, I have no instructions from God" (1 Cor. 7:25).

And you will say, "Why were genitals created? Why were we made in such a way by the most wise Creator, as to share passions for each other

1. *WBP*, 107–11.
2. Exact translation uncertain. The Latin is *Hac ratione nihil omnino erit, ne aliud esse desistat.*

and to long for natural copulation?"[3] My modesty in replying involves me in a risk, and I am caught between two rocks, the Symplegades of necessity and modesty, pulled this way and that, fearing the loss of my case or of my honor. I flush with shame to reply to the question, but if my modesty causes me to remain silent, I shall be thought to have given up my position, and will give my opponent the chance of beating me. Better to fight with one's eyes shut, like the gladiators who are blindfolded, than not to ward off his arrows with the shield of truth. Now I *could* say, "In the same way that the posterior section of the body and bowels, through which the excrement of the belly is removed, is hidden from the eyes, and is placed as it were behind one's back, similarly God has hidden away that which is beneath the stomach for bringing out the moistures and liquids which irrigate the veins of the body."

Since, however, the organs themselves and the construction of the genitals, the distinction between men and women, and the receptacles of the womb made to receive and nourish the foetus—since all these indicate the difference between the sexes, I will make this brief reply: Are we, then, never to cease from lust, so that we shouldn't have these limbs to no purpose? Why should a man abstain from his wife? Why should a widow keep herself chaste, if we were born only in order to live like animals? or, What harm will it do me, if my wife sleeps with someone else? For in the same way that the job of teeth is to chew, and to transmit what is chewed into the stomach, and there is no harm in anyone giving my wife bread, similarly, if it is the job of genitals always to follow their nature, then let someone else's virility surpass my lassitude, and let any chance lust quench my wife's eager appetite. What does the Apostle mean by exhorting continence, if it is against nature? Or God himself, by prescribing kinds of eunuchs (cf. Matt. 19:12)? The Apostle, who recommended his chastity to us, should constantly be assailed by this question, "Why do *you* have a tool, Paul? Why are you distinguished from the female sex by beard, hair, and other physical characteristics? Why don't your breasts swell, your hips spread out, your chest narrow? Your voice is older, your tone more fierce, and your brow shaggier. There is no point in your having all these male characteristics, if you do not have sexual intercourse." I have had to descend to a ridiculous kind of argument, but it was you who forced me to make this bold reply.

Our Lord and Savior, although in the form of God, deigned to take on the form of a servant, obedient to his Father, obedient till his death on the Cross. Why, then, was it necessary for him to be born with these limbs which he was not going to use?[4] For he was circumcised in order to indicate his sex. Why in his love did he castrate John the Apostle and John the Baptist, whom he had created as men? Therefore, let us, who believe in Christ, follow the example of Christ. * * * Certainly, at the Resurrection of the flesh our bodies will be of the same substance as now, though increased in glory. For the Savior had the same body after death as he had when he was crucified, to the extent that he showed his hands perforated by nails and the wound in his side. * * * "In the resurrection of the dead, they neither marry nor are given in marriage, but will

3. *WBP*, 115ff. The Wife seems to accept Jerome's argument but with a slightly different emphasis.
4. *WBP*, 139.

be like angels" (Matt. 22:30). What others are going to be in heaven, virgins have already begun to be on this earth. If we are promised the likeness of angels (who are not distinguished into sexes), either we shall lack sex, like the angels, or, what is clearly proved to be the case, we shall arise in our own sex, but not perform the offices of sex.

[He continues with an exposition of various statements of the Apostles, directed mainly to show that "living by the spirit" precludes marriage, and that the opposite is the way of death. In i, 39 (col. 265), he lists various precepts to chastity in the writings of other Apostles (notably 2 Pet. 2:9–22). In i, 40 (col. 267), he gives a description of the vicious life and habits of Jovinian himself, "a dog returning to his vomit" (2 Pet. 2:22). He summarizes the teachings of the early church:]

[i, 40, col. 270] The church does not condemn marriage, it relegates it; it does not reject it, but weighs it, knowing that in a great house there are not only gold and silver containers, but ones of wood and clay;[5] some are to our honor, some to our shame; whoever purifies himself will be an honorable container, prepared as is necessary for every good work.

[(i, 41, col. 270) Jerome realizes that his opponents may argue that this "new religion" (Christianity) is recommending a dogma which runs counter to nature; he therefore turns to pagan history and literature to produce examples of the honor in which virginity is held even by non-Christians. His examples include Atalanta, Harpalice, Camilla, Leo, Iphigeneia, the Sibyl, pagan priestesses and Vestal Virgins, the sign of the Zodiac, etc. He lists examples of women who have committed suicide rather than lose their virginity. (i, 42, col. 273-) He gives examples of pagan stories of virgin birth, including the Buddha, Athene, Bacchus, Plato (born of Apollo by Perictione), etc.

(i, 43, col. 273) He continues with examples of famous widows from pagan literature who would not take a second husband, including Dido (!), etc. (i, 46, col. 275) He lists famous Roman women, beginning with Lucretia. After this he quotes at length from Theophrastus in i, 47, cols. 276–78 (see above, pp. 395–97).]

[i, 48, cols. 278–80] Does the co-heir of Christ really want a human heir?[6] Does he long to have children, and to delight in a succession of descendants who may be seized by Antichrist? We read that Moses and Samuel set others before their own sons, and did not regard as their own children those whom they saw offending God.

After his divorce from Terentia Cicero was asked by Hirtius to marry the latter's sister; Cicero refused, and said that it was not possible to give attention both to philosophy and a wife. This fine wife, who had drunk wisdom from the Ciceronian spring, then married Sallust, his enemy, and her third husband was Messala Corvinus—she devolved down the ladder of eloquence, so to speak.

Socrates had two wives, Xantippe and Myron, niece of Aristeides. They used to quarrel frequently, and Socrates used to laugh at them because they quarreled over such a terrible picture of a man, snub-nosed, bald-headed,

5. *WBP*, 99–101.
6. This picks up the final remarks of Theophrastus (see above, p. 397).

shaggy-armed, and bow-legged; finally they turned their rage on him, and made him pay heavily—from then on he was put to flight and persecuted by them. On one occasion Xantippe was standing above him and wouldn't stop shouting at him; suddenly he found himself deluged by dirty water; he merely wiped his head and said, "I knew this thunder was sure to be followed by rain."[7]

Lucius Sylla the Lucky (if he hadn't been married) had a wife Metella who was openly unfaithful, and, because we are always the last to hear of our own misfortunes, Sylla didn't know about it even when it was common gossip in Athens; he finally learnt the secrets of his own home through the abuse of an enemy.

Pompey also had an unfaithful wife, Mutia, who was always surrounded by Easterners and crowds of eunuchs from the Pontus; everyone thought he knew about her and was suffering in silence, but a fellow-soldier mentioned it to him on an expedition, and by this sad message shook the conqueror of the world.

Cato the Censor had a lowly born wife, Actoria Paula, who was a drunkard, violent, and, what is hard to credit, arrogant towards Cato: I mention this in case anyone thinks that by marrying a poor woman he ensures married bliss for himself.

Philip, King of Macedon (the object of Demosthenes' tirades, the *Philippics*), was once shut out of his bedroom by his angry wife: he suffered in silence, and consoled himself for his misfortune with tragic verses. At Olympia the orator Gorgias once recited a book "On Concord" to the Greeks who were quarreling amongst themselves. His opponent Melanthius retorted: "Here is a man preaching to us about concord, who can't get concord in one house between his wife, his serving-wench and himself!"—his wife was jealous of the serving-girl's good looks, and was continually abusing her husband (in fact the most pure of men).

All Euripides' tragedies are indictments of women: Hermione, for instance, says "the counsels of evil women deceived me." * * *[8] We read of a noble at Rome who was defending himself among his friends for divorcing a rich, chaste, and beautiful wife; he stretched out his foot, and said, "This shoe that you see here looks fine and new to you: I alone know where my own shoe pinches." Herodotus writes that a woman takes off her chastity with her clothes.[9] Our Comic says that no one is fortunate who has married. Need I mention Pasiphae, Clytemnestra, Eriphyle?[1] The first was deep in luxury, being a king's wife, but is said to have sought the embrace of a bull; the second killed her husband for the love of her paramour; the third betrayed Amphiareus, by putting a golden necklace above her husband's safety. The tragedies are full of it, cities, kingdoms, homes are overthrown by it—the quarrel between wives and sweethearts. Parents take up weapons against their children; poisonous feasts are set out; for the rape of one woman Europe and Asia endured a ten-year war. We hear of some women married one day, divorced on the second day, and married again on the third: both husbands deserve censure, the one

7. *WBP*, 727–32.
8. The omitted passage explains the point of a somewhat obscure mother-in-law joke by Terence.
9. *WBP*, 782–83.
1. *WBP*, 733–46.

for being too quickly displeased, the other for being too quickly pleased. Epicurus, the prophet of pleasure (although his pupil Metrodorus married Leontia), said that few wise men should undertake marriage, because there were many disadvantages in it. In the same way that riches, honors, bodily health, and the other things which we call "morally indifferent" are in themselves neither good nor bad, and become good or bad only according to the way they are used and their result, so women are in this category of "both good and bad." Now it is a serious thing for a wise man to be in doubt whether he is going to marry a good wife or a bad one! Jokingly Chrysippus told the Romans to marry in order not to offend the "Jupiter of Marriage and Birth," for by this they would not marry at all, because they do not have a "Jupiter of Marriage"! * * *[2]

[i, 49, col. 280] Some of the above remarks are taken from writings on marriage by Aristotle, Plutarch, and Seneca. I here add some more: Love of beauty is loss of reason, and is the neighbor to insanity, a foul and inappropriate blemish on a blessed spirit. It destroys wise counsel, breaks high and noble spirits, drags them down from the loftiest to the meanest thoughts; it makes men quarrelsome, angry, rash, roughly imperious, servilely fawning, useless to everyone, and finally useless to love itself; for when it rages insatiably in the lust for enjoyment, it wastes many hours in suspicions, tears, and complaints. It makes one hate oneself, and finally hate love itself. The whole condemnation of love is set out by Plato [in the *Phaedro*], and Lysias expounds all its disadvantages—one takes a wife in madness, not in judgment; above all, the beauty of women needs the most strict guard. Further, Seneca tells us that he knew a fine man, who, when he was going out used to wrap his wife's girdle round his breast; not for a moment could he do without her presence; husband and wife would not drink anything unless both their lips had touched it; they did many equally foolish things, into which the sudden passion of burning love forced them. The origin of their love was honorable, but its size became monstrous. But in any case it makes no difference from what fine cause a man goes insane. Xystus says in his *Sentences* "the too eager lover of his own wife is an adulterer."[3] All love for another man's wife is disgraceful, but so is too great love for one's own wife[?].[4] A wise man should take a wife out of careful consideration, not out of love. He should keep a check on the urge of pleasure, not be rushed headlong into intercourse. Nothing is worse than to love a wife as one would a mistress. There are some who say that they couple with their wives and produce children for the sake of the state and the human race; they should at any rate imitate the animals, and not destroy their sons once their wife's womb has begun to swell. Let them behave to their wives as husbands, not as lovers. * * *[5] Thus satiety dissolves marriage of that sort swiftly. As soon as the pander of lust has gone, what once pleased is now cheapened. "What," says Seneca, "should I say of the poor men who for the most part marry to acquire the name of 'husband' in order to avoid the laws against celibacy?"

2. Jerome's comment on this joke is obscure.
3. See C. S. Lewis, *The Allegory of Love* (London: Oxford UP, 1936), p. 15 and n. 5.
4. Translation uncertain.
5. The omitted passage is difficult and obscure.

How can a married man control morals, order chastity, and keep the authority of a husband? The wisest of men says that chastity should be kept above all: once it is lost, all virtue tumbles. In this consists the chief of women's virtues. Chastity honors the poor woman, extolls the rich, redeems the ugly, adorns the beautiful: she deserves well of her ancestors because she has not soiled their line with a furtive conception; she deserves well of her children, who need have no shame of their mother nor doubt about who their father is, and most of all from herself, since she protects herself from insults on her outer body [?].[6] Captivity brings no greater misfortune than to be the object of another's lust. Men are honored by the consulship, eloquence extols their name forever, military glory and the triumph over a new people ennobles them. There are many things which bring glory to fine minds: a woman's virtue is properly her chastity. This made Lucretia the equal of Brutus—or even his superior, for he learnt from this woman that it is not possible to be a slave. It made Cornelia equal of Gracchus, Portia of the second Brutus. Tanaquilla is more famous than her husband—age has buried him among the names of kings, but her virtue (rare among all women) has fixed her name too firmly in the memory of all ages ever to be erased. Therefore let married women imitate Theano, Celobulina, Gorguntes, Timoclia, the Claudias and the Cornelias, and although they may see Paul pardoning evil women for their bigamy, let them read that even before the Christian religion shone forth in the world, faithful wives had glory among their sex: through virgins it was the custom to honor the goddess Fortune; no priest married twice or committed bigamy. Even today the High Priests at Athens are still castrated by a draught of hemlock; after they have been selected for the priesthood, they cease to be men.

End of Book One

WALTER MAP

From The Letter of Valerius to Ruffinus, against Marriage[†]

[This letter was written by the celebrated Walter Map, archdeacon of Oxford, probably before 1180; it was an early work and was not at first credited to him (because of the pseudonyms). Map therefore inserted it in his much longer work *De Nugis Curialium* (1181–93). Here he firmly asserted his authorship. The tone of the antifeminism is more akin to that of Theophrastus than of Jerome: it is philosophical rather than religious. It is referred to by the Wife of Bath as *Valerie*. I have made a few omissions.]

* * *

6. Translation uncertain.

† Prepared for an earlier edition of this volume by A. G. Rigg; see note, p. 395. The present translation is based on the 1914 edition by M. R. James in *Anecdota Oxoniensia* 14 (Oxford: Clarendom P, 1914), pp. 142–58. Since then the James edition has been revised by C. M. L. Brooke and R. A. B. Mynors as Walter Map, *De nugis curialium; Courtiers' Trifles* (Oxford: Clarendon P, 1983). The new edition includes a revised translation and will be useful to anyone desiring access to the full text.

I had a friend who lived the life of a philosopher; after many visits over a long time I once noticed that he had changed in his dress, his bearing and his expression: he sighed a lot, his face was pale and his dress vulgarly ostentatious; he said little and was sombre, but was arrogant in a strange way; he had lost his old wit and jollity. He said he was not well, and indeed he wasn't. I saw him wandering about alone, and in so far as respect for me allowed he refused to speak to me. I saw a man in the grip of Venus's paralysis: he seemed all suitor, not at all a philosopher. However, I hoped that he would recover after his lapse: I pardoned what I didn't know; I thought it was a joke, not something brutally serious: he planned not to be loved but to be wived—he wanted to be not Mars but Vulcan. My mind failed me; because he was bent on death, I began to die with him. I spoke to him, but was repulsed. I sent people to talk to him, and when he wouldn't listen to them I said "An evil beast hath devoured him" (Gen. 37:33). To fulfill all the good turns of friendship I sent him a letter in which I altered the names, and called myself (Walter) Valerius and him (John, a redhead [Lat. *rufus*]) Ruffinus, and called the letter "the letter of Valerius to Ruffinus the philosopher, against marrying."

I am forbidden to speak, and I cannot keep silent. I hate the cranes, the voice of the night-owl, the screech-owl and the other birds which gloomily predict with their wails the sadness of foul winter, and you mock the prophesies of disaster which will surely come true if you continue as you are. Therefore I am forbidden to speak, for I am a prophet not of pleasure but of truth.

I love the nightingale and the blackbird, for with their soft harmony they herald the joy of the gentle breeze, and above all the swallow,[1] which fills the season of longed-for joy with its fulness of delights, and I am not deceived. You love parasites and hangers-on with their sweet flatteries, and above all Circe who pours on you joys full of sweet-scented delight, to deceive you: I cannot keep silent, lest you are turned into a pig or an ass.[2]

The servant of Babel pours out for you honeyed poison, which "moveth itself aright" (Prov. 23:31) and delights and leads astray your spirit: therefore I am forbidden to speak. I know that "at the last it biteth like a serpent" (ibid.) and will give a wound which will suffer no antidote: therefore I cannot keep silent.

You have many to persuade you to pleasure, and they are pleasant to hear; I am a stumbling speaker of bitter truth which makes you vomit: therefore I am forbidden to speak. The voice of the goose among swans is held to be a poor delight for men to hear, but it taught the senators to save the city from fire, the treasure-houses from plunder, and themselves from the arrows of their foes. Perhaps you too will realize with the senators, for you are no fool, that the swans sing death, and the goose screeches safety: therefore I cannot keep silent.

1. This word also usually means "nightingale," but clearly Map had a different bird in mind from the first.
2. I.e., by Circe.

You are all afire with longing, and, seduced by the nobility of its fine head do not realize that you are seeking the chimaera,[3] you refuse to recognize that that three-formed monster is graced with the face of a noble lion, is sullied by the belly of a stinking goat, and is armed in its tail with a poisonous serpent: therefore I am forbidden to speak.

Ulysses was enticed by the harmony of the Sirens, but, because he knew the voices of the sirens and the drinks of Circe, he restrained himself with the chains of virtue, so that he avoided the whirlpool. I trust in the Lord and hope that you will imitate Ulysses, not Empedocles who was overcome by his philosophy (or rather, melancholy), and chose Etna as his tomb. In order that you may take notice of the parable you hear, I cannot keep silent.

But your present flame, by which the worse choice pleases you, is stronger than the flame which draws you to me; therefore, lest the greater flame draws the lesser to it, and I myself perish, I am forbidden to speak. That I may speak with the spirit by which I am yours, let the two flames be weighed in any scale, equal or not, and let your decision, whatever it is, be at my risk: you must pardon me, for the impatience of the love I have for you will not let me keep silent.

After the first creation of man the first wife of the first Adam sated the first hunger by the first sin, against God's command. The sin was the child of Disobedience, which will never cease before the end of the world to drive women tirelessly to pass on to the future what they learned from their mother. Friend, a disobedient wife is dishonor to a man: beware.

The Truth which cannot be deceived said of the blessed David, "I have found a man according to my heart" (1 Sam. 13:14). But by love of a woman he fell conspicuously from adultery to homicide, to fulfil the saying "scandals never come singly" (Matt. 18:7). For every iniquity is rich in followers, and whatever house it enters, it hands over to be soiled by abuse. Friend, Bathsheba was silent, and has never been criticized for anything; yet she became the spur which caused the fall of her perfect husband, the arrow of death for her innocent spouse. Is she innocent who strives with both eloquence, like Sampson's Delilah, and beauty, like Bathsheba, when the latter's beauty triumphed alone, even without intending to? If you are no closer than David to the heart of God, do not doubt that you too can fall.

Solomon, Sun of men, treasure of God's delights, singular home of wisdom, was clouded over by the cloud of darkness and lost the light of his soul, the smell of his glory, and the glory of his house by the witchery of women: finally, he bowed down before Baal, and from a priest of the Lord was turned into a servant of the Devil, so that he can be seen to have fallen from a higher precipice than Phoebus in the fall of Phaeton, when he became Admetus's shepherd instead of Jupiter's Apollo. Friend, if you are not wiser than Solomon—and no man is—you are not too great to be bewitched by a woman. Open your eyes and see.[4]

3. The image of the Chimaera (ultimately from Lucretius V. 903) was developed as an example against prostitutes by Marbod of Rennes (fl. 1100 C.E.) in his *Liber Decem Capitulorum,* ed. W. Bulst (Heidelberg, 1947), 3. 45–49, and came to be almost a proverb. The passage from Map was used by Lydgate, *Reson & Sensualyte*, ll. 3370–78, and is quoted in the margin of one MS at this point.

4. Cf. Chaucer, *Parson's Tale*, X, 955: "Ful ofte tyme I rede that no man truste in his owene perfeccioun, but he be stronger than Sampson, and hoolier than David, and wiser than Salomon." See also *Sir Gawain & the Green Knight*, ll. 2416–19. The list was used often: Map may be the direct source of many of the occurrences.

[Map continues his argument with a pun on *amare* "love" and *amarus* "bitter"; he says that chastity perished with Lucretia, Penelope, and the Sabine women. As examples of women's viciousness, he cites Scilla and Mirra. He quotes the stories of Jupiter, who became a bull in order to love Europa ("a woman will make you roar too"); Phoebus Apollo, whose light was eclipsed because of Leucithoe; Mars, who was put in chains by Vulcan when he was found sleeping with Venus, Vulcan's wife ("consider the chains which you cannot see but are beginning to feel, and tear yourself free while they can still be broken"). He notes that Paris passed an unfavorable judgment on Pallas Athene (when he preferred Helen), because she promised profit, not pleasure ("would you make the same decision?"). He reminds his friend of the fate of Julius Caesar, who did not heed the advice of the soothsayer on the day of his assassination. He then gives a series of anecdotes:]

King Phoroneus [famous for his legal innovations] on the day on which he went the way of all flesh said to his brother Leontius, "I would not have fallen short of the highest summit of good fortune, if only I had never had a wife." Leontius said, "How has a wife impeded you?" He replied, "All married men know!" Friend, would that you had experienced marriage, but were not married, so that you would know what an impediment it is to felicity!

The Emperor Valentius, eighty years old and still a virgin, when on the day of his death he heard the praises of his triumphs recounted—and he had had many—said that he was only proud of one victory. Asked "Which?" he said, "When I conquered my worst enemy, my own flesh." Friend, this emperor would have left the world without glory, if he had not boldly resisted that with which you have now made a pact.

After his divorce from Terentia, Cicero would not marry again; he said it was not possible to give one's attention both to a wife and to philosophy.* * *

Canius of Cadiz, a poet of a light and pleasant wit, was reproved by the sombre hen-pecked historian Livy of Phoenicia, because he enjoyed the loves of many women: "You cannot share in our philosophy when you yourself are shared by so many: Tityus does not love Juno with a liver torn into so many pieces by vultures!" Canius replied: "Whenever I slip, I get up more cautiously; when I am pushed down a little, I come up for air more quickly. The alternations of my nights make my days happier: a perpetuity of darkness is like hell. The first lilies of the springtime sun spread with a more effusive joy if they enjoy winds both from the South-east and the South-west—more than those which are blown over by the single blast of the fiery South wind. Mars broke his chains and sits at the heavenly banquet, from which hen-pecked Vulcan is excluded, held back by a long rope. Many threads bind less firmly than one chain: from philosophy I obtain pleasure—you go to it for relief!" Friend, I approve the words of both, but the lives of neither, but it is true that many diseases, which continually interrupt health, do less harm than a single disease which continually afflicts one with incurable illnesses.

Weeping, Pacuvius said to his neighbor Arrius, "Friend, I have in my garden an unlucky tree: my first wife hanged herself on it, then my second wife, and now the third." Arrius replied, "I'm surprised you find yourself able to weep in all these successes"; then he said, "Good Lord, think how many sorrows that tree has saved you!" Thirdly he said, "Friend, let me have some shoots of that tree to plant for myself." Friend, I'm afraid you may have to beg shoots of that tree when you won't be able to find any.[5]

Sulpicius, who had divorced a noble and chaste wife, knew where his own shoe pinched him. Friend, be careful that you don't have a pinching shoe which you can't take off.

Cato of Utica said, "If the world could exist without women, our company would not differ from that of the gods." Friend, Cato said nothing that he hadn't experienced and known; none of these men who attacked the deceits of women did so without having themselves been deceived—they were fully experienced and aware. You should believe them, for they tell the truth: they know that love pleases and then the loved one stabs [or: and stabs the loved one]; they know that the flower of Venus is a rose, but under its bright colour lie hidden many thorns.

Metellus would not marry the daughter of Marius, although she was rich in dowry, beautiful to look at, famous in birth, and of good reputation; he said, "I prefer to be mine than hers"; Marius said, "But she will be yours"; Metellus retorted, "A man has to be a woman's, because it is a point of logic that the predicates are only what the subject allows."[6] Thus by a joke Metellus turned away a load from his back. Friend, even if it is fitting to take a wife, it is not expedient. May it be love (and not blind love) that is in question, not income; may you choose beauty, not clothes; her mind, not her gold; may your bride be a wife, not a dowry. If it can possibly happen in this way, you may be able to be a predicate in such a way that you do not derive anger from the subject!

Lais of Corinth, a renowned beauty, only deigned to accept the embraces of kings and princes, but she tried to share the bed of the philosopher Demosthenes, so that she would seem, by breaking his notorious chastity, to have made rocks move by her beauty (as Amphion did with his lyre), and having attracted him by her blandishments treat him at her pleasure. When Demosthenes was enticed to her bedroom, Lais asked him for a hundred talents for the privilege; he looked up to heaven and said "I don't pay so much to feel penitent!" Friend, would that you might lift your attention to heaven, and avoid that which can only be redeemed by penitence.

Livia killed her husband whom she hated greatly; Lucilia killed hers, whom she loved to excess.[7] The former intentionally mixed poison, the latter was deceived and poured out madness as a cup of love. Friend, these women strove with opposite intentions, but neither was cheated of the end of female treachery, that is, their natural evil. Women walk by varying and diverse paths, but whatever the paths they wander, whatever the by-ways they take, there is one result, one finishing-post for all their routes, one head and point of agreement of all their ways—mischief. Take the example of these two women as evidence that woman, whether she loves or hates, is bold in everything—crafty, when she wants to do harm (which is always), and when she tries to help frequently gets in the way, and so turns out to do harm even unintentionally. You are placed in the furnace: if you are gold, you will come out gold.

5. *WBP*, 757–64 (with *Latumyus* inexplicably for *Pacuvius*).
6. Puns on *predicate* and *subject* (that which is literally "placed underneath" but logically governs the predicate) abound in medieval Latin antifeminist writers, both serious and frivolous.
7. *WBP*, 747–56 (with *Lucye* for *Lucilia*).

Deianeira clothed Hercules in a shirt, and brought vengeance on the "hammer of monsters" with the blood of a monster: what she had contrived to bring her happiness resulted in her tears * * * [women always look to their own pleasure, and never think of its effect on other people]. Hercules fulfilled twelve inhuman labors, but by the thirteenth, which surpassed all inhumanity, he was consumed. Thus the bravest of men lay dead, to be lamented like the most pitiful man,—he who had held up on his shoulders the span of the world without a groan.

Finally, what woman, among so many thousand thousands, ever saddened the eager and consistent suitor by a permanent refusal? Which one ever invariably cut off the words of a wooer? Her reply always savors of her favor, and however hard she may be she will always have hidden in her words some hint of encouragement for your plea. Any woman may say "No," but none say "No" for ever.

[His examples of unchastity[8] are inappropriately Jupiter's visit to Danae in a shower of gold and Perictione's virgin-birth of Plato out of Apollo: they are taken from Jerome (see above, p. 407) where they are used more appropriately. Map concludes his letter with a justification of his use of pagan examples, which may offer even a Christian a good example—in any case one should note that the pagans applied themselves to learning even without the promise of eternal felicity, simply to avoid ignorance—how much more should we pay attention to Scripture! He wants Ruffinus to marry not Venus but Pallas. The hand of the surgeon is hard, but it cures; the way to life is narrow and difficult, as was Jason's to the Golden Fleece. . . . Hard beginnings are rewarded by a sweet result. If you need any more evidence, read Theophrastus, or Seneca's *Medea*.]

From The Gospel According to St. John†

Chapter 4

* * *

5 He cometh therefore to a city of Samaria, which is called Sichar, near the land which Jacob gave to his son Joseph.

6 Now Jacob's well was there. Jesus therefore being wearied with his journey, sat thus on the well. It was about the sixth hour.

7 There cometh a woman of Samaria, to draw water. Jesus saith to her: Give me to drink.

8 For his disciples were gone into the city to buy meats.

9 Then that Samaritan woman saith to him: How dost thou, being a Jew, ask of me to drink, who am a Samaritan woman? For the Jews do not communicate with the Samaritans.

10 Jesus answered, and said to her: If thou didst know the gift of God, and who he is that saith to thee, Give me to drink; thou perhaps wouldst have asked of him, and he would have given thee living water.

8. Cf. *WBP*, 765ff.

† For this and the following Bible selections, we print the Douay/Rheims translation of the Latin Vulgate Bible, first published in 1582 and 1609, from the edition published by P. J. Kenedy and Sons (New York, 1914).

11 The woman saith to him: Sir, thou hast nothing wherein to draw, and the well is deep; from whence then hast thou living water?

12 Art thou greater than our father Jacob, who gave us the well, and drank thereof himself, and his children, and his cattle?

13 Jesus answered, and said to her: Whosoever drinketh of this water, shall thirst again; but he that shall drink of the water that I will give him, shall not thirst for ever:

14 But the water that I will give him, shall become in him a fountain of water, springing up into life everlasting.

15 The woman saith to him: Sir, give me this water, that I may not thirst, nor come hither to draw.

16 Jesus saith to her: Go, call thy husband, and come hither.

17 The woman answered, and said: I have no husband. Jesus said to her: Thou hast said well, I have no husband:

18 For thou hast had five husbands: and he whom thou now hast, is not thy husband. This thou hast said truly.

19 The woman saith to him: Sir, I perceive that thou art a prophet.

20 Our fathers adored on this mountain, and you say, that at Jerusalem is the place where men must adore.

21 Jesus saith to her: Woman, believe me, that the hour cometh, when you shall neither on this mountain, nor in Jerusalem, adore the Father.

22 You adore that which you know not: we adore that which we know; for salvation is of the Jews.

23 But the hour cometh, and now is, when the true adorers shall adore the Father in spirit and in truth. For the Father also seeketh such to adore him.

24 God is a spirit, and they that adore him, must adore him in spirit and in truth.

25 The woman saith to him: I know that the Messias cometh (who is called Christ); therefore, when he is come, he will tell us all things.

26 Jesus saith to her: I am he, who am speaking with thee.

27 And immediately his disciples came; and they wondered that he talked with the woman. Yet no man said: What seekest thou? or, why talkest thou with her?

28 The woman therefore left her water-pot, and went her way into the city, and saith to the men there:

29 Come, and see a man who has told me all things whatsoever I have done. Is not he the Christ?

30 They went therefore out of the city, and came unto him.

31 In the mean time the disciples prayed him, saying: Rabbi, eat.

32 But he said to them: I have meat to eat, which you know not.

33 The disciples therefore said one to another: Hath any man brought him to eat?

34 Jesus saith to them: My meat is to do the will of him that sent me, that I may perfect his work.

35 Do not you say, There are yet four months, and then the harvest cometh? Behold, I say to you, lift up your eyes, and see the countries; for they are white already to harvest.

36 And he that reapeth receiveth wages, and gathereth fruit unto life everlasting: that both he that soweth, and he that reapeth, may rejoice together.

37 For in this is the saying true: That it is one man that soweth, and it is another that reapeth.
38 I have sent you to reap that in which you did not labour: others have laboured, and you have entered into their labours.
39 Now of that city many of the Samaritans believed in him, for the word of the woman giving testimony: He told me all things whatsoever I have done.
40 So when the Samaritans were come to him, they desired that he would tarry there. And he abode there two days.
41 And many more believed in him because of his own word.
42 And they said to the woman: We now believe, not for thy saying: for we ourselves have heard him, and know that this is indeed the Saviour of the world.

* * *

From St. Paul to the Corinthians 1

Chapter 7

Now concerning the things whereof you wrote to me: It is good for a man not to touch a woman.
2 But for fear of fornication, let every man have his own wife, and let every woman have her own husband.
3 Let the husband render the debt to his wife, and the wife also in like manner to the husband.
4 The wife hath not power of her own body, but the husband. And in like manner the husband also hath not power of his own body, but the wife.
5 Defraud not one another, except, perhaps, by consent, for a time, that you may give yourselves to prayer; and return together again, lest Satan tempt you for your incontinency.
6 But I speak this by indulgence, not by commandment.
7 For I would that all men were even as myself: but every one hath his proper gift from God; one after this manner, and another after that.
8 But I say to the unmarried, and to the widows: It is good for them if they so continue, even as I.
9 But if they do not contain themselves, let them marry. For it is better to marry than to be burnt.
10 But to them that are married, not I but the Lord commandeth, that the wife depart not from her husband.
11 And if she depart, that she remain unmarried, or be reconciled to her husband. And let not the husband put away his wife.
12 For to the rest I speak, not the Lord. If any brother hath a wife that believeth not, and she consent to dwell with him, let him not put her away.
13 And if any woman hath a husband that believeth not, and he consent to dwell with her, let her not put away her husband.
14 For the unbelieving husband is sanctified by the believing wife; and the unbelieving wife is sanctified by the believing husband: otherwise your children should be unclean; but now they are holy.

15 But if the unbeliever depart, let him depart. For a brother or sister is not under servitude in such cases. But God hath called us in peace.

16 For how knowest thou, O wife, whether thou shalt save thy husband? Or how knowest thou, O man, whether thou shalt save thy wife?

17 But as the Lord hath distributed to every one, as God hath called every one, so let him walk: and so in all churches I teach.

18 Is any man called, being circumcised? let him not procure uncircumcision. Is any man called in uncircumcision? let him not be circumcised.

19 Circumcision is nothing, and uncircumcision is nothing: but the observance of the commandments of God.

20 Let every man abide in the same calling in which he was called.

21 Wast thou called, being a bondman? care not for it; but if thou mayest be made free, use it rather.

22 For he that is called in the Lord, being a bondman, is the free man of the Lord. Likewise he that is called, being free, is the bondman of Christ.

23 You are bought with a price; be not made the bondslaves of men.

24 Brethren, let every man, wherein he was called, therein abide with God.

25 Now concerning virgins, I have no commandment of the Lord; but I give counsel, as having obtained mercy of the Lord, to be faithful.

26 I think therefore that this is good for the present necessity, that it is good for a man so to be.

27 Art thou bound to a wife? seek not to be loosed. Art thou loosed from a wife? seek not a wife.

28 But if thou take a wife, thou hast not sinned. And if a virgin marry, she hath not sinned: nevertheless, such shall have tribulation of the flesh. But I spare you.

29 This therefore I say, brethren; the time is short; it remaineth, that they also who have wives, be as if they had none;

30 And they that weep, as though they wept not; and they that rejoice, as if they rejoiced not; and they that buy, as though they possessed not;

31 And they that use this world, as if they used it not: for the fashion of this world passeth away.

32 But I would have you to be without solicitude. He that is without a wife, is solicitous for the things that belong to the Lord, how he may please God.

33 But he that is with a wife, is solicitous for the things of the world, how he may please his wife: and he is divided.

34 And the unmarried woman and the virgin thinketh on the things of the Lord, that she may be holy both in body and in spirit. But she that is married thinketh on the things of the world, how she may please her husband.

35 And this I speak for your profit: not to cast a snare upon you; but for that which is decent, and which may give you power to attend upon the Lord, without impediment.

36 But if any man think that he seemeth dishonoured, with regard to his virgin, for that she is above the age, and it must so be: let him do what he will; he sinneth not, if she marry.

37 For he that hath determined being steadfast in his heart, having no necessity, but having power of his own will; and hath judged this in his heart, to keep his virgin, doth well.

38 Therefore, both he that giveth his virgin in marriage, doth well; and he that giveth her not, doth better.
39 A woman is bound by the law as long as her husband liveth; but if her husband die, she is at liberty: let her marry to whom she will; only in the Lord.
40 But more blessed shall she be, if she so remain, according to my counsel; and I think that I also have the spirit of God.

From St. Paul to the Ephesians

Chapter 5

Be ye therefore followers of God, as most dear children;
2 And walk in love, as Christ also hath loved us, and hath delivered himself for us, an oblation and a sacrifice to God for an odour of sweetness.
3 But fornication, and all uncleanness, or covetousness, let it not so much as be named among you, as becometh saints:
4 Or obscenity, or foolish talking, or scurrility, which is to no purpose; but rather giving of thanks.
5 For know you this and understand, that no fornicator, or unclean, or covetous person (which is a serving of idols), hath inheritance in the kingdom of Christ and of God.
6 Let no man deceive you with vain words. For because of these things cometh the anger of God upon the children of unbelief.
7 Be ye not therefore partakers with them.
8 For you were heretofore darkness, but now light in the Lord. Walk then as children of the light.
9 For the fruit of the light is in all goodness, and justice, and truth;
10 Proving what is well pleasing to God.
11 And have no fellowship with the unfruitful works of darkness, but rather reprove them.
12 For the things that are done by them in secret, it is a shame even to speak of.
13 But all things that are reproved, are made manifest by the light; for all that is made manifest is light.
14 Wherefore he saith: *Rise, thou that sleepest, and arise from the dead: and Christ shall enlighten thee.*
15 See therefore, brethren, how you walk circumspectly: not as unwise,
16 But as wise: redeeming the time, because the days are evil.
17 Wherefore become not unwise, but understanding what is the will of God.
18 And be not drunk with wine, wherein is luxury; but be ye filled with the holy Spirit,
19 Speaking to yourselves in psalms, and hymns, and spiritual canticles, singing and making melody in your hearts to the Lord;
20 Giving thanks always for all things, in the name of our Lord Jesus Christ, to God and the Father:
21 Being subject one to another, in the fear of Christ.
22 Let women be subject to their husbands, as to the Lord;

23 Because the husband is the head of the wife, as Christ is the head of the church. He *is* the saviour of his body.

24 Therefore as the church is subject to Christ, so also let the wives be to their husbands in all things.

25 Husbands, love your wives, as Christ also loved the church, and delivered himself up for it:

26 That he might sanctify it, cleansing it by the laver of water in the word of life:

27 That he might present it to himself a glorious church, not having spot or wrinkle, or any such thing; but that it should be holy, and without blemish.

28 So also ought men to love their wives as their own bodies. He that loveth his wife, loveth himself.

29 For no man ever hated his own flesh; but nourisheth and cherisheth it, as also Christ doth the church:

30 Because we are members of his body, of his flesh, and of his bones.

31 *For this cause shall a man leave his father and mother, and shall cleave to his wife, and they shall be two in one flesh.*

32 This is a great sacrament; but I speak in Christ and in the church.

33 Nevertheless let every one of you in particular love his wife as himself: and let the wife fear her husband.

From St. Paul to Timothy 1

Chapter 2

* * *

9 In like manner women also in decent apparel: adorning themselves with modesty and sobriety, not with plaited hair, or gold, or pearls, or costly attire,

10 But as it becometh women professing godliness, with good works.

11 Let the woman learn in silence, with all subjection.

12 But I suffer not a woman to teach, nor to use authority over the man: but to be in silence.

13 For Adam was first formed; then Eve.

14 And Adam was not seduced; but the woman being seduced, was in the transgression.

15 Yet she shall be saved through child-bearing; if she continue in faith, and love, and sanctification, with sobriety.

Chapter 5

* * *

3 Honour widows, that are widows indeed.

4 But if any widow have children, or grandchildren, let her learn first to govern her own house, and to make a return of duty to her parents: for this is acceptable before God.

5 But she that is a widow indeed, and desolate, let her trust in God, and continue in supplications and prayers night and day.

6 For she that liveth in pleasures, is dead while she is living.

7 And this give in charge, that they may be blameless.

8 But if any man have not care of his own, and especially of those of his house, he hath denied the faith, and is worse than an infidel.

9 Let a widow be chosen of no less than threescore years of age, who hath been the wife of one husband.

10 Having testimony for her good works, if she have brought up children, if she have received to harbour, if she have washed the saints' feet, if she have ministered to them that suffer tribulation, if she have diligently followed every good work.

11 But the younger widows avoid. For when they have grown wanton in Christ, they will marry:

12 Having damnation, because they have made void their first faith.

13 And withal being idle they learn to go about from house to house: and are not only idle, but tattlers also, and busy-bodies, speaking things which they ought not.

14 I will therefore that the younger should marry, bear children, be mistresses of families, give no occasion to the adversary to speak evil.

15 For some are already turned aside after Satan.

16 If any of the faithful have widows, let him minister to them, and let not the church be charged: that there may be sufficient for them that are widows indeed.

* * *

From St. Paul to Timothy 2

Chapter 2

* * *

14 Of these things put them in mind, charging them before the Lord. Contend not in words, for it is to no profit, but to the subverting of the hearers.

15 Carefully study to present thyself approved unto God, a workman that needeth not to be ashamed, rightly handling the word of truth.

16 But shun profane and vain babblings: for they grow much towards ungodliness.

17 And their speech spreadeth like a canker: of whom are Hymeneus and Philetus:

18 Who have erred from the truth, saying, that the resurrection is past already, and have subverted the faith of some.

19 But the sure foundation of God standeth firm, having this seal: the Lord knoweth who are his; and let every one depart from inquity who nameth the name of the Lord.

20 But in a great house there are not only vessels of gold and of silver, but also of wood and of earth: and some indeed unto honour, but some unto dishonour.

21 If any man therefore shall cleanse himself from these, he shall be a vessel unto honour, sanctified and profitable to the Lord, prepared unto every good work.

22 But flee thou youthful desires, and pursue justice, faith, charity,
and peace, with them that call on the Lord out of a pure heart.
23 And avoid foolish and unlearned questions, knowing that they beget
strifes.
24 But the servant of the Lord must not wrangle: but be mild towards
all men, apt to teach, patient,
25 With modesty admonishing them that resist the truth: if peradven-
ture God may give them repentance to know the truth,
26 And they may recover themselves from the snares of the devil, by
whom they are held captive at his will.

JOHN GOWER

The Tale of Florent†

* * *

Mi Sone, and I thee rede° this, *advise*
What so befalle of other weie,° *otherwise*
That thou to loves heste° obeie *command*
Als ferr as thou it myht suffise;° *be able*
For ofte sithe° in such a wise° *oftentimes / way*
Obedience in love availeth,
Wher al a mannes strengthe faileth.
Wherof, if that the list to wite° *it pleases thee to know*
In a cronique° as it is write, *chronicle*
A gret ensample° thou myht fynde, *example*
Which now is come to my mynde.

Ther was whilom° be° daies olde *once upon a time / in*
A worthi knyht, and as men tolde
He was nevoeu° to th'emperour *nephew*
And of his court a courteour.° *courtier*
Wifles° he was, Florent he hihte,° *Wifeless / was called*
He was a man that mochel myhte.° *could (do) a great deal*
Of armes he was desirous,
Chivalerous and amorous,
And for the fame of worldes speche,° *worldly reputation*
Strange aventures forto seche,° *seek*
He rod the Marches al aboute.
And fell° a time, as he was oute, *there befell*
Fortune, which may every thred
Tobreke° and knette° of mannes sped,° *Break apart / knit up / success*
Schop,° as this knyht rod in a pas,° *Arranged / at a walk*

† From *Confessio Amantis* I.1396–1871. Text based on *The English Works of John Gower*, ed. G. C. Macaulay, Early English Text Society, e.s. 81–82 (London, 1900–01; rpt. 1969), 1.74–86. The framing device in the *Confessio* is the lover-narrator's confession to Genius, who instructs him with many exempla organized according to the seven deadly sins. *The Tale of Florent* is told to counteract disobedience, one of the subdivisions of Pride. Gower completed the first version of the *Confessio* in 1390, having begun it some four years earlier. A revised version was completed in 1392–93. On Gower's relationship to Chaucer, see footnote, p. 375, and the Introduction to the *Man of Law's Tale*, pp. 99–102.

That he be strengthe° take was, *by force*
And to a castell thei him ladde,° *led*
Wher that he fewe frendes hadde;
For so it fell that ilke stounde° *at that same time*
That he hath with a dedly wounde,
Feihtende, his oghne hondes slain° *Fighting, (with) his own hands slew*
Branchus, which to the Capitain
Was sone and heir, wherof ben wrothe° *angry*
The fader and the moder bothe.
That knyht Branchus was of his hond
The worthieste of al his lond,
And fain° thei wolden do vengance° *willingly / take revenge*
Upon Florent, bot° remembrance *except for*
That thei toke of his worthinesse
Of knyhthod and of gentilesse,
And how he stod of cousinage° *was related*
To th'emperour, made hem° assuage,° *them / abate (their anger)*
And dorsten° noght slen° him for fere.° *(they) dared / slay / out of fear*
In gret desputeisoun° thei were *argumentation*
Among hemself, what was the beste.
Ther was a lady, the slyheste° *most clever*
Of alle that men knewe tho,° *then*
So old sche myhte unethes go,° *could scarcely walk*
And was grantdame° unto the dede;° *grandmother / dead (man)*
And sche with that began to rede,° *counsel*
And seide how sche wol bringe him inne,
That° sche schal him to dethe winne° *So that / bring to*
Al only of his oghne grant,° *by his own consent*
Thurgh strengthe of verray° covenant *a true*
Withoute blame of eny wiht.° *person*
Anon° sche sende for this kniht, *Immediately*
And of hire sone sche alleide° *alleged, cited*
The deth, and thus to him sche seide:
"Florent, how so thou be to wyte° *blame*
Of Branchus deth, men schal respite° *delay*
As now° to take vengement,° *Just now / revenge*
Be so° thou stonde in juggement *If*
Upon certein condicioun—
That thou unto a questioun
Which I schal axe° schalt ansuere; *ask*
And over this thou schalt ek° swere, *also*
That if thou of the sothe° faile, *truth*
Ther schal non other thing availe,
That thou ne schalt thi deth receive.
And for men schal thee noght deceive,
That thou therof myht ben avised,° *take counsel*
Thou schalt have day and tyme assised° *fixed, appointed*
And leve° saufly° forto wende,° *permission / safely / depart*
Be so that° at thi daies ende *If*
Thou come ayein° with thin avys."° *again / conclusion*
This knyht, which worthi was and wys,

This lady preith° that he may wite,° *beseeches / know*
And have it under seales write,
What question it scholde be,
For which he schal in that degree
Stonde of his lif in jeupartie.° *jeopardy*
With that sche feigneth compaignie,° *friendliness*
And seith: "Florent, on love it hongeth° *depends, concerns*
Al that to myn axinge° longeth:° *asking, question / belongs*
What alle wommen most desire,
This wole I axe, and in th'empire
Wher as° thou hast most knowlechinge° *Where / largest acquaintance*
Tak conseil upon this axinge."
Florent this thing hath undertake,
The day was set, the time take;
Under his seal he wrot his oth° *oath*
In such a wise,° and forth he goth *way*
Hom to his emes° court ayein;° *uncle's / again*
To whom his aventure plein
He tolde, of that him is befalle.
And upon that thei weren alle
The wiseste of the lond asent,° *sent for*
Bot natheles° of on° assent *nevertheless / one*
Thei myhte noght acorde plat.° *plainly*
On° seide this, an othre that. *One*
After° the disposicioun *According to*
Of naturel complexioun,° *temperament*
To som womman it is plesance° *a pleasure*
That to an other is grevance,° *a vexation*
Bot such a thing in special,° *particular*
Which to hem alle in general
Is most plesant, and most desired
Above alle othre and most conspired,° *sighed after*
Such o thing conne° thei noght finde *could*
Be constellacion ne kinde.° *Through astrological or natural investigation*
And thus Florent withoute cure° *remedy*
Mot stonde upon his aventure,° *Must endure his fortune*
And is al schape° unto the lere,° *prepared / loss*
As in defalte of his answere.
This knyht hath levere° forto dye *rather*
Than breke his trowthe° and forto lye *vow*
In place ther as he was swore,
And schapth him gon ayein° therfore. *prepares himself to return again*
Whan time cam he tok his leve,
That lengere° wolde he noght beleve,° *longer / remain*
And preith° his em he be noght wroth, *begs*
For that is a point of his oth,
He seith, that noman schal him wreke,° *avenge*
Thogh afterward men hiere speke° *hear (it) said*
That he par aventure° deie.° *by chance / die*
And thus he wente forth his weie° *way*
Alone as knyht aventurous,

And in his thoght was curious
To wite° what was best to do;   *know*
And as he rod al one° so,   *all alone*
And cam nyh° ther° he wolde be,   *nigh (near) / where*
In a forest under a tre
He syh° wher sat a creature,   *saw*
A lothly° wommannysch figure,   *loathly, loathsome*
That forto speke of fleisch and bon°   *flesh and bone*
So foul yit° syh° he nevere non.   *yet, until then / saw*
This knyht behield hir redely,°   *intently*
And as he wolde have passed by,
Sche cleped° him and bad abide;   *called*
And he his horse heved° aside   *pulled*
Tho° torneth, and to hire he rod,   *Then*
And there he hoveth° and abod,   *remained*
To wite° what sche wolde mene.°   *know / say*
And sche began him to bemene,°   *speak*
And seide: "Florent, be° thi name,   *by*
Thou hast on honde such a game,
That bot° thou be the betre avised,   *unless*
Thi deth is schapen° and devised,   *arranged*
That al the world ne mai the save,
Bot if that° thou my conseil have."   *Unless*
Florent, whan he this tale herde,
Unto this olde wyht° answerde   *person*
And of hir conseil° he hir preide.°   *advice / begged*
And sche ayein° to him thus seide: *again, in turn*
"Florent, if I for the° so schape,   *thee*
That thou thurgh me thi deth ascape°   *escape*
And take worschipe of° thi dede,   *receive honor for*
What schal I have to my mede?"°   *for my reward*
"What° thing," quod he, "that thou wolt axe."°   *Whatever / ask*
"I bidde° nevere a betre taxe,"°   *ask / no better fee*
Quod sche, "bot ferst, er° thou be sped,°   *before / have hastened off*
Thou schalt me leve° such a wedd,°   *leave / pledge*
That I wol have thi trowthe° in honde   *troth, promise*
That thou schalt be myn housebonde."
"Nay," seith Florent, "that may noght be."
"Ryd thanne forth thi wey," quod sche,
"And if thou go withoute red,°   *advice*
Thou schalt be sekerliche° ded."   *surely*
Florent behihte° hire good ynowh°—   *promised / goods enough*
Of lond, of rente,° of park,° of plowh°—   *income / forest / plowland*
Bot al that compteth sche at noght.°   *she considers worth nothing*
Tho° fell this knyht in mochel° thoght;   *Then / much*
Now goth he forth, now comth ayein,
He wot° noght what is best to sein,°   *knows / say*
And thoghte, as he rod to and fro,
That chese he mot on of the tuo,°   *That he must choose one of the two*
Or° forto take hire to his wif   *Either*
Or elles° forto lese° his lif.   *else / lose*

And thanne he caste° his avantage, *considered*
That sche was of so gret an age,
That sche mai live bot a while,
And thoghte° put hire in an ile,° *thought to / on an island*
Wher that noman hire scholde knowe,
Til sche with deth were overthrowe.
And thus this yonge lusti° knyht *vigorous*
Unto this olde lothly° wiht° *loathly / person*
Tho seide: "If that non other chance
Mai make° my deliverance, *bring about*
Bot only thilke same° speche *that same*
Which, as thou seist, thou schalt me teche,
Have hier myn hond, I schal thee wedde."
And thus his trowthe° he leith to wedde.° *troth, pledge / sets forth*
With that sche frounceth° up the browe: *wrinkles*
"This covenant I wol allowe,"° *accept*
Sche seith: "if eny other thing
Bot° that° thou hast of my techyng *Except / what*
Fro deth thi body mai respite,° *delay, put off*
I woll thee of thi trowthe acquite,° *release*
And elles° be non other weie. *otherwise*
Now herkne me what I schal seie:° *say*
Whan thou art come into the place,
Wher now thei maken gret manace° *show great hostility*
And upon thi comynge abyde,
Thei wole anon° the same tide° *at once / time*
Oppose thee of° thin answere. *Demand from thee*
I wot° thou wolt nothing° forbere° *know / not at all / hold back*
Of that° thou wenest° be thi beste,° *With what / thinkest / best (answer)*
And if thou myht so finde reste,° *peace*
Wel is,° for thanne is ther nomore. *it is*
And elles this schal be my lore,° *teaching*
That thou schalt seie, upon this molde° *earth*
That alle wommen lievest° wolde *most dearly*
Be soverein of° mannes love; *sovereign over, master of*
For what° womman is so above, *whatever*
Sche hath, as who seith,° al hire wille; *as it is said*
And elles may sche noght fulfille
What thing hir were lievest have.
With this answere thou schalt save
Thiself, and other wise noght.
And whan thou hast thin ende wroght,
Com hier ayein, thou schalt me finde,
And let nothing out of thi minde."° *escape thy memory*

He goth him forth with hevy chiere,° *sad countenance, mood*
As he that not° in what manere *knows not*
He mai this worldes joie atteigne;° *attain*
For if he deie,° he hath a peine, *die*
And if he live, he mot him binde
To such on° which of alle kinde° *a one / the species*
Of wommen is th'unsemlieste.° *the unseemliest, ugliest*

Thus wot° he noght what is the beste, *knows*
Bot be him lief° or be him loth,° *dear, desirable / loathsome, distasteful*
Unto the castell forth he goth,
His full answere forto yive,° *give*
Or° forto deie° or forto live. *Either / die*
Forth with his conseil° cam the lord, *council*
The thinges° stoden of record;° *Everything / as previously arranged*
He sende up for the lady sone,° *immediately*
And forth sche cam, that olde mone.° *crone*
In presence of the remenant° *rest*
The strengthe of al the covenant
Tho° was reherced openly, *Then*
And to Florent sche bad forthi° *therefore*
That he schal tellen his avis,° *conclusion*
As he that woot° what is the pris. *knows*
Florent seith al that evere he couthe,° *knew*
Bot such word cam ther non to mowthe,° *mouth*
That he for yifte° or for beheste° *by any gift / promise*
Mihte eny wise° his deth areste.° *in any way / prevent*
And thus he tarieth longe and late,
Til that this lady bad° algate° *commanded / finally, at last*
That he schal for the dom° final *judgment*
Yive° his answere in special° *Give / particular*
Of that sche hadde him ferst opposed:° *first put to him*
And thanne he hath trewly supposed
That he him may of nothing yelpe,° *boast*
Bot if° so be tho° wordes helpe *Unless / those*
Whiche as the womman hath him tawht° *taught*
Whereof he hath an hope cawht° *caught, conceived*
That he schal ben excused so,
And tolde out plein° his wille tho.° *plainly / then*
And whan that this matrone herde
The manere how this knyht ansuerde,
Sche seide: "Ha, treson!° Wo thee be,° *treason / Woe be to thee*
That hast thus told the privite,° *the secret knowledge*
Which° alle wommen most desire! *What*
I wolde that thou were afire!"
Bot natheles° in such a plit° *nevertheless / plight*
Florent of° his answere is quit,° *for / released*
And tho° began his sorwe newe, *then*
For he mot gon, or ben untrewe,
To hire which his trowthe hadde.
Bot he, which alle schame dradde,° *feared*
Goth forth in stede of° his penance, *to the place of*
And takth the fortune of his chance,
As he that was with trowthe affaited.° *governed by truth*
This olde wyht° him hath awaited *person*
In place wher as° he hire lefte. *where*
Florent his wofull heved° uplefte° *head / uplifted*
And syh° this vecke° wher sche sat, *saw / hag, old woman*
Which was the lothlieste what° *thing*

That evere man caste on his yhe.°	*eye*
Hire nase° bass,° hire browes hyhe,°	*nose / low, long / high*
Hire yhen° smale and depe set,	*eyes*
Hire chekes ben with teres wet	
And rivelen° as an emty skyn°	*shriveled / skin*
Hangende doun unto the chin;	
Hire lippes schrunken ben for age,	
Ther was no grace in the visage;	
Hir front° was nargh,° hir lockes°	*forehead / narrow / locks (of hair)*
hore,°	*hoary*
Sche loketh forth° as doth a More;°	*looks / Moor*
Hire necke is schort, hir schuldres courbe,°	*stooped*
That myhte a mannes lust destourbe;°	*trouble, destroy*
Hire body gret° and nothing° smal,	*large / not at all*
And schortly to descrive° hire al,	*describe*
Sche hath no lith° withoute a lak,°	*limb / defect, fault*
Bot lich° unto the wollesak°	*like / woolsack*
Sche proferth hire° unto this knyht,	*proffers herself*
And bad him, as he hath behyht,°	*promised*
So as° sche hath ben his warrant,°	*Since / protection*
That he hire holde covenant,°	*keep the covenant with her*
And be° the bridel sche him seseth.°	*by / seizes*
Bot Godd wot how that sche him pleseth	
Of° suche wordes as sche spekth.	*By*
Him thenkth° welnyh° his herte brekth	*It seems to him / almost*
For° sorwe that he may noght fle,	*Out of*
Bot if° he wolde untrewe be.	*Unless*
Loke how° a sek° man for his hele°	*Just as / sick / health*
Takth baldemoine° with canele,°	*gentian (a medicinal root) / cinnamon*
And with the mirre° takth the sucre,°	*myrrh / sugar*
Ryht upon such a maner lucre°	*kind of profit, reward*
Stant° Florent, as in this diete:	*Stands*
He drinkth the bitre° with the swete,	*bitter*
He medleth° sorwe with likynge,°	*mixes / pleasure (at being alive)*
And liveth, as who seith, deyinge;	
His youthe schal be cast aweie°	*away*
Upon such on,° which as the weie°	*a one / like the road*
Is old and lothly° overal.	*loathly*
Bot nede he mot that nede schal:°	*i.e., there's no denying necessity*
He wolde algate his trowthe holde,°	*keep his troth, promise*
As every knyht therto is holde,°	*beholden, bound*
What happ° so evere him is befalle.	*fortune, chance*
Thogh sche be the fouleste of alle,	
Yet to th'onour of wommanhiede°	*womanhood*
Him thoghte he scholde taken hiede,°	*heed*
So that for pure gentilesse,°	*nobility, courtesy*
As he hire couthe best adresce,°	*knew best how to position her*
In ragges as sche was totore°	*all torn*
He set hire on his hors tofore°	*before (him)*
And forth he takth his weie° softe;°	*way / gently*
No wonder thogh he siketh° ofte.	*sighs*

Bot as an oule° fleth° by nyhte — *owl / flies*
Out of alle othre briddes syhte,° — *sight*
Riht so° this knyht on daies brode° — *Just so / in broad daylight*
In clos° him hield, and schop° his rode° — *hiding / arranged / ride*
On nyhtes time, til the tyde° — *time*
That he cam there° he wolde abide. — *there where*
And prively° withoute noise — *secretly*
He bringth this foule grete coise° — *hag (lit., rump, thigh)*
To his castell in such a wise° — *way*
That noman myhte hire schappe° avise,° — *form / discern*
Til sche into the chambre cam:
Wher he his prive conseil° nam° — *private counsel / took*
Of suche men as he most troste,° — *trusted*
And tolde hem that he nedes moste° — *needs must*
This beste° wedde to his wif, — *beast*
For elles hadde he lost his lif.

The prive° wommen were asent,° — *confidential / sent for*
That scholden ben of his assent.
Hire ragges thei anon of drawe,° — *take off*
And, as it was that time lawe,
She hadde bath, sche hadde reste,
And was arraied to the beste;
Bot with no craft of combes brode° — *wide combs*
Thei myhte hire hore lockes schode,° — *part*
And sche ne wolde noght be schore° — *shorn*
For no conseil;° and thei therfore, — *On anyone's advice*
With such atyr° as tho° was used, — *attire / then*
Ordeinen° that it was excused, — *Ordained*
And hid so crafteliche° aboute, — *skillfully*
That noman myhte sen hem oute.° — *discern them (the locks of her hair)*
Bot when sche was fulliche arraied
And hire atyr was al assaied,° — *examined, inspected*
Tho was sche foulere on to se;° — *fouler to look on*
Bot yit° it may non other° be, — *yet / not otherwise*
Thei were wedded in the nyht.
So wo begon° was nevere knyht — *woebegone*
As he was thanne of mariage.
And sche began to pleie° and rage,° — *play / carry on wantonly, foolishly*
As who° seith, I am wel ynowh;° — *Like one who / happy enough*
Bot he thereof nothing ne° lowh,° — *not at all / laughed*
For° sche tok thanne chiere on honde° — *So / became more cheerful*
And clepeth° him hire housebonde, — *calls*
And seith, "My lord, go we to bedde,
For I to that entente° wedde, — *for that reason*
That thou schalt be my worldes blisse";
And profreth° him with that to kisse, — *proffers*
As° sche a lusti° lady were. — *As if / jolly*
His body myhte wel be there,
Bot as of° thoght and of memoire° — *for / memory*
His herte was in purgatoire.° — *purgatory*
Bot yit for strengthe of matrimoine

He myhte make non essoine,° — *excuse*
That he ne mot algates plie° — *could not in any way comply*
To gon to bedde of° compaignie. — *in*
And whan thei were abedde naked,
Withoute slep he was awaked;° — *Sleepless, he lay awake*
He torneth on that other side,
For that he wolde hise yhen° hyde — *eyes*
Fro lokynge on that foule wyht.° — *creature*
The chambre was al full of lyht,
The courtins were of cendal° thinne; — *a kind of silk*
This newe bryd° which lay withinne, — *bride*
Thogh it be noght with his acord,
In armes sche beclipte° hire lord, — *embraced*
And preide,° as° he was torned fro,° — *begged / since / away*
He wolde him torne ayeinward° tho; — *around*
"For now," sche seith, "we ben bothe on."° — *one*
And he lay stille as eny ston,
Bot evere in on° sche spak and preide, — *continually*
And bad him thenke on that° he seide, — *what*
Whan that he tok hire be the hond.
  He herde and understod the bond,
How he was set to his penance,
And as it were a man in trance
He torneth him al sodeinly,° — *suddenly*
And syh° a lady lay him by — *saw*
Of eyhtetiene wynter age,° — *i.e., eighteen years old*
Which was the faireste of visage° — *appearance*
That evere in al this world he syh.
And as he wolde have take hire nyh,° — *nigh, close*
Sche put hire hand and be his leve° — *by his leave, with his permission*
Besoghte him that he wolde leve,° — *leave off*
And seith that forto wynne or lese° — *lose*
He mot on of tuo thinges chese:° — *choose*
Wher° he wol have hire such on nyht,° — *Whether / at night*
Or elles upon daies lyht,° — *by day's light*
For he schal noght have bothe tuo.
And he began to sorwe tho
In many a wise, and caste his thoght,° — *pondered*
Bot for al that yit cowthe he noght° — *he didn't know how to*
Devise himself° which was the beste. — *Decide (for) himself*
And sche, that wolde his hertes reste,
Preith° that he scholde chese algate,° — *Begs / nevertheless*
Til ate laste longe and late
He seide: "O ye my lyves hele,° — *health, prosperity*
Sey what you list° in my querele,° — *pleases you / on my behalf*
I not° what ansuere I schal yive;° — *know not / give*
Bot evere whil that I may live,
I wol that ye be my maistresse,
For I can noght miselve gesse° — *guess, determine*
Which is the beste unto my chois.
Thus grante I yow myn hole vois:° — *my whole voice, my full assent*

Ches for ous bothen,° I you preie, — *both*
And what as evere that ye seie,
Riht as ye wole,° so wol I." — *Just as you wish*
"Mi lord," sche seide, "grant merci,° — *many thanks*
For of this word that ye now sein,° — *say*
That ye have made me soverein,
Mi destine° is overpassed,° — *destiny, fate / overcome*
That° nevere hierafter schal be lassed° — *So that / lessened*
Mi beaute, which that I now have,
Til I be take into my grave;
Bot nyht and day as I am now
I schal alwey be such to yow.
The kinges dowhter of Cizile° — *Sicily*
I am, and fell bot siththe awhile,° — *it happened but a while ago*
As I was with my fader late,° — *recently*
That my stepmoder for an hate,° — *hatred*
Which toward me sche hath begonne,° — *established, nurtured*
Forschop me,° til I hadde wonne — *Changed my shape*
The love and sovereinete
Of what knyht that in his degre
Alle othre passeth of good name.
And, as men sein,° ye ben the same; — *say*
The dede proeveth it is so—
Thus am I youres evermo."
Tho was plesance° and joye ynowh,° — *delight / enough*
Echon° with other pleide° and lowh;° — *Each one / played / laughed*
Thei live longe and wel thei ferde,° — *fared*
And clerkes that this chance° herde — *happening, story*
Thei writen it in evidence,
To teche how that obedience
Mai wel fortune° a man to love — *bring about*
And sette him in his lust above,° — *give him happiness, delight*
As it befell unto this knyht.
Forthi,° my Sone, if thou do ryht, — *Therefore*
Thou schalt unto thi love obeie,
And folwe hir will be alle weie.° — *in all ways*
Min holy fader, so I wile:
For ye have told me such a skile° — *reason*
Of° this ensample° now tofore,° — *By / example / foregoing*
That I schal evermo therfore
Hierafterward myn observance
To love and to his obeissance° — *obedience*
The betre kepe.

* * *

The Friar's Prologue and Tale

Many analogues to the *Friar's Tale* exist in many countries of Europe, not only from the Middle Ages but from later centuries as well. All of them feature an evil protagonist who meets and converses with a devil; the protagonist then encounters someone he has wronged, one whose heartfelt curse permits the devil to seize the evildoer. The story functioned as an illustrative moral tale or exemplum and appears both in medieval sermons and in collections of exempla. We print one of the closest analogues to Chaucer's version, from a sermon by Robert Rypon, an English Benedictine monk, probably composed around the turn of the fifteenth century.

ROBERT RYPON

A Greedy Bailiff†

* * * Thirdly, in the first main part [of this sermon], it remains to say in what way sin is observed in the devil. But some good men and women might perhaps dislike hearing the devil named. But it should be noted that there are two ways to speak about the devil, one of which is pleasing to him and the other displeasing. They displease him who preach about and expose the evils that he inflicts upon mankind so that these can be avoided. But those who name the name of the one whose naming pleases him, either by cursing out of negligence or rancor or in conjurations and such, give him pleasure with their speech, and more often than it is sought, the devil is permitted to carry out such curses and oaths.

So it is told of a certain bailiff, who in collecting rents for his lord was excessively greedy and eager for his own profit, being less merciful to the poor in particular. One day as he was riding to a certain village because of his duties, it happened that the devil in the form of a young man became his companion on his journey. The devil asked him, "Where are you going?", and he replied, "To the next village, on the business of my lord." The devil asked, "Is it true that you wish to gain for yourself and for your lord as much as you can and to take whatever they might wish to give to you?" The bailiff answered, "Yes, so I wish, if the gift is free." "Good," the devil said to him; "you do justly." "And who are you?" the bailiff asked, "and where do you come from?" "I," said his companion, "am the devil, and I go about for my profit just as you do for yours and for your lord's. And I too do not wish to take just anything that men might give to me,

† Translated for the second Norton Critical Edition by Peter Nicholson. Reprinted by permission of the translator. For the Latin original and a more literal translation, see Professor Nicholson's chapter on analogues to the *Friar's Tale* in *Sources and Analogues of the* Canterbury Tales, vol. 1, ed. Robert M. Correale and Mary Hamel, pp. 87–99.

but only what they give me freely with heart and will will I accept." "You do most justly," the bailiff replied. Going on together, they approached the village, and they saw coming towards them some nearly untamed oxen pulling a plough, and since they were going more often crookedly and off the track, the farmer commended them to the devil. "Here," said the bailiff; "these are yours." "No," was the response, "because they are not given from the heart." Then coming into the village, they heard a baby cry, and the angry mother, not able to calm it down, said, "Be quiet or let the devil have you!" The bailiff said, "This is yours." The devil answered, "Not at all, because she has no wish to give up her child." Finally reaching the edge of the village, they saw a poor widow whose only cow the bailiff had seized the day before, and when she saw the bailiff, she fell on her knees and stretched out her hands and cried, "To all the devils of hell I commend you!" Then said the devil, "Surely this one is mine, because it is given to me sincerely. And so I wish to have you." And he led the bailiff that he had received off to hell.

This story, though partly humorous, also provides a warning against certain evils. For it teaches first that one should not name the devil out of negligence or rancor, and second, that one should never commend anything to him, for such an offer might be carried out. Third, it teaches that the officers of lords should not be too greedy, and fourth, that they should do no wrong to the poor or to others either by harming their persons or extorting their goods, lest perhaps it happen to them in the end as it happened to this bailiff.

The Clerk's Prologue and Tale

The *Clerk's Tale* is a close translation of Petrarch's Latin version of the story of Griselda, although Chaucer relied on a French translation of Petrarch as well. Petrarch had expanded the story from the final tale of Boccaccio's *Decameron*, and his narrative became highly popular in the late fourteenth century. Petrarch wrote to Boccaccio about his interest in the story and also recorded the responses of some friends. Further evidence of medieval reaction to it can be found in the comments of an anonymous Parisian citizen (probably like the Franklin in social status) who included a French translation of the tale in a book that he wrote for his fifteen-year-old bride to instruct her in the duties of a good wife.

GIOVANNI BOCCACCIO

From The Decameron, Day 10[†]

Story 10

INDUCED BY THE ENTREATIES OF HIS VASSALS TO TAKE A WIFE, THE MARQUIS OF SALUZZO, WANTING TO CHOOSE ONE HIS OWN WAY, SELECTS THE DAUGHTER OF A PEASANT. AFTER HE HAS HAD TWO CHILDREN WITH HER, HE MAKES IT LOOK TO HER AS THOUGH THEY HAVE BEEN PUT TO DEATH. LATER ON, PRETENDING TO HAVE GROWN WEARY OF HER, HE CLAIMS HE HAS MARRIED ANOTHER WOMAN AND ARRANGES TO HAVE HIS OWN DAUGHTER BROUGHT HOME AS THOUGH SHE WERE HIS BRIDE, MEANWHILE HAVING TURNED HIS WIFE OUT OF DOORS WEARING NOTHING BUT HER SHIFT. ON FINDING THAT SHE HAS BORNE EVERYTHING WITH PATIENCE, HOWEVER, HE TAKES HER BACK HOME AGAIN, DEARER TO HIM THAN EVER, SHOWS HER THEIR GROWN-UP CHILDREN, AND HONORS HER AS MARCHIONESS AND CAUSES EVERYONE ELSE TO DO SO AS WELL.[1]

* * *

My gentle ladies, the way I see it, we have given this entire day over to kings and sultans and people of that ilk, and therefore, lest I stray too far away from the path you are on, I want to tell you about a Marquis whose

† From *The Decameron: A Norton Critical Edition*, trans. and ed. Wayne Rebhorn (New York: W. W. Norton, 2015), pp. 331-39. Copyright © 2016 by W. W. Norton & Company, Inc. Translation copyright © 2013 by Wayne A. Rebhorn. Used by permission of W. W. Norton & Company, Inc. We have omitted some of Rebhorn's notes. The narrator of this story is Dioneo, and with it—the last of 100 tales—the storytelling ends and the young people return to Florence. See the Conclusion to Day 10, reprinted above, pp. 363–64.

1. Although there are many examples of faithful wives put to harsh tests in medieval literature, the clearest source for this story is that of Job in the Bible. No scholar has been able to find anyone in the historical record who resembles Griselda. Indeed, her name seems to have been invented by Boccaccio, possibly as an ironic variation of Criseida, the notably unfaithful lover of Troilo (Troilus) in his romance *Il Filostrato*.

behavior was not an example of magnanimity, but of senseless brutality.[2] And even though things turned out well for him in the end, I would not recommend that you follow his lead, because it is a real shame that he derived any benefit from it at all.

A long time ago, there was a young man named Gualtieri who, as the head of the family, had succeeded to the Marquisate of Saluzzo, and being unmarried and childless, spent all of his time out hawking and hunting. He never gave a thought to finding a wife and starting a family, for which he should have been considered very wise, but his vassals were not content with this and repeatedly begged him to get married so that he would not be left without an heir and they without a lord. Moreover, they offered to find him a woman whose character and parents were such that there would be every reason to feel hopeful about the match and he could expect to be quite happy with her. In response Gualtieri said:

"My friends, you are forcing me to do something I had absolutely resolved never to do, considering how hard it is to find a person whose character will be a fit for your own, how very many of the other sort there are out there, and how miserable life will be for a man if he stumbles upon a wife who is not well suited to him. Furthermore, it's foolish of you to believe that you can figure out what daughters will be like by considering how their fathers and mothers behave and on that basis to argue that you are going to find one who will please me. For I don't know how you can get any information about the fathers, let alone find out the secrets of the mothers, and even if you could, daughters are often very different from either one of their parents. But look, since you want to bind me in these chains, I'm willing to do it. Nevertheless, so that I won't have anybody to blame except myself if it turns out badly, I want to be the one who's responsible for finding her. And let me assure you that no matter what woman I choose, if you fail to honor her as your lady, you will learn to your great misfortune just how serious a matter it was for you to have begged me to take a wife against my will."

The gentlemen replied that they were satisfied, as long as he was amenable to taking a wife.

For quite some time Gualtieri had been impressed with the behavior of a poor girl who lived in a village not far from his home, and since she was also very beautiful, he thought that life with her ought to be rather agreeable. Thus, without searching any further, he resolved to marry her, and having summoned her father, who was very poor indeed, he made arrangements with him to take her as his wife.

This done, Gualtieri called all his friends in the area together and said to them: "My friends, since it continues to be your pleasure that I should agree to take a wife, I'm prepared to do it, though more to gratify you than from any interest I have in getting married. You know what you promised me, namely, that you would be content with whatever woman I chose and would honor her as your lady. Now the time has arrived for me to keep my promise to you and for you to keep yours to me. I've located a young woman after my own heart who lives quite close by, and just a few

2. Dioneo's phrase here, *matta bestialità* ("insane bestiality," literal trans.), echoes Dante, who uses it to sum up the two types of sins in the lowest regions of Hell (see *Inferno* 11.82–83). The concept was developed by Saint Thomas Aquinas in his commentary on Aristotle's *Nicomachean Ethics*, 7.1.1.

days from now I intend to marry her and lead her home as my bride. So, see to it that the wedding feast is splendid and that you give her an honorable reception. That way I'll be able to pronounce myself satisfied that you've kept your word to me just as you'll be satisfied that I've kept mine to you."

The gentlemen all replied joyfully that they were very pleased with this decision and that no matter whom he chose, they would accept her as their lady and would honor her as such in every way they could. After that, they got everything ready so that the feast would be as grand and lavish and happy as possible, and Gualtieri did likewise, arranging for the most magnificent and beautiful wedding, to which he invited a host of his friends and relations as well as many great noblemen and others from the area round about. In addition, he had them make a fair number of beautiful dresses out of expensive material, all tailored to fit a girl who seemed to him the same size as the one he intended to marry. Finally, he ordered belts and rings, a lovely, costly crown, and everything else a new bride would require.

On the day set for the wedding, halfway between prime and tierce, Gualtieri mounted his horse, as did all those who had come to honor him, and after everything necessary had been seen to, he announced, "Gentlemen, it's time to go and fetch the new bride." Then off he rode with the entire company. Before long they reached the little village, and when they got to the house belonging to the girl's father, they spotted her carrying water back from the spring, hurrying so that she could go with the other women to see Gualtieri's spouse as she arrived. The moment Gualtieri saw her, he called her by her name, which was Griselda, and asked her where her father was, to which she bashfully replied, "He's in the house, my lord."

Gualtieri dismounted and told everyone to wait for him while he went into the hovel by himself. There he found her father, whose name was Giannucole, and said to him: "I've come to marry Griselda, but first, here in your presence, there are certain things I need to find out from her." Then he asked her whether, if he were to wed her, she would do her best to please him and never get upset at anything he ever said or did, and whether she would be obedient, and many other things of this sort, to all of which she replied that she would.

At this point Gualtieri, taking her by the hand, led her outside and in the presence of his entire company as well as all the other people living there, he had her stripped naked. Then he called for the clothing and shoes he had ordered for her and quickly had them dress her, after which he had them place a crown on her hair, disheveled though it was. And as everyone looked on in wonder, he proclaimed: "My lords, this is the woman I intend to take as my wife, provided that she wants to marry me." Then, turning to her as she stood there, feeling stunned and quite embarrassed, he asked her: "Griselda, will you have me as your husband?"

"Yes, my lord," she replied.

"And I," he said, "will take you as my wife." Then, right there, in the presence of the entire assembly, he married her, after which he had her seated on a palfrey and led her, honorably attended, to his house where the wedding was celebrated in as beautiful, festive, and magnificent a style as if he had married the daughter of the King of France.

The young bride appeared to change her mind and her manners along with her clothes. As we have already said, she had a fine figure and lovely features, and in keeping with her beauty, she now became so charming, so pleasant, and so well mannered that she did not seem like a shepherdess and the daughter of Giannucole, but like the child of some noble lord, leading everyone who had known her earlier to marvel at her transformation. Moreover, she was so obedient and attentive to her husband that he thought himself the happiest, most contented man in the world. At the same time she was so gracious and kind to her husband's subjects that they all loved her with utter devotion, honored her of their own free will, and prayed for her well-being, her prosperity, and her advancement. And whereas they used to say that Gualtieri had shown some lack of discretion in marrying her, now they declared him to be the wisest, most discerning man on earth because no one else could have ever perceived her lofty virtues, which were hidden under the poor rags of her peasant's clothing. In short, she comported herself so well that before long she had everyone talking, not only in her husband's domain, but far and wide, about how fine her character was and how virtuous her behavior, and she got people to change their minds if they had ever criticized her husband on her account at the time of his marriage.

She had not lived with Gualtieri very long before she became pregnant and in time, to his great happiness, gave birth to a little girl. But a little while later the strange idea popped into his head to test her patience by subjecting her to constant tribulations and generally making life intolerable for her. Consequently, he started by goading her with words, pretending to be angry and telling her that his vassals were thoroughly disgruntled with her because of her base origin, especially now that they saw her bearing children, and that, furthermore, they were upset about the little girl who had just been born and were doing nothing but grumbling about it.

The lady did not change her expression or show the least resentment when she heard these words. "My lord," she said, "do with me whatever you think best for your honor and your peace of mind, and I will be entirely content with it, for I know that I'm socially inferior to your vassals and that I'm unworthy of the honor that you have so graciously bestowed on me."[3] This reply was very gratifying to Gualtieri, for he realized that she had not gotten puffed up with pride because of the honors that he or the others had paid her.

Some time later, having already given her to understand in general terms that his subjects could not endure the little girl she had given birth to, he gave certain instructions to one of his servants and sent him to her. "My lady," said the servant, with the most sorrowful expression on his face, "if I don't want to be put to death, I have to do what my lord has commanded, and he has commanded me to take this daughter of yours and to . . ." And at this point he could say no more.

When the lady heard the servant's words and saw his face, and when she recalled what her husband had said to her, she concluded that the man had been ordered to put her child to death. In response, although

3. Griselda's response here echoes what Mary says to the Angel Gabriel: *Fiat mihi secundum verbum tuum* (Luke 1.38: "be it unto me according to thy word").

she was desperately sick at heart, she immediately took her daughter from the cradle, and without ever changing her expression, she kissed her and blessed her and placed her in the servant's arms. "There," she said to him, "do exactly what your lord, who is my lord as well, has ordered, but don't leave her to be devoured by the beasts and the birds unless he's told you to do so."

The servant took the child and reported what the lady had said to Gualtieri, who, marveling at her constancy, sent him away with the baby to one of his relatives in Bologna, asking her to raise and educate the child with some care, but never to reveal whose daughter she was.

Shortly afterward, the lady became pregnant once again, and when she came to term, she gave birth to a baby boy, which made Gualtieri very happy. Nevertheless, not content with what he had already done, he wounded his wife even more deeply. One day, glowering at her with feigned fury, he said: "Woman, ever since you gave birth to this boy, I've found it completely impossible to live with my vassals, so bitterly do they complain that one of Giannucole's grandsons is to succeed me as their lord. So, if I don't want to be deposed by them, I'm afraid that I'll have to do in this case what I did in the other one, and that I'll also eventually have to leave you and find another wife."

The lady listened patiently, and her only reply was: "My lord, you should think about your own happiness and about how to satisfy your desires. Don't waste another thought on me, for nothing is of any value to me unless I see that it gives you pleasure."

Not many days after that, Gualtieri sent for his son the same way he had for his daughter, and having likewise pretended to have him put to death, he sent him to be brought up in Bologna just as he had done with the girl. In response, his wife said nothing more and did not change the expression on her face any more than she had in her daughter's case, all to Gualtieri's great astonishment, who told himself that no other woman could do what she did. And if it were not for the fact that he saw her treat the children with the utmost tenderness as long as he permitted her to do so, he would have concluded that she acted as she did because she had stopped caring for them. He knew, however, that her behavior was the product of her wisdom.

Since Gualtieri's subjects believed he had arranged to have his two children murdered, they condemned him, blaming it all on his cruelty, whereas they felt nothing but the most profound pity for his wife. But to the women who mourned with her for her children because they had suffered such a death, she never said anything except that if such was the pleasure of the man who had conceived them, then it was her pleasure as well.

Finally, many years after the birth of his daughter, Gualtieri decided the time had come to put his wife's patience to the ultimate test. Accordingly, he spoke with a large company of his vassals and told them that under no circumstances could he put up with Griselda as his wife any longer. He said that he had come to realize just how bad and immature a decision he had made when he chose her, and that he would therefore do everything he could to procure a dispensation from the Pope so that he could leave Griselda and take another wife. A large number of the worthy men took him to task over this plan, but his only reply was that it had to be done that way.

Upon learning of her husband's intentions, the lady grieved bitterly inside, for it seemed to her that what she had to look forward to was returning to her father's house and perhaps tending his sheep as she had done before, while being forced to see the man she loved with all her heart in another woman's embrace. But still, just as she had borne all of Fortune's other afflictions, she was determined to keep her countenance unchanged and endure this one as well.

A little later Gualtieri arranged to have counterfeit letters sent to him from Rome and led his subjects to believe that they contained the Pope's dispensation, which allowed him to leave Griselda and take another wife. Hence, he summoned her to appear, and in the presence of a large number of people, he said to her: "Woman, through the concession granted me by the Pope I am now free to leave you and choose another wife. Since my ancestors have always been great noblemen and rulers in these parts, whereas yours have always been peasants, I no longer want you as my wife. You should return to Giannucole's house with the dowry you brought me, and I will bring home another woman I've found who is a more appropriate match for me."

When she heard these words, the lady managed to hold back her tears only by making an enormous effort that went well beyond the normal capacity of women.

"My lord," she said, "I have always known that my lowly condition and your nobility were in no way suited to one another, just as I have acknowledged that the position I have held with you was a gift from you and from God, nor have I taken what was given to me and treated it as if it were my own rather than as something lent to me. So, if it pleases you to have it back, then it must also please me—and it does—to return it to you. Look, here's the ring with which you married me: take it. As for your ordering me to carry away the dowry I brought here, to do that will not require a paymaster on your part, nor a purse, let alone a packhorse on mine, for I haven't forgotten that I was completely naked when you took me.[4] And if you think it proper to let everybody see this body that bore the children you sired, I will depart naked as well, but I beg you, in return for the virginity I brought here and cannot take away again, that it may please you to let me take away at least one single shift in addition to my dowry."

Although Gualtieri had a greater desire to weep than anything else, he maintained his stony expression and said: "You may take a shift with you."

The people standing about there begged him to give her a dress so that the woman who had been his wife for thirteen years or longer should not suffer the shame of leaving his house wearing only a shift like a pauper. All their pleading was in vain, however, and thus she left the house in her shift, barefoot, and with nothing to cover her head. After having said goodbye to them all, she returned to her father's home, accompanied by the weeping and wailing of everyone who saw her.

Since Giannucole never really believed it possible for his daughter to last very long as Gualtieri's wife, he had been expecting just such a

4. Cf. Job's words: *nudus egressus sum de utero matris meae et nudus revertar illuc Dominus dedit Dominus abstulit sit nomen Domini benedictum* (Job 1.21: "Naked came I out of my mother's womb, and naked shall I return thither: the Lord gave, and the Lord hath taken away; blessed be the name of the Lord").

development every day and had kept the clothes that she had taken off the morning Gualtieri married her. He brought them to her, and after she had put them on, she devoted herself to all the menial chores in her father's house just as she had been accustomed to do, bravely enduring the fierce assault of a hostile Fortune.

As soon as he had sent Griselda away, Gualtieri led his vassals to believe that he had chosen as his wife a daughter of one of the counts of Panago. And having ordered great preparations to be made for the wedding, he sent for Griselda to come to him. When she appeared, he said to her:

"I'm going to bring home the lady whom I have recently chosen to marry, and I want her to be given an honorable reception the moment she arrives. Since you know that I don't have any women in my house who can prepare the rooms properly and do many of the things that a festive occasion of this sort requires, and since you understand such household matters better than anyone else, I want you to see to it that all the arrangements are taken care of and that you invite as many ladies as you think necessary and receive them as though you were the mistress of the house. Then, when the wedding celebration is over, you can return home."

Gualtieri's words pierced Griselda's heart like so many knives, for she had not been able to put aside the love she bore him in the same way that she had relinquished the good fortune she once had. Nevertheless, she replied: "My lord, I am ready and willing."[5] And so, clad in homespun garments of coarse wool, she entered the house, which only a little while before she had left in a shift. Then she began sweeping and tidying up the rooms, had bed curtains and bench coverings put in place throughout the great halls, got the kitchen ready to go, and turned her hand to everything just as if she were some little household serving wench, never stopping until it was all as neat and trim as the occasion called for. Finally, after having invitations sent to all the women in those parts on Gualtieri's behalf, she stopped and waited for the celebration to begin. When the wedding day arrived, though the clothes she had on were poor, she displayed the spirit and bearing of a lady, receiving, with a happy smile on her face, all the women who came to the feast.

Gualtieri had seen to it that his children were brought up with care in Bologna by his kinswoman, who had married into the house of the counts of Panago. His daughter, who had now reached the age of twelve, was the most beautiful creature ever seen, and his son was six. Gualtieri sent word to his kinswoman's husband, asking him if he would be so kind as to accompany his daughter and her brother to Saluzzo, to arrange a noble, honorable escort for her, and not to reveal to anyone who she was in reality, but simply to tell them that he was bringing her there as Gualtieri's bride.

The nobleman did everything the Marquis requested, and a few days after he set out on his journey with the girl and her brother and their noble retinue, he reached Saluzzo, arriving around the dinner hour, where he found that all the people there, as well as many others from neighboring communities, were waiting for Gualtieri's new bride. She was received by the ladies, and as soon as she entered the hall where the

5. Another biblical allusion, this time to Mary's *Ecce ancilla Dei* (Luke 1.38: "Behold the handmaid of the Lord").

tables were set up, Griselda, dressed just as she was, happily went to meet her, and said: "You are welcome here, my lady."

The ladies had begged Gualtieri, earnestly but in vain, either to have Griselda remain in another room or to lend her one of the dresses that had once been hers, so that she would not appear in front of the guests looking as she did. But she was nevertheless seated at the tables along with all the rest of them, after which dinner was served. As everyone stared at the girl, they said that Gualtieri had done well by the exchange, and Griselda joined in, praising her warmly, and her little brother, too.

It seemed to Gualtieri that he had now seen as much as he could have ever desired of his wife's patience, for he had observed that no event, however outrageous, had produced any sort of change in her at all. Moreover, he felt sure that her reaction was not the result of obtuseness, since he knew just how wise she was. He therefore decided that it was time to deliver her from the bitter sorrow he guessed she was keeping hidden beneath her impassive exterior, and having summoned her, he smiled and asked her in the presence of all the assembled people: "What do you think of our bride?"

"My lord," replied Griselda, "she seems very fine to me, and if, as I believe, her wisdom matches her beauty, I have no doubt whatsoever that living with her will make you the happiest gentleman in the world. However, I beg you with all my heart not to inflict on her the same wounds you once gave the other spouse you used to have, because I find it hard to believe she'll be able to endure them, considering how much younger she is and also how refined an upbringing she has had, whereas the other one experienced continual hardships from the time she was a little girl."

Seeing that she firmly believed the girl was going to be his wife, and yet had nothing but good things to say, Gualtieri had her sit down beside him.

"Griselda," he said, "the time has finally come both for you to taste the fruit of your long patience, and for those who have thought me cruel, unjust, and brutish to realize that what I've done I've done with a deliberate end in view. For I wanted to teach you how to be a wife, to teach them how to manage one, and at the same time to beget for myself perpetual peace and quiet for the rest of my life with you. When I was at the point of taking a wife, I really feared I'd have no peace, and that's why I decided to choose one by means of a test and have, as you know, inflicted so much pain and suffering on you.

"And since I've never seen you deviate from my wishes in either word or deed, and since it seems to me that you will provide me with all the happiness I've desired, I intend to restore to you in an instant that which I took from you over such a long time, and with the sweetest of cures to heal the wounds I gave you. Receive this girl, then, with a glad heart, the one you believed to be my wife, along with her brother, for they are, in fact, our children, yours as well as mine, the very ones whom you and many others believed for a long time I had cruelly ordered to be put to death. And I am your husband, who loves you more than anything else, since I believe I may boast[6] that there is no one else who could be as content with his wife as I am with you."

6. This phrase (*credendomi poter dar vanto*) is a formula used by medieval knights who would boast, often at the dinner table, of some heroic deed they had done or some extraordinary possession they had, challenging the others present to match their claim.

When he finished speaking, he embraced her and kissed her, and while she wept for joy, they both got up and went over to where their daughter sat, listening in amazement to what they were saying. Both of them embraced her and her brother tenderly, thus dispelling any confusion that they, like many others present, were feeling. The ladies were overjoyed, and getting up from the tables, they went with Griselda into a chamber where, with a more auspicious view of her future, they divested her of her old clothes and dressed her in one of her own stately gowns. Then, like the lady of the castle, which she always appeared to be even when clad in rags, they led her back into the hall, where her rejoicing with her children was simply wonderful. Indeed, everyone was so happy about what had happened that the feasting and the celebrating were redoubled and continued unabated for many more days. They all declared that Gualtieri was very wise, although they thought that the tests to which he had subjected his wife were harsh and intolerable, but they considered Griselda to be the wisest of them all.

A few days later the Count of Panago returned to Bologna, and Gualtieri, having taken Giannucole away from his drudgery, set him up in a position befitting the man who was his father-in-law, so that he was treated with honor and lived in great comfort during his last remaining years. As for Gualtieri himself, having arranged a noble match for his daughter, he lived a long, contented life with Griselda, always honoring her in every way he could.

What more is there left to say except that divine spirits may rain down from the heavens even into the houses of the poor, just as there are others in royal palaces who might be better suited to tending pigs than ruling men. Who, aside from Griselda, would have suffered, not merely dry eyed, but with a cheerful countenance, the cruel, unheard-of trials to which Gualtieri subjected her? Perhaps it would have served him right if, instead, he had run into the kind of woman who, upon being thrown out of the house in her shift, would have found some guy to give her fur a good shaking and got a nice new dress in the bargain.

FRANCIS PETRARCH

The Story of Griselda (*Historia Griseldis*)†

In the chain of the Apennines, in the west of Italy, stands Mount Viso, a very lofty mountain, whose summit towers above the clouds and rises into the bright upper air. It is a mountain notable in its own nature, but most notable as the source of the Po, which rises from a small spring

† From Robert Dudley French, *A Chaucer Handbook*, 2nd ed. (Englewood Cliffs, NJ: Prentice-Hall, 1947), pp. 291–311. French's translation, originally made from a much earlier text of Petrarch's story, was changed in his second edition to reflect the more accurate version edited by J. Burke Severs, which appears both in *Sources and Analogues of Chaucer's* Canterbury Tales, ed. W. F. Bryan and Germaine Dempster (Chicago: U of Chicago P, 1941), pp. 296–330, and in Severs's own *The Literary Relationships of Chaucer's* Clerkes Tale (New Haven: Yale UP, 1942). As the letters on pp. 453–55 make clear, Petrarch translated and adapted Boccaccio's story in 1373. New texts and translations of the chief sources of the *Clerk's Tale*, by Thomas J. Farrell and Amy W. Goodwin, are available in *Sources and Analogues of the* Canterbury Tales, vol. 1, ed. Robert M. Correale and Mary Hamel, pp. 101–67.

upon the mountain's side, bends slightly toward the east, and presently, swollen with abundant tributaries, becomes, though its downward course has been but brief, not only one of the greatest of streams but, as Vergil called it, the king of rivers. Through Liguria its raging waters cut their way, and then, bounding Aemilia and Flaminia and Venetia, it empties at last into the Adriatic sea, through many mighty mouths. Now that part of these lands, of which I spoke first, is sunny and delightful, as much for the hills which run through it and the mountains which hem it in, as for its grateful plain. From the foot of the mountains beneath which it lies, it derives its name; and it has many famous cities and towns. Among others, at the very foot of Mount Viso, is the land of Saluzzo, thick with villages and castles. It is ruled over by noble marquises, the first and greatest of whom, according to tradition, was a certain Walter, to whom the direction of his own estates and of all the land pertained. He was a man blooming with youth and beauty, as noble in his ways as in his birth; marked out, in short, for leadership in all things,—save that he was so contented with his present lot that he took very little care for the future. Devoted to hunting and fowling, he so applied himself to these arts that he neglected almost all else; and—what his subjects bore most ill—he shrank even from a hint of marriage. When they had borne this for some time in silence, at length they came to him in a company; and one of their number, who had authority and eloquence above the rest and was on more familiar terms with his overlord, said to him, "Noble Marquis, your kindness gives us such boldness that we come separately to talk with you, with devoted trust, as often as occasion demands, and that now my voice conveys to your ears the silent wishes of us all; not because I have any especial privilege, unless it be that you have shown by many signs that you hold me dear among the others. Although all your ways, then, justly give us pleasure and always have, so that we count ourselves happy in such an overlord, there is one thing in which we should assuredly be the happiest of all men round about, if you would consent to it and show yourself susceptible to our entreaties; and that is, that you should take thought of marriage and bow your neck, free and imperious though it be, to the lawful yoke; and that you should do this as soon as possible. For the swift days fly by, and although you are in the flower of your youth, nevertheless silent old age follows hard upon that flower, and death itself is very near to any age. To none is immunity against this tribute given, and all alike must die; and just as that is certain, so is it uncertain when it will come to pass. Give ear, therefore, we pray you, to the entreaties of those who have never refused to do your bidding. You may leave the selection of a wife to our care, for we shall procure you such an one as shall be truly worthy of you, and sprung of so high a lineage that you may have the best hope of her. Free all your subjects, we beseech you, of the grievous apprehension that if anything incident to our mortal lot should happen to you, you would go leaving no successor to yourself, and they would remain deprived of a leader such as their hearts crave."

Their loyal entreaties touched the man's heart, and he made answer: "My friends, you constrain me to that which never entered my thoughts. I have had pleasure in complete liberty, a thing which is rare in marriage. Nevertheless, I willingly submit to the wishes of my subjects, trusting in your prudence and your devotion. But I release you from the task, which you have offered to assume, of finding me a wife. That task I lay on my own shoulders. For what benefit can the distinction of one confer upon another? Right often, children are all unlike their parents. Whatever is good in a man comes not from another, but from God. As I entrust to Him all my welfare, so would I entrust to Him the outcome of my marriage, hoping for His accustomed mercy. He will find for me that which shall be expedient for my peace and safety. And so, since you are resolved that I should take a wife, so much, in all good faith, I promise you; and for my part, I will neither frustrate nor delay your wishes. One promise, in your turn, you must make and keep: that whosoever the wife may be whom I shall choose, you will yield her the highest honor and veneration; and let there be none among you who ever shall dispute or complain of my decision. Yours it was that I, the freest of all the men you have known, have submitted to the yoke of marriage; let it be mine to choose that yoke; and whoever my wife may be, let her be your mistress, as if she were the daughter of a prince of Rome."

Like men who thought it hardly possible that they should see the wished-for day of the nuptials, they promised with one accord and gladly that they should be found in nothing wanting; and with eager alacrity they received the edict from their master, directing that the most magnificent preparations be made for a certain day. So they withdrew from conference; and the marquis, on his part, laid care upon his servants for the nuptials and gave public notice of the day.

Not far from the palace, there was a village, of few and needy inhabitants, one of whom, the poorest of all, was named Janicola. But as the grace of Heaven sometimes visits the hovels of the poor, it chanced that he had an only daughter, by name Griseldis, remarkable for the beauty of her body, but of so beautiful a character and spirit that no one excelled her. Reared in a frugal way of living and always in the direst poverty, unconscious of any want, she had learned to cherish no soft, no childish thoughts; but the vigor of manhood and the wisdom of age lay hidden in her maiden bosom. Cherishing her father's age with ineffable love, she tended his few sheep, and as she did it, wore her fingers away on the distaff. Then, returning home, she would prepare the little herbs and victuals suited to their fortune and make ready the rude bedchamber. In her narrow station, in fine, she discharged all the offices of filial obedience and affection. Walter, passing often by that way, had sometimes cast his eyes upon this little maid, not with the lust of youth, but with the sober thoughts of an older man; and his swift intuition had perceived in her a virtue, beyond her sex and age, which the obscurity of her condition concealed from the eyes of the common throng. Hence it came about that he decided, at one and the same time, to take a wife—which he had never before wished to do—and to have this woman and no other.

The day of the nuptials drew on, but no one knew whence the bride should come, and there was no one who did not wonder. Walter himself, in the meanwhile, was buying golden rings and coronets and girdles, and was having rich garments and shoes and all necessities of this kind made to the measure of another girl, who was very like Griseldis in stature. The longed-for day had come, and since not a word about the bride was to be heard, the universal bewilderment had risen very high. The hour of the feast arrived; and already, the whole house was in a great ferment of preparation. Then Walter came out of the castle, as if he were setting out to meet his approaching bride, and a throng of noble men and matrons followed in his train.

Griseldis, ignorant of all the preparations which were being made on her account, had performed what was to be done about her home; and now, with water from the distant well, she was crossing the threshold of her father's house, in order that, free from other duties, she might hasten, with the girls who were her comrades, to see her master's bride. Then Walter, absorbed in his own thoughts, drew near and, calling her by name, asked her where her father was; and when she had replied, reverently and humbly, that he was within, "Bid him," he said, "come hither."

When the old man was come, Walter took him by the hand and drew him a little aside; and lowering his voice, he said, "Janicola, I know that I am dear to you. I have known you for my faithful liegeman, and I believe you wish whatever suits my pleasure. One thing in particular, however, I should like to know: whether you would take me, whom you have as your master, for a son-in-law, giving me your daughter as a wife?"

Stupefied at this unlooked-for matter, the old man went rigid. At length, hardly able to stammer out a few words, he replied, "It is my duty to wish or to deny nothing, save as it pleases you, who are my master." "Let us, then, go in alone," said the marquis, "that I may put certain questions to the girl herself in your presence." They entered the house, therefore, while the populace stood expectant and wondering, and found the maiden busying herself about her father's service and abashed by the unexpected advent of so great a throng of strangers. Walter, approaching her, addressed her in these words: "It is your father's pleasure and mine that you shall be my wife. I believe that this will please you, too. But I have one thing to ask you: when that is done which shortly shall take place, will you be prepared, with consenting mind, to agree with me in all things; so that you dispute my wish in nothing, and permit me, with mind consenting, and without remonstrance of word or look, to do whatever I will with you?"

Trembling at this marvelous thing, the girl made answer: "I know myself unworthy, my lord, of so great an honor; but if it be your will, and if it be my destiny, I will never consciously cherish a thought, much less do anything, which might be contrary to your desires; nor will you do anything, even though you bid me die, which I shall bear ill."

"It is enough," said he; and so, leading her out before the throng, he showed her to the people, and said, "This is my wife, this is your lady; cherish her and love her; and if you hold me dear, hold her most dear of all." Then, lest she carry into her new home any relic of her former fortune, he commanded her to be stripped, and clad from head to heel with new garments; and this was done, reverently and swiftly, by matrons who stood around her and who embraced her each in turn. So this simple peasant girl, new clad, with her dishevelled tresses collected and made smooth, adorned with gems and coronet, was as it were suddenly transformed, so that the people hardly knew her. And Walter solemnly plighted her his troth with a precious ring, which he had brought with him for that purpose; and having placed her on a snow-white horse, he had her conducted to the palace, the populace accompanying her and rejoicing. In this way, the nuptials were celebrated, and that most happy day was passed.

Shortly thereafter, so much did God's favor shine upon the lowly bride, it seemed she was reared and bred, not in a shepherd's cottage, but in the imperial court; and to all she became dear and venerable beyond belief. Even those who had known her from her birth could hardly be persuaded she was Janicola's daughter; such was the graciousness of her life and of her ways, the gravity and sweetness of her speech, by which she had bound the hearts of all the people to her with the bond of a great love. And already her name, heralded by frequent rumor, had spread abroad, not only within the confines of her fatherland, but through every neighboring province; so that many men and matrons, with eager desire, came flocking to see her. So, graced by a marriage, which, however humble, was distinguished and prosperous, Walter lived in the highest peace and honor at home; and abroad he was held in the highest esteem; and because he had so shrewdly discovered the remarkable virtue hidden under so much poverty, he was commonly held to be a very prudent man. Not only did his wife attend adroitly to those domestic matters which pertain to women; but when occasion demanded, in her husband's absence, she undertook state affairs, settling and composing the country's law-suits and disputes among the nobles, with such weighty opinions and so great a maturity and fairness of judgment, that all declared this woman had been sent down from heaven for the public weal.

Not long time had passed ere she became pregnant; and after she had held her subjects for a time in anxious expectation, at length she bore the fairest of daughters. Though they had preferred a son, nevertheless she made both her husband and her country happy by this proof of the fertility they longed for. In the meanwhile, it so happened, when his little daughter had been weaned, that Walter was seized with a desire more strange than laudable—so the more experienced may decide—to try more deeply the fidelity of his dear wife, which had been sufficiently made known by experience, and to test it again and again. Therefore, he called her alone into his chamber and addressed her thus, with troubled brow:

"You know, Griseldis—for I do not think that amid your present good fortune you have forgotten your former state—you know, I say, in what manner you came into this house. To me, indeed, you are dear enough and well beloved; but to my nobles, not so; especially since you have begun to bear children. For they take it most ill that they should submit to a low-born mistress. Since, therefore, I desire peace with them, I must follow another's judgment, not my own, in the case of your daughter, and do that which is most grievous to me. But I would never do it without letting you know, and I wish you to accommodate your will to mine and to show that obedience which you promised at the outset of our married life."

She listened without a protesting word or glance. "You are our master," she said, "and both this little girl and I are yours. Do, therefore, as you will with your own; for nothing can please you which would displease me. There is absolutely nothing which I wish to have or fear to lose, save you. This is fixed in the very center of my heart, and never, either by lapse of years or by death, will it be torn away. Anything can happen ere I shall change my mind."

Happy in her reply, but feigning sadness in his looks, he left her; and a little later, he sent to her one of his underlings, a most faithful man, whose services he was wont to use in his most weighty affairs, and whom he instructed in the task before him. The fellow, coming to Griseldis by night, said to her, "Spare me, my lady, and do not lay to my blame what I am forced to do. You are right knowing, and you understand what it is to be subject to a master; nor is the harsh necessity of obedience unknown to one endowed with so much sense, though inexperienced. I am bidden to take this little baby girl, and—" Here, breaking off his speech, he ceased, as if he would indicate his cruel business by his silence. Suspect was the reputation of the man, suspect his face, suspect the hour, suspect his words. By these tokens, she clearly knew her sweet daughter was to be killed; yet she shed no tear, she breathed no sigh,—a thing most hard, even for a nurse, much more so for a mother. But taking up the little girl, with tranquil brow, she looked at her a little, and kissing her, blessed her and made the sign of the Holy Cross upon her. Then she gave the child to the fellow, and said, "Go; and whatever our lord hath laid upon you, see that you perform it. One thing I beg of you: take care lest beasts or birds tear her little body; and this, only if no contrary orders have been laid upon you."

The fellow returned to his master and told him what he had said and how Griseldis had replied; and when he had given him his daughter, paternal pity touched the marquis to the heart. Nevertheless, he did not relax the rigor of his purpose. He ordered his slave to wrap the child in cloths, to place it in a wickerwork basket upon a beast of burden, and carry it, secretly and with all the diligence he could command, to Bologna, to Walter's sister, who had married the Count of Panago. He should hand the child over to her, to be cherished with maternal care, to be reared in gentle ways, and to be concealed, moreover, with so much care that no one could know whose daughter she was. The slave journeyed thither and fulfilled with care what had been laid upon him.

Walter, in the meanwhile, though he often studied his wife's face and words, never detected any sign of a change of feeling: equal alacrity and diligence, her accustomed complaisance, the same love, no sadness, no mention of her daughter! Never did the girl's name fall from her mother's lips, either by design or by chance. In this way, four years went by; and being again with child, behold she brought forth a most excellent son, a great delight to his father and all their friends. But when, after two years, this child had been weaned, the father fell back into his former caprice. And again he said to his wife, "Once before you have heard that my people bear our marriage ill, especially since they knew you capable of bearing children; but it has never been so bad as since you gave birth to a son. For they say—and the murmur of it comes often to my ears, 'So, when Walter dies, Janicola's grandson shall rule over us, and so noble a land will be subject to such a master.' Each day many things of this tenor are current among my people; and I, eager for peace and—to say sooth—fearing for myself, am therefore moved to dispose of this infant as I disposed of his sister. I tell you this beforehand, lest the unexpected and sudden grief disturb you."

To which she made answer: "I have said, and I say again, that I can have no wishes save yours. In these children, indeed, I have no share, beyond the pangs of labor. You are my master and theirs: use your power over your own. Nor seek my consent; for when I entered your house, as I put off my clothes, so I put off my wishes and desires, and put on yours. Whatever you wish to do, therefore, about anything whatsoever, that is what I wish, too. Nay, if I could foresee your future wishes, I should begin beforehand, whatever it might be, to wish and desire what you wish. Now I gladly follow your desire, which I cannot anticipate. Suppose it pleased you that I should die, I would die gladly; nor is there any other thing—not death itself—to equal our love."

Marvelling at the steadfastness of the woman, he took his departure, his face agitated with emotion; and straightway he sent to her the servant whom he had sent before. The latter, with many a plea of the necessity of obedience, and with many an entreaty for forgiveness, if he had done or was doing her a wrong, demanded her child, as one who is about to commit a monstrous crime. But she, with unchanged mien, whatever might be passing in her mind, took up in her arms the son who was so well beloved, not only by his mother but by everyone, for the beauty of his body and his disposition; and she made upon him the sign of the Cross, blessing him, as she had blessed her daughter, clinging to him just a little while with her eyes, and bending down to kiss him; but she gave absolutely no other sign of her grief. Then she gave him to the fellow who had come to seek him, and she said, "Take him, too, and do what you are bidden. But one thing I beg of you: that if it can be done, you will protect the tender limbs of my beautiful baby against the ravages of birds and beasts."

The man, returning to his master with these words of hers, drove him to yet greater wonder, so that if he had not known her for the most loving of mothers, he might have had some faint suspicion that the strength of the woman came from a certain hardness of heart; but while she was strongly attached to all that were hers, she loved no one better than her husband. The servant was then bidden to set out for Bologna and to take the boy where he had taken his sister.

These trials of conjugal affection and fidelity would have been sufficient for the most rigorous of husbands; but there are those who, when once they have begun anything, do not cease; nay, rather, they press on and cling to their purpose. Keeping his eyes upon his wife, therefore, Walter watched continually for any change in her behavior toward him, and he was not able to find any at all, save that she became each day more devoted and more obedient to his wishes; so that it seemed there was but one mind between them, and that not common to them both, but, to say truth, the husband's alone; for the wife had declared, as has been said, that she had no wishes of her own.

Little by little, an ugly rumor about Walter had begun to spread abroad; namely, that with savage and inhuman cruelty, out of regret and shame for his humble marriage, he had ordered his children slain; for neither did his children appear, nor had anyone heard where in the world they were. Wherefore, he who had once been a man of spotless reputation, dear to his people, had become in the eyes of many men infamous and hateful. Not on that account, however, was his stern purpose altered, but he persevered in the severity which he had assumed and in his harsh caprice of testing his wife. And so, when twelve years had passed since the birth of his daughter, he sent envoys to Rome to bring back thence documents bearing the appearance of a papal bull, which should cause the rumor to circulate among the people that license had been granted him by the Roman pontiff, with a view to his own peace and that of his people, to annul his first marriage and to take another wife; nor was it difficult, in fact, to convince those untutored Alpine folk of anything you pleased. When this rumor reached Griseldis, she was sad, I think; but as one who had made her decision, once and for all, about herself and her destiny, she stood unshaken, awaiting what should be decreed for her by him to whom she had submitted herself and all that was hers.

Walter had already sent to Bologna and had asked his kinsman to send him his children, spreading the story in every quarter that this maiden was to be Walter's bride. His kinsman faithfully performed these orders and set out upon his journey on the appointed day, bringing with him, amid a brilliant throng of noblemen, the young maiden, who was now of marriageable age, of excellent beauty, and adorned with magnificent attire; and with her he brought her brother, who was now in his seventh year.

Walter, in the meanwhile, with his accustomed inclination to try his wife, even to the heights of grief and shame, led her forth before the multitude and said, "I have been wont to take ample delight in our marriage, having regard for your character, not your lineage; but now, since I perceive that great place is always great servitude, it is not permitted me to do what any peasant may. My people compel me—and the Pope consents—to take another wife. Already my wife is on her way, and presently she will be here. Therefore, be of stout heart, and yielding your place to another, take back your dowry and return to your former home with equal mind. No good fortune lasts forever."

She made answer: "My lord, I have always known that there was no proportion between your greatness and my lowly station. I have never considered myself worthy to be—I will not say, your wife, but your servant; and in this house, in which you have made me mistress, I call God to witness that I have remained in spirit as a handmaid. For these years, therefore, that I have dwelt with you in honor far beyond my deserts, I give thanks to God and you. For the rest, I am ready, with good heart and peaceful mind, to return to my father's house, to pass my age and to die where I have passed my youth, always happy in the honorable estate of widowhood, since I have been the wife of such a man. I readily yield place to your new bride—and may her coming bring you joy!—and I will not take away any ill feeling from this place, where I was wont to live most happily, while it so pleased you. But as for my dowry, which you bid me take back with me, I see of what sort it is, and it has not been lost; for as I came to you long since, stripped at my father's threshold of all my clothes and clad in yours, I had no other dowry but nakedness and devotion. Lo, therefore, I strip off this dress and restore this ring, with which you wed me. And the other rings and finery, with which your gifts have enriched me to the point of envy, are in your chamber. Naked I came from my father's house, and naked shall I return again—save that I think it unseemly that this belly, in which the children you begot were shaped, should appear naked before the people. Wherefore, if it please you—but not otherwise—I pray and beseech you, as the price of the maidenhood which I brought hither and do not take hence, bid me keep one shift, out of those I have been wont to wear, that I may cover therewith the belly of her who was once your wife."

The tears welled into her husband's eyes, so that they could no longer be restrained; and so, turning his face aside, "Take your one shift," he said, and his voice trembled so that he could scarcely say it. So, weeping, he took his departure. Before them all, she stripped off her clothes, keeping upon her only her shift; and covered with that alone, she went forth before them with feet and head quite bare. Followed by many, who wept and railed at fortune, she alone dry-eyed and to be honored for her noble silence, returned to her father's house. The good man, who had always held his daughter's marriage in suspicion and had never allowed himself high hopes, ever expecting it to turn out that so high-born a husband, proud after the fashion of noblemen, would one day be sated with so lowly a bride and send her home, had kept her coarse and well-worn gown hidden away in some corner of his narrow dwelling. Hearing the uproar, not of his daughter, who returned in silence, but of the accompanying throng, he ran to meet her at the threshold and covered her, half naked as she was, with the old gown. She remained with her father a few days, showing marvelous equanimity and kindness; for she gave no sign of the sadness of her heart and showed no trace of her more favorable lot, since, forsooth, she had always dwelt amid riches with lowly and humble spirit.

Now the Count of Panago was drawing near; and, on every hand, rumors of the new nuptials were rife. Sending forward one of his train, he announced the day on which he would arrive at Saluzzo. The day before, therefore, Walter sent for Griseldis, and when she had come with all fidelity, he said to her, "It is my desire that the maiden who is coming on the morrow to dine with us should be received sumptuously, as well as the men and matrons who come with her and such of our own people as are present at the feast, so that honor of place and welcome may be preserved unspotted, according to the dignity of each and all. But I have no women in the house who are suited to cope with this task; therefore, though your garments are but poor, you may best assume the duty of receiving and placing my guests, for you know my ways."

"I will do this," said she, "and whatever else I see will please you, not only willingly, but eagerly. Nor shall I grow weary or sluggish in this labor, so long as the least remnant of my spirit shall last." And when she had said this, straightway she caught up the implements of servant's toil and set to work, sweeping the house, setting the tables, making the beds, and urging on the others, like the best of handmaids.

At the third hour of the next day, the count arrived; and all the people vied in commending the manners and the beauty of the maiden and her youthful brother. There were those who said that Walter had been fortunate and prudent in the change he made, since this bride was more delicate and of nobler breeding, and had so fine a kinsman into the bargain. So, while the preparations for the feast went feverishly on, Griseldis, who had been present everywhere and solicitous of all—not cast down by so grievous a lot nor confused with shame for her old-fashioned clothing, but serene of countenance—came to meet the maiden as she entered. Bending the knee before her, after the manner of servants, with eyes cast reverently and humbly down, she said, "Welcome, my lady." Then she greeted others of the guests with cheerful face and marvelous sweetness in her words, and she managed the vast household with great skill; so that everyone greatly wondered—especially the newcomers—whence came that dignity of manner and that discretion beneath such a dress.

She, in her turn, could not grow weary of praising the maiden and the boy: now she extolled the maiden's beauty, now the boy's.

Just as they were to sit down at the tables, Walter turned toward her and said before them all, as if he were making game of her, "What think you, Griseldis, of this bride of mine? Is she pretty and worthy enough?"

"Surely," said she, "no prettier or worthier could be found. Either with her or with no one, can you lead a life of tranquillity and happiness; and that you may find happiness is my desire and my hope. One thing, in all good faith, I beg of you, one warning I give you: not to drive her with those goads with which you have driven another woman. For since she is younger and more delicately nurtured, I predict she would not be strong enough to bear so much."

Walter, seeing the cheerfulness with which she spoke, and turning over in his mind the steadfastness of the woman, who had been so often and so bitterly injured, took pity on the unworthy fate that had befallen her so unjustly. Able to bear it no longer, he cried out, "It is enough, my Griseldis! Your fidelity to me is made known and proved; nor do I think that under heaven there is another woman who has undergone such trials of her conjugal love." And saying this, with eager arms he embraced his dear wife, who stood all overcome with stupor and as if waking from a troubled sleep. "And you," he said, "are my only wife. I have no other, nor ever shall have. This maiden, whom you think to be my bride, is your daughter; and he, who is thought to be my kinsman, is your son. They whom you believed you had lost, each in turn, you get back both together. Let all know, who thought the contrary, that I am curious and given to experiments, but am not impious: I have tested my wife, not condemned her; I have hidden my children, not destroyed them."

Almost out of her wits for joy and beside herself with maternal love, on hearing these words, Griseldis rushed into her children's arms, shedding the most joyous tears. She wearied them with kisses and bedewed them with her loving tears. And straightway the ladies gathered about her with alacrity and affection; and when her vile apparel had been stripped off her, they clothed her in her accustomed garments and adorned her. The most joyous plaudits and auspicious words from all the throng resounded all about; and the day was the most renowned that ever was for its great joy and sorrow,—more renowned, even, than the day of her nuptials had been.

Many years thereafter they lived in great peace and concord; and Walter, who had appeared to neglect his father-in-law, lest he should stand in the way of the experiment he had conceived, had the old man moved into his palace and held him in honor. His own daughter he gave in noble and honorable marriage, and his son he left behind him as his heir, happy in his wife and in his offspring.

This story it has seemed good to me to weave anew, in another tongue, not so much that it might stir the matrons of our times to imitate the patience of this wife—who seems to me scarcely imitable—as that it might stir all those who read it to imitate the woman's steadfastness, at least; so that they may have the resolution to perform for God what this woman performed for her husband. For He cannot be tempted by evil, as saith James the Apostle, and He himself tempts no man. Nevertheless, He often proves us and suffers us to be vexed with many a grievous scourge; not that He may know our spirit, for that He knew ere we were made, but that our own frailty may be made known to us through notable private signs. Therefore I would assuredly enter on the list of steadfast men the name of anyone who endured for his God, without a murmur, what this obscure peasant woman endured for her mortal husband.

FRANCIS PETRARCH

[Two Letters to Boccaccio]†

I

Your book, written in our mother tongue and published, I presume, during your early years, has fallen into my hands, I know not whence or how. If I told you that I had read it, I should deceive you. It is a very big volume, written in prose and for the multitude. I have been, moreover, occupied with more serious business, and much pressed for time. You can easily imagine the unrest caused by the warlike stir about me, for, far as I have been from actual participation in the disturbances, I could not but be affected by the critical condition of the state. What I did was to run through your book, like a traveller who, while hastening forward, looks about him here and there, without pausing. I have heard somewhere that your volume was attacked by the teeth of certain hounds, but that you defended it valiantly with staff and voice. This did not surprise me, for not only do I well know your ability, but I have learned from experience of the existence of an insolent and cowardly class who attack in the work of others everything which they do not happen to fancy or be familiar with, or which they cannot themselves accomplish. Their insight and capabilities extend no farther; on all other themes they are silent.

My hasty perusal afforded me much pleasure. If the humour is a little too free at times, this may be excused in view of the age at which you wrote, the style and language which you employ, and the frivolity of the subjects, and of the persons who are likely to read such tales. It is important to know for whom we are writing, and a difference in the character of one's listeners justifies a difference in style. Along with much that was light and amusing, I discovered some serious and edifying things as well, but I can pass no definite judgment upon them, since I have not examined the work thoroughly.

As usual, when one looks hastily through a book, I read somewhat more carefully at the beginning and at the end. At the beginning you have, it seems to me, accurately described and eloquently lamented the condition of our country during that siege of pestilence which forms so dark and melancholy a period in our century. At the close you have

† From *Petrarch: The First Modern Scholar and Man of Letters*, trans. James Harvey Robinson and Henry Winchester Rolfe (New York: G. P. Putnam's Sons, 1914), pp. 191–96. Although Robinson and Rolfe print these two selections as parts of one letter, the first was written in 1373 as the preface to Petrarch's translation, the second in 1374, when Petrarch found that his original letter had not reached Boccaccio and sent him another copy of his translation. He begins by referring to *The Decameron* as a whole.

placed a story which differs entirely from most that precede it, and which so delighted and fascinated me that, in spite of cares which made me almost oblivious of myself, I was seized with a desire to learn it by heart, so that I might have the pleasure of recalling it for my own benefit, and of relating it to my friends in conversation. When an opportunity for telling it offered itself shortly after, I found that my auditors were delighted. Later it suddenly occurred to me that others, perhaps, who were unacquainted with our tongue, might be pleased with so charming a story, as it had delighted me ever since I first heard it some years ago, and as you had not considered it unworthy of presentation in the mother tongue, and had placed it, moreover, at the end of your book, where, according to the principles of rhetoric, the most effective part of the composition belongs. So one fine day, when, as usual, my mind was distracted by a variety of occupations, discontented with myself and my surroundings, I suddenly sent everything flying, and, snatching up my pen, I attacked this story of yours. I sincerely trust that it will gratify you that I have of my own free-will undertaken to translate your work, something I should certainly never think of doing for anyone else, but which I was induced to do in this instance by my partiality for you and for the story. Not neglecting the precept of Horace in his *Art of Poetry*, that the careful translator should not attempt to render word for word, I have told your tale in my own language, in some places changing or even adding a few words, for I felt that you would not only permit, but would approve, such alterations.

Although many have admired and wished for my version, it seemed to me fitting that your work should be dedicated to you rather than to anyone else; and it is for you to judge whether I have, by this change of dress, injured or embellished the original. The story returns whence it came; it knows its judge, its home, and the way thither. As you and everyone who reads this knows, it is you and not I who must render account for what is essentially yours. If anyone asks me whether this is all true, whether it is a history [*historia*] or a story [*fabula*], I reply in the words of Sallust, "I refer you to the author"—to wit, my friend Giovanni. With so much of introduction, I begin.

* * *

II

My affection for you has induced me to write at an advanced age what I should hardly have undertaken even as a young man. Whether what I have narrated be true or false I do not know, but the fact that you wrote it would seem sufficient to justify the inference that it is but a tale. Foreseeing this question, I have prefaced my translation with the statement that the responsibility for the story rests with the author; that is, with you. And now let me tell you my experiences with this narrative [*historia*], or tale [*fabula*], as I prefer to call it.

In the first place, I gave it to one of our mutual friends in Padua to read, a man of excellent parts and wide attainments. When scarcely half-way through the composition, he was suddenly arrested by a burst of tears. When again, after a short pause, he made a manful attempt to continue, he was again interrupted by a sob. He then realized that he could go no farther himself, and handed the story to one of his companions, a man of education, to finish. How others may view this occurrence I cannot, of course, say; for myself, I put a most favourable construction upon it, believing that I recognise the indications of a most compassionate disposition; a more kindly nature, indeed, I never remember to have met. As I saw him weep as he read, the words of the Satirist came back to me:

> Nature, who gave us tears, by that alone
> Proclaims she made the feeling heart our own;
> And 't is our noblest sense.[1]

Some time after, another friend of ours, from Verona (for all is common between us, even our friends), having heard of the effect produced by the story in the first instance, wished to read it for himself. I readily complied, as he was not only a good friend, but a man of ability. He read the narrative from beginning to end without stopping once. Neither his face nor his voice betrayed the least emotion, nor a tear or a sob escaped him. "I too," he said at the end, "would have wept, for the subject certainly excites pity, and the style is well adapted to call forth tears, and I am not hard-hearted; but I believed, and still believe, that this is all an invention. If it were true, what woman, whether of Rome or any other nation, could be compared with this Griselda? Where do we find the equal of this conjugal devotion, where such faith, such extraordinary patience and constancy?" I made no reply to this reasoning, for I did not wish to run the risk of a bitter debate in the midst of our good-humoured and friendly discussion. But I had a reply ready. There are some who think that whatever is difficult for them must be impossible for others; they must measure others by themselves, in order to maintain their superiority. Yet there have been many, and there may still be many, to whom acts are easy which are commonly held to be impossible. Who is there who would not, for example, regard a Curtius, a Mucius, or the Decii, among our own people, as pure fictions; or, among foreign nations, Codrus and the Philæni; or, since we are speaking of woman, Portia, or Hypsicratia, or Alcestis, and others like them?[2] But these are actual historical persons. And indeed I do not see why one who can face death for another, should not be capable of encountering any trial or form of suffering.

* * *

1. Juvenal, xv., 131–33, as translated by William Gifford [*Translators*].
2. All these examples from classical history and legend involve stories of acts of extraordinary courage or self-sacrifice. The first three are Roman: Marcus Curtius leapt into a chasm in order to close it; Gaius Mucius Scaevola, captured by enemies, put his hand into a fire to show that he did not fear their threats; the Decii—father, son, and grandson—all died in battle for Rome. Codrus was the last king of Athens and sacrificed himself because of a prophecy that success in battle would come to the side whose king died. The Philæni were two brothers who consented to being buried alive in order to secure extended territory for Carthage. The three women Petrarch cites are more directly related to his story of wifely devotion: Portia killed herself when she learned of the death of Brutus; Hypsicratia so loved Mithridates that she accompanied him everywhere, even in battle; Alcestis gave up her life so that Admetus could live.

From Le Ménagier de Paris†

* * *

Dear sister [dear wife], this story was translated by master Francis Petrarch, the poet crowned at Rome,[1] not in order to move good women to have patience amid the tribulations which their husbands cause them solely because of their love for those husbands. It was translated to show that since God, the Church, and Reason would have them be obedient; and since their husbands would have them endure a great deal; and since, to avoid worse, it is necessary that they submit themselves completely to their husbands' wills, enduring patiently whatever their husbands desire; and what is more, since these good women must conceal such troubles, keep silent about them, and indeed come to terms with them while seeking always, with a happy spirit, to draw closer to the favor and love of those mortal husbands: how much greater then the reason for which men and women ought to suffer in patience the tribulations which God, who is immortal and eternal, sends to them. Whether it be the death of friends; the loss of goods, children, or kinfolk; the distress brought about by enemies, captures, slaughters, destruction, fire, tempest, thunderstorms, floods or other unexpected disasters: one ought always to endure it patiently and turn oneself again, with love and solicitude, to the love of the immortal Sovereign, eternal and everlasting God. This we may learn by the example of this pitiable woman, born into poverty among simple people without rank or learning, who suffered so much for her mortal husband [*ami*].

I have set down this story here only in order to instruct you, not to apply it directly to you, and not because I wish such obedience from you. I am in no way worthy of it. I am not a marquis, nor have I taken in you a shepherdess as my wife. Nor am I so foolish, arrogant, or immature in judgment as not to know that I may not properly assault or assay you thus, nor in any such fashion. God keep me from testing you in this way or any other, under the color of lies and dissimulations. Nor do I wish to test you in yet some other manner, for I am fully satisfied by the proof already established through the good name of your ancestors and of yourself, along with what I feel and see and know from direct experience.

I apologize if this story deals with too great cruelty—cruelty, in my view, beyond reason. Do not credit it as having really happened; but the story has it so, and I ought not to change it nor invent another, since someone wiser than I composed it and set it down. Because other people have seen it, I want you to see it too, so that you may be able to talk about everything just as they do.

* * *

† Translated for this volume's first edition by Glending Olson and V. A. Kolve from: *Le Ménagier de Paris*, ed. Jérôme Pichon, 2 vols. (Paris: Crapelet, 1846), 1. 124–26. The book was written by a wealthy householder of Paris—a member of the upper bourgeoisie—for the instruction of his young wife, sometime between 1392 and 1394. His paraphrase of Petrarch's version of the Griselda story is one of several tales through which he discusses the obedience and humility a wife should show her husband.

1. In 1341, Petrarch was given the laurel crown for poetry, in imitation of ancient custom. Cf. *Clerk's Prologue*, ll. 31–33.

The Merchant's Prologue and Tale

Chaucer draws upon a great variety of literary texts and genres in the making of this tale, as its many allusions suggest. Here we print only the closest analogue for its concluding action, one of several medieval versions of what is known as the pear-tree story. It is taken from the *Novellino*, the first major collection of tales and anecdotes in Italian, whose earliest version dates from late in the thirteenth century (ca. 1280). For other versions of the pear-tree story, and for analogues to the tale's discussion of marriage and its portrayal of an old husband with a young wife, see N. S. Thompson's chapter on the *Merchant's Tale* in *Sources and Analogues of the* Canterbury Tales, vol. 2, ed. Robert M. Correale and Mary Hamel (Woodbridge: D. S. Brewer, 2005), pp. 479–534. For other material relevant to the tale's treatment of women, marriage, and the battle of the sexes, see the Sources and Backgrounds we provide for the *Wife of Bath's Prologue and Tale* and the section on lechery and its remedy in Chaucer's *Parson's Tale*, also printed in this Norton Critical Edition, pp. 333–44.

The Woman and the Pear-Tree†

There was once a rich man who had a very beautiful woman as his wife; he loved her ardently and was very jealous of her. Now, as God would have it, an illness befell this man's eyes and made him blind; he saw the light of day no more. And so it happened that this man would not leave his wife nor ever let her out of his reach, for he feared she might go astray.

Now it chanced that a man of the neighborhood fell in love with this woman, and not seeing how he could find an opportunity to converse with her—for her husband was always at her side—he made signs indicating he was dying of love. The woman, seeing him so enamored, felt sorry for him, and gave him to understand in return, "You see I can do nothing, for this man never leaves me." So the good man did not know what to do or say, and looked as thought he wanted to die. He could find no way of meeting the woman alone.

The woman, seeing this behavior, took pity on him and thought of a way of helping him. She had a long tube made from a reed, and put it to the ear of this man, and by that means spoke to him so that her husband could not hear. She said to the gentleman, "I am sorry for you, and have

† Translation freely adapted from *Il Novellino, the Hundred Old Tales,* trans. Edward Storer (New York: Dutton, 1925), pp. 130–33; for the original, see *Le novelle antiche dei codici panciatichiano-palatino 138 e laurenziano-gaddiano 193,* ed. Guido Biagi (Florence: Sansoni, 1880), pp. 199–201. Biagi's text is reprinted in *Sources and Analogues of Chaucer's* Canterbury Tales, ed. W. F. Bryan and Germaine Dempster (Chicago: U of Chicago P, 1941), pp. 342–43, and (with a more literal translation) in *The Literary Context of Chaucer's Fabliaux*, ed. Larry D. Benson and Theodore M. Andersson (Indianapolis: Bobbs-Merrill, 1971), pp. 238–41. This story appears in only one manuscript of the *Novellino*, dating from the fourteenth century, and is not thought to be part of the original collection.

thought of a way of helping you. Go into our garden and climb up a pear-tree that has many fine pears, and wait for me there, and I will come up to you." The good man went at once into the garden and climbed up the pear-tree, and waited for the woman.

Now came the time when the woman was in the garden, wishing to help the good man—but her husband was still by her side. And so she said, "I feel a desire for those pears at the top of that pear-tree, for they are very fine." The husband said, "Call someone to pick them for you." And the woman said, "I will pick them myself—otherwise I would not enjoy them." Then the woman went to the tree to climb it, and her husband came with her to its foot, putting his arms around its trunk so that no one could follow her up it.

Thus it happened that the woman climbed up the pear-tree to the friend who was awaiting her. They gave each other great happiness, and the pear-tree shook with their weight, and the pears fell down on top of the husband. Then he said, "What are you doing, woman, that you don't come back down? You are knocking down all the pears!" And the woman replied, "I wanted the pears off a certain branch, and that was the only way I could get them."

Now you should know that the Lord God and Saint Peter saw this happening, and Saint Peter said to the Lord God, "Do you not see the trick that woman is playing on her husband? Lord, cause the husband to see the light again, so he may see what his wife is doing." And the Lord God said, "I tell you, Saint Peter, no sooner will he see the light than the woman will find an explanation—an excuse. And so I will make the light return to his eyes, and you shall see what she will say."

Then the light returned to him, and he looked up and saw what the woman was doing. "What are you doing with that man? You honor neither yourself nor me, nor is this the loyalty proper in a woman." And the woman replied at once, "If I had not done so with him, you would not have seen the light." And the husband, hearing this, was satisfied. So you see how women and females are loyal, and how quick they are to find an excuse.

The Franklin's Prologue and Tale

The story told in the *Franklin's Tale* appears twice in Boccaccio: first in Book 4 of the *Filocolo* as one of the questions of love debated by a group of young men and women at their leisure; second in *The Decameron*, in a shorter version told on the final day as one of the tales illustrating the theme of generosity. Critics have argued for Chaucer's indebtedness to one or the other, or both, of these stories. We print the *Decameron* version here, along with Boccaccio's description, at the start of the following tale, of the listeners' responses to the issues posed by the narrative. We also include as background to some of the Franklin's thinking about love and marriage a passage discussing these topics from a fourteenth-century English translation of a popular thirteenth-century Latin encyclopedia, Bartholomaeus Anglicus's *De proprietatibus rerum*. Some of the biblical and antifeminist material printed above as background to the *Wife of Bath's Prologue and Tale* is also pertinent to this one; for example, Dorigen's long soliloquy about women who have preferred death to dishonor is drawn from St. Jerome's *Against Jovinian*.

GIOVANNI BOCCACCIO

From The Decameron, Day 10†

Story 5

Madonna Dianora asks Messer Ansaldo for a garden in January as beautiful as it would be in May, and he provides it for her by hiring a magician. Her husband then gives her permission to satisfy Messer Ansaldo's desires, but upon hearing of her husband's generosity, Messer Ansaldo releases her from her promise, and the magician releases Messer Ansaldo from his, refusing to accept any sort of payment from him.

Every member of the merry company praised Messer Gentile to the skies, after which the King ordered Emilia to continue, and as if she just could not wait to speak, she boldly began as follows:

Delicate ladies, no one can reasonably deny that Messer Gentile acted with generosity, but if anyone should argue that doing more than he did is impossible, it will perhaps not be all that difficult to prove that his accomplishments can indeed be surpassed, as I propose to show you in a little story of mine.

† From *The Decameron*, trans. Wayne Rebhorn (New York: W. W. Norton, 2014), pp. 779–85, 938. Copyright © 2013 by Wayne Rebhorn. Used by permission of W. W. Norton & Company, Inc. We have omitted some of Rebhorn's notes. For texts and translations of both this tale and the *Filocolo* version, as well as other source material, see Robert R. Edwards's chapter in *Sources and Analogues of the* Canterbury Tales, vol. 1, ed. Robert M. Correale and Mary Hamel (Woodbridge: D. S. Brewer, 2002), pp. 211–65.

In Friuli, which is a cold province, but one happily endowed with beautiful mountains, numerous rivers, and clear springs, there is a town called Udine where there once lived a beautiful, noble lady called Madonna Dianora, the wife of a very wealthy man named Gilberto who was exceptionally pleasant and amiable. Such was this lady's worth that she attracted the most fervent love of a noble lord named Messer Ansaldo Gradense, an important man of exalted station who was known everywhere for his feats of arms and his courtesy. Although he loved her passionately and did everything he could to get her to return his affection, sending her frequent messages to this end, all his efforts were in vain. Eventually, the lady found the gentleman's solicitations wearisome, and realizing that despite refusing everything he asked of her, he nevertheless persisted in loving her and would not stop importuning her, she came up with a novel and, to her mind, impossible request as a way to get rid of him. So one day she spoke to a woman who often came to her on his behalf.

"My good woman," she said, "you've assured me many times that Messer Ansaldo loves me more than anything else, and you've frequently offered me marvelous gifts on his behalf, which I'd prefer he kept for himself, because they could never induce me to love him or satisfy his desires. Were I certain, however, that he really did love me as much as you say he does, then I should undoubtedly bring myself to return his affection and do whatever he wished. Consequently, if he were willing to provide me with proof by doing what I intend to ask of him, I shall be only too ready to obey his commands."

"And just what is it, my lady, that you want him to do?" said the good woman.

"What I desire is this," she replied. "In the month of January that is now approaching, I want a garden, close to town here, that will be full of green grass and flowers and leafy trees just the way it would be in May. And if he can't produce it, then he's not to send you or anyone else to me ever again, because if he bothers me any more, I won't keep it a secret, as I have up to now, but instead, I'll seek to rid myself of him by complaining to my husband and my relatives."

When the gentleman heard what his lady was demanding as well as what she was offering in return, he felt that she was really asking him to do something quite difficult, indeed virtually impossible, and realized that the only reason she had for making such a request was to dash his hopes. Nevertheless, he resolved to try everything he could to fulfill it and had inquiries made throughout many parts of the world to see whether anyone could be found who might provide him with assistance or advice. Finally, he got hold of a man who offered to do what he wanted by means of necromancy, provided he was well paid for his services.

Having agreed to pay the magician a very large sum of money, Messer Ansaldo waited contentedly for the appointed time to arrive. On the night before the calends[1] of January, when it was extremely cold and everything was covered with snow and ice, the worthy man went to work with his arts, and the very next morning, in a quite lovely meadow not far from the town, there appeared, according to the testimony of those who saw it, one of the most exquisite gardens anyone has ever seen, with grass and trees and fruit of every kind.

1. The calends is the first of the month.

After the ecstatic Messer Ansaldo had looked over it, he arranged for some of the finest fruit and the most beautiful flowers growing there to be picked and presented in secret to the lady, along with an invitation for her to come and see the garden that she had asked for. Thus she would not only realize how much he loved her, but she would remember the promise she had given him, which she had sealed with an oath, and would thus, as a woman of honor, find a way to keep her word.

The lady had already heard many reports about the wonderful garden, and when she saw the flowers and fruit, she began to repent of the promise she had made. Nevertheless, for all her repentance, being curious to see such novelties, she set off with a large group of ladies from the town to have a look at the garden, and after according it great praise and expressing no small astonishment over it, she returned home, the saddest woman alive as she thought of what it obliged her to do. So intense was her grief that she was unable to conceal it, and her husband, noticing how she looked, insisted on knowing the reason why. Deeply ashamed, she maintained her silence for a long time, but finally felt compelled to tell him everything down to the last detail.

As he listened to her story, Gilberto was initially enraged, but then, upon mature reflection, considering the purity of his wife's intentions, he cast off his anger and said: "Dianora, it's not the part of a discreet and honorable lady to listen to messages of that sort, or to make a bargain about her chastity with any man, under any condition. The power of words that the heart receives by way of the ears is greater than many people believe, and for those who are in love there's almost nothing they can't accomplish. Thus, you did wrong, first of all by listening to him, and then by making that bargain. But because I know how pure your heart is, I'll allow you to do something to fulfill the promise you made, something that perhaps no other man would permit, albeit I'm also moved by my fear of the magician, for Messer Ansaldo might ask him to harm us if you played him for a fool. I therefore want you to go to him, and using any means at your disposal, I want you to do what you can to preserve your chastity and get him to release you from your promise. However, if that's not possible, then just this once you may yield your body, but not your heart, to him."

As she listened to her husband, the lady wept and insisted that she did not want such a favor from him. But no matter how vehemently she refused it, Gilberto remained adamant, and so, the next morning around dawn the lady set out, not having bothered to get especially dressed up, and made her way to Messer Ansaldo's house, preceded by just two of her servants and followed by a single chambermaid.

Messer Ansaldo was utterly astonished when he heard that his lady had come to him, and as soon as he got out of bed, he sent for the magician. "I want you to see for yourself what a wonderful prize your art has procured for me," he said. The two of them then went to meet her, and far from displaying anything like unbridled passion, Messer Ansaldo welcomed her with courtesy and reverence. After that, they went into a lovely room where a great fire was burning, and having offered her a place to sit, he said: "My lady, if the long love I have borne for you merits any sort of reward, I beseech you to do me the kindness of revealing the truth about what has brought you here at such an hour and with such a small escort as this."

Ashamed, her eyes welling up with tears, the lady replied: "Sir, I have not been led here because of any love I feel for you or because of the promise I gave you, but rather, because I was ordered to do so by my husband, who has more regard for the labors you've undertaken to satisfy your unbridled passion than he does for his own honor or for mine. And it is at his command that I am furthermore disposed, just this once, to satisfy your every desire."

If Messer Ansaldo had been astonished by the lady's coming to his house, his astonishment was much greater when he heard what she had to say, and he was so moved by Gilberto's liberality that his ardor gradually changed into compassion.

"My lady," he said, "things being the way you say they are, God forbid that I should mar the honor of a man who takes pity on my love. And so, for as long as you choose to stay here, you will be treated as if you were my sister, and whenever you please, you shall be free to depart, provided that you convey to your husband such thanks as you deem appropriate for the immense courtesy he has displayed and that from now on you always look upon me as your brother and servant."

Upon hearing his words, the lady was happier than she had ever been. "From what I've noted of your conduct," she replied, "nothing could ever make me believe that my coming here would have produced any result other than the response I see you've made to it, and for that, I will be eternally in your debt." The lady then took her leave and returned, now with an honorable escort, to Gilberto. She told him what had occurred, with the result that he and Messer Ansaldo became faithful friends, attached to one another by the closest of bonds.

The magician had observed Gilberto's liberality toward Messer Ansaldo as well as Messer Ansaldo's toward the lady, and so, just as Messer Ansaldo was preparing to give him the reward he had been promised, he declared: "Now that I've seen how generous Gilberto has been with regard to his honor and you with regard to your love, God forbid that I shouldn't also be equally generous as far as my remuneration is concerned. And considering how you deserve it, I intend to let you keep it for yourself."

This embarrassed the gentleman, who did everything he could to make him take either the entire sum, or at least part of it, but all his efforts were in vain. Consequently, when the magician, having removed his garden on the third day, expressed a wish to depart, Messer Ansaldo bid him Godspeed. And from then on, any carnal desire he felt for the lady having been extinguished in his heart, Messer Ansaldo burned only with honorable affection for her.

What, then, shall we conclude, loving ladies? Shall we take the case of a lady who was almost dead and a man's love for her that had already grown lukewarm because his hopes had waned, and shall we place it above the generosity of Messer Ansaldo, whose love was more fervent than ever, who burned, as it were, with even more hope than before, and who held the prey he had pursued for so long right there in his hands? It strikes me as foolish to believe that first example of generosity could be compared to this one.[2]

* * *

2. In her conclusion, Emilia is referring, of course, to the previous story.

Story 6

* * *

It would take too long to give a full account of all the varied discussions among the ladies as to whether Gilberto, Messer Ansaldo, or the necromancer had displayed the greater liberality in the case of Madonna Dianora. After the King had allowed them to debate the question for a while, however, he looked over at Fiammetta and ordered her to put an end to their dispute by telling her story.

BARTHOLOMAEUS ANGLICUS

[On Love and Marriage]†

De viro.

A man hatte° *vir* in latyn, and hath that name *is called*
of° myght and vertu° and strengthe. So seith *because of / power*
Isidre.[1] For in myght and strengthe a man pas-
sith° a womman, and a man is the hed of a wom- *surpasses*
man, as the apostil seith.[2] Therfore a man is
holde° to rule his wif, as the heed hath the cure° *bound / care*
and reule of al the body. And a man hatte *maritus*,
as it were wardinge° and defendinge the modir, *keeping*
for he taketh so the charge, the warde,° and the *guardianship*
kepinge of his wif that is modir of children, and
hatte *sponsus* also, and hath that name of *spondere*,° *from "to betroth"*
for a behotith° and oblegith himsilf. For in the *he promises*
contract of weddinge he plightith his treuthe,° *troth*
and oblegith himsilf to lede his lif with his wif
withoute departinge,° and to paye dettis to *parting from her*
here° and to kepe to here feith and companie, and *pay his (sexual) debts to her*
that he schal leve hire for none othir. A man hath
so gret love to his wif that because of here he
aventurith him° to al perilus,° ande settith [here] *himself / perils*
love tofore° his modir love,° and for to dwelle with *before / love for his mother*
his wif he forsaketh his fadir and modir and his
contray, as oure lord seith: Herefore a man schal
forsake fadir and modir and abide with his wif.[3]

Tofore the weddinge the spouse fondith° to *strives*
winne the love of hise spouse that° he wowith° *whom / woos*
with giftis, and certifieth of his wille° with lettres *makes known his intentions*
and messingeres and with divers sondes,° and *messages*

† Text based on *On the Properties of Things: John Trevisa's Translation of Bartholomaeus Anglicus de Proprietatibus Rerum*, ed. M. C. Seymour et al., 2 vols. (Oxford: Oxford UP, 1975), 1. 307–09. Reprinted by permission of Oxford University Press.

1. Isidore of Seville (d. 636), author of a popular medieval encyclopedia, the *Etymologies*. The explanations of the meanings of the Latin words *vir* (man), *maritus* (husband), and *sponsus* (bridegroom) in this paragraph are based on Latin etymologies that the English translation cannot reproduce.
2. St. Paul, in Ephesians 5:23; see p. 420.
3. Ephesians 5:31; see p. 420.

geveth many giftis and meche good and catelle,° and behotith° wel more. And to plese hire he puttith hym° to divers pleyes and games among gedderinge° of puple, and usith° ofte dedis of myght and of maistrie,° and maketh hym gay° and semeliche° in divers clothinge and aray. And alle that he is i-prayed° to geve othir° to doo for here love he geveth and doth anon with alle his myght, and werneth none bone° that is i-prayed in here name and for here love. He spekith to here plesingeliche,° and beholdith hire in the face with plesinge and glad chere° and with a scharp eye, and assentith° to hire at the laste, and tellith openliche his wille and his assent° in presence of hire frendes, and spousith° hire with a ring and taketh hire to wif, and geveth hire grete giftis in tokene of the contract of weddinge, and maketh to hire chartres and dedes° of graunt° and of giftis, and maketh revels and festis of spousailes,° and geveth many goode giftis to frendis and gestis, and comfortith and gladith his gestis with songis and pipis and with instrumentis of musik. And hereaftir he bryngith his spouse into the privetees° of his chambre, and fongith hire to felawe° and maketh hire felawe in bedde and at bourde.[4] And thanne he maketh hire lady of his money and of his meyne.° Thanne he hath hire cause as moche to herte as his owne, and taketh the charge and keping of here. And for special love he amendith° hire yif sche doth amys,° and taketh hede° of here beringe and goynge,° of spekinge and lokynge, and of here passinge° and agencomynge° and entringe.

No man hath more welthe than he that hath a good womman to wif. Ne no man is more wrecche nothir° hath woo and sorwe than he that hath an yvel wif, crienge, jangelinge,° chidinge and skoldinge, drunkelew° and unstedefast and contrarye° to hym, costlew,° stoute and gay,[5] envyous, noyful,° and lepinge ouer londes and contrayes, and mychinge,° suspicious, and wrethful. Fulgencius touchith al this matere in a certeyn sermon *de nupciis in Chana Galile*.[6] And so he likneth° Crist to the goode man, and holy chirche to a goode wif, and the synagoge to an evel wif that breketh spousehode.° In a goode spouse and wif nedith thes condicions: that sche be busy and

many goods and possessions
promises
himself
gathering / practices
prowess / well dressed
comely
asked / or
refuses no boon, request
pleasantly
countenance
submits
intent
espouses, marries
deeds / allowance
wedding feasts
privacy
takes her as a companion
household
corrects
wrong / heed
behavior
departing / returning
nor
chattering
prone to drunkenness
hostile / extravagant
troublesome
thieving
likens, compares
commits adultery

4. Literally "at table," but the phrase "bed and board" refers to the full range of a wife's sexual and domestic responsibilities and privileges.
5. Haughty and ostentatiously dressed.
6. We have not been able to find a sermon on the marriage at Cana (John 2:1–11) in the extant works of either Fulgentius, bishop of Ruspe, or Fulgentius the mythographer.

devoute in goddes servyse; meke° and servisable to here housbonde, and faire spekinge and goodlich° to here meyne;° merciable and good to wrecchis that beth nedy; esi° and pesible° to here neighbores; redy, ware,° and wys in thinges that schal be i-voided; rightful and pacient in soffringe;° besi [and] diligent in here doinge and dedis; manerliche in clothinge; sobre in movinge; ware in spekinge; chast° in lokinge; honest in beringe; sad° in goynge,° schamfast° among the puple; meri and glad with here housbonde; and chast in privete. Such a wif is worthi to be i-preised,° that fondith° more to plese here housbonde with heer° homliche i-wounde° than with heer gailiche i-pinchid,° and i-wrolled° more with vertues than with faire and gay clothinge. Sche usith the goodnes of matrimoni more bicause of children than of fleischliche likynge,° and hath more likinge in spousehod in children of grace than of kynde.[7] Of a goode wif be this inowgh° at this tyme.

meek

kind / household
agreeable / peaceful
wary, careful

suffering

chaste, modest
steady / behavior / modest

praised / strives
hair / simply braided
gaily curled / wrapped

physical pleasure

enough

7. For spiritual than for earthly reasons.

The Pardoner's Prologue and Tale

As in the case of the Wife of Bath, the relationship between the Pardoner's prologue and his tale is exceptionally provocative. The Pardoner's open revelation of his own hypocrisy and avarice, which frames the narrative, has precedent in the speech of False Seeming (*Faus Semblant*) from *The Romance of the Rose.* The basis of the story of the rioters and the treasure is an exemplum found in various forms in the Middle Ages and Renaissance, known in its fullest version as *The Hermit, Death, and the Robbers.* The Pardoner's discussion of the tavern sins owes much to traditional lore, such as Thomas of Cantimpré's exemplum about swearing. The grim atmosphere of death and its arbitrariness that permeates the tale is due in great part to the impact of the plague on late medieval consciousness, and the most substantial contemporary description of the Black Death is in the introduction to Boccaccio's *Decameron*, printed on pp. 350–63.

JEAN DE MEUN

From The Romance of the Rose†

[*False Seeming's Speech*]

* * *

False Seeming began his lecture and said to all in hearing:

"Barons, hear my theme: he who wants to become acquainted with False Seeming must seek him in the world or in the cloister. I dwell in no place except these two, but more in one and less in the other. Briefly, I am lodged where I think that I am better hidden. The safest hiding place is under the most humble garment. The religious are very covert, the worldly more open. I do not want to blame or defame the religious calling, in whatever habit one may find it. I shall not, as I may, blame the humble and loyal religious life, although I do not love it.

"I have in mind the false religious, the malicious criminals who want to wear the habit but do not want to subdue their hearts. The religious are all compassionate; you will never see a spiteful one. They do not care to follow pride, and they all want to live humbly. I never dwell with such

† From Guillaume de Lorris and Jean de Meun, *The Romance of the Rose*, trans. Charles Dahlberg (Princeton: Princeton UP, 1971), pp. 194–98, 202–205, 208–209. Jean de Meun wrote his vast conclusion to Guillaume's poem ca. 1275. In this passage, False Seeming (*Faus Semblant*) offers his service to the God of Love in an assault upon the Castle wherein Jealousy has imprisoned the Rose and Fair Welcoming (*Bel Accueil*), the object of the Lover's quest. False Seeming (who personifies an aspect of the Lover's mind and a part of his erotic strategy) here presents his credentials—an extended self-portrait of hypocrisy exultant—to the God of Love and his assembled barons. On Chaucer's knowledge of this poem, see p. 387 of this volume.

people, and if I do, I pretend. I can indeed assume their habit, but I would rather let myself be hanged than desert my main business, whatever face I put on it.

"I dwell with the proud, the crafty, the guileful, who covet worldly honors and who carry out large dealings, who go around tracking down large handouts and cultivating the acquaintance of powerful men and becoming their followers. They pretend to be poor, and they live on good, delicious morsels of food and drink costly wines. They preach poverty to you while they fish for riches with seines and trammel nets. By my head, evil will come of them. They are neither religious nor worldly. To the world they present an argument in which there is a shameful conclusion: this man has the robe of religion; therefore he is a religious. This argument is specious, not worth a knife of privet; the habit does not make the monk. Nevertheless no one knows how to reply to the argument, no matter how high he tonsures his head, even if he shaves with the razor of the *Elenchis*, that cuts up fraud into thirteen branches.[1] No man knows so well how to set up distinctions that he dare utter a single word about it. But whatever place I come to, no matter how I conduct myself, I pursue nothing except fraud. No more than Tibert the cat has his mind on anything but mice and rats do I think of anything except fraud. Certainly by my habit you would never know with what people I dwell, any more than you would from my words, no matter how simple and gentle they were. You should look at actions if your eyes have not been put out; for if people do something other than what they say, they are certainly tricking you, whatever robes they have or whatever estate they occupy, clerical or lay, man or woman, lord, sergeant, servant, or lady.

* * *

"But indeed I want to promise you to further the causes of all your friends, provided that they want my companionship. They are dead if they don't receive me, and they will serve my friend, or, by God, they will never succeed! Without fail, I am a traitor, and God has judged me a thief. I am perjured, but one hardly knows before the end what I am bringing to an end, for several who never recognized my fraud have received their deaths through me, and many are receiving them and will receive them without ever recognizing it. The man who does so, if he is wise, protects himself from it, or it will be his great misfortune. But the deception is so strong that it is very difficult to recognize it. For Proteus, who was accustomed to change into whatever form he wished, never knew as much fraud or guile as I practice; I never entered a town where I was recognized, no matter how much I was heard or seen. I know very well how to change my garment, to take one and then another foreign to it. Now I am a knight, now a monk; at one time I am a prelate, at another a canon; at one hour a clerk, at another a priest; now disciple, now master, now lord of the manor, now forester. Briefly I am in all occupations. Again I may be prince or page, and I know all languages by heart. At one hour I am old and white, and then I have become young again. Now I am Robert, now Robin, now Cordelier, now Jacobin. And in order to follow my companion, Lady Constrained Abstinence, who comforts me and

1. The allusion is to scholastic subtlety in argumentation; an *elenchus* is a procedure of refutation.

goes along with me, I take on many another disguise, just as it strikes her pleasure, to fulfill her desire. At one time I wear a woman's robe; now I am a girl, now a lady. At another time I become a religious: now I am a devotee, now a prioress, nun, or abbess; now a novice, now a professed nun. I go through every locality seeking all religions. But, without fail, I leave the kernel of religion and take the husk. I dwell in religion in order to trick people; I seek only its habit, no more. What should I tell you? I disguise myself in the way that pleases me. The time is very much changed in me; my deeds are very different from my words."

At this point False Seeming wanted to stay silent, but Love did not pretend that he was annoyed at what he heard; instead, to delight the company, he said to him:

"Tell us more especially in what way you serve disloyally. Don't be ashamed to speak of it, for, as you tell us of your habits, you seem to be a holy hermit."

"It is true, but I am a hypocrite."

"You go around preaching abstinence."

"True, indeed, but I fill my paunch with very good morsels and with wines such as are suitable for theologians."

"You go around preaching poverty."

"True, abundantly richly. But however much I pretend to be poor, I pay no attention to any poor person. I would a hundred thousand times prefer the acquaintance of the King of France to that of a poor man, by our lady, even though he had as good a soul. When I see those poor devils all naked, shivering with cold on those stinking dunghills, crying and howling with hunger, I don't meddle in their business. If they were carried to the Hôtel-Dieu, they wouldn't get any comfort from me, for they wouldn't feed my maw with a single gift, since they have nothing worth a cuttlefish. What will a man give who licks his knife? But a visit to a rich usurer who is sick is a good and pleasant thing. I go to comfort him, for I expect to bring away money from him. And if wicked death stifles him, I will carry him right up to his grave. And if anyone comes to reprove me for avoiding the poor, do you know how I escape from him? I give out behind my cloak that the rich man is more stained with sin than the poor, and has greater need of counsel, and that that is the reason that I see him and advise him.

* * *

"Working can give me no pleasure: I have nothing to do with it, for there is too great difficulty in working. I prefer to pray in front of people and cover my foxlike nature under a cloak of pope-holiness."

"What's this?" said Love. "The devil! What are your words? What have you said here?"

"What?"

"Great and open disloyalty. Don't you fear God then?"

"Certainly not. The man who wants to fear God can hardly attain anything great in this world, for the good, who avoid evil, live legitimately on what they have, and keep themselves according to God, scarcely get from one loaf to the next. Such people drink too much discomfort; there is no life that displeases me so much.

"But consider how usurers, counterfeiters, and loan sharks have money in their storehouses. Bailiffs, beadles, provosts, mayors, all live practically by rapine. The common people bow to them, while they, like wolves, devour the commoners. Everybody runs over the poor; there isn't anyone who does not want to despoil them, and all cover themselves with their spoil. They all snuff up their substance and pluck them alive without scalding. The strongest robs the weakest. But I, wearing my simple robe and duping both dupers and duped, rob both the robbed and the robbers.

"By my trickery I pile up and amass great treasure in heaps and mounds, treasure that cannot be destroyed by anything. For if I build a palace with it and achieve all my pleasures with company, the bed, with tables full of sweets—for I want no other life—my money and my gold increases. Before my treasure can be emptied, money comes to me again in abundance. Don't I make my bears tumble? My whole attention is on getting. My acquisitions are worth more than my revenues. Even if I were to be beaten or killed, I still want to penetrate everywhere. I would never try to stop confessing emperors, kings, dukes, barons, or counts. But with poor men it is shameful; I don't like such confession. If not for some other purpose, I have no interest in poor people; their estate is neither fair nor noble.

"These empresses, duchesses, queens, and countesses; their high-ranking palace ladies; these abbesses, beguines, and wives of bailiffs and knights; these coy, proud bourgeois wives, these nuns and young girls; provided that they are rich or beautiful, whether they are bare or well turned out, they do not go away without good advice.

"For the salvation of souls, I inquire of lords and ladies and their entire households about their characteristics and their way of life; and I put into their heads the belief that their parish priests are animals in comparison with me and my companions. I have many wicked dogs among them, to whom I am accustomed to reveal people's secrets, without hiding anything; and in the same way they reveal everything to me, so that they hide nothing in the world from me.

"In order that you may recognize the criminals who do not stop deceiving people, I will now tell you here the words that we read of Saint Matthew, that is to say, the evangelist, in the twenty-third chapter: 'Upon the chair of Moses' (the gloss explains that this is the Old Testament), 'the scribes and pharisees have sat.' These are the accursed false people that the letter calls hypocrites. 'Do what they say, but not what they do. They are not slow to speak well, but they have no desire to do so. To gullible people they attach heavy loads that cannot be carried; they place them on their shoulders, but they dare not move them with their finger.'"

"Why not?" asked Love.

"In faith," replied False Seeming, "they don't want to, for porters' shoulders are often accustomed to suffer from their burdens, and these hypocrites flee from wanting to do such a thing. If they do jobs that may be good, it is because people see them. They enlarge their phylacteries and increase their fringes; since they are haughty, proud, and overbearing, they like the highest and most honorable seats at tables and the first in the synagogues. They like people to greet them when they pass along the street, and they want to be called 'master,' when they shouldn't be called, for the gospel goes against this practice and shows its unlawfulness.

"We have another custom toward those that we know are against us. We want to hate them very strongly and attack them all by agreement among ourselves. He whom one hates, the others hate, and all are bent on ruining him. If we see that he may, through certain people, win honor in the land, income, or possessions, we study to find out by what ladder he may mount up, and the better to capture and subdue him, we treacherously defame him to those people, for we do not love him. We cut the rungs from his ladder, and we strip him of his friends in such a way that he will never know by a word that he has lost them. If we troubled him openly, we would perhaps be blamed for it and thus miss out in our calculation; if he knew our worst intention, he would protect himself against it so that we would be reprimanded for it.

"If one of us has done something very good, we consider that we have all done it. Indeed, by God, if he was pretending it, or if he no more than condescends to brag that he has advanced certain men, we make ourselves partners in the deed and, as you should well know, we say that these people have been helped on by us. In order to win people's praise we tell lies to rich men and get them to give us letters bearing witness to our goodness, so that throughout the world people will think that every virtue abounds in us. We always pretend to be poor, but no matter how we complain, we are the ones, let me tell you, who have everything without having anything.

"I also undertake brokerage commissions, I draw up agreements, I arrange marriages, I take on executor's duties, and I go around doing procurations. I am a messenger and I make investigations, dishonest ones, moreover. To occupy myself with someone else's business is to me a very pleasant occupation. And if you have any business to do with those whom I frequent, tell me, and the thing is done as soon as you have told me. Provided that you have served me well, you have deserved my service. But anyone who wanted to punish me would rob himself of my favor. I neither love nor value the man by whom I am reproved for anything. I want to reprove all the others, but I don't want to hear their reproof, for I, who correct others, have no need of another's correction.

* * *

"But to you I dare not lie. However, if I could feel that you would not recognize it, you would have a lie in hand. Certainly I would have tricked you, and I would never have held back on account of any sin. And I would indeed desert you if you were to treat me poorly."

The god smiled at this wonder, and everyone laughed with amazement and said, "Here is a fine sergeant, of whom people should indeed be proud!"

"False Seeming," said Love, "tell me: since I have brought you so near to me that your power in my court is so great that you will be king of camp followers here, will you keep your agreement with me?"

"Yes, I swear it and promise you; neither your father nor your forefathers ever had sergeants more loyal."

"How! It is against your nature."

"Take your chances on it, for if you demand pledges, you will never be more sure, in fact, not even if I gave hostages, letters, witnesses, or security. I call on you as witness of the fact that one can't take the wolf out of his hide until he is skinned, no matter how much he is beaten or curried. Do you think that I do not deceive and play tricks because I wear a simple robe, under which I have worked many a great evil? By God! I shall never turn my heart from this kind of life. And if I have a simple, demure face, do you think that I may cease doing evil? My sweetheart Constrained Abstinence has need of my providence. She would long ago have been dead and in a bad plight if she hadn't had me in her power. Grant that we two, she and I, may carry out the task."

"So be it," said Love, "I believe you without guarantee."

And the thief with the face of treachery, white without and black within, knelt down on the spot and thanked him.

* * *

The Hermit, Death, and the Robbers†

Here is the story of a hermit who, walking through a forest, found a very great treasure.

One day a hermit, walking through a forest, found a cave that was very large and well hidden, and went toward it to rest for he was very tired. Just as he reached the cave, he saw at a certain place within it a great brightness, because there was much gold there. As soon as he recognized what it was, he swiftly took his leave, and began running through the desert as fast as he could go. While running thus, this hermit happened upon three bold thieves who haunted that forest to rob anyone who passed through it, and who had not yet realized that this gold was there. As they stood in hiding, they saw this man running away with no one in pursuit, and were a little frightened. But they came out of hiding nevertheless, in order to learn why he was fleeing, for they marveled greatly at it. And he answered, "My brothers, I flee death, who comes after me, pursuing me." Seeing neither man nor beast chasing him, they said, "Show us who is pursuing you, and lead us to the place where he is." Then the hermit said to them, "Come with me, and I will show him to you," while begging them every step of the way not to go seeking death, whom he himself was fleeing. But they, wishing to find death, and to see how he was made, would not settle for anything else. The hermit, seeing he could not do otherwise, and being frightened of them, led them to the cave from which he had fled, and said to them, "Here is death, which pursued me," and showed them the gold that was there.

They immediately knew what it was, and began to rejoice greatly and to make merry together. They dismissed the good man, who went away about his own affairs, and remarked to each other on what a great simpleton he was. The three robbers stayed together, guarding the treasure and discussing what they wished to do with it. One said, "It seems to me, since God has given us this great good fortune, that we should not leave here until we carry away all this treasure." Another said, "Let us do otherwise.

† Translated for this volume's first edition by V. A. Kolve. The tale survives in a Renaissance collection of stories—Borghini's 1572 *Libro di novelle e di bel parlar gentile*—but materials in that collection have been traced back to the thirteenth century. For the Italian text and reference to the antecedents, see *Sources and Analogues of Chaucer's* Canterbury Tales, ed. W. F. Bryan and Germaine Dempster (Chicago: U Chicago P, 1941), pp. 416–19. This and other relevant texts are now edited and translated by Mary Hamel in *Sources and Analogues of the* Canterbury Tales, vol. 1, ed. Robert M. Correale and Mary Hamel (Woodbridge: D. S. Brewer, 2002), pp. 267–319.

Let one of us take a part of it and go to town and sell it, and get some bread and some wine and whatever else is necessary; and let him be as clever about this as he can, until he has obtained what we need." All three agreed to this together.

Now the Devil, who is crafty and inclined always to do as much evil as he can, put this thought into the heart of him who was going into town for provisions: "As soon as I am in town," he said to himself, "I want to eat and drink my fill, provide myself with certain things that have become necessary to me, and then poison the food which I carry back to my fellows. Once they are both dead, I shall be Lord of all that treasure. It seems so great, I think I shall be the richest man in this whole region." He did all those things, just as they had come into his mind. He took as much food for himself as he needed, poisoned all the rest, and brought it thus to his friends.

But while he went to town in the fashion I have told you, thinking evil and plotting to kill his friends so that everything would remain to himself, they were thinking no better of him. They said to each other, "As soon as this friend of ours returns with the bread and the wine and the other things we need, we will murder him, and then eat as much as we want, and afterward we'll have this great treasure just between the two of us. Since there will be fewer of us, each one will have a larger part of the treasure." When the one who had gone to town to buy the things they needed came back, his friends attacked him, as soon as they saw him, with lances and knives, and murdered him. When he was dead, they ate what he had brought, and as soon as they were full, both fell dead. And thus they died all three, for each killed the other, as you have heard, and did not possess the treasure.

Thus does our Lord God repay traitors: they went seeking death, and found it in such manner as they deserved. The wise man fled from it wisely. The gold remained free as before.

THOMAS OF CANTIMPRÉ

From Liber de Apibus†

Exemplum 103

In the city of Louvain, within the boundaries of Brabant we saw a noble and worthy citizen who, rising to go to matins on the holy night of Good Friday, passed in front of a tavern in which dissolute young men were sitting, playing at dice and vying with one another in blasphemies and oaths. Continuing on his way, this citizen found men in the street near the tavern who were making loud lamentation over a certain stranger who was badly

† Trans. Carleton Brown, *The Pardoner's Tale*, by Geoffrey Chaucer (Oxford: Oxford UP, 1935), pp. xvii–xviii. Reprinted by permission of the Estate of Carleton F. Brown. Thomas of Cantimpré (or Chantimpré) was born in Brabant (modern Belgium) ca. 1200 and died ca. 1270; the story here translated was written sometime before 1263. As an exemplum, it is less a tale in its own right than a narrative abstract that a preacher could use to illustrate and make vivid his theme and that he would characteristically expand in the telling through further dialogue and detail to the level of his ability and the needs of his sermon audience.

wounded and bleeding. When he asked the men who had inflicted these wounds they answered: "Those young men who are playing dice." Entering the tavern, the citizen upbraided the young men for playing on that night and asked them sternly why they had so cruelly beaten the stranger who had been with them. Much astonished, the young men denied that anyone had come in since they had sat down, and protested that they had wounded no one either by word or blow. Going forth quickly with the citizen, they sought for the bleeding stranger but could not find him. Having now recovered their senses, each of them realized that by their terrible oaths they had again insulted the Lord Christ and by their taunts had crucified him afresh.

man beaten is supposed to be Jesus/God!!

The Prioress's Prologue and Tale

Stories of the miracles performed by the Virgin Mary constitute one of the most familiar genres in medieval literature, and there are many analogues, in a variety of languages, to the particular miracle, known as the "lily miracle," recounted in the *Prioress's Tale*. Perhaps the most substantial is a fifteenth-century Latin version in a Trinity College, Cambridge, manuscript, here translated into English by A. G. Rigg. We also include a shorter Middle English verse analogue from the Vernon manuscript, an important fourteenth-century collection of religious and didactic literature. Laurel Broughton considers the Vernon version to be the closest analogue to the *Prioress's Tale*. She prints it, along with several other lily miracle stories (including Rigg's translation of the Trinity version), in her chapter in *Sources and Analogues of the* Canterbury Tales, vol. 2, ed. Robert M. Correale and Mary Hamel (Woodbridge: D. S. Brewer, 2005), pp. 583–647.

We print the song sung by Chaucer's "litel clergeoun," the *Alma Redemptoris Mater*, both in Latin and in Cardinal Newman's English translation. Finally, the historical context of the tale's anti-Semitism is indicated by a thirteenth-century papal bull concerned with claims of Jewish murder of Christian children, such as the one described by the Prioress in her story. For further discussion of Jewish-Christian relationships in the Middle Ages, see the appendix to Stephen Spector's "Empathy and Enmity in the *Prioress's Tale*," pp. 641–48.

The Story of the *Alma Redemptoris Mater*†

The Mother of Grace never forgets those who remember her, and so the memory of her should be continually brought to mind; praise should be lavished upon her, and we should preach her mighty works as often as possible. Although the treasure-chest of all goodness has no need of our good offices, nevertheless it is beneficial and salutary for us to heap praises on her goodness. I have, therefore, decided to take care to entrust the following chapter to writing, so that the story may come to the notice

† Translated and annotated for this volume's first edition by A. G. Rigg. Reprinted by permission of the translator. The original Latin is printed in *Sources and Analogues of Chaucer's* Canterbury Tales, ed. W. F. Bryan and Germaine Dempster (Chicago: U of Chicago P, 1941), pp. 480–85, from the unique MS Trinity College, Cambridge 0.9.38. The MS was compiled ca. 1450, mainly from material written much earlier; on the other hand, several stylistic features of this story resemble those of another Latin narrative in the MS, and both of them may have been "retouched" by the scribe with his own rhetorical embellishments (such as frequent biblical quotation for purely literary effect, not always aptly). There is, however, no *a priori* reason for saying that Chaucer could not have known the story in a version very close to this. The punctuation in *Sources and Analogues* is frequently deficient, and the following corrections should be made: p. 480 / l. 28 for *precanere* read *precauere*; 481/n.3 MS reads *diffitetur*; 481/22 delete *animis*; 482/41 *cunque* read *scilicet*; 483/22 *quanto* read *quanta*; 483/32 *suo* read *sue*; 484/20 *monumentum* read *monimentum*. Several unneccessary emendations of typical MS spellings are made in *Sources and Analogues*. The following emendations are necessary: 480/11 for *figura* read *figuram*; 481/6–7 *doctam* read *docta*; 483/22 *que* read *qui*; 484/9 *excitato* read *excitatus*.

of future generations, and so that those who hear it may be inspired all the more deeply and firmly to remember the Virgin.

There was once a certain boy born and bred in the city of Toledo; by the diligence of his mother he was sent to be instructed at school; he learned to dot his "i"s and to make the forms of letters; he learned the alphabet, and how to marry letter to letters and figure to figures properly. When he had learned how to join letters, he gladly passed on to music, in order that the understanding of the voice might be open to him as well as knowledge acquired by words.

Every day he dutifully made his reading, according to what the authority of his teacher required of him. Each day, when he had fulfilled his educational duty, the hour of mealtime followed, and this little boy then used to go to the house of a canon of Mother Church; by the help of this canon the boy relieved his hunger and cheated the demands of that most importunate of debt-collectors, his stomach. He went there in hope of satisfying his hunger with the rich man's crumbs; every day he was given a measure of the crumbs which fell from the table of his masters and of the fragments left over by those who had eaten. He carefully collected everything that was given him, not in a shepherd's bag but in a little pocket at his breast; for his own use he kept the smallest and most worthless scraps, setting aside the bigger and better portions for his mother. O Lord, you who look into and know our hearts—you know what lies within man!

One day the boy was assigned as his daily schoolwork that sweet and delightful antiphon in praise of the Virgin Mother, whose opening line is "Alma Redemptoris Mater."[1] The boy was anxious not to suffer the terrifying taunts of his schoolmaster, and so he carefully learned the antiphon by heart, and meditated on it, both because it was difficult to learn and because it is a delightful song to sing. In my opinion, however, he learned and sang the antiphon so often not so much because of the sweetness of the song as because of the memory and love of the Virgin Mother. For more worthy than the string of the harp is the heart of the player who prays out of love.[2] The judge who judges the hearts of men is more affected by the love from the heart than by the loudness of the harp, more by the prayer than by the voice which makes the prayer: when one learns to pray in faith one also learns to speak with beauty. Why is this? Because the voice never sounds pleasant unless the spirit leads the voice and prayer in the singing.

One day, when the hour of breakfast had arrived, the boy, who had earned rest by his hard work, was released from school; he practiced with effect what he had learned from usage, like the calf of Ephraim who was taught to love treading.[3] He proceeded in the direction of the house of the canon by whose mercy he used to relieve his own misfortune. By chance he happened to go into the courtyards of Jewry where that stiff-necked race lives, that detestable family—the race which objects to the fruitfulness of the Virgin Mary and denies that the Son of God was made

1. The hymn was probably composed in the eleventh century; for text and translation, see p. 484.
2. *Sources and Analogues* notes the presence of a rhyme on which this conceit is based in another MS, but in fact a later hand has added it in this text also; the rhyme puns on *amor, clamor, vox, volum*, etc.
3. Hosea 10:11 (all quotations are from the Vulgate): the line is not clarified by the biblical passage.

incarnate in her womb. A great number of the sons of the synagogue had gathered together in a house there, strengthening by their number that brotherhood of iniquity, that oppressive branch of sin. The boy arrived close by the house, singing the antiphon we have mentioned above, the *Alma Redemptoris Mater.* His intention was to pass through the area, but he did not get through unharmed. Among the Jews was a certain young Hebrew boy who had been taught a little Latin and understood the Latin idiom. They heard the song, and wondered what it was; Satan came among them, and one of them asked the Hebrew who knew Latin what the Christian boy was singing. The Hebrew replied that the boy was singing an antiphon composed in praise of the Virgin Mary; its delightful sweetness was intended to inspire the minds of the listeners to the memory of Mary. At the mention of the name of the Virgin, the Jew cried out; Satan put it into his heart to betray and kill the innocent boy.

He therefore treacherously asked his colleague to bring the boy in: if he couldn't do what was required simply by asking, he was to offer the boy a bribe. So the innocent boy was summoned and brought in, introduced—or, rather, traduced. They took firm hold of him; "their rejoicing was as that of him who eats the poor in secret."[4] Without delay they made themselves ready for the murder, and prepared to condemn the innocent boy to death. The lamb was seized by the wolves; one of them set a knife to his throat, and his tongue was cruelly cut out; his stomach was opened and his heart and liver taken out. They imagined that they were offering a double sacrifice, firstly by cutting the throat from which emerged the voice of praise, and secondly by tearing out the heart which incessantly meditated on the memory of the Virgin. They thought they were obeying God, but in fact they were making a sacrifice not to God but to the devils of hell. It is usual for malice to cease after death, but although they had killed the boy, their malice did not come to an end: they threw his corpse into a place of the coarsest filth, where nature purges itself in secret.

Immediately the blessed mother of the Redeemer arrived by his side; her gracious mercy was present; she appeared to place a pebble (which looked very like a stone) on and within the mouth of the dead boy. When the pebble had been put in place, the boy's heart and throat opened up; his voice and power of speech returned, and he began to sing the *Alma Redemptoris Mater.*

In the meantime the boy's mother was anxious at his delay: he was her only son. She was alarmed at his unusually long delay, and suddenly began to be afraid and frightened at his daylong absence. For a mother does not easily forget the child of her womb and the joy that a man is born into the world. Thus, scarcely in control of herself, she set aside her domestic task, and went out into the courtyards and walked through the streets of the town; everywhere she looked at the passersby, and carefully scrutinized everyone she met. But nowhere did she see the face of her son. She walked on and on, into the Jewish quarter, scarcely able to support herself for her grief: her soul slept for weariness when she pictured as dead the child whom she had loved in life. She was now close to the house where the progeny of vipers had committed the crime. Suddenly she heard her son singing the *Alma Redemptoris Mater*: that is, she heard his voice, but she

4. Habakkuk 3:14.

saw no one. She stopped in amazement, but just as a sheep recognizes its lamb by its bleat alone, so this mother recognized her own son by the uniqueness of his singing voice: she was in labour close to death when she bore him, and so now she was in labour again, shouting and not sparing her voice. She could not put a guard on her mouth; however hoarse her throat became through her shouting, she incessantly cried out at the doors of her bloody enemies, "Give me back my son! Give me back my son!" As she repeated the words again and again, her grief was opened up. Time and again, as she stood outside the house she begged the Jews for her son, but the cruel and treacherous Jews would not give her any satisfaction; on stumbling feet she went to the house of the canon, and told him the whole sequence of events. In great grief and sorrow for the boy, the canon came to the house and demanded back the body from the murderers, but the perfidious Jews still refused to satisfy his demand in any way. Nevertheless he also heard and recognized the voice of the innocent child sweetly singing the *Alma Redemptoris Mater.*

Together they ran to the Archbishop of the city of Toledo and told him the sequence of events. He gathered a huge company of men and quickly went to investigate. He entered the guilty and treacherous house, breaking down the doors in his way, and roughly ordered the killer to produce the remains of the murdered innocent as quickly as possible—for he was sure that the boy was dead, in view of the great secrecy with which the malicious Jews had hidden him. All of them had conspired in the murder, but the main culprit in the murder, fearing the majesty of the Archbishop, confessed the truth of all his wickedness—how, out of envy at the mother of the Redeemer, he had extinguished the life of an innocent child, just because he had sung such a sweet song in honour of the Virgin Mother. After his confession of the crime—or rather his conviction—he put himself under the judgment of the Archbishop, and asked him for his mercy rather than his condemnation. He led the Archbishop by the hand, for all was darkness and gloom where the boy lay dead in the depths. The singing voice was their leader and guide, and at last they arrived where the dead boy miraculously continued to sing the *Alma Redemptoris Mater* without ceasing—for when the dead boy's voice had finished the end of the antiphon, it would begin the same song over again throughout the whole day.

The boy was lifted out, like a second Joseph out of the pit;[5] with speed and rejoicing he was taken to the church. The song to the Virgin did not leave his lips; continually he sang the *Alma Redemptoris Mater.* The people were summoned, and the clergy sat down in complete devotion. The Archbishop began to celebrate the divine office in honour of the blessed Virgin. The moment came when the congregation was ordered to be silent; the preacher began to speak, bringing a message of salvation through the gospel. At this moment the boy also became quiet, and placed "a door of circumstance"[6] on his lips, so that the words of the gospel would not be misheard or misunderstood because of the sound of his voice.

The congregation listened with faith and devotion to the reading, and when the message of salvation was over, once again the boy miraculously

5. Genesis 37:28.
6. Psalms 140:3.

began to sing the antiphon. How great then was the pious devotion of the clergy's prayers! How great was the effusion of tears among the congregation in its place, when the dead boy began again what he had just stopped, going through in his song what he had just passed over in silence! The health-giving Host was offered devoutly on the altar and the memory of the Lord's Passion worshipped, and all this time the boy's voice continued to sing of the purity of Mary. When the mysteries of our Redemption had been performed, the Archbishop turned to the congregation and delivered a sermon in praise of the innocence of the Virgin—though while he reverently called to memory the mother, of course he did not neglect to honour Christ as well. At the end of the sermon he wept and encouraged the clergy and people altogether to beseech the Virgin's son with the aroma of devotion and the sweet scent of pious prayer, and to pray by the merits of his mother and the prayers of the precious Virgin that Christ should deign to restore the boy to life, and breathe the breath of life into the dead corpse.

The clergy and the people poured out their souls within themselves, giving out their hearts like water in the sight of the Lord, letting their tears flow in a willing shower in the evening, a shower of tears, for their tears "were on their cheeks."[7] They prayed in supplication; in faith they beseeched; they were not beset by a cloud of mistrust about the efficacy of their prayer, for it went straight up to the Trinity: their faith swiftly penetrated to heaven, and their blessed trust was faithfully and joyfully repaid. In reply to their public and private prayers, the Virgin Mother (as I imagine) looked into the face of Christ and beseeched him in what I picture as a familiar fashion; and immediately the boy's cut throat was allowed to breathe again, his previously torn flesh was restored fully, and his tongue, which sang divine praise, was given back to him; his heart and liver which had been removed were put back again, or were created anew by divine aid. His soul was summoned back again into its vessel and vehicle, and the boy became whole again; the immortal spirit was again married to the dead flesh. He who was dead came to life again and returned; the boy awoke, aroused, as it were, from a deep sleep. Even now he did not cease his praise of Mary, and his sweet voice continued to sing the *Alma Redemptoris Mater*. Truly blessed are you, Mother of the Redeemer, for coming to the help of the dead boy who lacked the power to rise again: she who, to the amazement of Nature,[8] gave birth to her own creator, again astonished Nature by pouring back the vital spirit into the dead child through the intercession of her prayer.

At the sight of this amazing miracle, the congregation of the faithful rejoiced, and at the sight they dissolved into tears: they still wondered if it was an illusion. When they looked at the revived boy's face, they discovered the pebble which Mary had placed in his mouth; they removed it, and immediately he stopped his singing of the antiphon. He lost the impelling power of speech which before had not allowed him to be silent. The pebble was placed as a sign in the cathedral church, to act as a monument of the event and as evidence of the miracle, to be kept there for ever.

7. Lamentations 1:2; cf. Joel 2:23.
8. The phrase *Natura mirante*, "to Nature's amazement," is taken from the antiphon *Alma Redemptoris Mater.*

The Archbishop now asked the boy to tell him the whole sequence and order of the affair, and he answered the pontiff to his satisfaction, giving him a full and true account of the whole series of events—the crime of the Jews, his own martyrdom and the assistance of the Virgin Mary. He attributed everything to the Mother of God: whatever had happened to him was done by the Mother of Grace, who had thus aided his wretchedness from the abundance of her mercy. As he told his story, he pointed with his finger at the murderer, but this boy, who had been raised from death, prayed humbly but insistently that his murderer should not be condemned to die for the crime. At last the boy rose, and gave thanks fully to his saviour, the Virgin, and, now made whole in every particular, lived long after in the city of Toledo.

The Jew was more sure of his punishment than hopeful for mercy, but after seeing the miracle he confessed himself guilty and worthy of execution; nevertheless, he asked first to be bathed by the saving water of baptism. The Archbishop was more eager for the saving of a soul than for the punishment of the crime; he baptized the Jew and entrusted him to the church; having marked him with the sign of our faith, he remitted the penalty and pardoned the crime. Afterward the Jew, who had before been the most impious persecutor of the name of the Virgin, became her most pious devotee. There was also an infidel who witnessed the miracle and who became a member of the Christian faith. Thus, in the faith of Christ, the two walls of the cornerstone, from both circumcised and uncircumsised,[9] were joined together. The second man, now a believer instead of an infidel, was prosperous and very rich: he built a church in honour of the Virgin Mother, where her memory is memorably celebrated. Thus the kindly Mother of the Redeemer helps everyone with success; by her deserts may she commend to God those of us who are mindful of her, and help them by her good actions. AMEN.

A Miracle of Our Lady[†]

"Hou the Jewes, in despit° of Ure Lady, threwe a chyld in a gonge"° — *scorn* / *privy*

Wose° loveth wel Ure Ladi, *Whoever*
Heo° wol quiten his wille wel whi,[1] *She*
Othur° in his lyf or at his ende, *Either*
The ladi is so freo° and hende.° *generous / gracious*
Hit fel sumtyme° in Parys,° *It happened once / Paris*

9. The image of the two walls meeting at the cornerstone comes from Ephesians 2:11–22 and Psalms 117:22, the antiphon for the Magnificat on December 22. The passage was interpreted in this way, as the union of circumcised and uncircumcised, by Pope Gregory the Great: see *The Christ of Cynewulf*, ed. A. S. Cook (1900; Hamden, CT: Archon Books, 1964), p. 75.

† Text based on *The Minor Poems of the Vernon MS*, ed. Carl Horstmann and F. J. Furnivall, Early English Text Society, original series 98, 117 (London, 1892, 1901), I. 141–45. The MS was made in the late fourteenth century, sometime after 1382, and is a vast miscellany of religious or didactic pieces written in Middle English and Anglo-Norman. It once included a comprehensive collection of Miracles of the Virgin—the index lists forty-two—but most of that part of the MS was destroyed long ago. Only eight Miracles, of which this is the second, survive in full; a ninth is fragmentary.

1. She will for that (reason) repay well his determination.

As witnesseth in Holy Writ storys,
In the cite bifel this cas:° *case, adventure*
A pore child was° of porchas,° *there was / income*
That with the beggeri that he con wynne[2]
He fond° sumdel what of° his kinne— *supported / certain of*
His fader, his moder, and eke himself.
He begged in cite bi everi half.° *in every section*
The child non othur craftus° couthe° *skills / knew*
But winne hys lyflode° with his mouthe. *livelihood*
The childes vois was swete and cler;
Men lusted° his song with riht good cher. *listened to*
With his song that was ful swete
He gat mete° from strete to strete. *obtained food*
Men herked° his song ful likyngly.° *listened to / pleasurably*
Hit was an antimne° of Ure Lady; *anthem*
He song that antimne everiwher,
I-called Alma Redemptoris Mater,
That is forthrightly° to mene° *plainly, simply / mean*
"Godus° moder, mylde and clene,° *God's / chaste*
Hevene gate and sterre of se,° *star of the sea*
Save thi peple from synne and we."° *woe*
That song was holden deynteous;° *considered precious*
The child song hit from hous to hous.
For° he song hit so lykynglye,° *Because / pleasingly*
The Jewes hedde° alle to hym envye. *had*
Til hit fel on a Setersday° *Saturday*
The childes wey thorw the Jewerie° lay; *the Jewish quarter*
The Jewes hedden that song in hayn,° *hate*
Therfore thei schope° the child be slayn. *made plans that*
So lykingly the child song ther,
So lustily song he never er.° *before*
On° of the Jewes malicious *One*
Tilled° the child in to his hous. *Enticed*
His malice there he gan to kuythe:° *show*
He cutte the childes throte alswithe.° *quickly*
The child ne spared nout° for that wrong *did not cease*
But never-the-latere° song forth his song. *nevertheless*
Whon he hedde endet, he eft° bigon; *again*
His syngyng couthe stoppe no mon.° *no man knew how to stop*
Therof the Jeuh was sore anuyet,° *annoyed, troubled*
Leste his malice mihte ben aspyet.° *spied out, discovered*
The Jeuh bithouhte him of a gynne.° *stratagem*
Into a gonge-put° fer withinne *privy pit*
The child adoun therinne he throng;° *thrust*
The child song evere the same song.
So lustily the child con crie,
That song he never er so hyghe.° *loudly*

2. Who with the money that he earned by begging.

Men mihte him here fer and neer,
The childes vois was so heigh and cleer.
The childes moder was wont to abyde° *wait (for him)*
Every day til the non-tyde;° *noontime*
Then was he wont to bring heom° mete *them*
Such as he mihte with his song gete.
Bote that day was the tyme apast;
Therfore his moder was sore agast.° *afraid*
With syk° and serwe° in everi strete *sighing / sorrow*
Heo souhte wher° heo mihte with him mete. *She sought (the place) where*
Bote whon heo com in to the Jewery,
Heo herde his vois so cler of cry.
Aftur that vois his modur dreuh;° *drew, followed*
Wher he was inne, therbi heo kneuh.° *knew*
Then of hire child heo asked a siht.° *sight*
The Jew withnayted° him anon-riht° *denied / promptly*
And seide ther nas non such child thrinne.° *therein*
The childes moder yit nolde not blinne,° *cease*
But ever the moder criede in on.° *continually*
The Jeuh seide evere ther nas such non.
Then seide the wommon, "Thou seist wrong.
He is herinne, I knowe his song."
The Jeuh bigon to stare° and swere *glare*
And seide ther com non such child there.
But never-the-latere men mihte here
The child song evere so loude and clere,
And ever the lengor, herre° and herre, *higher, louder*
Men mihte him here bothe fer and nerre.
The modur coude° non othur won:° *knew / hope*
To meir° and baylyfs° heo is gon. *mayor / bailiffs*
Heo pleyneth° the Jeuh hath don hire wrong *complains*
To stelen hire sone so for his song.
Heo preyeth to don hire lawe and riht,° *justice*
Hire sone don° come bifore heore siht. *To cause her son to*
Heo preyeth the meir par charite° *in the name of charity*
Of him to have freo lyveré.° *to take legal custody*
Thenne heo telleth the meir among° *the mayor along with others*
Hou heo lyveth bi hire sone song.
The meir then hath of hire pite,
And sumneth° the folk of that cite. *summons*
He telleth hem of that wommons sawe° *story*
And seith he mot don° hire the lawe, *enforce (for)*
And hoteth° hem with hym to wende,° *orders / go*
To bringe this wommons cause to ende.
Whon thei cum thider, for al heore noyse
Anon thei herde the childes voyse.
Riht as an angeles vois hit were,
Thei herde him never synge so clere.
Ther the meir maketh entré,
And of the child he asketh lyveré.° *delivery (into his possession)*

The Jeuh may nought the meir refuse,
Ne of the child hym wel excuse;
But nede he moste knouleche° his wrong, *acknowledge*
Ateynt° bi the childes song. *Convicted*
The meir let serchen hym° so longe *had him searched for*
Til he was founden in the gonge,° *privy*
Ful depe i-drouned in fulthe° of fen.° *filth / muck, dung*
The meir het drawe the child° up then, *ordered the child raised*
With fen and fulthe riht foule biwhorven,° *bespattered*
And eke the childes throte i-corven.° *carved, cut*
Anon-riht, er thei passede forthere,
The Jeuh was jugget° for that morthere.° *judged / murder*
And er the peple passede in sonder,° *dispersed*
The bisschop was comen to seo that wonder.
In presence of bisschop and alle ifere,° *together*
The child song evere iliche° clere. *continually*
The bisschop serchede with his hond;
Withinne the childes throte he fond
A lilie flour, so briht and cler,
So feir a lylie nas nevere seyen er,
With guldene° lettres everiwher: *golden*
"Alma Redemptoris Mater."
Anon° that lilie out was taken, *As soon as*
The childes song bigon to slaken.
That swete song was herd no more,
But as a ded cors° the child lay thore.° *corpse / there*
The bisschop with gret solempnete° *ceremony*
Bad bere the cors° throw al the cite; *Ordered the body carried*
And hymself with processioun
Com with the cors thorw al the toun,
With prestes and clerkes that couthen° syngen. *knew how to*
And alle the belles he het hem ryngen,
With torches brennynge and clothus riche;
With worschipe thei ladden that holi liche.° *body*
In to the munstre° whon thei kem,° *minster, church / came*
Bigonne the masse of requiem,° *Requiem Mass*
As for the dede men is wont.° *customary*
But thus sone thei weren i-stunt:° *astounded*
The cors aros in heore° presens, *their*
Bigon then "Salve sancta parens."° *"Hail, holy parent" (antiphon)*
Men mihte wel witen° the sothe° therbi: *know / truth*
The child hedde i-servet Ur Swete Ladi,
That worschipede° him so on erthe her° *honored / here*
And broughte his soule to blisse al cler.
Therfore I rede° that everi mon *advise*
Serve that ladi wel as he con,
And love hire in his beste wyse.° *way*
Heo wol wel quite° him his servise. *repay*
Now, Marie, for thi muchele° miht, *great*
Help us to hevene that is so briht!

Alma Redemptoris Mater[†]

Alma Redemptoris Mater quae pervia coeli
Porta manes, et stella maris, succurre cadenti,
Surgere qui curat, populo; tu quae genuisti,
Natura mirante, tuum sanctum Genitorem,
Virgo prius ac posterius, Gabrielis ab ore,
Sumens illud Ave, peccatorum miserere.

Kindly Mother of the Redeemer, who art ever of heaven
The open gate, and the star of the sea, aid a fallen people,
Which is trying to rise again; thou who didst give birth,
While Nature marveled how, to thy Holy Creator,
Virgin both before and after, from Gabriel's mouth
Accepting the All hail, be merciful toward sinners.
(trans. John Henry Newman)

POPE GREGORY X

[On Christian Mistreatment of Jews][‡]

Gregory, bishop, servant of the servants of God, extends greetings and the apostolic benediction to the beloved sons in Christ, the faithful Christians, to those here now and to those in the future. Even as it is not allowed to the Jews in their assemblies presumptuously to undertake for themselves more than that which is permitted them by law, even so they ought not to suffer any disadvantage in those [privileges] which have been granted them. Although they prefer to persist in their stubbornness rather than to recognize the words of their prophets and the mysteries of the Scriptures, and thus to arrive at a knowledge of Christian faith and salvation; nevertheless, inasmuch as they have made an appeal for our protection and help, we therefore admit their petition and offer them the shield of our protection through the clemency of Christian piety. In so doing we follow in the footsteps of our predecessors of blessed memory, the popes of Rome—Calixtus, Eugene, Alexander, Clement, Celestine, Innocent, and Honorius.

We decree moreover that no Christian shall compel them or any one of their group to come to baptism unwillingly. But if any one of them shall take refuge of his own accord with Christians, because of conviction, then, after his intention will have been manifest, he shall be made a

† This is one of four antiphons of the Blessed Virgin Mary used to conclude Compline, the final hour of the canonical day. Each is assigned to a different portion of the church year, the present antiphon being sung from the Saturday before the first Sunday of Advent through February 1. Cardinal Newman's translation is printed from *Tracts for the Times* 75 (3.23 in the bound editions of 1840–42, rpt. New York: AMS Press, 1969).

‡ From Jacob Rader Marcus, *The Jew in the Medieval World: A Source Book: 315–1791*, rev. ed., intro. Marc Saperstein (Cincinnati: Hebrew Union College P, 1999), pp. 170–72. Reprinted with the permission of Hebrew Union College Press. We have omitted Marcus's historical commentary. Gregory's bull is dated October 7, 1272. The first four paragraphs repeat language from earlier papal bulls that attempted to protect Jews. For the historical context of this letter and an edition of the Latin text, see Solomon Grayzel, *The Church and the Jews in the XIIIth Century*, vol. 2, ed. Kenneth R. Stow (New York: Jewish Theological Seminary of America, 1989), pp. 1–45, 116–20.

Christian without any intrigue. For, indeed, that person who is known to have come to Christian baptism not freely, but unwillingly, is not believed to possess the Christian faith.

Moreover no Christian shall presume to seize, imprison, wound, torture, mutilate, kill, or inflict violence on them; furthermore no one shall presume, except by judicial action of the authorities of the country, to change the good customs in the land where they live for the purpose of taking their money or goods from them or from others.

In addition, no one shall disturb them in any way during the celebration of their festivals, whether by day or by night, with clubs or stones or anything else. Also no one shall exact any compulsory service of them unless it be that which they have been accustomed to render in previous times.

Inasmuch as the Jews are not able to bear witness against the Christians, we decree furthermore that the testimony of Christians against Jews shall not be valid unless there is among these Christians some Jew who is there for the purpose of offering testimony.

Since it happens occasionally that some Christians lose their Christian children, the Jews are accused by their enemies of secretly carrying off and killing these same Christian children and of making sacrifices of the heart and blood of these very children. It happens, too, that the parents of these children or some other Christian enemies of these Jews secretly hide these very children in order that they may be able to injure these Jews, and in order that they may be able to extort from them a certain amount of money by redeeming them from their straits. And most falsely do these Christians claim that the Jews have secretly and furtively carried away these children and killed them, and that the Jews offer sacrifice from the heart and the blood of these children, since their law in this matter precisely and expressly forbids Jews to sacrifice, eat, or drink the blood, or to eat the flesh of animals having claws. This has been demonstrated many times at our court by Jews converted to the Christian faith: nevertheless very many Jews are often seized and detained unjustly because of this.[1]

We decree, therefore, that Christians need not be obeyed against Jews in a case or situation of this type, and we order that Jews seized under such a silly pretext be freed from imprisonment, and that they shall not be arrested henceforth on such a miserable pretext, unless—which we do not believe—they be caught in the commission of the crime. We decree that no Christian shall stir up anything new against them, but that they should be maintained in that status and position in which they were in the time of our predecessors, from antiquity till now.

We decree, in order to stop the wickedness and avarice of bad men, that no one shall dare to devastate or to destroy a cemetery of the Jews or to dig up human bodies for the sake of getting money. Moreover, if any one, after having known the content of this decree, should—which we

1. On the child-murder libel, see Gavin I. Langmuir, *Toward a Definition of Antisemitism* (Berkeley: U of California P, 1990), chaps. 9–11, and esp. chap. 12; also *The Blood Libel Legend: A Casebook in Anti-Semitic Folklore*, ed. Alan Dundes (Madison: U of Wisconsin P, 1991). It should be noted that this papal bull, like others before it, had little effect overall on Christian attitudes toward Jews in the Middle Ages.

hope will not happen—attempt audaciously to act contrary to it, then let him suffer punishment in his rank and position, or let him be punished by the penalty of excommunication, unless he makes amends for his boldness by proper recompense. Moreover, we wish that only those Jews who have not attempted to contrive anything toward the destruction of the Christian faith be fortified by the support of such protection.

* * *

The Prologue and Tale of Sir Thopas

Chaucer's *Tale of Sir Thopas* is a parody of popular Middle English romances, particularly those written in tail-rhyme stanzas (rhyming couplets bound together by shorter lines ending in a single repeated rhyme). Almost every feature of *Thopas*—its metrics, its conventional diction, its scenes of the hero's questing, arming, encountering a giant, and falling in love—can be found in one or another of the many romances that it sports with. Joanne A. Charbonneau (in *Sources and Analogues of the* Canterbury Tales, vol. 2, ed. Robert M. Correale and Mary Hamel [Woodbridge: D. S. Brewer, 2005], pp. 649–714) has gathered nearly 200 short excerpts from over two dozen romances that make clear how *Thopas* is a patchwork of their idioms and themes. As an example of what Chaucer drew on, we print a very small portion of a very long poem, *Guy of Warwick*, alluded to in line 899 of Chaucer's tale. Guy's military and amorous successes represent the typical exploits of romance heroes and thus suggest a norm against which to consider how Thopas conducts himself in battle and in love.

From Guy of Warwick†

God graunt hem heven blis to mede°   *heaven's bliss as a reward*
That herken to mi romaunce rede,°   *Who listen to my tale readily*
  Al of a gentil° knight.   *noble*
The best bodi° he was at nede°   *person / in (times of) need*
That ever might bistriden stede,°   *sit on a horse*
  And freest° founde in fight.   *most valorous*
The word of him ful wide it ran.
Over al this warld the priis he wan°   *he took the prize*
  As man most° of might.   *greatest*
Balder bern° was non in bi.°   *A bolder man / in any place (literally, in town)*
His name was hoten sir Gii°   *called Sir Guy*
  Of Warwick, wise and wight.°   *valiant*

Wight he was, for sothe to say,°   *to tell the truth*
And holden for priis° in everi play°   *considered worthy / i.e., activity*
  As knight of gret bounte.°   *goodness*

† Text adapted from *The Romance of Guy of Warwick*, ed. Julius Zupitza, Early English Text Society, e.s. 49 (London, 1887; rpt. 1966), pp. 384–88, 394–96. There are various Middle English versions of this thirteenth-century Anglo-Norman historical romance. We print a passage from the tail-rhyme portion of the version in the Auchinleck manuscript, written in the 1330s in London and conceivably read by Chaucer. This passage occurs in the second half of the poem; Guy is returning to England after many displays of heroism in adventures overseas, thus proving his worthiness to marry the woman he loves, Felice, daughter of the Earl of Warwick.

Out of this lond he went his way
Thurch° mani divers cuntray° *Through / countries*
That was biyond the see.° *sea*
Sethen° he com into Inglond *Afterward*
And Athelston° the king he fond,° *Athelstan / sought*
That was bothe hende° and fre.° *courteous / generous*
For his love, ich° understond, *I*
He slough° a dragoun in Northumberlond, *slew, killed*
Ful fer in the north cuntre.° *region*

He and Herhaud,[1] for sothe to say,
To Wallingforth° toke the way, *Wallingford (in south-central England)*
That was his faders toun.° *father's town*
Than was his fader, sothe to say,
Ded and birid° in the clay. *buried*
His air was sir Gioun.° *Sir Guy was his heir*
Alle that held of° him lond or fe° *received from / payment for service*
Deden him omage° and feute° *Gave him homage / fealty (feudal loyalty)*
And com to his somoun.° *came (to court) at his summons*
He tok alle his faders lond
And yaf it hende Herhaud in hond° *gave it to courteous Herhaud to control*
Right to his warisoun.° *As a proper reward (for Herhaud's service)*

And alle that hadde in his servise be° *been*
He yaf hem gold and riche fe° *splendid payment*
Ful hendeliche° on honde. *courteously*
And sethen° he went with his meyne° *afterward / retinue*
To th'Erl Rohaud° that was so fre.° *Earl Rohaud (Guy's feudal lord) / noble*
At Warwike° he him fond. *Warwick*
Alle than were thai glad and blithe
And thonked God a thousand sithe° *times*
That Gii was comen° to lond. *had returned*
Sethe on hunting thai gun ride° *did ride*
With knightes fele° and miche pride *many*
As ye may understond.

On a day Sir Gii gan fond,° *decided to act*
And feir Felice he tok bi hond
And seyd to that bird° so blithe:° *lady / glad, merry*
"Ichave,"° he seyd, "thurch Godes sond° *I have / gift*
Won the priis° in mani lond *Taken the honors*
Of° knightes strong and stithe,° *From / valiant, stalwart*
And me is boden gret anour° *great honor has been offered me*
Kinges douhter and emperour° *emperor's*
To have to mi wive.° *take as my wife*
Ac,° swete Felice," he seyd than,° *But / then*
"Y no schal never spouse wiman° *I shall never marry (any other) woman*
Whiles thou art olive."° *alive*

1. Guy's foster-father, teacher, and constant companion on his adventures.

Than answerd that swete wight° *person*
And seyd ogain° to him ful right:° *in reply / directly*
"Bi him that schope mankinne,° *created mankind*
Icham° desired day and night *I am*
Of° erl, baroun, and mani a knight, *By*
For nothing wil thai blinne.° *They will not cease for anything*
Ac Gii," sche seyd, "hende and fre,
Al mi love is layd on they;° *given to thee*
Our love schal never twinne.° *be parted*
And bot ich have the to make° *unless I have thee as my mate*
Other lord nil y non take,° *I will accept no other lord*
For al this warld to winne."

Anon to hir than answerd Gii,
To fair Felice that sat him bi,° *sat by him*
That semly was of sight.° *Who was pleasing to look upon*
"Leman,"° he seyd, "gramerci."° *Lover / thank you*
With joie and with melodi
He kist° that swete wight. *kissed*
Than was he bothe glad and blithe.° *merry*
His joie couthe he noman kithe
For that bird so bright.[2]
He no was never therbiforn° *He had never before been*
Half so blithe sethe° he was born, *since*
For nought that man him hight.° *For anything anyone had promised him*

* * *

When he hadde spoused° that swete wight, *married*
The fest° lasted a fourtennight,° *feast / fortnight (two weeks)*
That frely° folk in fere° *noble / together*
With erl, baroun, and mani a knight,
And mani a levedy° fair and bright, *lady*
The best in lond that were.
Ther wer giftes for the nones,° *for the occasion*
Gold and silver and precious stones
And druries° riche and dere.° *treasures / valuable*
Ther was mirthe and melody
And al maner menstracie° *every sort of minstrelsy (i.e., entertainment)*
As ye may fortheward here:° *hear next*

Ther was trumpes° and tabour,° *trumpets / drum*
Fithel, croude, and harpour,
Her craftes for to kithe;[3]
Organisters° and gode stivours,° *Organ players / bagpipers*
Minstrels of mouthe° and mani dysour° *i.e., Singers / storytellers*
To glade tho bernes blithe.° *To gladden those merry folk*
Ther nis no tong° may telle in tale *tongue*
The joie that was at that bridale° *wedding party (literally, bride-ale)*

2. He knew no way of expressing to anyone the joy he took in such a beautiful lady.
3. Fiddle, crowd [a stringed instrument played with a bow], and harper, (all) showing their skill.

With menske° and mirthe to mithe,° *courtesy / to be seen*
For ther was al maner of gle° *music, entertainment*
That hert might thinke other eyghe se,° *or the eye see*
As ye may list and lithe.° *As it may please and soothe you*

Herls,° barouns hende and fre *Earls*
That ther war gadred° of mani cuntre, *Who were gathered there*
That worthliche were in wede,° *Who were nobly dressed*
Thai yoven glewemen° for her gle *They gave to the entertainers*
Robes riche, gold, and fe.° *fee (payment)*
Her giftes were nought gnede.° *stingy*
On the fiften° day, ful yare,° *fifteenth / fully prepared*
Thai toke her leve for to fare° *journey*
And thonked hem her gode dede.° *i.e., for their hospitality*
Than hadde Gii, that gentil knight,
Feliis° to his wil day and night, *Felice*
In gest also we rede.° *As we read in the story*

The Nun's Priest's Prologue and Tale

Beast fables were popular throughout the Middle Ages. The preface to William Caxton's translation of Aesop's fables provides a summary of conventional views about the genre and its purposes. Sometime around 1200 Marie de France wrote a collection of fables in Anglo-Norman; one of them, "The Cock and the Fox," tells the story that is the nucleus of the *Nun's Priest's Tale*. For the expansion of fable into beast-epic, Chaucer knew of the tales of Reynard the Fox, which circulated widely in France and elsewhere. Robert A. Pratt has argued that the confrontation of Reynard and Chanteclere in branch 2 of the *Roman de Renart* is one of Chaucer's direct sources. The learned and mock-heroic inflations of the *Nun's Priest's Tale* derive from many places; we include Macrobius's authoritative chapter on dreams and Geoffrey of Vinsauf's rhetorical lament on the death of King Richard I. The courtly elements of Chaucer's story may even have been suggested by the encyclopedic tradition, as may be seen in a portion of Bartholomaeus Anglicus's description of the cock, here printed in John of Trevisa's fourteenth-century English translation.

WILLIAM CAXTON

From Aesop's Fables†

[Book I]

Here begyneth the preface or prologue of the fyrst book of Esope.

I, Romulus, son of Thybere[1] of the cyte of Atyque,° gretyng. Esope, man of Grece, subtyll and ingenyous, techeth in his fables how men ought to kepe and rewle them° well. And to th'ende that he shold shewe the lyf and customes of al maner of men, he induceth° the byrdes, the trees and the beestes spekynge, to th'ende that the men may knowe wherfore the fables were found.° In the whiche he hath wreton the malyce of the evylle people and the argument of the improbes.° He techeth also to be humble and for to use wordes, and many other fayr ensamples

Attica · *themselves* · *introduces* · *invented* · *wicked*

† Text based on Caxton's 1484 edition as printed in *The Fables of Aesop*, ed. Joseph Jacobs, 2 vols. (London: David Nutt, 1889), 2.3.

1. Tiberius. The "Romulus" version of Aesop's fables circulated widely in the Middle Ages; the author is unknown, but it was certainly not the Roman emperor's son.

reherced and declared here after, the whiche I, Romulus, have translated oute of Grekes tongue in to Latyn tongue, the which yf thou rede them, they shalle aguyse° and sharp thy wytte and shal gyve to the cause of joye. *adorn*

MARIE DE FRANCE

The Cock and the Fox†

This is the story of a cock, who was standing on a dunghill, singing. A fox came up alongside and spoke to him with pleasant words: "How very handsome you are, sir," he said. "I've never seen such a noble bird; you have the clearest voice of any creature. Except for your father, whom I knew well, no bird has sung better—but he was better at it than you, because he kept his eyes closed." "I can do it that way," said the cock. He flapped his wings and shut his eyes, thinking that he would sing all the more beautifully. The fox jumped, seized him, and fled toward the forest with him.

As the fox passed through a field, all the shepherds ran to catch him, and the dogs all around ran barking after him. So here is the fox holding the cock: he will lose what he's won if he comes too close to them. "Go ahead," the cock said, "call out to them that you've got me and will never let me go." The fox was determined to shout loudly, at which point the cock bolted out of his mouth and flew up to a tall trunk of a tree. When the fox realized what had happened, he knew he had been completely fooled by the cock's clever trickery. In vexation and sheer anger at himself he began to curse his own mouth for speaking when it should have been silent. The cock said in response: "I should do likewise: curse the eye that would close when it ought to keep watch and be alert that no evil comes to its lord."

This is how many foolish people act: they speak when they should be silent and stay silent when they should speak.

From Le Roman de Renart, Branch 2‡

How Chanteclere Makes a Fool of Reynard

It happened on a day that Reynard the Fox, well-versed in evil arts and guile, came trotting up to a farm set in the woods. The farm possessed many chickens, ducks, and geese. The lord of that land was Constantine of Noyes, a farmer of great wealth. His house was full to the bursting with fowl and bacon and salted meat. He also had plenty of grain set by, and the orchards

† Translated by Glending Olson from Marie de France, *Les Fables*, 2nd ed., ed. Charles Brucker (Paris and Leuven: Peeters, 1998), pp. 238–41. Reprinted with authorization of Peeters Publishers, Leuven. For a complete text and English translation, see Marie de France, *Fables*, ed. and trans. Harriet Spiegel (Toronto: U of Toronto P, 1987). For translations of other works by Marie, see *Marie de France: Poetry: A Norton Critical Edition*, ed. and trans. Dorothy Gilbert (New York: W. W. Norton, 2015).

‡ Translated for this volume's first edition by Elizabeth Hanson-Smith from *Le Roman de Renart*, ed. Ernest Martin (Strasbourg: Trübner, 1882), 1. 91–104. Reprinted by permission of the translator. For texts and translations of this and other sources of the *Nun's Priest's Tale*, see Edward Wheatley's chapter in *Sources and Analogues of the* Canterbury Tales, vol. 1, ed. Robert M. Correale and Mary Hamel (Woodbridge: D. S. Brewer, 2002), pp. 449–89.

bore their many and various fruits in season. It was here that Reynard came for his own amusement.

The courtyard was enclosed by a palisade of sharp oak stakes and spiny hawthorn, and there Sir Constantine had placed his hens, as in a kind of fortress. Reynard addressed himself to the palisade, but though his resourcefulness was great, the spines were sharper still. At last he squatted in the road, angry and upset, yet not wanting to abandon the hens. If he tried to leap the stockade wall, he would be seen, and the hens that pecked the dirt not two feet beyond would disappear. The fox paced angrily up and down, until he spied a broken stake. At once he plunged through the wall. Where the stockade was broken, the farmer had planted cabbages, and Reynard dropped down among them, hoping he had not been seen. But the chickens had heard the noise of his fall, and every one of them took flight.

Master Chanteclere the Cock, who had been scratching in a dusty path, came toward the band of chickens. Plumes spread and neck outstretched, he demanded haughtily why they had fled. Pinte of the Large Eggs, who roosted at the cock's right hand, was the wisest, and she told him what had happened: "We were all terrified," she said.

"But why?" the rooster demanded. "What have you seen?"

"Some kind of wild beast, who would have done great harm, if we hadn't fled the garden."

"I beg your pardon," Chanteclere replied, "but this is just a trifle. Don't worry yourself about it further."

"By my faith," said Pinte, "I loyally swear to you I saw him clearly."

"And how did you catch sight of whatever it was?"

"How? I saw the enclosure shake and the cabbage leaf tremble where he lies in wait."

"Pinte," exclaimed the cock, "you're a fool! I don't know of any fox or polecat strong enough to breach our walls. I promise you by the loyalty I owe you, there is nothing there. Go on back!" And the rooster returned to his dust.

He who fears nothing, except a dog or fox, will always be quite confident—as long as he thinks himself safe. And thus Chanteclere acted quite disdainfully, for he feared nothing but the fox.

As one bored with both singing and scratching, one eye open, the other shut, the cock at last flew up under the eaves and took his rest. Roosting there in delicious sleep, Chanteclere began to dream. (Now don't think I'm making this up—it's the whole truth, and you can find it written down.) He dreamed that something entered the courtyard, although it was securely locked, and came up to him, face to face. Chanteclere shuddered at this. The creature had a fur mantle of red and white, its collar trimmed in bone. Here Chanteclere tossed and turned in his sleep. Suddenly the cloak was wrapped about him, by force. And most strange, he was forced into it through the narrow collar, so that his head was at the creature's tail. Great was the pain that Chanteclere suffered for that dream, and he thought himself cursed in that vision. At last he struggled into wakefulness and heaved a sigh, saying "Holy Spirit, save my body from that prison, and keep me safe!" Off he rushed, no longer quite so secure, and came upon the hens, who pecked beside the hawthorn. He did not cry out to them at once, but called Pinte aside to take counsel with her first.

"Pinte," he said, for he trusted her, "I can't hide my sorrow and despair. And fear. I think some bird of prey or wild beast is going to harm us."

"Dear sweet lord," cried Pinte, "never say that aloud! For shame! You'll frighten us all. You betray yourself in saying you are afraid. By all the saints to whom we pray, you're like the dog who whines before the stone is cast. Why are you frightened? What's the matter with you?"

"You don't know," he answered, "what a strange dream I've had. It seemed to me there was an evil apparition within the enclosure of this very farm. That is why you see me pale and trembling. It seemed to me some animal came in, wearing a mantle of red fur, sown together without scissors or seam, trimmed in bone, all white and hard. He forced me to dress in his mantle, and I had to put it on over my head, collar first. When I awoke I was no longer wrapped up in fur, but I marvel still at the tightness of that collar, and at the tail that seemed to be in front of my face. That is why I despair. Pinte, I am tormented by this dream. By the loyalty you owe me, tell me, do you know what this signifies?"

Pinte, his trusted one, answered then, "You have told me your dream, but please God, it won't come true. If you wish an explanation of it, I know well what it is, for what you have seen while dreaming, that thing dressed in a red cloak—that is the fox. He's easily known by his red fur coat. The trim of bone, that was his teeth, by which he forced you inside him. The collar that did not fit, that was so horribly tight for you—that is the gullet of the beast, that's how you entered his belly. The tail means, no doubt—by all the saints in all the world!—that when the fox has swallowed you, his tail will be before your nose! Now you know the meaning of your dream, God help me. Gold and silver can't save you. And it will all come to pass before high noon. But if you still don't believe me, take a look over there, for he lies in wait, quietly, in the cabbage patch, ready to betray and deceive you."

When Chanteclere had heard this interpretation of his dream, he said, "Pinte, these are traitorous words! You say I'll be conquered by a beast who is even now inside our stockade. Cursed is the man who believes that! You've told me nothing I care to hear. No matter what, I won't believe I'll suffer for this dream."

"Sire," she answered, "God forbid it should be so, but I swear to you, if things don't turn out as I've predicted, I am no longer your true love."

"Oh, Pinte," said Chanteclere, "never mind!"

Chanteclere considered that interpretation a wild tale, and walked back to take his pleasure in his patch of dust, where he soon began to slumber again.

Meanwhile, Reynard had waited patiently and looked on, much amused. Once certain the cock had fallen asleep, Reynard crept up, one paw after another, soundlessly. If once the fox had Chanteclere in his teeth, he would make a meal of him. He longed for chicken dinner, but when he sprang, heavy-handed, he missed. While Chanteclere flew to the top of a dungheap, well out of reach, Reynard cursed himself for failing. But at once the fox began again to plot a way to trick poor Chanteclere. If he did not eat that rooster, his time was wasted.

"Dear Chanteclere," he called, "don't fly away for this trifle. After all, you and I are first cousins, quite closely related."

Chanteclere gained confidence at this, and sang a little song for joy.

Reynard said to his cousin, "Do you remember Chanteclin, your dear father, who begot you? No other cock could sing the way he did. The country folk miles away could hear him. When he sang, he took a good deep breath and closed his eyes tight. Ah, but his voice was grand. He wasn't always peering about him, when he let go in the pleasures of song."

"Reynard, cousin," said Chanteclere, "are you trying to pull a trick?"

"Of course . . ." answered Reynard, "I am not. But now, please sing! Shut those eyes and go to it! You know we are of one flesh, one blood—and I would rather lose a leg than see you come to grief."

Said Chanteclere, "I don't believe you. Remove yourself a little way before I sing a song. There won't be a neighbor far or near who cannot hear my falsetto!"

Reynard smiled broadly: "Well, do it loudly, then! Sing, cousin! Let it be known you were born of my uncle Chanteclin."

The cock began quite loudly, letting out a terrific din, but with only one eye closed, and the other open, watching Reynard, whom he strongly suspected of mischief.

Reynard said, "This is nothing. Chanteclin sang far differently. He'd close his eyes tight and his great crowing could be heard for miles beyond the palisade."

Chanteclere at last believed him, and screwing his eyes up tight in the effort, he sent forth his melody. Reynard did not hesitate a moment, but seized the cock by the neck, and off he raced in high spirits, for he'd won his prey.

Pinte saw that Reynard had her love, and she fell into a frenzied despair when she saw the cock being carried off. She wailed after them, "Sire, I told you so! But you scorned my words and called me a fool. Now those words are proven true and it is your own reasoning that brought you to ruin. I was a fool to cry 'fox' before you had actually seen him. Now Reynard has you and bears you off. Alas! Misery! I shall die! For if I lose my lord and master, my honor too is lost forever!"

The good old woman of the manor opened the door to her yard, for it was evening, and she wished to put her hens back in the coop. "Come, Pinte, Bise, Rosette!" she called, but none of them answered. She wondered what was wrong, until she heard her cock yelling, as best he could, and saw the fox running off with him. She knew she couldn't catch them and raised a cry for help. All the peasants on the farm came running when they heard her bawling so. They asked her what was wrong.

"Alas," she sighed heavily, "what a wicked thing has happened!"

"But what is it?" they demanded.

"I have lost my rooster—the fox has him!"

"You foul old hag!" shouted Constantine. "Didn't you stop him?"

"Sire," she replied, "You do me wrong. By holy God, I couldn't catch him. He wouldn't wait for me."

"Why didn't you hit him?"

"I couldn't find a stick. But anyway, he ran so fast, a Breton hound couldn't have caught up with him."

"Where did he go?"

"That way."

And off the peasants ran in great haste, shouting, "Over there, he's over there!"

Reynard leaped through the hole in the palisade and bore the cock to earth with him, but the noise he made was heard by all. "After him!" Constantine shouted, and called his mastiffs: "Mauvoisin! Bardol! Travers! Humbaut! Rebors! After him! After Renard the Red!"

Now Chanteclere was in great peril if he didn't think of some trick. And so he said, "Lord Reynard, don't you hear the shameful things those peasants say? Constantine recognized you and called you all sorts of names. When he shouts, 'Reynard is stealing my rooster!' you should say, 'In spite of all your efforts!' There's nothing that would annoy him more."

No one is so wise that he can't be fooled sometime: Reynard had tricked all the world, but this time he himself was deceived. The peasants raised the cry again, and Reynard turned to shout back, "In spite of all your efforts! I'll steal him any time I please!"

But with these words, Chanteclere felt those terrible jaws go slack, and beating his wings with all his might, he flew into an apple-tree. Reynard sat down on a dung-heap below him, chagrined, enraged, tormented by the cock who had escaped. Chanteclere just laughed: "Reynard," he said, "how's the world treating you these days?"

The traitor shook with rage and in sheer bad humor said, "Cursed be the mouth that speaks when it should be silent."

"Amen, amen," said the rooster. "Yes, and I wish him every evil who shuts his eyes and goes to sleep when he should stay awake. Cousin Reynard," he continued, "no one should ever trust you. Cursed be your cousinage! It almost ruined me. Reynard, you liar, get out of here! If you wait around, you'll lose your hide!"

Reynard was always very careful of his fur coat. He spoke not a word more, but turned at once and ran. Through the hedge beside the plain, straight down the road he fled. But his heart was heavy because of the rooster, who had escaped when he'd had him in his hands.

MACROBIUS

[On Dreams][†]

* * *

After these prefatory remarks, there remains another matter to be considered before taking up the text of *Scipio's Dream*. We must first describe the many varieties of dreams recorded by the ancients, who have classified and defined the various types that have appeared to men in their sleep, wherever they might be. Then we shall be able to decide to which type the dream we are discussing belongs.

All dreams may be classified under five main types: there is the enigmatic dream, in Greek *oneiros*, in Latin *somnium*; second, there is the prophetic vision, in Greek *horama*, in Latin *visio*; third, there is the oracular dream, in Greek *chrematismos*, in Latin *oraculum*; fourth, there is the nightmare, in Greek *enypnion*, in Latin *insomnium*; and last, the apparition, in Greek

† From *Commentary on the Dream of Scipio*, trans. William Harris Stahl (New York: Columbia UP, 1952), pp. 87–90. Copyright © 1952 Columbia University Press. Reprinted by permission of the publisher. Stahl's notes have been omitted.

phantasma, which Cicero, when he has occasion to use the word, calls *visum*.

The last two, the nightmare and the apparition, are not worth interpreting since they have no prophetic significance. Nightmares may be caused by mental or physical distress, or anxiety about the future: the patient experiences in dreams vexations similar to those that disturb him during the day. As examples of the mental variety, we might mention the lover who dreams of possessing his sweetheart or of losing her, or the man who fears the plots or might of an enemy and is confronted with him in his dream or seems to be fleeing him. The physical variety might be illustrated by one who has overindulged in eating or drinking and dreams that he is either choking with food or unburdening himself, or by one who has been suffering from hunger or thirst and dreams that he is craving and searching for food or drink or has found it. Anxiety about the future would cause a man to dream that he is gaining a prominent position or office as he hoped or that he is being deprived of it as he feared.

Since these dreams and others like them arise from some condition or circumstance that irritates a man during the day and consequently disturbs him when he falls asleep, they flee when he awakes and vanish into thin air. Thus the name *insomnium* was given, not because such dreams occur "in sleep"—in this respect nightmares are like other types—but because they are noteworthy only during their course and afterwards have no importance or meaning.

Virgil, too, considers nightmares deceitful: "False are the dreams (*insomnia*) sent by departed spirits to their sky." He used the word "sky" with reference to our mortal realm because the earth bears the same relation to the regions of the dead as the heavens bear to the earth. Again, in describing the passion of love, whose concerns are always accompanied by nightmares, he says: "Oft to her heart rushes back the chief's valour, oft his glorious stock; his looks and words cling fast within her bosom, and the pang withholds calm rest from her limbs." And a moment later: "Anna, my sister, what dreams (*insomnia*) thrill me with fears?"

The apparition (*phantasma* or *visum*) comes upon one in the moment between wakefulness and slumber, in the so-called "first cloud of sleep." In this drowsy condition he thinks he is still fully awake and imagines he sees specters rushing at him or wandering vaguely about, differing from natural creatures in size and shape, and hosts of diverse things, either delightful or disturbing. To this class belongs the incubus, which, according to popular belief, rushes upon people in sleep and presses them with a weight which they can feel. The two types just described are of no assistance in foretelling the future; but by means of the other three we are gifted with the powers of divination.

We call a dream oracular in which a parent, or a pious or revered man, or a priest, or even a god clearly reveals what will or will not transpire, and what action to take or to avoid. We call a dream a prophetic vision if it actually comes true. For example, a man dreams of the return of a friend who has been staying in a foreign land, thoughts of whom never enter his mind. He goes out and presently meets his friend and embraces him. Or in his dream he agrees to accept a deposit, and early the next day a man runs anxiously to him, charging him with the safekeeping of his money and committing secrets to his trust. By an enigmatic dream we mean one that conceals with strange shapes and veils with ambiguity the true meaning of the information being offered, and requires an interpretation for its understanding. We need not explain further the nature of this dream since everyone knows from experience what it is. There are five varieties of it: personal, alien, social, public, and universal. It is called personal when one dreams that he himself is doing or experiencing something; alien, when he dreams this about someone else; social, when his dream involves others and himself; public, when he dreams that some misfortune or benefit has befallen the city, forum, theater, public walls, or other public enterprise; universal, when he dreams that some change has taken place in the sun, moon, planets, sky, or regions of the earth.

* * *

GEOFFREY OF VINSAUF

[Lament on the Death of Richard I]†

Once defended by King Richard's shield, now undefended, O England, bear witness to your woe in the gestures of sorrow. Let your eyes flood with tears, and pale grief waste your features. Let writhing anguish twist your fingers, and woe make your heart within bleed. Let your cry strike the heavens. Your whole being dies in his death; the death was not his but yours. Death's rise was not in one place only but general. O tearful day of Venus! O bitter star! That day was your night; and that Venus your venom. That day inflicted the wound; but the worst of all days was that other—the day after the eleventh—which, cruel stepfather to life, destroyed life. Either day, with strange tyranny, was a murderer. The besieged one pierced the besieger; the sheltered one, him without cover; the cautious one pierced the incautious; the well-equipped soldier pierced an unarmed man—his own king! O soldier, why, treacherous soldier, soldier of treachery, shame of the world and sole dishonour of warfare; O soldier, his own army's creature, why did you dare this against him? Why did you dare this crime, this hideous crime? O sorrow! O greater than sorrow! O death! O truculent death! Would you were dead, O death! Bold agent of a deed so vile, how dare you recall it? You were pleased to remove our sun, and condemn day to darkness. Do you realize whom you snatched from us? To our eyes he was light; to our ears, melody; to our minds an amazement. Do you realize, impious death, whom you snatched from us? He was the lord of warriors, the glory of kings, the delight of the world. Nature knew not how to add any further perfection; he was the utmost she could achieve. But that was the reason you snatched him away: you seize precious things, and vile things you leave as if in disdain. And Nature, of you I complain: for were you not, when the world was still young, when you lay new-born in your cradle, giving zealous attention to him? And that zeal did not flag before your old age. Why did such strenuous effort bring this wonder into

† From the *Poetria Nova of Geoffrey of Vinsauf*, trans. Margaret F. Nims (Toronto: Pontifical Institute of Mediaeval Studies, 1967), pp. 29–31. Copyright © 1967 by Pontifical Institute of Mediaeval Studies, Toronto. Reprinted by permission of the publisher. This passage is one of several examples given by Geoffrey (fl. 1200) to illustrate the use of apostrophe as a device of amplification.

the world, if so short an hour stole the pride of that effort away? You were pleased to extend your hand to the world and then to withdraw it; to give thus, and then to recall your gift. Why have you vexed the world? Either give back to us him who is buried, or give us one like him in excellence. But you have not resources for that; whatever you had that was wondrous or precious was expended on him. On him were exhausted your stores of delight. You were made most wealthy by this creature you made; you see yourself, in his fall, most impoverished. If you were happy before, in proportion to happiness then is your misery now. If heaven allow it, I chide even God. O God, most excellent of beings, why do you fail in your nature here? Why, as an enemy would, do you strike down a friend? If you recall, your own Joppa gives evidence for the king—alone he defended it, opposed by so many thousands. Acre, too, gives evidence—his power restored it to you. The enemies of the cross add their witness—all of them Richard, in life, inspired with such terror that he is still feared now he is dead. He was a man under whom your interests were safe. If, O God, you are, as befits your nature to be, faithful and free of malice, just and true, why then did you shorten his days? You could have shown mercy to the world; the world was in need of him. But you choose to have him with you, and not with the world; you would rather favour heaven than the world. O Lord, if it is permissible to say it, let me say—with your leave—you could have done this more graciously, and with less haste, if he had bridled the foe at least (and there would have been no delay to that end; he was on the verge of success). He could have departed more worthily then to remain with you. But by this lesson you have made us know how brief is the laughter of earth, how long are its tears.

BARTHOLOMAEUS ANGLICUS

[On the Cock][†]

* * * Also the kok is hoot and drie of complexioun,° and therfore he is ful bolde and hardy, and so fightith boldeliche for his wyfes agenst his adversaries and assaileth and resith on° hem and tereth and woundeth ham with bile° and with spores.° And whan he hath the maistrie he singeth anon, and or° he singeth he betith himself with his wynges to make him the more able to singe. And he usith° fer in the nyght to singe moost cleereliche and strongliche, and aboute the morwetyde° he schapith° lyght voys and song, as Ambrose saith. The cok bereth a comb on his hede in stede of a crowne, and yif he lesith° his comb he lesith his hardinesse and is the more slow and coward to assaile his adversarie. And he loveth cherliche° his wyves. And whenne he

complexioun: i.e., temperament; resith on: attacks; bile: beak; spores: spurs; or: before; usith: is accustomed; morwetyde / schapith: morning / produces; lesith: loses; cherliche: tenderly

† Text based on *On the Properties of Things: John Trevisa's Translation of Bartholomaeus Anglicus De Proprietatibus Rerum*, ed. M. C. Seymour et al., 2 vols. (Oxford: Oxford UP, 1975), I. 627. Reprinted by permission of Oxford University Press. Bartholomaeus was an early 13th-century scholastic.

fyndeth mete° he clepith his wifes togedres with a *food*
certeyn voys and spareth his owne mete to fede
therwith his wifes. And settith next to him on
rooste the henne that is most fatte and tendre
and loveth hire best and desireth most to have
hire presence. In the morwetide whanne he fleeth° *flies*
to gete his mete, furst he leith his side to hire side
and bi certeyne tokenes and beckes,° as it were *gestures*
love tacchis,° a woweth° and prayeth hire to *indications / he woos*
tredinge;° and fightith for hire specialliche as *copulation*
though he were jelous, and with byle and spores
he chacith and dryveth awey from him cokkes
that cometh nyghe° his wifes. And in fightinge he *near*
smytith the grounde with his bile and rereth up
the weyes° aboute his necke to maken him the *feathers*
more bolde and hardy, and meveth the fetheres of
his taile upwarde and donwarde that he mowe so
the more abilliche° come to the bataile. *ably*

* * *

The Manciple's Prologue and Tale

Ovid's *Metamorphoses* is the most important source for western medieval versions of the story about the punishment of a truth-telling bird. We print a translation of Ovid's story of Phoebus, Coronis, and the raven. The *Metamorphoses* was widely translated, adapted, and commented on in the Middle Ages; these texts usually treat the story of Phoebus and Coronis as a lesson about the dangers of indiscreet speech. It is not certain which, if any, of these medieval versions Chaucer relied on. We include a brief adaptation by his acquaintance John Gower as an example of how the tale could be reworked for didactic purpose.

OVID

[The Story of Phoebus and Coronis]†

[At that time] the shining white wings of the chattering raven had been suddenly changed to dusky black.

This bird was once of a silvery hue, with such snowy feathers that it could rival any spotless dove. It was no less white than the geese who were one day to save the Capitol with their wakeful voices, as white as the swan that haunts rivers. But its tongue brought about the raven's downfall. Thanks to its chattering tongue, its plumage, once white, is now the very opposite.

In all Thessaly there was no one lovelier than Coronis of Larissa. At any rate, she won the heart of the god of Delphi [i.e., Phoebus Apollo], while she remained true to him, or at least while her faults passed unobserved. But the bird of Phoebus detected her in wrongdoing, and, a pitiless informer, hurried to its master, determined to reveal her guilt. * * * [It] went and told its master, Phoebus, that it had seen Coronis lying with a young Thessalian.

When her lover heard this charge against Coronis, the wreath of laurel slipped from his head, his face changed, his colour ebbed away, and the plectrum fell from his fingers. His heart was in a fever of swelling rage. Seizing his customary weapons, he strung his bow, bending it from its horns, and, with the arrow that none can avoid, pierced the breast he had so often clasped to his own. As the shaft struck home, Coronis groaned; when she drew it out, scarlet blood welled over her fair white limbs. "O Phoebus," she cried, "you could have let me bear your child, and then have punished me. Now, in my one person, two will perish." That was all

† *Metamorphoses* 2. 534–57, 598–632. From *The Metamorphoses of Ovid,* trans. Mary M. Innes (London: Penguin Books Ltd.), pp. 64–67. Copyright © Mary M. Innes, 1955. Reprinted by permission of Penguin Books Ltd. We have omitted a tale embedded within the story of Phoebus and Coronis that includes another instance of a truthful revelation angrily received.

she said, before her spirit ebbed out with her blood. A deathly chill crept over her lifeless body.

Too late, the lover repented of the cruel punishment he had exacted, and hated himself for listening to the tale, for allowing his anger to blaze up in such a way. He hated the bird, whose officiousness had forced him to learn of Coronis' guilt, forced him to know that he had cause for indignation; and no less did he hate his bow, his hands, his arrows too, shafts he had so rashly launched. Fondling her lifeless frame, he tried to thwart the fates, but he employed his healing art without avail: his aid came too late.

When he saw that his attempts were vain, that the pyre was being got ready, and that her limbs were about to be consumed by the funeral fires, then indeed Apollo groaned from the very depths of his heart—tears are forbidden to the gods. Even so does a heifer mourn when, before her eyes, the mallet is poised close to the slaughterer's right ear, and then brought crashing down with a resounding blow upon the hollow forehead of her unweaned calf. Then he poured upon Coronis' breast perfumes which she could never enjoy, clasped her to him for the last time, and performed all too soon the rites that death demands.

That his own seed should perish in those same ashes was more than he could bear. He snatched his son from his mother's womb, saved him from the flames, and carried him to the cave of Chiron, the centaur.

As for the raven, which was hoping for a reward for revealing the truth, Phoebus decreed that never again should it be numbered among white birds.

JOHN GOWER

The Tale of Phoebus and Cornide†

* * *

And over this, my sone diere,° *furthermore, my dear son*
Of° othre men, if thou might hiere° *Concerning / hear, learn of*
In privete° what thei have wroght,° *Privately, secretly / done*
Hold conseil° and descoevere° it noght, *Be silent / reveal*
For Cheste° can no conseil hele° *Chiding / conceal no secret*
Or be it wo or be it wele.° *Whether it be bad or good*
And tak a tale into thi mynde,° *memory*
The which of olde ensample I finde.° *Which I derive from (an) old story*
   Phebus,° which makth the daies lihte, *Phoebus Apollo (god of the sun)*
A love he hadde, which tho hihte° *who then was called*

† *Confessio Amantis* 3.775–835. Text based on *The English Works of John Gower*, ed. G. C. Macaulay, Early English Text Society, e.s. 81–82 (London, 1900–1901; rpt. 1969), 1. 247–48. Notes and glosses are by the editors of this Norton Critical Edition. The speaker of this passage is the priest and counsellor Genius, who instructs his "son" Amans, the lover-protagonist, about the sins he should avoid. Here Genius discusses a subdivision of the sin of wrath, Cheste (chiding, contentiousness), personified as a creature whose mouth is always open, spewing forth whatever bad things he knows, fomenting strife. After telling the story of the raven, Genius adds a second short example of ill-fated tale-bearing (ll. 818–27), drawn from Ovid's *Fasti* 2.585–616. On the *Confessio* see further the note on p. 422, and on Chaucer's relationship to Gower see the note on p. 375. It is not certain that Chaucer knew Gower's version, though some critics think that the Manciple's repetitious invocation of his mother's advice to "my sone" is a parody of the way Genius addresses Amans throughout the *Confessio* and, by implication, of an approach to fiction that is purely instructional.

Cornide,° whom aboven alle — *Coronis*
He pleseth. Bot° what schal befalle° — *But / befall, happen*
Of° love ther is noman° knoweth, — *In regard to / no person (who)*
Bot° as fortune hire happes throweth.° — *Except / disposes by chance*
So it befell upon a chaunce° — *by chance*
A yong kniht° tok hire aqueintance° — *knight / made her acquaintance*
And hadde of hire al that he wolde,° — *all that he desired (sexually)*
Bot a fals bridd,° which sche hath holde — *false, untrustworthy bird*
And kept in chambre of pure yowthe,° — *i.e., because she was young*
Discoevereth° all that ever he cowthe.° — *Reveals / knew*
This briddes name was as tho° — *at that time*
Corvus,° the which was thanne also — *Raven (Latin)*
Welmore° whyt than eny swan, — *Much more*
And he, that schrewe,° al that he can° — *scoundrel / knows*
Of° his ladi to Phebus seide.° — *About / spoke, revealed*
And he for wraththe° his swerd outbreide,° — *in anger / drew out*
With which Cornide anon° he slowh.° — *immediately / slew*
Bot after him was wo ynowh,° — *But afterwards he was very sorrowful*
And tok a full gret repentance,
Wherof—in tokne° and remembrance — *as a sign*
Of hem whiche usen wicke speche°— — *those who engage in evil speech*
Upon this bridd he tok this wreche.° — *vengeance*
That ther° he was snow whyt tofore,° — *whereas / before*
Ever afterward colblak° therfore — *coal black*
He was transformed, as it scheweth.° — *is evident*
And many a man yit° him beschreweth° — *still / curses*
And clepen° him into° this day — *call(s) / to*
A raven, be° whom yit° men mai — *by / still*
Take evidence° whan he crieth — *Take as a sign*
That som mishapp it signefieth.° — *it signifies some misfortune*
Be war° therfore and sei° the beste — *Be careful / speak*
If thou wolt be thiself° in reste, — *keep thyself*
My goode sone, as I the rede.° — *advise thee*
  For in an other place I rede° — *read*
Of thilke Nimphe which Laar hihte.° — *that nymph called Lara*
For° sche the privete be nyghte° — *Because / the nighttime secret*
(How Jupiter lay be Jutorne°) — *with Juturna (a naiad)*
Hath told, god° made hire overtorne.° — *i.e., Jupiter / come to grief*
Hire tunge he kutte, and into helle
For evere he sende° hir forto duelle, — *sent*
As sche that was noght worthi hiere° — *here (on earth)*
To ben of love a chamberere,° — *chambermaid, servant*
For sche no conseil couwthe hele.° — *could keep no secret*
And suche adaies be now fele° — *(there) are many such nowadays*
In loves court, as it is seid,
That lete here tunges gon unteid.° — *let their tongues go untied, loose*
  Mi sone, be thou non of tho° — *do not be one of those*
To jangle° and telle tales so,° — *speak indiscreetly / in such a way*
And namely that thou ne chyde,° — *chide, reproach (someone else)*
For Cheste° can no conseil hide, — *Chiding*
For Wraththe seide nevere wel.° — *Since Anger never spoke well (of another)*

CRITICISM

MAURICE KEEN

From Social Hierarchy and Social Change†

If one looks back into the past, beyond the time when Rousseau sent out his clarion call for liberty, equality and fraternity, one looks back into what we nowadays call a deference society. Deference implies an ordered gradation of society, its hierarchic arrangement by scales which regulate the respect and the kind of services which one man or woman may expect of another, or may expect to pay another. It would not be the case, though, that the further one looks back the more such scales of deference one should expect to find. In the very last days of the Ancien Régime in Europe, the niceties of social rank were probably more refined in their definition than they had ever been before. The processes of refinement which reached their apogee in the rules of precedence of the courts of Versailles and Vienna had their origins in the late middle ages. That is one of the reasons why the later medieval period is an important and formative one in social history: it is also the reason why, if one is to understand the history of that period, even in England where social grades were more flexible and less sharply defined than they were in other European lands, one must know something about the contemporary hierarchy as men then saw it. For in the minds of the men of that age, the relations of deference and service that persisted between the grades were the basis of social order, of its essence: they had not yet come to regard social distinctions as divisive, as forces with the potential to tear society apart, as Rousseau and later Marx were to do.

'You know that there be three estates of men,' said John Gower, Chaucer's fellow poet and contemporary. To him the statement was a truism. In his time it was traditional wisdom that society was composed of three orders, functionally defined in their relation to one another: the clergy whose business was with prayer and spiritual well-being; the warriors who defended the land and people with their arms; and the labourers whose toil supported the other two 'orders' or 'estates'. In England this view of society was first given expression (as far as we know) by King Alfred in an aside in his translation of Orosius. A king needs tools to help him in his work, he says: he must have men who will pray, men who will fight and men who will work the land to support these others. But the idea is certainly older: it has echoes, clearly, of Plato's tripartite division of the inhabitants of his ideal *Republic*, into philosopher rulers, warriors and workers, and is reminiscent too of the Hindu caste system that identifies separate castes of priests (Brahmins), warriors and peasants. Some have argued that the quest for its origins leads back into the remote history of the Indo-European past.

About the medieval version of the idea perhaps the first thing to stress is its specifically Christian framework. 'In the church there be needful these three offices,' says a fourteenth-century homilist, 'priesthood, knighthood, and labourers': to him the church, the community of Christian people, *was*

† From *English Society in the Later Middle Ages 1348–1500* (London: Allen Lane/The Penguin Press, 1990), pp. 1–8, 23–24, 306.

society, and the performance of the tasks of his station a man's Christian duty:

> And one thing I dare well say, that he that is not labouring in this world on studying, on prayers, on preaching for help of the people—as it falleth to priests; nor in ruling the people, maintaining them and defending them from enemies, as it falleth to knights; nor labouring on earth in divers crafts, as it falleth to labourers: when the day of reckoning cometh, right as he lived here without labour, so he shall there lack the reward of 'the penny', that is, the endless joy of heaven.

Laborare est orare, to work is to pray, that is the message, and that attention to the duties of one's station discharges simultaneously obligation to God and to one's neighbour. William Langland caught this last point beautifully in the terms of the deal struck by his personified labourer Piers the Plowman with the knight:

> By St Paul quoth Perkin you proffer so freely
> That I'll swink and sweat and sow for us both,
> And other labours do for thy love all my lifetime.
> In covenant that thou keep Holy Church and myself
> From wasters and wicked men that this world destroy,
> And go hunt hardily for hares and for foxes,
> For boars and for badgers that break down my hedges,
> And go train thy falcons wildfowls to kill,
> For such come to my croft and crop off my wheat.

The medieval view of the three estates thus had a Christian framework, and a functional approach to their relationship to one another. Two other aspects require emphasis also. First it must be stressed that it was explicitly hierarchic: the priest had primacy in order of dignity, the knight or warrior came second and the place of the labourer was in social subjection to these other two. The functions of the first two estates involved them in the exercise of authority, each one in its own sphere; the labourer's did not. 'To the knight it sufficeth not that he be given the best arms and the best beast,' says the fifteenth-century translation of Ramon Lull's *Order of Chivalry*, 'but also that he be given *seignory*', that is, lordship over lesser men. The estates view of society was thus firmly anti-egalitarian. The second point that I must stress is connected to this first one; it is that it was no warmer towards social mobility than it was to social equality. Principally because hierarchical ordering was seen in terms of divine intention, the relationship between the three orders was viewed in a static way. 'When God could have made all men strong, wise and rich,' wrote Master Ralph Acton, 'he was unwilling to do so . . . He willed these men to be strong and healthy, wise or rich, that they might save their own souls by helping others through love of them: those others he willed to be weak or foolish or in want, that they might save their souls by enduring hardship in patience. Hence God says, the poor ye have always with you.'

The social quietism of the preacher's message here may ring strangely on the ear of the modern age which has been so thoroughly attuned to the notion of social progress; but it had the authority of St Paul behind it: 'Let each man abide in the same calling wherein he was called.'

The conception of the three estates and their relations to one another was of course an ideal vision: it never did and never could have corresponded to reality. No doubt that is part of the reason why some thinkers sought to explain the relationships of different degrees or callings in the body politic in more complex, analogical terms. Thus John of Salisbury (d. 1180) used the symbol of the human body in his analogy: the priesthood is the soul (the animating principle without which the body cannot live) of the community; the prince is the head; the senate (or council) the heart; the judges the eyes; the warriors the armed hands; the tax-gatherers the intestines; the labourers and craftsmen the feet. But for a very long period the straight three-estates view held the field as the commonest and most basic mode of expressing a hierarchic, functionally structured social ideal; and it did so, no doubt, because for a long time it could be seen as relating well enough, if rather roughly and approximately, to real social conditions.

That was in the earlier, predominantly rural period of the middle ages, when independent towns were mere islets in the great sea of feudal lordship, when commercial exchange was at its slackest and slightest, and the merchant most often a stranger; when, also, the need for protection that only expensively armed warriors could provide (against marauding Vikings or Welshmen in England; against Vikings, Hungarians and Saracens in other parts of Europe) was at a premium. These times were also the great age of the monasteries, those powerhouses of prayer whose liturgical round of services offered up a steady stream of intercession for the *patria* and for all Christian people dead and living, and which were protected and sustained in this vital task by the arms and endowments of nobles and the toil of peasants. In these conditions the three-estates view, if somewhat ideal, could and did seem a not inappropriate model of social relations.

Even as late as the early fourteenth century, at the eve of the period that this book seeks to examine, this traditional view had not yet entirely lost all semblance of appropriateness to contemporary English conditions. Things had changed a great deal, it is true, since the end of what might be called the 'age of invasions' of the eleventh and preceding centuries (the last of them had been, for England, the Norman Conquest of 1066). The Normans had settled down and become anglicized. The pace of trade had quickened: towns had grown in number and in population density. Government had become more stable, and also more complex and bureaucratic. In the religious sphere, the monastic movement had found no fresh impetus since the end of the twelfth century, and by 1300 the vigour even of the new orders of religion of the thirteenth century, the mendicant friars, was beginning to look tarnished. Nevertheless, England was still a predominantly rural society. The wealth and influence of her ecclesiastical aristocracy (the bishops, the greater monasteries, and the richer among the beneficed clergy) depended on land and a pre-emptive right to a lion's share of the fruits of the labour of those who tilled and tended it: and the same was true of the secular aristocracy of barons and knights. Though a good many knights (and other substantial freeholders) had lost most of their taste for martial activity and were beginning to look more like country gentlemen than cavaliers, the reckoning of their social obligations, as landholders, in terms of military service (owed either to the king directly or mediately in respect of tenures held of some baronial overlord), stood as a reminder of the traditional relations between martial function and secular privilege. All this was still true, as I say, around 1300, even perhaps for a little longer, and in these conditions the three-estates description of social relations could still enjoy some appearance of relevance to real circumstances.

A hundred and fifty or so years later, at the end of the fifteenth century, this was no longer so. Things had by then changed too much. Traditional views die hard, and as we have seen, at the end of the fourteenth century Gower could still refer to the tripartite division of society as if it were a truism, and some clung to the view much longer, into the sixteenth century and even beyond. But by the late fourteenth century it was already fast losing what had been at least a seeming relation to reality, and by the end of the fifteenth, long before Henry VIII finally laid secular hands on monastic wealth, it had lost it. The changes in the structure of society that took place during the period between around 1350 and around 1500 were vast ones, and are what make the intervening years so important in the social history of England.

As Dr Jonathan Hughes has recently said, 'the period between the Black Death and the Wars of the Roses was a social and cultural watershed in English history'. The forces underlying the great shifts of these times were multiplex and many faceted: pride of place may however be given to three principal factors. First, there were the effects of the great Hundred Years War between England and France, which broke out in 1337 and rumbled on till 1453, when the English lost their last footholds on the soil of France, bar Calais. This war and the strains that it engendered had a profound impact on the relations of government and governed in England, and contributed significantly to the development of a new consciousness of national identity. A second factor was the spread of literacy, especially of vernacular literacy, to a much broader cross-section of society. To quote Hughes again, 'narrative poems were written that offered a broader and more realistic perspective on human nature . . . Chaucer's *Canterbury Tales* celebrated the new diversity of English society . . . more people than ever before were reading books for instruction and entertainment'. The third factor, the most dramatic and the most wide-ranging in its consequences, was the demographic recession that followed the onset in the mid fourteenth century of the great plagues—in the first outbreak, the Black Death of 1348–9, up to a third of the population of England may, it is thought, have perished.

It is not irrelevant to what has gone before in this chapter that the impact of the third of these factors, of plague and demographic decline, though it affected all and sundry, was particularly significant for the labouring sectors of the population. The effects of the French war were likewise felt at all levels of society, but inevitably most of all by the nobles, knights and gentry who provided the leadership for the hosts that fought in France and were the agents of their recruitment; and whose representatives voted in Parliament the taxes that paid for the fighting. The spread of literacy and the rise of the vernacular affected in a particular way the clerical estate, whose influence and privileged position had been previously so firmly buttressed by the clerks' near monopoly of any sophisticated degree of literacy, especially of literacy in Latin, the traditional language not only of intellectual debate and of Christian liturgy but also of administration. It is thus clear why the forces that in this period were effecting major changes in society were such as inevitably to affect also the relation of the three-estates view to the realities of living.

Hughes describes Chaucer's *Canterbury Tales* as celebrating 'the new diversity of English society'. If one looks carefully at the vivid pen portraits of his pilgrims that Chaucer offers in the 'General Prologue' to the *Tales*, the enduring influence of the three-estates approach is still visible: it can be no accident that the three most clearly idealized figures in his company are the knight, the parson and the ploughman. Nevertheless the new diversity is also very clearly there. Leaving aside for a moment his clerical characters, into which of the three estates, one may ask, is one to fit his man of law, his franklin, his merchant, his shipman, his wife of Bath? If one looks again, and more carefully, something else appears too. Most (though not perhaps all) of his figures are based on stereotypes, often adverse stereotypes of persons untrue to what ought to be the principles of their calling (and so the key to its position in the social whole)—the uncloistered monk, the friar too familiar with women and taverns, the partial judge, the reeve who knows how to cheat his master, the domineering female. Chaucer has concealed the stereotyping by the skill with which he has individualized his description of each, giving the monk a bald head 'that shone as any glass', telling of how the friar's eyes twinkled when he took the harp, of the franklin's sanguine countenance that reflected his prodigal hospitality, of the wife of Bath's red stockings. But the stereotypes are there, and one can find their analogues, shorn of the measure of personality that Chaucer gave them, in more pedestrian works, say in Gower's *Mirour de l'omme* or in the invective of contemporary homilists who seek to review the typical shortcomings of particular sectors of society. My point here is that even if a good many of Chaucer's figures are hard to fit into a three-estates scheme, he is still trying to relate each to a specific place and a specific function in the social hierarchy, following the same principle as that in which the three-estates view was based. Indeed, Chaucer is quite explicit that this is what he is trying to do. He is going, he says at the beginning of the 'Prologue', to tell of each of his pilgrims what was his 'condition' and his 'degree'; and at the end of it he apologizes for not putting them in the right hierarchic order, in 'here degree . . . as thei schulde stonde'. Rather as the far-sighted John of Salisbury in an earlier age, Chaucer has not reacted to 'new diversity' by breaking with a functional hierarchic view of the ordering of society, but by multiplying the number of 'degrees' or 'estates' that must be fitted into their place in the body politic. The reaction to overt signs of changing conditions is not to conclude that the framework needs loosening, but almost the opposite, to seek to define more narrowly and relate more carefully functions and 'degrees' within the social whole.

* * *

All through this chapter so far, I have talked in terms of men, of male degrees of worship, masculine qualifications. This has been deliberate. This was an age when, by and large, most men and most women, if they survived long enough, married. The physiological aspects of life apart, what principally dictated the pattern of living, of leisure preoccupations and work for a woman was not her sex, but rather the degree and standing of her male connections, her husband, her father, her brothers. Whether the wife as well as the husband was or was not expected actually to labour (as opposed to merely busying herself in the family interest) probably marked the sharpest of all dividing lines in society, in countryside and town alike, separating the genteel and those that might be equated with them from all others. For this reason, in this chapter, * * * it has seemed to me better not to treat womankind separately, but in the context of the class, standing and preoccupations into which their partnerships with their menfolk drew them.

All the same, there has probably been too little said so far of women. There were callings, in this age as in all others, that were purely female, those of the nun, the midwife, the 'wise woman', the prostitute (there were plenty of these). There were also avenues of living that were not open to women: they could not become priests or go to university, hold offices or practise at law. But they could retain men, employ workers, administer their own estates and sue at law in their own right; if they were born into wealthy or genteel condition they could play a powerful role personally. If their chattels were deemed at law to be their husband's property (while he lived), lands that they brought him were not by any means in his free disposal, even though the income from them might be. As heiresses, well-born girls could often be the victims of arranged marriages (so indeed could rich young men), but they could also be the vital agents in the advancement of their husbands. Perhaps most importantly of all, women as widows, in almost every rank of society, enjoyed a great degree of independence and significant legal rights. They were virtually always assured of a share at least in their dead husbands' goods or property, whether by way of dower, or through a joint settlement of lands, or under the rules of *free bench* (the widow's right to a share of the marital home) or *legitim* (the woman's legitimate share in the chattels of her deceased husband). In widowhood, a woman might have to shoulder significant responsibilities, the raising of her late husband's children, the management of his holding, his business or his estates. But widows also enjoyed a large measure of free choice not only in the discharge of these responsibilities, but as to how they should live and, above all, whether they should remarry. Marriage, by her agreement, to a well-placed widow, could be a very important step in the upward progress of an aspiring man. Though the historical record usually does not leave much evidence of it, she no doubt often made a man of him in more than one other sense as well.

BIBLIOGRAPHIC NOTE [ABRIDGED]

In writing on the estates in this chapter I found two books particularly useful: G. R. Owst, *Literature and Pulpit in Medieval England* (Cambridge, 1933), and Jill Mann, *Chaucer and Medieval Estates Satire: The Literature of Social Classes and the General Prologue of the Canterbury Tales* (Cambridge, 1973). [Keen's references to Jonathan Hughes are to *Pastors and Visionaries: Religion and Secular Life in Late Medieval Yorkshire* (Woodbridge, 1988).]

WINTHROP WETHERBEE

An Introduction to Chaucer and His Poem†

For most readers the *Canterbury Tales* mean the General Prologue, with its gallery of portraits, and a few of the more humorous tales. What we retain is a handful of remarkable personalities, and such memorable moments as the end of the Miller's tale. These are worth having in themselves, but it requires an extra effort to see the significant relationship among them, and to recognize that their bewildering variety is Chaucer's technique for representing a single social reality. We may compare the first part of Shakespeare's *Henry IV*, where our impressions can be so dominated by Falstaff, Hotspur and Hal as to leave Henry and the problems of his reign in shadow. The comparison is the more suggestive in that Shakespeare has recreated the England of Chaucer's last years, when a society that is essentially that of the *Canterbury Tales* was shaken by usurpation, regicide and civil war. Both poets describe a nation unsure of its identity, distrustful of traditional authority, and torn by ambition and materialism into separate spheres of interest. For both, the drives and interactions of individual personalities express a loss of central control, a failure of hierarchy which affects society at all levels.

Shakespeare's focus is always on a single "body politic," and though his characters span all levels of society, their situations are determined by a central crisis of monarchical authority. Chaucer's project is harder to define. He shows us nothing of Shakespeare's royal Westminster, and gives us only a glimpse of his chaotic Eastcheap; and though profoundly political in their implications, the *Tales* offer no comment on contemporary politics. But the Canterbury pilgrims, too, are a society in transition, their horizons enlarged by war and commerce, their relations complicated by new types of enterprise and new social roles. What holds them together is a radically innovative literary structure, a fictional world with no center, defined by oppositions between realistic and idealistic, worldly and religious, traditionalist and individualist points of view.

The plot of the *Tales* is simple enough. In early April, the narrator is lodged at the Tabard in Southwark, ready to make a pilgrimage to the shrine of St. Thomas à Becket at Canterbury, when a group of twenty-nine pilgrims arrive at the inn. The narrator is admitted to their number and provides portraits of most of the group, each of whom embodies a different aspect of English society. The host of the Tabard, Harry Baily, decides to join the pilgrims, and proposes a game to divert them on the road: all will tell stories, and the best tale will be rewarded at journey's end with a supper at the Tabard. The bulk of the poem consists of the tales of twenty-three pilgrims, interspersed with narrative and dialogue which link their performances to the frame of the pilgrimage journey.

The literary form of the story collection, in which narratives of diverse kinds are organized within a larger framing narrative, had a long history,

† From *Geoffrey Chaucer: The Canterbury Tales* (Cambridge: Cambridge UP, 1989), pp. 1–16. 2nd ed. 2004.

and had been treated with new sophistication in Chaucer's own time. But neither the *Confessio Amantis* of his friend John Gower, which was in progress during the early stages of his own project, nor Boccaccio's *Decameron*, which he almost certainly knew, exhibits anything like the complexity of the *Tales*. The social diversity of Chaucer's pilgrims, the range of styles they employ, and the psychological richness of their interaction, both with one another and with their own tales, are a landmark in world literature. In no earlier work do characters so diverse in origin and status as Chaucer's "churls" and "gentles" meet and engage on equal terms. In the *Decameron* "churls" exist only as two-dimensional characters in stories told by an aristocratic company. In the *Romance of the Rose*, the thirteenth-century love-allegory which was the greatest single influence on Chaucer's poetry, the low social status and coarse behavior of "Evil-Tongue" and "Danger" is allegorical, defining them as threats to the progress of the poem's courtly lover. But Chaucer's churls exist on the same plane of reality as the Knight and Prioress. Some are undeniably beyond the pale in ordinary social terms, and their membership in the pilgrim company gives them a voice they could acquire in no other way. Under the rough authority of the Host, and the wide-eyed, uncritical gaze of the narrator, characters as mean or unsavory as the Manciple and Summoner take part in a dialogue in which no point of view is exempt from criticism and conventional social values have frequently to be laid aside.

The narrator is one of the most remarkable features of the *Tales*. He is at once the most innocent and most knowing of men, seemingly guileless as he points to the revealing traits of speech and behavior in his fellow pilgrims, yet astute in filling the gaps created by their reticence, and placing them in relation to the issues affecting their world. Naiveté aside, this narrator must resemble the historical Geoffrey Chaucer, a poet uniquely qualified by background and experience to produce a work so broad in its social vision. He was the son of a successful merchant who had served the crown as a customs official. As an adolescent he entered the service of Elizabeth, Countess of Ulster and wife of Lionel, Duke of Clarence, second son of Edward III. Still in his teens, he was captured while serving with Edward's invading army in France, and ransomed by the King. From the mid-1360s until his death around 1400 he served the crown, visiting France and Italy on diplomatic missions, working as a customs official, sitting on various commissions and for a term as a Member of Parliament, and acting as Clerk of the Works, in charge of the maintenance of various royal buildings. He was in close touch with the worlds of law, commerce, diplomacy, and warfare, and with the life of the court and aristocracy. He was also one of the most learned laymen of his day, and one of the most European in outlook, fully at home with French culture, and ahead of his time in appreciating the brilliant achievements of fourteenth-century Italy. And though his poetry rarely says so directly, he was acutely aware of the grim realities of English politics.

In the last years of Edward III, the heavy taxation required by long and unsuccessful wars, charges of corruption against high officials, and hostility to the wealth and power of the Church were dividing the country. The "Good Parliament" of 1376 indicted several prominent courtiers and financiers, but its attempted reforms had little effect. In the late 1370s a series of poll taxes brought to a head the longstanding grievances of the laboring classes, who, since the labor shortages caused by the terrible plagues of 1348–49, had seen repeated attempts to control their wages and mobility. In 1381, under the pressures of taxation, anxiety about foreign competition in the cloth trade, and a concern for legal rights, the Peasants' Revolt broke out in several parts of southern England. In London many buildings were burned, including the sumptuous palace of Chaucer's patron John of Gaunt, and a mob killed dozens of Flemish merchants and cloth-workers. Richard II, who had assumed the throne at the age of ten in 1377, showed courage and judgment in negotiating with the rebels, but his later years were marred by favoritism and financial irresponsibility. The Parliament of 1386, in which Chaucer sat as a member for Kent, demanded many reforms, and when Richard refused to accede, battle was joined between the king's supporters and his chief opponents. The rebel lords, who included the future King Henry IV, having gained a victory at Radcot Bridge in Oxfordshire and marched on London, became the so-called Lords Appellant of the "Merciless Parliament" of 1388, in the course of which a number of Richard's friends and financial backers were sentenced to death.

Chaucer seems to have maintained good relations with the Court through three troubled decades, though his friends included men deeply involved in the conflicts of the time, some of whom lost their lives. And apart from two disparaging references to the Peasants' Revolt, his poetry never addresses contemporary political issues. He was clearly troubled by the effects of commerce and social mobility: restlessness, ambition, and a concern with power are pervasive among the Pilgrims, and are always suspect. But in matters of practical politics, his view of established authority seems to have been fundamentally conservative.

On religious questions, too, Chaucer is reticent. In a period of mounting hostility to the established Church, he confines his criticism to the specific excesses of the Friar, Pardoner, and Monk. He never addresses the condition of the episcopal hierarchy, or urges any reform more radical than the renewal of fundamental Christian values outlined in the Parson's tale. However, it is likely that he was responsive to evangelical tendencies at work among the lower clergy and laity. Throughout the later fourteenth century the reformers known to their opponents as "Lollards" (mumblers [of prayers]?), inspired by the largely anti-establishment theology of John Wycliffe, sought to free religious practice from the sanctions of the Church hierarchy, and placed a new emphasis on the individual conscience. Though attacked as heretics, their concern to distance religion from worldly institutions had a broad appeal. Chaucer's clear preference for the simple, private piety promoted by the Nun's Priest and the Parson, as against the elaborately self-dramatizing religiosity of the Man of Law and the Prioress, would be fully consonant with Lollard sympathies. We may note that in the "Epilogue" that follows the Man of Law's tale in several manuscripts, the Parson is openly accused of Lollardy, and makes no attempt to deny the charge. The accusation is based on his aversion to the swearing of religious oaths, a typical Lollard attitude with which Chaucer shows sympathy elsewhere. It is possible, too, that the capping of the tale-telling game with the Parson's austere penitential treatise indicates sympathy with the reformers. Certainly Chaucer's friends included the so-called "Lollard Knights," courtiers and men of affairs who gave protection to Lollard preachers and maintained certain distinctive practices and beliefs. The extent of their Lollardy is hard to gauge, but several in their wills requested simple funerals and graves, and asked that money from their estates be given to the poor rather than providing rich funeral feasts or bequests to religious institutions. Such austerity did not prevent their pursuing successful careers as soldiers, diplomats and land-owners, but the contradiction is no greater than that presented by Chaucer's own "Retraction" to the *Canterbury Tales*, in which much of that work and the bulk of his earlier poems are repudiated as "worldly vanitees."

But if Chaucer's position on major questions remains elusive, the form of his poem and its treatment of character are themselves vehicles of serious social criticism. A major project of the *Tales* is the testing of traditional values. In the General Prologue a hierarchical model of society, defined by traditional obligation and privilege, provides a tentative framework, but few of the pilgrims can be said to embody traditional roles in a recognizable form, and theirs are the least palpably real of Chaucer's portraits. More often the rejection or usurpation of traditional roles provides an index to social mobility: again and again such "modern" tendencies as the secularizing of the religious life, or the aspirations of the professions and guilds, take the form of an emulation or appropriation of the style and prerogatives of gentility. Such pretensions are often only a veil for self-interest, but they point up the inadequacy of traditional categories to define the hierarchical position of newly powerful commercial and professional groups concerned to claim a status and dignity of their own. Faced with so many forms of "worthiness," the narrator must finally concede his inability to set his characters "in their degree," the place where they "stand" in traditional social terms.

Chaucer was well situated to appreciate this crisis of values. Familiar as he was with many areas of his society, he was primarily a courtier and a gentleman, for whom courtesy, honor and truth constituted social norms. He would have agreed with the Wife of Bath that gentility bears no inherent relation to birth or fortune, but he clearly saw it as more readily compatible with some ways of life than with others. Hence his portraits of such emergent "gentles" as the Merchant and the Man of Law mix respect for their professional and public functions with a keen awareness of how easily these can coexist with covert or self-deceiving materialism and self-aggrandizement. He would probably have conceded them the status of gentlemen, but there is no clear line between their world and that of the equally professional Shipman and Physician, though the one is perhaps a pirate and the other something of a charlatan.

But if the usurpation of gentility and its prerogatives disturbs Chaucer, the chivalric and courtly ideals are themselves scrutinized in the course of the poem, and it is made clear that they harbor their own inherent contradictions. In keeping with Chaucer's concern for hierarchy, the Knight, highest in rank among the pilgrims, opens the competition with a tale that promotes the virtues of Theseus, conqueror and knightly hero *par excellence*. Unabashedly an argument for chivalry as the basis of social order, the tale nevertheless shows chivalry repeatedly unable to contain or subdue disorder, largely because its only resource is authority imposed from above and reinforced by armed power. Ultimately, the tale is a searching exploration of the limits of the chivalric ethic as a political instrument. Other tales extend this critique to courtly values in general, not only by parody, as in the Miller's rejoinder to the Knight, but by focusing on them directly, as when the Wife of Bath uses the standard of *gentilesse* to expose an Arthurian knight's failure to exhibit true courtly conduct. The Squire's tale, the imaginative vision of a knight in embryo, shows naiveté and confusion coexisting with real virtues in a young mind that takes courtly values wholly for granted. And the Franklin, a man (like Chaucer) at home on the border between the courtly and practical worlds, subjects the ethical contradictions of the courtly code to a peculiarly modern scrutiny, showing that much of what seems foolish in the Squire's performance is inherent in the courtly ideal itself.

And of course the world of the *Tales* includes a number of characters who are not courtly, for whom the narrator feels a need to apologize and whose coarseness he carefully disowns. The importance of the opposition of "churls" to "gentles" is established by the opening cluster of tales, in which the Knight's cumbersome celebration of order is challenged by the brilliant and broadly salutary parody of the Miller, and this in turn by the largely *ad hominem* thrust of the Reeve. The descent from highly serious poetry to parody to personal attack implies a breakdown of social order that ends in the flight of the Cook's wayward apprentice; as the Cook's narrative disintegrates into the random particulars of London lowlife, we are left at an immense distance from the ceremonial world of Theseus. The social oppositions defined in this opening sequence do not appear again in so clear-cut a form, but their implications pervade the entire poem.

The tension between large, public concerns like those of the Knight and the narrower vision of the churls is also expressed in a contrast of literary genres. Like the Knight, the gentle Squire and Franklin tell tales that can be defined as *romance*, centered on the world of chivalry and courtly idealism. The typical mode of the churls, brilliantly exemplified by the Miller's and Reeve's tales, is the *fabliau*, a short comic tale, often deliberately coarse, which normally deals with a bourgeois or lower-class world and emphasizes action, cleverness, and the gratification of instinct. This opposition of genres, too, is clearest in the opening sequence; in later tales romance and fabliau elements are often combined with one another, or adapted to other concerns. In the Merchant's history of the marriage of January a grotesque attempt at romance is gradually transformed into the fabliau of the elderly hero's betrayal. The Wife of Bath describes her own marital history in terms that are very much those of the world of fabliau, but then, through her intense imagining of a life in which women would be valued at their true worth and treated with real *gentilesse*, she transcends that world. From the rough-and-tumble of her fifth marriage she emerges into an equilibrium of mutual respect, and the passage from her prologue to her tale is simultaneously a passage from fabliau to romance. Romance becomes self-critical in the hands of the Franklin, and fabliau is a vehicle for satire in the Summoner's rejoinder to the Friar. And the tale of the Shipman, who dwells on the border between the world of the professionals and that of the churls, is in effect an upper-class fabliau, pragmatic and mechanical in treating economic and sexual motivation, but deceptively subtle in presenting the private world of its merchant protagonist.

There is a broad pattern in the interaction of romance and fabliau in the *Tales*, an increasing tendency to expose the contradictions and absurdities of the one accompanied by a perceptible rise in the dignity of the other. The shift expresses an increasingly pragmatic approach to the social reality the poem engages, an uneasiness with traditional categories and a desire to bring emerging social forces into confrontation. A broadly similar opposition can be observed among the tales of religion. The first of these, the Man of Law's tale, presents itself as a religious counterpart to the Knight's, comparable in solemnity and historical perspective, and similarly committed to affirming order in the face of the uncertainties of earthly life. The Man of Law's Custance is an emperor's daughter and the "mirror of all courtesy," and her story has been aptly described as "hagiographic romance." The rich rhetoric of prayer and sentiment in the Prioress's tale is similarly indebted to courtly poetry. At the opposite pole are the Nun's Priest's Aesopian fable of the cock and the fox and the spare penitential treatise of the Parson. Together they present a daunting challenge to religious emotionalism and high style, as the blunt colloquialism and materialist skepticism of the churls debunk the ideals of romance.

But the tales of Man of Law and Prioress, whatever their effect as vehicles of religious sentiment, also express distinctive points of view toward the world. The Man of Law's horror of the familial tensions that continually threaten his Custance, and the broader anxiety about earthly justice that pervades his tale, at times getting the better of his faith in Providence, are the preoccupations of a man who knows these problems at first hand. The Prioress's tale is marred by a violence and anti-Semitism that are no less horrible for being virtually invisible to the Prioress herself, and expose the emotional privation behind her façade of genteel and complacent piety. The social and spiritual complexities revealed in the process of tale-telling are the real focus of both performances, and remind us of the importance of character as a vehicle of social criticism, the extent to which we must rely on the often distorted vision of the pilgrims themselves to gauge the bearing of great issues on their lives.

Chaucer goes to extraordinary lengths to show the obstacles to vision and knowledge posed by the pilgrims' existential situations, and we may compare his perspective to that of the great Franciscan philosopher of the previous generation, William of Ockham. "Ockham's razor" is often said to have severed philosophy from theology: this is an exaggeration, but his denial of the necessity of natural secondary causes (since there is nothing God might effect through a secondary cause that He is not equally able to accomplish directly), and his confinement of *scientia*, or real knowledge, to the sphere of observation and logical inference, tend in this direction. They allow us to affirm little about the relation of created life to God beyond the acknowledgment, through faith, of his omnipotence and goodness, and the ethical imperative of obeying his commands. Chaucer accepts similar constraints for his characters. Theseus' evocation of the benevolent "First Mover," insofar as it is more than a political gesture, is a leap of faith, and a pervasive concern of the *Tales* as a whole is the psychological effect of living with no more immediate confirmation of order and providence than such a leap provides. Some characters simply refuse to consider "Who hath the world in honde"; others reveal their anxiety in such neurotic forms as the Man of Law's vacillating attitude toward

Providence or the Pardoner's compulsive blasphemy; and the Nun's Priest, apparently after serious thought, seems to have made peace with the likelihood that the large questions of providence and self-determination are unanswerable.

Cut off from a sure sense of relation to the divine, or of their place in a traditional hierarchy, the pilgrims question their own status. Many of the tales are essays in self-definition, attempts to establish values and goals that lead to startling revelations. The Knight, whose tale begins as an apology for chivalry, finds himself unable to bring it to a satisfying resolution, and is carried steadily toward a confrontation with the horror of violence and death which challenges his chivalric values. The Wife of Bath, trying to justify a life of striving for mastery in marriage, becomes half-aware that her deepest need is to be recognized and valued as a woman, something of which her society seems incapable. The Pardoner flaunts his success as a religious huckster and defies the taboo effect of his sexual abnormality, but gradually reveals a religious inner self that accepts the paradoxical guilt of the scapegoat, an agonizing display that illustrates the intolerance of a Christian society. In all these cases the tale-tellers' struggles are rendered more painful by a vision of order or harmony or forgiveness that seems to hover just out of reach.

The elaborate context in which Chaucer's characters live and think is again a landmark in literary history. To compare the Wife of Bath or the Pardoner with the embodiments of lechery and hypocrisy in the *Romance of the Rose* on whom they are modeled is to see at once the greater depth and complexity of Chaucer's creations. The noble company who tell the tales of the *Decameron* are social equals with no personal history, charming but limited by their very urbanity. Their relations with one another and with the tales they tell exhibit none of the interplay that gives the *Canterbury Tales* their rich complexity. The closest equivalent to the dense social and psychological medium in which Chaucer's characters function is the *Inferno* of Dante, and their self-revelations are often as powerful as those of Dante's sinners. But Dante's characters are necessarily static, fixed forever in the attitudes defined by their besetting sins; Chaucer's are alive, able to exercise their imaginations in ways which unexpectedly open up new dimensions in their lives. Their condition is one of radical uncertainty and vast possibility.

The project of tale-telling is of course what keeps the lives of the pilgrims open-ended, and the juxtaposition and interaction of the tales are the basis of the poem's structure. To address the difficult question of the pattern that emerges as the sequence of tales runs its course, we may divide the poem into a series of broad movements. The first is bracketed by the tales of the Knight and the Man of Law, the two major attempts in the poem to address the problem of order. The Knight's tale, as I have suggested, is undone by contradictions inherent in the chivalric code. In the Man of Law's tale commitment is undermined by personal anxiety. He loudly affirms God's abiding concern for Custance, but feels a need to supplement Providence with an officiousness of his own which ensures that her contact with the world is minimal. Custance never becomes real, her human constancy is never tried, and the narrator remains torn between commitment to faith in God and an irrepressible fear of imminent danger. Thus this first group of tales calls into question the authoritarian models proposed by the two highest-ranking pilgrims. The challenge to order which surfaces in the Knight's tale and is elaborated in the descending movement of the tales that follow, as social vision is increasingly narrowed by personal concerns, is recapitulated in the Man of Law's tale as a conflict in the narrator's own view of the world.

In the broad central area of the poem, social criticism is on a smaller scale. The problem of authority in marriage, introduced in spectacular fashion by the Wife of Bath, is a recurring theme, punctuated by the naming of the Wife in the tales of both Clerk and Merchant, and climaxed by the Franklin's exhaustive catalogue of the things that make for success in marriage. The astute perceptions of the Shipman likewise center on domestic relations. Otherwise the tales of this section are largely fueled by private concerns. The social conflict dramatized in the first fragment reappear on a reduced scale in the mutual hostility of Friar and Summoner, which combines criticism of institutions with *ad hominem* malevolence, and the closest equivalents to the institutional commitments of the Knight and Man of Law are the Squire's breathless and abortive flight of courtly idealism and the tormented piety of the Prioress's miracle story. The tales of Merchant and Physician are circumscribed by the materialism of their tellers, and the Wife and Pardoner are concerned as much with their status as human beings as with the issues implied by their social roles.

In the midst of the varied company of this central group, the Clerk's tale stands out with stark clarity. The story of patient Griselde and her tyrannical husband has been explained as answering the Wife of Bath's challenge to male authority in marriage by vindicating the traditional, misogynistically conceived institution as a proving-ground of virtue. But in the end, as the intensity of Griselde's suffering forces its way to the surface, what we learn is that the constraints imposed on her are indeed "importable" (unbearable). The Clerk's story is a searching comment on power and authority, not only in the social context implied by the role of Walter, an Italian minor tyrant of a kind Chaucer may have observed at first hand, but in the institutionalizing of moral values and the creation of moral fiction. The almost perversely beautiful style which sets off the prolonged sufferings of Griselde cannot wholly conceal a substructure of sado-masochistic fantasy. The appropriation of her femininity to an ostensibly moral and spiritual purpose is at times perilously close to the fetishistic treatment of emblematic figures in other tales. This tendency is present in the Man of Law's overprotection of Custance, and is carried to extremes in the cases of the twelve-year-old Virginia of the Physician's tale or the Prioress's child-martyr. The Clerk's tale has superficial affinities with these tales of sainthood, but its purpose is humane rather than hagiographical. The convoluted irony of his performance is finally unfathomable, but a number of features of his tale hint at an underlying sympathy with the Wife's attempt to redefine sexual relations, and it is perhaps the most fully achieved of all the tales in its rendering of the complexities it addresses.

The four tales which follow are concerned with the value of fiction itself, and the project of the *Canterbury Tales* in particular. The pilgrim narrator's paired tales, *Sir Thopas* and *Melibee*, present a polar opposition of form and style. *Sir Thopas*, a comic romance rendered almost chaotic by a proliferation of incident and the confusion of its hero's motives, reflects the array of problems Chaucer has set himself in the *Tales* as a whole by his deliberate indulgence of the eccentric energies of his pilgrims. In the *Melibee,* a moral argument is expounded with virtually no regard for narrative or personality, and the result is a cumbersome tale whose human significance never emerges. The opposition between the brilliant parody of the one tale and the ponderous moral eloquence of the other show Chaucer aware of the difficulty of synthesizing his brilliant and varied gifts and adapting them to the presentation of a coherent world view.

The tales of the Monk and the Nun's Priest form a similar pairing, one that invites us to ponder the relevance of epic and tragedy to the concrete and often homely world of the *Tales.* The Monk's collection of nineteen stories of the falls of great men represents a form Chaucer's own collection might have taken, a group of exemplary stories organized by a common concern with the workings of fortune. But like the *Melibee,* the Monk's tale attains coherence only at the price of fragmenting history and falsifying character to reduce its material to simple moral terms. The contrasting tale of the Nun's Priest is the Aesopian fable of the cock and the fox, lavishly embellished with epic and tragic rhetoric, vivid stories illustrating the truth and value of dreams, and speculation on the theological meaning of Chauntecleer's capture by the fox. The implicit suggestion that such materials, the resources of some of Chaucer's most serious poetry, are as applicable to the story of a rooster as to human affairs poses in a new way the question of how literature engages reality.

A third pairing, between the tales of the Second Nun and the Canon's Yeoman, develops the spiritual implications of Chaucer's concern with the problems of tale-telling, and points forward toward the religious emphasis of the poem's conclusion. There is a precise thematic contrast between the Yeoman's largely confessional tale of the desperate, failed, and finally specious project of "translation" undertaken by his alchemists, and the Second Nun's impersonal and authoritative depiction of the religious transformations wrought by St. Cecilia. The alchemists' murky world of fumes, toil, and blind obsession is the antithesis of the tranquil assurance and radiant spirituality with which Cecilia and her companions are vested. The balancing of these tales defines the absolute limits of human art, and the necessity of spiritual authority as a supplement to earthly vision. The two tales that conclude the poem reinforce this point in a way that directly implicates the project of the *Canterbury Tales.* Both are dismissive of fiction, but their messages are sharply opposed. The Manciple's anti-moral—that it is better not to speak than to risk the consequences of doing so—seems to deny and mock the very idea of serious fiction, and the Parson's total rejection of "fable" presents the same lesson in a positive form. For the expected verse tale he substitutes a treatise in prose, designed to aid penitents in considering the state of their souls, and including a detailed analysis of the deadly sins and their remedies. As the last of the tales, the Parson's treatise is a part of the larger economy of the poem. But its effect is to withdraw us to another plane of reality, enabling us to see the world of the previous tales in perspective, and encouraging us to turn our minds to higher things.

* * * No poem lends itself better to oral presentation, and we can be sure that it was read aloud, but it shows none of the conventional signs of address to a mixed audience of courtly aristocrats that mark Chaucer's

earlier poetry. The *Canterbury Tales* are a boldly experimental work, and it is probable that the audience to whom Chaucer looked for a fully appreciative reception were those most involved in the changes affecting the world the poem describes. In a verse *envoy* (letter) to his friend Bukton, Chaucer urges him to "rede" the Wife of Bath before entering into marriage; the word can bear several meanings, but it is probable that what is being suggested is a private rereading of the Wife's Prologue, and probable too that the poem as a whole was aimed most directly at readers capable of thoughtful engagement with the issues raised by Chaucer's poetry. Though a new insight into the condition of women is one of the chief rewards the poem offers, its audience was no doubt largely male. Whether knights, civil servants or men of learning, law, or commerce, they are likely to have been gentlemen who, like Chaucer himself, had learned to function in several worlds, and had few illusions about the workings of justice, commerce, or aristocratic and ecclesiastical power. Such men would recognize clearly the difference between "churl" and "gentle," and the Peasants' Revolt may have sharpened their sense of it; but in an age of social mobility they would also recognize that such distinctions were not absolute, and in some cases might even have been drawn by Lollard sympathies into a closer sense of relation to those of lower station. We may assume that the *Canterbury Tales* did for them what they can still do for us, making them more aware and more tolerant of human diversity, and so, in a sense of the word important to Chaucer, more gentle.

WINTHROP WETHERBEE

The Reception of the *Canterbury Tales*†

Chaucer was the major poet of his time, and it is clear from the number of surviving manuscripts and Caxton's two early printings that the *Canterbury Tales* were his most popular work, but they were not widely imitated, and in a time when the proprietary claims of authorship were treated very casually, remarkably few attempts were made to augment them, beyond the construction by scribal editors of links among existing tales. In some manuscripts the Cook's abortive tale is supplemented by *Gamelyn*, a popular romance in loose accentual verse about a young man of noble birth forced by adversity to become a sort of Robin Hood. A single manuscript includes the broadly similar but inferior tale of *Beryn*, adapted to the structure of the *Tales* by way of a long prologue which narrates the doings of the various pilgrims after their arrival in Canterbury. The narrator is careful to make the behavior of the different pilgrims conform superficially to their Chaucerian characters, and develops a sort of fabliau around the Pardoner, who is led by an ill-considered display of sexual bravado into a nocturnal adventure that ends in his being beaten by the lover of a barmaid at his inn. John Lydgate's *Siege of Thebes*, though clearly

† From *Geoffrey Chaucer: The Canterbury Tales* (Cambridge: Cambridge UP, 1989), pp. 129–33. 2nd ed. 2004. The translations of Chaucer mentioned at the end of Wetherbee's summary of reception are from Nevill Coghill, trans., *The Canterbury Tales* (Harmondsworth: Penguin, 1952) and Theodore Morrison, trans., *The Portable Chaucer*, 2nd ed. (New York: Viking, 1975).

intended as an independent work, has a similar preface which begins with a humorous imitation of the opening of the General Prologue (the main verb shows up in line 66), and describes Lydgate's encounter with the pilgrims at Canterbury.

That the relatively crude *Gamelyn* and *Beryn* were incorporated into the *Tales* suggests that the poem was seen as being of a lower order than Chaucer's other works. Such distinctions were important in the fifteenth century, when literacy was expanding to include a middle class respectful of high culture and eager to assimilate the tastes of the upper classes. England was politically isolated, French was in decline, and the vast projects of fifteenth-century writers like Lydgate and Malory reflect the desire for English versions of the major texts of continental courtly culture. In such circumstances Chaucer's realism and comic irony were bound to be undervalued, and he was regarded chiefly as a moralist, court poet, and translator. The tales that appear most often in manuscript anthologies are those of the Clerk and Prioress, and we may assume that they were read as straightforward examples of religious eloquence. Poets endlessly imitated Chaucer's earlier poems, drew courtly motifs from the tales of Knight and Squire, and echoed Chaucer's moral rhetoric, but, apart from certain of Henryson's *fables*, none directly engaged the *Tales* in their fullness and variety.

An anonymous *Plowman's Tale*, a satire on the Church establishment whose title probably owes more to Langland's Piers than to Chaucer's pilgrim, was incorporated into the *Tales* in William Thynne's edition of 1542, highlighting for post-Reformation readers the traces of anti-clericalism in the poem. Other such works were attributed to Chaucer, and he enjoyed a brief vogue as a political radical. But the "scurrility" of the *Tales* was also noted, and "Canterbury Tale" came to denote any trivial, outrageous, or bawdy story. Throughout the sixteenth century, moreover, Chaucer's language and meter were growing steadily more obscure; the situation was not improved by the attempts of Renaissance editors to correct them, and it was inevitably the more colloquial, less conventional tales that suffered most, and were least read as a result.

The traditional view of an essentially courtly Chaucer was inherited and perpetuated by Wyatt and Sidney. Even Spenser, who read Chaucer with care, and assimilated his style and language to an extraordinary degree, is remarkably sparing in his use of the non-courtly tales. The *Shepheardes Calendar* at several points evokes Chaucer in his largely misattributed role as proto-Reformer, and the social criticism of *Mother Hubberds Tale* is broadly reminiscent of several of Chaucer's non-courtly tales, but Book Four of the *Faerie Queene*, explicitly conceived as the completion of the Squire's tale, represents both Spenser's most elaborate use of Chaucer and the fullest flowering of the tradition of the courtly Chaucer.

A similarly one-sided view of Chaucer appears in the early drama. The Elizabethan period saw plays based broadly on the Clerk's, Physician's, Knight's, Man of Law's, and Franklin's tales, and even one *De Meliboeo Chauceriano*, but only Shakespeare seems to have drawn on the comic tales. In addition to the clear debt of *A Midsummer Night's Dream* and *The Two Noble Kinsmen* to the Knight's tale, it is very likely that the quarrel of Oberon and Titania in the *Dream* owes something to the figures of Pluto and Proserpina in the Merchant's tale, and that the Wife of Bath's prologue was an important model for the Falstaff of *The Merry Wives of Windsor*. Allusions to most of the *Tales* have been discovered in the plays, and it seems clear that Shakespeare was better read in Chaucer than any writer of his time save Spenser.

The courtly Chaucer is still a canonical figure for Milton's *Penseroso*, but his importance seems to have dwindled over the course of the seventeenth century. Perhaps the first post-Elizabethan writer to take Chaucer seriously, and certainly one of the first to regard the *Canterbury Tales* as his major achievement, was John Dryden, whose *Fables* (1700) include modern versions of the Knight's, Nun's Priest's, and Wife of Bath's tales. His famous Preface credits Chaucer with a representation of the world of his time, and of human nature in general, so complete and so accurate that "'Tis sufficient to say, according to the proverb, that *here is God's Plenty*." For Dryden Chaucer's verse is irredeemably rough, a product of the "infancy of our [English] poetry," and his tone unnecessarily coarse, but he did not hesitate to declare Chaucer superior to Ovid, both in his representation of character and in the disciplined simplicity of a style in which fidelity to nature always takes precedence over "the turn of words." In Dryden's renderings his own Augustan style tends to contaminate this simplicity with unnecessary epithets, but his appreciation of the *Tales* did much to define later views of Chaucer. After Dryden it was the poet's realism that was valued above all, a complete reversal of the Renaissance view of the poet. An early nineteenth-century biographer dismissed *Troilus and Criseyde* as "merely a love-tale," and though the *Troilus* has survived this slight, the modern editor F. N. Robinson could still place the courtly Chaucer in perspective by declaring that the love-allegory of his early poetry was "essentially foreign to his genius," a fashion which he outgrew as his work matured. In effect Chaucer came to be seen as having evolved, rather abruptly, from a medieval poet to a harbinger of the modern novel. Only in the last thirty years, and with the help of Charles Muscatine's *Chaucer and the French Tradition*, have we come to recognize the essential continuity of Chaucer's work, and the importance for the *Canterbury Tales* of the continual interplay between courtly romance and fabliau, high and low styles.

Chaucer's popularity in our own day is largely due to the scholarly enterprise of the past century, which has given us a reliable version of Chaucer's text and language, but this subject cannot be dealt with briefly. Suffice it to say that the work of the Chaucer Society, founded by F. J. Furnivall in 1867, led to the landmark editions of W. W. Skeat (1894) and F. N. Robinson (1933, 1957), and we now take for granted a range of well-annotated texts which enable us to read Chaucer in "the original," and give us a fair approximation of the sound and rhythm of his verse.

Under these fortunate circumstances we need not accept Dryden's view of Chaucer as a "rough diamond" who requires the polish of modern verse in order to be appreciated, and it can be asked whether English-speaking readers have any use for translations. These inevitably tend less to facilitate access to the original than to replace it, offering canned peaches when fresh ones are ready to hand. Setting a passage you have enjoyed, however imperfectly, in Middle English side by side with a modern rendering of it is bound to heighten the effect of the one by showing how much the other has failed to deliver.

An interesting test case is Wordsworth's rendering of the Prioress's tale, in one sense surely the most faithful translation of Chaucer ever made. Wordsworth's feeling for the special qualities of the tale was good (though one might wish to rephrase his prefatory remark that "the fierce bigotry of the Prioress forms a fine background for her tender-hearted sympathies with the Mother and Child"), and he took great pains to make his version as nearly as possible a transparent medium. With the help of accent-marks Wordsworth created a remarkable approximation of Chaucer's meter, and he deliberately preserves archaic words (what he calls "sprinklings of antiquity") when their sense is still clear. The result is a version that sounds superficially very much like Chaucer. But as Theodore Morrison remarks (in an excellent introduction to his own volume of translations), it is somehow stuffy. What comes across most clearly is the scholarly effort involved in the recreation, and its final effect is to make Chaucer himself sound pedantic.

Morrison's own freer verse renderings, and those of Nevill Coghill, reflect the translators' appreciation of Chaucer in a more spontaneous way. Both are artistic achievements in their own right, and a reader who knows the *Canterbury Tales* well can gain real pleasure from seeing what they have done. But the most useful service my own little book could perform would be to help persuade those reading the *Tales* for the first time that the use of any translation whatever is more likely to hinder than to enhance their appreciation of Chaucer.

E. TALBOT DONALDSON

Chaucer the Pilgrim†

Verisimilitude in a work of fiction is not without its attendant dangers, the chief of which is that the responses it stimulates in the reader may be those appropriate not so much to an imaginative production as to an historical one or to a piece of reporting. History and reporting are, of course, honourable in themselves, but if we react to a poet as though he were an historian or a reporter, we do him somewhat less than justice. I am under the impression that many readers, too much influenced by Chaucer's brilliant verisimilitude, tend to regard his famous pilgrimage to Canterbury as significant not because it is a great fiction, but because it seems to be a remarkable record of a fourteenth-century pilgrimage. A remarkable record it may be, but if we treat it too narrowly as such there are going to be certain casualties among the elements that make up the fiction. Perhaps first among these elements is the fictional reporter, Chaucer the pilgrim, and the role he plays in the Prologue to the *Canterbury Tales* and in the links between them. I think it time that he was rescued from the comparatively dull record of history and put back into his poem. He is not really Chaucer the poet—nor, for that matter, is either the poet, or the poem's protagonist, that Geoffrey Chaucer frequently mentioned in contemporary historical records as a distinguished civil servant, but never as a poet. The fact that these are three

† From *PMLA* 69 (1954): 928–36. Reprinted by permission of the copyright owner, the Modern Language Association.

separate entities does not, naturally, exclude the probability—or rather the certainty—that they bore a close resemblance to one another, and that, indeed, they frequently got together in the same body. But that does not excuse us from keeping them distinct from one another, difficult as their close resemblance makes our task.

The natural tendency to confuse one thing with its like is perhaps best represented by a school of Chaucerian criticism, now outmoded, that pictured a single Chaucer under the guise of a wide-eyed, jolly, rolypoly little man who, on fine Spring mornings, used to get up early, while the dew was still on the grass, and go look at daisies. A charming portrait, this, so charming, indeed, that it was sometimes able to maintain itself to the exclusion of any Chaucerian other side. It has every reason to be charming, since it was lifted almost *in toto* from the version Chaucer gives of himself in the Prologue to the *Legend of Good Women*, though I imagine it owes some of its popularity to a rough analogy with Wordsworth—a sort of *Legend of Good Poets*. It was this version of Chaucer that Kittredge, in a page of great importance to Chaucer criticism, demolished with his assertion that 'a naïf Collector of Customs would be a paradoxical monster'. He might well have added that a naïve creator of old January would be even more monstrous.

Kittredge's pronouncement cleared the air, and most of us now accept the proposition that Chaucer was sophisticated as readily as we do the proposition that the whale is a mammal. But unhappily, now that we've got rid of the naïve fiction, it is easy to fall into the opposite sort of mistake. This is to envision, in the *Canterbury Tales*, a highly urbane, literal-historical Chaucer setting out from Southwark on a specific day of a specific year (we even argue somewhat acrimoniously about dates and routes), in company with a group of persons who existed in real life and whom Chaucer, his reporter's eye peeled for every idiosyncrasy, determined to get down on paper—down, that is, to the last wart—so that books might be written identifying them. Whenever this accurate reporter says something especially fatuous—which is not infrequently—it is either ascribed to an opinion peculiar to the Middle Ages (sometimes very peculiar), or else Chaucer's tongue is said to be in his cheek.

Now a Chaucer with tongue-in-cheek is a vast improvement over a simple-minded Chaucer when one is trying to define the whole man, but it must lead to a loss of critical perception, and in particular to a confused notion of Chaucerian irony, to see in the Prologue a reporter who is acutely aware of the significance of what he sees but who sometimes, for ironic emphasis, interprets the evidence presented by his observation in a fashion directly contrary to what we expect. The proposition ought to be expressed in reverse: the reporter is, usually, acutely unaware of the significance of what he sees, no matter how sharply he sees it. He is, to be sure, permitted his lucid intervals, but in general he is the victim of the poet's pervasive—not merely sporadic—irony. And as such he is also the chief agent by which the poet achieves his wonderfully complex, ironic, comic, serious vision of a world which is but a devious and confused, infinitely various pilgrimage to a certain shrine. It is, as I hope to make clear, a good deal more than merely fitting that our guide on such a pilgrimage should be a man of such naïveté as the Chaucer who tells the tale of *Sir Thopas*. Let us accompany him a little distance.

It is often remarked that Chaucer really liked the Prioress very much, even though he satirized her gently—very gently. But this is an understatement: Chaucer the pilgrim may not be said merely to have liked the Prioress very much—he thought she was utterly charming. In the first twenty-odd lines of her portrait (A118 ff.) he employs, among other superlatives, the adverb *ful* seven times. Middle English uses *ful* where we use *very*, and if one translates the beginning of the portrait into a kind of basic English (which is what, in a way, it really is), one gets something like this: 'There was also a Nun, a Prioress, who was very sincere and modest in the way she smiled; her biggest oath was only "By saint Loy"; and she was called Madame Eglantine. She sang the divine service very well, intoning it in her nose very prettily, and she spoke French very nicely and elegantly'—and so on, down to the last gasp of sentimental appreciation. Indeed, the Prioress may be said to have transformed the rhetoric into something not unlike that of a very bright kindergarten child's descriptive theme. In his reaction to the Prioress Chaucer the pilgrim resembles another—if less—simple-hearted enthusiast: the Host, whose summons to her to tell a tale must be one of the politest speeches in the language. Not 'My lady Prioresse, a tale now!' but, 'as curteisly as it hadde been a maide',

> My lady Prioresse, by youre leve,
> So that I wiste I sholde you nat greve,
> I wolde deemen that ye telle sholde
> A tale next, if so were that ye wolde.
> Now wol ye vouche sauf, my lady dere? (B^2 1636–41)

Where the Prioress reduced Chaucer to superlatives, she reduces the Host to subjunctives.

There is no need here to go deeply into the Prioress. Eileen Power's illustrations from contemporary episcopal records show with what extraordinary economy the portrait has been packed with abuses typical of fourteenth-century nuns. The abuses, to be sure, are mostly petty, but it is clear enough that the Prioress, while a perfect lady, is anything but a perfect nun; and attempts to whitewash her, of which there have been many, can only proceed from an innocence of heart equal to Chaucer the pilgrim's and undoubtedly directly influenced by it. For he, of course, is quite swept away by her irrelevant *sensibilité*, and as a result misses much of the point of what he sees. No doubt he feels that he has come a long way, socially speaking, since his encounter with the Black Knight in the forest, and he knows, or thinks he knows, a little more of what it's all about: in this case it seems to be mostly about good manners, kindness to animals, and female charm. Thus it has been argued that Chaucer's appreciation for the Prioress as a sort of heroine of courtly romance *manquée* actually reflects the sophistication of the living Chaucer, an urbane man who cared little whether amiable nuns were good nuns. But it seems a curious form of sophistication that permits itself to babble superlatives; and indeed, if this is sophistication, it is the kind generally seen in the least experienced people—one that reflects a wide-eyed wonder at the glamour of the great world. It is just what one might expect of a bourgeois exposed to the splendours of high society, whose values, such as they are, he eagerly accepts. And that is precisely what Chaucer the pilgrim is, and what he does.

If the Prioress's appeal to him is through elegant femininity, the Monk's is through imposing virility. Of this formidable and important prelate the pilgrim does not say, with Placebo,

> I woot wel that my lord can more than I:
> What that he saith, I holde it ferm and stable, (E1498–99)

but he acts Placebo's part to perfection. He is as impressed with the Monk as the Monk is, and accepts him on his own terms and at face value, never sensing that those terms imply complete condemnation of Monk *qua* Monk. The Host is also impressed by the Monk's virility, but having no sense of Placebonian propriety (he is himself a most virile man) he makes indecent jokes about it. This, naturally, offends the pilgrim's sense of decorum: there is a note of deferential commiseration in his comment, 'This worthy Monk took al in pacience' (B3155). Inevitably when the Monk establishes hunting as the highest activity of which religious man is capable, 'I saide his opinion was good' (A183). As one of the pilgrim's spiritual heirs was later to say, Very like a whale; but not, of course, like a fish out of water.

Wholehearted approval for the values that important persons subscribe to is seen again in the portrait of the Friar. This amounts to a prolonged gratulation for the efficiency the deplorable Hubert shows in undermining the fabric of the Church by turning St Francis's ideal inside out:

> Ful swetely herde he confessioun
> And plesant was his absolucioun.
>
> For unto swich a worthy man as he
> Accorded nat, as by his facultee,
> To have with sike lazars aquaintaunce. (A221–22, 243–45)

It is sometimes said that Chaucer did not like the Friar. Whether Chaucer the man would have liked such a Friar is, for our present purposes, irrelevant. But if the pilgrim does not unequivocally express his liking for him, it is only because in his humility he does not feel that, with important people, his own likes and dislikes are material: such importance is its own reward, and can gain no lustre from Geoffrey, who, when the Friar is attacked by the Summoner, is ready to show him the same sympathy he shows the Monk (see D1265–67).

Once he has finished describing the really important people on the pilgrimage the pilgrim's tone changes, for he can now concern himself with the bourgeoisie, members of his own class for whom he does not have to show such profound respect. Indeed, he can even afford to be a little patronizing at times, and have his little joke at the expense of the too-busy lawyer. But such indirect assertions of his own superiority do not prevent him from giving substance to the old cynicism that the only motive recognized by the middle class is the profit motive, for his interest and admiration for the bourgeois pilgrims is centred mainly in their material prosperity and their ability to increase it. He starts, properly enough, with the out-and-out moneygrubber, the Merchant, and after turning aside for that *lusus naturae*, the non-profit-motivated Clerk, proceeds to the Lawyer, who, despite the pilgrim's little joke, is the best and best-paid ever; the Franklin, twenty-one admiring lines on appetite, so expensively catered to; the Gildsmen, cheered up the social ladder, 'For catel hadde they ynough and rente' (A373); and the Physician, again the best and richest. In this series the portrait of the Clerk is generally held to be an ideal one, containing no irony; but while it is ideal, it seems to reflect the pilgrim's sense of values in his joke about the Clerk's failure to make money: is not this still typical of the half-patronizing, half-admiring *un*understanding that practical men of business display towards academics? But in any case the portrait is a fine companion-piece for those in which material prosperity is the main interest both of the characters described and of the describer.

Of course, this is not the sole interest of so gregarious—if shy—a person as Chaucer the pilgrim. Many of the characters have the additional advantage of being good companions, a faculty that receives a high valuation in the Prologue. To be good company might, indeed, atone for certain serious defects of character. Thus the Shipman, whose callous cruelty is duly noted, seems fairly well redeemed in the assertion, 'And certainly he was a good felawe' (A395). At this point an uneasy sensation that even tongue-in-cheek irony will not compensate for the lengths to which Chaucer is going in his approbation of this sinister seafarer sometimes causes editors to note that *a good felawe* means 'a rascal'. But I can find no evidence that it ever meant a rascal. Of course, all tritely approbative expressions enter easily into ironic connotation, but the phrase *means* a good companion, which is just what Chaucer means. And if, as he says of the Shipman, 'Of nice conscience took he no keep' (A398), Chaucer the pilgrim was doing the same with respect to him.

Nothing that has been said has been meant to imply that the pilgrim was unable to recognise, and deplore, a rascal when he saw one. He could, provided the rascality was situated in a member of the lower classes and provided it was, in any case, somewhat wider than a barn door: Miller, Manciple, Reeve, Summoner, and Pardoner are all acknowledged to be rascals. But rascality generally has, after all, the laudable object of making money, which gives it a kind of validity, if not dignity. These portraits, while in them the pilgrim, prioress-like conscious of the finer aspects of life, does deplore such matters as the Miller's indelicacy of language, contain a note of ungrudging admiration for efficient thievery. It is perhaps fortunate for the pilgrim's reputation as a judge of men that he sees through the Pardoner, since it is the Pardoner's particular tragedy that, except in Church, every one can see through him at a glance; but in Church he remains to the pilgrim 'a noble ecclesiaste' (A708). The equally repellent Summoner, a practising bawd, is partially redeemed by his also being a good fellow, 'a gentil harlot and a kinde' (A647), and by the fact that for a moderate bribe he will neglect to summon: the pilgrim apparently subscribes to the popular definition of the best policeman as the one who acts the least policely.

Therefore Chaucer is tolerant, and has his little joke about the Summoner's small Latin—a very small joke, though one of the most amusing aspects of the pilgrim's character is the pleasure he takes in his own jokes, however small. But the Summoner goes too far when he cynically suggests that purse is the Archdeacon's hell, causing Chaucer to respond with a fine show of righteous respect for the instruments of spiritual punishment. The only trouble is that his enthusiastic defence of them carries *him* too far, so that after having warned us that excommunication will indeed damn our souls—

> But wel I woot he lied right in deede:
> Of cursing oughte eech gilty man him drede,
> For curs wol slee right as assoiling savith— (A659–61)

he goes on to remind us that it will also cause considerable inconvenience to our bodies: 'And also war him of a *Significavit*' (A662). Since a *Significavit* is the writ accomplishing the imprisonment of the excommunicate, the line provides perhaps the neatest—and most misunderstood—Chaucerian anticlimax in the Prologue.

I have avoided mentioning, hitherto, the pilgrim's reactions to the really good people on the journey—the Knight, the Parson, the Plowman. One might reasonably ask how his uncertain sense of values may be reconciled with the enthusiasm he shows for their rigorous integrity. The question could, of course, be shrugged off with a remark on the irrelevance to art of exact consistency, even to art distinguished by its verisimilitude. But I am not sure that there is any basic inconsistency. It is the nature of the pilgrim to admire all kinds of superlatives, and the fact that he often admires superlatives devoid of—or opposed to—genuine virtue does not inhibit his equal admiration for virtue incarnate. He is not, after all, a bad man; he is, to place him in his literary tradition, merely an average man, or mankind: *homo*, not very *sapiens* to be sure, but with the very best intentions, making his pilgrimage through the world in search of what is good, and showing himself, too frequently, able to recognize the good only when it is spectacularly so. Spenser's Una glows with a kind of spontaneous incandescence, so that the Red Cross Knight, mankind in search of holiness, knows her as good; but he thinks that Duessa is good, too. Virtue concretely embodied in Una or the Parson presents no problems to the well-intentioned observer, but in a world consisting mostly of imperfections, accurate evaluations are difficult for a pilgrim who, like mankind, is naïve. The pilgrim's ready appreciation for the virtuous characters is perhaps the greatest tribute that could be paid to their virtue, and their spiritual simplicity is, I think, enhanced by the intellectual simplicity of the reporter.

The pilgrim belongs, of course, to a very old—and very new—tradition of the fallible first person singular. His most exact modern counterpart is perhaps Lemuel Gulliver who, in his search for the good, failed dismally to perceive the difference between the pursuit of reason and the pursuits of reasonable horses: one may be sure that the pilgrim would have whinnied with the best of them. In his own century he is related to Long Will of *Piers Plowman*, a more explicit seeker after the good, but just as unswerving in his inability correctly to evaluate what he sees. Another kinsman is the protagonist of the *Pearl*, mankind whose heart is set on a transitory good that has been lost—who, for very natural reasons, confuses earthly with spiritual values. Not entirely unrelated is the protagonist of Gower's *Confessio Amantis*, an old man seeking for an impossible earthly love that seems to him the only good. And in more subtle fashion there is the teller of Chaucer's story of *Troilus and Criseide*, who, while not a true protagonist, performs some of the same functions. For this unloved 'servant of the servants of love' falls in love with Criseide so persuasively that almost every male reader of the poem imitates him, so that we all share the heartbreak of Troilus and sometimes, in the intensity of our heartbreak, fail to learn what Troilus did. Finally, of course, there is Dante of the *Divine Comedy*, the most exalted member of the family and perhaps the immediate original of these other first-person pilgrims.

Artistically the device of the *persona* has many functions, so integrated with one another that to try to sort them out produces both oversimplification and distortion. The most obvious, with which this paper has been dealing—distortedly, is to present a vision of the social world imposed on one of the moral world. Despite their verisimilitude most, if not all, of the characters described in the Prologue are taken directly from stock and recur again and again in medieval literature. Langland in his own Prologue and elsewhere depicts many of them: the hunting monk, the avaricious friar, the thieving miller, the hypocritical pardoner, the unjust stewards, even, in little, the all-too-human nun. But while Langland uses the device of the *persona* with considerable skill in the conduct of his allegory, he uses it hardly at all in portraying the inhabitants of the social world: these are described directly, with the poet's own voice. It was left to Chaucer to turn the ancient stock satirical characters into real people assembled for a pilgrimage, and to have them described, with all their traditional faults upon them, by another pilgrim who records faithfully each fault without, for the most part, recognizing that it is a fault and frequently felicitating its possessor for possessing it. One result—though not the only result—is a moral realism much more significant than the literary realism which is a part of it and for which it is sometimes mistaken; this moral realism discloses a world in which humanity is prevented by its own myopia, the myopia of the describer, from seeing what the dazzlingly attractive externals of life really represent. In most of the analogues mentioned above the fallible first person receives, at the end of the book, the education he has needed: the pilgrim arrives somewhere. Chaucer never completed the *Canterbury Tales*, but in the Prologue to the Parson's Tale he seems to have been doing, rather hastily, what his contemporaries had done: when, with the sun nine-and-twenty degrees from the horizon, the twenty-nine pilgrims come to a certain—unnamed—*thropes ende* (112), then the pilgrimage seems no longer to have Canterbury as its destination, but rather, I suspect, the Celestial City of which the Parson speaks.

If one insists that Chaucer was not a moralist but a comic writer (a distinction without a difference), then the device of the *persona* may be taken primarily as serving comedy. It has been said earlier that the several Chaucers must have inhabited one body, and in that sense the fictional first person is no fiction at all. In an oral tradition of literature the first person probably always shared the personality of his creator: thus Dante of the *Divine Comedy* was physically Dante the Florentine; the John Gower of the *Confessio* was also Chaucer's friend John Gower; and Long Will was, I am sure, some one named William Langland, who was both long and wilful. And it is equally certain that Chaucer the pilgrim, 'a popet in an arm t'enbrace' (B1891), was in every physical respect

Chaucer the man, whom one can imagine reading his work to a courtly audience, as in the portrait appearing in one of the MSS of *Troilus*. One can imagine also the delight of the audience which heard the Prologue read in this way, and which was aware of the similarities and dissimilarities between Chaucer, the man before them, and Chaucer the pilgrim, both of whom they could see with simultaneous vision. The Chaucer they knew was physically, one gathers, a little ludicrous; a bourgeois, but one who was known as a practical and successful man of the court; possessed perhaps of a certain diffidence of manner, reserved, deferential to the socially imposing persons with whom he was associated; a bit absent-minded, but affable and, one supposes, very good company—a good fellow; sagacious and highly perceptive. This Chaucer was telling them of another who, lacking some of his chief qualities, nevertheless possessed many of his characteristics, though in a different state of balance, and each one probably distorted just enough to become laughable without becoming unrecognizable: deference into a kind of snobbishness, affability into an over-readiness to please, practicality into Babbittry, perception into inspection, absence of mind into dimness of wit; a Chaucer acting in some respects just as Chaucer himself might have acted but unlike his creator the kind of man, withal, who could mistake a group of stock satirical types for living persons endowed with all sorts of superlative qualities. The constant interplay of these two Chaucers must have produced an exquisite and most ingratiating humour—as, to be sure, it still does. This comedy reaches its superb climax when Chaucer the pilgrim, resembling in so many ways Chaucer the poet, can answer the Host's demand for a story only with a rhyme he 'lerned longe agoon' (B1899)—*Sir Thopas*, which bears the same complex relation to the kind of romance it satirizes and to Chaucer's own poetry as Chaucer the pilgrim does to the pilgrims he describes and to Chaucer the poet.

Earlier in this paper I proved myself no gentleman (though I hope a scholar) by being rude to the Prioress, and hence to the many who like her and think that Chaucer liked her too. It is now necessary to retract. Undoubtedly Chaucer the man would, like his fictional representative, have found her charming and looked on her with affection. To have got on so well in so changeable a world Chaucer must have got on well with the people in it, and it is doubtful that one may get on with people merely by pretending to like them: one's heart has to be in it. But the third entity, Chaucer the poet, operates in a realm which is above and subsumes those in which Chaucer the man and Chaucer the pilgrim have their being. In this realm prioresses may be simultaneously evaluated as marvellously amiable ladies and as prioresses. In his poem the poet arranges for the moralist to define austerely what ought to be and for his fictional representative—who, as the representative of all mankind, is no mere fiction—to go on affirming affectionately what is. The two points of view, in strict moral logic diametrically opposed, are somehow made harmonious in Chaucer's wonderfully comic attitude, that double vision that is his ironical essence. The mere critic performs his etymological function by taking the Prioress apart and clumsily separating her good parts from her bad; but the poet's function is to build her incongruous and inharmonious parts into an inseparable whole which is infinitely greater than its parts. In this complex structure both the latent moralist and the naïve reporter have important positions, but I am not persuaded that in every case it is possible to determine which of them has the last word.[1]

ARTHUR W. HOFFMAN

Chaucer's Prologue to Pilgrimage: The Two Voices[†]

Criticism of the portraits in Chaucer's General Prologue to *The Canterbury Tales* has taken various directions: some critics have praised the portraits especially for their realism, sharp individuality, adroit psychology, and vividness of felt life; others, working in the genetic direction, have pointed out actual historical persons who might have sat for the portraits; others, appealing to the light of the medieval sciences, have shown the portraits to be filled, though not burdened, with the lore of Chaucer's day, and to have sometimes typical identities like case histories. Miss Bowden,[1] in her recent study of the Prologue, assembles the fruits of many earlier studies and gives the text an impressive resonance by sketching historical and social norms and ideals, the facts and the standards of craft, trade, and profession, so that the form of the portraits can be tested in the light of possible conformities, mean or noble, to things as they were or to things as they ought to have been.

It is not unlikely that the critics who have explored in these various directions would be found in agreement on one commonplace, a metaphor which some of them indeed have used, the designation of the portraits in the General Prologue as figures in a tapestry. It is less likely that all of the critics would agree as to the implications of this metaphor, but it seems to me that the commonplace deserves to be explored and some of its implications tested. The commonplace implies that the portraits which appear in the General Prologue have a designed togetherness, that the portraits exist as parts of a unity.

Such a unity, it may be argued, is partly a function of the exterior framework of a pilgrimage to Canterbury; all the portraits are portraits of pilgrims:

> At nyght was come into that hostelrye
> Wel nyne and twenty in a compaignye,
> Of sondry folk, by aventure yfalle
> In felaweshipe, and pilgrimes were they alle (23–26)[2]

But the unity of the Prologue may be also partly a matter of internal relationships among the portraits, relationships which are many and various

1. Books referred to or cited in this paper are G. L. Kittredge, *Chaucer and His Poetry* (Cambridge, Mass., 1915), p. 45; Eileen Power, *Medieval People* (London, 1924), pp. 59–84. Robinson's note to A650 records the opinion that *a good felawe* means a 'rascal'. The medieval reader's expectation that the first person in a work of fiction would represent mankind generally and at the same time would physically resemble the author is commented on by Leo Spitzer in an interesting note in *Traditio*, iv. (1946), 414–22.

† From *ELH* 21 (1954): 1–16.

1. Muriel Bowden, *A Commentary on the General Prologue to the Canterbury Tales* (New York, 1948).

2. All references to the text of *The Canterbury Tales* are to *The Poetical Works of Chaucer*, ed. F. N. Robinson (Cambridge, Mass., 1933).

among "sondry folk." One cannot hope to survey all of these, but the modest objective of studying some of the aesthetically important internal relationships is feasible.

If one begins with the unity that is exterior to the portraits, the unity that contains them, one faces directly the question of the nature of pilgrimage as it is defined in this dramatic poem. What sort of framework does the Prologue in fact define? Part of the answer is in the opening lines, and it is not a simple answer because the definition there ranges from the upthrust and burgeoning of life as a seasonal and universal event to a particular outpouring of people, pilgrims, gathered briefly at the Tabard Inn in Southwark, drifting, impelled, bound, called to the shrine of Thomas à Becket at Canterbury. The pilgrimage is set down in the calendar of seasons as well as in the calendar of piety; nature impels and supernature draws. "Go, go, go," says the bird; "Come," says the saint.

In the opening lines of the Prologue springtime is characterized in terms of procreation, and a pilgrimage of people to Canterbury is just one of the many manifestations of the life thereby produced. The phallicism of the opening lines presents the impregnating of a female March by a male April, and a marriage of water and earth. The marriage is repeated and varied immediately as a fructifying of "holt and heeth" by Zephirus, a marriage of air and earth. This mode of symbolism and these symbols as parts of a rite of spring have a long background of tradition; as Professor Cook[3] once pointed out, there are eminent passages of this sort in Aeschylus and Euripides, in Lucretius, in Virgil's *Georgics*, in Columella, and in the *Pervigilium Veneris*, and Professor Robinson cites Guido delle Colonne, Boccaccio, Petrarch, and Boethius. Zephirus is the only overt mythological figure in Chaucer's passage, but, in view of the instigative role generally assigned to Aphrodite in the rite of spring, she is perhaps to be recognized here, as Professor Cook suggested, in the name of April, which was her month both by traditional association and by one of the two ancient etymologies.[4] Out of this context of the quickening of the earth presented naturally and symbolically in the broadest terms, the Prologue comes to pilgrimage and treats pilgrimage first as an event in the calendar of nature, one aspect of the general springtime surge of human energy and longing. There are the attendant suggestions of the renewal of human mobility after the rigor and confinement of winter, the revival of wayfaring now that the ways are open. The horizon extends to distant shrines and foreign lands, and the attraction of the strange and faraway is included before the vision narrows and focusses upon its English specifications and the pilgrimage to the shrine at Canterbury with the vows and gratitude that send pilgrims there. One way of regarding the structure of this opening passage would emphasize the magnificent progression from the broadest inclusive generality to the firmest English specification, from the whole western tradition of the celebration of spring (including, as Cook pointed out, such a non-English or very doubtfully English detail as "the droghte of March") to a local event of English society and English Christendom, from natural forces in their most general operation to a very

3. Albert S. Cook, "Chaucerian Papers—1: 1. Prologue 1–11," *Transactions of the Connecticut Academy of Arts and Sciences*, XXIII (New Haven, 1919), pp. 5–21.
4. Cook, pp. 5–10.

specific and Christian manifestation of those forces. And yet one may regard the structure in another way, too; if, in the calendar of nature, the passage moves from general to particular, does it not, in the calendar of piety, move from nature to something that includes and oversees nature? Does not the passage move from an activity naturally generated and impelled to a governed activity, from force to *telos*? Does not the passage move from Aphrodite and *amor* in their secular operation to the sacred embrace of "the hooly blisful martir" and of *amor dei*?

The transition from nature to supernature is emphasized by the contrast between the healthful physical vigor of the opening lines and the reference to sickness that appears in line 18. On the one hand, it is physical vitality which conditions the pilgrimage; on the other hand, sickness occasions pilgrimage. It is, in fact, rather startling to come upon the word "seeke" at the end of this opening passage, because it is like a breath of winter across the landscape of spring. "Whan that they were seeke" may, of course, refer literally to illnesses of the winter just past, but, in any event, illness belongs symbolically to the inclement season. There is also, however, a strong parallelism between the beginning and end of this passage, a parallelism that has to do with restorative power. The physical vitality of the opening is presented as restorative of the dry earth; the power of the saint is presented as restorative of the sick. The seasonal restoration of nature parallels a supernatural kind of restoration that knows no season; the supernatural kind of restoration involves a wielding and directing of the forces of nature. The Prologue begins, then, by presenting a double view of the Canterbury pilgrimage: the pilgrimage is one tiny manifestation of a huge tide of life, but then, too, the tide of life ebbs and flows in response to the power which the pilgrimage acknowledges, the power symbolized by "the hooly blisful martir."

After line 18 the process of particularizing is continued, moving from "that seson" just defined to a day and to a place and to a person in Southwark at the Tabard, and thence to the portraits of the pilgrims. The double view of pilgrimage is enhanced and extended by the portraits where it appears, in one aspect, as a range of motivation. This range of motivation is from the sacred to the secular and on to the profane—"profane" in the sense of motivations actually subversive of the sacred. All the pilgrims are, in fact, granted an ostensible sacred motive; all of them are seeking the shrine. The distances that we are made aware of are both *within* some of the portraits, where a gulf yawns between ostensible and actual motivation, and *between* the portraits, where the motivation of the Knight and the Parson is near one end of the spectrum, and the motivation of the Summoner and the Pardoner near the other end. There is such an impure but blameless mixture as the motivation of the Prioress; there is the secular pilgrimage of the Wife of Bath, impelled so powerfully and frankly by Saint Venus rather than drawn by Saint Thomas, and goaded by a Martian desire to acquire and dominate another husband; in the case of the Prioress, an inescapable doubt as to the quality of *amor* hesitates between the sacred and secular, and in the case of the thoroughly secular Wife of Bath, doubt hesitates between the secular and the profane while the portrait shows the ostensible motive that belongs to all the pilgrims shaken without ever being subverted, contradicted perhaps, brazenly opposed, but still acknowledged and offered, not, at any rate, hypocritically betrayed. In the area of motivation, the portraits seem to propose, ultimately, a fundamental, inescapable ambiguity as part of the human condition; prayer for the purification of motive is valid for all the pilgrims. And the pilgrims who move, pushed by impulse and drawn by vows, none merely impelled and none perfectly committed, reflect, in their human ambiguity, the broad problem of origins and ends, the stubbornness of matter and the power of spirit, together with ideas of cosmic resolution and harmony in which source and end are reconciled and seem to be the same, the purposes of nature and supernature found to be at one, the two restorative powers akin, the kinds of love not discontinuous, Saint Venus and Saint Thomas different and at odds yet not at war, within the divine purpose which contains both.

The portraits of the Knight and the Squire have a particular interest. The relationships between these two portraits are governed by and arise out of the natural relationship of father and son. Consanguinity provides the base for a dramatic relationship, and at the same time is the groundwork for a modestly generalized metaphor of age and youth. Each portrait is enhanced and defined by the presence of the other: the long roll of the Knight's campaigns, and the Squire's little opportunity ("so litel space"), a few raids enumerated in one line; a series of past tenses, a history, for the Knight, and for the Squire a present breaking forth in active participles; the Knight not "gay," wearing fustian soiled by his coat of mail, "bismotered," the Squire bright and fresh and colorful; the Knight meek and quiet,—or so the portrait leaves him—beside the Squire, who sings and whistles all the day. The Knight's love is an achieved devotion, a matter of pledges fulfilled and of values, if not completely realized, yet woven into the fabric of experience (ideals—"trouthe," "honour," "fredom," "curteisie"). The Squire is a lover, a warm and eager lover, paying court to his lady and sleeping no more than the nightingale. In the one, the acquired, tutored, disciplined, elevated, enlarged love, the piety; and in the other, the love channelled into an elaborate social ritual, a parody piety, but still emphatically fresh and full of natural impulse. One cannot miss the creation of the Squire in conventional images of nature, and meadow, the flowers, the freshness like May, the lover like the nightingale,—comparisons that are a kind of re-emergence of the opening lines of the Prologue, the springtime surge of youthful, natural energy that animates the beginning. "Go, go, go," the bird's voice, is a major impulse in the portrait of the Squire and in the Squire's pilgrimage; the Knight's pilgrimage is more nearly a response to the voice of the saint. Yet the Squire is within the belt of rule, and learning the calendar of piety. The concluding couplet of the portrait

> Curteis he was, lowely and servysable,
> And carf biforn his fader at the table. (99–100)

has the effect of bending all the youth, energy, color, audibleness, and high spirit of the Squire to the service of his father, the Knight, and to attendance on his pilgrimage, with perhaps a suggestion of the present submitting to the serious and respected values served and communicated by the past, the natural and the imposed submitting of the son to his natural father, and beyond him to the supernatural goal, the shrine to which the father directs his pilgrimage.

The portraits of the Knight and the Squire represent one of the ways in which portraiture takes into account and develops the double definition of pilgrimage which is established at the beginning. The double definition of pilgrimage is involved in a different way in the portrait of the Prioress; there it appears as a delicately poised ambiguity. Two definitions appear as two faces of one coin. Subsequently, when the portrait of the Prioress is seen together with the portraits of the Monk and the Friar, a sequence is realized, running from ambiguity to emphatic discrepancy, and the satire that circles the impenetrable duality of sacred and secular impulse in the case of the Prioress knifes in as these impulses are drawn apart in the case of the Monk and strikes vigorously in the still wider breach that appears in the case of the Friar. What is illustrated within the portraits is amplified by a designed sequence.

The delicate balance in the picture of the Prioress has been generally recognized and has perhaps been only the more clearly exhibited by occasional seesawing in the critical interpretation of the portrait in which the satiric elements are sometimes represented as heavy, sometimes as slight, sometimes sinking the board, and sometimes riding light and high. There is, perhaps, no better illustration of the delicacy of the balance than the fact that the Prioress's very presence on a pilgrimage, as several commentators have pointed out, may be regarded as the first satiric touch. The very act of piety is not free from the implication of imperfection; the Prioress is obligated to a cloistered piety that serves and worships God without going on a journey to seek a shrine, and prioresses were specifically and repeatedly enjoined from going on pilgrimages. Prioresses did, nevertheless, go as pilgrims, so that Chaucer's Prioress is not departing from the norm of behavior of persons in her office so much as she is departing from the sanctioned ideal of behavior.[5] In the case of the Prioress, the blemish is sufficiently technical to have only faint satiric coloring; it is not the notable kind of blemish recognized in all times and all places. Nevertheless, it is precisely this kind of hint of a spot that places the Prioress at one end of a sequence in which the more obviously blemished Monk and Friar appear. If we pose a double question—What kind of woman is the Prioress, and what kind of prioress is the woman?—the portrait responds more immediately to the first part of the question, and leaves the answer to the second part largely in the area of implication. The portrait occupies forty-five lines, and more than three-fourths of the lines have to do with such matters as the Prioress's blue eyes, her red mouth, the shape of her nose and width of her forehead, her ornaments and dress, her table manners, her particular brand of French, her pets and what she fed them, and her tenderness about mice. It is, of course, one of the skilful arts of these portraits to work with surfaces and make the surfaces convey and reveal what lies beneath, but it should be observed that in the case of the Parson—or even in the case of the Knight—a character is arrived at almost entirely without physical and superficial detail. One need not take the emphatic surface in the portrait of the Prioress as necessarily pejorative in its implication; it need not follow that the Prioress is a shallow and superficial person, and, in consequence, sharply satirized. But the portrait does seem, by means of its

5. The relevance of the ideal sanctioned character of an office to the portrait of a person will appear again strikingly in the case of the Summoner and the Pardoner.

emphasis on surfaces, to define the Prioress as woman, and strongly enough so that tension between the person and her office, between the given human nature and the assumed sacred obligation is put vividly before us, and rather as the observation of a fact than as the instigation of a judgment. In the cases of the Monk and the Friar, the tension is so exacerbated that judgment is, in the case of the Monk, incited, and in the case of the Friar, both incited and inflamed to severity.

In the portrait of the Prioress the double view of pilgrimage appears both in an ambiguity of surfaces, and in an implied inner range of motivation. In the surfaces there is a sustained hovering effect: the name, Eglentyne, is romance, and "simple and coy" is a romance formula, but she *is* a nun, by whatever name, and "simple" and "coy," aside from their romance connotations have meanings ("simple" and "modest") appropriate enough to a nun; there are the coral beads and the green gauds, but they *are* a rosary; there are the fluted wimple and the exposed forehead, but the costume *is* a nun's habit; there is the golden brooch shining brightly, but it *is* a religious emblem. Which shall be taken as principal, which as modifying and subordinate? Are the departures or the conformities more significant of her nature? Are her Stratford French and her imitation of court manners more important than the fact that she sings well and properly the divine service? Do we detect vanity in her singing well, or do we rely on what she sings and accept her worship as well performed—to the glory of God? The ambiguity of these surface indications leads into the implied range of motivation; this implied range has been generally recognized in the motto—"*Amor vincit omnia*"—on the Prioress's golden brooch, and the implications set up in the portrait as a whole seem to be clustered and tightly fastened in this ornament and symbol.

The motto itself has, in the course of history, gone its own double pilgrimage to the shrine of Saint Venus and to sacred shrines; the original province of the motto was profane, but it was drawn over to a sacred meaning and soon became complexly involved with and compactly significant of both. Professor Lowes comments on the motto as it pertains to the Prioress:

> Now is it earthly love that conquers all, now heavenly; the phrase plays back and forth between the two. And it is precisely that happy ambiguity of the convention—itself the result of an earlier transfer—that makes Chaucer's use of it here . . . a master stroke. *Which of the two loves does "amor" mean to the Prioress?* I do not know; but I think she thought she meant love celestial.[6]

Professor Lowes, presumably, does not really expect to see the matter concluded one way or the other and finds this very inconclusiveness, hovering between two answers, one of the excellences of the portrait. There is, however, a certain amount of illumination to be gained, though not an answer to the question as formulated by Professor Lowes, by asking the question another way and considering an answer in terms that lie outside of the Prioress's motivation. Put the question in this form: Which of the two loves does the *portrait* in the context of the Prologue mean by *amor*? The answer to this question, of course, is *both*. On the one hand, profane love or the

6. John Livingston Lowes, *Convention and Revolt* (Boston and New York, 1919), p. 66.

love of earthly things does overcome all; the little vanities and pretensions, the love of color and decoration and dress, the affection squandered in little extravagances toward pets, the pity and tender emotion wasted upon a trapped mouse—the multiplicity of secular, impulsive loves threatens to and could ultimately stifle the dedication to the celestial love. This answer is, in fact, a version of the Prioress's character and motivation sometimes offered. It actually implies one half of the view of pilgrimage—the natural powers that move people and that may usurp the whole character. But the other answer—celestial love conquers all things—also applies to the portrait, though it is not very easily arrived at in terms of the Prioress's motivation. Here we are dealing with the ostensible meaning of the motto, the ideal meaning of the motto as worn by a prioress—what it ought to mean in terms of her office. And, no matter what the impurity of the Prioress's motives, no matter what she means or thinks she means by the motto, the motto does, in the calendar of piety, mean that God's love is powerful over all things, powerful in this case over the vanity that may be involved in the wearing of the brooch, powerful over all the shallowness and limitation and reduction and misdirection of love that the Prioress may be guilty of, powerful over all her departures from or misunderstandings of discipline and obligation and vow, powerful over all inadequacy, able to overcome the faults of God's human instruments and make this woman's divine office valid. The motto and the portrait of which it is the conclusion appreciate both the secular impulses and the sacred redemptive will, but there is no doubt which love it is that is crowned with ultimate power.

Chaucer has found ways, as in the case of the Prioress, of making an ideal or standard emerge within a portrait. The standard may be ambiguously stated or heavily involved in irony, but it is almost always present, and nowhere with greater effectiveness than in the most sharply satiric portraits. This, I take it, is the effect of the formula of worthiness which is applied to so many of the pilgrims. A character is declared to be "worthy" or "the best that ever was" of his craft or profession or office, and frequently under circumstances that make the statement jarring and the discrepancy obvious. There is a definite shock, for example, when Friar Huberd is declared to be a "worthy lymytour," or the Pardoner "a noble ecclesiaste." Even when the satiric thrust has two directions, striking both at the individual and at the group to which he belongs, the implication has nevertheless been lodged in the portrait that there could be, for example, a worthy friar, or a pardoner who was indeed a noble ecclesiastic. The reader is, as it were, tripped in the act of judging and reminded that if he condemns these figures, if they appear culpable, there must be some sort of standard by which they are so judged, by which they appear so.

Chaucer has also adopted the method of including ideal or nearly ideal portraits among the pilgrims. There are, for example, the Knight and the Plowman, figures at either end of the secular range, and among the clerical figures there is the Parson. A host of relative judgments, of course, are set up by devices of sequence and obvious pairing and contrasting of portraits. It is the ideal portraits, however, that somehow preside over all these judgments and comparisons, and it is to them that the relative distinctions are presented for a kind of penultimate judgment. Prioress, Monk, and Friar, and all the other clerical figures are reckoned with the Parson who is, in fact, made to speak in an accent of judgment upon the clerical figures who go astray—". . . if gold ruste, what shal iren do?" (We may remember the Prioress's shining gold brooch, the Monk's gold pin, and, among the secular figures, the Physician who so doubly regarded gold as a sovereign remedy.)

Chaucer has used an interesting device for undergirding the ideal portrait of the Parson. He employs consanguinity with metaphorical effect. After the assertions which declare that the Parson "first . . . wroghte, and afterward . . . taughte," the actualizing of Christian ideals is supported by the representation of the Parson as brother to the Plowman. It is the Parson's Christian obligation to treat men as brothers, and the portrait abundantly affirms that he does so. Making him actually the brother of the Plowman brilliantly insists that what supernature calls for is performed by the Parson and, more than that, comes by nature to him.[7] The achieved harmony both comes from above and rises out of the ground; sacred and secular are linked, the shepherd of souls and the tiller of the soil. This is a vantage point from which the conflicts of secular and sacred, of nature and supernature, are seen in a revealing light, a point at which one sees reflected in the clear mirror of ideal characters and an actual-ideal relationship the fundamental double view of pilgrimage established in the beginning.

The double definition of pilgrimage is differently but nonetheless revealingly illuminated by the portraits of another fraternizing pair, the Summoner and Pardoner, who conclude the sequence of pilgrims. The illumination here is not clarified by way of ideal characters but somehow refracted and intensified by the dark surfaces upon which it falls. The darkness is most visible in connection with the theme of love, which appears here in a sinister and terrible distortion. The hot and lecherous Summoner, the type of sexual unrestraint, is represented as harmonizing in song with the impotent Pardoner, the eunuch; the deep rumbling voice and the thin effeminate voice are singing, "Com hider, love, to me!" The song, in this context, becomes both a promiscuous and perverted invitation and an unconscious symbolic acknowledgment of the absence of and the need for love, love that comes neither to the grasping physical endeavor of the Summoner nor to the physical incapacity of the Pardoner—nor to their perverted spirits. Love has been treated in the Prologue from the beginning as dual in character, a matter both of the body and the spirit, the *amor* symbolized by Venus, sung by the Squire, equivocally illustrated by the Prioress, lustily celebrated by the Wife of Bath; and the *amor dei*, the love shadowily there beyond all the secular forms of love, a hovering presence among the pilgrims and sometimes close, as to the Knight and the Parson and the Plowman, and symbolized in the saint's shrine which is the goal of all of them. On this view, the song of the Summoner and the Pardoner is a superb dramatic irony acknowledging the full extent of their need and loss, the love of God which they ought to strive for, the love which they desperately need.

The office which each of these men is supposed to fulfill should be taken into account. The Summoner is, ostensibly, an instrument through whom divine justice, in a practical way, operates in the world. There are, in the

7. There is, of course, plenty of actual basis for representing a parson as a son of the soil; the connection is not merely an artistic and symbolic device.

portrait, a few touches that may be reminders of the ultimate source of his authority and function: his "*Questio quid iuris*," though it is represented satirically as the sum and substance of his knowledge, and posed as a question, *is* legitimately the substance of his knowledge—his province is law, especially the divine law; "*Significavit*" is the opening word of a legal writ, a dreaded worldly pronouncement of divine judgment, excommunication; he is physically a fearful figure from whom children run (not the divine love which suffers them to come), and some of the physical details may be reminders of noble and awesome aspects of divine justice—his "fyr-reed cherubynnes face" and the voice described in a significant analogy as like a trumpet, "Was nevere trompe of half so greet a soun." The Pardoner, on the other hand, is the ostensible instrument of divine mercy and love. Many of the pardoners, as Miss Bowden points out, went so far as to pretend to absolve both *a poena* and *a culpa*, thereby usurping, in the pretended absolution *a culpa*, a function which theological doctrine reserved to God and His grace. In any case, their legitimate functions were an appeal for charity and an extension of God's mercy and love. The Pardoner, it should be observed, is, compared to the Summoner, an attractive figure. We may be reminded of the superior affinity of the Pardoner's office by the veil which he has sewed upon his cap, the copy of St. Veronica's veil which is supposed to have received the imprint of Christ's face.[8]

The justice and love[9] of which the Summoner and Pardoner are emissaries are properly complementary and harmoniously, though paradoxically and mysteriously, related, so that the advances that are being made both of persons and of values are, in a very serious sense, proper to this pair. The radical physical distinctness of Summoner and Pardoner is at this level the definition of two aspects of supernature; there is the same employment of physical metaphor here that there is in the portraits of the Parson and the Plowman, but with the difference that light comes out of darkness, and out of the gravest corruption of nature the supernatural relationship emerges clarified in symbol. The Summoner cannot finally pervert, and the Pardoner's impotence cannot finally prevent; the divine justice and love are powerful even over these debased instruments—*Amor vincit omnia.* Beyond their knowing, beyond their power or impotence, impotently both Pardoner and Summoner appeal for the natural love—melody of bird-song and meadows of flowers—and both pray for the celestial love, the ultimate pardon which in their desperate and imprisoned darkness is their only hope: "Com hider, love, to me!"

The exterior unity achieved by the realistic device and broadly symbolic framework of pilgrimage is made stronger and tighter in the portraits, partly by local sequences and pairings, but most impressively by the

8. Later, in telling his story, the Pardoner acknowledges that his pardons are inferior versions of the supreme pardon which is Christ's. See *The Pardoner's Tale*, 915–18.

9. This statement of the symbolic values behind the Summoner and the Pardoner is not a disagreement with, but merely an addition to, the point made by Kellogg and Haselmayer (Alfred L. Kellogg and Louis A. Haselmayer, "Chaucer's Satire of the Pardoner," *PMLA LXVI* [March 1951], 215–77) when they assert: "In this paradox, this ironic portrait of justice and crime singing in close harmony, we reach the center of Chaucer's satire" (p. 275). There is, indeed, the strongest satiric impact in this affiliation of the man who should apprehend the wrong-doer with the criminal. In addition, however, if we are to see beyond the Summoner's disabilities to his representation of justice, we see in parallel vision beyond the Pardoner's disabilities a representation of love.

illustration, the variation and enrichment by way of human instances, of a theme of love, earthly and celestial, and a general complex intermingling of the consideration of nature with the consideration of supernature. The note of love is sounded in different keys all through the portraits:

The Knight
. . . he loved chivalrie,
Trouthe and honour, fredom and curteisie (45–46)
The Squire
A lovyere and a lusty bacheler . . . (80)
So hoote he lovede that by nyghtertale
He sleep namoore than dooth a nyghtyngale. (97–98)
The Prioress
. . . *Amor vincit omnia.* (162)
The Monk
A Monk . . . that lovede venerie, . . . (166)
He hadde of gold ywroght a ful curious pyn;
A love-knotte in the gretter ende ther was. (196–97)
A fat swan loved he best of any roost. (206)
The Friar
In love-dayes ther koude he muchel help . . . (258)
Somewhat he lipsed, for his wantownesse, . . . (264)
The Clerk
For hym was levere have at his beddes heed
Twenty bookes, clad in blak or reed,
Of Aristotle and his philosophie,
Than robes riche, or fithele, or gay sautrie. (293–96)
The Frankelyn
Wel loved he by the morwe a sop in wyn;
To lyven in delit was evere his wone,
For he was Epicurus owene sone . . . (334–36)
The Physician
He kepte that he wan in pestilence.
For gold in phisik is a cordial,
Therefore he lovede gold in special. (442–44)
The Wife of Bath
Of remedies of love she knew per chaunce,
For she koude of that art the olde daunce. (475–76)
The Parson
But rather wolde he yeven, out of doute,
Unto his povre parisshens aboute
Of his offryng and eek of his substaunce. (487–89)
. . . Cristes loore and his apostles twelve
He taughte, but first he folwed it hymselve. (527–28)
The Plowman
With hym ther was a Plowman, was his brother, . . . (529)
Lyvynge in pees and parfit charitee.
God loved he best with al his hoole herte
At alle tymes, thogh him gamed or smerte,
And thanne his neighebor right as hymselve. (532–35)
The Summoner and The Pardoner
. . . "Com hider, love, to me!" (672)

The theme of restorative power attends upon the theme of love. It is, of course, announced at the beginning and defined in terms both of nature and supernature. Both the Physician, concerned with natural healing, and the Pardoner, the agent of a supernatural healing, appear under the rubric of "Physician, heal thyself." The worldly Physician is disaffected from God; the Pardoner is naturally impotent. Serious inadequacy in either realm appears as counterpart of inadequacy in the other. It is the Parson who both visits the sick and tends properly to the cure of souls; he works harmoniously in both realms, and both realms are in harmony and fulfilled in him.

The pilgrims are represented as affected by a variety of destructive and restorative kinds of love. Their characters and movement can be fully described only as mixtures of the loves that drive and goad and of the love that calls and summons. The pilgrims have, while they stay and when they move, their worldly host. They have, too, their worldly Summoner and Pardoner who, in the very worst way, move and are moved with them. Nevertheless, the Summoner and Pardoner, who conclude the roll of the company, despite and beyond their appalling personal deficiency, may suggest the summoning and pardoning, the judgment and grace which in Christian thought embrace and conclude man's pilgrimage and which therefore, with all the corrosions of satire and irony, are also the seriously appropriate conclusion to the tapestry of Chaucer's pilgrims.

JILL MANN

From Suffering Woman, Suffering God†

[On the *Man of Law's Tale* and the *Clerk's Tale*]

'Wommen are born to thraldom and penance,
And to ben under mannes governance.'
(*Man of Law's Tale* 286–7)

The marriage that begins the *Man of Law's Tale* is not the culmination of a romantic courtship; instead, Constance, its heroine, is the instrument of a politico-religious alliance. Although he has never set eyes on her, the Sultan of Syria falls so passionately in love with her by reputation alone that he engages that he and all his baronage will embrace Christianity if he can have her as his bride. The matter is settled, not by the delicate negotiation of feeling, but 'by tretys and embassadrie, / And by the popes mediacioun / And al the chirche, and al the chivalrie' (233–5)—everyone, it appears, being consulted but Constance herself. She accepts her fate without protest, but also without enthusiasm. The day of her departure for Syria is a

† From *Feminizing Chaucer* (Woodbridge, Suffolk, and Rochester, NY: D. S. Brewer, 2002), pp. 100–28. Reprinted by permission of Boydell & Brewer Ltd. Indented block quotations of Chaucer's poetry from *The Riverside Chaucer*, ed. Larry D. Benson (Boston: Houghton Mifflin, 1987), have been replaced with quotations from this Norton Critical Edition. The spelling within short quotations from Chaucer's poetry has been modified to reflect this change. Abbreviated references to the *MED* and the *OED* are to the *Middle English Dictionary* (see our Selective Bibliographies, p. 674) and the *Oxford English Dictionary*. Unless otherwise indicated, the notes are the author's. We have omitted Mann's discussion of the *Physician's Tale*, glossed in brackets some of the Middle English in her citations of Julian of Norwich, and drawn the bibliography for this selection from the complete bibliography at the end of her book.

day of sorrow, for both Constance and the members of her family, which on Constance's side at least represents not only regret at what she is leaving behind, but also fear of what she is going to.

> Allas, what wonder is it though she wepte,
> That shal be sent to strange nacioun
> Fro freendes that so tendrely hir kepte,
> And to be bounden under subjeccioun
> Of oon, she knoweth not his condicioun?
> Housbondes been alle goode, and han ben yore;
> That knowen wyves—I dar say yow no more. (267–73)

An everyday tragedy, one might say. Constance's fate must have been the fate suffered by multitudes of medieval women (and men too) whose marriages were dictated not by individual choice but by the accumulation of landed estates or the forging of political alliances. The narratorial comment encourages us to see the situation in its most bleakly depressing aspect, but Constance herself renounces the protest for which its cynicism seems to make room, accepting her fate with Stoic resignation as the general lot of women, as she takes leave of her parents for the last time:

> 'Allas, unto the Barbre nacioun
> I moste anon, sin that it is your wille.
> But Crist, that starf for our redempcioun,
> So yeve me grace his hestes to fulfille.
> I, wrecche womman—no fors though I spille.
> Wommen are born to thraldom and penance,
> And to ben under mannes governance.' (281–7)

Constance's view of woman's fate derives from Genesis, where God decrees that as a punishment for Eve's sin in eating the apple, women should suffer the pains of childbirth and subjection to their husbands (Gen. 3:15–16).

The mask of romantic fiction here seems to fall away, leaving the bleak visage of reality. Woman's fate is not to be the 'lady' whose word is law to her submissive lover, it is 'thraldom' to her father and her husband. The aspirations of the *Franklin's Tale*—'Wommen, of kynde, desiren libertee, / And nat to been constreyned as a thral'—seem here to be brought down to earth. Power is male, submission and suffering are female. In this context, patience seems to dwindle into nothing more than the opium of the oppressed, a convenient means of persuading them to accept the inevitability of 'thraldom'.

And indeed such is the view of the Sultan's mother, whose vigorous resistance to her son's marriage is in marked contrast with Constance's resignation. Indignantly she protests to her council her unwavering loyalty to Mohammed:

> 'What shulde us tyden of this newe lawe
> But thraldom to our bodies and penance,
> And afterward in helle to be drawe
> For we reneyed Mahoun our creance?' (337–40)]

The Sultaness's rejection of Christianity is also a rejection of the 'thraldom and penance' that for Constance is woman's lot. And this rejection of the womanly condition is emphasized in the narrative comment that follows:

> O Sowdanesse, rote of iniquitee!
> Virago, thou Semyram the secounde!
> O serpent under femininitee,
> Lyk to the serpent depe in helle y-bounde!
> O feyned womman, al that may confounde
> Vertu and innocence, thurgh thy malyce,
> Is bred in thee, as nest of every vyce!
>
> O Sathan, envious sin thilke day
> That thou were chased from our heritage,
> Wel knowestow to wommen the olde way:
> Thou madest Eva bringe us in servage.
> Thou wolt fordoon this Cristen mariage.
> Thyn instrument—so weylawey the whyle!—
> Makestow of wommen, whan thou wolt bigyle. (358–71)][1]

The Sultaness is not only an evil woman, she is also, it seems, a *counterfeit* woman. The immediate meaning of 'feyned' is 'feigning, false' (*MED* 6b), but the pressure from 'virago', with its implications of 'mannishness', and the suggestion of counterfeit in 'serpent under femininitee' also activate the sense 'feigned' (*MED* 5d; cf. Delany, [1974–5] 1983, 42). That this is Chaucer's intention here is confirmed by the similar outburst against Constance's second wicked mother-in-law, Donegild, who is called 'mannysh' (782). The Sultaness and Donegild are 'masculine' in their choice of action over suffering; in contrast to Constance, who suffers her fate with a Stoic dignity, they assert themselves in active opposition to whatever they do not like. The Sultaness murders her son and his guests at the wedding feast, and sends Constance out to sea in a rudderless boat; Donegild invents false letters to and from Alla, Constance's second husband, which lead to Constance being set adrift a second time with her child.

The obvious cruelty of their actions seems to tip the scales unfairly against the active self-assertion that fuels them, and so to endorse Constance's passive resignation as the only acceptable feminine ideal. Yet to read the tale in this way is to endorse a simplistic opposition between 'active' and 'passive' that the tale is precisely designed to question; in context, the terms dissolve into each other, as we have seen them do in the representations of love and marriage. The active independence of the two 'mannish' women, seen from another perspective, appears as mere illusion. In imposing her will on events, the Sultaness acts as the 'instrument' of Satan's will; her independence becomes the tool of his designs. Donegild likewise is presented as a mere receptacle for the 'feendlych spirit' that makes use of her body ('Thogh thou heere walke, thy spirit is in helle!': 784). What makes this more than a dramatically articulated endorsement of feminine

1. *The Riverside Chaucer* puts the 'so' in line 370 outside the parenthetical exclamation, but comparison with other uses of this traditional formula in Chaucer (e.g., line 632) show that it is an integral part of it: I have emended the punctuation accordingly. (As does the *Riverside Canterbury Tales.*)

submissiveness is that it is not only female power that is presented as illusory and limited in this way, it is also the 'mannes governance' to which Constance is subjected. Immediately after the expression of resignation to her father's will, there follows an extraordinary passage of cosmic vision which represents him as a helpless pawn in the play of forces far greater than his own.

> O firste moevyng, cruel firmament,
> With thy diurnal sweigh that crowdest ay
> And hurlest al from Est til Occident,
> That naturelly wolde holde another way,
> Thy crowding set the heven in swich array
> At the beginning of this fiers viage
> That cruel Mars hath slayn this mariage.
>
> Infortunat ascendent tortuous
> Of which the lord is helples falle, allas,
> Out of his angle into the derkest hous!
> O Mars, O atazir as in this cas!
> O feble mone, unhappy been thy pas!
> Thou knittest thee ther thou art nat receyved.
> Ther thou were weel, fro thennes artow weyved.
>
> Imprudent Emperour of Rome, allas!
> Was ther no philosophre in al thy toun?
> Is no tyme bet than other in swich cas?
> Of viage is ther noon eleccioun,
> Namely to folk of heigh condicioun,
> Nat whan a rote is of a birthe y-knowe?
> Allas! we ben to lewed or to slowe. (295–315)

The power of the Emperor is annihilated beneath the crushing weight of astral influence. The summit of human power is merely the lowest rung on the ladder of cosmic hierarchy.

But there is more to this passage than that, for the vision of the cosmos in these stanzas is of a quite extraordinary character. The mechanics of it are orthodox enough: the 'natural' movement of the planetary spheres from West to East is counteracted by the East–West movement of the Primum Mobile, the 'first moving' sphere whose outermost position in the system gives it greatest influence, so that it imposes its own motion on the heavenly bodies beneath it. Scientifically, this theory of a double motion in the cosmos accounted for the precession of the equinoxes—that is, the slight shift to the east in the annual return of the stars to their original position in relation to the sun. Poetically, the double motion was often interpreted as a reflection of moral hierarchy—for example, of the proper subjection of the senses to reason (Mann, 1983a, 170–1). In striking contrast to other medieval writers, Chaucer makes it expressive of a violence and cruelty in the cosmos as a whole. The Primum Mobile is a 'cruel firmament'; it 'crowds' and 'hurls' the planets away from their natural course. The planets whose influence blights Constance's marriage are thus themselves helpless victims of a greater force; their power, like the Emperor's, is limited and thwarted of its effect. The 'lord of the ascendant' is not powerful but 'helples', the moon is 'feble'. Images of power ('cruel Mars') resolve themselves strangely into images of impotence. When probed for precise scientific information on the state of the heavens, this passage is revealed as 'technical but unspecific' (Eade, 1982, 82)—suggesting that Chaucer chose such technical terms as 'tortuous' and 'derkeste hous' less for their informative value than for their emotional colouring. The universe we see here is not a harmoniously ordered whole; it is crooked, awry, at odds with itself, held together only by violence.

The question of 'mannes governance' is thus no sooner introduced than it is expanded on to a cosmic scale. Woman is subject to man; man is subject to the planets, the planets to the Primum Mobile. And the Primum Mobile—? Beyond the first moving sphere, there is only the First Mover—that is, God, the invisible presence behind this cosmic scheme. Silently but inexorably this passage raises the question of God's 'governance' of the cosmos, which seems, like that of man over woman, to express itself as cruelty and tyranny. This is a question that is central to Boethius's *Consolation of Philosophy*, in translating which Chaucer constantly used the words 'governance' and its associates—'governe', 'government', 'governor'—to express God's control over his creation. Boethius's crushing personal misfortunes cause him to doubt the divine governance that seems to punish the innocent and allow the guilty to go free: 'O thou governour, governynge alle thynges by certein ende, whi refusestow oonly to governe the werkes of men by duwe manere?' (I m.5.31–3). Philosophy diagnoses Boethius as having 'foryeten by which governementz the werld is governed, forthy weenestow that thise mutacions of fortunes fleten withouten governour'; she undertakes to bring him to 'the sothe sentence of governance of the werld, that thou bylevest that the governynge of it nis nat subgit ne underput to the folye of thise happes aventurous, but to the resoun of God' (I pr.6.79–92). But for Boethius, the ordered governance of the heavens—the regular motions of the wheeling stars, the waxing and waning of the moon, and the unfailing succession of day and night, summer and winter—is precisely the criterion against which the anarchy in human affairs can be measured (I m.5). In the *Man of Law's Tale*, the operations of the cosmos provide no such reassuring vision of governance; instead they repeat and intensify the human sense of 'thraldom and penance', of helpless subjection to powerful cruelty. Woman's subjection to 'mannes governance' thus becomes in this tale a paradigm of the human condition. Woman's 'thraldom' to man is replicated in man's 'thraldom' to God.

The parallel has been recognized by Sheila Delany: Chaucer, she says, represents through Constance's marriage 'the relation of humanity at large to an apparently arbitrary and inscrutable God'. Constance 'suffers because that is the human condition. Her passivity is what orthodox Christianity of the period recommended as a response to the human condition' ([1974–5] 1983, 37). But it is perhaps already apparent here that for Delany, 'the human condition' is equivalent to the social status quo; she sees Constance's 'extreme humility and silent endurance' (36) as designed to encourage an attitude of passive acceptance in the victims of social injustice. 'Constance seems to exist in order to suffer; yet it is unclear why she suffers', she protests, with the confidence of one who is sure the answer to such questions can be found in an inadequate social welfare programme or a lack of revolutionary commitment. The 'why' that Chaucer turns on the problem of suffering in the *Man of Law's Tale* is larger than that. And so far from trying to suppress this question, it is the function of the tale to raise it. Constance's bleak obedience to her father's will focusses the human sense of pain and bewilderment in the recognition that the power exercised by a supposedly loving Father should make itself felt as cruelty (Kirk, 1978, 96–7). It raises the question of whether fatherhood is simply a mask worn by tyranny; whether human beings are not God's children but his thralls (Mann, 1983a, 171).

There is, of course, no final answer to the 'why' of suffering on a metaphysical level, and Chaucer does not try to give one. Faith in the 'purveiaunce' of God does nothing to dispel or deny the darkness of man's 'ignorance' (479–83). The *Man of Law's Tale* 'answers' the question it so movingly raises only on the emotional, experiential level of Christianity itself, by locating God *in* the suffering. Boethius's question about divine justice is echoed by the constable who is charged with sending Constance out to sea for the second time:

> 'O mighty God, if that it be thy wille,
> Sith thou art rightful juge, how may it be
> That thou wolt suffren innocents to spille
> And wikked folk regne in prosperitee?' (813–16)

Like the Emperor of Rome and the planetary bodies, the constable is a figure who unites power and impotence:

> 'O good Custance, allas, so wo is me
> That I mot be thy tormentour, or deye
> On shames deeth—ther is noon other weye.' (817–19)

And the same combination of power and helplessness is found in the God he assumes to be all-powerful, as we see in Constance's immediately following prayer to Mary; the ruler of the cosmos is incarnated in the child slain on the cross.

> 'Moder,' quod she, 'and mayde bright, Mary,
> Sooth is that thurgh wommannes eggement
> Mankind was lorn and damned ay to dye,
> For which thy child was on a croys y-rent.
> Thy blisful eyen sawe al his torment.
> Than is ther no comparisoun bitwene
> Thy wo and any wo man may sustene.' (841–7)

Divine power dissolves into powerlessness; the human victim becomes the tormentor. In the Crucifixion, the 'why' of human suffering is turned back on human kind: it is to mankind and not to God that the 'why' of divine suffering is to be addressed.

The cruelty of which mankind complains in the divine Father is nowhere more apparent than in the Crucifixion of his own Son. Constance's identification with Mary's maternal sufferings teaches us to see that her sorrowful questioning of Alla's paternal cruelty would fit equally well on the lips of Mary at the foot of the cross (Mann, 1983a, 174):[2]

2. The Marian parallel is recognized (with illustration from the Pseudo-Bonaventuran *Meditations*) by Weissman (1979, 151–2), but is interpreted as an instance of Chaucer's ridicule of 'late Gothic piety' in the tale.

'O litel child, allas! What is thy gilt,
That never wroughtest sinne as yet, pardee,
Why wil thyn harde fader han thee spilt?' (855–7)

Deguileville's 'Piteous complaint of the Virgin Mary for the death and passion of her son', which I quote in Hoccleve's translation, makes the implicit parallel evident:[3]

'O fadir god, how fers & how cruel,
In whom thee list or wilt, canst thow thee make.
Whom wilt thow spare, ne wot I neuere a deel,
Syn thow thy sone hast to the deeth betake,
That the offendid neuere, ne dide wrake,
Or mystook him to the, or disobeyde,
Ne to noon othere dide he harm or seide.'
(ed. Seymour, 1–7)

Yet the very framing of this question is enough to make it clear that the division between cruel Father and suffering Son is, once again, an illusion; the Father *is* the Son who suffers, united in singleness of godhead. The Father's cruelty is the vehicle for the Son's love. And just as power dissolves into powerlessness, so powerlessness assumes power; it is through the suffering of the cross that mankind is redeemed. Thus Constance invokes the 'holy croys', not only as symbol of suffering, 'reed of the Lambes blood', but also as a source of strength and power, 'Victorious tree, proteccioun of trewe' (451–62).

The *Man of Law's Tale* deconstructs power, showing that it does not exist as a separate, self-contained entity, like a parcel that can be transferred from one possessor to another. Instead, it is diffused into its operations, where it is qualified by the complex relationships of which it forms part. The tale contemplates the question of what power is or could be—a question that feminism, in the struggle for urgent and immediate objectives, sometimes fails to bring into focus. I quote a recent example, which there is no advantage in attributing: 'What the women's movement wanted (and still wants) is for women themselves to have power so that they do not need to depend on men granting it to them.' It is hard to disagree with this. But then we may ask: power over whom? over what? If women identify male power as repression, how can they wish to acquire such power? 'Power over their own lives' might be the safe answer; the question is, how great can that power be? The cosmic scale of the *Man of Law's Tale* means that it moves on the plane where the writ of human power over human lives ceases to run. To ignore the existence of this plane is to fall prey to delusions about power whose function is precisely to foster masculine self-importance. There is a telling moment in the *Second Nun's Tale* where the Roman prefect Almachius attempts to subdue Cecilia by boasting of his power:

'Han noght our mighty princes to me yeven,
Ye, bothe power and auctoritee
To maken folk to dyen or to liven?
Why spekestow so proudly than to me?' (470–3)

3. The lament forms part of the debate between the green tree and the dry tree in Deguileville's *Pèlerinage de l'ame* (6353ff.), the continuation of the *Pèlerinage de la vie humaine*, from which Chaucer translated a hymn to the Virgin (*An ABC*).

Unimpressed, Cecilia reveals the hollowness of this claim:

> 'Thou seyst thy princes han thee yeven might
> Bothe for to sleen and for to quiken a wight.
> Thou, that ne mayst but only lyf bireve,
> Thou hast non other power ne no leve.' (480–3)

Almachius is no more than a 'ministre of deeth' (485); his vaunted power is only the power to destroy. This is a power already available to women, as the Sultaness and Donegild show. The *Man of Law's Tale*, so far from endorsing this kind of power, turns against it the full force of its indignation, calling it 'tirannye' (779).

Constance's 'silent endurance' does not imply limpness or inertia; when attacked on board ship by a would-be rapist, she resists so vigorously that she throws him overboard 'with hir struglyng wel and myghtily', so that he is drowned (921–2)—the only instance, this, in Chaucer, of a woman fending off rape by her own physical efforts. Still less does it imply masochism, as Delany suggests; there is no sign that she takes pleasure in the sufferings inflicted on her. As Eugene Clasby puts it:

> Her acceptance of what she cannot change is not to be construed as submission to the rule of those who have contrived her situation. Her womanhood is not a sign of human bondage, but an image of human freedom. It is an image of independence from circumstances and worldly authority, of the human capacity to live and to give life, even in the most desperate of situations. (1978–9, 225–6)

For Chaucer, this Boethian freedom from the bondage of Fortune was the highest ideal of Christian philosophy, and it is a sign of the importance he gives to women that it is not in a man, but in two women—Constance and Griselda—that he embodies this ideal.

The operations of power in this tale are not, however, restricted to the machinations of the destructive figures—the Sultaness, Donegild, and the knight who engineers Constance's accusation for murder. Power is manifested in a very different way in pity, which works throughout the tale to counteract the machinations of 'tirannye'. It prompts the constable and Hermengild to take Constance in and shelter her (528–9). It is likewise the agent of Constance's release from the charge of murdering Hermengild, when her plight arouses the pity of her judge, King Alla:

> The kinges herte of pitee gan agryse
> Whan he saugh so benigne a creature
> Falle in disese and in misaventure . . .
>
> This Alla king hath swich compassioun,
> As gentil hert° is fulfild of pitee,
> That from his eyen ran the water doun. (614–16, 659–61)

Pity is the pressure brought to bear by the sufferer on the beholder; it is the invisible strength which acts as the 'champioun' Constance lacks (631). The appeal to Christ to be her 'stronge champioun' (635) is answered by Alla's pity, which is the vehicle for God's power as the Sultaness's intransigence is the vehicle for Satan's: he makes the knight swear the truth of his accusation on the Gospels, provoking the hand of heaven to strike him down and a divine voice to proclaim Constance's innocence. Here as in the *Franklin's Tale* pity is a *dynamic* power.

Alla's power to save Constance is thus qualified on the one hand by its role as a surrogate for God's power, and on the other by the fact that it is pity for Constance's suffering that calls it into action. Pity cancels power, uniting beholder with sufferer—a union enacted in the Middle English word 'pitous' itself, which means both 'pitiable' and 'pitying'. It is a union we can see also in the language of Constance's prayer to the Virgin:

> 'Thou glorie of wommanhede, thou faire may,
> Thou haven of refut, brighte sterre of day,
> Rewe on my child, that of thy gentillesse
> Rewest on every rewful in distresse.' (851–4)

'Rewe' and 'rewest' are called into existence as a response to 'rewful', but are also presupposed by it; the pitier is absorbed into the state of the pitied, the pitiable create pity. Pity submerges the Creator in his creation, uniting power and suffering in the image of the cross, 'Reed of the Lambes blood ful of pitee' (452). It unites Mary with the suffering of her child, in fulfilment of Simeon's prophecy that 'a sword shall pierce through thy own soul also' (Luke 2:35). The Middle English lyric 'Stond well, moder, under Rode' (ed. Davies, no. 24) reflects the common belief that the pains Mary suffered at her son's Crucifixion stood in place of the pangs of childbirth that she had been spared at the Nativity (Keiser, 1985, 171):

> 'Moder, now thou might well leren
> Whet sorewe haveth that children beren,
> Whet sorewe it is with childe gon.' (37–9)

Her pain is the common pain of women. So Constance sees in Mary's pain the mirror of her own; the community of suffering creates the community of pity. Constance's support is not in the bland assurance of a divine plan, but in her imagined identification with another woman's pain. The *Man of Law's Tale* does not produce Christianity like a rabbit out of a hat to 'answer' the problems of human existence; instead, it grounds Christianity in human experience, painfully feeling its way through cruelty to the pity that beholds and suffers.

Most important of all, the circle of pity reaches beyond the bounds of the story to embrace the reader (Gray, 1979, 185). The *Man of Law's Tale* is, one might say, the literary counterpart of the Pietà—a form developed in the visual arts at exactly this period, and for which the Middle English name was 'a pite' (*MED* 5)[4]—in which Mary's pity for her dead son, Christ's pity for mankind, and the beholder's pity for their suffering, are realized as a single emotion.[5] Nothing could be further from the truth than Morton Bloomfield's claim that 'the tragedy of victimization'

4. The earliest examples are early fifteenth-century, but there is no reason to suppose that the term is not as old as the form itself, which developed in late fourteenth-century Germany. Pinder (1920) argues that the roots of the Pietà are literary; the *Man of Law's Tale* is a good example of the general sensibility that stimulated its development.

5. The Pietà is an example of the pictorial aids to devotion to which art historians apply the term 'Andachtsbild' ('meditational image'); Panofsky comments on such images that they encourage in the beholder a contemplative immersion in the subject represented, a spiritual fusion of subject and object (1927, 264).

represented in this tale distances the reader from the narrative because we 'perpetually feel superior to' the suffering victim (1972, 385). On the contrary, Chaucer appeals to the power of pity to work on the reader as it does on Alla, obliterating distance in an intense identification of feeling:

> Have ye nat seyn somtyme a pale face
> Among a prees, of him that hath be lad
> Toward his deeth, wher as him gat no grace,
> And swich a colour in his face hath had
> Men mighte knowe his face that was bistad
> Amonges alle the faces in that route?
> So stant Custance, and loketh hir aboute. (645–51)

The appeal in the next stanza to 'queenes, lyvynge in prosperitee / Duchesses, and ye ladyes everichone' to have 'som routhe' on Constance (652–4), is an appeal to submerge the difference represented by their own 'prosperitee' in an imaginative identification with the fate threatening this 'Emperoures doghter'. The pathetic mode of the tale is thus a means by which the reader can be 'educated' into pity, can relinquish neutrality and independence in an imaginative surrender to the story.

Precisely because it asks for such a surrender, the power of pathos is often resisted by modern readers (e.g. Weissman, 1979), but it is for all that a power of which the women's movement has freely availed itself. What legitimates its use here is the tale's representation of the *strength* necessary to surrender. It is a strength we feel in Constance's unshaken dignity, in her equally calm acceptance of disaster and of good fortune, in her unconscious influence on those around her. The twice-repeated motif of the rudderless boat is at the heart of this tale because it expresses the courage needed to hazard the self to the flux of events, bereft of all supports to selfhood save selfhood alone. And it also expresses the power that is released as a result of this surrender, in the shape of the mysterious force that preserves Constance from death and carries her to unforeseen destinations. This is a power that is guaranteed poetically, as the fussy machinations of 'tirannye' are not, in the two great series of rhetorical questions which confront the miracle of Constance's preservation. I quote only a part:

> Now sith she was not at the feste y-slawe,
> Who kepte hir fro the drenching in the see?
> Who kepte Jonas in the fisshes mawe
> Til he was spouted up at Ninivee?
> Wel may men knowe it was no wight but he
> That kepte peple Ebraik from hir drenchinge,
> With drye feet thurghout the see passinge.
>
> Who bad the foure spirits of tempest,
> That power han t'anoyen land and see
> Bothe north and south and also west and est,
> 'Anoyeth neither see, ne land, ne tree'?
> Sothly, the comaundour of that was he
> That fro the tempest ay this womman kepte
> As wel whan she wook as whan she slepte.

Wher mighte this womman mete and drinke have
Three yeer and more? How lasteth hir vitaille?
Who fedde the Egipcien Marie in the cave
Or in desert? No wight but Crist, sans faille.
Fyve thousand folk it was as gret mervaille
With loves fyve and fisshes two to fede.
God sente his foison at hir grete nede. (484–504)

The brilliance of this lies in the way that the continuity of form disguises a reversal of function: as the flow of questions extends itself, we realize that they are coming back to us as answers, like a wave breaking and returning on itself. Like the 'why' of suffering, the 'why' of salvation is answered only by multiplied images of itself. It is a tautology that constitutes a frank acknowledgement that to answer either question by saying 'it is God's will' is to reformulate the enigma without solving it. But if the questions multiply enigma, they turn it into a source of strength; the confidence that sustains their rhetoric lifts and carries the reader forward on its billowing waves as Constance is lifted and carried on the sea. The reader is summoned to surrender to the tale, to be carried by it rather than to resist it with sceptical interrogation, and to feel this surrender not as cowardly inertia but as the absorption into the movement of a greater power. Constance's surrender to God is re-enacted as literary experience in our own surrender to Chaucer.

The surrender is not, however, rewarded by easy reassurance, and the withholding of this reassurance is another source of the tale's strength. As the tale deconstructs power, so it deconstructs the 'happy ending'; the points where Constance seems to have come finally to an end of suffering—her peaceful life with Hermengild and the constable, her marriage with Alla—prove to be only temporary halting-places before the turbulent movement of events carries her on again. Even at the end of the tale, finality is resisted; no sooner has the joyful reunion between Constance, her father and her husband knotted up the narrative threads into a happy conclusion than Chaucer sets to work to unravel it:

This king Alla, whan he his tyme sey,
With his Custance, his holy wyf so swete,
To Engelond been they come the righte wey,
Wher as they live in joye and in quiete.
But litel whyl it lasteth, I yow hete,
Joye of this world, for tyme wol nat abyde.
Fro day to night it changeth as the tyde.

Who lived ever in swich delyt o day
That him ne moeved outher conscience,
Or ire, or talent, or som kin affray,
Envye, or pryde, or passion, or offence?
I ne seye but for this ende this sentence:
That litel whyl in joye or in plesance
Lasteth the blisse of Alla with Custance. (1128–41)

These beautiful and moving lines—some of the most moving in Chaucer's poetry—dissolve the illusion of the 'happy ending' into the momentary fluctuations of lived existence; happiness is not a fixed state but a series of discrete moments brought on the tide of life, with 'sodeyn wo' always hard behind (421–7). This time the rhetorical question is not a dramatic challenge, but a quiet appeal to the common knowledge that comes from a shared humanity—a knowledge of the inevitable instabilities of mood and feeling that make change an ineradicable part of human experience, and patience, here as in the *Franklin's Tale*, a necessary response. Resignation is not a matter of pious platitudes that blanket out the realities of suffering; rather, it lies in the matter-of-fact simplicity of tone in these lines, in the unblinking steadiness of vision with which they focus on the inevitability of change. The possibility of suffering disappears only with the possibility of happiness; it is only when Constance returns to her father after Alla's death, in a circular movement that shows her life to have run its worldly course, that she is said to have 'scaped al hire aventure' (1151). To live in the world is to be borne on the flux of 'aventure'; patience and pity follow its movement.

* * *

The *Clerk's Tale* has proved even harder for the modern reader to accommodate than the *Physician's Tale*. Medieval readers were uncomfortable with Walter's cruelty, but they seem to have had no difficulty in admiring Griselda, only in believing that such extreme patience could exist (Middleton, 1980). From the nineteenth century onwards, however, readers have found it difficult to give her the sympathetic approval that the tale requires (Morse, 1985, 54). And on the face of it, their response is reasonable. Griselda acquiesces not only in her own 'subjeccioun' to her husband, but also in the death which she supposes him to inflict on her children. She endures without protest his dismissal of her in favour of a new wife, and obeys his command to set the house in order for the marriage. In all this she is praised for her steadfast calm and uncomplaining patience. The *Merchant's Tale*'s conception of the ideal wife as a doormat, a creature without will or feeling of her own, here seems to be realized in the flesh.

Paying attention to the narrative detail of the tale will go some way towards avoiding misinterpretation. It is important to note, for example, that Griselda's unquestioning obedience to her husband is not the simple result of her marriage vow, but something that she takes upon herself with the unique promise that is the special condition of her marriage. It is this promise, not her wifely duty, that exacts Griselda's cheerful compliance with Walter's every wish. As in the *Franklin's Tale*, a fairy-tale promise claims an absolute adherence that the practical common-sense of everyday life could not tolerate. And as in the *Franklin's Tale*, adherence to it becomes a test of 'trouthe', of the integrity of selfhood invested in the promise; to deny one's promise is to deny oneself. It is in this steady maintenance of selfhood that Griselda's strength makes itself felt in the very act of self-denial.

The second thing that must play a part in interpretation of this tale is that this marriage, like that of Dorigen and Arveragus, is in its early stages forged by a complicated interaction of 'lordshipe' and 'servage'. Walter's marriage is not the result of his own initiative; it is imposed upon him by his tenants' wishes. To Walter, marriage appears 'servage':

'Ye wol,' quod he, 'myn owene peple dere,
To that I never erst thoghte streyne me.
I me rejoysed of my libertee
That selde tyme is founde in mariage;
Ther I was free, I moot been in servage.' (143–7)

His tenants represent it, however, in the terms of the *Franklin's Tale*—that is, as a paradoxical fusion of 'servage' and 'lordshipe':

'Boweth youre nekke under that blisful yok
Of soveraynetee, noght of servyse,
Which that men clepeth spousaille or wedlok.' (113–15)

Despite his regret for his lost liberty, Walter assents 'of [his] free wyl' to their demands (150), but he in turn lays an imposition on them: instead of letting them find for him one of the highest-born in the land, he will choose his own wife, and whoever she may be, they are to agree to accept her with the honour and reverence fitting for an emperor's daughter, and never to grumble at his choice (162–70). To this demand, his people agree 'with hertely wyl' (176).

The process of negotiation by which the marriage is agreed on is thus a classic example of the combination of 'lordshipe' and 'servage'. Each of the parties involved yields in one respect in order to assert their will in another. The natural expectation is that the marriage will bear the same character as the negotiations that have brought it about—that it will indeed be a 'blisful yok / Of soveraynetee' for both partners. The expectation is strengthened by the fact that Walter's response to his tenants shows the 'pitee' that subordinates the wishes of a great lord to those of his inferiors:

Hir meke preyere and hir pitous chere
Made the markis herte han pitee. (141–2)

It also shows the trust that embodies a willingness to hazard the self to the control of others: 'I see youre trewe entente, / And truste upon youre wit, and have doon ay' (148–9). Trust is evident likewise in his refusal of the high-born wife that they would choose for him:

'For God it woot, that children ofte been
Unlyk hir worthy eldres hem bifore;
Bountee comth al of God, nat of the streen
Of which they been engendred and y-bore.
I truste in Goddes bountee and therfore
My mariage and myn estaat and reste
I him bitake; he may don as him leste.' (155–61)

The choice of a low-born wife, which in hindsight we read as allowing Walter more room for dictatorship, appears at this moment—with perfect validity—as a surrender of the self to divine providence. It is not an insurance policy designed to minimize the loss of liberty as far as possible, but on the contrary, a leap in the dark, an act of faith in the individual virtue buried by obscure circumstances.

The promise that Walter exacts from Griselda is a call for a similar leap in the dark on her part, a similar exercise of trust. It seems, on the face of it, like the last link in the chain of acts combining 'lordshipe' and 'servage': Griselda's elevation to power and riches is twinned with her subordination to her husband. Yet from this point on, trust fails and mutuality ceases. Walter is obsessed with the desire to actualize the total commitment which has been promised, to see whether in fact it has limits or secret reservations. Mutuality is swallowed up in the one-sided exercise of his will. The marital unanimity which in the *Franklin's Tale* flows spontaneously from the shifts and adaptations of each partner to the other is here achieved by painful grinding effort, as Griselda must bend all her own desires to the shape that Walter imposes on them.

For which it semed thus, that of hem two
Ther nas but o wil; for, as Walter leste,
The same lust was hire plesance also;
And, God be thanked, al fil for the beste.
She shewed wel for no worldly unreste
A wyf, as of hirself, no thing ne sholde
Wille in effect but as hir housbond wolde. (715–21)

It is a picture that seems to call for the acerbic scorn with which Defoe's Roxana greets her lover's attempts to persuade her that marriage involves no loss of liberty, for 'where there was a mutual Love, there could be no Bondage; but that there was but one Interest, one Aim, one Design; and all conspir'd to make both very happy':

> Ay, said I, *that is the Thing I complain of*; the Pretence of Affection, takes from a Woman every thing that can be call'd *herself*; she is to have no Interest; no Aim; no View; but all is the Interest, Aim, and View, of the Husband . . . you, that are now upon even Terms with me, and I with you, *says I*, are the next Hour sat up upon the Throne, and the humble Wife plac'd at your Footstool; all the rest, that you call Oneness of Interest, Mutual Affection, *and the like*, is Curtesie and Kindness then, and a Woman is indeed, infinitely oblig'd where she meets with it; but can't help herself where it fails. (149–51)

The *Clerk's Tale* goes beyond the picture of mutual affection presented in the *Franklin's Tale* to ask, as does Roxana, what happens when it fails. In this tale, patience is shorn of its quality of movement, its role as reciprocal response, and is frozen into the marble stillness of endurance. Walter's summons to Griselda to 'Shewe now youre pacience' (495) is as cynical as, if less comic than, the Wife of Bath's exhortations to her old husbands to practise the patience they preach (*Wife of Bath's Prologue* 434–9). He even has the audacity to *pretend* to experience 'lordshipe' as 'servage' as a pretext for tormenting her:

'But now knowe I in verray soothfastnesse
That in gret lordshipe, if I wel avyse,
Ther is gret servitute in sondry wyse.

I may nat don as every plowman may.
My peple me constreyneth for to take
Another wyf, and cryen day by day.' (796–801)

There is no shred of support for Walter's behaviour in the narrative; on the contrary, Chaucer carefully adds to it explicit condemnations of his obsessive desire to test Griselda.

> But as for me, I seye that yvel it sit
> T'assaye a wyf whan that it is no nede,
> And putten hire in anguish and in drede.
>
> O needles was she tempted in assay!
> But wedded men ne knowe no mesure
> Whan that they finde a pacient creature. (460–2, 621–3)

Where Petrarch asks whether the loss of her children did not sufficiently prove Griselda's obedience and fidelity without further testing, Chaucer explicitly refers this same question to women:

> But now of wommen wolde I axen fayn,
> If thise assayes mighte nat suffyse?
> What coude a sturdy housbond more devyse
> To preve hir wyfhod and hir stedfastnesse,
> And he continuinge evere in sturdinesse? (696–700)

Admiration for Griselda's patience in no way implies the sanctioning of Walter's right to test her. Bernard Levy's suggestion that the test is designed 'in order to prove her worthy of complete acceptance into the royal society' by revealing her innate 'gentilesse' (1986, 403) is completely alien to the spirit of the tale, both in its complacent snobbery (what proves *Walter's* 'gentilesse'?) and in its denial of Chaucer's insistence that Walter's testing of his wife is 'needles'. The *Clerk's Tale*, so far from being, as Kittredge claimed ([1911–12] 1959, 198), an answer to the *Wife of Bath's Tale*, shares with it—and with the *Franklin's Tale* and the *Melibee*—the same vision of a marital ideal, founded on the surrender of masculine 'maistrye'. The monstrous perversion of this ideal created by Walter's tyranny merely proves the point from a negative direction.

We know, then, how the women will judge Walter, but how are they to judge Griselda? Whereas Roxana's imaginary wife 'can't help herself', Griselda *could* help herself but renounces the attempt. She could, that is, protest and remonstrate, or appeal to outside agencies for the protection of her children. The fairy-tale absolutes of the story of course teach the reader to renounce such impulses towards practical solutions along with the realism they imply. Yet realism is not a mode entirely alien to this tale, as Elizabeth Salter has shown (1962, 50–9); on the contrary, some of its finest moments reside in the vivid immediacy of speech and thought which realizes Griselda's sufferings as lived experience. Nor is the cynicism that pervades the comic tales entirely absent; behind the bland assurance that 'A wyf, as of hirself, no thing ne sholde / Wille in effect but as hir housbonde wolde' (720–1), there flickers briefly the kind of irony that runs through the mock-encomium of the *Merchant's Tale*—an irony that accommodates the protest Griselda renounces. The protest suppressed throughout the tale finally breaks loose in its Envoy, where husbands are warned not to repeat Walter's experiment, for modern women are made in a different mould, and 'noble wyves' are exhorted to take care that they show no such patience and humility.

Folweth Ekko, that holdeth no silence,
But evere answereth at the countretaille;
Beth nat bidaffed for your innocence,
But sharply tak on yow the governaille.
Emprinteth wel this lesson in youre minde
For commune profit, sith it may availle.

Ye archewyves, stondeth at defence!
Sin ye be stronge as is a greet camaille,
Ne suffreth nat that men yow doon offence.
And sclendre wyves, feble as in bataille,
Beth egre as is a tygre yond in Inde;
Ay clappeth as a mille, I yow consaille.

Ne dreed hem nat, doth hem no reverence;
For though thyn housbonde armed be in maille,
The arwes of thy crabbed eloquence
Shal perce his brest, and eek his aventaille.
In jalousye I rede eek thou him binde,
And thou shalt make him couche as dooth a quaille.

If thou be fair, ther folk ben in presence,
Shew thou thy visage and thyn apparaille;
If thou be foul, be free of thy dispence;
To gete thee freendes ay do thy travaille.
Be ay of chere as light as leef on linde,
And lat him care, and wepe, and wringe, and waille!
(1189–1212)

As in the *Merchant's Tale* and the *Wife of Bath's Prologue*, female shrewishness is seen as the natural punishment for masculine bullying. But if the Envoy shows us this as the most obvious response to behaviour such as Walter's (and what else is there, given that the 'Mutual Affection' of the *Franklin's Tale* is ruled out by the very terms of the problem?), it also shows us that it leads straight back into the impasse of marital hostility: '*Oon* of us two moste bowen, doutelees', as the Wife of Bath tells her husbands (440). Mutuality disappears as a possibility. So the *Clerk's Tale* refuses the obvious option of Griselda's rebellion, as the *Franklin's Tale* refuses the obvious narrative option of Dorigen's suicide. And our consciousness of this refusal goes towards creating our sense of the strength in Griselda's patience. 'The energy that would animate a crime is not more than is wanted to inspire a resolved submission', as George Eliot observes in *Middlemarch*. The energy released in the Envoy is our measure of the energy involved in Griselda's submission.

But the most obvious testimony to Griselda's strength is the tale's ending. It is an ending often ignored in critical accounts of the tale, yet it is crucial to its meaning. For it is not Griselda who gives way under the pressures of her trial, but Walter. As in the *Franklin's Tale*, the story does not simply illustrate the virtue of patience; it shows that patience *conquers*. And here, as there, it conquers through pity. The 'pitee' that had marked Walter at the beginning of the tale reasserts itself, already threatening to break forth as he inaugurates her final test:

> But wel unnethes thilke word he spak
> But wente his wey for rewthe and for pitee. (892–3)

The 'rewthe' that prompts his final change of heart ('This sturdy markys gan his herte dresse / To rewen upon hire wyfly stedfastnesse': 1049–50) blossoms into the 'pitous joye' of the reconciliation scene (1080), calling forth 'many a teere on many a pitous face' (1104).

Through pity, suffering realizes itself as power. Griselda's patience—her 'sadnesse', in Chaucer's term—constitutes an unrelenting pressure on Walter. It is a pressure felt by the reader of the tale in the form of narrative suspense; like Walter, the reader is driven by curiosity, the desire to know at what point Griselda will give way. Thwarted of satisfaction on this side by Griselda's unvarying self-consistency ('She was ay oon in herte and in visage': 711), the forward pressure of narrative suspense turns instead to Walter for release, finding relief, as does Walter himself, in his capitulation. The 'variance' he looks for in Griselda he realizes in himself. The 'ynogh' with which he closes her trials corresponds in one sense to the 'ynogh' with which the Knight halts the unrelenting stream of woe which is the *Monk's Tale* (2768); human nature resists sameness, seeks the relief of change. It is the pressure of Griselda's sameness that eventually issues in Walter's change.

The word 'ynogh' is of central significance in this tale, as I have shown in detail elsewhere (1983b). Walter's response to Griselda's promise to obey him—"This is ynogh, Grisilde myn'—is repeated verbatim as he puts an end to her testing. The repetition raises the question of what *is* enough; so far from being satisfied by Griselda's first promise, Walter succumbs to the insatiable desire to test her 'alwey moore and moore' (458). Walter's insatiability is answered by Griselda's 'sadnesse', a word coloured in this context by its oldest English meaning (still active in Chaucer's usage), 'satisfied, sated, full' (*MED* 1). Griselda's 'sadnesse'—steadfastness, constancy—reflects her 'suffisaunce', the Boethian self-sufficiency that creates her willingness to relinquish wealth, status, children and husband, in the knowledge that none of these things ever belonged to her of right. How deeply Boethian a heroine she is, we can see in the speech that Philosophy imagines Fortune as addressing to Boethius, for it contains the plot of the *Clerk's Tale* in embryo, with Walter as surrogate of Fortune:

> 'Whan that nature brought the foorth out of thi modir wombe, I resceyved the nakid and nedy of alle thynges, and I norissched the with my richesses, and was redy and ententyf thurwe my favour to sustene the—and that maketh the now inpacient ayens me; and I envyrounde the with al the habundance and schynynge of alle goodes that ben in my ryght. Now it liketh me to withdrawe myn hand. Thow hast had grace as he that hath used of foreyne goodes; thow hast no ryght to pleyne the, as though thou haddest outrely forlorn alle thy thynges. Why pleynestow thanne? I have doon the no wrong.' (II pr.2.14–28)

The difference is that Griselda is *not* 'inpacient' at the loss of Fortune's goods; what Philosophy teaches Boethius through Fortune's speech, she expresses in her actions. Her patience is thus not specifically or exclusively a feminine ideal, despite the special relationship women are (as we shall see) given to it. It represents the Stoic 'suffisaunce' which meets 'with evene herte' 'the strook of Fortune or of aventure' (811–12). As in the *Man of Law's Tale*, woman's subjection to man is the experience in which the human subjection to God's 'purveiaunce' is focussed and explored.

Chaucer's concluding comments on the *Clerk's Tale*, which he borrowed from Petrarch, encourage us to see this, and not a moral about proper wifely behaviour, as its true meaning. It is not designed to encourage wives to imitate Griselda, 'for it were inportable, though they wolde', but to encourage all human beings to be 'constant in adversitee'.

> For sith a womman was so pacient
> Unto a mortal man, wel more us oghte
> Receyven al in gree that God us sent.
> For greet skile is he preve that he wroghte,
> But he ne tempteth no man that he boghte—
> As seith Seint Jame, if ye his pistel rede.
> He preveth folk al day, it is no drede,
>
> And suffreth us, as for our excercyse,
> With sharpe scourges of adversitee
> Ful ofte to be bete in sondry wyse,
> Nat for to knowe oure wil; for certes he,
> Er we were born, knew al oure freletee.
> And for our beste is al his governaunce:
> Lat us than live in vertuous suffraunce. (1149–62)

Rather than solving the difficulties inherent in the *Clerk's Tale*, this reading of it has in general only been found to increase them, for in paralleling God's role with Walter's, it seems to make of God a sadistic bully. Yet it is precisely this vision of God that the tale wishes us to confront. Like the *Man of Law's Tale*, it asks if his 'governaunce' is mere tyranny, and if mankind's belief in his fatherly kindness is a mere delusion. In her challenging interpretation of the *Clerk's Tale*, Elizabeth Salter drew attention to the jarring note struck by Griselda's reference to Walter as 'benigne fader':

> 'O tendre, o dere, o yonge children myne,
> Your woful mooder wende stedfastly
> That cruel houndes or som foul vermyne
> Hadde eten yow; but God of his mercy,
> And youre benigne fader, tendrely
> Hath doon yow kept;' and in that same stounde
> Al sodeynly she swapte adoun to grounde. (1093–9)

Griselda's thankfulness to Walter and to God would be, Salter believes, appropriate 'in isolation'; the difficulty comes in Chaucer's failure to keep the tale on the general and abstract plane of its religious meaning. Walter's actions are 'not sufficiently mysterious and inexplicable'; we know too much about his cruelty (1962, 60).

So far from representing a failure in narrative control, however, the jarring reference to Walter as 'benigne fader' is the very nub of the tale's meaning. For the difficulty in reconciling Walter's evident cruelty with his claimed benignity is the very problem that the tale transposes on to its religious level. If Walter appears to kill his children, God does so in sober earnest. Griselda's words of renunciation to Walter—'Naked out of my fadres hous . . . / I cam, and naked moot I turne agayn' (871–2)—echo Job's response to the news of his children's death: 'Naked came I out of my mother's womb, and naked shall I return thither: the Lord gave, and the Lord hath taken away; blessed be the name of the Lord' (1:21). Job's words are the model for the response of the earthly mother whose children are taken from her by death; like Griselda, she must trust in the benignity of the divine Father whose actions seem both senseless and cruel (Mann, 1983a, 179–80). Griselda's dignified speeches of resignation to Walter's will are, we are told, appropriate for the deity, but inappropriate for her husband. But it is this very inappropriateness that raises the question of their appropriateness for God, the question that orthodox piety effectively suppresses; it forces us to experience just what is asked of human beings in their submission to the divine will.

As in the *Man of Law's Tale*, the religious level of the *Clerk's Tale* does not 'answer' the problem of suffering but finds an imaginative form within which it can be apprehended as a mystery. The gulf between cruelty and benignity cannot be bridged by explanation; it can only be bridged by faith—the 'feith' that Griselda brought to Walter as her marriage dowry.

> 'To yow broghte I noght elles, out of drede,
> But feyth and nakednesse and maydenhede.' (865–6)

Trust fails in Walter, but it never falters in Griselda, however sharp her awareness of the disparity between the 'gentil and kynde' aspect he wore at their wedding and his later harshness. It is in the words 'benigne fader' that we can plumb the depth of this trust, and thus take true measure of the depth of trust needed to have faith in the benignity of the divine will. Like Arveragus's trust in Dorigen, Griselda's trust erases the need for explanations and recriminations; it finds 'suffisaunce' in the restoration of what has been lost, a restoration as gratuitous, as little to be claimed by right, as the original gift.

The 'sadnesse' that had seemed to suppress emotion in Griselda releases itself *as* emotion in the tightness of her embrace:

> And in her swough so sadly holdeth she
> Hire children two, whan she gan hem t'embrace,
> That with greet sleighte and greet difficultee
> The children from hire arm they gonne arace. (1100–3)

The religious meaning of the *Clerk's Tale* lies not in the revelation of a sanctioning explanation for Griselda's suffering, but in the imagined participation in this ecstatic moment when it is obliterated by joy. It is a moment which is strangely and movingly illuminated by a passage in the autobiography of the nineteenth-century writer Margaret Oliphant—a passage concentrating all the sufferings she endured over the years in the loss, one by one, of the children she struggled to support. I quote it because it not only shares the same imagined vision as the end of the *Clerk's Tale*, but because it too shows the power of the feelings that can be released into the simple word 'enough'.

> Ah me, alas! pain ever, for ever, God alone knows what was the anguish of these years. And yet now I think of *ces beaux jours quand j'étais si malheureuse*, the moments of relief were so great and so sweet that they seemed compensation for the pain,—I remembered no more the anguish. Lately in my many sad musings it has been brought very clearly before my mind how often all the horrible tension, the dread, the anxiety which there are no words strong enough to describe,—which devoured me, but which I had to conceal often behind a smiling face,—would yield in a moment, in the twinkling of an eye, at the sound of a voice, at the first look, into an ineffable ease and the overwhelming happiness of relief from pain, which is, I think, our highest human sensation, higher and more exquisite than any positive enjoyment in this world. It used to sweep over me like a wave, sometimes when I opened a door, sometimes in a letter,—in all simple ways. I cannot explain, but if this should ever come to the eye of any woman in the passion and agony of motherhood, she will more or less understand. I was thinking lately, or rather, as sometimes happens, there was suddenly presented to my mind, like a suggestion from some one else, the recollection of these ineffable happinesses, and it seemed to me that it meant that which would be when one pushed through that last door and was met—oh, by what, by whom?—by instant relief. The wave of sudden ease and warmth and peace and joy. I felt, to tell the truth, that it was one of them who brought that to my mind, and I said to myself, 'I will not want any explanation, I will not ask any question,—the first touch, the first look, will be enough, as of old, yet better than of old.' (146–7)

To see Walter as an image of God's cruelty and Griselda as an image of human suffering is not, however, to exhaust the religious meaning of this tale. It is merely the first step that leads, through *engagement* with the problem of suffering, to an even deeper level of the tale, where the symbolic associations of the two central characters astonishingly reverse themselves. For as in the *Man of Law's Tale*, we see that it is not humanity only that suffers, but also God. Griselda's suffering reaches beyond the human, figuring forth the divine. It is this realisation of the divine in woman's form that is Chaucer's most original development of the meaning of this traditional story.

It is the word 'enough' that leads us on to this deeper level. Its numerous uses in the tale show Chaucer exploiting a double meaning in the Middle English adverb 'ynogh', which means not only 'sufficiently, moderately', but also 'extremely, . . . fully, completely, entirely . . . as much as well could be'.[6] 'Enough', that is, does not represent merely a limited satisfaction; it also represents complete fulfilment. It is not only a mean, a half-way house between the extremes of 'too little' and 'too much', but is also itself an extreme, finding its limit only in the completeness of perfection. So the 'enough' that Griselda bestows on Walter knows no limitation; it is an inexhaustible outpouring that out-distances even his insatiability. And in this boundless will to suffer until satisfaction is reached, Griselda images the Christ who speaks in vision to Julian of Norwich, offering more and yet more:

6. See *OED* 1, 2a, and *MED* b, d, e. For more detailed analysis of this word and its associates in the *Clerk's Tale*, see Mann, 1983b, on which the following discussion draws.

> Then seide oure good lorde askyng: Arte thou well apayd [satisfied] that I sufferyd for thee? I seyde: ȝe, good lorde, gramercy; ye, good lorde, blessyd moet þow be. Then seyde Jhesu our good lord: If thou arte apayde, I am apayde. It is a joy, a blysse, an endlesse lykyng to me that evyr I sufferd passion for the; and yf I myght suffer more, I wolde suffer more . . .
>
> And in these wordes: If I myght suffer more I wolde suffer more, I saw truly þat as often as he myght dye, as often he wolde, and loue shulde nevyr lett hym haue rest tille he hath done it. And I behelde with gret diligence for to wet [know] how often he wolde dye yf he myght. And truly the nomber passyd my vnderstandyng and my wittes so ferre that my reson myght nott nor cold nott comprehende it ne take it.
>
> And whan he had thus ofte dyed or shuld die, yet he wolde sett it at nought for loue; for alle thynkyth hym but lytylle in regard of his loue.
>
> (Long Text, Chap. 22)

As Julian's Christ shares Griselda's limitless suffering, so Walter's desire to have 'more and more' from Griselda is paralleled in Julian's insatiable longing for the divine:

> This saw I bodely, swemly and darkely, [physically, (yet) faintly and obscurely] and I desyred mor bodely light to haue seen more clerly. And I was answeryde in my reason: If god will shew thee more, he shal be thy light; thou nedyth none but him. For I saw him and sought him, for we be now so blynde and so vnwyse that we can never seke god till what tyme þat he of his goodnes shewyth hym to vs. And whan we see owght of hym graciously, then are we steryd [guided] by the same grace to seke with great desyer to see hym more blessedfully. And thus I saw him and sought him, and I had hym and wantyd hym; and this is and should be our comyn workyng in this life, as to my syght.
>
> (Long Text, Chap. 10)

Julian of Norwich enables us to see that the religious interpretation of the *Clerk's Tale* that identifies Walter's role with God's is only half of the picture. God is more truly imaged in Griselda's boundless suffering than in Walter's tyrannical cruelty. And in Walter we can see the image of man making endless trial of the patience of God, endlessly testing to see how far it will go. How much man asks of God—and receives from him—can be seen in Griselda's words to Walter:

> 'For wiste I that my deeth wolde do yow ese,
> Right gladly wolde I dyen, yow to plese.
>
> Deth may noght make no comparisoun
> Unto youre love.' (664–7)

Griselda's words do not figure human resignation to God—it is not man who dies to do God 'ese'—but God's self-sacrifice for love of man. In Walter's unworthiness of the flood of love here unstintingly poured out for him, we can gauge man's unworthiness of the divine love that he takes for granted. Like Griselda, God meets man's endless demands with a limitless abundance that man must finally acknowledge as satisfaction. So, like the *Clerk's Tale*, Julian of Norwich finds repose in the simple word 'enough':

> tendyrly oure lorde towchyth vs and blysydfully callyth vs, seyeng in oure soule: Lett [Listen to] me aloone, my derwurdy [beloved] chylde, intende to me. I am inogh to þe, and enjoy in thy sauiour and in thy saluation. (Long Text, Chap. 36)

In Griselda, human suffering and divine patience are united in one person, as Christ united manhood and Godhead. And it is her 'wommanhede' that is the ground of the union. Patience, like pity, is a *womanly* quality.

> Men speke of Job and most for his humblesse,
> As clerkes, whan hem list, can wel endyte,
> Namely of men; but as in soothfastnesse,
> Thogh clerkes preyse wommen but a lyte,
> Ther can no man in humblesse him acquyte
> As womman can, ne can ben half so trewe
> As wommen been, but it be falle of newe. (932–8)

Job, type of human suffering, was also interpreted in the Middle Ages as a type of Christ. Griselda's patience, like Job's, mirrors the divine in human experience, and mirrors it in female form.

The feminist reader is immediately suspicious: is the assurance that women excel in patient suffering merely a means of confining them in their traditionally subordinate role by praising them for their meek acceptance of it?[7] Reassurance may come from the fact that patience is not, for Chaucer, a gender-specific virtue in the sense that it is a feminine ideal only; on the contrary, it is an ideal for both sexes alike. Activity is not reserved for men, passivity for women; the celebration of patience in the *Franklin's Tale* shows each sex active and passive by turns. But the ideal that governs this alternation is derived from female experience. What makes patience a specifically female quality for Chaucer is not, I think, the conventional expectations of his society about female behaviour. It is rather its intimate connection with female sexuality, and in particular with childbirth. In Latin, *patior* and *patientia* are technical terms for the female role in intercourse (Adams, 1982, 189–90), a usage that gives a punning quality to Chaucer's comments on Constance's wedding night in the *Man of Law's Tale*:

> They goon to bedde, as it was skile and right.
> For thogh that wyves been ful holy thinges,
> They moste take in pacience at night
> Swich maner necessaries as been plesinges
> To folk that han y-wedded hem with ringes,
> And leye a lyte hir holinesse asyde
> As for the tyme—it may no bet bityde. (708–14)

7. Lesley Johnson objects to the use of the word 'merely' here, asking 'why should the putative response of a feminist be constructed in unfairly reductive terms?' (1994, 203) So far from wishing to be 'unfairly reductive' to a putative feminist, by the 'feminist reader' here I meant *myself*; the question posed here is one I pose seriously to myself. Johnson argues that even if patience is accepted as an ideal for both sexes, 'a valuable question still remains about the masochistic qualities of the kind of spirituality on offer here and why it might be especially appropriate to realize the figure of a suffering God in female form' (ibid.). The second of these questions I try to answer above; the first would need a larger exposition of the word 'masochistic' which itself seems unfairly reductive. As I have argued in connection with Constance, there is no sign at all that Griselda *enjoys* suffering—quite the reverse.

Constance's patience derives not only from her holiness but also from her sexuality, and it expresses both.

To object to the identification of woman's sexual role as 'passivity' is, paradoxically, to endorse the masculine ideology that defines activity as superior. Chaucer himself is free of any such ideology. For him, it is the 'passive' role that is superior; we must never forget that patience *conquers*. It is 'rigour', the attempt to dominate and control, that is impotent and sterile. So woman's sexual activity expresses itself as acceptance; she is not violated or subordinated by male penetration, but absorbs it into her own essential rhythm, making it part of her own movement.

The quality of acceptance is even more important in childbirth, the crucial demarcation between male and female. In the same passage of the *Man of Law's Tale* we can see how the processes of parturition involve the will in cooperative responsiveness rather than initiatory decision.

> Now faire Custance, that is so humble and meke,
> So longe is goon with childe til that stille
> She halt hir chambre, abyding Cristes wille.
>
> The tyme is come a knave child she ber . . .
> (*Man of Law's Tale* 719–22)

The space between the stanzas enacts the quiet space in which the self is subordinated to the workings of nature. 'The tyme is come'; the moment of birth is determined not by human decree but by natural maturation, the 'fullness of the time' in which Mary brought forth her son (Gal. 4: 4). So Griselda's 'sadnesse', her 'fullness' of self-sufficiency, is linked with 'ripeness' ('rype and sad courage': 220; cf. 438). The acceptance of the slow maturation of another being within one's own is a fundamental image of patience. But the acceptance called for in childbirth is greater than this: it is above all the acceptance of pain. When Griselda is called upon to relinquish the second of her children, she expresses her resignation in Petrarch's Latin version of the tale by saying 'truly, I have no part in these children beyond the bearing of them' ('preter laborem'; Bryan and Dempster, 1941, 316). Chaucer intensifies her resignation into a strange poignancy:

> 'I have noght had no part of children tweyne
> But first siknesse, and after wo and peyne.' (650–1)

The strangeness lies in the first impression that Griselda is saying her children are nothing but a nuisance, and the oddity of this response from one whom we see elsewhere to be a tenderly loving mother concentrates attention on the words to find their meaning and the source of their ability to move. It lies, I think, in the acceptance of suffering that unites the bearing of children with the endurance of their loss. The 'siknesse, wo and peyne' of pregnancy and childbirth teach the self-surrender that is the very essence of patience.

Childbirth is not simply an image of suffering; it is an image of 'suffraunce' in the dual Middle English sense of 'suffering-and-allowing'. The woman in childbirth becomes the vehicle of a power that she can control only by full identification with it, by ceasing to resist it. It is the dual sense of 'suffraunce' that gives new meaning to the final statement that God

> . . . *suffreth* us, as for our excercyse,
> With sharpe scourges of adversitee
> Ful ofte to be bete in sondry wyse, . . .
> And for our beste is al his governaunce:
> Lat us than live in vertuous *suffraunce*.
> (1156–8, 1161–2; my italics)

'Allowing' here seems to be allocated to God; 'suffering' to mankind. But as in the *Man of Law's Tale*, the tale shows that the suffering that God 'allows' is visited on himself. Griselda, as she bids her daughter what she thinks is a last farewell, marks her with the sign of the cross 'Of thilke Fader—blessed moote he be!— / That for us deyde upon a croys of tree' (557–8). She does not refer, as she most naturally might, to the Son who died on the cross, but to the Father (Engle, 1989, 450); the Father who decreed the death of his Son is also the Son who suffered death at the will of his Father. For God to 'allow' the world to be as it is is for him also to suffer it, to endure the pain of its cruelty.

Julian of Norwich identifies the nature of the Second Person of the Trinity as 'moderhede', grounding the identification in the quality of mercy that unites Christ with human mothers, but also in the experience of suffering. The suffering of the Cross is assimilated to the pains of childbirth:

> We wytt [know] that alle oure moders bere vs to payne and to dyeng. A, what is that? But oure very moder Jhesu, he alone beryth vs to joye and to endlesse levyng, blessyd mot he be. Thus he susteyneth vs with in hym in loue and traveyle, in to the full tyme þat he wolde suffer the sharpyst throwes [torments] and grevous paynes that evyr were or evyr shalle be, and dyed at the last. And whan he had done, and so borne vs to blysse, yett myght nott all thys make a seeth [bring satisfaction] to his mervelous loue. And that shewd he in theyse hye ovyrpassyng wordes of loue: If I myght suffer more I wold suffer more. He myght no more dye, but he wolde nott stynte werkyng. (Long Text, Chap. 60)[8]

The love that embraces the pain of birth sustains and informs the mother's 'allowing' of her child to be chastised for its own good:

> The kynde lovyng moder that woot and knowyth the neyde of hyr chylde, she kepyth it full tenderly, as the kynde and condycion of moderhed wyll. And evyr as it waxith in age and in stature, she channgyth her werkes, but nott her loue. And when it is wexid of more age, she sufferyth it that it be chastised in brekynge downe of vicis, to make the chylde receyve vertues and grace. This werkyng with all þat be feyer and good, oure lord doth it in hem by whome it is done. (ibid.)

8. I adopt the variant reading 'throwes' in place of 'thornes'; Colledge and Walsh admit it is 'attractive', and it is in addition a clear example of *difficilior lectio* [the more difficult reading (and thus more likely to be authorial)—*Editors*].

The *Clerk's Tale* shares with Julian's *Showings* this relatively rare vision of divinity in female as well as male form.[9] For Chaucer, as for Julian, the suffering of childbirth is the mirror in which divine patience is reflected. It is the quintessential image of conquering patience, of powerful suffering, and one which validates the notion of patience as a female quality. If Walter's tyranny caricatures God's 'governaunce', Griselda's patience *truly* reflects God's suffering. Her 'vertuous suffraunce' is not opposed to God's 'governaunce'; it is one with it.

BIBLIOGRAPHY

Primary Works

Davies, R. T., ed. *Medieval English Lyrics: A Critical Anthology* (London: Faber and Faber, 1963).

Defoe, Daniel. *Roxana: The Fortunate Mistress*, ed. J. Jack (London: Oxford University Press, 1969).

Deguileville, Guillaume de. *Le Pèlerinage de l'âme*, ed. J. J. Stürzinger, Roxburghe Club (London: Nichols and Sons, 1895).

Hoccleve, Thomas. *Selections from Hoccleve*, ed. M. C. Seymour (Oxford: Clarendon Press, 1981).

Julian of Norwich. *A Book of Showings to the Anchoress Julian of Norwich*, ed. E. Colledge and J. Walsh, 2 vols. (Toronto: Pontifical Institute of Mediaeval Studies, 1978).

Oliphant, Margaret. *Autobiography and Letters of Mrs Margaret Oliphant*, ed. Mrs H. Coghill ([originally published 1899] Leicester: Leicester University Press, 1974).

Secondary Works

Adams, J. N. *The Latin Sexual Vocabulary* (London: Duckworth, 1982).

Bloomfield, M. W. 'The Man of Law's Tale: A Tragedy of Victimization and a Christian Comedy', *PMLA* 87 (1972): 384–90.

Bryan, W. F., and G. Dempster. *Sources and Analogues of Chaucer's Canterbury Tales* (Chicago: University of Chicago Press, 1941; repr. New York: Humanities Press, 1958).

Bynum, C. W. *Jesus as Mother: Studies in the Spirituality of the High Middle Ages* (Berkeley: University of California Press, 1982).

Cabassut, A. 'Une dévotion médiévale peu connue: la dévotion à "Jésus notre mère"', *Revue d'ascétique et de mystique* 25 (1949): 234–45.

Clasby, E. 'Chaucer's Constance: Womanly Virtue and the Heroic Life', *Chaucer Review* 13 (1978–9): 221–33.

Delany, S. 'Womanliness in the *Man of Law's Tale*' [originally published 1974–5], pp. 36–46 in her *Writing Woman: Women Writers and Women in Literature, Medieval to Modern* (New York: Schocken Books, 1983).

9. For documentation and discussion of the tradition, see Cabassut, 1949, Bynum, 1982 and Heimmel, 1982.

Eade, J. C. '"We ben to lewed or to slowe": Chaucer's Astronomy and Audience Participation', *Studies in the Age of Chaucer* 4 (1982): 53–85.

Engle, L. 'Chaucer, Bakhtin, and Griselda', *Exemplaria* 1 (1989): 429–59.

Gray, D. 'Chaucer and "Pite"', pp. 173–203 in *J. R. R. Tolkien, Scholar and Storyteller: Essays in Memoriam*, ed. M. Salu and R. T. Farrell (Ithaca, N.Y.: Cornell University Press, 1979).

Heimmel, J. P. *'God is Our Mother': Julian of Norwich and the Medieval Image of Christian Feminine Divinity* (Salzburg: Institut für Anglistik und Amerikanistik, University of Salzburg, 1982).

Johnson, L. 'Reincarnations of Griselda: Contexts for the *Clerk's Tale*?', pp. 195–220 in *Feminist Readings in Middle English Literature: The Wife of Bath and all Her Sect*, ed. R. Evans and L. Johnson (London and New York: Routledge, 1994).

Keiser, G. R. 'The Middle English *Planctus Mariae* and the Rhetoric of Pathos', pp. 167–93 in *The Popular Literature of Medieval England*, ed. T. J. Heffernan (Knoxville: University of Tennessee Press, 1985).

Kirk, E. D. '"Who Suffreth More Than God?": Narrative Redefinition of Patience in *Patience* and *Piers Plowman*', pp. 88–104 in *The Triumph of Patience: Medieval and Renaissance Studies*, ed. G. J. Schiffhorst (Orlando: University Presses of Florida, 1978).

Kittredge, G. L. 'Chaucer's Discussion of Marriage' [originally published 1911–12], pp. 188–215 in *Chaucer: Modern Essays in Criticism*, ed. E. Wagenknecht (New York: Oxford University Press, 1959).

Levy, B. S. 'The Meanings of *The Clerk's Tale*', pp. 385–409 in *Chaucer and the Craft of Fiction*, ed. L. A. Arrathoon (Rochester, Mich.: Solaris Press, 1986).

Mann, J. 'Parents and Children in the *Canterbury Tales*', pp. 165–83 in *Literature in Fourteenth-Century England*, ed. P. Boitani and A. Torti (Tübingen: Gunter Narr; Cambridge: D. S. Brewer, 1983) [1983a].

Mann, J. 'Satisfaction and Payment in Middle English Literature', *Studies in the Age of Chaucer* 5 (1983): 17–48 [1983b].

Middleton, A. 'The Clerk and his Tale: Some Literary Contexts', *Studies in the Age of Chaucer* 2 (1980): 121–50.

Morse, C. C. 'The Exemplary Griselda', *Studies in the Age of Chaucer* 7 (1985): 51–86.

Panofsky, E. '"Imago Pietatis": Ein Beitrag zur Typengeschichte des "Schmerzenmanns" und der "Maria Mediatrix"', pp. 261–308 in *Festschrift für Max J. Friedländer zum 60. Geburtstage* (Leipzig: E. A. Seemann, 1927).

Pinder, W. 'Die dichterische Würzel der Pietà', *Repertorium für Kunstwissenschaft* 42 (1920): 145–63.

Salter, E. *The Knight's Tale and The Clerk's Tale* (London: Edward Arnold, 1962).

Weissman, H. P. 'Late Gothic Pathos in *The Man of Law's Tale*', *Journal of Medieval and Renaissance Studies* 9 (1979): 133–53.

SUSAN SCHIBANOFF

From Worlds Apart: Orientalism, Antifeminism, and Heresy in Chaucer's *Man of Law's Tale*†

Although the *Man of Law's Tale* comes fifth in the order of the Canterbury tales in all but one manuscript,[1] readers often detect something initiatory about this performance. The Host's astronomical calculation of date and time in the Introduction to the tale sounds like a "new beginning" to Derek Pearsall,[2] and Cooper speculates that the Introduction, which implies that the storytelling has not yet begun, may once have stood at the head of all the tales, following the *General Prologue*.[3] Cooper also finds that the lawyer's tale of Custance, the Christian missionary bride, "certainly makes a new start":

> after the ever more sexually active women of the first fragment comes the saintly Emperor's daughter . . . [;] after the vagaries of Fortune and the frenzied human disorder of the preceding tales comes a story that insists throughout on the providential control of events.[4]

V. A. Kolve has also written on the initiatory nature of the Man of Law's tale, arguing, as does Cooper, that it provides the overall work "a new beginning"[5]: in contrast to the secular romance and bawdy fabliaux that constitute the first four tales told by the Knight, Miller, Reeve, and Cook, the austere story of Custance's trials and tribulations reorients the direction of the *Canterbury Tales*, heading it for the first time towards its pilgrimage goal. In Kolve's view, the Man of Law's tale encodes a Chaucerian "self-correction,"[6] a kind of interim palinode before the final Retraction, which serves the end of "clarification and renewal—for the *communitas* as much as for the individual Christian soul."[7] As Chaucer's spokesperson, Kolve's Man of Law rallies the faithful by presenting them the narrative of Custance's spiritual journey to emulate in their own travel to Canterbury.

The reading I shall develop here also detects something new and initiatory about the Man of Law's tale, but proceeds from my perception of a different kind of novelty in the narrative: the story of Custance presents Chaucer's sole textual confrontation with medieval Christianity's strongest religious rival, Islam, and it contains his only reference to the prophet Muhammad and to the Qur'an. My question from the start has been to

† From *Exemplaria* 8.1 (Spring 1996): 59–92. Reprinted by permission of Taylor & Francis Ltd., http://www.tandfonline.com. We have omitted pp. 92–96 of this essay because they deal with a problematic "Epilogue" not printed in this volume. We have made some corresponding adjustments in the text and notes as needed.

1. As Helen Cooper, *The Structure of the Canterbury Tales* (Athens: University of Georgia Press, 1984), 121, notes, "the manuscripts, with remarkable consistency, place [the Man of Law's Tale] after fragment I and the Cook's Tale, whether the tale ascribed to the Cook is the Chaucerian fragment or *The Tale of Gamelyn*." The one exception appears to be Hengwrt, but, Cooper observes (121 n11), Hengwrt "has a misplaced quire at this point."
2. Pearsall, *The Canterbury Tales* (London: Unwin Hyman, 1985), 286.
3. Cooper, *Structure*, 63, 120.
4. Ibid., 121.
5. V. A. Kolve, *Chaucer and the Imagery of Narrative: The First Five Canterbury Tales* (Stanford: Stanford University Press, 1984), 296.
6. Ibid., 368.
7. Ibid., 297.

interrogate why, at this particular juncture in the *Canterbury Tales* and nowhere else, Chaucer turns our attention to an alien faith, to a faraway place, to a distant time.

I shall argue that the Man of Law uses a discourse of orientalism[8] to issue a clarion call for unity—not among the general *communitas* of the faithful but specifically among the Christian men of his audience. What the lawyer endeavors to remedy by means of his tale is not so much the licentious disorder that characterizes the opening stories as it is the overt divisiveness that has broken out among their narrators, starting with the Miller's "quiting" of the Knight and continuing into the Reeve's angry retort to the Miller and the Cook's possible jab at the Host. As Lee Patterson notes,[9] this dissension takes the form of class antagonism, and the Miller's disruption proves to be the most "explicitly threatening" of all the discord that occurs on the pilgrimage.

The lawyer's strategy, I shall maintain, is to deflect attention from potentially explosive class rivalry by confronting the fractious men of fragment I with another world, another time, ultimately with the Other, in order to forge a sense of community—that is, fraternity—among them. Gradually but inexorably the Man of Law works to build an airtight case against the Other. It is a project that Chaucer eventually subverts by exposing its self-interested hypocrisy; like Patterson, I hear in the Man of Law "the voice of orthodoxy"[1] from which Chaucer dissociates himself. Yet, in the remaining Canterbury tales, Chaucer creates no subsequent voice persuasive enough to undermine the Man of Law's authority, discredited as it may be.

My reading also proceeds from my observation that the Man of Law constructs the Other in tightly intertwined guises in his tale—as Saracen or Muslim, as woman, and as heretic—and that the lawyer repeatedly performs a reductive rhetorical maneuver in order to induce Christian fraternity among the pilgrims. In locating orientalism at the heart of the Man of Law's treatment of the Muslim, I must take issue with such critics as Morton W. Bloomfield, who in 1952 judged the tale to be tolerant of cultural and religious diversity. Focussing on Chaucer's sense of history, Bloomfield also remarks that the narrative of Custance goes beyond its source to present matters from the "Mohammedan point of view" and to give credibility to Saracen deliberations concerning the sultan's impending conversion and marriage.[2] Elaborating upon Bloomfield's reading, Roger Ellis more recently argues that the tale offers a "sympathetic presentation of Islam" by virtue of Chaucer's "heterodox understanding" that the "experience of faith [is] remarkably *similar* no matter what the formal system created to contain it":

8. I use the term "orientalism" in the sense that Edward W. Said does, to indicate "a Western style for dominating, restructuring, and having authority over the Orient," *Orientalism* (New York: Pantheon Books, 1978), 3.
9. Lee Patterson, "'No Man His Reson Herde': Peasant Consciousness, Chaucer's Miller, and the Structure of the *Canterbury Tales*," in *Literary Practice and Social Change in Britain, 1380–1530* (Berkeley: University of California Press, 1990), 124. Patterson reiterates the nature of the Miller's explicit threat in *Chaucer and the Subject of History* (Madison: University of Wisconsin Press, 1991), 246.
1. Patterson, "No Man His Reson Herde," 124.
2. Bloomfield, "Chaucer's Sense of History," *JEGP* 51 (1952): 309. Note the use of "Mohammedan" even in modern scholarly discourse.

> The [Man of Law's] narrative hints at this heterodox understanding when it gives *similar* terms to Christian and Muslim to describe the experience of their own faith. The Muslim law is "sweete" [II.223], and the Christian "deere" [II.237], to its followers.[3]

Contra Bloomfield and Ellis, I maintain that the Man of Law is not sympathetic but hostile to Islam and that an altogether orthodox antipathy rather than "heterodox understanding" motivates the lawyer's implication that Islam imitates Christianity. The Man of Law renders Islam threatening not by depicting it as different from Christianity—as idolatrous—but by revealing its dangerous closeness to his own religion. He employs what I shall call the "rhetoric of proximity" to figure Islam as an insidious heresy that mimics Christianity.[4] In doing so, the lawyer avails himself of a popular medieval tradition regarding Islam's relationship to Christianity, albeit one unsupported by canon law.

I shall further argue that the Man of Law's hostility extends beyond religion to gender—specifically, to woman. In holding this view, I join with feminist critics who have commented upon the tale's misogyny for several decades now. Their analyses have largely centered upon Custance's passivity. Although for many readers Custance's lack of action and agency constitutes her Christian virtue, Sheila Delany has defined the problematic nature of this behavior: in the Man of Law's handling, it becomes less an emblem of laudable Christian suffering than a model for female submission.[5] Similarly, Priscilla Martin sees the tale as one of decidedly female—rather than Christian—suffering that endorses the tyranny of husband over wife.[6] So too does Elaine Tuttle Hansen remark upon Custance's resemblance to the "archetypally passive" woman who "put[s] the love of a man above all other responsibilities, even above life itself," in direct consequence of which she must endure "great suffering."[7]

Custance's passivity indeed offers little cause for feminist celebration, but my concern here will be to define the functional role it is made to play in the Man of Law's narrative. Not only does Custance's behavior provide a model of female submission, but it helps the Man of Law reach a more fundamental goal in his tale: to establish and maintain woman's difference from (inferiority to) man, her otherness. The Man of Law's overriding aim, I shall suggest, is to preserve and enhance such difference—between women and men, East and West, Islam and Christianity, ultimately between western patriarchal culture and the Other. That his rhetoric renders Muslims and women interchangeable and thus dehumanizes them is of no consequence to the lawyer; indeed, such reductiveness facilitates his creation

3. Roger Ellis, *Patterns of Religious Narrative in the Canterbury Tales* (Totowa, N.J.: Barnes & Noble, 1986), 146; italics mine.
4. Recent exploration of Chaucer's treatment of Islam is similarly skeptical concerning Chaucer's (or the Man of Law's) sympathy. See, for instance, Glory Dharmaraj, "Multicultural Subjectivity in Reading Chaucer's *Man of Law's Tale*," *Medieval Feminist Newsletter* 16 (1993): 4–8. Sheila Delany, *The Naked Text: Chaucer's Legend of Good Women* (Berkeley: University of California Press, 1994), remarks that Chaucer availed himself of the "patristic/popular mythos of the ever-threatening Orient" in the *Legend* (230), even though the poet is not a "raving warmonger" on the subject of the forced conversion of Muslims (185–86).
5. Sheila Delany, "Womanliness in the *Man of Law's Tale*," *ChauR* 9 (1974): 62.
6. Priscilla Martin, *Chaucer's Women: Nuns, Wives, and Amazons* (Iowa City: University of Iowa Press, 1990), 139.
7. Elaine Tuttle Hansen, *Chaucer and the Fictions of Gender* (Berkeley: University of California Press, 1992), 196.

of Christian fraternity. And what this tale-teller most fears—similitude—he exploits to realize this objective.

I

In his exploration of the homosexual as Other, Jonathan Dollimore establishes that such anxiety concerning sameness or proximity and such appropriation often go hand in hand in western culture.[8] Dollimore argues that the system of binary oppositions, so basic to western thought, finds similarity the "most disturbing of all forms of transgression": "the outlaw . . . as inlaw, and the other as proximate [prove] more disturbing than the other as absolute difference."[9] At the same time, ironically, the most effective way to maintain this system of polar opposition, which always favors the dominant party, is to figure its collapse—in particular, to depict the Other as potentially similar, the outlaw-as-inlaw.

The roots of this strategy of threatening proximity lie in patristic thought. In Augustine's theodicy, Dollimore notes, the figuration of evil as proximate to good—indeed, as intimate with good—leads to a strengthening of their binary opposition, for it means that "one must necessarily and always seek to distinguish the good from the evil": "as Augustine says, one knows evil only through good. From here it is a short step to knowing good by always and vigilantly distinguishing it from evil."[1] The perception that evil may masquerade as good causes the vigilant Christian continually to separate the two, to redefine and resituate evil as absolutely other. What I call the rhetoric of proximity, which draws the Other dangerously near by suggesting its similitude or "intimacy," ultimately serves the monitory purpose of displaying evil's disturbing likeness to good; it sounds the alarm, so to speak, that mobilizes the faithful to repel evil into a clearly delimited position as Other. The rhetoric of proximity thus plays an indispensable role in maintaining rigid binary oppositions by temporarily destabilizing them.

The simultaneous fear and exploitation of similitude that Dollimore detects in Augustine's theodicy surfaces in two later medieval discourses of domination, those of heresy and of antifeminism. Heresy was perceived—and represented—as an attack on the religious community from *within* itself as opposed to the challenge posed by the non-belief of those who

8. Jonathan Dollimore, *Sexual Dissidence: Augustine to Wilde, Freud to Foucault* (Oxford: Clarendon Press, 1991), 131–48. In Dollimore's terms, "similarity" or "proximity" indicates the intimate relationship that exists between supposedly opposite binaries. Such "intimacy" ultimately stems from the Christian anti-dualistic notion of evil as good's privation, not good's opposite, of vice as the perversion rather than antithesis of virtue. Evil and vice are thus "the more dangerous and potentially subversive for being in intimate relation with good" (141).

While I employ Dollimore's ideas of "transgressive proximity" and the "perverse dynamic" to theorize issues of gender, race, and religion in Chaucer, Glenn Burger has applied these concepts to (homo)sexuality; see his "Kissing the Pardoner," *PMLA* 107 (1992): 1142–56. Just as the Man of Law conflates the Muslim, woman, and the East, so are homosexuality, heresy, and Islam frequently coalesced in medieval thought. See, for instance, John Boswell, *Christianity, Social Tolerance, and Homosexuality* (Chicago: University of Chicago Press, 1980); Michael Camille, *The Gothic Idol: Ideology and Image-Making in Medieval Art* (Cambridge: Cambridge University Press, 1989), 90–92; Steven F. Kruger, "Claiming the Pardoner: Toward a Gay Reading of Chaucer's Pardoner's Tale," *Exemplaria* 6 (1994): 133 n45; Jeffrey Richards, *Sex, Dissidence and Damnation: Minority Groups in the Middle Ages* (London: Routledge, 1990), 148; and my "Mohammed, Courtly Love, and the Myth of Western Heterosexuality," *Medieval Feminist Newsletter* 16 (1993): 27–32.

9. Dollimore, 15.

1. Ibid., 138.

subscribed to contrary religious doctrines.[2] In canon law, the heretic (from Greek *haerein*, to choose) is one who keeps the name of Christian but chooses to doubt or deny some part of the faith, whereas the infidel rejects a religion never professed and the pagan remains ignorant of Christian religion.[3]

As "outlaws" rather than "inlaws," non-believers—pagans or infidels—posed the lesser threat to Christianity. Clearly defined as Other, non-Christians occupied a stable, unambiguous position. Ironically but perhaps logically, medieval Christianity could show an ecumenical and charitable attitude to virtuous heathens and good pagans, preferably long dead ones; Langland, Dante, and Chaucer all accord such figures as Trajan and Troilus a final resting place in heaven, if not ultimate salvation.[4] Good Saracens, the heroic figures of the *chansons de geste*, are dubbed "pagans," and, Norman Daniel observes, "there is a persistent effort to link them with the pagans of the ancient world,"[5] while evil Saracens are denied this relatively benign status.

By their definition as wayward "insiders," heretics, however, evoked a different response. Their insidious proximity to the dominant faith created a dangerous instability that demanded resolution, not complacency or tolerance. Typically, that resolution took one of two forms: the heretic was either reassimilated into the fold or altogether driven from it, clearly branded as other through excommunication or a worse fate. Condemned as a relapsed heretic, Joan of Arc, for instance, had but two choices: abjuration or the stake.[6] The heretic's "perversion"—or choice to turn away from true belief or doctrine—must either be eliminated (made orthodox or "straightened out") or exaggerated for all to recognize clearly.

While actual heretics such as Joan of Arc were subjected to attempts to clarify (and nullify) their ambiguous position, the concept of heresy, personified in Satan, might also serve useful ends and thus remained integral to Christian thought. As Augustine argued in the *City of God*, "heresies are necessary, to show which of you are in sound condition."[7] The archheretic, Satan, was similarly "necessary" to strengthen the faithful by

2. See Bernard Cullen, "Heresy," *Dictionary of the Middle Ages*, ed. Joseph R. Strayer (New York: Charles Scribner's Sons, 1985) 6: 202–4.
3. Ellen C. Shannon, *A Layman's Guide to Christian Terms* (New York: A. S. Barnes, 1969), s.v. "heresy."
4. On the virtuous pagan and salvation of the heathen in medieval literature, see R. W. Chambers, "Long Will, Dante, and the Righteous Heathen," *Essays and Studies* 9 (1923): 50–69; T. P. Dunning, "Langland and the Salvation of the Heathen," *Medium Aevum* 12 (1943): 45–54; Thomas G. Hahn, *God's Friends: Virtuous Heathens in Later Medieval Thought and English Literature* (Ph.D. thesis, University of California Los Angeles, 1974); and A. J. Minnis, *Chaucer and Pagan Antiquity* (Cambridge, England: D. S. Brewer, 1982), 55–56 and 61–67.
5. Norman Daniel, *Heroes and Saracens: An Interpretation of the Chansons de Geste* (Edinburgh: Edinburgh University Press, 1984), 263. Daniel notes exceptions to the treatment of Islam as heresy in the poetic tradition (*chansons de geste*) which calls Saracens "pagans" and views them as "non-Christian communities" (131). See also Antonio Franceschetti, "On the Saracen in Early Italian Chivalric Literature," *Comparative Literature East and West: Traditions and Trends; Selected Conference Papers*, ed. Cornelia N. Moore and Raymond A. Moody (Honolulu: College of Languages, Linguistics and Literature, University of Hawaii, 1986), 203–11. More typically, however, the Saracen is misrepresented not as heroic pagan but as evil heretic, as I discuss below. On this latter depiction, see William Wistar Comfort, "The Literary Role of the Saracens in the French Epic," *PMLA* 55 (1940): 628–59, and C. Meredith Jones, "The Conventional Saracen of the Songs of Geste," *Speculum* 17 (1942): 201–25.
6. Joan's "heresy" was her wearing of male attire, deemed idolatry, as I discuss in "True Lies: Transvestism and Idolatry in the Trial of Joan of Arc" (*Fresh Verdicts on Joan of Arc*, ed. Bonnie Wheeler and Charles T. Wood, Garland, 1996).
7. *City of God* 16.2, cited and translated by Dollimore, *Sexual Dissidence*, 139.

reminding them of unseen enemies that lurked nearby. Of the two high-water periods of Christian heresy, the earlier centuries of the patristic era and the last three centuries of the Middle Ages, the first no doubt resulted from the historical struggle that took place to define Christian dogma and defend it against its competitors. The second period, however, may have resulted from the Church's attempt to envision itself as persecuted, as "imitator Christi," when in fact it no longer had strong rivals in western Europe.

Steven Kruger has suggested that the Church sought to downplay its situation as "an enormously powerful institution" in the later Middle Ages by imagining itself as beset by enemies bent on its destruction, thus "deny[ing] its own power and claim[ing] the moral high ground of the persecuted."[8] If the late medieval Church did seek to present itself as marginalized, then the heretic, by definition a foe so similar as to be nearly invisible, offered it a unique opportunity, for the Church might posit the threat of heresy with impunity and thus rally the faithful to its defense. As Augustine had earlier noted, heresies are "necessary" for delimiting and preserving the Christian *communitas*.

The discourse of medieval antifeminism also feared yet traded upon similitude, specifically, woman's proximity to man. Patristic interpretation of the dual account of woman's creation in Genesis provides an early example of this simultaneous anxiety and exploitation. Genesis contains two etiologies of woman, the first in 1:27: "And God created man [*hominem*] to his own image: to the image of God he created him, male and female he created them."[9] As R. Howard Bloch observes, this passage implies the contemporaneous "creation of man and woman, undifferentiated with respect to their humanness, and whose equality is attested by a common designation [*homo*]."[1] The second—and more familiar—account of Eve's creation from Adam's rib (Genesis 2:7–22) accords man chronological and ontological priority over woman, who is called "*virago*" "because she was taken out of man" (Genesis 2:23). Despite the apparent differences between these accounts, both could be (and were) interpreted by medieval exegetes as arguments for woman's essential lack of similitude (hence inferiority) to man.

For instance, in *De Genesi ad litteram*, Augustine couples the egalitarian creation story of Genesis 1:27 with Genesis 1:28, which expresses God's

8. Steven Kruger, "Racial/Religious and Sexual Queerness in the Middle Ages," *Medieval Feminist Newsletter* 16 (1993): 35. Late medieval heresy, of course, did more than offer the church an excuse to self-marginalize; it voiced social protest and called for reform, particularly of the institution it attacked as overly materialistic or endowed. With respect to the Man of Law's seemingly irrelevant tirade against poverty in the prologue to his tale, it is interesting to note that scholars now see voluntary poverty as the common practice of late medieval heresies, including Lollardy. For instance, Gordon Leff, *Heresy in the Later Middle Ages: The Relation of Heterodoxy to Dissent, c. 1250–c. 1450* (New York: Barnes & Noble, 1969), 1:9, calls the veneration of poverty "one of the hallmarks of most heretical movements." The Man of Law castigates involuntary rather than elective poverty, yet any kind of anti-materialism may well be a threatening "heresy" to this lawyer who specializes in real estate transactions. Heretical or not, poverty evokes the lawyer's self-serving contempt; see Chauncey Wood, *Chaucer and the Country of the Stars* (Princeton: Princeton University Press, 1970), 192–244, and Paul A. Olson, *The Canterbury Tales and the Good Society* (Princeton: Princeton University Press, 1986), 90–91.

9. I cite the Douay-Rheims translation of the Old Testament (New York: P. J. Kennedy, 1950).

1. R. Howard Bloch, *Medieval Misogyny and the Invention of Western Romantic Love* (Chicago: University of Chicago Press, 1991), 22.

command about fecundity ("increase and multiply"). Genesis 1:28 defines the purpose of woman's creation (in 1:27) as generative, Augustine argues. Woman was created to help Adam beget children, and woman's role in generation is passive, opposite from and inferior to man's active role. Therefore, woman is different from (less perfect than) man, regardless of the cotemporality of their creation. So too, of course, in Augustine's interpretation of the second creation story of Adam's rib, Eve—*virago*—has a status dependent upon Adam, formed from his body and after him. Aquinas and other later medieval authorities also read both creation accounts as justification of the binary opposition of man and woman, expressing the widespread anxiety about similitude that fuels antifeminist discourse.[2]

At the same time, however, the story of Adam's rib was expropriated to implicate woman's alarming propensity to elide differences between the sexes and encroach upon male status. While the term "*virago*" initially indicated Eve's derivational and inferior status, her "otherness" from Adam, by the later Middle Ages it could also refer to woman's perverse desire to take over male roles and claim similitude to him. Throughout the Middle Ages, the term occurs pejoratively to denote a "mannish" woman, as the OED records, a bold, impudent, or wicked woman, a termagant and scold. And the reason the virago evoked such cultural scorn was because, as Gavin Douglas phrased it, she transgressed traditional gender roles by "exersand a mannis office."[3]

The virago became a standard monitory topos of later medieval antifeminist satire and discourse. Boccaccio's *Corbaccio*, for instance, warns its (implied) male audience that women's "appetite for mastery" knows no bounds. Women desire the accoutrements of power—crowns, girdles, ermines, and costly clothes—as ill-disguised "weapons to combat [their husbands'] mastery and vanquish it," "contriving with all their might to seize control" from their "wretched husbands" and become "mistress and ruler" of the house.[4] Like man or "mannish" but not quite man—"mistress and ruler": Boccaccio thus situates his virago in the disturbingly unstable position of proximity to man, the "outlaw" posing as "inlaw." Such ambiguous intimacy, Dollimore argues, leads to calls for resolution by the dominant party. Unlike the heretic, who theoretically might abjure the status of outlaw or Other and rejoin the faithful, medieval woman could not put aside her sex and literally become male. Thus, the patriarchal solution to the threat of her proximity was to reestablish woman's distance from man, to reinscribe her as inferior and subordinate to him, which Augustine, Aquinas, and others repeatedly did.

Ultimately, the rhetoric of proximity that devolves from patristic thought serves the agenda of western binary ideology, for its figuration of woman and heretic as, respectively, "mannish" and pseudo-Christian creates intense

2. Kari Elisabeth Borresen, *Subordination and Equivalence: The Nature and Role of Woman in Augustine and Aquinas*, trans. Charles H. Talbot (Washington, D.C.: University Press of America, 1981), 17–21 and 157, discusses both Augustine's reading of Genesis 1:27 in the context of 1:28 and Aquinas's use of *De Genesi ad litteram*. See also Prudence Allen, *The Concept of Woman: The Aristotelian Revolution, 750 BC–AD 1250* (Montreal: Eden Press, 1985), 223–25, on the dual creation account.
3. Cited by Larry D. Benson, ed., *The Riverside Chaucer*, 3rd ed. (Boston: Houghton Mifflin, 1987), 860 n359. All quotations of Chaucer's text are from this edition and cited parenthetically by fragment and line number in my text.
4. Boccaccio, *The Corbaccio*, trans. and ed. Anthony K. Cassell (Urbana: University of Illinois Press, 1975), 25.

pressure to resituate them as clearly distant or Other, be it passive helpmate or member of Satan's perverse legions. As I shall next argue, so too does medieval orientalism employ the discourse of similitude to misrepresent Islam as a crisis of proximity—as a Christian heresy—that demands response and resolution, not tolerance.[5]

II

In Said's view, the discourse of medieval orientalism sought to "domesticate the exotic" through analogy:

> since Christ is the basis of Christian faith, it was assumed—quite incorrectly—that Mohammed was to Islam as Christ was to Christianity. Hence the polemic name "Mohammedanism" given to Islam, and the automatic epithet "imposter" applied to Mohammed.[6]

The purpose of such rhetoric, Said maintains, was to establish Islam as both a misguided and inferior "version of Christianity," the "Orient and the Oriental [as] repetitious pseudo-incarnations of some great original (Christ, Europe, the West) they were supposed to have been imitating."[7]

Said speculates that the strangeness of Islam was deliberately rendered familiar—analogized—by western Europeans in the Middle Ages in order to mute and hence control the threat of this new religion:

> If the mind must suddenly deal with what it takes to be a radically new form of life—as Islam appeared to Europe in the early Middle Ages—the response on the whole is conservative and defensive. Islam is judged to be a fraudulent new version of some previous experience, in this case, Christianity. The threat is muted, familiar values impose themselves, and in the end the mind reduces the pressure upon it by accommodating things to itself as either "original" or "repetitious."[8]

Said bases his paradigm of domestication on European response to Islam in the early Middle Ages, yet Dollimore's theory of transgressive proximity would appear to illuminate more satisfactorily the dynamics of orientalism in the high and later medieval periods.[9] That is, the western rhetoric of proximity troped the familiarity of Islam in these latter eras not to mute the threat of the new religion to Europe, but to intensify it, to increase rather than reduce the "pressure" it created upon the occidental mind. Islam was commonly misrepresented as a heresy, a viper all the more dangerous for its proximity to Christianity's bosom, its intimacy with the

5. In addition to the work of Said, Daniel, Southern, and others cited specifically in these notes, several studies generally inform my discussion of medieval western attitudes to Islam: Jeremy Jones, "Christianity and Islam," *The Oxford Illustrated History of Christianity*, ed. John McManners (Oxford: Oxford University Press, 1990), 163–95; Rana Kabbani, *Europe's Myths of Orient* (Bloomington: Indiana University Press, 1986); Benjamin Z. Kadar, *Crusade and Mission: European Approaches Toward the Muslims* (Princeton: Princeton University Press, 1984); Bernard Lewis, *The Arabs in History* (1950; rpt. New York: Harper, 1967); Maria Rosa Menocal, *The Arabic Role in Medieval Literary History: A Forgotten Role* (Philadelphia: University of Pennsylvania Press, 1987); and W. Montgomery Watt, *The Influence of Islam on Medieval Europe* (Edinburgh: Edinburgh University Press, 1972).
6. Said, *Orientalism*, 60.
7. Ibid., 61–62.
8. Ibid., 59.
9. The period of the Crusades might well produce a different dynamic of orientalism, yet Norman Zacour, *Jews and Saracens in the Consilia of Oraldus de Ponte* (Toronto: PIMS, 1990), 22, maintains that "even during periods of truce with Islamic states, the tension between Christians and those Muslims who lived within Christian territory remained severe."

"true" faith.[1] To heresy, the medieval Christian mind could never accommodate itself; in one way or another—by conversion or extinction—the pressure posed by the heretic as proximate Other had to be released.

The creation of such pressure through the falsification of Islam as a Christian heresy appears to have taken on a new urgency in the period of the Crusades. Although such earlier authorities as John of Damascus (ca. 675–ca. 749) viewed Islam as the last and greatest of the Christian heresies,[2] it was Peter the Venerable (1092–1156) who made a concerted attempt to forge Christian "weapons" against the heresy of Islam, as Southern phrases it (39). In theological terms, canon law denied that Islam was a heresy. Norman Daniel clarifies the issue: canon law recognized that, unlike a heretic, a Muslim had not been baptized and therefore was "not liable to penalties for leaving the church."[3] In what Sheila Delany calls the "rational-scholarly approach" to Islam, this distinction is sometimes observed; Mark of Toledo, for instance, regards Islam as a *legem tertiam* that combines features of Judaism and Christianity yet evidently remains a separate religion.[4] And respect for the rationality of Islam, if not a willingness to grant its autonomous status, would seem to undergird the repugnance some Christians experienced over the forced conversion of Muslims. Delany cites William of Tripoli and thirteenth-century Dominican and Franciscan missionaries who "believed in the principle that God is not pleased by forced worship."[5] And Dana Carleton Munro charts the development of a generally more positive and accurate European approach to Muslims beginning in the thirteenth century, due in part, he speculates, to increased contact between East and West and to the appearance of a new enemy, the Byzantines.[6]

Yet, Munro notes, a stronger counter-tradition of antipathy to Islam exists throughout the Middle Ages: the majority of Christian clergy remained hostile, especially during the high propaganda periods preceding new Crusades.[7] And Delany discusses the deep roots of later medieval (Chaucerian) orientalism. Founded on patristic and popular attitudes "older than the rationalistic one that had developed since the twelfth century," this antipathetic tradition "maintained the idea of a sinister, immoral, insidious Orient."[8] The notion of an "insidious" Orient had as its corollary, I would argue, the premise that Islam was a Christian heresy, an

1. R. W. Southern, *Western Views of Islam in the Middle Ages* (Cambridge: Harvard University Press, 1962), 39, observes that Islam, in fact, "never made the slightest appeal in Europe," and, if accurate, one of the reasons for this failure, I would suggest, is the success of the rhetoric of proximity.
2. Cf. Daniel J. Sahas, *John of Damascus on Islam* (Leiden: Brill, 1972).
3. Norman Daniel, *Islam and the West: The Making of an Image* (Edinburgh: Edinburgh University Press, 1960), 187. In *The Arabs and Medieval Europe* (London: Longmans, 1975), 254, Daniel further notes that "although theoretically Islam was identified as the sum of ancient heresies, it was never actually treated as a heresy until the sixteenth-century Inquisition was able to lay its hands on *baptized* Moriscos" (italics mine). Daniel also observes that Islam was never associated specifically with particular heresies of the high Middle Ages, e.g., Albigensians, Waldensians (*Arabs*, 246–47). The charges of heresy against Islam are painted broadly—"sum of all heresies," "sink of all heresies," etc. These accusations are rhetorical, not theological, meant for popular consumption, not for ecclesiastical court (cf. Daniel, *Arabs*, 246).
4. Delany, *Naked Text*, 184.
5. Ibid., 185.
6. Munro, "The Western Attitude toward Islam during the Period of the Crusades," *Speculum* 6 (1931): 329–43.
7. Ibid., 343.
8. Delany, *Naked Text*, 186.

internal perversion of the putatively true faith. Learned men promoted this view, and some apparently recognized at the same time that it was a falsification, as is the case with Peter the Venerable. Peter, who wrote his *Summa totius haeresis Saracenorum* for the purpose of acquainting Europeans with Islam so that they might resist it, opens his work by arguing that Islam is the greatest, the most formidable, of all the Christian heresies, as had his predecessor, John of Damascus. But, James Kritzeck notes, Peter immediately subjects his choice of terms to scrutiny, questioning whether a body of religious doctrine that originated outside, not within, the Church could be called a "heresy":

> I cannot clearly decide whether the Mohammedan error must be called a heresy and its followers heretics, or whether they are to be called pagans. For I see them, now in the manner of heretics, take certain things from the Christian faith and reject other things; then—a thing which no heresy is described as ever having done—acting as well as teaching according to pagan customs.[9]

In the end, Kritzeck comments, while Peter left the decision up to his readers whether to call Islam a Christian heresy or a distinct pagan faith, he himself chose to view it as a heresy.

Daniel maintains that the western image of Islam as the "culmination or summit of all heresy" was widespread, if by no means universal, for many of Peter's contemporaries adopted the term casually and carelessly in spite of canon law: "neither at Cluny nor elsewhere did polemists take the canonical position into account."[1] Some authorities saw no real distinction between the Muslim and the heretic and treated them as equivalents, even if they were aware that Muslims had not entered the Catholic faith and thus could not renounce it.[2] The popular western notion that Islam was carved out of Christian dogma took different literary forms, often fantastic in conception:

> [T]here were stories that associated Muhammad with the New Testament heresiarch Nicholas; others that supposed him to have been under the influence of, or actually to have been, a Roman cardinal or cleric, frustrated in his ambition, who perverted his own converts to spite the Roman Church; together with the poems of Waltherius, du Pont, and before them Hildebert, all these presuppose that Islam arose in a Christian people, "derelicta fide catholica."[3]

The effect of the polemical decision by Peter and others to mischaracterize Islam as a Christian heresy was, in Daniel's words, to find a place for it *within* the "family of Christian error,"[4] to present it as an erroneous faith

9. Text and translation are from James Kritzeck, *Peter the Venerable and Islam* (Princeton: Princeton University Press, 1964), 143–44.
1. Daniel, *Islam*, 187. The notion of Islam as Christian heresy lingers, implicitly or explicitly, in some of the earlier scholarship I have cited above, as, for instance, in Southern's statement: "But in fact the heresy of Mahomet—if it was a heresy—never made the slightest appeal in Europe" (*Western Views*, 39).
2. Norman Zacour, *Jews and Saracens*, 42, cites the lack of distinction between Muslims and heretics in Oraldus's consilium 51. Oraldus (d. 1337?) also equates Jews with Saracens and heretics. See also Peter Herde, "Christians and Saracens at the Time of the Crusaders: Some Comments of Contemporary Medieval Canonists," *Studia Gratiana* 12 (1967): 359–76.
3. Daniel, *Islam*, 83–84.
4. Ibid., 184.

that Christians could see only as a perversion of their *own* truth. In particular, Islam's denial of Christ's divinity was considered the most blasphemous part of its heretical falsehood. Yet Islam did accept Christ as a prophet, and the western rhetoric of proximity contained several tropes to acknowledge that the Qur'an mixed truth with untruth, honey with poison. Perhaps more than anything else, this recognition of the Qur'an's "sweetness," its "truth" about Christ, positioned Islam in what Dollimore would call the "permanently unstable" position of intimacy with Christianity and hence demanded resolution. Typically, Christian polemicists and other western writers suggested that the problem posed by Islam's proximity might be solved in one of two related ways: either by fully assimilating Islam to Christianity or by exposing it as a diabolical plot and altogether rejecting it. In either case, the intent was to eradicate Islam from the West and insure Christian hegemony. Even the relatively more benign "scholarly" tradition, Delany observes, "was as determined as any other to extirpate Islam."[5]

An example of what Daniel sees as the assimilative approach occurs in William of Tripoli's *Tractatus de statu Saracenorum* (ca. 1271), which encourages Muslims to think that "they themselves were in a fair way to becoming Christians."[6] A later work expressing the same viewpoint but addressed to a Christian audience is Mandeville's *Travels*. It opens its discussion of the Saracens with an enumeration of the beliefs and doctrines shared by the Qur'an and the Scriptures, stressing the infancy narrative and Christ's status as a prophet. It then solves the "problem" of Islam's proximity to Christianity by seeing in it an opportunity for evangelizing:

> because [the Saracens] go so nigh our faith, they be lightly converted to Christian law when men preach them and shew them distinctly the law of Jesu Christ, and when they tell them of the prophecies.[7]

Daniel points out that favorable western commentary on the closeness of Islam to Christianity always had the ulterior motive of conversion, just as praise of a Saracen—usually the token figure, Saladin—served the satirical purpose of exhorting Christians to live up to the ideals of their own faith. After all, the rationale went, if a Muslim could achieve virtue, a Christian should strive to do at least as much.

The inverse western response to the challenge of the Qur'an's "truth" was to expose it as Muhammad's trick to deceive innocent Christians, as does an anonymous Cluniac commentator:

> In the first chapter (i.e., surah II) [Muhammad] immediately praises prayers and alms, that is, under the appearance of seeming good he may entice the unwary to believe him. Notice throughout the whole book that, with marvellous cunning, when he is going to say something ungodly, or recalls having said it, he soon puts in something about fasting, or about prayer, or praising God.[8]

5. Delany, *Naked Text*, 185.
6. *Islam*, 263. Munro, "Western Attitude," 341–42, summarizes William's account.
7. *The Travels of Sir John Mandeville*, ed. A. W. Pollard (New York: Dover, 1964), 91.
8. Translated by Daniel, *Islam*, 164.

Yet another metaphor that unmasks Muhammad's fraud, in which he is characterized as offering the unwary "deadly poison" within a "sweet apple," analogizes the Prophet to the ultimate instigator of the heresy of Islam: Satan. Often, the link between Christianity's arch-heresiarch, its first and chief pervert, and Muhammad is asserted more baldly. For Peter the Venerable, Muhammad is simply "this Satan," one who advanced all previous heresies, a nefarious task to be "wholly completed by Antichrist, according to diabolical intention." William of Tyre phrases the relationship in familial terms: Muhammad is the "first-born of Satan." As Satan had seduced Eve, Muhammad "seduced" the Orient. Jacques de Vitry combines all these motifs in his condemnation of Muhammad:

> [L]ike another Antichrist and the first-born son of Satan, transfigured like Satan into an angel of light, Muhammad, upheld by God's great anger and special displeasure, with the co-operation of the enemy of the human race, perverted . . . more people than any other heretic before his time.[9]

In this case, the difficulty posed by Islam's proximity to Christianity was not soluble by subsuming its followers within the community. Instead, Islam's "poison" had to be exposed and expelled. Characterized as the first-born son of Christianity's initial and chief pervert, Muhammad was distinctly cordoned off as absolutely Other, beyond the pale, even if the rhetoric of proximity would continue its inherent work of resituating Islam dangerously close to Christianity only to inspire yet more intense acts of resolution. In practice, these acts were often violent: "it is evident that Christendom recognized a relationship which aimed primarily at the destruction of Islam, and in which missionary endeavor held a subordinate place."[1] Even as late and supposedly liberal a cleric as Robert Holcot (d. 1349) argued the right to kill Muslims who refused to convert. If Christian attempts at conversion fail, Holcot reasons, then the community is justified in protecting itself from the dangerous element that threatens its integrity, just as "a putrid member must be cut off from the natural body."[2]

Holcot's diction figures Islam not as an external foe, but as *in*fection, an internal corruption of the natural body of the community; and the communal body must act to rid itself of this deadly venom. As I shall next trace, the narrative movement of the *Man of Law's Tale* enacts a similarly oscillating paradigm of medieval orientalism, for it tropes Islam's "sweetness"—its intimately heretical relationship with Christianity—only to reveal the poison within that calls for a communal act of expulsion. Although Paul E. Beichner has concluded that Chaucer's secular lawyer "must have known much canon law in so far as it touched upon civil law and things temporal,"[3] such knowledge would not necessarily have impeded the Man of Law's orientalist project, for any number of medieval religious authorities chose to ignore canon law and present Islam as a heresy. I shall further argue that the lawyer constructs woman's otherness on the same model. * * *

9. This passage from Jacques de Vitry, and the preceding quotations of Peter and William, are translated by Daniel, *Islam*, 185.
1. Daniel, ibid., 123.
2. Translated by Daniel, *Islam*, 322.
3. Paul E. Beichner, "Chaucer's Man of Law and *Disparitas Cultus*," *Speculum* 23 (1948): 75.

III

Based upon a section of Nicholas Trevet's Anglo-Norman *Chronique* (ca. 1334) and, probably, John Gower's adaptation of it in his *Confessio amantis*, the lawyer's narrative of Custance follows the main outlines of its sources.[4] In all three versions, the saint-like Christian woman is first pledged in marriage to the sultan of Syria on condition that he, a Muslim, convert to her religion. The sultan's mother takes deep offense at her son's conversion and has him murdered, exiling Custance at sea. Custance eventually washes ashore in Northumbria and in due course weds its pagan monarch, Aella, who also converts. Fiercely opposed to her son's action, Aella's mother engineers Custance's second exile. Set adrift again, this time with her infant son, Custance makes her way back to Rome, and her lot finally begins to improve as she and her child are reunited with Aella and with her father, the emperor of Rome.

Although Trevet, Gower, and Chaucer relate the same basic set of events, each shapes the narrative to different ends—respectively, to biography, moral exemplum, and orientalist polemic—and this molding is foreshadowed in each version's development of the initial episode. Taking the role of biographer, albeit of a pseudo-historical narrative, Trevet opens his life of Constance with claims to historical accuracy; he alludes to the different sources (various chronicles, including the ancient one of the Saxons) he has drawn upon, some of which conflict with one another concerning Constance's genealogy. Trevet sorts out the matter and then reconstructs Constance's family tree, identifying her father, mother, and son, and recounting details of Constance's early years with her parents.[5]

Gower's narrator, Genius, however, characterizes his tale in advance as moral exemplum, not as history or biography. Genius terms the Constance narrative a "tale of gret entendement" (*CA* 2.584)[6] and offers it as an example of correct behavior in response to envy and detraction. He too begins the tale with reference to Constance's early years in Rome, but truncates the discussion of sources and focusses instead on the worthiness of Constance's father, the emperor Tiberius Constantius, and Constance's own good name, setting the stage for the attacks by Envy and Backbiting in the guise of the two evil mothers.

Unlike Trevet and Genius, whose first episodes feature Constance, the Man of Law initially ignores her, casting his opening focus instead upon the group of Syrian merchants that has travelled to the Christian community

4. The extensive scholarship on the sources of Chaucer's tale of Custance is summarized by David Raybin, "Custance and History: Woman as Outsider in Chaucer's *Man of Law's Tale*," SAC 12 (1990): 72–73, and by A. S. G. Edwards, "Critical Approaches to the *Man of Law's Tale*," in *Chaucer's Religious Tales*, ed. C. David Benson and Elizabeth Robertson (Cambridge, England: D. S. Brewer, 1990), 87–90. See also Peter Nicholson, "The *Man of Law's Tale*: What Chaucer Really Owed to Gower," *ChauR* 26 (1991): 153.

5. For lack of a better text of Trevet, which is under preparation by the Chaucer Library, I have relied upon Margaret Schlauch's edition of Oxford MS Magdalen 45 in W. F. Bryan and Germaine Dempster, eds., *Sources and Analogues of Chaucer's Canterbury Tales* (1941; rpt. New York: Humanities Press, 1958), 165–81, and Edmund Brock's dual-language edition of British Museum Arundel 56 in F. J. Furnivall, Edmund Brock, and W. A. Clouston, eds., *Originals and Analogues of Some of Chaucer's Canterbury Tales* (1872; rpt. London: N. Trubner, 1887), 1–53. Quotations from Trevet, or Brock's translations, in my text are cited as *Chron* by page number from Brock's edition.

6. For Gower's *Confessio amantis*, I use the edition by Russell A. Peck (New York: Holt, Rinehart, Winston, 1968), cited by book and line number in my text as *CA*.

of Rome either for business or leisure ("for chapmanhood or for disport," II. 143). Whatever the merchants' motivation, their passage from Syria to Rome is unremarkable, historically no doubt a commonplace occurrence given the physical proximity of the two Mediterranean locations. Their merchandise ("chaffare," II.138) may be novel, but in themselves the merchants evoke little curiosity. In fact, the Man of Law goes out of his way—beyond Trevet and Gower—to underline the extent to which the Syrians exhibit western values and attitudes. He observes that the merchants are not merely rich and successful, but trustworthy and honest ("sadde and trewe," II.135). These are indeed good men, as seen through western eyes. Like Mandeville, the Man of Law searches for commonalities; at least at the outset of his tale, he makes no mention of the cultural and religious differences—the *disparitas cultus*[7]—between Syrians and Romans. Instead, the Man of Law works to establish the closeness, both geographically and culturally, between the two as his opening act.

His next move is to recount how these merchants come to learn of Custance's reputation for goodness and beauty and carry word of it back to their ruler, the sultan. Here the lawyer's emphasis is more upon the "traffic" between the groups of men—the Romans who sing Custance's praises and the Syrians who heed it—than it is upon Custance herself, who has not yet actually appeared in the tale.[8] No cultural or other barriers prevent the Syrians from recognizing and appreciating western—Roman—goodness and beauty as soon as they hear reports of them. Forthwith, the merchants load their ships, catch a glimpse of the "blisful mayden" (II.172) for themselves, and return home as Custance's ambassadors.

In contrast, Trevet and Genius's merchants are clearly delineated as Other the moment we encounter them: they are presented as pagan or heathen traders who have arrived in Rome. Trevet identifies their origin as the great Saracenland, wherever that vague region might be ("marchauntz paens hors de la graunde sarazine," *Chron.* 5), while Genius specifies their homeland as "Barbarie" (*CA* 2.599),[9] and both narrators maintain an emphasis upon the foreignness of the newcomers. Indeed, the merchants' visit to Rome immediately arouses Constance's curiosity, and she seeks them out to learn of their land and of their religious beliefs. Upon discovering that the merchants are heathens ("paens," *Chron.* 5), she sets to preaching them the Christian faith. Her instruction is so forceful that in short course the foreign merchants renounce, in Genius's words, their "false goddes" (*CA* 2.610), convert, and receive baptism. They then return to their land. The episode is brief and aptly summed up in the marginal annotation of Trevet's manuscript (Arundel 56): "conuersio paganorum" (*Chron.* 5). Significantly (and accurately, according to canon law), Trevet considers his Saracens to be pagans, unbaptized non-believers, rather than heretics—unambiguous outlaws rather than outlaws posing as inlaws.

As the Chaucerian narrative continues, however, so does its emphasis upon the commonalities between Syrians and Romans, culminating in

7. See Beichner, "*Disparitas Cultus*," 72.
8. In somewhat different contexts, R. A. Shoaf, "'Unwemmed Custance': Circulation, Property, and Incest in the Man of Law's Tale," *Exemplaria* 2 (1990): 287–302, and Laurel L. Hendrix, "'Pennannce profytable': The Currency of Custance in Chaucer's Man of Law's Tale," *Exemplaria* 6 (1994): 141–66, view Custance as a token of exchange between men, as does Patterson, *History*, 285.
9. The Man of Law's Custance echoes this place name, II.281.

the voluntary and altogether effortless conversion of the former to the latter's faith. Hearing from the merchants of Custance's great "noblesse" (II.185), the sultan sets his heart upon the emperor's daughter and to that end assigns his privy council the task of discovering some remedy for his lovesickness.[1] His advisors consider several cures, including magic and deception, but conclude that the only relief for the sultan's malady is to wed Custance. At this point, the issue of cultural diversity throws a brief shadow across the lawyer's narrative: the sultan's councillors doubt that a Christian emperor would allow his daughter to marry under "Mahoun's" law "by cause that ther was swich diversitee / Bitwene hir bothe lawes" (II.220–21).

But the hurdle raised by this "diversitee" is easily overcome, for the sultan soon waves aside his own faith and vows to convert in order to wed Custance. Like Mandeville, whose Saracens may be "lightly converted," the Man of Law stresses the ease with which the sultan comes to terms with Custance's religious differences by speeding the narrative along: "what nedeth gretter dilitacioun?" (II.232), the narrator asks as he quickly runs through the negotiations that take place between Syrians and Romans, condensing greatly this part of Trevet's story. In short space, the Man of Law brings both sides to agreement—"they been accorded" (II.238). Sounding again the note of commonality between Muslims and Christians—"this same accord was sworn on eyther side" (II.244)—the Man of Law succinctly draws this section of his narrative to a close: "this is th' ende" (II.255). The followers of Muhammad's "lawe sweete" take up the parallel "lawe deere" of Christ, and every Christian is instructed to pray that Christ look favorably upon the union between the new convert and his bride. By implication, the Man of Law figures the sultan's religious faith as but a variation of Christianity, and his conversion requires little effort. The sultan's conversion also seems not to demand the sacrament of baptism; or, if it does, the lawyer has the ceremony performed discreetly offstage in order to mute the actual differences between Islam and Christianity as the canonists saw them.

The unique congruity that Chaucer's narrator establishes between the law of Islam and Christianity, Syrians and Romans, in the first part of the story of Custance gains emphasis from the disparity he creates between different religions and cultures in the second part, which relates Custance's further adventures in sixth-century England, specifically, in the Northumberland ruled by King Aella upon whose shores Custance's boat washes up after her exile from Syria. The first note the Man of Law strikes in this second episode is one of cultural difference: upon her discovery by the Saxon constable, Custance begs for mercy "in hir langage" (II.516), which, of course, is not the tongue of Saxon Britain, but a "maner Latyn corrupt" (II.519), or Italian.[2]

1. The sultan's sudden and intense passion for Custance, a woman he has never seen, is an orientalist motif in that it analogizes the sultan to the lovesick knight of western romance whose beloved remains afar, although it might also be seen to stereotype the sultan as the sensualist eastern potentate.
2. *Riverside Chaucer*, 861 n519. See John A. Burrow, "'A Maner Latyn Corrupt,'" *Medium Aevum* 30 (1961): 33–37. The Man of Law earlier finessed the problem of how Custance spoke with her new compatriots and inlaws-to-be, implying that Syrian and Roman understood one another unaided.

By contrast, Gower's Genius altogether sidesteps the matter of linguistic difference at this point in the narrative and takes poetic license to allow the Roman woman to communicate with her Saxon hosts. Trevet's Constance knows several languages, including Saxon, and she speaks the constable's tongue ("en sessoneys," *Chron.* 13) so well that she raises his hopes that perhaps she is one of his own race, maybe the daughter of a Saxon king from abroad, from Germany, Saxony, Sweden, or Denmark. Speaking her own language and no other, the lawyer's Custance, however, is too foreign-sounding to excite such expectations in her hosts. By unexplained means, she manages to make herself understood, yet the Man of Law establishes the dominant note of diversity between Latin and Saxon culture early in this episode.

Evidently, Custance is also foreign-looking to her new Saxon acquaintances. Aella's mother, Donegild, opposes the marriage of her son to Custance not because, as in Trevet, she envies her daughter-in-law's marvellous beauty ("merueilouse beaute," *Chron.* 25), goodness and purity, or, as in Gower, because she fears her new in-law will displace her (*CA* 2.648), but because it seems to her an insult that her son should wed "so straunge a creature" (II.700) as Custance. Unlike the Syrian sultan, who was smitten with Custance's physical beauty, or at least with the report of it, Aella appears largely unaware of or unaffected by Custance's charms. The Saxon king marries Custance, the Man of Law explains, because Christ wills it, a motivation unique to the lawyer's version of the tale:

> And after this Jhesus, of his mercy,
> Made Alla wedden ful solempnely
> This hooly mayden, that is so bright and sheene;
> And thus hath Crist ymaad Custance a queene.
> II.690–93

The Man of Law sounds the note of cultural estrangement again as he turns his attention to the religion of Custance's Saxon hosts. Unlike Trevet and Gower's accounts, which merely remark that Constance comes to shore in a heathen land, the *Man of Law's Tale* depicts sixth-century England in greater detail as a land conquered by pagans ("payens," II.534, 542), who have driven all but a few Christian Britons into Wales. Those native Christians who do remain must practice their religion secretly, shielding it from the "hethen folk" (II.549) who now rule the realm. Unlike the parallels between the "sweete lawe" of Islam and the "deere" one of Christianity that the lawyer created earlier, he establishes no close ties between Custance's faith and that of Aella's people. Indeed, as the Man of Law comments, the constable's wife Hermengyld takes a liking to Custance in spite of her religion, not because of it:

> This constable and dame Hermengyld, his wyf,
> Were payens, and that contree everywhere,
> *But* Hermengyld loved [Custance] right as hir lyf.
> II.533–35; italics mine

The Saxon conversion to Christianity in the second part of the Man of Law's narrative is also configured differently than was that of the Syrians in the first part. In the earlier episode, the sultan's councillors "by wey of resoun" (II.219) lead their lord to see that he must convert in order to have

Custance; however inadvertently, the sultan's advisors themselves further the Christian agenda. The pagan Saxons, however, require overt external agency to persuade them to accept the truth of Custance's faith, and Custance herself helps effect the initial conversions. After Christ converts Hermengyld (II.538–39), Custance emboldens her to perform his will and restore sight to the blind Briton (II.566). When the astonished constable questions this miracle, Custance expounds upon "oure lay" (II.572) until he too converts. Aella's conversion also requires acts of divine intervention, in the form of the mysterious hand that knocks down Custance's accuser and a disembodied voice that declares her innocent of his false charge of murder. These two events lead the Saxon king (and "many another," II.685) to convert, followed by Aella's marriage to Custance. Unlike the Syrians, the pagan Saxons do not bring about their own conversion; rather, they capitulate to a wondrous and frightening display of divine power and might, abetted by Custance herself.

Thus, in contrast to the distant pagan Saxons, the Muslims of the Man of Law's tale indeed appear "nigh" unto Christianity, as Mandeville would have phrased it, and the lawyer's efforts to situate Islam close to Christianity culminate in the proposed dynastic merger between Romans and Syrians when Custance and the sultan are to marry. But, as the rhetoric of proximity dictates, at exactly this juncture the Man of Law reveals the corruption within Islam that calls for its violent repositioning as Other. Upon learning of her son's conversion and negotiations to wed Custance, the sultaness herself feigns conversion and requests the honor of holding a banquet for her son and his Roman guests. At the banquet, the sultaness reveals her malice; her men slay all the Christians, both Syrian converts and Roman visitors, and set Custance adrift. Not only is the impending union between Custance and the sultan averted in this act, but it leads to the separation of the two cultures and religions, for Custance's father, emperor of Rome, later retaliates against the sultaness and her entire country of Muslims. Roman forces invade Syria and "brennen, sleen, and brynge [its inhabitants] to meschaunce / Ful many a day" (II.964–65). As the Man of Law observes, it is certainly "heigh vengeance" (II.963) that Christians exact upon Muslims.

In their retaliation upon Islamic Syria, the Romans reverse—and thus complete—the lawyer's narrative paradigm that began in similitude. They enact his warning that proximity may harbor and disguise danger, and they model one extreme resolution of the unsettling ambiguities they perceive in such intimacy. This solution takes the form of eradicating the corruption that lurks near Christianity, if not within its very family, and resituating Islam in its radically opposite (and inferior) position as Other. The Syrians literally disappear from the Man of Law's narrative at this point, enabling the tale to proceed to its joyous conclusion of reuniting Custance with her *western* family, her Saxon husband, Aella, and her Roman father, and to end on a note of dynastic succession in the observation that Custance and Aella's son, Maurice, became a model Christian emperor. As Margaret Schlauch identifies it, this "recognition scene" is typical of Greek romance,[3] but I would suggest that it functions in the

3. Bryan and Dempster, *Sources and Analogues*, 160.

Man of Law's narrative to draw round the wagons—western Christian defenses—against a now clearly defined oriental Other.

If the Man of Law partly shapes his narrative to provide an etiology of British Christianity, aligning its origins with the dynastic line that begins in the new emperor, Maurice, he also contrasts this successful merger with the disastrous and aborted union between East and West. Whether or not many fourteenth-century English people had actually met Muslims, or so-called Saracens, such narratives as the Man of Law's must have informed their response to them. But this reinscription of the oriental as Other does not complete the lawyer's cultural work, for he also employs the cautionary discourse of transgressive proximity to create a second outsider in his tale, this one, however, known personally to every Englishman: woman.

IV

Islam may stalk the boundaries of Christianity in the *Man of Law's Tale*, but closest to its center lurks the primal transgressor, Satan, the heresiarch of whom Muhammad is but a shadow, or, as medieval writers phrased it, "first-born son." Furthermore, the lawyer's narrative couples Satan with an equally alarming figure to the medieval patriarchal mind, woman, through whose agency the "father of lies" exclusively operates to undermine Christianity. Woman, Syrian as well as Saxon, not only imitates Satan's deceptive means but, as the Man of Law exposes her, presents the ultimate menace: although distanced and putatively stabilized in ancient and medieval philosophy and science as man's binary opposite, she schemes to obscure these differentiating marks and become, if not actually male, like man—"mannysh" (II.782), as the lawyer phrases it. Such "mannishness" is the more threatening transgression the Man of Law wishes to reveal, for he presents it as having plagued the entire world—Occident as well as Orient—from its inception, from Eve through Semiramis to the sultaness and Donegild, and, by extension, to the lawyer's own era.[4] Compared to woman, Islam is an analogous but localized and recent problem.

As Satan's agents, women in the *Man of Law's Tale* work against both Christianity and patriarchy through deception and infiltration. In both the Syrian and Saxon episodes, women are in-laws—actual or intended mothers-in-law of Custance—who are at the same time Dollimore's "outlaws." Their transgressive acts originate in response to Custance's intrusion of a foreign religion into their worlds, but, as the Man of Law presents it, these women also plot to usurp the traditionally masculine power of rulership for themselves.

Outraged that her son has abandoned "Makometes lawe" (II.336) in order to marry Custance, the sultaness vows to die rather than also take up the "newe lawe" (II.337) of Christianity. She wishes to reestablish the Qur'an as the law of the land and thus to escape the pains of hell for renouncing Muhammad. So too does Trevet's sultaness act out of concern that her son's conversion imperils the future of Islam in Syria (*Chron.* 8). Yet the Man of Law alone creates a desire for conventionally male power in

4. My interpretation is indebted to Delany's important early reading of the way in which women define one another in the Man of Law's tale ("Womanliness," 67–71), and to Jill Mann, *Geoffrey Chaucer* (Atlantic Highlands, N.J.: Humanities Press, 1991), 130–31, for a similar reading of how "mannishness" is made to gloss "womanliness" in the tale. [See above, p. 545—*Editors.*]

his sultaness, inventing for her a scene that anticipates the council in hell in book 2 of Milton's *Paradise Lost*, with the sultaness playing the role of Satan as he schemes to regain his former might and glory. She assembles her Syrian "conseil" and harangues its members with rhetorical questions about the evils of forsaking "Mahoun," promising to keep them safe if they swear allegiance to her (II.330–43) and recruit their friends to do so. Unlike Trevet and Gower's figure, the lawyer's sultaness works to establish a political power base in opposition to that of her son. Albeit smaller, her council rivals her son's, for, the Man of Law pointedly observes, in her murderous enterprise the sultaness means to usurp her son's rule: "she hirself wolde al the contree lede" (II.434).

Like Satan, the sultaness enacts her transgressive desire deceptively, feigning conversion to Christianity and good will to Custance in order to entrap and assassinate the sultan and his retinue of converts. Such counterfeit proximity comes in for its share of rhetorical vituperation by the Man of Law, who castigates the sultaness as the scorpion who, for all her flattery of Christianity and Custance, fully intends to "stynge" them (II.403–5). So too does the Man of Law associate the sultaness with the primal transgressor, the source of all evil: she is the "welle of vices" (II.323), "roote of iniquitee" (II.358), "nest of every vice" (II.364), and a serpent disguised as woman "lik to the serpent depe in helle ybounde" (II.360–61). Yet the sultaness's most egregious sin is not that she impersonates Satan, for, the Man of Law remarks, it is Satan who makes women his instrument when he wishes to beguile, as he did with Eve (II.365–71). Instead, the sultaness's ultimate danger is that she would be like man; she is, as the Man of Law alone styles her, "Virago," "Semyrame the secounde" (II.359).

In the Middle Ages, Semiramis was known as the militant queen of ancient Syria (or Assyria) who built Babylon's walls and later became notorious for sexual depravity, including incest with her son, the sin for which Dante consigns her to the second circle of hell. As Johnstone Parr argues, however, more pertinent to the *Man of Law's Tale* than Semiramis's sexual aberration is the legend that she usurped the throne from her husband, King Ninus, whom she had assassinated after he attended a banquet she arranged for him.[5] Alternatively, as Boccaccio relates the legend in *De claris mulieribus*, after King Ninus had died from an arrow wound, Semiramis prevented her young son from ruling and "retain[ed] for herself the great kingdom of her husband."[6]

Boccaccio also offers a detailed account of how Semiramis managed to expropriate unto herself the conventionally masculine prerogative of rulership after Ninus's death. With "feminine wiles," Boccaccio explains, she "masqueraded as a man and pretended to be her own son":

> Semiramis's face looked very much like her son's; both were beardless; her woman's voice sounded no different from her young son's; and she was just a trifle taller, if at all. Taking advantage of this resemblance, she always wore a turban and kept her arms and legs covered. . . . Lest the novelty of her garb shock her countrymen, Semiramis decreed that everyone should dress in this fashion.

5. Johnstone Parr, "Chaucer's Semiramis," *ChauR* 5 (1970): 57–61.
6. Boccaccio, *Concerning Famous Women*, trans. Guido A. Guarino (New Brunswick, N.J.: Rutgers University Press, 1963), 5. All subsequent quotations of this translation are from pages 5 and 6.

Having proven her abilities as a ruler, Semiramis later revealed her actual sex, almost as if, Boccaccio speculates, "she wanted to show that in order to govern it is not necessary to be a man, but to have courage." For this "marvelous subterfuge," Semiramis gained the admiration of all those who looked upon her, and she not only retained the lands acquired by her husband, but added Ethiopia and India to them, restored Babylon, and built other new cities, Boccaccio concludes.

Semiramis's pretense as a man and her usurpation of masculine privilege do not, however, finally escape Boccaccio's censure, for he ends his portrayal of her with a dire warning concerning the sexual confusion such masquerades cause in men. It is believed, Boccaccio reports, that the "manly-spirited" Semiramis, "constantly burning with carnal desire," gave herself to many men, including her own son, Ninus, "a very handsome young man," by which description Boccaccio means to suggest the son's effeminacy: "as if he had changed sex with his mother, Ninus rotted away idly in bed, while she sweated in arms against her enemies." Women who take over traditionally male roles, Boccaccio implies, not only threaten men's power and prerogatives but confuse their very sexual identities, indeed, confound even sexual perversity itself. Like the woman-man of medieval homophobic discourse,[7] Ninus plays the passive or female role, yet he does so in heterosexual intercourse with his mother, the man-woman: "Oh, what a wicked thing this is!" Boccaccio complains, "something more beastly than human."

The Man of Law points to the sultaness's relationship to Boccaccio's figure in the epithet "virago" that he couples with "Semiramis" (II.359). As the fifteenth-century poet Gavin Douglas defined the term, a "virago" is not simply a large or quarrelsome woman, but like Juturna in the *Aeneid*, "a woman exersand a mannis office."[8] To be sure, the lawyer's sultaness is but "Semiramis the secounde," a pale reflection of the cross-dressed transgressor Boccaccio had constructed. Unlike her notorious predecessor, the sultaness does not literally impersonate a male ruler, nor does she commit incest (the "unkynde abhomynacion," II.88, the Man of Law earlier ruled out as potential subject matter for his tale), but she too would take "mannis office" of rulership into her own hands.

Impersonation does occur, however, in the second episode of female deception in the Man of Law's narrative, that in which King Aella's mother, Donegild, masquerades in writing as her son.[9] Having intercepted a letter to Aella informing him that Custance has given birth to their child, Donegild substitutes a letter proclaiming Custance to have borne a monstrous creature. (Such offspring implies that Custance is an "elf," II.745, an evil spirit in the form of a woman.) Donegild next intercepts the return letter from Aella, which voices his compassionate acceptance of the fabricated news, and substitutes her own missive, which directs that Custance and her son are to be exiled from the country, set adrift in the sea. On the authority of this forged letter, the constable sadly carries out what he believes to be Aella's wishes and banishes

7. On the topos of the woman-man, see Monica McAlpine, "The Pardoner's Homosexuality and How It Matters," *PMLA* 95 (1980): 8–22.
8. Cited in *Riverside Chaucer,* 860 n359.
9. On the forged letter as female stratagem, see Joan Ferrante, "Public Postures, Private Maneuvers: Roles Medieval Women Play," in *Women and Power in the Middle Ages*, ed. Mary Erler and Maryanne Kowaleski (Athens: University of Georgia Press, 1988), 217–18.

Custance and her child. For her traitorous male masquerade, the Man of Law excoriates Donegild and rhetorically links her perverse "mannishness" to the ultimate pervert, Satan: "Fy, mannysh, fy!—o nay, by God, I lye— / Fy, feendlych spirit . . . !" (II.782–83).

Donegild's arrogation of male power extends beyond the fact that she impersonates King Aella to the mode by which she actually does so: she takes up the pen, traditionally a male instrument in the Middle Ages, and forges a letter from him. Trevet's narrative also specifies that his Domild intercepts and reads Aella's message and substitutes the counterfeit one she writes herself. Gower, whose interest is to exemplify the evils of envy, not of "mannishness," suppresses Domilde's literal inscription of the letters. She commissions others to do the actual writing: "Sche hath [Aella's] lettres overseie / And formed in an other weie" (*CA* 2.1011–12). But the Man of Law restores the proscribed "mannish" agency of Trevet's Domild, putting the pen back into his Donegild's hand, so to speak. When Aella returns and finds his wife and child exiled contrary to his express orders, his supposed letter of banishment is reexamined and the hand that wrote it identified (II.890). Presumably this hand is Donegild's, for Aella at once slays his mother for her "cursed dede" (II.891).

The Man of Law also recasts Donegild's motivation for opposing Custance into the virago's, rather than invoking the traditionally female reasons earlier writers named. Trevet imputes Domild's hostility to her envy and jealousy of Constance's "goodness and holiness and marvellous beauty" (*Chron.* 24), and Gower ascribes it to the conventionally female verbal sins associated with envy—"bacbitinge" (*CA* 2.1281) and "false tunge" (*CA* 2.1299). The Man of Law, however, names malice and tyranny (the latter implicated twice, II.696 and 779) as the dominant causes of Donegild's hostility to Custance. Tyranny in particular is an "unwomanly" trait to the Man of Law's way of thinking. Earlier in his narrative, he established that it stands opposed to humility, the Virgin Mary's preeminent virtue in the later Middle Ages,[1] and perhaps Custance's dominant quality as well: "Humblesse hath slayn in [Custance] al tirannye" (II.165), the lawyer observes early in his tale.

As male impersonator, writer, and would-be tyrant, Donegild is indeed "mannish" to patriarchal eyes, like the sultaness, another "Semiramis the secounde." In the Man of Law's deployment, the rhetoric of proximity brings these two maternal figures perilously close to man, blurring the traditional hierarchical arrangement of distinct binary opposition between the sexes. As was the case with the proximate Muslim, such ambiguous "intimacy" calls for violent clarification, which in due course the lawyer's narrative supplies: both the Roman emperor, who dispatches the sultaness, and Aella, who kills Donegild, move decisively to reestablish male dominance over—distance from—woman.

Yet the sultaness and Donegild's attempted appropriation of so-called male roles evokes a further—and perhaps more forceful—resituation of woman as man's submissive opposite. Against these viragoes and the transgressive women who serve as their exemplars, from Semiramis back to Eve, the Man of Law advances Custance. Unlike the "mannish" woman, who

1. On the figure of the humility Madonna in medieval art and thought, see my "Botticelli's *Madonna del Magnificat:* Constructing the Woman Writer in Early Humanist Italy," *PMLA* 109 (1994): 196–97.

crowds the preserve of maleness, Custance is repeatedly differentiated as female Other throughout the narrative. In fact, I would argue that Custance plays an integral role in the Man of Law's project to construe and expose woman's insidious desire to achieve similitude to man. Custance is not only an emblem of submissiveness, as Delany observes, but a reassuring symbol of all that is not-man. At crucial points in his narrative, the lawyer uses Custance to reinforce woman's proper difference from man, a task he has rendered urgent by his exposure of woman's perverse desire and ability to mask her outlaw status and masquerade as inlaw, as man.

V

The Man of Law shapes his presentation of Custance not to offer a biography of her but to focus on her relationship to male power, divine and human. Unlike Trevet's history and Gower's exemplum, which start with the birth and early years of Constance and end with her death, the lawyer's narrative truncates this cradle-to-grave coverage and frames our exposure to Custance between two scenes: her departure from and eventual return to Rome, where Custance is reunited with her husband and her father. In the first episode, in which Custance bids farewell to her parents, she arises "ful pale" (II.265) and weeps at the prospect of leaving her home for a strange land and an arranged marriage to a husband whose "condicioun" (II.271) she does not know. Furthermore, marriage itself is presented pejoratively here: Custance is to "be bounded under subjeccioun" (II.270) to a husband. If we expect any active resistance on Custance's part to the designs patriarchal authorities—father, husband-to-be, church, or state—have on her life, we soon find that Custance serves a different purpose in the Man of Law's narrative. She stands to articulate reassuring asymmetries between the sexes, not troubling congruities. Accordingly, Custance's first words in the lawyer's narrative not only signal her acquiescence to her father's plans to marry her to the sultan, but enunciate the basic dissimilitude between men, born to rule, and women, destined to serve:

> "Wommen are born to thraldom and penance,
> And to been under mannes governance,"

Custance remarks (II.286–87). The Man of Law's tale ends with an image of subjection that mirrors this opening scene. Upon the death of her husband, Aella, Custance returns to Rome to live with her father. Finding him, "doun on hir knees falleth she to grounde" (II.1153). By word and by gesture, Custance's role in the lawyer's tale is to represent and validate woman's difference from man, her humble position literally beneath him.

Accordingly, Custance's response to the adversities that men—her father, the false knight who accuses her of murdering Hermengyld, and, as she is tricked into believing, Aella—visit upon her is silence or submission. To the emperor's wish that she marry the sultan, Custance quickly succumbs: "I moste anoon, syn that is youre wille" (II.282), a sentiment the Man of Law echoes ("But forth she moot," II.320). In the face of the false accusation that Custance has murdered Hermengyld, Custance loses her voice altogether, and the Man of Law must speak for her:

> Alias! what myghte she seye?
> For verray wo hir wit was al aweye. II.608–9

As the lawyer points out, Custance cannot defend herself; she has no mortal "champion," and unlike "mannish" women such as Semiramis, she does not know how to "fighte" (II.631–32). Instead, Custance assumes her properly female—submissive—posture. She falls upon her knees and prays for Christ's aid, which is forthcoming. Exiled with her son by, she believes, Aella's decree, Custance takes it all in "good entente" (II.824), once again kneeling down to request Christ's succor. Reunited in Rome with Aella, whom she still believes commanded her and her child's cruel exile, Custance stands as "dumb as a tree" (II.1055), only to swoon twice at Aella's feet before he clears himself of guilt. Throughout the narrative, Custance's silence and her humble postures—kneeling, fainting—implicitly reiterate her different status from man.[2]

So too does Custance explicitly assert the difference between human and divine. As she is about to be exiled from England, Custance, again kneeling, first prays to Christ and then to Mary to take pity on her infant son, Maurice, also condemned to banishment. Despite the clear parallels between these two mothers, Custance emphasizes that there is "no comparison" (II.846) between the Virgin's woe and her own:

> "Thow sawe thy child yslayn bifore thyne yen,
> And yet now lyveth my litel child parfay!" II.848–49

It is, of course, Custance's very refusal to analogize her experience—to man or to god—that distinguishes her from the virago, be it the sultaness, Donegild, Semiramis, or, ultimately, Eve, through whose "eggement / Mankynde was lorn, and damned ay to dye" (II.842–43), Custance prompts us to recall.

Yet at the same time that Custance stands opposed to the sultaness and Donegild, she is allied to them, for together these female figures define the full range of woman in medieval antifeminist thought, from Eve to the second Eve, Mary. Accordingly, the Man of Law never brings Custance into actual confrontation with her female opponents the way she is brought into conflict with her male adversaries.[3] Instead, Custance is yoked in juxtaposition to the viragoes, her humble and "womanly" behavior serving as a corrective gloss on their "mannishly" tyrannical actions. Thus, following the farewell scene (invented for the Man of Law) in which Custance declares woman to be born to slavery and man's governance (II.246–322), the lawyer inserts the episode in which the sultaness plots to usurp the governance of her country from her son (II.323–85). And with the account of Custance's wedding night (including the narrator's sententious decree that wives must suffer "in pacience," II.710, their husbands' sexual advances[4]) and of the subsequent birth of Maurice, the Man of Law pairs the scene in which

2. On the one occasion when Custance does act physically to defend herself, against a would-be rapist, the Man of Law mutes her personal agency and emphasizes God's role in protecting her (II.918–45). Significantly, this aggressor who has hidden himself on Custance's ship is a heretic, "a theef, that had reneyed oure creaunce" (II.915).

3. After Trevet's sultaness assassinates her son and all the Saracen converts, she first tempts and tortures Constance, who refuses to renounce her faith, and eventually exiles her (*Chron.* 11). Gower's Genius compresses this episode, but personally involves the sultaness in arranging Constance's banishment (*CA* 2.705–6), whereas unspecified Syrians, appearing to act on their own volition, set Custance adrift in the Man of Law's tale.

4. Neither Trevet nor Gower's Genius mentions the need for female submission to male sexual desire.

Donegild employs a traditionally masculine agent—the phallic pen—to enact her own desires and "depaternalize" her son by misleading him into thinking Maurice was fathered by a demon.

Neither the sultaness nor Donegild slays Custance, for the obvious reason that her absence would halt the tale. At the same time, however, one might observe in this narrative pattern the interdependence of the female characters as the Man of Law situates them. In their "mannishness," their transgressive proximity to man, the sultaness and Donegild provide patriarchal interests justification for creating and venerating the figure of Custance, the clearly distanced female Other. The former figure, the virago, is used to promote the establishment of the latter, and while both the sultaness and Donegild are eventually eradicated from the narrative, the rhetoric of proximity might readily supply a host of substitutes, beginning with Eve, to continue justifying a Custance.

* * *

LOUISE O. [ARANYE] FRADENBURG

"Fulfild of Fairye": The Social Meaning of Fantasy in the *Wife of Bath's Prologue* and *Tale*†

The Wife of Bath has captivated, and sometimes offended, readers of the *Canterbury Tales* in very special ways. She has been considered astonishingly "lively" and realistic—so much so that she is more commonly spoken of as a person than as a literary character. To many readers she has seemed more "modern" than Chaucer's other pilgrims—especially "alive" to us, especially able to speak to our contemporary moment. A critic named D. W. Robertson has even suggested that the Wife is typically "feminine" (330). But other critics, including Robertson himself, have seen the Wife as only deceptively modern and vital. These critics argue that Chaucer did not mean the Wife to be a vivacious modern "character" (Robertson 330). Instead, they suggest, the Wife is meant to embody a profoundly medieval idea, that of "carnal understanding" (Robertson 330)—of pleasurable, but lethal, abuses of reason, which lead to the kinds of mistaken understandings of Scripture the Wife proposes in her prologue.

Critics have argued over whether the Wife is medieval or modern; over whether her prologue is an exemplification of bad readings of Scripture or an autobiography. I am interested in why the question of the Wife's modernity has been so important to literary critics. I am also interested in why the question of the Wife's modernity is so often linked to the Wife's pursuit of carnal pleasure. The Wife impresses some readers as lively, as modern, as a "personality," in part because she defends bodily pleasure, and in part because she tells us the story of her life. For other readers, she only *impresses* us as full of life, and is really a very old figure, a medieval way of imaging carnal misunderstanding. For such readers

† From *Geoffrey Chaucer: The Wife of Bath*, ed. Peter G. Beidler. Case Studies in Contemporary Criticism (Boston: Bedford Books of St. Martin's Press, 1996), pp. 205–20. Reprinted by permission of the author. On pp. 189–204 Beidler provides introductory and bibliographic material and an essay on psychoanalytic criticism by Ross C. Murfin.

the Wife is so far from being full of life as to be dangerous to life, or desperate for it. In her critical tradition, then, she appears a little bit like the old woman of her tale: now young (or at least full of energy), now old; now a frightening reminder of death and the limits of human knowledge, now a beneficent donor of life and happiness. Why have critics argued so much over what we might call the Wife of Bath's "temporality"—over whether, when, and how she lives and addresses us?

In this essay I will explain some of the ways in which anxieties about mortality have shaped criticism of the *Wife of Bath's Prologue* and *Tale*. I will also show how concerns about the mortal body and its pleasures are at work in the prologue and tale themselves. First, it will be helpful to understand how the problem of pleasure is linked to that of mortality. The body is often understood to be the part of us that dies, even if we believe that the body will ultimately be resurrected. Moreover, the vulnerability of our bodies to time can make them seem frightening to us. Distrust of the body's pleasures and appetites has been a long tradition in Western thought, perhaps because our appetites remind us so forcefully of how material our bodies are. When we feel hunger, for example, and can think of little other than satisfying our hunger as pleasantly as possible, we are very much aware that we are embodied creatures, not pure spirit. And when our appetites remind us of our corporeality, they remind us also of our bodies' vulnerability to time: we know that all flesh is grass.

In discussing how awareness of mortality shapes the Wife's *Prologue* and *Tale*, I will be exploring a long-standing association of the romance genre with fantasy. Fantasy inspires anxieties similar to those linked with the mortal body and its pleasures. For example, most of us are familiar with the idea that supermarket romance novels are escapist fantasy. We fear fantasy will be so pleasurable that it will separate us from truth or reality, and thereby endanger us. We fear that, by isolating us from reality, fantasy can leave us vulnerable to the perils of reality, among which are aging and death. For example, we often speak of people who live in "a world of their own." Such people can seem "out of touch with reality." Although these figures can be enormously charismatic—gurus, dreamers, saints—we often hesitate to adopt their example. We fear that if we live in a world of our own, we may not notice that the world around us is changing, and making different demands on us. We may not adapt to those demands, and may thus lose friends, lovers, money, life. So fantasy, like bodily appetite and pleasure, can make us anxious, partly because we fear that fantasy may become *too* pleasurable, a preferable alternative to reality.

Class and gender are also important to my argument in this essay. I will not be discussing class and gender as explicitly as some of the other topics I've already mentioned, since my chief task in this essay is to explore psychoanalytic methods of reading. But critical methods rarely work in isolation, and it will be helpful to readers of this essay to understand some of the ways in which class and gender relate to my concerns about mortality and pleasure.

In medieval as well as modern culture, women are sometimes associated with death, pleasure, and fantasy. Women are sometimes thought to be especially dangerous to life, especially sensual, or especially rebellious with respect to the demands of reality and truth. Perhaps the most obvious example is the myth of Eve's desire for the apple and her consequent responsibility for bringing death into the world. Another example would be the damsel-in-distress story, in which the hero must risk his life to save a woman who has gotten into trouble through her stubbornness or helplessness. These plots are as popular now—for example, in action and adventure movies and in supermarket romances—as they were during the Middle Ages.

The idea that the Wife of Bath commits "carnal misunderstanding" likewise associates the Wife with danger and with an unwillingness to accept truth. According to some critics, the Wife interprets Scripture the way she wants to—according to her fantasies or wishes—instead of the way theologians say it should be read. These critics suggest that when the Wife argues that Scripture encourages sex, she is arguing a point of view that could endanger her spiritual life, and the spiritual lives of her audience. Moreover, her desire to dominate her husbands seems to many commentators a clear inversion of what, in the Middle Ages, were supposed to be the proper relations between husband and wife: the husband was to rule the wife, just as reason ought to rule the appetites. If this structure of rule was upset, then the proper order of things was upset, with dangerous consequences for all.

The Wife's class position is also relevant to the ways in which she can seem dangerous. The Wife is a wealthy commoner. She is successful in cloth-making, one of the most active sectors of the late-medieval English economy, and she is an able manipulator of the ways the late-medieval marriage market could also be a financial market. Critics have argued over the significance of the Wife's class and economic positioning, but most agree that her sexual appetite is somehow connected to her economic appetite: she seems to want property as much as she wants carnal pleasure or rule over husbands. Some critics have seen her as astray because she regards her own sexuality *as* a commodity. To these critics, she seems to accept the idea that women can be turned into objects of exchange in the marriage market. Other critics have regarded her economic enterprise as a clear sign of her dedication to false idols, analogous to her pursuit of love in all the wrong places. It is certainly easy to conclude from her prologue that the Wife is ambitiously determined to do well for herself in a number of ways, as a woman but also as a businesswoman. She thus might seem to threaten not only medieval gender hierarchies, in which husbands were ideally to rule wives, but social hierarchies as well—in which the lower classes were also ideally to stay in their "place."

The central thesis of my argument is that the *Wife of Bath's Prologue* and *Tale* ask us to analyze and undo these associations among women, commoners, death, pleasure, and fantasy. In particular, I will argue that the *Wife of Bath's Prologue* and *Tale* ask us to reevaluate fantasy. In the Wife's prologue and tale, Chaucer asks us to consider the possibility that fantasies do not simply separate us from reality. Instead, Chaucer suggests, fantasies can have the power to remake the social realities in which we live and desire. This means not that fantasies are inevitably benign, but that, far from being illusions powerless to affect reality, fantasies affect the way people and societies feel and act.

I. TRUE ROMANCE

By way of beginning to think about how psychoanalysis can help us address the questions about fantasy raised in the *Wife of Bath's Prologue* and *Tale*, we might turn to Freud's "The Theme of the Three Caskets," an essay concerned partly with Shakespeare's *The Merchant of Venice* and *King Lear*. In *The Merchant of Venice*, three suitors vying for the hand of Portia must choose among three caskets—one of lead, one of silver, and one of gold. The successful suitor, Bassanio, chooses the lead casket—the least valuable and beautiful of the three. In *King Lear*, Lear asks his three daughters to declare their love for him, so that he can evaluate which of them loves him most. On the basis of their declarations, he will decide how much of his kingdom each will inherit. Cordelia, the youngest, gives the plainest speech, and is disinherited; but she is eventually revealed to be Lear's only truly faithful and loving daughter.

Freud suggests that these literary examples can be related to a mythic scene whose workings he detects in a wide variety of stories and beliefs: "a scene of choosing between three women, of whom the youngest is the best, the supreme one" (65). Freud argues, however, that in this scene the youngest and most beautiful of the three women represents death; to choose her is to choose death, or, to put it another way, is to accept the fact of death, to accept the fact that all living things must die. For most of us, the thought of our own death is a sad, even horrible, one. Indeed, Freud argues that unconsciously we cannot believe we will die. But the scene he analyzes in "Three Caskets" makes Death appear fair, not horrible. It depicts the masculine hero as choosing death, rather than fantastically refusing to believe in this powerful fact of life. Through a defensive reversal—"replacement by the opposite"—death appears as the "fairest, best, most desirable and the most lovable among women" (72).

For Freud, the purpose of this scene of choice is twofold. The scene "warns man that he too is a part of nature and therefore subject to the immutable law of death" (72). But the scene also eases, makes palatable, the terror and sense of unfreedom produced by this warning. It does so by representing the hero as *choosing* death rather than simply submitting to its necessity. Indeed, the scene makes the choice of death seem a free and heroic one, one that will bring good fortune, at least of a certain kind. The element of choice transforms unfreedom (no one can escape death) into an experience of freedom (the hero chooses to recognize the truth that he will not escape death). Thus the element of choice transforms warning and terror into pleasure. As Freud puts it:

> Choice stands in the place of necessity, of destiny. Thus man overcomes death, which in thought he has acknowledged. No greater triumph of wish-fulfillment is conceivable. Just where in reality he obeys compulsion, he exercises choice; and that which he chooses is not a thing of horror, but the fairest and most desirable thing in life. (73)

How might we make use of this passage in interpreting the Wife's tale? First, the nameless knight commits the crime of rape and is sentenced to death. But instead of losing his life, he is rewarded with "the most lovable among women"—the ideal wife, who is both beautiful and faithful. At the end of the tale, his power and freedom are restored: "And she obeyed him in every thing / That mighte doon him plesance or liking" (1255–56). But, as in Freud's scene, this transformation is accomplished through the knight's *submission.* At the beginning of the tale, the knight is mortally ignorant of what women want. We might say that he is out of touch with certain realities. His experiences in the world of "fairye," however, offer him a magical, redemptive knowledge that turns multifarious and confusing data about women's preferences into a single truth about a species. That truth is women's wish for sovereignty—which, if the knight willingly submits to it, will be transformed into his freedom. Thus a death sentence is transformed into its reverse, a new lease on life, and necessity is transformed into its reverse, freedom of choice. The obligation to submit to reality, once met, turns magically into new powers and freedoms.

These reversals of necessity into freedom and of mortality into the promise of enduring life are also at work in the relations between the Wife's prologue and her tale. Most critics accept the idea that the old woman beside the forest is a figure for the Wife of Bath herself, or at least of some part of her. The Wife describes herself in her prologue as a troublesomely appetitive woman who is willing to scheme against and injure her husbands to get what she wants. In her tale, however, she transforms herself into a loving rescuer of man.

The kind of time that characterizes the prologue is also transformed, even reversed, in the tale. In the prologue we are made aware of the passage of time as the Wife laments the loss of her beauty brought on by the aging process. But the tale is characterized by the magical timing of "fairye," in which bodies can choose their age—can choose to be young again. The transition from prologue to tale converts sex and violence into loving rescue, a movement repeated within the tale itself. Interestingly, Freud interprets rescue fantasies as renegotiations of mortality: the fantasy is that if we can save someone, we might perhaps have power over life and death (see his essay "A Special Type of Object Choice Made by Men"). Moreover, in the transition from prologue to tale vulnerability to the passing of time is changed into magical power *over* time. Despite these conversions of sex and violence into a fantasy of rescue, however, the Wife's tale ends with her curse and with a reminder of the fact (dwelt on in her prologue, but forgotten until the end of her tale) that men grow old: "And olde and angry nigardes of dispence, / God sende hem soone verray pestilence!" (1263–64). It would seem from this ending that the enchantment of romance—its promise of wish fulfillment—is fragile and transitory; the Wife's curse seems designed to make us feel that we are back in the real world and that we had better be aware of its power conflicts if we are going to survive in it. The Wife's performance appears to suggest, then, that romance fantasy is distinct from, even opposed to, the real world. This idea is also commonly expressed in scholarly and critical writing on the romance.

The romance genre has often been associated with the marvelous and has been contrasted to genres, like history writing or the novel, that seem more committed to the truthful depiction of reality. In one of the most influential twentieth-century accounts of the romance genre, Eric Auerbach argues that "the courtly romance is not reality shaped and set forth by art, but an escape into fable and fairy tale" which has a "restrictive" effect on the development of "literary realism" (138). Bishop Richard Hurd also contrasts the romance with more truthful kinds of discourse.

He wrote his *Letters on Chivalry and Romance* in the later eighteenth century, at a time when English literary culture was taking a certain pride in throwing off what it regarded as the superstitions and unreasonable fancies of older literary forms like the romance. Hurd's own estimation of the romance is ambivalent. He seems nostalgic for it. He writes, "we have lost . . . a world of fine fabling" (120). But he identifies the "*lying wonders*" of romance with the female figure of "Fancy." And he writes that Fancy, who "had wantoned it so long in the world of fiction," was "now constrained . . . to ally herself with strict truth, if she would gain admittance into reasonable company" (120).

Like Bassanio in *The Merchant of Venice*, who chooses the lead rather than the gold or silver casket, critics of romance seem perpetually to be preferring plain truth, however dull, to glitter. And in order to present themselves as preferring plain truth to glitter, they must first insist on the distinction between truth and glitter. They must convince us, and themselves, that there is a huge difference between reality and fantasy. What do they gain by doing so? The simple answer is, in Hurd's words, "strict truth"—now in the form of critical or scholarly wisdom. And the truths revered by this "reasonable company" of scholars promise new life just as much as the truth offered by the old woman of the Wife's tale. Hurd, for example, implies that anyone in the eighteenth century who preferred romance to strict truth would have been regarded as hopelessly old-fashioned. But, as we have seen, the idea that we will be rewarded with a better life if we "choose" reality is an idea with which the romance genre is very much at home. Critics of romance shake their heads over the alluring frivolities of the genre and admit that after all reality is a better thing: Bassanio gives up the gold casket, and the knight in the Wife's tale chooses to obey his elderly but wise wife.

So although critics of romance may think they are analyzing the genre's fantastic failings at realism, they may really be repeating the very wish that romance promises to fulfill: that necessity could be turned into choice, death into a better life. This tells us that romance is not just wish-fulfillment fantasy; it is instead a genre that helps, in a variety of ways, to persuade its readers that submitting to necessity might be almost as pleasant as a dream—maybe even more pleasant. Sometimes romance lets us dream that we might live happily ever after in fairyland. One medieval romance, *Launfal*, actually lets its hero vanish into fairyland, never returning to the real world. More often, though, romance fulfills a slightly different wish: the wish that, by renouncing fairyland, we will live better lives in a world we can securely believe is reality. The romance can thus be a very powerful agent in persuading us to accept our lives as they are, rather than as they might be.

Like Eric Auerbach and Bishop Hurd, the Wife of Bath also tells a story about the demise of romance. But she tells this story in a way that nonetheless suggests the continuing relevance of the romance to her real world of bickering and brokering. What can we learn further about the romance, and about the Wife's romance, from the way psychoanalysis itself narrates the loss of a "world of fine fabling"? In the section following I will show a few ways psychoanalysis can help us to understand the timing of sexuality and death, and the relation of such timing to historical and autobiographical narration, in the Wife's prologue and tale.

II. MORTALITY AND THE SUBJECT

One of the chief intellectual contributions of psychoanalytic theory has been its approach to the way human subjectivity takes shape in time. From the perspective of psychoanalysis, human subjectivity is profoundly historical and mortal. It is also structured by, and seeks structural change through, language. In psychoanalytic therapy, every subject has her own story to tell. Every subject explains herself by telling a story about the past. It is through the process of speaking, listening to, and transforming this kind of historical narrative that psychoanalysis aims to restore the subject to happiness. Moreover, for Freud—and for one of his most influential followers, Jacques Lacan—the subject learns, through telling her story, that she *has* a history, even that she *is* her history. The subject learns to recognize the ego's fantastic structure, its limitations, its mortality. In some strains of psychoanalysis this lesson can unfortunately take the form of a normalization; that is, some psychoanalysts, just like romance critics, would like us to believe that we must accept the truth of death if we are to be realistic, normal people. But psychoanalytic theory has also offered a different, much more interesting formulation: by telling the story of her pleasures and pains, her living and dying, as a mortal creature, the subject can remake her chances for happiness in this world and in the body. In doing so the subject does not so much accept reality as come to recognize that there are different definitions and experiences of reality, some of which are indeed unacceptable.

One of the narratives that psychoanalysis itself uses to explain the formation of the subject is the story of the subject's movement from the "polymorphous perverse" of infancy to the regulated sexual and emotional styles of later years. The term "polymorphous perverse" refers to the notion that in infancy our pleasures are varied because we do not yet have a sense of the "normal" way to experience pleasure. We are born without an identity, an ego; the infant enjoys, and suffers from, a multiple and shifting array of wishes, pleasures, and pains. Only later will these pleasures and pains be organized into an "I" who feels separate from its own sensations and the objects of its desires—an "I" who wants "this" and not "that." This multifarious play of desires is shaped through repression and other processes into an "I" who eats socially approved foods at socially approved times, spends wisely, and engages in genital sexuality. Or, conversely, it may be shaped into an "I" who has eating "disorders," or gambles "compulsively," or engages in sexual "perversion." Incidentally, while the term "perversion" has too often been used as a disciplinary or derogatory term, Freud's work argues that the desires at stake in "perversion" are common to us all, because we have all experienced the polymorphous pleasures of infancy.

Whether a given identity has been styled in such a way as to produce genital sexuality or perversion, eating disorders or balanced meals, psychoanalysis contends that all such identities mourn the loss of pleasures and experiences they have learned to forget. All identities are haunted by the traces of memories of proscribed pleasures. And because of such psychic losses, none of us will find happiness easy to achieve. Both the multifariousness of human pleasures and their fragility are registered in the Wife of Bath's performance. She remarks:

I ne loved nevere by no descrecioun,
But evere folwede mine appetit,
All were he short, or long, or blak, or whit.
I took no kepe, so that he liked me,
How poore he was, ne eek of what degree. (622–26)

The Wife's language here suggests something of the range and mobility of desire as psychoanalysis understands it. This "appetite" that refuses "discretion" cares little for considerations of class, wealth, shape, complexion. But even as the Wife of Bath speaks of her transgressive appetite and searches for her next husband, she is telling the story, the history, of her pleasures and pains, and she speaks of her loves as past loves—as fond memories from a past quite separate from her uncertain present and future. Psychoanalysis helps us understand why this sense of loss is registered at the very moment the Wife of Bath declares the range and extent of her appetite: she says "I ne loved nevere by no descrecioun" in the past tense.

The Wife's sensitivity to the passage of time is expressed perhaps most strongly in the following lines of her prologue:

But, Lord Crist, whan that it remembreth me
Upon my youthe and on my jolitee,
It tikleth me aboute mine herte roote.
Unto this day it dooth mine herte boote
That I have had my world as in my time.
  But age, allas, that all wole envenyme,
Hath me biraft my beautee and my pith.
Lat go. Farewell. The devel go therwith! (469–76)

The haunting, recognized by psychoanalysis, of our moments of greatest happiness by the memory of something lost is one way of accounting for the frequently elegiac tone of the Wife of Bath's exuberant defense of embodied pleasures. The importance of loss and pleasure to questions of identity, to the very question of what identity is, is enacted in the prominence of the "I" in the *Wife of Bath's Prologue*, and in the extraordinary length and complexity of its autobiographical mode. *The Wife of Bath's Prologue* is *about* the historical nature of the subject and the shaping of the subject's identity through the history of its losses and pleasures.

If the subject is historical she is also always social. Psychoanalytic theory recognizes that the individual subject's feelings are always mediated by the structures of the family and the larger social world. Freud's notion of the Oedipus complex is perhaps the most famous instance of the idea that the family works to manage the desire of the subject. Freud named the Oedipus complex after the protagonist of the Greek play *Oedipus Rex*, by Sophocles, in which Oedipus, abandoned at birth, later mistakenly kills his father and marries his mother (discussed in Freud's essay "A Special Type of Object Choice Made by Men"). Through the Oedipus complex, the subject's complicated networks of desire are triangulated into the relations among father, mother, and child. The various ways in which the parents feel, perform, and embody desire in front of the child and for the child help to shape how, what, and whom she desires. In turn, the parents' desires include traces of the histories and communities that shaped them, traces that will be felt and relayed by their children and their children's children.

Not all these desires are conscious, and this fact has important implications for psychoanalytic understandings of the social nature of desire. As theorized by Freud and Lacan, the unconscious is not only that most private of places where the individual ego keeps its most shameful and exciting secrets; it is also a part of the subject that the subject does not know precisely because the unconscious is social. For example, some of the unconscious desires that shape the subject are secrets transmitted unknowingly from one generation to another. Lacanian psychoanalysis in particular has emphasized that the subject participates in an unconscious social structuring of desires and demands, sometimes called the symbolic order. The symbolic order is the network of language, kinship, and power that names and identifies us as "I," as "you," as a "person" with a proper name, and so on. We are not fully conscious of our dependence on and participation in these networks.

At this point it might seem that the subject is carefully structured indeed—shaped and disciplined by family, by family history, and by the symbolic order more generally. But the social nature of desire also means that desire is unpredictable. So much information comes from so many different directions, and terms can shift their meanings so readily, that the subject's desire can never be managed completely. For example, the Oedipus complex seems often designed to produce the transgression of its own careful structures. The child might wish to explode her parents' marriage by murdering one member and carrying off the other. Or the child might give up on both parents as hopeless or lethal or inaccessible, and seek pleasure elsewhere—although often from an elsewhere powerfully reminiscent of these past loves and hatreds. One way in which the *Wife of Bath's Prologue* suggests both the weaknesses and disciplinary power of family and social structures is through the account the Wife gives of her marital history. Her marital statistics—the way they reflect, but also exaggerate, the frequency of multiple marriage in the Middle Ages—would suggest to a psychoanalytic critic that the role of the family in structuring, and failing to structure, desire is being addressed in the *Wife of Bath's Prologue* and *Tale*.

Having recognized the openness of the social structuring of the subject's desire, we must also remind ourselves that the subject's desire is *never* not social. The moment the subject is born, with all the apparent freedom of her polymorphous perversities, the subject is already plunged into the social relationships that will shape her desire. But the social nature of the subject's desire is often itself repressed. The idea that the child simply wants things that she must learn, for her own safety, not to want defends against recognition of the broad social function of the family as transmitter of desire and loss through and across generations. To misrecognize the unconscious as individual rather than social is part of the workings of a repression that tries to locate infantile pleasure safely in the past and to equate maturity with increasing respect for reality—as though the subject's acquaintance with social realities had not always been at stake in its desire.

Freud's notion of the relationship between the pleasure principle and the reality principle can be interpreted as just such a misrecognition. Infancy is seen as a time when the search for pleasure is so dominant that the infant will seek satisfaction in fantastic and, possibly, injurious scenarios when it encounters the obstacles posed by reality. As the subject is shaped and regulated through those very encounters, the subject learns to submit to the discipline of reality, seeking pleasure by more roundabout and safer means. This narrative has much in common with the romance structures discussed above. It makes the following assumptions: reality is a given, and pleasure is not itself a way of knowing or shaping reality; pleasure blocks, rather than results from, maturation; pleasure, not reality, can be dangerous, partly because it is insufficiently aware of death. But psychoanalysis also complicates these assumptions. It insists that desire is always social—always interacting with reality—*and* that past pleasures never leave us. For Freud, the past is always with us. And Freud insists that if we are to remake ourselves and our world for happiness, an embrace of the past (and of its continuing presence) is essential. In the next section I will show how the *Wife of Bath's Tale* offers a similar insight. While the Wife's tale depicts the power of the romance wish that we could better our lives by choosing to submit to reality, it does something else as well, something more interesting: it proposes that we might contend with necessity by changing it.

III. FANTASY MAKES THE WORLD

The *Wife of Bath's Tale* begins by lamenting the passing of the days of King Arthur and "fairye." The opening lines also lament the disenchanted nature of modern times, when the only fairies to be found are friars hiding behind bushes, waiting to assault the objects of their desire:

> In th'olde dayes of the king Arthour,
> Of which that Britons speken greet honour,
> All was this land fulfild of fairye.
> The elf-queene with her joly compaignye
> Daunced ful ofte in many a grene mede.
> This was the olde opinion, as I rede—
> I speke of many hundred yeres ago.
> But now kan no man seen none elves mo. (857–64)

In this passage, the Wife recounts a history of Britain by developing a contrast between past and present, between the "olde dayes" (857) and "now" (864). This past and present, moreover, are different not just because they represent different times; they are distinct worlds.

The old world—which the Wife knows about only through "olde opinion" (862)—is spoken of with respect, is "fulfild of fairye" (859) and of "joly" women (860). It is a world in which pleasure and women are not opposed to truth or honor, but are rather their inseparable companions or even embodiments. The romance genre is thus presented from the very beginning of the *Wife of Bath's Tale* as the trace of a lost world, strange now but once very familiar, indeed once reality itself, the archaic reality of England. The passage thus reminds us that one person's fantasy may once have been another person's reality. Reality shifts over time and space, and what can seem the very touchstone of reality in one context will seem an elaborate dream in another.

Any power structure will find it useful to be able to represent *as past* (for example, as "primitive") kinds of people, pleasures, or viewpoints that are threatening. Social realities persuade us that they are real, that they are all there is, by distinguishing themselves from lost, absent pleasures, from a fantastic past. But the ability to *offer* pleasure is equally crucial to power. Medieval archaisms often function in this way for contemporary U.S. culture. Medieval or Renaissance banquets and fairs, medieval motifs in movies and theme parks (*Braveheart,* Cinderella's castle) and in family hotels in Las Vegas (Excalibur), Dungeons and Dragons, and Goth fashion are examples of how archaisms can be used to signify pleasurable alternatives to the weary disenchantments of modern life.

The Wife of Bath shows us that associating the past with happiness and wish fulfillment was also a medieval practice. She moves us sharply away from fairyland to her modern world, fulfilled not of "fairye" but of the inventoried objects of a disenchanted reality:

> For now the grete charitee and prayeres
> Of limitours and othere hooly freres,
> That serchen every lond and every streem
> As thikke as motes in the sonne-beem,
> Blessinge halles, chambres, kichenes, boures,
> Citees, burghes, castels, hye toures,
> Thropes, bernes, shipnes, dairyes.
> This maketh that there been no fairyes.
> For there as wont to walken was an elf
> There walketh now the limitour himself. (865–74)

The Wife laments that women are now safe from those pleasurable elves of old, and that their replacements, the friars, give women dishonor, not excitement:

> Wommen may go now saufly up and doun.
> In every bussh or under every tree
> Ther is noon oother incubus but he,
> And he ne wol doon hem but dishonour. (878–81)

This world has been thoroughly demystified. There is no time for reflection—no time, literally, for old-fashioned visions, for stories, for the elf queen and her "joly compaignye." We are made to feel that this new world is intensely realistic in contrast to its predecessor. Chaucer achieves this feeling partly by a technique of proliferation; instead of "a grene mede" the new world is full of proliferating manmade structures like "halles, chambres, kitchenes, boures" and "citees, burghes, castels, hye toures" and "thropes, bernes, shipnes, dairyes" (869–71). The rhythm and tumble of these lines suggest that this new world is all moving too fast. For the Wife of Bath, the world of "now" (864, 865, 874, 878) measures its distance from the past by evoking, through a kind of material chaos, the loss of archaic beauty. In the welter of all that man-made hustle and bustle, who could possibly see an elf?

Through such masterful strokes as the rhyming of "dairyes / fairyes" (871–72), the Wife calls attention to the incommensurability of the marvelous and the everyday. Her prologue also evokes a world that feels concrete and everyday and "now" to the reader because it is full of scarlet cloth, moths, books, slaps, wine, money, calculation. But this world gives way to the romance and "th'olde dayes of the king Arthour" (857). Chaucer seems to distinguish sharply between prologue and tale, between transitory and lasting happiness, between the everyday world of time and work and the romance world.

But the Wife of Bath's performance calls attention to the *dependence* of the everyday on the marvelous. This insight is similar to psychoanalytic formulations of the way reality and desire transform one another. For example, the Wife's tale seems clearly to be produced by the desires and anxieties registered in the prologue. This implies that romance fantasy is for the Wife a contemporary practice. The Wife might be dreaming of the good old days, but we see that she is doing so *because* her modern world is troublesome.

Moreover, "fairye" turns out in the end to be absolutely central to the tale's ambitious politics, not an escape from them. The old woman's magical changeability works to reassure the knight—and by extension, the aristocracy—that it can mingle, even in marriage, with the common (poor, ugly) body without losing its own identity. Thus alliances between commoners and aristocrats are made to look not only safe, but desirable. Magical transformations of the common people into fairy-tale brides serve to reassure the aristocracy of its immortality. Crucial to this reassurance are the oscillations between fantasy and harsh reality *within* the romance. The knight rides

> In all this care under a forest side
> Wher as he saugh upon a daunce go
> Of ladyes foure and twenty and yet mo.
> Toward the whiche daunce he drow ful yerne,
> In hope that some wisdom sholde he lerne.
> But certeinly, er he came fully there,
> Vanisshed was this daunce, he nyste where.
> Ne creature saugh he that bar lif,
> Save on the grene he saugh sittinge a wif.
> A fouler wight there may no man devise. (990–99)

The twenty-four ladies whom the old woman replaces clearly offer a vision of happiness. Their disappearance, in turn, offers a vision of the fragility of happiness, of its tendency to vanish. Thus the promise of happiness is transformed, through a rude awakening, into an ugly truth about aging and death: "a fouler wight there may no man devise" (999). Romance has become a mere dream. And yet the ugly truth that replaces it—think, for example, of the old woman's truth-telling powers (the answer to the knight's quest, and the sermon on gentillesse)—is itself a marvel, an ugly old woman who can turn herself into a youthful, beautiful blessing for her noble knight.

Given the Wife's own social circumstances—a rebellious sexual ideologue, a successful participant in one of the most aggressive sectors of the late fourteenth-century English economy—one might have expected from her a tale more obviously critical of powerful male aristocrats. But, at least when considered in tandem with psychoanalytic understandings of fantasy, the Wife's performance offers something more subtle: a reading of how social change is made possible by fantasy. It's true that, through the old woman's transfiguration, the threat of change represented by the Wife herself is domesticated: "love in a cottage" will be enough. An image of death is made into an image of life when the tale promises that the aristocracy will be able to keep its fabulous body of perpetual youth and beauty, its entitlement to privilege, so long as it is willing to forge alliances with the wealth and knowledge of the commons. And the tale promises that, in the process, the social and sexual threat posed by aging and ambitious women will be completely controlled and tamed. But the Wife's closing curse suggests the extent to which this promise is indeed a fairy tale. And her tale registers an even more powerful message: that the transformation and preservation of relations of power depend on the fantastic pleasure of imagining the world otherwise.

WORKS CITED

Auerbach, Eric. *Mimesis: The Representation of Reality in Western Literature.* 1953. Trans. Willard R. Trask. Princeton: Princeton UP, 1968, 1974.

Freud, Sigmund. *On Creativity and the Unconscious: Papers on the Psychology of Art, Literature, Love, Religion.* Ed. Benjamin Nelson. New York: Harper, 1958.

———. "A Special Type of Object Choice Made by Men." *On Creativity* 162–72.

———. "The Theme of the Three Caskets." *On Creativity* 63–75.

Hurd, Bishop Richard. *Letters on Chivalry and Romance.* 1762. Ed. Hoyt Trowbridge. Los Angeles: Augustan Reprint Society / Clark Memorial Library, 1963.

Robertson, D. W. *A Preface to Chaucer: Studies in Medieval Perspectives.* Princeton: Princeton UP, 1962.

HELEN COOPER

From The Pardoner's Prologue and Tale†

The Prologue: Structure, Themes, and Style

The structure and the main theme of the Pardoner's Prologue are indicated by his triple allusion to his text:

> My theme is alwey oon, and evere was—
> *Radix malorum est Cupiditas.*
>
> (333–4; cf. 425–6)

It is his own personal theme as well as the text of his sermon—the vice that he both preaches against and practises (427–8). The first section of his 'confession' is devoted to expounding his techniques (335–99); the second, to making quite clear what his 'entente' is in preaching—to make money, or if the going gets rough, to 'spitte out venim', but certainly not to save souls (400–34); the third section extends his avarice to cover his whole way of life, and also relates his vice to the processes of storytelling (435–62).

There is a superficial similarity of imagery throughout the Prologue that at once masks and expresses a deeper perversion. Part of the Pardoner's success lies in the fact that he deals in the everyday concerns of rural life: cows and oxen, cocks crowing, wheat, oats, wells, soup, mittens. It is a world of material fact, not religious doctrine; but he never moves

† From *Oxford Guides to Chaucer: The Canterbury Tales*, 2nd ed. (New York: Oxford UP, 1996), pp. 262–64, 266–71. Reprinted by permission of Oxford University Press. We have reorganized and sometimes expanded Cooper's bibliographic information. Indented block quotations of Chaucer's poetry from *The Riverside Chaucer*, ed. Larry D. Benson (Boston: Houghton Mifflin, 1987), have been replaced with quotations from this Norton Critical Edition. The spelling within short quotations from Chaucer's poetry has been modified to reflect this change.

beyond the material to the spiritual. His relics are likewise mere physical objects, bones and rags. He uses Latin 'to saffron with my predicacioun', an image drawn from gourmet food; he looks like a dove as he addresses people, stretching out his neck to look around—brilliant as a visual comparison, but, in the context of preaching the Word of God, a ludicrously animalistic downgrading of the dove of the Holy Ghost. Damnation is similarly trivialized into the commonplace in the image of souls going blackberrying. He rejects in so many words the apostolic life of labour and poverty, preferring the solid gains of 'money, wolle, chese, and whete', wine and wenches. If doves are a normal part of the life of every village or great household, the serpent that stings with the venom of its tongue is biblical (Jas. 3:8). The speech that starts, in fact, with a concern for the merely physical, turns into an overt rejection of religious values.

The Pardoner's high regard for storytelling is of a piece with his skill as a preacher. That 'lewed peple loven tales olde' was a fact acknowledged in all handbooks on the art of preaching, and there were numerous collections of such *ensamples* made for preachers' use. The Pardoner may even, as a side-effect, bring people to repentance through his sermons. His main concern, however, is to line his own pockets. Stories in sermons—fiction in general—were supposed to be morally profitable; the Pardoner has discovered that they can also be financially profitable. It is yet another instance of his determined conversion of the spiritually valuable into material wealth, of God into Mammon. His Tale can thus both be morally abhorrent, as a cynical exploitation of religion for his own financial advantage, and yet draw men away from evil. It is at once an image of how one should not live, and how he himself does.

> For though myself be a ful vicious man,
> A moral tale yet I yow telle can. (459–60)

Knowledge of evil in the Pardoner works to enable him not to choose the good but to exploit it.

The line of argument that declares the Pardoner to be a congenital eunuch and, by interpretation, spiritually sterile, has also seen in the Prologue an image of utter evil on the Augustinian model, of sin feeding upon sin in a tortured agony of despair. Such a reading can only, however, be imposed when one starts from Augustine. The text of the Prologue as Chaucer wrote it shows no signs whatever of despair or torture on the part of its speaker. Its self-congratulatory complacency is indeed one of the most horrific things about it—and the source of much of its comedy: it is an anti-authoritarian flouting of Christian principle that has touches of carnival licence in it as well as plenty of the devil. Like most Chaucerian satire, it condemns by wit and sheer outrageousness rather than by invective. It is in any case an absurdity to argue that the Pardoner ought to show the Augustinian pattern of tortured sinfulness; the point of the Prologue is that he ought not to be behaving like this at all.

The Tale: Genre

'Lo, sires, thus I preche', declares the Pardoner at the end of his tale (915), and it does indeed have a good deal in common with a sermon—a biblical text; an indictment of sin; the main story as illustrative exemplum;

the application of the story to the congregation; and a concluding prayer. These elements do not altogether fit the formula for sermon construction, however, and a number of other features fail to match such a generic model. The biblical text precedes the Prologue, not the sermon; the exemplum dominates over everything else; the application has more to do with the Pardoner's acquisitiveness than with the substance of the tale; the prayer appears to fall outside the sermon and into the frame. None the less, given that vernacular sermons were often more loosely constructed than Latin ones, and given the particular requirements here of the context—that the Pardoner has been asked for a story, and so the extent of the exemplum is justified by the *Tales* rather than the genre—the category of sermon is elastic enough to serve.

Chaucer may have thought of it in the looser terms of homily: when the Pardoner has run through the opening didactic sections with their short exemplary anecdotes, he announces,

> But, sires, now wol I telle forth my tale. (660)

This line could simply mark the next section of the address, but the dominant impression is not of the structural unity of a single sermon, but of homiletic prefatory matter leading up to a story that fulfils both a function within the sermon and also the Pardoner's obligation in the storytelling competition.

* * *

Structure

The Pardoner's Tale shows less similarity in structure to the sermon it has been claimed to be than to other tales in the Canterbury sequence, notably the Merchant's and Manciple's, where a brief narrative introduction (here, of the 'compaignye' of rioters) is followed by a long moralistic digression before the story gets properly under way. Many tales (the Summoner's, the Nun's Priest's) put these digressions into the mouth of a character; here, they are presented as part of the Pardoner's address to his congregation—he himself is a character within his own tale.

The structure of the Tale cannot finally be separated from the Prologue. It is not just that the text for the sermon precedes the Prologue and that the theme of avarice and evil is expounded there in the Pardoner's own practices: the Prologue also acts as frame for the Tale. Once again, Chaucer is offering different ways of articulating successive stories so that their connection is something other than linear. Here, the Pardoner tells about himself preaching, and the sermon is inset within that as part of the story of his own life; and inset within the sermon is the story of the rioters. The structure is emphasized by repetitions of *tell* and *tale*. He declares at the start, 'I can al by rote that I telle' (332), and proceeds to expound what he tells to his congregation. After describing his abuses, he announces,

> A moral tale yet I yow telle can,
> Which I am wont to preche for to winne.
> Now holde youre pees, my tale I wol beginne. (460–2)

It is a story, in fact, of himself telling a tale. When the moralizing on the tavern sins is over, he signals the start of the main story:

> But, sires, now wol I telle forth my tale. (660)

It scarcely matters by this time whether the 'sires' are his congregation or the pilgrim audience.

It does matter, however, at the end. 'Lo, sires, thus I preche' (915) must be addressed to the pilgrims: but the lines that follow sound like the closing formula of a sermon—of this sermon, since he has ended by offering pardons:

> And Jesu Crist, that is our soules leche,
> So graunte yow his pardon to receyve,
> For that is best; I wol yow nat deceyve. (916–18)

The lines need not spoil his sales pitch: they add to his illusion of sincerity ('I wol yow nat deceyve', for once palpably true, but no doubt for the wrong reasons), and in any case Christ's pardon seems to be offered as an extra to his own rather than an alternative. The formula is certainly powerful, but it is none the less a formula, and it lacks the compelling particularity of

> Cometh up, ye wyves, offreth of youre wolle!
> Youre names I entre heer in my rolle anon:
> Into the blisse of hevene shul ye gon. (910–12)

Christ's pardon can at best be prayed for in the subjunctive; the Pardoner can give salvation for the medieval equivalent of cash down and a certificate of authenticity.

There follows, however, the oddest line of the whole performance:

> But sires, o word forgat I in my tale: (919)

and he proceeds to offer the pilgrims the relics and pardons he has already declared to be spurious. The much-debated reasons for the con-man's overreaching himself may lie not in the psychological complexity of the Pardoner, but in the phrasing of that particular line. The sermon should be finished by now; the Pardoner has returned to the autobiographical frame ('thus I preche'). But in the single overwhelming *entente* of avarice, the two have got mixed up. The interlocking of tale and frame is visible even in the story layout: all the manuscripts divide off the 'Host's words' from the Prologue, and the Prologue from the Tale, but there is no single point at the end where such a separation can be made. The sermon is addressed through the congregation to the pilgrim audience, and the two sets of hearers will interpret it in opposite ways. But the Pardoner is accustomed to listeners he can treat with contempt. Here, I think, he has confused the two audiences, 'forgat' that he has in fact moved outside his 'tale' to the point where the fiction has broken down. He is trying to get back in to that fiction of sincerity, to reach an audience who will serve his overriding desire for acquisition.

Within this larger structure, the 'moral thing' that he tells has a structural logic of its own. As befits an oral delivery, its stages are clearly announced—except for the first, where the transition from the narrative setting of the 'compaignye | Of yonge folk' to the invective against drunkenness is elided so smoothly that the audience is given no opportunity to switch off their attention. After that, the shifts of subject from gluttony to gambling (589–90), to blasphemy (629–30), and to the main story (660) are all clearly signalled.

One difference of this tale from all the others of the *Canterbury Tales* is that the characters introduced in the first few lines are not particularized.

The Pardoner later appears to recall 'thise ryotoures three of which I telle' (661), but this is in fact the first time they have been distinguished from the 'compaignye'. The revellers mentioned at the beginning are there to introduce not so much the story as the preaching against the tavern sins. The effect is to reinforce the exemplary and the sinister qualities of the story when it does get under way: almost every one of the rioters' speeches and actions has been exposed in advance as damnable.

The exemplum of the rioters manages to combine a high proportion of direct speech with a strong sense of narrative speed, especially up to the buying of the poison. The rioters start up from their places in the tavern to search for death, they run to the treasure when they are directed to it. This literal speed of movement halts only for the eerie quietness of the old man's speech, and for their contemplation of the gold. The deaths are accomplished almost in parenthesis—'what nedeth it to sermone of it more?' (879). Most of the space in this later part of the story is devoted not to events but to the rioters' plans for their own destruction.

The move back to the congregation is accomplished smoothly. First comes the rhetorical climax—

> O cursed sinne of alle cursednesse! (895)

—then the transition to the listeners' need to avoid avarice and to seek forgiveness. The offer of pardon follows easily and with spurious logic. It is in the next transition, from imagined congregation to the immediate audience of the pilgrims, that the Pardoner's smooth talk turns into a banana-skin.

Themes

The Pardoner's Tale embodies two contradictory sets of meanings. In itself, it is a powerful moral tale against avarice and the tavern sins. Spoken by the Pardoner, it becomes deeply immoral—not only as a revelation of his own vice, but as a means to advance his own love of money; and moreover he chooses this tale while drinking in the tavern setting he so fiercely condemns. Its two sets of significances are in direct opposition; but they reinforce each other rather than cancelling each other out. The Pardoner's vices become all the more unpardonable for being laid bare in the tale, and the message of the tale is all the clearer by virtue of the perversion of its purpose.

The themes of the story itself are clear enough, as befits the moral purpose of a sermon. The condemnation of the tavern sins is resounding, and, in the case of gluttony, revolting. The tale of the rioters emphasizes the power of evil to bring about its own destruction: only in Chaucer's version do the malefactors set out to seek death, the treasure being no more than a catalyst for the forces of destruction already within them. Their swearing by 'Cristes blessed body al to-rente' that 'deeth shal be deed' constitutes a blasphemy in the substance as well as the uttering of the oaths: they are arrogating to themselves a power shown only by God in the Redemption.

The threat is also a powerful example of a pervasive motif of the tale—the reduction of the spiritual to the physical, such as has been shown already by the Pardoner in his Prologue. The destruction of Death is taken as a material quest. The condemnation of the tavern sins likewise allows the Pardoner to concentrate on the physical. Gluttony is the sin that has most to do with the body, and the physiological processes of eating, defecating, and letting off wind are described with horrible relish. Cooking becomes the material obverse of transubstantiation, in which the substance of the eucharistic elements of bread and wine are transformed, while the outward appearance, the accidents, remain the same; cooks, by contrast, 'turnen substance into accident' (539). The Fall is described in terms of gluttony alone, physical abuse, rather than as a spiritual rejection of God. The physical effects of drunkenness are brilliantly evoked. Blasphemy consists of the tearing to pieces of 'our blissed Lordes body' (474, cf. 651–4, 692, 695). Even the dice are 'bones' (656). Bread and wine are potentially the redemptive elements of the Eucharist; when the youngest rioter—the Son of this unholy Trinity, though that is unstressed in the text—fetches them from the town, it is to turn them into the vehicle of bodily death. Even the treasure of the traditional tale becomes, in the mouth of the Pardoner, an ironic transmutation into the material of the *infinitum thesaurum*, the infinite treasury of grace stored up by Christ and the saints on which pardoners were supposedly able to draw cheques in the form of indulgences.

The one figure in the tale who can see beyond this materialism to God is the old man. He envisages death, it is true, in corporeal terms—the death of the body rather than the salvation of the soul—but he can pray for the rioters' salvation by the Redemption (766).

What is the old man? His equivalent in the analogues is a wise man or philosopher, even Christ: here he keeps the wisdom, now associated also with old age, and the virtue—a reading of him as evil has to ignore the way Chaucer presents him. He cannot be Death, since death is his greatest desire, and part of the point of the tale, paradoxically, is that death is not a material thing that can be found—the gold is death to the rioters, but only by metonymy for the self-destruction they bring with them. He is not the Wandering Jew, though he has something of the same compelling mythic power. Nor is he *vetus homo*, unredeemed or sinful man, since he knows all about the Redemption, quotes Holy Writ, and sees himself as following 'Goddes wille' (726). He is what the text says he is: an old man seeking death. The implications of that, however, are extensive.

In the first place, he is a familiar medieval type, though more familiar in visual than literary art. Allegorical pictures of the universality of death invariably show Death leading away the young, the beautiful, the rich, the carefree, and leaving behind cripples, beggars, and the aged, who reach towards him with outstretched hands. The theme had gained extra poignancy at the time of the Black Death, when the plague struck most viciously at the young and healthy—and it is 'pestilence' that is Death's weapon in this story (679). At one level, the tale is giving verbal form to the pictorial allegory of death. The particular power associated with the old man, however, which has prompted so many attempts to explain him, comes in part at least from his most literal meaning. He is the truth of what the rioters are seeking: life without death. He is not immortal (725–6), but like the Wandering Jew or Swift's Struldbrugs, he is cursed with that most terrible of human myths, an infinitely prolonged old age. He has learnt that earthly treasure is valueless compared with a pauper's shroud (734–6); the rioters chase off after the gold and find in the gift of Fortune the death they had scorned.

The rioters are 'exemplary' characters: the point of their appearance in a sermon is to warn the congregation off similar vices. They are accordingly never given individual names, and are often referred to by their degree of sinfulness—'the proudeste', 'the worste'. The figure outside the Tale who most nearly resembles them is however the Pardoner himself. He too is on a quest for treasure, and the quest becomes explicit at the end of the tale, in his double appeal to his congregation and to his pilgrim audience. The Pardoner makes it quite clear why he has come on the pilgrimage: he has only one *entente*, of acquisition (403), and when he turns to the pilgrims he is aiming to put it into practice. Just as his spurious pardons are a corruption and perversion of penance, so the penitential aim of pilgrimage is corrupted to pecuniary ends. The morality of his tale is similarly perverted for his own unethical purposes.

The rioters find Death at the end of their quest; the Pardoner finds a threat of castration—'Lat cutte hem of!'. It is at this point, if anywhere, that the image of the Pardoner as spiritual eunuch is suggested: his Prologue and Tale have insistently deprived things of their potential spiritual meanings, and the Host's threat would show in physical form his lack of spiritual fruitfulness. But the passage is not allegory, nor is the threat given literal expression. All that happens is that the Pardoner's quest for income is guaranteed unfruitful, and he has to perform his one act of charity and reconciliation in the entire work, in exchanging a kiss with Harry Bailly. The two elder rioters had killed the third 'as in game' (829, 880–1); the Knight turns aside the violence that threatens their own 'pleye'. That the Pardoner is so angry, however (957), adds the final sin of wrath to complete the list: pride, in his contempt for God and his fellowmen; gluttony, in his fondness for wine, and which he himself has associated with the Fall; lechery, in his boasting about wenches, and his other more doubtful sexual practices; envy, in backbiting and defamation (415); sloth, in his spiritual deadness; and above all, avarice—the sin that was seen as the most threatening of the later Middle Ages by many moralists, including the Parson, who repeats the Pardoner's own text: 'The rote of alle harmes is Coveitise' (X(I) 739).

There is one last irony in the tale, in Harry Bailly's outburst,

> 'Thou woldest make me kisse thyn olde breech
> And swere it were a relik of a seint,
> Thogh it were with thy fundement depeint!' (948–50)

It is the last, and potentially the most damaging, reduction of the spiritual to the earthly, for one of the most prized relics of the shrine of St Thomas at Canterbury, to which the pilgrims were making their way, was the saint's filthy breeches, unchanged over the years as part of the process of his mortification of the flesh. A little over a century later another Catholic pilgrim, Erasmus, was appalled by both the unspirituality of the relics and the avarice of their custodians. Chaucer almost certainly knew Langland's valuing of spiritual pilgrimage, the search for truth in the heart, above geographical pilgrimage, and the thought was by no means original with Langland. Chaucer's Pardoner is a forerunner of the Reformation, not only as an instance of corruption within the Church and as a peddler of false pardons, but because he opens the way to questioning the connections between outward forms and spiritual meaning. He threatens the harmony of this pilgrimage: what he stands for will destroy the whole basis of pilgrimage, and any possibility of the harmony of a universal church.

* * *

BIBLIOGRAPHIC NOTES

for the Pardoner's Prologue:

Dewey R. Faulkner (ed.), *Twentieth Century Interpretations of the Pardoner's Tale* (Englewood Cliffs, NJ, 1973), is a very useful collection of essays on the Prologue and Tale.

C. W. R. D. Moseley's capable edition of the Prologue and Tale (Penguin Masterstudies, Harmondsworth, 1987) notes the biblical parallel at 413; A. C. Spearing's edition of *The Pardoner's Tale* (Cambridge, 1965) is also useful.

Alastair Minnis, 'Chaucer's Pardoner and the Office of Preacher', in Piero Boitani and Anna Torti (eds.), *Intellectuals and Writers in Fourteenth-century Europe: The J. A. W. Bennett Memorial Lectures 1984* (Tübingen and Cambridge, 1986), pp. 88–119, is the fullest discussion of the implications of a vicious man telling a moral tale.

Alfred L. Kellogg, 'An Augustinian Interpretation of Chaucer's Pardoner', in his *Chaucer, Langland, Arthur: Essays in Middle English Literature* (New Jersey, 1972), pp. 245–68 (repr. from *Speculum*, 26 [1951], 465–81), and Robert P. Miller, 'Chaucer's Pardoner, the Scriptural Eunuch, and the Pardoner's Tale', in Richard J. Schoeck and Jerome Taylor (eds.), *Chaucer Criticism I: The Canterbury Tales* (Notre Dame, 1960), pp. 221–44 (repr. from *Speculum*, 30 [1955], 180–99), are the classic exegetical studies of the Pardoner. For a critique, see the articles by C. David Benson and Richard Firth Green in *Mediaevalia*, 8 (1985 for 1982), 'Chaucer's Pardoner: His Sexuality and Modern Critics' (pp. 337–49) and 'The Sexual Normality of Chaucer's Pardoner' (pp. 351–8), and Gabriel Josipovici, 'Fiction and Game in *The Canterbury Tales*', excerpted in Faulkner (above) from *Critical Quarterly*, 7 (1965), 193–7. For psychoanalytic and historical versions of the 'despair' interpretation, see respectively H. Marshall Leicester, Jr., *The Disenchanted Self: Representing the Subject in The Canterbury Tales* (Berkeley, Los Angeles and Oxford, 1990), pp. 35–64, and Lee Patterson, *Chaucer and the Subject of History* (Madison, Wis., and London, 1991), pp. 374–86.

for the Pardoner's Tale:

Robert P. Merrix, 'Sermon Structure in the *Pardoner's Tale*', *Chaucer Review*, 17 (1982–3), 235–49, contains a useful critique of attempts to fit the Tale into the sermon mould.

Faulkner's *Twentieth Century Interpretations* (above) assembles many of the notable studies.

Good general studies include Janet Adelman, 'That We May Leere Som Wit', in Faulkner, pp. 96–106; and Ian Bishop, 'The Narrative Art of the Pardoner's Tale', *Medium Ævum*, 36 (1967), 15–24.

On the old man I have developed the line indicated by John M. Steadman, 'Old Age and *Contemptus mundi* in *The Pardoner's Tale*', reprinted in

Faulkner from *Medium Ævum*, 33 (1964), 121–30, and Elizabeth R. Hatcher, 'Life without Death: The Old Man in Chaucer's *Pardoner's Tale*', *Chaucer Review*, 9 (1975), 248–52.

John M. Steadman, 'Chaucer's Pardoner and the *Thesaurus meritorum*', *ELN* 3 (1965–6), 4–7, notes the connection of the Pardoner's office with the rioters' treasure.

Daniel Knapp, 'The Relyk of a Seint: A Gloss on Chaucer's Pilgrimage', *ELH* 39 (1972), 1–27, discusses the possible allusion to the relics of St Thomas in the Host's words. For a fabliau connection in the lines, see Richard Firth Green, 'The Pardoner's Pants (and Why they Matter)', *Studies in the Age of Chaucer*, 15 (1993), 131–45.

John Halverson, 'Chaucer's Pardoner and the Progress of Criticism', *Chaucer Review*, 4 (1970), 184–202, contains a useful survey of criticism.

CAROLYN DINSHAW

Eunuch Hermeneutics†

[On the *Pardoner's Tale*]

Very early in her *Prologue*, just as she is warming to her theme, the Wife of Bath is interrupted by the Pardoner on the road to Canterbury. He initially bristles at her images of "tribulacion in mariage" (173), but after she orders him to hear her out, he in fact urges her to teach him the tricks of her trade. It might seem as though there couldn't be a more unlikely pair: the Wife, flamboyantly arrayed and ostentatiously heterosexual, "carping" and in good fellowship with the company, and the Pardoner, that defective man, who makes the "gentils" cry out even before he begins his tale. But pilgrims are never only coincidentally brought together in the *Canterbury Tales*, and we begin to sense similarities between these two even on the superficial level of clothing. The Pardoner is as clothes-conscious as is the Wife of Bath in her "hosen . . . of fyn scarlet reed" (I.456): wearing no hood, with only a cap, "Hym thoughte he rood al of the newe jet" (I.682).[1] The emphasis on the apparel of these two pilgrims leads us to deeper connections between them. As I shall argue, the body is the field on which issues of representation and interpretation are literally and metaphorically played out. The eunuch Pardoner, focusing anxiety about the use of language on the road to Canterbury, embodies a truth about language that explains why the Wife's fantasy of the perfect marriage—analogous, in her *Prologue* and *Tale*, to the perfect glossing of a text—remains but a dream that can never be fully satisfied.

The Wife, so concerned in her *Prologue* with the question of how to read texts, presents in herself a perfect image of a text—a fictional or pagan one, as medieval writers from Macrobius to Richard of Bury imaged it. The fictional text, they write, is like a woman, extravagantly and seductively arrayed. Richard of Bury, for example, writes in his

† From *ELH* 55.1 (1988): 27–51. Copyright © 1988 The John Hopkins University Press. Reprinted with permission of The Johns Hopkins University Press. We have abridged some of the author's notes. In revised form this article appears in Professor Dinshaw's *Chaucer's Sexual Poetics* (Madison: U of Wisconsin P, 1989), pp. 156–84.

1. All quotations of Chaucer's poetry are from *The Works of Geoffrey Chaucer*, ed. F. N. Robinson, 2nd ed. (Boston: Houghton Mifflin, 1957). Citations are given parenthetically.

Philobiblon that the pagan classics are texts which, like females, appeal to the "wanton minds of men" with their seductive garments, their "masks of pleasure."[2] But the proper way to read such a text is to strip it of those garments, to penetrate to what Richard calls "the naked truth" (*nuda veritas*). I call such an approach to the text a "heterosexual hermeneutic": the text is woman's body, to be stripped and penetrated (or "glossed," from Greek *glossa*, "tongue") by male interpreters.

But this orthodox, "straight" hermeneutic will not work for the Pardoner, that sexually peculiar figure. The Pardoner's fashionable clothes do not, in fact, mask his body: without a hood, his cap reveals his carefully styled but thin and lifeless hair, and that hair, taken with the other details of his appearance, proclaims the unfortunate facts of his anatomy. As critics since W. C. Curry have noted, the Pardoner's "secret" is no secret at all: he appears to be a eunuch, either congenital or castrated.[3] The Pardoner's sense of his own physical lack not only informs his social behavior, but the thematics and narrative strategies of his tale as well. And most important, it represents the nature of language itself. It is not only modern theorists who analyze language as radically fragmentary: medieval writers too were preoccupied with the fundamental incompleteness of human language. The Pardoner enunciates the only possible strategy of using language in a postlapsarian world, cut off from primary wholeness and unity: he acts according to what I call the hermeneutrics of the partial, or, for short, eunuch hermeneutics.

The Pardoner surrounds himself with objects—relics, sealed documents, even language, regarded as a kind of object—that he substitutes for his own lacking parts. But these objects are themselves fragments, and cannot properly fill the lack that hollows the Pardoner's being. To be a eunuch is, as R. P. Miller has demonstrated, a spiritual condition as well as a physical one, and that spiritual condition has a psychological valence which I propose to analyze here: the substitute objects the Pardoner adopts cannot convert his bottomless *cupiditas*, that state of radical wanting, radical desire, into *caritas*, a state of oneness with the Father.[4] Nevertheless, even though the Pardoner knows that his relics, documents, words are defective substitutes—they are fakes, and he tells us so—he holds on to the belief that they can make him whole, part of the body of pilgrims, and

2. Richard of Bury, *Philobiblon*, ed. and trans. Ernest C. Thomas (London: Kegan Paul, Trench, and Co., 1887), 13.180: "Accordingly the wisdom of the ancients devised a remedy by which to entice the wanton minds of men by a kind of pious fraud, the delicate Minerva secretly lurking beneath the mask of pleasure" (trans. Thomas).
3. "The Secret of Chaucer's Pardoner" was W. C. Curry's groundbreaking article in *Journal of English and Germanic Philology* 18 (1919): 593–606, later appearing in his *Chaucer and the Medieval Sciences* (rev. ed., New York: Barnes and Noble, 1960), 54–90. Curry was the first to bring the inference of eunuchry (from the narrator's statement in the *General Prologue*, "I trowe he were a geldyng or a mare") under critical scrutiny, providing evidence from classical and medieval scientific discourse. Curry's particular interpretation of this evidence—his conclusion that the Pardoner is a congenital eunuch, a *eunuchus ex nativitate*—has come under attack, but there has been a broad consensus among Chaucerians that the Pardoner is a eunuch, either congenital or castrated. I address this issue in more detail below, in note 9.
4. See Robert P. Miller's classic article, "Chaucer's Pardoner, the Scriptural Eunuch, and the Pardoner's Tale," *Speculum* 30 (1955): 180–99. Augustine's analyses of spiritual conditions are powerful psychological analyses as well, as Donald R. Howard comments in his discussion of the Pardoner in his *Idea of the Canterbury Tales* (Berkeley: U of California P, 1976), 355–56. Janet Adelman ("'That We May Leere Som Wit,'" in *Twentieth-Century Interpretations of the Pardoner*, ed. Dewey R. Faulkner [Englewood Cliffs, N.J.: Prentice-Hall, 1973], 96–106) discusses aesthetic implications of *cupiditas*, seeing in the *Tale*'s use of parody and analogy a pattern of false substitution.

of the larger body of Christians. If we express this in terms of the problematics of interpretation, we can say that the eunuch's hermeneutics proceeds by double affirmations, double truths, the incompatible affirmations of knowledge and belief. A heterosexual hermeneutic penetrates and discards fiction for the truth, but the eunuch suggests that the relationship between fiction and truth is not so easy to discern: the eunuch holds on to the fiction, knowing that it is false but wanting to believe that it is true. That desire to believe is everyone's: the eunuch Pardoner, wanting to believe in his own wholeness, plays on his audience's desire to believe in theirs; he exposes everyone's radical longing for completeness.[5]

I

Richard of Bury provides an image for the heterosexual reading act, but he nonetheless associates reading with eunuchs as well. As I have said, he images reading as a seduction by the wanton letter of the text, a penetration to the naked body of woman. But he also—and somewhat contradictorily—emphasizes, with St. Paul, that the reader must leave behind the carnal letter to get to the text's spirit. Thus he suggests elsewhere in the *Philobiblon* that the end of reading is, finally, asexual: he commends Origen as an exemplary reader, one who was not distracted by any improper lusts of the flesh; and he cites the eunuch mentioned by St. Paul in the *Acts* as an example to all those who would learn to read properly: reading the Scriptures without understanding, the eunuch asked Philip to guide him; Philip "preached unto him Jesus" (Acts 8:35), and the eunuch was baptised.[6] To pursue this association of eunuchry with spiritual understanding beyond these citations in Richard of Bury, we need only turn to Abelard, perhaps the most famous of medieval castrati. Abelard built his career as a Christian philosopher upon his castration. He writes in the *Historia calamitatum* that in order to gain spiritual understanding—to read properly—it was necessary not only that he cease reading as he had been with Heloise (a literally heterosexual use of reading), but that he be castrated—although he admits that this was not among the *remedia amoris* he would have chosen—so that he would be freed for the work of the true philosopher. The eunuch, untempted by and discontinuous in the flesh, is the perfect reader.[7]

But Chaucer's eunuch, the Pardoner, is hardly the perfect, "spiritual" reader. There is an extraordinary focus on the body in his portrait, *Prologue*, and *Tale*. He is preoccupied by, chained to, the flesh, never rising out of it to reach the spirit. It is no coincidence that the Pardoner follows the Physician in telling his tale; the Physician is the pilgrim most

5. Here I wish to acknowledge a general indebtedness throughout this essay to R. Howard Bloch, *The Scandal of the Fabliaux* (Chicago: U of Chicago P, 1986).

6. About the eunuch in the *Acts*, Richard remarks: "Love of his book alone had wholly engrossed this domicile of chastity, under whose guidance he soon deserved to enter the gate of faith" (trans. Thomas). *Philobiblon* 15.203. See also 15.193, for citation of Origen.

7. "Abelard's Letter of Consolation to a Friend," ed. J. T. Muckle, *Mediaeval Studies* 12 (1950): 182 and passim. For remarks regarding Origen, see letter 4, from Abelard to Heloise, ed. Muckle, *Mediaeval Studies* 15 (1953): 89–90. R. Howard Bloch's discussion in *Etymologies and Genealogies: A Literary Anthropology of the French Middle Ages* (Chicago: U of Chicago P, 1983), "Philosophy and the Family: Abelard," suggests ways in which castration informs Abelard's theological formulations and his radical break from philosophical tradition.

Abelard's castration was not voluntary, of course, however salutary he later found it. He notes that Origen acted impetuously and was worthy of blame: "Yet Origen is seriously to be

concerned with the body—he is professionally dependent upon it. The tale the Physician tells, the story of Appius and Virginia, is taken from the *Roman de la rose*, and its narrative position there is significant: the story is told by Raison after her account of Saturn's castration. Raison's point is that justice was lost when Jupiter castrated his father; in the *Roman de la rose*, castration marks the loss of the Golden Age, the loss of an ideal.[8] And it does so, I shall argue, in the *Canterbury Tales* as well. The Pardoner follows the Physician's redaction of this tale as if to explain the sordid world of the *Physician's Tale*: it's an unjust world, a world cut off from natural justice, natural love—a castrated world.

Harry Bailly's garbled oath in calling for a tale to follow the Physician's ("By corpus bones!" [VI.314]) is a response to both the Physician's occupation and the sense of the corporal that surrounds the Pardoner. But the focus on the body in the Pardoner's portrait, *Prologue*, and *Tale* might more properly be said to be a focus on fragments of the body. First on the list of these fragments is, of course, the Pardoner himself. The narrator expresses some uncertainty about the Pardoner's sexuality in the *General Prologue*—"I trowe he were a geldyng or a mare" (I.691)—but the pieces of information he gives there—thin hair, glaring eyes, high voice, beardlessness—clearly suggest a eunuch, either congenital or castrated.[9] The narrator's uncertainty stems from his perception that something is lacking, either the physical equipment or masculine gender-identification, and, in fact, the categories of eunuchry and other physical and sexual conditions were often conflated in the Middle

blamed because he sought a remedy for blame in punishment of his body. True, he has zeal for God, but an ill-informed zeal, and the charge of homicide can be proved against him for his self mutilation" (trans. Betty Radice, *The Letters of Abelard and Heloise* [New York: Penguin, 1974], 149). See letter 4, 90. Similarly, John of Salisbury, one of Abelard's students in Paris, commends Origen for his zeal but remarks on his lack of good sense (*Polycraticus* 8.6, in *Patrologia latina* ed. J.-P. Migne, [Paris, 1855], 199: cols. 724D–725D. The idea that self-castration was blameworthy was current throughout the Middle Ages. Voluntary self-castration was not approved of even by the Early Church: opposing Gnostic opinion regarding self-castration, the Council of Nicea (325 A.D.) enunciated the belief that nature should not be mutilated. Aquinas summed up medieval opinion when he stressed that God intended, through nature, that the human body be integral in all its members; see *Summa theologica* 2.2 quaest. 65 ("De mutilatione membrorum"), art i–ii (*Opera omnia* [Parma, 1852–73; reprint, New York: Musurgia, 1948], 3: 244–45). In the *Roman de la rose* (ed. Félix Lecoy, Classiques français du moyen âge, 98 [Paris: Honoré Champion, 1970]), Nature (17022–29) and Genius (20007–52) similarly stress the natural integrity of the body. See John T. Noonan, Jr., *Contraception: A History of Its Treatment by the Catholic Theologians and Canonists* (Cambridge: Harvard UP, 1966), 95, 246, for summary discussion of medieval attitudes toward castration. Richard of Bury does, it is true, acknowledge that Origen's self-castration was a hasty remedy ("repugnant alike to nature and to virtue" in Thomas's emphatic translation), but ends the chapter with his vigorous commendation of the New Testament castrato; the metaphoric charge of Richard's discourse is most important here.

8. *Roman de la rose*, 5505ff.; Genius also explicitly connects castration to the loss of the Golden Age (20007 ff). For a detailed analysis of the Golden Age in reference to these passages in the *Rose* divergent from the one I will propose here, see John V. Fleming, *Reason and the Lover* (Princeton: Princeton UP, 1984), 97–135.
9. Curry's diagnosis (note 3) has been criticized by Muriel Bowden, *A Commentary on the General Prologue to the Canterbury Tales* (New York: Macmillan, 1957), 274–76; Beryl Rowland, "Chaucer's Idea of the Pardoner," *Chaucer Review* 14 (1979): 140–54; Monica E. McAlpine, "The Pardoner's Homosexuality and How It Matters," *PMLA* 95 (1980): 8–22; and C. David Benson, "Chaucer's Pardoner: His Sexuality and Modern Critics," *Mediaevalia* 8 (1982): 337–49. Curry's conclusion that the Pardoner is a congenital eunuch (rather than a castrated one) is arguable, since he bases this on his own interpretation of the Pardoner's character and not on the medieval physiognomists (according to whom all eunuchs look alike). But, as McAlpine concedes, he reveals that Chaucer does accurately use the physical stereotype of the eunuch in details of the Pardoner's portrait. R. P. Miller (note 4) has provided the Scriptural background that supports the diagnosis *eunuchus*: Chaucer's detailing of the Pardoner's physical condition, as Lee Patterson puts it, renders it meaningful in both realms of science and religious symbol ("Chaucerian Confession: Penitential Literature and the Pardoner," *Medievalia et Humanistica*, n.s., 7 [1976]:

Ages.[1] As I see it, an enormous lack—the Pardoner's unquenchable *cupiditas*, repeatedly expressed in his Prologue as "I wol . . . I wol . . . I wol"—and a disjunct sexual identity are objectified in his defective, lacking, fragmented physique.

"This fragmented body," writes Jacques Lacan, the modern theorist of the *corps morcelé*, "usually manifests itself in [images] when . . . analysis encounters a certain level of aggressive disintegration in the individual. It then appears in the form of disjointed limbs."[2] Body parts move grotesquely, almost surrealistically, through the *Prologue* and *Tale*. "Myne handes and my tonge goon so yerne / That it is joye to se my bisynesse" (398–99); "Thanne peyne I me to strecche forth the nekke" (395). "The shorte throte, the tendre mouth" (517) are the loci of gluttony; the "womb, belly, stinking cod" are sites of sin. "Oure blissed Lordes" body (474) is torn, by swearing, into "herte," "nayles," "blood," and "armes" (651–54). Tongues, noses, gullets freely animate the Pardoner's sermon. The Old Man in the exemplum wails that he is nothing but "flessh, and blood, and skyn" (732); his "bones" await their final rest.

But relics are perhaps the things that we remember the best about the Pardoner, even though, as Alfred L. Kellogg has shown, they are not conventional characteristics of abusive pardoners.[3] Relics are holy fragments, scraps and chips of saints, and it is wholly appropriate that the Pardoner claims to have many. He has "a gobet of the seyl / That Seint Peter hadde" (696–97), a jar of "pigges bones," a "shoulder-boon / Which that was of an hooly Jewes sheep" (350–51), a "miteyn" (the shape of a hand), and a "pilwebeer" (supposed to be Our Lady's veil). I want to consider the nature of sacred fragments for a moment.[4] The Pardoner's relics are not the most fragmentary of medieval relics on record: the relics that would seem to be paradigms of the fragmentary are splinters of the True Cross ("the croys which that Seint Eleyne fond" [951], by which the Host swears in response

153–73). As I hope to demonstrate, eunuchry has a powerfully determining psychological value as well in the *Prologue* and *Tale*. None of the other suggestions about the Pardoner's sexuality—that he is homosexual (Bowden, McAlpine), or a "testicular pseudo-hermaphrodite of the feminine type" (Rowland, "Animal Imagery and the Pardoner's Abnormality," *Neophilologus* 48 [1964]: 56–60), or a combination pervert (Eric W. Stockton, "The Deadliest Sin in The Pardoner's Tale,'" *Tennessee Studies in Literature* 6 [1961], who argues that the Pardoner is "a manic depressive with traces of anal eroticism, and a pervert with a tendency toward alcoholism" [47])—are supported by such a dense pattern of signification on so many levels.

1. The narrator's perception of lack is what Donald R. Howard (note 4) stresses in his reading of the line, "I trowe he were a geldyng or a mare" (343). Howard seeks to restore the sense of the Pardoner's inexplicably strange presence among the pilgrims but accepts, nonetheless, Curry's determination that he is a eunuch. McAlpine (note 9) briefly documents the conflation of sexual categories in the Middle Ages. For more on medieval homosexuality and its conflation with other sexual categories, see John Boswell, *Christianity, Social Tolerance, and Homosexuality: Gay People in Western Europe from the Beginning of the Christian Era to the Fourteenth Century* (Chicago: U of Chicago P, 1980).
2. Jacques Lacan, "The mirror stage as formative of the function of the I as revealed in psychoanalytic experience," in his *Ecrits: A Selection*, trans. Alan Sheridan (New York: W. W. Norton & Company, 1977), 4.
3. Alfred L. Kellogg, *Chaucer, Langland, Arthur: Essays in Middle English Literature* (New Brunswick: Rutgers UP, 1972), 212–44.
4. I have found Jonathan Sumption, *Pilgrimage: An Image of Mediaeval Religion* (London: Faber, 1975), especially useful—well documented and lively—on the subject of relics. Other interesting, general treatments I have used include Hippolyte Delehaye, *Les Origines du culte des martyrs*, 2nd ed., rev. (Brussels: Société des Bollandistes, 1933); P. Séjourné "Reliques," in *Dictionnaire de théologie catholique* (Paris: Librairie Letouzey et Ané, 1937), 13: 2311–75; and Peter Brown, *The Cult of the Saints: Its Rise and Function in Latin Christianity* (Chicago: U of Chicago P, 1981). In the brief discussion that follows, I cite sources from the early through the late Middle Ages; veneration of relics of course varied through the age, but the essential theological idea of relics remained fairly constant: Sumption suggests that the early Church's defenses of relics are echoed in every major apologist of the Middle Ages (23).

to the Pardoner). Pilgrims, according to several sources from the early and the high Middle Ages, kissed the Cross and surreptitiously carried the splinters away in their teeth.[5] Other holy monuments, such as tombs and gilded shrines, were broken into bits by pilgrims eager to bring back tokens. Body parts, however, were the medieval relics valued most highly: heads, arms, fingers of saints were severed and boxed in jeweled reliquaries. The efficacy of the whole body of the saint was powerful in these parts: synecdochically, in the divided body grace survived undivided.[6] Interestingly, dismemberment of saints' bodies was not allowed originally by the early Church, but the great demand for relics made more relics necessary: by the eighth century, relics had come to be regarded as requirements for the consecration of a church, and private collectors, from the very early years of Christianity, were greedy for them. In the face of this demand, dismemberment was eventually allowed. (Fortunately, the saints themselves approved of dismemberment, as the story of St. Mammas attests: a finger of that saint detached itself of its own accord when a priest came to the body to collect relics.)[7]

But it was the very practice of fragmentation that led to widespread frauds. Once the bodies were divided into pieces and translated from one church to another, it was impossible to verify their authenticity. And the fragments proliferated: if all the claims were to be believed, there were, by the twelfth century, at least three heads of John the Baptist, innumerable arms and fingers of various saints, five or six foreskins of Christ.[8] Despite growing concern in the late Middle Ages about "multiple" relics—Guibert of Nogent's arguments about the absurdity of some claims to authenticity, very unusual in the twelfth century, began to be echoed by fifteenth-century pilgrims—the cult of relics in itself was not questioned. In *Mandeville's Travels* (c. 1357), for example, the history of John the Baptist's head is carefully recounted (the head was first enclosed in a wall of a church in Sebaste, then translated to Constantinople, where the "hynder partye" remains, the "forpartie" is in Rome, the jaws and platter in Genoa), but then put in question by the claim that the whole head might in fact be at Amiens. But the hesitancy this competing claim provokes is overwhelmed by devotion:

> And summen seyn that the heed of seynt John is at Amyas in Picardye. And other men seyn that it is the heed of seynt John the bysshop; I wot nere, but god knoweth. But in what wyse that men worschipen it the blessed seynt John holt him apayd.[9]

5. See A. Frowlow, *La Relique de la vrai croix: recherches sur le développement d'un culte,* Archives de l'orient chrétien, 7 (Paris: Institut français d'études byzantines, 1961), 60–61, 161–65.
6. See Theodoret of Cyrus, *Graecarum affectionum curatio* 8, quoted in Sumption (note 4 above), 28. See also Victricius of Rouen, *De laude sanctorum* 10–11, *Patrologia latina,* 20: col. 454B, who speaks of saints' bodies, wherein every fragment "is linked by a band to the whole stretch of eternity," as Brown elegantly translates it. See Brown's (note 4 above) discussion of Victricius, 78–79.
7. See Sumption, 28.
8. Guibert of Nogent traces corruption and fraudulent claims to the practice of dismemberment and translation: "All the evil of contention (over relics) originates in the fact that the saints are not permitted the repose of a proper and immutable burial place" (*Gesta Dei per Francos* 1.5, *PL* 156: col. 695A, my translation). In *De pignoribus sanctorum,* Guibert points to the competing claims of Constantinople and Angeli to the head of the Baptist and remarks: "What, therefore, is more ridiculous than to suppose that this great man had two heads?" (1.3.2, in *PL* 156: col. 624D; my translation). See Delehaye (note 4 above), 82–83, for a specific history of the head; Sumption summarizes the history of Christ's foreskin (46).
9. *Mandeville's Travels,* ed. from British Museum Ms. Cotton Titus C. XVI by P. Hamelius, Early English Text Society, old series, 153 (London: Kegan Paul, 1919 for 1916), chap. 13, p. 71.

Indeed, there is more than a suggestion that competing claims to the same body part could be believed. A plurality of bodies seems to have been not only plausible, but preferable to a single one in the case of the Blessed Virgin: Our Lady of Coutances was a different entity from Our Lady of Bayeux, and some preferred the former, some the latter.[1] And in the case of Christ's foreskins, the multiplicity was perhaps even cultivated, as an index of virility—"humanation," as Leo Steinberg would call it.[2]

But the Pardoner's scraps and chips of saints substitute for his lack of natural virility. As free-floating body parts, they are both reifications of his own fragmentariness and substitutes for his own lacking parts. He can't increase and multiply literally or spiritually, as R. P. Miller stresses.[3] But he uses the proliferating relics as the means by which he unnaturally increases and multiplies: his relics, he claims, will make grain and cattle multiply; he increases the number of believers (even though "that is nat my principal entente" [432]); and he makes his income multiply outrageously.

His other artifacts, those sealed documents from Rome, are closely associated with his own dismemberment as well. I will consider the pardons' more complicated psychological value later, but already we can see the substitution that has been made. We are told in the *General Prologue* that he carries his pardons in his lap: "His walet lay biforn hym in his lappe, / Bretful of pardoun, comen from Rome al hoot" (I.686–87). As rolled-up parchments with seals dangling from them, the Pardoner's documents and bulls, placed conspicuously in his bulging "male" (IV.920), present an iconographic substitute for his own lacking genitals. He emphatically declares that these bulls validate, make potent and unquestionable, his fractured body:

> my bulles shewe I, alle and some.
> Oure lige lordes seel on my patente,
> That shewe I first, my body to warente.
> (336–38)

So written documents and relics both function as body parts for the Pardoner. Historically, they were sometimes assimilated to one another: in the early Middle Ages, a book such as the *Lindisfarne Gospels* was itself a relic and a shrine, because of its association with Saint Cuthbert. Documents were kept along with relics in early treasure stores, and relics, to insure their authenticity, were sometimes sealed with bulls.[4]

Fragmentary and partial themselves, relics and documents also function for the Pardoner as "partial objects," to adapt a psychoanalytic idea to my purposes here. A "partial object," as I shall employ the term, is used by the subject in the attempt to fill the lack brought into being by the loss of an original ideal, an original wholeness and plenitude.[5] In the

1. See Sumption, 50–51.
2. Leo Steinberg, *The Sexuality of Christ in Renaissance Art and in Modern Oblivion* (New York: Pantheon, 1983).
3. Miller (note 4, p. 613), 185–86 and passim.
4. M. T. Clanchy, *From Memory to Written Record: England, 1066–1307* (Cambridge: Harvard UP, 1979), 125. See also Delehaye (note 4, p. 616).
5. My "partial object" is different from Melanie Klein's "part-object." As Harry Guntrip explains, in his *Personality Structure and Human Interaction* (New York: International Universities P, 1961), 226 ff., Klein establishes that in early infancy "all the baby knows or experiences is a breast (a 'part-object') and that it takes time and development for the baby to become aware of the mother in her completeness (a 'whole-object')." The "part-object," to the infant, is not

psychoanalytic economy, the loss of such an ideal of fullness and plenitude is always associated with castration: the original fullness of continuity with the mother is lost as the child, first perceiving physical differentiation from the mother, fears for the integrity of its own body. With the father's interruption of the mother-child union, the child perceives sexual difference and, specifically, the mother's lack of a penis. According to the Freudian analysis of the male castration complex, when the boy-child perceives the mother's lack, and the lacks of other females around him, he fears his own castration. "If a woman ha[s] been castrated, then his own possession of a penis [is] in danger": this threat of castration puts an end to the boy's Oedipus complex, as he (ideally) detaches himself from the mother and submits to the father.[6] Lacan, reinterpreting Freud, argues that the child not only fears his own castration upon recognition of physical differentiation, but *is* castrated at this moment, precisely because he is cut off from primary nondifferentiation, primary identification with the mother. In this sense, everyone is castrated, male and female alike; everyone is separated from the realm of primary union and continuity. Law and language, symbolic forms associated with the father, are imposed in the castrated realm of difference: the distance opened up by the entrance of the father creates the distinction between subjects and objects, signifiers and signifieds.[7]

Because of the loss of that ideal, the castrated subject forever seeks the realm of original fullness but must be content with substitutes only partially sufficient. These substitutes by their very nature signify the loss of an ideal, and therefore signify castration, even as they are—because they are—accepted as substitutes for lost genitals. So written documents, as the eunuch Pardoner's partial objects, fill his "male" (I.694) while deceiving no one, and relics provide the means by which he increases and multiplies. That his relics perform this genital role for the Pardoner is made explicit at the end of the *Tale*, when Harry Bailly wishes that he could make the ultimate relic for the Pardoner's collection out of the Pardoner's

partial; it is a whole-object to the baby, and is partial only in the adult's eyes. In my adaptation of the term, the partialness of the object, from the subject's point of view, is important: the object is a substitute for a formerly known whole, and is recognized to be defective in relation to that lost whole. Klein stresses that part-objects remain active as representations of the mother even after the infant has perceived her as a whole, and analysts following Klein have pointed to situations in which older children treat people as part-objects. See, for example, Emilio Rodrigue, "An Analysis of a Three-Year-Old Mute Schizophrenic," in Klein, Heimann, and Money-Kyrle, eds., *New Directions in Psycho-Analysis* (New York: Basic Books, 1955), 140–79. It is this afterlife of the Kleinian part-object that led me to the idea that the part has an important function after perception of and loss of the whole: that it is, in fact, fetishized.

6. Sigmund Freud, "Fetishism," in *The Standard Edition of the Works of Sigmund Freud*, ed. and trans. James Strachey (London: Hogarth P, 1953–56), 21:153. See also "The Dissolution of the Oedipus Complex," *Standard Edition*, 19:173–79. The fear of castration, according to Freud, does not apply to the girl-child; she already has been castrated, and her Oedipus complex is the result of her castration. The resolution of the female Oedipus complex remains rather unclear.

7. Lacan, in "The function and field of speech and language in psychoanalysis" (note 2, p. 616, 102–04), reinterprets Freud's analysis of his grandson's game of Fort!/Da!, analyzing the partial object as itself conveying absence: as Anthony Wilden puts it, "The partial object conveys the lack which created the desire for unity from which the movement toward identification springs—since identification is itself dependent upon the discovery of *difference,* itself a kind of absence" (Anthony Wilden, "Lacan and the Discourse of the Other," in Jacques Lacan, *The Language of the Self,* translated and with commentary by Anthony Wilden [Baltimore: Johns Hopkins UP, 1968], 163). The partial object attempts to fill a lack created by a loss of ideal plenitude; Lacan analyzes the restless movement of desire opened up by the loss of the *objet a*, the loss of the relation to an other who is not conceived of as an object. The substitutes will always be partial. This lost object *a* is in particular the mother's body; in Lacan's interpretation

"coillons" (balls): he would cut them off and enshrine them in a hog's turd. But he can't, for reasons evident to all.

Harry Bailly's response to the Pardoner's invitation to "kiss the relikes everychon" is surprising in its vehemence: that final moment between the two pilgrims is highly charged with sexual repugnance. But I find Harry's response interesting in another way as well: in its explicit association of relics and balls, it refers to another medieval discussion wherein relics, balls, and writing are all brought together in a discussion of castration. Relics, testicles, and language are not, as far as I know, common bedfellows in medieval literature; we must, therefore, investigate how and why they are brought together in a passage in the *Roman de la rose*—the text commonly acknowledged to contain, in Faux-Semblant, a source for the characterization of the Pardoner—and from the *Rose* into the *Canterbury Tales*.

II

In the *Roman de la rose*, Raison's narration of the story of Saturn's castration, the event that she identifies as the moment at which the Golden Age, the original ideal community, was lost, leads to a discussion of her use of language (6898–7200). Amant quibbles with Raison's free naming of "coilles" in her narration. "Balls are not of good repute in the mouth of a courteous lady," he protests, perhaps referring to dirty sex as well as to dirty language.[8] Her language goes against Amors's "clean speech commandment," as John V. Fleming has put it.[9] If such things as balls must be mentioned, Amant insists, Raison should at least provide a gloss. The word is dirty, he clearly implies, because the thing is dirty.

Raison counters by protesting that neither word nor thing is dirty. Both word and thing are good, and she can name a thing which is good—made by God—openly and by its own name. Her words are proper names of things; they are perfectly adequate to, share in the *propre* of, the things they name. Amant protests further that even if God made the things, he still didn't make the words, which are unspeakably nasty. But Raison goes on to declare that God could have made the words at the time of creation; instead he deputized her to do it at her leisure. Her comment traces language to the time before the Fall: her view here is an essentially prelapsarian view of language, an Adamic view that words share in the nature of the things they signify.

Raison then goes on to say that if she had called "reliques coilles" and "coilles reliques," Amant would have objected that "reliques" is a base word. Clearly, she implies, "reliques" is a good word because "reliques" are holy things. But even in Raison's suggestion that she could have named "reliques coilles" and vice versa, there is an implication of the arbitrariness of signs:

---

of the Oedipal situation, the father interrupts the symbiotic relationship of mother and child; the phallus represents sexual difference and thus is a sign of castration. See "Of the Gaze as *Objet Petit a*," in *Four Fundamental Concepts of Psychoanalysis*, ed. J.-A. Miller, trans. Alan Sheridan (New York: W. W. Norton & Company, 1981), 67–119, esp. 67–77.

8. *Roman de la rose*, 6898–6901).

9. Fleming (note 8, p. 615) 101. Fleming has written the most recent analysis of this scene in his chapter "Words and Things." He identifies Augustine as the most important influence here (the "supertext," to use his term), as I also do; but our conclusions are somewhat different. My discussion coincides more closely with Bloch, *Etymologies and Genealogies*, 137–41.

the original relation between word and thing, between *signans* and *signatum*, was, in fact, arbitrary. She could have named the things anything. And her comments on "custom" that follow develop this protonominalist point: names are set by custom, by convention.

These are two distinct and contradictory positions on language: the one "naturalistic," the other "conventional." The issue of the naturalness or conventionality of the relationship between word and thing, sign and signified, had been debated since Plato's *Cratylus*, and both positions are found in medieval writers on language. Medieval writers explicitly adopted Hermogenes' position, asserting that the sign's relation to the signified is determined by convention, but at the same time, their linguistic and analytical habits imply a belief in the natural fitness of signs to things. Socrates too, of course, had it both ways: he judged that there is a natural resemblance between word and thing, but he acknowledged the conventional establishment of meaning as well. This dichotomous or ambivalent position, R. Howard Bloch has suggested, can be seen in writers from the late Latin grammarians (Varro, Priscian) to writers of the high Middle Ages (Abelard, John of Salisbury).[1] Such ambivalence may be very clearly seen in Augustine, whose discussions of sign theory proved fundamental throughout the entire Middle Ages, and whose thought informs this passage in the *Roman de la rose*.

Augustine accepts the anti-Cratylistic notion that the relation between *signans* and *signatum* is conventionally established. Very clearly (even simplistically, as some critics have suggested) he explains in the *De doctrina*:

> the single sign *beta* means a letter among the Greeks but a vegetable among the Latins. When I say *lege*, a Greek understands one thing by these two syllables, a Latin understands another. Therefore just as all of these significations move men's minds in accordance with the consent of their societies, and because their consent varies, they move them differently, nor do men agree upon them because of an innate value, but they have a value because they are agreed upon.[2]

Verbal signs do not have innate referential values. Augustine suggests to Adeodatus in *De magistro* that one cannot even know that a word is a sign until one knows what it means: the decision to attend to it as a sign is set by convention, as is its meaning.[3] Language is a social phenomenon and there cannot be, according to this position, any constitutive similarity between thing and sign.

Nevertheless, there is in Augustine's writing a deep strain of belief in the natural relation of words and their referents. *De dialectica* includes a chapter on the origins of words: there Augustine argues against the Stoics' claim that *all* words can be traced to their natural origins, but he endorses

1. Bloch, *Etymologies and Genealogies*, 44–53.
2. St. Augustine, *De doctrina christiana*, ed. J. Martin, Corpus christianorum (hereafter cited as CC), series latina, 32 (Turnholt: Brepols, 1962), 2.24, pp. 59–60. Trans. as *On Christian Doctrine* by D. W. Robertson, Jr. (Indianapolis: Bobbs-Merrill, 1958), 60–61. For a critique of Augustine's position here, see R. A. Markus, "St. Augustine on Signs," in *Augustine: A Collection of Critical Essays*, ed. R. A. Markus (New York: Doubleday Anchor, 1972), 78.
3. St. Augustine, *De magistro*, ed. K.-D. Daur, CC, 29 (Turnholt: Brepols, 1970), 11.36, p. 194.

and practices etymological analysis of many words, tracing them back to find an essential, constitutive similarity between sound and thing.[4] Origins of words are essential to his argument in *De civitate Dei*: the names of the founders of the two cities express the whole program of human history.[5] His fascination with the infant's process of learning language in the *Confessiones* (I.6, 8) suggests a profound desire for verbal signs rooted in the physical, in the body, a language understood by all humans. Even though he is careful, always, to distinguish natural signs from conventional signs and to put language in the latter category, he expresses a definite linguistic nostalgia—a desire for a language in which word and thing are again one.

This nostalgia is a symptom of his desire to escape from the problems that the conventionality of language poses, problems of language's unreliability. For language, established by convention, is radically limited. Augustine's *De magistro* is an extended treatise on the limitations of verbal signs. The conventions that link *signans* to *signatum* can be changed, disregarded, broken. Words are capable only of reminding, not teaching, Augustine says to Adeodatus; they are able to point to the truth but do not possess it. And consequently, all kinds of slips are possible between the speaker, his language, and his audience.[6]

Theologically speaking, the problem of language's defectiveness was solved by the Incarnation. As God took on humanity in a Word made flesh, so can human language express divinity; language is redeemed.[7] The Incarnation restores man to God, the word to the Word: the continuity of language and being, disrupted at the Fall, is reestablished. Nevertheless, the problem of language's defectiveness, exemplified most profoundly by its inability to express the divine, remains. Augustine begins the *Confessiones* by lamenting the poverty of language and asserting the ultimate ineffability of God, and he ends the *De trinitate* similarly—even

4. *De dialectica* is a work whose authorship has been disputed, but one which has been taken by its most recent translator and by Fleming (note 8, p. 615) as genuinely Augustinian. See the introduction to *De dialectica*, ed. Jan Pinborg, trans. with introduction and notes by B. Darrell Jackson (Boston and Dordrecht, Holland: D. Reidel, 1975). Augustine begins the chapter by suggesting that a word's origin may indeed be a matter of indifference, as long as its meaning is understood; he suggests that the pursuit of the origin of words is a potentially endless task, dependent on the researcher's own ingenuity, and that some words' origins can't ever be accounted for. But he asserts, in the same chapter, that there are many cases of natural resemblance between word and referent: the impressions made on the senses by the sounds of such words as *lene* and *asperitas* are in harmony (*concordarent*) with the impressions made by the referents themselves. Further on, Augustine specifically discusses the *vis* of words—their affective power—suggesting that the sensible qualities of words convey a meaning that is in accord with the referent itself. Sound and referent, physical property of word and physical property of thing, are linked: the word shares the natural property of the thing.
5. Bloch (*Etymologies and Genealogies*, 36) makes this observation and cites *De civitate Dei* 15.17: "Now as Cain, signifying possession, the founder of the earthly city, and his son Enoch, meaning dedication, in whose name it was founded, indicate that this city is earthly both in its beginning and in its end—a city in which nothing more is hoped for than can be seen in this world—so Seth, meaning resurrection, and being the father of generations registered apart from the others, we must consider what this sacred history says of his son." *De civitate Dei*, CC, 47 (Turnholt: Brepols, 1955), 480; trans. M. Dods, in *Basic Writings of Saint Augustine*, ed. Whitney J. Oates (New York: Random House, 1948), 2:300.
6. *De magistro* 13.43 and passim.
7. Critical in Augustine's intellectual movement toward Christianity is his understanding of the Incarnation: as Marcia Colish demonstrates, the rhetorician's whole conversion experience can be traced by following this idea of the redemption of language. See Marcia Colish, *The Mirror of Language* (New Haven: Yale UP, 1968), 8–81.

though it is in this latter treatise that he delineates the mimetic relation of the inner word of the mind to the Word.[8]

So human language is essentially partial. This is why Raison's narration of castration leads to a discussion of language and relics: "coilles," "reliques," "paroles"—all are fragments. A sign itself, Augustine sees, is accurate, but by definition it is only a partial representation of the thing it signifies. The word we speak is only a fragment of what we think (*De magistro* 14.46). And that inner word is only a partial representation of the Word (*De trinitate* 15.10–11). Words are, physically, fragments, one giving way to another in the construction of a whole message (*Confessiones* 4.11). And there is always something left over, unexpressed: language always lags behind the mind (*De catechizandis rudibus*, 2.3).[9] Augustine's awareness of linguistic inadequacy, even as he formulated the idea of a redeemed rhetoric, reflects, as Bloch puts it, an "anguished ambiguity provoked by a deep split between what medieval writers knew about verbal signs and what they desired to believe about them."[1]

The Pardoner, with his "hauteyn speche" (330), missing "coillons," and fake relics, is the focus of anxiety about language in the *Canterbury Tales*. Late-medieval fears about language's instability and unreliability focused, at least in part, on the use of language by self-seeking preachers (especially friars); and the Pardoner is, of course, a false preacher. Fourteenth-century treatises on preaching stress, on the one hand, that preaching is mandated by Christ: it is both necessary and possible with a "redeemed rhetoric" such as Augustine describes, a rhetoric based on the "unity of substance" in the Word, as Robert of Basevorn puts it in his *Forma praedicandi* (1322). Christ preached and ordered his followers to preach; indeed, in so doing, he was following a tradition of preaching that dated from the Creation, when, as Robert writes, God first preached to Adam. Preaching is thus linked to unfallen language.[2] Also associating preaching with Creation, Humbert of

8. *Confessiones* 1.4; see *De trinitate*, ed. W. J. Mountain, CC, 50 (Turnholt: Brepols, 1968), 11 and 15 for the explication of the relationship between word and Word; and 15.28 (Oratio), 533–35, for the final protestation of the ineffability of God and the shortcomings of language: "When the wise man spake of Thee in his book, which is now called by the special name of *Ecclesiasticus*, 'We speak,' he said, 'much, and yet come short; and in sum of words, He is all.' When, therefore, we shall have come to Thee, these very many things that we speak, and yet come short, will cease; and Thou, as One, wilt remain 'all in all.'" Trans. A. W. Haddan, rev. by W. G. T. Shedd, in *Basic Writings of Saint Augustine* (note 5, p. 622), 2:878.
9. St. Augustine, *De catechizandis rudibus*, ed. I. B. Bauer, CC, 46 (Turnholt: Brepols, 1969), 122–23.
1. Bloch, *Etymologies and Genealogies*, 44.
2. Robert of Basevorn, *Forma Praedicandi* 6, in *Artes praedicandi*, ed. Th.-M. Charland, O.P., Publications de l'Institut d'Etudes Médiévales d'Ottawa (Paris and Ottawa, 1936): "After creating man, God preached (if we extend the word 'preaching'), saying to Adam (Gen. 2:17): *For in what day soever thou shalt eat of it, thou shalt die the death.* This was the first persuasion of which we read in Scripture. . . . And at last He Himself, taking on a human soul and body in the unity of substance, came preaching the same theme which his precursor had preached before, as is seen in Matt. 4:17." Trans. Leopold Krul, O.S.B., in *Three Medieval Rhetorical Arts*, ed. James J. Murphy (Berkeley: U of California P, 1971), 126–27. See also Thomas Waleys, *De modo componendi sermones cum documentis* 1, in Charland, 329–41. I have benefitted from the surveys of sermon rhetoric in James J. Murphy, *Rhetoric in the Middle Ages: A History of Rhetorical Theory from St. Augustine to the Renaissance* (Berkeley and Los Angeles: U of California P, 1974), 269–355; Etienne Gilson, "Michel Menot et la technique du sermon médiévale," in his *Les Idées et les lettres*, 2nd ed. (Paris: J. Vrin, 1955), 93–154; and Margaret Jennings, C.S.J., "The *Ars componendi sermones* of Ranulph Higden," in *Medieval Eloquence: Studies in the Theory and Practice of Medieval Rhetoric*, ed. J. J. Murphy (Berkeley: U of California P, 1978), 112–26.

Romans states in his mid-thirteenth-century treatise on preaching that it functions to "scatter the word of God like seed."[3]

But on the other hand, language was understood to be partial and fragmentary; abuses of language in preaching were perceived as not only possible but rampant. The widespread uneasiness about false preaching had as its ultimate preoccupation the defective, shifting relationship of the spoken word to the Word. Wycliffe charged again and again that false preachers—abusive friars—had obfuscated the true Word.[4] Wycliffe's literalism was extreme and unorthodox, but protests against friars who "redefined" or altogether discarded the Word to serve their own ends in sermons were rife: Chaucer's Summoner paints a perfect portrait of the "glosying" friar; Richard FitzRalph, Archbishop of Armagh in the mid-fourteenth century, exclaims against friars who complain of his insistence on textual proof. Such charges against preaching friars as hypocrites point directly to a deep split between the speaker's intention, his spoken word, and the Word.[5]

So false preachers represent not just a threat to language; they represent a truth about language, in fact, language's "double truth." Language is at best a fragment, and, like "coilles" and "reliques," can be cut off altogether from the Significator. Yet people nostalgically believe in it, must believe in it; they necessarily affirm by speaking and listening that the spoken word can adequately express the inner word, and the inner word, the Word. Faux-Semblant, false preacher of the *Roman de la rose*, embodies the uneasy possibility of the breakdown of all coherence and stability in that narrative. As an unfixed, shape-shifting being, putting on

3. Humbert of Romans, *De eruditione praedicatorum* 1.3, ed. J. J. Berthier (Rome: A. Befani, 1889), 2:377: "Without preaching, through which the word of God is sown, all the world would be sterile and without fruit" (my translation).

4. This accusation is a fundamental one in Wycliffe's continual antifraternal polemic. For examples in English, see his vernacular version of his Latin *De officio pastorali* (c. 1377), chap. 26:

> thus ther ben many causis that letten goddis word to renne. . . . the fourthe cause is bringing in of false freris bi many cuntreys; for, as it is seid bifore, thei letten trewe preching to renne and maken curatis bi many weyes to leeue this moost worthy offiss. First they robben hem many weyes and maken hem bisy for to lyue, for they deprauen hem to ther parischens bi floriyshid wordis that they bringen yn; and no drede they shapen ther sermouns by dyuysiouns and othere iapis that they maken moost plese the puple. And thus they erren in bileue and maken the puple to trowe to hem that sermouns ben nought but in ther foorme.

The English Works of Wyclif, Hitherto Unprinted, ed. F. D. Mathew, Early English Text Society, n.v. (London: Trubner, 1880), 445–46. Another example is sermon III, on the Feast of the Seven Brethren:

> Thes wordis of Crist ben scorned of gramariens and devynes. Gramariens and filosophris seien, that Crist knewe not his gendris; and bastard dyvynes seien algatis that thes wordis of Crist ben false, and so no wordis of Crist bynden, but to the witt that gloseris tellen. But here we seien to thes trowauntis that thei blaiberen thus for defaute of witt. Leeve we thes heretikes as foolis, and seie we sum witt that God hath yovon us.

Select English Works of John Wyclif, ed. Thomas Arnold (Oxford: Clarendon P, 1869), 1:375–76. See G. R. Owst, *Preaching in Medieval England: An Introduction to Sermon Manuscripts of the Period, c. 1350–1450* (New York: Russell and Russell, 1965), for a discussion of fraternal preaching, and *Literature and Pulpit in Medieval England* (Oxford: Basil Blackwell, 1961), 56–109, for literal and allegorical uses of Scripture in sermons. Dom David Knowles, *The Religious Orders of England* (Cambridge: Cambridge UP, 1957), 2:61–73, 90–115, provides a good discussion of mendicant orders and their critics.

5. Arnold Williams cites a sermon by FitzRalph (British Museum Ms. Lansdowne 393, fol. 108) in which FitzRalph remarks that "when he challenged the friars to produce one scriptural text commanding poverty or proving that Christ ever begged voluntarily or spontaneously, they complained that he respected only the text of Scripture, not the gloss" ("Chaucer and the Friars," *Speculum* 28 [1953]: 511). Even some friars themselves admitted that they preached sometimes with hatred in their hearts, not with the *caritas* that is the proper significator of all language: see G. R. Owst, *Preaching in Medieval England,* 77.

clothes without a body beneath, he is a sign without a Significator, a spoken word without a Word. And he is sexually indeterminate: he can adopt both genders, and is neither. If one truth about language associates it with prelapsarian times, a time of perfect sexual relations, gendered but uncorrupted, the other truth cuts it off from perfect sexuality. The breakdown of language and determinate sexuality are of a piece, as it were; and the Pardoner, false preacher, of a broken, corrupted sexuality, is Faux-Semblant's descendant in every way.

III

The Pardoner both exposes and is caught in language's double truth. He uses language as he does his relics and his documents, as a partial object, a substitute for his absent genitals, and for what their absence represents: a lost Golden Age in which there is no differentiation between self and other, signifier and signified—the realm of the Word. His partial objects are flawed; they are inadequate substitutes, and he knows it. In fact he tells the pilgrims again and again that his relics are fakes; he insists that his words and his intentions are discrepant; he admits that Christ's pardon, not his, "is best." Yet he adopts these partial objects in the knowledge of their insufficiency. The psychologic of knowingly accepting such faulty substitutes is succinctly expressed by O. Mannoni in his discussion of the fetish: "Je sais bien, mais quand même . . . [I know, but even so . . .]. This is the logic of the eunuch that informs the hermeneutics of the partial.[6]

Mannoni is, of course, following Freud here, who writes that the fetish "is a substitute for the woman's (the mother's) penis that the little boy once believed in, and . . . does not want to give up." The fetish allows the child to retain the idea of the maternal phallus even after he has perceived sexual difference; it allows him to remain in the realm of nondifferentiation and plenitude (his mother and he are not separate) even after he knows that she doesn't have an organ like his, even after mother and child are cut off from each other by the interruption of the father. But such a substitute is inevitably inadequate; the child *knows* that the mother is separate and other, and anxiously tries to fill that unfillable emptiness. The fetish is precisely what I have been calling a partial object: it admits the fact of castration even as it refuses to admit it. Thus the fetish is constituted of contrary ideas, of "two mutually incompatible assertions": the mother has her penis and she has been castrated; the child is united with the mother and is cut off from her.[7] The fetishist maintains a conceptual fiction, a fiction of nondifferentiation and plenitude, in the face of perceptual knowledge.[8] "I know, but even so . . .": the fetish is the first model of all repudiations of reality.[9] Thus the medieval theorists of language know about the fallenness of language, but hold on

6. O. Mannoni, *Clefs pour l'imaginaire* (Paris: Seuil, 1969), 9–33.
7. Freud (note 6, p. 619), 21:152–53, 157.
8. D. W. Winnicott, "Transitional Objects and Transitional Phenomena: A Study of the First Not-Me Possession," *International Journal of Psycho-Analysis* 34 (1953): 95–96, contrasts the fetish with the transitional object in order to emphasize the abnormality of the fetishist. The fetish, based as it is on a delusion of a maternal phallus, is not a normal phenomenon, whereas the transitional object, based on illusion (an area between primary creativity and objective reality based on reality testing), is healthy and universal. Phyllis Greenacre, "The Fetish and the Transitional Object," *Psychoanalytic Study of the Child* 24 (1969): 144–65, also stresses the arrest of development of the fetishist.
9. See Mannoni, 12.

to the belief otherwise. Just as the fetishist knows that a foot is just a foot—but even so . . .

The Pardoner, using his partial objects as substitute genitals, is a fetishist. His verbal arts, documents, relics are all entirely transparent substitutes: they are admissions, signs of his lack even as they guard against his acknowledgment of it. He knows that they are only partial, that they are fakes, but even so he uses them—aggressively, desperately—in the belief that they can make him whole, somehow part of the body of pilgrims. And his *Tale*, a sample sermon, is a narrative representation of the fetishist's conflicted psyche. The world of the *Tale* is an Old Testament one, punitive and unredeemed; the "riotoures thre" are dispatched by "Deeth" in a terrifyingly immediate judgment of their sin. Yet the "olde man," embodying mutually incompatible assertions, has, along with a knowledge of this implacable "Deeth," a belief in redemption, "even so."[1]

The tavern world of the riotors is the world of the Law. Most of the Pardoner's exempla are drawn from the Old Testament, and he seems in fact to prefer the Old Testament to the New in setting the scene: "Witnesse on Mathew; but in special / Of sweryng seith the hooly Jeremye" (634–35). Christ's Redemption is duly acknowledged, but our original corruption and consequent damnation, imposed by an angry God the Father at the Fall, vividly endure in the Pardoner's rhetoric:

O glotonye, ful of cursednesse!
O cause first of oure confusioun!
O original of oure dampnacioun,
Til Crist hadde boght us with his blood agayn!
Lo, how deere, shortly for to sayn,
Aboght was thilke cursed vileynye!
Corrupt was al this world for glotonye.
(498–504)

"Heighe Goddes heestes" (640), the tables of the Law, govern, and sin is inexorably punished: its wages are death. "Deeth," in fact, presides over "this contree"; he has slain "al the peple" (676) and will inevitably prevail over those who seek to slay him. In the emotional economy of the tale, this ineluctable Death is the same force as the Father, "verray God, that is omnipotent" (576). When the Pardoner assigns the three riotors, three stumbling, swearing drunks, to overcome Death, it becomes clear that to his mind redemption from the Law, from this forbidding "verray God," is impossible. "'Deeth shal be deed!'" the riotors yell, "al dronken in this rage" (710, 705): the three inebriated ruffians are incapable—obviously, lugubriously—of this salvific mission. Death gets them in the end, and there is no thought of salvation.

Indulging in all the sins of which the Pardoner says he is himself guilty, the three riotors are a representation of the Pardoner's belief in the impossibility of atonement with the Father. The "olde man," whom they accost in the search for Death, is another representation of the Pardoner himself: he

1. Among the many recent critics who have discussed narrative elements of the *Tale* as representations or projections of the Pardoner himself, see H. Marshall Leicester, Jr., "'Synne Horrible': The Pardoner's Exegesis of His Tale, and Chaucer's," in *Acts of Interpretation: The Text in Its Contexts, 700–1600*, ed. Mary J. Carruthers and Elizabeth D. Kirk (Norman, Okla.: Pilgrim Books, 1982), 25–50; Alfred David, *The Strumpet Muse* (Bloomington: Indiana UP, 1976), 193–204; Patterson (note 9, p. 615), 166–67; and Howard (note 4, p. 613), 357–63.

is an incarnation of the Pardoner's anguished knowledge of his fragmentariness: "Lo how I vanysshe, flessh, and blood, and skyn!" (732). The old man wails for some redemption from his defective and dying corpse, and he expresses this desire not in terms of atonement with the Father but of reunion with his "leeve mooder":

> Thus walke I, lyk a resteless kaityf,
> And on the ground, which is my moodres gate,
> I knokke with my staf, bothe erly and late,
> And seye "Leeve mooder, leet me in!"
>
> (728–31)

Between the old man and his "leeve mooder," that lost ideal realm of unity and plenitude, stands "Goddes wille." To be "at reste" in the "ground" with his mother would provide a return to nondifferentiation, a reunion of subject and object, a redemption from the torments of age and separation. Even though he knows of Christ's atonement for the loss of original plenitude—he tells the riotors of it—he remains unredeemed by Him "that boghte agayn mankynde" (766): he walks continually "lyk a restelees kaityf" (728). The old man has an image and a hope of fullness and plenitude—"Deeth" to him is reunion, not separation, and he states that he has not been reunited with his mother "yet"—but the way to this plentitude is not through the Father: "Goddes wille" blocks it.

The figure of the old man in particular articulates the Pardoner's own "incompatible assertions." The Pardoner's world as he imagines it is dominated by a jealous, unforgiving Old Testament God, a castrating Father; Christ's pardon is acknowledged but the Pardoner is still convicted by the image of the forbidding Father, and under the Law there is no redemption, nothing but death as the wages of sin. Cut off, the Pardoner obsessively desires wholeness, and wholeness is what he repeatedly claims his pardons will deliver: he promises his rustic audiences again and again that their cows, calves, sheep will be made "hool" (357, 359), and they themselves will remain a part of the body of Christians (377–88). And he comments to the pilgrims that "Paraventure ther may fallen oon or two / Doun of his hors, and breke his nekke atwo" (935–36), but, he boasts and somehow believes, he is "suffisant" to the task of making them whole again. The Pardoner is an enormous success as a swindler precisely because he truly believes in his own false relics.[2]

So the Pardoner believes in the possibility of the restoration of lost plenitude, and he successfully plays on the fetishism of his audiences as well. His promises of wholeness make him richer by far than any parish priest. And the Pardoner knows that the pilgrims desire wholeness: when he interrupts the Wife of Bath to claim that he was about to wed a wife, when he later proclaims in his *Prologue* that he wants a jolly wench in every town, he is not simply trying to enter the heterosexual world of the pilgrims; he is cannily playing on their desire to believe in the integrity of the body, their desire to believe in the integrity of *his* body, and of their

2. "We have already seen that there are several ways to believe and not to believe" (Mannoni, 24; my translation). The swindler believes, in a certain fashion, in his admittedly false inventions, using the fetishist's belief "even so." Belief is the key to the creation of illusion or of the successful swindle, and as Mannoni suggests, it is the swindler's own belief that makes the job work. "Clearly there is no doubt that disavowal is enough to create magic" (29; my translation).

own pilgrim body. He is exploiting their fetishistic ability to admit his oddity even while they refuse the practical consequences of their admission. They know (that he is sexually weird), but even so (they demand a "moral thyng" from him). Their desire for an edifying tale is well described by this fetishistic logic: even out of the mouth of a ribald figure they insist that it will be a "moral thyng"; even though it is fiction, they will find it true. Fiction is not just for "lewed peple" to "holde" onto (438); it is for everyone, a partial object par excellence. Made of flawed language, fiction is not literally true, we know, but it plays on our desire for truth. To paraphrase John of Garland's definition of "realistic fiction" (*argumentum*), "I know that it didn't happen, but even so, it could have . . ."—and we will find the ways in which it can be said to tell the truth.[3]

The particular form of the exemplum is perfectly suited to the Pardoner's, and his audiences', fetishistic purposes. It is not only a lie that tells the truth; it formally demonstrates the psychological stagnation of the fetishist, caught between incompatible affirmations.[4] The exemplum is unnecessary to the logical argument of the sermon; it doesn't develop or complicate a point, but merely demonstrates it. *Radix malorum est cupiditas*: the three riotors are greedy and unscrupulous, and evil befalls them. The wages of sin are death: they set out to find death, and they find it. The plot is nothing but the rigorous working out of what is announced at the outset: how the riotors find death remains to be seen, but that they will find it is certain. The tale itself is, from this standpoint, superfluous—we already know the outcome—and thus it is no coincidence that "superfluytee abhomynable" (471)—drinking, gambling, cursing—motivates the narrative. Yet despite its excessive status there is nothing left over. The admirable neatness of the tale, the clever reification of the *radix malorum* into "under a tree," is a function of its essentially resolved form. Everyone and everything is consumed in the turns of the narrative, either dying or fading out, going "thider as I have to go" (749), as the old man says.

Fetishism is, finally, a conservative behavior: it allows one to maintain a fiction of plenitude even in the face of loss and dislocation. The Pardoner is fixed between knowledge of his fragmentation and belief that he can be made whole; knowledge of Death, God's Law, and judgment, and belief in the possibility of reunion and redemption; knowledge that his pardons are fraudulent, and belief that they can restore him to an original unity. He is neither hopeful nor despairing, but is somewhere between the two. In its stuck quality, this mechanism of disavowal is similar to the cyclical mechanism, as Augustine analyzes it, of sinning that leads to despair that leads to further sinning.[5] But despair is finally destructive,

3. See John of Garland, *Parisiana poetria*, ed. and trans. Traugott Lawler (New Haven: Yale UP, 1974), 5.327–31: "Argumentum est res ficta que tamen fieri potuit, ut contingit in comediis [A Realistic Fiction is a fictitious event which nevertheless could have happened, as is the case in comedies]" (Lawler's translation). This description of *argumentum* was made as early as the *Rhetorica ad herennium* 1.8.13, to which John was indebted. See Ernst Robert Curtius, *European Literature and the Latin Middle Ages*, trans. Willard R. Trask (Princeton: Princeton UP, 1953), for the classical background of the distinction among *historia*, *fabula*, and *argumentum*.

4. Bloch analyzes the psychologically and socially conservative functions of the *fabliau* in similar ways in his *Scandal of the Fabliaux*, 101–28.

5. See Augustine, *Contra Julianum Pelagianum*, *Patrologia latina*, 44: col. 787: "Thus concupiscence of the flesh . . . is at once sin . . . and punishment of sin . . . and cause of sin" (my translation). Quoted in Kellogg (note 3, p. 616), 245–68. See also Howard (note 4, p. 613), 355–57.

whereas the Pardoner will continue to "go . . . as I have to go," neither destroying himself nor finding redemption.

The Pardoner's coup de grace—or, better, *coupure de grace*—at the end of the tale is the final gesture of the fetishist among his peers: "I have relics and pardon in my male / As fair as any man in Engelond" (920–21), he boasts to the pilgrims. In other words: "I know that they're phony substitutes, but even so, I believe they're 'as fair' as any other man's. And you know that they're frauds, but even so, you want to believe in the grace of absolution. So step right up and kiss them." The Host's threat to castrate the eunuch Pardoner makes sense in this context: "I know that you don't have the balls to be cut off, but even so, I posit the fiction to increase the power of my threat." But it is only a fiction: the Host's language, like all language, is itself castrated; it is a partial object, itself a fragment. The Knight's intervention can only return the company to the beginning: "And, as we diden, lat us laughe and pleye" (1967), he exhorts them. As before in Fragment I (856), they again "ryden forth hir weye."

STEPHEN SPECTOR

Empathy and Enmity in the *Prioress's Tale*†

Midway through the impassioned prayer that precedes her tale, Chaucer's Prioress alludes to the Incarnation in terms of joined contraries conveying sublime paradox:

O moder mayde! o mayde moder free!
O bush unbrent, brenninge in Moyses sighte,
That ravysedest doun fro the deitee,
Thurgh thyn humblesse, the goost that in th'alighte,
Of whos vertu, whan he thyn herte lighte,
Conceived was the Fadres sapience. . . . (467–72)[1]

The force and economy with which these contradictions are joined are rhetorically heightened by the chiastic structure of the first of these lines, "O mother Virgin, O virgin Mother noble." The following line too is structurally compressed, juxtaposing contraries in the "unburnt, burning" bush, a familiar type of Mary, who "was fyred brente not, for she was moder without losse of maydenhod."[2] In the next two lines, the Prioress astonishingly transforms the Gospel account of the Incarnation, in which Gabriel tells Mary that the Holy Spirit will come upon her, and the power of the Most High will overshadow her (Luke 1.35). In the nun's fervent reworking, it is instead the Virgin who ravishes the Holy Ghost down from the Deity! Yet the heat and energy suggested in the word *ravysedest*

† From *The Olde Daunce: Love, Friendship, Sex, and Marriage in the Medieval World*, ed. Robert R. Edwards and Stephen Spector (Albany: State U of New York P, 1991), pp. 211–28, 289–300. Reprinted by permission of the State University of New York Press.

1. Indented block quotations of Chaucer's poetry from *The Riverside Chaucer*, ed. Larry D. Benson (Boston: Houghton Mifflin, 1987), have been replaced with quotations from this Norton Critical Edition. The spelling within short quotations from Chaucer's poetry has been modified to reflect this change.
2. *The Myroure of oure Ladye,* Early English Text Society, e.s. 19 (1873), ed. John Henry Blunt, p. 296.

are paradoxically contained, like the flames of the burning bush, within the chastity of the Conception.[3] And the fact that Mary ravishes the Holy Ghost through her humility, compelling or possessing through acquiescence, further extends the paradox in this prayer. The joining of contraries in paradox is thus as crucial to the Prioress's prayer as the joining of contradictions in irony is to her *General Prologue* portrait. But there is still another contradiction here: that the Prioress, whose faith and emotion seem so shallow and misplaced in the *General Prologue*, should utter so ardent a prayer at all.

Much of the mystery and delight of Chaucer's poetry issues from the marriage of such contraries, the reconciliation of the apparently irreconcilable, often in wonder and surprise, if not in peace. As much as any of Chaucer's pilgrims, the Prioress embodies a juxtaposition of such polarized qualities. A bride of Christ, she is nonetheless described as if she had stepped out of an Old French romance. Her ecclesiastical authority seems subverted in the *General Prologue* by her spiritual superficiality. Yet this shallowness is later shown, in her prayer, to conceal a burning religious fervor. And her genteel spotlessness in the *General Prologue* is shockingly contrasted in her tale by the bloody child cast in a dungpit. She is undeniably a creature of love, however compromised, and yet she embeds in her tale an animosity, directed toward Jews, that is as passionate as her prayer. Wordsworth observed that her tender-hearted sympathies are set off against her fierce bigotry, and D. S. Brewer says that the Prioress is the gentlest of the pilgrims who tells the only cruel and fanatical tale.[4] Talbot Donaldson notes in her tale a "strange mixture of delicacy and horror."[5] "Jewels and jakes," says Alan Gaylord, "charm and depravity," says Ian Robinson.[6] And, we must add, love and hate.

This essay is an exploration of the intersection of love and hate, and of the unresolved play between these and other contradictions in Chaucer's presentation of the Prioress. I attempt here to discover the connectedness in her contraries, and to deconstruct the moral dichotomy in her depiction of Christian and Jew. In the process, I review historical scholarship on Christian-Jewish relations in the late medieval period in order to challenge the assertion that Chaucer himself necessarily participated in a universal intolerance toward Jews.

Long before the advent of post-structuralism, critics detected the subversions that pervade the Prioress's description and problematize her tale. The Prioress's intention is not complex: she attempts to illustrate the simple beauty of her faith by offering a beautiful and simple Miracle of

3. The word *ravysedest* in its primary senses suggests "took by force," and, most extremely, "raped." James Winny, for example, glosses the word as "seized, took possession of" (*The Prioress' Prologue and Tale* [Cambridge: Cambridge University Press, 1975]). Even rendered in its mildest sense as "drew, attracted," this word attributes a far more active role to Mary than she has in the Gospel story (compare Latin *raptus* and Paul's use of the word in 2 Cor. 12. 1–4). The verb *lighten* means not only "make light, render cheerful" or "illumine," the possible renderings in Robinson, or "cheer, gladden," the gloss in the *Chaucer Glossary*, but also "set on fire." These senses, following the image of the burning bush, sustain the paradox of sexualized asexuality that characterizes the passion of the prayer.
4. D. S. Brewer, *Chaucer* (London: Longmans, 1953; reprint ed. 1961), p. 151.
5. E. T. Donaldson, *Chaucer's Poetry* (New York: Ronald Press, 1958; reprint ed. 1975), p. 1096.
6. Alan T. Gaylord, "The Unconquered Tale of the Prioress," *Papers of the Michigan Academy of Science, Arts, and Letters* 47 (1962): 632; Ian Robinson, *Chaucer and the English Tradition* (Cambridge: Cambridge University Press, 1972), p. 153.

the Virgin. In so doing, she valorizes innocent faith while rejecting the cursed Jews, whom she presents as the enemies of naive devotion. Her tale is thus intended to represent and vindicate her own qualities. For most of this century, however, critics have observed the ways in which the Prioress's qualities differ from themselves. And in recent decades, they have debated the degree to which these differences complicate and undermine her simple intention. In consequence, the profound conflicts in so shallow a pilgrim have been reproduced as conflicts in readings of the text.

Chaucer's description of the Prioress is itself a matter of spirited debate. Despite nearly general critical agreement that he wrote this portrait with restraint and even affection, virtually every line has provoked conflict among readers. The Prioress's age and appearance are an extreme case: some critics regard her as young and beautiful, others as old and overgrown. True, beautiful medieval foreheads were large, but D. W. Robertson, Jr., says that the Prioress's signified stupidity or lack of discretion.[7] Gordon Harper says that a forehead a span broad would scarcely conform to any notion of beauty.[8] And F. N. Robinson's note on this line questions whether a nun's forehead shouldn't have been covered in any case. Harper, in an essay titled "Chaucer's Big Prioress," takes the fact that the Prioress "was nat undergrowe" to mean that she was unusually large, even fat, and he makes a dastardly reference to her as bulbous. But Muriel Bowden says that being "nat undergrowe" means that she is well proportioned, and Talbot Donaldson and John Block Friedman assume that the Prioress's figure is good.[9] The gentle Prioress threatens to become a different creature for each reader, so that for Sister M. Madeleva, a sensible, mature nun, the Prioress is one too.[1] And for G. K. Chesterton, the Prioress is a spinster, but particularly English, with a special kindness to animals so much valued by the English gentry today.[2] The Prioress's tale has, as we shall see, undergone similar shapeshifting.

John Livingston Lowes gave classic expression to the contradictions and subversions in the Prioress's portrait by observing that she is a religious who is described by language appropriate to a romance heroine. The manner of her smile, the choice of her name, and indeed her entire description, are, said Lowes, "steeped in reminiscences of the poetry of courtly love," creating a "delightfully imperfect submergence of the woman in the nun."[3] The *General Prologue* portrait, in fact, is constituted of qualities that seem mislocated and misdirected. The Prioress's concern for physical spotlessness, for example, parodies the true interest of a religious, the safeguarding of spiritual spotlessness. Worse, this passage is modelled on the advice of the sinful figure La Vieille in the *Roman de la Rose,* who recommends such table manners among women's wiles to attract men. Sister Madeleva, one of the staunchest defenders of the

7. D. W. Robertson, Jr., *A Preface to Chaucer* (Princeton, N.J.: Princeton University Press, 1962), p. 246.
8. Gordon H. Harper, "Chaucer's Big Prioress," *Philological Quarterly* 12 (1933): 310.
9. Muriel Bowden, *A Commentary on the General Prologue to the Canterbury Tales* (London: Macmillan & Co., 1948; 2nd ed. 1969), p. 95; Donaldson, *Chaucer's Poetry,* p. 1044; John Block Friedman, "The Prioress's Beads 'Of Smal Coral,'" *Medium Aevum,* 39 (1970): 301; cf. Thomas Blake Clark, "Forehead of Chaucer's Prioress," *Philological Quarterly,* 9 (1930): 312–14.
1. Sister M. Madeleva, "Chaucer's Nuns" in *Chaucer's Nuns and Other Essays* (New York: D. Appleton, 1925), pp. 21 ff.
2. G. K. Chesterton, *Chaucer* (London: Faber & Faber, 1932; reprint ed. 1965), pp. 202–3.
3. John Livingston Lowes, "Simple and Coy," *Anglia* 33 (1910): 440–51.

Prioress, denies irony in the portrait, arguing that her table manners, for instance, reflect the nun's natural desire to keep her habit clean.[4] Arguments of this kind are valid in themselves, but they fail to consider the context of the passage, both in the portrait and its source. And they account neither for the manner of presentation, the language employed, nor what is left unsaid.

There is further misdirection and mislocation in the Prioress's *conscience and tendre herte.* The irony is conveyed, as Bowden points out, by the fact that it is a mouse that calls forth the Prioress's sympathy, not the suffering of her fellow man.[5] God and neighbor are the true objects of charity, adds John Steadman, who observes that the falseness of the Prioress's choice of objects is made obvious by contrast with the Plowman.[6] Robertson notes that this passage, like much of the portrait, proceeds by anticlimax, raising expectations by referring to conscience, charity, and pity, and then descending to the trapped mouse that benefits from those qualitites.[7] And Chauncey Wood, developing Stanley Fish's idea that readers make anticipatory judgments, or partial closures, says that the reference to conscience is one of many instances in this portrait in which the reader is teased into a false expectation, only to be surprised by what follows.[8]

The reader's expectations are similarly misled by the portrait as a whole. It does not, for instance, prepare us for the passion of Eglentyne's prayer, which is presumably concealed beneath the "chere of court." We are similarly surprised by her tale. Critics have often found the Prioress of the *General Prologue* to be charming, possibly beautiful, but spiritually superficial, oversentimental, conflicted, and, to some scholars, stupid. Yet there is no hint within the portrait of the outburst of intolerance that will follow. Quite the contrary, the focus is on love. This love is misdirected and made pathetic, as in the Prioress's tears for suffering mice. And sacred and profane love are conflated, as emblematized in the Prioress's motto. But the central theme remains love, not hate, and the newcomer to Chaucer, having read the *General Prologue* description, may well expect the Prioress's tale to speak of love, however confused, and perhaps of the rescue of nuns in distress.

In fact, the Prioress does tell a tale of love, and of rescue, a Miracle of the Virgin. The story begins with a *litel clergeoun.* This *litel child* attends a *litel scole* where, while studying his primer one day, he hears the older children singing the antiphon *Alma redemptoris mater.* He does not understand the Latin, and fails in his attempts to have it explained to him, but it is sufficient for him to know that the song is in praise of Mary. This innocent learns the song by rote, and sings it twice a day as he passes through the city's Jewry, a place

4. Madeleva, pp. 13–15.
5. Bowden, p. 99; Jill Mann adds that medieval satirists traditionally contrasted excessive tenderness for animals with indifference to human suffering (*Chaucer and Medieval Estates Satire* [Cambridge: Cambridge University Press, 1973], p. 132).
6. John M. Steadman, "The Prioress' Dogs and Benedictine Discipline," *Modern Philology* 54 (1956): 3.
7. Robertson, p. 246.
8. Chauncey Wood, "Chaucer's Use of Signs in His Portrait of the Prioress," in *Signs and Symbols in Chaucer's Poetry,* eds. John P. Hermann and John J. Burke, Jr. (University, Alabama: University of Alabama Press, 1981), pp. 89–91.

Sustened by a lord of that contree
For foule usure and lucre of vileynye,
Hateful to Crist and to his compaignye;
(490–92)

The Jews are provoked, and the Prioress evokes both their traditional association with the devil and their assumed willingness to kill in defense of their law:

Oure firste fo, the serpent Sathanas,
That hath in Jewes herte his waspes nest,
Up swal and seide, "O Hebraik peple, allas!
Is this to yow a thing that is honest,
That swich a boy shal walken as him lest
In youre despyt, and singe of swich sentence,
Which is agayn oure lawes reverence?"
(558–64)

With allusions recalling the conspiracy against Christ and the Slaughter of the Innocents, the Prioress tells that the Jews hire a murderer, another cursed Jew, who seizes the child, cuts his throat, and casts him into a privy. Referring to Herod (another allusion to the Slaughter of the Innocents), then to Cain's killing of Abel, the nun reaches an emotional pitch reminiscent of her prayer:

I seye that in a wardrobe they him threwe
Where as these Jewes purgen hir entraille.
O cursed folk of Herodes al newe,
What may youre yvel entente yow availle?
Mordre wol out, certein, it wol nat faille,
And namely ther th'onour of God shal sprede,
The blood out cryeth on your cursed dede.
(572–78)

The Jews wickedly lie to the child's mother, denying that the boy ever passed through the Jewry. But through the intercession of the Virgin, the dead child, his throat cut, sings the *Alma redemptoris mater*. The Christian folk hear the song, and send for the provost. With torment and shameful death, the provost kills the Jews who knew of the murder, dragging them by horses, then hanging them, acts of which the gentle Prioress implicitly approves. The child then explains that Mary herself, the "welle of mercy," has brought about the miracle, placing a grain under his tongue, bidding him to sing the anthem, and then expressing a distinctly maternal consolation and assurance:

My litel child, now wol I fecch thee
Whan that the greyn is fro thy tongue y-take;
Be nat agast, I wol thee nat forsake.
(667–69)

The martyr's "litel body swete" is finally buried in a tomb of clear marble. The Prioress concludes by beseeching young Hugh of Lincoln, slain by "cursed Jewes" in a ritual blood slaughter, to intercede, so that merciful God, because of his mercy, will multiply his mercy on us "sinful folk unstable." This juxtaposition of condemnation and mercy, the damned and the saved, the objects of hate and of sentimentality, crystallizes the contraries that inform her tale.

Many early critics took no notice of any such contraries. Instead, they spoke of the tale as a perfect illustration of the Miracle of the Virgin genre. George Lyman Kittredge, praising the Prioress's dignity and daintiness, speaks of the tale as "infinitely pathetic," never mentioning the Jews.[9] Chesterton says that the Prioress's tale is beautiful, and Nevill Coghill calls it one of the sweetest expressions of Chaucer's special feeling for the Blessed Virgin, conveying the beauty of holiness and of Christian triumph.[1] Wordsworth did speak of the bigotry set off against tenderness in the tale; but, as Florence Ridley notes, this did not stop him from rendering the tale in modern English.[2] Even Lowes, who so elegantly expressed the incongruities in the Prioress's portrait, speaks of her in ways that suggest affection and delight, betraying no sign of disturbance: he characterizes her description as "delicately ironical," "exquisitely sympathetic," "delightfully imperfect."[3]

The fact is that before the Holocaust much informed opinion about the *Prioress's Tale* was undisturbed by her treatment of the Jews, which was often not noticed at all.[4] Instead, her tale was praised for its beauty and perfection. This is significant and must be given full weight, for if it was so in our own century, one cannot expect Chaucer to have necessarily felt differently. For Kittredge and the others, and perhaps for Chaucer too, the Prioress's stereotyping of vicious Jews was no more serious a matter than the Man of Law's treatment of the heathen Surryens, who also commit murder to defend their law, instigated by Satan's instrument, the Sowdanesse.

Since the Holocaust, by contrast, the question of anti-Semitism has been a central point of discussion about the Prioress. R. J. Schoeck argues that Chaucer presented the tale in order to denounce the ritual murder libel, and George K. Anderson calls the Prioress a vapid anti-Semite.[5] Several scholars, including Talbot Donaldson, Ian Robinson, Alfred David, and Donald R. Howard, have distinguished Chaucer's own views from the Prioress's, citing his greater awareness of Christianity and the posture of the

9. George Lyman Kittredge, *Chaucer and His Poetry* (Cambridge, Mass.: Harvard University Press, 1925), pp. 175–78.
1. Chesterton, p. 171; Nevill Coghill, *The Poet Chaucer* (London: Oxford University Press, 1949), pp. 22, 138.
2. Florence H. Ridley, *The Prioress and the Critics* (Berkeley and Los Angeles: University of California Press, 1965), p. 2.
3. John Livingston Lowes, "The Prioress's Oath," *Romanic Review* 5 (1914): 368; "Simple and Coy," 442.
4. Sister Madeleva says that the tale tells just the sort of story "that Sisters are telling to the smaller and even the grown children in Catholic boarding schools the world over to-day . . . that the children clamor for again and again and never tire of hearing" (pp. 37–38). Robert Kilburn Root, in discussing the Prioress's tale in 1906, attributed the "senseless persecution" of the Jews in European history to the "fact" that the Jews were rich while the Christians were poor. He added that the Christians' belief in the Jews' murderous practices "could hardly have sprung up without some sort of foundation" in fact (*The Poetry of Chaucer* [Boston: Houghton Mifflin, 1906], p. 191)! Thomas R. Lounsbury, by contrast, as early as 1891 denounced the "folly and fanaticism" that underlie the tale (*Studies in Chaucer* [New York: Harper & Brothers, 1891; reprint ed. 1962], 2:490–91).
5. R. J. Schoeck, "Chaucer's Prioress: Mercy and Tender Heart," in *Chaucer Criticism*, eds. Richard Schoeck and Jerome Taylor (Notre Dame: Notre Dame Books, 1960; reprint ed. 1965), I, 245–58; George K. Anderson, "*Beowulf*, Chaucer, and Their Backgrounds," in *Contemporary Literary Scholarship*, ed. Lewis Leary (New York: Appleton-Century-Crofts, 1958), p. 41. The term "antisemitism" is appropriate to a modern rather than a medieval context; see n. 6, p. 642.

Church, or his other personal qualities.[6] Others, notably Ridley and Albert B. Friedman, have refuted these assertions about the reputed tolerance of the Church, noting the ubiquity of anti-Jewishness at the time, and its pervasiveness in Christian piety.[7] Under such cultural circumstances, this line of argument suggests, the Prioress's bigotry loses significance. Her cruelty is manifest only from a point of view impossible to the Middle Ages, says Brewer, and David questions whether any medieval reader would have perceived the ironies in miracles of the Virgin that are apparent to the modern mind.[8] Ridley (p. 5) argues that the Prioress "and the rest of her credulous countrymen" regarded Jews "as strange, mysterious, and therefore sinister." Hardy Long Frank asserts that Jews were universally considered to be devils in late medieval Christendom.[9] And Friedman (p. 120) considers it foolish to expect Chaucer to have been above the narrow beliefs of his age when broadmindedness was impossible for Pascal, 250 years later.

This critical impasse over the horizons of Chaucer's possible attitude toward Jews illustrates with particular clarity the influence of history and ideology on critical perspective. Readers' responses, already divided by the contraries in the Prioress's portrait, have been further distanced by recent experience. Several post-Holocaust scholars, sensitized by the barbarism of the twentieth century, have looked for greater civility in the fourteenth, at least in the transcendent person of Chaucer. They implicitly view earlier assessments of the tale as naive and insensitive (like the Prioress herself) precisely because those views were conceived in innocence of the horrific consequences of intolerance that we have seen in our time. Other scholars have challenged the validity of applying such a modern sensibility to a medieval text. Their position is reinforced by more radical contemporary critical claims that broadly dismiss the notion of Chaucer as a man who transcended the influences of his period—who was in his time but not of it. The possibility that Chaucer escaped conventional prejudices will be rejected by some advocates of this view as a relic of a discredited Whig historiography.[1]

Both sides of this debate deserve reexamination. The assumption of an inescapable and constant medieval hatred of Jews in which Chaucer

6. Donaldson notes that unlike the narrowly limited Prioress, Chaucer, an intelligent man and a great poet, was in no way limited (*Chaucer's Poetry*, p. 1097). Ian Robinson (p. 152) says that it would be surprising if a responsible public servant like Chaucer were as simple-minded and savage as the Prioress. Alfred David, drawing the valid analogy between the tale and a fairy story, says that Chaucer, unlike the Prioress, is "very much aware that fairy-tale justice and Christian mercy are incompatible" (*The Strumpet Muse* [Bloomington: Indiana University Press, 1976], p. 209); Donald R. Howard in *The Idea of the Canterbury Tales* (Berkeley: University of California Press, 1976), p. 277, says that it is out of the question that the tolerant, open-minded, and empathetic Chaucer could have failed to note the Prioress's moral blindness.

7. Ridley, pp. 5ff.; Albert B. Friedman, "The *Prioress's Tale* and Chaucer's Anti-Semitism," *Chaucer Review* 9 (1974–75): 118–29.

8. Brewer, p. 151; David, p. 207; Robert Worth Frank, Jr., observes that anti-Semitism is a standard constituent element in the Miracle of the Virgin genre ("Miracles of the Virgin, Medieval Anti-Semitism, and the 'Prioress's Tale,'" in *The Wisdom of Poetry: Essays in Early English Literature in Honor of Morton W. Bloomfield*, eds. Larry D. Benson and Siegfried Wenzel [Kalamazoo: Medieval Institute Publications, 1982]), p. 179.

9. Frank also cites examples of tolerance and benevolence toward Jews, however. See his "Chaucer's Prioress and the Blessed Virgin," *Chaucer Review* 13 (1978–79): 355, 358. Compare Schoeck, pp. 255–56, and Howard, p. 279.

1. See Lee Patterson, *Negotiating the Past* (Madison: University of Wisconsin Press, 1987), ch. 1. Patterson asserts (p. 74) that the *Canterbury Tales* stood in ideological opposition to the dominant formations of its period. I take this to support the contention I develop below that Chaucer need not have shared in the prevailing intolerance of his time.

necessarily shared is drastically oversimplified. The actual historical picture across Europe over a period of centuries was far more complex. Many prominent medieval Jewish historians have concluded that enmity toward Jews, though widespread and often calamitous, was not universal. As the appendix below demonstrates, along with official oppression and popular hatred, there were many recorded gestures and declarations of respect and amity between individual Gentile and Jew. These interactions often occurred in spite of formal proscriptions, which themselves help document the behavior they were designed to suppress.

On the other hand, Chaucer's own attitude toward Jews is probably irretrievable. Beliefs and prejudices of this sort are often prelogical, and are not always discernible from an author's writing. This is particularly true of the portrayal of the Jews, which since the patristic period had typically been axiomatic rather than observed or deduced.[2] In the *Canterbury Tales,* the issue is further complicated, of course, by the fact that narratives are assigned to taletellers and often colored by irony. Moreover, to address the question of how Chaucer felt about Jews, one must interrogate the actions neither of Chaucer the pilgrim, nor even of Chaucer the poet, whose masked and fragmented qualities, to the extent that they can be inferred, are part of a posture offered to public view. Rather, one must investigate the inner life of Chaucer the private individual.[3] And there are reasons for skepticism that in issues of this kind a man's personal qualities are necessarily identical with the public ones suggested in his work. Barring new documentary discoveries, we cannot even establish that the issue was in any sense significant to Chaucer. What we can address, however, is the artistic function of the intolerance within the text.

The issue I wish to consider here, therefore, is not whether Chaucer was anti-Jewish, but rather how he transformed the conventional intolerance in a traditional Miracle of the Virgin in his presentation of the Prioress: why, in short, such an unexpected outburst of hatred is attributed

2. James Parkes observes that Christian texts had, since the early days of the Church, portrayed Jews not in terms of their contemporary relationships or circumstances, but rather in accordance with their Scriptural roles (*The Conflict of the Church and the Synagogue* [New York: Atheneum, 1969; reprint ed. 1977], pp. 220, 374f.). In Augustine's formulation, the Jew remained doctrinally "stationary in useless antiquity." This characterization of the Jew as frozen in time applied, of course, to the characterization itself. By the thirteenth century, however, Church scholars had to respond to the realization that Judaism had in fact evolved since the first century; see Jeremy Cohen's "Scholarship and Intolerance in the Medieval Academy: The Study and Evaluation of Judaism in European Christendom," *American Historical Review* 91 (1986): 592–613.
3. This argument differs in emphasis from Donaldson's in his famous essay "Chaucer the Pilgrim," which reaches somewhat different conclusions about the distinctions between Chaucer the pilgrim, the poet, and the man. Though these three figures bore a close resemblance to one another and "frequently got together in the same body," Donaldson says, Chaucer the poet subsumed the other two. Interestingly, much of this discussion treats the portrayal of the Prioress. Donaldson asserts that Chaucer the man, like his pilgrim persona, would have found the Prioress charming; Chaucer the poet, by contrast, noted her many imperfections, and incorporated her inharmonious parts into an inseparable whole (*Publications of the Modern Language Society* 69 [1954]: 928–36; reprinted in *Speaking of Chaucer* [New York: W. W. Norton, 1970], pp. 1–12). [Reprinted above, pp. 525–33.] Responses to Donaldson have included the observation that writers project some element of themselves into any character, and the question as to whether anyone knows his "real" self well enough to present or conceal it (see Donald R. Howard, "Chaucer the Man," *PMLA* 80 [1965]: 337–43; reprinted in *Chaucer's Mind and Art,* ed. A. C. Cawley [New York: Barnes and Noble, 1970], pp. 31–45). But the disjunction between the suggestion of the poet's personality in the text and the historical indications about Chaucer the man has also been noted. See, for example, George Kane, *Chaucer* (Oxford: Oxford University Press, 1984), pp. 9–10.

to so gentle a nun.[4] The Parson's references to Jews are merely incidental. But the Jews of the Prioress's tale play, as I shall try to show, a particularized role that is specifically relevant to Eglentyne. Merely to assert that the Prioress participates in a general hostility toward Jews ignores the context in which they appear in her tale, and the function that they serve. Such an approach recalls the important but self-limiting work of the early critics of the *General Prologue* portrait, who documented historical practices and infractions resembling the Prioress's, but failed to account for the context and the manner of presentation of these elements in the Prioress's description. Moreover, this approach allows a divorce between the tale and the Prioress's character as it emerges in the *General Prologue* description. This, in fact, is precisely what John Lawlor recommends: he warns that attempting to fit the tale to the *General Prologue* description must call into play our modern suspicions, so that we will "view dourly any essay into that commonest of medieval modes, the pathetic."[5] But as Edward H. Kelly observes, in order to "more fully appreciate the poet's art of creation, it is necessary to see the description in the *General Prologue* as artistically functional in understanding the tale."[6]

Critics who have explored the unity of the *General Prologue* and the tale have in several instances emphasized the Prioress's unscrutinized sensibility or sentimentality, or the inherent association between these qualities and cruelty. Bowden (pp. 99–100) says that the implication of the Prioress's sympathy for mice rather than men is reinforced in her tale, in which she tells with perfect blandness of the tortures visited upon the Jews. Donaldson says that "Emotionalism that excludes the intellect—as it does in the *Prioress' Tale*—can be a dangerous thing, for the psychological transition from exquisite sensibility to bloodshed is an easy one."[7] Bertrand Bronson also puts the blame on the nun's "shallow sensibility," which, he says, is the obverse of cruelty.[8] Gaylord links sentimentality and brutality in describing the Prioress's actions, and Ian Robinson says that the Prioress's sentimentality is so thoughtless as to become wicked.[9] Ridley, taking a different approach, considers the tale a humorless display of naiveté, ignorance, blind vehement devotion, and (following Kittredge) suppressed maternal longing (p. 29).

Questions remain, however. Bowden's point about the Prioress's misplaced sympathy in the *General Prologue* does not explain the nun's explosion of enmity, or her abundant sympathy with the clergeon. And though

4. Gaylord (p. 631) cites the brutality of attitude, action, and imagery in the tale, and observes that the brutality of the Prioress's language in the tale "tends to belie the total softness and sweetness of the lady who swears by Saint Loy." Albert B. Friedman denies this, and argues that the line "I seye that in a wardrobe they hym threwe" (572) reveals the Prioress's "fastidious hesitation in mentioning this unpleasant but necessary detail" (p. 126). I disagree: the line can equally well be read as charged with indignation.
5. John Lawlor, *Chaucer* (London: Hutchinson University Library, 1968), p. 131.
6. Edward H. Kelly, "By Mouth of Innocentz: The Prioress Vindicated," *Papers on Language and Literature,* 5 (1969): 363. In this essay I attempt to occupy a middle ground between Kittredge's claim (p. 155) that the tales exist for the sake of developing the pilgrims as characters, and more recent arguments that the pilgrims are not recognizably motivated characters. I contend that in portraying the Prioress, Chaucer developed a stock literary figure in surprising ways, in part by matching her with a tale that both inspired and complicated his characterization of her.
7. Donaldson, *Chaucer's Poetry,* p. 1097. Cf. Howard, who says that the Prioress's simplicity and air of elegance lead her into a deplorable frame of mind (p. 276).
8. Bertrand H. Bronson, *In Search of Chaucer* (Toronto: University of Toronto Press, 1960), p. 78.
9. Gaylord, p. 632; Robinson, p. 150.

sentimentality and shallow (or heightened) sensibility can accompany and conceal cruelty, they need not cause it, and are not invariably associated with it. The same is true of the naiveté, ignorance, and blind devotion that Ridley mentions. Current psychoanalytical thinking about intolerance proceeds, as we shall see, along very different lines. As for Kittredge's notion of thwarted motherhood, I think that it is mistaken, a "partial closure" inspired by the Prioress's sympathy for small animals and the little boy. For in her prayer, the Prioress emphatically adopts the perspective not of a mother, but of a child, with motherhood relegated to the nurturant Virgin Mother, whose guidance and strength Eglentyne beseeches.

The prayer, which serves as prologue to her tale, is the key to reconciling the Prioress's contraries. Beautiful and moving when considered in itself, this rarely examined prayer provides the missing elements that connect the portrait and the tale. And it reveals how the empathy and enmity in her tale are precisely suited to her character—or, rather, how her character is suited to the tale. The prayer begins with a versifying of Psalm 8:

O Lord, oure Lord, thy name how merveillous
Is in this large worlde y-sprad–quod she—
For noght only thy laude precious
Parfourned is by men of dignitee,
But by the mouth of children thy bountee
Parfourned is, for on the brest soukinge
Somtyme shewen they thyn heryinge.
(453–59)

This psalm, Sister Madeleva informs us (p. 30), is the first of several allusions in the prayer to the Little Office of the Blessed Virgin. The psalm also appears in the Mass for the Feast of the Holy Innocents, and so links the prayer to the liturgical and Scriptural reminiscences of the Slaughter of the Innocents in the tale.[1] Beyond that, the psalm serves as the text, as it were, for her tale, which illustrates praise from the mouth of a child. But, just as in our reading of the *General Prologue* portrait, we are surprised by what follows: the significance of these lines is transformed in light of the final stanza of this prayer, for the image of the nursing child refers not to the clergeon but to the Prioress herself:

My conning is so wayk, o blisful Quene,
For to declare thy grete worthinesse,
That I ne may the weighte nat sustene;
But as a child of twelf monthe old, or lesse,
That can unnethes any word expresse,
Right so fare I, and therfor I yow preye,
Gydeth my song that I shal of yow seye.
(481–87)

The clergeon is seven years old, beyond infancy, but the Prioress images herself as still an infant. These lines display, in fact, the specificity with

1. See Marie Padgett Hamilton, "Echoes of Childermas in the Tale of the Prioress," in *Chaucer: Modern Essays in Criticism*, ed. Edward Wagenknecht (New York: Oxford University Press, 1959), 88–97.

which the Prioress's qualities are reproduced in her tale. As a child of twelve months old or less, she places herself at the age of the Innocents to whose slaughter her tale refers. Moreover, she mirrors herself in that other innocent, the clergeon. The simple, faithful child becomes the repository of her own simple, childlike faith. Like her, he is *souded to virginitee* "made fast in virginity," because he dies a virgin. His devotion, like hers in the *General Prologue,* is expressed only in song. And just as the clergeon is unaware of the meaning of his song, knowing only that it praises Mary, so we are told only of the *sound* of hers, and her manner of singing.[2] Both the nun and the child are filled with devotion for Mary, and for both, fervor substitutes for substantial understanding. Both are untutored in the suffering and compassion that inform Christianity. The child, after all, is only beginning to learn his Primer. And, significantly, the Primer is a source of the Prioress's prayer. For the Primer contains the Little Office of the Blessed Virgin, which the Prioress paraphrases in the prayer.[3]

The nun's frailty and vulnerability also reemerge in the child. In her prayer, Eglentyne stresses her childlike weakness, her frail inability to sustain her song.[4] And in her tale, the helpless child has his throat cut so that he can no longer sing. The treatment of his body also recalls the Prioress's portrait: she is obsessed with cleanliness, and the clergeon is killed by the forces of foulness and defilement, who cast his body in the uncleanest of places. Mary's intervention in the tale further identifies the Prioress with the clergeon, for he is saved by a miracle that answers the nun's own request of Mary: declaring that she is like a child, scarcely able to speak, Eglentyne prays that Mary will guide her song. In the tale, this actually happens to the child: he is rendered literally unable to speak, and Mary does guide his song. And the Prioress realizes her own desire for spotlessness through him by placing him among the 144,000 virgins of Apocalypse 14, who are *sine macula* "without spot," and who, as she says, follow the "white lamb celestial."

The function of the Jews in the tale lends specific meaning to the Prioress's outburst of enmity. By assigning this tale to the Prioress, or, more correctly, by creating the Prioress and matching her so precisely with the tale, Chaucer introduced a detailed self-referentiality between teller and tale. In consequence, the Jews in the tale are not generalized bogeymen, as they may appear to be in the analogues, or in the tale considered in isolation. Rather, in signifying threats to childlike innocence, to virginal spotlessness, and to simple faith, the Jews are made to endanger the very qualities that Chaucer embodied in the nun. They are the foul representatives not only of spiritual stain, but also of physical defilement, which issues from their entrails. As such, they symbolize the most offensive possible contrary to the immaculate Eglentyne. The non-specific

2. Audrey Davidson notes the unusual beauty of the *Alma redemptoris mater* and its emphasis on the motherliness of Mary, factors that make the anthem appropriate in a tale told by Madame Eglentyne ("*Alma Redemptoris Mater*: The Little Clergeon's Song," *Studies in Medieval Culture* 4 [1974]: 459–66). [For a text and translation of the *Alma*, see above, p. 484.]
3. See Beverly Boyd, "Young Hugh of Lincoln and Chaucer's 'The Prioress's Tale,'" *The Radford Review* 14 (1960): 1–5.
4. Donald W. Fritz interprets this assertion in terms of the topos of the "inexpressible" in "The Prioress's Avowal of Ineptitude," *Chaucer Review* 9 (1974–75): 166–81.

anti-Jewishness of the tale and its analogues is thus translated into the Prioress's revulsion at the qualities that constitute her own negation.[5]

This treatment of the Jews offers a striking parallel to the dominant psychoanalytical model of intolerance, in which the bigot localizes in the Jew the unwanted or threatening elements of his internal or external world.[6] A similar paradigm informs the cycle drama, in which the Jews represent precisely those qualities that the good figures must expel from themselves.[7] In terms of literary rather than psychological projection, the Jew in the Prioress's tale, as in the cycles, is a highly specific figure signifying a precise danger to the Christian. Deconstructed in this way, the conflict *between* faith and disbelief in these texts is seen as a conflict *within,* and the radically marginalized figure of the Jew emerges as central.[8]

Madame Eglentyne's enmity is aimed, then, at figures whose role is profoundly relevant to her. The same is true of her empathy. And this reveals the self-referentiality of the sentiment in which the Prioress bathes the clergeon: her loving approbation of the child with whom she shares so many qualities is, finally, love of self. Her love is thus misdirected, just as her pity and tenderness are in the *General Prologue.* But this does not negate her love of Mary, as is only fitting in a pilgrim so thoroughly composed of contraries, who reconciles in her nature such various expressions of love. In fact, this joining of personal and spiritual love recreates the ambiguity of the Prioress's love in the *General Prologue,* reenacting the imperfect submergence of the woman in the nun. In the end, though, it is Mary's perfect love that prevails in the tale, drawn down from heaven by the child's simple, unthinking, but ardent devotion. The nun thus

5. Other scholars have also noted the Prioress's affinity with the child, but have reached different conclusions from mine. Gaylord, in his perceptive and good-humored "The Unconquered Tale of the Prioress" (p. 634), says that the Prioress keeps the tale at the emotional and intellectual level of a child, evidencing her "arrested development." Maurice Cohen says that Eglentyne's sado-masochism toward the Jews is anal-erotic ("Chaucer's Prioress and Her Tale, A Study of Anal Character and Anti-Semitism," *Psychoanalytic Quarterly* 31 [1962]: 232–49). Sherman Hawkins takes her spiritual childishness as the starting point for the clergeon too, and develops a learned patristic argument about the child's spiritual growth: the pit and the murder represent, he says, the literal understanding of Scripture and death to the law ("Chaucer's Prioress and the Sacrifice of Praise," *Journal of English and Germanic Philology* 63 [1964]: 599–624). Albert B. Friedman (pp. 124–25) concludes that the Prioress's sentimental sympathy with the clergeon leads her to enter too completely into the child's world and to identify with him. He attributes this only to a lack of mature judgment, however, and rejects Gaylord's interpretation of arrested development; he adds that Bronson's assertion that sentimentality is the obverse of cruelty is not relevant here. George J. Engelhardt conjectures that the Prioress, assuming the persona of the child, imagines herself singing unto death the plaint of litigation over the redemption of her convent's liberties ("The Ecclesiastical Pilgrims of the *Canterbury Tales:* A Study in Ethology," *Mediaeval Studies* 37 [1975]: 292–93). And Robert W. Hanning adopts a very interesting feminist perspective, in which the Jews and the child's teachers represent male domination and authority, and the tale expresses the Prioress's vulnerability to men ("From *Eva* and *Ave* to Eglentyne and Alisoun: Chaucer's Insight into the Roles Women Play," *Signs* 2 [1977]: 580–99). I attribute to the Jews their more traditional religious significance.

6. As Gavin I. Langmuir says, psychological (as opposed to cognitive) explanations of intolerance rely heavily on the Freudian concepts of displacement and projection ("Prolegomena to Any Present Analysis of Hostility against Jews," *Social Science Information* 15 [1976]: 701). For a review of Sartre's use of this theory and its application to medieval Biblical drama, see Stephen Spector, "Anti-Semitism and the English Mystery Plays," in *The Drama of the Middle Ages,* eds. Clifford Davidson, C. J. Gianakaris, John H. Stroupe (New York: AMS Press, 1982), pp. 329–30. Freud himself proposed that anti-Semitism is projected resentment against the Church by the "badly christened": those who had Christianity forced on them and deal with their own hostility by identifying similar sentiments in the Jews and vilifying them for it. See Sigmund Freud, *Moses and Monotheism,* trans. Katherine Jones (New York: Vintage Books, 1939; reprint ed. 1967), pp. 116–17.

7. Spector, "Anti-Semitism and the English Mystery Plays," pp. 328–41.

8. One could argue in Derridean terms that the invagination of the text creates a marginal graft, thereby dislocating the text and undermining the narrative intention.

vindicates her own qualities by having Mary reward them with the maternal love that the Prioress, in her spiritual infancy, requires.

Ultimately, much of the unresolved tension in the presentation of the Prioress centers on the question of love. The nun's love is confused, compromised. In the prayer and tale, by contrast, Mary's abundant love is unambiguous. And so in the tale Eglentyne, the humble, thorny, brier rose, has Mary, the noble "white lylye flour" of her prayer, bestow her love to redeem virginal innocence from the forces that endanger it.[9] In so doing, Mary redeems the Prioress too, and vanquishes ambiguity from the motto *"Amor vincit omnia."* This is the triumph of love in the Prioress's tale. But it occurs only within the tale. In this regard, Eglentyne recalls the Wife of Bath, whose magical tale of marital peace and accord is incongruous with her own experience of marriage.[1] Similarly, the Prioress is assigned a tale that appears to miraculously transcend the misdirections and ambiguities in her portrait. The tale does not negate the contradictions in her makeup, however, but rather completes the restless Chaucerian marriage of contraries.

APPENDIX
THE HORIZONS OF TOLERANCE

Anti-Jewishness was inherent in Christian doctrine, and hostility toward Jews was widespread even a century after they had been expelled, as was the case in England when Chaucer wrote. Viewed telescopically, the official and popular intolerance toward Jews was generally progressive, and the principal events concerning them during the fourteenth century were marked by persecution, violence, and expulsion.[2] Having been expelled from England in 1290, they were evicted from all royal possessions in France in 1306. After returning to France in 1315, they were attacked in 1320 by the so-called Pastoureaux, or Shepherd crusaders, and were expelled again in 1322 after being accused of conspiring with lepers to poison wells. They were reinvited to France in 1359, but expelled definitively from most districts in 1394. In Germany at the time of the Black Death (1348–49), Jews were charged with well poisoning and burned *en masse*. Some cities, like Ratisbon and Vienna, successfully defended their Jews. But most German cities were emptied of Jews, many of whom went to Poland. Those who returned to their towns in Germany often did so under less favorable economic and political agreements than had previously obtained. And in 1391 in Spain, a pogrom movement

9. Hardy Long Frank, in his fine discussion of the ambiguity in Madame Eglentyne's name, cites two figurative references to the Virgin as the eglantine in the poetry of Gautier de Coinci. In the present context, however, the contrast between the floral symbols is appropriate to the dichotomy between the Prioress and Mary.

1. The Wife's impulse to join in marriages that inevitably result in struggle recalls the joining of restless elements in Chaucer's art itself.

2. Salo Wittmayor Baron comments that when considered as "a single list of pogroms and expulsions, the attacks on Jews appear indeed as an uninterrupted succession of catastrophes. But one must realize that during the thirteenth century (until 1290 in England and 1298 in Germany) there were but relatively few local anti-Jewish attacks with little bearing on Jewish conditions elsewhere. . . . Only the Black Death generated a mass hysteria . . . which had ominous implications for the very survival of European Jewry. . . . However, the then most populous Jewish settlements in Spain, Sicily, southern France, and the Papal States, as well as in Bohemia, Hungary, and Poland, suffered relatively little" (*A Social and Religious History of the Jews*, 2nd ed. [New York: Columbia University Press; Philadelphia: Jewish Publication Society of America, 1967], 11:281–82).

accompanied by forced conversions anticipated events of a century later, when the Jews were expelled from that nation in 1492.

By Chaucer's lifetime (*ca.* 1343–1400), the European Jews had been widely abused and oppressed. Nationalist and economic pressures in concert with religious fervor, popular prejudice, and pogromist violence, had spurred many communities to degrade and ultimately expel the Jews.[3] Theologically, their guilt and spiritual infirmity had by then long been a commonplace. Chaucer would have been well aware that in both religious literature and popular belief, the Jews were traditional symbols of evil, perfidious and threatening allies of the devil.[4] Did he and all other Gentiles inevitably share this view? As recent criticism asserts, people are ineluctably affected by the ideology and social determinants of their time. But the specific responses to such influences are always individual and incalculable. The issue of intolerance provides a test case. Modern experience teaches that the reaction to highly propagandized prejudice can be contradictory, labile, even uncanny.[5] Medieval anti-Judaism differed in important ways from the racially based anti-Semitism practiced in the twentieth century.[6] But along with that earlier hostility too, and despite the proscriptions and condemnations that it engendered, there are many signs of a crosscurrent of mutual tolerance between Christian and Jew. Moreover, the evidence suggests the existence of more than mere formal tolerance, which could, after all, be negotiated on the basis of self-interest, or purchased, or grudgingly conceded on theological grounds: there are in addition gestures and expressions of mutual respect and personal regard.[7] As Salo Baron (11:120–21) observes, Jews were often despised and haunted, especially at critical moments in history. But despite it all, Jews and Christians

3. Guido Kisch argues, however, that nationalism in the modern sense of the word did not influence the treatment of the medieval Jew (*The Jews in Medieval Germany* [Chicago: University of Chicago Press, 1949], pp. 335–37).
4. The Jews and the devil were represented as having a common interest in maintaining the old law. For popular beliefs about the Jews' supposed association with the devil and the Antichrist, see especially Joshua Trachtenberg, *The Devil and the Jews* (New Haven: Yale University Press, 1943).
5. Not all angels wear halos: Gentiles who risked their lives to save Jews during the 1940s sometimes seemed to be unlikely choices for their roles. Many Jews survived the Holocaust because of the protection of the German industrialist Oskar Schindler, for example. They had good reason to be grateful that the brave and resourceful—but not conventionally moral or religious—Schindler was more faithful to his Jews than to his wife; see Thomas Keneally, *Schindler's List* (New York: Simon and Schuster, 1982). The influence of the Protestant pastor André Trocmé constitutes a partial explanation of why the people of Le Chambon courageously protected Jewish children while other French villagers took no such risk; see Philip P. Hallie, *Lest Innocent Blood Be Shed* (New York: Harper & Row, 1979).
6. The etiology of modern anti-Semitism is complex and disputed, but I use the term here as a means of distinction from medieval anti-Jewishness. Langmuir (p. 691) asserts that the hostility against Jews about 1900 was very similar to the hostility about 1400; and to the recipient, hostility no doubt does feel the same regardless of its rationalization. But medieval hostility to Jewishness was in large measure theologically inspired: the putative defects it attributed to the Jew could, at least in theory, be washed away by baptism. The most virulent modern "anti-Semitism," by contrast, postulates Jewish racial inferiority that cannot be effaced. Hitler, for example, denounced religiously based political anti-Jewishness as sham anti-Semitism (Lucy S. Dawidowicz, *The War against the Jews 1933–1945* [New York: Bantam Books, 1975; reprint ed. 1978], ch. 1). The term "anti-Semitism," in the sense that Hitler used it, would be anachronistic in discussing medieval attitudes. Another term, "Ritual Blood Libel," is also inappropriate to the Prioress's tale, which does not refer to the ritualized slaughter of a Christian child at Passover. The genre of the tale is Miracle of the Virgin.
7. One cannot discover the essence of Jewish-Christian relations in a brief survey of the present kind, and that is not my purpose here in any case. I intend only to refute the globally negative assertions about the possibility of amity and respect toward Jews during the period under consideration. I therefore present chiefly positive evidence.

> often maintained far closer social relations (even in the obscure realm of sex) than one might expect in the light of the stringent segregationist laws and preaching on both sides.
>
> [11:119–20]

Baron (11:187) adds that friendly daily exchanges often went unreported. But the closeness of relations between the groups can be inferred, as, for example, from the lavish efforts that had to be expended in order to cut off such contacts.

An explicit doctrine tolerating Jewish residence in Christian communities had been evolved in the patristic period and developed by Bernard of Clairvaux and Thomas Aquinas. From the thirteenth century, the Jews were technically *servi camerae,* or the king's serfs.[8] Jacob Katz notes that many Jews achieved high political standing, as evidenced by the fact that they were permitted to bear arms in France and Germany well into the thirteenth century.[9] Baron (11:114) adds that Jews were never prohibited from carrying arms in Italy or Spain. Katz asserts that despite oppressive rules and ideologies of separateness on both sides, neighborly and even friendly relations between Jews and Christians always occurred. The religious symbolism that permeated each community was a further barrier to social penetration, but, says Katz, Jews and Christians nevertheless often met in a friendly spirit.

Although the two communities remained socially unintegrated, common features marked their social life. Jews and Gentiles shared practices and beliefs and sometimes enjoyed common literary interests.[1] And in large measure, depending on the time and place, they dressed alike and spoke alike.[2] From the thirteenth century, Jews were required to wear a

8. Neither legislators nor jurists attempted to define Jewish serfdom clearly. Jews were also referred to as *servitus Judaeorum* and as chests (*cofres*) or treasures of the King (Baron, 11:4–5).
9. Jacob Katz, *Exclusiveness and Tolerance* (New York: Behrman House, 1961), p. 6. In this argument Katz depends on Kisch, *Germany,* pp. 119–28.
1. Israel Abrahams says that twelfth-century Jews read Christian love songs and ballads (*Jewish Life in the Middle Ages* [Philadelphia: Jewish Publication Society of America, 1896; reprint ed. New York: Atheneum, 1978], p. 361). H. H. Ben-Sasson adds that the influence of Christian romances led the author of the *Sefer Hasidim* to draw a comparison between service to God and a knight's loyalty to his lord (*A History of the Jewish People* [Cambridge, Mass.: Harvard University Press, 1969; English translation, 1976], p. 555). It is worth noting in a study of the *Prioress's Tale* that despite its negative stereotypes about Christian morality, the *Sefer Hasidim* holds the life of Gentiles sacred. It adds that if a Jew is conspiring against a Gentile, every other Jew must foil the plot (see Katz, p. 101, who follows F. Y. Baer in his discussion of this book). Katz (p. 93) and Ben-Sasson (p. 546) note shared, or at least parallel, religious movements between Jews and Christians.
2. Kisch observes that Jews in northern France dressed indistinguishably from Christians from the twelfth to the fourteenth century, and typically walked bare-headed. In Germany and the rest of central Europe, by contrast, Jews were distinguished by their horned hats, which they wore of their own free will according to old tradition, as well as by their beards. The famous thirteenth-century miniature of the Jewish minnesinger Süsskind von Trimberg, for example, shows him in fashionable dress except for his pointed hat and beard. In Spain and Italy, Jews had assimilated in dress, though Johannes Purgoldt's early sixteenth-century German lawbook asserts that Italian Jews were required to wear different clothes from those of Christians. See Kisch, *Germany,* pp. 296–98, and *Forschungen zur Rechts-, Wirtschafts- und Sozialgeschichte der Juden* (Sigmaringen: Thorbecke, 1979), pp. 119–20; also Baron, 11:101, 137. For their own safety, Jews wore the same clothes as Gentiles when travelling, and sometimes even dressed as priests and nuns! (See Ben-Sasson, p. 623; also Kisch, *Forschungen,* p. 118.) Jews achieved a high degree of linguistic assimilation in their host countries, though dialectic differences eventually emerged under the influence of Hebrew and talmudic thinking (Baron, 11:188, 377n). Bernhard Blumenkranz observes that Rashi used some 2,000 French words in his Biblical and talmudic commentaries and demonstrated a perfect mastery of French (*Histoire des Juifs en France,* ed. Edouard Privat [Toulouse: Collection Franco-Judaïca, 1972], p. 26. Kisch says that Jews employed the German language of their native province to annotate and translate Scripture (*Germany,* p. 309). Abrahams (p. 425) notes that Jews in the late Middle Ages also bore the same names as Christians. But compare Blumenkranz, pp. 27–28.

badge, undoubtedly an important step in their social degradation. The badge was not uniformly enforced during the medieval period, however.[3] And Baron (11:187) notes that it was imposed on Jews precisely because it was needed to distinguish them from Christians, with whom they had close relations.

Social interaction occurred in direct defiance of segregative laws. During the famous disputation in Paris in 1240, the Jewish spokesman is reported to have said that contrary to talmudic prescription,

> we do sell cattle to Gentiles, we enter into companionship with them, we stay with them alone, we entrust our infants to them to be suckled in their own homes, and we do teach *Torah* to a Gentile, for there are many clerics able to read Jewish books. [quoted from Katz, p. 108]

Despite formal prohibitions, Gentile and Jew gave gifts to one another until the end of the period.[4] Close personal ties appear to have developed. Israel Abrahams reports, for example, that Immanuel of Rome, Dante's Jewish imitator, required special consolation on Dante's death in 1321. Abrahams observes that no theological prejudice stood in the way of the mutual regard between the Christian poet and the Jew, and notes that Immanuel wrote in an Italian sonnet:

> Love has never read the *Ave Maria,* Love knows no law or creed. Love cannot be barred by a *Paternoster,* but to all who question his supreme power Love answers, "It is my will."[5]

Friendships between the groups, according to Abrahams (pp. 420, 426) were especially notable in Italy, where Jews and Christians played cards together and ate, drank, and danced together. Sentimental attachment is attested elsewhere in Europe as well during Chaucer's lifetime. Guido Kisch notes, for example, that German lawbooks reveal outspokenly friendly attitudes between individual Jews and Gentiles in the late fourteenth and the fifteenth centuries. Such utterances, Kisch concludes, gain weight because they were evidently free expressions, made openly in court, of popular sentiment in favor of Jews (*Germany,* p. 326). Abrahams (p. 426) cites the isolated but piquant instance of a Christian in Frankfurt who in 1377 applied the friendly epithet *selig* to a deceased Jew. Relationships between the sexes in this century often went well beyond friendship. Though formal marriage was not recognized unless one of the parties converted, affairs, common law marriage, and concubinage between Christian and Jew were frequent. So many Mediterranean Jews kept Christian

3. The Jew Badge was required in 1215 because in many provinces Jews were indistinguishable from Christians, and so might "by error" have intercourse with them (see Baron, 9:28). The badge was not generally worn in France until 1269, and in Castile until the mid-fourteenth century. In Italy, distinguishing marks were common only in the fifteenth century (though earlier in Sicily). In Germany the distinctive Jewish hat was made obligatory in the thirteenth century; the hat obviated the need for a badge, and no mention is made of the red or yellow wheel as Jewish badge until the fifteenth century. See Kisch, *Forschungen,* pp. 126–27, and *Germany,* pp. 296–97; also Cecil Roth, *A History of the Jews* (New York: Schocken, 1954; revised ed. 1970), p. 277.

4. See Baron, 11:186. In Provence, c. 1300, R. Menahem Ha-Me'iri said that giftgiving to Christians was not only permissible but meritorious (Katz, p. 117). See R. Israel Isserlein's similar position, discussed below.

5. Quoted from Abrahams, p. 420. It is worth noting that Dante expressed an antagonistic position toward Jews as a people when he urged Pope Boniface VIII to make war on the Jews and Saracens rather than on the Colonnas (Baron, 11:131).

concubines that this practice was often attacked by Jewish moralists.[6] Illicit relationships between Jews and Gentiles are also documented in France, Zurich, and Constance.[7] Each side tended to be more permissive if its own males had relations with females of the other religion, and Baron (11:82–84) observes that Christian popular literature in some cases sympathetically depicted the seduction of Jewish girls.

Expressions of personal respect and evidently of friendship—or at least of personal diplomacy—are documented from the fifteenth century as well. Despite longstanding warnings from both sides about defilement through exposure to the other's religious ceremonies, for example, social contact did occur at such events. A Sicilian Christian, to cite one instance, served as godfather at a Jewish circumcision in 1484. Baron observes that friendly acts of this sort were normally taken for granted, and so passed unnoticed by official documents.[8] In Germany, friendly exchanges of gifts in connection with religious rituals caused frequent problems. In Wiener Neustadt, for example, the eating of cakes that a Christian had brought to a Jewish wedding was officially permitted by R. Israel Isserlein. Isserlein also approved of Jews' giving gifts to Christians, including clerics, for New Year's, as well as on a Jewish holiday, the *Lag be–'omer.*[9] German Gentiles and Jews were sufficiently friendly, in fact, to provoke a Church council to forbid them to bathe, eat, or drink together.[1] Numerous similar prohibitions in German secular lawbooks further witness the amicable relationships that then existed (Kisch, *Germany,* p. 326). Sexual relations between Gentile and Jew are also documented from the fifteenth century: in the Orthodox German community of Ratisbon, for example, three Jews were prosecuted within the space of seven years (1460–67) on that charge, and several were reported awaiting trial.[2] In Italy in 1418, Jewish leaders complained about the sexual laxity of Italian Jews, many of whom considered Gentile women "permitted to them." And in Spain, personal associations with Gentiles were so close, and sexual relations so common, that some Jews attributed their downfall in that country to their excessive rapprochement with their Christian neighbors. A final illustration of trusting relationships between Christian and Jew in defiance of official regulation is the fact that fifteenth-century popes employed Jewish doctors in spite of papal decrees opposing such services.[3]

6. Baron, 11:81. In Spain the Church too tried to prevent such illicit relations (see Baron, 9:26).
7. In one noteworthy case, the provost of Paris, Hughes Aubriot, was denounced in 1381 for alleged sexual relations with Jewish women, as well as for allowing baptized Jewish children to be returned to the Jews (see Baron, 11:85, who concedes that such allegations could have been political; also 11:80). Noting that sexual contacts between Jews and Christians were often cited to demonstrate "la tendance habituelle des Juifs à la débauche," Blumenkranz cites the act of contrition presented in 1300 by Bonfils, "Juif de la Grasse, pour s'excuser des 'crimes quil avoit commis iusqua ce iour la en iouant ou en baisant, embrassant ou connoissant les femmes chrestiennes'" (p. 49).
8. Baron, 11:186. Abrahams (p. 425) cites the instance of a German knight who reportedly removed the crucifix from his mantel on the frequent occasions that he received Jewish visitors. This, of course, may represent nothing more than an isolated case of politic behavior.
9. Isserlein's ruling on the cakes gave Jews general permission to eat bread prepared by Gentile bakers, except during the Ten Days of Repentance between the New Year and the Day of Atonement (Baron, 11:186–87).
1. See Abrahams, p. 409, and Baron, 9:26.
2. Baron, 11:85. Such illicit relationships continued in Germany: one German lawbook of c. 1500 provided that children born to a Jewish father and a Christian mother be removed from the father, baptized, and educated at the father's expense (Kisch, *Germany,* p. 207).
3. Baron, 11:81, 241; Abrahams, p. 428.

Most of the acts and gestures cited above were inspired by actual social contact between the groups. Whether Chaucer ever met Jews is purely speculative.[4] But even where personal interaction was unlikely, thoughtful people were capable of assessing Jews on their merits, rather than as a stereotypically damned and demonic people. In fourteenth-century England, for example, several religious and literary figures acknowledged the piety and ethicality in Jewish behavior.[5] Langland conceded, albeit grudgingly, that Jews were kinder to their needy fellows than were Christians.[6] The homilies of John Bromyard praise the Jews' piety, care for the poor, and heroic suffering for their faith, as well as their avoidance of swearing.[7] Thomas Brunton's printed sermons consider Jews superior to Christians in moral and religious practice.[8] Richard Rex notes that Wyclif and others argued that Jews, Saracens, and pagans could be saved on the basis of their virtuous acts.[9]

4. Chaucer's response, if he did meet Jews, would also be wholly conjectural. He might have had contact with Jews in 1366, when he was granted a three-month safe conduct in Navarre. This trip may have been connected with the Black Prince's alliance with King Pedro in the civil war in Castile, and perhaps concerned the recall of English mercenaries serving Pedro's opponent, Henry of Trastamara. If Chaucer had dealings with either party, he may well have had contact with Jews. Pedro's court physician and royal treasurer were Jewish, and Henry called Pedro the "Judaized king," who confided only in Jews. Henry for his part was later noted for having many Jewish officials and intimates, and during his reign Jews were accorded great liberty and power in the royal household. Chaucer could also have encountered Jews in France, where one Jewish family was received with esteem at the court of Charles V at the time of Chaucer's diplomatic missions to Paris, Montreuil, and "parts of France" (if, in fact, Chaucer did conduct these missions in 1377, as Froissart reports). Chaucer could have met Jews in Italy, where, Abrahams tells us, friendships between Christians and Jews extended into literary circles. And he may even have come into contact with Jews in England, where they occasionally came to the attention of the court. In 1390 a Sicilian Jew was baptized in the presence of Richard II. In 1392, according to Montagu Frank Modder, a Jewish physician was called to the court to attend Richard. And during most of Chaucer's lifetime, a *domus conversorum* was occupied by converted Jews on the street now known as Chancery Lane in London. Essentially a royal institution, the *domus*, at least earlier in the century, had attracted the warm interest of the king. See Baron, 11:122, 231; Heinrich Graetz, *History of the Jews* (Philadelphia: Jewish Publication Society of America, 1894; reprint ed. 1941), 4:129, 150; *Chaucer Life-Records*, eds. Martin M. Crow and Clair C. Olson (Oxford: Oxford University Press, 1966), pp. 44–53; Haldeen Braddy, "Froissart's Account of Chaucer's Embassy in 1377," *Review of English Studies* 14 (1938): 63–67; Martin M. Crow and Virginia E. Leland, "Chaucer's Life," in *Riverside Chaucer*, pp. xvii–xviii; Leon Poliakov, *The History of Anti-Semitism* (New York: Vanguard Press, 1961; reprint ed. 1973), 2:150–51; John A. Crow, *Spain* (New York: Harper & Row, 1963), p. 110; Michael Adler, *Jews of Medieval England* (London: Jewish Historical Society of England, 1939), pp. 307–39; Albert M. Hyamson, *A History of the Jews in England* (London: Jewish Historical Society of England, 1908), pp. 127, 130–31; and Montagu Frank Modder, *The Jew in the Literature of England* (Philadelphia: Jewish Publication Society of America, 1944), p. 12 (cited by Ridley, p. 13).
5. For a more developed argument that the Jews "were not viewed as ministers of Satan by those Englishmen capable of moral reflection," see Richard Rex, "Chaucer and the Jews," *Modern Language Quarterly* 45 (1984): 107–22.
6. See Schoeck, p. 256; *Piers the Plowman*, ed. Walter W. Skeat (London: Oxford University Press, 1886; reprint ed., 1965), B. IX. 81–88. Ridley (p. 10) correctly points out that in this passage, Langland cites the Jews' virtue in order to shame Christians for failing to behave as well as "Iudas felawes" did (IX. 84).
7. See G. R. Owst, *Literature and Pulpit in Medieval England* (Oxford: Basil Blackwell, 1933; reprint ed., 1966), pp. 177, 418; and his letter to *The Jewish Guardian* (London), 6 August 1926, p. 5 (cited by Rex, pp. 115–16).
8. Cf. Rex, who says (p. 115) that Chaucer must have heard Brunton sermonize on numerous occasions. Rex observes that Gower praised Jews for observing the Sabbath. In response to claims that the *Confessio Amantis* is anti-Jewish, Rex cites Ruth M. Ames, "The Source and Significance of 'The Jew and the Pagan,'" *Mediaeval Studies* 19 (1957): 37–47, and notes Gower's praise for "the good Jew Mordecai" in *Mirour de l'Omme*.
9. Rex's admirable and well-intentioned survey attributes this view of salvation to *Mandeville's Travels* and the *Parson's Tale*, but the passages he cites from these texts do not explicitly demonstrate this point. Compare Ridley's discussion (pp. 10–11) of Langland's position on the salvation of the Jews. R. W. Southern considers the growing concern to include unbelievers in the scheme of salvation to be "one of the most attractive features of the period" (*Western Views of Islam in the Middle Ages*, 2nd. ed. [Cambridge, Mass.: Harvard University Press, 1978], p. 76; cited by Rex, p. 118).

At least some fourteenth-century continental poets viewed the Jews more sympathetically than did religious polemic, treating them as human beings who were victimized by their historical circumstances. The German poet Heinrich der Teichner, who was active from about 1340 to 1375, wrote, for example, that "Many a man, who is himself much worse, bears an unjust grudge against the poor Jew." Jan van Boendale (de Clerk), a Flemish poet of the first half of the fourteenth century, wrote of the Jews:

> Want mi dunct emmer dat si
> also wel menschen syn als wi
> ende oec comen van Adame.

> [It always seems to me that they are human beings like us and have also come from Adam].[1]

Respect toward Jews and the potential for friendship with them is prominently portrayed in the *Decameron,* the most suggestive analogue to the *Canterbury Tales.*[2] In the second tale of the first day, Neifile describes an intimate friendship between a Christian and a Jewish merchant named Abraham. The tale repeatedly emphasizes Abraham's integrity, goodness, learning, and modesty. It is his wisdom, in fact, that ultimately leads him to convert, for he realizes that a religion that can survive the spiritual decadence of its princes in Rome must be favored by God! The subsequent tale also portrays a wise Jew, Melchisedech, whose actions illustrate the declared lesson of the tale: that good sense can save a man from danger. In the process, Melchisedech compares Judaism, Christianity, and Islam to three rings. Originally there was only one ring, which signified that the son who was given it would inherit the wealth of his family. But in one generation a man had three virtuous and obedient sons whom he loved equally. So he had two more rings made, each virtually indistinguishable from the first. According to this parable, God gave the three religions to equally beloved peoples; each carries out God's commandments, and, says Melchisedech, the question of which is the true heir remains unsettled. These tales demonstrate the possibility of displaying Jews in a distinctly positive light. Melchisedech's contentions about the status of Judaism, though placed in a distant setting, are nonetheless remarkable. And the affection between the Christian and the Jew in Neifile's tale is represented emphatically and without apology, firmly suggesting that Boccaccio's audience would have regarded such a relationship as unexceptionable.

A caveat: though some of the instances cited here evidence longstanding patterns, others are isolated and possibly exceptional. At least some of them may belie private conviction. Their cumulative testimony demonstrates, however, that the historical position and experience of the Jews were far more complex than the simple assumptions of the *Prioress's Tale* and its literary and theological matrix suggest. The degradation of the Jews of medieval Europe was widespread and often agonizing. But there

1. See Kisch, *Germany,* pp. 325, 539–40.
2. Although there is no proof that Chaucer ever read the *Decameron,* it was, as Larry Benson observes, the most famous prose work of his favorite Italian poet. He must have heard of it, and it may well have offered suggestions that inspired the frame of the *Canterbury Tales* (*Riverside Chaucer,* p. 3).

were other views and other voices than the Prioress's, and several of them indicate that the horizons of potential tolerance were less drastically constricted than has sometimes been supposed.

PAUL STROHM

From A Mixed Commonwealth of Style†

A Literary Model of Social Diversity

* * *

A special property of the *Canterbury Tales* is the extent to which its generic and stylistic variety is couched in polyvocality, in its embrace of separate and distinctive voices as a means of asserting social difference. Chaucer's poetry was always polyphonic, permitting the juxtaposition of separate themes and generic structures within the external form of a given work, but it becomes increasingly polyvocalic in its capacity to contain unreconciled voices as we move from the avian disputants of the *Parliament* to the distinctive and ultimately incompatible voices of Troilus and Pandarus and Criseyde to the yet fuller degree of autonomy assigned to the diverse Canterbury speakers. The Canterbury tales are richly polyphonic *and* polyvocalic, in the sense that, like medieval music, they pursue autonomous lines of development, and in the twentieth-century sense that they remain independent and unmerged. The principal theorist of this latter sense is of course Bakhtin, who argues that the precondition for true polyphony is that its voices are never subject to dialectical resolution, but remain unmerged in "unceasing and irreconcilable quarrel."[1] Chaucer critics have long appreciated the senses in which his commitment to autonomous voices inspires debate, though critics of an earlier day regarded the principal debates of the *Canterbury Tales* as subject to dialectical resolution.[2] In recent years critics have moved to embrace more fully the concept of Chaucer's polyphony, as defined both by medieval practice and modern theory, and his poetry is now characterized by such terms as "contrastive," "exploratory," a repository of "partial truths," "pluralistic," "inconclusive," "plurivalent," and "disjunctive."[3]

† From *Social Chaucer* (Cambridge: Harvard UP, 1989), pp. 168–69, 171–78, 179–82, 225–27. We have slightly altered the author's notes.

1. *Problems of Dostoevsky's Poetics* (Minneapolis: U of Minnesota P, 1984), p. 30. Bakhtin would restrict total polyvocality, in which "every thought" is represented as "the position of a personality" (p. 9) to the capitalist era (pp. 20–21), and he may be correct in this most rigorous application of his term. But, even while recognizing that many passages of the *Canterbury Tales* bear meanings that cannot be attributed to their imaginary speakers, I would nevertheless argue for the general applicability of his concept to works by Chaucer, Langland, and other pre-nineteenth-century authors.
2. Especially in the influential formulation of G. L. Kittredge, who believed the *Franklin's Tale* to propose a solution with which "the whole debate has been brought to a satisfactory conclusion." "Chaucer's Discussion of Marriage," *MP* (1911–12): 467.
3. See Helen Cooper, *The Structure of the Canterbury Tales* (London: Duckworth, 1983), pp. 54–55; Larry Sklute, *Virtue of Necessity: Inconclusiveness and Narrative Form in Chaucer's Poetry* (Columbus: Ohio State UP, 1984), pp. 3–12; Jesse M. Gellrich, *The Idea of the Book in the Middle Ages* (Ithaca: Cornell UP, 1985), pp. 213–14.

Rather than repeating the work of the many critics who have set out to demonstrate the polyphonic presuppositions of the *Canterbury Tales*,[4] I wish instead to pose a related question: in what sense is Chaucer's commitment to polyvocality *itself* a socially significant gesture? I have asserted that the stylistic and generic variety sustained by Chaucer's varied speakers is a figure for social variety, within the more conciliatory sphere of literary language, and Bakhtin's own description of polyphony in Dostoevsky's novels specifies the dynamics of this process. Bakhtin argues that Dostoevsky's polyphony is a refraction, through available literary possibilities, of the "contradictory multi-leveledness" of his own society. He argues that, had Dostoevsky perceived multi-leveledness as residing only in the human spirit, he could have created an ultimately monologic novel that took as its subject the contradictory evolution of the human spirit; instead, since he found multi-leveledness in the objective social world, he brought it into his novels as an equivalent for irreducible social contradiction.[5] Bakhtin here points to the possibility of an ultimately monologic portrayal of diversity, as opposed to a portrayal of diversity that is polyphonic through and through and could not have been otherwise because of divisions in the author's experience of society. The *Canterbury Tales* is, I believe, polyphonic in this latter sense, and the polyphony is bound up in its identity as a social text.

* * *

Helen Cooper describes Chaucer's "house of fiction" as one that offers vantages through various windows, each presenting a perspective peculiar to a particular genre and each with its own partial truth,[6] and her metaphor is apt in its emphasis on Chaucer's rejection of a single, univalent "truth" and preference for truths embodied in multiple voices. This is not to say that the claims of different Canterbury narratives to validity go unchallenged. The Wife of Bath's inversion of traditional authority is promptly challenged by the Clerk's reassertion of the necessity for submissiveness, the Merchant's disenchanted account of an abuse of human trust is promptly challenged by the Franklin's assertion of human trustworthiness to do the right thing once freed of sterile agreements. But, just as no claims are permitted to stand unchallenged, so is no claim—however overidealized on the one hand or jaundiced on the other—presented to us as devoid of any truth at all. The polyphonic work is, as Bakhtin has reminded us, "dialogic through and through,"[7] and it is grounded not simply in a perverse human nature that refuses to recognize transcendent truth, but in an experience of a society constituted by various groups, each with its own version of reality.

Like Bakhtin's Dostoevsky, Chaucer may be viewed as having "participated in the contradictory multi-leveledness of his own time,"[8] and the form of his work as the expression of a socially determined view that presupposes irreconcilable difference. The form of the *Canterbury Tales*

4. For example, those critics listed in the previous note, together with David A. Lawton, *Chaucer's Narrators* (Cambridge: D. S. Brewer, 1985), and Paul Strohm, "Form and Social Statement in *Confessio Amantis* and the *Canterbury Tales*," *SAC*, 1 (1979): 17–40.
5. Bakhtin, *Dostoevsky's Poetics*, p. 27.
6. Cooper, p. 55.
7. Bakhtin, *Dostoevsky's Poetics*, p. 40.
8. Ibid., p. 27.

is not, of course, to be regarded as a direct reflection of a society riven by faction and socially based disagreement, but rather as a mediation of that view. "Mediation" is here taken not in its most traditional Marxist sense, in which the contradictions inherent in a given situation are restated at different cultural levels with added concealment but without any progress toward resolution. Mediation is, rather, conceived in an alternative—though, I would argue, still Marxist—sense, as a positive social process, which does not simply restate intractable situations but restates them *in terms more amenable to resolution.*[9] The potential of this restatement for socially constructive resolution lies in the receptivity of Chaucer's chosen form to the language of conflict. The socially creative form of the *Canterbury Tales* permits a relatively untroubled contemplation of extreme difference, a degree of difference that could not be acknowledged in the social sphere without danger to the participants. The literary language of the *Canterbury Tales* is thus "conciliatory" in the sense proposed by Macherey, in its ability to restate and to accommodate extremes of opinion as great as those of Chaucer's social reality, but to accommodate them "avec moins de risque," undangerously.[1] This accommodation is, as Macherey would be quick to point out, imaginary, since it has no necessary effect on social reality. Yet, in its literary reproduction of a social reality that embraces varied social tendencies for the good of all, Chaucer's work itself becomes a social agent in the constructive possibilities it imagines and poses.

The Silent Plowman and the Talkative Parson

Chaucer has used the vehicle of a temporally and socially defined pilgrimage to inscribe a community of mixed discourse that models the possible harmony of a mixed state. The space within which he imagines his discursive community has, however, been precariously maintained. It has, on the one hand, required an extreme stylization of actual social conditions in late fourteenth-century English society, including near erasure of the numerical preponderance (and the sometimes threatening claims) of those agricultural workers who comprised over nine tenths of the English populace. It has, on the other hand, required deferral of the claims of an authoritative spiritual system that minimizes the importance of secular society even as it somewhat paradoxically insists on the organization of secular society according to divinely ordained hierarchy. The complicated exclusions that render Chaucer's mixed commonwealth possible are epitomized in the silence of the Plowman, the single peasant participating in the pilgrimage. The deferral of a system of spiritual transcendence inimical to the natural and mixed temporal state is brought to an end by his suddenly loquacious brother, the Parson, with his rejection of the "draf" of fabulation in favor of the "whete" of unmediated doctrine (x. 35–36).

The Plowman is admitted to the *compaignye* of pilgrims, but without a tale. In this regard, Chaucer's practice is consistent with that of most commentators on the natural state, among whom even the relative

9. As in Claude Lévi-Strauss, "The Structural Study of Myth," *Structural Anthropology* (New York: Anchor Books, 1967), esp. pp. 217–27.
1. Etienne Balibar and Pierre Macherey, "On Literature as an Ideological Form," in *Untying the Text: A Post-Structuralist Reader*, ed. Robert Young (London: Routledge and Kegan Paul, n.d.).

democrats emphasize the participation of a *gravior pars* [more dignified part of society], noting the importance of the peasantry but assigning it no consequential role. John of Salisbury is typical in his praise of the *agricolae* he calls the *pedes* or feet of the commonwealth, classing them among those who are useful or profitable to the commonwealth but who have nothing to do with its governance ("quae nec ad praesidendi pertinent auctoritatem et uniuersitati rei publicae usquequaque proficiunt"—VI. 20). And even the democratic Marsilius[2] classes agricultural workers among the *officia* rather than the *partes* of the state—with the former exercising necessary functions and belonging to the *vulgi* and the latter participating in civic rule and belonging to the *honorabilitates* (I.5). Hierarchical theory tended to demand a single thing of these workers—obedient service or *obsequium*—while suggesting that this service would be repaid with other kinds of benign assistance ("Debent autem obsequium inferiora superioribus quae omnia eisdem uicissim debent necessarium subsidium prouidere"—*Polycraticus*, VI. 20). Organic theory tended to conceal this demand within broader assertions of reciprocity ("singula sint quasi aliorum ad inuicem membra"—*Polycraticus*, VI. 20). Often commingled, each justified major exactions from agricultural producers, while simultaneously expecting servitude and denying a consequential civic role. In this regard Chaucer's silent servitor is fully assimilated to an ideology that asks much of him in the way of willing work (he is a "trewe swynkere"—I.531), cheerful relinquishment of the surplus value of his toil ("His tithes payde he ful faire and wel"—I.539), and acceptance of broad communal obligation ("He wolde thresshe . . . for every povre wight"—I.536–37).

All preliminary indications suggest that the voice of the Plowman, when Chaucer came to give him one, would not have been a voice of complaint, as was the Plowman of the Chaucer apocrypha who decries clerical theories of agricultural labor ("They make us thralles at hir lust"[3]). But we are not finally to know. For, as Patterson has argued, the voice of peasant protest is effectively erased within the *Canterbury Tales*.[4] He finds that this voice is given limited articulation in the Miller's prologue and tale, and even more limited articulation in the case of the Wife of Bath, but that it is progressively suppressed in favor of a depoliticized and transhistorical subjectivity. Patterson's argument is plainly essentially correct, although one wonders if the exclusion of the peasantry might not be even more thoroughgoing than he supposes; the Miller and the Wife of Bath are rural small producers, but hardly peasants or *agricolae* in any meaningful sense of the word.[5]

But I agree that, certain traces notwithstanding, Chaucer has virtually excluded the peasantry and rural small production from the *Canterbury Tales*. Just as the peasantry is slighted both descriptively and functionally in medieval political theory, so does Chaucer suppress its numerical and economic importance in the process of establishing his commonwealth of

2. Marsilius of Padua (d. 1342), an important political theorist. John of Salisbury, for several years secretary to Archbishop Thomas Becket, sent him the *Polycraticus* in 1159 [*Editors*].
3. "The Plowman's Tale," in Chaucer, *Works*, ed. W. W. Skeat, vol. 7, 11. 41–42.
4. Lee Patterson, "'No man his reson herde': Peasant Consciousness, Chaucer's Miller, and the Structure of the *Canterbury Tales*," *South Atlantic Quarterly* 86 (1987): 457–95.
5. The Miller would, for example, be considered a prosperous "yoman" in the terms of the 1363 statute; an "artificer" in the 1379 poll tax; a "man of craft" in the Norwich guild ordinance.

mixed literary discourse. Briefly to venture an absurd reduction: just as Chaucer would have been unlikely to imagine a commonwealth that admitted to full participation the 90 or so percent of the populace in various states of peasantry or villeinage, so could he hardly have created a literary counterpart to his own civic experience while drawing some two dozen of his speakers from the ranks of peasants and villeins. A price has certainly been paid, in regard to accurate representation of the peasantry and to direct articulation of the voice of peasant protest. Yet this devaluation of peasant concerns is an act of exclusion that, paradoxically, opens a narrative space within which the mixed middle strata produce a literary model of social diversity.

Chaucer's literary model of social diversity is itself increasingly threatened by forces hostile to those practices of fabulation and artificial use of language on which his discursive community is founded. The reliability of fabulation as a means of embodying the truth is questioned as early as the Pardoner's prologue and tale. The dilemma is posed in the Pardoner's contention that a "vicious man" can nevertheless tell a "moral tale" (VI.459–460)—a dilemma that, as we have seen, creates discomfort for the pilgrim audience and for subsequent audiences as well. This mistrust of what might be called the uses of fabulation is extended in the *Manciple's Tale* to the act of tale telling itself (cautionarily represented in the silencing of the song of the crow as punishment for indiscriminate conversation or "false tale"—IX.293) and to the narrator's mistrust of language in relation to its referent (in his acknowledgment of the "loaded" judgment implied in his choice of the word "lemman" to describe Apollo's wife's lover—IX.205–222). That the *Manciple's Tale* is about "the failure of words" has been mentioned on several occasions.[6] What remains to be added here is that the failure in question is not only a general failure of reference but a failure of *socially charged* reference, of language in its capacity justly to represent the social implications of human action. *Lemman* is one of those courtly terms that, as Donaldson reminded us, slipped a good deal between the thirteenth and fourteenth centuries.[7] The narrator accordingly pauses to note its harsh, or at least drab and ordinary, connotations, informing us that nothing separates the misconduct of a "wyf" of "heigh degree" and a "povre wenche" except the words by which we describe their behavior:

> . . . the gentile, in estaat above,
> She shal be cleped his lady, as in love;
> And for that oother is a povre womman,
> She shal be cleped his wenche or his lemman. (IX.217–20)

Then follows a crude and assertively male observation, driving home the point that beneath the words the behavior is the same:

> And, God it woot, myn owene deere brother,
> Men leyn that oon as lowe as lith that oother. (IX.221–22)

Called into question here is the meaningfulness of social specification in language: "lady" (in the sense of "beloved") versus "lemman," and by

6. Most notably, James Dean, "Dismantling the Canterbury Book," *PMLA* 100 (1985): 746–59.
7. E. Talbot Donaldson, "Idiom of Popular Poetry in the Miller's Tale." *Speaking of Chaucer* (1970; rpt. New York: W. W. Norton & Company, 1972), pp. 13–29.

implication the broader categories of "wyf" and "lady" versus "wenche" and "womman." The *swyving* is all the same, regardless of social category, and the categories have begun to blur a bit too. But the idea that different discourses are appropriate to different social levels, that certain genres and even certain styles may be assigned to persons of certain social levels, has been one of the crucial enabling ideas of the *Canterbury Tales.* Once this equation of social level and discourse is called seriously into question, Chaucer's creation of a community of discourse as a figure for a mixed commonwealth loses a crucial underpinning. That this wound to Chaucer's narrative enterprise is essentially self-inflicted suggests a crucial shift in the status of narrative itself, and this shift is shortly to be confirmed in the words with which the Parson prefaces the penitential treatise that will be his "tale."

All the Canterbury tales that preceded the Parson's are *narrationes* and possessed of plots (even if, as in the case of *Melibee*, thinly so). But it is specifically plotted narrative (that is, fabulation itself and not just Aesopic fable) that the Parson rejects when he refuses to tell "fables and swich wrecchednesse" (x.34).[8] He will instead dispense the pure "whete" of doctrine directly, offering "moralitee and vertuous mateere" in the form of an unplotted *tretys* (x.35–38). And, even before he commences his tale, several conditions that have promoted the rampant narrativity and the stylistic variousness of this discursive community are decisively altered.

Immediately altered is the pilgrims' attitude toward temporality. Until now the pilgrimage itself has—along with the tales the pilgrims tell—unfolded in the temporal realm, in the space of Bakhtin's "historically productive horizontal."[9] An atmosphere congenial to the resolution of narrative conflict in time has, despite occasional openings to the eternal, prevailed. Now we are reminded—rather urgently—that time is at a premium; late afternoon has come and Harry Bailly tells us that his plan is complete for all tales but one and that haste is essential if the Pilgrims are to be fruitful before the setting of the sun. No longer invited to participate in a leisurely temporal unfolding of narrative events, the pilgrims are requested to give "space" (x.64) to the Parson, whose tale will in fact be a spatial rather than a temporal dilatation of various penitential themes. This is not to say that the Parson's tale is brief, which it is most assuredly not, but that its shape will follow the extratemporal demands of the project he sets for himself. The "haste" enjoined by Harry Bailly is a haste to begin his undertaking; once begun, its exposition of a timeless sacrament proceeds without the pressures or interruptions that would signify the passage of worldly time. Its ending in fact is not in temporality at all, but in a timeless vision of a realm of permanent "sikernesse" (x.1077) and in Chaucer's contemplation of Christ reigning in eternity, "per omnia secula."

Also signaled by the Parson's prologue is the end of the *compaignye* of Canterbury pilgrims as a socially varied body of speakers oriented toward pluralistic discourse. Until now the pilgrims have rarely agreed on anything (unless we are to take the sobriety that settles on "every man" at the end of the *Prioress' Tale* as a form of agreement). More often, responses lapse into

8. On *fable* as a narrative with invented plot, see Paul Strohm, "Some Generic Distinctions in the *Canterbury Tales*," *MP* 68 (1971–72): 321–28.
9. "Forms of Time and of the Chronotope in the Novel," *The Dialogic Imagination*, ed: Michael Holquist (Austin: U of Texas P, 1981), p. 157.

discord or blatant partiality of understanding, or else apparent unanimity turns out to mask varied response, as at the end of the *Knight's Tale* ("nas ther yong ne oold / That he ne seyde it was a noble storie / . . . And namely the gentils everichon"—I.3110–13). Now, however, we find the audience united in its assent to the Parson's austere intention of telling a moral tale, in prose, emphasizing unmediated doctrine, and redirecting this temporal pilgrimage to an atemporal home in "Jerusalem celestial" (x.51):

> Upon this word we han assented soone,
> For, as it seemed, it was for to doone—
> To enden in som vertuous sentence. (x.61–63)

Harry Bailly has "the wordes for us alle" (x.67) when he gives the Parson free rein and promises audience. For the implication is that the Parson's "sentence" will transcend division and social difference, addressing itself to all Christians without regard to condition, in its awareness of their bondage and need for spiritual repair. The pilgrims are unlikely to slip from this new vantage back into temporality and social dissension. For the *Parson's Tale* would subsume the world of varied temporality into its timeless categories.[1]

The Parson's analytical frame is thoroughly traditional in ways that suggest how far afield Harry Bailly was in judging him a "Lollere" in the canceled endlink to the *Man of Law's Tale*.[2] In marked contrast even to "The Two Ways" by Chaucer's friend Clanvowe, with its reliance on self-regulation, the *Parson's Tale* seeks full submission to church authority as embodied in its injunctions and sacraments. The existence of sin in the world is traced not to erroneous human choice but to failure of full obedience to God (x.338) and to a withdrawal from contemplation of God's timeless blessings into a world of temporal reward. As Chaucer notes, in free adaptation of Augustine: "Deedly synne . . . is whan a man turneth his herte fro God, which that is verray sovereyn bountee, that may nat chaunge, and yeveth his herte to thyng that may chaunge and flitte" (x.367). Chaucer's apparent addition here is the concept of the "sovereyn" nature of God's bounty—an addition that refers mainly to its universal excellence but that also arrays God in the attributes of a supreme ruler from whom beneficence flows and to whom obeisance is due.[3] Running through the *Parson's Tale* is an argumentative and imagistic strain suggesting that the errant Christian has failed to accept God's good lordship, has sought to be a free subject of history and choice who can pursue a variety of temporal options instead of submitting freely to God's singular and permanent sovereignty. This imagery solidifies around the most visible and traditional manifestation of God's eternal order, in the suggestion that the Christian become a vassal of God: the Christian must "yeven his body and al his herte to the service of Jhesu Crist, and therof doon hym hommage" (x.314). The *Parson's Tale* recommends, in effect, a refeudalization of relations, within that sphere of hierarchical transcendence that

1. Patterson observes that the *Parson's Tale* "cancels out . . . that which precedes." "The *Parson's Tale* and the Quitting of the *Canterbury Tales*," *Traditio* 34 (1978): 379.
2. On the orthodox proscription of swearing, see G. R. Owst, *Literature and Pulpit in Medieval England* (Cambridge: Cambridge UP, 1933), pp. 414–25.
3. With respect to Chaucer's source, see Kate Oelzner Peterson, *The Sources of the Parson's Tale* (1901; rpt. New York: AMS Press, 1973), n. to pp. 34–35.

afforded the original pattern for the descending ideology of high medieval feudalism.

* * *

If the polyphony of the *Canterbury Tales* is a figuration of the variety of the natural state, the monovocality of the Parson's closing treatise is appropriate to the announcement of a more rigid, descending order. The finality of the Parson's utterance is enhanced by its appeal to divine ordinance. Its finality is further enhanced by its status as the last of the tales, told by common consent and followed by the closely associated Retraction, in which Chaucer responds *in propria persona* to the Parson's admonition to repent. And, beyond any of these considerations, the practice of monovocality *itself* aspires to finality. As Bakhtin has observed, "Monologue pretends to be the *ultimate word*. It closes down the represented world and represented persons."[4] In a sense this monologue does close down the *Canterbury Tales*, by denying the autonomy of that natural and varied world of temporality to which the Canterbury pilgrimage offers a literary and stylistic counterpart.

In other important senses, however, the *Canterbury Tales* resists closure, denying to any one pilgrim the finality of utterance to which the voice of the Parson would aspire. One aspect of this denial resides in the manifestly unfinished and fragmentary nature of the *Tales* itself. For an element of the Parson's authority has been our acceptance of his tale's status as the "last word," the concluding utterance of a finished literary work.

His tale does, to be sure, enjoy undoubted status as the last of Chaucer's intended narratives, whether the "thropes ende" (x.12) that the pilgrims are entering as he begins to speak refers to the outskirts of Canterbury (on a "one-way" journey) or London/Southwark (on a "round trip"). But six centuries of scribes, editors, and critics have moved beyond this indisputable fact to a presumption of near-completion that lacks ultimate support in internal evidence. Starting with the activities of the earliest fifteenth-century scribes and editors,[5] this unifying enterprise reached a climax in the middle decades of this century, through a convergence of conclusions derived within two apparently incompatible critical tendencies. Ralph W. Baldwin, accepting the assumptions about organic unity inherent in the "new criticism," launched his argument for the conversion of the *Tales* from a literal to a symbolic journey to "Jerusalem celestial" (x.51).[6] Concurrently, D. W. Robertson and his associates launched their argument for the exegetical unity of the *Tales*, including the rather willful misreading of Chaucer's "this litel tretys or rede" (x.1081) as an application of his Retraction not only to the completed *Parson's Tale* but to the entire work.[7]

Against such claims for Chaucer's final intent must be weighed his own insistence on his work as open, provisional, and unfinished. Our

4. *Dostoevsky's Poetics*, p. 293.
5. For a discussion of the activities of the Ellesmere and Hengwrt scribes, with accompanying bibliography, see Derek Pearsall, *The Canterbury Tales* (London: Unwin Critical Library, 1985), pp. 1–23. An interesting account of the "bookish" pretensions of the Ellesmere manuscript has been given by Alan T. Gaylord (unpublished paper, 1982 NCS Congress).
6. Baldwin, *The Unity of the "Canterbury Tales," Anglistica* 5 (Copenhagen, 1955).
7. Robertson's argument that the "litel tretys" of the Retraction is the whole of the *Tales* occurs in *A Preface to Chaucer* (Princeton: Princeton UP, 1962), p. 369. For a corrective, see John W. Clark, "'This Litel Tretys' Again," *The Chaucer Review* 6 (1971–72): 152–56.

tendency to imagine Chaucer's tales as a "Canterbury book" must, in the first instance, minimize the provisional nature of any arrangement of its inner fragments.[8] Beyond this fact lie other indications of Chaucer's refusal to fix his tales in a definite scheme: his distribution of narratives among many voices, his refusal to invest authority in his often-befuddled narrator or to create a Gowerian genius figure as authoritative interpreter, his minimal interest in devices such as glosses by which Gower and other contemporary authors promoted ultimate monovocality.[9]

Just as Chaucer's text announces its own unfinished nature, so does the evidence of early reception argue for random and piecemeal dissemination. Chaucer's immediate audience would have encountered his work not in presentation volumes, or any volumes at all, or even necessarily in manuscript form.[1] Rather, Chaucer's most immediate and most prized audience must have known his poetry in a discontinuous and segmented way, largely through oral rendition and occasionally, at best, through fragmentary manuscripts. To the extent that we can reconstruct a contemporary response to Chaucer, we must imagine that response less as contemplation of a finished order and more as an awareness of local juxtaposition, of ideas placed side by side, in unresolved contention.

The Parson therefore presents us with a paradox: with a voice that would transcend worldly fragmentation and division, situated in a work that treats fragmentation and division as inevitable aspects of life in the world. Chaucer's own Retraction may offer a partial resolution of this paradox, in its suggestion that the proper response to the Parson's admonitions lies beyond the temporal sphere and beyond works that imitate that sphere—in sacramental time, in "omnia secula." To the limited extent that the Parson's views about hierarchy and transcendence refer back to that temporal and mutivoiced site of personal and ideological contention offered by the *Canterbury Tales*, they must take their chances, among a multitude of contending conceptions.

In situating the Parson's voice at the end of his pilgrimage, Chaucer has shown respect for its special claims. But, at the same time, in *deferring* the Parson's voice to the end of the pilgrimage, Chaucer has opened a discursive space within which various conceptions of social reality can coexist. The impetus behind the Parson's voice is assertively utopian, in the sense that it would deny division and faction by transcending it. But another, more modestly directed but no less utopian, impulse infuses

8. Pearsall observes that the text should ideally be presented to modern readers "partly as a bound book (with first and last fragments fixed) and partly as a set of fragments in folders, with the incomplete information as to their nature and placement fully displayed" (*The Canterbury Tales*, p. 23).

9. For arguments that some manuscript glosses may ultimately be authorial, see Daniel S. Silvia, "Glosses to the *Canterbury Tales* from St. Jerome's *Epistola Adversus Jovinianum*," *SP* 62 (1965): 28–39; Robert E. Lewis, "Glosses to the *Man of Law's Tale* from Pope Innocent III's *De Miseria Humane Conditionis*," *SP* 64 (1967): 1–16. On the scribal origin of the glosses as an enhancement of the prestige of Chaucer's compilation, see A. I. Doyle and M. B. Parkes, "The Production of Copies of the *Canterbury Tales* and the *Confessio Amantis* in the Early Fifteenth Century," *Medieval Scribes, Manuscripts and Libraries: Essays Presented to N. R. Ker*, ed. Parkes and A. G. Watson (London: Scolar P, 1978), pp. 190–91.

1. Though manuscript circulation of individual tales and fragments prior to Chaucer's death remains a possibility. An argument for the circulation of individual tales in his lifetime, based on independent textual traditions as inferred from textual variants in fifteenth-century manuscripts, is advanced by Charles A. Owen, Jr., "The *Canterbury Tales:* Early Manuscripts and Relative Popularity," *JEGP* 54 (1955): 104–110.

Chaucer's later poetry as well, in his exploitation of the conciliatory possibilities of literary language to offer his audience a mixed commonwealth of discourse.

Chaucer's commonwealth is implicitly utopian in its accommodation of varied socially and vocationally defined voices and points of view, its opening of existing hierarchies to infiltration by new classes of people and categories of discourse, its treatment of heterogeneity as a normal condition of civic life.[2] A commonwealth so conceived obviously had much to offer Chaucer himself and that new group of fellow gentlepersons "en service" so prominent in his immediate audience. Yet, however densely implicated in its own historical situation and however charged its significance for its original audience, Chaucer's work continues to command the attention of succeeding readers. Its appeal is not that it exists on an aesthetic plane beyond the social fray. Rather, its appeal owes much to its rich situation between contending social models, its subtle poise at the boundaries of rank and class awareness. The comprehensiveness and argumentative energy with which Chaucer's work opens itself to its historical moment allow readers in posterity a continuing opportunity to refresh their own belief in social possibility.

LEE PATTERSON

From The *Parson's Tale* and the Quitting of the *Canterbury Tales*†

* * *

In closing the *Canterbury Tales* with a work of this generality [i.e., the *Parson's Tale*], * * * Chaucer forces us to look beyond the specific world that has so far occupied our attention. He concludes, in other words, with something of the same dismissive withdrawal to a higher, more inclusive perspective as occurs at the end of the *Troilus*. In both cases Chaucer himself emerges at the end, replacing the narratorial voice, dramatic, engaging, and multivalent, with his own identifiably historical tone. In the *Troilus* he invokes the judgment of his friends Gower and Strode and in the *Canterbury Tales* he provides us with an account of his past and a promise for the future. The effect of this gradual withdrawal from fiction to history is to devalue fiction, and the specific reductions occasioned by these endings are in effect extensions of the larger reduction implied by the form itself. The elaborately contrived fictional world is brought into contact with a reality, both divine and human, which exposes simply by its presence the factitiousness of what has preceded it. The effect, then, is not to invite a reinterpretation or even revaluation of the fiction but to declare it

2. Paul Olson's *The Canterbury Tales and the Good Society* (Princeton: Princeton UP, 1986) also argues for the social significance of Chaucer's literary text. Readers of both studies will note, however, my essential point of difference with Olson's conviction that Chaucer's reconstruction of society depends on a reassertion of hierarchy and a discouragement of pervasively "epicurean" tendencies.

† From *Traditio* 34 (1978): 370–80. Copyright © Fordham University. Published by and reproduced with permission of Cambridge University Press. We have added publication information to some of the author's notes.

transcended. Having once been granted his vision of the insignificance of earth, Troilus can hardly return, and the certainties of the *Parson's Tale* render the complexities of the tales inconsequential and even sophistical. Indeed, to argue that the Parson's view of human character provides the standard by which we should measure what we have just read is to encourage us to reread precisely that which Chaucer now dismisses as unworthy.

Yet while the *Parson's Tale* issues into the clear light of reality it takes its beginning in the imprecision of fiction, and it is itself a part of the whole it dismisses. This is the paradox the Parson himself expresses when he promises to 'telle a myrie tale in prose' that will 'knytte up al this feeste, and make an ende' (46–47). On the one hand, the *Parson's Prologue* stands securely within the limited dramatic world of the pilgrimage; but on the other, despite its air of agreeable consensus, it radically redefines the nature of the tale-telling itself. As the sun descends and the shadows lengthen the Host moves confidently toward the completion, oddly enough, not of the journey but of the tale-telling game he has initiated and presided over:

> Lordynges everichoon,
> Now lakketh us no tales mo than oon.
> Fulfilled is my sentence and my decree;
> I trowe that we han herd of ech degree;
> Almoost fulfild is al myn ordinaunce. (15–19)

The note of self-satisfaction is clearly heard here, and it is continued in his direction to the final participant in the game. 'Be what thou be, ne breke thou nat our pley' (24), he warns him, and advises him that in order to 'knytte up wel a greet mateere' he should 'Telle us a fable anoon' (28–29). In rejecting fables the Parson rejects more than the Ovidian form chosen by the Manciple and more than the 'gesta, poemata vel fabulas extra corpus scripturae' [stories, verses or fables outside Scripture] that (according to Wyclif) infected the popular preaching of the day.[1] He rejects both the Host's game and its tales, the *fabulae Chauceri*, as one manuscript labels them.[2] The Parson invokes Paul's exhortation to Timothy: 'preach the word, be urgent in season and out of season, convince, rebuke, and exhort, be unfailing in patience and in teaching. For the time is coming when people will not endure sound teaching'—*sanam doctrinam*, the Parson's 'moralitee and vertuous mateere' (38)—'but having itching ears they will accumulate for themselves teachers to suit their own likings, and will turn away from listening to the truth and wander into myths [*fabulas*]. As for you, always be steady, endure suffering, do the work of an evangelist, fulfil your ministry' (2 Timothy 4.2–5). When the Host proposed the tale-telling game in the *General Prologue* he presented it as a pastime 'to shorte with oure weye' (791), a means of 'confort' and 'myrthe' (773) to while away the journey. Far from an extension or expression of the pilgrimage, the tale-telling is in fact an alternative, a distraction from both the tedium of the journey and, inevitably and even deliberately, its significance. As we

1. On *fabula* as designating specifically a beast fable, see Vincent of Beauvais, *Speculum doctrinale* 3.113 in *Bibliotheca Mundi* (Douai 1624) II col. 289; and Bromyard, *Summa praedicantium* 6.14 (Antwerp 1614). Wyclif's strictures are quoted by H. Simon in 'Chaucer a Wycliffite: An Essay on Chaucer's Parson and *Parson's Tale*,' *Essays on Chaucer* Part 3 (Chaucer Society, 2nd series 16; London 1876), 239.
2. See John Norton-Smith, *Geoffrey Chaucer* (London 1974), 146.

approach the end the Host is proud of the fulfillment of 'my sentence and my decree,' of 'al myn ordinaunce.' But as he fails to realize, this completion is possible only because the tale-telling has been simply 'pley,' a game that is by definition enclosed and delimited. The Parson rightly understands that their journey is linear and not circular, and that it extends further than they can easily see, into a darkness of which the approaching night is a mere symbol. In its ultimate terms, the opposition between Host and Parson is between literalist and symbolist, between an attitude that accepts the here and now as a sufficient reality and one that perceives human experience as only the foreground to a larger horizon. In literary terms it is an opposition between *fabulae* and *sana doctrina*, and between two concepts of form: an additive, self-generating, and almost extemporaneous seriality on the one hand, and on the other a carefully organized action with beginning, middle, and end.[3]

Everybody agrees that the *Canterbury Tales* has a coherent beginning and end, but the large, undistributed middle remains to challenge the ingenuity of the exegete. Any reading that presents the tales as providing, as a recent writer puts it, 'most of all a way of expressing the developing pilgrimage,' is compromised by several unavoidable facts.[4] First, it is not enough to show that there is a beginning, middle, and end, to all of which the concept of pilgrimage is relevant, since it is indeed relevant to all medieval action. Rather, we must show how the middle develops from the beginning and requires the end: we can go from A to Z easily enough, but how are all the other letters to be fitted into their appropriate order? To my knowledge, nobody has even attempted this kind of progressive reading of the tales; but if one is to argue that they are meaningful primarily ('most of all') in terms of pilgrimage, then this timely and specific relevance must be demonstrated.[5] Second, a reading that invokes the pilgrimage metaphor as continuously relevant must confront the fact that it is never explicitly invoked throughout the tales. It is present at the beginning of the *General Prologue*, momentarily in Egeus' speech in the *Knight's Tale*, and in the *Parson's Prologue and Tale*, but it is absent from everything in between. Professor Donaldson is surely right when he reminds us that the medieval reader would have been most struck by Chaucer's 'avoidance throughout most of the Canterbury Tales of the expected implications of the pilgrimage.'[6] For Chaucer's poem bears only an oblique relationship to pilgrimage allegories such as Deguileville's *Pèlerinage de la vie humaine* or Jean de Coucy's *Chemin de vaillance*, and to describe the *Canterbury Tales* as 'linked a priori to the great body of pilgrimage literature written during the

3. These two kinds of medieval narrative form are discussed by Charles Singleton, 'Meaning in the *Decameron*,' *Italica* 21 (1944): 117–24; in *The Unity of the* Canterbury Tales (*Anglistica* 5; Copenhagen 1955), Ralph Baldwin discusses Singleton's distinction in relation to the *Canterbury Tales* and attempts to see the pilgrimage frame as providing a *sovrasenso* equivalent to that of the *Divine Comedy*.
4. The phrase is used by Edmund Reiss, 'The Pilgrimage Narrative and the *Canterbury Tales*,' *Studies in Philology* 67 (1970): 295–305.
5. Paul Ruggiers, 'The Form of *The Canterbury Tales: Respice Fines*,' *College English* 17 (1956): 439–44, does discuss the relevance of the *Knight's Tale* and the *Man of Law's Tale* as providing, respectively, a philosophical and religious guide for the pilgrimage, with the *Parson's Tale* then as a final admonition to those who have not followed this advice and have gone astray; see also his comments in *The Art of the Canterbury Tales* (Madison 1965), 5–11, 247–57. There are many discussions of the appropriateness of beginning with the classical values of the *Knight's Tale*, e.g., Joseph Westlund, 'The *Knight's Tale* as an Impetus for Pilgrimage,' *Philological Quarterly* 43 (1964): 526–37.
6. *Chaucer's Poetry* (2nd ed.; New York, 1975), 1113.

late Middle Ages'[7] is to allow one contingent and carefully limited theme to become the sole determinant of genre.[8] It would of course be excessive on the other side to say that the pilgrimage theme is irrelevant. One of the major differences between Chaucer's formal conception and those of Boccaccio and Sercambi is that Chaucer's travellers are not simply wandering in an effort to escape from reality but actually journeying toward it. But the tale-telling game in which they engage is in a radical way opposed to the concerns of their journey. Indeed, that the game comes so near to completion is a testimony to the success with which the meaning of the pilgrimage has been repressed throughout.

The degree of this repression can be gauged by recalling how narrow is the scope granted to the tales of 'moralitee and devocioun' in the course of the narrative. The narrator's division of the tales into 'sentence' and 'solaas,' despite its limitations, has the advantage of sorting out Chaucer's complicated blendings of *utile dulci* [profit and pleasure] into opposed categories. The serious tales of the Knight, Man of Law, Clerk, Physician, Prioress, Monk, and Second Nun, and the *Tale of Melibee*, provide not merely recreation for those sophisticated enough to enjoy them but absolutes that are uplifting and urgent. They present to their audience imperatives that go beyond appreciation to self-scrutiny and moral action. In this sense, each of the serious tales is at odds with the holiday mood that is the context and foundation of the tale-telling, and much of the *Canterbury Tales* is concerned with disarming this threat to its continuance. Hence we should notice that the serious tales are never allowed to impose their tone or perspective upon the pilgrimage but are consistently countered and limited.

The most obvious instances of this limitation are the refusals by the comic characters to allow the sober Knight and Man of Law to be followed by the equally sober Monk and Parson. These interruptions are perhaps judgment enough, but a finally more telling critique is provided by the new and severely limiting contexts which the interjected comic tales establish for their dour predecessors. This limitation is enforced by the narrative strategy of the *Canterbury Tales* itself: the inclusion of the teller with the tale personalizes the meanings that emerge and encourages a dramatic reading that discounts any authoritative significance. The Truth that each teller labors to express is rendered simply as an individual truth or the truth for an individual. The total effect, then, of the *Miller's Tale* on the Knight's is to suggest that the Knight's Boethian wisdom is as much a function of his class consciousness as are his preferred ways of making love and war. Similarly, while the uncertainties of order make it difficult to provide the same context for the *Man of Law's Tale*, it is easy enough to see how the faithless wife of the *Shipman's Tale* or the Wife of Bath herself provides a sufficient foil for the otherworldly Constance. Further, in re-invoking the dominant dramatic and psychological mode of the *Tales* either of these succeeding tales serves to foreground the unseemly personal qualities of the Man of Law that have been allowed a presence in his tale. The same kind of deflation and even satiric

7. Reiss 297.
8. In responding to Reiss's article, Siegfried Wenzel, 'The Pilgrimage of Life as a Late Medieval Genre,' *Mediaeval Studies* 35 (1973): 370–88, discusses these, and other, pilgrimage allegories and shows to just how substantial a degree Chaucer's poem differs from them.

dismissal is brought to bear upon the Physician, Prioress, and Monk, whose personalities stand in awkward contrast to their proffered values and indecorously intrude into their tales. Finally, the *Second Nun's Tale*, while secure in its anonymity, is revealed as providing at best only a partial antidote to the problem of sloth and despair when set next to the hectic confession of the Canon's Yeoman; and the *Clerk's Tale*, by far the most assured of Chaucer's creations in this mode, carries an epilogue that ironically limits its relevance. In sum, the *Canterbury Tales* provides various prospects on and versions of the truth, but no one is allowed authority or even an unchallenged assertion. Indeed it seems that truth fares best when, as in the *Nun's Priest's Tale*, it is pared down to the limitations of a proverb and hidden within the sharp perspectives of irony.

While this circumscription of the serious and the demanding is characteristic of Chaucer's urbane good humor, it also implies an unorthodox and even subversive poetics. The full range of medieval literary theory can hardly be dealt with on this occasion, but we should note that Chaucer's poetic practice more often reflects the internally determined values of a rhetorical poetics than the external strategies prescribed by the allegorists. As the exegete discovers when he tries to specify the full meaning of a Chaucerian poem, Chaucerian *sententiae* are less the conclusion which all the elements of the text express than occasions for writing which the complexities of the text rapidly transcend. Theme figures as only one element among many, not the *res* [things, realities] which the *verba* [words] labor to express but a ground of significance upon which the variables of fable, personality, and language display themselves. Like the Pardoner's sermon, Chaucer's poems use traditional truths as *themae* upon which to play variations, and we can no more define the significance of the whole by reference to its rhetorical origins than we can say that the *Pardoner's Tale* means *radix malorum est cupiditas* [avarice is the root of all evil; see *PardT* 333–34]. When located within a rhetorical perspective, then, the *Canterbury Tales* reveals itself not as a progression toward a goal—parts that signify a unifying whole—but as a series of poetic experiments in various styles, a witty compendium of late medieval literary fashion embellished with the appropriate personalities.

Indeed, not only does the progressive and coherent form of the pilgrimage frame not extend to the inner organization of the tales, but the form this great, undistributed middle *does* display is minimal, additive, and arbitrary. It is a form required by the tale-telling game; the Host, in his role of *magister ludi*, defines it as *quitting* (I.3119). Its workings are demonstrated in Fragment I: Miller quits Knight, Reeve quits Miller, Cook (presumably) quits Reeve, but not before warning the Host, 'But er we parte, ywis, thou shalt be quit' (4362) in turn. The form is thus one of the most common of medieval narrative structures, bipartition or binarism.[9]

9. An account of the bipartite or 'diptych' form, with examples, is provided by William W. Ryding, *Structure in Medieval Narrative* (The Hague 1971): 116–137. Donald Howard, *The Idea of the Canterbury Tales* (Berkeley 1976), 224–25, 322–24, discusses binary structure, with interesting comments on its source in the relationship of the Old to the New Testament. It is worth remembering that the single most important source for the *Canterbury Tales*, the *Roman de la Rose*, is itself binary, the second part functioning as a revision and hence a gloss on the first: Jean de Meun promises 'si la chose espondre / que riens ne s'i porra repondre' [to explain the matter so that none of it can stay concealed] (10573–574); ed. Félix Lecoy (CFMA 95; Paris 1966), II 72.

The tales proceed two-by-two, and a mere listing of the pairs (appropriately annotated) is sufficient to indicate the binary form: Man of Law/Wife of Bath; Friar/Summoner; Wife of Bath/Clerk; Clerk/Merchant; Squire/Franklin; Physician/Pardoner; Shipman/Prioress; *Tale of Sir Thopas/Tale of Melibee*; Monk/Nun's Priest; Second Nun/Canon's Yeoman; Manciple/Parson.[1] Certainly larger thematic patterns exist, but in relying upon binarism for his basic narrative structure Chaucer reduces form to a bare minimum. Indeed, as the tales proceed even the use to which this form is put is simplified. Fragment I displays a relatively sophisticated use, in which the second member of each pair provides the first member of the next (Knight/Miller, Miller/Reeve), and this pattern is repeated, with an interruption, in Fragments II–IV: Man of Law/Wife of Bath, Wife of Bath/Clerk, Clerk/Merchant. Is the *Franklin's Tale* then the conclusion to the Marriage Group? Perhaps, but the Franklin is in the first instance responding to the Squire, a tale-teller who has, his gracious opponent admits, 'yquit' himself well (V.673).[2] The quitting pattern is thus explicitly reinvoked in Fragment V, and from then on the binary form continues in its simplest mode. It is the *first instance* that is crucial: the binary pattern provides Chaucer with a clearly defined structure upon which to play variations, but it also enforces the discreteness of each pair and so foregrounds their merely sequential relationship. Tied to each other, they look inward rather than out to the tales as a whole. As our reading proceeds, then, the variations fall away to reveal the repetitive pattern beneath. Uncontrolled by any larger purpose, there is no reason the pattern should not repeat itself endlessly, extending itself even beyond the one hundred and twenty tales envisioned by the Host: any ending is arbitrary for a form that is merely additive. The form itself, in other words, is no more meaningful than the ten-by-ten scheme of the *Decameron*. Nor should we expect it to be: the rules of every game are arbitrary.[3]

1. My list assumes the Ellesmere order, convincingly defended by E. Talbot Donaldson, 'The Ordering of the *Canterbury Tales*,' in *Medieval Literature and Folklore Studies: Essays in Honor of Francis Lee Utley*, ed. Jerome Mandel and Bruce A. Rosenberg (New Brunswick 1970), 193–204; but it can easily be accommodated to the Bradshaw shift. Indeed, nothing could more tellingly demonstrate the absence of a coherent, sequential order in the tales than the fact that readers are still arguing about the proper placement of over 3000 lines. What other masterpiece could survive such uncertainty? The point is that the different placements require only local adjustments, i.e., they make no difference to the total meaning of the poem because the 'poem' has no total meaning. Hence Donaldson is right to argue that the question of order is properly an editorial one, and to opt for Ellesmere because it has greater manuscript authority.

   The thematic connections between the Man of Law and the Wife of Bath have often been discussed: see, e.g., Lee Sheriden Cox, 'A Question of Order in the *Canterbury Tales*,' *Chaucer Review* 1 (1966–67): 228–52. More important is the formal pairing: these two tales are the first of four pairs that are generically linked by the pattern of hagiography and confession, the other three being Clerk/Merchant, Physician/Pardoner and Second Nun/ Canon's Yeoman. For discussions of this pattern in the last pair of the sequence, see Joseph E. Grennen, 'Saint Cecilia's "Chemical Wedding": The Unity of the *Canterbury Tales*, Fragment VIII,' *Journal of English and Germanic Philology* 65 (1966): 466–81, and Bruce A. Rosenberg, 'The Contrary Tales of the Second Nun and the Canon's Yeoman,' *Chaucer Review* 2 (1967–68): 278–91. Of the other pairs listed, the only problematical one is the Shipman/Prioress, a difficulty that arises, I suppose, because of the incompleteness of the revisions. For the Squire/Franklin, see below, n. 2.
2. For this linking of Squire and Franklin, see Harry Berger, Jr. 'The F-Fragment of the *Canterbury Tales*,' *Chaucer Review* 1 (1966–67): 88–102, 135–56.
3. The reader will have noticed that the brevity of my discussion has allowed me to beg several important questions. The most recent and most ambitious attempt to demonstrate that a premeditated and fully articulated form lies 'behind' the *Canterbury Tales* is Donald Howard's *The Idea of the Canterbury Tales*; I have offered a fuller critique of this project, both particularly and in general, in the *University of Toronto Quarterly* 48 (1978–9).

The Parson's final contribution to the game is thus a formal alternative that in effect renders the game unplayable: the monolithic articulation of his *summa* reveal how inconsequent and even random are the self-generated oppositions of the tales. But there are compensations, for it is only by such an interruption that the tales can be brought to any conclusion. The Parson destroys the poem, in other words, in order to release the poet from his fiction-making, to turn him finally from shadows to reality. The beneficence the Parson offers can be fully appreciated only when we recognize how persistently Chaucer has asked the moral questions raised by his kind of poetry, and how persistently he has refused to answer them. Of course poetry can never tell the truth in quite the way that the allegorical literary theory of Chaucer's day prescribed, and his conventionalized gestures toward authenticity, whether moral or historical, are more appeasements of this expectation than real claims to truthfulness.[4] The traditional justifications are offered but they are never pressed home, for Chaucer's unwillingness to define a poetics that is anything more than *ad hoc* is a prerequisite for his most striking formal innovations. But it leaves him vulnerable to moralistic attacks, such as that which (as Alfred David has shown) lies behind the autobiographical comments in the *Man of Law's Prologue*.[5] Chaucer's response to these Gower-like criticisms is typically delimited. Rather than providing a comprehensive defense of his stylistic eclecticism and complex *modus significandi*, Chaucer is content with an *ad hominem* and local victory. He gently parodies Gower in the fussy moral narrowness of the Man of Law and then out-Gowers Gower by retelling, more effectively, one of his opponent's own stories. This is not a defense, in short, but an avoidance of attack, and the problem of the morality of Chaucer's kind of poetry remains unresolved. It is raised again, in a particularly telling form, by the *Manciple's Tale*. Indeed, the Manciple prepares for the Parson not just by rehearsing one of the fables the Parson is going to reject but by casting doubt upon the whole poetic enterprise. Superficially, his tale is simply a bitter commentary on the contretemps of his prologue: the crow is to Phoebus as he himself is to the Cook. Just as he was rebuffed in his attempt to admonish a public drunkard, so the crow is a truth-teller who is punished for his honesty. The concluding litany of homely saws and proverbial wisdom serves then as the Manciple's mocking celebration of the trimmer's motto that silence is the best policy. The disdain and self-regard of his rebuke to the Cook, mirrored in the tale by the crow's cruelly elaborate account to Phoebus of

4. As Robert O. Payne, *The Key of Remembrance: A Study of Chaucer's Poetics* (New Haven 1963), has shown, Chaucer is fascinated with the relation of poetry to scientific and moral wisdom, to dreams, and to experience itself. But none of these relationships is anything less than complex and ambiguous, and in no case does the poem resolve itself into one pole of the dialectic. At the end of the *General Prologue*, for instance, the narrator defends the salty language he is going to use by reference to the demands of *mimesis* (731–36). Far from being a statement of theoretical intent, however, this passage is in fact a way of assuring a courtly audience that the bourgeois literature they are about to enjoy is authentic and gratifyingly vulgar. Chaucer is asserting not a realistic relationship of life to literature but defining the relation of one form of literature to another. Similarly local purposes are served by the other quasi-theoretical statements in the *Canterbury Tales*. The Physician's boast that the tale of Virginia 'is no fable, / But knowen for historical thyng notable' (155–56) is part of his larger effort at self-authorization; and when the Second Nun says that she is simply recording 'the wordes and sentence / Of hym that at the seintes reverence / The storie wroot' (81–83) she is defining a stance of spiritual humility rather than a poetics relevant to Chaucer, as the subtlety and elegance of the tale suggest.

5. 'The Man of Law vs. Chaucer: A Case in Poetics,' *Publications of the Modern Language Association* 82 (1967): 217–25.

his wife's adultery, allows the reader to see the Manciple's pose as an injured moralist in an ironic light. But the severity of the charge implicitly levelled against poetry is not diminished by the Manciple's own moral inadequacy. On the contrary, the *Manciple's Prologue and Tale* provides a bitter parody of the tale-telling game. The festivity in which it began and by which it has been sustained has by this time degenerated into the Bacchic excesses of the Cook, and the balancing pressure of a larger vision, never granted its full scope throughout the course of the tales, is now reduced to the querulous cynicism of the Manciple.[6] Further, the Manciple implicitly calls into question the artful use of language itself.[7] His tale is a set of evasions that offers an opinion only to withdraw it and that mouths moralisms but remains in fact deeply cynical. He asserts with harsh realism that man is dominated by an animal nature, but the only redemption he offers is expediency dressed as integrity—the verbal equivalent to the wine with which the Cook is put back to sleep and a version of the poetic encomium by which the self-deluded Phoebus reconciles himself to the wife he has murdered. In sum, the Manciple's refusal to give a serious answer to the complex moral issues raised by his tale stands as a dark parody of Chaucer's dispassionate withdrawal from assertion, and we are invited to see in the cynical Manciple a sour self-portrait of the ironic poet.[8]

These doubts about the moral integrity of poetic language have been raised throughout the *Canterbury Tales*. The dismissal of the tales that the *Parson's Tale* effects consists not merely in the reduction of the rich complexity of personality to seven types of misbehavior, nor in the transcendence of the various truths of the preceding tales with an authoritative Truth. Rather, by choosing as his final work a treatise on confession Chaucer redefines in an irremediable way the very act of speaking. Poetic speech in its largest definition, as the artful use of language, is the most general target of this redefinition, and the *Manciple's Tale* exists precisely to present poetic speech in its most morally offensive form. But there is as well a more local target, specific to the *Canterbury Tales*, in the self-expressiveness that runs through the tales and that in characters such as the Wife of Bath, Pardoner, and Canon's Yeoman becomes virtually confessional.[9] While the degree of this self-expressiveness is a matter of critical dispute, the very form of the narrative forces the issue upon us. By

6. Norton-Smith, 150–51, connects the Cook to Bacchus, but sees the relationship as wholly comic. As a further link, see the passage quoted by Pamela Gradon, *Form and Style in Early English Literature* (London 1971), 54, from Holcot, *In Librum Sapientiae*: 'Someone feigns the image of Drunkenness to have been thus depicted, the image of a child, having in his hand a horn and on his head a crown of [vine]. He was a boy in token that (drunkenness) makes a man speechless and senseless, in the manner of a child. He had a horn in his hand as a token that (the drunken man) conceals no secret but reveals (it) with clamour and clangour. He has a [vine] crown, because he considers himself glorious and wealthy, he who is drunk, whereas he has nothing.'
7. V. J. Scattergood, 'The Manciple's Manner of Speaking,' *Essays in Criticism* 24 (1974): 124–46.
8. Scattergood points out the parallel between the Manciple as a servant to lawyers and Chaucer as patronized by the court, and adds: 'Chaucer is particularly interested in the Manciple because the Manciple's way of using words bears some relation to the strategies he himself uses as a poet' (143).
9. See my 'Chaucerian Confession: Penitential Literature and the Pardoner,' *Medievalia et Humanistica* 7 (1976): 153–73, and Lawrence V. Ryan, 'The Canon's Yeoman's Desperate Confession,' *Chaucer Review* 8 (1973–74): 297–310. The paratactic and digressive style in which these confessional prologues are couched provides a paradigm for the form of the *Canterbury Tales* as a whole, and, as the extent of the critical literature suggests, the Wife of Bath and Pardoner express literary values that are recognized as quintessentially Chaucerian.

including within his poem the tellers as well as their tales, Chaucer manages to achieve the same poetic range as in his dream visions: the total meaning of each tale extends beyond its narrative to include its relationship with its teller, just as the experience of the poet-dreamer provides a crucial element of the total significance of those poems. To some extent, then, each of the tales is self-expressive, and it is this process of self-expression that the *Parson's Tale* serves to redefine. For his sober and prosaic treatise is a rejection of all personal speaking that does not confront, in the sacramental language of penance, the sinfulness of the human condition. It is not merely the qualifying complexities of the personality that are to be abandoned, but any language that does not deal with sin in the terms defined by the Parson. 'Why sholde I sowen draf out of my fest, / Whan I may sowen whete, if that me lest?' (35–36): his question draws its authority less from medieval arguments about the validity of literature than from its immediate context, the shadows that lengthen about him. The tales were told as a pastime to 'shorte with the weye,' but now the time has passed and the way must be attended to. So the Parson redefines not only the journey but the tale-telling itself: he gives not so much directions to the heavenly Jerusalem as the prior and more radical knowledge that 'this viage' itself, the specific journey to Canterbury, can be so undertaken that it can itself become a 'parfit glorious pilgrymage,' a pilgrimage that does not merely lead to but in fact constitutes— 'is highte'— 'Jerusalem celestial.' And for this to happen the various voices of the tales must give way to the penitential speaking defined by the Parson.

It is necessary, then, that the *Parson's Tale* should provide not a fulfillment to the tales but an alternative, a complete and exclusive understanding of character, action, and even language. But in concluding we must return to the paradox in which the tale is grounded. If it cancels out rather than completes that which precedes, its position at once enforces and weakens its authority. His tale takes its origin in the very dramatic and realistic context which it will dismiss, and it is a denial of the tale-telling game that in the first instance quits the Manciple. In sum, while the Parson has the last word he must wait until last to say it, and although the transcendence of his message is never in doubt he must wait until the imperfect and even immoral expressions of merely verbal art have been passed in review. Chaucer and the pilgrims have it both ways, but this should lead us to question neither their nor Chaucer's sincerity. The evidence is that the *Parson's Tale* was written late in the poet's career, and there seems no reason not to accept the obvious biographical implication that it was his last work. Furthermore, its very nature is terminal. It begins within the fictional construct but becomes the tale to end all tales, and its conclusion inevitably escapes from the narrative frame and now refers to the larger context of biography. The tale becomes not simply the last element of a sustained poetic enterprise but a crucial and even decisive piece of evidence about the moral worth of Chaucer himself. As the *licentia auctoris* [authorial license] informs us, it is to be measured by the standards not of literary fame but of eternal salvation. Indeed, the *Parson's Tale* itself shows Chaucer already beginning to respond to these new imperatives. The writing of an edifying treatise as an act of penance is a not uncommon medieval habit. Chaucer would certainly have known the treatise on *The Two Ways* written by his friend Sir John Clanvowe just before he died in 1391, and would probably also have been familiar with *Le Livre de seyntz medicines* by Henry, Duke of Lancaster, written in 1354. Both the *licentia* and the medieval habit of the repentance of old age encourage us to see the *Parson's Tale* as another instance of literary penance. This is a penance that is neither perfunctory, as the care with which the tale is composed suggests, nor unexpected. Rather it is a part of the fitting shape of the Christian life, hardly a hypocritical *volte-face* but an inevitable and gratifying process of change and fulfillment. 'Young devil, old saint' runs one of the proverbs that express this conception, and its cynicism is tempered with a benign assurance that each man's history is concluded with a reversal that is both fulfillment and justification. It is in this radically linear awareness of the range of human action in its response to divine requirements that we should locate the paradox of a tale that can at once 'knytte up al this feeste, and make an ende.'

Geoffrey Chaucer: A Chronology†

1327	Reign of Edward III begins.
1337–1453	The Hundred Years' War with France.
1340–45	Birth of Geoffrey Chaucer, son of Agnes and John Chaucer, a successful wine merchant in London.
1348–50	The Black Death. Epidemics of plague recur throughout Chaucer's lifetime.
1357	Chaucer in service as a page in the household of Elizabeth de Burgh, countess of Ulster.
1360	Edward III contributes to Chaucer's ransom after his capture in France. Chaucer carries letters to England from Calais for Lionel, earl of Ulster.
1365–67	Chaucer marries Philippa Roet, a lady-in-waiting to Queen Philippa; they have a son, Thomas, who later becomes a prosperous landholder and respected member of Parliament.
1366	Chaucer in Spain, perhaps on a diplomatic mission.
1367	Edward III grants to Chaucer, his "valet," an annuity of twenty marks for life. (A mark is worth two-thirds of a pound. Cf. Chaucer's financial rewards for service to the king in 1381, 1393, and 1394.)
1369	Chaucer in service as an esquire in the royal household. Takes part in John of Gaunt's campaign in northern France.
1370	Chaucer travels on the Continent in the king's service.
1372–73	Chaucer commissioned to establish an English seaport for Genoese trade; to this end and for other matters of the king's business, travels to Genoa and Florence.
1374	Edward III grants Chaucer a pitcher of wine daily. Chaucer leases a house above Aldgate. Appointed Controller of Wool Custom and Subsidy for the Port of London.
1377	Chaucer goes to France and Flanders on the king's secret business. Assists at the negotiations at Montreuil-sur-Mer for peace and in Paris for the marriage of Prince Richard. Reign of Richard II begins.
1378	Chaucer sent to Lombardy on a mission concerning the war.
1381	Chaucer receives a gift of twenty-two pounds from Richard II for his diplomatic service in France. Peasants' Revolt.
1385–86	Chaucer sits as Justice of the Peace for Kent.

† The principal source for Chaucer's biography is the *Chaucer Life-Records*, ed. Martin M. Crow and Clair C. Olson (Austin: U of Texas P, 1966). The standard biography is Derek Pearsall, *The Life of Geoffrey Chaucer* (Oxford: Blackwell, 1992). A few of these dates are conjectural.

1386	Chaucer elected to Parliament as Knight of the Shire for Kent. Retires as Controller of the Port of London. Richard II's power is weakened.
1389	Richard II regains power. Chaucer appointed Clerk of the King's Works, with responsibility for construction at Westminster, the Tower of London, and several castles and manors.
1390	Chaucer is among those charged with responsibility for the walls, ditches, and other works on the Thames between Woolwich and Greenwich.
1391	Chaucer retires from the clerkship. Appointed deputy forester of the Royal Forest of North Petherton, Somerset.
1393	Richard II awards Chaucer ten pounds for "good service."
1394	Richard II grants Chaucer an annuity of twenty pounds for life.
1397	Richard II's final gift to Chaucer: a "tonel" (252 gallons) of wine a year for life.
1399	Richard II deposed. Henry IV, upon his accession to the throne, renews Richard's gifts to Chaucer and grants him an additional annuity of forty marks. Chaucer leases a residence in the garden of the Lady Chapel of Westminster Abbey.
1400	A sixteenth-century tomb in Westminster Abbey records Chaucer's death as occurring on October 25 of this year.

A Short Glossary

This glossary is a brief reference source for common words in Chaucer's vocabulary. These terms are usually glossed marginally at the beginning of tales but not always when they appear subsequently. The glossary also suggests the range of meaning or implication of some of Chaucer's most resonant terms.

agayn, ayein, ayeyn: again; against; facing; in return
al (conj.): although; albeit
al, alle (adj.): all; every
anon: promptly; quickly; soon
aventure: chance; luck; fortune; circumstance
  per aventure: perhaps
ay: always; ever; all the time; continually
been: (to) be; are; exist
bet: better
bountee: goodness; kindness
brenne(n): burn (p.t. **brente**)
cas: case; instance; situation; circumstance; example
certein (adj., adv.): certain(ly); sure(ly); a certain (quality or number)
certes: certainly
chambre: chamber; room; bedroom
cheer: face; expression; attitude; friendliness; enjoyment
clepe(n): call; name
clerk: student; scholar; learned authority; cleric
comth: comes
conne(n): know; know how to; be able to; can
  (p.t. **coude:** knew; was able; could)
conseil: advice; counsel; council of advisors; secret; confidant
corage: heart; spirit; mood; disposition; will
curteisye: courtliness; courtesy; civility; kindness
dere: dear; beloved
devyse: describe; tell; narrate; think about; imagine
doon: do; make; cause to happen
douteles: doubtless; certainly
eek: and; also; moreover
eft: again
  eftsone: soon after (this)
elles: also; else
eve: evening
everich: every; each
  everichon: everyone; each one
faire (adj., adv.): fair; lovely; elegant(ly); courteous(ly)
feend: fiend; devil; Satan
fer: far
  ferre: farther
ferforth: as far as; to the extent that

folye: folly; foolishness
for: because
free: generous; liberal; noble
fro: from
ful, full(e): very; complete(ly); intently
fy: fie
gan: began; often a signal of past tense, e.g.,
  gan aryse: did rise; rose
gentilesse: nobility of rank; nobility of behavior; kindness; graciousness
han: have
heigh: high; tall; high in social rank; noble; heavenly
hem: them
hente(n): seize; take; catch; caught
hight(e): named; called; was called; promised
hir, hire: her; their
honest: honorable; decent; proper; suitable; honest
ilke: that same
lette(n): hinder; prevent; cease
lewed: ignorant; uneducated
list(e): it pleases; it pleased
  me list(e): it pleases me (to); i.e., I wish (to), I like (to)
lordynges: lords (respectful address to an audience regardless of class)
lust: pleasure; desire; delight; lust
lyte: little; slight
manere: manner; way
matere: matter; subject; material
mayde: maiden; virgin
mene: mean; signify; intend (to say)
mete (n.): food; meal
mo: more
moot, mote: must; shall; may
mowe(n): be able (to); can; may (p.t. **mighte**)
namely: especially
nas (contraction of **ne was**): was not
natheles: nevertheless
nis: is not
noblesse: nobility; high rank; noble character; splendor
nolde (contraction of **ne wolde**): did not want (to)
nyce: foolish; silly
o, oo, oon: one; a single (one)
ones: once
pardee: by God; indeed
payne: pain; punishment; suffering; grief
pitous: full of pity; compassionate; pitiable; pious
pleyn (adj., adv.): plain; plainly; clear(ly); simple; straightforward; openly
pray(en), prey(en): request; beg; pray
prively: privately; quietly; secretly
quod: said; spoke
rede(n): read; read aloud; interpret; advise
regne: realm; kingdom; rule; reign
saugh: saw
save: except; except for
sely: holy; innocent; simple; pitiable; wretched; foolish
sey, seyn, seyen: say (p.t. **sayde, seyde**: said)
  seistow: thou sayest
sin, sith: since; because of

sith, sithen: since; afterward; then
sooth (n., adj.): truth; true
specially: especially; in particular
spede: go quickly; prosper; succeed (p.t. **sped, spedde**)
swich: such; such a
than, thanne, thenne: then; than
ther: there; where; when
  ther as: where; there where
thilke: this; this same
thinke(n): think; seem; often used as impersonal verb, e.g.,
  him/hire/hem thoughte: it seemed to him/her/them
  me thinketh: it seems to me; I think
tho: then
thurgh: through; throughout; because of
til: until; to; into
tro(u)th(e): truth; troth; pledge of faith; loyalty; truthfulness
trowe(n): believe; think; imagine
verraily: truly
verray: true; real; exact; faithful
war: aware; wary; careful
werche(n), werk(en): make; perform; do; work; cause
  (p.t. **wroghte, wroghten**)
weylawey: alas
whan: when
wher, wher as: where; wherever
wight: person; man; creature
wolde (p.t. of **willen**): willed, wished, or wanted (to); would have
wood: mad; furious; crazy
wot, woot: know; knows
wyse: way; manner
yeve(n): give (p.t. **yaf**)
yif: if
ylich(e) (adj. and adv.): alike; equal; equally
yno(u)gh, ynowe: enough; sufficient(ly); plenty
ywis: indeed; certainly

Selective Bibliographies

• indicates works included or excerpted in this Norton Critical Edition.

The amount of published material devoted to Chaucer and *The Canterbury Tales* is enormous, and these selective bibliographies are meant only as starting points for undergraduate and graduate students. We include both general areas of Chaucer scholarship and work focused specifically on each tale we print—chiefly critical studies but also editions and background material. The bibliographies of individual tales include, when available, volumes in the Variorum Chaucer and the Toronto Chaucer Bibliographies series; these volumes provide thoughtful surveys of criticism published up to a few years of the date of their own publication. Within each bibliography the arrangement is generally chronological rather than alphabetical.

There are now many online resources for studying Chaucer. Teachers at several universities have created websites for their students that are publicly available, some of which offer rich sets of links to other sites on Chaucer and the Middle Ages. The *Harvard Geoffrey Chaucer Website* (chaucer.fas.harvard.edu) offers a variety of background material and a complete *Canterbury Tales* in Middle English with an interlinear modern English translation. The New Chaucer Society provides a substantial number of links to bibliographical and historical work at its website, newchaucersociety.org/resources/. So do the sites at labyrinth.georgetown.edu and the medieval literature section of luminarium.org. The "Chaucer Metapage" looks outdated as we write this in 2017, but many of its links still work. In the bibliographies that follow we include URLs for online resources; since life in cyberspace changes constantly and quickly, this information may well date equally fast.

INDEX OF BIBLIOGRAPHIES

MODERN EDITIONS AND FACSIMILES

Skeat, W. W., ed. *The Works of Geoffrey Chaucer.* 7 vols. Oxford: Clarendon P, 1894–97.

Manly, John M., and Edith Rickert, eds. *The Text of the* Canterbury Tales, *Studied on the Basis of All Known Manuscripts.* 8 vols. Chicago: U of Chicago P, 1940.

Robinson, F. N., ed. *The Works of Geoffrey Chaucer.* 2nd ed. Boston: Houghton Mifflin, 1957.

Baugh, Albert C., ed. *Chaucer's Major Poetry.* New York: Appleton-Century-Crofts, 1963.

Pratt, Robert A., ed. *The Tales of Canterbury.* Boston: Houghton Mifflin, 1974.

Donaldson, E. Talbot, ed. *Chaucer's Poetry: An Anthology for the Modern Reader.* 2nd ed. New York: Ronald Press, 1975.

Ruggiers, Paul G., and Donald C. Baker, eds. *The* Canterbury Tales: *A Facsimile and Transcription of the Hengwrt Manuscript, with Variants from the Ellesmere Manuscript.* Norman: U of Oklahoma P, 1979.

Benson, Larry D., gen. ed. *The Riverside Chaucer.* 3rd ed. Boston: Houghton Mifflin, 1987. Rpt. Oxford and New York: Oxford UP, 2008. Includes a full glossary.
Fisher, John H., ed. *The Complete Poetry and Prose of Geoffrey Chaucer.* New York: Holt, Rinehart and Winston, 1977. 2nd ed., 1989.
Hanna, Ralph, III, intro. *The Ellesmere Manuscript of Chaucer's* Canterbury Tales: *A Working Facsimile.* Rochester, NY: Boydell and Brewer, 1989.
Stubbs, Estelle, ed. *The Hengwrt Chaucer Digital Facsimile.* Leicester: Scholarly Digital Editions, 2000 [facsimiles and transcriptions of Hengwrt MS and Merthyr fragment of *The Canterbury Tales,* with marginalia].
Bowers, John M., ed. *The Canterbury Tales: Fifteenth-Century Continuations and Additions.* Kalamazoo: Medieval Institute Publications, 1992.
Woodward, Daniel, and Martin Stevens, eds. *The* Canterbury Tales *by Geoffrey Chaucer: The New Ellesmere Chaucer Facsimile.* San Marino, CA: Huntington Library, 1995.
———. *The* Canterbury Tales *by Geoffrey Chaucer: The New Ellesmere Chaucer Monochromatic Facsimile.* San Marino, CA: Huntington Library, 1997.
Partridge, Stephen. *The Manuscript Glosses to the* Canterbury Tales. Woodbridge, Suffolk: Boydell and Brewer, 2001.
Caxton's Chaucer. London: British Library, 2003. www.bl.uk/treasures/caxton/homepage.html [facsimiles of William Caxton's 1476 and 1483 editions of *The Canterbury Tales*].
Mann, Jill, ed. *The Canterbury Tales.* New York: Penguin, 2005. Includes a full glossary.
Fisher, John A., and Mark Allen, eds. *The Complete Canterbury Tales of Geoffrey Chaucer.* Boston: Thomson, 2006.
Boenig, Robert, and Andrew Taylor, eds. *The Canterbury Tales.* 2nd ed. Peterborough, Ontario, and Buffalo: Broadview P, 2012.
———. *The Canterbury Tales: A Selection.* 2nd ed. Peterborough, Ontario, and Buffalo: Broadview P, 2013.

TRANSLATIONS

Raffel, Burton, trans. *The Canterbury Tales.* New York: Modern Library, 2009.
Fisher, Sheila, trans. *The Selected Canterbury Tales: A New Verse Translation.* New York: Norton, 2011 [with Middle English text].
Wright, David, trans. *The Canterbury Tales.* Intro. Christopher Cannon. Oxford: Oxford UP, 2011.
Hopper, Vincent F., trans. *Chaucer's* Canterbury Tales (Selected): *An Interlinear Translation.* 1948. Rev. ed. Andrew Galloway. Hauppauge: Barron, 2012.
Harvard's *Geoffrey Chaucer Website.* chaucer.fas.harvard.edu. Click on "Canterbury Tales" and then on "Text and Translations." This online source offers interlinear translations for all of the verse tales and linking passages, using the Middle English text of the *Riverside Chaucer.* The translation of the *Tale of Melibee* is available both interlinearly and as an independent text. The *Parson's Tale,* followed by *Chaucer's Retraction,* appears in translation only; a full Middle English text is available in any complete edition of *The Canterbury Tales* listed above, notably the recent editions of Benson; Fisher and Allen; Mann; and Boenig and Taylor.

DICTIONARIES, GLOSSARIES, CONCORDANCES

Kurath, Hans, et al., eds. *Middle English Dictionary.* Ann Arbor: U of Michigan P, 1952–2001. Online edition accessible at quod.lib.umich.edu/m/med.
Tatlock, John S. P., and Arthur G. Kennedy. *A Concordance to the Complete Works of Chaucer and to the Romaunt of the Rose.* 1927. Gloucester: Peter Smith, 1963.
Davis, Norman, Douglas Gray, Patricia Ingham, and Anne Wallace-Hadrill. *A Chaucer Glossary.* Oxford: Clarendon P, 1979.
Oizumi, Akio, ed. Programmed by Kunihiro Miki. *A Complete Concordance to the Works of Geoffrey Chaucer.* 10 vols. New York: Olms-Weidmann, 1991.
Harvard's *Geoffrey Chaucer Website.* chaucer.fas.harvard.edu. Click on "Resources" and then on "Glossary."
Benson, Larry D. *A Glossarial DataBase of Middle English: Canterbury Tales.* hti.umich.edu/english/gloss/.
NeCastro, Gerard. *eChaucer: Chaucer in the Twenty-First Century.* ummutility.umm.maine.edu/necastro/chaucer/. The Concordance allows vocabulary searches of both individual tales and the entire *Canterbury Tales.*

CHAUCER'S LANGUAGE

Kökeritz, Helge. *A Guide to Chaucer's Pronunciation*. 1954. Toronto: U of Toronto P, 1978.
Burnley, David. *A Guide to Chaucer's Language*. Norman: U of Oklahoma P, 1983.
Sandved, Arthur O. *Introduction to Chaucerian English*. Cambridge: D. S. Brewer, 1985.
Blake, N. F., ed. *The Cambridge History of the English Language: Volume 2, 1066–1476*. Cambridge: Cambridge UP, 1992.
Burrow, J. A., and Thorlac Turville-Petre. *A Book of Middle English*. 2nd ed. Oxford: Basil Blackwell, 1996.
Fisher, John H. *The Emergence of Standard English*. Lexington: UP of Kentucky, 1996.
Cannon, Christopher. *The Making of Chaucer's English: A Study of Words*. Cambridge: Cambridge UP, 1998.
Trotter, D. A., ed. *Multilingualism in Later Medieval Britain*. Cambridge: D. S. Brewer, 2000.
Horobin, Simon. *Chaucer's Language*. Basingstoke and New York: Palgrave Macmillan, 2007.
Lerer, Seth. "Lord of This Langage. Chaucer's English." *Inventing English: A Portable History of the Language*. New York: Columbia UP, 2007. 70–84.
Butterfield, Ardis. *The Familiar Enemy: Chaucer, Language, and Nation in the Hundred Years War*. Oxford and New York: Oxford UP, 2009.
Yerkes, David. "Chaucer's Twelve 'Long' and 'Short' Vowels: The Evidence from the Rhymes in *Troilus and Criseyde*." *Chaucer Review* 45 (2011): 252–74.
Machan, Tim William. "Chaucer and the History of English." *Studies in Philology* 87 (2012): 147–76.

CHAUCER BIBLIOGRAPHIES

Allen, Mark, ed. "An Annotated Chaucer Bibliography." *Studies in the Age of Chaucer*. Annual bibliographies begin in volume 1 (1979). The complete Chaucer Bibliography Online, maintained by Allen, is a compilation of these; it offers thorough coverage of work on Chaucer (since 1975, easily accessible by subject heading, author, or title, at http://uchaucer.utsa.edu).
Hammond, Eleanor P. *Chaucer: A Bibliographic Manual*. 1908. New York: Peter Smith, 1933.
Griffith, Dudley D. *Bibliography of Chaucer 1908–1953*. Seattle: U of Washington P, 1955.
Crawford, William R. *Bibliography of Chaucer 1954–63*. Seattle: U of Washington P, 1967.
Baird, Lorrayne Y. *A Bibliography of Chaucer, 1964–73*. Boston: Hall, 1977.
Leyerle, John, and Anne Quick. *Chaucer: A Selected Bibliography*. Toronto: U of Toronto P, 1986.
Allen, Mark, and John H. Fisher. *The Essential Chaucer: An Annotated Bibliography of Major Modern Studies*. Boston: G. K. Hall, 1987.
Baird-Lange, Lorrayne Y., and Hildegard Schnuttgen. *A Bibliography of Chaucer, 1974–1985*. Hamden, CT: Archon, 1988.
Allen, Mark, and Bege K. Bowers. *Annotated Chaucer Bibliography, 1986–96*. Notre Dame: U of Notre Dame P, 2002.
———, and Stephanie Amsel. *Annotated Chaucer Bibliography: 1997–2010*. Manchester: Manchester UP, 2016.

SOURCES, BACKGROUNDS, BIOGRAPHIES

Bryan, W. F., and Germaine Dempster, eds. *Sources and Analogues of Chaucer's* Canterbury Tales. Chicago: U of Chicago P, 1941. Rpt. New York: Humanities Press, 1958.
Rickert, Edith. *Chaucer's World*. Ed. Clair C. Olson and Martin M. Crow. New York: Columbia UP, 1948.
Magoun, Francis P., Jr. *A Chaucer Gazetteer*. Chicago: U of Chicago P, 1961.
Loomis, Roger S. *A Mirror of Chaucer's World*. Princeton: Princeton UP, 1965.
Crow, Martin M., and Clair C. Olson, eds. *Chaucer Life-Records*. Austin: U of Texas P, 1966.
Benson, Larry D., and Theodore M. Andersson, eds. *The Literary Context of Chaucer's Fabliaux*. Indianapolis: Bobbs-Merrill, 1971.

Du Boulay, F. R. H. "The Historical Chaucer." *Writers and Their Background: Geoffrey Chaucer.* Ed. Derek Brewer. Athens: Ohio UP, 1975. 33–57.

Brewer, Derek. *Chaucer and His World.* New York: Dodd, Mead, 1977. 2nd ed. 1992.

Miller, Robert P., ed. *Chaucer: Sources and Backgrounds.* New York: Oxford UP, 1977.

Howard, Donald R. *Chaucer: His Life, His Work, His World.* New York: E. P. Dutton, 1987.

Besserman, Lawrence. *Chaucer and the Bible: A Critical Review of Research, Indices, and Bibliography.* New York: Garland, 1988.

De Weever, Jacqueline. *A Chaucer Name Dictionary: Guide to Astrological, Literary, and Mythological Names in the Works of Geoffrey Chaucer.* New York: Garland, 1988. Rpt. London and New York: Routledge, 2013.

Blamires, Alcuin, ed., with Karen Pratt and C. W. Marx. *Woman Defamed and Woman Defended: An Anthology of Medieval Texts.* Oxford: Clarendon P, 1992.

Pearsall, Derek. *The Life of Geoffrey Chaucer: A Critical Biography.* Oxford: Blackwell, 1992.

Ashby, Cristina, Geoff Couldrey, and Susan Dickson. *Chaucer: Life and Times.* CD-ROM. Woodbridge, CT: Primary Source Media, 1995 [provides access to searchable texts, translations, glossary, critical essays, images, and other background information].

Foster, Edward E., and David H. Carey. *Chaucer's Church: A Dictionary of Religious Terms in Chaucer.* Aldershot, Hants., and Burlington, VT: Ashgate, 2002.

Correale, Robert M., gen. ed., with Mary Hamel. *Sources and Analogues of the* Canterbury Tales. 2 vols. Woodbridge, Suffolk, and Rochester, NY: D. S. Brewer, 2002–2005.

Andrew, Malcolm. *The Palgrave Literary Dictionary of Chaucer.* Basingstoke and New York: Palgrave Macmillan, 2006.

Amtower, Laurel, and Jacqueline Vanhoutte, eds. *A Companion to Chaucer and His Contemporaries: Texts and Contexts.* Peterborough, Ontario: Broadview P, 2009.

Collette, Carolyn P., and Harold Garrett-Goodyear, eds. *The Later Middle Ages: A Sourcebook.* Basingstoke and New York: Palgrave Macmillan, 2011.

Barron, Caroline M. "Chaucer the Poet and Chaucer the Pilgrim." *Historians on Chaucer: The 'General Prologue' to the* Canterbury Tales. Ed. Stephen H. Rigby, with Alastair Minnis. Oxford: Oxford UP, 2014. 24–41.

Strohm, Paul. *Chaucer's Tale: 1386 and the Road to Canterbury.* New York: Viking, 2014.

COLLECTIONS OF CRITICAL ESSAYS

Burrow, J. A., ed. *Geoffrey Chaucer: A Critical Anthology.* Baltimore: Penguin, 1969.

Arrathoon, Leigh A., ed. *Chaucer and the Craft of Fiction.* Rochester, MI: Solaris Press, 1986.

Fein, Susanna Greer, David Raybin, and Peter C. Braeger, eds. *Rebels and Rivals: The Contestive Spirit in* The Canterbury Tales. Kalamazoo: Medieval Institute Publications, Western Michigan U, 1991.

Benson, C. David, and Elizabeth Robertson, eds. *Chaucer's Religious Tales.* Cambridge: D. S. Brewer, 1990.

Andrew, Malcolm, ed. *Critical Essays on Chaucer's Canterbury Tales.* Toronto: U of Toronto P, 1991.

Stevens, Martin, and Daniel Woodward, eds. *The Ellesmere Chaucer: Essays in Interpretation.* San Marino, CA: Huntington Library, 1997.

Beidler, Peter G., ed. *Masculinities in Chaucer: Approaches to Maleness in the* Canterbury Tales *and* Troilus and Criseyde. Cambridge: D. S. Brewer, 1998.

Brown, Peter, ed. *A Companion to Chaucer.* Oxford: Blackwell, 2000.

Koff, Leonard Michael, and Brenda Deen Schildgen, eds. *The Decameron and the Canterbury Tales: New Essays on an Old Question.* Madison, NJ: Fairleigh Dickinson UP, 2000.

Saunders, Corinne, ed. *Chaucer.* Blackwell Guides to Criticism. Oxford: Blackwell, 2000.

Yeager, Robert F., and Charlotte C. Morse, eds. *Speaking Images: Essays in Honor of V. A. Kolve.* Asheville, NC: Pegasus P, 2001.

Lynch, Kathryn L., ed. *Chaucer's Cultural Geography.* London and New York: Routledge, 2002.

Boitani, Piero, and Jill Mann, eds. *The Cambridge Chaucer Companion.* Cambridge: Cambridge UP, 1986. *The Cambridge Companion to Chaucer.* 2nd ed. 2003.

Delany, Sheila, ed. *Chaucer and the Jews: Sources, Contexts, Meanings.* New York and London: Routledge, 2002.
Ellis, Steve, ed. *Chaucer: An Oxford Guide*. Oxford: Oxford UP, 2005.
Burton, T. L., and John F. Plummer, eds. *"Seyd in forme and reverence": Essays on Chaucer and Chaucerians in Memory of Emerson Brown, Jr.* Provo, UT: Chaucer Studio P, 2006.
Butterfield, Ardis, ed. *Chaucer and the City.* Cambridge: D. S. Brewer/Boydell and Brewer, 2006.
Lerer, Seth, ed. *The Yale Companion to Chaucer.* New Haven and London: Yale UP, 2006.
Patterson, Lee, ed. *Geoffrey Chaucer's* The Canterbury Tales*: A Casebook*. Oxford and New York: Oxford UP, 2007.
Epstein, Robert, and William Robins, eds. *Sacred and Profane in Chaucer and Late Medieval Literature: Essays in Honour of John V. Fleming.* Toronto: U of Toronto P, 2010.
Fein, Susanna Greer, and David Raybin, eds. *Chaucer: Contemporary Approaches.* University Park, PA: Pennsylvania State UP, 2010.
Phillips, Helen, ed. *Chaucer and Religion.* Cambridge and Rochester, NY: D. S. Brewer/Boydell and Brewer, 2010.
Carney, Clíodhna, and Frances McCormack, eds. *Chaucer's Poetry: Words, Authority and Ethics.* Dublin and Portland, OR: Four Courts P, 2013.
Travis, Peter W., and Frank Grady, eds. *Approaches to Teaching Chaucer's* Canterbury Tales. 2nd ed. New York: Modern Language Association of America, 2014.

GENERAL CRITICAL STUDIES

Kittredge, George Lyman. *Chaucer and His Poetry.* Cambridge, MA: Harvard UP, 1915, 1970.
Baldwin, Ralph. *The Unity of the* Canterbury Tales. *Anglistica* 5. Copenhagen: Rosenkilde and Bagger, 1955.
Muscatine, Charles. *Chaucer and the French Tradition.* Berkeley: U of California P, 1957.
Robertson, D. W., Jr. *A Preface to Chaucer: Studies in Medieval Perspectives.* Princeton: Princeton UP, 1963.
Jordan, Robert M. *Chaucer and the Shape of Creation: The Aesthetic Possibilities of Inorganic Structure.* Cambridge: Harvard UP, 1967.
Burrow, J. A. *Ricardian Poetry.* New Haven: Yale UP, 1971.
David, Alfred. *The Strumpet Muse: Art and Morals in Chaucer's Poetry.* Bloomington: Indiana UP, 1976.
Howard, Donald R. *The Idea of the* Canterbury Tales. Berkeley: U of California P, 1976.
Owen, Charles A., Jr. *Pilgrimage and Storytelling in the* Canterbury Tales. Norman: U of Oklahoma P, 1977.
Middleton, Anne. "Chaucer's 'New Men' and the Good of Literature in the *Canterbury Tales." Literature and Society. Selected Papers from the English Institute.* Ed. Edward W. Said. Baltimore: The Johns Hopkins UP, 1980. 15–56.
Benson, Larry D. "The Order of *The Canterbury Tales." Studies in the Age of Chaucer* 3 (1981): 77–120. Rpt. in *Contradictions: From* Beowulf *to Chaucer: Selected Studies of Larry D. Benson.* Ed. Theodore M. Andersson and Stephen A. Barney. Aldershot, Hants: Scolar, 1995.
Olson, Glending. *Literature as Recreation in the Later Middle Ages.* Ithaca and London: Cornell UP, 1982.
Kolve, V. A. *Chaucer and the Imagery of Narrative: The First Five* Canterbury Tales. Stanford: Stanford UP, 1984. *Telling Images: Chaucer and the Imagery of Narrative II*. Stanford: Stanford UP, 2009.
Bowers, John M. *"The Tale of Beryn* and *The Siege of Thebes:* Alternative Ideas of *The Canterbury Tales." Studies in the Age of Chaucer* 7 (1985): 23–50.
Ferster, Judith. *Chaucer on Interpretation.* Cambridge: Cambridge UP, 1985.
Pearsall, Derek. *The* Canterbury Tales. London: Allen & Unwin, 1985.
Aers, David. *Chaucer.* Atlantic Highlands, NJ: Humanities Press International, 1986.
Benson, C. David. *Chaucer's Drama of Style: Poetic Variety and Contrast in the* Canterbury Tales. Chapel Hill: U of North Carolina P, 1986.
Ellis, Roger. *Patterns of Religious Narrative in the* Canterbury Tales. Totowa, NJ: Barnes & Noble, 1986.
Knight, Stephen. *Geoffrey Chaucer.* Oxford: Blackwell, 1986.

Olson, Paul A. *The* Canterbury Tales *and the Good Society.* Princeton: Princeton UP, 1986.

Howard, Donald R. *Chaucer: His Life, His Works, His World.* New York: E. P. Dutton, 1987.

Jordan, Robert M. *Chaucer's Poetics and the Modern Reader.* Berkeley: U of California P, 1987.

Lindahl, Carl. *Earnest Games: Folkloric Patterns in the Canterbury Tales.* Bloomington: Indiana UP, 1987.

Patterson, Lee. *Negotiating the Past: The Historical Understanding of Medieval Literature.* Madison: U of Wisconsin P, 1987.

Kendrick, Laura. *Chaucerian Play: Comedy and Control in the* Canterbury Tales. Berkeley: U of California P, 1988.

Koff, Leonard Michael. *Chaucer and the Art of Storytelling.* Berkeley: U of California P, 1988.

• Dinshaw, Carolyn. *Chaucer's Sexual Poetics.* Madison: U of Wisconsin P, 1989.

• Strohm, Paul. *Social Chaucer.* Cambridge, MA: Harvard UP, 1989.

• Wetherbee, Winthrop. *Chaucer: The Canterbury Tales.* Cambridge: Cambridge UP, 1989; 2nd ed. 2004.

Ganim, John M. *Chaucerian Theatricality.* Princeton: Princeton UP, 1990.

Georgianna, Linda. "The Protestant Chaucer." *Chaucer's Religious Tales.* Ed. C. David Benson and Elizabeth Robertson. Cambridge: D. S. Brewer, 1990. 55–69.

• Keen, Maurice. *English Society in the Later Middle Ages 1348–1500.* London: Allen Lane/The Penguin P, 1990.

Knapp, Peggy. *Chaucer and the Social Contest.* New York: Routledge, 1990.

Leicester, H. Marshall, Jr. *The Disenchanted Self: Representing the Subject in the* Canterbury Tales. Berkeley: U of California P, 1990.

Brown, Peter, and Andrew Butcher. *The Age of Saturn: Literature and History in the Canterbury Tales.* Oxford: Basil Blackwell, 1991.

Hill, John M. *Chaucerian Belief: The Poetics of Reverence and Delight.* New Haven: Yale UP, 1991.

Kiser, Lisa J. *Truth and Textuality in Chaucer's Poetry.* Hanover, NH: UP of New England, 1991.

• Mann, Jill. *Geoffrey Chaucer.* Feminist Readings. Atlantic Heights, NJ: Humanities Press International, 1991. New ed. *Feminizing Chaucer.* Rochester, NY: D. S. Brewer, 2002.

Patterson, Lee. *Chaucer and the Subject of History.* Madison: U of Wisconsin P, 1991.

Hansen, Elaine Tuttle. *Chaucer and the Fictions of Gender.* Berkeley: U of California P, 1992.

Lerer, Seth. *Chaucer and His Readers: Imagining the Author in Late-Medieval England.* Princeton: Princeton UP, 1993.

Brown, Peter. *Chaucer at Work: The Making of the* Canterbury Tales. New York: Longman, 1994.

Crane, Susan. *Gender and Romance in Chaucer's* Canterbury Tales. Princeton: Princeton UP, 1994.

• Cooper, Helen. *Oxford Guides to Chaucer: The Canterbury Tales.* New York: Oxford UP, 1989. 2nd ed. 1996.

Wallace, David. *Chaucerian Polity: Absolutist Lineages and Associational Forms in England and Italy.* Stanford: Stanford UP, 1997.

Condren, Edward I. *Chaucer and the Energy of Creation: The Design and Organization of the Canterbury Tales.* Gainesville: UP of Florida, 1999.

Dinshaw, Carolyn. *Getting Medieval: Sexualities and Communities, Pre- and Postmodern.* Durham: Duke UP, 1999.

Olson, Glending. "Geoffrey Chaucer." *The Cambridge History of Medieval English Literature.* Ed. David Wallace. Cambridge: Cambridge UP, 1999. 566–88.

Bowers, John M. "Chaucer after Smithfield: From Postcolonial Writer to Imperialist Author." *The Postcolonial Middle Ages.* Ed. Jeffrey Jerome Cohen. New York: St. Martin's P, 2000. 53–66.

Ellis, Steve. *Chaucer at Large: The Poet in the Modern Imagination.* Minneapolis: U of Minnesota P, 2000.

Phillips, Helen. *An Introduction to the* Canterbury Tales: *Fiction, Writing, Context.* New York: St. Martin's P, 2000.

Collette, Carolyn P. *Species, Phantasms, and Images: Vision and Medieval Psychology in "The Canterbury Tales."* Ann Arbor, MI: U of Michigan P, 2001.

Schildgen, Brenda Deen. *Pagans, Tartars, Moslems and Jews in Chaucer's Canterbury Tales."* Tampa: U of South Florida P, 2001.

Shoaf, R. Allen. *Chaucer's Body: The Anxiety of Circulation in the* Canterbury Tales. Gainesville: UP of Florida, 2001.

Hirsh, John. *Chaucer and the* Canterbury Tales*: A Short Introduction*. Oxford: Blackwell Publishers, 2002.
Trigg, Stephanie. *Congenial Souls: Reading Chaucer from Medieval to Postmodern*. Minneapolis: U of Minnesota P, 2002.
Burger, Glenn. *Chaucer's Queer Nation*. Minneapolis: U of Minnesota P, 2003.
Fletcher, Alan J. "Chaucer the Heretic." *Studies in the Age of Chaucer* 25 (2003): 53–121.
Mitchell, J. Allan. *Ethics and Exemplary Narrative in Chaucer and Gower*. Cambridge and Rochester, NY: D. S. Brewer/Boydell and Brewer, 2004.
Miller, Mark. *Philosophical Chaucer: Love, Sex, and Agency in the* Canterbury Tales. Cambridge: Cambridge UP, 2005.
Spearing, A. C. *Textual Subjectivity: The Encoding of Subjectivity in Medieval Narratives and Lyrics*. Oxford and New York: Oxford UP, 2005.
Blamires, Alcuin. *Chaucer, Ethics, and Gender*. Oxford and New York: Oxford UP, 2006.
Patterson, Lee. *Temporal Circumstances: Form and History in the* Canterbury Tales. New York: Palgrave Macmillan, 2006.
Brown, Peter. *Chaucer and the Making of Optical Space*. Oxford: Peter Lang, 2007.
Turner, Marion. *Chaucerian Conflict: Languages of Antagonism in Late Fourteenth-Century London*. Oxford: Clarendon P; New York: Oxford UP, 2007.
Foster, Michael. *Chaucer's Narrators and the Rhetoric of Self-Representation*. Oxford: Peter Lang, 2008.
Knapp, Peggy A. *Chaucerian Aesthetics*. New York: Palgrave Macmillan, 2008.
Woods, William F. *Chaucerian Spaces: Spatial Poetics in Chaucer's Opening Tales*. Albany: State U of New York P, 2008.
Gust, Geoffrey W. *Constructing Chaucer: Author and Autofiction in the Critical Tradition*. New York: Palgrave, 2009.
Heffernan, Carol Falvo. *Comedy in Chaucer and Boccaccio*. Cambridge: D. S. Brewer, 2009.
Cawsey, Kathy. *Twentieth-Century Chaucer Criticism: Reading Audiences*. Farnham, Surrey, and Burlington, VT: Ashgate, 2011.
Clarke, K. P. *Chaucer and Italian Textuality*. New York and Oxford: Oxford UP, 2011.
Higl, Andrew. *Playing the* Canterbury Tales*: The Continuations and Additions*. Farnham, Surrey, and Burlington, VT: Ashgate, 2012.
McTaggart, Anne. *Shame and Guilt in Chaucer*. New York: Palgrave Macmillan, 2012.
Pitcher, John A. *Chaucer's Feminine Subjects: Figures of Desire in the* Canterbury Tales. New York: Palgrave Macmillan, 2012.
Spearing, A. C. *Medieval Autographies: The "I" of the Text*. Notre Dame: U of Notre Dame P, 2012.
Meyer-Lee, Robert J. "Abandon the Fragments." *Studies in the Age of Chaucer* 35 (2013): 47–83.
Bahr, Arthur. "Constructing Compilations of Chaucer's *Canterbury Tales*." *Fragments and Assemblages: Forming Compilations of Medieval London*. Chicago: U of Chicago P, 2013. 155–207.
Minnis, Alastair. *The Cambridge Introduction to Chaucer*. Cambridge: Cambridge UP, 2014.

THE GENERAL PROLOGUE

Bowden, Muriel. *A Commentary on the General Prologue to the* Canterbury Tales. New York: Macmillan, 1948.
Cunningham, J. V. "The Literary Form of the Prologue to the *Canterbury Tales*." *Modern Philology* 49 (1952): 172–81.
• Donaldson, E. Talbot. "Chaucer the Pilgrim." *PMLA* 69 (1954): 928–36. Rpt. in *Speaking of Chaucer*. New York: W. W. Norton & Company, 1970, 1–12.
• Hoffman, Arthur W. "Chaucer's Prologue to Pilgrimage: The Two Voices." *ELH: A Journal of English Literary History* 21 (1954): 1–16.
Brooks, Harold F. *Chaucer's Pilgrims: The Artistic Order of the Portraits in the* Prologue. London: Methuen, 1962.
Jordan, Robert M. "Chaucer's Sense of Illusion: Roadside Drama Reconsidered." *ELH: A Journal of English Literary History* 29 (1962): 19–33.
Mann, Jill. *Chaucer and Medieval Estates Satire*. Cambridge: Cambridge UP, 1973.
Sumption, Jonathan. *Pilgrimage: An Image of Mediaeval Religion*. Totowa, NJ: Rowman and Littlefield, 1975.

Zacher, Christian K. *Curiosity and Pilgrimage: The Literature of Discovery in Fourteenth-Century England.* Baltimore: The Johns Hopkins UP, 1976.
Leicester, H. Marshall, Jr. "The Art of Impersonation: A General Prologue to the *Canterbury Tales.*" *PMLA* 95 (1980): 213–24.
Eberle, Patricia J. "Commercial Language and the Commercial Outlook in the *General Prologue.*" *Chaucer Review* 18 (1983): 161–74.
Nolan, Barbara. "'A Poet Ther Was': Chaucer's Voices in the General Prologue to *The Canterbury Tales.*" *PMLA* 101 (1986): 154–69.
Cooper, Helen. "Langland's and Chaucer's Prologues." *Yearbook of Langland Studies* 1 (1987): 71–81.
Eckhardt, Caroline D. *Chaucer's* General Prologue *to the* Canterbury Tales: *An Annotated Bibliography, 1900–1984.* Toronto: U of Toronto P, 1990.
Georgianna, Linda. "Love So Dearly Bought: The Terms of Redemption in *The Canterbury Tales.*" *Studies in the Age of Chaucer* 12 (1990): 85–116.
Leicester, H. Marshall, Jr. "Structure as Deconstruction: 'Chaucer and Estates Satire' in the *General Prologue.*" *Exemplaria* 2 (1990): 241–61.
Andrew, Malcolm, Charles Moorman, and Daniel J. Ransom, eds., with Lynne Hunt Levy. *The General Prologue.* 2 vols. The Variorum Chaucer, II:IA and IB. Norman: U of Oklahoma P, 1993.
Lambdin, Laura C., and Robert T. Lambdin, eds. *Chaucer's Pilgrims: An Historical Guide to the Pilgrims in the* Canterbury Tales. Westport: Greenwood, 1996.
Stevens, Martin, and Daniel Woodward, eds. *The Ellesmere Chaucer: Essays in Interpretation.* San Marino, CA: Huntington Library, 1997 [essays on pilgrim portraits by Betsy Bowden, Richard K. Emmerson, and Alan T. Gaylord].
Bowers, John M. "Chaucer's Canterbury Tales—Politically Corrected." *Rewriting Chaucer: Culture, Authority, and the Idea of the Authentic Text, 1400–1602.* Ed. Thomas A. Prendergast and Barbara Kline. Columbus: Ohio State UP, 1999. 13–44.
Blamires, Alcuin. "Chaucer the Reactionary: Ideology and the 'General Prologue' to *The Canterbury Tales.*" *Review of English Studies* ns 51 [204] (2000): 523–39.
Hodges, Laura F. *Chaucer and Costume: The Secular Pilgrims in the General Prologue.* Cambridge: D. S. Brewer, 2000.
Solopova, Elizabeth, ed. *The General Prologue on CD-ROM.* Cambridge: Cambridge UP, 2000 [digital images and transcriptions of manuscripts and early printed editions, with a user guide, databases, and essays].
Dyas, Dee. *Pilgrimage in Medieval English Literature 700–1500.* Cambridge: D. S. Brewer, 2001.
Hodges, Laura F. *Chaucer and Clothing: Clerical and Academic Costume in the General Prologue to* The Canterbury Tales. Cambridge: Brewer, 2005.
Farrell, Thomas J. "Hybrid Discourse in the *General Prologue* Portraits." *Studies in the Age of Chaucer* 30 (2008): 39–93.
Mack, Peter, and Chris Walton, eds. *General Prologue to the Canterbury Tales, by Geoffrey Chaucer.* Rev. ed. Oxford: Oxford UP, 2008.
Rigby, Stephen H., ed., with Alastair Minnis. *Historians on Chaucer: The 'General Prologue' to the* Canterbury Tales. Oxford: Oxford UP, 2014.
Carlin, Martha. "The Host." *Historians on Chaucer: The 'General Prologue' to the* Canterbury Tales. Ed. Stephen H. Rigby, with Alastair Minnis. Oxford: Oxford UP, 2014. 460–80.

THE KNIGHT AND HIS TALE

Muscatine, Charles. "Form, Texture, and Meaning in Chaucer's *Knight's Tale.*" *PMLA* 65 (1950): 911–29.
Owen, Charles A., Jr. "Chaucer's *Canterbury Tales:* Aesthetic Design in the Stories of the First Day." *English Studies* 35 (1954): 49–56.
Salter, Elizabeth. *Chaucer: The* Knight's Tale *and the* Clerk's Tale. London: Edward Arnold, 1962.
Hanning, Robert W. "'The Struggle between Noble Design and Chaos': The Literary Tradition of Chaucer's *Knight's Tale.*" *Literary Review* 23 (1980): 519–41.
Jones, Terry. *Chaucer's Knight: The Portrait of a Medieval Mercenary.* 1980. 2nd. ed. London: Methuen, 1994.
Minnis, A. J. *Chaucer and Pagan Antiquity.* Woodbridge, Suffolk: Boydell and Brewer, 1982.
Burrow, J. A. "Chaucer's *Knight's Tale* and the Three Ages of Man." *Essays on Medieval Literature.* Oxford: Clarendon P, 1984. 27–48.

Kolve, V. A. "*The Knight's Tale* and Its Settings: The Prison/Garden and the Tournament Amphitheatre." *Chaucer and the Imagery of Narrative.* Stanford: Stanford UP, 1984. 85–157.

Fowler, Elizabeth. "The Afterlife of the Civil Dead: Conquest in the Knight's Tale." *Critical Essays on Geoffrey Chaucer.* Ed. Thomas C. Stillinger. New York: G. K. Hall, 1987. 59–81.

Leicester, H. Marshall, Jr. "The Institution of the Subject: A Reading of the *Knight's Tale.*" *The Disenchanted Self: Representing the Subject in the* Canterbury Tales. Berkeley: U of California P, 1990. 219–382.

Wetherbee, Winthrop. "Romance and Epic in Chaucer's *Knight's Tale.*" *Exemplaria* 2 (1990): 303–28.

McAlpine, Monica. *Chaucer's Knight's Tale: An Annotated Bibliography 1900–1985.* Toronto: U of Toronto P, 1991.

Nolan, Barbara. *Chaucer and the Tradition of the Roman Antique.* Cambridge: Cambridge UP, 1992.

Fradenburg, Louise O. "Sacrificial Desire in Chaucer's *Knight's Tale.*" *Journal of Medieval and Early Modern Studies* 27 (1997): 47–75. Rpt. in L. O. Aranye Fradenburg, *Sacrifice Your Love: Psychoanalysis, Historicism, Chaucer.* Minneapolis: U of Minnesota P, 2002. 155–75.

Ingham, Patricia Clare. "Homosociality and Creative Masculinity in the Knight's Tale." *Masculinities in Chaucer: Approaches to Maleness in the* Canterbury Tales *and* Troilus and Criseyde. Ed. Peter G. Beidler. Cambridge: D. S. Brewer, 1998. 23–35.

Pratt, John H. *Chaucer and War.* Lanham, MD: UP of America, 2000.

Jones, Terry. "The Image of Chaucer's Knight." *Speaking Images: Essays in Honor of V. A. Kolve.* Ed. Robert F. Yeager and Charlotte C. Morse. Asheville, NC: Pegasus P, 2001. 205–36.

Morgan, Gerald. "The Worthiness of Chaucer's Worthy Knight." *Chaucer Review* 44 (2009): 115–58.

Rack, Melissa J. "'I nam no divinistre': Heterodoxy and Disjunction in Chaucer's *Knight's Tale.*" *Medieval Perspectives* 25 (2010): 89–102.

Grimes, Jodi. "Arboreal Politics in the *Knight's Tale.*" *Chaucer Review* 47 (2012): 340–64.

Withers, Jeremy. "'A beest may al his lust fulfille': Naturalizing Chivalric Violence in Chaucer's *Knight's Tale.*" *Rethinking Chaucerian Beasts.* Ed. Carolynn Van Dyke. Basingstoke and New York: Palgrave Macmillan, 2012. 173–84.

Fumo, Jamie C. "The Pestilential Gaze: From Epidemiology to Erotomania in *The Knight's Tale.*" *Studies in the Age of Chaucer* 35 (2013): 85–136.

Rigby, Stephen H. "The Knight." *Historians on Chaucer: The 'General Prologue' to the* Canterbury Tales. Ed. Stephen H. Rigby, with Alastair Minnis. Oxford: Oxford UP, 2014. 42–62.

Corrigan, Nora. "The Knight's Earnest Game in Chaucer's *The Canterbury Tales.*" *Games and Gaming in Medieval Literature.* Ed. Serina Patterson. Basingstoke and New York: Palgrave Macmillan, 2015. 147–68.

THE MILLER AND HIS TALE

Donaldson, E. Talbot. "Idiom of Popular Poetry in the *Miller's Tale.*" *English Institute Essays 1950.* Ed. Alan S. Downer. New York: Columbia UP, 1951. 116–40.

Harder, Kelsie B. "Chaucer's Use of the Mystery Plays in the *Miller's Tale.*" *Modern Language Quarterly* 17 (1956): 193–98.

Olson, Paul A. "Poetic Justice in the *Miller's Tale.*" *Modern Language Quarterly* 24 (1963): 227–36.

Rowland, Beryl. "The Play of the *Miller's Tale:* A Game Within a Game." *Chaucer Review* 5 (1970): 140–46.

Beidler, Peter G. "Art and Scatology in the *Miller's Tale.*" *Chaucer Review* 12 (1977): 90–102.

Ross, Thomas W., ed. *The Miller's Tale.* The Variorum Chaucer, II:3. Norman: U of Oklahoma P, 1983.

Kolve, V. A. "The Miller's Tale: Nature, Youth, and Nowell's Flood." *Chaucer and the Imagery of Narrative.* Stanford: Stanford UP, 1984. 158–216.

Patterson, Lee. "'No Man His Reson Herde': Peasant Consciousness, Chaucer's Miller, and the Structure of the *Canterbury Tales.*" *South Atlantic Quarterly* 86 (1987): 457–95. Rpt. as "The *Miller's Tale* and the Politics of Laughter" in *Chaucer and the Subject of History.* Madison: U of Wisconsin P, 1991. 244–79.

Farrell, Thomas J. "Privacy and the Boundaries of Fabliau in the *Miller's Tale.*" *ELH* 56 (1989): 773–95.

Lochrie, Karma. "Women's 'Pryvetees' and Fabliau Politics in the *Miller's Tale.*" *Exemplaria* 6 (1994): 287–304.

Burton, T. L., and Rosemary Greentree, eds. *Chaucer's* Miller's, Reeve's, *and* Cook's Tales. Chaucer Bibliographies. Toronto: U of Toronto P, 1997.

Miller, Mark. "Naturalism and Its Discontents in the *Miller's Tale.*" *ELH* 67 (2000): 1–44.

Mann, Jill. "Speaking Images in Chaucer's 'Miller's Tale.'" *Speaking Images: Essays in Honor of V. A. Kolve.* Ed. Robert F. Yeager and Charlotte C. Morse. Asheville, NC: Pegasus P. 2001. 237–53.

Nolan, Barbara. "Playing Parts: Fragments, Figures and the Mystery of Love in "The Miller's Tale.'" *Speaking Images: Essays in Honor of V. A. Kolve.* Ed. Robert F. Yeager and Charlotte C. Morse. Asheville, NC: Pegasus P, 2001. 255–99.

Bullón-Fernández, María. "Private Practices in Chaucer's *Miller's Tale.*" *Studies in the Age of Chaucer* 28 (2006): 141–74.

Blamires, Alcuin. "Philosophical Sleaze? The 'Strok of Thoght' in the Miller's Tale and Chaucerian Fabliau." *Modern Language Review* 102 (2007): 621–40.

Heyworth, Gregory. "Ineloquent Ends: *Simplicitas*, Proctolalia, and the Profane Vernacular in the Miller's Tale." *Speculum* 84 (2009): 956–83.

Knight, Stephen. "'Toward the fen': Church and Churl in Chaucer's Fabliaux." *Chaucer and Religion.* Ed. Helen Phillips. Cambridge: D. A. Brewer, 2010. 41–51.

Morgan, Gerald. "Obscenity and Fastidiousness in The Miller's Tale." *English Studies* 91 (2010): 492–518.

Stanbury, Sarah. "Derrida's Cat and Nicholas's Study." *New Medieval Literatures* 12 (2010): 155–67.

Freedman, Paul. "The Miller." *Historians on Chaucer: The 'General Prologue' to the* Canterbury Tales. Ed. Stephen H. Rigby, with Alastair Minnis. Oxford: Oxford UP, 2014. 368–85.

THE REEVE AND HIS TALE

Tolkien, J. R. R. "Chaucer as a Philologist: *The Reeve's Tale.*" *Transactions of the Philological Society* (1934): 1–70.

Copland, Murray. "*The Reeve's Tale*: Harlotrie or Sermonyng?" *Medium Aevum* 31 (1962): 14–32.

Olson, Paul A. "The *Reeve's Tale*: Chaucer's *Measure for Measure.*" *Studies in Philology* 59 (1962): 1–17.

Delany, Sheila. "Clerks and Quiting in the *Reeve's Tale.*" *Mediaeval Studies* 29 (1967): 351–56.

Friedman, John B. "A Reading of Chaucer's *Reeve's Tale.*" *Chaucer Review* 2 (1967): 8–19.

Brewer, Derek. "The *Reeve's Tale* and the King's Hall, Cambridge." *Chaucer Review* 5 (1971): 311–17.

Plummer, John F. "'Hooly Chirches Blood': Simony and Patrimony in Chaucer's *Reeve's Tale.*" *Chaucer Review* 18 (1983): 49–60.

Burton, T. L., and Rosemary Greentree, eds. *Chaucer's* Miller's, Reeve's, *and* Cook's Tales. Chaucer Bibliographies. Toronto: U of Toronto P, 1997.

Kolve, V. A. "The Reeve's Prologue and Tale: Death-as-Tapster and the Horse Unbridled." *Chaucer and the Imagery of Narrative.* Stanford: Stanford UP, 1984. 217–56.

Fein, Susanna Greer. "'Lat the Children Pleye': The Game Betwixt the Ages in The Reeve's Tale." *Rebels and Rivals: The Contestive Spirit in* The Canterbury Tales. Ed. Susanna Greer Fein, David Raybin, and Peter C. Braeger. Kalamazoo: Medieval Institute Publications, 1991. 73–104.

Harwood, Britton J. "Psychoanalytic Politics: Chaucer and Two Peasants." *ELH* 68 (2000): 1–27.

Crocker, Holly A. "Affective Politics in Chaucer's *Reeve's Tale*: 'Cherl' Masculinity After 1381." *Studies in the Age of Chaucer* 29 (2007): 225–58.

Epstein, Robert. "'Fer in the north; I kan nat telle where': Dialect, Regionalism, and Philologism." *Studies in the Age of Chaucer* 30 (2008): 95–124.

Sidhu, Nicole Nolan. "'To Late for to Crie': Female Desire, Fabliau Politics, and Classical Legend in Chaucer's Reeve's Tale." *Exemplaria* 21 (2009): 3–23.

Taylor, Joseph. "Chaucer's Uncanny Regionalism: Rereading the North in *The Reeve's Tale.*" *Journal of English and Germanic Philology* 109 (2010): 468–89.

Stone, David. "The Reeve." *Historians on Chaucer: The 'General Prologue' to the* Canterbury Tales. Ed. Stephen H. Rigby, with Alastair Minnis. Oxford: Oxford UP, 2014. 399–420.

THE COOK AND HIS TALE

Stanley, E. G. "'Of this cokes tale maked Chaucer na moore.'" *Poetica* (Tokyo) 5 (1976): 36–59.

Kolve, V. A. "The Cook's Tale and the Man of Law's Introduction: Crossing the Hengwrt/Ellesmere Gap." *Chaucer and the Imagery of Narrative*. Stanford: Stanford UP, 1984. 257–96.

Scattergood, V. J. "Perkyn Revelour and the *Cook's Tale*." *Chaucer Review* 19 (1984): 14–23. Rpt. in *Reading the Past: Essays on Medieval and Renaissance Literature*. Portland, OR: Four Courts P, 1996. 83–91.

Burton, T. L., and Rosemary Greentree, eds. *Chaucer's* Miller's, Reeve's, *and* Cook's Tales. Chaucer Bibliographies. Toronto: U of Toronto P, 1997.

Wallace, David. "Chaucer and the Absent City." *Chaucer's England: Literature in Historical Context*. Ed. Barbara A. Hanawalt. Minneapolis: U of Minnesota P, 1991. 59–90. Rpt. in *Chaucerian Polity* (Stanford: Stanford UP, 1997). 156–81.

Strohm, Paul. "'Lad with Revel to Newegate': Chaucerian Narrative and Historical Meta-Narrative." *Art and Context in Late Medieval English Narrative: Essays in Honor of Robert Worth Frank, Jr.* Ed. Robert R. Edwards. Cambridge: D. S. Brewer. 1994. 163–76. Rpt. in *Theory and the Premodern Text*. Minneapolis: U of Minnesota P, 2000. 51–64.

Kang, Ji-Soo. "The (In)completeness of the Cook's Tale." *Medieval English Studies* 5 (1997): 145–70.

Bertolet, Craig E. "'Wel Bet is Roten Appul Out of Hoord': Chaucer's Cook, Commerce, and Civic Order." *Studies in Philology* 99 (2002): 229–46.

Casey, Jim. "Unfinished Business: The Termination of Chaucer's *Cook's Tale*." *Chaucer Review* 41 (2006): 185–96.

Fulton, Helen. "Cheapside in the Age of Chaucer." *Medieval Cultural Studies: Essays in Honour of Stephen Knight*. Eds. Ruth Evans, Helen Fulton, and David Matthews. Cardiff: U of Wales P, 2006. 138–51.

Pigg, Daniel F. "Imagining Urban Life and Its Discontents: Chaucer's Cook's Tale and Masculine Identity." *Urban Space in the Middle Ages and the Early Modern Age*. Ed. Albrecht Classen. New York: Walter de Gruyter, 2009. 395–408.

Woolgar, Christopher M. "The Cook." *Historians on Chaucer: The 'General Prologue' to the* Canterbury Tales. Ed. Stephen H. Rigby, with Alastair Minnis. Oxford: Oxford UP, 2014. 262–76.

THE MAN OF LAW AND HIS TALE

Schlauch, Margaret. *Chaucer's Constance and Accused Queens*. New York: New York UP, 1927.

Wood, Chauncey. "Astrology in the *Man of Law's Tale*." *Chaucer and the Country of the Stars: Poetic Uses of Astrological Imagery*. Princeton: Princeton UP, 1970.

Kolve, V. A. "*The Man of Law's Tale*: The Rudderless Ship and the Sea." *Chaucer and the Imagery of Narrative*. Stanford: Stanford UP, 1984. 297–358.

Astell, Ann W. "Apostrophe, Prayer, and the Structure of Satire in *The Man of Law's Tale*." *Studies in the Age of Chaucer* 13 (1991): 81–97.

• Schibanoff, Susan. "Worlds Apart: Orientalism, Antifeminism, and Heresy in Chaucer's *Man of Law's Tale*." *Exemplaria* 8.1 (1996): 59–96.

Allen, Elizabeth. "Chaucer Answers Gower: Constance and the Trouble with Reading." *ELH* 64 (1997): 627–55.

Lynch, Kathryn L. "Storytelling, Exchange and Constancy: East and West in Chaucer's *Man of Law's Tale*." *Chaucer Review* 33 (1999): 409–22.

Spearing, A. C. "Narrative Voice: The Case of Chaucer's 'Man of Law's Tale.'" *New Literary History* 32 (2001): 715–46. Revised rpt. in *Textual Subjectivity: The Encoding of Subjectivity in Medieval Narratives and Lyrics*. Oxford and New York: Oxford UP, 2005. 101–36.

Lavezzo, Kathy. "Beyond Rome: Mapping Gender and Justice in *The Man of Law's Tale*." *Studies in the Age of Chaucer* 24 (2002): 149–80. Revised rpt. in *Angels on the Edge of the World*. Ithaca, NY: Cornell UP, 2006. 93–113.

Nolan, Maura. "'Acquiteth yow now': Textual Contradiction and Legal Discourse in the Man of Law's Introduction." *The Letter of the Law: Legal Practice and Literary Production in Medieval England*. Ed. Emily Steiner and Candace Barrington. New York: Cornell UP, 2002. 136–53.

Heng, Geraldine. "Beauty and the East, a Modern Love Story: Women, Children, and Imagined Communities in The Man of Law's Tale and Its Others." *Empire of Magic: Medieval Romance and the Politics of Cultural Fantasy*. New York: Columbia UP, 2003. 181–237.

Barlow, Gania. "A Thrifty Tale: Narrative Authority, and the Competing Values of the *Man of Law's Tale*." *Chaucer Review* 44 (2010): 397–420.

Nelson, Ingrid. "Premodern Media and Networks of Transmission in the *Man of Law's Tale*." *Exemplaria* 25 (2013): 211–30.

Musson, Anthony. "The Sergeant of Law." *Historians on Chaucer: The 'General Prologue' to the* Canterbury Tales. Ed. Stephen H. Rigby, with Alastair Minnis. Oxford: Oxford UP, 2014. 206–26.

THE WIFE OF BATH AND HER TALE

Silverstein, Theodore. "The Wife of Bath and the Rhetoric of Enchantment; or, How to Make a Hero See in the Dark." *Modern Philology* 58 (1960–61): 153–73.

Pratt, Robert A. "The Development of the Wife of Bath." *Studies in Medieval Literature*. Ed. MacEdward Leach. Philadelphia: U of Pennsylvania P, 1961. 45–79.

———. "Jankyn's Book of Wikked Wyves: Medieval Antimatrimonial Propaganda in the Universities." *Annuale Mediaevale* 3 (1962): 5–27.

Matthews, William. "The Wife of Bath and All Her Sect." *Viator* 5 (1974): 413–43.

Carruthers, Mary. "The Wife of Bath and the Painting of Lions." *PMLA* 94 (1979): 209–22.

Robertson, D. W., Jr. "'And for My Land Thus Hastow Mordred Me?': Land Tenure, the Cloth Industry, and the Wife of Bath." *Chaucer Review* 14 (1980): 403–20.

Patterson, Lee. "'For the Wyves love of Bathe': Feminine Rhetoric and Poetic Resolution in the *Roman de la Rose* and the *Canterbury Tales*." *Speculum* 58 (1983): 656–95.

Fradenburg, Louise O. "The Wife of Bath's Passing Fancy." *Studies in the Age of Chaucer* 8 (1986): 31–58.

Knapp, Peggy A. "Alisoun Weaves a Text." *Philological Quarterly* 65 (1986): 387–401. Rpt. in *Chaucer and the Social Contest*. New York: Routledge, 1990. 114–28.

Crane, Susan. "Alison's Incapacity and Poetic Instability in the Wife of Bath's Tale." *PMLA* 102 (1987): 20–28.

Beidler, Peter G., and Elizabeth M. Biebel. *Chaucer's* Wife of Bath's Prologue and Tale: *An Annotated Bibliography, 1900 to 1995*. Chaucer Bibliographies. Toronto: U of Toronto P, 1998.

Hansen, Elaine Tuttle. "The Wife of Bath and the Mark of Adam." *Women's Studies* 15 (1988): 399–416. Rpt. in *Chaucer and the Fictions of Gender*. Berkeley: U of California P, 1992. 26–57.

Blamires, Alcuin. "The Wife of Bath and Lollardy." *Medium Aevum* 58 (1989): 224–42.

Dinshaw, Carolyn. "'Glose/bele chose': The Wife of Bath and Her Glossators." *Chaucer's Sexual Poetics*. Madison: U of Wisconsin P, 1989. 113–31.

Leicester, H. Marshall, Jr. *The Disenchanted Self: Representing the Subject in the* Canterbury Tales. Berkeley: U of California P, 1990. Chapters 2–5.

Crane, Susan. "The Writing Lesson of 1381." *Chaucer's England: Literature in Historical Context*. Ed. Barbara A. Hanawalt. Minneapolis: U of Minnesota P, 1991. 201–21.

Galloway, Andrew. "Marriage Sermons, Polemical Sermons, and *The Wife of Bath's Prologue*: A Generic Excursus." *Studies in the Age of Chaucer* 14 (1992): 3–30.

Strohm, Paul. "Treason in the Household." *Hochon's Arrow: The Social Imagination of Fourteenth-Century Texts*. Princeton: Princeton UP, 1992. 121–44.

Beidler, Peter G., ed. *Geoffrey Chaucer: The Wife of Bath*. Case Studies in Contemporary Criticism. Boston: Bedford Books of St. Martin's P, 1996 [text and critical essays by Laurie Finke, Louise O. (Aranye) Fradenburg, Elaine Tuttle Hansen, H. Marshall Leicester, Jr., and Lee Patterson].

• Fradenburg, Louise O. [Aranye]. "'Fulfild of Fairye': The Social Meaning of Fantasy in the Wife of Bath's Prologue and Tale." *Geoffrey Chaucer: The Wife of Bath*. Ed. Peter G. Beidler. Boston: Bedford Books of St. Martin's P, 1996. 205–20.

Robinson, Peter, ed. *The Wife of Bath's Prologue on CD-ROM*. Cambridge: Cambridge UP, 1996 [digital images and transcriptions of manuscripts and early printed editions, with a user guide, databases, and essays].

Hanna, Ralph, III, and Traugott Lawler, eds. and trans. *Jankyn's Book of Wikked Wyves*, vol. 1: *The Primary Texts*. The Chaucer Library. Athens, GA: U of Georgia P,

1997. Vol. 2: *Seven Commentaries on Walter Map's Dissuasio Valerii*. Athens, GA: U of Georgia P, 2014.

Friedman, John B. "Alice of Bath's Astral Destiny: A Re-Appraisal." *Chaucer Review* 35 (2000–2001): 166–81.

Minnis, A. J. *Fallible Authors: Chaucer's Pardoner and Wife of Bath*. Philadelphia: U of Pennsylvania P, 2008.

Scala, Elizabeth. "Desire in the *Canterbury Tales*: Sovereignty and Mastery Between the Wife and Clerk." *Studies in the Age of Chaucer* 31 (2009): 81–108.

Tinkle, Theresa. "The Wife of Bath's Marginal Authority." *Studies in the Age of Chaucer* 32 (2010): 67–101.

Allen, Mark, and John H. Fisher, eds., with Joseph Traherne. *The Wife of Bath's Prologue and Tale*. The Variorum Chaucer, II:5a, 5b. 2 vols. Norman: U of Oklahoma P, 2012.

Parsons, Ben. "Beaten for a Book: Domestic and Pedagogic Violence in *The Wife of Bath's Prologue*." *Studies in the Age of Chaucer* 37 (2015): 163–94.

Karras, Ruth Mazo. "The Wife of Bath." *Historians on Chaucer: The 'General Prologue' to the* Canterbury Tales. Ed. Stephen H. Rigby, with Alastair Minnis. Oxford: Oxford UP, 2014. 319–33.

THE FRIAR AND HIS TALE

Birney, Earle. *"After His Ymage*—The Central Ironies of the *Friar's Tale*." *Mediaeval Studies* 21 (1959): 17–35.

Mroczkowski, Przemyslaw. "The *Friar's Tale* and Its Pulpit Background." *English Studies Today*. Ed. G. A. Bonnard. Berne: Franke, 1961. 107–20.

Richardson, Janette. "Hunter and Prey: Functional Imagery in Chaucer's *Friar's Tale*." *English Miscellany* 12 (1961): 9–20. Rpt. in *Blameth Nat Me: A Study of Imagery in Chaucer's Fabliaux*. The Hague: Mouton, 1970. 73–85.

Szittya, Penn R. "The Green Yeoman as Loathly Lady: The Friar's Parody of the *Wife of Bath's Tale*." *PMLA* 90 (1975): 386–94.

Bloomfield, Morton W. "The *Friar's Tale* as a Liminal Tale." *Chaucer Review* 17 (1983): 286–91.

Hahn, Thomas, and Richard W. Kaeuper. "Text and Context: Chaucer's *Friar's Tale*." *Studies in the Age of Chaucer* 5 (1983): 67–101.

Kolve, V. A. "'Man in the Middle': Art and Religion in Chaucer's *Friar's Tale*." *Studies in the Age of Chaucer* 12 (1990): 5–46. Rpt. in *Telling Images: Chaucer and the Imagery of Narrative II*. Stanford: Stanford UP, 2009. 66–92.

Ridley, Florence H. "The Friar and the Critics." *The Idea of Medieval Literature: New Essays on Chaucer and Medieval Culture in Honor of Donald R. Howard*. Ed. James M. Dean and Christian Zacher. Newark: U of Delaware P, 1992. 160–72.

Wallace, David. "The Powers of the Countryside." *Chaucerian Polity*. Stanford: Stanford UP, 1997. 136–44.

Kline, Daniel T. "'Myne by Right': Oath Making and Intent in *The Friar's Tale*." *Philological Quarterly* 77 (1998): 271–93.

Somerset, Fiona. "'Mark him wel for he is on of þo': Training the 'Lewed' Gaze to Discern Hypocrisy." *ELH* 68 (2001): 315–34.

Phillips, Helen. "'A gay yeman, under a forest side': 'The Friar's Tale' and the Robin Hood Tradition." *Medieval Cultural Studies: Essays in Honour of Stephen Knight*. Ed. Ruth Evans, Helen Fulton, and David Matthews. Cardiff: U of Wales P, 2006. 123–37.

Bryant, Brantley L. "'By Extorcions I Lyve': Chaucer's Friar's Tale and Corrupt Officials." *Chaucer Review* 42 (2007): 180–95.

Homar, Katie. "Chaucer's Novelized, Carnivalized Exemplum: A Bakhtinian Reading of the Friar's Tale." *Chaucer Review* 45 (2010): 85–105.

Weiskott, Eric. "Chaucer the Forester: The Friar's Tale, Forest History, and Officialdom." *Chaucer Review* 47 (2013): 323–36.

Geltner, G. "The Friar." *Historians on Chaucer: The 'General Prologue' to the* Canterbury Tales. Ed. Stephen H. Rigby, with Alastair Minnis. Oxford: Oxford UP, 2014. 156–69.

THE SUMMONER AND HIS TALE

Fleming, John V. "The Antifraternalism of the *Summoner's Tale*." *Journal of English and Germanic Philology* 65 (1966): 688–700.

———. "The Summoner's Prologue: An Iconographic Adjustment." *Chaucer Review* 2 (1967): 95–107.

Levitan, Alan. "The Parody of Pentecost in the *Summoner's Tale*." *U of Toronto Quarterly* 40 (1971): 236–46.

Szittya, Penn R. "The Friar as False Apostle: Antifraternal Exegesis and the *Summoner's Tale*." *Studies in Philology* 71 (1974): 19–46. Rpt. in *The Antifraternal Tradition in Medieval Literature*. Princeton: Princeton UP, 1986. 231–46.

Clark, Roy Peter. "Doubting Thomas in Chaucer's *Summoner's Tale*." *Chaucer Review* 11 (1976): 164–78.

Fleming, John V. "Anticlerical Satire as Theological Essay: Chaucer's *Summoner's Tale*." *Thalia* 6:1 (1983): 5–22.

Hanning, Robert W. "Roasting a Friar, Mis-taking a Wife, and Other Acts of Textual Harassment in Chaucer's *Canterbury Tales*." *Studies in the Age of Chaucer* 7 (1985): 3–21.

Mann, Jill. "Anger and 'Glosynge' in the *Canterbury Tales*." *Proceedings of the British Academy* 76 (1990): 203–23.

Kolve, V. A. "Chaucer's Wheel of False Religion: Theology and Obscenity in the *Summoner's Tale*." *The Centre and Its Compass: Studies in Medieval Literature in Honor of Professor John Leyerle*. Ed. Robert Taylor, James F. Burke, Patricia J. Eberle, Ian Lancashire, and Brian S. Merrilees. Kalamazoo: Medieval Institute Publications, 1993. 265–96.

Cox, Catherine S. "'Grope Wei Bihynde': The Subversive Erotics of Chaucer's Summoner." *Exemplaria* 7 (1995): 145–77.

Plummer, John F., ed. *The Summoner's Tale*. The Variorum Chaucer, II:7. Norman: U of Oklahoma P, 1995.

Wallace, David. "The Powers of the Countryside." *Chaucerian Polity*. Stanford: Stanford UP, 1997. 144–52.

Olson, Glending. "The End of *The Summoner's Tale* and the Uses of Pentecost." *Studies in the Age of Chaucer* 21 (1999): 209–45.

Somerset, Fiona. "'As just as is a squyre': The Politics of 'Lewed Translacion' in Chaucer's *Summoner's Tale*." *Studies in the Age of Chaucer* 21 (1999): 187–207.

Bowers, John M. "Queering the Summoner: Same-Sex Union in Chaucer's *Canterbury Tales*." *Speaking Images: Essays in Honor of V. A. Kolve*. Ed. Robert F. Yeager and Charlotte C. Morse. Asheville, NC: Pegasus P, 2001. 301–24.

Travis, Peter W. "Thirteen Ways of Listening to a Fart: Noise in Chaucer's Summoner's Tale." *Exemplaria* 16 (2004): 323–48.

Olson, Glending. "Demonism, Geometric Nicknaming, and Natural Causation in Chaucer's Summoner's and Friar's Tales." *Viator* 42 (2011): 247–82.

Raybin, David. "'Goddes Instrumentz': Devils and Free Will in the Friar's and Summoner's Tales." *Chaucer Review* 46 (2011): 93–110.

Crane, Susan. "Cat, Capon, and Pig in *The Summoner's Tale*." *Studies in the Age of Chaucer* 34 (2012): 319–24.

Forrest, Ian. "The Summoner." *Historians on Chaucer: The 'General Prologue' to the* Canterbury Tales. Ed. Stephen H. Rigby, with Alastair Minnis. Oxford: Oxford UP, 2014. 421–42.

THE CLERK AND HIS TALE

Sledd, James. "The *Clerk's Tale*: The Monsters and the Critics." *Modern Philology* 51 (1953–54): 73–82.

Salter, Elizabeth. *Chaucer: The* Knight's Tale *and the* Clerk's Tale. London: Edward Arnold, 1962.

McCall, John P. "The *Clerk's Tale* and the Theme of Obedience." *Modern Language Quarterly* 27 (1966): 260–99.

Utley, Francis Lee. "Five Genres in the *Clerk's Tale*." *Chaucer Review* 6 (1972): 198–228.

Frese, Dolores W. "Chaucer's *Clerk's Tale*: The Monsters and the Critics Reconsidered." *Chaucer Review* 8 (1973): 133–46.

Middleton, Anne. "The Clerk and His Tale: Some Literary Contexts." *Studies in the Age of Chaucer* 2 (1980): 121–50.

Wimsatt, James I. "The Blessed Virgin and the Two Coronations of Griselda." *Mediaevalia* 6 (1980): 187–207.

Morse, Charlotte C. "The Exemplary Griselda." *Studies in the Age of Chaucer* 7 (1985): 51–86.

Ganim, John M. "Carnival Voices and the Envoy to the *Clerk's Tale*." *Chaucer Review* 22 (1987): 112–27. Rpt. in *Chaucerian Theatricality*. Princeton: Princeton UP, 1990. 79–91.

Dinshaw, Carolyn. "Griselda Translated." *Chaucer's Sexual Poetics*. Madison: U of Wisconsin P, 1989. 132–55.

Morse, Charlotte C. "Critical Approaches to the 'Clerk's Tale'." *Chaucer's Religious Tales*. Ed. C. David Benson and Elizabeth Robertson. Cambridge: D. S. Brewer, 1990. 71–83.

Wallace, David. "'Whan She Translated Was': A Chaucerian Critique of the Petrarchan Academy." *Literary Practice and Social Change in Britain, 1380–1530*. Ed. Lee Patterson. Berkeley: U of California P, 1990. 156–215. Rpt. in *Chaucerian Polity*. Stanford: Stanford UP, 1997. 261–98.

Bronfman, Judith. *Chaucer's* Clerk's Tale: *The Griselda Story Received, Rewritten, Illustrated*. New York: Garland. 1994.

Georgianna, Linda. "The Clerk's Tale and the Grammar of Assent." *Speculum* 70 (1995): 793–821.

Stanbury, Sarah. "Regimes of the Visual in Premodern England: Gaze, Body, and Chaucer's *Clerk's Tale*." *New Literary History* 28 (1997): 261–89.

Morse, Charlotte C. "Griselda Reads Philippa de Coucy." *Speaking Images: Essays in Honor of V. A. Kolve*. Ed. Robert F. Yeager and Charlotte C. Morse. Asheville, NC: Pegasus P, 2001. 347–92.

Olson, Glending. "The Marquis of Saluzzo and the Marquis of Dublin." *Speaking Images: Essays in Honor of V. A. Kolve*. Ed. Robert F. Yeager and Charlotte C. Morse. Asheville, NC: Pegasus P, 2001. 325–45.

Denny-Brown, Andrea. "*Povre* Griselda and the All-Consuming *Archewyves*." *Studies in the Age of Chaucer* 28 (2006): 77–115.

Sidhu, Nicole Nolan. "Weeping for the Virtuous Wife: Laymen, Affective Piety and Chaucer's 'Clerk's Tale.'" *Medieval Domesticity: Home, Housing and Household in Medieval England*. Ed. Maryanne Kowaleski and P. J. P. Goldberg. Cambridge and New York: Cambridge UP, 2008. 177–208.

Morgan, Gerald. "The Logic of the Clerk's Tale." *Modern Language Review* 104 (2009): 1–25.

Stavsky, Jonathan. "John Lydgate Reads The Clerk's Tale." *Studies in the Age of Chaucer* 34 (2012): 209–46.

Schwebel, Leah. "Redressing Griselda: Restoration through Translation in the Clerk's Tale." *Chaucer Review* 47 (2013): 274–99.

Briggs, Charles F. "The Clerk." *Historians on Chaucer: The 'General Prologue' to the* Canterbury Tales. Ed. Stephen H. Rigby, with Alastair Minnis. Oxford: Oxford UP, 2014. 187–205.

Sun, Hee-Jung. "The Clerk's Ironic Storytelling in the Clerk's Tale." *Medieval and Early Modern English Studies* 23 (2015): 31–59.

Narinsky, Anna. "Anti-Dualism and Social Mind in Chaucer's Clerk's Tale." *Partial Answers: Journal of Literature and the History of Ideas* 14 (2016): 187–216.

Normandin, Shawn. "'Non Intellegant': The Enigmas of the Clerk's Tale." *Texas Studies in Literature and Language* 58 (2016): 189–223.

THE MERCHANT AND HIS TALE

Burrow, J. A. "Irony in the *Merchant's Tale*." *Anglia* 75 (1957): 199–208.

Olson, Paul A. "Chaucer's Merchant and January's 'hevene in erthe heere.'" *ELH* 28 (1961): 203–14.

Jordan, Robert M. "The Non-Dramatic Disunity of the Merchant's Tale." *PMLA* 78 (1963): 293–99. Rpt. in *Chaucer and the Shape of Creation*. Cambridge, MA: Harvard UP, 1967. 132–51.

Donaldson, E. Talbot. "The Effect of the Merchant's Tale." *Speaking of Chaucer*. New York: W. W. Norton & Company, 1970. 30–45.

Brown, Emerson, Jr. "Chaucer, the Merchant, and Their Tale: Getting Beyond Old Controversies." Parts I and II. *Chaucer Review* 13 (1978–79): 141–56, 247–62.

Wentersdorf, Karl P. "Imagery, Structure, and Theme in Chaucer's *Merchant's Tale*." *Chaucer and the Craft of Fiction*. Ed. Leigh A. Arrathoon. Rochester, MI: Solaris Press, 1986. 36–52.

Mandel, Jerome. "The Unity of Fragment IV (Group E): The *Clerk's Tale* and the *Merchant's Tale*." *Hebrew University Studies in Literature and the Arts* 16 (1988): 27–50.

Edwards, A. S. G. "*The Merchant's Tale* and Moral Chaucer." *Modern Language Quarterly* 51 (1990): 409–26.

Jager, Eric. "The Carnal Letter in Chaucer's Earthly Paradise." *The Tempter's Voice: Language and the Fall in Medieval Literature*. Ithaca: Cornell UP, 1993. 241–98.

Jost, Jean. "May's Mismarriage of Youth and Elde: The Poetics of Sexual Desire in Chaucer's *Merchant's Tale.*" *Feminea Medievalia 1: Representations of the Feminine in the Middle Ages.* Ed. Bonnie Wheeler. Cambridge: Academia P, 1993. 117–38.

Rose, Christine. "Women's 'Pryvete,' May, and the Privy: Fissures in the Narrative Voice in the *Merchant's Tale,* 1944–86." *Chaucer Yearbook* 4 (1997): 61–77.

Lucas, Angela M. "The Mirror in the Marketplace: Januarie Through the Looking Glass." *Chaucer Review* 33 (1998): 123–45.

Crocker, Holly A. "Performative Passivity and Fantasies of Masculinity in the Merchant's Tale." *Chaucer Review* 38 (2003): 178–98.

Kolve, V. A. "Of Calendars and Cuckoldry." *Telling Images: Chaucer and the Imagery of Narrative II.* Stanford: Stanford UP, 2009. 93–170.

Blamires, Alcuin. "May in January's Tree: Genealogical Configuration in the Merchant's Tale." *Chaucer Review* 45 (2010): 106–17.

McDonie, R. Jacob. "'Ye get namoore of me': Narrative, Textual, and Linguistic Desires in Chaucer's 'Merchant's Tale.'" *Exemplaria* 24 (2012): 313–41.

O'Byrne, Theresa. "'To Take a Wyf It Is a Glorious Thing': Januarie's Thesis on Marriage in the Merchant's Tale." *English Studies* 93 (2012): 150–68.

Schrock, Chad. "The Ends of Reading in the Merchant's Tale." *Philological Quarterly* 91 (2012): 591–609.

Seal, Samantha Katz. "Pregnant Desire: Eyes and Appetites in the Merchant's Tale." *Chaucer Review* 48 (2014): 284–306.

Goddard, Richard. "The Merchant." *Historians on Chaucer: The 'General Prologue' to the* Canterbury Tales. Ed. Stephen H. Rigby, with Alastair Minnis. Oxford: Oxford UP, 2014. 170–86.

Zedolik, John. "'The Gardyn Is Enclosed Al Aboute': The Inversion of Exclusivity in the Merchant's Tale." *Studies in Philology* 112 (2015): 490–503.

THE FRANKLIN AND HIS TALE

Blenner-Hassett, Roland. "Autobiographical Aspects of Chaucer's Franklin." *Speculum* 28 (1953): 791–800.

Gaylord, Alan T. "The Promises in *The Franklin's Tale.*" *ELH: A Journal of English Literary History* 31 (1964): 331–65.

David, Alfred. "Sentimental Comedy in *The Franklin's Tale.*" *Annuale Mediaevale* 6 (1965): 19–27.

Mann, Lindsay A. "'Gentilesse' and the Franklin's Tale." *Studies in Philology* 63 (1966): 10–29.

Berger, Harry, Jr. "The F-Fragment of the *Canterbury Tales.*" *Chaucer Review* 1 (1966–67): 88–102, 135–56.

Peck, Russell. "Sovereignty and the Two Worlds of the *Franklin's Tale.*" *Chaucer Review* 1 (1967): 253–71.

Kearney, A. M. "Truth and Illusion in *The Franklin's Tale.*" *Essays in Criticism* 19 (1969): 245–53.

Knight, Stephen. "Ideology in *The Franklin's Tale.*" *Parergon* 28 (1980): 3–31.

Saul, Nigel. "The Social Status of Chaucer's Franklin: A Reconsideration." *Medium Aevum* 52 (1983): 10–26.

Kolve, V. A. "Rocky Shores and Pleasure Gardens: Poetry vs. Magic in Chaucer's *Franklin's Tale.*" *Poetics: Theory and Practice in Medieval English Literature.* Ed. Piero Boitani and Anna Torti. Cambridge: D. S. Brewer, 1991. 165–95. Rpt. in *Telling Images: Chaucer and the Imagery of Narrative II.* Stanford: Stanford UP, 2009. 171–98.

Riddy, Felicity. "Engendering Pity in the *Franklin's Tale.*" *Feminist Readings in Middle English Literature: The Wife of Bath and All Her Sect.* Ed. Ruth Evans and Lesley Johnson. London: Routledge, 1994. 54–71.

Edwards, Robert R. "Source, Context, and Cultural Translation in the *Franklin's Tale.*" *Modern Philology* 94 (1996): 141–62.

Green, Richard Firth. "Rash Promises." *A Crisis of Truth: Literature and Law in Ricardian England.* Philadelphia: U of Pennsylvania P, 1999. 293–335.

Lightsey, Scott. "Chaucer's Secular Marvels and the Medieval Economy of Wonder." *Studies in the Age of Chaucer* 23 (2001): 289–316.

Staley, Lynn. *Languages of Power in the Age of Richard II.* University Park, PA: Pennsylvania State UP, 2005. 62–73 [on courtly rhetoric in the *Franklin's Tale*].

Cartlidge, Neil. "'Nat that I chalange any thyng of right': Love, Loyalty, and Legality in the Franklin's Tale." *Writings on Love in the English Middle Ages*. Ed. Helen Cooney. New York: Palgrave Macmillan, 2006. 115–30.

Ganze, Alison. "'My trouth for to holde—Allas, Allas!': Dorigen and Honor in the *Franklin's Tale*." *Chaucer Review* 42 (2008): 312–29.

Hume, Kathy. "'The name of soveraynetee': The Private and Public Faces of Marriage in The Franklin's Tale." *Studies in Philology* 105 (2008): 284–303.

Kao, Wan-Chuan. "Conduct Shameful and Unshameful in *The Franklin's Tale*." *Studies in the Age of Chaucer* 34 (2012): 99–139.

Carruthers, Leo. *Reading the Middle English Breton Lays and Chaucer's* Franklin's Tale. Paris: Atlande, 2013.

Narinsky, Anna. "'The Road Not Taken': Virtual Narratives in *The Franklin's Tale*." *Poetics Today* 34 (2013): 53–118.

Coss, Peter. "The Franklin." *Historians on Chaucer: The 'General Prologue' to the* Canterbury Tales. Ed. Stephen H. Rigby, with Alastair Minnis. Oxford: Oxford UP, 2014. 227–46.

THE PARDONER AND HIS TALE

Kellogg, Alfred L. "An Augustinian Interpretation of Chaucer's Pardoner." *Speculum* 26 (1951): 465–81.

Miller, Robert P. "Chaucer's Pardoner, the Scriptural Eunuch, and the Pardoner's Tale." *Speculum* 30 (1955): 180–99.

Steadman, John M. "Old Age and *Contemptus Mundi* in the *Pardoner's Tale*." *Medium Aevum* 33 (1964): 121–30.

Howard, Donald R. "The Pardoner and the Parson." *The Idea of the* Canterbury Tales. Berkeley: U of California P, 1976. 333–87.

Patterson, Lee W. "Chaucerian Confession: Penitential Literature and the Pardoner." *Medievalia et Humanistica* n.s. 7 (1976): 153–73. Rpt. in *Chaucer and the Subject of History*. Madison: U of Wisconsin P, 1991. 367–421.

Minnis, A. J. "Chaucer's Pardoner and the 'Office of Preacher'." *Intellectuals and Writers in Fourteenth-Century Europe*. Ed. Piero Boitani and Anna Torti. Tubingen: Narr; Cambridge: Brewer, 1986. 88–119.

• Dinshaw, Carolyn. "Eunuch Hermeneutics." *ELH* 55 (1988): 27–51. Rpt. in *Chaucer's Sexual Poetics*. Madison: U of Wisconsin P, 1989. 156–84.

• Cooper, Helen. "The Pardoner's Prologue and Tale." *Oxford Guides to Chaucer: The Canterbury Tales*. New York: Oxford UP, 1989. 2nd ed. 1996. 260–75.

Leicester, H. Marshall, Jr. *The Disenchanted Self: Representing the Subject in the* Canterbury Tales. Berkeley: U of California P, 1990. Chapters 1, 6, 7.

Burger, Glenn. "Kissing the Pardoner." *PMLA* 107 (1992): 1143–56. Rpt. in *Chaucer's Queer Nation*. Minneapolis: U of Minnesota P, 2003. 140–59.

Frantzen, Allen J. "*The Pardoner's Tale*, the Pervert, and the Price of Order in Chaucer's World." *Class and Gender in Early English Literature: Intersections*. Ed. Britton J. Harwood and Gillian R. Overing. Bloomington: Indiana UP, 1994. 131–48.

Kruger, Steven F. "Claiming the Pardoner: Toward a Gay Reading of Chaucer's *Pardoner's Tale*." *Exemplaria* 6 (1994): 115–39.

Dinshaw, Carolyn. "Chaucer's Queer Touches/A Queer Touches Chaucer." *Exemplaria* 7 (1995): 75–92. Rpt. in *Getting Medieval: Sexualities and Communities, Pre- and Postmodern*. Durham: Duke UP, 1999. 100–43.

Sutton, Marilyn. *Chaucer's* Pardoner's Prologue and Tale: *An Annotated Bibliography. 1900 to 1995*. Chaucer Bibliographies. Toronto: U of Toronto P, 2000.

Sturges, Robert S. *Chaucer's Pardoner and Gender Theory: Bodies of Discourse*. New York: St. Martin's P, 2000.

Kelly, Henry Ansgar. "The Pardoner's Voice: Disjunctive Narrative and Modes of Effemination." *Speaking Images: Essays in Honor of V. A. Kolve*. Ed. Robert F. Yeager and Charlotte C. Morse. Asheville, NC: Pegasus P, 2001. 411–44.

Lynch, Kathryn L. "The Pardoner's Digestion: Eating Images in *The Canterbury Tales*." *Speaking Images: Essays in Honor of V. A. Kolve*. Ed. Robert F. Yeager and Charlotte C. Morse. Asheville, NC: Pegasus P, 2001. 393–409.

Patterson, Lee. "Chaucer's Pardoner on the Couch: Psyche and Clio in Medieval Literary Studies." *Speculum* 76 (2001). 638–80.

Minnis, Alastair. *Fallible Authors: Chaucer's Pardoner and Wife of Bath*. Philadelphia: U of Pennsylvania P, 2008.

———. "Once More into the Breech: The Pardoner's Prize 'Relyk.'" *Through a Classical Eye: Transcultural and Transhistorical Visions in Medieval English, Italian, and Latin Literature in Honour of Winthrop Wetherbee*. Ed. Andrew Galloway and R. F. Yeager. Toronto: U of Toronto P, 2009. 287–315.

Horrox, Rosemary. "The Pardoner." *Historians on Chaucer: The 'General Prologue' to the* Canterbury Tales. Ed. Stephen H. Rigby, with Alastair Minnis. Oxford: Oxford UP, 2014. 443–59.

THE PRIORESS AND HER TALE

Lowes, John Livingston. "Simple and Coy: A Note on Fourteenth-Century Poetic Diction." *Anglia* 33 (1910): 440–51.

Schoeck, Richard J. "Chaucer's Prioress: Mercy and Tender Heart." *The Bridge: Yearbook of Judaeo-Christian Studies* 2 (1956): 239–55.

Beichner, Paul E., C.S.C. "The Grain of Paradise." *Speculum* 36 (1961): 302–307.

Gaylord, Alan T. "The Unconquered Tale of the Prioress." *Papers of the Michigan Academy of Science, Arts, and Letters* 47 (1962): 613–36.

Ridley, Florence H. *The Prioress and the Critics*. U of California English Studies 30. Berkeley and Los Angeles: U of California P, 1965.

Langmuir, Gavin I. "The Knight's Tale of Young Hugh of Lincoln." *Speculum* 47 (1972): 459–82.

Wood, Chauncey. "Chaucer's Use of Signs in His Portrait of the Prioress." *Signs and Symbols in Chaucer's Poetry*. Ed. John P. Hermann and John J. Burke, Jr. University, AL: U of Alabama P, 1981. 81–101.

Frank, Robert Worth, Jr. "Miracles of the Virgin, Medieval Anti-Semitism, and the 'Prioress's Tale.'" *The Wisdom of Poetry: Essays in Early English Literature in Honor of Morton W. Bloomfield*. Ed. Larry D. Benson and Siegfried Wenzel. Kalamazoo: Medieval Institute Publications, 1982. 177–88.

Boyd, Beverly, ed. *The Prioress's Tale*. The Variorum Chaucer, II:20. Norman: U of Oklahoma P, 1987.

Fradenburg, Louise O. "Criticism, Anti-Semitism and the *Prioress's Tale*." *Exemplaria* 1 (1989): 69–115.

Ferster, Judith. "'Your Praise Is Performed by Men and Children': Language and Gender in the *Prioress's Prologue and Tale*." *Exemplaria* 2 (1990): 149–68.

Robertson, Elizabeth. "Aspects of Female Piety in the *Prioress's Tale*." *Chaucer's Religious Tales*. Ed. C. David Benson and Elizabeth Robertson. Cambridge: D. S. Brewer, 1990. 145–60.

• Spector, Stephen. "Empathy and Enmity in the *Prioress's Tale*." *The Olde Daunce: Love, Friendship, Sex and Marriage in the Medieval World*. Ed. Robert R. Edwards and Stephen Spector. Albany: State U of New York P, 1991. 211–28. Rpt. in *Geoffrey Chaucer's* The Canterbury Tales: *A Casebook*. Ed. Lee Patterson. Oxford and New York: Oxford UP, 2007. 183–209.

Rex, Richard. *"The Sins of Madame Eglentyne" and Other Essays on Chaucer*. Newark: U of Delaware P, 1995.

Kelly, Henry Ansgar. "A Neo-Revisionist Look at Chaucer's Nuns." *Chaucer Review* 31 (1996): 115–32.

Tomasch, Sylvia. "Postcolonial Chaucer and the Virtual Jew." *The Postcolonial Middle Ages*. Ed. Jeffrey Jerome Cohen. New York: St. Martin's Press, 2000. 243–60.

Patterson, Lee. "'The Living Witnesses of Our Redemption': Martyrdom and Imitation in Chaucer's Prioress's Tale." *Journal of Medieval and Early Modern Studies* 31 (2001): 507–60.

Delany, Sheila, ed. *Chaucer and the Jews: Sources, Contexts, Meanings*. New York: Routledge, 2002.

Dahood, Roger. "The Punishment of the Jews, Hugh of Lincoln, and the Question of Satire in Chaucer's Prioress's Tale." *Viator* 36 (2005): 465–91.

Kruger, Steven. *The Spectral Jew: Conversion and Embodiment in Medieval Europe*. Minneapolis: U of Minnesota P, 2005.

Lochrie, Karma. "Close to Lollardy: Chaucer's Prioress." *Heterosyncracies: Female Sexuality When Normal Wasn't*. Minneapolis: U of Minnesota P, 2005. 60–70.

Dahood, Roger. "English Historical Narratives of Jewish Child-Murder, Chaucer's *Prioress's Tale*, and the Date of Chaucer's Unknown Source." *Studies in the Age of Chaucer* 31 (2009): 125–40.

Dahood, Roger. "The Anglo-Norman 'Hugo de Lincolnia': A Critical Edition and Translation from the Unique Text in Paris, Bibliothèque nationale de France MS fr. 902." *Chaucer Review* 49 (2014): 1–38.

Lewis, Katherine J. "The Prioress and the Second Nun." *Historians on Chaucer: The 'General Prologue' to the* Canterbury Tales. Ed. Stephen H. Rigby, with Alastair Minnis. Oxford: Oxford UP, 2014. 94–113.

CHAUCER'S TALE OF SIR THOPAS

Loomis, Laura Hibbard. "Chaucer and the Auchinleck MS: *Thopas* and *Guy of Warwick.*" *Essays and Studies in Honor of Carleton Brown.* [no editor]. New York: New York UP, 1940. 111–28.

Gaylord, Alan T. "Chaucer's Dainty 'Dogerel': The 'Elvyssh' Prosody of *Sir Thopas.*" *Studies in the Age of Chaucer* 1 (1979): 83–104. Rpt. in *Chaucer's Humor: Critical Essays.* Ed. Jean E. Jost. New York: Garland, 1994. 271–94.

Scattergood, V. J. "Chaucer and the French War: *Sir Thopas* and *Melibee.*" *Court and Poet.* Ed. Glyn S. Burgess et al. Liverpool: Cairns, 1987. 287–96.

Benson, C. David. "Their Telling Difference: Chaucer the Pilgrim and His Two Contrasting Tales." *Chaucer Review* 18 (1983); 61–76. Rpt. *Chaucer's Drama of Style: Poetic Variety and Contrast in the* Canterbury Tales. Chapel Hill: U of North Carolina P, 1986. 26–43.

Gaylord, Alan T. "The 'Miracle' of *Sir Thopas.*" *Studies in the Age of Chaucer* 6 (1984): 65–84.

Patterson, Lee. "'What Man Artow?': Authorial Self-Definition in *The Tale of Sir Thopas* and *The Tale of Melibee.*" *Studies in the Age of Chaucer* 11 (1989): 117–75.

Lerer, Seth. "'Now Holde Youre Mouthe': The Romance of Orality in the *Thopas-Melibee* Section of the *Canterbury Tales.*" *Oral Poetics in Middle English Poetry.* Ed. Mark C. Amodio. New York: Garland, 1994. 181–205.

Burrow, J. A. "Elvish Chaucer." *The Endless Knot: Essays on Old and Middle English in Honor of Marie Borroff.* Ed. M. Teresa Tavormina and R. F. Yeager. Cambridge: D. S. Brewer, 1995. 105–11.

Askins, William. "All That Glisters: The Historical Setting of the *Tale of Sir Thopas.*" *Reading Medieval Culture: Essays in Honor of Robert W. Hanning.* Ed. Robert M. Stein and Sandra Pierson Prior. Notre Dame: U of Notre Dame P, 2005. 271–89.

Børch, Marianne. "Writing Remembering Orality: Geoffrey Chaucer's *Sir Thopas.*" *European Journal of English Studies* 10 (2006): 131–48.

Jager, Katharine. "'Som deyntee thyng': Poetry and Possibility in Chaucer's *Tale of Sir Thopas.*" *Medieval Perspectives* 24 (2009): 22–45.

Cannon, Christopher. "Chaucer and the Auchinleck Manuscript Revisited." *Chaucer Review* 46 (2011): 131–46.

Brantley, Jessica. "Reading the Forms of *Sir Thopas.*" *Chaucer Review* 47 (2013): 416–38.

CHAUCER'S TALE OF MELIBEE

Askins, William. "*The Tale of Melibee* and the Crisis at Westminster, November, 1387." *Studies in the Age of Chaucer, Proceedings, No. 2 (1986).* Ed. John V. Fleming and Thomas J. Heffernan. Knoxville, TN: New Chaucer Society, 1987. 103–12.

Yeager, R. F. "'Pax Poetica': On the Pacifism of Chaucer and Gower." *Studies in the Age of Chaucer* 9 (1987): 97–121.

Kempton, Daniel. "Chaucer's *Melibee*: 'A lytel thyng in prose.'" *Genre* 21 (1988): 263–78.

Johnson, Lynn Staley. "Inverse Counsel: Contexts for the *Melibee.*" *Studies in Philology* 87 (1990): 137–55. See also David Aers and Lynn Staley, *The Powers of the Holy.* University Park, PA: The Pennsylvania State UP, 1996. 217–33.

Collette, Carolyn P. "Heeding the Counsel of Prudence: A Context for the *Melibee.*" *Chaucer Review* 29 (1995): 416–33.

Ferster, Judith. "Chaucer's *Tale of Melibee:* Advice to the King and Advice to the King's Advisers." *Fictions of Advice: The Literature and Politics of Counsel in Late Medieval England.* Philadelphia: U of Pennsylvania P, 1996. 89–107.

Blamires, Alcuin. *The Case for Women in Medieval Culture.* Oxford: Clarendon P, 1997.

Wallace, David. "Household Rhetoric: Violence and Eloquence in the *Tale of Melibee.*" *Chaucerian Polity.* Stanford: Stanford UP, 1997. 212–46.

Burger, Glenn. "Mapping a History of Sexuality in *Melibee.*" *Chaucer and Language: Essays in Honour of Douglas Wurtele.* Ed. Robert Myles and David Williams. Montreal: McGill-Queen's UP, 2001. 61–70, 198–203.

Walling, Amanda. "'In Hir Tellyng Difference': Gender, Authority, and Interpretation in the *Tale of Melibee*." *Chaucer Review* 40 (2005): 163–81.
DeMarco, Patricia. "Violence, Law, and Ciceronian Ethics in Chaucer's *Tale of Melibee*." *Studies in the Age of Chaucer* 30 (2008): 125–69.
Spencer, Alice. "Dialogue, Dialogics, and Love: Problems of Chaucer's Poetics in the Melibee." The Canterbury Tales *Revisited—21st Century Interpretations*. Ed. Kathleen A. Bishop. Newcastle: Cambridge Scholars, 2008. 228–55.
Taylor, Jamie. "Chaucer's *Tale of Melibee* and the Failure of Allegory." *Exemplaria* 21 (2009): 83–101.

THE NUN'S PRIEST AND HIS TALE

Curry, Walter Clyde. "Chauntecleer and Pertelote on Dreams." *Englische Studien* 58 (1924): 24–60.
Young, Karl. "Chaucer and Geoffrey of Vinsauf." *Modern Philology* 41 (1943–44): 172–82.
Donovan, Mortimer J. "The *Moralite* of the Nun's Priest's Sermon." *Journal of English and Germanic Philology* 52 (1953): 498–508.
Manning, Stephen. "The Nun's Priest's Morality and the Medieval Attitude toward Fables." *Journal of English and Germanic Philology* 59 (1960): 403–16.
Allen, Judson B. "The Ironic Fruyt: Chauntecleer as Figura." *Studies in Philology* 66 (1969): 25–35.
Pratt, Robert A. "Three Old French Sources of the Nonnes Preestes Tale." *Speculum* 47 (1972): 424–44, 646–68.
Donaldson, E. Talbot. "The Nun's Priest's Tale." *Chaucer's Poetry: An Anthology for the Modern Reader.* 2nd ed. New York: Ronald Press, 1975. 1104–108.
Gallacher, Patrick. "Food, Laxatives, and Catharsis in Chaucer's Nun's Priest's Tale." *Speculum* 51 (1976): 49–68.
Pearsall, Derek, ed. *The Nun's Priest's Tale.* The Variorum Chaucer, II:9. Norman: U of Oklahoma P, 1984.
Scanlon, Larry. "The Authority of Fable: Allegory and Irony in the 'Nun's Priest's Tale.'" *Exemplaria* 1 (1989): 43–68.
McAlpine, Monica E. "The Triumph of Fiction in the Nun's Priest's Tale." *Art and Context in Late Medieval English Narrative: Essays in Honor of Robert Worth Frank, Jr.* Ed. Robert R. Edwards. Cambridge: D. S. Brewer, 1994. 79–92.
Kempton, Daniel. "The Nun's Priest's Festive Doctrine: 'Al That Written Is.'" *Assays* 8 (1995): 101–18.
Wheatley, Edward. "Commentary Displacing Text: *The Nun's Priest's Tale* and the Scholastic Fable Tradition." *Studies in the Age of Chaucer* 18 (1996): 119–41. Rev. rpt. in *Mastering Aesop: Medieval Education, Chaucer, and His Followers*. Gainesville: UP of Florida, 2000. 97–123.
Varty, Kenneth. *Reynard, Renart, Reinaert and Other Foxes in Medieval England: The Iconographic Evidence*. Amsterdam: Amsterdam UP, 1999.
Finlayson, John. "Reading Chaucer's *Nun's Priest's Tale*: Mixed Genres and Multi-Layered Worlds of Illusion." *English Studies* 86 (2005): 493–510.
Thomas, Paul, ed. *The Nun's Priest's Tale on CD-ROM*. Birmingham, UK: Scholarly Digital Editions, 2006 [digital images and transcriptions of all pre-1500 manuscripts and editions, with a user guide, databases, and essays].
Mann, Jill. "The Nun's Priest's Tale as Reynardian Tale." *From Aesop to Reynard: Beast Literature in Medieval England*. Oxford and New York: Oxford UP, 2009. 250–61.
Travis, Peter W. *Disseminal Chaucer: Rereading* The Nun's Priest's Tale. Notre Dame: U of Notre Dame P, 2010.
Oliva, Marilyn. "The Nun's Priest." *Historians on Chaucer: The 'General Prologue' to the* Canterbury Tales. Ed. Stephen H. Rigby, with Alastair Minnis. Oxford: Oxford UP, 2014. 114–36.

THE SECOND NUN AND HER TALE

Giffin, Mary. "'Hir hous the chirche of Seinte Cecilie highte.'" *Studies on Chaucer and His Audience*. Hull, Québec: Éditions "L'Éclair," 1956. 29–48.
Clogan, Paul M. "The Figural Style and Meaning of *The Second Nun's Prologue* and *Tale*." *Medievalia et Humanistica* 3 (1972): 213–40.

Reames, Sherry L. "The Cecilia Legend as Chaucer Inherited It and Retold It: The Disappearance of an Augustinian Ideal." *Speculum* 55 (1980): 38–57.

Kolve, V. A. "The Second Nun's Tale and the Iconography of St. Cecilia." *New Perspectives in Chaucer Criticism*. Ed. Donald M. Rose. Norman, OK: Pilgrim Books, 1981. 137–74. Rpt. in *Telling Images: Chaucer and the Imagery of Narrative II*. Stanford: Stanford UP, 2009. 199–222.

Hagen, Susan K. "Feminist Theology and *The Second Nun's Tale*: Or, St. Cecilia Laughs at the Judge." *Medieval Perspectives* 4–5 (1989–90): 42–52.

Reames, Sherry L. "A Recent Discovery Concerning the Sources of Chaucer's *Second Nun's Tale*." *Modern Philology* 87 (1989–90): 337–61.

Hirsh, John C. "The *Second Nun's Tale*." *Chaucer's Religious Tales*. Ed. C. David Benson and Elizabeth Robertson. Cambridge: D. S. Brewer, 1990. 161–70.

Johnson, Lynn Staley. "Chaucer's Tale of the Second Nun and the Strategies of Dissent." *Studies in Philology* 89 (1992): 314–33. Rpt. in David Aers and Lynn Staley. *The Powers of the Holy: Religion, Politics and Gender in Late Medieval English Culture*. University Park, PA: Pennsylvania State UP, 1996. 198–213.

Raybin, David. "Chaucer's Creation and Recreation of the 'Lyf of Seynt Cecile.'" *Chaucer Review* 32 (1997): 196–212.

Reames, Sherry L. "The Second Nun's Prologue and Tale." *Sources and Analogues of The Canterbury Tales, Volume I*. Ed. Robert M. Correale and Mary Hamel. Cambridge: D. S. Brewer, 2002. 491–527.

Sanok, Catherine. "Performing Feminine Sanctity in Late Medieval England: Parish Guilds, Saints' Plays, and the *Second Nun's Tale*." *Journal of Medieval and Early Modern Studies* 32 (2002): 269–303.

Little, Katherine C. "Images, Texts, and Exegetics in Chaucer's *Second Nun's Tale*." *Journal of Medieval and Early Modern Studies* 36 (2006): 103–34.

Robertson, Elizabeth. "Apprehending the Divine and Choosing to Believe: Voluntarist Free Will in Chaucer's *Second Nun's Tale*." *Chaucer Review* 46 (2011): 111–30.

Lewis, Katherine J. "The Prioress and the Second Nun." *Historians on Chaucer: The 'General Prologue' to the* Canterbury Tales. Ed. Stephen H. Rigby, with Alastair Minnis. Oxford: Oxford UP, 2014. 94–113.

THE MANCIPLE AND HIS TALE

Shumaker, Wayne. "Chaucer's Manciple's Tale as Part of the Canterbury Group." *University of Toronto Quarterly* 22 (1953): 147–56.

Hazelton, Richard. "The *Manciple's Tale:* Parody and Critique." *Joumal of English and Germanic Philology* 62 (1963): 1–31.

Scattergood, V. J. "The Manciple's Manner of Speaking." *Essays in Criticism* 24 (1974): 124–46.

Dean, James. "The Ending of the *Canterbury Tales*." *Texas Studies in Language and Literature* 21 (1979): 17–33.

Baker, Donald C., ed. *The Manciple's Tale*. The Variorum Chaucer, II.10. Norman: U of Oklahoma P, 1984.

Fradenburg, Louise O. "The Manciple's Servant Tongue: Politics and Poetry in *The Canterbury Tales*." *ELH* 52 (1985): 85–118.

Burrow, J. A. "Chaucer's Canterbury Pilgrimage." *Essays in Criticism* 36 (1986): 97–119.

Allen, Mark. "Penitential Sermons, the Manciple, and the End of *The Canterbury Tales*." *Studies in the Age of Chaucer* 9 (1987): 77–96.

Grudin, Michaela Paasche. "Chaucer's Manciple's Tale and the Poetics of Guile." *Chaucer Review* 25 (1991): 329–42.

Ginsburg, Warren. "Chaucer's Canterbury Poetics: Irony, Allegory, and the *Prologue* to *The Manciple's Tale*." *Studies in the Age of Chaucer* 18 (1996): 55–89.

Kensak, Michael. "Apollo Exterminans: The God of Poetry in Chaucer's Manciple's Tale." *Studies in Philology* 98 (2001): 143–57.

Mann, Jill. "The Manciple's Tale." *From Aesop to Reynard: Beast Literature in Medieval England*. Oxford and New York: Oxford UP, 2009. 206–19.

Fumo, Jamie C. "Domestic Apollo: Crises of Truth in the *Manciple's Tale*." *The Legacy of Apollo: Antiquity, Authority and Chaucerian Poetics*. Toronto: U of Toronto P, 2010. 202–28.

Kordecki, Lesley. "Mythological Censorship and the Manciple's Tale." *Ecofeminist Subjectivities: Chaucer's Talking Birds*. Basingstoke and New York: Palgrave Macmillan, 2011. 121–42.

Bertolet, Craig E. "The Anxiety of Exclusion: Speech, Power, and Chaucer's Manciple." *Studies in the Age of Chaucer* 33 (2011): 183–218.

Lim, Hyunyang. "Transgression and Containment: Language, Defamation, and *The Manciple's Tale.*" *Medieval and Early Modern English Studies* 21 (2013): 193–214.

Ramsay, Nigel. "The Manciple." *Historians on Chaucer: The 'General Prologue' to the* Canterbury Tales. Ed. Stephen H. Rigby, with Alastair Minnis. Oxford: Oxford UP, 2014. 386–98.

THE PARSON AND HIS TALE

Allen, Judson Boyce. "The Old Way and the Parson's Way: An Ironic Reading of the *Parson's Tale.*" *Journal of Medieval and Renaissance Studies* 3 (1973): 255–71.

Howard, Donald R. "The Pardoner and the Parson." *The Idea of the* Canterbury Tales. Berkeley: U of California P, 1976. 333–87.

Delasanta, Rodney. "Penance and Poetry in the *Canterbury Tales.*" *PMLA* 93 (1978): 240–47.

• Patterson, Lee. "The *Parson's Tale* and the Quitting of the *Canterbury Tales.*" *Traditio* 34 (1978): 331–80.

Wurtele, Douglas J. "The Penitence of Geoffrey Chaucer." *Viator* 11 (1980): 335–61.

Taylor, Paul Beekman. "The Parson's Amyable Tongue." *English Studies* 64 (1983): 401–409.

Wenzel, Siegfried, ed. and trans. *Summa Virtutum de Remediis Anime*. The Chaucer Library. Athens, GA: U of Georgia P, 1984.

Lawton, David. "Chaucer's Two Ways: The Pilgrimage Frame of *The Canterbury Tales.*" *Studies in the Age of Chaucer* 9 (1987): 3–40.

Bestul, Thomas H. "Chaucer's Parson's Tale and the Late-Medieval Tradition of Religious Meditation." *Speculum* 64 (1989): 600–619.

Raybin, David, and Linda Tarte Holley, eds. *Closure in* The Canterbury Tales: *The Role of* The Parson's Tale. Kalamazoo: Medieval Institute Publications, 2000 [critical essays plus extensive bibliography].

Pitard, Derrick. "Sowing Difficulty: The Parson's Tale, Vernacular Commentary, and the Nature of Chaucerian Dissent." *Studies in the Age of Chaucer* 26 (2004): 299–330.

Smith, Nicole D. "The Parson's Predilection for Pleasure." *Studies in the Age of Chaucer* 28 (2006): 117–40.

McCormack, Frances. *Chaucer and the Culture of Dissent: The Lollard Context and Subtext of the "Parson's Tale."* Dublin and Portland, OR: Four Courts P, 2007.

Winstead, Karen. "Chaucer's Parson's Tale and the Contours of Orthodoxy." *Chaucer Review* 43 (2008): 239–59.

Thomas, Arvind. "What's 'Myrie' About the Prose of the Parson's Tale?" *Chaucer Review* 46 (2012): 419–38.

Lepine, David. "The Parson." *Historians on Chaucer: The 'General Prologue' to the* Canterbury Tales. Ed. Stephen H. Rigby, with Alastair Minnis. Oxford: Oxford UP, 2014. 334–51.

CHAUCER'S RETRACTION

Gordon, James D. "Chaucer's Retraction: A Review of Opinion." *Studies in Medieval Literature in Honor of Professor Albert Croll Baugh.* Ed. MacEdward Leach. Philadelphia: U of Pennsylvania P, 1961. 81–96.

Campbell, A. P. "Chaucer's 'Retraction': Who Retracted What?" *University of Ottawa Quarterly* 35 (1965): 35–53.

Sayce, Olive. "Chaucer's 'Retraction': The Conclusion of the *Canterbury Tales* and Its Place in Literary Tradition." *Medium Aevum* 40 (1971): 230–48.

McGerr, Rosemarie Potz. "Retraction and Memory: Retrospective Structure in the *Canterbury Tales.*" *Comparative Literature* 37 (1985): 97–113.

Travis, Peter W. "Deconstructing Chaucer's Retraction." *Exemplaria* 3 (1991): 135–58.

Vaughan, Micéal F. "Creating Comfortable Boundaries: Scribes, Editors, and the Invention of the Parson's Tale." *Rewriting Chaucer: Culture, Authority, and the Idea of the Authentic Text, 1400–1602.* Ed. Thomas A. Prendergast and Barbara Kline. Columbus: Ohio State UP, 1999. 45–90 [on the connection of the Retraction to the *Parson's Tale*].

Fumo, Jamie C. "The God of Love and Love of God: Palinodic Exchange in the Prologue of the *Legend of Good Women* and the *Retraction*." *The Legend of Good Women: Context and Reception*. Ed. Carolyn P. Collette. Cambridge: D. S. Brewer, 2006. 157–75.

Kerby-Fulton, Kathryn. "'Non Fabulas Poetarum': Chaucer's 'Retraction,' Pluralist Puritanisms, and 'Lollard Knights.'" *Books Under Suspicion: Censorship and Tolerance of Revelatory Writing in Late Medieval England*. Notre Dame: U of Notre Dame P, 2006. 350–57.

Johnson, Ian. "The Ascending Soul and the Virtue of Hope: The Spiritual Temper of Chaucer's *Boece* and *Retracciouns*." *English Studies* 88 (2007): 245–61.

Partridge, Stephen B. "'The Makere of this Boke': Chaucer's *Retraction* and the Author as Scribe and Compiler." *Author, Reader, Book: Medieval Authorship in Theory and Practice*. Ed. Partridge and Eric Kwakkel. Toronto: U of Toronto P, 2012. 106–53.